. B S

.ed Bibliography

1971–1980

HERBS

An Indexed Bibliography

1971–1980

The Scientific Literature
on Selected Herbs,
and Aromatic and Medicinal Plants
of the Temperate Zone

James E. Simon
Alena F. Chadwick
Lyle E. Craker

ARCHON BOOKS

1984

© 1984 James E. Simon, Alena F. Chadwick, Lyle E. Craker. All rights reserved.
First published in 1984 as an Archon Book, an imprint of
The Shoe String Press, Inc., Hamden, Connecticut 06514

Printed in the United States of America

Library of Congress Cataloging in Publication Data

Simon, James E.
  Herbs: an indexed bibliography, 1971–1980.

  Includes index.
  1. Herbs–Indexes. 2. Aromatic plants–
Indexes. 3. Medicinal plants–Indexes.
4. Herbs. 5. Aromatic plants. 6. Medicinal
plants. I. Chadwick, Alena F. II. Craker,
Lyle E. III. Title. [DNLM: 1. Herbs–
Bibliography. ZQV 767 S595h 1971–80]
Z5996.H37S56 1983 [SB351.H5] 016.582′063 82-24493
ISBN 0-208-01990-1

WARNING: The traditional medicinal and folk uses of each herb have been
included for informational purposes only. The authors and publishers do not
advocate nor prescribe the use of any herb for medicinal or other purposes. Please
note that some herbs included in this reference work are poisonous. The authors and
publishers assume no liability for omissions or for use or misuse of information
contained herein.

To Robin and Daniella, and to the memory
of my father.

J.E.S.

To my ever-patient family and friends.

A.F.C.

To the love of my family.

L.E.C.

CONTENTS

PREFACE

The writing of this book was undertaken to fill what we perceived to be a serious gap in a growing area of science, the study of herbs. For those working in research and development, access to accurate and recent information is critical. Yet scientific knowledge about the plants represented in this volume is spread throughout numerous journals, agricultural research reports, and 'in-house' publications, making it extremely difficult to retrieve, review, and use. The problem is especially acute in countries where international journals and reference aids are unavailable or too costly for libraries to maintain.

The idea of preparing a comprehensive bibliography on the major commercially significant herbs of the temperate zone was conceived by the first author several years ago while studying the adaptation of domesticated and wild herbs to marginal and mountainous land in Israel. The other authors recognized the need for a convenient reference source while doing a feasibility study on growth and production of herb and spice crops in the northeastern United States. It is our hope that this book will save others the laborious and time-consuming effort of searching scattered literature for details on the science of herbs.

This bibliography is written for professional horticulturists, chemists, food scientists, pharmacologists, administrators, researchers, students, plus others with either a technical or commercial interest in herbs and related plants. Additionally, we trust that agricultural research and development groups, food-processing companies, pharmaceutical industries, and government planners will find this reference useful as both a technical and planning aid. As a reference source, we feel it will stimulate an exchange of scientific information, allowing the researcher and student easy and complete access to pertinent work in a wide variety of subject categories related to these herbs.

Every article in this book has been painstakingly verified by reference to the original article or an abstracting source. We have tried to include all material from the body of world literature that was relevant to the theme of the book. Although we will have undoubtedly missed some sources, we hope that these omissions are neither numerous nor prominent.

James E. Simon
Alena F. Chadwick
Lyle E. Craker
October 1982

ACKNOWLEDGEMENTS

If we have met our goal of compiling an accurate and complete bibliographic reference on herbs, our success is due to the extensive help we have received from many sources. Linda Chatfield entered the references and narratives onto the computer accurately and with an eagle eye for our errors and inconsistencies. Renita Ballard programmed the filing systems necessary for precisely knowing where each reference was located. Their skill and involvement were most valuable.

The student assistants listed here treated their long and arduous task of article verification with an enthusiasm that made them real partisans in the project. We thank John Bujaucius, Christine Cassidy, Ginger Jones, Michelle Kelley, Mary Kennedy, Channing Lefebvre, Susan Radovsky, and members of the Massachusetts chapter of Alpha Zeta. Many people donated their time to assist us with library and language needs. For this we thank Jan Chadwick, May Chadwick, Janina Chadwick, Hiroyasu Toriumi, John Lydon, Zhao Shuying, and Andrea Wawra. We give special thanks to Michael Fayer and Gerald Litchfield for their assistance in computer programming.

Each chapter has been reviewed by Dennis Decoteau and to him we owe a great deal for his valuable comments. We would like to thank both the Interlibrary Loan Department of the University of Massachusetts/Amherst Library for their efficient handling of the enormous workload we generated, and the Reference Department of the Mann Library at Cornell University for their invaluable skill and patient assistance.

We also wish to express our gratitude to our publisher, especially to Patty Bernblum and James Thorpe of Archon Books, whose encouragement and concern for high standards of quality, have been much appreciated. Our appreciation also goes to the following publishers for giving their permission for us to verify references from their publications: Chemical Abstracts Service, Commonwealth Agricultural Bureaux, Oryx Press, and Macmillan Co. (for Bibliography of Agriculture).

In all such projects, there are many other people who have been involved indirectly and without whom the book might never have evolved. Dr. Paul Buck, of Cornell University, introduced James Simon to culinary herbs more than a decade ago. Thanks are also due to Drs. Dan Palevitch and Eli Putievsky, who initiated research on culinary herbs in Israel, and to Mr. Herzl Almon, who spent countless hours in the Galilee Mountains studying these plants with the first author.

Last, and most important, we are grateful for the patience, support, and encouragement of our families and friends.

INTRODUCTION

Herbs, a broad class of aromatic, dye, spice, medicinal, and other useful plants generally associated with the temperate zone, have contributed to the quality of human life for thousands of years. From ancient texts and scriptures associated with the centers of early civilizations, it is apparent that, before the modern chemical revolution, these plants served as the principal and often the only components of seasonings, flavorings, cosmetics, dyes, and medicines. While the food plants give basic subsistance for survival, the unique role of herbs and their extracts has been to provide physical psychological pleasure, the feeling of well-being and diversion from the daily tasks and necessities of life.

Traditionally, herbs have been added to food and beverages to spice up a monotonous diet, disguise or mask the odor and taste of spoiled food, and act as natural food perservatives. Thye have served as fragrances and cosmetics, applied to the body for delectation, adornment, and beautification or to appease the deities in religious rituals. Some herbs have supplied the pigments needed to create colorful fabrics and cloth. Herbs have been used to relieve pain and discomfort, to heal wounds and other human afflictions, to refresh the mind in tonics, and to bring solace and comfort through narcotic and other biological actions that induce altered states of consciousness.

Through these historical and traditional uses of herbs we gain some clues and insights into each plant's chemical constituents, biological activity, and aroma and fragrance characteristics. The long, close association between herbs and human activity, however, has resulted in an abundance of folk and ethnobotanical lore passed through the ages but of questionable accuracy. To be useful, the traditional information must be screened and reevaluated scientifically to separate the fact from the fiction, to identify and provide a true analysis of each plant's cultural and chemical potential. The problems associated with misidentification of plant material, untested biological or medicinal activities, and handed-down cultural practices are unacceptable as demands for new and improved flavoring agents, fragrances, and medicinal products increase.

The ease with which many herb plants can be grown, the limited requirements for space and care, and most important, the multitude of aromatic oils and other extractable chemicals available for use in the food, cosmetic, perfume, and pharmaceutical industries, make herbs attractive and important contributors to human life. The demand for information and informational exchange on herbs is illustrated by the many symposia, conferences, and marketing surveys on herb, spice, and medicinal plants conducted in the past few years, and by the more than seven thousand references from 1971 to 1980 that are included in this book. Unfortunately, access to recent information is often limited. Companies with a commercial interest in herbs often withhold proprietary technical information. The scientific research on herbs is published in many languages and scattered in numerous professional journals and reports. Developing countries interested in herb production frequently lack libraries with extensive scientific journal collections or reference aids necessary for information retrieval.

Poor access to scientific information on the herb plants has resulted in a proliferation of popular guides and books that rely almost completely on previously published guides, which in turn are based on other popular guides. A multitude of written materials has therefore grown from a few old, standard herbals. Commercial growers, government planners, researchers, students, and other individuals interested in the production and chemistry of herbs have generally had no quick or dependable method of gaining accurate information. A reference source providing easy access to the scientific literature will offer those in need of facts a ready and complete means of reviewing experimental data.

Our primary purpose with this bibliography is to facilitate entry into the scientific and technical literature on herbs, aromatics, and medicinal plants by both the professional and nonprofessional. To accomplish this goal, we have searched primary and secondary sources, collecting and indexing references on herbs of the temperate zone. Bowing to the extensiveness of the publications and to avoid duplication of previous bibliographies, we limited our coverage to the years 1971 through 1980 and to sixty-four plant groups.

To give a complete perspective on the plants, we have included a short, detailed description summarizing the botanical, ecological, cultural, and chemical uses of each herb. The material in these descriptions comes from the authors' personal observations and experiences, from standard reference texts, and from selected articles in the scientific literature. Subject coding of articles is based on the main or central theme of the reported work. Considerable overlap of the subject areas occurs in some articles, and since each article is listed only once the reader should always review related subject areas, which may contain additional information. It was not our objective to review each article in the bibliography critically, determining whether the herbs are correctly identified and the research accurately reported. We left this judicial evaluation to others as we concentrated on producing a comprehensive compilation of the literature of the last decade on herb, aromatic, and medicinal plants.

Citations are referenced, with only minor alterations dictated by limits of the computer, according to the format recommended in the CBE Style Manual, 3rd ed., 1973. Journal abbreviations follow those listed in the Chemical Abstracts Source Service Index. The subdivisions of the individual subject areas were modified from the Universial Decimal Classification by the British Standards Institution (B.S.1000A: 1961 F.I.D. No. 289, Abridged English Edition). When the original article was not used to verify the citation, the source from which it was checked or obtained is given after the reference.

This book allows easy entry into the scientific literature on herbs and aromatic and medicinal plants. A number of access points where users with specific or general needs can initiate their search are provided.

The book has been divided into three major parts: The Herbs, Subject Classifications, and Other References. Part 1, The Herbs, provides in alphabetical order a narrative description of each herb, giving information on plant chemistry, botany, horticulture, pharmacology, and utilization. Each herb narrative is followed by a list of bibliographical references that can be found in Part 2, Subject Classifications. The bibliographical entries in Part 2 are arranged in subject areas alphabetically by author. Each entry was placed in one of sixty-three subject categories according to the main emphasis of the particular reference. Part 3, Other References, contains the bibliographical entries for books; bibliographies; reports, conferences, and symposia; and general references. These entries were separated from Part 2 because they contain many plant species and/or cover many subject areas.

Searchers interested in individual herbs should start in Part 1 where general information and bibliographical citations for each herb are supplied. Access to specific subject areas is gained by scanning the classifications (i.e. 2.0 Botany) and subclassifications (i.e. 2.1 Biology) in Part 2. Titles are in English with the original language indicated, except for monographs where the original language has been retained.

Subject and Author Indexes are included in the book. The Subject Index references the herb narratives in Part 1, the subject categories in Part 2, and the section titles in Part 3. Common and scientific plant names, plant families, and cultivars, are listed in the Subject Index. The author index lists the bibliographic citation(s) authored by an individual or corporate source. Since references were gathered from several secondary sources, transliteration of non-Roman names may differ. When the original article was used as a source, the author was transliterated according to the CBE Style Manual, 1978. Some names like those beginning with "Mac" and "Mc" or "St." and "Saint", are separated because of constraints in computer alphabetizing.

KEYS AND ABBREVIATIONS

When the original article was not available to verify a citation, a

secondary source was used. This source is included with the reference in
Part 2. Abbreviations are listed below.

    AA = Apicultural Abstracts
    AEA = Agricultural Engineering Abstracts
    AGRICOLA = National Agricultural Library database
    ALA = Arid Lands Abstracts
    Bib.Ag. = Bibliography of Agriculture
    CA = Chemical Abstracts
    CFR = U.S. Code of Federal Regulations
    CIM = Cumulated Index Medicus
    DSA = Dairy Science Abstracts
    FA = Forestry Abstracts
    FCA = Field Crops Abstracts
    FSTA = Food Science and Technology Abstracts
    GRAI = Government Reports Announcements and Index
    HA = Horticultural Abstracts
    HELM AB-A = Helminthological Abstracts Ser. A
    HELM AB-B = Helminthological Abstracts Ser. B
    HERB AB = Herbage Abstracts
    INB = Indian National Bibliography
    IV = Index Veterinarius
    LC-S = Library of Congress Subject Catalog-Books
    MC = Monthly Catalog (U.S. Superintendent of Documents)
    NALC = National Agricultural Library Catalog
    NAR = Nutrtition Abstracts and Reviews
    NAR-A = Nutrition Abstracts and Reviews Ser. A
    NAR-B = Nutrition Abstracts and Reviews Ser. B
    NLMCC = National Library of Medicine Current Catalog
    NUC = National Union Catalog
    RAE-A = Review of Applied Entomology Ser. A
    RAE-B = Review of Applied Entomology Ser. B
    RMVM = Review of Medical and Veterinary Mycology
    RPP = Review of Plant Pathology
    SF = Soils and Fertilizers
    WA = Weed Abstracts
    WAERSA = World Agricultural Economics and Rural Sociology

Part 1: The Herbs

ANGELICA (Angelica archangelica L.)

Family: Apiaceae (Umbelliferae)

French: Angelique   Italian: Angelica (f)
German: Angelika (f);   Spanish: Angelica (f)
        Engelwurz (f)

Angelica, Angelica archangelica L., is a herbaceous, aromatic herb
native to Eurasia and commercially cultivated in Belgium, Germany,
France, and several other countries. Also known as archangel, European
angelica, garden angelica, and wild parsnip, the species has sometimes
been classified as Angelica officinalis Moench or Angelica officinalis
(Moench) Hoffm. Reaching a height of 2 meters, the plant has compound
leaves, a hollow stem, a long, thick, fleshy root, and a compound umbel
with greenish-white flowers.

The reported life zone of angelica is 5 to 19 degrees centigrade
with an annual precipitation of 0.5 to 1.3 meters and a soil pH of 4.5
to 7.3 (4.1-31). The hardy plant thrives best on rich, well drained
loam soils. Considered a biennial or short-lived perennial, the plant
dies after flowering. Cross-pollination is by bees.

Roots intended for flavoring agents are often harvested in fall of
the first year. Leaves and stalks are generally harvested in the spring
of the second year. Seeds are harvested when ripe. Under cultivation,
tops are usually pruned to prevent bloom and thus allow root growth to
continue.

The essential oils obtained from the seeds and roots by steam
distillation are known to contain d-alpha-phellandrene, alpha-pinene,
osthenole, osthole, angelicin, alpha-thujene, camphene, and numerous
other compounds (1.1-242, 1.2-112). The fruits of angelica contain a
higher percentage of oil and are rich in coumarins (1.2-113, 8.2-52,
14.1-35). Root oil is considered superior to the oils obtained from
other parts of the plant.

As flavoring agents, roots and seeds of angelica are widely used in
alcoholic liqueurs such as benedictine and chartreuse, and in gin and
vermouth. The fruit is used in herbal teas. The leaves are sometimes
blanched, boiled, and eaten in salads or as a garnish with vegetables
and meats. Leaf stalks may be candied and used in cakes and other
desserts. The essential oil of angelica is used in perfumes, creams,
soaps, salves, oils, shampoos, and cigarettes.

As a medicinal plant, angelica was considered to have 'angelic'
healing powers. It was used as a carminative, expectorant, stimulant,
stomachic, and tonic. The plant has been used as a remedy for nervous
headaches, fever, skin rashes, wounds, rheumatism, and toothaches.
Seeds have been used as a diaphoretic and diuretic. Angelica has
exhibited some antimicrobial activity (8.2-80).

Several other Angelica species have traditional medicinal uses. The
roots and rhizomes of Angelica pubescens are employed in Chinese herbal

preparations for arthritis, rheumatism, headache, toothache, abscesses, and carminative activity (11.1-10). Angelica sinensis (Oliv.) Diels is used in treatment of such acute abdominal conditions as appendicitis and against psoriasis (7.7-6, 11.1-97). This plant has been shown to induce uterine contractions and relaxation, act as a sedative, and overcome symptoms induced by vitamin-E deficiency (11.1-96, 11.1-97). Toki, the root of Angelica acutiloba (Siebold and Zucc.) Kitag, has been shown to be an effective analgesic and to have anti-inflammatory effects (7.6-206). Lahnophyllum lactone and osthol isolated from Angelica kiusiana have been shown to repel sea snails (1.8-115).

Wild angelica is the common name for Angelica sylvestris L., a small plant native to Bulgaria. The angelica tree is Aralia spinosa L., grown primarily for its ornamental value. The Japanese angelica tree, Aralia eleta Miq. is native to northwest Asia. The Chinese angelica tree, Aralia chinensis L. (Aralia sinensis Hort.), is native to China.

The Angelica species are generally recognized as safe for human consumption as natural seasonings/flavorings, and Angelica archangelica L. is also safe as a natural extractive/essential oil (21 CFR sections 182.10, 182.20 [1982]).

BIBLIOGRAPHIC REFERENCES

1.0 CHEMISTRY 1.1-19, 1.1-49, 1.1-70, 1.1-74, 1.1-137, 1.1-139, 1.1-171, 1.1-176, 1.1-231, 1.1-242, 1.1-260, 1.2-4, 1.2-80, 1.2-112, 1.2-113, 1.3-4, 1.4-6, 1.4-42, 1.4-44, 1.4-445, 2.1-47, 2.1-53, 2.1-58, 2.1-59, 2.1-68, 2.1-76, 2.1-78, 2.1-79, 2.1-82, 2.1-121, 2.1-139, 2.1-147, 2.1-151, 2.2-13, 2.2-26, 2.2-82, 2.2-85, 2.2-88, 2.2-98, 2.2-107, 2.2-130, 2.3-4, 2.3-18, 2.3-20, 2.3-22, 2.3-29, 2.3-30, 2.3-31, 2.3-40, 2.3-41, 2.3-42, 2.3-51, 2.3-52, 2.3-61, 2.3-81, 2.3-87, 2.3-92, 2.3-110, 2.3-123, 2.3-137, 2.3-142, 2.3-150, 2.3-165, 2.3-168, 2.3-171, 2.3-180, 2.3-185, 2.3-191, 2.3-194, 2.3-197, 2.3-202, 2.3-209, 2.3-211, 2.3-212, 2.3-218, 2.3-220, 2.3-222, 2.3-228, 2.3-230, 2.3-245, 2.4-26, 2.4-43, 2.4-44, 2.4-51, 2.4-93, 2.4-95, 2.4-108, 2.4-116, 2.4-133, 2.4-138, 2.5-25, 2.5-61, 2.5-69, 2.5-78, 2.5-85, 2.5-89, 2.5-91, 2.5-104, 2.6-8, 2.6-28, 2.6-59, 2.6-69, 2.7-15, 2.7-30, 2.7-47, 2.7-48, 2.7-49, 2.7-51, 2.7-82, 2.7-111, 2.8-41, 2.8-48, 2.8-66, 2.8-79, 2.8-82, 2.8-86, 2.8-88, 2.9-2, 2.9-12, 2.9-13, 2.9-31, 2.9-32, 2.9-36, 2.9-43, 2.9-65, 2.9-66, 2.9-67, 2.9-117, 2.9-124, 2.9-126, 2.9-131, 2.9-134, 2.9-135.

3.0 BIONOMICS 3.1-17, 3.1-27, 3.1-28, 3.1-31, 3.1-46, 3.1-63, 3.1-66, 3.3-4, 3.3-7, 3.3-10, 3.3-17, 3.3-34, 3.3-42, 3.3-49, 3.3-52, 3.3-55, 3.3-64, 3.3-65, 3.3-66, 3.3-67, 3.3-68, 3.3-72, 3.3-94, 3.3-103, 3.3-104, 3.3-108, 3.3-113, 3.3-116, 3.3-120, 3.3-130, 3.3-131, 3.3-142, 3.3-160, 3.3-162, 3.3-163, 3.3-176, 3.3-178, 3.3-180, 3.3-189, 3.3-193, 3.3-200, 3.3-204, 3.3-212, 3.3-220, 3.3-229, 3.4-26, 3.4-31, 3.4-32, 3.4-41, 3.4-70, 3.4-86, 3.4-88, 3.4-106, 3.4-138, 3.5-2, 3.5-15, 3.6-12.

4.0 HORTICULTURE 4.1-9, 4.1-19, 4.1-31, 4.1-76, 4.2-89, 4.2-103, 4.2-122, 4.2-132, 4.2-156, 4.2-184, 4.2-197, 4.2-210, 4.2-211, 4.2-276, 4.2-298, 4.2-320, 4.2-372, 4.3-19, 4.3-42, 4.3-85, 4.3-118, 4.3-208, 4.4-39, 4.4-108, 4.5-20, 4.5-33, 4.5-78, 4.5-131, 4.5-167, 4.5-171, 4.5-242, 4.5-243, 4.6-3, 4.6-23, 4.6-27, 4.6-28, 4.6-75, 4.6-79, 4.6-97, 4.9-10, 4.9-67, 4.9-70, 4.9-87, 4.9-88, 4.9-128, 4.9-137, 4.9-166.

5.0 PRODUCTION ECOLOGY 5.1-15, 5.1-16, 5.2-32, 5.2-37, 5.3-22, 5.3-23, 5.3-61, 5.3-63, 5.4-9, 5.4-39, 5.4-42, 5.4-57, 5.4-59, 5.4-79,

5.4-90, 5.4-94, 5.4-147, 5.4-165, 5.4-166, 5.4-167, 5.4-168, 5.5-19, 5.5-108, 5.5-123, 5.5-126, 5.5-185, 5.5-200, 5.5-217, 5.5-257, 5.5-316, 5.5-352, 5.5-369, 5.6-18, 5.6-39, 5.6-40, 5.6-41, 5.6-44, 5.6-45, 5.6-54, 5.6-64, 5.6-67, 5.6-87, 5.7-23, 5.7-78, 5.7-231, 5.8-118, 5.8-137, 5.9-42, 5.9-51.

6.0 CULINARY STUDIES 6.1-17, 6.1-94, 6.2-4, 6.2-43, 6.2-58, 6.2-71, 6.3-14, 6.3-20, 6.3-28, 6.3-36, 6.3-37, 6.3-38, 6.3-44, 6.3-47, 6.3-55, 6.3-59, 6.3-61, 6.3-62, 6.3-65, 6.4-1, 6.4-4, 6.4-6, 6.4-16, 6.4-36, 6.4-71, 6.4-73, 6.4-74, 6.4-93, 6.4-108, 6.5-21, 6.5-43, 6.5-54, 6.5-55, 6.5-91, 6.5-107, 6.5-114, 6.5-125, 6.5-134, 6.5-153.

7.0 PHARMACOLOGY 7.2-19, 7.2-29, 7.2-47, 7.2-78, 7.2-87, 7.3-10, 7.3-19, 7.3-20, 7.3-25, 7.3-49, 7.3-55, 7.3-73, 7.3-161, 7.4-12, 7.4-42, 7.4-54, 7.4-55, 7.5-7, 7.5-25, 7.5-26, 7.5-38, 7.5-40, 7.5-48, 7.5-56, 7.5-57, 7.5-73, 7.5-99, 7.5-100, 7.5-107, 7.5-110, 7.5-113, 7.5-116, 7.5-125, 7.6-24, 7.6-29, 7.6-59, 7.6-64, 7.6-87, 7.6-100, 7.6-101, 7.6-118, 7.6-122, 7.6-130, 7.6-142, 7.6-181, 7.6-185, 7.6-186, 7.6-193, 7.6-199, 7.6-206, 7.6-207, 7.7-6, 7.7-17, 7.7-25, 7.8-15, 7.8-20, 7.8-29, 7.8-30, 7.8-32, 7.8-52, 7.8-62, 7.8-64.

8.0 PERFUMERY 8.2-52, 8.2-61, 8.2-79, 8.2-80, 8.2-87, 8.2-91, 8.3-2, 8.3-58, 8.3-75, 8.3-83, 8.3-89, 8.3-106, 8.4-3.

10.0 COMMERCE 10.1-20.

ANISE (Pimpinella anisum L.)

Family: Apiaceae (Umbelliferae)

French: Anis (m)   Italian: Anice
German: Anis (m)   Spanish: Anis (m)

Anise, Pimpinella anisum L., a herbaceous annual native to the Mediterranean region and Egypt, is cultivated in Europe, Asia Minor, India, Mexico, North Africa, and the USSR. The plant reaches a height of about 0.5 meters and requires a warm and long frost-free growing season of 120 days (11.1-128). The reported life zone for anise production is 8 to 23 degrees centigrade with 0.4 to 1.7 meters of precipitation and a soil pH of 6.3 to 7.3.

Anise develops best in deep, friable soils and appears to respond favorably to nitrogen fertilization by yielding a greater quantity of high-quality fruit (4.3-158). The small white flowers bloom in midsummer, and seed maturation usually occurs one month after pollination, when the oil content is the dried fruit is about 2.5 percent. The major constituent in oil of anise is anethole. Methyl chavicol and para-methoxyphenylacetone are also present, but in smaller amounts.

While the entire plant is fragrant, it is the fruit of anise, commercially called anise seed, that has been highly valued since antiquity. The delicate fragrance is widely used for flavoring curries, breads, soups, cakes, candies, desserts, nonalcoholic beverages, and such liqueurs as anisette and arak. The volatile or essential oil, obtained by steam distillation of the crushed anise seed, is valuable in perfumery and soaps and has been used in toothpastes, mouthwashes, and skin creams (11.1-96). Anise oil is sometimes used as an adulterant in the essential oil of licorice. The oil is sometimes used as sensitizer for bleaching colors in photography (11.1-128).

As a medicinal plant, anise has been used as a carminative, antiseptic, antispasmodic, expectorant, stimulant, and stomachic. In addition, it has been used to promote lactation in nursing mothers and as a medicine against bronchitis, indigestion and lice. Oil of anise is used today as an ingredient in cough medicine and lozenges and is reported to have diuretic and diaphoretic properties (11.1-136). If ingested in sufficient quantities, anise oil may induce nausea, vomiting, seizures, and pulmonary edema (11.1-136). Contact of the concentrated oil with the skin can cause irritation (11.1-136).

Star anise, _Illicium verum_ Hook. f., of the Magnoliaceae family, is a small evergreen tree or bush, native to China. This plant, produced commercially in the People's Republic of China, is distinctly different from the herb anise and is commercially important for its star-shaped fruits that can be sold or distilled for their essential oil. The volatile oil of star anise is very much like that of anise, having a similar odor, flavor, and utilization. Anise oil is sometimes adulterated with star anise oil, fennel oil, or synthetic anethole (14.1-9). Anise-hyssop (_Agastache foeniculum_ formerly _Agastache anethiodora_), is a perennial plant of the Lamiaceae, native to the United States, which has a characteristic anise scent and flavor. Common names for this plant include Korean mint or anise mint.

Anise and oil of anise are generally regarded as safe for human consumption as a spice/natural flavoring and plant/oil extract (21 CFR sections 182.10, 182.20 [1982]).

BIBLIOGRAPHIC REFERENCES

1.0 CHEMISTRY 1.1-34, 1.1-47, 1.1-68, 1.1-119, 1.1-204, 1.1-236, 1.1-239, 1.2-26, 1.2-110, 1.3-10, 1.3-24, 1.3-43, 1.4-84, 1.5-9, 1.5-59, 1.5-65, 1.5-81, 1.5-98, 1.5-125, 1.5-126, 1.6-2, 1.6-43, 1.6-50, 1.6-56, 1.7-101, 1.7-102, 1.8-17, 1.8-43, 1.8-69, 1.8-100, 1.8-132, 1.8-151, 1.8-158, 1.8-184.

2.0 BOTANY 2.1-132, 2.1-133, 2.1-149, 2.2-122, 2.3-61, 2.3-214, 2.4-7, 2.4-93, 2.5-37, 2.5-109, 2.5-110, 2.6-75, 2.6-76, 2.6-79, 2.6-81, 2.7-16.

3.0 BIONOMICS 3.1-47, 3.2-82, 3.3-68, 3.3-82, 3.4-31, 3.4-32, 3.7-11.

4.0 HORTICULTURE 4.2-79, 4.2-117, 4.3-125, 4.3-158, 4.4-98, 4.5-132, 4.5-167, 4.6-50, 4.6-89, 4.9-81, 4.9-94, 4.9-111, 4.9-113, 4.9-136.

5.0 PRODUCTION ECOLOGY 5.1-84, 5.2-84, 5.4-1, 5.4-155, 5.5-241, 5.5-344, 5.6-89.

6.0 CULINARY STUDIES 6.1-6, 6.1-30, 6.3-9, 6.3-10, 6.3-46, 6.4-35, 6.4-36, 6.4-45, 6.4-49, 6.4-99, 6.5-31, 6.5-45, 6.5-88, 6.5-126.

7.0 PHARMACOLOGY 7.1-6, 7.3-84, 7.3-156, 7.4-5, 7.5-3, 7.5-27, 7.5-102, 7.6-57, 7.6-169, 7.7-17, 7.7-32, 7.8-12, 7.8-47, 7.8-51.

8.0 PERFUMERY 8.1-17, 8.2-34, 8.2-41, 8.2-44, 8.2-79, 8.2-85, 8.3-94, 8.3-104, 8.4-3.

6.2-61, 6.3-54, 6.4-93, 6.4-101, 6.4-102, 6.4-104, 6.4-120, 6.5-23, 6.5-41, 6.5-88, 6.5-134, 6.5-153.
   7.0 PHARMACOLOGY 7.1-5, 7.1-20, 7.1-62, 7.5-25, 7.5-26, 7.5-45, 7.5-74, 7.6-142, 7.7-21, 7.7-29, 7.7-31, 7.7-39, 7.8-12, 7.8-51.
   8.0 PERFUMERY 8.1-17, 8.1-25, 8.1-29, 8.2-20, 8.2-21, 8.2-39, 8.2-78, 8.2-85, 8.2-88, 8.2-104, 8.3-52, 8.3-75, 8.3-87, 8.3-88, 8.4-4, 8.4-5.
   9.0 NATURAL DYES AND ORNAMENTAL APPLICATIONS 9.2-9, 9.2-16.
   10.0 COMMERCE 10.1-15.

BAY LAUREL (Laurus nobilis L.)

Family: Lauraceae

French: Laurier (m)   Italian: Alloro (m); Lauro (m)
German: Lorbeer (m)   Spanish: Laurel (m)

   Bay laurel, sweet laurel, laurel, or sweet bay, Laurus nobilis L., an evergreen shrub or small tree native to the Mediterranean region and Asia Minor, has been admired for its beauty and aromatic leaves since Greek and Roman times. Currently, the plant is both cultivated and collected from the wild in many Mediterranean countries. Commercial production centers include areas of Turkey, Algeria, Belgium, France, Greece, Mexico, Morocco, Portugal, Spain, the Canary Islands, Central America, and the southern United States (11.1-128, 14.1-9).
   The reported life zone of bay laurel is 8 to 25 degrees centigrade with an annual precipitation of 0.3 to 2.2 meters and a soil pH of 4.5 to 8.3 (4.1-31). Best development occurs in full sun and deep soils. The plant can withstand several degrees of frost (14.1-4).
   The oil of laurel, accumulated in the palisade and mesophyll cells of leaves, reaches a content of 1 to 3 percent on a fresh-weight basis. There appears to be a seasonal periodicity in oil synthesis and accumulation with significant oil increases in leaves occurring during early summer and maximizing in mid-summer (1.2-117). The main constituent of the essential oil includes cineole, alpha- and beta-pinene, sabinene, l-linalool, eugenol, eugenol acetate, methyl eugenol, l-alpha-terpineol acetate, alpha-phellandrene, plus other esters and terpenoids (1.2-20, 1.2-120, 3.1-65, 14.1-9). The high concentrations of oil catechins in bay laurel leaves are maintained by drying (6.3-55).
   The dark to bright green leaves are very fragrant, and after drying they are broken, cracked, or cooked to release the characteristic aroma. Dried leaves are used as a flavoring for soups, fish, meats, stews, puddings, vinegars, and beverages. Oil of bay or oil of laurel leaves, the essential or volatile oil obtained by steam distillation, and an oleoresin have replaced dry leaves in some food preparations. Several varieties and leaf forms of bay laurel are available for growing as ornamentals. The plant can readily be sheared into distinctive shapes and is adaptable to outdoor gardens and container growth. Leaves and branches are used for garlands and wreaths.
   As a medicinal plant, bay leaves and berries have been employed against rheumatism, skin rashes, and earaches. In addition, it has been used as a stomachic, astringent, carminative, diaphoretic, stimulant, emetic, emmenagogue, abortifacient, and insect repellant. The essential oil is used by the cosmetic industry in creams, perfumes, and soaps.
   There are several other plants referred to as bay, and the essential

oils of some of these plants are also known as oil of bay. An essential
oil from mountain laurel, Umbellularia californica Nutt., an aromatic
tree native to California and Oregon in the United States, has been used
as both a condiment and as an insecticide (14.1-9). Umbellulone, a
chief constituent of this plant's essential oil, is a mucous irritant
and has shown toxicological properties (14.1-9). Safrole, another
constituent in the essential oil, has carcinogenic and hallucinogenic
activity (11.1-96). Mountain laurel (Kalmia latifolia L.), sheep laurel
(Kalmia angustifolia L.), cherry laurel (Prunus laurocerasus L.), bull
bay (Magnolia grandiflora L.), bayberry (Myrica pennsylvanica Loisel),
and loblolly bay (Gordonia lasianthus Ellis) should not be confused with
true bay laurel, as some are poisonous. Oil of bay obtained from the
bay rum tree or West Indian bay tree is actually from Pimenta racemosa
J. W. Moore.

Laurel is generally recognized as safe for human consumption as both
a spice/natural flavoring and a plant/essential oil extract (21 CFR
sections 182.10, 182.20 [1982]).

BIBLIOGRAPHIC REFERENCES

1.0 CHEMISTRY 1.1-66, 1.1-113, 1.1-147, 1.1-200, 1.1-204, 1.1-240,
1.2-8, 1.2-20, 1.2-52, 1.2-53, 1.2-70, 1.2-114, 1.2-117, 1.2-119,
1.2-120, 1.4-91, 1.4-94, 1.5-3, 1.5-7, 1.5-46, 1.5-139, 1.5-148, 1.7-17,
1.8-76, 1.8-96.

2.0 BOTANY 2.1-72, 2.1-87, 2.3-35, 2.3-67, 2.3-119, 2.3-217,
2.3-225, 2.3-226, 2.3-227, 2.4-49, 2.7-78, 2.8-22, 2.9-105.

3.0 BIONOMICS 3.1-7, 3.1-65, 3.4-26, 3.4-31, 3.4-88, 3.4-125,
3.4-136, 3.4-137.

4.0 HORTICULTURE 4.1-31, 4.2-304, 4.3-167, 4.5-31, 4.6-28, 4.7-3,
4.8-78, 4.8-92.

5.0 PRODUCTION ECOLOGY 5.1-90, 5.2-49, 5.4-9, 5.4-13, 5.4-18,
5.4-44, 5.4-82, 5.4-98, 5.4-106, 5.4-146, 5.4-148, 5.5-55, 5.7-3,
5.7-59, 5.7-137, 5.7-141, 5.8-159, 5.8-178.

6.0 CULINARY STUDIES 6.1-54, 6.1-62, 6.1-84, 6.1-87, 6.3-55,
6.4-45, 6.4-81, 6.5-41, 6.5-88, 6.5-103.

7.0 PHARMACOLOGY 7.2-60, 7.2-67, 7.5-74, 7.7-32, 7.8-5, 7.8-40,
7.8-51.

8.0 PERFUMERY 8.1-17, 8.2-36, 8.2-43, 8.2-75, 8.2-78, 8.2-79,
8.4-4.

9.0 NATURAL DYES AND ORNAMENTAL APPLICATIONS 9.2-1.

10.0 COMMERCE 10.1-13, 10.2-5.

BERGAMOT (Monarda didyma L.)

Family: Lamiaceae (Labiatae)

French: Monarde (f)   Italian: Menta (f) rosa
German: Monarde (f);   Spanish: Monarda (f)
        Goldmelisse (m)

Bergamot, bee balm, Oswego tea, scarlet monarda, red balm, American
melissa, Indian's plume, and mountain balm all generally refer to
Monarda didyma L., a plant native to North America and naturalized in
Europe. This perennial herb, sometimes reported as Monarda coccinea
Hort. and Monarda kalmiana, is called bergamot because of its pungent
lemony scent, reminiscent of bergamot oil extracted from Citrus

aurantium L. subspecies bergamia Wright et Asn. Bergamot reaches a height of about one meter and has scarlet flowers. Many cultivars and forms exist, providing a wide variety of growth habits and flower colors. The plant is adaptable to a broad range of growth environments.

The Monarda species are generally known for an extractable oil high in thymol, with smaller amounts of para-cymene, d-limonene, carvacrol, linalool, and hydrothymoquinone (11.1-136, 14.1-8). Total phenol content of the essential oil ranges from 60 to 80 percent, and chemotypes differing in concentrations of carvacrol and thymol have been identified (14.1-8).

The plant has been valued for ornamental, culinary, and medicinal uses. Young leaves are dried and used in herbal teas, such as Oswego tea, or as flavoring in wines, jellies and fruit dishes. Leaves are used in potpourris. The blossoms, appearing in dense clusters at the stem terminal, last for several weeks and make the plant an attractive addition to gardens. Bees are especially attracted to the blossoms, hence the name bee balm.

Bergamot has been used as a carminative, rubefacient, stimulant, and relaxant, and as medicine against colds. Extractable thymol from Monarda is a strong antiseptic and is used against fungi, bacteria, and such parasites as hookworm (14.1-35). The toxicological effects of thymol include gastric pain, nausea, vomiting, convulsions, and external rashes, although there have been no reports of toxic ingestions of plants or extracts of the Monarda species (11.1-136, 14.1-35).

Monarda punctata L., known as horsemint and sometimes referred to as Monarda lutea, is a perennial of North America that grows to 0.7 meters and has a strong aromatic odor because of its high concentration of thymol. The flowers have a yellow corolla and are spotted with purple flecks. Similar to Monarda didyma L. in its medicinal uses, Monarda punctata L. has also been used as a diaphoretic, diuretic, emmenagogue, and antiemetic, and as a cure for backaches. In addition, it is believed to act as a cardiac stimulant. Although once considered a potential source of thymol, horsemint was not economically competitive.

Wild bergamot, Monarda fistulosa L., is a perennial herb native to the eastern United States. The plant reaches a height of about one meter and has a wider geographical distribution than other Monarda species. Wild bergamot has been used for medicinal purposes similar to those of Monarda didyma L. and Monarda punctata L. Lemon bergamot, Monarda citriodora Cerv. (formerly classified as Monarda pectinata Nutt, or lemon mint) is an annual or short-lived perennial native to the midwestern and western United States. As the common name suggests, the plant is noted for a lemony scent, which comes from the citral and carvacrol in its volatile oil. Monarda menthaefolia, a species similar to Monarda fistulosa, is native to North America and has an essential oil high in carvacrol rather than in thymol. Bergamot mint refers to Mentha gentilis L. (red mint), Mentha citrata Ehrh., or Mentha odorata.

Monarda punctata L., horsemint, is generally recognized as safe for human consumption as a plant extract/essential oil/oleoresin (21 CFR section 182.20 [1982]).

BIBLIOGRAPHIC REFERENCES

1.0 CHEMISTRY 1.1-58, 1.2-93, 1.3-38, 1.4-6, 1.4-90, 1.6-15, 1.7-70.

2.0 BOTANY 2.1-23, 2.1-50, 2.1-100, 2.2-60, 2.6-31, 2.6-32, 2.6-33, 2.6-83, 2.8-76, 2.9-53.

3.0 BIONOMICS 3.1-20, 3.1-82, 3.2-4, 3.2-45, 3.2-58, 3.2-69, 3.2-79, 3.3-18, 3.3-19, 3.3-79, 3.3-114, 3.3-125, 3.3-180, 3.4-135, 3.5-27, 3.5-28, 3.5-29.

4.0 HORTICULTURE 4.1-65, 4.4-5, 4.4-104.

5.0 PRODUCTION ECOLOGY 5.4-34, 5.4-169, 5.5-227.
6.0 CULINARY STUDIES 6.1-15.
7.0 PHARMACOLOGY 7.5-27, 7.5-28, 7.5-108.
8.0 PERFUMERY 8.1-17, 8.2-6, 8.2-22, 8.2-25, 8.3-11, 8.3-1
8.4-8.
9.0 NATURAL DYES AND ORNAMENTAL APPLICATIONS 9.2-12.
10.0 COMMERCE 10.2-3.

BORAGE (Borago officinalis L.)

Family: Boraginaceae

French: Bourrache (f)   Italian: Borrana (f)
German: Boretsch (m)   Spanish: Borraja (f)

Borage, Borago officinalis L., an annual herb considered native
Europe, Asia Minor, northern Europe, and Africa, has blue to purpl
flowers that appear throughout the growing season. The plan
naturalized in North America. The reported life zone for borage is 5
21 degrees centigrade with an annual precipitation of 0.3 to 1.3 met
and a soil pH of 4.5 to 8.3 (4.1-31). Reaching a height of one met
borage thrives in most soil types and is adaptable to a wide range
environmental conditions.

The borage plant is cultivated primarily as a decorative ornamen
that is attractive to bees, although it is sometimes used locally
culinary and purported medicinal value. The taste of borage foliage
flowers is reminiscent of cucumber and are used in selected sala
soups, and some vegetable and meat dishes. The pubescent and pric
stems, however, make it somewhat undesirable as a culinary plant. Dr
flowers have been used in potpourris. Parts of the plant are someti
used as a flavoring agent in wine, gin, and other alcoholic
nonalcoholic beverages. Flowers are often candied and added
confections.

Traditional medicinal uses of borage include the treatment
jaundice, coughs, fever, dermatitis, and kidney ailments. It has a
been used to stimulate lactation and employed as a tonic, diaphoret
diuretic, demulcent, and emollient. Although little information
available on chemical constituents and biological activity of bor
extracts, investigations have indicated that borage conta
pyrrolizidine alkaloids, such as lasiocarpine, which have been repor
to cause liver damage and induce cancer in laboratory anim
(11.1-154).

Borago laxiflora, a purple-flowering perennial native to Corsica,
suitable as an ornamental in rock gardens (14.1-3).

BIBLIOGRAPHIC REFERENCES

1.0 CHEMISTRY 1.8-158.
2.0 BOTANY 2.1-110, 2.2-108, 2.3-183, 2.5-111, 2.6-54, 2.7-1
2.8-10, 2.8-87, 2.9-130, 2.9-134.
3.0 BIONOMICS 3.1-53, 3.3-213, 3.4-31, 3.4-32.
4.0 HORTICULTURE 4.1-31, 4.2-40, 4.2-167, 4.3-146.
5.0 PRODUCTION ECOLOGY 5.6-49.
6.0 CULINARY STUDIES 6.1-76, 6.5-101.
7.0 PHARMACOLOGY 7.2-14, 7.5-25, 7.5-26, 7.5-71.
9.0 NATURAL DYES AND ORNAMENTAL APPLICATIONS 9.2-12.

CAPER (Capparis spinosa L.)

Family: Capparidaceae

German: Kapernstrauch (m)   Spanish: Cabriola (m)
French: Capre (f)   Italian: Cappero (m)

Caper, Capparis spinosa L., a shrub native to the Mediterranean region, is a tender perennial plant with deep roots and a long stem that reaches a height of 1.5 meters. Two forms of caper exist, a spiny and a nonspiny (var. inermis)., The reported life zone of capers is 13 to 27 degrees centigrade with 0.3 to 2.6 meters annual precipitation and a soil pH of 6.3 to 8.3 (4.1-31, 14.1-4). Capers thrive best in dry soil with plenty of drainage. Detailed studies on horticultural and chemical aspects of capers have not been completed.

In commercial operations, unopened flower buds are generally collected by hand from wild plants and pickled to produce a pungent taste and smell before being used in salads and in tartar and other sauces. Recent research has indicated that extracts of capers are an effective treatment for enlarged capillaries and for improving dry skin (7.5-66). Leaves of the related species Capparis horrida are used as rubefacients. Capparis flexuosa is reported to be useful in treating general skin diseases (11.1-96). Capparis fascicularis and Capparis tumentosa are poisonous (11.1-96).

Capers are generally recognized as safe when used as spices or natural seasonings/flavorings (21 CFR section 182.10 [1982]).

BIBLIOGRAPHIC REFERENCES

1.0 CHEMISTRY 1.1-101.
2.0 BOTANY 2.8-69, 2.8-70.
3.0 BIONOMICS 3.4-7, 3.4-31, 3.4-96, 3.4-119.
4.0 HORTICULURE 4.1-31.
5.0 PRODUCTION ECOLOGY 5.4-47, 5.4-84, 5.4-110.
6.0 CULINARY STUDIES 6.1-45.
7.0 PHARMACOLOGY 7.5-66, 7.6-135.

CAPSICUM PEPPER (Capsicum species)

Family: Solanaceae

Capsicum annuum L.

French: Poivre (m) rouge   Italian: Pepe (m) di caienna
German: Roter Pfeffer (m)   Spanish: Pimenton (m); Aji (m)

Capsicum frutescens L.

French: Poivre (m) de quince   Italian: Peperane (m)
German: Paprika (m)   Spanish: Pimenton (m)

Capsicum pepper refers primarily to Capsicum annuum L. and Capsicum frutescens L., plants used in the manufacture of selected commercial products known for their pungency and color. Capsicum annuum L. is a herbaceous annual that reaches a height of one meter and has glabrous or pubescent lanceolate leaves, white flowers, and fruit that vary in length, color, and pungency depending upon the cultivar. Native to America, this plant is cultivated almost exclusively in Europe and the

United States. Capsicum frutcens L. is a short-lived perennial with
woody stems that reach a height of two meters, glabrous or pubescent
leaves, has two or more greenish-white flowers per node, and extremely
pungent fruit. This plant is cultivated in the tropics and warmer
regions of the United States.

The reported life zone for capsicum peppers is 7 to 29 degrees
centigrade with an annual precipitation of 0.3 to 4.6 meters and a soil
pH of 4.3 to 8.7 (4.1-31). Capsicum species are cold sensitive and
generally grow best in well-drained, sandy or silt-loam soil. Plantings
are established by seeding or transplanting. Flowering usually occurs
three months after planting. Hot and dry weather is desirable for fruit
ripening. Fruit is generally handpicked as it ripens, and then allowed
to dry in the sun, although artifical drying is often employed in Europe
and the United States. The fruit may be ground intact or after the
removal of seeds, placenta parts, and stalks, increasing the fruit color
and lowering the pungency (4.6-66, 4.6-67).

The level of pungency of the Capsicum species depends upon the
concentration of capsaicinoids, primarily of capsaicin, in the fruit.
Capsicum peppers are classified commercially by the concentration of
capsaicinoids, since confusion about the biological identities of some
varieties has made other methods unreliable. Paprika comes from plants
with 10 to 30 parts per million capsaicinoids, chili peppers from plants
with 30 to 600 parts per million, and red peppers from plants with 600
to 13,000 parts per million (1.5-152). The chemical composition of the
Capsicum species includes a fixed oil, pungent principles, volatile oil,
and carotenoid, mostly capsanthin, pigments (6.1-65, 2.8-45). An
oleoresin is obtained by solvent extraction. Capsicum frutescens L. is
much more pungent than Capsicum annuum L.

Capsicum species are used fresh or dried, whole or ground, and alone
or in combination with other flavoring agents. Capsicum annuum L. is
used in sweet bell peppers, paprika, pimento, and other red pepper
products. Capsicum frutescens L. is used in tabasco, tabasco sauce,
and other red chili pepper. Fruits of Capsicum annuum L., paprika
types, are widely used as coloring agents. The extracts of Capsicum
species have been reported to have antioxidant properties (11.1-126).
Paprika is derived from Capsicum annuum L. and is used primarily in the
flavoring of garnishes, pickles, meats, barbecue sauces, ketchup,
cheese, snack food, dips, chili con carne, salads, and sausages
(11.1-128). Spanish paprika is called pimento and is generally used for
coloring purposes (14.1-10). Chilies and chili pepper from cultivars of
Capsicum annuum L. and Capsicum frutescens L. are employed as a
flavoring in many foods, such as curry powder and tabasco sauce. Chili
powder is a blend of spices that includes ground chilies. Red or hot
peppers from Capsicum annuum L. and Capsicum frutescens L. are the
most pungent peppers and are used extensively in Mexican and Italian
foods. Cayenne pepper is the ground product derived from the smaller,
most pungent Capsicum species.

As a medicinal plant, the Capsicum species has been used as a
carminative, digestive irritant, stomachic, stimulant, rubefacient, and
tonic. The plants have also been used as folk remedies for dropsy,
colic, diarrhea, asthma, arthritis, muscle cramps, and toothache.
Capsicum frutescens L. has been reported to have hypoglycemic
properties (7.1-21). Prolonged contact with the skin may cause
dermatitis and blisters, while excessive consumption can cause
gastroenteritis and kidney damage (11.1-101). Paprika and cayenne
pepper may be cytotoxic to mammalian cells in vitro (7.8-25).
Consumption of red pepper may aggravate symptons of duodenal ulcers
(7.8-55). High levels of ground hot pepper have induced stomach ulcers
and cirrhosis of the liver in laboratory animals (6.1-65). Body

temperature, flow of saliva, and gastric juices may be stimulated by capsicum peppers (14.1-35).

Other Capsicum species of some importance include Capsicum chinense, Capsicum pendulum, Capsicum pubescens, and Capsicum minimum. Black and white pepper come from Piper nigrens L., of the Piperaceae family. The name pimento is sometimes used in reference to allspice, Pimento dioica (L.) Merrill, a native of the West Indies and a member of the Myrtaceae family.

Capsicum annuum L. and Capsicum frutescens L. are generally recognized as safe for human consumption as spices/natural flavorings and as plant extracts/oleoresins (21 CFR sections 182.10, 182.20 [1982]).

BIBLIOGRAPHIC REFERENCES

1.0 CHEMISTRY 1.0-0, 1.0-0, 1.1-17, 1.1-69, 1.1-80, 1.1-118, 1.1-130, 1.1-155, 1.1-139, 1.1-199, 1.1-200, 1.1-209, 1.1-237, 1.2-45, 1.2-50, 1.2-111, 1.3-1, 1.3-14, 1.3-32, 1.3-33, 1.3-35, 1.3-44, 1.4-5, 1.4-72, 1.4-102, 1.5-4, 1.5-19, 1.5-25, 1.5-46, 1.5-53, 1.5-62, 1.5-73, 1.5-80, 1.5-87, 1.5-89, 1.5-97, 1.5-101, 1.5-109, 1.5-110, 1.5-131, 1.5-152, 1.5-155, 1.6-12, 1.6-13, 1.6-26, 1.6-33, 1.6-48, 1.7-8, 1.7-35, 1.7-46, 1.7-48, 1.7-85, 1.7-137, 1.8-1, 1.8-33, 1.8-50, 1.8-59, 1.8-60, 1.8-88, 1.8-156, 1.8-157, 1.8-171, 1.8-178.

2.0 BOTANY 2.1-28, 2.1-62, 2.1-85, 2.1-89, 2.1-148, 2.2-37, 2.2-38, 2.3-14, 2.3-27, 2.3-30, 2.3-59, 2.3-65, 2.3-82, 2.3-90, 2.3-97, 2.3-97, 2.3-100, 2.3-115, 2.3-123, 2.3-134, 2.3-140, 2.3-141, 2.3-143, 2.3-146, 2.3-167, 2.3-174, 2.3-185, 2.3-188, 2.3-194, 2.3-195, 2.3-206, 2.3-229, 2.3-231, 2.3-238, 2.3-242, 2.4-19, 2.4-22, 2.4-23, 2.4-24, 2.4-25, 2.4-37, 2.4-37, 2.4-41, 2.4-62, 2.4-73, 2.4-77, 2.4-90, 2.4-112, 2.4-128, 2.4-140, 2.4-149, 2.4-150, 2.4-152, 2.4-167, 2.5-26, 2.5-40, 2.5-44, 2.5-51, 2.5-65, 2.5-92, 2.5-108, 2.6-15, 2.6-16, 2.6-20, 2.6-69, 2.6-72, 2.6-74, 2.7-7, 2.8-31, 2.8-45, 2.9-72, 2.9-78, 2.9-105, 2.9-145.

3.0 BIONOMICS 3.0-0, 3.2-2, 3.2-10, 3.2-28, 3.2-36, 3.2-51, 3.2-54, 3.3-68, 3.3-84, 3.3-85, 3.3-95, 3.3-106, 3.3-182, 3.3-198, 3.4-89, 3.5-0, 3.5-20, 3.5-21, 3.5-33, 3.5-38, 3.6-7, 3.7-9.

4.0 HORTICULTURE 4.1-2, 4.1-31, 4.1-33, 4.1-38, 4.1-53, 4.1-63, 4.1-78, 4.1-84, 4.1-85, 4.1-97, 4.1-109, 4.1-111, 4.1-114, 4.1-115, 4.2-6, 4.2-14, 4.2-15, 4.2-20, 4.2-21, 4.2-22, 4.2-28, 4.2-66, 4.2-74, 4.2-75, 4.2-77, 4.2-91, 4.2-104, 4.2-118, 4.2-135, 4.2-140, 4.2-156, 4.2-161, 4.2-162, 4.2-183, 4.2-194, 4.2-213, 4.2-238, 4.2-255, 4.2-261, 4.2-265, 4.2-278, 4.2-283, 4.2-290, 4.2-291, 4.2-298, 4.2-299, 4.2-321, 4.2-321, 4.2-343, 4.2-345, 4.2-355, 4.2-363, 4.2-364, 4.2-368, 4.2-386, 4.3-7, 4.3-8, 4.3-9, 4.3-18, 4.3-25, 4.3-71, 4.3-78, 4.3-79, 4.3-81, 4.3-103, 4.3-106, 4.3-109, 4.3-118, 4.3-141, 4.3-154, 4.3-155, 4.3-174, 4.3-177, 4.3-185, 4.3-196, 4.3-197, 4.3-205, 4.3-213, 4.3-216, 4.4-22, 4.4-26, 4.4-29, 4.4-30, 4.4-34, 4.4-50, 4.4-61, 4.4-67, 4.4-73, 4.4-97, 4.4-101, 4.5-4, 4.5-12, 4.5-15, 4.5-17, 4.5-18, 4.5-19, 4.5-35, 4.5-44, 4.5-46, 4.5-61, 4.5-64, 4.5-72, 4.5-80, 4.5-83, 4.5-86, 4.5-87, 4.5-91, 4.5-92, 4.5-93, 4.5-94, 4.5-101, 4.5-103, 4.5-106, 4.5-127, 4.5-137, 4.5-139, 4.5-145, 4.5-158, 4.5-190, 4.5-191, 4.5-221, 4.5-222, 4.5-226, 4.5-227, 4.5-228, 4.5-233, 4.5-234, 4.5-235, 4.5-247, 4.6-5, 4.6-7, 4.6-19, 4.6-25, 4.6-36, 4.6-37, 4.6-38, 4.6-41, 4.6-44, 4.6-47, 4.6-49, 4.6-63, 4.6-65, 4.6-66, 4.6-67, 4.6-86, 4.6-94, 4.7-4, 4.7-4, 4.7-8, 4.7-10, 4.7-10, 4.7-11, 4.7-12, 4.7-14, 4.8-2, 4.8-5, 4.8-17, 4.8-28, 4.8-34, 4.8-37, 4.8-38, 4.8-45, 4.8-46, 4.8-50, 4.8-60, 4.8-64, 4.8-65, 4.8-70, 4.8-76, 4.8-81, 4.8-83, 4.8-86, 4.8-88, 4.8-97, 4.8-100, 4.9-55, 4.9-105, 4.9-107, 4.9-112, 4.9-124, 4.9-138.

5.0 PRODUCTION ECOLOGY 5.1-6, 5.1-11, 5.1-17, 5.1-31, 5.1-40, 5.1-45, 5.1-58, 5.1-62, 5.1-65, 5.1-68, 5.1-86, 5.1-88, 5.1-94, 5.2-3,

5.2-11, 5.2-12, 5.2-13, 5.2-29, 5.2-30, 5.2-31, 5.2-36, 5.2-52, 5.2-67,
5.2-68, 5.2-75, 5.2-81, 5.2-89, 5.3-21, 5.3-36, 5.3-54, 5.4-8, 5.4-25,
5.4-29, 5.4-43, 5.4-64, 5.4-66, 5.4-81, 5.4-100, 5.4-109, 5.4-138,
5.4-140, 5.4-149, 5.4-151, 5.4-154, 5.4-172, 5.5-6, 5.5-8, 5.5-22,
5.5-36, 5.5-40, 5.5-48, 5.5-76, 5.5-77, 5.5-78, 5.5-80, 5.5-84, 5.5-88,
5.5-103, 5.5-119, 5.5-128, 5.5-133, 5.5-134, 5.5-137, 5.5-146, 5.5-147,
5.5-156, 5.5-158, 5.5-164, 5.5-167, 5.5-170, 5.5-171, 5.5-173, 5.5-178,
5.5-182, 5.5-191, 5.5-193, 5.5-202, 5.5-203, 5.5-204, 5.5-208, 5.5-210,
5.5-211, 5.5-212, 5.5-213, 5.5-230, 5.5-235, 5.5-244, 5.5-265, 5.5-270,
5.5-273, 5.5-279, 5.5-280, 5.5-281, 5.5-298, 5.5-301, 5.5-304, 5.5-313,
5.5-323, 5.5-333, 5.5-342, 5.5-344, 5.5-357, 5.5-373, 5.6-4, 5.6-6,
5.6-8, 5.6-13, 5.6-15, 5.6-19, 5.6-23, 5.6-24, 5.6-31, 5.6-32, 5.6-36,
5.6-37, 5.6-39, 5.6-40, 5.6-41, 5.6-47, 5.6-54, 5.6-67, 5.6-74, 5.6-85,
5.6-93, 5.7-11, 5.7-13, 5.7-13, 5.7-19, 5.7-20, 5.7-21, 5.7-23, 5.7-27,
5.7-30, 5.7-43, 5.7-46, 5.7-61, 5.7-63, 5.7-66, 5.7-79, 5.7-81, 5.7-86,
5.7-87, 5.7-88, 5.7-93, 5.7-96, 5.7-97, 5.7-98, 5.7-99, 5.7-100,
5.7-104, 5.7-110, 5.7-111, 5.7-113, 5.7-116, 5.7-131, 5.7-136, 5.7-142,
5.7-143, 5.7-144, 5.7-148, 5.7-162, 5.7-163, 5.7-167, 5.7-168, 5.7-179,
5.7-180, 5.7-182, 5.7-183, 5.7-186, 5.7-195, 5.7-195, 5.7-198, 5.7-200,
5.7-202, 5.7-208, 5.7-209, 5.7-217, 5.7-219, 5.7-220, 5.7-225, 5.7-226,
5.7-227, 5.7-228, 5.7-229, 5.7-230, 5.7-236, 5.7-239, 5.8-5, 5.8-7,
5.8-15, 5.8-18, 5.8-23, 5.8-25, 5.8-26, 5.8-28, 5.8-28, 5.8-29, 5.8-35,
5.8-36, 5.8-39, 5.8-40, 5.8-41, 5.8-41, 5.8-42, 5.8-44, 5.8-52, 5.8-58,
5.8-60, 5.8-64, 5.8-66, 5.8-69, 5.8-73, 5.8-79, 5.8-82, 5.8-83, 5.8-85,
5.8-86, 5.8-87, 5.8-88, 5.8-89, 5.8-91, 5.8-96, 5.8-98, 5.8-106,
5.8-108, 5.8-111, 5.8-115, 5.8-117, 5.8-120, 5.8-145, 5.8-146, 5.8-148,
5.8-150, 5.8-158, 5.8-163, 5.8-182, 5.8-187, 5.8-188, 5.8-189, 5.8-190,
5.9-4, 5.9-7, 5.9-10, 5.9-16, 5.9-18, 5.9-19, 5.9-19, 5.9-25, 5.9-28,
5.9-35, 5.9-53, 5.9-55.
     6.0 CULINARY STUDIES 6.1-1, 6.1-2, 6.1-4, 6.1-5, 6.1-7, 6.1-8,
6.1-9, 6.1-20, 6.1-43, 6.1-46, 6.1-48, 6.1-50, 6.1-54, 6.1-59, 6.1-65,
6.1-67, 6.1-68, 6.1-85, 6.1-87, 6.1-88, 6.1-90, 6.1-101, 6.2-16, 6.2-29,
6.2-48, 6.2-49, 6.2-56, 6.2-60, 6.2-72, 6.3-7, 6.3-11, 6.3-17, 6.3-28,
6.3-31, 6.3-32, 6.3-34, 6.3-35, 6.3-43, 6.3-45, 6.3-49, 6.3-51, 6.3-64,
6.3-70, 6.3-71, 6.3-74, 6.4-1, 6.4-2, 6.4-5, 6.4-9, 6.4-10, 6.4-11,
6.4-13, 6.4-14, 6.4-15, 6.4-17, 6.4-26, 6.4-28, 6.4-30, 6.4-31, 6.4-32,
6.4-35, 6.4-38, 6.4-39, 6.4-44, 6.4-45, 6.4-47, 6.4-54, 6.4-55, 6.4-56,
6.4-68, 6.4-69, 6.4-71, 6.4-72, 6.4-73, 6.4-74, 6.4-76, 6.4-83, 6.4-84,
6.4-87, 6.4-94, 6.4-97, 6.4-98, 6.4-99, 6.4-102, 6.4-105, 6.4-110,
6.4-116, 6.4-124, 6.5-1, 6.5-3, 6.5-7, 6.5-9, 6.5-13, 6.5-14, 6.5-29,
6.5-36, 6.5-37, 6.5-43, 6.5-45, 6.5-52, 6.5-54, 6.5-55, 6.5-65, 6.5-72,
6.5-74, 6.5-83, 6.5-86, 6.5-90, 6.5-93, 6.5-96, 6.5-103, 6.5-106,
6.5-107, 6.5-108, 6.5-117, 6.5-118, 6.5-129, 6.5-135, 6.5-136, 6.5-137,
6.5-143.
     7.0 PHARMACOLOGY 7.1-21, 7.1-40, 7.1-62, 7.3-47, 7.3-97, 7.4-23,
7.4-23, 7.5-38, 7.5-82, 7.5-107, 7.5-110, 7.5-122, 7.6-27, 7.6-43,
7.6-93, 7.6-133, 7.6-139, 7.6-145, 7.6-147, 7.6-162, 7.6-170, 7.6-183,
7.7-18, 7.7-34, 7.7-39, 7.8-6, 7.8-9, 7.8-12, 7.8-13, 7.8-24, 7.8-25,
7.8-25, 7.8-38, 7.8-41, 7.8-42, 7.8-43, 7.8-44, 7.8-51, 7.8-55.
     8.0 PERFUMERY 8.1-17, 8.2-3, 8.2-56.
     9.0 NATURAL DYES AND ORNAMENTAL APPLICATIONS 9.1-1, 9.1-2, 9.1-6,
9.2-7.
     10.0 COMMERCE 10.1-1,10.1-5,10.1-7,10.1-17,10.1-22, 10.2-4.

CARAWAY (Carum carvi L.)

Family: Apiaceae (Umbelliferae)

French: Carvi (m);   Italian: Carvi (m)
      Cumin (m) des pres
German: Kuemmel (m)   Spanish: Hinojo (m) de prado;
                                              Alcaravea (f)

Caraway, Carum carvi L., is a slender annual or biennial herb native to Asia Minor and Europe and naturalized in North America. The plant, reaching a height of approximately one meter, has long been prized as a flavoring agent or condiment. Caraway seeds are actually the mericarps of ripe fruit borne in compound umbels. Principal production areas are located in Egypt, the Netherlands, Poland, Spain, Turkey, the USSR, the United States, and Morocco.

The reported life zone for caraway is 6 to 19 degrees centigrade with an annual precipitation of 0.4 to 1.3 meters and a soil pH of 4.8 to 7.8 (4.1-31). The plant can grow in a wide range of soil conditions, but probably does best on upland well-tilled soils (14.1-29). The plant is sensitive to frost, plant competition, and mechanical injury.

Since maturity requires about 15 months, the biennial caraway is usually intercropped with vegetables that are harvested the first year. In the Netherlands, caraway is typically seeded at the end of March and blossoms during the following year, in May. For the annual variety grown in the United States, planting is done in early spring, and the plants mature in late summer. Harvesting begins when the seed color changes to brown, as shattering is a problem with late harvests. Fall planting allows caraway to be grown in regions with shorter growing seasons.

Caraway fruit contains 3 to 6 percent essential oil on a dry weight basis, with carvone being the main constituent (50 to 60 percent). Other volatile oil compounds include and to a lessor extent dihydrocarvone, dihydrocarveol, carveol, d-perillyl alcohol, and d-dihydropinol (1.5-118, 14.1-9). The oils of caraway grown in different locations differ from each other in quantity, quality, and composition. An inferior oil, caraway chaff oil, is obtained from husks and stalks and used for scenting soaps (14.1-9).

The aromatic seeds are used for flavoring breads, cakes, fish, meats, sausages, cheeses, soups,, sauerkraut, and confectionery products. Leaves can be added to salads, soups and stews. Roots of the plant can be eaten as a winter vegetable. Oils are used in liqueurs, mouthwashes, toothpastes, soaps, and perfumes. The German liqueur kummel gets its flavor from caraway oil.

As a medicinal plant, caraway has been used against indigestion, colic, and nausea. Additionally, it has been employed as an antispasmodic, appetizer, carminitive, emmenagogue, expectorant, stomachic, and stimulant. The oil is sometimes used as a flavoring agent with other medicinal preparations. Most activity of caraway comes from the volatile oil, which is a mucuous-membrane irritant (11.1-136). Oil of caraway has antibacterial properties (1.8-130). The ketone carvone and terpene limonene, ingredients of the essential oil, can cause contact dermatitis (11.1-96).

Black caraway is actually from Nigella sativa L.

Caraway is generally recognized as safe for human consumption both as a spice/natural flavoring and plant extract/essential oil (21 CFR sections 182.10, 182.20 [1982]).

BIBLIOGRAPHIC REFERENCES

1.0 CHEMISTRY 1.1-34,   1.1-50,   1.1-75,   1.1-227,   1.1-262,   1.2-6,
1.2-27,   1.2-70, 1.2-99, 1.3-24, 1.3-28, 1.3-39, 1.4-35, 1.4-77, 1.4-84,
1.5-28,   1.5-46,   1.5-67,   1.5-118,   1.6-22,   1.6-50,   1.7-34,   1.7-122,
1.7-125, 1.7-126, 1.8-130, 1.8-172.

2.0 BOTANY 2.1-119,   2.1-149,   2.2-39,   2.2-41,   2.2-75,   2.2-76,
2.2-82,   2.2-129,   2.3-7,   2.3-36,   2.3-37,   2.3-38,   2.3-66,   2.3-158,
2.3-180, 2.3-240, 2.4-5, 2.4-7, 2.4-61, 2.4-93, 2.5-37, 2.6-12,   2.6-64,
2.8-36, 2.9-31, 2.9-117, 2.9-118, 2.9-123.

3.0 BIONOMICS 3.2-42,   3.2-73,   3.2-79,   3.3-12,   3.4-31,   3.4-32,
3.7-7.

4.0 HORTICULTURE 4.1-7, 4.1-31,   4.1-95,   4.2-48,   4.2-64,   4.2-65,
4.2-79,   4.2-117,   4.2-273,   4.3-14,   4.3-94,   4.3-95, 4.3-145, 4.3-171,
4.3-178, 4.3-217, 4.4-58,   4.5-185,   4.5-187,   4.6-42,   4.8-33, 4.8-59,
4.9-4, 4.9-5, 4.9-6, 4.9-7, 4.9-161.

5.0 PRODUCTION ECOLOGY 5.1-70, 5.1-71,   5.4-79,   5.4-116,   5.4-136,
5.4-166,   5.5-31,   5.5-64,   5.5-75,   5.5-116,   5.5-241, 5.6-89, 5.7-23,
5.7-72, 5.7-112, 5.7-211, 5.8-57, 5.8-137, 5.8-164, 5.9-50.

6.0 CULINARY STUDIES 6.1-14,   6.1-21,   6.1-64,   6.1-87,   6.4-35,
6.4-45, 6.4-111, 6.5-12, 6.5-52, 6.5-97, 6.5-138.

7.0 PHARMACOLOGY 7.3-93, 7.4-12,   7.4-54,   7.5-2,   7.5-22,   7.5-23,
7.5-25, 7.5-26, 7.6-52, 7.7-17, 7.8-51.

8.0 PERFUMERY 8.2-31,   8.2-41,   8.2-44,   8.2-77,   8.2-79,   8.3-83,
8.4-4.

10.0 COMMERCE 10.2-4.

CATNIP (Nepeta cataria L.)

Family: Lamiaceae (Labiatae)

French: Cataire (f); Herbe a chat   Italian: Erba dei gatti (f)
German: Katzenminze (f)   Spanish: Gatera (f); Calamento (m);
                                            Calaminta (f)

Catnip, Nepeta cataria L., a perennial herb native to Eurasia and
widely naturalized in North America, is well known as an attractant and
behavior modifying drug for both domestic and wild members of the cat
family.   Indeed, the species name cataria is from the latin word for
cat, indicating an early recognition of the special attraction of cats
to catnip (14.1-3). This erect-growing plant, which can reach a height
of one meter, has pubescent leaves and a spike-like inflorescent with
purple-spotted white flowers.

The reported life zone of catnip is 7 to 19 degrees centigrade with
an annual precipitation of 0.4 to 1.3 meters and a soil pH of 4.9 to 7.5
(4.1-31). The plant thrives in well-drained soils and is commonly
considered a weed when growing in gardens of the northeastern United
States. The flowering tops, attractive to bees, are harvested during
full bloom and allowed to dry in the shade for preservation of color and
fragrance. When harvesting catnip for cats, all parts of the plant are
utilized.

Catnip contains volatile oils, sterols, acids, and tannins.
Specific chemical compounds include nepetalactone, nepetalic acid,
nepetalic anhydride, alpha- and beta-citral, limonene, dispentine,
geraniol, citronella, nerol, beta-caryophyllene, and valeric acid
(11.1-138, 14.1-8). Although now replaced by less expensive synthetic

products, the oil from catnip has been used as an attractant scent for baiting wild animal traps (14.1-8, 14.1-29).

Catnip has been used for ornamental and culinary purposes and as a domestic folk-medicine remedy. The leaves and shoots have been used in sauces, soups, and stews. Leaves and flowers are used in herbal teas. Medicinally, catnip has been used as an antispasmodic, carminative, diaphoretic, emmenagogue, nervine, stomachic, stimulant, and mild sedative. The herb has also found use in treatment of diarrhea, colic, the common cold, and cancer (16.1-16). Extract of catnip is reported to exhibit juvenile hormone activity (1.8-162). Smoking catnip can produce a euphoria and visual hallucinations thought to be caused by the nepetalactone content (6.8-54, 11.1-96). Catnip, in combination with Eugenia caryophyllata, and Sassafras albidum, has been used as poultice for aching teeth in the American Ozark Mountains (11.1-96).

Several other Nepeta species are commercially available for use as ornamental and ground-cover plants.

BIBLIOGRAPHIC REFERENCES

1.0 CHEMISTRY 1.1-142, 1.1-229, 1.1-241, 1.2-82, 1.2-92, 1.4-23, 1.4-29, 1.5-120, 1.5-154, 1.8-125, 1.8-162, 1.8-173.
2.0 BOTANY 2.1-57, 2.1-150, 2.4-31, 2.4-66, 2.4-97, 2.6-83, 2.7-86, 2.9-41, 2.9-54, 2.9-61.
3.0 BIONOMICS 3.1-17, 3.1-82, 3.2-40, 3.2-43, 3.2-55, 3.3-61, 3.3-79, 3.3-109, 3.3-136, 3.3-190, 3.4-31, 3.4-32, 3.4-97, 3.7-13.
4.0 HORTICULTURE 4.1-31, 4.2-11, 4.3-101, 4.5-104, 4.7-2, 4.9-49, 4.9-132.
5.0 PRODUCTION ECOLOGY 5.4-150, 5.7-45, 5.8-80, 5.9-24.
6.0 CULINARY STUDIES 6.4-93, 6.8-54.
7.0 PHARMACOLOGY 7.1-59, 7.4-21, 7.4-22, 7.5-37, 7.5-103, 7.5-108, 7.6-65, 7.6-66, 7.6-73, 7.6-189, 7.8-54.
8.0 PERFUMERY 8.1-16.
9.0 NATURAL DYES AND ORNAMENTAL APPLICATIONS 9.2-12.

CELERY (Apium graveolens L.)

Family: Apiaceae (Umbelliferae)

French: Celeri (m);   Italian: Sedano (m)
        Celeri (m) a couper
German: Sellerie (m);   Spanish: Apio (m) para cortar
        Schnittselerie

Celery, Apium graveolens L., is a biennial plant native to North America, South America, and Eurasia. Although extensively cultivated as a vegetable, the dried ripe fruit are produced as a spice in the People's Republic of China, France, India, Italy, Pakistan, the United States, and Great Britain (11.1-75, 11.1-76).

The reported life zone of celery is 5 to 27 degrees centigrade with an annual precipitation of 0.3 to 4.6 meters and a soil pH of 4.2 to 8.3 (4.1-31). The plants thrive in deep sandy or loamy soils but require irrigation because of their shallow root systems. Plants are seeded or transplanted, and the compound white umbels, cross-pollinated by insects, are developed in the second year. Harvested plants are allowed to dry and are then threshed to remove seeds.

An essential oil is obtained from seeds or seed chaff by a process of crushing and steam distillation. The essential oil of celery seed includes d-limonene, selinene, sesquiterpene alcohols, sedanolide, and sedanonic anhydride (14.1-9). A fixed oil includes the fatty acids petroselinic, oleic, linoleic, myristic, palmitic, palmitoleic, stearic, and myristoleic (1.2-6). Oil of celery seed is sometimes adulterated with celery chaff oil or di-limonene and other terpenes from less expensive essential oils.

The brown, characteristically aromatic, pungent seed is used in salads, soups, stews, vegetable dishes, meat dishes, and celery salt (a mixture of table salt and ground celery seed). The essential oil and oleoresin of celery seed are used as a flavoring or fragrance in liqueurs, perfumes, and cosmetics, such as soaps, creams, and lotions. The odor is produced by the anhydrides, sedanoid, and sedanomic (11.1-136). As a vegetable, celery is cultivated for the green and blanched leaf stalks (Apium graveolens L. var. dulce [Mill.] Pers.), or, to a limited extent, the edible thickened roots and crowns (Apium graveolens L. var. rapaceum [Mill.] Gaud.-Beaup).

As a medicinal plant, celery has been used as an aphrodisiac, anthelmintic, antispasmodic, carminative, diuretic, emmenagogue, laxative, sedative, stimulant, and tonic. The plant is used against asthma, bronchitis, and rheumatism. Large amounts of the volatile oil can produce sedation and irritation that may be responsible for attributed antispasmodic properties. Celery is known to cause photodermatitis and contact dermatitis (8.2-79, 11.1-96). Celery has also shown hypoglycemic activity (7.1-21, 11.1-96). Myristicin found in the seed is chemically related to known carcinogens (7.8-12). Wild celery usually refers to Vallisneria spiralis L., an aquatic perennial plant of the Hydrocharitaceae family (14.1-3).

Celery seed is generally recognized as safe for human consumption as a spice, natural seasoning, and plant extract/essential oil (21 CFR sections 182.10, 182.20 [1982]).

BIBLIOGRAPHIC REFERENCES

1.0 CHEMISTRY 1.1-7, 1.1-84, 1.1-86, 1.1-87, 1.1-88, 1.1-89, 1.1-90, 1.1-91, 1.1-114, 1.1-171, 1.1-177, 1.1-200, 1.1-223, 1.2-6, 1.2-8, 1.2-17, 1.2-30, 1.2-31, 1.5-23, 1.5-24, 1.6-24, 1.7-51, 1.7-79, 1.8-72.

2.0 BOTANY 2.1-75, 2.2-5, 2.2-6, 2.2-7, 2.2-20, 2.2-43, 2.2-62, 2.2-65, 2.2-66, 2.2-67, 2.2-68, 2.2-69, 2.2-73, 2.2-74, 2.2-104, 2.2-105, 2.2-110, 2.2-111, 2.2-112, 2.2-113, 2.2-114, 2.4-107, 2.9-28, 2.9-29, 2.9-31, 2.9-43, 2.9-75.

3.0 BIONOMICS 3.2-3, 3.3-82, 3.4-32, 3.5-18.

4.0 HORTICULTURE 4.1-31, 4.1-67, 4.1-110, 4.2-114, 4.2-117, 4.2-166, 4.2-176, 4.2-177, 4.2-178, 4.2-179, 4.2-180, 4.2-181, 4.2-198, 4.2-310, 4.3-11, 4.3-12, 4.3-108, 4.4-23, 4.4-102, 4.5-133, 4.5-134, 4.6-55, 4.6-79, 4.6-82, 4.8-42.

5.0 PRODUCTION ECOLOGY 5.1-48, 5.1-82, 5.5-144, 5.5-231, 5.5-232, 5.5-329, 5.5-375, 5.6-11, 5.7-35, 5.8-70, 5.8-71, 5.8-169.

6.0 CULINARY STUDIES 6.1-31, 6.1-50, 6.1-87, 6.2-43, 6.3-12, 6.3-68, 6.4-45, 6.4-90, 6.4-99, 6.4-104, 6.5-29, 6.5-41, 6.5-112, 6.5-125, 6.5-143.

7.0 PHARMACOLOGY 7.1-21, 7.5-25, 7.5-26, 7.5-27, 7.5-53, 7.5-74, 7.7-17, 7.8-12, 7.8-51.

8.0 PERFUMERY 8.1-17, 8.2-41, 8.2-42, 8.2-79, 8.4-4.

10.0 COMMERCE 10.1-15, 10.1-18.

CHAMOMILE

Family: Asteraceae (Compositae)

ROMAN CHAMOMILE (Chamaemelum nobile [L.] All.)
French: Chamomile (f)   Italian: Camomilla romana (f)
German: Gartenkamille (f)   Spanish: Manzanilla romana (f)

GERMAN CHAMOMILE (Matricaria recutita L.)
French: Matricaire camomille (f)   Italian: Camomilla nostrale (f)
German: Kamille (f)   Spanish: Matricaria species

Roman chamomile, Chamaemelum nobile (L.) All., and German chamomile, Matricaria recutita, are two different species of plant commonly known as the same herb.

Formerly classified as Anthemis nobilis L. and called English or Russian chamomile, Roman chamomile is a creeping, herbaceous perennial native to western Europe and North Africa. Reaching a height of about 0.3 meters, the aromatic plant is characterized by downy stems and yellow-disc, white-ray flowers that appear in late spring or early July. Roman chamomile is cultivated in Europe, especially in Belgium, France, and England.

German chamomile, Matricaria recutita L., is also known as matricaria, wild chamomile, Hungarian chamomile, and sweet false chamomile. This many-branched, erect-growing annual, formerly classified as Matricaria chamomilla L., reaches a height of about 0.3 meter and has yellow disc white ray flowers. Cultivated in Germany, Hungary, Russia, and several other European countries, German chamomile is native to Europe and western Asia and naturalized in North America.

The reported life zone for the chamomiles is 7 to 26 degrees centigrade with an annual precipitation of 0.4 to 1.4 meters and a soil pH of 6.5 to 8.0 (Roman) or 4.8 to 8.3 (German) (4.1-31). Seeded or transplanted into the field for cultivation, Roman chamomile requires full sun but will grow in most soils having good drainage. Cultivated from seed, German chamomile grows in poor, clay soils. With Roman chamomile, the flower heads are hand picked and dried at the height of bloom about five times each growing season. The short, two-month growing season of German chamomile allows it to be interplanted with other biennial herbs or planted as an early or late crop.

The essential oil of Roman chamomile consists chiefly of chamazulene, angelic acid, tiglic acid, and several sesquiterpene lactones (1.4-34, 14.1-10). Other constituents of Roman chamomile include anthemic acid, athesterol, anthemene, resin and tannin (14.1-35). The essential oil of German chamomile contains chamazulene, alpha-bisabolol, alpha-bisabololoxides A and B, spathulenol and farnesene (1.7-121, 2.3-74). Other constituents of German chamomile include a volatile oil, anthemic acid, antheminidine, tannin, matricarin, and apigenin (11.1-136, 14.1-35).

Dried flowers from Roman and German chamomile are employed in herbal teas. Flower heads of Roman chamomile have been used in the manufacture of herb beers (11.1-49). The essential oils are used as agents in alcoholic beverages, confections, desserts, perfumes, and cosmetics. Roman chamomile is often grown as a ground cover or as an ornamental in flower gardens.

As medicinal plants, the chamomiles have been traditionally considered to be antispasmodics, carminatives, diaphoretics, emmenagogues, sedatives, and stomachics. The plants have been used as bitters, tonics, insect repellents, and as a folk remedies against asthma, colic, fevers, inflammations, and cancer (14.1-13). German chamomile has been used to induce sleep and as an anthelmintic. Roman chamomile is a pharmaceutical aromatic bitter, and chamazulene, obtained from German chamomile, is a pharmaceutical anti-inflammatory and antipyretic agent (14.1-35). Extracts of Roman chamomile have shown antitumor activity and extracts of German chamomile are reported to have antiseptic, antibacterial, and antifungal properties (1.4-34, 1.8-13, 7.2-19). Chamomile in tea may cause toxic reactions in individuals sensitive to ragweed or allergens (11.1-96). The chamomiles can also cause contact dermititis (11.1-96)

Roman and German chamomile are generally recognized as safe for human consumption as natural seasonings/flavorings and as plant extracts/essential oils from the flowers (21 CFR sections 182.10, 182.20 [1982]).

BIBLIOGRAPHIC REFERENCES

1.0 CHEMISTRY 1.1-1, 1.1-21, 1.1-31, 1.1-71, 1.1-73, 1.1-108, 1.1-143, 1.1-162, 1.1-177, 1.1-187, 1.2-28, 1.2-86, 1.2-90, 1.2-97, 1.2-120, 1.3-28, 1.4-20, 1.4-34, 1.4-96, 1.4-100, 1.5-26, 1.5-34, 1.5-55, 1.5-102, 1.5-108, 1.5-124, 1.5-150, 1.6-8, 1.6-43, 1.6-49, 1.6-51, 1.7-50, 1.7-75, 1.7-120, 1.7-121, 1.7-127, 1.7-139, 1.8-2, 1.8-13, 1.8-42, 1.8-44, 1.8-114, 1.8-125, 1.8-140, 1.8-159, 1.8-160.

2.0 BOTANY 2.1-4, 2.1-5, 2.1-21, 2.1-38, 2.1-42, 2.1-71, 2.1-83, 2.1-91, 2.1-92, 2.1-107, 2.1-123, 2.1-144, 2.2-29, 2.3-60, 2.3-70, 2.3-74, 2.3-211, 2.3-228, 2.3-233, 2.4-43, 2.4-135, 2.5-21, 2.5-26, 2.5-58, 2.5-82, 2.5-88, 2.5-104, 2.5-115, 2.7-51, 2.7-69, 2.7-70, 2.7-92, 2.7-107, 2.7-110, 2.8-20, 2.9-73, 2.9-102, 2.9-107, 2.9-137.

3.0 BIONOMICS 3.2-53, 3.3-107, 3.3-187, 3.4-31, 3.4-32, 3.4-37, 3.4-40, 3.4-55, 3.4-63, 3.4-100, 3.5-29, 3.6-0.

4.0 HORTICULTURE 4.1-23, 4.1-31, 4.1-80, 4.2-0, 4.2-70, 4.2-110, 4.2-111, 4.2-112, 4.2-118, 4.2-162, 4.2-201, 4.2-300, 4.2-315, 4.2-319, 4.2-334, 4.2-335, 4.2-355, 4.2-358, 4.2-370, 4.3-26, 4.3-27, 4.3-36, 4.3-95, 4.3-99, 4.3-111, 4.3-151, 4.3-189, 4.3-203, 4.3-220, 4.4-54, 4.4-88, 4.4-103, 4.5-57, 4.5-68, 4.5-97, 4.5-167, 4.5-187, 4.5-190, 4.5-201, 4.5-220, 4.5-244, 4.6-15, 4.6-32, 4.6-33, 4.6-40, 4.6-50, 4.6-91, 4.6-92, 4.6-96, 4.7-15, 4.8-41, 4.8-90, 4.9-34, 4.9-45, 4.9-112, 4.9-124, 4.9-138, 4.9-154, 4.9-170, 4.9-171, 4.9-172, 4.9-173.

5.0 PRODUCTION ECOLOGY 5.2-60, 5.2-69, 5.2-70, 5.3-4, 5.3-16, 5.3-25, 5.3-27, 5.3-28, 5.4-50, 5.4-51, 5.4-52, 5.4-53, 5.4-99, 5.4-135, 5.4-151, 5.5-344, 5.5-372, 5.6-66, 5.6-87, 5.7-112, 5.7-151, 5.7-205, 5.7-223, 5.8-92, 5.8-94, 5.8-117, 5.8-121, 5.8-125, 5.8-137, 5.8-151, 5.8-154, 5.8-181, 5.8-183, 5.9-36, 5.9-39, 5.9-40.

6.0 CULINARY STUDIES 6.1-63, 6.1-92, 6.3-18, 6.4-99, 6.5-16, 6.5-26, 6.5-31, 6.5-49, 6.5-109, 6.5-111, 6.5-127.

7.0 PHARMACOLOGY 7.1-14, 7.1-25, 7.1-27, 7.1-32, 7.1-56, 7.1-59, 7.1-60, 7.2-19, 7.2-30, 7.2-82, 7.2-86, 7.3-39, 7.3-44, 7.3-84, 7.3-94, 7.3-149, 7.3-150, 7.4-8, 7.4-11, 7.4-12, 7.4-26, 7.4-30, 7.5-4, 7.5-7, 7.5-8, 7.5-13, 7.5-32, 7.5-74, 7.5-108, 7.6-40, 7.6-52, 7.6-57, 7.6-60, 7.6-81, 7.6-82, 7.6-92, 7.6-200, 7.7-32, 7.8-23, 7.8-34, 7.8-40, 7.8-45.

8.0 PERFUMERY 8.1-17, 8.1-24, 8.2-1, 8.2-53, 8.2-79, 8.4-1, 8.4-3, 8.4-4.

10.0 COMMERCE 10.1-20, 10.2-12.

CHERVIL (Anthriscus cerefolium Hoffm.)

Family: Apiaceae (Umbelliferae)

French: Cerfeuil (m)   Italian: Cerfoglio (m)
German: Kerbel (m)   Spanish: Perifollo (m)

Chervil, Anthriscus cerefolium Hoffm., Scandix cerefolium L., or Cerefolium cerefolium Britt., is native to the Caucasus Mountains, south Russia, and western Asia, and is naturalized in the United States. Known as garden chervil, salad chervil, gourmet parsley, and French parsley, this small, hardy plant reaches a height of 0.5 meters. An annual, chervil develops pinnate leaves with deeply cut ovate segments, producing a foliage that is very finely divided in appearance (14.1-4). Small white flowers are borne in compound umbels. The herb is produced commercially in France and the western United States.

The reported life zone of chervil is 7 to 21 degrees centigrade with an annual precipitation of 0.5 to 1.3 meters and a soil pH of 5.0 to 8.2 (4.1-31). The plant grows best in cool, shaded or partially shaded locations on well-drained soils. It is usually grown as a spring or autumn crop because high temperatures cause rapid bolting. The leaves can be harvested 8 to 12 weeks after seeding and must be carefully dried to prevent significant loss of flavor.

Fresh leaves of chervil are parsley-flavored with an anise-like fragrance. The leaves, used to intensify the flavor of other herbs, are employed in salads, soups, garnishes, meats, fish, sauces, eggs, and vinegar. Chervil is perhaps best noted for use in combination with herbs such as basil, chives, and tarragon. The collective blend is called "fine herbes" and used in French cuisine. As a kitchen spice, chervil is often substituted for French tarragon where the latter is unavailable.

As a medicinal plant, chervil is considered a diuretic, expectorant, and stimulant. It has been used against eczema and to lower blood pressure. Another Anthriscus species, hedge parsley, is suspected of causing allergic reactions, such as hay fever, resulting from contact with the flowers (11.1-96).

Chaerophyllum bulbosum L., called chervil or tuberous chervil, is a hardy biennial that produces an edible root. A member of the Apiaceae family, this plant is native to southern Europe. Its culture is similar to that of carrots, and it produces an externally grey or blackish root that has a yellowish-white, sweet-tasting flesh. The roots are used as a vegetable.

Chervil is generally recognized as safe for human consumption as a natural seasoning/flavoring and plant extract (21 CFR sections 182.10, 182.20 [1982]).

BIBLIOGRAPHIC REFERENCES

1.0 CHEMISTRY 1.1-43, 1.3-49.

2.0 BOTANY 2.9-117.

3.0 BIONOMICS 3.1-8, 3.3-171, 3.3-213, 3.4-31, 3.4-32, 3.5-2, 3.7-13.

4.0 HORTICULTURE 4.1-31, 4.3-146, 4.5-81, 4.8-99.

5.0 PRODUCTION ECOLOGY 5.4-28, 5.4-92, 5.5-71, 5.5-72, 5.5-73, 5.6-60, 5.6-61, 5.6-62, 5.7-126, 5.8-99, 5.8-137.

6.0 CULINARY STUDIES 6.2-14, 6.5-41, 6.5-101, 6.5-105.

7.0 PHARMACOLOGY 7.5-27, 7.7-17, 7.8-51.

10.0 COMMERCE 10.1-15.

CHICORY (Cichorium intybus L.)

Family: Asteraceae (Compositae)

Chicory
French: Chicoree (f)   Italian: Cicoria (f)
German: Zichorienwurzel (f)   Spanish: Achichoria (f) de raiz

Witloof Chicory
French: Chicoree-witloof (m)   Italian: Cicoria (f)
German: Zichoriensalat (m)   Spanish: Achicoria (f) de
                                                 barba gruesa;
                                                 Achicoria (f) de Bruselas

Chicory, Cichorium intybus L., is a perennial herb native to Europe, North Africa, and Western Asia, and naturalized in North America. Also known as common chicory, blue-sailor's succory, and witloof, this long-time cultivated plant reaches a height of 1 to 2 meters and has bright blue flowers. Several distinct cultivars of chicory exist, developed from breeding programs designed to meet the different commercial uses of the plant. Centers of chicory production are located in Belgium, Holland, France, and the United States.

The reported life zone of chicory is 6 to 27 degrees centigrade with 0.3 to 4 meters of annual precipitation and a soil pH of 4.5 to 8.3 (4.1-31). The plant does best in cool weather and calcareous soils. Cultivated chicory is planted in the spring and the harvested or harvested and crowns are harvested in autumn. The harvested material is stored until winter and then placed in an environment conducive to "forcing" growth in the off-season. A blanched, highly desirable, creamy-colored head develops in 2 to 4 weeks.

Chicory is a source of the natural taste modifier maltol, known to intensify the flavor of sugar (11.1-96). The crop is also a potential source of fructose for the flavor industry (5.1-10, 11.1-96). The fresh roots contain large amounts of inulin , vitamins A and C, chicoric acid, esculitin, esculin, chichociim, and several other bitter compounds (1.1-72, 1.1-203, 11.1-136).

Cultivars of chicory developed for use as coffee substitutes have large, thickened roots that are externally yellow and internally white. The roots of these plants are dried, chopped, roasted, and ground for addition to coffee, imparting a strong, bitter flavor. Cultivars of chicory developed for use in salads have more and larger leaves than other cultivars. Salad leaves are often blanched in the field to reduce possible bitterness. Young and tender roots can be boiled and eaten as a vegetable. Chicory extracts are used in alcoholic and nonalcoholic beverages.

As a medicinal plant, chicory root has been used as a digestive aid, diuretic, laxative, tonic, and mild sedative. The root has also been used against jaundice, inflammations, warts, tumors, and cancer (14.1-13). Chicory was thought to purify the liver and spleen. Extracts from the roots have been shown to affect heart tissue isolated from toad (7.5-96).

Cichorium endiva L., commonly called endive, is cultivated as a salad plant.

Chicory is generally recognized as safe for human consumption when used as a plant extract (21 CFR section 182.20 [1982]).

BIBLIOGRAPHIC REFERENCES

1.0 CHEMISTRY 1.1-72, 1.1-203, 1.4-74, 1.7-124, 1.8-172.
2.0 BOTANY 2.1-13, 2.1-86, 2.1-103, 2.1-106, 2.1-142, 2.2-100, 2.3-18, 2.3-102, 2.3-103, 2.3-104, 2.3-144, 2.3-145, 2.3-149, 2.3-150, 2.3-153, 2.3-232, 2.4-40, 2.4-88, 2.4-116, 2.4-133, 2.5-34, 2.5-74, 2.5-79, 2.5-80, 2.8-21, 2.9-114.
3.0 BIONOMICS 3.3-29, 3.4-31, 3.4-32.
4.0 HORTICULTURE 4.1-11, 4.1-25, 4.1-31, 4.1-32, 4.1-49, 4.1-66, 4.1-89, 4.1-90, 4.1-91, 4.2-60, 4.2-119, 4.2-173, 4.2-239, 4.2-240, 4.2-241, 4.2-263, 4.2-311, 4.2-390, 4.3-132, 4.3-148, 4.3-152, 4.3-161, 4.3-214, 4.4-18, 4.4-19, 4.4-31, 4.4-57, 4.4-84, 4.4-107, 4.5-5, 4.5-240, 4.6-6, 4.6-13, 4.6-26, 4.6-45, 4.6-51, 4.8-3, 4.8-10, 4.8-11, 4.8-12, 4.8-22, 4.8-23, 4.8-30, 4.8-32, 4.8-44, 4.8-47, 4.8-48, 4.8-51, 4.8-66, 4.8-67, 4.8-68, 4.8-69, 4.8-74, 4.8-91, 4.8-94, 4.9-20, 4.9-21, 4.9-64, 4.9-65, 4.9-117, 4.9-118, 4.9-120, 4.9-126, 4.9-127, 4.9-128, 4.9-140, 4.9-181, 4.9-182.
5.0 PRODUCTION ECOLOGY 5.1-10, 5.1-91, 5.1-92, 5.2-7, 5.2-21, 5.4-141, 5.5-14, 5.5-61, 5.5-219, 5.5-247, 5.5-259, 5.5-300, 5.5-335, 5.5-355, 5.5-360, 5.5-361, 5.5-362, 5.5-363, 5.5-364, 5.6-10, 5.6-90, 5.7-47, 5.7-62, 5.7-149, 5.8-30, 5.8-45, 5.8-95, 5.8-126, 5.8-127, 5.8-128, 5.8-129, 5.8-175.
6.0 CULINARY STUDIES 6.2-13, 6.2-57, 6.3-2, 6.3-19, 6.3-24, 6.3-39, 6.3-59, 6.3-69, 6.4-6, 6.4-58, 6.4-60, 6.4-67, 6.4-100, 6.5-18, 6.5-27, 6.5-28, 6.5-75, 6.5-132, 6.5-145, 6.5-150.
7.0 PHARMACOLOGY 7.5-6, 7.5-8, 7.5-88, 7.5-96, 7.7-27, 7.8-40.

CLARY SAGE (Salvia sclarea L.)

Family: Lamiaceae (Labiatae)

French: Toute-bonne (f);   Italian: Sclarea (f)
       Sauge (f) sclaree
German: Scharlei (m)   Spanish: Hierba (f) de los ojos

Clary sage, Salvia sclarea L., is an erect herbaceous biennial, native to southern Europe and the Mediterranean region. Also known as clary, clear eye, eyebright, clarywort, and muscatel sage, the species is widely cultivated throughout the temperate regions of the world. Principal production centers include France, the USSR and Hungary (14.1-8). Reaching a height of 1 to 1.5 meters during flowering, the plant is characterized by broad-ovate, green, pubescent leaves, and the economically important lilac to blue-colored flowers. The name sclarea is Latin for clear or bright, in reference to the color of the flowers, and the name "clear eye" refers to the traditional use of the plant for clearing the eyes (14.1-3).

The reported life zone of clary is 7 to 19 degrees centigrade with an annual precipitation of 0.7 to 2.6 meters and a soil pH of 4.8 to 7.5 (4.1-31). The plant grows in dry calcareous soils of high elevation, and is sensitive to poorly drained soils. Rich, excessively fertilized soils produce tall plants with few flowers and low yields.

The biennial is sometimes cultivated as a short-lived perennial (up to six years) by fall planting, which satisfies the flower-inducing chill requirements the first winter. Flowers are harvested at the end of the blooming period and steam-distilled immediately to minimize volatilization of essential oil. Occasionally, two harvests a year are obtained.

The yield of essential oil ranges from 0.1 to 0.34 percent of fresh material, depending upon environmental conditions and plant genotype. The essential oil, known as clary oil or muscatel sage, contains l-linalyl acetate, linalool, and nerol (8.4-4, 14.1-8). The concrete and absolute of clary sage include linalyl acetate, linalool, sclareol, and sesquiterpenes (14.1-8).

Fresh and dried leaves of clary sage have been used as flavoring agents in adulteration of wine, in substitution for hops, and in adulteration of digitalis (11.1-50). The flowers are used in herbal teas, sachets, potpourris, and beverages. The essential oil is used as a fragrance and fixative in the perfume industry. The concrete and absolute, often blended with lavender, jasmine, or other scents, are used in soaps, detergents, creams, powders, perfumes, and lotions (14.1-8). Clary sage is also grown as an ornamental.

As a medicinal plant, clary sage is known for the mucilaginous seeds used to clear the sight and reduce inflammation of the eye. The plant has reportedly been used for its antispasmodic, astringent, and carminative properties. Clary sage has been used in treatment of cancer (14.1-16). The plant displays lecithinic properties (11.1-96), and the seed contains anti-Tn-specific agglutinins (7.2-4, 7.2-5). Antispasmodic activity is probably attributable the presence of nerol (8.2-69).

Wild clary or vervain are the common terms for Salvia verbenaca L., an erect perennial, native to southern and western Europe, Israel, and Syria (14.1-4). The plant has medicinal uses similar to those of clary sage (11.1-50).

Clary sage is generally recognized as safe for human consumption as both a natural seasoning/flavoring and as a plant extract/essential oil (21 CFR sections 182.10, 182.20 [1982]).

BIBLIOGRAPHIC REFERENCES

1.0 CHEMISTRY 1.1-175, 1.1-191, 1.1-213, 1.2-96, 1.3-23, 1.5-111, 1.5-144, 1.6-19, 1.7-140, 1.8-177.

2.0 BOTANY 2.1-102, 2.1-121, 2.1-140, 2.2-2, 2.2-19, 2.2-42, 2.3-43, 2.3-108, 2.3-114, 2.3-168, 2.3-199, 2.4-71, 2.5-4, 2.5-5, 2.5-31, 2.5-53, 2.5-70, 2.5-90, 2.6-6, 2.6-56, 2.6-57, 2.6-67, 2.7-100, 2.9-7.

3.0 BIONOMICS 3.2-33, 3.2-52, 3.2-60, 3.2-66, 3.4-31, 3.4-69.

4.0 HORTICULTURE 4.1-31, 4.1-46, 4.1-47, 4.1-103, 4.1-117, 4.2-10, 4.2-83, 4.2-84, 4.2-120, 4.2-122, 4.2-154, 4.2-307, 4.2-360, 4.2-361, 4.2-391, 4.2-392, 4.2-393, 4.3-121, 4.5-50, 4.5-88, 4.5-89, 4.5-147, 4.6-89.

5.0 PRODUCTION ECOLOGY 5.2-72, 5.3-23, 5.3-53, 5.4-21, 5.5-64, 5.5-81, 5.5-284, 5.5-286, 5.5-344, 5.8-76, 5.8-81, 5.8-122.

6.0 CULINARY STUDIES 6.2-69, 6.5-7.

7.0 PHARMACOLOGY 7.1-3, 7.1-47, 7.2-4, 7.2-5, 7.2-6, 7.5-4, 7.5-74, 7.5-108, 7.6-20, 7.6-116.

8.0 PERFUMERY 8.1-4, 8.1-5, 8.1-32, 8.2-1, 8.2-29, 8.2-34, 8.2-69, 8.2-79, 8.3-98, 8.4-4.

COMFREY (Symphytum officinale L.)

Family: Boraginaceae

French: Grande Consoude (f)   Italian: Consolida (f) maggiore
German: Schwarzmarz (f)   Spanish: Consuelda

Comfrey, Symphytum officinale L., is a hardy perennial herb native to Eurasia and naturalized in North America. Also known as common comfrey, blackwort, boneset, bruisewort, gum plant, healing herb, salsify, and slippery root, this erect-growing herb can reach a height of one meter. Characteristically covered with a prickly pubescence, the plant develops flowers colored from white to purple, a thick, externally black root, and relatively large leaves.

The reported life zone of comfrey is 6 to 25 degrees centigrade with an annual precipitation of 0.5 to 2.7 meters and a soil pH of 5.3 to 8.7 (4.1-31). The plant grows best in a moist environment and is found wild along rivers.

Although long grown for medicinal and nutritional properties, comfrey is sometimes used as an ornamental and culinary herb. Fresh leaves are used as a salad green, and the dried roots can be combined with dandelion and chicory for use as a noncaffinated coffee. Symphytum officinale L. cv. variegatum is a commercially available ornamental with white variegated leaves. Comfrey can be used as a fodder crop for livestock.

The roots and leaves of the plant have been used medicinally as an astringent, demulcent, emollient, and expectorant, and against digestive disturbances, ulcers, internal inflammations, bleeding, and cancer (14.1-13). The "healing herb" name comes from the traditional external application of comfrey to heal injured tissue and bones. The plant root has a large content of mucilage, allantoin, symphytine, echimidine, isobauerenol, beta-sitosterol, tannins, and lasiocarpine (11.1-136). The tannins are undoubtedly responsible for astringent properties of the plant parts, and the allantoin in the mucilage accounts for the demulcent activity. The pyrrolizidine alkaloids are potentially toxic, known to cause hepatotoxicity and to be carcinogenic (11.1-154). Whether the small to moderate amounts ingested by humans are harmful is still under debate. Comfrey leaves have been used as an adulterant with foxglove leaves (11.1-50).

Russian comfrey, Symphytum uplandicum Nym. (formerly Symphytum peregrinum), is the result of a cross between Symphytum officinale and Symphytum asperum (prickly comfrey) and is a tall herb growing up to two meters in height. Its life zone is between 12 and 18 degrees centigrade, with an annual precipitation of 0.5 to 2 meters and a soil pH of 5.3 to 6.8 (4.1-31). The plant likes a moist environment and is found growing wild along rivers. Considered a hardy perennial, Russian comfrey can be grown in colder northern temperate climates. Symphytum caucasicum is a commercially available ornamental herb with blue flowers.

BIBLIOGRAPHIC REFERENCES

1.0 CHEMISTRY 1.1-185, 1.2-51, 1.5-30, 1.5-112, 1.6-9, 1.8-107.
2.0 BOTANY 2.1-29, 2.1-84, 2.3-0, 2.6-17, 2.7-23, 2.8-10, 2.9-17, 2.9-44, 2.9-45, 2.9-46, 2.9-47, 2.9-48, 2.9-50. 2.9-140.
3.0 BIONOMICS 3.1-73, 3.2-48, 3.3-63, 3.4-31, 3.4-32,
4.0 HORTICULTURE 4.1-31, 4.2-192, 4.3-43, 4.3-44, 4.3-187, 4.3-219, 4.9-175, 4.9-186.
5.0 PRODUCTION ECOLOGY 5.1-85.
6.0 CULINARY STUDIES 6.1-49, 6.1-91, 6.2-38.

7.0 PHARMACOLOGY 7.1-53, 7.2-11, 7.2-22,   7.3-143,   7.5-7,   7.5-25,
7.5-26, 7.5-108, 7.6-55, 7.8-16, 7.8-29, 7.8-30, 7.8-31, 7.8-45, 7.8-60.

CORIANDER (Coriandrum sativum L.)

Family: Apiaceae (Umbelliferae)

French: Coriandre (f)   Italian: Coriandolo (m)
German: Koriander (m)   Spanish: Cilantro (m)

Coriander, Coriandrum sativum L., also known as Chinese parsley or
cilantro, is an annual herb native to the eastern Mediterranean region
and southern Europe. Valued for the dry ripe fruits, called coriander
seeds, the herb is produced in Morocco, Romania, Mexico, Argentina, the
People's Republic of China, Bangladesh, Bulgaria, Canada, Egypt, India,
Indonesia, Nigeria, Poland, Syria, the United States, the USSR, and
Yugoslavia (11.1-95, 11.1-96). Reaching a height of 1 meter, the plant
has strong smelling pinnately or ternately decompound leaves and
produces compound umbels with small white or pinkish flowers that are
attractive to bees.

The reported life zone of coriander is 7 to 27 degrees centigrade
with an annual precipitation of 0.3 to 2.6 meters and a soil pH of 4.9
to 8.3 (4.1-31). Coriander thrives in full sun and grows best in deep
fertile loams with adequate drainage. The plant is tolerant to cold,
heat and drought stresses (14.1-7).

Usually sown in early spring, the adromonoecious plant flowers in
July and August. Since seeds shatter soon after maturity, timeliness of
harvest and weather conditions greatly influence yield. Young, immature
fruit have a characteristic disagreeable odor and lack the desirable
spicy aroma associated with mature fruit.   Harvesting in the early
morning, while the dew is on the plant, reduces seed loss caused by
shattering. The seed is dried and stored for later use.

For essential oil extraction, the seed is ground immediately before
distillation to increase oil yield and minimize distillation time. The
essential oil content of dried fruit ranges from 0.5 to 1 percent and
the   oil   contains   d-linalool, camphor, d-alpha-pinene, camphene,
beta-pinene, sabinene, myrcene, alpha-terpinene, gamma-terpinene,
limonene, and other compounds (1.5-141, 14.1-9). Coriander fruit also
contain a fixed or fatty oil.

Coriander seeds, available whole or ground, are used primarily as a
flavoring agent in the food industry or as spice in the home kitchen for
breads, cheeses, curry, fish, meats, sauces, soups, pastries, and
confections.   The seeds are also used to flavor alcoholic beverages,
such as gin, and in liqueurs. Fresh leaves are especially popular where
the plant is produced locally for use as a flavoring agent in soups and
stews. The essential oil is used in perfumes, soaps, and other
cosmetics. The fruit has been used to flavor cigarette tobacco.

As a medicinal plant, coriander has been used as an antispasmodic,
carminative, stimulant, and stomachic.   Coriander has also exhibited
hypoglycemic activity (7.1-21). At one time, coriander was used in love
potions and considered to be an aphrodisiac. Chinese herbal medicine
includes the use of coriander for measles, stomachache, nausea, hernia,
and as a tonic (11.1-10). The linalool in coriander oil is known to
cause contact dermatitis (11.1-96). Seeds are sometimes used as a
flavoring agent to improve taste in other medicinal preparations.

Coriander is generally recognized as safe for human consumption as a spice/natural flavoring and for use as an essential oil or oleoresin (21 CFR sections 182.10, 182.20 [1982]).

BIBLIOGRAPHIC REFERENCES

1.0 CHEMISTRY 1.1-50, 1.1-100, 1.1-115, 1.1-119, 1.1-157, 1.1-186, 1.1-200, 1.1-205, 1.2-62, 1.2-63, 1.2-74, 1.2-75, 1.2-76, 1.2-108, 1.3-24, 1.3-25, 1.5-9, 1.5-17, 1.5-46, 1.5-132, 1.5-141, 1.6-22, 1.6-35, 1.6-50, 1.7-83, 1.8-2, 1.8-31, 1.8-56, 1.8-57, 1.8-65, 1.8-69, 1.8-163, 1.8-172, 1.8-184.

2.0 BOTANY 2.1-40, 2.1-74, 2.1-77, 2.1-79, 2.1-116, 2.1-149, 2.2-2, 2.2-8, 2.2-11, 2.2-23, 2.2-46, 2.2-76, 2.2-109, 2.2-123, 2.2-124, 2.3-4, 2.3-5, 2.3-19, 2.3-128, 2.3-133, 2.3-176, 2.3-180, 2.3-209, 2.3-212, 2.4-61, 2.4-93, 2.5-1, 2.5-23, 2.5-29, 2.5-37, 2.5-50, 2.5-73, 2.5-81, 2.5-99, 2.5-105, 2.6-23, 2.6-28, 2.7-105, 2.7-106, 2.8-7, 2.8-11, 2.8-24, 2.8-41, 2.9-15, 2.9-49, 2.9-50, 2.9-123, 2.9-142.

3.0 BIONOMICS 3.1-18, 3.2-0, 3.2-17, 3.2-49, 3.2-50, 3.2-79, 3.3-68, 3.3-82, 3.3-213, 3.3-222, 3.3-225, 3.4-16, 3.4-17, 3.4-31, 3.4-32, 3.4-79, 3.4-100, 3.4-109, 3.7-3, 3.7-10.

4.0 HORTICULTURE 4.1-28, 4.1-29, 4.1-31, 4.1-95, 4.1-116, 4.2-4, 4.2-9, 4.2-12, 4.2-23, 4.2-24, 4.2-61, 4.2-71, 4.2-79, 4.2-96, 4.2-115, 4.2-116, 4.2-117, 4.2-160, 4.2-170, 4.2-188, 4.2-260, 4.2-280, 4.2-281, 4.2-294, 4.2-314, 4.2-351, 4.2-390, 4.3-65, 4.3-99, 4.3-110, 4.3-125, 4.3-132, 4.3-150, 4.3-179, 4.3-180, 4.3-181, 4.3-221, 4.4-2, 4.4-6, 4.4-40, 4.4-64, 4.5-5, 4.5-79, 4.5-84, 4.5-120, 4.5-167, 4.5-169, 4.5-187, 4.5-215, 4.5-237, 4.5-246, 4.6-9, 4.6-33, 4.6-54, 4.6-89, 4.6-90, 4.8-57, 4.9-18, 4.9-113, 4.9-128.

5.0 PRODUCTION ECOLOGY 5.1-30, 5.2-25, 5.2-58, 5.2-71, 5.2-73, 5.3-9, 5.3-32, 5.3-57, 5.4-19, 5.4-76, 5.4-76, 5.4-94, 5.4-114, 5.4-125, 5.4-140, 5.5-9, 5.5-10, 5.5-16, 5.5-42, 5.5-48, 5.5-58, 5.5-122, 5.5-123, 5.5-140, 5.5-144, 5.5-149, 5.5-190, 5.5-195, 5.5-223, 5.5-252, 5.5-254, 5.5-310, 5.5-318, 5.5-319, 5.5-320, 5.5-330, 5.5-334, 5.5-344, 5.5-354, 5.6-10, 5.6-14, 5.6-26, 5.6-33, 5.6-59, 5.6-63, 5.6-64, 5.6-69, 5.6-71, 5.6-77, 5.6-87, 5.6-88, 5.7-22, 5.7-76, 5.7-78, 5.7-95, 5.7-107, 5.7-108, 5.7-112, 5.7-129, 5.7-149, 5.7-161, 5.7-170, 5.7-207, 5.7-235, 5.8-100, 5.8-101, 5.8-134, 5.8-137, 5.8-177, 5.9-20.

6.0 CULINARY STUDIES 6.1-17, 6.1-54, 6.1-87, 6.1-94, 6.2-13, 6.2-15, 6.2-25, 6.2-26, 6.2-47, 6.2-61, 6.2-65, 6.3-1, 6.3-14, 6.3-15, 6.3-16, 6.3-44, 6.3-52, 6.3-54, 6.3-63, 6.3-67, 6.4-13, 6.4-35, 6.4-45, 6.4-49, 6.4-58, 6.4-67, 6.4-78, 6.4-93, 6.4-97, 6.4-104, 6.4-108, 6.4-111, 6.5-7, 6.5-16, 6.5-18, 6.5-29, 6.5-30, 6.5-33, 6.5-74, 6.5-97, 6.5-119, 6.5-122, 6.5-124, 6.5-133, 6.5-144.

7.0 PHARMACOLOGY 7.1-21, 7.1-56, 7.2-42, 7.2-43, 7.5-13, 7.5-27, 7.5-74, 7.5-88, 7.7-17, 7.7-27, 7.8-35.

8.0 PERFUMERY 8.1-17, 8.2-41, 8.2-44, 8.2-47, 8.2-77, 8.3-45, 8.3-52.

10.0 COMMERCE 10.2-3.

CUMIN (Cuminum cyminum L.)

Family: Apiaceae (Umbelliferae)

French: Cumin (m)   Italian: Comino (m)
German: Kreuzkuemmer (m);   Spanish: Comino (m)
        Roemischer Kuemmel (m)

Cumin, Cuminum cyminum L., also known as Cuminum odorum Salisb., is
a small annual herb native to the Mediterranean region. Primary
cultivation of cumin is in Europe, Asia, the Middle East, and North
Africa with India and Iran as the largest cumin exporters. The valued
portion of the plant is the dried fruit called cumin seed, which is
esteemed as a condiment.
The reported life zone of cumin is 9 to 26 degrees centigrade with
an annual precipitation of 0.3 to 2.7 meters and a soil pH of 4.5 to 8.3
(4.1-31). Cumin thrives on rich, well-drained sandy loam soil. The
plant, which needs mild temperatures during a three to four month
growing season, is intolerant of long periods of dry heat (11.129,
14.1-29).
In the Middle East, cumin is grown as a winter crop, sown and
harvested between April and May. Seeds are usually collected and
threshed by hand, since the small, tender plants are difficult to
harvest mechanically. The seeds become hard, the fruit changes color,
and the vegetative material withers as the plant matures. The three
major types of cumin seed on the market, Iranian, Indian, and Middle
Eastern, differ in seed color, quantity of essential oil, and flavor.
The odor and flavor of cumin is derived largely from the essential
oil, which contains cuminaldehyde as the main constituent. Other
ingredients of the oil are dihydrocuminaldehyde, d,l-pinene, d-alpha-
pinene, para-cymene, beta-pinene, dipentene, and cuminyl alcohol
(14.1-7). Synthetic cuminaldehyde is an adulterant to cumin oil and can
not be detected chemically. The dried seed of cumin has 2.5 to 5
percent essential oil on a dry weight basis and is obtained by steam
distillation. The characteristic odor of cumin is caused primarily by
aldehydes that are present in the oil (6.4-114).
Cumin is used as a flavoring agent in cheeses, pickles, sausages,
soups, stews, stuffings, rice and bean dishes, and liqueurs. Cumin is
the key ingredient in all types of curries and chili powders. Oil of
cumin is used in fragrances. As a medicinal plant, cumin has been
utilized as an antispasmodic, carminative, sedative, and stimulant.
Cumin oil has been reported to have antibacterial activity (1.8-130).
Distinct phototoxic effects have been reported from undiluted cumin oil
(8.2-79).
Black cumin, Bunium persicum B. Fedtsch., has smaller and sweeter
seeds than Cuminum cyminum L. This plant, which grows wild in the
Middle East, especially Iran, is not commercially significant
(11.1-128). Black cumin, Nigella sativa L., which is sometimes called
black caraway, is a herb native to the Mediterranean region and not
related to cumin. The black seeds are used in seasonings.
Cumin is generally recognized as safe for human consumption as a
spice/flavoring and plant extract/oleoresin (21 CFR sections 182.10,
182.20 [1982]).

BIBLIOGRAPHIC REFERENCES

1.0 CHEMISTRY 1.1-72, 1.1-119, 1.1-200, 1.1-267, 1.2-16, 1.2-80,
1.3-19, 1.3-34, 1.3-37, 1.4-4, 1.4-29, 1.5-119, 1.5-127, 1.6-22, 1.6-29,
1.7-63, 1.7-124, 1.8-17, 1.8-39, 1.8-95, 1.8-130, 1.8-154.

2.0 BOTANY 2.1-55, 2.1-64, 2.1-86, 2.1-96, 2.1-106, 2.1-142,
2.2-11, 2.2-40, 2.2-78, 2.2-79, 2.2-80, 2.2-81, 2.2-95, 2.2-100, 2.3-18,
2.3-54, 2.3-104, 2.3-120, 2.3-144, 2.3-145, 2.3-149, 2.3-150, 2.3-153,
2.3-181, 2.3-189, 2.3-191, 2.3-193, 2.3-230, 2.3-232, 2.4-7, 2.4-13,
2.4-40, 2.4-53, 2.4-63, 2.4-88, 2.4-116, 2.4-127, 2.4-132, 2.5-18,
2.5-19, 2.5-24, 2.5-26, 2.5-34, 2.5-43, 2.5-79, 2.5-112, 2.5-119,
2.6-48, 2.6-66, 2.7-109, 2.9-9, 2.9-15, 2.9-63, 2.9-123, 2.9-142.
    3.0 BIONOMICS 3.1-15, 3.2-23, 3.3-42, 3.3-82, 3.3-113, 3.3-114,
3.4-31, 3.4-32, 3.4-93, 3.5-44.
    4.0 HORTICULTURE 4.1-31, 4.1-73, 4.1-74, 4.1-99, 4.1-107, 4.2-31,
4.2-33, 4.2-61, 4.2-115, 4.2-117, 4.2-139, 4.2-165, 4.2-173, 4.2-187,
4.2-193, 4.2-218, 4.2-219, 4.2-220, 4.2-225, 4.2-228, 4.2-239, 4.2-241,
4.2-279, 4.2-282, 4.2-301, 4.2-306, 4.2-316, 4.2-348, 4.2-349, 4.2-350,
4.2-366, 4.3-3, 4.3-82, 4.3-85, 4.3-127, 4.3-160, 4.3-184, 4.3-207,
4.4-57, 4.4-92, 4.5-44, 4.5-51, 4.5-63, 4.5-156, 4.5-160, 4.5-198,
4.5-242, 4.5-243, 4.6-13, 4.6-20, 4.6-27, 4.8-39, 4.8-67, 4.8-68,
4.9-20, 4.9-21, 4.9-34, 4.9-64, 4.9-65, 4.9-84, 4.9-85, 4.9-110,
4.9-120, 4.9-126, 4.9-127, 4.9-140, 4.9-163, 4.9-182.
    5.0 PRODUCTION ECOLOGY 5.1-3, 5.1-14, 5.1-21, 5.1-63, 5.1-81,
5.2-8, 5.2-21, 5.3-18, 5.3-63, 5.4-1, 5.4-46, 5.4-63, 5.4-76, 5.4-114,
5.4-125, 5.4-141, 5.5-3, 5.5-18, 5.5-25, 5.5-48, 5.5-68, 5.5-95, 5.5-96,
5.5-146, 5.5-187, 5.5-188, 5.5-195, 5.5-245, 5.5-263, 5.5-293, 5.5-300,
5.5-330, 5.5-335, 5.5-337, 5.5-524, 5.6-1, 5.6-28, 5.6-29, 5.6-88,
5.7-37, 5.7-47, 5.7-109, 5.7-120, 5.7-122, 5.7-128, 5.7-129, 5.7-145,
5.7-159, 5.7-184, 5.7-188, 5.7-190, 5.7-193, 5.7-194, 5.7-196, 5.7-197,
5.7-201, 5.7-206, 5.8-45.
    6.0 CULINARY STUDIES 6.1-71, 6.2-33, 6.2-51, 6.2-55, 6.2-57,
6.2-64, 6.2-67, 6.2-68, 6.2-71, 6.3-24, 6.3-57, 6.4-82, 6.4-90, 6.4-93,
6.4-99, 6.4-104, 6.4-114, 6.5-31, 6.5-41, 6.5-74, 6.5-97, 6.5-116,
6.5-144, 6.5-145, 6.5-151.
    7.0 PHARMACOLOGY 7.4-20, 7.4-42, 7.5-6, 7.5-25, 7.5-26, 7.5-30,
7.5-74, 7.5-82, 7.5-101, 7.6-57, 7.6-103, 7.6-136, 7.6-208, 7.6-216,
7.7-17, 7.8-8, 7.8-51, 7.8-63.
    8.0 PERFUMERY 8.1-17, 8.2-46, 8.2-79.

DANDELION (Taraxacum officinale, Wiggers)

Family: Asteraceae (Compositae)

French: Pissenlit (m);   Italian: Dente (m) di leone;
        Dent (f) de lion   Soffione (m)
German: Loewenzahn (m);   Spanish: Diente (m) de leon
        Kuhblume (f)

    Common dandelion, Taraxacum officinale Wiggers, is believed to be
native to Europe. Naturalized in many parts of the world, the plant is
sometimes classified as Leontodon taraxacum L. and known as blowball,
cankerwort, Irish daisy, priest's crown, swine's snout, lion's tooth,
puffball, white endive, or wild endive. A developing plant   is
characterized by a long, thick taproot, a rosette of short leaves, and a
single hollow stem bearing a yellow flower, which turns into a round
fluffy seed head at maturity. Upon injury, the plant exudes a milky
latex or juice.
    The reported life zone of dandelion is 5 to 26 degrees centigrade
with an annual precipitation of 0.3 to 2.7 meters and a soil pH of 4.2
to 8.3 (4.1-31). The plant is a hardy perennial, adaptable to most soil

conditions.   Strong   regenerative   properties   make   it   difficult   to
eradicate, and it is therefore a common weed in many locations.
   Horticultural varieties of dandelion differing in morphological and
chemical characteristics are available for cultivation.   Roots are
generally harvested in spring or fall of the second year, while leaves
and flower heads are gathered from cultivated and wild plants throughout
the growing season.
   The bitter plant resin found in both roots and above-ground parts
contains taraxacin, taraxerin, taraxerol, taraxasterol, inulin, gluten,
gum, potash, choline, levulin, and putin (11.1-136, 14.1-35). The plant
itself is nutritious, being high in vitamins A, C, and niacin
(11.1-136).
   Dried and ground roots are used for noncaffinated, coffee-like
beverages, as a flavoring agent in coffee and cocoa, and as an addition
to salad dishes. Dandelion wine can be made from the leaves and flower
heads. Young, tender leaves are used in salads and soups. Roots stored
in fall may be stimulated under suitable enviromental conditions to
produce leaves for use in winter salads.
   As a medicinal plant, dandelion has been considered to be an
aperient,   diuretic,   stimulant,   stomachic, tonic, and detoxicant.
Dandelion tea has been used against fever, insomnia, jaundice,
rheumatism, eczema and other skin diseases, and constipation. Common
dandelion and other Taraxacum species have also been used against warts,
cancers, and tumors (14.1-14). The dried root constitutes a crude drug,
taraxacum, but appears to lack any real therapeutic value (7.5-19,
14.1-23). Taraxacin in the plant resin may stimulate gastric secretions
(11.1-136).   Hypoglycemic effects have been noted in animals fed
dandelions (7.1-21).
   Taraxacum kok-saghyz Rodin, or Russian dandelion, is from Turkestan
and can be used for production of rubber (14.1-3). Taraxacum mongolicum
Hand.-Mazz. is employed in Chinese herbal medicine for detoxification,
fevers,   external   wounds,   congestion, stomach strengthening, and
lactation stimulation. The resin of the plant contains taraxacin,
taraxacerin, taraxasterol, taraxerol, pectinum, and choline (11.1-10,
11.1-97).
   Extracts of common dandelion and Taraxacum laevigatum D.C.   are
generally recognized as safe for human consumption (21 CFR section
182.20 [1982]).

BIBLIOGRAPHIC REFERENCES

   1.0 CHEMISTRY 1.1-102, 1.1-194, 1.5-42, 1.5-101, 1.5-105, 1.6-38,
1.7-103, 1.8-82, 1.8-107.
   2.0 BOTANY 2.1-14, 2.1-18, 2.1-44, 2.1-61,   2.1-65,   2.1-115,
2.1-135, 2.1-142, 2.2-10, 2.2-31, 2.2-56, 2.2-59, 2.2-63, 2.2-91, 2.3-8,
2.3-116, 2.3-241, 2.4-8, 2.4-28, 2.4-43, 2.4-57, 2.4-58, 2.4-70,
2.4-100, 2.4-106, 2.4-134, 2.4-136, 2.4-138, 2.5-11, 2.5-39, 2.5-61,
2.5-85, 2.5-100, 2.5-120, 2.6-2, 2.6-40, 2.7-17, 2.7-18, 2.7-39, 2.7-79,
2.8-57, 2.9-14, 2.9-25, 2.9-93, 2.9-114, 2.9-139.
   3.0 BIONOMICS 3.1-2, 3.1-58, 3.3-79, 3.4-3, 3.4-21, 3.4-23, 3.4-27,
3.4-32, 3.4-42, 3.4-57, 3.4-72, 3.4-84, 3.4-87, 3.4-116, 3.4-117,
3.4-118, 3.4-130, 3.4-138, 3.4-139, 3.5-14, 3.5-17, 3.5-19, 3.5-39,
3.6-9, 3.6-13.
   4.0 HORTICULTURE 4.1-28, 4.1-29, 4.1-31, 4.2-54, 4.2-189, 4.1-31,
4.2-250, 4.2-320, 4.4-12, 4.4-40, 4.4-56, 4.4-90, 4.5-9, 4.5-26, 4.5-40,
4.5-100, 4.5-159, 4.5-212, 4.9-19, 4.9-22, 4.9-23, 4.9-24, 4.9-100,
4.9-104.
   5.0 PRODUCTION ECOLOGY 5.1-29, 5.2-17, 5.2-26, 5.2-37, 5.2-39,
5.2-51, 5.3-10, 5.3-15, 5.3-52, 5.4-2, 5.4-3, 5.4-6, 5.4-17, 5.4-50,

5.4-51, 5.4-52, 5.4-53, 5.4-65, 5.4-135, 5.4-136, 5.5-57, 5.5-126, 5.5-160, 5.5-161, 5.5-264, 5.5-321, 5.5-326, 5.8-90, 5.9-46.
6.0 CULINARY STUDIES 6.1-19, 6.1-22, 6.1-26, 6.1-27, 6.1-93, 6.2-24, 6.2-53.
7.0 PHARMACOLOGY 7.1-1, 7.1-21, 7.4-12, 7.5-19, 7.5-50, 7.5-51, 7.6-167, 7.6-184, 7.8-2, 7.8-26, 7.8-40, 7.8-45.
8.0 PERFUMERY 8.2-15, 8.4-1, 8.4-3, 8.4-4.

DILL (<u>Anethum graveolens</u> L.)

Family: Apiaceae (Umbelliferae)

French: Aneth (m)   Italian: Aneto (m)
German: Dill (m)   Spanish: Eneldo (m); Aneldo (m)

Dill, <u>Anethum graveolens</u> L., an annual or biennial aromatic herb native to Europe, is naturalized to North America and the West Indies. Also known as common dill, American dill, European dill, and Danish dill, this widely cultivated species has sometimes been classified as <u>Peucedanum graveolens</u> (L.) C.B. Clarke. Principal dill production areas are India and Pakistan, but Egypt, Fiji, Mexico, the Netherlands, the United States, England, Hungary, Germany, and Holland also have commercially productive areas. The plant grows erect and can reach a height of one meter. It is characterized by hollow stems, blue-green leaves, and yellow-flowering compound umbels, which produce a dried ripe fruit commonly called seeds.

The reported life zone is 6 to 26 degrees centigrade with an annual precipitation of 0.5 to 1.7 meters and a soil pH of 5.3 to 78 (4.1-31). The hardy plant requires long days and cool weather, and is sensitive to environmental stresses, such as low moisture, hail, high temperatures, strong winds, and hard rains during the flowering and seed maturation period. The plant grows best in deep, fertile loam soils.

Grown best as an annual crop, timeliness of harvest is crucial to maximize seed yield, because seeds tend to ripen at different times and seed shattering is a potential problem. Generally, harvesting for dill weed or the essential oil of dill weed is done before the plant flowers. Harvesting for seed is initiated when the bulk of the seed crop is physiologically mature. Plants used for essential oil production are steam distilled on the day of harvest to minimize volatilization losses.

The essential oils of dill differ in flavor and odor depending upon whether they are obtained from mature seed or dill weed. The seed oil resembles the essential oil of caraway because of the high carvone content (reaching 50 to 60 percent) in mature seeds (14.1-9). Dill seed oil includes d-carvone, d-limonene, d-phellandrene, alpha-pinene, diterpene, d-dihydrocarvone, beta-phellandrene, beta-pinene, 1,8-cineole, beta-myricene, para-cymene, and alpha-thujone (3.3-44, 14.1-7). Dill herb oil contains d-alpha-phellandrene, terpinene, limonene, carvone, dillapiole, isomyristicin, and myristicin (3.3-44, 14.1-9). The actual quality of dill oil can fluctuate greatly, depending on the percentage of seed oil, the physiological maturity of the seeds used for oil. The time of harvest may also be significant, because carvone is synthesized during the day from alpha-phellandrene breakdown (4.6-97). Dill herb oil is sometimes adulterated with terpenes from other sources (14.1-9).

Dill seeds are used whole or ground as a condiment for flavoring meats, sauces, stews, breads, vinegars, pastries, and vegetables. Dried and fresh leaves are used in sauces, salads, soups, stews, and vinegars. Dill is an important flavoring agent in the pickling of cucumbers. Some dill oil is used in cosmetics and perfumes. Dried dill foliage is commonly called dill weed.

As a medicinal plant, dill has been used as an antispasmodic, carminative, diuretic, stimulant, and stomachic. It has also been used as a remedy for colic and insomnia and as a stimulant for lactation. The name 'dill' may come from the Norwegian word dill (to lull), referring to the plant's alleged carminative properties (11.1-50). Dill will provoke photodermatitis and contact dermatitis in humans (11.1-96). Myristicin, apiol, and dillapiol present in dill oil are effective naturally occurring insecticides (1.8-90). Myristicin is also known to be responsible for psychoactive and hallucinogenic properties in some other plants, and the apiol content may be responsible for diuretic properties (7.2-62, 7.8-12).

Indian dill or East Indian dill, Anethum sowa Roxb., is a perennial herb grown and utilized similarly to dill. Indian dill has a higher specific gravity than common dill, attributed to the presence of dillapiole and a lower carvone content (14.1-9). The high dillapiole content may make Indian dill a source of pyrethrum synergists (1.8-166).

Dill and Indian dill are generally recognized as safe for human consumption (21 CFR sections 172.510, 184.1282 [1982]).

BIBLIOGRAPHIC REFERENCES

1.0 CHEMISTRY 1.1-12, 1.1-15, 1.1-105, 1.1-119, 1.1-140, 1.1-186, 1.1-200, 1.1-207, 1.1-223, 1.1-228, 1.1-230, 1.1-236, 1.1-244, 1.1-262, 1.2-3, 1.2-7, 1.2-11, 1.2-12, 1.2-13, 1.2-44, 1.2-51, 1.2-69, 1.2-83, 1.2-95, 1.2-104, 1.2-107, 1.3-21, 1.4-66, 1.5-11, 1.5-12, 1.5-13, 1.5-14, 1.5-29, 1.5-48, 1.5-67, 1.5-81, 1.5-98, 1.5-103, 1.5-122, 1.6-12, 1.6-19, 1.7-92, 1.7-101, 1.7-102, 1.7-108, 1.8-20, 1.8-43, 1.8-48, 1.8-69, 1.8-90, 1.8-100, 1.8-131, 1.8-141, 1.8-143, 1.8-149, 1.8-150, 1.8-154, 1.8-158, 1.8-166, 1.8-184.

2.0 BOTANY 2.1-47, 2.1-75, 2.1-131, 2.1-153, 2.1-154, 2.2-50, 2.2-76, 2.2-116, 2.2-117, 2.3-34, 2.3-64, 2.3-129, 2.3-131, 2.3-198, 2.3-203, 2.3-244, 2.5-101, 2.6-68, 2.6-71, 2.6-77, 2.6-78, 2.7-52, 2.8-21, 2.8-52, 2.9-16, 2.9-43.

3.0 BIONOMICS 3.2-3, 3.2-21, 3.2-22, 3.2-79, 3.3-44, 3.3-82, 3.3-165, 3.3-189, 3.3-213, 3.3-228, 3.4-31, 3.4-32, 3.7-1, 3.7-13.

4.0 HORTICULTURE 4.1-31, 4.1-61, 4.1-94, 4.2-69, 4.2-90, 4.2-317, 4.2-363, 4.3-38, 4.3-76, 4.3-108, 4.3-121, 4.3-126, 4.3-146, 4.3-222, 4.4-28, 4.4-112, 4.4-113, 4.4-114, 4.5-9, 4.5-64, 4.5-84, 4.5-85, 4.5-122, 4.5-167, 4.5-212, 4.6-82, 4.6-97, 4.8-54, 4.8-57, 4.9-59, 4.9-94, 4.9-152, 4.9-153, 4.9-158.

5.0 PRODUCTION ECOLOGY 5.1-1, 5.1-29, 5.2-29, 5.2-30, 5.2-38, 5.2-40, 5.2-46, 5.2-94, 5.2-95, 5.3-52, 5.4-74, 5.4-75, 5.4-118, 5.5-130, 5.5-153, 5.5-185, 5.5-195, 5.5-330, 5.5-375, 5.5-376, 5.7-12, 5.7-17, 5.7-205, 5.7-234, 5.8-16, 5.8-50, 5.8-70, 5.8-71, 5.8-94, 5.8-99, 5.8-122, 5.8-137, 5.8-171, 5.8-176, 5.8-186.

6.0 CULINARY STUDIES 6.1-5, 6.1-6, 6.1-15, 6.1-83, 6.1-87, 6.2-14, 6.2-25, 6.2-26, 6.2-61, 6.3-9, 6.3-20, 6.3-28, 6.3-73, 6.3-77, 6.4-4, 6.4-45, 6.4-90, 6.4-99, 6.5-17, 6.5-41, 6.5-92, 6.5-97, 6.5-101, 6.5-121, 6.5-141, 6.5-154.

7.0 PHARMACOLOGY 7.1-64, 7.2-62, 7.2-87, 7.2-97, 7.2-98, 7.3-43, 7.3-120, 7.5-3, 7.5-16, 7.5-25, 7.5-26, 7.5-86, 7.5-110, 7.6-57, 7.6-162, 7.6-168, 7.6-189, 7.7-17, 7.7-31, 7.7-32, 7.8-12, 7.8-51.

8.0 PERFUMERY 8.2-36, 8.2-44, 8.2-69.

9.0 NATURAL DYES AND ORNAMENTAL APPLICATIONS 9.2-12.

10.0 COMMERCE 10.1-15, 10.2-2.

DITTANY OF CRETE (Origanum dictamnus L.)

Family: Lamiaceae (Labiatae)

French: Dictame (m) de Crete   Italian: Dittamo(m) cretico
German: Kretischer Diptam (m)   Spanish: Dictamo(m) cretico

Dittany of Crete, Origanum dictamnus L. (formerly Amaracus dictamnus Benth. or Amaracus tomentosus Moench.), is one of the best-known healing herbs of folklore. Native to the mountains of Crete and also called dittany or dictamnus, this perennial plant can reach a height of 0.3 meters. Procumbent white, woolly stems, usually trailing, develop pink or purplish flowers in the summer. The small gray leaves have a velvety texture.

Of minor importance today, dittany of Crete is primarily used as a potted plant or as an ornamental plant in garden borders. The flowers have been used in herbal teas, but the plant has no culinary value. As a medicinal plant, the herb has been utilized to heal wounds, soothe pain, cure snake bites, and ease childbirth. In addition, it has been used as a remedy against gastric or stomach ailments and rheumatism.

Dictamnus albus L. (Dictamnus fraxinella Pers.), known as dittany and fraxinella, is often confused with dittany of Crete. This perennial plant is of the Rutaceae family and reaches a height of approximately one meter. Grown as a garden plant with showy pink, purple or white flowers, its dried leaves can be used in teas. The plant has been used medicinally as a diuretic, emmenagogue, and expectorant. However, the seed pods can cause contact dermatitis. The plant is known as the gas plant because it will often give a burst of flame when a lighted match is held beneath the flower cluster (14.1-3).

Cunila origanoides Britt. is called dittany, Maryland dittany, and stone-mint. This low-growing perennial with a minty flavor is native to the eastern United States. The plant, which has been classified as Satureja origanoides L. and Cunila mariana L., is primarily used as an ornamental border in gardens, although the leaves may be used in herbal teas.

Dittany of Crete is generally recognized as safe for human consumption as a natural flavoring (21 CFR section 172.510 [1982]).

BIBLIOGRAPHIC REFERENCES

1.0 CHEMISTRY 1.2-101, 1.8-173.
2.0 BOTANY 2.7-51.
4.0 HORTICULTURE 4.3-199.
7.0 PHARMACOLOGY 7.5-13, 7.7-20.
9.0 NATURAL DYES AND ORNAMENTAL APPLICATIONS 9.2-12.

FENNEL (Foeniculum vulgare Mill.)

Family: Apiaceae (Umbelliferae)

French: Fenouil (m)   Italian: Finocchio (m)
German: Fenchel (m)   Spanish: Hinojo (m)

Fennel, Foeniculum vulgare Mill., is an erect growing perennial herb
native to southern Europe and the Mediterranean area. Reaching a height
of 1.5 meters, the plant has yellow flowers on a compound umbel. Sweet
or Roman fennel is thought to originate from Foeniculum vulgare Mill.
subspecies capillaceum (Galib.) Holmboe var. dulce Mill., whereas
bitter or wild fennel is from Foeniculum vulgare Mill. subspecies
capillaceum (Galib.) Holmboe var. vulgare Mill. (8.2-53). Sweet
fennel has also been classified as Foeniculum vulgare Mill. subspecies
vulgare var. dulce Batt. and Trab., and as Foeniculum dulce Mill.
(14.1-4). The subspecies of bitter fennel has been classified as
piperitum rather than capillaceum (4.3-38). Principal fennel production
areas are located in India, the People's Republic of China, Egypt,
Argentina, Indonesia, and Pakistan. The word foeniculum is from the
latin word for fragrant hay, reflecting the plant's odor (11.1-14.1-3).
     The reported life zone of fennel is 4 to 27 degrees centigrade with
an annual precipitation of 0.3 to 2.6 meters and a soil pH of 4.8 to 8.3
(4.1-31). Fennel thrives on well drained loam soil.
     Although a perennial, fennel is generally grown as an annual or
biennial crop. Yields of the dried fruit, commonly thought of as fennel
seed, are low in the first year but increase in the second. The umbels
do not mature uniformly, and several harvests are therefore necessary to
maximize yield. Mechanical harvesting of commercial stands must be
carefully timed to obtain high yields. Approximately 60 percent of the
essential oil is located in the fruit, with the rest in the rays of the
umbel and other green plant parts.
     The oils of both sweet and bitter fennel seed, obtained by steam
distillation, contain anethole, fenchone, alpha-pinene, camphene,
beta-pinene, sabenine, myrcene, alpha-phellandrene, limonene,
cis-ocimene, para-cymene, camphor, and several other chemical compounds,
including a fixed oil (8.2-53). Bitter fennel oil is thought to contain
more fenchone (a bitter mixture with a camphor-like odor and flavor) and
less anethole than sweet fennel oil. Sweet fennel oil is of a superior
quality with a more pleasing aroma and flavor (14.1-9). Some analyses
have indicated a lack of fenchone in sweet fennel and high
concentrations of limonene in bitter fennel (8.2-53).
     Fennel seed is used in the food and flavor industry for addition to
meats, vegetable products, fish sauces, soups, salad dressings, stews,
breads, pastries, teas, and alcoholic beverages. Crushed seed has been
used as a substitute for juniper in flavoring gin. The essential oil
and the oleoresin of fennel are used in condiments, soaps, creams,
perfumes, and liqueurs. Several types of fennel differing in morphology
and leaf color are available for ornamental use and as a fresh
vegetable.
     As a medicinal plant, fennel seed has been used as an antispasmodic,
carminative, diuretic, expectorant, laxative, stimulant, and stomachic.
Fennel has also been used to stimulate lactation, as a remedy against
colic, and to improve the taste of other medicines. Chinese herbal
medicine includes the use of fennel for gastroenteritis, hernia,
indigestion, abdominal pain, and to resolve phlegm and stimulate milk
production (11.1-10). Fennel is known to provoke both photodermatitis
and contact dermatitis in humans (11.1-96). The volatile oil may cause
nausea, vomiting, seizures, and pulmonary edema (1.8-100). The

2.2-80, 2.2-81, 2.2-84, 2.2-106, 2.2-107, 2.2-119, 2.3-0, 2.3-9, 2.3-10, 2.3-19, 2.3-83, 2.3-96, 2.3-147, 2.3-157, 2.3-161, 2.3-176, 2.3-181, 2.3-219, 2.3-224, 2.3-235, 2.4-1, 2.4-14, 2.4-15, 2.4-91, 2.4-92, 2.4-98, 2.4-110, 2.4-122, 2.4-123, 2.4-124, 2.4-125, 2.4-126, 2.4-127, 2.5-46, 2.5-47, 2.5-52, 2.5-76, 2.6-25, 2.6-48, 2.6-65, 2.7-35, 2.7-43, 2.7-44, 2.7-45, 2.7-103.

   3.0 BIONOMICS 3.2-79, 3.4-31, 3.4-52, 3.4-53, 3.4-104, 3.4-109, 3.4-120.

   4.0 HORTICULTURE 4.2-16, 4.2-24, 4.2-125, 4.2-328, 4.3-37, 4.3-112, 4.3-136, 4.4-36, 4.4-79, 4.4-86, 4.5-71, 4.5-78, 4.5-126, 4.6-11, 4.6-68, 4.6-77, 4.9-8, 4.9-25, 4.9-46, 4.9-62, 4.9-73, 4.9-86, 4.9-97, 4.9-98, 4.9-101, 4.9-102, 4.9-103, 4.9-109, 4.9-122, 4.9-123, 4.9-151, 4.9-159, 4.9-164, 4.9-180.

   5.0 PRODUCTION ECOLOGY 5.1-78, 5.2-47, 5.2-57, 5.2-61, 5.4-19, 5.4-45, 5.4-46, 5.4-70, 5.4-91, 5.4-125, 5.4-174, 5.5-24, 5.5-82, 5.5-90, 5.5-121, 5.5-129, 5.5-226, 5.5-249, 5.5-359, 5.6-3, 5.7-84, 5.7-121, 5.7-127, 5.8-3, 5.8-49, 5.9-47.

   6.0 CULINARY STUDIES 6.1-31, 6.1-50, 6.2-3, 6.2-6, 6.2-7, 6.2-20, 6.2-21, 6.2-47, 6.2-51, 6.2-58, 6.2-65, 6.3-13, 6.3-23, 6.4-45, 6.4-99, 6.5-40, 6.5-74. 6.5-144.

   7.0 PHARMACOLOGY 7.1-9, 7.1-42, 7.1-64, 7.2-13, 7.2-19, 7.2-23, 7.2-45, 7.2-46, 7.2-79, 7.2-93, 7.3-3, 7.3-12, 7.3-28, 7.3-32, 7.3-51, 7.3-52, 7.3-53, 7.3-54, 7.3-67, 7.3-68, 7.3-69, 7.3-70, 7.3-79, 7.3-106, 7.3-112, 7.3-116, 7.3-122, 7.3-126, 7.3-152, 7.4-13, 7.4-51, 7.5-98, 7.5-101, 7.8-51.

   8.0 PERFUMERY 8.2-86.

FOXGLOVE (Digitalis species)

Family: Scrophulariaceae

French: Digitale (f)   Italian: Digitale (f)
German: Fingerhut (m)   Spanish: Digital (f)

   Foxglove is the common name for plants of the Digitalis species, primarily represented by common foxglove, Digitalis purpurea L., and Grecian foxglove, Digitalis lanata J. F. Ehrh. These biennial or per- ennial plants, native to the Mediterranean region, reach heights of 1.2 to 2 meters. The plants have lanceolate to ovate leaves and showy bell-shaped flowers in racemes. Foxglove, almost always produced under commercial contract, has traditionally been grown in Germany, England, India, and several eastern European countries.
   The reported life zone for common foxglove is 6 to 21 degrees centigrade with an annual precipitation of 0.3 to 2.1 meters and a soil pH of 4.5 to 8.3 (4.1-31). The hardy, easy to grow plant flourishes in well-drained loam soil. Because of the small seed size and nonuniform germination of the typical heterogenous seed lots, plants are usually transplanted into the field to obtain the desired plant density. Leaves are harvested late in the first fall or in the following spring. Plants are dried in the shade or with artificial heat. Exposure to sunlight or moisture decreases the medicinal value of the leaves.
   There are many natural, secondary, and other derived compounds from Digitalis species. The important cardenolides or cardiac glycosides include digitoxin, digoxin, gitoxin, from the lanatosides A, B. and C, and from purpurea glycoside A and B. The important saponins include digitonin, tigonin and gitonin. Additional medicinally useful steroids

and cortical hormones can be made from the plant steroids. The
glycoside content of tissue varies with the individual plant, the stage
of development, the growth environment, and the time and method of
harvest. Comfrey leaves have been reported to be used as an adulterant
(11.1-50).

There are several varieties of ornamental foxglove available,
differing in size and flower color. The primary value of foxglove,
however, is as a source of the medicinally important glycosides found in
the plant. Digitalis, a cardiovascular drug extracted from the leaves,
is the most effective drug available for heart failure caused by
hypertension or arteriosclerosis (11.1-96). It is also used medicinally
as a heart regulator, a diuretic, and an expectorant. Digoxin and
lanatoside C from foxglove are effective in the correction of
arrhythmias (11.1-96). Folk remedies use foxglove as a cardiac tonic
and in the treatment of circulatory failures (11.1-154). The
cardenolides slow and strengthen the heart beat.

Digitalis is poisonous, and symptoms include vomiting, headache,
irregular heartbeat, and convulsions (11.1-96). Overdoses can be fatal.

Several wild strains and cultivated varieties of foxglove exist and
are collected or produced for their ornamental and medicinal values.

BIBLIOGRAPHIC REFERENCES

1.0 CHEMISTRY 1.1-57, 1.1-85, 1.1-212, 1.1-257, 1.1-258, 1.2-8,
1.2-16, 1.3-48, 1.4-51, 1.4-75, 1.5-121, 1.5-136, 1.5-137, 1.6-53,
1.7-56, 1.7-69, 1.7-72, 1.7-82, 1.7-116, 1.7-129, 1.7-138, 1.8-74,
1.8-109, 1.8-136.

2.0 BOTANY 2.1-32, 2.1-41, 2.1-108, 2.1-138, 2.1-144, 2.2-18,
2.2-27, 2.2-87, 2.2-90, 2.2-94, 2.3-72, 2.3-84, 2.3-159, 2.3-179,
2.3-184, 2.4-112, 2.4-127, 2.4-153, 2.4-154, 2.5-20, 2.5-21, 2.5-27,
2.5-58, 2.5-59, 2.5-83, 2.5-106, 2.5-107, 2.5-118, 2.6-10, 2.6-62,
2.7-24, 2.8-34, 2.8-40, 2.9-19, 2.9-70, 2.9-115, 2.9-131, 2.9-142.

3.0 BIONOMICS 3.1-32, 3.1-39, 3.3-13, 3.3-25, 3.3-171, 3.4-22,
3.4-31, 3.4-32, 3.4-49, 3.4-58, 3.6-2, 3.6-6, 3.6-7.

4.0 HORTICULTURE 4.1-31, 4.2-41, 4.2-151, 4.2-195, 4.2-196, 4.3-2,
4.3-27, 4.3-45, 4.3-70, 4.3-95, 4.3-112, 4.3-122, 4.3-195, 4.3-208,
4.4-82, 4.4-83, 4.5-170, 4.5-183, 4.5-184, 4.5-186, 4.5-187, 4.6-4,
4.7-15, 4.9-3, 4.9-45, 4.9-47, 4.9-51, 4.9-57, 4.9-66, 4.9-75, 4.9-76,
4.9-90, 4.9-91, 4.9-92, 4.9-93, 4.9-108, 4.9-134, 4.9-143, 4.9-144,
4.9-145, 4.9-147, 4.9-148, 4.9-149, 4.9-155, 4.9-156, 4.9-167, 4.9-174,
4.9-185.

5.0 PRODUCTION ECOLOGY 5.2-33, 5.4-33, 5.4-61, 5.4-107, 5.5-32,
5.5-90, 5.5-114, 5.5-115, 5.5-157, 5.5-168, 5.6-44, 5.6-45, 5.7-71,
5.7-115, 5.7-185, 5.8-5, 5.8-67, 5.8-123, 5.8-137, 5.8-140, 5.9-29,
5.9-51.

6.0 CULINARY STUDIES 6.2-33, 6.3-30, 6.4-88, 6.5-47.

7.0 PHARMACOLOGY 7.1-1, 7.1-6, 7.1-18, 7.1-22, 7.1-24, 7.1-45,
7.1-48, 7.1-55, 7.1-56, 7.2-3, 7.2-57, 7.2-58, 7.2-64, 7.2-92, 7.3-4,
7.3-11, 7.3-16, 7.3-27, 7.3-34, 7.3-35, 7.3-40, 7.3-41, 7.3-66,
7.3-72, 7.3-75, 7.3-76, 7.3-82, 7.3-83, 7.3-86, 7.3-87, 7.3-92, 7.3-104,
7.3-117, 7.3-135, 7.3-136, 7.3-137, 7.4-4, 7.4-56, 7.5-11, 7.5-18,
7.5-21, 7.5-27, 7.5-33, 7.5-34, 7.5-36, 7.5-38, 7.5-50, 7.5-51, 7.5-82,
7.5-105, 7.5-109, 7.5-110, 7.6-63, 7.6-134, 7.6-150, 7.6-151, 7.7-9,
7.7-12, 7.7-18, 7.7-31, 7.8-2, 7.8-14, 7.8-17, 7.8-36, 7.8-50, 7.8-56,
7.8-67.

9.0 NATURAL DYES AND ORNAMENTAL APPLICATIONS 9.1-4, 9.1-5.

HENNA (Lawsonia inermis L.)

Family: Lythraceae

French: Henne (m)   Italian: Enne (m)
German: Farbemittel (m)   Spanish: Arbusto (m)

Henna, Lawsonia inermis L., a perennial shrub native to northern Africa, Asia, and Australia, is naturalized and cultivated in the tropics of America, Egypt, India, and parts of the Middle East. Also known as El-Henna, Egyptian priest, and mignonette tree, the species is sometimes classified as Lawsonia alba Lam. or Lawsonia ruba. Reaching a height of up to 6 meters, the plant has fragrant white or rose-red flowers.

The reported life zone of henna is 19 to 27 degrees centigrade with an annual precipitation of 0.2 to 4.2 meters and a soil pH of 4.3 to 8.0 (4.1-31). Henna is planted today primarily as an ornamental hedge, but is probably best known for the dried, ground leaves (called henna) traditionally used to produce colorfast orange, red, and brown dyes. Dried, powdered leaves of henna contain about 0.5 to 1.5 percent lawsone, the chief constituent responsible for the dyeing properties of the plant (1.1-273, 14.1-35). Henna also contains mannite, tannic acid, mucilage, gallic acid, and napthaquinone (7.6-192).

The leaves of henna have been used in Asia since antiquity as a hair, nail, and skin dye. In the West and the Middle East, henna is used in hair shampoos, dyes, conditioners, and rinses. Henna dye products are mixed with indigo or other plant material to obtain a greater color range. Extracts of henna are also used to stain wood and to dye fabrics and textiles.

As a medicinal plant, henna has been used for astringent, antihemorrhagic, intestinal antineoplastic, cardio-inhibitory, hypotensive, and sedative effects (7.6-192, 11.1-154). It has also been used as a folk remedy against amoebiasis, headache, jaundice, and leprosy (11.1-154). Henna extracts show antibacterial, antifungal, and ultraviolet light screening activity (1.8-169, 7.2-21, 14.1-21, 14.1-35). Henna has exhibited antifertility activity in animals and may induce menstruation (7.5-76, 11.1-154).

The dried leaf and petiole of henna are generally recognized as safe when used as a color additive for hair (21 CFR section 73.2190 [1982].)

BIBLIOGRAPHIC REFERENCES

1.0 CHEMISTRY 1.1-24, 1.1-25, 1.1-26, 1.1-48, 1.1-158, 1.1-273, 1.8-15, 1.8-58, 1.8-134, 1.8-145, 1.8-146, 1.8-168, 1.8-169, 1.8-170, 1.8-176, 1.9-0.

3.0 BIONOMICS 3.1-1, 3.2-1, 3.2-31, 3.2-47, 3.2-56, 3.2-59, 3.4-31, 3.4-32.

4.0 HORTICULTURE 4.1-31, 4.4-63, 4.5-69, 4.5-163, 4.6-58.

5.0 PRODUCTION ECOLOGY 5.4-47, 5.5-17.

7.0 PHARMACOLOGY 7.2-21, 7.3-8, 7.3-77, 7.5-1, 7.5-15, 7.5-24, 7.5-25, 7.5-26, 7.5-31, 7.5-63, 7.5-70, 7.5-76, 7.6-21, 7.6-192, 7.7-29, 7.8-15.

8.0 PERFUMERY 8.4-5.

HOREHOUND (Marrubium vulgare L.)

Family: Lamiaceae (Labiatae)

French: Marrube (m)   Italian: Marrubio (m)
German: Weisser Andorn (m)   Spanish: Marrubio (m)

Horehound, Marrubium vulgare L., is a spreading perennial herb native to central and western Asia, southern Europe, and northern Africa and naturalized in parts of North America. Also known as common horehound, white horehound, and hoarhound, the plant reaches a height of almost 0.7 meters and is characterized by white, pubescent leaves, woolly stems, and continually blooming white flowers. Commercial production is centered in France. The name "marrubium" refers to the bitter qualities of the herb, and "hoar" refers to the white pubescence covering the plant (14.1-3).

The reported life zone of horehound is 7 to 24 degrees centigrade with an annual precipitation of 0.3 to 1.3 meters and a soil pH of 4.5 to 8.3 (4.1-31). The hardy plant grows in full sun on poor, dry calcareous soils having good drainage.

Although still collected from the wild, horehound is primarily grown in cultivated plantations for commercial uses. The crop is harvested and dried just prior to open bloom. Cultivated stands, which generally last from four to five years, can be cut two or three times each year (4.3-48).

The chief constituent of horehound is the bitter principle marrubium. Tannins, resins, waxes, and a volatile oil containing monoterpenes and a sesquiterpene have also been isolated from the plant (1.1-181, 11.1-50, 11.1-136).

The leaves and stems of horehound are often boiled and used in the preparation of candied products, cough drops, and syrups. Extracts of horehound are used in bitters and liqueurs. The plant is also grown for its ornamental value and is attractive to bees.

As a medicinal plant, horehound has traditionally been used against asthma, coughs, colds, bronchitis, sore throats, and skin irritations. The plant has also been used as a diaphoretic, diuretic, expectorant, laxative, stimulant, stomachic, tonic, and vermifuge. Horehound has been used in treatment of tumors (14.1-16). The volatile oil is a carminative and expectorant, while the bitter principle results in gastric activity (7.5-52, 11.136). Consumption of large quantities of horehound can induce diarrhea and nausea (11.1-136).

Black horehound is the common name for the perennial herb Ballota nigra L., another member of the Lamiaceae family distinguished by its offensive odor, and is used as an antispasmodic, stimulant, and vermifuge (11.1-50).

Horehound is generally recognized as safe for human consumption as a natural flavoring and plant extract (21 CFR sections 182.10, 182.20 [1982]).

BIBLIOGRAPHIC REFERENCES

1.0 CHEMISTRY 1.1-138, 1.1-181, 1.3-12, 1.4-73, 1.5-23, 1.5-24, 1.5-71, 1.5-93.

2.0 BOTANY 2.1-102, 2.1-103, 2.2-103, 2.4-84, 2.7-77, 2.7-86, 2.7-90, 2.9-29, 2.9-101, 2.9-136, 2.9-141.

3.0 BIONOMICS 3.1-54, 3.1-59, 3.1-69, 3.3-53, 3.4-31, 3.4-32.

4.0 HORTICULTURE 4.1-31, 4.3-23, 4.3-48.

5.0 PRODUCTION ECOLOGY 5.2-62, 5.4-78.

6.0 CULINARY STUDIES 6.1-97.

HORSERADISH (Armoracia rusticana P. Gaertn., B. Mey. & Scherb.)

Family: Brassicaceae (Cruciferae)

French: Raifort (m)   Italian: Ramolaccio (m)
German: Meerrettich (m)   Spanish: Rabano(m) rusticano

Horseradish, Armoracia rusticana P. Gaertn., B. Mey. & Scherb.,
is a perennial herb native to Europe and Asia and naturalized in North
America. This species has also been classified as Cochlearia armoracia
L., Nasturtium armoracia (L.) Fries, Radicula armoracia (L.) B. L.
Robinson, Rorippa armoracia (L.) A. S. Hitch., and Armoracia
lapathiofolia Gilib. Reaching a height of one meter, the plant has
deep, fleshy roots and bears white flowers on terminal panicles in late
spring. Horseradish may be an interspecific hybrid and is generally
reported to be sterile. However, viable seed has been produced
(14.1-7). Principal production areas are located in the United States
and, to a lesser extent, in Europe.

The reported life zone of horseradish is 5 to 19 degrees centigrade
with an annual precipitation of 0.5 to 1.7 meters and a soil pH of 5.0
to 7.5 (4.1-31). The hardy horseradish thrives in moist, semi-shaded
environments of the north-temperate regions of North America. Although
the plant will grow on any soil type, best growth is in deep, rich loam
soil high in organic matter.

Horseradish is planted with root crowns and root cuttings.
Traditionally grown as a perennial in eastern Europe, the plant is
cultivated as an annual in the United States. The originally planted
root cuttings are harvested for market and the newly developed lateral
roots are broken off and stored in the dark for planting during the
following season. The planted roots increase in diameter, but not
length, by the end of the growing season (October or November). Of the
two types of horseradish produced, the crinkled-leaf or common
horseradish is thought to be of higher quality but more susceptible to
disease than the smooth-leaved Bohemian type.

The intense pungency and aroma of horseradish is the result of
isothiocyanates released from the glucosinolates sinigrin and
2-phenylethylglucosinolate by the naturally occurring enzyme myrosinase
(6.4-103, 14.1-7). Though the undisturbed root has little odor,
pungency develops upon crushing or grinding the tissue. The roots are
usually processed under refrigeration immediately after dicing, because
of the high volatility of the oil (6.4-103).

As a condiment the horseradish root is usually grated or minced and
mixed with vinegar, salt, or other flavorings to make sauce or relish.
These are often used with fish or other seafood or as an appetizer with
meats. The plant material is also employed as an ingredient in some
catsups and mustards. Horseradish is available in a dehydrated form.

The fresh root of horseradish has been considered an antiseptic,
diaphoretic, diuretic, rubefacient, stimulant, stomachic, and vermifuge.
The material has also been used as a remedy for asthma, coughs, colic,
rheumatism, scurvy, toothache, ulcers, venereal diseases, and cancer
(14.1-14). Peroxidase enzyme is extracted from the plant root and used
as an oxidizer in chemical tests, such as blood glucose determinations.
Horseradish has strong irritant activity and ingestion of large amounts
can cause bloody vomiting and diarrhea (11.1-136). Livestock feeding on
tops or roots of horseradish may be poisoned (11.1-96). The volatiles
of horseradish root are reported to have herbicidal and microbial
activity (1.8-127, 11.1-136).

Japanese horseradish, Wasabia japonica (Miq) Matsum., a glabrous
perennial herb with creeping pungent rhizomes, is found wild along

streams in Japan. Like regular horseradish, it is cultivated and used as a condiment (14.1-25). The horseradish tree, _Moringa pterygosperma_ C. F. Gaertin (formerly _Moringa oleifera_ Lam.), is a fragrant, flowering native of India with edible roots and fruits that belongs to the Moringaceae family (14.1-4).

Horseradish is generally recognized as safe for human consumption as a natural seasoning and flavoring (21 CFR section 182.10 [1982]).

BIBLIOGRAPHIC REFERENCES

1.0 CHEMISTRY 1.1-65, 1.1-109, 1.1-179, 1.1-202, 1.1-223, 1.1-232, 1.3-18, 1.3-26, 1.4-0, 1.4-0, 1.4-88, 1.4-98, 1.5-49, 1.5-76, 1.5-77, 1.6-23, 1.6-31, 1.7-30, 1.7-94, 1.8-127, 1.8-170, 1.8-175.

2.0 BOTANY 2.1-46, 2.1-55, 2.1-101, 2.3-8, 2.4-35, 2.4-63, 2.4-96, 2.4-141, 2.5-16, 2.5-31, 2.6-18, 2.6-78, 2.7-41, 2.7-113, 2.7-114, 2.8-53.

3.0 BIONOMICS 3.3-70, 3.4-31, 3.7-6.

4.0 HORTICULTURE 4.1-31, 4.1-41, 4.1-104, 4.2-288, 4.2-356, 4.2-357, 4.3-35, 4.3-64, 4.3-124, 4.3-139, 4.3-169, 4.3-173, 4.3-202, 4.4-4, 4.4-10, 4.4-11, 4.4-27, 4.4-62, 4.4-71, 4.5-41, 4.5-172, 4.5-225, 4.6-0, 4.9-60, 4.9-61.

5.0 PRODUCTION ECOLOGY 5.3-24, 5.3-59, 5.3-60, 5.4-11, 5.4-35, 5.4-102, 5.4-104, 5.4-129, 5.5-26, 5.5-27, 5.5-91, 5.5-104, 5.5-151, 5.5-232, 5.5-237, 5.5-303, 5.5-341, 5.5-347, 5.7-65, 5.7-102, 5.7-153, 5.7-215, 5.8-34, 5.9-3.

6.0 CULINARY STUDIES 6.1-41, 6.1-50, 6.1-56, 6.1-57, 6.1-58, 6.1-66, 6.1-74, 6.3-18, 6.3-22, 6.3-36, 6.3-48, 6.4-37, 6.4-57, 6.4-103, 6.4-104, 6.5-38, 6.5-48, 6.5-66, 6.5-67, 6.5-68, 6.5-69, 6.5-70, 6.5-71, 6.5-110.

10.0 COMMERCE 10.1-3.

HYSSOP (_Hyssopus officinalis_ L.)

Family: Lamiaceae (Labiatae)

French: Hysope (f)	Italian: Issopo (m)
German: Ysop (m)	Spanish: Hisopo (m)

Hyssop, _Hyssopus officinalis_ L., is a perennial subshrub native to southern Europe, the Mediterranean region, and temperate Asia and naturalized in the United States. Sometimes classified as _Hyssopus aristata_ Godr. or _Hyssopus vulgaris_ Bubani, hyssop is produced commercially in France and several other European countries. The plant reaches a height of 0.5 to 1 meter and bears small blue flowers on a terminal spike.

The reported life zone of hyssop is 7 to 21 degrees centigrade with an annual precipitation of 0.6 to 1.5 meters (4.1-31). The plant grows on dry, rocky, calcareous soils. Traditionally, hyssop seedlings are transplanted into the field with the first harvest occurring two years later, immediately after bloom.

The essential oil is extracted by steam distillation. The oil contains pinocamphone, isopinocamphone, beta-pinene, alpha-pinene, camphene, alpha-terpinene, pinocampheol, cineole, linalool, terpineol, and other compounds (1.2-56, 2.1-68). Hyssop oil may be adulterated with spike, lavandin, lavender, rosemary, and camphor oils (14.1-8).

The flowering tops and leaves of hyssop are used as flavoring agents in such beverages as teas, tonics, and bitters, and to a limited extent in vegetable dishes, soups, salads, and candied products. The essential oil is used in liqueurs, perfumes, soaps, creams, and other cosmetics. The erect growth habit and showy flowers make hyssop a favorite ornamental plant which is also attractive to bees.

As a medicinal plant, hyssop has been used as a carminative, diaphoretic, emmenagogue, expectorant, stimulant, stomachic, and tonic. Leaves have been used as a poultice to remove discoloration around bruised eyes and as a remedy for asthma, rheumatism, sore throats, wounds, ulcers, and tumors (11.1-96, 14.1-16).

Several varieties, differing in flower color and leaf shape, exist; alba (white flowers), grandiflora (large flowers), rosea (rose flowers), and rubia (red flowers) are commercially available (14.1-4). Hedge hyssop refers to the perennial Gratiola officinalis L., a medicinal and potentially poisonous plant of the Scrophulariaceae family. Giant hyssop refers to several perennial Agastache species of the Lamiaceae family (14.1-4).

Hyssop is generally recognized as safe for human consumption as a natural flavoring and plant extract/essential oil (21 CRF sections 182.10, 182.20 [1982]).

BIBLIOGRAPHIC REFERENCES

1.0 CHEMISTRY 1.1-120, 1.1-175, 1.1-190, 1.2-56, 1.7-114, 1.8-69, 1.8-112.

2.0 BOTANY 2.1-68, 2.2-15, 2.2-58, 2.2-107, 2.3-10, 2.3-53, 2.3-112, 2.3-157, 2.4-89, 2.4-128, 2.5-90, 2.8-85.

3.0 BIONOMICS 3.1-80, 3.2-81, 3.3-190, 3.4-31, 3.4-32, 3.5-20, 3.5-213, 3.7-13.

4.0 HORTICULTURE 4.1-31, 4.2-191, 4.3-62, 4.3-112, 4.5-167, 4.6-50, 4.9-96.

5.0 PRODUCTION ECOLOGY 5.6-23, 5.8-26, 5.8-33, 5.8-36, 5.8-37, 5.8-39, 5.8-64, 5.8-86, 5.8-114, 5.8-174, 5.9-5, 5.9-7, 5.9-10, 5.9-11, 5.9-12, 5.9-14, 5.9-19, 5.9-20, 5.9-21, 5.9-23, 5.9-29, 5.9-33, 5.9-35, 5.9-37, 5.9-40, 5.9-41, 5.9-42, 5.9-44, 5.9-46, 5.9-47, 5.9-49, 5.9-50, 5.9-52, 5.9-54, 5.9-55.

6.0 CULINARY STUDIES 6.2-14.

7.0 PHARMACOLOGY 7.4-21, 7.5-105, 7.6-70, 7.7-4, 7.7-24, 7.7-26, 7.8-57.

8.0 PERFUMERY 8.1-5, 8.2-45, 8.2-86.

9.0 NATURAL DYES AND ORNAMENTAL APPLICATIONS 9.2-12.

INDIGO (Indigofera species)

Family: Fabaceae (Leguminosae)

French: Indigotier (m)   Italian: Anile (m)
German: Indigostrauch (m)   Spanish: Anil (m); Indigo (m)

Indigo refers to several species of Indigofera, famous for the natural blue colors obtained from leaflets and branches of this herb. Of primary importance are French indigo, Indigofera tinctoria L., and Guatemalan indigo, Indigofera suffruticosa Mill., which was formerly classified as Indigofera anil L. These plants are perennial shrubs with an erect stem reaching a height of 1 to 2 meters. The French and Guatemalan indigo differ in size and shape of the leaflets and pods (14.1-3). Prior to the development of synthetic aniline and indigo dyes, the indigo species were grown commercially in the East Indies, India, and parts of North, South, and Central America for export and domestic use. Popularity and economic value of the plant reached a peak during the Middle Ages, when indigo was the most important dye plant for blue color in the western portion of the world (9.1-5).

The reported life zone of Indigofera tinctoria is 16 to 27 degrees centigrade with an annual precipitation of 0.7 to 4.2 meters and a soil pH of 5.0 to 7.3 (4.1-31). Indigo is generally grown as a perennial shrub, although in Morocco it grows as a biennial herbaceous plant (13.1-76).

The blue dyestuff is produced during fermentation of the leaves, commonly with caustic soda or sodium hydrosulfite. A paste that exudes from fermenting plant material is processed into cakes and finely ground. The blue color develops as the material is exposed to air (13.1-76). The indigo dye is a derivative of indican, a natural constituent of several of the Indigofera species (14.1-19). Indican is enzymatically converted to blue indigotin (14.1-35). The colorfast dye is mixed with different mordants and other plant materials to produce a wide range of colorants. The species name tinctoria refers to tinctorius, meaning "of dyes" or "belonging to dyes" (14.1-3). Today almost all indigo for dyeing cotton and wool is synthesized commercially.

As a medicinal plant, indigo has been used as an emetic. The Chinese use Indigofera tinctoria L. to clean the liver, detoxify the blood, reduce inflammation, alleviate pain, and reduce fever (11.1-10). The powdered root of Indigofera cf. patens is used in South Africa to alleviate toothache (11.1-96). Indigofera spirata is known as a plant teratogen because of the presence of indospicine (11.1-96). Indigofera endecaphylla plant, creeping indigo, is poisonous and has been responsible for livestock death (11.1-96). Indigofera arrecta Hochst. ex A. Rich and Indigofera caroliniana Mill. are used as dye plants (9.1-5).

False, wild, and bastard indigo are names for Baptisia tinctoria L., a native North-American member of the Leguminosae family, whose leaves, pods, and bark are used to make a blue color. Medicinally, it is employed as an astringent, emetic, stimulant, and antiseptic. Fake indigo and Baptisia leucantha are reported to have caused poisonings, diarrhea, vomiting, and loss of appetite (11.1-96, 11.1-136). Strobilanthes flaccidifolis and Dalea emoryi L., known as indigo bush, have been used as indigo dye plants.

BIBLIOGRAPHIC REFERENCES

1.0 CHEMISTRY 1.2-8, 1.2-16, 1.8-135, 1.9-0.
2.0 BOTANY 2.2-87, 2.4-127, 2.9-19, 2.9-142.

countries, the plant reaches a height of about one meter, has linear, lanceolate leaves covered with a velvety pubescence, and develops blue or purple flowers. French lavender, also known as fringed lavender, and formerly classified as Lavandula delphinensis Hort., is native to Spain. Grown as a popular ornamental, plants have long, linear, toothed, tomentose leaves that are a gray color and flowers that are a purplish color.

The reported life zone of lavender is 7 to 21 degrees centigrade with an annual precipitation of 0.3 to 1.3 meters and a soil pH of 5.8 to 8.3 (4.1-31). Lavender grows in well drained, dry, calcareous soils located in full sun. Plants can be directly seeded, but are usually transplanted from vegetative cuttings. Growth is slow, and it takes a few years for the crop to develop fully. Some varieties have been bred to display their terminal inflorescence high above the foliage to facilitate hand and mechanized harvesting. Established plantings can last as long as thirty years. Lavender oil is obtained by the immediate steam distillation or solvent extraction of flowers harvested at full bloom. The essential oil contains linalyl acetate, linalool, 1,8-cineole, camphor, alpha-pinene, and several other compounds (8.3-78, 14.1-8). The concrete and absolute are commercially available.

The leaves and flowers of lavender are used in regions where the plant is grown as a flavoring in salads, dressings, fruit desserts, jellies, and wines (14.1-23). The plant and oil are used in herbal teas and as a flavoring mixed with black teas. Flowers and leaves are sometimes used in sachets, potpourris, and dried bouquets. The plant material is used to perfume linen and scent tobacco. The oil is used in perfumes, toilet water, and cosmetics. The plants are grown as ornamentals along garden borders, in rock gardens, and as potted outdoor plants. The plants are also grown near highways for beautification and stabilization of soil. Lavender plants are attractive to bees.

As a medicinal plant, the lavenders have traditionally been considered antispasmodics, carminatives, diuretics, nervines, stimulants, and tonics. They have been used as a folk remedy against colic and headaches. The essential oil of lavender is reported to have antiseptic, carminative, and spasmolytic activity (11.1-154). The leaves are considered to be an insect repellant (14.1-23).

Cultivated for perfumery and ornamental purposes, Spanish lavender, Lavandula stoechas L., also known as French lavender, has narrow tomentose leaves and purplish flowers. Spike or broad-leaved lavender, Lavandula latifolia Medic., has wide, gray-green tomentose leaves and is collected in the countryside of Spain for use in perfume. Lavandin, Lavandula hybrida Reverchon, is a hybrid of English and spike lavender and is reported to supply one of the most important essential oils in the fragrance industry (8.2-48). The plants produce a high yield of lower quality lavender oil, which is used in the less expensive perfumes, in scenting soaps, and in the adulteration of other higher-quality lavender oils (14.1-8).

English lavender is generally recognized as safe for human consumption as a natural flavoring, and spike lavender and lavandin are generally recognized as safe for use as natural plant extracts/essential oils (21 CFR sections 182.10, 182.20 [1982]).

BIBLIOGRAPHIC REFERENCES

1.0 CHEMISTRY 1.1-131, 1.1-229, 1.7-15, 1.7-64, 1.7-65.
2.0 BOTANY 2.1-9, 2.1-35, 2.2-13, 2.2-82, 2.2-89, 2.3-26, 2.3-201, 2.4-94, 2.5-16, 2.5-31, 2.5-96, 2.5-104, 2.6-63, 2.7-12, 2.7-101, 2.8-26, 2.8-56, 2.9-20, 2.9-58.
3.0 BIONOMICS 3.1-59, 3.1-80, 3.2-68, 3.3-9, 3.3-11, 3.3-53, 3.3-58, 3.4-32, 3.4-39, 3.4-95, 3.4-99.

4.0 HORTICULTURE 4.1-31, 4.2-83, 4.2-185, 4.2-197, 4.2-224, 4.2-276, 4.2-286, 4.5-13, 4.5-14, 4.5-53, 4.5-163.
    5.0 PRODUCTION ECOLOGY 5.1-37, 5.1-61, 5.5-55, 5.5-100, 5.5-101, 5.5-179, 5.5-180, 5.5-192, 5.5-340, 5.5-380, 5.6-68, 5.7-124, 5.7-174, 5.7-238, 5.8-161.
    6.0 CULINARY STUDIES 6.5-102.
    7.0 PHARMACOLOGY 7.7-29.
    8.0 PERFUMERY 8.1-3, 8.1-11, 8.2-16, 8.2-23, 8.2-45, 8.2-48, 8.2-53, 8.2-93, 8.2-97, 8.3-2, 8.3-13, 8.3-21, 8.3-30, 8.3-33, 8.3-39, 8.3-62, 8.3-78, 8.3-86, 8.3-96.

LEMON BALM (Melissa officinalis L.)

Family: Lamiaceae (Labiatae)

French: Melisse (f) officinale;   Italian: Cedrina (f)
        Melisse (f) citronnelle
German: Zitronemelisse (f)
                                     Spanish: Melisa (f); Toronjil (m)

    Lemon balm, Melissa officinalis L., a perennial herb native to southern climates of Europe and North America, is presently found in both wild and cultivated states. Several other species of Melissa have been reported from the Mediterranean and central Asian areas, but only Melissa officinalis L. is cultivated. The plant grows erect and reaches a height of 0.5 to 1 meter.
    The reported life zone of balm is 7 to 23 degrees centigrade with 0.5 to 1.3 meters annual precipitation and a soil pH of 4.5 to 7.8 (4.1-31). The plant, which develops best in full sun and deep soil, is sensitive to cold temperature and excessive or inadequate water levels in the soil.
    Horticulturally, lemon balm is grown as an annual or perennial, harvested only once at flowering during the first year and twice in subsequent years. Significant loss of aroma sometimes occurs during drying. Both the white and pink flowers, which blossom from middle to late summer, and the vegetative portion of the plant are known to attract honeybees (1.8-38). The name of the genus, Melissa, comes from the Greek word meaning "bee," attesting to the early recognition of this characteristic (14.1-3). Irrigation does not appear to alter the essential oil in balm (4.5-167).
    The volatile oil, obtained by steam distillation of plant material immediately after harvest, is used only limitedly in perfumery because of perfumers are able to simulate the odor of lemon balm with less expensive extracts of other aromatic plants. The oil content of fresh leaves averages 0.1 percent or less with a large range between 0.01 and 0.13 percent (14.1-8). Multiple harvests and optimum horticultural practices have been reported to increase the percent of extractable essential oil (4.3-15). The highest levels of essential oil have been extracted in late summer from the lower parts of the plants (4.3-15). The essential oil contains geraniol, citronellol, cintronellal, linalool, eugenol acetate, and nerol. The essential oil is often adulterated with mixtures of lemongrass, citronella, or lemon oil (14.1-8).
    The green, lemony-scented, aromatic leaves are used both fresh and dried as a seasoning in salad dressings, sauces, soups, meats, vegetables, desserts, and confections. Dried leaves are often used in potpourris. As a flavoring agent, balm is used in some alcoholic

beverages and liqueurs and in herbal teas. Several varieties, including a variegated type, are available for ornamental uses, especially as border plants in gardens.

As a medicinal plant, lemon balm has traditionally been employed against catarrh, fever, flatulence, headaches, influenza, and toothaches. It has also been used as a carminative, diaphoretic, and sedative. Recent evidence suggests that lemon balm has a depressant or sedative action on the central nervous systems of laboratory mice (7.5-90). Oil of balm has also been shown to have antiviral, antibacterial, and antispasmodic activity. Lemon balm has been reported to be an insect repellant (11.1-96).

Bee balm (Monarda spp.), often confused with lemon balm, is a separate member of the Labiatae family.

Lemon balm is generally considered safe for human consumption as a spice/natural flavoring and a plant/oil extract (21 CFR sections 182.10, 182.20 [1982]).

BIBLIOGRAPHIC REFERENCES

1.0 CHEMISTRY 1.1-37, 1.1-175, 1.1-250, 1.4-84, 1.5-68, 1.8-38.

2.0 BOTANY 2.1-114, 2.2-58, 2.3-73, 2.3-86, 2.3-237, 2.5-31, 2.6-83.

3.0 BIONOMICS 3.1-16, 3.2-77, 3.3-98, 3.4-31, 3.4-32.

4.0 HORTICULTURE 4.1-31, 4.3-15, 4.3-112, 4.3-128, 4.3-146, 4.3-168, 4.3-170, 4.4-50, 4.5-166, 4.5-167, 4.8-4.

5.0 PRODUCTION ECOLOGY 5.4-16, 5.4-34, 5.4-107, 5.5-64, 5.5-290.

6.0 CULINARY STUDIES 6.1-26, 6.5-32, 6.5-60, 6.5-111.

7.0 PHARMACOLOGY 7.1-41, 7.3-93, 7.3-130, 7.5-25, 7.5-26, 7.5-90, 7.5-108, 7.6-52, 7.6-212, 7.7-29.

8.0 PERFUMERY 8.2-38.

LEMONGRASS (Cymbopogon species)

Family: Poaceae (Gramineae)

French: Jonc (m) odorant   Italian: Citronella (f)
German: Cymbopogon species   Spanish: Cymbopogon species

Lemongrass, a perennial herb widely cultivated in the tropics and subtropics, designates two different species, East Indian, Cymbopogon flexuosus (DC.) Stapf., and West Indian, Cymbopogon citratus (DC. ex Nees) Stapf. East Indian lemongrass, also known as cochin or Malabar grass is native to India, while West Indian lemongrass is native to southern India and Ceylon. The lemongrasses are cultivated commercially in Guatemala, India, the People's Republic of China, Paraguay, England, Sri Lanka, and other parts of Indochina, Africa, Central America, and South America (11.1-73). The plant grows in dense clumps up to 2 meters in diameter and has leaves up to 1 meter long.

The reported life zone for lemongrass is 18 to 29 degrees centigrade with an annual precipitation of 0.7 to 4.1 meters with a soil pH of 5.0 to 5.8 (East Indian) or 4.3 to 8.4 (West Indian) (14.1-9). The plants need a warm, humid climate in full sun. They grow well in sandy soils with adequate drainage. Since the plants rarely flower or set seed, propagation is by root or plant division. The plants are harvested mechanically or by hand about four times each year with the productive populations lasting between four and eight years (14.1-9). Extensive breeding programs have developed many varieties of lemongrass.

The quality of lemongrass oil is generally determined by the content of citral, the aldehyde responsible for the lemon odor. Some other constituents of the essential oils are alpha-terpineol, myrcene, citronellol, methyl heptenone, dipentene, geraniol, limonene, nerol, and farnesol (14.1-9). West Indian oil differs from East Indian oil in that it is less soluble in 70 percent alcohol and has a slightly lower citral content (14.1-9).

Lemongrass is used in herbal teas and other nonalcoholic beverages, in baked goods, and in confections. Oil from lemongrass is widely used as a fragrance in perfumes and cosmetics, such as soaps and creams. Citral, extracted from the oil, is used in flavoring soft drinks, in scenting soaps and detergents, as a fragrance in perfumes and cosmetics, and as a mask for disagreeable odors in several industrial products. Citral is also used in the synthesis of ionones used in perfumes and cosmetics (11.1-73, 14.1-9).

As a medicinal plant, lemongrass has been considered a carminative and insect repellant. West Indian lemongrass is reported to have antimicrobial activity (1.8-84, 1.8-130). Oil of West Indian lemongrass acts as a central nervous system depressant (7.6-187). Oil of East Indian lemongrass has antifungal activity (1.8-132). The volatile oils may also have some pesticide and mutagenic activities (11.1-96, 11.1-136).

Cymbopogon nardus is a source of citronella oil. Cymbopogon martinii is reportedly toxic to fungi (1.8-53).

Lemongrass is generally recognized as safe for human consumption as a plant extract/essential oil (21 CFR section 182.20 [1982]).

BIBLIOGRAPHIC REFERENCES

1.0 CHEMISTRY 1.2-80, 1.4-19, 1.5-8, 1.6-5, 1.8-22, 1.8-24, 1.8-53, 1.8-54, 1.8-64, 1.8-84, 1.8-121, 1.8-130, 1.8-132, 1.8-152.

2.0 BOTANY 2.4-55, 2.4-56, 2.5-82, 2.6-60, 2.9-42.

3.0 BIONOMICS 3.2-9, 3.2-69, 3.3-6, 3.3-31, 3.3-147, 3.4-15, 3.4-25, 3.4-30, 3.4-32.

4.0 HORTICULTURE 4.1-71, 4.1-92, 4.2-336, 4.3-153, 4.3-200, 4.5-174, 4.5-175, 4.6-12, 4.6-14, 4.8-53.

5.0 PRODUCTION ECOLOGY 5.5-70, 5.5-221, 5.5-242, 5.5-287, 5.7-112.

6.0 CULINARY STUDIES 6.4-40, 6.4-99, 6.5-133.

7.0 PHARMACOLOGY 7.1-62, 7.5-74, 7.6-58, 7.6-187.

8.0 PERFUMERY 8.2-47, 8.2-72, 8.2-73, 8.2-79, 8.2-81, 8.2-84, 8.2-98, 8.2-99, 8.3-45, 8.3-67, 8.3-104.

10.0 COMMERCE 10.2-2, 10.2-4.

LEMON VERBENA (Aloysia triphylla (L'Her.) Britt.)

Family: Verbenaceae

French: Vervein (f) citronelle;   Italian: Erba (f) luisa;
      Vervein (f) odorante   Limoncina (f); Cedrina (f)
German: Zitronenkraut (n);   Spanish: Luisa (f); Hierba luisa (f);
      Punschkraut (n)   Yerbaluisa (f)

Lemon verbena, Aloysia triphylla (L'Her.) Britt., is an aromatic shrub native to Argentina and Chile. Also known as herb Louisa and formerly classified as Aloysia citriodora (Cav.) Ort., Lippia citriodora (Ort.) HBK, Verbena citriodora Cav., and Verbena triphylla

L'Her., the deciduous plant is commonly cultivated in the tropics and Europe. It is produced commercially in France and North Africa. Reaching heights of 1 to 3 meters, the plants are characterized by fragrant, lemon-smelling, narrow leaves and small white flowers borne in terminal panicles.

Lemon verbena prefers full sun and a light loam soil. The plant is sensitive to cold and has high water requirements. Either seeds or vegetative cuttings are used for generating new plants. Commercial areas are generally harvested in early summer at full bloom and in the autumn just prior to cold, killing temperatures. Essential oil is extracted by steam distillation as soon as possible to minimize volatilization, because yields of the oil are very low (14.1-11).

The essential oil, known as oil of verbena, contains alpha-citral, beta-citral, methyl heptenone, carvone, l-limonene, dipentene, linalool, alpha-terpineol, borneol, nerol, geraniol, and other compounds (14.1-11). Because of the its high price, oil of verbena is often adulterated with distillates from other plant material. Extraction of verbena with petroleum ether and alcohol gives the concrete and absolute of verbena (14.1-11).

The leaves and flowering tops of lemon verbena are used in teas and to flavor alcoholic beverages. The plant is also an ingredient in some desserts, fruit salads, and jams. It is used in perfumery, especially in making toilet water and eau de cologne. The plant is often grown as an ornamental, but it needs to be kept indoors during winter months in northern regions.

As a medicinal plant, the leaves and flowers of lemon verbena have been used as an antispasmodic, antipyretic, sedative, and stomachic.

Lemon verbena is generally recognized as safe for human consumption in alcoholic beverages (21 CFR section 172.510 [1982]).

BIBLIOGRAPHIC REFERENCES

1.0 CHEMISTRY 1.1-58, 1.1-142, 1.1-190, 1.2-58, 1.2-84, 1.3-31, 1.5-114, 1.5-154, 1.7-65.
2.0 BOTANY 2.1-53, 2.6-57, 2.7-21, 2.8-15, 2.8-28.
3.0 BIONOMICS 3.1-76, 3.3-53, 3.3-114.
4.0 HORTICULTURE 4.3-36, 4.4-35, 4.4-38, 4.6-53.
5.0 PRODUCTION ECOLOGY 5.5-291.
6.0 CULINARY STUDIES 6.1-12, 6.5-111.
7.0 PHARMACOLOGY 7.5-108, 7.7-32.
8.0 PERFUMERY 8.1-5, 8.1-17, 8.1-30.

LICORICE (Glycyrrhiza glabra L.)

Family: Fabaceae (Leguminosae)

French: Reglisse (f)   Italian: Liquirizia (f)
German: Suessholz (n)   Spanish: Regaliz (m)

Licorice, Glycyrrhiza glabra L., has long been prized for the roots and rhizomes (collectively called roots), which are used for flavoring and medicinal purposes. Native to the Mediterranean region and to central through southwest Asia, the plant is produced principally in Spain, France, Italy, Greece, Iran, Iraq, Turkey, and Syria (11.1-74). Reaching a height of 1 to 1.5 meters, the perennial plant has dark green leaflets, yellow, blue, or violet flowers, and sweet-flavored rhizomes.

The reported life zone of licorice is 6 to 25 degrees centigrade with an annual precipitation of 0.3 to 1.1 meters and a soil pH of 5.5 to 8.2 (4.1-31). The plant prefers deep sandy oil located in warm regions that have long photoperiods.

Although the plant can be grown from seed, commercial plantings are usually propagated from vegetative cuttings of rhizomes, suckers, or crowns (14.1-29). Marketable-size rhizomes develop in three to five years. Harvesting takes place in the autumn, after the foliage has dried. Commercial licorice is available in many forms, including sticks, peeled or unpeeled, solid extract, and block juice.

Licorice contains glycyrrhizin, saponin, asparagine, sugars, resin, bitter principles, a volatile oil, and other compounds (6.1-29, 11.1-136, 14.1-35). Commercial glycyrrhizin is the ammoniated form of glycyrrhzic acid, which tends to intensify other flavors, such as chocolate and maple (11.1-74).

Glycyrrhizin, the main constituent of licorice, is more than fifty times sweeter than cane sugar (11.1-74). The powdered licorice root is employed as a natural sweetner in alcoholic and nonalcoholic beverages, confections, and pharmaceuticals. Licorice is often mixed with anise oil, which has a licorice-like scent, for use as candy or in flavoring of other candies, pastries or baked goods. Licorice extract has been used as a foaming agent in fire extinguishers (11.1-67).

As a medicinal plant, licorice has been considered a demulcent, diuretic, emollient, expectorant, laxative, pectoral, and stomachic. Folk remedies call for licorice to be used against asthma, bronchitis, coughs, fevers, ulcers, and cancers (11.1-97, 14.1-17). Licorice is known to have mineralocorticoid, spasmolytic, and estrogenic properties (7.8-10). The bark of licorice plants contains a hemolytically active saponin. Glycyrrhetinic acid, a constituent of glycyrrhizin, is used in the commercial preparation of carbenoxolone, employed as an anti-inflammatory agent against gastric ulcers and in the treatment of Addison's disease (11.1-74). Excessive licorice is known to promote cardiovascular toxicity, hypertension, and edema (11.1-136). Metabolic effects may occur in individuals consuming only modest amounts (7.8-20).

The licorice of commerce is derived from several varieties of Glycyrrhiza glabra L., including var. typica (Spanish), var. glandulifera (Russian), and beta-ulolacea (Persian). Glycyrrhiza uralensis Fisch., Chinese licorice, has long been used in treatment of ulcers and Addison's disease (11.1-97). Wild licorice refers to Aralia nudicaulis L. of the Araliaceae family.

Licorice is generally recognized as safe for human consumption as a natural flavoring and plant extract (21 CFR sections 182.10, 182.20 [1982]).

BIBLIOGRAPHIC REFERENCES

1.0 CHEMISTRY 1.1-4, 1.1-22, 1.1-23, 1.1-27, 1.1-28, 1.1-30, 1.1-61, 1.1-63, 1.1-64, 1.1-83, 1.1-128, 1.1-129, 1.1-132, 1.1-133, 1.1-134, 1.1-135, 1.1-136, 1.1-144, 1.1-152, 1.1-169, 1.1-196, 1.1-197, 1.1-198, 1.1-215, 1.1-216, 1.1-253, 1.1-263, 1.2-8, 1.3-7, 1.3-30, 1.3-47, 1.4-15, 1.4-37, 1.4-38, 1.4-99, 1.5-2, 1.5-16, 1.5-39, 1.5-63, 1.5-72, 1.5-135, 1.7-7, 1.7-86, 1.8-29, 1.8-30, 1.8-70, 1.8-105, 1.8-106, 1.8-129, 1.8-172, 1.8-179.

2.0 BOTANY 2.1-25, 2.2-45, 2.2-51, 2.2-87, 2.2-96, 2.3-1, 2.3-3, 2.3-6, 2.3-75, 2.3-101, 2.3-154, 2.3-239, 2.4-2, 2.4-3, 2.4-4, 2.4-81, 2.5-71, 2.5-87, 2.6-3, 2.9-91.

3.0 BIONOMICS 3.1-42, 3.1-50, 3.1-74, 3.2-63, 3.3-39, 3.3-101, 3.3-102, 3.3-156, 3.3-185, 3.3-194, 3.4-1, 3.4-6, 3.4-12, 3.4-13, 3.4-24, 3.4-123.

4.0 HORTICULTURE 4.1-31, 4.1-70, 4.1-105, 4.2-1, 4.2-157, 4.3-4, 4.3-52, 4.3-88, 4.3-96, 4.3-104, 4.3-115, 4.3-116, 4.3-117, 4.3-144, 4.8-73, 4.9-9, 4.9-160, 4.9-169, 4.9-174, 4.9-188.

5.0 PRODUCTION ECOLOGY 5.1-87, 5.2-2, 5.2-17, 5.3-1, 5.3-15, 5.3-39, 5.4-83, 5.5-3, 5.5-145, 5.7-36, 5.8-156.

6.0 CULINARY STUDIES 6.1-16, 6.1-23, 6.1-29, 6.3-60, 6.4-3, 6.4-63, 6.4-91, 6.4-95, 6.4-115, 6.5-152.

7.0 PHARMACOLOGY 7.1-2, 7.1-7, 7.1-30, 7.1-57, 7.1-65, 7.2-16, 7.2-40, 7.2-48, 7.2-66, 7.2-81, 7.2-83, 7.3-1, 7.3-5, 7.3-15, 7.3-29, 7.3-50, 7.3-63, 7.3-86, 7.3-88, 7.3-91, 7.3-98, 7.3-99, 7.3-100, 7.3-103, 7.3-108, 7.3-109, 7.3-114, 7.3-115, 7.3-128, 7.3-129, 7.3-133, 7.3-138, 7.3-141, 7.3-147, 7.3-159, 7.3-163, 7.4-14, 7.4-25, 7.4-33, 7.4-35, 7.4-38, 7.4-39, 7.4-40, 7.4-43, 7.4-52, 7.4-53, 7.5-5, 7.5-39, 7.5-59, 7.5-62, 7.5-77, 7.5-97, 7.5-104, 7.5-117, 7.5-126, 7.6-15, 7.6-16, 7.6-17, 7.6-18, 7.6-19, 7.6-24, 7.6-25, 7.6-37, 7.6-47, 7.6-48, 7.6-49, 7.6-50, 7.6-68, 7.6-83, 7.6-86, 7.6-87, 7.6-90, 7.6-119, 7.6-132, 7.6-157, 7.6-163, 7.6-164, 7.6-171, 7.6-188, 7.6-203, 7.6-208, 7.6-216, 7.6-217, 7.6-222, 7.7-11, 7.7-14, 7.7-22, 7.7-30, 7.7-35, 7.8-4, 7.8-10, 7.8-20, 7.8-33, 7.8-46, 7.8-61, 7.8-62, 7.8-63.

8.0 PERFUMERY 8.4-7, 8.4-10, 8.4-11.

LOBELIA (Lobelia inflata L.)

Family: Campanulaceae

French: Lobelie (f)   Italian: Lobelia (f)
German: Lobelie (f)   Spanish: Lobelia (f)

Lobelia, Lobelia inflata L., is typically an annual plant that reaches a height of one meter. Sometimes called Indian tobacco, wild tobacco, asthma weed, gagroot, vomitroot, pulseweed, emetic herb, bladder pod, low belia, and eyebright, this native North American plant is poisonous (14.1-28).

The reported life zone of lobelia is 7 to 19 degrees centigrade with an annual precipitation of 0.7 to 1.3 meters and a soil pH of 4.8 to 6.8 (4.1-31). The cultivated plant grows well on a rich, moist loam soil in full sun or partial shade (14.1-29). Pale blue flowers appear in summer and last until frost. The plant develops two-celled, capsuled capsule fruits. The leaves, tops, and fruit are collected during seed formation as the fruit capsules begin to enlarge (14.1-28).

Several alkaloids are found in the plant. The main alkaloid is lobeline, and others include lobelidine, lobelanine, nor-lobelaine, lobelanidine, nor-lobelanidine, lobeline and isolobenine, as well as fourteen pyridine alkaloids, which give the plant a total alkaloid content of up to 0.63 percent (11.1-96, 11.1-136, 14.1-34).

Lobelia has been used medicinally as an expectorant, emetic, anti-asthmatic, stimulant, antispasmodic, diaphoretic, diuretic, and nervine. In addition, the plant or its extracts have served to induce vomiting, to encourage and to stimulate respiration in cases of general and pelvic-musculature muscle relaxation during childbirth, narcotic overdose and newborn infants (11.1-96, 11.1-154). Lobeline has been of some benefit in commercial preparations of antismoking products (11.1-96). Lobelia, after it has been chewed, tastes similar to tobacco and produces effects like those of nicotine. These similarities account for the plant's having been called Indian tobacco and for reports of its stimulatory and depressant activity. Toxicological properties of

lobelia   include   dizziness,   nausea,   hypotension,   vomiting,   stupor,
tremors,   paralysis,   convulsions,   coma,   and   death   (11.1-136,   14.1-35).
Use of lobelia in some products, such as cigarettes and herb teas, could
account   for   the   psychoactive   effects   of   these   herbal   preparations
(7.8-54).

Lobelia nicotianaefolia is used   in   India   to   treat   bronchitis,
asthma, and insect and scorpion bites and to induce nausea and vomiting.
(11.1-96).   Lobelia erinus L., an annual used extensively   as   a   garden
border plant, has numerous varieties that vary in foliage color, flower
size, and growth habit.   The plant has also   been   used   medicinally   to
treat   cancer, syphilis, and other venereal diseases (11.1-50).   Chinese
herbal medicine employs Lobelia radicans Thunb.   to   treat   sores   and
abscesses, poisonous snakebites, tooth abscesses, ascites, and traumatic
injuries (11.1-10).

BIBLIOGRAPHIC REFERENCES

1.0 CHEMISTRY 1.1-272.
3.0 BIONOMICS 3.1-9, 3.2-16, 3.4-31.
4.0 HORTICULTURE 4.1-31, 4.3-95, 4.4-3, 4.4-38, 4.4-70, 4.8-40.
5.0 PRODUCTION ECOLOGY 5.5-163, 5.5-315, 5.7-118.
7.0 PHARMACOLOGY 7.1-35, 7.2-50, 7.2-68,   7.2-85,   7.3-74,   7.5-38,
7.5-106, 7.8-54.
9.0 NATURAL DYES AND ORNAMENTAL APPLICATIONS 9.2-4.

LOVAGE (Levisticum officinale W.D.J. Koch.)

Family: Apiaceae (Umbelliferae)

French: Liveche (f)   Italian: Levistico (m)
German: Liebstoeckel (n);   Spanish: Apio (m) de montana
        Maggikraut (n)

Lovage, Levisticum officinale W.D.J. Koch., a perennial herb   native
to   the   mountainous   regions   of northern Europe and naturalized in the
eastern United States,   has   been   grown   over   the   centuries   for   its
aromatic fragrance,   its   fine   ornamental   qualities,   and to a lesser
extent, its medicinal values.   All parts of   the   plant,   including   the
roots,   are   strongly   aromatic   and contain extractable essential oils.
The plant has been alternatively classified as Ligusticum levisticum L.,
Hipposelinum levisticum,   Britt.   and   Rose,   and   Angelica levisticum
Baillon.

Ecologically, the reported life zone is 6 to 18   degrees   centigrade
with 0.5 to 1.5 meters annual precipitation and a soil pH of 5.0 to 7.8
(4.1-31).   Lovage thrives in deep, moist, rich soils   and   can   grow   in
full sun or lightly shaded areas.

Centers of lovage cultivation are   located   principally   in   central
Europe,   where the plants are collected and the essential oils extracted
by steam distillation.   The fresh roots, which produce an oil similar to
angelica's   when   crushed   and   distilled,   are generally first harvested
from two- to three-year-old plants.   Subsequent   harvests   take   place
every   third   year.   Chemical   constituents   of   lovage oil are mainly
phthalides   and   terpenoids,   including   n-butylidene   phthalide,
n-butyl-phthalide,   sedanonic   anhydride,   d-alpha-terpineol,   carvacrol,
eugenol, and volatile acids (14.1-9).

The variations in aroma and fragrance among the different   parts   of the plant allow each portion of the plant to be utilized somewhat differently. The volatile oil extracted from the roots is highly valued for use in perfumery, soaps, and creams,and it has been used for flavoring tobacco products. The seeds and seed oil are used as flavoring agents in confectionery and liqueurs. The stems are used for candied products, and leaves are added to salads, soups, and stews because of their pungent, celery-like flavor.

As a medicinal plant, lovage has been used as a carminative, diaphoretic, diuretic, emmenagogue, expectorant, stimulant, and stomachic; and also as a treatment for jaundice. Current medicinal applications include use as a diuretic and for regulation of menses. Several coumarins have been identified in lovage oil (1.1-94, 7.2-2, 14.1-9).

Scotch lovage, Ligusticum scoticum or Levisticum scoticum, native to coastal areas of northwest Europe and England, is sometimes used as a vegetable, but is not economically important. Because of similar development, black lovage, Smyrnium olisatrum L., and bastard lovage, Laserpitium latifolium L., are sometimes mistaken for lovage. Water lovage, Oenanthe crocata L., is a poisonous plant of the Apiaceae family (11.1-49).

Lovage is generally recognized as safe for human consumption as a natural seasoning and flavoring agent (21 CFR section 172.510 [1982]).

BIBLIOGRAPHIC REFERENCES

1.0 CHEMISTRY 1.1-74, 1.1-94, 1.1-177, 1.2-43, 1.5-91, 1.5-145.

2.0 BOTANY 2.1-29, 2.1-31, 2.1-71, 2.1-73, 2.1-125, 2.2-26, 2.3-121, 2.3-126, 2.3-228, 2.6-72, 2.7-110, 2.8-29, 2.8-64, 2.9-43.

3.0 BIONOMICS 3.1-31, 3.2-28, 3.3-73, 3.3-120, 3.3-165, 3.4-31, 3.4-32, 3.4-55, 3.5-6, 3.5-7.

4.0 HORTICULTURE 4.1-31, 4.1-84, 4.1-85, 4.2-265, 4.2-293, 4.3-63, 4.3-93, 4.3-151, 4.4-43, 4.5-90, 4.5-100, 4.6-80, 4.6-86, 4.6-91, 4.6-92, 4.8-41, 4.8-45, 4.8-81.

5.0 PRODUCTION ECOLOGY 5.2-26, 5.2-81, 5.3-27, 5.3-28, 5.3-30, 5.4-94, 5.5-32, 5.5-168, 5.5-232, 5.5-250, 5.8-90, 5.8-118, 5.8-137, 5.8-174, 5.9-37.

6.0 CULINARY STUDIES 6.1-31, 6.1-79, 6.2-14, 6.4-30, 6.4-31, 6.5-45, 6.5-153.

7.0 PHARMACOLOGY 7.1-27, 7.2-2, 7.2-9, 7.2-12, 7.2-53, 7.5-49, 7.5-74, 7.5-110, 7.5-118, 7.6-195, 7.7-17.

8.0 PERFUMERY 8.2-43, 8.2-62, 8.2-86, 8.3-58.

9.0 NATURAL DYES AND ORNAMENTAL APPLICATIONS 9.1-2, 9.2-10.

MARJORAM (Origanum majorana L.)

Family: Lamiaceae (Labiatae)

French: Marjolaine (f)   Italian: Maggiorana (f)
German: Majoran (m)   Spanish: Mejorana (f)

Marjoram, Origanum majorana L., is a tender perennial herb native to North Africa and southwest Asia and naturalized in southern Europe. Formerly clasified as Majorana hortensis Moench. and also known as sweet or knotted marjoram, the plant reaches a height of 0.5 meters and has small, gray-green, ovate leaves, pink or purple flowers, and erect, glabrous to tomentose stems. Marjoram is cultivated in France, Greece,

Hungary, the United States, Egypt, and several other Mediterranean countries.

The reported life zone of marjoram is 6 to 28 degrees centigrade with an annual precipitation of 0.5 to 2.7 meters and a soil pH of 4.9 to 8.7 (4.1-31). The plant is adapted to well-drained, fertile loa soils. The cold-sensitive plant cannot survive northern climates. For cultivation, marjoram is both seeded directly and transplanted into fields. Harvesting is generally accomplished at full bloom and can be done two or three times per year, depending upon the growing region Plant material is often dried in drying sheds to avoid direct sunlight and thus preserve the green color and the aroma.

The essential oil obtained by steam distillation contains terpen-4-ol, gamma-terpinene, alpha-terpineol, alpha-terpinene, cis-sabinene hydrate, linalool, and several other compounds (1.5-51, 1.5-142). Dried marjoram, imported into the United States, has been reported to contain thymol and carvacrol (6.4-101). Marjoram seeds contain about 37 percent fixed oil (6.1-60). An oleoresin is also available.

The highly aromatic leaves and flowering tops are used fresh, dried, and ground to flavor salads, stews, stuffings, soups, eggs, vegetables, fish, meat, and sausages. Fresh leaves are added to vinegars, and seeds are added to confections. Marjoram has been used in bouquet garni. Leaves and flowering tops are used in sachets and potpourris (14.1-16). Oil is used in place of plant material and in perfumes and cosmetics. The plant has been noted to exhibit antioxidant and antifungal properties (1.8-8, 6.4-104, 11.1-126). Marjoram is sometimes grown as an ornamental plant.

As a medicinal plant, marjoram has traditionally been used as a stimulant and tonic. As a folk remedy it has been used against asthma, indigestion, headache, rheumatism, and toothache. Marjoram has been employed in the treatment of cancer (14.1-16). The plant exhibits some antifungal activity (11.1-126).

There are a wide range of ecotypes and chemotypes of marjoram, and the plant is often confused with other Origanum species. Pot marjoram, Origanum onites L., is a short perennial with papillose, hirsute stems, ovate leaves, and white or purple flowers. Formerly classified as Majorana onites (L.) Benth., this plant is native to southeast Europe, Turkey, and Syria. Wild marjoram refers to several plants, generally of Origanum species that are collected and used as oregano. Thymus mastichina L., a native of Spain and North Africa, is the source of the an essential oil known as Spanish wild marjoram oil (14.1-8).

Marjoram and pot marjoram are both generally recognized as safe for human consumption as natural flavorings/seasonings, and marjoram is generally recognized as safe as an extract/essential oil (21 CFR sections 182.10, 182.20 [1982]).

BIBLIOGRAPHIC REFERENCES

1.0 CHEMISTRY 1.1-200, 1.1-234, 1.2-10, 1.2-24, 1.2-61, 1.2-116, 1.5-51, 1.5-64, 1.5-142, 1.7-41, 1.8-8, 1.8-9, 1.8-10, 1.8-11, 1.8-12, 1.8-158.

2.0 BOTANY 2.2-19, 2.2-57, 2.2-58, 2.3-2, 2.3-62, 2.3-63, 2.4-100, 2.5-31, 2.5-72, 2.5-116, 2.9-96, 2.9-97.

3.0 BIONOMICS 3.3-213, 3.4-31, 3.7-13.

4.0 HORTICULTURE 4.1-31, 4.2-6, 4.2-68, 4.2-264, 4.3-15, 4.3-67, 4.3-131, 4.3-163, 4.3-164, 4.3-165, 4.3-169, 4.3-170, 4.5-27, 4.5-42, 4.5-70, 4.5-82, 4.5-187, 4.6-0, 4.6-89, 4.9-99.

5.0 PRODUCTION ECOLOGY 5.2-29, 5.5-39, 5.7-216, 5.8-105, 5.8-135, 5.8-137.

MINT (Mentha species)

Family: Lamiaceae (Labiatae)

French: Menthe (f) poivree   Italian: Menta (f) piperita
German: Pfefferminze (f)   Spanish: Menta (f)

Mint is the common name for a highly aromatic group of perennial herbs prized for their fragrant foliage and essential oil. Of prime commercial importance are Japanese mint (Mentha arvensis L.), peppermint (Mentha x piperita L.), and spearmint (Mentha spicata L.). Formerly classified as Mentha austriaca Jacq. and known as cornmint and field mint, Japanese mint is an erect plant that reaches a height of one meter and has a pubescent stem, ovate to elliptic leaves, and lilac colored flowers. The mint of commercial importance is var. piperescens Malinv., native to Asia and cultivated extensively in Japan, Taiwan, the People's Republic of China, Paraguay, Brazil, Argentina, and India. This plant is the chief source of menthol, one of the most widely used flavors in the world.

Peppermint is an erect, branching plant cultivated for its essential oil and, to a lesser extent, its aromatic leaves. A hybrid of Mentha aquatica L. and Mentha spicata L., the plant is sterile. Although different types of peppermint exist, the majority of peppermint oil in the United states comes from English mint, var. vulgaris L., a plant characterized by dark red stems, dark green leaves, and high oil yields. American mint has green stems that are sometimes purple tinged, light green leaves, and a lower oil yield. White mint, var. officinalis L., is a smaller, less hardy plant grown around Mitchum, England, that is considered to produce the finest of all peppermint oils (14.1-8). In the United states, black Mitchum, var. piperita, is extensively cultivated. Peppermint is cultivated in many other countries throughout the world.

Spearmint is an erect, strong-scented plant widely cultivated for its essential oil and scented leaves. Formerly classified as Mentha viridis L., spearmint is grown primarlily in the United States, the People's Republic of China, and India.

The reported life zone of the mints is 6 to 27 degrees centigrade, with an annual precipitation of 0.3 to 4.2 meters and a soil pH of 4.5 to 8.3 (4.1-31). Peppermint and spearmint are found wild in damp fields and are cultivated in mucklands as well as in well-drained fertile soils. The plants are propagated by suckers and stolons, and by use of vegetative cuttings and crown division. Transplants are set in rows in the spring and the growth of plants will cover the ground by fall. Fields usually need irrigation during the growing season. Harvesting begins when the plant is in full bloom with fields of mint productive for about three years. Quality of the oil is dependent upon several genetic and evironmental variables (4.5-35, 5.1-11, 5.2-11, 5.2-12, 14.1-8).

The essential oil of peppermint is approximately 50 percent menthol, with menthone, menthyl acetate, pulegone, limonene, cineole, and other compounds comprising the rest of the oil (2.9-68, 4.5-35, 5.2-11, 14.1-8). The essential oil of spearmint contains approximately 60 percent carvone, plus limonene, beta-pinene, dihydrocarvone, linalool, 1,8-cineole, alpha-pinene, phellandrene, and other compounds (1.2-39, 1.2-88, 4.6-61, 14.1-8). The essential oil of Japanese mint is approximately 60 percent menthol, in addition to containing menthone, isomenthone, menthyl acetate, alpha- and beta-pinene, limonene, neomenthol, caryophyllene, pulegone, and several other compounds (1.2-106, 3.2-20, 14.1-8). Oils are generally rectified prior to use in the flavor and food industry.

Peppermint is one of the most extensively used flavoring agents and is added to foods, beverages, confections, chewing gums, toothpastes, mouthwashes, perfumes, cosmetics, and medicinal cough preparations. The plant or essential oil flavors tobacco and masks undesirable odors in industrial products and medicines. Dried leaves of peppermint are used in herbal teas, fruit jams, and dessert dishes. Except for medicinal purposes, spearmint is used similarly to peppermint. Fresh and dried leaves and oil are used to flavor salads, sauces, soups, vegetables, jellies, fruit desserts, confections, ice cream, vinegars, beverages, chewing gums, toothpastes, and mouthwashes. Menthol, expecially from Japanese mint, is used in alcoholic beverages, confections, perfumes, tobacco, cough drops, and food products. Many mints are cultivated as ornamentals.

For medicinal purposes, mint has traditionally been considered an antispasmodic, diuretic, stomachic, tonic, and digestive stimulant. Mint plants have also been used in folk remedies against colic, cramps, colds, coughs, headaches, nausea, nervousness, and rheumatism. Some mint varieties have been used in the treatment of warts and cancer (14.1-16). Japanese mint has been thought to function as an antifertility agent, but laboratory experiments have failed to demonstrate this property (7.5-55). Peppermint oil has been reported to be a natural carminative with antispasmodic properties, effective in the treatment of irritable bowel syndrome (7.6-170). Volatile oil of mint may have acaricidal and antimicrobial activity (1.8-130, 1.8-152, 7.4-22, 7.5-88, 11.1-126). Spearmint may cause contact dermatitis because of the presence of phellandrene and other constituents in the essential oil (11.1-96).

Bergamot mint, Mentha x piperita L. var. citrata (J. F. Ehrh.) Briq., is a culinary and ornamental herb with a lemon aroma and taste that was formerly classified as Mentha citrata Ehrh. Water mint, cross mint, or curled mint refers to Mentha aquatica L., a strong-scented mint used in flavoring foods and beverages. Scotch or red ment, Mentha x gentilis L., is a hybrid of Japanese mint and spearmint which has an apple-mint flavor and is cultivated as a culinary and ornamental herb. Pineapple mint, Mentha x gentilis var. variegata plant, is a cultivar with a pineapple-like aroma. Corsican mint, menthella, or creme-de-menthe, Mentha requienii Benth., is a small prostrate-growing herb with very small orbiscular leaves, native to Corsica and Sardinia and highly valued for its strong mint odor.

Peppermint and spearmint are generally recognized as safe for human comsumption as seasonings/flavorings, and other mints used for menthol are generally recognized as safe as plant extracts/essential oils (21 CFR sections 182.10,182.20 [1982]).

BIBLIOGRAPHIC REFERENCES

1.0 CHEMISTRY 1.1-46, 1.1-51, 1.1-69, 1.1-72, 1.1-105, 1.1-145,

1.1-146, 1.1-172, 1.1-189, 1.1-199, 1.1-208, 1.1-209, 1.1-214, 1.1-220,
1.1-235, 1.1-237, 1.2-14, 1.2-22, 1.2-23, 1.2-37, 1.2-38, 1.2-39,
1.2-40, 1.2-46, 1.2-47, 1.2-48, 1.2-50, 1.2-59, 1.2-68, 1.2-77, 1.2-82,
1.2-87, 1.2-88, 1.2-89, 1.2-94, 1.2-106, 1.2-111, 1.3-22, 1.3-26,
1.3-27, 1.3-28, 1.3-31, 1.3-36, 1.3-44, 1.3-45, 1.4-0, 1.4-5, 1.4-57,
1.4-61, 1.4-62, 1.4-63, 1.4-83, 1.4-84, 1.4-85, 1.4-102, 1.5-1, 1.5-10,
1.5-19, 1.5-22, 1.5-25, 1.5-26, 1.5-33, 1.5-35, 1.5-58, 1.5-67, 1.5-75,
1.5-82, 1.5-85, 1.5-86, 1.5-94, 1.5-99, 1.5-100, 1.5-102, 1.5-129,
1.5-131, 1.5-143, 1.5-155, 1.6-7, 1.6-14, 1.6-20, 1.6-30, 1.6-37,
1.6-42, 1.6-43, 1.6-45, 1.6-46, 1.6-49, 1.7-1, 1.7-2, 1.7-3, 1.7-6,
1.7-9, 1.7-10, 1.7-12, 1.7-19, 1.7-26, 1.7-33, 1.7-34, 1.7-35, 1.7-36,
1.7-46, 1.7-48, 1.7-83, 1.7-93, 1.7-98, 1.7-112, 1.7-119, 1.7-124,
1.7-133, 1.7-134, 1.8-2, 1.8-15, 1.8-22, 1.8-25, 1.8-26, 1.8-40, 1.8-42,
1.8-44, 1.8-54, 1.8-69, 1.8-77, 1.8-88, 1.8-95, 1.8-130, 1.8-140,
1.8-143, 1.8-151, 1.8-152, 1.8-168.

2.0 BOTANY 2.1-28, 2.1-43, 2.1-51, 2.1-55, 2.1-57, 2.1-85, 2.1-86,
2.1-88, 2.1-95, 2.1-99, 2.1-105, 2.1-106, 2.1-118, 2.1-122, 2.1-142,
2.1-146, 2.1-147, 2.1-148, 2.1-150, 2.2-10, 2.2-38, 2.2-77, 2.2-93,
2.2-100, 2.3-18, 2.3-22, 2.3-27, 2.3-28, 2.3-47, 2.3-48, 2.3-55, 2.3-58,
2.3-59, 2.3-81, 2.3-82, 2.3-89, 2.3-90, 2.3-104, 2.3-115, 2.3-117,
2.3-123, 2.3-135, 2.3-144, 2.3-145, 2.3-146, 2.3-148, 2.3-149, 2.3-150,
2.3-153, 2.3-160, 2.3-169, 2.3-181, 2.3-184, 2.3-188, 2.3-194, 2.3-195,
2.3-204, 2.3-205, 2.3-210, 2.3-232, 2.3-242, 2.3-243, 2.4-10, 2.4-22,
2.4-23, 2.4-24, 2.4-25, 2.4-30, 2.4-40, 2.4-41, 2.4-60, 2.4-63, 2.4-73,
2.4-74, 2.4-77, 2.4-78, 2.4-80, 2.4-85, 2.4-88, 2.4-89, 2.4-101,
2.4-116, 2.4-132, 2.4-135, 2.4-140, 2.4-142, 2.4-143, 2.4-144, 2.4-145,
2.4-156, 2.4-167, 2.5-8, 2.5-34, 2.5-79, 2.5-93, 2.6-1, 2.6-11, 2.6-15,
2.6-34, 2.6-45, 2.6-59, 2.6-80, 2.7-2, 2.7-7, 2.7-20, 2.7-77, 2.7-86,
2.8-8, 2.8-17, 2.8-27, 2.8-54, 2.8-55, 2.8-58, 2.8-66, 2.8-82, 2.8-84,
2.9-5, 2.9-23, 2.9-61, 2.9-64, 2.9-68, 2.9-69, 2.9-71, 2.9-76, 2.9-81,
2.9-82, 2.9-83, 2.9-87, 2.9-88, 2.9-92, 2.9-94, 2.9-106, 2.9-109,
2.9-111, 2.9-119, 2.9-120, 2.9-122, 2.9-143.

3.0 BIONOMICS 3.0-0, 3.1-4, 3.1-5, 3.1-11, 3.1-12, 3.1-18, 3.1-19,
3.1-29, 3.1-33, 3.1-35, 3.1-38, 3.1-41, 3.1-56, 3.1-59, 3.1-60, 3.1-62,
3.1-65, 3.1-68, 3.1-71, 3.1-82, 3.2-5, 3.2-6, 3.2-7, 3.2-12, 3.2-13,
3.2-15, 3.2-17, 3.2-18, 3.2-20, 3.2-25, 3.2-26, 3.2-27, 3.2-30, 3.2-36,
3.2-43, 3.2-51, 3.2-58, 3.2-64, 3.2-69, 3.2-71, 3.2-79, 3.2-84, 3.2-86,
3.3-9, 3.3-11, 3.3-14, 3.3-20, 3.3-22, 3.3-23, 3.3-26, 3.3-28, 3.3-30,
3.3-32, 3.3-49, 3.3-50, 3.3-50, 3.3-51, 3.3-60, 3.3-61, 3.3-71, 3.3-77,
3.3-79, 3.3-92, 3.3-93, 3.3-100, 3.3-106, 3.3-112, 3.3-114, 3.3-122,
3.3-128, 3.3-129, 3.3-149, 3.3-150, 3.3-151, 3.3-152, 3.3-153, 3.3-154,
3.3-155, 3.3-161, 3.3-177, 3.3-183, 3.3-191, 3.3-198, 3.3-207, 3.3-211,
3.3-217, 3.3-218, 3.3-219, 3.3-223, 3.3-228, 3.4-31, 3.4-32, 3.4-93,
3.4-121, 3.4-136, 3.5-11, 3.5-37, 3.6-6, 3.6-7, 3.7-11.

4.0 HORTICULTURE 4.1-3, 4.1-5, 4.1-18, 4.1-20, 4.1-24, 4.1-30,
4.1-31, 4.1-38, 4.1-44, 4.1-45, 4.1-55, 4.1-59, 4.1-60, 4.1-83, 4.1-86,
4.1-95, 4.1-97, 4.1-105, 4.1-114, 4.1-115, 4.1-116, 4.2-17, 4.2-18,
4.2-19, 4.2-26, 4.2-27, 4.2-28, 4.2-29, 4.2-30, 4.2-47, 4.2-72, 4.2-78,
4.2-82, 4.2-98, 4.2-100, 4.2-101, 4.2-103, 4.2-105, 4.2-106, 4.2-107,
4.2-118, 4.2-129, 4.2-130, 4.2-131, 4.2-133, 4.2-134, 4.2-136, 4.2-137,
4.2-150, 4.2-156, 4.2-162, 4.2-163, 4.2-168, 4.2-169, 4.2-171, 4.2-173,
4.2-174, 4.2-199, 4.2-204, 4.2-207, 4.2-208, 4.2-209, 4.2-210, 4.2-211,
4.2-212, 4.2-213, 4.2-214, 4.2-215, 4.2-222, 4.2-224, 4.2-230, 4.2-239,
4.2-241, 4.2-243, 4.2-244, 4.2-245, 4.2-246, 4.2-247, 4.2-248, 4.2-253,
4.2-254, 4.2-255, 4.2-256, 4.2-257, 4.2-259, 4.2-266, 4.2-283, 4.2-284,
4.2-285, 4.2-291, 4.2-296, 4.2-298, 4.2-299, 4.2-322, 4.2-339, 4.2-341,
4.2-342, 4.2-343, 4.2-346, 4.2-353, 4.2-355, 4.2-362, 4.2-368, 4.2-376,
4.2-382, 4.2-383, 4.2-384, 4.2-385, 4.2-386, 4.2-394, 4.3-2, 4.3-7,
4.3-13, 4.3-22, 4.3-28, 4.3-36, 4.3-40, 4.3-50, 4.3-53, 4.3-58, 4.3-71,

4.3-75,   4.3-81,   4.3-90,   4.3-91,   4.3-95,   4.3-97,   4.3-98,   4.3-112,
4.3-121,   4.3-130,   4.3-133,   4.3-141,   4.3-145,   4.3-155,   4.3-162,   4.3-166,
4.3-176,   4.3-185,   4.3-188,   4.3-190,   4.3-193,   4.3-194,   4.3-198,   4.3-211,
4.3-216,   4.3-223,   4.4-5,   4.4-7,   4.4-26,   4.4-30,   4.4-50,   4.4-57,   4.4-65,
4.4-73, 4.4-76, 4.4-85, 4.4-104, 4.5-1, 4.5-1,   4.5-1,   4.5-12,   4.5-15,
4.5-16,   4.5-21, 4.5-26, 4.5-26, 4.5-35, 4.5-38, 4.5-46, 4.5-47, 4.5-49,
4.5-56, 4.5-58, 4.5-65, 4.5-72, 4.5-76, 4.5-82, 4.5-83, 4.5-84,   4.5-99,
4.5-101,   4.5-104, 4.5-137, 4.5-165, 4.5-167, 4.5-181, 4.5-186, 4.5-187,
4.5-189, 4.5-190, 4.5-191, 4.5-193, 4.5-196, 4.5-200, 4.5-203,   4.5-204,
4.5-205,   4.5-206,   4.5-207, 4.5-208, 4.5-210, 4.5-217, 4.5-226, 4.6-10,
4.6-13, 4.6-25, 4.6-29, 4.6-33, 4.6-39, 4.6-43, 4.6-44, 4.6-60,   4.6-61,
4.6-69,   4.6-72,   4.6-78, 4.6-93, 4.7-13, 4.7-14, 4.8-4, 4.8-26, 4.8-27,
4.8-28, 4.8-63, 4.8-67, 4.8-68, 4.8-88, 4.9-20, 4.9-21, 4.9-26, 4.9-27,
4.9-28, 4.9-42, 4.9-43, 4.9-44, 4.9-54, 4.9-64, 4.9-65, 4.9-89, 4.9-105,
4.9-113, 4.9-114, 4.9-120, 4.9-126, 4.9-127, 4.9-140, 4.9-168, 4.9-176,
4.9-182.

    5.0 PRODUCTION ECOLOGY 5.1-8, 5.1-11,   5.1-17,   5.1-18,   5.1-34,
5.1-58,   5.1-62,   5.1-68, 5.1-69, 5.2-5, 5.2-11, 5.2-12, 5.2-13, 5.2-14,
5.2-15, 5.2-21, 5.2-29, 5.2-67, 5.2-68, 5.2-77, 5.2-90, 5.2-91,   5.2-92,
5.3-14,   5.3-30,   5.3-36,   5.3-48, 5.3-53, 5.4-6, 5.4-8, 5.4-16, 5.4-23,
5.4-25, 5.4-29, 5.4-32, 5.4-66, 5.4-71, 5.4-86, 5.4-88, 5.4-90, 5.4-100,
5.4-127,   5.4-132, 5.4-135, 5.4-141, 5.4-145, 5.4-154, 5.4-158, 5.4-161,
5.4-162,   5.4-169,   5.5-22,   5.5-30,   5.5-39,   5.5-58,   5.5-59,   5.5-66,
5.5-85,   5.5-90,   5.5-107,   5.5-113, 5.5-119, 5.5-125, 5.5-148, 5.5-172,
5.5-177, 5.5-179, 5.5-180, 5.5-200, 5.5-201, 5.5-202, 5.5-203,   5.5-204,
5.5-205,   5.5-220, 5.5-221, 5.5-236, 5.5-242, 5.5-253, 5.5-283, 5.5-288,
5.5-289, 5.5-294, 5.5-300, 5.5-312, 5.5-325, 5.5-327, 5.5-335,   5.5-336,
5.5-338, 5.5-344, 5.5-380, 5.6-6, 5.6-8, 5.6-10, 5.6-15, 5.6-18, 5.6-20,
5.6-25, 5.6-36, 5.6-52, 5.6-53, 5.6-58, 5.7-18, 5.7-19, 5.7-20,   5.7-21,
5.7-47,   5.7-64, 5.7-69, 5.7-73, 5.7-74, 5.7-75, 5.7-79, 5.7-80, 5.7-89,
5.7-90, 5.7-91,   5.7-92,   5.7-94,   5.7-96,   5.7-100,   5.7-112,   5.7-113,
5.7-116,   5.7-123, 5.7-125, 5.7-130, 5.7-132, 5.7-132, 5.7-133, 5.7-134,
5.7-140, 5.7-143, 5.7-148, 5.7-151, 5.7-162, 5.7-163, 5.7-185,   5.7-189,
5.7-214, 5.7-217, 5.7-219, 5.7-233, 5.8-6, 5.8-7, 5.8-8, 5.8-15, 5.8-22,
5.8-27, 5.8-32, 5.8-45, 5.8-53, 5.8-55, 5.8-56, 5.8-60, 5.8-61,   5.8-73,
5.8-74,   5.8-75,   5.8-77,   5.8-78,   5.8-93,   5.8-97,   5.8-107,   5.8-117,
5.8-120, 5.8-133, 5.8-137, 5.8-144, 5.8-157, 5.8-155, 5.8-166,   5.8-167,
5.8-170, 5.8-182, 5.8-188, 5.8-189, 5.9-1, 5.9-4, 5.9-23, 5.9-43,
5.9-53.

    6.0 CULINARY STUDIES 6.1-7, 6.1-81, 6.2-25, 6.2-57, 6.2-71, 6.3-6,
6.3-24, 6.4-10, 6.4-45, 6.4-49, 6.4-75, 6.4-99, 6.4-101, 6.5-1, 6.5-6,
6.5-6, 6.5-8, 6.5-13, 6.5-14, 6.5-23, 6.5-32, 6.5-41, 6.5-45, 6.5-47,
6.5-49, 6.5-63, 6.5-72, 6.5-88, 6.5-109, 6.5-111, 6.5-128, 6.5-133,
6.5-145, 6.5-149.

    7.0 PHARMACOLOGY 7.1-1, 7.1-5, 7.1-6, 7.1-14, 7.1-20, 7.1-40,
7.1-46, 7.1-56, 7.2-82, 7.3-21, 7.3-43, 7.3-44, 7.3-84, 7.3-125, 7.4-6,
7.4-11, 7.4-12, 7.4-22, 7.5-4, 7.5-6, 7.5-8, 7.5-25, 7.5-26, 7.5-27,
7.5-28,   7.5-29, 7.5-54, 7.5-55, 7.5-86, 7.5-87, 7.5-88, 7.5-105,
7.5-108, 7.5-118, 7.6-21, 7.6-40, 7.6-52, 7.6-102, 7.6-133, 7.6-139,
7.6-162, 7.6-168, 7.6-170, 7.6-184, 7.7-2, 7.7-7, 7.7-8, 7.7-10, 7.7-31,
7.7-32, 7.7-34, 7.8-45, 7.8-59, 7.8-65.

    8.0 PERFUMERY 8.1-5, 8.1-17, 8.1-27, 8.1-31, 8.2-6, 8.2-8, 8.2-19,
8.2-22, 8.2-35, 8.2-39, 8.2-40, 8.2-44, 8.2-46, 8.2-56, 8.2-57, 8.2-58,
8.2-59, 8.2-77, 8.2-79, 8.2-86, 8.3-17, 8.3-18, 8.3-25, 8.3-28, 8.3-45,
8.3-48,   8.3-49, 8.3-54, 8.3-56, 8.3-59, 8.3-94, 8.3-99, 8.3-101,
8.3-102, 8.3-103, 8.3-104, 8.4-1, 8.4-4, 8.4-8.

    10.0 COMMERCE 10.1-4,10.1-6,10.1-12,10.1-20,10.2-4, 10.2-7.

MUSTARD (Brassica species)

Family: Brassicaceae (Cruciferae)

French: Moutarde (f)   Italian: Brassica (f)
German: Senf (m)   Spanish: Mostaza (f)

Mustard refers to several Brassica species that are valued for their spicy and pungent dried seeds. Native to Eurasia, the species is widely cultivated in Europe and North America. Black mustard, Brassica nigra (L.) W. D. J. Koch, is a many-branched annual with yellow flowers. Formerly classified as Sinapis nigra L., the plant, whose seeds are used in table mustard, reaches a height of 2 meters. Brown mustard, Brassica juncea (L.) Czerniak, is an annual with yellow flowers. Also known as Indian mustard, leaf mustard, and mustard greens, the plant was formerly classified as Brassica rugosa Hort. and Sinapis juncea L. Seeds of this species are used for table mustard and leaves are used as salad greens. White mustard, Brasssica hirta Moench., is an annual with yellow flowers and hairy seed pods. Formerly classified as Brassica alba (L.) Rabenh. and Sinapis alba L., the plant is cultivated for seeds used in table mustard and leaves used as salad greens. Rape refers to Brassica napus L., colza or Argentine rape, and Brassica rapa L., field mustard. Reaching a height of 1 meter, these plants have branching stems, yellow flowers, brown fruit, and brown-black seeds. The seeds are the source of rapeseed or colza oil, used as industrial lubricating oil and edible salad oil.

The reported life zone for mustard and rape is 5 to 27 degrees centigrade with an annual precipitation of 0.3 to 4.2 meters and a soil pH of 4.2 to 8.3 (4.1-31). The mustards are best adapted to sandy loam soils with limited rainfall. Rape is a cool-season crop that grows best in clay or clay-loam soils. Cultivation of mustard and rape crops is completely mechanized. The crops are sown in the spring and harvested in the fall. Fully ripe fruit shatters, and the crop must therefore be harvested before the plants reach this growth stage.

The aroma and flavor of mustard comes from the essential oils (which can now be made synthetically) contained as glucosides inside the seeds (14.1-11). Powdered mustard has essentially no aroma until it is moistened. The enzymatic action of myrosin on the glucoside sinigrin in black and brown mustard or on sinalbin in white mustard releases the mustard oil, which consists principally of allyl isothiocyanate in black and brown mustards and of p-hydroxybenzyl isothiocyanate in white mustard, the compounds responsible for the pungency (1.5-151, 1.6-41). The steam-extracted volatile oil of black and brown mustard is about 94 percent allyl isothiocyanate, and it also contains some allyl cyanide and carbon disulfide (14.1-11). The essential oil of white mustard is extracted from seeds with solvents (14.1-11).

Mustard seed and seed products are used extensively in the food industry, in meats, sausages, processed vegetables, and relishes. White mustard is generally used for flavoring, and black and brown mustards are generally used for aroma (14.1-11). Mustard seeds are processed to yield mustard flour, from which table mustard and other condiments are made. Ground mustard, powdered dry mustard, prepared mustard, mustard paste, and whole seeds are commercially available. White, brown, and black mustards are blended to secure the desired flavor and aroma. White mustard seed is used as a spice in cucumber pickling. Prepared English and French mustards are usually made from brown mustard seeds, to which are added capers, white wine, and vinegar. Mustards are used in mayonnaise and other products as emulsion stabilizers, antioxidants, and antifungal agents (11.1-126). In addition to providing seed oil for industry and food products, rape plants are grown as forage crops for livestock and to produce seed for bird feed.

As a medicinal plant, mustard has traditionally been considered a digestive irritant, rubefacient, and stimulant. Mustard has been used as a folk remedy against arthritis, rheumatism, inflammation, and toothache. The powdered seeds act as a stimulant to gastric mucosa and increase pancreatic secretions (11.1-96). Contact of mustard extract with skin can cause blistering. Isothiocyanate in mustard oil, considered poisonous and mutagenic, has induced goiter in laboratory animals (7.6-5). Pharmaceutically, mustards are considered emetics and counterirritants in humans and animals, and are used as carminatives in veterinary practices (14.1-35).

Brassica juncea (L.) Czerniak var. crispifolia L. H. Bailey, curled mustard, var. foliosa L. H. Bailey, broad-leaved mustard, and other Brassica species are commonly used as mustard greens.

Black, brown, and white mustard are generally recognized as safe for human consumption as spices/natural flavorings and as plant extracts (21 CFR sections 182.10, 182.20 [1982]).

BIBLIOGRAPHIC REFERENCES

1.0 CHEMISTRY 1.1-59, 1.1-62, 1.1-109, 1.1-119, 1.1-174, 1.1-178, 1.1-202, 1.1-249, 1.1-268, 1.2-15, 1.2-21, 1.2-45, 1.3-15, 1.4-54, 1.5-6, 1.5-18, 1.5-27, 1.5-36, 1.5-61, 1.5-63, 1.5-77, 1.5-90, 1.5-116, 1.5-149, 1.5-151, 1.6-27, 1.6-28, 1.6-41, 1.7-4, 1.7-32, 1.7-52, 1.7-62, 1.7-84, 1.7-110, 1.7-111, 1.7-115, 1.7-144, 1.8-16, 1.8-81, 1.8-94, 1.8-142, 1.8-171.

2.0 BOTANY 2.1-19, 2.1-22, 2.1-26, 2.1-36, 2.1-56, 2.1-66, 2.1-81, 2.1-93, 2.1-93, 2.1-94, 2.1-97, 2.1-129, 2.1-130, 2.2-1, 2.2-9, 2.2-22, 2.2-44, 2.2-47, 2.2-55, 2.2-61, 2.2-70, 2.2-82, 2.2-83, 2.2-88, 2.2-101, 2.2-127, 2.2-130, 2.3-0, 2.3-15, 2.3-20, 2.3-39, 2.3-51, 2.3-52, 2.3-78, 2.3-85, 2.3-98, 2.3-110, 2.3-111, 2.3-122, 2.3-139, 2.3-148, 2.3-171, 2.3-197, 2.3-213, 2.4-11, 2.4-18, 2.4-29, 2.4-32, 2.4-44, 2.4-54, 2.4-64, 2.4-75, 2.4-95, 2.4-103, 2.4-104, 2.4-109, 2.4-111, 2.4-115, 2.4-117, 2.4-139, 2.4-146, 2.4-148, 2.4-160, 2.4-164, 2.5-9, 2.5-10, 2.5-22, 2.5-52, 2.5-54, 2.5-55, 2.5-57, 2.5-64, 2.5-91, 2.5-94, 2.6-27, 2.6-37, 2.6-42, 2.6-43, 2.7-4, 2.7-5, 2.7-10, 2.7-49, 2.7-50, 2.7-55, 2.7-85, 2.7-87, 2.8-6, 2.8-18, 2.8-35, 2.8-59, 2.8-67, 2.9-38, 2.9-51, 2.9-77, 2.9-79, 2.9-90, 2.9-100, 2.9-101, 2.9-110, 2.9-136, 2.9-141.

3.0 BIONOMICS 3.1-25, 3.2-32, 3.2-49, 3.3-32, 3.3-123, 3.3-166, 3.3-171, 3.4-4, 3.4-15, 3.4-32, 3.5-0, 3.5-5, 3.5-6, 3.5-34, 3.5-35, 3.5-41, 3.6-1, 3.6-3.

4.0 HORTICULTURE 4.1-31, 4.1-50, 4.1-82, 4.1-98, 4.2-7, 4.2-13, 4.2-43, 4.2-44, 4.2-46, 4.2-57, 4.2-67, 4.2-108, 4.2-109, 4.2-159, 4.2-164, 4.2-164, 4.2-167, 4.2-175, 4.2-227, 4.2-229, 4.2-242, 4.2-252, 4.2-258, 4.2-270, 4.2-271, 4.2-272, 4.2-280, 4.2-292, 4.2-295, 4.2-312, 4.2-313, 4.2-318, 4.2-323, 4.2-324, 4.2-325, 4.2-325, 4.2-326, 4.2-330, 4.2-332, 4.2-347, 4.2-365, 4.2-374, 4.2-375, 4.2-381, 4.3-2, 4.3-41, 4.3-105, 4.4-58, 4.4-72, 4.5-2, 4.5-6, 4.5-8, 4.5-22, 4.5-23, 4.5-24, 4.5-77, 4.5-98, 4.5-107, 4.5-121, 4.5-131, 4.5-135, 4.5-136, 4.5-140, 4.5-171, 4.5-194, 4.5-199, 4.5-209, 4.5-213, 4.5-214, 4.5-259, 4.6-17, 4.6-31, 4.6-43, 4.6-81, 4.8-15, 4.8-62, 4.8-79, 4.8-85, 4.8-93, 4.9-83, 4.9-106, 4.9-157.

5.0 PRODUCTION ECOLOGY 5.1-5, 5.1-7, 5.1-12, 5.1-13, 5.1-24, 5.1-26, 5.1-28, 5.1-33, 5.1-41, 5.1-47, 5.1-49, 5.1-50, 5.1-51, 5.1-66, 5.1-72, 5.1-79, 5.1-80, 5.1-95, 5.2-6, 5.2-10, 5.2-18, 5.2-19, 5.2-31, 5.2-41, 5.2-42, 5.2-76, 5.2-82, 5.3-5, 5.3-17, 5.3-29, 5.3-41, 5.3-43, 5.3-46, 5.3-50, 5.3-62, 5.4-14, 5.4-15, 5.4-30, 5.4-68, 5.4-70, 5.4-96,

5.4-103, 5.4-103, 5.4-114, 5.4-116, 5.4-121, 5.4-139, 5.4-170, 5.5-12,
5.5-17, 5.5-38, 5.5-93, 5.5-124, 5.5-224, 5.5-241, 5.5-262, 5.5-305,
5.5-365, 5.6-5, 5.6-38, 5.6-65, 5.6-70, 5.6-82, 5.7-9, 5.7-9, 5.7-10,
5.7-28, 5.7-29, 5.7-42, 5.7-51, 5.7-53, 5.7-56, 5.7-60, 5.7-92, 5.7-101,
5.7-103, 5.7-126, 5.7-146, 5.7-157, 5.7-165, 5.7-165, 5.7-178, 5.7-199,
5.8-1, 5.8-10, 5.8-31, 5.8-38, 5.8-63, 5.8-104, 5.8-132, 5.8-154, 5.9-8,
5.9-11, 5.9-12, 5.9-26, 5.9-31, 5.9-38, 5.9-52.
     6.0 CULINARY STUDIES 6.1-18, 6.1-36, 6.1-50, 6.1-56, 6.1-57, 6.2-9,
6.2-37, 6.2-41, 6.2-44, 6.2-59, 6.3-29, 6.3-36, 6.3-65, 6.4-19, 6.4-45,
6.4-66, 6.4-70, 6.4-77, 6.4-99, 6.4-118, 6.5-48, 6.5-51, 6.5-70, 6.5-71,
6.5-78, 6.5-79, 6.5-80, 6.5-81, 6.5-82, 6.5-100, 6.5-103, 6.5-139,
6.5-151.
     7.0 PHARMACOLOGY 7.2-71, 7.4-18, 7.5-21, 7.5-25, 7.5-26, 7.5-38,
7.5-45, 7.5-52, 7.5-70, 7.5-75, 7.5-105, 7.5-106, 7.6-5, 7.6-172,
7.6-203, 7.8-48, 7.8-51.
     10.0 COMMERCE 10.2-5.

ONION (Allium species)

Family: Liliaceae

Chives (Allium schoenoprasum L.)
French: Ciboulette (f)   Italian: Cipollina (f)
German: Schnittlauch (m)   Spanish: Cebolleta (f)

Garlic (Allium sativum L.)
French: Ail   Italian: Aglio (m)
German: Knoblauch (m)   Spanish: Ajo (m)

Shallot (Allium cepa var. aggregatum)
French: Echalote (f)   Italian: Scalogno (m)
German: Schalotte (f)   Spanish: Chalote ascolonia (f)

     Onion is the general name for herbs of the genus Allium and includes
chives, Allium schoenoprasum L., garlic, Allium sativum L., and
shallots, Allium cepa var. aggregatum. Chives, native to Eurasia,
have light green, hollow, cylindrical leaves that reach a height of 0.3
meters. Dense clumps of bulbs are clustered on a very small rhizome and
the plant has purple, lavender, or rose flowers and small gray fruit
with fertile black seeds. Garlic, formerly classified as Allium
controversum Schrad., Allium sativum var. controversum (Schrad.)
Regel, and Allium sativum var. ophioscorodon (Link) Doll, has flat
leaves that reach a height of 1 meter. Its ovoid bulbs are usually
divided into several cloves, that bear bulblets, and terminal umbels,
that have bulbils. The plant has white flowers, that later abscise.
Shallots, formerly classified as Allium ascalonicum L., have hollow
cylindrical leaves that reach a height of 0.3 meters, flowers that are
colored from pink to purple and are generally sterile, and cloves of
bulbs produced from a parent bulb. Chives are usually produced locally
in window boxes, gardens, and pots for consumption and decorative
purposes. Garlic plants are grown commercially in the western United
States, Egypt, Italy, Bulgaria, Hungary, and Taiwan (11.1-128).
Shallots are traditionally produced in the southern United States.
     The reported life zone for Allium species is 6 to 27 degrees
centigrade with an annual precipitation of 0.3 to 4.0 meters and a soil
pH of 4.5 to 8.3 (4.1-31). Bulbs are produced in response to warm

temperatures and long days of spring. Chives, hardy plants adapted to most soils, require full sunlight for best growth. They can be harvested several times each year. Garlic, a hardy perennial, grows best in fertile, well-drained clay loams.

For production, garlic cloves are separated from underground parent bulbs or from bulbils of the inflorescences and then planted in the spring or from autumn to mid-winter in the westen United States. The underground bulbs are harvested when the leaves wither. Traditionally, early emerging garlic has cloves that are enclosed in white scales of the parent bulb while late garlic has cloves that are enclosed in pinkish scales of the parent bulb. Shallot culture is similar to that of garlic with lateral bulbs or shoots generally used to establish plantings. Artificial drying of harvested material is preferred, as this results in smaller losses of allyl sulfide, total sulfur, antibacterial activity, and aroma (11.1-126).

The volatile oils of _Allium_ include disulfides and trisulfides (1.1-53). Garlic oil includes alliin, s-methyl-L-cysteine sulfoxide, s-propyl-L-cysteine sulfoxide, alliinase, mucilage, albumin, and other compounds (2.3-236, 14.1-11, 14.1-35). The characteristic flavor, aroma, and active principle in garlic are found only upon rupture of the cell membranes, which allows the enzyme alliinase to produce the disulfide of the characteristic garlic odor.

Chives are grown for their delicate, mild, onion-flavored leaves. Available fresh, dried, and freeze-dried, they are used in soups, stews, egg dishes, salads, cheese, cream cheese and garnishes. Chive bulbs are sometimes pickled. The chive plant is grown as an ornamental, especially a long garden borders. Garlic bulbs are available fresh or dried and as cloves, powdered, crushed, dehydrated, or as an ingredient in table salt. The oil and the oleoresin from garlic are used extensively in the food industry as a flavoring in soups, stews, sauces, breads, cheeses, vinegars, pickles, processed foods, meats, sausages, and other dishes. Shallots are used in salads, sauces, soups, stews, and vinegars.

Medicinally, chives have traditionally been considered a digestive and used to improve the appetite (11.1-101). Garlic has been traditionally considered an antiseptic, anthelmintic, antispasmodic, carminative, cholagogue, diaphoretic, digestive, diuretic, expectorant, febrifuge, and insect repellent. The plant has also been used as a folk remedy against asthma, colds, coughs, ulcers, high blood pressure, poor circulation, tumors, and leprosy (11.1-126, 14.1-17). The plant is reported to have strong microbial activity, to reduce blood sugar, and to affect cholesterol levels and arteriosclerosis (7.6-17, 7.6-21, 7.6-24, 7.6-88, 7.5-90, 7.6-91, 11.1-126). Raw extracts of garlic are reported to be anthelmintic (7.6-40). Allicin, the active chemotherapeutic compound, may be an important neoplastic drug (11.1-96). Contact with garlic can cause dermatitis, and garlic preparations have been fatal to children (11.1-136).

Chinese chives, garlic chives, and oriental chives are _Allium_ tuberosum Rottl. ex K. Spreng., native to southeast Asia; the leaves and flower stalks of these are used as vegetables. Elephant or great-headed garlic, _Allium_ _ampeloprasum_ L. Ampeloprasum Group, is a mild novelty-type, large-bulbed garlic used as a seasoning.

BIBLIOGRAPHIC REFERENCES

    1.0 CHEMISTRY 1.1-9, 1.1-53, 1.1-60, 1.1-77, 1.1-79, 1.1-79, 1.1-109, 1.1-117, 1.1-203, 1.1-226, 1.1-233, 1.1-256, 1.4-1, 1.6-17, 1.6-56, 1.8-1, 1.8-3, 1.8-4, 1.8-5, 1.8-6, 1.8-7, 1.8-14, 1.8-19, 1.8-21, 1.8-27, 1.8-29, 1.8-30, 1.8-32, 1.8-34, 1.8-35, 1.8-37, 1.8-46,

1.8-51, 1.8-53, 1.8-61, 1.8-75, 1.8-93, 1.8-98, 1.8-99, 1.8-102, 1.8-103, 1.8-104, 1.8-108, 1.8-110, 1.8-113, 1.8-122, 1.8-139, 1.8-148, 1.8-157, 1.8-158, 1.8-161, 1.8-164, 1.8-174, 1.8-181.

2.0 BOTANY 2.2-98, 2.3-24, 2.3-33, 2.3-40, 2.3-41, 2.3-42, 2.3-44, 2.3-45, 2.3-46, 2.3-53, 2.3-71, 2.3-73, 2.3-106, 2.3-125, 2.3-136, 2.3-137, 2.3-175, 2.3-215, 2.3-216, 2.3-236, 2.4-76, 2.4-120, 2.4-158, 2.5-32, 2.5-67, 2.5-77, 2.5-88, 2.6-26, 2.6-46, 2.6-87, 2.7-8, 2.7-9, 2.7-13, 2.7-14, 2.7-15, 2.7-16, 2.7-22, 2.7-25, 2.7-31, 2.7-32, 2.7-36, 2.7-37, 2.7-38, 2.7-40, 2.7-46, 2.7-54, 2.7-61, 2.7-64, 2.7-65, 2.7-71, 2.7-72, 2.7-73, 2.7-83, 2.7-88, 2.7-96, 2.7-97, 2.7-104, 2.8-19, 2.8-49, 2.8-50, 2.8-64, 2.9-30, 2.9-49, 2.9-84, 2.9-86, 2.9-89, 2.9-95, 2.9-124, 2.9-125, 2.9-127, 2.9-129, 2.9-132, 2.9-138.

3.0 BIONOMICS 3.2-11, 3.2-79, 3.3-105, 3.3-114, 3.3-171, 3.3-196, 3.3-197, 3.3-198, 3.3-213, 3.4-31, 3.2-32, 3.5-9, 3.7-4, 3.7-9.

4.0 HORTICULTURE 4.1-1, 4.1-14, 4.1-15, 4.1-31, 4.1-34, 4.1-35, 4.1-42, 4.1-48, 4.1-51, 4.1-53, 4.1-58, 4.1-68, 4.1-75, 4.1-81, 4.1-109, 4.2-25, 4.2-35, 4.2-39, 4.2-86, 4.2-95, 4.2-145, 4.2-149, 4.2-152, 4.2-190, 4.2-202, 4.2-203, 4.2-231, 4.2-352, 4.2-359, 4.2-363, 4.2-373, 4.2-389, 4.3-1, 4.3-21, 4.3-42, 4.3-54, 4.3-66, 4.3-74, 4.3-83, 4.3-138, 4.3-140, 4.3-147, 4.3-210, 4.4-1, 4.4-20, 4.4-51, 4.4-52, 4.4-53, 4.4-53, 4.4-68, 4.4-69, 4.4-109, 4.5-3, 4.5-28, 4.5-29, 4.5-32, 4.5-54, 4.5-62, 4.5-74, 4.5-109, 4.5-113, 4.5-115, 4.5-116, 4.5-117, 4.5-130, 4.5-141, 4.5-157, 4.5-158, 4.5-179, 4.5-180, 4.5-194, 4.5-195, 4.5-211, 4.5-223, 4.5-224, 4.5-238, 4.5-239, 4.5-241, 4.5-245, 4.6-34, 4.6-52, 4.6-73, 4.6-75, 4.7-1, 4.7-9, 4.8-1, 4.8-9, 4.8-17, 4.8-29, 4.8-72, 4.9-1, 4.9-52, 4.9-95, 4.9-116, 4.9-137, 4.9-184.

5.0 PRODUCTION ECOLOGY 5.1-35, 5.1-36, 5.1-42, 5.1-52, 5.1-53, 5.1-54, 5.1-55, 5.1-59, 5.1-60, 5.1-93, 5.2-1, 5.2-9, 5.2-79, 5.2-85, 5.2-86, 5.2-93, 5.3-17, 5.3-22, 5.3-37, 5.4-19, 5.4-24, 5.4-36, 5.4-58, 5.4-60, 5.4-69, 5.4-80, 5.4-117, 5.4-123, 5.4-165, 5.5-4, 5.5-23, 5.5-34, 5.5-37, 5.5-38, 5.5-45, 5.5-56, 5.5-85, 5.5-89, 5.5-97, 5.5-102, 5.5-108, 5.5-109, 5.5-110, 5.5-166, 5.5-175, 5.5-181, 5.5-206, 5.5-225, 5.5-228, 5.5-238, 5.5-240, 5.5-249, 5.5-267, 5.5-269, 5.5-274, 5.5-275, 5.5-277, 5.5-283, 5.5-283, 5.5-299, 5.5-307, 5.5-308, 5.5-322, 5.5-345, 5.5-350, 5.5-353, 5.5-356, 5.5-370, 5.5-377, 5.6-2, 5.6-7, 5.6-9, 5.6-12, 5.6-35, 5.6-43, 5.6-48, 5.6-51, 5.6-78, 5.6-94, 5.7-6, 5.7-7, 5.7-8, 5.7-16, 5.7-31, 5.7-32, 5.7-33, 5.7-41, 5.7-48, 5.7-55, 5.7-67, 5.7-68, 5.7-82, 5.7-110, 5.7-118, 5.7-142, 5.7-160, 5.7-164, 5.7-175, 5.7-176, 5.7-203, 5.7-221, 5.8-2, 5.8-4, 5.8-10, 5.8-20, 5.8-33, 5.8-103, 5.8-109, 5.8-131, 5.8-132, 5.8-141, 5.8-143, 5.8-149, 5.8-156, 5.8-160, 5.8-172, 5.8-179, 5.8-180, 5.8-185, 5.8-191, 5.8-192.

6.0 CULINARY STUDIES 6.1-5, 6.1-18, 6.1-32, 6.1-50, 6.1-50, 6.1-74, 6.1-89, 6.2-46, 6.2-72, 6.3-21, 6.3-25, 6.3-26, 6.3-27, 6.3-28, 6.3-33, 6.3-38, 6.3-42, 6.3-50, 6.3-53, 6.3-60, 6.3-73, 6.3-77, 6.4-7, 6.4-19, 6.4-24, 6.4-29, 6.4-59, 6.4-86, 6.4-93, 6.4-99, 6.4-106, 6.4-115, 6.4-119, 6.5-6, 6.5-17, 6.5-41, 6.5-74, 6.5-87, 6.5-116, 6.5-117, 6.5-143.

7.0 PHARMACOLOGY 7.1-20, 7.1-64, 7.3-105, 7.5-12, 7.5-12, 7.5-27, 7.5-46, 7.5-51, 7.5-108, 7.5-109, 7.6-11, 7.6-12, 7.6-17, 7.6-21, 7.6-22, 7.6-23, 7.6-24, 7.6-25, 7.6-40, 7.6-53, 7.6-85, 7.6-86, 7.6-87, 7.6-88, 7.6-89, 7.6-90, 7.6-91, 7.6-105, 7.6-119, 7.6-136, 7.6-150, 7.6-151, 7.6-176, 7.6-188, 7.7-32, 7.7-39, 7.8-51.

9.0 NATURAL DYES AND ORNAMENTAL APPLICATIONS 9.2-15.

10.0 COMMERCE 10.1-10, 10.1-15, 10.1-16.

OREGANO (Origanum species and Lippia species)

Family: Origanum; Lamiaceae (Labiatae)
         Lippia; Verbenaceae

French: Origan (m)   Italian: Origano (m)
German: Dost (m)   Spanish: Oregano (m)

Oregano is the common name for a general aroma and flavor primarily derived from several species of Origanum and Lippia. European oregano, which is sometimes called wild marjoram, winter marjoram, oregano, and organy, is derived principally from Origanum vulgare L. Greek oregano, which is sometimes called winter sweet marjoram or pot marjoram, is derived from Origanum heracleoticum L., formerly classified as Origanum hirtum Link. Mexican oregano, also known as Mexican sage, origan, oregamon, wild marjoram, Mexican marjoram, or Mexican wild sage, is derived principally from Lippia graveolens H.B.K. European and Mexican oregano are often mixed to produce particular spice blends.

The Origanum species are perennial herbs native to the dry, rocky calcareous soils in the mountainous areas of southern Europe and southwest Asia, and the Mediterranean countries. The perennial, erect plants reach a height of 0.8 to 1 meter and have pubescent stems, ovate, dark green leaves, and white or purple flowers. European oregano is primarily produced in Greece, Italy, Spain, Turkey, and the United States. The Lippia species are small shrubs with larger leaves than the Origanum species and come primarily from Mexico.

The reported life zone for Origanum vulgare L. is 5 to 28 degrees centigrade with an annual precipitation of 0.4 to 2.7 meters and a soil pH of 4.5 to 8.7 (4.1-31). Although much of the commercial material is collected from wild plants, fields can be seeded or established from transplants on light, dry, well-drained soils that are somewhat alkaline. Harvesting can take place two to six times per year. The Lippia species are predominantly collected as wild plants in Mexico.

The essential oil of European oregano is composed mainly of the phenols carvacrol and thymol (8.4-4, 14.1-8). Greek oregano oil has carvacrol, thymol, alpha-terpineol, beta-caryophyllene, terpinen-4-ol, d-linalool, and other compounds (6.4-101). Mexican oregano oil contains approximately equal amounts of carvacrol and thymol and smaller amounts of 1,8-cineole and other compounds. The basic composition of the oil varies with the plant source and geographical growth area.

European oregano is used as a flavoring in meat and sausage products, salads, stews, sauces, and soups. Prior to the introduction of hops, oregano was used to flavor ale and beer (14.1-23). The essential oil and oleoresin, used extensively in place of the plant material, are found in food products, cosmetics, and alcoholic liqueurs. Mexican oregano is used predominantly in flavoring Mexican foods, pizza, and barbecue sauces. Mexican oregano has a somewhat sharper and more pungent flavor than European oregano.

As a medicinal plant, European oregano has traditionally been used as a carminative, diaphoretic, expectorant, emmenagogue, stimulant, stomachic, and tonic. In addition, it has been used as a folk remedy against colic, coughs, headaches, nervousness, toothaches, and irregular menstrual cycles (11.1-101). Origanum oil is a powerful disinfectant, and carvacrol and thymol are considered to be anthelmintic and antifungal agents (14.1-8, 14.1-35).

It is estimated that over forty plant species can contribute to the commercial product oregano (14.1-6). Other important species collected and marketed as European oregano include Thymus capitatus Hoffm. & Link, formerly classified as Coridothymus capitatus Rchb. and sometimes

called Spanish oregano; Origanum syriacum L., formerly classified as
Origanum maru L. and called Syrian marjoram or zatar; and Origanum
virens Hoffm. & Link. Additional species used in Mexican oregano
include Lippia palmeri Wats. and Lippia origanoides H.B.K.

The Lippia species of oregano are generally recognized as safe for
human consumption as natural flavorings/seasonings, and the Origanum
species are generally recognized as safe as natural extracts/essential
oils (21 CFR sections 182.10, 182.20 [1982]).

BIBLIOGRAPHIC REFERENCES

1.0 CHEMISTRY 1.1-105, 1.1-145, 1.2-10, 1.2-18, 1.2-19, 1.2-33,
1.2-58, 1.2-61, 1.2-78, 1.2-79, 1.2-80, 1.2-101, 1.2-114, 1.4-64,
1.5-64, 1.5-114, 1.6-54, 1.7-118, 1.8-8, 1.8-9, 1.8-10, 1.8-39, 1.8-49,
1.8-137.

2.0 BOTANY 2.1-7, 2.1-20, 2.1-67, 2.1-127, 2.1-134, 2.2-19, 2.2-58,
2.3-62, 2.3-142, 2.4-138, 2.5-31, 2.5-42, 2.5-62, 2.5-78, 2.5-114,
2.5-116, 2.5-117, 2.5-120, 2.6-11, 2.7-11, 2.7-21, 2.7-80, 2.7-86,
2.8-8, 2.8-23, 2.8-37, 2.8-38, 2.8-63, 2.8-83, 2.9-89, 2.9-96, 2.9-97.

3.0 BIONOMICS 3.1-29, 3.1-65, 3.1-76, 3.2-5, 3.2-14, 3.2-50,
3.2-79, 3.3-3, 3.3-16, 3.3-22, 3.3-25, 3.3-35, 3.3-40, 3.3-60, 3.3-61,
3.3-81, 3.3-87, 3.3-98, 3.3-114, 3.3-117, 3.3-121, 3.3-137, 3.3-138,
3.3-139, 3.3-140, 3.3-143, 3.3-144, 3.3-157, 3.3-158, 3.3-159, 3.3-168,
3.3-169, 3.3-173, 3.3-175, 3.3-186, 3.3-189, 3.3-213, 3.3-221, 3.3-226,
3.4-31, 3.4-32, 3.4-126, 3.5-26, 3.7-13.

4.0 HORTICULTURE 4.1-31, 4.2-62, 4.2-68, 4.2-76, 4.2-289, 4.3-2,
4.3-15, 4.3-67, 4.3-95, 4.3-146, 4.3-163, 4.3-169, 4.3-199, 4.4-50,
4.4-78, 4.5-42, 4.5-70, 4.5-176, 4.6-72.

5.0 PRODUCTION ECOLOGY 5.2-66, 5.4-31, 5.4-92, 5.5-39, 5.5-79,
5.5-92, 5.5-136, 5.5-209.

6.0 CULINARY STUDIES 6.1-5, 6.1-12, 6.1-50, 6.1-51, 6.1-80, 6.1-87,
6.4-11, 6.4-45, 6.4-93, 6.4-99, 6.4-101, 6.4-104, 6.4-119, 6.5-15,
6.5-41, 6.5-47, 6.5-56, 6.5-88, 6.5-103, 6.5-104, 6.5-111, 6.5-143.

7.0 PHARMACOLOGY 7.1-5, 7.1-20, 7.1-34, 7.2-56, 7.2-69, 7.4-22,
7.5-13, 7.5-25, 7.5-26, 7.5-50, 7.5-51, 7.5-74, 7.5-81, 7.5-89, 7.5-105,
7.5-107, 7.5-108, 7.5-109, 7.5-110, 7.5-120, 7.6-115, 7.6-209, 7.7-16,
7.7-21, 7.8-51.

8.0 PERFUMERY 8.1-5, 8.2-18, 8.2-36, 8.2-79, 8.4-4.

9.0 NATURAL DYES AND ORNAMENTAL APPLICATIONS 9.2-12, 9.2-16.

10.0 COMMERCE 10.1-13.

PARSLEY (Petroselinum crispum (Mill.) Nyman ex A. W. Hill)

Family: Apiaceae (Umbeliiferae)

French: Persil (m)   Italian: Prezzemolo (m);
        Petrosello (m)
German: Petersilie (f)   Spanish: Perejil (m)

Parsley, Petroselinum crispum (Mill.) Nyman ex A. W. Hill, is a
biennial herb native to Europe and western Asia. Formerly known as
Petroselinum hortense Hoffm., Petroselinum sativum Hoff., or Carum
petroselinum (L.) Benth. and Hook. f., the plant is extensively
cultivated throughout many parts of the world for its aromatic and
attractive leaves. Common or curly-leaf parsley, var. crispum, and
Italian parsley, var. neapolitanum Danert, are characterized

respectively by curled, crisped leaves and flat, noncrisped leaves.
Italian parsley was formerly classified as Petroselinum crispum var.
latifolium Airy-Shaw. Parsley is grown in the western United States,
Germany, France, Hungary, and several other European countries. The
erect-growing parsley reaches a height of 0.3 to 0.7 meters and has
green leaves and greenish-yellow flowers in compound umbels. Seeds are
smooth, ribbed, and ovate.

The reported life zone for parsley is 5 to 26 degrees centigrade
with an annual precipitation of 0.3 to 4.6 meters and a soil pH of 4.9
and 8.3 (4.1-31). The plant prefers a rich, moist soil with good
drainage. Seeds germinate very slowly, and therefore a pretreatment
soaking is usually employed to hasten germination. The plant can be
either seeded directly or transplanted. Only a rosette of leaves is
produced in the first year with a flowering stem appearing early in the
second year. Several harvests a year are feasible. Commercially
produced parsley seeds are actually mericarps.

Parsley is a rich source of vitamin C and yields a fixed oil, an
essential oil, and tannins. The seeds contain both a fixed and volatile
oil, the latter being comprised of apiol, myristicin, tetramethoxy-
benzene, alpha-pinene, and other compounds (1.2-35, 14.1-9, 14.1-35).
The leaf or herb oil is considered superior to seed oil, as the volatile
characteristics are more similar to parsley leaves. The fixed oil of
parsley contains petroseline plus oleic, linoleic, palmatic, and other
fatty acids (1.2-6).

The seeds, leaves, and essential oils of parsley are utilized as
condiments or seasonings. Fresh leaves are used for garnishing such
food dishes as meat, fish, and vegetables. Fresh, dried, and dehydrated
leaves flavor a wide array of food products, including salads, sauces,
soups, stews, eggs, and processed foods. Parsley-seed oil is employed
as a fragrance in perfumes, soaps, and creams. The plant is sometimes
grown as an ornamental edging plant.

As a medicinal plant, parsley has traditionally been used as an
antispasmodic, carminative, diuretic, emmenagogue, and stomachic
(11.1-101). The plant has also been used as a remedy for asthma,
conjunctivitis, dropsy, fever, and jaundice. The essential oil of
parsley seed has been reported to stimulate hepatic regeneration
(7.6-57).

New plant forms similar to parsley and of potential economic
significance have been obtained by hybridization of parsley and celery,
Apium graveolens L. (4.2-179). Turnip-rooted parsley, Petroselinum
crispum (Mill.) Nyman ex A. W. Hill var. tuberosum (Bernh.) Crov.,
formerly known as Petroselinum hortense var. radicosum (Alef.), is
grown for its enlarged edible roots.

Parsley is generally recognized as safe as a natural
seasoning/flavoring and plant extract (21 CFR sections 182.10, 182.20
[1982]).

BIBLIOGRAPHIC REFERENCES

1.0 CHEMISTRY 1.1-13, 1.1-78, 1.1-80, 1.1-84, 1.1-105, 1.1-114,
1.1-119, 1.1-124, 1.1-141, 1.1-151, 1.1-168, 1.1-203, 1.1-221, 1.1-223,
1.1-252, 1.2-2, 1.2-5, 1.2-6, 1.2-34, 1.2-35, 1.2-108, 1.3-41, 1.4-22,
1.4-56, 1.5-23, 1.5-24, 1.5-30, 1.5-43, 1.5-70, 1.5-92, 1.5-95, 1.5-112,
1.6-21, 1.7-51, 1.7-66, 1.7-79, 1.7-90, 1.7-91, 1.7-95, 1.7-96, 1.7-106,
1.7-128, 1.7-149, 1.8-20, 1.8-44.

2.0 BOTANY 2.1-6, 2.1-34, 2.1-75, 2.1-125, 2.2-17, 2.2-72, 2.2-102,
2.2-131, 2.3-13, 2.3-73, 2.3-76, 2.3-80, 2.3-107, 2.3-234, 2.3-241,
2.4-46, 2.4-51, 2.4-59, 2.4-157, 2.5-15, 2.5-36, 2.7-6, 2.7-30, 2.7-62,
2.7-63, 2.7-84, 2.7-85, 2.9-28, 2.9-29, 2.9-37, 2.9-43, 2.9-75, 2.9-85,
2.9-121, 2.9-128.

3.0 BIONOMICS 3.1-55, 3.2-2, 3.2-3, 3.3-33, 3.3-69, 3.3-161,
3.3-165, 3.3-171, 3.4-31, 3.4-32, 3.4-80, 3.5-2, 3.5-10, 3.5-12, 3.5-13,
3.5-15, 3.5-25, 3.5-32, 3.5-36, 3.7-9.
4.0 HORTICULTURE 4.1-4, 4.1-19, 4.1-31, 4.1-54, 4.1-110, 4.2-58,
4.2-79, 4.2-114, 4.2-146, 4.2-166, 4.2-176, 4.2-177, 4.2-178, 4.2-179,
4.2-180, 4.2-181, 4.2-310, 4.2-363, 4.3-59, 4.3-60, 4.3-80, 4.3-130,
4.3-146, 4.3-156, 4.3-182, 4.4-24, 4.4-37, 4.5-81, 4.5-90, 4.5-167,
4.6-30, 4.6-55, 4.6-79, 4.6-82, 4.6-94, 4.6-95, 4.8-42, 4.8-43, 4.8-56,
4.8-57, 4.8-96, 4.8-99, 4.9-14, 4.9-50, 4.9-67, 4.9-68, 4.9-69, 4.9-70,
4.9-71, 4.9-72, 4.9-74, 4.9-78, 4.9-79, 4.9-96, 4.9-110, 4.9-119,
4.9-121, 4.9-125, 4.9-129, 4.9-130, 4.9-139, 4.9-146, 4.9-166, 4.9-176.
5.0 PRODUCTION ECOLOGY 5.2-29, 5.2-30, 5.2-64, 5.2-65, 5.4-74,
5.4-75, 5.4-92, 5.5-13, 5.5-14, 5.5-15, 5.5-33, 5.5-35, 5.5-42, 5.5-44,
5.5-46, 5.5-51, 5.5-71, 5.5-72, 5.5-86, 5.5-87, 5.5-127, 5.5-130,
5.5-149, 5.5-154, 5.5-231, 5.5-260, 5.5-329, 5.5-331, 5.5-376, 5.6-34,
5.6-57, 5.6-59, 5.6-60, 5.6-72, 5.7-10, 5.7-17, 5.7-35, 5.7-135,
5.7-220, 5.8-16, 5.8-47, 5.8-70, 5.8-71, 5.8-130, 5.8-152, 5.8-153,
5.8-155, 5.8-186, 5.9-6, 5.9-32, 5.9-50.
6.0 CULINARY STUDIES 6.1-5, 6.2-1, 6.2-8, 6.2-22, 6.2-25, 6.2-26,
6.2-27, 6.2-32, 6.2-36, 6.2-39, 6.2-40, 6.2-42, 6.2-43, 6.2-50, 6.2-52,
6.2-56, 6.2-61, 6.2-63, 6.2-66, 6.2-71, 6.2-76, 6.3-3, 6.3-12, 6.3-28,
6.3-47, 6.3-53, 6.3-58, 6.3-62, 6.3-68, 6.3-70, 6.3-73, 6.3-75, 6.3-77,
6.4-8, 6.4-22, 6.4-45, 6.4-64, 6.4-93, 6.4-99, 6.4-102, 6.4-123, 6.5-6,
6.5-9, 6.5-11, 6.5-17, 6.5-41, 6.5-42, 6.5-44, 6.5-46, 6.5-57, 6.5-58,
6.5-59, 6.5-61, 6.5-64, 6.5-76, 6.5-83, 6.5-94, 6.5-105, 6.5-114,
6.5-116, 6.5-125, 6.5-130, 6.5-142, 6.5-154.
7.0 PHARMACOLOGY 7.1-53, 7.2-62, 7.5-25, 7.5-26, 7.5-27, 7.5-60,
7.5-92, 7.6-44, 7.6-57, 7.7-17, 7.8-11, 7.8-12, 7.8-32, 7.8-47, 7.8-58.
8.0 PERFUMERY 8.2-80.
10.0 COMMERCE 10.1-15.

PENNYROYAL (Hedeoma pulegioides (L.) Pers. and Mentha pulegium L.)

Family: Lamiaceae (Labiatae)

French: Pouliot (m)   Italian: Puleggio (m)
German: Polei (f)   Spanish: Poleo (m)

Pennyroyal represents plants of two genera, Mentha pulegium L.,
European pennyroyal, and Hedeoma pulegioides (L.) Pers., American
pennyroyal. European pennyroyal is a low, prostrate, and spreading
perennial herb, native to Europe and western Asia. Reaching a height of
0.3 meters, the plant has ovate to nearly orbicular leaves and lilac
flowers. American pennyroyal is a low-growing annual plant, native to
the eastern part of the United States. Reaching a height of 0.3 meters,
the plant has multibranched pubescent stems, small, narrow, elliptic
leaves, and light blue to purple flowers that appear in the summer
months.
The reported life zone of European pennyroyal is 7 to 26 degrees
centigrade with an annual precipitation of 0.3 to 1.2 meters and a soil
pH of 4.8 to 8.3 (4.1-31). The plant is found in humid, low-coastal
regions along the Mediterranean Sea, and grows best in fertile, moist
soils with partial shade (14.1-8). American pennyroyal grows on dry,
sandy soils and is commercially cultivated to only a very limited
extent.
The essential oil of pennyroyal is obtained by steam distillation

from leaves and flowering tops.The oil consists chiefly of pulegone but also contains menthone, isomenthone, l-alpha-pinene, l-limonene, dipentene, menthol, and other compounds (14.1-35). American pennyroyal has a similar essential oil. Other chemical constituents include bitter principle and tannin (14.1-35).

The leaves of pennyroyal have a strong mint-like odor and are used fresh or dried in culinary preparations, especially puddings from which it derives the name 'pudding grass.' The essential oil is used as a fragrance in cosmetics. Pulegone from the essential oil is used as a starting material for the manufacture of synthetic menthol.

As a medicinal plant, pennyroyal has traditionally been used as an antispasmodic, carminative, diaphoretic, emmenagogue, sedative, stimulant, aromatic, and stomachic. It has been used to promote menstruation, induce abortion, cure headaches, and relieve colds (11.1-101). The essential oil can be toxic, causing nausea, vomiting, diarrhea, depression, stimulation, and convulsions (8.2-19, 11.1-136). Pennyroyal is pharmaceutically classified as a diaphoretic and emmenagogue (14.1-35). The plant has been used as an insect repellent against fleas and other pests. Plants and oil can cause contact dermatitis (11.1-96).

European and American pennyroyal are generally recognized as safe for human consumption (21 CFR section 172.50 [1982]).

BIBLIOGRAPHIC REFERENCES

1.0 CHEMISTRY 1.2-38, 1.5-1, 1.5-10, 1.5-100, 1.7-1, 1.7-3, 1.7-12, 1.8-88, 1.8-183.
2.0 BOTANY 2.1-105, 2.7-77, 2.7-86.
3.0 BIONOMICS 3.1-5, 3.1-11, 3.1-12, 3.1-60, 3.3-74, 3.3-161, 3.4-31, 3.4-73, 3.4-110, 3.4-139.
4.0 HORTICULTURE 4.1-31, 4.2-215, 4.3-95, 4.3-223.
5.0 PRODUCTION ECOLOGY 5.4-71, 5.4-162.
7.0 PHARMACOLOGY 7.5-108, 7.6-117, 7.7-7, 7.8-59.
8.0 PERFUMERY 8.2-19, 8.2-79.

PLANTAIN SPECIES (Plantago species)

Family: Plantaginaceae

French: Plantain (m)   Italian: Piantaggine (f);
        Cinquenervi (f)
German: Wegerich (m)   Spanish: Llanten (m); Zaragatona (f)

Plantain is the general name for several small herbs used medicinally because of their mucilaginous properties. Spanish psyllium or fleawort, Plantago psyillium; Indian or blood plantago, Plantago ovata Forsk; common plantain, Plantago major L.; and narrow-leaved plantain, Plantago lanceolata L., are representatives of the species. Spanish psyllium, an annual native to the eastern Mediterranean region and naturalized in the eastern United States, is about 0.6 meters tall with hairy leaves, a dense spike of flowers, and a dehiscent seed capsule. Common plantain and narrow-leaved plantain are perennial low-growing herbs.

Indian plantago, Spanish psyllium, and black psyllium (Plantago indica), are cultivated in India, the United States, France, and Spain. Little cultural information on plantain exists, although planting takes place in the southwestern United States during mid-autumn. Plantain grows as a weed in most places.

Psyllium seed gum, a natural gum or mucilage, is extracted from the seed coat and husk with hot water and used as a bulk laxative or purgative. The material hydrates slowly with the addition of water, forming a viscous mass (14.1-26). Some Plantago species are not suitable for the extraction of mucilage because of anatomical differences within the seed.

The plant has been traditionally used as a remedy against insect bites, toothaches, fevers, ulcers, and wounds (11.1-918). Other medicinal applications of the plantain species have included use as an astringent, demulcent, and diuretic. Extracts of common plantain have been reported to exhibit antibacterial activity. Plantago species have also been used in the treatment of cancer (14.1-6). The plant may be an aeroallergen, causing rhinitis or hay fever (11.1-96).

Hoary plantain, Plantago media,, is a perennial used as a natural laxative.

BIBLIOGRAPHIC REFERENCES

1.0 CHEMISTRY 1.1-5, 1.1-57, 1.1-111, 1.1-148, 1.1-149, 1.1-150, 1.1-159, 1.1-160, 1.1-161, 1.1-162, 1.1-238, 1.2-8, 1.2-109, 1.4-76, 1.5-37, 1.5-42, 1.5-71.

2.0 BOTANY 2.1-16, 2.1-18, 2.1-74, 2.1-90, 2.2-8, 2.2-21, 2.2-56, 2.2-64, 2.2-106, 2.2-120, 2.2-121, 2.3-88, 2.3-99, 2.3-128, 2.4-82, 2.4-86, 2.4-87, 2.4-155, 2.5-50, 2.6-5, 2.6-7, 2.6-24, 2.6-47, 2.6-58, 2.6-84, 2.7-28, 2.7-34, 2.7-51, 2.7-57, 2.7-76, 2.8-1, 2.8-7, 2.8-11, 2.8-39, 2.9-49, 2.9-144.

3.0 BIONOMICS 3.1-13, 3.1-14, 3.1-18, 3.1-23, 3.1-43, 3.1-49, 3.1-60, 3.1-77, 3.1-81, 3.3-79, 3.3-107, 3.3-205, 3.3-211, 3.3-212, 3.4-16, 3.4-17, 3.4-25, 3.4-54, 3.4-57, 3.4-59, 3.4-80, 3.4-98, 3.4-100, 3.4-122, 3.4-132, 3.4-134, 3.5-39, 3.5-42, 3.6-11, 3.6-13.

4.0 HORTICULTURE 4.2-201, 4.2-319, 4.3-2, 4.5-52, 4.5-108, 4.9-184.

5.0 PRODUCTION ECOLOGY 5.1-43, 5.2-39, 5.3-9, 5.3-10, 5.3-32, 5.3-33, 5.3-42, 5.3-49, 5.4-5, 5.4-30, 5.4-39, 5.4-54, 5.5-1, 5.5-2, 5.5-19, 5.5-29, 5.5-65, 5.5-67, 5.5-78, 5.5-111, 5.5-126, 5.5-184, 5.5-246, 5.5-251, 5.5-256, 5.5-257, 5.5-258, 5.5-276, 5.5-326, 5.5-367, 5.6-46, 5.6-56, 5.7-24, 5.7-36, 5.7-151, 5.8-24, 5.8-92, 5.8-137, 5.8-181, 5.9-9, 5.9-21, 5.9-22, 5.9-30, 5.9-51.

6.0 CULINARY STUDIES 6.2-77, 6.5-32, 6.5-51.

7.0 PHARMACOLOGY 7.1-1, 7.1-60, 7.2-89, 7.2-90, 7.3-145, 7.4-26, 7.5-13, 7.5-61, 7.5-67, 7.5-107, 7.5-110, 7.5-121, 7.7-5, 7.7-24, 7.7-25, 7.7-28, 7.7-33, 7.8-49.

POPPY (Papaver somniferum L.)

Family: Papaveraceae

French: Pavot (m)   Italian: Papavero (m)
German: Mohn (m)   Spanish: Adormidera (f)

Poppy, Papaver somniferum L., is an annual herb native to southeastern Europe and western Asia. Also known as opium poppy, the species is cultivated extensively in many countries, including Iran, Turkey, Holland, Poland, Romania, Czechoslovakia, Yugoslavia, India, Canada, and many Asian and Central and South American countries.

Reaching a height of 1.2 meters, the erect plant can have white, pink, red, or purple flowers. Seeds range in color from white to a slate shade that is called blue in commercial classifications.

The reported life zone of poppy is 7 to 23 degrees centigrade with an annual precipitation of 0.3 to 1.7 meters and a soil pH of 4.5 to 8.3 (4.1-31). The plants grow best in rich, moist soil and tend to be frost sensitive.

A latex containing several important alkaloids is obtained from immature seed capsules one to three weeks after flowering. Incisions are made in the walls of the green seed pods, and the milky exudation is collected and dried. Opium and the isoquinoline alkaloids morphine, codeine, noscapine, papaverine, and thebaine are isolated from the dried material. The poppy seeds and fixed oil that can be expressed from the seed are not narcotic, because they develop after the capsule has lost the opium-yielding potential (11.1-128). Total yield of alkaloids is dependent on light, temperature, the plant species, and the time of harvest (5.2-4).

Poppy seeds are used as a condiment with baked goods and pastries for their nutty odor and flavor. Poppy oil is widely used as an edible cooking oil. The oil is also used in the manufacture of paints, varnishes, and soaps (14.1-35). Opium is used in the production of morphine, codeine, other alkaloids, and deodorized forms of opium (14.1-35). Morphine is the raw material from which heroin is obtained. Poppy plants are important as ornamental plants in flower gardens.

Poppy is one of the most important medicinal plants. Traditionally, the dry opium was considered an astringent, antispasmodic, aphrodisiac, diaphoretic, expectorant, hypnotic, narcotic, and sedative. Poppy has been used against toothaches and coughs. The ability of opium from poppy to serve as an analgesic is well known. Opium and derivatives of opium are used in the pharmaceutical industry as narcotic analgesics, hypnotics, and sedatives. These compounds are also used as antidiarrheals, antispasmodics, and antitussives (14.1-35). Opium and the drugs derived from opium are addictive and can have toxicological effects.

The poppy has had a tremendous impact on several societies as an opiate. Currently, there is interest in developing a poppy plant rich in thebaine and low in morphine as the former could be converted to codeine and other legal pharmaceutical products with less morphine available for illegal conversion into heroin.

Papaver rhoeus L., known as corn or field poppy, is an annual herb native to Europe and Asia. Extracts of the plant are used in medicine and beverages. The alkaloids rhoeadine, morphine, and papaverine have been reported in this species (14.1-32). Papaver orientale L., formerly Papaver bracteatum Lindl., is a morphine-free alkaloid source used for medicinal purposes. Mexican or prickly poppy, Argemone mexicana L., has been reported to have toxicological properties but no substantial medicinal uses have been recorded (11.1-136).

Poppy seed is generally recognized as safe for human consumption as a spice or a natural flavoring (21 CFR section 182.10 [1982]).

BIBLIOGRAPHIC REFERENCES

1.0 CHEMISTRY 1.1-62, 1.1-112, 1.1-116, 1.1-119, 1.1-180, 1.1-188, 1.1-264, 1.1-269, 1.2-85, 1.2-102, 1.4-7, 1.4-10, 1.4-18, 1.4-33, 1.4-35, 1.4-46, 1.4-50, 1.4-54, 1.4-70, 1.6-3, 1.7-4, 1.7-5, 1.7-13, 1.7-14, 1.7-16, 1.7-18, 1.7-20, 1.7-21, 1.7-22, 1.7-23, 1.7-24, 1.7-57, 1.7-58, 1.7-73, 1.7-77, 1.7-87, 1.7-89, 1.7-103, 1.7-105, 1.7-107, 1.7-113, 1.7-136, 1.7-145, 1.8-47, 1.8-125, 1.8-144.
2.0 BOTANY 2.1-1, 2.1-2, 2.1-3, 2.1-11, 2.1-12, 2.1-16, 2.1-26,

1.5-115, 1.5-123, 1.6-1, 1.6-4, 1.6-34, 1.6-39, 1.6-40, 1.6-56, 1.7-15,
1.7-34, 1.7-49, 1.7-65, 1.7-79, 1.7-95, 1.7-114, 1.8-25, 1.8-26, 1.8-45,
1.8-118, 1.8-119, 1.8-121, 1.8-132, 1.8-138.

2.0 BOTANY 2.1-34, 2.1-118, 2.1-120, 2.1-145, 2.2-58, 2.3-68,
2.3-177, 2.3-178, 2.3-237, 2.4-94, 2.5-26, 2.7-30, 2.7-81, 2.8-12,
2.8-15, 2.8-17, 2.8-41, 2.8-44, 2.8-47, 2.8-78, 2.9-21, 2.9-41, 2.9-50,
2.9-58, 2.9-75.

3.0 BIONOMICS 3.1-22, 3.1-45, 3.1-59, 3.1-65, 3.1-85, 3.2-60,
3.3-45, 3.3-53, 3.3-88, 3.3-114, 3.3-127, 3.3-161, 3.3-206, 3.3-213,
3.4-31, 3.4-32, 3.4-48, 3.4-60, 3.4-81, 3.4-108, 3.4-129, 3.6-10,
3.6-12, 3.7-5, 3.7-9.

4.0 HORTICULTURE 4.1-18, 4.1-31, 4.2-79, 4.2-110, 4.2-153, 4.2-166,
4.2-167, 4.2-193, 4.2-310, 4.2-363, 4.3-0, 4.3-69, 4.3-212, 4.4-100,
4.6-69, 4.8-42, 4.9-67, 4.9-125.

5.0 PRODUCTION ECOLOGY 5.2-49, 5.5-33, 5.5-371, 5.6-30, 5.7-177.

6.0 CULINARY STUDIES 6.1-3, 6.1-42, 6.1-61, 6.1-70, 6.2-17, 6.4-12,
6.4-25, 6.4-35, 6.4-45, 6.4-48, 6.4-80, 6.4-99, 6.4-101, 6.4-104,
6.4-109, 6.4-117, 6.4-119, 6.5-23, 6.5-41, 6.5-88.

7.0 PHARMACOLOGY 7.1-20, 7.2-71, 7.2-82, 7.5-25, 7.5-26, 7.5-27,
7.5-28, 7.5-74, 7.5-89, 7.5-112, 7.6-52, 7.6-210, 7.7-17, 7.7-32,
7.7-34, 7.8-32, 7.8-51.

8.0 PERFUMERY 8.1-5, 8.1-17, 8.2-15, 8.2-30, 8.2-46, 8.2-48,
8.2-50, 8.2-53, 8.2-63, 8.2-71, 8.2-79, 8.2-100, 8.3-22, 8.3-35, 8.3-82,
8.3-89, 8.4-1, 8.4-4.

9.0 NATURAL DYES AND ORNAMENTAL APPLICATIONS 9.2-2, 9.2-12, 9.2-16.

10.0 COMMERCE 10.1-13, 10.2-3.

SAFFRON (Crocus sativus L.)

Family: Iridaceae

French: Safran (m)   Italian: Zafferano (m)
German: Safran (m)   Spanish: Azafran (m)

Saffron, Crocus sativus L., is a perennial herb known only in
cultivation. The plant has been prized since antiquity for the
yellow-colored dyestuff that comes from the flower stigmas. Also known
as saffron crocus, the species is principally grown in Spain, but is
also cultivated in Greece, Turkey, India, France, Italy, and the
People's Republic of China. The low-growing, cormous plant, whose
linear upright leaves reach heights of 0.15 to 0.3 meters, has fragrant
flowers.

The reported life zone of saffron is 6 to 19 degrees centigrade with
an annual precipitation of 0.1 to 1.1 meter and a soil pH of 5.8 to 7.8
(4.1-31). The crop grows best in well-drained soils of medium fertility
(14.1-31). Planted from early spring to autumn from corms, the plants
can remain undisturbed for three to five years before they need to be
divided. Blossoming lasts only a few weeks, and flowers must be
collected daily as they open in order to remove the stigmas.
Approximately 210,000 dried stigmas from 70,000 flowers make one pound
of true saffron (11.1-128).

Saffron contains a volatile oil, picrococin, crocin, a fixed oil,
and wax (1.1-275, 14.1-35). The volatile oil consists of safranal,
oxysafranal, pinene, cineole isophorone, napthalene, and other compounds
(1.1-275). Extracted saffron is a red-orange color, and has an aromatic
odor and a bitter taste. Principal coloring pigments of saffron include

crocin, crocetin, carotene, lycopene, zeaxanthin, and picrocrocin (11.1-126).

Saffron, available commercially as individual stigmas, ground, or crushed, is used in cookery as a spice, in flavoring aperitif beverages, and to color such foods as butter, cheese, rice, sauces, and soups (11.1-75). The high cost of saffron production encourages the use of turmeric and the synthetic colorant tartrazine as alternatives to saffron (11.1-75).

As a medicinal plant, saffron has traditionally been considered an anodyne, antispasmodic, aphrodisiac, diaphoretic, emmenagogue, expectorant, and sedative (11.1-101). The plant has been used as a folk remedy against scarlet fever, smallpox, colds, insomnia, asthma, tumors, and cancer (14.1-16). Saffron is reported to contain a poison of the central nervous system and kidneys that can prove fatal (11.1-136, 11.1-101).

Autumn or meadow crocus, Colchicum autumnale L., is a poisonous plant not related to saffron. Fake or American saffron actually refers to safflower, Carthamus tinctorius L., whose flower heads yield a dye used as an adulterant to true saffron.

Saffron is generally recognized as safe as a natural seasoning or flavoring and plant extract (21 CFR sections 182.10, 182.20 [1982]).

BIBLIOGRAPHIC REFERENCES

1.0 CHEMISTRY 1.1-55, 1.1-274, 1.1-275, 1.2-1, 1.4-14, 1.7-104, 1.7-143, 1.8-155.
2.0 BOTANY 2.1-27, 2.3-31, 2.3-105, 2.4-6, 2.4-12, 2.5-33, 2.5-38, 2.7-19, 2.7-82, 2.7-99, 2.8-60, 2.9-80, 2.9-103.
3.0 BIONOMICS 3.2-19, 3.3-73, 3.3-79, 3.3-146, 3.4-31, 3.4-32, 3.4-131.
4.0 HORTICULTURE 4.1-31, 4.2-3, 4.2-4, 4.2-5, 4.3-51, 4.3-134, 4.3-175, 4.3-201, 4.5-114, 4.9-10.
5.0 PRODUCTION ECOLOGY 5.4-113, 5.5-278, 5.5-381, 5.6-27.
6.0 CULINARY STUDIES 6.1-17, 6.1-25, 6.1-47, 6.1-50, 6.1-69, 6.1-72, 6.1-98, 6.4-45, 6.4-83, 6.5-86, 6.5-89, 6.5-99.
7.0 PHARMACOLOGY 7.3-33, 7.5-106, 7.7-29, 7.8-51.
10.0 COMMERCE 10.2-1, 10.2-9.

SAGE (Salvia officinalis L.)

Family: Lamiaceae (Labiatae)

French: Sauge (f)   Italian: Salvia (f)
German: Salbei (f)   Spanish: Salvia (f)

Sage, Salvia officinalis L., is a perennial shrub native to southern Europe and Asia Minor. Also known as common or garden sage, the growing herb reaches a height of 0.6 meters, has gray to silver-green leaves with a velvety texture, and white, blue, or purple flowers that bloom from late winter to early summer. The plant is cultivated and collected from the wild in Yugoslavia, Albania, Turkey, Italy, Greece, the United States, Spain, and Crete (11.1-128).

The reported life zone of sage is 5 to 26 degrees centigrade with an annual precipitation of 0.3 to 2.6 meters and a soil pH of 4.2 to 8.3 (4.1-31). The species is well suited to warm dry regions and grows best on a nitrogen-rich, clay loam soil located in the full sun. The plant is sensitive to extended dry periods with excessively high temperatures, and it will winter-kill when the temperature reaches about -10 degrees centigrade.

For commercial cultivation, the plant can be established from seeds, by plant division, by layering, or from cuttings. Vegetative propagation is preferred for ensuring a rapid harvest and specific plant clones. The plantings last from two to six years, and the initial harvest is made in the first year. Generally, two or three harvests are taken just prior to bloom in subsequent years. Leaves and vegetative tops are harvested and dried in the shade or with low artificial heat to ensure retention of the color and the quality and content of the volatile oil (3.3-43, 14.1-8).

The essential oil, extracted by steam distillation, ranges from 1.2 to 2.5 percent of dry leaves. Constituents of sage oil include alpha-thujone, camphor, linalool, 1,8-cineole, cis-ocimene, beta-thujone, sabinyl acetate and several other compounds (1.2-73, 6.4-102). The quality of the essential oil of sage differs by geographic region, but this may be attributable to the use of different sage species or types (2.9-116). The most common adulterant to sage oils is thujone, from the leaves of Juniperus virginiana L., red cedar. An oleoresin is obtained by organic solvent extraction.

The dried leaves and essential oil of sage are employed as seasonings for sausages, ground meats, stuffings, fish, honey, salads, soups, and stews. Sage is also used as a flavoring and antioxidant in cheeses, pickles, vegetables, processed foods, and beverages (6.4-104). The oil is used to extend the keeping quality of fats and meats (6.4-12). The plant is used in perfumes and cosmetics and as a natural insect repellant. Sage can be purchased as whole leaf, ground, rubbed, sliced, or cut.

As a medicinal plant, sage has traditionally been considered an antispasmodic, antiseptic, astringent, diaphoretic, expectorant, nervine, and tonic. The plant has also been used as a folk remedy against colds, diarrhea, enteritis, venereal disease, excessive perspiration, snake bites, sore throats, toothaches, and cancer (11.1-96, 14.1-16). The plant was thought to improve the memory. Sage has been reported to act as a bactericide and is used in mouthwashes and gargles (7.5-68, 11.1-128). The plant is also used as a convulsant and antisecretory agent, and as Salvin, a preparation of leaves used as an antimicrobial, anti-inflammatory agent in treating oral cavity disease (7.6-224, 14.1-8, 14.1-35). The name Salvia is from the Latin salvere, meaning "to heal," or "to be safe and unharmed" (11.1-128, 14.1-3).

Although five hundred species of Salvia and many varieties and chemotypes exist, only a few types of sage are commercially important. Dalmation sage, a type of Salvia officinalis L., serves as the standard sage to which others are compared, as it is considered to possess the finest and most characteristic sage aroma. Salvia fructicosa Mill., formerly known as Salvia triloba L. f., and native to some of the Mediterranean and Middle Eastern countries, may account for more than 50 percent of the culinary sage imported into the United States as common sage (6.5-140). This species is commonly referred to as Greek, Mediterranean, or wild sage. Salvia lavandulifolia Vahl., Spanish sage, is a small shrub sold as sage but of minor commercial importance. Salvia miltiorrhiza L. is used as a Chinese herbal medicine for treatment of menstrual irregularities, uterine bleeding, abdominal pain, neurasthenia, insomnia, hepatitis, mastitus, and hives (11.1-97). Leaves from Salvia lyrata L., wild sage or cancerweed, an herb native to the eastern section of the United States, are used as a folk remedy in the treatment of warts (11.1-101). Salvia tomentosa Mill., a native of the Mediterranean region, has been traditionally used to reduce

abdominal pain and heal warts (7.1-63).   Leaves of Salvia divinorum,
Yerba de Maria, are used in some religious ceremonies because of their
hallucinogenic properties (11.1-96).

Salvia elegans Vahl, formerly Salvia rutilans Carriere and known as
pineapple sage, is a perennial shrub cultivated as an annual. Reaching
heights of over one meter, the plant is characterized by decorative,
fragrant leaves, which are employed in bouquets, and by scarlet flowers
that bloom in autumn and are used in potpourris.   Salvia leucophylla
Greene, a perennial shrub native to the western United States, has been
used as sage but is considered very inferior and not acceptable in
commercial markets. Volatile monoterpenes emitted from the species are
reported to have growth-inhibitory activity (1.8-93).

Indian and wild sage refers to Eupatorium perfoliatum L., a plant
native to North America.   Sage of Bethlehem actually refers to
spearmint, Mentha spicata L. The sagebrush native to western portions
of the United States and northern Mexico is of the Artemisia species.

Sage, as Salvia officinalis L. or Salvia triloba L., is generally
recognized as safe for human consumption as a natural seasoning and as a
plant extract/essential oil (21 CFR sections 182.10, 182.20 [1982]).
Spanish sage is also recognized as safe for human consumption as a plant
extract (21 CFR section 182.20 [1982]).

BIBLIOGRAPHIC REFERENCES

1.0 CHEMISTRY 1.1-35, 1.1-36, 1.1-38, 1.1-39, 1.1-41, 1.1-190,
1.1-191, 1.1-200, 1.1-213, 1.2-19, 1.2-54, 1.2-73, 1.2-80, 1.2-96,
1.3-23, 1.3-28, 1.4-69, 1.5-31, 1.5-111, 1.5-144, 1.6-1, 1.6-32, 1.6-36,
1.6-50, 1.7-15, 1.7-34, 1.7-37, 1.7-38, 1.7-39, 1.7-40, 1.7-43, 1.7-44,
1.7-60, 1.7-114, 1.7-140, 1.8-25, 1.8-26, 1.8-41, 1.8-44, 1.8-88,
1.8-91, 1.8-92, 1.8-93, 1.8-94, 1.8-125, 1.8-158, 1.8-177.

2.0 BOTANY 2.1-69, 2.1-95, 2.1-118, 2.1-121, 2.1-140, 2.2-2,
2.2-19, 2.2-42, 2.2-58, 2.2-71, 2.3-43, 2.3-108, 2.3-113, 2.3-114,
2.3-168, 2.3-199, 2.4-44, 2.4-71, 2.5-4, 2.5-5, 2.5-31, 2.5-53, 2.5-70,
2.5-93, 2.6-4, 2.6-6, 2.6-7, 2.6-56, 2.6-57, 2.6-67, 2.6-83, 2.7-100,
2.8-56, 2.8-80, 2.9-6, 2.9-7, 2.9-8, 2.9-26, 2.9-27, 2.9-41, 2.9-116.

3.0 BIONOMICS 3.1-25, 3.1-65, 3.1-67, 3.1-72, 3.1-82, 3.2-33,
3.2-52, 3.2-66, 3.2-79, 3.3-2, 3.3-43, 3.3-53, 3.3-88, 3.3-91, 3.3-132,
3.3-213, 3.3-214, 3.3-215, 3.3-216, 3.3-228, 3.4-31, 3.4-32, 3.4-108,
3.5-2.

4.0 HORTICULTURE 4.1-31, 4.1-46, 4.1-47, 4.1-116, 4.1-117, 4.2-10,
4.2-76, 4.2-83, 4.2-84, 4.2-120, 4.2-122, 4.2-154, 4.2-285, 4.2-294,
4.2-307, 4.2-360, 4.2-361, 4.2-391, 4.2-392, 4.2-393, 4.3-15, 4.3-24,
4.3-27, 4.3-89, 4.3-121, 4.3-131, 4.3-168, 4.3-170, 4.3-209, 4.3-212,
4.5-30, 4.5-34, 4.5-50, 4.5-88, 4.5-89, 4.5-147, 4.6-0, 4.7-13, 4.8-4,
4.9-66.

5.0 PRODUCTION ECOLOGY 5.1-75, 5.2-16, 5.2-53, 5.2-72, 5.3-23,
5.4-21, 5.4-107, 5.4-162, 5.4-169, 5.5-81, 5.5-134, 5.5-179, 5.5-180,
5.5-284, 5.5-286, 5.5-295, 5.5-344, 5.6-20, 5.7-114, 5.7-234, 5.8-76,
5.8-81, 5.8-122.

6.0 CULINARY STUDIES 6.1-15, 6.1-17, 6.1-28, 6.1-39, 6.1-77,
6.1-87, 6.4-12, 6.4-20, 6.4-45, 6.4-49, 6.4-93, 6.4-99, 6.4-101,
6.4-102, 6.4-104, 6.4-109, 6.4-117, 6.5-20, 6.5-23, 6.5-25, 6.5-37,
6.5-41, 6.5-45, 6.5-47, 6.5-50, 6.5-60, 6.5-91, 6.5-98, 6.5-105,
6.5-109, 6.5-111, 6.5-140, 6.5-141.

7.0 PHARMACOLOGY 7.1-3, 7.1-5, 7.1-17, 7.1-20, 7.1-47, 7.1-63,
7.2-4, 7.2-5, 7.2-6, 7.2-82, 7.3-30, 7.4-8, 7.5-4, 7.5-20, 7.5-25,
7.5-26, 7.5-54, 7.5-55, 7.5-68, 7.5-89, 7.5-105, 7.5-109, 7.5-119,
7.5-121, 7.6-122, 7.6-224, 7.7-6, 7.7-8, 7.7-32, 7.7-36, 7.8-51, 7.8-57.

8.0 PERFUMERY 8.1-4, 8.1-7, 8.1-17, 8.1-32, 8.2-5, 8.2-29, 8.2-34,

8.2-36, 8.2-41, 8.2-42, 8.2-45, 8.2-69, 8.2-79, 8.3-7, 8.3-28, 8.3-45, 8.3-98, 8.4-1, 8.4-4.
9.0 NATURAL DYES AND ORNAMENTAL APPLICATIONS 9.2-12.
10.0 COMMERCE 10.1-4,10.1-15.

SAVORY (Satureja species)

Family: Lamiaceae (Labiatae)

Summer Savory (Satureja hortensis L.)
French: Sarriette (f)   Italian: Satureia (f); Peverella (f)
German: Bohnenkraut (n)   Spanish: Ajedrea (f) de jardin

Winter Savory (Satureja montana L.)
French: Sarriette (f) vivace   Italian: Santoreggia (f) invernale
German: Winterbohnenkraut (n)   Spanish: Hisopillo (m);
        Guisopillo (m)

There are two important species of Satureja used as culinary herbs. Satureja hortensis L., known as summer savory, comprises the principle savory of commerce. It is a herbaceous annual, native to southern Europe and naturalized to sections of North America. Satureja montana L., or winter savory, is a hardy, woody perennial, native to Europe and North Africa, and used only limitedly. Flowers of both savory species are pink to blue-white and are known to attract bees.

The reported life zone of summer savory is 7 to 21 degrees centigrade with 0.3 to 1.3 meters of annual precipitation and a soil pH of 5.6 to 8.2 (4.1-31). Reaching a height of 0.5 meter, summer savory develops best in full sunlight and is quite tolerant of different soil types and different moisture regimes. Winter savory, a plant slightly smaller than summer savory, grows between 7 and 23 degrees centigrade with 0.7 to 1.7 meters annual precipitation and a soil pH of 6.5 to 7.3 (4.1-31).

The plants are generally harvested during the first flowering season and if grown as short-lived perennials, harvested twice in subsequent years. Uniformity of plant material for processing is usually questionable as a combination of plant types of similar botanical origin and fragrances are frequently collected and bulked together.

The main constituents of the essential oil in summer savory are the phenols carvacrol and thymol, as well as para-cymene, beta-caryophyllene, linalool, alpha-terpineol, camphene, myrcene, and other terpenoids (6.4-102, 14.1-8). Essential oil from winter savory includes the phenols carvacrol and thymol, as well as para-cymene, l-linolool, l-terpineol, d-borneol, dihydrocuminyl alcohol, l-carvone, l-menthone, and various organic acids (14.1-8). Oil from Coridothymus capitatus Fchb. f., a type of origanum, and Thymus vulgaris L. are sometimes used as adulterants in savory oil (14.1-8).

The green leaves and herbaceous sections of stems from both species are used fresh and dried as flavoring agents in seasonings, stews, meat dishes, poultry, sausages, and vegetables. Summer savory has a sweeter and more delicate aroma and fragrance than does winter savory, and is therefore the more popular of the two species. Both the essential oil, obtained by steam distillation, and the oleoresin are used in the food industry. In addition, the essential oils of both species have been used in the perfume industry, either alone or blended with other essential oils.

As a medicinal plant, summer savory has been traditionally used as a stimulant, stomachic, carminative, expectorant, antidiarrheic, and aphrodisiac. The essential oil has demonstrated antimicrobial and antidiarrheic activity because of the phenols in the oil (14.1-8). Savory have been used in the treatment of cancer (14.1-16).

Calamintha hortensis, Hort. and C. montana Lam. have been mistakenly cited as summer and winter savory, respectively (14.1-3, 14.1-4). Satureja intricata, a savory from Spain, has recently been reclassified as Satureja montana and Satureja nepeta, of Europe and Asia, has been reclassified as Calamintha nepeta (14.1-3). Satureja thymbra, of which there are several chemotypes, grows wild in some Mediterranean and Middle Eastern countries and is known for its high carvacrol or thymol content. This plant is picked and used locally in herbal teas, in culinary preparations, and as an oregano when other plants normally used as oregano are unavailable. Satureja douglasii, an evergreen perennial, is also used in western United States as a tea.

Summer and winter savory are generally recognized as safe for human consumption as both spices/natural flavorings and plant/oil extracts (21 CFR sections 182.10, 182.20 [1982]).

BIBLIOGRAPHIC REFERENCES

1.0 CHEMISTRY 1.7-118, 1.8-69, 1.8-138, 1.8-158.

2.0 BOTANY 2.2-58, 2.3-50, 2.3-218, 2.3-220, 2.3-221, 2.5-37, 2.5-98, 2.8-4, 2.8-32, 2.8-33, 2.9-5, 2.9-122.

3.0 BIONOMICS 3.1-82, 3.2-14, 3.2-79, 3.3-62, 3.3-99, 3.3-115, 3.3-119, 3.3-126, 3.3-133, 3.3-141, 3.3-165, 3.3-172, 3.3-174, 3.3-213, 3.3-220, 3.3-227, 3.4-31, 3.4-85, 3.4-105, 3.7-13.

4.0 HORTICULTURE 4.1-31, 4.1-113, 4.2-76, 4.3-146, 4.5-167, 4.6-79, 4.6-87, 4.6-88, 4.8-57.

5.0 PRODUCTION ECOLOGY 5.2-44, 5.2-45, 5.3-20, 5.4-126, 5.5-39, 5.5-106, 5.5-159, 5.5-177, 5.8-137, 5.8-139.

6.0 CULINARY STUDIES 6.1-15, 6.1-35, 6.1-75, 6.1-100, 6.2-25, 6.2-26, 6.2-61, 6.4-96, 6.4-101, 6.4-102.

7.0 PHARMACOLOGY 7.1-5, 7.1-20, 7.1-58, 7.2-71, 7.5-86, 7.5-120, 7.6-137, 7.6-162, 7.8-51.

8.0 PERFUMERY 8.1-22, 8.2-69.

10.0 COMMERCE 10.1-14.

YARROW (Achillea millefolium L.)

Family: Compositae

French: Millefeville (f)   Italian: Achillea (f);
       Millefoglie (m)
German: Schafgarbe (f)   Spanish: Milenrama (f)

Yarrow, Achillea millefolium L., is native to Europe and Asia and naturalized in North America. Also known as milfoil, thousand-leaf, green arrow, wound wort, nosebleed, and yarroway, this perennial herb can reach heights of 0.6 meters. The flowers are white, pink, or reddish, and the leaves are divided into many segments.

The reported life zone of yarrow includes most of the temperate zone, and the plant grows wild along roadways and in fields and pastures. Often considered a weed, yarrow is a hardy perennial and grows on many soil types if there is adequate drainage. Tops of the plant are collected when the plant is in flower, from early to late summer. Maximum oil content is found in dried buds and flowers (2.3-196).

The chemical constituents of yarrow include a volatile oil comprised of azulene and, in smaller amounts, caryophyllene, eucalyptol, alpha- and beta-pinene, and borneol (2.3-196). Lactones, such as achilleic or aconitic acid, and achillene are also present, as are tannins, caledivain, and alkaloids (11.1-136). The proazulene content can be used to separate chemotypes.

Many Achillea species, differing in growth, flower color, and leaf shape, are available for ornamental purposes as border plants and in rock gardens. Dried flowers can be utilized in flower arrangements. Leaves and flowers have a bitter, astringent taste when used in culinary applications. Yarrow has been used in the manufacture of beer and can be found as an ingredient in herbal teas (11.1-50). Yarrow oil has been traditionally used in hair shampoos (11.1-96).

As a medicinal plant, yarrow and other Achillea species have been used as antispasmodics, astringents, carminatives, diaphoretics, stimulants, and tonics. In addition, yarrow has been used against colds, cramps, fevers, kidney disorders, toothaches, skin irritations, and hemorrhages, and to regulate menses, stimulate the flow of bile, and purify the blood. Chinese herbal medicine specifies the use of Achillea sibirica Ledeb. for stomach ulcers, amenorrhea, abdominal cramps, abscesses, snakebites, traumatic falls and bleeding, and to reduce inflammation (11.1-10). The alkaloids present in yarrow have decreased the required blood clotting time in rabbits (11.1-136). Extracts of of yarrow exhibit antibiotic activity and may also act as antineoplastic drugs (7.2-51, 7.8-37). Contact with yarrow has been reported to cause dermatitis (7.8-1).

Yarrow is generally recognized as safe in beverages only if the finished beverage is thujone-free (21 CFR section 172.510 [1982]).

BIBLIOGRAPHIC REFERENCES

1.0 CHEMISTRY 1.1-14, 1.1-16, 1.1-17, 1.1-31, 1.1-94, 1.1-121, 1.1-127, 1.1-173, 1.1-182, 1.1-251, 1.1-270, 1.2-8, 1.2-29, 1.2-32, 1.2-103, 1.3-8, 1.4-20, 1.5-42, 1.5-52, 1.7-50, 1.8-28, 1.8-55, 1.8-68, 1.8-87, 1.8-130, 1.8-158, 1.8-167.

2.0 BOTANY 2.1-11, 2.1-16, 2.1-30, 2.1-38, 2.1-109, 2.1-141, 2.2-10, 2.2-49, 2.2-86, 2.3-6, 2.3-23, 2.3-57, 2.3-138, 2.3-196, 2.4-84, 2.4-138, 2.5-11, 2.5-120, 2.6-7, 2.6-30, 2.6-36, 2.7-3, 2.7-60, 2.8-14, 2.8-29, 2.9-10, 2.9-21, 2.9-25, 2.9-33, 2.9-34, 2.9-39, 2.9-52, 2.9-98, 2.9-106, 2.9-107, 2.9-137.

3.0 BIONOMICS 3.1-3, 3.1-17, 3.1-34, 3.1-48, 3.1-61, 3.1-75, 3.2-4, 3.2-65, 3.3-184, 3.3-199, 3.3-211, 3.3-212, 3.4-8, 3.4-29, 3.4-57, 3.4-61, 3.4-74, 3.4-78, 3.4-103, 3.4-132, 3.4-133, 3.4-136, 3.4-137, 3.4-139, 3.5-24, 3.6-4, 3.6-11.

4.0 HORTICULTURE 4.1-103, 4.2-254, 4.3-2, 4.3-88, 4.3-95, 4.5-100, 4.5-185, 4.7-4.

5.0 PRODUCTION ECOLOGY 5.1-43, 5.2-54, 5.3-4, 5.3-12, 5.3-42, 5.4-7, 5.4-16, 5.4-57, 5.4-73, 5.4-77, 5.4-93, 5.4-95, 5.4-112, 5.5-105, 5.5-264, 5.8-137, 5.8-147, 5.9-13, 5.9-48.

6.0 CULINARY STUDIES 6.2-24, 6.4-93, 6.4-99, 6.5-45, 6.5-109, 6.5-115.

7.0 PHARMACOLOGY 7.1-12, 7.1-27, 7.1-32, 7.1-37, 7.1-53, 7.1-56, 7.2-51, 7.3-148, 7.5-64, 7.5-106, 7.5-108, 7.6-25, 7.6-46, 7.8-1, 7.8-37, 7.8-40.

8.0 PERFUMERY 8.2-37, 8.4-3, 8.4-4.

Part 2: Subject Classifications

1.0 CHEMISTRY

1.1 Plant Composition

1.1-1 Abou-Zied, E.N., and Rizk, A.M. 1973. Phytochemical investigation of Anthemis nobilis L. growing in Egypt. Qual. Plant. Mater. Veg. 22: 141-144. HA 44: 678.

1.1-2 Abyshev, A.Z., Denisenko, P.P., Abyshev, D.Z., and Kerimov, Yu.B. 1977. Chemical study of some species of the Caucasus flora of the umbellate family [in Russian]. Farmatsiya (Moscow) 26{2}: 42-44. CA 87: 2351.

1.1-3 Abyshev, D.Z., Damirov, I.A., and Abyshev, A.Z. 1976. Foeniculum vulgare as new source of biologically active coumarins [in Russian]. Azerb. Med. Zh. 53{6}: 34-37. CA 86: 2357.

1.1-4 Afchar, D., Cave, A., and Vaquette, J. 1980. A study of liquorice plants of Iran. Flavonoids of Glycyrrhiza glabra var. glandulifera (licuraside 1 (2-0-glucosyl-apiosyl-4 isoliquiritigenin), glucosyl-apiosyl-4'-liquiritigenin 2, isoliquiritin 3 and liquiritin 4) [in French]. Plant. Med. Phytother. 14: 46-50. HA 51: 2108.

1.1-5 Ahmad, M.S., Ahmad, M.U., and Osman, S.M. 1980. A new hydroxyolefinic acid from Plantago major seed oil. Phytochemistry 19: 2137-2139.

1.1-6 Ahmed, Z.F., Rizk, A.M., Hammouda, F.M., and Seif El-Nasr, M.M. 1972. Glucosinolates of Egyptian Capparis species. Phytochemistry 11: 25-256.

1.1-7 Ahuja, M.M., and Nigam, S.S. 1971. Constituents of a new acid isolated from the essential oil of Apium graveolens (celery seed oil) [in German]. Riechst., Aromen, Koerperpflagem. 21: 281-282, 284. CA 76: 144746.

1.1-8 Akhmedov, I.S., Kasymov, Sh.Z., and Sidyakin, G.P. 1972. Arabsin - A new lactone from Artemisia absinthium. Chem. Nat. Compd. (Engl. Transl.) 8: 245. Translation of Khim. Prir. Soedin. 1972{2}: 245-246.

1.1-9 Alexander, M.M., and Sulebele, G.A. 1973. Pectic substances in onion and garlic skins. J. Sci. Food Agric. 24: 611-615.

1.1-10 Alyukina, L.S., and Ryakhovskaya, T.V. 1980. Flavonoids in the genus Artemisia of the Kazakhstan flora [in Russian]. Rastit. Resur. 16: 187-192. HA 51: 1499.

1.1-11 Antos, K., Nemec, P. Jun., and Hrdina, M. 1972. 4-Substituted beta-phenylethylisothiocyanate [in German]. Collect. Czech. Chem. Commun. 37: 3339-3341.

1.1-12 Ashraf, M., and Bhatty, M.K. 1975. Studies on the essential oils of the Pakistani species of the family Umbelliferae. II. Foeniculum vulgare Miller (fennel) seed oil. Pak. J. Sci. Ind. Res. 18: 236-240. HA 48: 5873.

1.1-13 Ashraf, M., Sandra, P.J., Saeed, T., and Bhatty, M.K. 1979. Studies on the essential oils of the Pakistani species of the family Umbeliferae. Part XXXIII. Petroselinum crispum, Miller (parsley) seed oil. Pak. J. Sci. Ind. Res. 22: 262-264. CA 92: 127171.

1.1-14 Bagni, N. 1975. Polyamines in halophilous and calcicolous plants [in Italian]. G. Bot. Ital. 109: 308 (Abstr.).

1.1-15 Bandyukova, V.A. 1972. The distribution of flavonoids in certain families of higher plants. Part 6. The Umbelliferae [in Russian]. Rastit. Resur. 8: 436-450. HA 43: 3340.

1.1-16 Bandyukova, V.V., and Avanesov, E.T. 1975. On the probability of finding certain aglycones in the families of higher plants [in Russian]. Rastit. Resur. 11: 334-342.

1.1-17 Banh-Nhu, C., Gacs-Baitz, E., Radics, L., Tamas, J., Ujszaszy, K., and Verzar-Petri, G. 1979. Achillicin, the first proazulene from Achillea millefolium. Phytochemistry 18: 331-332.

1.1-18 Banthorpe, D.V., Baxerndale, D., Gatford, C., and Williams, S.R. 1971. Monoterpenes of some Artemisia and Tanacetum species grown in England. Planta Med. 20: 147-152. CA 76: 23048.

1.1-19 Basa, S.C., Basu, D., and Chatterjee, A. 1971. Occurrence of flavonoid in Angelica: archagelenone, a new flavanone from the root of Angelica archangelica Linn. Chem. Ind. (London) 13: 355-356. AGRICOLA.

1.1-20 Basu, A.K. 1975. Phospholipids of some Indian seeds. Page 50 in V.S. Motial, ed. Seminar on recent advances in plant sciences. Abstracts of papers. Association for Advancement of Plant Sciences, Kalyani, India.

1.1-21 Bekers, A.G.M., and Kroh, M. 1978. Carbohydrate composition of the mucilage on Ocimum basilicum L. seeds. Acta Bot. Neerl. 27: 121-123.

1.1-22 Bharadwaj, D.K. [i.e. Bhardwaj, D.K.], Murari, R., Seshadri, T.R., and Singh, R. 1976. Occurrence of 2-methylisoflavones in Glycyrrhiza glabra. Phytochemistry 15: 352-353.

1.1-23 Bhardwaj, D.K., Seshadri, T.R., and Singh, R. 1977. Glyzarin, a new isoflavone from Glycyrrhiza glabra. Phytochemistry 16: 402-403.

1.1-24 Bhardwaj, D.K., Seshadri, T.R., and Singh, R. 1977. Xanthones from Lawsonia inermis. Phytochemistry 16: 1616-1617.

1.1-25 Bhardwaj, D.K., Jain, R.K., Jain, B.C., and Mehta, C.K. 1978. 1-Hydroxy-3,7-dimethoxy-6-acetoxyxanthone, a new xanthone from Lawsonia inermis. Phytochemistry 17: 1440-1441.

1.1-26 Bhardwaj, D.K., Murari, R., Seshadri, T.R., and Radhika Singh. 1976. Lacoumarin from Lawsonia inermis. Phytochemistry 15: 1789.

1.1-27 Bhardwaj, D.K., Murari, R., Seshadri, T.R., and Singh, R. 1976. Liqcoumarin, a novel coumarin from Glycyrrhiza glabra. Phytochemistry 15: 1182-1183.

1.1-28 Bhardwaj, D.K., and Singh, R. 1977. 'Glyzaglabrin', a new isoflavone from Glycyrrhiza glabra. Curr. Sci. 46: 753.

1.1-29 Bishnoi, S. 1975. Localization of PAS positive substances in Foeniculum ovule. Indian Sci. Cong. Assoc. Proc. 62 (pt. III Sect. VI): 77-78 (Abstr.).

1.1-30 Bogatkina, V.F., Murav'ev, I.A., Stepanova, E.F., and Kir'yalov, N.P. 1975. Triterpenic compounds from the epigeal mass of Glycyrrhiza glabra. Chem. Nat. Compd. (Engl. Transl.) 11: 114-115. Translation of Khim. Prir. Soedin. 1975{1}: 101-102.

1.1-31 Bohlmann, F., Zdero, Ch., and Suwita, A. 1974. Polyacetylenic compounds. 225. Further amides from the tribe Anthemideae [in German]. Chem. Ber. 107: 1038-1043.

1.1-32 Boida, A., Sparatore, F., and Binieka, M. 1975. N-Substituted derivatives of rosmaricine [in Italian]. Studi Sassar. Sez. 2 53: 383-393. CA 88: 69046.

1.1-33 Borisov, M.I. 1974. Coumarins of the genera Asperula and Galium. Chem. Nat. Compd. (Engl. Transl.) 10: 78. Translation of Khim. Prir. Soedin. 1974{1}: 82.

1.1-34 Brieskorn, C.H., Hagen, P., and Mosandl, A. 1972. o-Diphenol proteins from the fruits of anise and caraway [in German]. Z. Lebensm.-Unters.-Forsch. 148: 83-89. CA 76: 152260.

1.1-35 Brieskorn, C.H., and Kapadia, Z. 1979. Constituents of Salvia officinalis. XXIII. 5-Methoxysalvigenin in leaves of Salvia officinalis. Planta Med. 35: 376-378.

1.1-36 Brieskorn, C.H., and Kapadia, Z. 1980. Constituents of Salvia officinalis. XXIV. Triterpene alcohols, triterpenes and pristane in leaves of Salvia officinalis [in German]. Planta Med. 38: 86-90.

1.1-37 Brieskorn, C.H., and Krause, W. 1974. Further triterpenes from Melissa officinalis L. [in German]. Arch. Pharm. (Weinheim, Ger.) 307: 603-612. AGRICOLA

1.1-38 Brieskorn, C.H., and Biechele, W. 1971. Flavones from Salvia officinalis. Components of Salvia officinalis. Arch. Pharm. (Weinheim, Ger.) 304: 557-561. CA 75: 148543.

1.1-39 Brieskorn, C.H., Michel, H., and Biechele, W. 1973. Flavones of rosemary leaves [in German]. Deut. Lebensm.-Rundsch. 69: 245-246. CA 79: 102803.

1.1-40 Brieskorn, C.H., and Kabelitz, L. 1971. Hydroxy fatty acids from the cutin of the leaf of Rosmarinus officinalis [in German]. Phytochemistry 10: 3195-3204.

1.1-41 Brieskorn, C.H., and Buchberger, L. 1973. Diterpenquinones from Labiatae roots [in German]. Planta Med. 24: 190-195.

1.1-42 Brieskorn, C.H. 1973. Lipids of plant peelings [in German]. Wiss. Veroeff. Deut. Ges. Ernaehr. 24: 66-73. CA 80: 130482.

1.1-43 Brown, S.O., Hamilton, R.J., and Shaw, S. 1975. Hydrocarbons from seeds. Phytochemistry 14: 2726.

1.1-44 Buffa, M., Congui, G., Lombard, A., and Tourn, M.L. 1980. A homologous series of non-reducing oligosaccharides in Artemisia absinthium L. roots. J. Chromatogr. 200: 309-312.

1.1-45 Bukhbinder, A.A. 1974. Free amino acids in pelargonium hybrid cultivars grown on alluvial soils of the Kolkhida lowland [in Russian]. Subtrop. Kul't. 1974{4}: 86-90. HA 45: 10001.

1.1-46 Canova, L. 1972. The composition of Scotch spearmint oil. An. Acad. Bras Cienc. 44(Suppl.): 273-277.

1.1-47 Carter, G.T., Schnoes, H.K., and Lichtenstein, E.P. 1977. 4-Methoxy-2-(trans-1-propenyl) phenyl(plus or minus)-2-methylbutanoate from anise plants. Phytochemistry 16: 615-616.

1.1-48 Chakrabortty, T., Podder, G., and Deshmukh, S.K. 1977. Triterpenoids and other constiuents of Lawsonia alba Lam. syn. L. inermis Linn. Indian J. Chem. Sect. B. 15: 96-97.

1.1-49 Chi, H.J. 1975. Bisabolangelone from Angelica spp. Yakhak Hoe Chi 19{3}: 115-117. CA 84: 102257.

1.1-50 Chou, J.S.T. 1974. Analytical results on the volatile components of cardamon, caraway, and coriander oils by gas chromatography, irspectroscopy, and other methods. Koryo 106: 55-60. CA 81: 82235.

1.1-51 Clarke, A.E., Gleeson, P.A., Jermyn, M.A., and Knox, R.B. 1978. Characterization and localization of beta-lectins in lower and higher plants. Aust. J. Plant Physiol. 5: 707-722.

1.1-52 Dalakishvili, Ts.M., Angelaeva, N.V., Kemertelidze, E.P., Slepyan, L.I., M Ikhailova, N.V., and Vysotskaya, R.I. 1980. Composition of fatty acids in Panax ginseng roots and in some tissue culture strains of certain members of the Araliaceae [in Russian]. Rastit. Resur. 16: 118-123. HA 51: 1527.

1.1-53 Dembele, S., and Dubois, P. 1973. The composition of essential oils from shallots, Allium cepa var. aggregatum [in French]. Ann. Technol. Agric. 22: 121-129. HA 44: 9647.

1.1-54 Dermanovic, M., Mladenovic, S., and Stefanovic, M. 1976. Chemical investigation of Yugoslav species of Artemisia absinthium. Glas. Hem. Drus. Biograd. 41: 287-292. CA 87: 98796.

1.1-55 Dhingra, V.K., Seshadri, T.R., and Mukerjee, S.K. 1975. Minor carotenoid glycosides from saffron (Crocus sativus). Indian J. Chem. 13: 339-341.

1.1-56 Divakar, N.G., Subramanian, V., Sugumaran, M., and Vaidyanathan, C.S. 1979 Indole oxygenase from the leaves of Jasminum grandiflorum. Plant Sci. Lett. 15: 177-181.

1.1-57 Dolya, V.S., Taldykin. O.E., and Shkurupii, E.N. 1976. Fatty oil of four plants, of the Digitalis and Plantago genera [in Ukrainian]. Farm. Zh. (Kiev) 31{4}: 83-84. CA 85: 166478.

1.1-58 Dominguez, X.A., and Chacon, I. 1971. Beta-sitosterol and other substances from Monarda citriodora. Phytochemistry 10: 1691.

1.1-59 Durkee, A.B., and Thivierge, P.A. 1975. Bound phenolic acids in Brassica and Sinapis oilseeds. J. Food Sci. 40: 820-822.

1.1-60 Du, C.T., and Francis, F.J. 1975. Anthocyanins of garlic (Allium sativum L.). J. Food Sci. 40: 1101-1102.

1.1-61 Dzhumamuratova, A., Seitmuratov, E., Rakhimov, D.A., and Ismailov, Z.F. 1978. Polysaccharides of some species of Glycyrrhiza. Chem. Nat. Compd. (Engl. Transl.) 14: 437-439. Translation of Khim. Prir. Soedin. 1978{4}: 513-514.

1.1-62 Eklund, A. 1975. The contents of phytic acid in protein concentrates prepared from nigerseed, sunflower seed, rapeseed and poppy seed. Upsala J. Med. Sci. 80{1}: 5-6. NAR 46: 3505.

1.1-63 Elgamal, M.H.A., and El-Tawil, B.A.H. 1975. Constituents of local plants. XVIII. 28-Hydroxyglycyrrhetic acid, a new triterpenoid isolated from the roots of Glycyrrhiza glabra. Planta Med. 27: 159-163.

1.1-64 Elgamal, M.H.A., and Fayez, M.B.E. 1975. A new triterpenoid from the roots of Glycyrrhiza glabra L. Constituents of local plants XXI. Naturwissenschaften 62: 183.

1.1-65 Eloesser, W., and Herrmann, K. 1975. Flavonols and flavones of vegetables. V. Flavonols and flavones of root vegetables [in German]. Z. Lebensm.-Unter. -Forsch. 159: 265-270. HA 46: 9252.

1.1-66 El-Feraly, F.S., and Benigni, D.A. 1980. Sesquiterpene lactones of Laurus nobilis leaves. J. Nat. Prod. 43: 527-531. HA 51: 2969.

1.1-67 El-Khrisy, E.A.M., Mahmoud, A.M., and Abu-Mustafa, E.A. 1980. Chemical constituents of Foeniculum vulgare fruits. Fitoterapia 51: 273-275. AGRICOLA.

1.1-68 El-Moghazi, A.M., Ali, A.A., Ross, S.A., and Mottaleb, M.A. 1979. Flavonoids of Pimpinella anisum L. growing in Egypt. Fitoterapia 50: 267-268. CA 93: 66107

1.1-69 Embong, M.B., Steele, L., Hadziyev, D., and Molnar, S. 1977. Essential oils from herbs and spices grown in Alberta. Peppermint oil, Mentha piperita var. Mitchum, L. Can. Inst. Food Sci. Technol. J. 10: 247-256.

1.1-70 Escher, S., Keller, U., and Willhalm, B. 1979. New phellandrene derivatives from the root oil of Angelica archangelica L. [in German]. Helv. Chim. Acta 62: 2061-2072.

1.1-71 Exner, J., Reichling, J., and Becker, H. 1980. Flavonoids in Matricaria chamomilla [in German]. Planta Med. 39: 219 (Abstr.).

1.1-72 Fedorin, G.F., Dem'yanenko, V.G., Georgievskii, V.P., Dranik, L.I., and Prokopenko, A.P. 1974. Cichorium intybus a source of esculetin [in Russian]. Rastit. Resur. 10: 573-574. HA 45: 4864.

1.1-73 Felklova, M., and Jasicova, M. 1978. Substances contained in Matricaria chamomilla L. [in Czech]. Cesk. Farm. 27: 359-366. CIM 20{2}: 1171.

1.1-74 Fischer, F.C., and Baerheim Svendsen, A. 1976. Apterin, a common furanocoumarin glycoside in the Umbelliferae. Phytochemistry 15: 1079-1080.

1.1-75 Florya, V.N. 1972. The content of biologically active substances in some Umbelliferae species [in Russian]. Izv. Akad. Nauk Mold. SSR Ser. Biol. Khim. Nauk 1972{4}: 84-85.

1.1-76 Fowden, L., Pratt, H.M., and Smith, A. 1973. 4-Hydroxyisoleucine from seed of Trigonella foenum-graecum. Phytochemistry 12: 1707-1711.

1.1-77 Freeman, G.G., and Whenham, R.J. 1976. Nature and origin of volatile flavour components of onion and related species. Int. Flavours Food Addit. 7: 222-227, 233.

1.1-78 Freeman, G.G., Whenham, R.J., Self, R., and Eagles, J. 1975. Volatile flavour components of parsley leaves (Petroselinum crispum (Mill.) Nyman). J. Sci. Food Agric. 26: 465-470.

1.1-79 Freeman, G.G., and Whenham, R.J. 1975. A survey of volatile components of some Allium species in terms of S-alk(en)yl-L-cysteine sulphoxides present as flavour precursors. J. Sci. Food Agric. 26: 1869-1886.

1.1-80 Fukuda, M., and Yamaguchi, T. 1977. Free hydroxyproline content of vegetables [in Japanese]. Mukogawa Joshi Daigaku Kiyo Shokumotsu-hen. 25: 29-31. CA 89: 213815.

1.1-81 Fursa, N.S. Phenolic compounds of the epigeal part of valerian. II. Composition of the phenolic compounds of Valeriana amurensis. Chem. Nat. Compd. (Engl. Transl.) 15: 356. Translation of Khim. Prir. Soedin. 1979{3}: 407.

1.1-82 Fursa, N.S. 1980. Study of the flavonoid composition of common valerian of the Asian part of the USSR [in Ukrainian]. Farm. Zh. (Kiev) 1980{3}: 72-73. CA 93: 120314.

1.1-83 Furuya, T., Ayabe, S.-I., and Kobayashi, M. 1976. Licodione, a new dibenzoylmethane derivative from cultured cells of Glycyrrhiza echinata. Tetrahedron Lett. 1976{29}: 2539-2540.

1.1-84 Galkina, S.N., and Markh, A.T. 1978. Organic acids and trace elements of celery, parsnips, and parsley [in Russian]. Konservn. Ovoshchesush. Prom-st. 1978{3}: 26-27. CA 88: 168664.

1.1-85 Garbuzova, V.M., Bogacheva, N.G., Pakaln, D.A., Monina, O.I., Bezukladniko Va, N.F., and Libizov, N.I. 1973. Content of lanatoside a, b and c in some foxglove species introduced in Krasnodar Krai [in Russian]. Rastit. Resur. 9{1}: 41-44.

1.1-86 Garg, S.K., Gupta, S.R., and Sharma, N.D. 1979. Minor phenolics of Apium graveolens seeds. Phytochemistry 18: 352.

1.1-87 Garg, S.K., Gupta, S.R., and Sharma, N.D. 1978. Apiumetin - a new furanocoumarin from the seeds of Apium graveolens. Phytochemistry 17: 2135-2136.

1.1-88 Garg, S.K., Gupta, S.R., and Sharma, N.D. 1979. Coumarins from Apium graveolens seeds. Phytochemistry 18: 1580-1581.

1.1-89 Garg, S.K., Gupta, S.R., and Sharma, N.D. 1979. Apiumoside, a new furanocoumarin glucoside from the seeds of Apium graveolens. Phytochemistry 18: 1764-1765.

1.1-90 Garg, S.K., Gupta, S.R., and Sharma, N.D. 1980. Celerin, a new coumarin from Apium graveolens. Planta Med. 38: 186-188.

1.1-91 Garg, S.K., Gupta, S.R., and Sharma, N.D. 1980. Glucosides of Apium graveolens. Planta Med. 38: 363-365.

1.1-92 Gorovoi, P.G., Uvarova, N.I., Oshitok, G.I., and Elyakov, G.B. 1975. Betulafolientriol in the leaves of four far eastern Betula L. species [in Russian]. Rastit. Resur. 11: 97-98.

1.1-93 Gozin, A.A. 1972. The chemical composition of Artemisia absinthium growing in the Smolensk region [in Russian]. Rastit. Resur. 8: 571-573. HA 43: 6246.

1.1-94 Grandi, R., Marchesini, A., Pagnoni, U.M., and Trave, R. 1972. Beta-elemen-9 beta-ol from Achillea ageratum. Phytochemistry 11: 3363-3365.

1.1-95 Granger, R., Passet, J., and Girard, J.P. 1972. 2-Methyl-6-methylene-2,7-octadienol of Thymus vulgaris [in French]. Phytochemistry 11: 2301-2305.

1.1-96 Greger, H. 1979. Aromatic acetylenes and dehydrofalcarinone derivatives within the Artemisia dracunculus group. Phytochemistry 18: 1319-1322. HA 50: 491.

1.1-97 Greger, H., and Bohlmann, F. 1979. 8-Hydroxycapillarine - a new isocoumarin from Artemisia dracunculus [in German]. Phytochemistry 18: 1244-1245. HA 49: 8821.

1.1-98 Greger, H., Bohlmann, F., and Zdero, C. 1977. New isocoumarins from Artemisia dracunculus [in German]. Phytochemistry 16: 795-796.

1.1-99 Greger, H. 1978. A new acetylenic ester from Artemisia absinthium. Phytochemistry 17: 806. HA 48: 8529.

1.1-100 Gupta, G.K., Dhar, K.L., and Atal, C.K. 1977. Chemical constituents of Coriandrum sativum seeds. Indian Perfum. 21: 86-90. CA 88: 177009.

1.1-101 Hammouda, F.M., El-Nasr, M.M.S., and Rizk, A.M. 1975. Constituents of Egyptian Capparis species. Pharmazie 30: 747-748. HA 46: 7934.

1.1-102 Hansel, R., Kartarhardja, M., Huang, J.-T., and Bohlmann, F. 1980. A sesquiterpene lactone-beta-D-glucopyranoside and a new eudesmanolide from Taraxacum officinale [in German]. Phytochemistry 19: 857-861.

1.1-103 Hansen, H. 1974. The content of glucosinolates in horse-radish [in Danish]. Tidsskr. Planteavl 78: 408-410. HA 45: 6788.

1.1-104 Hanson, S.W., Crawford, M., Koker, M.E.S., and Menezes, F.A. 1976. Cymbopogonol, a new triterpenoid from Cymbopogon citratus. Phytochemistry 15: 1074-1075.

1.1-105 Hardh, J.E. 1978. The aromatic compounds of spice plants in Nordic environment. Acta Hortic. 1978{73}: 269-271.

1.1-106 Hardman, R., and Abu-Al-futuh, I.M. 1976. The occurrence of 4-hydroxyisoleucine in steroidal sapogenin-yielding plants. Phytochemistry 15: 325.

1.1-107 Hendriks, H., Smith, D., and Hazelhoff, B. 1977. Eugenlyl isovalerate and isoeugenyl isovalerate in the essential oil of valerian root. Phytochemistry 16: 1853-1854.

1.1-108 Herisset, A., Paris, R.R., and Chaumont, J.-P. 1971. The flavonoids of Roman chamomile (Anthemis nobilis L.). Plant. Med. Phytother. 5: 234-239.

1.1-109 Herrmann, K. 1977. Review of non-essential constituents of vegetables. II. Cruciferae (brassicas, radish, turnip, rutabaga and horse-radish) and Monocotyledons (onion, leek, chive, garlic and asparagus) [in German]. Z. Lebensm.-Unters.-Forsch. 165: 151-164. HA 48: 6451.

1.1-110 Hikino, H., Kato, T., and Takemoto, T. 1975. Sesquiterpenoids. 48. Constituents of wild Japanese valerian roots [in Japanese]. Yakugaku Zasshi 95: 243-245. CA 83: 10456.

1.1-111 Hino, T., and Kametaka, M. 1978. Sterols in white clover and other plants. Nippon Sochi Gakkai-Shi 19: 379-388. HERB AB 786.

1.1-112 Hodkova, J., Vesely, Z., Koblicova, Z., Holubek, J., and Trojanek, J. 1972. On alkaloids. XXV. Minor alkaloids of poppy capsules. Lloydia 35: 61-68.

1.1-113 Hogg, J.W., Terhune, S.J., and Lawrence, B.M. 1974. Dehydro-1,8-cineole: a new monoterpene oxide in Laurus nobilis oil. Phytochemistry 13: 868-869.

1.1-114 Innocenti, G., Dall'Acqua, F., and Caporale, G. 1976. Investigations of the content of furocoumarins in Apium graveolens and in Petroselinum sativum. Planta Med. 29: 165-170. HA 46: 10444.

1.1-115 Iqbal, M.L., Raie, M.Y., Gilani, D.H., and Bhatty, M.K. 1977. The fatty acid composition of the triglycerides of the Pakistani Coriandrum sativum of the family Umbelliferae. Pak. J. Sci. Ind. Res. 20: 124-125.

1.1-116 Itoh, T., Tamura, T., and Matsumoto, T. 1974. Sterols and methylsterols in some tropical and subtropical vegetable oils. Oleagineux 29: 253-258. HA 45: 1926.

1.1-117 Itoh, T., Tamura, T., Mitsuhashi, T., and Matsumoto, T. 1977. Sterols of Liliaceae. Phytochemistry 16: 140-141.

1.1-118 Itoh, T., Jeong, T.M., Hirano, Y., Tamura, T., and Matsumoto, T. 1977. Occurrence of lanosterol and lanostenol in seeds of red pepper (Capsicum annuum). Steroids 29: 569-577.

1.1-119 Janicki, J., Warchalewski, J., Sobkowska, E., Nowakowska, K., and Stasinska, B. 1972. Amino acid composition of proteins in seeds of some oil-bearing plants [in Polish]. Rocz. Technol. Chem. Zywn. 22: 251-260. NAR 43: 6530.

1.1-120 Joulain, D. 1976. Study of the chemical composition of hyssop (Hyssopus officinalis Linnaeus) essential oil [in French]. Riv. Ital. Essenze, Profumi, Piante Off., Saponi, Cosmet., Aerosol 58{9}: 479-485. CA 86: 95852.

1.1-121 Kaloshina, N.A., and Neshta, I.D. 1973. Flavonoids of Achillea millefolium. Chem. Nat. Compd. (Engl. Transl.) 9: 261. Translation of Khim. Prir. Soedin. 1973{2}: 273.

1.1-122 Karawya, M.S., Wassel, G.M., Baghdadi, H.H., and Ammar, N.M. 1980. Mucilagenous contents of certain Egyptian plants. Planta Med. 38: 73-78.

1.1-123 Kartnig, T., Bohm, J., and Hiermann, A. 1977. Flavonoids in the leaves of Digitalis purpurea [in German]. Planta Med. 32: 347-349.

1.1-124 Kasting, R., Andersson, J., and Von Sydow, E. 1972. Volatile constituents in leaves of parsley. Phytochemistry 11: 2277-2282.

1.1-125 Kasymov, Sh.Z., Abdullaev, N.D., Sidyakin, G.P., and Yagudaev, M.R. 1979. Anabsin - a new diguanolide from Artemisia absinthium. Chem. Nat. Compd. (Engl. Transl.) 15: 430-435. Translation of Khim. Prir. Soedin. 1979{4}: 495-501.

1.1-126 Kasymov, Sh.Z., Abdullaev, N.D., Zakirov, S.Kh., Sidyakin, G.P., and Yagudaev, M.R. 1979. Artemolin - a new guaianolide from Artemisia absinthium. Chem. Nat. Compd. (Engl. Transl.) 15: 577-579. Translation of Khim. Prir. Soedin. 1979{5}: 658-661.

1.1-127 Kasymov, Sh.Z., and Sidyakin, G.P. 1972. Lactones of Achillea millefolium. Chem. Nat. Compd. (Engl. Transl.) 8: 246. Translation of Khim. Prir. Soedin. 1972{2}: 246-247.

1.1-128 Kattaev, N.Sh., and Nikonov, G.K. 1974. Flavonoids of Glycyrrhiza glabra. Chem. Nat. Compd. (Engl. Transl.) 10: 94-95. Translation of Khim. Prir. Soedin. 1974{1}: 93.

1.1-129 Kattaev, N.Sh., and Nikonov, G.K. 1972. Glabranin - a new flavanone from Glycyrrhiza glabra. Chem. Nat. Compd. (Engl. Transl.) 8: 790-791. Translation of Khim. Prir. Soedin. 1972{6}: 805-806.

1.1-130 Kehayoglou, A.H., and Manoussopoulos, C.I. 1977. Amino acid composition of red pepper. J. Agric. Food Chem. 25: 1260-1262.

1.1-131 Khalil, A.M., Ashy, M.A., El-Tawil, B.A.H., and Tawfiq, N.I. 1979. Constituents of local plants. Part 5. The coumarin and triterpenoid constituents of Lavandula dentata L. plant. Pharmazie 34: 564-565. HA 50: 7318.

1.1-132 Kinoshita, T., Saitoh, T., and Shibata, S. 1976. The occurrence of an isoflavene and the corresponding isoflavone in licorice root. Chem Phar Bull. (Tokyo) 24: 991-994.

1.1-133 Kinoshita, T., Saitoh, T., and Shibata, S. 1978. A new

3-arylcoumarin from licorice root. Chem. Pharm. Bull. (Tokyo) 26: 135-140. AGRICOLA.

1.1-134 Kinoshita, T., Saitoh, T., and Shibata, S. 1978. A new isoflavone from licorice root. Chem. Pharm. Bull. (Tokyo) 26: 141-143. AGRICOLA.

1.1-135 Kir'yalov, N.P., Murav'ev, I.A., Stepanova, E.F., and Bogatkina, V.F. 1973. Triterpene compounds of the herbage of Glycyrrhiza glabra. Chem. Nat. Compd. (Engl. Transl.) 6: 787. Translation of Khim. Prir. Soedin. 1970{6}: 770-771.

1.1-136 Kir'yalov, N.P., Bogatkina, V.F., and Barkaeva, E.Yu. 1974. Triterpenoids of the roots of Glycyrrhiza uralensis. Chem. Nat. Compd. (Engl. Transl.) 10: 112. Translation of Khim. Prir. Soedin. 10{1}: 102-103.

1.1-137 Kis, I., Tibori, G., and Racz, G. 1980. Volatile terpenes from the roots of Angelica archangelica [in Romanian]. Rev. Med. (Tirgu-Mures, Rom.) 26{1}: 79-82. CA 94: 117799.

1.1-138 Kowalewski, Z., and Matlawska, I. 1978. Flavonoids in Marrubium vulgare herbage [in Polish]. Herba Pol. 24: 183-186. 50: 547.

1.1-139 Kozawa, M., Bab, K., and Imisui, M. 1973. Chemical components of the roots of Ligusticum hultenii Fernald and Angelica shikokiana Makino [in Japanese]. Yakugaku Zasshi 93: 248-251. AGRICOLA.

1.1-140 Kozawa, M., Baba, K., Arima, T., and Hata, K. 1976. New xanthone glucoside, dillanoside from dill, the fruits of Anethum graveolens L. [in German]. Chem. Pharm. Bull. (Tokyo) 24: 220-223.

1.1-141 Krebs, D., and Weigert, E. 1972. Flavonoid compounds, especially rutin, found in Santa Maria flowers [in Portuguese]. Rev. Cent. Cienc. Biomed. 1: 77-82. CA 81: 68418.

1.1-142 Kudrzycka-Bieloszabska, F.W., and Szaniawska-Dekundy, D. 1976. A comparative analysis of some species of Nepeta [in Polish]. Ann. Univ. Mariae Curie-Sklodowska Sect. D. Med. 31: 187-189. CIM 19{13}: 9665.

1.1-143 Kunde, R., and Isaac, O. 1979. On the flavones of chamomile (Matricaria chamomilla L.) and a new acetylated apigenin-7-glucoside [in German]. Planta Med. 37: 124-130.

1.1-144 Kuz'min, E.V., Kashkarova, N.F., and Golovenko, K.A. 1975. The glycyrrhizinic acid content in the roots of liquorice from the valley of the river Ural [in Russian]. Tr. Inst. Bot. Akad. Nauk Kaz. SSR 34: 98-113. HA 47: 1893.

1.1-145 Lawrence, B.M., Terhune, S.J., and Hogg, J.W. 1974. 4,5-Epoxy-p-menth-1-ene: a new constituent of Origanum heracleoticum. Phytochemistry 13: 1012-1013.

1.1-146 Lawrence, B.M. 1972. Some trace constituents in the oil of Mentha piperita L. An. Acad. Bras. Cienc. 44(Suppl.): 191-197.

1.1-147 Lawrence, B.M. 1979. Chemical evaluation of various bay oils. Int. Congr. Essent. Oils, [Pap.], 7th, 1977. 7: 172-179. CA 92: 64511.

1.1-148 Lebedev-Kosov, V.I. 1976. Flavonoids of Plantago major. Chem. Nat. Compd. (Engl. Transl.) 12: 730. Translation of Khim. Prir. Soedin. 1975{6}: 812-813.

1.1-149 Lebedev-Kosov, V.I. 1980. Flavonoids and iridoids of Plantago major and P. asiatica [in Russian]. Rastit. Resur. 16: 403-406. HA 51: 4941.

1.1-150 Lebedev-Kosov, V.I., Bykov, V.I., and Glyzin, V.I. 1978. Flavonoids of Plantago major. Chem. Nat. Compd. (Engl. Transl.) 14: 223. Translation of Khim. Prir. Soedin. 1978{2}: 266.

1.1-151 Leienbach, K.-W., Heeger, V., and Barz, W. 1976. Metabolism of nicotinic acid in plant cell suspension cultures. IV. Occurrence and metabolism of nicotinic acid N-alpha-arabinoside [in German]. Hoppe Seylers Z. Physiol. Chem. 357: 1089-1095.

1.1-152 Litvinenko, V.I., and Nadezhina, T.P. 1972. The flavonoids of the above-ground part of Glycyrrhiza glabra L. [in Russian]. Rastit. Resur. 8: 35-42. AGRICOLA.

1.1-153 Lombard, A., Nano, G.M., and Rossetti, V. 1972. On the free amino acids, soluble carbohydrates and terpenes of Artemisia dracunculus [in French]. An. Acad. Bras. Cienc. 44(Suppl.): 211-215.

1.1-154 Lombard, A., Belliardo, F., Buffa, M., and Tourn, M.L. 1975. Oligosaccharides of Artemisia dracunculus L. roots [in Italian]. Atti Accad. Sci. Torino, Cl. Sci. Fis., Mat. Nat. 109: 439-446. CA 85: 74938.

1.1-155 Luhadiya, A.P., and Kulkarni, P.R. 1978. Polyphenoloxidase of Capsicum frutescens var. grossa Sendt. J. Food Sci. Technol. 15: 214-215.

1.1-156 MacLeod, A.J., and Islam, R. 1975. Volatile flavour components of watercress. J. Sci. Food Agric. 26: 1545-1550.

1.1-157 MacLeod, A.J., and Islam, R. 1976. Volatile flavour components of coriander leaf. J. Sci. Food Agric. 27: 721-725.

1.1-158 Mahmoud, Z.F., Salam, N.A.A., and Khafagy, S.M. 1980. Constituents of henna leaves (Lawsonia inermis L.) growing in Egypt. Fitoterapia 51: 153-155. HA 51: 8033.

1.1-159 Maksiutina, N.P. 1972. Polyphenol compounds of Plantago major L. leaves [in Ukrainian]. Farm. Zh. (Kiev) 27: 59-63.

1.1-160 Maksyutina, N.P. 1971. Hydroxycinnamic acids of Plantago major and Plantago lanceolata. Chem. Nat. Compd. (Engl. Transl.) 7: 795. Translation of Khim. Prir. Soedin. 1971{6}: 824-825.

1.1-161 Maksyutina, N.P., and Lebedev-Kosov, V.I. 1974. Polysaccharides of some Plantago species [in Ukrainian]. Farm. Zh. (Kiev) 29: 60-62.

1.1-162 Maksyutin, G.V. 1972. Amino acids in Plantago (plantain) major leaves and Matricaria recutita inflorescences [in Russian]. Rastit. Resur. 8: 110-112. CA 76: 138160.

1.1-163 Mallabaeva, A., Saitbaeva, I.M., and Sidyakin, G.P. 1971. The isocoumarin artemidinal from <u>Artemisia dracunculus</u>. Chem. Nat. Compd. (Engl. Transl.) 7: 248-249. Translation of Khim. Prir. Soedin. 1971{3}: 257-259.

1.1-164 Mallabaev, A., Yagudaev, M.R., Saitbaeva, I.M., and Sidyakin, G.P. 1973. The isocoumarin artemidin from <u>Artemisia dracunculus</u>. Chem. Nat. Compd. (Engl. Transl.) 6: 479. Translation of Khim. Prir. Soedin. 1970{4}: 467-468.

1.1-165 Mallabaev, A., and Sidyakin, G.P. 1976. Artemidinol -- a new isocoumarin from <u>Artemisia dracunculus</u>. Chem. Nat. Compd. (Engl. Transl.) 12: 729. Translation of Khim. Prir. Soedin. 1976{6}: 811-812.

1.1-166 Mallabaev, A., and Sidyakin, G.P. 1974. Artemidiol -- a new isocoumarin from <u>Artemisia dracunculus</u>. Chem. Nat. Compd. (Engl. Transl.) 10: 743-745. Translation of Khim. Prir. Soedin. 1974{6}: 720-723, 1974.

1.1-167 Mangaldzhiev, N. 1972. Flavonoids of <u>Jasminum fructicants</u>. I. [in Bulgarian]. Farmatsiya (Sofia) 22{2}: 46-49. CA 77: 105555.

1.1-168 Medrano, M.A., and Bartolome, E.R. 1978. Flavonoid glycosides in parsley <u>Petroselinum crispum</u> Mill. seeds [in Spanish]. An. Asoc. Quim. Argent. 66{3}: 169-172. CA 92: 18813.

1.1-169 Muchnik, Zh.S. 1976. The contents of glycyrrhizic acid, sugars and extractives in the underground organs of <u>Glycyrrhiza glabra</u> grown in Moldavia [in Russian]. Rastit. Resur. 12: 78-84. HA 46: 8674.

1.1-170 Mukhamedova, Kh.S., Akbarov, R.R., and Akramov, S.T. 1978. Amounts of phospholipids and phytin in seeds of various plants. Part 2. Chem. Nat. Compd. (Engl. Transl.) 114: 330-331. Translation of Khim. Prir. Soedin. 1978{3}: 395-396.

1.1-171 Murray, R.D.H. 1978. Naturally occurring plant coumarins. Fortschr. Chem. Org. Naturst. 35: 199-429.

1.1-172 Nagell, A., and Hefendehl, F.W. 1974. Composition of the essential oil of <u>Mentha rotundifolia</u> [in German]. Planta Med. 26: 1-8.

1.1-173 Neshta, I.D., Kaloshina, N.A., Zapesochnaya, G.G., and Ban'kovskii, A.I. 1972. Rutin from <u>Achillea millefolium</u>. Chem. Nat. Compd. (Engl. Transl.) 8: 664. Translation of Khim. Prir. Soedin. 1972{5}: 676-677.

1.1-174 Noda, M., and Umeda, Y. 1973. Neutral diol lipids in plant seeds [in Japanese]. Kyoto-furitsu Daigaku Gakujutsu Hokoku, Nogaku 1973{25}: 53-60. FCA 27: 3603.

1.1-175 Panekina, T.V., Gusakova, S.D., Zalevskaya, E.M., and Umarov, A.U. 1979. Composition of the triacylglycerols of the seeds of some representatives of the family Labiatae. Chem. Nat. Compd. (Engl. Transl.) 15: 538-545. Translation of Khim. Prir. 1979{5}: 618-625.

1.1-176 Patra, A., Ghosh, A., and Mitra, A.K. 1976. Triterpenoids and furocoumarins of the fruits of <u>Angelica archangelica</u>. Indian J. Chem. Sect. B. 14: 816-817.

1.1-177 Pattenden, G. 1978. Natural 4-ylidenebutenolides and 4-ylidenetetronic acids. Fortschr. Chem. Org. Naturst. 35: 133-198.

1.1-178 Pojarova, H., and Sasek, A. 1974. Presence of haemagglutinins in the seeds of legumes, maize and mustard [in Czech]. Sb. UVTIZ Genet. Slechteni 10: 261-266. FCA 31: 2754.

1.1-179 Poniedzialek, M. 1977. The content of some selected components in the roots of 5 types of horseradish (Armoracia rusticana Gaertn.) [in Polish]. Zesz. Nauk. Ogrod. Akad. Roln. Krakow. 1977{5}: 111-130.

1.1-180 Pontovich, V.E., and Sedova, L.V. 1976. Gibberellin-like substances in the placenta and seeds of developing fruit of opium poppy. Sov. Plant Physiol. (Engl. Transl.) 23: 629-633. Translation of Fiziol. Rast. (Moscow) 23: 747-752.

1.1-181 Popa, D.P., and Salei, L.A. 1973. Diterpenoids of the genus Marrubium [in Russian]. Rastit. Resur. 9: 384-387. HA 44: 2750.

1.1-182 Popescu, H., and Katz, E. 1978. Volatile oil in Achillea millefolium flowers from the Salaj district (Romania) [in Romanian]. Farmacia (Bucharest) 26{1}: 51-54. HA 49: 6124.

1.1-183 Poplawski, J., Wrobel, J.T., and Glinka, T. 1980. Panaxydol, a new polyacetylenic epoxide from Panax ginseng roots. Phytochemistry 19: 1539-1541.

1.1-184 Racusen, D., and Foote, M. 1974. The hexosamine content of leaves. Can. J. Bot. 52: 2111-2113.

1.1-185 Ramshaw, J.A.M., Brown, R.H., Scawen, M.D., and Boulter, D. 1973. Higher plant plastocyanin. Biochim. Biophys. Acta 303: 269-273.

1.1-186 Rasmussen, S., Rasmussen, K.E., and Baerheim Svendsen, S.A. 1972. Occurrence of anethole in the volatile oil of Coriandrum sativum. Terpenes and related compounds. Medd. Nor. Farm. Selsk. 34{3-4}: 33-36. CA 80: 124564.

1.1-187 Redaelli, C., Formentini, L., and Santaniello, E. 1980. Apigenin 7-glucoside and its 2"- and 6"-acetates from ligulate flowers of Matricaria chamomilla. Phytochemistry 19: 985-986.

1.1-188 Roberts, M.F. 1971. Polyphenolases in the 1000g fraction of Papaver somniferum latex. J. Pharm. Pharmacol. 23 (Suppl.): 234S (Abstr.).

1.1-189 Rojahn, W., Hammerschmidt, F.J., Ziegler, E., and Hefendehl, F.W. 1977. Presence of viridiflorol in peppermint oil (Mentha piperita L.) [in German]. Dragoco Rep. (Ger. Ed.) 24{10}: 230-232. CA 88: 141478.

1.1-190 Romanova, A.S., Pribylova, G.F., Patudin, A.V., Leskova, E.S., Pakaln, D.A., and Ban'kovskii, A.I. 1972. The quinones of some species of sage. Chem. Nat. Compd. (Engl. Transl.) 8: 231-232. Translation of Khim. Prir. Soedin. 1972{2}: 237.

1.1-191 Romanova, A.S., Patudin, A.V., Pervykh, L.N., and Zobenko, L.P. 1978. Quinones of Salvia sclarea. Chem. Nat. Compd. (Engl. Transl.) 14: 439-440. Translation of Khim. Prir. Soedin. 1978{4}: 515-516.

1.1-192 Rossignol, M. 1976. Lipid composition of the roots of various cultivated species [in French]. Phytochemistry 15: 1893-1896.

1.1-193 Ruecker, G., and Tautges, J. 1976. Beta-ionon and patchouli alcohol from the underground parts of Valeriana officinalis [in German]. Phytochemistry 15: 824.

1.1-194 Rutherford, P.P., and Deacon, A.C. 1972. Beta-fructofuranosidases from roots of dandelion (Taraxacum officinale Weber). Biochem.J. 126: 569-573.

1.1-195 Rybal'chenko, A.S., Fursa, N.S., and Litvinenko, V.I. 1976. Phenolic compounds of the epideal part of valerian. I. Phenolic carboxylic acids and flavonoids. Chem. Nat. Compd. (Engl. Transl.) 12: 98. Translation of Khim. Prir. Soedin. 1976{1}: 106-107.

1.1-196 Saitoh, T., and Shibata, S. 1975. New type chalcones from licorice root. Tetrahedron Lett. 1975{50}: 4461-4462.

1.1-197 Saitoh, T., Kinoshita, T., and Shibata, S. 1976. New isoflavan and flavanone and licorice root. Chem. Pharm. Bull. (Tokyo) 24: 752-755.

1.1-198 Saitoh, T., Kinoshita, T., and Shibata, S. 1976. Flavonols of licorice root. Chem. Pharm. Bull. (Tokyo) 24: 1242-1245.

1.1-199 Sakata, I., and Koshimizu, K. 1978. Occurrence of L-menthyl-B-D-glucoside and methyl palmitate in rhizoma of Japanese peppermint. Agric. Biol. Chem. 42: 1959-1960.

1.1-200 Salzer, U.-J. 1975. Fatty acid composition of lipids of some spices [in German]. Fette Seifen Anstrichm. 77: 446-450.

1.1-201 Sarkar, S. 1977. Occurrence of arachidic esters in Foeniculum vulgare. Indian J. Chem. Sect. B 15B: 583.

1.1-202 Schmidtlein, H., and Herrmann, K. 1975. The phenolic acids of vegetables. 1. Hydroxycinnamic acids and hydroxybenxoic acids of Brassica- species and leaves of other Cruciferae [in German]. Z. Lebensm.-Unters.-Forsch. 159: 139-148. HA 46: 8410.

1.1-203 Schmidtlein, H., and Herrmann, K. 1975. The phenolic acids of vegetables. IV. Hydroxycinnamic acids and hydroxybenzoic acids of vegetables and potatoes [in German]. Z. Lebensm.-Unters.-Forsch. 159: 255-263. HA 46: 9251.

1.1-204 Schulz, J.M., and Herrmann, K. 1980. Occurrence of catechins and proanthocyanidins in spices [in German]. Z. Lebensm. Unters. Forsch. 171: 278-280.

1.1-205 Sergeeva, N.V. 1974. Rutin and other polyphenols of the herbage of Coriandrum sativum. Chem. Nat. Compd. (Engl. Transl.) 10: 98. Translation of Khim. Prir. Soedin. 1974{1}: 94-95.

1.1-206 Seshadri, T.R., Varshney, I.P., and Sood, A.R. 1973. Study of glycosides from Trigonella corniculata Linn. and T. foenum-graecum Linn. seeds. Curr. Sci. 42: 421-422.

1.1-207 Shah, C.S., Qadry, J.S., and Chauhan, M.G. 1972. Dillapiole-free Indian dill. Indian J. Pharm. 34: 77-78. AGRICOLA.

1.1-208 Shakhova, M.F., and Dedneva, A.L. 1972. Sterols of Mentha piperita [in Russian]. Farmatsiya (Moscow) 21{5}: 19-21. CA 78: 40427.

1.1-209 Shakova, M.F. 1971. Anthocyanins and leucoanthocyanins of peppermint inflorescences [in Russian]. Rastit. Resur. 7: 407-410. HA 44: 660.

1.1-210 Shankaracharya, N.B., and Natarajan, C.P. 1972. Fenugreek - chemical composition and use. Indian Spices 9{1}: 2-12. NAR 43: 4438.

1.1-211 Shankaracharya, N.B., Anadaraman, S., and Natarajan, C.P. 1973. Chemical composition of raw and roasted fenugreek seeds. J. Food Sci. Technol. 10: 179-181. NAR 44: 7756.

1.1-212 Shchelokova, L.G., Glumov, G.A., and Garbuzova, V.M. 1975. Content of lanatosides ABC in yellow foxglove in the Cis Ural region USSR [in Russian]. Rastit. Resur. 11: 358-362.

1.1-213 Shevchenko, S.V., and Tikhomirova, L.I. 1973. Some data on the essential oil composition of Salvia sclarea [in Russian]. Rastit. Resur. 9: 391-395. HA 44: 2707.

1.1-214 Shibata, H., and Shimizu, S. 1974. Synthesis of a new tautomer diosphenol (buccocamphor). Agric. Biol. Chem. 38: 1741.

1.1-215 Shibata, S., and Saitoh, T. 1978. Flavonoid compounds in licorice root. J. Indian Chem. Soc. 55{11}: 1184-1191. CA 91: 154399.

1.1-216 Shibata, S., and Saitoh, T. 1973. Chemical constituents of licorice roots [in Japanese]. Taisha 10: 619-625. CA 81: 101792.

1.1-217 Simonyan, A.V., and Litvinenko, V.I. 1972. Rosmarinic acid in representatives of the genus Thymus. Chem. Nat. Compd. (Engl. Transl.) 8: 776. Translation of Khim. Prir. Soedin. 1972{6}: 797.

1.1-218 Simonyan, A.V., and Litvinenko, V.I. 1971. Flavone aglycons of some Thymus species from the Caucasus [in Russian]. Rastit. Resur. 7: 580-582. CA 76: 70055.

1.1-219 Simonyan, A.V., Shinkarenko, A.L., and Litvinenko, V.I. 1973. Flavone glycosides of certain Thymus spp. growing in the Caucasus [in Russian]. Rastit. Resur. 9: 395-399. HA 44: 1806.

1.1-220 Singh, S.B., Goswami, A., Nigam, M.C., and Thakur, R.S. 1980. 1-Vinylmenth-4{8}-ene, a terpenoid hydrocarbon from Mentha citrata. Phytochemistry 19: 2466.

1.1-221 Sirnik, V. 1979. Important constituents of parsley (Petroselinum hortense) from different sources [in Serbo-Croatian]. Zb. Bioteh. Fak. Univ. Ljublj. Kmetijstvo 33: 409-416. HA 51: 7223.

1.1-222 Skopp, K., and Horster, H. 1976. Sugar-bound regular monoterpenes. Part I. Thymol and carvacrol glycosides in Thymus vulgaris [in German]. Planta Med. 29: 208-215. HA 47: 1851.

1.1-223 Skorikova, Yu.G., and Gavrilishina, L.I. 1979. Polyphenol composition of the leaves of horseradish, celery, parsley, and dill [in Russian] Konservn. Ovoshchesush. Prom-st. 1979{2}: 31-34. CA 90: 164722.

1.1-224 Sood, A.R. 1975. Chemical components from the leaves of Trigonella foenum-graecum Linn. Indian J. Pharm. 37: 100-101. HA 46: 7986.

1.1-225 Sood, A.R., Boutard, B., Chadenson, M., Chopin, J., and Lebreton, P. 1976. A new flavone C-glycoside from Trigonella foenum-graecum. Phytochemistry 15: 351-352.

1.1-226 Starke, H., and Herrmann, K. 1976. Flavonols and flavones of vegetables. 7. Flavonols of leeks, chives and garlic [in German]. Z. Lebensm.-Unters. -Forsch. 161: 25-30. NAR-A 47: 8685.

1.1-227 Stepanenko, G.A., Gusakova, S.D., and Umarov, A.U. 1980. Lipids of Carum carvi and Foeniculum vulgare seeds. Khim. Prir. Soedin. 1980{6}: 827-828. HA 51: 7220.

1.1-228 Stepanenko, G.A., Umarov, A.U., and Markman, A.L. 1974. Fatty acid composition of the oils of the seeds of Anethum graveolens during their ripening. Chem. Nat. Compd. (Engl. Transl.) 10: 515-516. Translation of Khim. Prir. Soedin. 1974{4}: 513.

1.1-229 Stepanenko, G.A., Gusakova, S.D., and Umarov, A.U. 1980. Composition of the coats and kernels of the seeds of Nepeta pannonica and Lavandula vera. Chem. Nat. Compd. (Engl. Transl.) 16: 434-437. Translation of Khim. Prir. Soedin. 1980{5}: 614-620.

1.1-230 Stepanenko, G.A., Umarov, A.U., and Markman, A.L. 1974. Fatty-acid composition of the oils of the seeds of Anethum graveolens during their ripening. Chem. Nat. Compd. (Engl. Transl.) 10: 515-516. Translation of Khim. Prir. Soedin. 1974{4}: 513.

1.1-231 Stepanenko, G.A., Umarov, A.U., and Markman, A.L. 1975. Oils of the family Umbelliferae. Chem. Nat. Compd. (Engl. Transl.) 11: 86-87. Translation of Khim. Prir. Soedin. 1975{1}: 86-87.

1.1-232 Stoehr, H., and Herrman, K. 1975. The phenolic acids of vegetables. III. Hydroxycinnamic acids and hydroxybenzoic acids of root vegetables [in German]. Z. Lebensm.-Unters. -Forsch. 159: 219-224. HA 46: 9247.

1.1-233 Stoianova-Ivanova, B., and Tzutzulova, A.M. 1974. On the composition of higher fatty acids in the scales and the interior of Allium sativum L. bulbs. Dokl. Bolg. Akad. Nauk 27: 503-506. HA 45: 362.

1.1-234 Subramanian, S.S., Nair, A.G.R., Rodriguez, E., and Mabry, T.J. 1972. Polyphenols of the leaves of Majorana hortensis. Curr. Sci. 41: 202-204.

1.1-235 Subramanian, S.S., and Nair, A.G.R. 1972. Flavonoids of the leaves of Mentha spicata and Anisochilus carnosus. Phytochemistry 11: 452-453

1.1-236 Sud'eva, N.G., Senich, V.Ya., Popova, S.A., and Polyakov, A.F. 1973. Composition of anise seeds [in Russian]. Izv. Vyssh. Ucheb. Zaved. Pishch. Tekhnol. 1973{2}: 131-132. CA 79: 41113.

1.1-237 Sviderskaya, Z.I. 1971. Alcohol composition of essential oils of individual varieties of peppermint [in Russian]. Tr. Vses. Nauchno-Issled. Inst. Efirnomaslichn. Kul't. 3: 47-51. CA 78: 62052.

1.1-238 Swiatek, L. 1977. Phenolic acids and iridoid glucosides in some indigenous medicinal species of Plantago [in Polish]. Herba Pol. 23: 201-210. HA 48: 8568.

1.1-239 Szegfu, A., Novak, I., and Szendrei, K. 1972. Proazulenes of Anisi fructus [anise fruit] [in Hungarian]. Acta Pharm. Hung. 42: 162-170. CA 77: 111449.

1.1-240 Tada, H., and Takeda, K. 1976. Sesquiterpenes of Lauraceae plants. IV. Germacranolides from Laurus nobilis L. Chem. Pharm. Bull. (Tokyo) 24: 667-571.

1.1-241 Tagawa, M., and Murai, F. 1980. A new iridoid glucoside, nepetoglucosylester from Nepeta cataria. Planta Med. 39: 144-147.

1.1-242 Taskinen, J. 1975. 12-Methyl-omega-tridecanolide, a new macrocyclic lactone from Angelica root oil. Acta Chem. Scand. Ser. B 29: 637-638.

1.1-243 Terhune, S.J., Hogg, J.W., and Lawrence, B.M. 1974. Bicyclosesquiphellandrene and 1-epibicyclosesquiphellandrene: two new dienes based the cadalene skeleton. Phytochemistry 13: 1183-1185.

1.1-244 Teuber, H., and Herrmann, K. 1978. Flavonol glycosides of leaves and fruit of dill (Anethum graveolens) [in German]. Z. Lebensm.-Unters.-Forsch. 167: 101-104. HA 50: 1351.

1.1-245 Thappa, R.K., Dhar, K.L., and Atal, C.K. 1979. Isointermedeol, a new sesquiterpene alcohol from Cymbopogon flexuosus. Phytochemistry 18: 571-672. HA 49: 6967.

1.1-246 Tharanathan, R.N., and Anjaneyalu, Y.V. 1972. Polysaccharides from the seed mucilage of Ocimum basilicum Linn. Curr. Sci. 41: 214.

1.1-247 Tharanathan, R.N., and Anjaneyalu, Y.V. 1974. Polysaccharides from the seed mucilage of Ocimum basilicum Linn. Indian J. Chem. 12: 1164-1165.

1.1-248 Tharanathan, R.N., and Shamanna, D. 1975. Composition of Ocimum gratissium (shrubby basil) seed mucilage. Indian J. Chem. 13: 307-308.

1.1-249 Theander, O., Aman, P., Miksche, G.E., and Yasuda, S. 1977. Carbohydrates, polyphenols, and lignin in seed hulls of different colors from turnip rapeseed. J. Agric. Food Chem. 25: 270-273.

1.1-250 Thieme, H., and Kitze, C. 1973. The occurrence of flavonoids in Melissa officinalis [in German]. Pharmazie 28: 69-70. HA 43: 7079.

1.1-251 Tillyaev, K.S., Khalmatov, Kh.Kh., Primukhamedov, I., and Talipova, M.A. 1973. The chemical characterization of Achillea millefolium grown in Uzbekistan [in Russian]. Rastit. Resur. 9: 58-62.

1.1-252 Tomas, F., Mataix, J.J., and Carpena, O. 1972. Flavonoid glucosides in Petroselinum sativum [in Spanish]. Rev. Agroquim. Tecnol. Aliment. 12{2}: 263-268. CA 77: 149671.

1.1-253 Toulemonde, B., Mazza, M., and Bricout, J. 1977. Composition of the aroma of the rhizome of Glycyrrhiza glabra L. [in French]. Ind. Aliment. Agric. 94: 1179-1182. AGRICOLA.

1.1-254 Tourn, M.L., and Lombard, A. 1974. Studies on the oligofructosans of Artemisia absinthium leaves [in Italian]. Atti Acad. Sci. Torino, Cl. Sci. Fis., Mat. Nat. 5-6: 941-950. CA 84: 177678.

1.1-255 Toyoda, T., Muraki, S., and Yoshida, T. 1978. Pyridine and nicotinate derivatives in jasmine. Agric. Biol. Chem. 42: 1901-1905.

1.1-256 Treutner, R., Jankovsky, M., and Hubacek, J. 1978. The content of some substances in selected varieties of garlic (Allium sativum L.) [in Czech]. Rostl. Vyroba 24: 1003-1008. PBA 49: 3165.

1.1-257 Tschesche, R., Seidel, L., Sharma, S.C., and Wulff, G. 1972. Steroid saponins with more than one sugar chain. VI. Lanatigoside and lanagitoside, two bisdemosidic 22-hydroxyfurostanol glycosides from the leaves of Digitalis lanata Ehrh. [in German]. Chem. Ber. 105: 3397-3406.

1.1-258 Tschesche, R., Javellana, A.M., and Wulff, G. 1974. Steroid saponins with more than one sugar chain. IX. Purpureagitoside, a bisdesmosidic 22-hydroxyfurostanol glycoside from the leaves of Digitalis purpurea [in German]. Chem. Ber. 107: 2828-2834.

1.1-259 Ul'chenko, N.T., Gigienova, E.I., Seitanidi, K.L., Yagudaev, M.R., and Umarov, A.U. 1979. Seed oil of Artemisia absinthium. Chem. Nat. Compd. (Engl. Transl.) 15: 409-414. Translation of Khim. Prir. Soedin. 1979{4}: 471-477

1.1-260 Valutskaya, A.H., and Tyurina, E.V. 1972. The coumarin content of Siberian representatives of the Umbelliferae [in Russian]. Rastit. Resur. 8: 547-554. HA 43: 6283.

1.1-261 Varshney, I.P., and Beg, M.F.A. 1978. Study of saponins from the seeds of Trigonella foenum-graecum Linn. Indian J. Chem. Sect. B. 16: 1134-1136.

1.1-262 Verghese, J. 1980. Dihydrocarvone. Perfum. Flavor. 5{6}: 23-26. CA 94: 103570.

1.1-263 Vondenhof, T., Glombitza, K.W., and Steiner, M. 1973. Soluble carbohydrates in licorice (Succus liquiritiae) [in German]. Z. Lebensm.-Unters. Forsch. 152{6}: 345-347. CA 79: 145020.

1.1-264 Vosa, C.G., D'Amato, G., Capineri, R., Marchi, P., and De Dominicis, G. 1972. Quinacrine-like fluorescence of extracts from Papaveraceae and Fumariaceae. Nature (London) 239: 405-406.

1.1-265 Wagner, H., Iyengar, M.A., and Horhammer, L. 1973. Vicenin-1 and -2 in the seeds of Trigonella foenumgraecum. Phytochemistry 12: 2548.

1.1-266 Wallbank, B.E., and Wheatley, G.A. 1976. Volatile constituents from cauliflower and other crucifers. Phytochemistry 15: 763-766.

1.1-267 Wankhede, D.B., and Tharanathan, R.N. 1976. Sesame (Sesamum indicum) carbohydrates. J. Agric. Food Chem. 24: 655-659.

1.1-268 Yamauchi, F. 1972. Complex compounds in cereals and their products. Glycolipids and phospholids [in Japanese]. Nippon Shokuhin Kogyo Gakkaishi 19: 327-333. NAR 46: 6681.

1.1-269 Yarosh, N.P., and Megorskaya, O.M. 1975. The composition of fatty acids in free and bound lipids of poppy seeds [in Russian]. Maslo-zhir. Promst. 41{7}: 10-12. FSTA 8: 7N275.

1.1-270 Yaskonis, Yu.A. 1971. Biological and biochemical characteristics of yarrow milfoil (2. Biochemical characteristics) [in Russian]. Liet. TSR Mokslu Akad. Darb. Ser. C 1971{1}: 81-87.

1.1-271 Yoshihara, K., and Hirose, Y. 1975. The sesquiterpenes of ginseng. Bull. Chem. Soc. Japan 48: 2078-2080.

1.1-272 Yoshitama, K. 1977. An acylated delphinidin 3-rutinoside-5,3',5'-triglucoside from Lobelia erinus. Phytochemistry 16: 1857-1858.

1.1-273 Youssef, A., Osman, M., Soliman, N.Z., Nakhla, A.M., and Said, T. 1979. Some chemical constituents of henna leaves. Isolation and estimation of lawsone. Ann. Agric. Sci. (Moshtohor) 11: 51-57. AGRICOLA.

1.1-274 Zarghami, N.S., and Heinz, D.E. 1971. The volatile constituents of saffron. Lebensm.-Wiss. Technol. 4: 43-45.

1.1-275 Zarghami, N.S., and Heinz, D.E. 1971. Monoterpene aldehydes and isophorone-related compounds of saffron. Phytochemistry 10: 2755-2761.

1.1-276 Zarghami, N.S., and Russell, G.F. 1973. The volatile constituents of tarragon (Artemisia dracunculus). Chem. Mikrobiol. Technol. Lebensm. 2: 184-186.

1.1-277 Zyczynska-Baloniak, I., Matuszelewska, H., and Dudzinska, J. 1971. Neutral constituents of the flowers of Anthemis nobilis L. Acta Pol. Pharm. (Engl. Transl.) 28: 625-634. Translation of Acta Pol. Pharm. 28: 625-634.

1.2 Essential Oils

1.2-1 Akhmedov, A.I., Goriaev, M.I., Chogovadze, Sh.K., and Dembitskii, A.D. 1972. An investigation of substance present in essential oils. 55. On the saffron essential oil (Crocus sativus L.) [in Russian]. Izv. Akad. Nauk Kaz. SSR Ser. Khim. 1972{5}: 56-59. AGRICOLA.

1.2-2 Alimukhamedov, S.A., Maksudov, N.A., Goryaev, M.I., and Sharipova, F.S. 1972 Investigation of the essential oil of garden parsley fruits. Pharm. Chem. J. (Engl. Transl.) 6: 572-574. Translation of Khim.-Farm. Zh. 6{9}: 15-17, 1972.

1.2-3 Ashraf, M., Aziz, J., and Bhatty, M.K. 1977. Studies on the essential oils of the Pakistani species of the family Umbelliferae. Part VI. Anethum graveolens (dill, sowa) seed oil. Pak. J. Sci. Ind. Res. 20: 52-54.

1.2-4 Ashraf, M., Ahmad, R., Mahmood, S., and Bhatty, M.K. 1980. Studies on the essential oils of the Pakistani species of the family Umbelliferae. XLVII. Angelica archangelica, Linn. var. Himalaica (Clarke), E. Nasir, seed oil. Pak. J. Sci. Ind. Res. 23{1-2}: 73-74. CA 94: 109075.

1.2-5 Ashraf, M., Ahmad, R., Mahmood, S., and Bhatty, M.K. 1980. Studies on the essential oils of the Pakistani species of the family Umbelliferae. XLVIII. Petroselinum crispum, (Miller), Hills (Eng. parsley) oil of the green plant. Pak. J. Sci. Ind. Res. 23: 128-129. CA 94: 71200.

1.2-6 Balbaa, S.I., Hilal, S.H., and Haggag, M.Y. 1975. A study of the fixed oils of the fruits of Carum copticum Benth. and Hook., Apium graveolens L. and Petroselinum sativum Hoffm. growing in Egypt. Egypt. J. Pharm. Sci. 16: 383-390. HA 48: 9276.

1.2-7 Bandopadhyay, M., Pardeshi, N.P., and Seshadri, T.R. 1972. Comparative study of Anethum graveolens and Anethum sowa. Curr. Sci. 41: 50-51.

1.2-8 Barclay, A.S., and Earle, F.R. 1974. Chemical analysis of seeds. III. Oil and protein content of 1253 seeds. Econ. Bot. 28: 178-236.

1.2-9 Baruah, A.K.S., and Bhagat, S.D. 1976. Oil of Indian wintergreen. Indian J. Pharm. 38: 56-57.

1.2-10 Basker, D., and Putievsky, E. 1976. Essential oils in three species of the Labiatae family [in Hebrew]. Hassadeh 57: 413-415.

1.2-11 Baslas, B.K., and Baslas, R.K. 1972. Chemistry of the essential oil obtained from the tops of Anethum graveolens [in German]. Riechst. Aromen Koerperpflegem. 22{6}: 200-202. CA 77: 85546.

1.2-12 Baslas, B.K., and Baslas, R.K. 1972. Chemistry of the oil from the herb Anethum graveolens [in German]. Riechst. Aromen Koerperflegem. 22: 155-156. CA 77: 66100.

1.2-13 Baslas, B.K., and Baslas, R.K. 1971. Chemical studies of the essential oils from the plants of Anethum graveolens and Anethum sowa (dill oils). Indian Perfum. 15{1}: 27-29. CA 76: 158207.

1.2-14 Baslas, B.K., Singh, B.R., and Baslas, R.K. 1973. Chemical composition of the essential oil of Mentha piperita. Indian Perfum. 17(pt. 2): 66-68. CA 82: 21710.

1.2-15 Basu, A.K., Ghosh, A., and Dutta, J. 1973. Fatty acid composition of mustard (Brassica nigra) seed oil by gas-liquid chromatography. J. Chromatogr. 86: 232-233.

1.2-16 Bhale, R., and Bokadia, M.M. 1979. Study of seed oils: component fatty acids of some Leguminosae seed fats. Acta Cienc. Indica [Ser.] Chem. 5{1}: 55-56. CA 91: 171659.

1.2-17 Bjeldanes, L.F., and Kim, I.-S. 1977. Phthalide components of celery essential oil. J. Org. Chem. 42: 2333-2335.

1.2-18 Bodrug, M.V. 1972. Origanum vulgare in Moldavia and its essential oil content [in Russian]. Izv. Akad. Nauk Mold. SSR Ser. Biol. Khim. Nauk 1972{2}: 81. CA 77: 85747.

1.2-19 Buil, P., Garnero, J., Guichard, G., and Konur, Z. 1977. The composition of some essential oils of Turkish origin [in French]. Riv. Ital. Essenze Profumi Piante Off. Aromi Saponi Cosmet. Aerosol 59: 379-384. HA 48: 8505.

1.2-20 Buttery, R.G., Black, D.R., Guadagni, D.G., Ling, L.C., Connolly, G., and Teranishi, R. 1974. California bay oil. I. Constituents, odor properties. J. Agric. Food Chem. 22: 773-777.

1.2-21 Chang, Q.-L., and Chang, W.-H. 1971. Fatty acid composition of some edible vegetable oils produced in Taiwan. Chung-kuo Nung Yeh Hua Hsueh Hui Chih 1971(Special Issue, Dec.): 51-58. FCA 26: 945.

1.2-22 Chladek, M., Stompfova, H., and Bublova, J. 1973. Composition of essential oils in various Mentha species [in German]. Pharmazie 28: 134. HA 43: 7081.

1.2-23 Chobanu, V.I. 1972. The essential oils of Mentha arvensis L. [in Russian]. Pages 83-90 in A.G. Nikolaev, ed. Khimicheskaia izmenchivost' rastenii. Shtiintsa, Kishinev, USSR. AGRICOLA.

1.2-24 Dayal, B., and Purohit, R.M. 1971. Chemical examination of the essential oil from the seeds of Majorana hortensis Moench. Flavour Ind. 2: 477-480.

1.2-25 Embong, M.B., Hadziyev, D., and Molnar, S. 1977. Essential oils from spices grown in Alberta. Fennel oil (Foeniculum vulgare var. Dulce.). Can. J. Plant Sci. 57: 829-837.

1.2-26 Embong, M.B., Hadziyev, D., and Molnar, S. 1977. Essential oils from spices grown in Alberta. Anise oil (Pimpinella anisum). Can. J. Plant Sci. 57: 681-688.

1.2-27 Embong, M.B., Hadziyev, D., and Molnar, S. 1977. Essential oils from spices grown in Alberta. Caraway oil (Carum carvi). Can. J. Plant Sci. 57: 543-549.

1.2-28 Evdokimoff, V., Bucci, B.T., and Cavazzutti, G. 1972. An analytical study of chamazulene from the essential oil of Matricaria chamomilla [in Italian]. Farmaco, Ed. Prat. 27: 163-173. HA 43: 3050.

1.2-29 Falk, A.J., Bauer, L., Bell, C.L., and Smolenski, S.J. 1974. The constituents of the essential oil from Achillea millefolium L. Lloydia 37: 598-602.

1.2-30 Fehr, D. 1974. The essential oil of celery leaves [in German]. Pharmazie 29: 349. HA 45: 1115.

1.2-31 Fehr, D. 1979. Investigation of aromatic substances in celery (Apium graveolens). Part 1. [in German]. Pharmazie 34: 658-662.

1.2-32 Fertman, G.I., and Lesnov, P.P. 1971. Identification of the composition of essential oils in plant raw materials [in Russian]. Izv. Vyssh. Ucheb. Zaved., Pishch. Tekhnol. 1971{5}: 165-167. CA 76: 63099.

1.2-33 Fleisher, A., Smir, N., Putievsky, E., and Orlan, Z. 1980. Essential oils of spice and fragrant plants (II) [in Hebrew]. Hassadeh 60: 1972-1974. HA 51: 2876.

1.2-34 Franz, C., and Glasl, H. 1974. Investigations of volatile oils in the leafs of some parsley varieties [in German]. Ind. Obst. Gemuseverwert. 59: 176. AGRICOLA.

1.2-35 Frattini, C., Belliardo, F., Reyneri, C., and Bicchi, C. 1978. Components of the essential oil of Piedmontese tarragon [in Italian]. Riv. Ital. Essenze Profumi Piante Off., Aromat., Syndets, Saponi, Cosmet., Aerosols 60{5}: 286-290. CA 89: 168947.

1.2-36 Friedrich, H. 1976. Phenylpropanoid constituents of essential oils Lloydia 39{1}: 1-7.

1.2-37 Fujita, S., Nakano, T., and Fujita, Y. 1977. Studies on the essential oils of the genus Mentha. Part IX. Biochemical study of the essential oils of Mentha japonica Makino [in Japanese]. Nippon Nogei Kagaku Kaishi 51: 405-408. HA 48: 2694.

1.2-38 Fujita, S., and Fujita, Y. 1972. Essential oils of the genus Mentha. VII. High-boiling components of the essential oil of Mentha pulegium L. [in Japanese]. Nippon Nogei Kagaku Kaishi 46: 303-307. CA 77: 105503.

1.2-39 Fujita, S., and Nezu, K. 1980. Studies on the essential oils of the genus Mentha. Part XII. On the components of the essential oils of Mentha spicata Linn. (a pilose form, longifolia type) [in Japanese] Nippon Nogei Kagaku Kaishi 54{5}: 341-344. CA 93: 225487.

1.2-40 Fujita, S.I., Nakano, T., and Fujita, Y. 1977. Studies on the essential oils of the genus Mentha. X. Components of the essential oils of Mentha rotundifolia [in Japanese]. Nippon Nogei Kagaku Kaishi 51: 699-702. HA 48: 7567.

1.2-41 Georgiev, E., and Genov, N. 1973. Gas-chromatographic study of the macrocomponents of basil oil [in Bulgarian]. Nauchni Tr. Vissh Inst. Khranit. Vkusova Prom-st. Plovidv 20: 209-217. CA 86: 8576.

1.2-42 Gigienova, E.I., Ul'chenko, N.T., and Umarov, A.U. 1974. alpha-Hydroxydienic acids of the seed oil of Artemisia absinthium. Chem. Nat. (Engl. Transl.) 10: 725-727. Translation of Khim. Prir. Soedin. 1974{6}: 701-704.

1.2-43 Gijbels, M.J.M., Scheffer, J.C.C., and Baerheim Svendsen, A. 1980. Z-butylidenephtalide in the essential oil from roots of Levisticum officinale. Planta Med. 1980(Suppl.): 41-47.

1.2-44 Gockeritz, D., Poggendorf, A., Schmidt, W., Schubert, D., and Pohloudek-Fabini, R. 1979. Essential oil from the roots of Anethum graveolens [in German]. Pharmazie 34: 426-429.

1.2-45 Golubev, M.I., and Kornilov, I.I. 1975. Seed oil contents of Indian mustard cultivars in the steppe regions of Volga and Rostov territory [in Russian]. Sb. Nauchn. Rab. Sarat. S-kh. Inst. 1975{33} 107-126. FCA 29: 5941.

1.2-46 Gora, J., Druri, M., Kaminska, J., and Kalemba, D. 1975. Chemical composition of oil from Mentha spicata spp. longifolia [in Polish]. Herba Pol. 21: 357-365. HA 47: 1844.

1.2-47 Gora, J., and Kalemba, D. 1979. Chemical composition of essential oil from Mentha spicata herbage [in Polish]. Herba Pol. 25: 269-275. HA 51: 4876.

1.2-48 Gora, J., Druri, M., Kaminska, J., and Kalemba, D. 1975. Chemical composition of essential oil from Mentha spicata L. subsp. longifolia (L) Tacik [in Polish]. Herba Pol. 20: 357-365. AGRICOLA.

1.2-49 Hazelhoff, B., Smith, D., Malingre, T.M., and Hendriks, H. 1979. The essential oil of Valeriana officinalis L. s.l. Pharm. Weekbl. 1{2}: 443-449. CA 91: 27173.

1.2-50 Hefendehl, F.W., and Ziegler, E. 1975. Analysis of peppermint oils [in German]. Deut. Lebensm.-Rundsch. 71: 287-290. HA 46: 10603.

1.2-51 Hodisan, V., Popescu, H., Fagarasan, E. 1980. Studies of Anethum graveolens L. II. Chemical composition of essential oil from fruits [in Romanian]. Contrib. Bot. Univ. Babes-Bolyai Gradina Bot. 1980: 263-266. Bib. Ag. 46: 27476.

1.2-52 Hogg, J.W., Terhune, S.J., and Lawrence, B.M. 1971. Essential oils and their constituents. VII. Epimeric 10-cadinols. Am. Perfum. Cosmet. 86{9}: 33-34.

1.2-53 Huergo, H.H., and Retamar, J.A. 1978. The essential oil of Laurus nobilis [in Spanish]. Riv. Ital. Essenze, Profumi, Piante Off., Aromat., Syndets, Saponi, Cosmet., Aerosols 60{11}: 635-636. Ca 90: 109789.

1.2-54 Ivanic, R., and Savin, K. 1976. A comparative analysis of essential oils from several wild species of Salvia. Planta Med. 30: 25-31. CA 85: 112651.

1.2-55 Ivanova, L.G., Chipiga, A.P., and Naidenova, V.P. 1977. Lactones from lavender oil production wastes. Chem. Nat. Compd. (Engl. Transl.) 13: 98-99. Translation of Khim. Prir. Soedin. 1976{1}: 111-112.

1.2-56 Joulain, D., and Ragault, M. 1976. Some new constituents of the essential oil of Hyssopus officinalis [in French]. Riv. Ital. Essenze Profumi Piante Off. Aromi Saponi Cosmet. Aerosol 58: 129-131.

1.2-57 Juell, S.M.-K., Hansen, R., and Jork, H. 1976. New substances from essential oils made from various species of Artemisia.

1. Spathulenol, an azolenogenic sesquiterpene alcohol [in German]. Arch. Pharm. (Weinheim) 309: 458-466.

1.2-58 Kaiser, R., and Lamparsky, D. 1976. Constituents of verbena oil. Part 2. Caryophyllane-2,6-beta-oxide, a new sesquiterpenoid compound from the oil of Lippia citriodora. Helv. Chim. Acta 59: 1803-1808.

1.2-59 Karasawa, D., and Shimizu, S. 1976. Sesquiterpene alcohols in the essential oils of Mentha aquatica L. and Mentha piperita L. Shin Shu Daigaku Nogakubu Kiyo 13{1}: 89-98. PBA 47: 10046.

1.2-60 Karawya, M.S., Hashim, F.M., and Hifnawy, M.S. 1974. Oils of Ocimum basilicum L. and Ocimum rubrum L. grown in Egypt. J. Agric. Food Chem. 22: 520-522.

1.2-61 Karawya, M.S., and Hifnawy, M.S. 1976. Egyptian marjoram oil. Egypt. J. Pharm. Sci. 17: 329-334. HA 50: 6517.

1.2-62 Karim, A., Ashraf, M., and Bhatty, M.K. 1979. Studies on the essential oils of the Pakistani species of the family Umbelliferae.

Part XXVIII. Coriandrum sativum Linn. (coriander, dhania) oil of the seeds and the whole plant. Pak. J. Sci. Ind. Res. 22: 205-207.

1.2-63 Karlsen, J., Chingova, B., Zwetkov, R., and Baerheim Svendsen, A. 1971. Essential oil of the fruits of Coriandrum sativum studied by means of gas liquid chromatography. Terpenes and related compounds. XI. Pharm. Weekbl. 106{12}: 293-300. CA 74: 136449.

1.2-64 Kasimovskaya, N.N., Red'ka, D.Ya., and Shkurat, D.F. 1972. Content and composition of the essential oil in parts of fennel plants [in Russian]. Tr. Vses. Nauchno-Issled. Inst. Efirnomaslichn. Kul't. 4{2}: 28-32. CA 78: 47646.

1.2-65 Kharebava, L.G., and Sardzhvedladze, G.P. 1979. Study of the essential oil of laurel with the capillary gas chromatography method (Preliminary report) [in Russian]. Subtrop. Kul't. 1979{2}: 98-102.

1.2-66 Konovalova, O.A., and Konon, N.T. 1978. Content of essential oil in the rhizomes and roots of the drug plant Valeriana officinalis cultivated in the Moscow region [in Russian]. Rastit. Resur. 14: 231-233. AGRICOLA.

1.2-67 Kosumov, F.Yu. 1980. Essential oils of thyme [in Russian]. Maslo-Zhir. Prom-st. 1980{1}: 31-32.

1.2-68 Lawrence, B.M., Hogg, J.W., and Terhune, S.J. 1972. Essential oils and their constituents. X. Some new trace constituents in the oil of Mentha piperita L. Flavour Ind. 3: 467-472.

1.2-69 Lawrence, B.M. 1978. Progress in essential oils. Perfum. Flavor. 3{2}: 45-50. HA 48: 10811.

1.2-70 Lawrence, B.M. 1980. Progress in essential oils. Perfum. Flavor. 4{5}: 31-32, 35-36. CA 92: 185700.

1.2-71 Lawrence, B.M., Terhune, S.J., and Hogg, J.W. 1971. Essential oils and their constituents. VI. The so-called "exotic" oil of Ocimum basilicum L. Flavour Ind. 2: 173-176.

1.2-72 Lawrence, B.M., Hogg, J.W., Terhune, S.J., and Pichitakul, N. 1972. Essential oils and their constituents. IX. The oils of Ocimum sanctum and Ocimum basilicum from Thailand. Flavour Ind. 3: 47-49.

1.2-73 Lawrence, B.M. 1971. Essential oils and their constituents. IV. Traces of new constituents in the essential oil of Salvia officinalis L. [in French]. Parfum. Cosmet. Savons Fr. 1{5}: 256-259. CA 75: 80186.

1.2-74 Lewis, Y.S., Krishnamurthy, N., Shivashankar, S., and Natarajan, C.P. 1978 Report on an unusual sample of coriander oil. Indian Arecanut, Spices and Cocoa Journal 2{1}: 1-2. HA 49: 4428.

1.2-75 Lewis, Y.S., Nambudiri, E.S., Krishnamurthy, N., and Amma, B.S.K. 1976. Essential oils in spices. Arecanut and Spices Bulletin 8: 5-8. HA 48: 6762.

1.2-76 Lishtvanova, L.N., and Moskalenko, L. 1971. Coriander essential oil [in Russian]. Tr. Vses. Nauchno-Issled. Inst. Efirnomaslichn. Kul't. 3: 45-47. CA 78: 62053.

1.2-77 Lupeanu, R., and Paun, E. 1974/1975. Studies on some essential oils of Mentha piperita L. [in Romanian]. An. Inst. Cercet. Cereale Plante Teh. Fundulea Acad. Stiinte Agric. Silvice Ser. C 42: 409-413. HA 48: 10051.

1.2-78 Maarse, H., and Os, F.H.L. van. 1973. Volatile oil of Origanum vulgare L. ssp. vulgare. I. Qualitative composition of the oil. Flavour Ind. 4: 477-481.

1.2-79 Maarse, H., and Os, F.H.L. van. 1973. Volatile oil of Origanum vulgare L. ssp. vulgare. II. Oil content and quantitative composition of the oil. Flavour Ind. 4: 481-484.

1.2-80 Malik, M.N., Imam, S.M., and Khan, F.W. 1971. The essential oils from the minor forest wealth of west Pakistan - an appraisal from the analytical data. Pak. J. For. 21: 159-168.

1.2-81 Minikeeva, A.S., Freiman, R.E., and Umarov, A.U. 1971. A study of the oils of Ocimum basilicum and Cardaria repens. Chem. Nat. Compd. (Engl. Transl.) 7: 5-7. Translation of Khim. Prir. Soedin. 1971{1}: 7-11.

1.2-82 Mishurova, S.S., and Abbasov, R.M. 1979. Studies of essential oil in the lemon variation of catmint in the Apsheron Peninsula [in Russian]. I Zv. Akad. Nauk Az. SSR Ser. Biol. Nauk 1979{4}: 24-26.

1.2-83 Miyazawa, M., and Kameoka, H. 1974. Constitution of the volatile oil from dill seed [in Japanese]. Yukagaku 23{11}: 746-749. CA 83: 136696.

1.2-84 Montes, M., Valenzuela, L., Wilkomirsky, T., and Arrive, M. 1973. The composition of the essential oil of Aloysia triphylla ("Cedron") [in French]. Planta Med. 23: 119-124. HA 43: 8991.

1.2-85 Morice, J., and Louarn, J. 1971. Study of morphine in the oil poppy (Papaver somniferum L.) [in French]. Ann. Amelior. Plant. 21:465-484. PBA 43: 2124.

1.2-86 Motl, O., Repcak, M., and Sedmera, P. 1978. Additional constituents of chamomile oil [in German]. Arch. Pharm. (Weinheim) 311: 75-76. CA 88: 141481.

1.2-87 Nagasawa, T., Umemoto, K., Tsuneya, T., and Shiga, M. 1976. Studies on the essential oil of Mentha spicata L. var. crispa Benth. Part IV. Essential oil of Mentha spicata var. crispa harvested in winter [in Japanese]. Nippon Nogei Kagaku Kaishi 50: 287-289. HA 47: 4899.

1.2-88 Nagasawa, T., Umemoto, K., Tsuneya, T., and Shiga, M. 1974. Essential oil of Mentha spicata var. crispa grown in Japan. 3. Components of peculiar odor in Japanese spearmint oil [in Japanese]. Koryo 108: 45-50. CA 82: 129171.

1.2-89 Nagell, A., Hefendehl, F.W., and Hoyer, J. 1974. Two stereoisomeric 1,2-epoxymenthyl acetates from an oil of Mentha rotundifolia X Mentha longifolia. Z. Naturforsch. Teil C 29: 294-295. PBA 46: 3034.

1.2-90 Nano, G.M., Sacco, J., and Frattini, C. 1973. Anthemis oils [in

Italian].   Pages   50-57 in Atti, convegno nazionale sugli olii
essenziali e sui derivati agrumari, 2nd, Reggio Calabria, Italy, Mr.
25-26, 1973. Stazione Sperimentale per l'Industria delle Essenze e
Derivate degli Agrumi, Reggio Calabria, Italy. CA 81: 111400.

1.2-91 Oliveros-Belardo, L., and Aureus, E. 1977. Essential oil from
Cymbopogon citratus (DC.) Stapf. growing wild in the Philippines.
Perfum. Flavor. 2{5}: 59-60 (Abstr.). HA 48: 5871.

1.2-92 Panekina, T.V., Gusakova, S.D., and Umarov, A.U. 1978. The seed
oil of Nepeta cataria. Chem. Nat. Compd. (Engl. Transl.) 14: 139-141.
Translation of Khim. Prir. Soedin. 1978{2}: 174-176.

1.2-93 Pfab, I., Heinrich, G., and Francke, W. 1980. Glycoside bound
components in the volatile oil of Monarda fistulosa [in German].
Biochem. Physiol. Pflanz. (BPP) 175: 194-207. HA 51: 2082.

1.2-94 Piper, T.J., and Price, M.J. 1975. Atypical oils from Mentha
arvensis var. piperascens (Japanese mint) plants grown from seed. Int.
Flavours Food Addit. 6: 196-198.

1.2-95 Poggendorf, A., Gockeritz, D., and Pohloudek-Fabini, R. 1977. The
essential oil content of Anethum graveolens L. [in German]. Pharmazie
32: 607-613.

1.2-96 Popa, D.P., and Salei, L.A. 1974. Manool from Salvia sclarea.
Chem. Nat. Compd. (Engl. Transl.) 10: 409. Translation of Khim. Prir.
Soedin. 1974{3}: 405.

1.2-97 Reichling, J., and Becker, H. 1977. Analysis of essential oils
from chamomile [in German]. Dtsch. Apoth. -Ztg. 117: 275-277. HA 48:
2691.

1.2-98 Richard, H.M.J., Miquel, J.D., and Sandret, F.G. 1975. The
essential oils of the thyme of Morocco and the thyme of Provence [in
French]. Parfums, Cosmet. Aromes 6: 69-72, 75-78. CA 85: 51614.

1.2-99 Rothbacher, H., and Suteu, F. 1975. The hydroxylic compounds in
caraway oil [in German]. Planta Med. 28: 112-123. HA 46: 6055.

1.2-100 Russell, G.F., and Olson, K.V. 1972. The volatile constituents
of oil of thyme. J. Food Sci. 37: 405-407.

1.2-101 Schaden, G., and Hesse, C. 1976. The essential oil of Origanum
dictamnus L. Monatsh. Chem. 107: 929-931.

1.2-102 Sengupta, A., and Mazumder, U.K. 1976. Triglyceride composition
of Papaver somniferum seed oil. J. Sci. Food Agric. 27: 214-218.

1.2-103 Shalabi, A., and Verzar-Petri, G. 1979. Cytological conditions
and composition of essential oil of the Hungarian millefolii herba.
Planta Med. 36: 291 (Abstr.).

1.2-104 Sharma, M.L., Shukla, S., Raina, R.M., and Srivastava, G.S.
1980. Essential oil from the seeds of Anethum graveolens Linn. raised
at Lucknow. Indian Perfum. 24: 124-125.

1.2-105 Slepetys, J. 1973. Essential oil in common wormwood [in
Russian]. Page s 289-293 in K. Jankevicius, ed. Polezny rasteniia

Pribaltiishikh respublik i Belorussii. Nauchnaia konferentsiia po issledovaniiu i obogashcheni, lu rastitel'nkyh resurov Pribaltiiskikh respublik i Belorussii, 2nd, Vilna, 1973. CA 81: 60957.

1.2-106 Srivastava, A.K., Lal, R.N., Siddiqui, M.S., and Nigam, M.C. 1976. Studies on the essential oil of Mentha arvensis Linn. subsp. haplocalyx Briq. var. piperescens Holmes in alkaline soils at Lucknow. Indian Perfum. 20(1-B): 61-65. CA 88: 141485.

1.2-107 Stahl, E., and Herting, D. 1976. The essential oil and coumarin content of single fruits of some Apiaceae [in German]. Planta Med. 29: 1-9. HA 46: 9607.

1.2-108 Stepanenko, G.A., Umarov, A.U., and Markman, A.L. 1974. Study of fine oils of plants of the family Umbelliferae. Part 3. Chem. Nat. Compd. (Engl. Transl.) 10: 31-33. Translation of Khim. Prir. Soedin. 1974{1}: 37-40.

1.2-109 Swiatek, L., Kurowska, A., and Gora, J. 1980. Chemical composition of seed oil from Plantago (including P. major, P. media and P. lanceolata). Page 26 in E. Mechler and E. Reinhard, eds. International research congress on natural products as medicinal agents. [The Congress], Strasbourg, France. HA 51: 627.

1.2-110 Tabacchi, R., Garnero, J., and Buil, P. 1974. Chemical composition of Turkish anise seed essential oil [in French]. Riv. Ital. Essenze Profumi Piante Off., Aromi, Saponi, Cosmet., Aerosol 56: 683-698. CA 83: 65303.

1.2-111 Takahashi, K., Someya, T., Muraki, S., and Yoshida, T. 1980. A new keto-alcohol, (-)-mintlactone, (+)-isomintlactone and minor components in peppermint oil. Agric. Biol. Chem. 44: 1535-1543.

1.2-112 Taskinen, J., and Nykanen, L. 1975. Chemical composition of Angelica root oil. Acta Chem. Scand. Ser. B 29: 757-764.

1.2-113 Taskinen, J. 1975. A new sesquiterpene alcohol of the copane series from Angelica archangelica root oil. Acta Chem. Scand. Ser. B 29: 999-1001.

1.2-114 Terhune, S.J., Hogg, J.W., Bromstein, A.C., and Lawrence, B.M. 1974. Interesting new components of common essential oils. Int. Congr. Essent. Oils [Pap.], 6th, 1974. 153, 9 pp. CA 84: 169540.

1.2-115 Ul'chenko, N.T., Gigienova, E.I., and Umarov, A.U. 1976. Epoxy acids of the seed oil of Artemisia absinthium. Chem. Nat. Compd. (Engl. Transl.) 12: 635-639. Translation of Khim. Prir. Soedin. 1976{6}: 705-710.

1.2-116 Vernon, F., Richard, H.M.J., and Sandret, F.G. 1978. Essential oil of marjoram (Majorana hortensis Moench.) from Egypt [in French]. Perfum. Cosmet. Aromes 21: 85-88. CA 89: 203993.

1.2-117 Yoshida, T. 1979. On the oil containing tissue, the essential oil contents and the chemical composition of essential oil in laurel leaf (Laurus nobilis L.) produced in Mediterranean countries [in Japanese]. Nettai Nogyo 23{1}: 6-10.

1.2-118 Zafar, R., Deshumkh, V.K., and Saoji, A.N. 1975. Studies on some papilionaceous seed oils. Curr. Sci. 44: 311-312. HA 46: 3658.

1.2-119 Zola, A., Le Vanda, J.P., and Guthbrod, F. 1977. Essential oils of bay laurel [in French]. Riv. Ital. Essenze Profumi Piante Off., Aromat., Syndets, Saponi, Cosmet., Aerosols 59: 374-378. CA 88: 11724.

1.2-120 Zola, A., Vanda, J.P. Le, and Guthbrod, F. 1977. Bay laurel essential oil [in French]. Plant. Med. Phytother. 11: 241-246. HA 48: 5874.

1.3 Extraction and Isolation

1.3-1 Awasthi, D.N., and Singh, B.P. 1973. Isolation and identification of capsaicin and allied compound in chilli. Proc. Indian Acad. Sci. Sect. B 77B: 196-201.

1.3-2 Batra, U.R., Deshmukh, M.G., and Joshi, R.N. 1976. Factors affecting extractability of protein from green plants. Indian J. Plant Physiol. 19: 211-216. FCA 30: 7994.

1.3-3 Bhardwaj, D.K., Murari, R., Seshadri, T.R., and Radhika Singh. 1977. Isolation of 7-acetoxy-4- methylcoumarin from Trigonella foenum-graecum. Indian J. Chem. Sect. B. 15: 94-95.

1.3-4 Chatterjee, A., Basa, S.C., and Basu, D. 1973. Isolation and structure of archangelenone: a flavonoid constituent of Angelica archangelica Linn. Indian J. Chem. 11: 407-409.

1.3-5 Clermont, S., and Percheron, F. 1979. Uridine diphosphogalactose-4 epimerase in fenugreek: studies on its purification and various properties [in French]. Phytochemistry 18: 1963-1965.

1.3-6 Damjanic, A., and Grzunov, K. 1973. Essential oil from Rosmarinus officinalis obtained by different methods of distillation [in Croatian]. Kem. Ind. 22: 497-501. AGRICOLA.

1.3-7 Elgamal, M.H.A., and Fayez, M.B.E. 1972. Isolation of formonometin from the roots of Glycyrrhiza glabra Linn. collected locally. Indian J. Chem. 10: 128.

1.3-8 Falk, A.J., Smolenski, S.J., Bauer, L., and Bell, C.L. 1975. Isolation and identification of three new flavones from Achillea millefolium L. J. Pharm. Sci. 64: 1838-1842. HA 46: 7952.

1.3-9 Ganchev, G., Georgiev, E., and Ognyanov, I. 1974. Distillation of basil oil (Ocimum basilicum). Int. Congr. Essent. Oils, [Pap.], 6th, 1974, 33, 4 pp. CA 84: 65164.

1.3-10 Garcia, L.A., and Gulden, E.E. 1972. Molecular distillation equipment for descending film [in Spanish]. SAFYBI (Soc. Argent. Farm. Bioquim. Ind.) 12{39}: 652-662. CA 79: 93767.

1.3-11 Georgiev, E., Genov, N., Lazarova, R., and Ganchev, G. 1978. On the distillation of annual wormwood (Artemisia annua Linnaeus). Riv. Ital. Essenze, Profumi, Piante Off., Aromat., Syndets, Saponi, Cosmet., Aerosols 60{5}: 302-306. CA 89: 135663.

1.3-12 Guerra, M.J., and Park, Y.K. 1975. Extraction of sesame seed protein and determination of its molecular weight by sodium dodecyl sulfate polyacrylamide gel electrophoresis. J. Am. Oil Chem. Soc. 52: 73-75.

1.3-13 Hardman, R., Kosugi, J., and Parfitt, R.T. 1980. Isolation and characterization of a furostanol glycoside from fenugreek. Phytochemistry 19: 698-700.

1.3-14 Houser, T.J., Biftu, T., and Hsieh, P.F. 1975. Extraction rate equations for paprika and turmeric with organic solvents. J. Agric. Food Chem. 23: 353-355.

1.3-15 Ivanov, S.A., and Konova, B. 1976. The composition of lipid 6-hydroxychromane fractions in some Umbelliferae [in German]. Dokl. Bolg. Akad. Nauk 29: 371-374. HA 47: 769.

1.3-16 Kamel, K.F. 1973. Effect of different solvents on the yield and the constituents of some edible oils. Egypt. J. Bot. 16: 337-343. FCA 29: 9039.

1.3-17 Karawya, M.S., Hashim, F.M., and Hifnawy, M.S. 1972. Colorimetric assay of citral and citronella in volatile oils. J. Assoc. Off. Anal. Chem. 55: 1183-1186.

1.3-18 Karowowska, K., and Tokarska, B. 1977. Isolation of horseradish flavor components [in Polish]. Pr. Inst. Lab. Badaw. Przem. Spozyw. 27{1}: 7-12. CA 88: 103422.

1.3-19 Khafagy, S.M., Sarg, T.M., Abdel Salam, N.A., and Gabr, O. 1978. Isolation of two flavone glycosides from the fruits of Cuminum cyminum L. growing in Egypt. Pharmazie 33: 296-297. CA 89: 103738.

1.3-20 Kim, J.P., Shim, W.M., and Kim, C.I. 1980. Separation and composition of sesame meal protein [in Korean]. Hanguk Nonghwa Hakhoe Chi 23: 14-22.

1.3-21 Koedam, A., Scheffer, J.J.C., and Baerheim Svendsen, A. 1979. Comparison of isolation procedures for essential oils. I. Dill (Anethum graveolens L.). Chem. Mikrobiol. Technol. Lebensm. 6: 1-7. AGRICOLA.

1.3-22 Kozhin, S.A., Moskvin, L.N., Fleisher, A.Yu., and Epifanova, I.O. 1973. Separation of essential oils by means of liquid-liquid partition chromatography with inverted liquid phase. J. Gen. Chem. USSR (Engl. Transl.) 43: 424-429. Translation of Zh. Obshch. Khim. 43: 428-434, 1973.

1.3-23 Kukhta, E.P., Chirva, V.Ya., Shadrin, G.N., and Stazaeva, L.P. 1979. Pectin substances of essential-oil crops. III. Isolation and characterization of the pectin of Salvia sclarea. Chem. Nat. Compd. (Engl. Transl.) 15: 189-191. Translation of Khim. Prir. Soedin. 1979{2}: 222.

1.3-24 Kunzemann, J., and Herrmann, K. 1977. Isolation and identification of flavon(ol)-O-glycosides in caraway (Carum carvi), fennel (Foeniculum vulgare), anise (Pimpinella anisum) and coriander (Coriandrum sativum) and of flavon-C-glycosides in anise. I. Phenolics of spices [in German]. Z. Lebensm.-Unters. -Forsch. 164: 194-200. HA 48: 2684.

1.3-25 Lee, L.T., and Wah, M.W. 1973. Extraction of 6-octadecenoic acid from Taiwan coriander [in Chinese]. Hua Hsueh 2: 52-54. CA 80: 45638.

1.3-26 Loomis, W.D., Lile, J.D., Sandstrom, R.P., and Burbott, A.J. 1979. Adsorbant polystyrene as an aid in plant enzyme isolation. Phytochemistry 18: 1049-1054.

1.3-27 Majak, W., and Towers, G.H.N. 1973. Methods for the isolation and purification of ethanol-insoluble, phenolic esters in Mentha arvensis. Phytochemistry 12: 1141-1147.

1.3-28 Mechler, E. 1979. The yield of essential oils according to the two different methods of European pharmacopoeia and German pharmacopoeia 7th edition. Planta Med 36: 278-279 (Abstr.).

1.3-29 Murav'ev, I.A., Ponomarev, V.D., and Pshukov, Yu.G. 1973. Diffusion coefficients of substances in the extraction of dry and swollen vegetable raw material. Pharm. Chem. J. (Engl. Transl.) 7: 242-244. Translation of Khim.-Farm. Zh. 7{4}: 42-45, 1973.

1.3-30 Murav'ev, I.A., and Zyubr, T.P. 1974. Study of the effect of several factors on extraction of roots and rhizomes of Uralian licorice [in Russian]. Aktual. Vopr. Farm. 2: 241-243. CA 84: 95563.

1.3-31 Narasimha, M.B., Kulkarni, T.G., and Deshmukh, V.N. 1977. Optimization studies on steam distillation of Mentha piperita and Eucalyptus citriodora. Pages 402-408 in C.K. Atal and B.M. Kapur, eds. Cultivation & utilization of medicinal and aromatic plants. Regional Research Laboratory, Jammu-Tawi, India.

1.3-32 Philip, T., and Francis, F.J. 1971. Isolation and chemical properties of capsanthin and derivatives. J. Food Sci. 36: 823-827.

1.3-33 Polesello, A., and Pizzocaro, F. 1976. Separation and determination of capsaicin in red peppers in thin layer chromatography [in Italian]. Sci. Tecnol. Alimenti 6: 305-306. AGRICOLA.

1.3-34 Prakash, V., and Nandi, P.K. 1978. Isolation and characterization of alpha-globulin of sesame seed (Sesamum indicum L.). J. Agric. Food Chem. 26: 320-323.

1.3-35 Rios, V.M., and Duden, R. 1971. Thin-layer chromatographic isolation and reflectance photometric determination of capsaicin [in German]. Lebensm. Wiss. Technol. 4{3}: 97-98. CA 76: 2596.

1.3-36 Sakata, I., and Mitsui, T. 1975. Isolation and identification of L-menthyl-beta-D-glucoside from shubi. Agric. Biol. Chem. 39: 1329-1330.

1.3-37 Sankarikutty, S., Sumathykutty, M.A., Bhat, A.V., and Mathew, A.G. 1978. Studies on extraction of oils and oleoresins from cumin, fennel and fenugreek. Indian Arecanut, Spices and Cocoa Journal 2{2}: 25-30. HA 49: 8818

1.3-38 Scora, R.W., and Tin, W. 1971. Isolation and identification of alkanes from three taxa of Monarda. Phytochemistry 10: 462-464.

1.3-39 Sen, A.R., Sardar, P.K., and Sengupta, P. 1977. Thin layer chromatographic detection of Carum bulbocastanum Koch in Carum carvi Linn. J. Assoc. Off. Anal. Chem. 60: 235-236.

1.3-40 Simonyan, A.V., Oganesyan, E.T., and Azaryan, R.A. 1973. Triterpene acids from the wastes from the production of thyme extract. Chem. Nat. Compd. (Engl. Transl.) 9: 122. Translation of Khim. Prir. Soedin. 1973{1}: 123.

1.3-41 Stermitz, F.R., and Thomas, R.D. 1973. Separation of furocoumarins by high-pressure liquid chromatography. J. Chromatogr. 77: 431-433. CA 79: 2193.

1.3-42 Sticher, O. 1971. Isolation of monotropein from Asperula odorata [in German]. Pharm. Acta Helv. 46: 121-128. CA 74: 130321.

1.3-43 Tabacchi, R., Garnero, J., and Buil, P. 1974. Isolation and identification of the sesquiterpene hydrocarbons from the essential oil of anise grains [in French]. Helv. Chim. Acta 57: 849-851.

1.3-44 Tanasienko, F.S., Kravets, T.I., and Kasimovskaia, N.N. 1975. Solubility of essential oil of peppermint in water [in Russian]. Tr. Vses. Nauchno-Issled. Inst. Efirnomaslichn. Kul't. 8: 250-255. AGRICOLA.

1.3-45 Tsuneya, T., Shibai, T., Yoshioka, A., and Shiga, M. 1973. Isolation of 6-hydroxycarvone from spearmint oil [in Japanese]. Koryo 104: 23-26. CA 80: 40925.

1.3-46 Ueda, J., and Kato, J. 1980. Isolation and identification of a senescence-promoting substance from wormwood (Artemisia absinthium L.). Plant Physiol. 66: 246-249.

1.3-47 Van Hulle, C., Braeckman, P., and Vandewalle, M. 1971. Isolation of two new flavonoids from the root of Glycyrrhiza glabra var. typica Planta Med. 20: 278-282. CA 76: 83552.

1.3-48 Yoshikawa, T., and Furuya, T. 1979. Purification and properties of sterol: UDPG glucosyltransferase in cell culture of Digitalis purpurea. Phytochemistry 18: 239-241.

1.3-49 Zwauing, J.H., Smith, D., and Bos, R. 1971. Essential oil of chervil, Anthriscus cerefolium. Isolation of 1-allyl-2,4-dimethoxybenzene. Pharm. Weekbl. 106: 182-189. CA 76: 1348.

1.4 Physical and Chemical Properties

1.4-1 Abdel-Fattah, A.F., and Edrees, M. 1972. A study on the composition of garlic skins and the structural features of the isolated pectic acid. J. Sci. Food Agric. 23: 871-877.

1.4-2 Akhmedov, I.S., Kasymov, Sh.Z., and Sidyakin, G.P. 1973. Structure of artabin. Chem. Nat. Compd. (Engl. Transl.) 6: 703-704. Translation of Khim. Prir. Soedin. 1970{6}: 691-694.

1.4-3 Anjaneyalu, Y.V., and Gowda, D.C. 1979. Structural studies of an acidic polysaccharide from Ocimum basilicum seeds. Carbohydr. Res. 75: 251-256.

1.4-4 Bai, N.J., Kumar, K.S., and Krishnamurthy, S. 1972. Studies of enzymes of oil seeds. Solubilization and properties of a lipase from seeds of Sesamum indicum (gingelly). Enzymologia 43: 345-351.

1.4-5 Bassani, C., and Morita, T. 1979. Study on chemical and physicochemical characteristics of Brazilian dementholized peppermint oil (Mentha arvensis var. IAC 701). Int. Congr. Essent. Oils, [Pap.], 7th, 1977. 7: 333-342. CA 92: 64529.

1.4-6 Bates, R.B., Eckert, D.J., Paknikar, S.K., and Thalacker, V.P. 1972. Structure and synthesis of archangelin. Spectral methods for distinguishing bergaptyl from isobergaptyl ethers. Tetrahedron Lett. 1972{36}: 3811-3814.

1.4-7 Battersby, A.R., Sheldrake, P.W., Staunton, J., and Summers, M.C. 1977. Stereospecificity in the biosynthesis of papaverine. Bioorg. Chem. 6: 43-47.

1.4-8 Beauhaire, J., Fourrey, J.L., Vuilhorgne, M., and Lallemand, J.Y. 1980. Dimeric sesquiterpene lactones: structure of absinthin. Tetrahedron Lett. 1980{21}: 3191-3194.

1.4-9 Belsten, J.C., Bramwell, A.F., Burrell, J.W.K., and Michalkiewicz, D.M. 1972. Structure and synthesis of a newly discovered terpenoid isolated from lavandin oil - Trans-5-hydroxy-2-isopropenyl-5--methylhex-3-enyl acetate. Tetrahedron 28: 3439-3440.

1.4-10 Benesova, M., Senkpiel, K., Kovacs, P., and Barth, A. 1980. Multiple molecular forms of aminopeptidases in poppy seedlings (Papaver somniferum L. cv. "Dubsky") [in German]. Biochem. Physiol. Pflanz. (BPP) 175: 252-262.

1.4-11 Birnbaum, G.I., Findlay, J.A., and Krepinsky, J.J. 1978. Stereochemistry of valerenane sesquiterpenoids. Crystal structure of valerenolic acid. J. Org. Chem. 43: 272-276.

1.4-12 Bogacheva, N.G., Sheichenko, V.I., and Kogan, L.M. 1977. Structure of the tetraside jamogenin from seeds of Trigonella foenum-graecum. Pharm. Chem. J. (Engl. Transl.) 11: 938-942. Translation of Khim.-Farm. Zh. 11{7}: 65-69, 1977.

1.4-13 Bouquelet, S., and Spik, G. 1976. Characterization and localization of four forms of N-acetyl-beta-D-hexosaminidase from fenugreek (Trigonella foenum graecum) germinated seeds. FEBS. Lett. 63: 95-101.

1.4-14 Buchecker, R., and Eugster, C.H. 1973. Absolute configuration of picrocrocin [in German]. Helv. Chim. Acta 56: 1121-1124.

1.4-15 Campsteyn, H., Dupont, L., Lamotte, J., Dideberg, O., and Vermeire, M. 1977 Crystal and molecular structure of glycyrrhetinic acid acetone monohydrate. Acta Crystallogr. Sect. B 33: 3443-3448.

1.4-16 Chialva, F., Doglia, G., Gabri, G., Aime, S., and Milone, L. 1976. Isolation and identification of cis- and trans-epoxyocimenes from the essential oil of Italian Artemisia absinthium Linnaeus [in Italian]. Riv. Ital. Essenze, Profumi, Piante Off., Aromi, Saponi, Cosmet., Aerosol 58: 522-526. CA 86: 161105.

1.4-17 Clermont, S., and Villarroya, E. 1973. Purification and enzymatic properties of alpha galactosidase of germinated fenugreek seeds [in French]. C.R. Hebd. Seances Acad. Sci. Ser. D 276: 1069-1070.

1.4-18 Cosovic, C., and Prostenik, M. 1974. Nature of polar lipids of poppy seeds (Papaver somniferum). Acta Pharm. Jugosl. 23: 207-212.

1.4-19 Crawford, M., Hanson, S.W., and Koker, M.E.S. 1975. The structure of cymbopogone, a novel triterpenoid from lemongrass. Tetrahedron Lett. 1975{35}: 3099-3102.

1.4-20 Cuong, B.N., Verzar-Petri, G., and Tamas, J. 1979. MS and H-NMR structural data of chamazulene carboxylic acid. Arch. Pharm. (Weinheim, Ger.) 312: 626-628.

1.4-21 Dabrowski, Z., Wrobel, J.T., and Wojtasiewicz, K. 1980. Structure of an acetylenic compound from Panax ginseng. Phytochemistry 19: 2464-2465.

1.4-22 Diesperger, H., and Sandermann, H., Jr. 1978. Evidence for an electrophilic intermediate in microsomal hydroxylation of cinnamic acid in plants. FEBS Lett. 85: 333-336. CA 88: 184742.

1.4-23 Eisenbraun, E.J., Brown, C.E., Irvin-Willis, R.L., McGurk, D.J., Elial, E.L., and Harris, D.L. 1980. Structure and stereochemistry of 4a beta, 7 alpha, 7a beta-nepetalactone from Nepeta mussini and its relationship to the 4a alpha, 7 alpha, 7a alpha- and 4a alpha, 7 alpha, 7a beta-nepetalactones from N. cataria. J. Org. Chem. 45: 3811-3814.

1.4-24 Endo, T., and Taguchi, H. 1977. The consituents of valerian root. The structures of four new iridoid glycosides, kanokoside A, B, C, and D from the root of "Hokkaikisso". Chem. Pharm. Bull. (Tokyo) 25: 2140-2142.

1.4-25 Fiad, S., and Osman, F. 1976. Glyceride structure of Egyptian vegetable oils. 8. Cruciferous seed oils. Egypt. J. Chem. 19: 1053-1061. FCA 33: 6550.

1.4-26 Foglietti, M.J. 1976. The purification of a plant galactokinase. The advantages of affinity chromatography [in French]. J. Chromatogr. 128: 309-312. HA 47: 5871.

1.4-27 Frazao, S., and Cunha, J. da. 1972. Comparative study of physical and chemical characteristics of essential oils of Portuguese and foreign rosemary [in Portuguese]. An. Acad. Bras. Cienc. 44(Suppl.): 351-354.

1.4-28 Greger, H., and Hofer, O. 1980. New unsymmetrically substituted tetrahydrofurofuran lignans from Artemisia absinthium. Assignment of the relative stereochemistry by lanthanide induced chemical shifts. Tetrahedron 36: 3551-3558. HA 51: 5726.

1.4-29 Gusakova, S.D., Umarov, A.U., and Panekina, T.U. 1978. Acylisomerization of triglycerides during their chromatography on aluminum oxide. Chem. Nat. Compd. (Engl. Transl.) 14: 257-263. Translation of Khim. Prir. Soedin. 1978{3}: 310-313.

1.4-30 Hardman, R., and Abu-Al-Futuh, I.M. 1979. The detection of isomers of 4-hydroxyisoleucine by the JEOL Amino Acid Analyser and by TLC. Planta Med. 36: 79-84.

1.4-31 Hasegawa, K., Murata, M., and Fujino, S. 1978. Characterization of subunits and temperature-dependent dissociation of 13S globulin of sesame seed. Agric. Biol. Chem. 42: 2291-2297.

1.4-32 Hiai, S., Oura, H., and Nakajima, T. 1976. Color reaction of some sapogenins and saponins with vanillan and sulfuric acid. Planta Med. 29: 116-122. CA 84: 155741.

1.4-33 Holloway, P.J., Jeffree, C.E., and Baker, E.A. 1976. Structural determination of secondary alcohols from plant epicuticular waxes. Phytochemistry 15: 1768-1770.

1.4-34 Holub, M., and Samek, Z. 1977. Isolation and structure of 3-epinobilin, 1,10-epoxynobilin and 3-dehydronobilin — other sesquiterpenic lactones from the flowers of Anthemis nobilis L. Revision of the structure of nobilin and eucannabinolide. Collect. Czech. Chem. Commun. 42: 1053-1064.

1.4-35 Hopf, H., and Kandler, O. 1977. Characterization of the 'reserve cellulose' of the endosperm of Carum carvi as a beta (1-4)-mannan. Phytochemistry 16: 1715-1717.

1.4-36 Ignatov, G., Dimitrov, D., and Rangelov, P. 1972. Thermophysical characteristics of some Bulgarian essential oils [in Bulgarian]. Nauchni Tr., Vissh Inst. Khranit. Vkusova Prom-st., Plovidiv 19: 341-346. CA 83: 168311.

1.4-37 Kaneda, M., Saitoh, T., Iitaka, Y., and Shibata, S. 1973. Chemical studies on the oriental plant drugs. XXXVI. Structure of licoricone, a new isoflavone from licorice root. Chem. Pharm. Bull. (Tokyo) 21: 1338-1341.

1.4-38 Kaneda, M., Iitaka, Y., and Shibata, S. 1973. Crystal and molecular structure of licoricone monobromacetate. Acta Crystallogr. Sect. B 29{pt. 12}: 2827-2832. CA 80: 53327.

1.4-39 Karimov, Z., Kasymov, Sh.Z., Yagudaev, M.R., and Sidyakin, G.P. 1980. Crystal structure of the sesquiterpene lactone absinthin (isolated from Artemisia absinthium) [in Russian]. Khim. Prir. Soedin. 1980{5}: 729-730. HA 51: 4900.

1.4-40 Karimov, Z., Kasymov, Sh.Z., Yagudaev, M.R., and Sidyakin, G.P. 1979. Crystal structure of the dilactone anabsin. Chem. Nat. Compd. (Engl. Transl.) 15: 648-649. Translation of Khim. Prir. Soedin. 1979{5}: 731-732.

1.4-41 Kir'yalov, N.P., and Bogatkina, V.F. 1975. Structure of glabric acid. Chem. Nat. Compd. (Engl. Transl.) 11: 123-124. Translation of Khi.x m. Prir. Soedin. 1975{1}: 105-107.

1.4-42 Kirtany, J.K., Paknikar, S.K., and Chatterjee, A. 1973. Revised structure of angelicain. Indian J. Chem. 11: 505.

1.4-43 Kondo, N., Marumoto, Y., and Shoji, J. 1971. Studies on the constituents of Panacis japonici Rhizoma. IV. The structure of chikusetsusaponin V. Chem. Pharm. Bull. (Tokyo) 19: 1103-1107.

1.4-44 Kondo, N., Shoji, J., and Tanaka, O. 1973. Studies on the constituents of Himalayan ginseng, Panax pseudoginseng. I. The structures of the saponins. (I). Chem. Pharm. Bull. (Tokyo) 21: 2705-2711.

1.4-45 Kondo, N., and Shoji, J. 1975. Studies on the constituents of Himalayan ginseng, Panax pseudoginseng. II. The structures of the saponins. 2. Chem. Pharm. Bull. (Tokyo) 23: 3282-3285.

1.4-46 Kovacs, P., and Benesova, M. 1976. Some properties of aminopeptidases from seedlings of Papaver somniferum L. cv. "Dubsky". Biologia Ser. C (Bratislava) 31: 423-430.

1.4-47 Kozawa, M., Morita, N., Baba, K., and Hata, K. 1978. Chemical components of the roots of Angelica keiskei Koidzumi. III. Structure of a new dihydrofurocoumarin [in Japanese]. Yakugaku Zasshi 98: 636-638. CA 89: 129431.

1.4-48 Kozawa, M., Morita, N., Baba, K., and Hata, K. 1977. The structure of xanthoangelol a new chalcone from the roots of Angelica keiskei (Umbelliferae). Chem. Pharm. Bull. (Tokyo) 25: 515-516.

1.4-49 Kozawa, M., Baba, K., Matsuyama, Y., and Hata, K. 1980. Studies on coumarins from the root of Angelica pubescens Maxim. III. Structure of various coumarins including angelin, a new premylcoumarin. Chem. Pharm. Bull. (Tokyo) 28{6}: 1782-1787. CA 93: 182785.

1.4-50 Kringstad, R., Jorgensen, A.-G., Jacobsen, E., and Nordal, A. 1978. Identif ication and quantitative determination of meconic acid by differential pulse polarography. Acta Pharm. Suec. 15: 147-149. CA 89: 86645.

1.4-51 Lazur'evskii, G.V., Kintya, P.K., Pukhal'skaya, E.C., and Sof'ina, Z.P. 1977. Structure and activity of steroidal glycosides. Pharm. Chem. J. (Engl. Transl.) 11(6 part 1): 749-757. Translation of Khim.-Farm. Zh. 11{6}: 19-29, 1977.

1.4-52 Lin, T.D., Kondo, N., and Shoji, J. 1976. Studies on the constituents of Panacis japonici rhizoma. V. The structures of chikusetsusaponin I, IA, IB, IVA and glycoside P1. Chem. Pharm. Bull. (Tokyo) 24: 253-261.

1.4-53 Lin, T.T., and Shoji, J. 1979. Constituents of Panacis japonici rhizoma VI. The structure of chikusetsu-saponin II, IVC. J. Chin. Chem. Soc. (Taipei) 2, 26{1}: 29-35. AGRICOLA.

1.4-54 Litynski, A., and Trzecki, S. 1973. Determination of several important physical properties of the seeds of oil producing plants [in Polish]. Biul. Inst. Hodowli Aklim. Rosl. 1973: 147-150. FCA 28: 2243.

1.4-55 Mitra, A.K., Patra, A., and Ghosh, A. 1979. Carbon-13 NMR spectra of some furocoumarins. Indian J. Chem. Sect. B 17B: 385.

1.4-56 Mitsuda, H., Takii, Y., Iwami, K., and Yasumoto, K. 1975. Purification and properties of thiamine pyrophosphokinase from parsley leaf. J. Nutr. Sci. Vitaminol. 21: 103-115. CA 83: 110329.

1.4-57 Muraki, S., Takahashi, K., Kato, T., Kabuto, C., Suzuki, T., Uyehara, T., Onhuma, T., and Yoshida, T. 1979. Isolation and X-ray

crystal structure of mintsulfide, a novel sulfur-containing
sesquiterpene. J. Chem. Soc. Chem. Commun. 1979{11}: 512-513.

1.4-58 Nagai, M., Ando, T., Tanaka, N., Tanaka, O., and Shibata, S.
1972. Chemical studies on the oriental plant drugs. XXVIII. Saponins
and sapogenins of ginseng: stereochemistry of the sapogenin of
ginsenosides -Rb1, -Rb2, and -Rc2. Chem. Pharm. Bull. (Tokyo) 20:
1212-1216.

1.4-59 Nagai, M., Tanaka, O., and Shibata, S. 1971. Chemical studies on
the oriental plant drugs. XXVI. Saponins and sapogenins of ginseng.
The absolute configurations of cinenic acid and panaxadiol. Chem.
Pharm. Bull. (Tokyo) 19: 2349-2353.

1.4-60 Nagai, Y., Tanaka, O., and Shibata, S. 1971. Chemical studies on
the Oriental plant drugs. XXIV. Structure of gensenoside-Rg1 a neutral
saponin of ginseng root. Tetrahedron 27: 881-892.

1.4-61 Nagasawa, T., Umemoto, K., Tsuneya, T., and Shiga, M. 1974.
Absolute configuration and conformation of a new terpenic alcohol
isolated from the essential oil of Mentha gentilis L. Studies on the
native mints of Tokai Districts. Part II. [in Japanese]. Nippon Nogei
Kagauku Kaishi 48: 467-472.

1.4-62 Nagasawa, T., Umemoto, K., Tsuneya, T., and Shiga, M. 1975.
Absolute configuration of (+)-1-acetoxy-P-menth-3-one isolated from
essential oil of Mentha gentilis (L.). Agric. Biol. Chem. 39:
2083-2084.

1.4-63 Nagell, A., and Hefendehl, F.W. 1972. Structure determination of
diosphenolene [in German]. Phytochemistry 11: 3359-3361.

1.4-64 Neidlein, R., and Daldrup, V. 1980. Isolation and structure of
substances in Lippia americana. II. [in German]. Arch. Pharm.
(Weinheim) 313: 97-108.

1.4-65 Nishimura, N., Okubo, K., and Shibasaki, K. 1979. Chemical and
physical properties of 13S globulin, the major protein in sesame
seeds. Cereal Chem. 56: 239-242.

1.4-66 Ohsawa, T., Tanaka, N., Tanaka, O., and Shibata, S. 1972.
Chemical studies on the oriental plant drugs. XXIV. Saponins and
sapogenins of ginseng: further study on the chemical properties of the
side chain of dammarane type triterpenes. Chem. Pharm. Bull. (Tokyo)
20: 1890-1897.

1.4-67 Okubo, K., Nishimura, N., and Shibasaki, K. 1979. Separation of
the 13S globulin in sesame seeds into two groups of acidic and basic
subunits, and their physicochemical properties. Cereal Chem. 56:
317-320.

1.4-68 Paknikar, S.K., and Kirtany, J.K. 1972. The structure of
Valeriana waalichi hydrocarbon. Chem. Ind. (London) 1972{20}: 803. CA
77: 164865.

1.4-69 Panenko, V.V., Shlyapnikov, V.A., and Morozova, S.B. 1973.
Dielectric constants of certain essential oils. J. Appl. Chem. USSR
(Engl. Transl.) 46: 1483-1485. Translation of Zh. Prikl. Khim.
(Leningrad) 46: 1385-1387

1.4-70 Paulsen, B.S., Johansen, B., and Wold, J.K. 1978. Identification of neutral oligosaccharides from a partial, acid hydrolysate of the water-soluble polysaccharide of the opium poppy. Carbohydr. Res. 65: 320-325.

1.4-71 Peter, H.H., and Remy, M. 1978. Basil oil, a comparative study [in French]. Parfum. Cosmet. Aromes 21: 61-64, 67-68. CA 90: 12155.

1.4-72 Philip, T., Nawar, W.W., and Francis, F.J. 1971. The nature of fatty acids and capsanthin esters in paprika. J. Food Sci. 36: 98-100.

1.4-73 Popa, D.P., and Pasechnik, G.S. 1975. The structure of vulgarol - a new diterpenoid from Marrubium vulgare. Chem. Nat. Compd. (Engl. Transl.) 11: 752-761. Translation of Khim. Prir. Soedin. 1975{6}: 722-728.

1.4-74 Proliac, A., and Blanc, M. 1976. Isolation and identification of two beta-carbolins in roasted chicory root [in French]. Helv. Chim. Acta 59: 2503-2505.

1.4-75 Raymakers, A., and Compernolle, F. 1973. Structure of cyclohexanone derivatives from Digitalis purpurea. Phytochemistry 12: 2287-2291.

1.4-76 Rohrer, D.C. 1972. The crystal and molecular structure of planteose dihydrate. Acta Crystallogr. Sect. B. 28: 425-433.

1.4-77 Rothbaecher, H., and Suteu, F. 1972. Isomers of carveol in the essential oil of Carum carvi of Rumanian origin [in German]. Pharmazie 27: 340-341. HA 43: 325.

1.4-78 Ruecker, G., and Tautges, J. 1974. The structure of jatamansic acid [in German]. Arch. Pharm. (Weinheim) 307{10}: 791-795. CIM 16{3}: 1956.

1.4-79 Sanada, S., Kondo, N., Shoji, J., Tanaka, O., and Shibata, S. 1974. Studies on the saponins of ginseng. II. Structures of ginsenoside Re, -Rf, and -Rg-2. Chem. Pharm. Bull. (Tokyo) 22: 2407-2412.

1.4-80 Sanada, S., Kondo, N., Shoji, J., Tanaka, O., and Shibata, S. 1974. Studies on the saponins of ginseng. I. Structures of ginsenoside-Ro, -Rb1, -Rb2, -Rc and -Rd. Chem. Pharm. Bull. (Tokyo) 22: 421-428.

1.4-81 Sano, K., Yosioka, I., and Kitagawa, I. 1973. Stereostructures of decursin, decursidin, and a new coumarin isolated from Angelica decursiva. Chem. Pharm. Bull. (Tokyo) 21: 2095-2097.

1.4-82 Sano, K., Yosioka, I., and Kitagawa, I. 1975. Studies on coumarins from the root of Angelica decursiva Fr. et Sav. II. Stereostructures of decursin, decursidin, and other new pyranocoumarin derivatives. Chem. Pharm. Bull. (Tokyo) 23: 20-28.

1.4-83 Schantz, M. von, Widen, K.G., and Granquist, L. 1975. Structures of some aliphatic compounds in the essential oil of Mentha X gentilis nm. hirtella. Phytochemistry 14: 2023-2024.

1.4-84 Schmidt, F., and Grolla, I. 1972. Boiling behavior of some essential oils [in German]. Krankenhaus-Apoth. 22{3}: 30. CA 79: 23495.

1.4-85 Shibata, H., and Shimizu, S. 1973. Absolute configuration of 1,2-epoxy menthyl acetate isolated from a new chemical strain of M. rotundifolia. Agric. Biol. Chem. 37: 2675-2676.

1.4-86 Sorochan, V.D., Dzizenko, A.K., and Ovodov, Yu.S. 1972. A study of the behavior of pectin substances in aqueous solutions by the light-scattering method. Chem. Nat. Compd. (Engl. Transl.) 8: 10-11. Translation of Khim. Prir. Soedin. 1972{1}: 12-14.

1.4-87 Sorochan, V.D., Dizizenko, A.K., Bodin, N.S., and Ovodov, Yu.S. 1971. Light-scattering studies of pectic substances in aqueous solution. Carbohydr. Res. 20: 243-249.

1.4-88 Stigbrand, T. 1971. Structural properties of umecyanin-A copper protein from horseradish root. Biochim. Biophys. Acta 236: 246-252.

1.4-89 Strigina, L.I., Remennikova, T.M., Isakov, V.V., Dzizenko, A.K., Elkin, Iu.N., Deshko, T.N., and Eliakov, G.B. 1975. Study of aglycone sterochemistry isolated in enzymatic hydrolysis of panaxoside A from Panax ginseng [in Russian]. Izv. Akad. Nauk SSSR Ser. Khim. 1975{3}: 638-643. AGRICOLA.

1.4-90 Swanson, C.L., and Otey, F.H. 1979. Molecular weights of natural rubbers from selected temperate zone plants. J. Appl. Polym. Sci. 23: 743-748.

1.4-91 Tada, H., and Takeda, K. 1971. Structure of the sesquiterpene lactone laurenobiolide. Chem. Commun. 1971{21}: 1391-1392.

1.4-92 Talvitie, A., Paasivirta, J., and Widen, K.-G. 1977. Structure proof of valeranone with NMR shift reagent. Finn. Chem. Lett. 1977{7}: 197-199.

1.4-93 Tharanathan, R.N., and Anjaneyalu, Y.V. 1975. Structure of the acid-stable core-polysaccharide derived from the seed mucilage of Ocimum basilicum. Aust. J. Chem. 28: 1345-1350. HA 46: 3691.

1.4-94 Tori, K., Horibe, I., Tamura, Y., Kuriyama, K., Tada, H., and Takeda, K. 1976. Re-investigation of the conformation of laurenobiolide, a ten-membered ring sesquiterpene lactone by variable-temperature carbon-13 NMR spectroscopy. Evidence for the presence of four conformational isomers in solution. Tetrahedron Lett. 1976{5}: 387-390.

1.4-95 Ul'chenko, N.T., Gigienova, E.I., and Umarov, A.U. 1976. Tautomerism of the alpha-hydroxydienic acids of seed oil of Artemisia absinthium. Chem. Nat. Compd. (Engl. Transl.) 12: 525-528. Translation of Khim. Prir. Soedin. 1976{5}: 584-588.

1.4-96 Vaverkova, S., and Herichova, A. 1980. Qualitative characteristics of secondary metabolites of Matricaria chamomilla L. after pyrimidine application. Acta Fac. Rerum Nat. Univ. Comenianae Physiol. Plant. 17: 47-54. HA 51: 7232.

1.4-97 Vernet, P. 1977. Genetic and ecological analysis of the variability of the essential oil of Thymus vulgaris L. (Labiatae) [in

French]. C. R. Seances Acad. Agric. Fr. 63: 645-646 (Abstr.). PBA 48: 6128.

1.4-98 Welinder, K.G. 1975. Covalent structure of the glycoprotein horseradish peroxidase (EC 1.11.1.7). FEBS. Lett. 72: 19-23.

1.4-99 Xu, R.-S., Wen, K.-L., Jiang, S.-F., Wang, C.-G., Jaing, F.-X., Xie, Y.-Y., and Gao, Y.-S. 1978. Isolation, structure and total synthesis of licochalcone [in Chinese]. Hua Hsueh Hsueh Pao 37{4}: 289-297. CA 92: 198060.

1.4-100 Yakovlev, A.I., and Gorin, A.G. 1977. Structure of the pectic acid of Matricaria chamomilla. Chem. Nat. Compd. (Engl. Transl.) 13: 160-162. Translation of Khim. Prir. Soedin. 1977{2}: 186-189.

1.4-101 Yang, T.I. 1971. Chemical studies on "Tan-kui". II. Lipids and fatty acids [in Chinese]. Chung-kuo Nung Yeh Hua Hsueh Hui Chih 9: 150-155. AGRICOLA.

1.4-102 Yaskonis, Yu.A., and Jaskonis, J. 1972. Biological and biochemical characteristics of peppermint 2. Biochemical characteristics [in Russian]. Liet. TSR Mokslu Akad. Darb. Ser. C. 1972{4}: 53-60. PBA 43: 5595.

1.4-103 Zakirov, S.Kh., Kasymov, Sh.Z., and Sidyakin, G.P. 1976. Structures of ashurbin and arabsin. Chem. Nat. Compd. (Engl. Transl.) 12: 492-493. Translation of Khim. Prir. Soedin. 1976{4}: 548-549.

1.5 Identification, Synthesis, and Characterization

1.5-1 Alpmen, G. 1975. Gas chromatographic studies on Mentha pulegium L. collected from several parts of Istanbul [in Turkish]. Istanbul Univ. Eczacilik Fak. Mecm. 11: 95-102.

1.5-2 Amirova, G.S. 1978. Products of the acetylation of triterpene hydroxy acids isolated from the roots of trifoliolate licorice (Glycyrrhiza triphylla Fish. et Mey.). J. Gen. Chem. USSR (Engl. Transl.) 48: 1728-1731. Translation of Zh. Obshch. Khim. 48: 1895-1898, 1978. CA 90: 6570.

1.5-3 Andersen, N.H., Syrdal, D.D., Lawrence, B.M., Terhune, S.J., and Hogg, J.W. 1973. Widespread occurrence of two heteroannular dienes of the cadalane skeleton. Phytochemistry 12: 827-833.

1.5-4 Andre, L. 1976. Determination of total pigment contents in powdered paprika by the Benedek method, with the use of a spectrophotometer. I. [in Hungarian]. Elelmiszervizgalati Kozl. 22: 229-234. AGRICOLA.

1.5-5 Anonymous. 1977. Application of gas-liquid chromatography to the analysis of essential oils. V. Determination of 1,8-cineole in oils of lavender and lavandin. Analyst (London) 102{1217}: 607-612. CA 88: 94664.

1.5-6 Appelqvist, L.-A., and Nair, B.M. 1977. Amino acid composition of some Swedish cultivars of Brasssica species determined by gas liquid chromatography. Qual. Plant. Plant Foods Hum. Nutr. 27: 255-263.

1.5-7 Artem'ev, B.V., Pekhov, A.V., Kas'yanov, G.I., and Dyuban'kova, N.F. 1980. Chromato-mass-spectrometric studies on the essential oil composition of Laurus nobilis leaves [in Russian]. Rastit. Resur. 16: 209-219. HA 51: 1479.

1.5-8 Baiswara, R.B., Chaurasia, L.O., Nair, K.N.G., and Mathew, T.V. 1976. Detection of gingergrass oil in lemongrass oil by thin layer chromatography. Res. Ind. 21: 39-40. AGRICOLA.

1.5-9 Balinova-Tsvetkova, A., and Kamburova, K. 1975. Determination of the essential oil content in the seed of some Umbelliferae [in Bulgarian]. Rastenievud. Nauki 12{5}: 40-45. HA 46: 3679.

1.5-10 Banthorpe, D.V., and Charlwood, B.V. 1972. The catabolism of biosynthetic precursors by higher plants. Planta Med. 22: 428-433.

1.5-11 Baslas, R.K., Gupta, R., and Baslas, K.K. 1971. Chemical examination of essential oils from plants of genus Anethum (Umbelliferae)--Oil of seeds of Anethum graveolens. (Part I). Flavour Ind. 2: 241-245.

1.5-12 Baslas, R.K., and Gupta, R. 1971. Chemical examination of essential oils from plants of genus Anethum (Umbelliferae)--Oil of seeds of East Indian dill. (Part II). Flavour Ind. 2: 363-366.

1.5-13 Belafi-Rethy, K., Kerenyi, E., and Kolta, R. 1974. Investigation of the composition of domestic and foreign essential oils. III. The components of dill oil [in German]. Acta Chim. Acad. Sci. Hung. 83: 1-13.

1.5-14 Belafi-Rethy, K., and Kerenyi, E. 1977. Investigation of indigenous and foreign essential oils. VI. Coumarene derivatives in the essential oil of dill [in German]. Acta Chim. Acad. Sci. Hung. 94: 1-9.

1.5-15 Belafi-Rethy, K., Iglewski, S., Kerenyi, E., and Kolta, R. 1973. Investigation of the composition of Hungarian and foreign volatile oils, I. Composite method for the analysis of volatile oils on the basis of efficient separation and component identification by large instruments. Acta Chim. Acad. Sci. Hung. 76: 1-11.

1.5-16 Bell, J.H. 1980. Determination of glycyrrhizic acid in licorice extracts and chewing tobaccos. Tob. Int. 182{21}: 68-71. CA 94: 2161.

1.5-17 Berstovaya, M.M. 1971. Effect of the moisture content of coriander on the accuracy of determination of essential oil [in Russian]. Tr. Vses. Nauchno-Issled. Inst. Efirnomaslichn. Kul't. 4{2}: 16-18. CA 78: 47648.

1.5-18 Bhattacharya, J., and Chaudhuri, D.K. 1974. Isolation and characterisation of a crystalline antithiamine factor from mustard seed, Brassica juncea. Biochim. Biophys. Acta 343: 211-214.

1.5-19 Bicchi, C., and Frattini, C. 1980. Quantitative determination of minor components in essential oils: determination of pulegone in peppermint oils. J. Chromatogr. 190: 471-474.

1.5-20 Bishay, D.W., and Gomaa, C.S. 1976. Comparative chromatographic studies of oils of some medicinal seeds. Egypt. J. Pharm. Sci. 17: 249-255. HA 49: 4447.

1.5-21 Bouquelet, S., and Spik, G. 1978. Properties of four molecular forms of N-acetyl-B-D-hexosaminidase isolated from germinating seeds of fenugreek (Trigonella foenum graecum). Eur. J. Biochem. 84: 551-559.

1.5-22 Bourwieg, D., Janistyn, B., Stocker, M., and Pohl, R. 1974. Detection of 5-hydroxychromone 7-rutinoside in Mentha longifolia [in German]. Arch. Pharm. (Weinheim, Ger.) 307: 131-136. CA 80: 133751.

1.5-23 Bubarova, M. 1980. Electrophoretic study of soluble proteins in new plant forms resulting from remote hybridization of Apium graveolens L. and Petroselinum hortense Hoffm. I. Acid proteins [in Bulgarian]. Genet. Sel. 13: 263-270. CA 94: 44201.

1.5-24 Bubarova, M. 1980. Electrophoretic study of soluble proteins in new plant forms resulting from remote hybridization of Apium graveolens L. and Petroselinum hortense Hoff. II. Basic proteins [in Bulgarian]. Genet. Sel. 13: 358-367. CA 94: 153576.

1.5-25 Burbott, A.J., Croteau, R., Shine, W.E., and Loomis, W.D. 1973. Biosynthesis of cyclic monoterpenes by cell-free enzymes from peppermint. Plant Physiol. 51 (Suppl.): 49 (Abstr.).

1.5-26 Burzanska-Hermann, Z. 1978. Isolation and identification of components of the flavonoid fraction of domestic species of Mentha L. section Verticillatae (M. arvensis L., M. sachalinensis Kudo, M. verticillata L., M. smithiana Graham, Mentha gentilis L.) [in Polish]. Acta Pol. Pharm. 35: 673-680.

1.5-27 Chikkaputtaiah, K.S., Shankaranarayana, M.L., and Natarajan, C.P. 1971. Volumetric determination of allyl isothiocyanate in black mustard (Brassica nigra). Flavour Ind. 2: 591-593.

1.5-28 Chladek, M., Machovicova, F., Tyllova, M., and Mesarosova, L. 1974. Investigations on the essential oil quality of annual caraway (Carum carvi S. annuum) by thin-layer chromatography [in Czech]. Bulletin Vuzkumny Ustav Zelinarsky Olomouc {18}: 73-81. HA 46: 4913

1.5-29 Chubey, B.B., and Dorrell, D.G. 1976. Changes in the chemical composition of dill oil during hydrodistillation. Can. J. Plant Sci. 56: 619-622.

1.5-30 Constantinescu, E., Popescu, M., and Denes, S. 1972. Chemical study of the saponifiable fraction of the fat oil from fruits of Petroselinum sativum [in French]. Riv. Ital. Essenze, Profumi, Piante Off., Aromi, Saponi, Cosmet., Aerosol 54: 419-421. CA 78: 20100.

1.5-31 Croteau, R., and Karp, F. 1976. Enzymatic synthesis of camphor from neryl pyrophosphate by a soluble preparation from sage (Salvia officinalis). Biochem. Biophys. Res. Commun. 72: 440-447.

1.5-32 Datta, D., Bose, P.C., and Ghosh, D. 1971. Thin layer chromatography and UV spectrophotometry of alcoholic extracts of Hydrastis canadensis [goldenseal]. Planta Med. 19: 258-263. CA 74: 91212.

1.5-33 Davies, D.D., Nascimento, K.H., and Patil, K.D. 1974. The distribution and properties of NADP malic enzyme in flowering plants. Phytochemistry 13: 2417-2425.

1.5-34 Debska, W., and Bartkowikowa, T. 1978. Determination of bisabolol, 'spiroether' (5-(hexa-2,4-diynylene) -2,2',3',4',5,5'-hexahydro-2,2'- spirobifuran) and chamazulene in Matricaria chamomilla flower-heads [in Polish]. Acta Pol. Pharm. 35: 699-700. HA 50: 4552.

1.5-35 Debska, W., Gnusowski, B., and Zygmunt, B. 1979. Determination of oxycarbon residues in medicinal plants. Analyst 104: 1191-1194.

1.5-36 Devani, M.B., Shishoo, C.J., Dadia, B.K., and Mody, H.J. 1978. Colorimetry of allylisothiocyanate in (black) mustard seed. J. Assoc. Off. Anal. Chem. 61: 167-168.

1.5-37 Dzyuba, N.P., and Chushenko, V.N. 1977. Determination of the qualitative and quantitative composition of polysaccharides in plant raw material and preparations by physiochemical methods. Communication II [in Ukrainian]. Farm. Zh. (Kiev) 2: 17-18. CA 86: 136342.

1.5-38 El-Obeid, H.A., and Hassan, M.M.A. 1979. NMR assay of essential oils. II. Assay of methylsalicylate in wintergreen oil. Spectrosc. Lett. 12: 555-557. CA 92: 28379.

1.5-39 Ferro, V. de O. 1979. Contribution to the chromatography and chemical analysis of Brazilian licorice - Periandra mediterranean (Velloso) Taubert [in Portuguese]. An. Farm. Quim. Sao Paulo 19{2}: 314-334. CA 94: 109403.

1.5-40 Festenstein, G.N. 1972. Water-soluble carbohydrates in extracts from large-scale preparation of leaf protein. J. Sci. Food Agric. 23: 1409-1415.

1.5-41 Festenstein, G.N. 1976. Carbohydrates associated with leaf protein. J. Sci. Food Agric. 27: 849-854.

1.5-42 Franke, W., and Lawrenz, M. 1980. On the contents of protein and its composition of amino acids in leaves of some medicinal and spice plants, edible as greens. Acta Hortic. 96{II}: 71-82.

1.5-43 Franz, C., and Glasl, H. 1974. Information on the essential oils of parsley. I. Thin layer chromatography and gas chromatography of the leaf oils of some parsley cultivars [in German]. Qual. Plant. Plant Foods Hum. Nutr. 24: 175-182.

1.5-44 Fruehwirth, H., and Krempler, F. 1979. Essential oils in spices-percentage and method of determination [in German]. Ernaehrung (Vienna) 3: 26-35. CA 90: 202324.

1.5-45 Garcia-Villanova, R., and Lopez Martinez, M.C. 1972. Determination of the fat in sesame seeds by indirect complexometry with magnesium II [in Spanish]. Grasas Aceites (Seville) 23: 224-225. AGRICOLA.

1.5-46 Genin, S.A., Korsungkaya, G.I., and Zoloedova, S.F. 1971. Gas chromatographic characteristics of spice oils [in Russian]. Vopr. Pitan. 1971{3}: 75-78. HA 43: 7066.

1.5-47 Glowniak, K. 1978. Investigation of the gasoline extracts of some Umbelliferae fruits. I. Sterols and fatty acids in angelica (Angelica officinalis) fruits [in Polish]. Acta Pol. Pharm. 35{3}: 353-357. CA 90: 36301.

1.5-48 Gockeritz, D., Poggendorf, A., Schmidt, W., Schubert, D., and Pohloudek-Fabini, R. 1979. The detection of 3,6-dimethyl-2,3,3a,4,5,7a-hexahydrobenzofuran in the essential oil of dill herbage [in German]. Pharmazie 34: 846-847.

1.5-49 Grob, K., Jr., and Matile, P. 1980. Capillary GC of glucosinolate-derived horseradish constituents. Phytochemistry 19: 1789-1793.

1.5-50 Grzunov, K., and Devetak, Z. 1978. Gas chromatography of rosemary oil isolated by various methods of distillation from rosemary leaves [in Serbo-Croatian]. Kem. Ind. 27{8}: 409-412. CA 92: 185711.

1.5-51 Hafez, H.N., Ashour, F.M., and Mahmoud, H. 1980. Studies on the physiochemical properties of Egyptian marjoram oil. Ann. Agric. Sci (Moshtohor) 13: 99-106. HA 51: 2877.

1.5-52 Haggag, M.Y., Shalaby, A.S., and Verzar-Petri, G. 1975. Thin layer and gas-chromatographic studies on the essential oil from Achillea millefolium. Planta Med. 27: 361-366. HA 46: 6083.

1.5-53 Haspel-Horvatovic, E. 1976. Spectrophotometrical determination of yellow and red paprika pigments from the total extract [in German]. Z. Lebensm.-Unters.-Forsch. 160: 275-276. CA 85: 3944.

1.5-54 Hendricks, H., and Bruins, A.P. 1980. Study of three types of essential oil of Valeriana officinalis L. S.L. by combined gas chromatography-negative ion chemical ionization mass spectrometry. J. Chromatogr. 190: 321-330.

1.5-55 Herisset, A., Jolivet, J., and Rey, P. 1972. Differentiation of some essential oils with similar composition, in particular by means of ultra-violet, infra-red and Raman spectroscopy. VI. Extracts of "camomille romaine" (Anthemis nobilis L.) and Matricaria (Matricaria chamomilla L.) [in French]. Plant. Med. Phytother. 6: 194-203

1.5-56 Herisset, A., Jolivet, J., and Rey, P. 1973. Differentiation of some essential oils with similar composition, in particular by means of ultra-violet, infra-red and Raman spectroscopy. VIII. Extracts of different Thymus spp. [in French]. Plant. Med. Phytother. 7: 37-47. HA 43: 7991.

1.5-57 Herisset, A., Jolivet, J., and Rey, P. 1973. Differentiation of some essential oils with similar composition. IX. Gas phase chromatography of Thymus extracts [in French]. Plant. Med. Phytother. 7: 114-120. HA 44: 2710.

1.5-58 Herisset, A., Jolivet, J., and Rey, P. 1971. Differentiation of some essential oils with similar structure (especially by examining their UV, IR, and Raman spectrum). I. Essences of Mentha piperita L. [in French]. Plant. Med. Phytother. 5: 188-198. AGRICOLA.

1.5-59 Herisset, A., Jolivet, J., and Rey, P. 1972. Differentiation of some essential oils presenting a related constitution (particularly by the analysis of their UV, IR, and Raman spectras). V. Essences from Chinese anise (Illicium verum Hook f.), green anise (Pimpinella anisum L.) and sweet fennel (Foeniculum dulce D.C.). Plant. Med. Phytother. 6: 137-148. AGRICOLA.

1.5-60 Hiai, S., Oura, H., Hamanaka, H., and Odaka, Y. 1975. A color reaction of panaxadiol with vanillan and sulfuric acid. Planta Med. 28: 131-138. HA 46: 6102.

1.5-61 Hils, A.K.A. 1979. Determination of allyl isothiocyanate in pungent mustard seeds and mustard [in German]. Deut. Lebensm-Rundsch. 75: 123-126 FCA 34: 1359.

1.5-62 Horvath, Gy., Filvig, Gy., and Varga, Zs. 1975. Investigation of the iron content of ground paprika by a spectrophotometric method [in Hungarian]. Elelmiszervizgalati Kozl. 21: 324-329. AGRICOLA.

1.5-63 Jeannes, A., and Tetau, M. 1971. Chromatographic evaluation of glycerrhetic acid concentrations in a product based on licorice paste [in French]. Plant. Med. Phytother. 5: 214-223. AGRICOLA.

1.5-64 Jolivet, J., Rey, P., and Boussarie, M.F. 1971. Differentiation of some essential oils with similar structure (especially by examining their UV, IR, and Raman spectrum). II. Essence of Origanum majorana L. and essence of Origanum vulgare L. [in French]. Plant. Med. Phytother. 5: 199-208. AGRICOLA.

1.5-65 Kaempf, R., and Steinegger, E. 1974. Thin layer and gas chromatographic studies of oleum anisi and oleum anisi stellati [in German]. Pharm. Acta Helv. 49: 87-93. CA 82: 7679.

1.5-66 Karawya, M.S., and Hifnawy, M.S. 1974. Analytical study of the volatile oil of Thymus vulgaris L. growing in Egypt. J. Assoc. Off. Anal. Chem. 57: 997-1001.

1.5-67 Karawya, M.S., Hifnawy, M.S., and El-Hawary, S.S. 1979. Colorimetric determination of carvone in volatile oils in the presence of menthone and pulegone. J. Assoc. Off. Anal. Chem. 62: 250-252.

1.5-68 Karlsen, J. 1972. Microanalysis of volatile compounds in biological material by means of gas liquid chromatography. J. Chromatogr. Sci. 10: 642-643. 1.5-69 Kato, Y. 1975. Effects of spice extracts on hydrolases. No. 1. On trypsin [in Japanese]. Koryo 113: 17-23. CA 84: 149393.

1.5-70 Kayukova, V.A., Rozov, N.F., and Shatilov, I.S. 1973. Spectrophotometric determination of vitamins B1, B2, and C in plants with simultaneous detection of a chromatogram in a thin layer of silica gel [in Russian]. Dokl. Vses. Akad. Sel'skokhoz. Nauk. 1973{2}: 10-12. CA 78: 144845.

1.5-71 Khuchua, G.N., and Stasyak, A.B. 1975. Electrophoretic determination of S-methylmethionine in plants [in Russian]. Prikl. Biokhim. Mikrobiol. 11: 914-921. CA 84: 56078.

1.5-72 Killacky, J., Ross, M.S.F., and Turner, T.D. 1976. The determination of beta-glycyrrhetinic acid in liquorice by high pressure liquid chromatography. Planta Med. 30: 210-216. CA 86: 86145.

1.5-73 Kim, J.C., and Rhee, J.S. 1980. Studies on processing and analysis of red pepper seed oil. Hanguk Sikp'un Kwahakhoe Chi 12: 126-132.

1.5-74 Kohda, H., and Tanaka, O. 1975. Enzymic hydrolysis of ginseng saponins and their related glycosides [in Japanese]. Yakugaku Zasshi 95: 246-249. CA 82: 134815.

1.5-75 Kohlmunzer, S., Grzybek, J., and Sodzawiczny, K. 1975. Polyphenolic compounds in post-distillation wastes of the Mentha piperita plants [in Polish]. Herba Pol. 21: 130-137.

1.5-76 Kojima, M. 1976. Studies on the volatile components of Wasabia japonica horseradish by gas chromatography using the head space technique [in Japanese]. Nippon Shokuhin Kogyo Gakkai-shi 23: 324-326. AGRICOLA.

1.5-77 Kojima, M., Uehida, M., and Akahori, Y. 1973. Studies on the volatile components of Wasabia japonica, Brassica juncea, and Cocholearia armoracia by gas chromatography- mass spectrometry. I. Determination of low mass volatile components [in Japanese]. Yakugaku Zasshi 93: 453-459. CA 79: 63527.

1.5-78 Kotlyarova, M.V., and Salakaya, V.K. 1971. Determination of eugenol in the oil of eugenol basil by adsorption spectrophotometry in the ultraviolet region [in Russian]. Tr. Sukhum. Opyt. St. Efirnomaslich. Kul't. 1971{10}: 165-172. CA 78: 47640.

1.5-79 Kotylarova, M.V., and Salakaya, V.K. 1971. Determination of eugenol in basil oil by ultraviolet absorption spectrophotometry [in Russian]. Pages 175-178 in P.V. Naumenko et al., eds. Mezhdunarodnyi kongress po efirnym maslam [Materialy], 4th, Tiflis, 1968, v.1. Pishchevaya Promyshlennost', Moscow, USSR. CA 78: 128340.

1.5-80 Kozma, L., Huszka, T., and Fekete, M. 1976. Spectrophotometric method for determining the pigment content of ground paprika. Z. Lebensm.-Unters. Forsch. 161: 31-33. AGRICOLA.

1.5-81 Kravets, T.I., Persidskaya, K.G., Karpacheva, A.N., Lishtvanova, L.N., and Mosalenko, L.M. 1971. Determination of anethole content in anise seed and fennel oils [in Russian]. Tr. Vses. Nauchno-Issled. Inst. Efirnomaslichn. Kul't 4{2}: 19-24. CA 78: 47649.

1.5-82 Lal, R.N., and Siddiqi, M.S. 1972. Determination of menthone present in dark coloured essential oils by potentiometric titration. Flavour Ind. 3: 418-419.

1.5-83 Lal, R.N., and Sen, T. 1971. Studies on the essential oils from the seeds of Indian varieties of Foeniculum vulgare Miller. Flavour Ind. 2: 544-545.

1.5-84 Lal, R.N., Sen, T.K., and Nigam, M.C. 1978. Gas chromatography of the essential oil of Ocimum sanctum L. [in German]. Parfuem. Kosmet. 59{7}: 230-321. CA 89: 94878.

1.5-85 Lassanyi, Z. 1971. Some microchemical identity reactions of Mentha species type carvone and menthol. Herba Pol. 17: 391-395. Bib. Ag. 37: 25552.

1.5-86 Lawrence, B.M., and Morton, J.K. 1972. 3-Dodecanone in Mentha X gentilis. Phytochemistry 11: 2639-2640.

1.5-87 Lee, S.W. 1979. Gas liquid chromatographic studies on sugars and organic acids in different portions of hot pepper fruit (Capsicum annuum L.). Hanguk Sikp'un Kwahakhoe Chi 11: 278-282.

1.5-88 Lemberkovics, E., Verzar-Petri, G., Pethes, E., and Mikita, K. 1977. Essential oils in leaf lamellae of Valeriana officinalis L. and their comparison with root oil [in German]. Sci. Pharm. 45: 281-289. CA 88: 197425.

1.5-89 Lippert, L.F., and Hall, M.O. 1973. Determination of total carotenoids in Capsicum. HortScience 8: 38-40.

1.5-90 Lundborg, T. 1980. Fractionation by centrifugation of leaf proteins in press juices from Brassica and other species as a function of pH. Physiol. Plant. 48: 186-192.

1.5-91 Lu, R.M., He, L.Y., Fang, H.J., and Zhan, X.Q. 1980. Thin layer chromatography and densitrometry of lingustilide in Umbelliferae plants [in Chinese]. Yao Hsueh Hsueh Pao 1980{6}: 371-374. CA 94: 71576.

1.5-92 Maksudov, N.Kh., Goriaev, M.I., and Alimukhamedov, S.A. 1973. Investigation of the fatty oils of garden parsley fruits [in Russian]. Dokl. Akad. Nauk Uzb. SSR 30{4}: 41-43. CA: 130494.

1.5-93 Mangoni, L., Adinolfi, M., Laonigro, G., and Caputo, R. 1972. Synthesis of marrubiin. Tetrahedron 28: 611-621.

1.5-94 Mannino, S., and Amelotti, G. 1979. Pulegone determination in essential oils of Mentha [in Italian]. Riv. Ital. Sostanze Grasse 56: 61-62. HA 50: 500.

1.5-95 Markham, K.R., Ternai, B., Stanley, R., Geiger, H., and Mabry, T.J. 1978. Carbon-13 NMR studies of flavonoids. III. Naturally occurring flavonoid glycosides and their acylated derivatives. Tetrahedron 34: 1389-1397.

1.5-96 Mateo, C. 1978. Analytical study of essential oils from Spanish plants. I. Species of the Thymus genus [in Spanish]. Riv. Ital. Essenze Profumi Piante Off. Aromat., Syndets, Saponi, Cosmet., Aerosols 60{11}: 621-627. CA 90: 127384.

1.5-97 Meerov, Ya.S., Katyuzhanskaya, A.N., and Dyuban'kova, N.F. 1974. Investigation of a CO2 extract of the fruit of Capsicum annuum. Chem. Nat. Compd. (Engl. Transl.) 10: 486-489. Translation of Khim. Prir. Soedin. 1974{4}: 481-485.

1.5-98 Mohamed, Y.A., Abdel Salam, N.A., El-Sayed, M.A., and Abdel Salam, M.A. 1976. Spectrophotometric determination of certain volatile oils. Part III. Assay of anethole in volatile oils of anise and fennel. Indian J. Pharm. 38: 117-119.

1.5-99 Nagasawa, T., Uemoto, K., Tsuneya, T., and Shiga, M. 1974. On the identification of dextro-1-2-epoxymenthol isolated from the essential oil of Mentha gentilis L. (Studies on the wild mints of Tokai Districts Part I.). Nippon Nogei Kagaku Kaishi 48: 39-42.

1.5-100 Nakanishi, O., Fujitani, M., Ichimoto, I., and Ueda, H. 1980. An improved process for the synthesis of piperitenone from mesityl oxide and methyl vinyl ketone. Agric. Biol. Chem. 44: 1667-1668.

1.5-101 Nakayama, R.M., and Matta, F.B. 1973. Extractable red color of chile peppers (Capsicum frutescens) as influenced by fruit maturity and alar, gibberellic acid and ethephon treatments. HortScience 8: 252 (Abstr.).

1.5-102 Nano, G.M., Fundaro, A., Calvino, R., and Cabella, P. 1972. The components of the sesquiterpenes of Mentha piperita Italo-Mitcham cultivated in Piedmont [in Italian]. Essenze Deriv. Agrum. 42: 325-332. CABF 73148307.

1.5-103 Narzieva, M.D., Stepanenko, G.A., Umarov, A.U., and Maksudov, N.Kh. 1974. Investigation of the oils of Anethum graveolens. Chem. Nat. Compd. (Engl. Transl.) 10: 248. Translation of Khim. Prir. Soedin. 1974{2}: 243.

1.5-104 Nishio, M., Zushi, S., Ishii, T., Furuya, T., and Syono, K. 1976. Mass fragmentographic determination of indole-3-acetic acid in callus tissues of Panax ginseng and Nicotiana tabacum. Chem. Pharm. Bull. (Tokyo) 24: 2038-2042.

1.5-105 Nitsche, H., and Pleugel, C. 1972. Neoxanthin from Helianthus, Taraxacum and Impatiens. Phytochemistry 11: 3383-3385.

1.5-106 Ognyanov, I.V., and Botcheva, D. 1972. On the acid catalyzed cleavage of oxypeucedanin. Dokl. Bolg. Akad. Nauk 25: 1061-1063. AGRICOLA.

1.5-107 Okubo, K., Nishimura, N., and Shibasaki, K. 1979. Composition of sesame seed protein components and purification of the main globulin. Cereal Chem. 56: 100-104.

1.5-108 Padula, L.Z., Rondina, R.V.D., and Coussio, J.D. 1976. Quantitative determination of essential oil, total azulenes and chamazulene in German chamomile (Matricaria chamomilla) cultivated in Argentina. Planta Med. 30: 273-280. HA 47: 5935.

1.5-109 Palacio, J.J.R. 1977. Spectrophotometric determination of capsaicin. J. Assoc. Off. Anal. Chem. 60: 970-972.

1.5-110 Palacio, J.J.R. 1979. Further study of the spectrophotometric determination of capsaicin. J. Assoc. Off. Anal. Chem. 62: 1168-1170.

1.5-111 Petri, G., and Then, M. 1974. Comparative thin layer and gas chromatographic investigations on Salvia officinalis and S. sclarea essential oil composition [in Hungarian]. Herba Hung. 13{3}: 51-60. HA 45: 10004.

1.5-112 Popesco, C.E., and Denes Steliana, M. 1972. Contributions to the chemical study of the saponifiable fraction of the fat oil from fruits of Petroselinum sativum Hoffm. [in Italian]. Riv. Ital. Essenze Profumi Piante Off. Aromi Saponi Cosmet. Aerosol 54: 419-421. AGRICOLA

1.5-113 Radosevic, B., Brnic, I., and Balzer, I. 1976. Gas chromatographic determinations of the volatile substances in honey [in Serbo-Croatian]. Poljopr. Znan. Smotra 37{47}: 5-10. AA 30: 1070/79.

1.5-114 Rao, C.B., Vijayakumar, E.K.S., and Krishna, R.R. 1979. Chemical examination of the stems of Lippia citriodora Linn. (yields stigmasterol, beta-amyrin and beta-sitosterol). Curr. Sci. 48: 534-535. HA 50: 3663.

1.5-115 Rasmussen, K.E., Rasmussen, S., and Baerheim Svendsen, A. 1972. Quantitative deviations in the composition of the volatile oils in individual leaves of Rosmarinus officinalis, studies with the help of direct gas chromatography of plant material. Terpenes and related substances. XX [in German]. Sci. Pharm. 40: 286-290. CA 78: 94884.

1.5-116 Romo, C.R., Lakin, A.L., and Rolfe, E.J. 1975. Properties of protein isolates prepared from ground seeds. I. Development and evaluation of a dye binding procedure for the measurement of protein solubility. J. Food Technol. 10: 541-546.

1.5-117 Saiki, Y., Uchida, M., Okegawa, O., and Fukushima, S. 1974. On the mass spectra of several furanocoumarins having various isoprenoidal residues. Chem. Pharm. Bull. (Tokyo) 22: 1227-1232.

1.5-118 Salveson, A., and Baerheim Svendsen, A. 1976. Gas liquid chromatographic separation and identification of the constituents of caraway seed oil. Planta Med. 30: 93-96. HA 47: 2895.

1.5-119 Salveson, A., and Baerheim Svendsen, A. 1978. Oxygen-containing monoterpenes. II. Gas chromatographic separation and identification of cumin oil constituents [in German]. Sci. Pharm. 46{2}: 93-100. CA 89: 160134.

1.5-120 Sastry, S.D., Springstube, W.R., and Waller, G.R. 1972. Identification of 5,9-dehydronepetalactone, a new monoterpene from Nepeta cataria. Phytochemistry 11: 453-455.

1.5-121 Satoh, D., and Hashimoto, T. 1976. Preparation of card-17 {20}-enolides from carda-16, 20 {22}-dienolide. Chem. Pharm. Bull. (Tokyo) 24: 1950-1953.

1.5-122 Scheffer, J.J.C., Koedam, A., and Baerheim Svendsen, A. 1977. Analysis of essential oils by combined liquid-solid and gas-liquid chromatography. II. Monoterpenes in essential seed oil of Anethum graveolens L. Meddelelser fra Norsk Farmaceutisk Selskap. 39: 161-187. HA 48: 5864.

1.5-123 Scheffer, J.J.C., Gijbels, M.J.M., Koedam, A., and Baerheim Svendsen, A. 1978. Analysis of essential oils by combined liquid-solid and gas-liquid chromatography. Part IV. Monoterpenes in the essential oil of Rosmarinus officinalis Linnaeus. Riv. Ital. Essenze, Profumi, Piante Off., Aromat., Syndets, Saponi, Cosmet., Aerosols 60: 591-600. CA 90: 92242.

1.5-124 Schilcher, H. 1972. Recent data on the qualitative evaluation of chamomile or chamomile oil. I. Determination of volatile oil in chamomile [in German]. Dtsch. Apothztg. 112: 1497-1500. HA 44: 1146.

1.5-125 Schulz, J.M., and Herrmann, K. 1980. Analysis of hydroxybenzoic and hydroxycinnamic acids in plant material. I. Sample preparation and thin-layer chromatography. J. Chromatogr. 195: 85-94.

1.5-126 Schulz, J.M., and Herrmann, K. 1980. Analysis of hydroxybenzoic and hydroxycinnamic acids in plant material. II. Determination by gas-liquid chromatography. J. Chromatogr. 195: 95-104.

1.5-127 Sen, A.R., Sardar, P.K., Sil, S., and Mathew, T.V. 1973. Importance of volatile oil and cold water extract estimation in analysis of cumin (jira). J. Food Sci. Technol. 10: 187.

1.5-128 Seoane, E., Canadell, E., Ribo, J.M., and Valls, N. 1975. Analysis of high-molecular-weight esters and ketones in (two species of) Thymus. Microchem. J. 20: 154-164. HA 46: 7947.

1.5-129 Sergeeva, N.V., and Zakharova, N.L. 1977. A qualitative and quantitative investigation of carotenoids in some galenic preparations [in Russian]. Farmatsiya (Moscow) 25{1}: 34-38.

1.5-130 Shigel'skii, O.A., Yashchenko, V.K., Butenko, R.G., and Vollosovich, A.G. 1974. Emission spectral analysis of the content of certain trace elements in cultures of isolated tissues and intact medicinal plants. Sov. Plant Physiol. (Engl. Transl.) 21: 74-77. Translation of Fiziol. Rast. 21{1}: 93-97, 1974.

1.5-131 Shine, W.E., and Loomis, W.D. 1974. Isomerization of geraniol and geranyl phosphate by enzymes from carrot and peppermint. Phytochemistry 13: 2095-2101.

1.5-132 Shtovkhan, N.P., Koshevoi, E.P., Maslikov, V.A., Kurnosov, A.G., and Troitskaia, N.S. 1977. Investigation of phase conditions of an essential coriander oil-fatty coriander oil-liquefied carbon dioxide system [in Russian]. Izv. Vyssh. Ucheb. Zaved Pishch. Tekhnol. 1979{3}: 123-124.

1.5-133 Simonyan, A.V., Shinkarenko, A.L., and Oganesyan, E.T. 1972. Quantitative determination of triterpenoids in plants of the genus Thymus. Chem. Nat. Compd. (Engl. Transl.) 8: 290-291. Translation of Khim. Prir. Soedin. 1972{3}: 293-295.

1.5-134 Sorochan, V.D., Gladkikh, R.V., and Dzizenko, A.K. 1976. Refractometric study of pectin substances. Chem. Nat. Compd. (Engl. Transl.) 12: 473-474. Translation of Khim. Prir. Soedin. 1975{4}: 534.

1.5-135 Steinegger, E., and Marty, S. 1976. Glycyrrhizic acid determination in Radix liquiritae. Comparison of existing methods. 1. [in German]. Pharm. Acta Helv. 51: 374-377. CA 87: 122833.

1.5-136 Stohs, S.J. 1975. Metabolism of 3-beta-hydroxy-5 alpha- and 3-beta-hydroxy-5-beta pregnan-20-one by leaf homogenates. Phytochemistry 14: 2419-2422.

1.5-137 Stohs, S.J., and El-Olemy, N.M. 1971. Delta-beta-sitosten-3-one from beta-sitosterol by leaf homogenates. Phytochemistry 10: 2987-2990.

1.5-138 Stothers, J.B., Stoessl, A., and Ward, E.W.B. 1978. A carbon-13 NMR study of the biological oxidation of capsidiol [in German]. Z. Naturforsch. C Biosci. 33: 149-150.

1.5-139 Strack, D., Proksch, P., and Guelz, P.G. 1980. Analysis of sesquiterpene lactones by high performance liquid chromatography. Z. Naturforsch. C. Biosci. 35: 915-918.

1.5-140 Strigina, L.I., Elkin, Yu.N., Isakov, V.V., Remennikova, T.M., Dzizenko, A.K., and Elyakov, G.B. 1973. The production of the native aglycone of panaxoside A from Panax ginseng C.A. Meyer by enzymatic hydrolysis Dokl. Biochem. (Engl. Transl.) 210: 208-211. Translation of Dokl. Akad. Nauk SSR 210: 727-730, 1973. AGRICOLA.

1.5-141 Taskinen, J., and Nykanen, L. 1975. Volatile constituents
obtained by the extraction with alcohol-water mixture and by steam
distillation of coriander fruit. Acta Chem. Scand. Ser. B 29: 425-429.

1.5-142 Taskinen, J. 1974. Composition of the essential oil of sweet
marjoram obtained by distillation with steam and by extraction and
distillation with alcohol water mixture. Acta Chem. Scand. Ser. B 28:
1121-1128.

1.5-143 Tateo, F. 1976. GLC characterization of Mentha essential oils
[in Italian]. Riv. Ital. Sostanze Grasse 53: 77-87. AGRICOLA.

1.5-144 Then, M., and Verzar-Petri, G. 1979. Analysis of volatile oils
in Salvia sclarea L. for the purpose of qualification. I. Thin layer
chromatography studies. Acta Agron. Acad. Sci. Hung. 28: 90-95.

1.5-145 Tibori, G., Csedo, C., and Racz, G. 1974. Gas chromatographic
identification of terpene compounds in the volatile oil of lovage
(Levisticum officinale) [in Romanian]. Rev. Med. (Tirgu-Mures, Rom.)
20{2}: 222-225. CA 82: 160093.

1.5-146 Tourn, M.L., Lombard, A., Cassone, M.C., and Damonte, A. 1971.
The low molecular weight carbohydrates of the Artemisias. Part 4. The
soluble carbohydrates of roots and leaves of some species of Artemisia
collected in Piedmont at the beginning of vegetative renewal [in
Italian]. Atti Accad. Sci. Torino Cl. Sci. Fis. Mat. Nat. 105:
367-382.

1.5-147 Trenkle, K. 1972. Recent investigations on fennel (Foeniculum
vulgare M.): 2. The essential oil of the fruit, herb and root of the
fruiting plants [in German]. Pharmazie 27: 319-324.

1.5-148 Urushadze, U.D., Chkaidze, D.Kh., and Sardzhveladze, G.P. 1975.
Determining the minimum possible content of essential oil in Laurus
nobilis leaves for the purposes of standardization [in Russian].
Subtrop. Kul't. 1975{2}: 91-94. FA 37: 3329.

1.5-149 VanEtten, C.H., McGrew, C.E., and Daxenbichler, M.E. 1974.
Glucosinolate determination in cruciferous seeds and meals by
measurement of enzymatically released glucose. J. Agric. Food Chem.
22: 483-487.

1.5-150 Verzar-Petri, G., Marczal, G., and Lemberkovics, E. 1976.
Studies on the elucidation of the composition of chamomile oil [in
German]. Pharmazie 31: 256-257. HA 46: 11657.

1.5-151 Vose, J.R. 1972. The fractionation of two glucosinolases from
Sinapis alba seed by isoelectric focusing. Phytochemistry 11:
1649-1653.

1.5-152 Woodbury, J.E. 1980. Determination of Capsicum pungency by high
pressure liquid chromatography and spectrofluorometric detection. J.
Assoc. Off. Anal. Chem. 63: 556-558.

1.5-153 Zakharov, P.I., Terent'ev, P.B., and Nikonov, G.K. 1976. A
mass-spectrometric study of the dihydrocoumarin sachalinin. Chem. Nat.
Compd. (Engl. Transl.) 12: 34-36. Translation of Khim. Prir. Soedin.
1976{1}: 41-43.

1.5-154 Zamureenko, V.A., Klyuev, N.A., Mumladze, M.G., Dmitriev, L.B., and Grandberg, I.I. 1980. Identification of the components of essential oil from Nepeta cataria var. citriodora Balb. [in Russian]. Izv. Timiryazevsk. S-kh. Akad. 1980{5}: 167-169. AGRICOLA.

1.5-155 Zamureenko, V.A., Klyuev, N.A., Dmitriev, L.B., and Grandberg, I.I. 1980. Study of the composition of the essential oil of peppermint using chromato-mass spectrometry [in Russian]. Izv. Timiryazevsk. S-kh. Akad. 1980{1}: 169-172. CA 92: 152870.

1.6 Analytical Techniques

1.6-1 Anonymous. 1973. Application of gas-liquid chromatography to the analysis of essential oils. Part II. Determination of 1,8-cineole in oils of cardamom, rosemary, sage and spike lavender. Analyst 98: 616-623.

1.6-2 Ballarian, C., and Ballarin, J. 1972. Thin-layer chromatographic differentiation of fennel and aniseed oil [in German]. Pharmazie 27: 544. CA 78: 7738.

1.6-3 Bruni, A., Dall'olio, G., and Mares, D. 1977. Use of fluorescent labeling methods in morphological and histochemical studies of latex "in situ". Caryologia 30: 486-487 (Abstr.).

1.6-4 Cabo Torres, T., Maldonado, R., Jimenez, J., Villar del Fresno, A., and Bravo Diaz, L. 1972. Chromatographic study of the essential oils of Spanish rosemary. III. Comparative analysis using gas chromatography [in Spanish]. Boll. Chim. Farm. 111: 573-578. CA 78: 62049.

1.6-5 Chandrasekharan Nair, K., and Nair, E.V.G. 1975. A study on the condensate flow during the distillation of lemongrass (Cymbopogon flexuosus). Agric. Res. J. Kerala 13: 209-210.

1.6-6 Collins, F.W., and Chandorkar, K.R. 1971. Thin-layer chromatography of fructo-oligosaccharides. J. Chromatogr. 56: 163-167.

1.6-7 Davies, A.M.C. 1975. The application of chromatographic data to commodity source identification. J. Chromatogr. 115: 293-298.

1.6-8 Debska, W., Wasiewiczowa, E., and Bartkowiakowa, T. 1978. Method for detecting and determining the contents of chamazulene, bisabolol and spiroether in Matricaria chamomilla inflorescences [in Polish]. Herba Pol. 24: 215-221. HA 50: 497.

1.6-9 Durand, M., and Laval-Martin, D. 1974. Thin layer chromatographic separation of tetrapyrrole type chlorophyll derivatives and application to research of these derivatives in fruit in the course of ripening [in French]. J. Chromatogr. 97: 92-98.

1.6-10 El-Sayed, M.A., Mohamed, Y.A., and Abdel Salam, N.A. 1976. Spectrophotometric determination of certain volatile oils. 1. Assay for phenols in volatile oils of clove and thyme. Pharmazie 31: 361-362.

1.6-11 Govindarajan, V., and Ananthakrishna, S. 1974. Paper chromatographic determination of capsaicin. Flavour Ind. 5: 176-178.

1.6-12 Grosman, A.M., Soloveva, E.I., and Berliant, O.R. 1971. Method of determining content of essential oils in sweet peppers and dill [in Russian]. Knoserv. Ovoshchesushilnaya Prom. 1971{1}: 30-32. AGRICOLA.

1.6-13 Harkayvinkler, M. 1975. Comparative investigation of the Benedek method and of the thin-layer chromatographic method for the determination of the pigment content of powdered spice paprika [in Hungarian]. Elelmiszervizgalati Kozl. 21: 195-201. AGRICOLA.

1.6-14 Hendriks, H. 1973. Description of an apparatus for the distillation of essential oils [in German]. Planta Med. 24: 158-164.

1.6-15 Herisset, A., Jolivet, J., Rey, P., and Lavault, M. 1973. Differentiation of some essential oils having a similar composition (in particular by the examination of their UV, IR, and Raman spectra). X. Essences of various citrus. Plant. Med. Phytother. 7: 306-318. AGRICOLA.

1.6-16 Iljin, S.G., Dzizenko, A.K., Elyakov, G.B., Tarnopolsky, B.L., and Safina, Z.S. 1978. X-ray analysis of panaxoside A progenin I acetate, a triterpene glycoside isolated from Panax ginseng C.A. Meyer. Tetrahedron Lett. 1978{6}: 593-594.

1.6-17 Isono, H., Tachinami, S., and Kurono, G. 1976. Studies on the constituents of Liliaceae plants. V. Convenient analytical method for the aliphatic compounds [in Japanese]. Yakugaku Zasshi 96: 86-90. CA 84: 132648.

1.6-18 Kashchenko, G.F., Akimov, Yu.A., Volchenkov, V.F., and Boitsov, E.N. 1971. Temperature conditions for the decantation of some essential oils [in Russian]. Maslo-Zhir. Prom. 37{10}: 24-25. CA 76: 37336.

1.6-19 Kernoczi, L., Tetenyi, P., Mincsovics, E., and Szejtli, J. 1978. Application of the "TAS" procedure to the testing of volatile oil-cyclodextrin complexes. Q.J. Crude Drug Res. 16: 153-157.

1.6-20 Kerven, G.L., Dwyer, W., Duriyaprapan, S., and Britten, E.J. 1980. A semimicro apparatus for essential oil determination of multiple mint samples by steam distillation. J. Agric. Food Chem. 28{1}: 162-164.

1.6-21 Kiper, M. 1978. A quick hydroxyapatite chromatography technique especially adapted for work with DNA networks. Anal. Biochem. 91: 70-74.

1.6-22 Koedam, A., Scheffer, J.J.C., and Baerheim Svendsen, A. 1979. Comparison of isolation procedures for essential oils. II. Ajowan, caraway, coriander and cumin. Z. Lebensm.-Unters. Forsch. 168: 106-111. CA 90: 150377.

1.6-23 Kojima, M. 1977. A simple method for quantitative determination of pungent components in the hydrolyzate of Wasabia japonica by head-space gas chromatography [in Japanese]. Nippon Shokuhin Kogyo Gakkaishi 24: 90-93. CA 91: 156172.

1.6-24 Lund, E.D. 1978. Thin layer and high pressure liquid chromatographic analysis of celery seed oil. J. Assoc. Off. Anal. Chem. 61: 1083-1088.

1.6-25 Lu, R.-M., He, L.Y., Fang, H.J., and Zhang, X.Q. 1980. Thin layer chromatography and densitometry of ligustilide in Umbelliferae plants [in Chinese]. Yao Hsueh Hsueh Pao 1980{6}: 371-374. CA 94: 71576.

1.6-26 Manuelian, Kh. 1979. Use of ethyl alcohol for the determination of pigment substances in red pepper [in Bulgarian]. Gradinar. Lozar. Nauka 15{1}: 91-96. AGRICOLA.

1.6-27 McGregor, D.I. 1977. A rapid and simple method of screening rapeseed and mustard seed for erucic acid content. Can. J. Plant Sci. 57: 133-142.

1.6-28 Medina, M.B., Kleyn, D.H., and Swallow, W.H. 1976. Protein estimation in sesame seed and rapeseed flours and meals by a modified UDY dye binding method. J. Am. Oil Chem. Soc. 53: 555-558.

1.6-29 Mino, Y., Ota, N., Sakao, S., and Shimomura, S. 1980. Determination of germanium in medicinal plants by atomic-absorption spectrometry with electrothermal atomisation. Chem. Pharm. Bull. (Tokyo) 28: 2687-2691 HA 51: 8919.

1.6-30 Mishurova, S.S. 1971. Oxydases of Mentha and a method for their determination [in Russian]. Izv. Akad. Nauk Az. SSR Ser. Biol. Nauk 1971{1}: 26-32. AGRICOLA.

1.6-31 Mullin, W.J. 1980. Potential errors in the measurement of oxazolidinethiones by UV. Lebensm.-Wiss. Technol. 13: 36-37.

1.6-32 Novotny, M., McConnell, M.L., and Lee, M.L. 1974. Some aspects of high-resolution gas chromatographic analysis of complex volatile samples. J. Agric. Food Chem. 22: 765-770.

1.6-33 Ohmacht, R. 1979. Simple mixing device for gradient elution in liquid chromatography [in German]. Chromatographia 12: 565-566.

1.6-34 Rasmussen, K.E., Rasmussen, S., and Baerheim Svendson, A. 1972. Terpenes and related substances. XVI. New technique for the quantitative determination of essential oils in plant material. Quantitative fluctuation of the content of essential oil in the leaves of Rosmarinus officinalis in the spring [in German]. Sci. Pharm. 40: 17-23. CA 77: 2766.

1.6-35 Redshaw, E.S., Hougen, F.W., and Baker, R.J. 1971. A distillation technique for isolation of volatile materials for gas chromatographic analysis and its application to coriander seed (Coriandrum sativum). J. Agric. Food Chem. 19: 1264-1266.

1.6-36 Romanova, A.S., Pervykh, L.N., and Pribylova, G.F. 1979. Method of quantitative determination of rouleanones in the roots of Salvia officinalis L. Pharm. Chem. J. (Engl. Transl.) 13: 213-214. Translation of Khim.-Farm. Zh. 13{2}: 108-110, 1979.

1.6-37 Ross, M.S.F. 1978. Application of high-performance liquid chromatography to the analysis of volatile oils. J. Chromatogr. 160: 199-204.

1.6-38 Sapozhnikov, D.I., Maslova, T.G., Popova, O.F., Popova, I.A., and Koroleva, O.Y. 1978. The method of fixation and keeping leaves for quantitative estimation of plastidia pigments [in Russian]. Bot. Zh. (Leningrad) 63: 1586-1592.

1.6-39 Scheffer, J.J.C., Koedam, A., and Baerheim Svendsen, A. 1976. Occurrence and prevention of isomerization of some monoterpene hydrocarbons from essential oils during liquid-solid chromatography on silica gel. Chromatographia 9: 425-432.

1.6-40 Scheffer, J.J.C., Koedam, A., and Baerham Svendsen, A. 1976. Fractionated column-chromatographic preparation of essential oil monoterpene hydrocarbons for gas chromatography [in German]. Sci. Pharm. 44: 119-128 CA 86: 47203.

1.6-41 Shankaranarayana, M.L., Nagalaskshmi, S., Raghavan, B., and Natarajan, C.P. 1972. Oxidimetric method of determination of allyl isothiocyanate in black mustard (Brassica nigra L.) with chloramine-T. Flavour Ind. 3: 75-77.

1.6-42 Staikov, V., and Kalaidzhiev, I. 1971. Fitting attached to the gas chromatograph for direct study of essential oil in plant raw materials. Dokl. Akad. Sel'skokhoz. Nauk Bolg. 4{3}: 251-256. CA 77: 39031.

1.6-43 Stanislas, E., Fouraste, I., and Moulis, C. 1973. On the determination of essential oils in plants. Improved apparatus for volumetric measurements [in French]. Plant. Med. Phytother. 7: 59-67.

1.6-44 Surholt, E., and Hoesel, W. 1978. Screening for flavonol 3-glycoside specific beta-glycosidases in plants using a spectrophotometric enyzmatic assay. Phytochemistry 17: 873-877.

1.6-45 Sviderskaya, I. 1971. Method for the chemical study of essential oils of some plants [in Russian]. Pages 308-311 in P.V. Naumenko, et al., eds. Mezhunarodnyi kongress po efirnym maslam, [Materialy], 4th, Tiflis, 1968, v. 1. Pishchevaya Promyshlennost', Moscow, USSR. CA 78: 140341

1.6-46 Svyshchuk, O.A., and Makhnovs'kyi, M.K. 1974. A method for obtaining 1-menthol [in Ukrainian]. Farm. Zh. (Kiev) 29: 94-95.

1.6-47 Taha, A.M., and Goma, C.S. 1972. Micro determination of thymol via oxidative coupling. Am. Cosmet. Perfum. 87{10}: 41-42a.

1.6-48 Teranishi, R., Keller, U., Flath, R.A., and Mon, T.R. 1980. Comparison of batchwise and continuous steam distillation-solvent extraction recovery of volatiles from oleoresin Capsicum, African type (Capsicum frutescens). J. Agric. Food Chem. 28: 156-157.

1.6-49 Varju, M. 1975. Some problems of dry-ashing sample preparation. Pages 207-216 in P. Kozma, D. Polyak and E. Hervay, eds. Le controle de l'alimentation des plantes cultivees. 34d Colloque Europeen et Mediterraneen, Budapest, Hungary, Sept. 4-7, 1972. Akademiai Kiado, Budapest, Hungary. vol. I.

1.6-50 Velea, St., Ciulei, I., Achimescu, V., and Anghelescu, O. 1973. The nondestructive determination of the oil content in Umbelliferae fruits by means of the nuclear magnetic resonance in a fast adiabatic passage with modulation. Int. Congr. Pharm. Sci. Abstr. 33: 228.

1.6-51 Verzar, Mrs. G.J.P., Marczal, G., and Lemberkovics, E. 1976. Analytical procedures in the examination of chamomile oil [in Hungarian]. Herba Hung. 15{2}: 69-76. AGRICOLA.

1.6-52 Verzar, Mrs. P., Pethes, E., and Lemberkovics, E. 1976. Thin layer and gas chromatographic studies on iridoidic compounds in Valeriana officinalis L. [in Hungarian]. Herba Hung. 15{3}: 79-91. AGRICOLA.

1.6-53 Weiler, E.W. 1977. Radioimmuno-screening methods for secondary plant products. Pages 266-277 in W. Barz, E. Reinhard and M.H. Zenk, eds. Plant tissue culture and its bio-technological application. Proceedings of the first international congress on medicinal plant research, Section B, Munich, Germany, Sept. 6-10, 1976. Springer-Verlag, New York, N.Y.

1.6-54 Younos, C., Mortier, F., and Pelt, J.M. 1972. A contribution to the chemical and pharmacological study of the essential oils of the Labiatae from Afghanistan. I. Analytical methods used in the analysis and fractionation of essential oils [in French]. Plant. Med. Phytother. 6: 171-177. HA 43: 3949.

1.6-55 Zholkevich, V.N., Butenko, R.G., Pitsetskaya, N.F., and Borisova, T.A. 1972. The relation between mitotic activity, respiration intensity, and heat emission in the culture of tissue isolated from Panax ginseng. Phytomorphology 22: 177-180.

1.6-56 Zuercher, K., and Hadorn, H. 1979. Improved apparatus for determination of essential oil in spices [in German]. Mitt. Geb. Libensmittelunters Hyg. 70: 278-282. FSTA 11{11}: 11T551.

1.7 Phytochemistry

1.7-1 Akhila, A., and Banthorpe, D.V. 1980. Biosynthesis of the skeleton of pulegone in Mentha pulegium. Z. Pflanzenphysiol. 99: 277-282.

1.7-2 Akhila, A., Banthorpe, D.V., and Rowan, M.G. 1980. Biosynthesis of carvone in Mentha spicata. Phytochemistry 19: 1433-1437.

1.7-3 Allen, K.G., Banthorpe, D.V., Charlwood, B.V., Ekundayo, O., and Mann, J. 1976. Metabolic pools associated with monoterpene biosynthesis in higher plants. Phytochemistry 15: 101-107.

1.7-4 Andersson, G. 1973. The fatty-acid pattern of various oil plants [in German]. Fette Seifen Anstrichm. 75: 7-13.

1.7-5 Antoun, M.D., and Roberts, M.F. 1976. Enzymes involved in norlaudanosoline biosynthesis in Papaver somniferum latex. Lloydia 39: 481 (Abstr.).

1.7-6 Aviv, D., and Galun, E. 1978. Biotransformation of monoterpenes by Mentha cell lines: conversion of pulegone to isomenthone. Planta Med. 33: 70-77.

1.7-7 Ayabe, S., Yoshikawa, T., Kobayashi, M., and Furuya, T. 1980. Biosynthesis of a retrochalcone, echinatin: involvement of O-methyltransferase to licodione. Phytochemistry 19: 2331-2336.

1.7-8 Baker, F.C., and Brooks, C.J.W. 1976. Biosynthesis of the sesquiterpenoid, capsidiol, in sweet pepper fruits inoculated with fungal spores. Phytochemistry 15: 689-694.

1.7-9 Banthorpe, D.V., Ekundayo, O., Mann, J., and Turnbull, K.W. 1975. Biosynthesis of monoterpenes in plants from 14C-labelled acetate and CO2. Phytochemistry 14: 707-715.

1.7-10 Banthorpe, D.V., Modawi, B.M., Poots, I., and Rowan, M.G. 1978. Redox interconversions of geraniol and nerol in higher plants. Phytochemistry 17: 1115-1118.

1.7-11 Banthorpe, D.V., Patourel, G.N.J. le, and Francis, M.J.O. 1972. Biosynthesis of geraniol and nerol and their beta-D-glucosides in Pelargonium graveolens and Rosa dilecta. Biochem. J. 130: 1045-1054.

1.7-12 Banthorpe, D.V., Charlwood, B.V., and Young, M.R. 1972. Terpene biosynthesis. Part IV. Biosynthesis of (+)-pulegone in Mentha pulegium L. J. Chem. Soc. Perkin Trans. I. 1972{12}: 1532-1534.

1.7-13 Battersby, A.R., Staunton, J., Wiltshire, H.R., Bircher, B.J., and Fuganti, C. 1975. Studies of enzyme-mediated reactions. Part V. Synthesis of (13S)- and (13R)-{13-3H1} scoulerine from stereospecifically labelled (R)- and (S)- [alpha-3H1] benzyl alcohols: sterochemistry of enzymic reactions at saturated benzylic carbon. J. Chem. Soc. Perkin Trans. I. 1975{12}: 1162-1171.

1.7-14 Battersby, A.R., Staunton, J., Wiltshire, H.R., Francis, R.J., and Southgate, R. 1975. Biosynthesis. Part XXII. The origin of chelidonine and of other alkaloids derived from the tetrahydroprotoberberine skeleton. J. Chem. Soc. Perkin Trans. I. 1975{12}: 1147-1156.

1.7-15 Battersby, A.R., Laing, D.G., and Ramage, R. 1972. Biosynthesis. Part XIX. Biosynthesis of (-)-camphor and (-)-borneol in Salvia officinalis. J. Chem. Soc. Perkin Trans. I 21: 2743-2748.

1.7-16 Boehm, H., Olesch, B., and Schulze, C. 1972. Further investigations on the biosynthesis of alkaloids in isolated latex from opium poppy (Papaver somniferum L.). Biochem. Physiol. Pflanz. (BPP) 163: 126-136.

1.7-17 Bondavalli, F., Schenone, P., Lanteri, S., and Ranise, A. 1977. Syntheses of 1,3,3-trimethyl-2- oxabicyclo[2.2.2]oct-5-ene (2,3-didehydro-1,8-cineole), 6,6-dimethyl-2-methylene-7-oxabicyclo [3.2.1]octane (isopinol), 2,6,6-trimethyl-7-oxabicyclo[3.2.1]oct-2-ene (pinol), and 1(3-isopropylidenecyclopentyl)ethanone (pinolone) from hydroxy- and bromo-derivatives of cineole. J. Chem. Soc. Perkin Trans. I 4: 430-433.

1.7-18 Borkowski, P.R., Horn, J.S., and Rapoport, H. 1978. Role of 1,2-dehydroreticulinium ion in the biosynthetic conversion of reticuline to thebaine. J. Am. Chem. Soc. 100{1}: 276-281.

1.7-19 Bosila, Kh. A., and Udalova, V.I. 1977. Dynamics of changes in the principal essential oil components of Mentha piperita and M. crispa treated with growth regulators [in Russian]. Nauk. Pr.-Ukr. Sel's'kogospod. Akad. 1977{196}: 173-177. HA 49: 2127.

1.7-20 Brochmann-Hanssen, E., Chen, C.Y., and Linn, E.E. 1980. Biosynthesis of unnatural papaverine derivatives in Papaver somniferum. J. Nat. Prod. 43: 736-738. CA 94: 61811.

1.7-21 Brochmann-Hanssen, E., and Okamoto, Y. 1980. Biosynthesis of opium alkaloids. Substrate specificity and aberrant biosynthesis: attempted detection of oripavine in Papaver somniferum. J. Nat. Prod. 43: 731-735. CA 94: 44058.

1.7-22 Brochmann-Hanssen, E. 1971. Aspects of chemistry and biosynthesis of opium alkaloids. Pages 347-369 in H. Wagner and L. Hoerhammer, eds. Pharmocognosy and phytochemistry. Springer Verlag, New York.

1.7-23 Brochmann-Hanssen, E., Fu, C.-C., and Misconi, L.Y. 1971. Opium alkaloids. XI: Biosynthesis of aporphines in Papaver somniferum. J. Pharm. Sci. 60: 1880-1883.

1.7-24 Brochmann-Hanssen, E., Chen, C.-H., Chen, C.R., Chiang, H.-C., Leung, A.Y., and McMurtrey, K. 1975. Opium alkaloids. Part XVI. The biosynthesis of 1-benzylisoquinolines in Papaver somniferum. Preferred and secondary pathways; stereo-chemical aspects. J. Chem. Soc. Perkin Trans. I 1975{16}: 1531-1537.

1.7-25 Brown, S.A. 1979. Biosynthetic studies on coumarins. Planta Med. 36: 299-310.

1.7-26 Bui Tkhi Ban, and Nikolaev, A.G. 1975. Mint species as the source of linalool [in Russian]. Rastit. Resur. 11: 104-109.

1.7-27 Canonica, L., Manitto, P., Monti, D., and Sanchez, A.M. 1971. Biosynthesis of allyphenols in Ocimum basilicum L. Chem. Commun. 1971{18}: 1108-1109.

1.7-28 Canonica, L., Gramatica, P., Manitto, P., and Monti, D. 1979. Biosynthesis of caffeic acid in Ocimum basilicum L. Chem. Commun. 1979{23}: 1073-1075

1.7-29 Chatterjee, A., Bhattacharya, S., Banerji, J., and Ghosh, P.C. 1977. A new synthesis of coumarins. Indian J. Chem. Sect. B 15B: 214-216.

1.7-30 Chisholm, M.D., and Matsuo, M. 1972. Biosynthesis of allyglucosinolate and 3-methylthiopropylglucosinolate in horseradish, Armoracia lapathifolia. Phytochemistry 11: 203-207.

1.7-31 Cole, R.A. 1976. Isothiocyanates, nitriles and thiocyanates as products of autolysis of glucosinolates in Cruciferae. Phytochemistry 15: 759-762.

1.7-32 Cole, R.A. 1975. 1-Cyanoepithiolkanes: major products of alkenylglucosinolate hydrolysis in certain Cruciferae. Phytochem istry 14: 2293-2294.

1.7-33 Croteau, R., and Loomis, W.D. 1975. Biosynthesis and metabolism of monoterpenes. Int. Flavours Food Addit. 6: 292-296.

1.7-34 Croteau, R. 1980. The biosynthesis of terpene compounds. Perfum. Flavor. 1980 (Special Issue, October): 35-38, 45-48, 50-52, 54-59. HA 51: 2868.

1.7-35 Croteau, R., Burbott, A.J., and Loomis, W.D. 1972. Biosynthesis of mono- and sesquiterpenes in peppermint from glucose-14C and 14CO2. Phytochemistry 11: 2459-2467.

1.7-36 Croteau, R., and Loomis, W.D. 1973. Biosynthesis of squalene and other triterpenes in Mentha piperita from mevalonate-2-14C. Phytochemistry 12: 1957-1965.

1.7-37 Croteau, R., and Karp, F. 1977. Biosynthesis of monoterpenes: partial purification and characterization of 1,8-cineole synthetase from Salvia officinalis. Arch. Biochem. Biophys. 179: 257-265.

1.7-38 Croteau, R., Hooper, C.L., and Felton, M. 1978. Biosynthesis of monoterpenes. Partial purification and characterization of a bicyclic monoterpenol dehydrogenase from sage (Salvia officinalis). Arch. Biochem. Biophys. 188: 182-193.

1.7-39 Croteau, R., and Karp, F. 1979. Biosynthesis of monoterpenes: preliminary characterization of bornyl pyrophosphate synthetase from sage (Salvia officinalis) (leaves) and demonstration that geranyl pyrophosphate is the preferred substrate for cyclization. Arch. Biochem. Biophys. 198: 512-522.

1.7-40 Croteau, R., and Karp, F. 1979. Biosynthesis of monoterpenes: hydrolysis of bornyl pyrophosphate, an essental step in camphor biosynthesis, and hydrolysis of geranyl pyrophosphate, the acyclic precursor of camphor, by enzymes from sage (Salvia officinalis) (leaves). Arch. Biochem. Biophys. 198: 523-532.

1.7-41 Croteau, R. 1977. Site of monoterpene biosynthesis in Majorana hortensis leaves. Plant Physiol. 59: 519-520.

1.7-42 Croteau, R., Felton, M., and Ronald, R.C. 1980. Biosynthesis of monoterpenes: preliminary characterization of I-endo-fenchol synthetase from fennel (Foeniculum vulgare) and evidence that no free intermediate is involved in the cyclization of geranyl phyrophosphate to the rearranged product. Arch. Biochem. Biophys. 200: 534-546.

1.7-43 Croteau, R., and Karp, F. 1977. Demonstration of a cyclic pyrophosphate intermediate in the enzymatic conversion of neryl pyrophosphate to borneol. Arch. Biochem. Biophys. 184: 77-86.

1.7-44 Croteau, R., and Karp, F. 1976. Biosynthesis of monoterpenes: Enzymatic conversion of neryl pyrophosphate to 1,8-cineole, alpha-terpineol, and cyclic monoterpene hydrocarbons by a cell-free preparation from sage (Salvia officinalis). Arch. Biochem. Biophys. 176: 734-746.

1.7-45 Croteau, R., Felton, M., and Ronald, R.C. 1980. Biosynthesis of monoterpenes: Conversion of the acyclic precursors geranyl pyrophosphate and neryl pyrophosphate to the rearranged monoterpenes fenchol and fenchone by a soluble enzyme preparation from fennel (Foeniculum vulgare). Arch. Biochem. Biophys. 200: 524-533.

1.7-46 Croteau, R., and Loomis, W.D. 1972. Biosynthesis of mono- and sesquiterpenes in peppermint from mevalonate-2-14C. Phytochemistry 11: 1055-1066.

1.7-47 Croteau, R., and Felton, N.M. 1980. Substrate specificity of

monoterpenol dehydrogenases from Foeniculum vulgare and Tanacetum
vulgare. Phytochemistry 19: 1343-1347.

1.7-48 Croteau, R., Burbott, A.J., and Loomis, W.D. 1973. Enzymatic
cyclization of neryl pyrophosphate to alpha-terpineol by cell-free
extracts from peppermint. Biochem. Biophys. Res. Commun. 50:
1006-1012.

1.7-49 Croteau, R., and Klattukudy, P.E. 1974. Biosynthesis of
pentahydroxystearic acid of cutin from linoleic acid in Rosmarinus
officinalis. Arch. Biochem. Biophys. 162: 458-470.

1.7-50 Cuong, B.N., Verzar-Petri, G., and Tamas, J. 1977. Study on
prochamazulenes of Achillea millefolium L. ssp. collina Becker Proc.
Hung. Annu. Meet. Biochem. 17: 127-128. AGRICOLA.

1.7-51 Dall' Acqua, Innocenti, G., and Caporale, G. 1975. Biosynthesis
of O-alkyl-furocoumarins. Planta Med. 27: 343-348.

1.7-52 Doernemann, D., Loeffelhardt, W., and Kindl, H. 1974. Chain
elongation of aromatic amino acids in the role of 2-benzyl-malic acid
in the biosynthesis of a C6C4 amino acid and a C6C3 mustard oil
glucoside. Can J. Biochem. 52: 916-921.

1.7-53 Ellis, B.E., and Amhrein, N. 1971. The 'Nih-shift' during
aromatic ortho-hydroxylation in higher plants. Phytochemistry 10:
3069-3072.

1.7-54 El-Moghazy, A.M., Ali, A.A., Ross, S.A., and Mohamed, A.A. 1980.
Phytochemical studies on Jasminum mesnyi H. Fitoterapia 51{4}:
197-199. CA 95: 21314.

1.7-55 Epstein, W.W., and Poulter, C.D. 1973. A survey of some irregular
monoterpenes and their biogenetic analogies to presqualene alcohol.
Phytochemistry 12: 737-747.

1.7-56 Evans, F.J., and Cowley, P.S. 1973. Incorporation of 14CO2 into
cardenolide and sapogenin steroids of Digitalis purpurea.
Phytochemistry 12: 791-794.

1.7-57 Evdokimova,L.I., Rat'kin, A.V., Andreen, V.S., and Zaprometov,
M.N. 1980. Characteristics of anthocyanidin and flavonol biosynthesis
in opium poppy flowers. Sov. Plant Physiol. (Engl. Transl.) 27:
399-405. Translation of Fiziol. Rast. (Moscow) 27: 536-543, 1980.

1.7-58 Floria, F.G., and Ghiorghita, G.I. 1980. The influence of the
treatment with alkylating agents on Papaver somniferum L., in M1. Rev.
Roum. Biol. Ser. Biol. Veg. 25: 151-155.

1.7-59 Foglietti, M.-J., and Persheron, F. 1974. Occurrence of
galactokinase in fenugreek seedlings [in French]. Biochimie 56:
473-475.

1.7-60 Gambliel, H., and Croteau, R. 1980. Biosynthesis of alpha-pinene
and beta-pinene. Plant Physiol. 65 (6 Suppl.): 96 (Abstr.).

1.7-61 Games, D.E., and James, D.H. 1972. The biosynthesis of the
coumarins of Angelica archangelica. Phytochemistry 11: 868-869
(Abstr.).

1.7-62 Gerhardt, B. 1974. Studies on the formation of glycolate oxidase in developing coytledons of Helianthus annuus L. and Sinapis alba L. Z. Pflanzenphysiol. 74: 14-21.

1.7-63 Gleeson, P.A., and Jermyn, M.A. 1977. Leguminous seed glycoproteins that interact with concanavalin A. Aust. J. Plant Physiol. 4: 25-37.

1.7-64 Granger, R., Passet, J., and Teulade-Arbousset, G. 1973. Biogenesis of camphor and of fenchone in Lavandula stoechas L. [in French]. C.R. Hebd. Seances Acad. Sci. Ser. D 276{20}: 2839-2842.

1.7-65 Granger, R., Passet, J., and Arbousset, G. 1971. Biogenesis of bicyclic monoterpenes in Rosmarinus officinalis and Lavandula stoechas [in French]. Bull. Tech., Gattefosse SFPA 66: 25-26. CA 78: 1952.

1.7-66 Hahlbrock, K., Sutter, A., Wellmann, E., Ortmann, R., and Griesebach, H. 1971. Relationship between organ development and activity of enzymes involved in flavone glycoside biosynthesis in young parsley plants. Phytochemistry 10: 109-116.

1.7-67 Harrison, P.G., Bailey, B.K., and Steck, W. 1971. Biosynthesis of furano-chromosomes. Can. J. Biochem. 49: 964-970.

1.7-68 Hartmann, E., and Kilbinger, H. 1974. Occurrence of light-dependent acetylcholine concentrations in higher plants. Experientia 30: 1387-1388.

1.7-69 Hashimoto, T., Shibahara, H., Yamahara, Y., Toyooka, K., and Satoh, D. 1977 Studies on Digitalis glycosides. XXXIV. Transformation of gitoxigenin to digitoxigenin 3-acetate. Chem. Pharm. Bull. 25: 2468-2470.

1.7-70 Heinrich, G. 1973. The essential oil of Monarda fistulosa and the incorporation of labelled CO_2 into its components [in German]. Planta Med. 23: 201-212. HA 43: 9002.

1.7-71 Hewgill, F.R. 1978. Oxidation of alkoxyphenols - XXIV. A dipheno-2,2'-quinone from sesamol. Tetrahedron 34: 1595-1596.

1.7-72 Hirotani, M., and Furuya, T. 1977. Restoration of cardenolide-synthesis in redifferentiated shoots from callus cultures of Digitalis purpurea. Phytochemistry 16: 610-611.

1.7-73 Hodges, C.C., Horn, J.S., and Rapoport, H. 1977. Morphinan alkaloids in Papaver bracteatum biosynthesis and fate. Phytochemistry 16: 1939-1942.

1.7-74 Hoelzl, J. 1973. Preparation of 14C-administered valepotriates with Valeriana wallichii [in German]. Planta Med. 24: 66-72. CIM 15{8}: 9581.

1.7-75 Hoelzl, J., Franz, C., Fritz, D., and Voemel, A. 1975. Biosynthesis of the essential oil of Matricaria chamomilla L. 1. 14C-Labelling of the substances of the essential oil [in German]. Z. Naturforsch. C: Biosci. 30: 853-854.

1.7-76 Holland, H.L., Jeffs, P.W., Capps, T.M., and MacLean, D.B. 1979. The biosynthesis of protoberberine and related isoquinoline alkaloids. Can. J. Chem. 57: 1588-1597.

1.7-77 Horn, J.S., Paul, A.G., and Rapoport, H. 1978. Biosynthetic conversion of thebaine to codeinone. Mechanism of ketone formation from enol ether in vivo. J. Am. Chem. Soc. 100: 1895-1898.

1.7-78 Innocenti, G., Dall'Acqua, F., Rodighiero, P., and Caporale, G. 1978. Biosynthesis of O-alkylfurocoumarins in Angelica archangelica. Planta Med. 34: 167-171.

1.7-79 Innocenti, G., Dall'acqua, F., Guiotto, A., and Caporale, G. 1977. Investigations on the role of 7-demethylsuberosin in the biosynthesis of linear furocoumarins. Atti Ist. Veneto Sci. Lett. Arti. Cl. Sci. Mat. Nat. 135: 37-47. CA 90: 51485.

1.7-80 Inouye, H., Ueda, S., Inoue, K., and Takeda, Y. 1974. Monoterpene glucosides and related natural products. XXIII. Biosynthesis of the secoiridoid glucosides, gentiopicroside, morroniside, oleuropein, and jasminin. Chem. Pharm. Bull. 22{3}: 676-686. CA 81: 1326.

1.7-81 Inouye, H., Ueda, S., Inoue, K., and Takeda, Y. 1971. Biosynthesis of oleuropein-type secoiridoid glucosides by Oleaceae [in German]. Tetrahedron Lett. 1971{43}: 4073-4076. CA 76: 44028.

1.7-82 Jacobsohn, M.K., and Jacobsohn, G.M. 1976. Annual variation in the sterol content of Digitalis purpurea L. seedlings. Plant Physiol. 58: 541-543. 1.7-83 Jaskonis, J. 1972. Biological and biochemical characteristics of peppermint. 1. Biological characteristics [in Russian]. Liet. TSR Mokslu Akad. Darb. Ser. C 1972{2}: 61-70. AGRICOLA.

1.7-84 Josefsson, E. 1972. Conversion of indole-3-acetaldehyde oxime to 3-indolylmethylglucosinolate in Sinapis alba. Physiol. Plant. 27: 236-239.

1.7-85 Kanner, J., Mendel, H., and Budowski, P. 1976. Carotene oxidizing factors in red pepper fruits (Capsicum annuum L.). Ascorbic acid. J. Food Sci. 41: 183-185.

1.7-86 Kerbabaev, B.B., and Gladyshev, A.I. 1972. Changes in the glycyrrhizin and extractives content of licorice growing in the mid-Amudaria region [in Russian]. Izv. Akad. Nauk Turkm. SSR Ser. Biol. Nauk 1972{4}: 28-32 HA 43: 7108.

1.7-87 Kirby, G.W., Massey, S.R., and Steinreich, P. 1972. Biosynthesis of unnatural morphine derivatives in Papaver somniferum. J. Chem. Soc. C 13: 1642-1647.

1.7-88 Klischies, M., Stoeckigt, J., and Zenk, M.H. 1975. Biosynthesis of the allylphenols eugenol and methyleugenol in Ocimum basilicum L. J. Chem. Soc. Chem. Commun. 1975{21}: 879-880.

1.7-89 Kovacs, P., Jindra, A., Nemec, P., and Benesova, M. 1974. Enzymological aspects of opium alkaloid biosynthesis. Pharmazie 29: 74 (Abstr.).

1.7-90 Kreuzaler, F., and Hahlbrock, K. 1975. Enzymatic synthesis of aromatic compounds in higher plants. Formation of bis-noryangonin (4-hydroxy-6-[4-hydroxystyrl]-2-pyrone) from p-coumaroyl-CoA and malonyl-CoA. Arch. Biochem. Biophys. 169: 84-90.

1.7-91 Kreuzaler, F., and Hahlbrock, K. 1972. Enzymatic synthesis of aromatic compounds in higher plants: formation of naringenin (5,7,4'-trihydroxyflavanone) from p-coumaroyl coenzyme A and malonyl coenzyme A. FEBS Lett. 28: 69-72.

1.7-92 Kurlyanchik, I.A., Suprunov, N.I., Skokova, A.A., Syshchikova, N.M., and Deren'ko, S.A. 1979. Accumulation of carotenoids and ascorbic acid in Anethum graveolens. Chem. Nat. Compd. (Engl. Transl.) 15: 767-768. Translation of Khim. Prir. Soedin. 1979{6}: 861.

1.7-93 Lawrence, B.M. 1979. A fresh look at the biosynthetic pathways for most compounds found in Mentha oils. Int. Congr. Essent. Oils, [Pap.], 7th, 1977. 7: 121-126. CA 92: 37669.

1.7-94 Lew, J.Y., and Shannon, L.M. 1973. Incorporation of carbohydrate residues into peroxidase isoenzymes in horseradish roots. Plant Physiol. 52: 462-465.

1.7-95 Light, R.J., and Hahlbrock, K. 1978. Biosynthesis of flavonoids. Direction of cyclization of the A ring determined by C-13 NMR. Fed. Proc. 37: 1714 (Abstr.).

1.7-96 Luckner, M. 1978. Plant biochemistry. Trends Biochem. Sci. (Pers. Ed.) 3{7}: N148, N150-N151. CA 89: 126085.

1.7-97 Macleod, A.J., and Macleod, G. 1977. Synthesis and natural occurrence of 8-methylthiooctanonitrile and 9-methylthiononanitrile. Phytochemistry 16: 907-909.

1.7-98 Majak, W., and Towers, G.H.N. 1973. Incorporation of 14CO2, 14C-phenylalanine and 14C-cinnamate into soluble and insoluble cinnamic derivatives in Mentha arvensis. Phytochemistry 12: 2189-2195

1.7-99 Manitto, P., Gramatica, P., and Monti, D. 1975. Biosynthesis of phenylpropanoid compounds. Part II. Incorporation of specifically labelled cinnamic acids into eugenol. J. Chem. Soc. Perkin Trans. I. 1975{16}: 1548-1551.

1.7-100 Manitto, P., Monti, D., and Gramatica, P. 1974. Biosynthesis of phenylpropanoid compounds. Part I. Biosynthesis of eugenol in Ocimum basilicum L. J. Chem. Soc. Perkin Trans. I. 1974{14}: 1727-1731.

1.7-101 Manitto, P., and Monti, D. 1978. Incorporation of 2-14C, 2-3H cinnamic acid into anethole in Pimpinella anisum L. Gazz. Chim. Ital. 108(9/10): 579-580

1.7-102 Manitto, P., Monti, D., and Gramatica, P. 1974. Biosynthesis of anethole in Pimpinella anisum L. Tetrahedron Lett. 1974{17}: 1567-1568.

1.7-103 May, D.S., and Villarreal, H.M. 1974. Altitudinal differentiation of the Hill reaction in populations of Taraxcum officinale in Colorado. Photosynthetica 8: 73-77.

1.7-104 Melotte, R. 1973. Evolution of the concentration of valtrates in Valeriana procurrens Wallr. cultivated in conditioned media [in French]. J. Pharm. Belg. 28: 373-383. CIM 15{8}: 9580.

1.7-105 Misconi, L.Y. 1973. Synthesis and biosynthesis of the opium alkaloid isoboldine. Proc. Aust. Biochem. Soc. 6: 74 (Abstr.).

1.7-106 Mitsuda, H., Takii, Y., Iwami, K., and Yasunoto, K. 1975. Enzymic formation of thiamine pyrophosphate in plants. J. Nutr. Sci. Vitaminol. 21: 19-26. CA 83: 92808.

1.7-107 Mouranche, A., and Costes, C. 1978. Mechanism and enzymes in morphine biosynthesis [in French]. Ann. Technol. Agric. 27: 715-731. AGRICOLA.

1.7-108 Mujumdar, A.S., and Usgaonkar, R.N. 1974. Benzodipyrans. Part V. Synthesis of a linear dihydrobenzodipyrandione isolated from dill and of other similar benzodipyrandiones. J. Chem. Soc. Perkin Trans. I 19: 2236-2239.

1.7-109 Nadkarni, D.R., and Usgaonkar, R.N. 1977. Synthesis of artemidinal (3-formyl-isocoumarin) and a new synthesis of isocoumarin-3-carboxylic acid. Indian J. Chem. Sect. B. 15: 185-186.

1.7-110 Nakabayashi, H., Ohira, K., and Fujiwara, A. 1972. On the content of isothiocyanate and oxazolidinethione in Brassica seeds [in Japanese]. Bull. Coll. Agric. Utsunomiya Univ. 8{2}: 1-7. FCA 26: 5853.

1.7-111 Ngo, T.T., and Shargool, P.D. 1974. The enzymatic synthesis of L-cysteine in higher plant tissues. Can. J. Biochem. 52: 435-440.

1.7-112 Nuss, R.F., and Loewus, F.A. 1978. Further studies on oxalic acid biosynthesis in oxalate-accumulating plants. Plant Physiol. 61: 590-592.

1.7-113 Parker, H.I., Blaschke, G., and Rapoport, H. 1972. Biosynthetic conversion of thebaine to codeine. J. Am. Chem. Soc. 94: 1276-1282.

1.7-114 Patudin, A.V., and Romanova, A.S. 1977. Amounts of royleanones in the roots of some species of sage and the dynamics of the accumulation during the vegetation period. Pharm. Chem. J. (Engl. Transl.) 11: 84-87. Translation of Khim.-Farm. Zh. 11{1}: 90-94, 1977.

1.7-115 Pihakaski, K., and Iversen, T.-H. 1976. Myrosinase in Brassicaceae. I. Localization of myrosinase in cell fractions of roots of Sinapis alba L. J. Exp. Bot. 27: 242-258. 1.4.

1.7-116 Pilgrim, H. 1972. Cholesterol side-chain cleaving enzyme activity in seedling and in vitro tissue of Digitalis purpurea [in German]. Phytochemistry 11: 1725-1728.

1.7-117 Poulose, A.J., and Croteau, R. 1978. Biosynthesis of aromatic monoterpenes. Conversion of gamma-terpinene to p-cymene and thymol in Thymus vulgaris L. Arch. Biochem. Biophys. 187: 307-314.

1.7-118 Poulose, A.J., and Croteau, R. 1978. Gamma-terpinene synthetase: a key enzyme in the biosynthesis of aromatic monoterpenes. Arch. Biochem. Biophys. 191{1}: 400-411.

1.7-119 Rao, P.G., Zutshi, U., Pushpangadah, P., Sobti, S.N., and Atal, C.K. 1979. Biosynthetic studies of linalooel & linalyl acetate in Ocimum canum Sims & Mentha citrata Ehrh. Indian J. Exp. Biol. 17: 530-532.

1.7-120 Reichling, J., Beiderbeck, R., and Becker, H. 1979. Comparative studies on secondary products from tumors, flowers, herb and roots of Matricaria chamomilla L. [in German]. Planta Med. 36: 322-332.

1.7-121 Repcak, M., Halasova, J., Honcariv, R., and Podhradsky, D. 1980. The content and composition of the essential oil in the course of anthodium development in wild camomile (Matricaria chamomilla L.). Biol. Plant. 22: 183-191.

1.7-122 Rothbacher, H., and Suteu, F. 1974. Origin and formation of carvenone in caraway oil [in German]. Planta Med. 26: 283-288.

1.7-123 Saitoh, T., Shibata, S., Sankawa, U., Furuya, T., and Ayabe, S. 1975. Biosynthesis of echinatin. A new biosynthetical scheme of retrochalcone. Tetrahedron Lett. 1975{50}: 4463-4466.

1.7-124 Sato, M., and Hasegawa, M. 1972. Transglucosylases in Cichorium intybus converting cichoriin to esculin. Phytochemistry 11: 3149-3156

1.7-125 Schantz, M. von, and Ek, B.S. 1971. On the formation of essential oil in caraway, Carum carvi [in German]. Sci. Pharm. 39{2}: 82-101.

1.7-126 Schantz, M. von, and Huhtikangas, A. 1971. On the formation of limonen and carvone in caraway, Carum carvi [in German]. Phytochemistry 10: 1787-1793.

1.7-127 Schilcher, H. 1977. Biosynthesis of (-)-alpha- bisabolol nad bisabololoxides. 1st Report; in-vivo tracer studies with 14C-precursors [in German]. Planta Med. 31: 315-321. HA 48: 802.

1.7-128 Schroeder, J., Heller, W., and Hahlbrock, K. 1979. Flavanone synthase: simple and rapid assay for the key enzyme of flavonoid biosynthesis. Plant Sci. Lett. 14: 281-286.

1.7-129 Siqueira, N.S. de, Alice, C.B., Silva, G.A. de A.B., Bauer, L., and Santana, B.S. 1975. Digitalis purpurea L. in Rio Grande do Sul, Brazil. I. Biochemistry [in Portuguese]. Trib. Farm. 43: 18-22. AGRICOLA.

1.7-130 Slepetys, J. 1974. Biology and biochemistry of wormwood, Artemisia absinthium. 8. Accumulation dynamics of tannic substances, ascorbic acid and carotene [in Russian]. Liet. TSR Mokslu Akad. Darb. Ser. C 1974{1}: 43-48. AGRICOLA.

1.7-131 Srivastava, G.C., and Pandey, M. 1977. Level of glutamic aminotransferase and glutamic dehydrogenase enzymes in seed. Curr. Sci. 46: 316-317.

1.7-132 Steck, W., and Brown, S.A. 1971. Comparison of (+)- and (-)-marmesin as intermediates in the biosynthesis of linear furano-coumarins. Can J. Biochem. 49: 1213-1216.

1.7-133 Stocker, M., and Pohl, R. 1976. Formation of 5,7-dihydroxychromone-7-rutinoside Mentha longifolia after the death of the plant [in German]. Phytochemistry 15: 571-572.

1.7-134 Suga, T., Shishibori, T., and Morinaka, H. 1980. Preferential participation of linaloyl pyrophosphate rather than neryl pyrophosphate in biosynthesis of cyclic monoterpenoids in higher plants. J. Chem. Soc. Chem. Commun. 1980{4}: 167-168.

1.7-135 Trenkle, K. 1971. New research in Foeniculum vulgare organic acids, specifically phenylcarboxylic acids [in German]. Planta Med. 20: 289-301. CA 76: 70092.

1.7-136 Uprety, H., Bhakuni, D.S., and Kapil, R.S. 1975. Biosynthesis of papaverine. Phytochemistry 14: 1535-1537.

1.7-137 Valadon, L.R.G., and Mummery, R.S. 1977. Carotenoids of lilies and of red pepper: Biogenesis of capsonthin and capsorubin. Z. Pflanzenphysiol. 82: 407-416.

1.7-138 Valcavi, U., and Innoenti, S. 1974. Synthesis of digitoxigenin 3-acete [in Italian]. Farmaco. Ed. Sci. 29: 194-203.

1.7-139 Vaverkova, S. 1979. Changes in growth and content of secondary metabolites of the true camomile (Matricaria chamomilla L.) after application of flurenol. Biologia (Bratislava) 34: 295-302. HA 50: 498.

1.7-140 Verzar-Petri, G., and Then, M. 1974. Biosynthesis of volatile oils in Salvia sclarea in the course of germination. Part I. Planta Med. 25: 366-372.

1.7-141 Verzar-Petri, G. 1974. Biosynthesis and localization of biologically active substances in Valeriana officinalis L. Pharmazie 29: 71 (Abstr.).

1.7-142 Verzar-Petri, G. 1974. Biosynthesis of alkaloids, valtrates and volatile oils in the roots of Valeriana officinalis L. from radioactive precursors [in Hungarian]. Acta Pharm. Hung. (Suppl).: 54-65 CIM 15{8}: 9581.

1.7-143 Weber, F., and Grosch, W. 1976. Co-oxidation of a carotenoid by the enzyme lipoxygenase: Influence on the formation of linoleic acid byhydroperoxides. Z. Lebensm.-Unters. Forsch. 161: 223-230. CA 85: 118631.

1.7-144 Wojciechowski, Z.A., Zimowski, J., and Zielanska, M. 1976. Biosynthesis and metabolism of steryl glycosides in Sinapis alba seedlings. Phytochemistry 15: 1681-1683.

1.7-145 Wold, J.K., Paulsen, B.S., and Nordal, A. 1977. Precursor incorporation experiments in Papaver alkaloid biosynthesis. II. Papaver somniferum L. Acta Pharm. Suec. 14: 403-408. CA 88: 19085.

1.7-146 Wuest, J.D., Madonik, A.M., and Gordon, D.C. 1977. Vinylketenes synthesis of (+)-actinidine. J. Org. Chem. 42: 2111-2113.

1.7-147 Wuu, T.-Y., and Baisted, D.J. 1973. Non-uniform labelling of geraniol biosynthesized from $^{14}CO_2$ in Pelargonium graveolens. Phytochemistry 12: 1291-1297.

1.7-148 Yosioka, I., Sugawara, T., Imai, K., and Kitagawa, I. 1972. Soil bacterial hydrolysis leading to genuine aglycone. V. On ginsenosides-Rb1, Rb2, and Rc of the ginseng root saponins. Chem. Pharm. Bull. (Tokyo) 20: 2413-2421.

1.7-149 Zelenin, V.M. 1974. Biochemical characteristics of parsley in the Permsk Region [in Russian]. Tr. Permsk. Gos. S-kh. Inst. 106: 92-100. CA 84: 132644.

1.8 Biological Activity

1.8-1 Abdou, I.A., Abou-Zeid, A.A., El-Sherbeeny, M.R., and Abou-El-Gheat, Z.H. 1972. Antimicrobial activities of Allium sativum, Allium cepa, Raphanus sativus, Capsicum frutescens, Eruca sativa, All kurrat on bacteria. Qual. Plant. Mater. Veg. 22: 29-35. HA 43: 5168.

1.8-2 Abivardi, C. 1971. Studies on the effects of nine Iranian anthelmintic plant extracts on the root-knot nematode Meloidogyne incognita. Phytopathol. Z. 71: 300-308.

1.8-3 Abou-Hussein, M.R., Fadl, M.S., and Wally, Y.A. 1975. Effect of garlic bulb crude extract on flowering, sex ratio and yield of squash. Egypt. J. Hortic. 2: 129-130. HA 46: 8426.

1.8-4 Abou-Hussein, M.R., Fadl, M.S., and Wally, Y.A. 1974. Regulatory effects of garlic bulb extract on gradual changes in relative activities of endogenous growth active materials in squash (Cucurbita pepo L.). Egypt. J. Hortic. 1: 113-125. HA 46: 5725.

1.8-5 Abou-Hussein, M.R., Fadl, M.S., and Wally, Y.A. 1974. Some biological properties of garlic bulb extract. Egypt. J. Hortic. 1: 127-136. HA 46: 5726.

1.8-6 Abou-Hussein, M.R., Fadl, M.S., and Wally, Y.A. 1975. Effect of garlic bulb extract on flowering, sex ratio, and yield of squash. I. Effect of different fractions of partitioned garlic bulb extract on flowering in squash. Egypt. J. Hortic. 2: 3-9. HA 46: 8424.

1.8-7 Abou-Hussein, M.R., Fadl, M.S., and Wally, Y.A. 1975. Effect of garlic bulb extract on flowering, sex ratio and yield of squash. II. Modulation of sex ratio by application of different fractions of garlic bulb extract. Egypt. J. Hortic. 2: 11-22. HA 46: 8425.

1.8-8 Afifi, A.F., and Dowidar, A.E. 1976. Effect of volatile materials produced by some members of Labiatae on spore germination and spore respiration of some soil fungi. Egypt. J. Physiol. Sci. 3: 81-92. HA 48: 9285.

1.8-9 Afifi, A.F. 1978. Effect of volatile substances released from Origanum majorana and Ocimum basilicum on the rhizosphere and phyllosphere fungi of Phaseolus vulgaris. Folia Microbiol. (Prague) 23: 399-405.

1.8-10 Afifi, A.F., and Dowidar, A.E. 1978. Effect of volatile substances from Origanum majorana and Ocimum basilicum on spore respiration and germination of some soil fungi. Folia Microbiol. (Prague) 23: 489-492.

1.8-11 Afifi, A.F. 1975. Effect of the volatile substances emanated from some members of Labiatae on the rhizospheric and phyllospheric fungi of the associated plant Phaseolus vulgaris. Ann. Microbiol. Enzimol. 25: 9-17. SF 40: 120.

1.8-12 Afifi, A.F. 1975. Effect of volatile substances from species of Labiatae on rhizospheric and phyllospheric fungi of Phaseolus vulgaris. Phytopathol. Z. 83: 296-302.

1.8-13 Aggag, M.E., and Yousef, R.T. 1972. Study of antimicrobial activity of chamomile oil. Planta Med. 22: 140-144. HA 43: 4770.

1.8-14 Agrawal, P. 1978. Effect of root and bulb extracts of Allium spp. on fungal growth. Trans. Br. Mycol. Soc. 70: 439-441.

1.8-15 Ahmed, S.R., and Agnihotri, J.P. 1977. Antifungal activity of some plant extracts. Indian J. Mycol. Plant Pathol. 7: 180-181. HA 49: 2877.

1.8-16 Alam, M.M., Kirmani, M.R., and Khan, A.M. 1976. Studies on the role of root-exudates for nematode control by the interculture of mustard and rocket-salad with wheat and barley. Fert. Technol. 13: 289-292. SF 41: 2591.

1.8-17 Ali, A.D., Donia, A.R., and El-Sawaf, S.K. 1972. The influence of natural food on the development and reproductive rate of Lasioderma serricorne Fab. (Coleopt., Anobiidae). Z. Angew. Entomol. 72: 212-220. RAE 63: 1897.

1.8-18 Allegrini, J., DeBouchberg, S., and Boillot, A. 1972. Essential oil antibacterial power [in French]. Prod. Probl. Pharm. 29{9}: 819-827. CA 78: 75830.

1.8-19 Amonkar, S.V., and Banerji, A. 1971. Isolation and characterization of larvicidal principle of garlic. Science 174: 1343-1344.

1.8-20 Apliak, I.V. 1972. Antimicrobial effect of essential oils from certain spice plants [in Russian]. Pages 258-259 in B.E. Aizenmann, ed. Fitontsidy; rezul'taty ierspektivy: zadachi issledovanii. Soveschanie po probleme fitontisidov, 6th, Kiev, 1969. AGRICOLA.

1.8-21 Appleton, J.A., and Tansey, M.R. 1975. Inhibition of growth of zoopathogenic fungi by garlic extract. Mycologia 67: 882-885. HA 46: 4467.

1.8-22 Arora, R., and Pandey, G.N. 1977. The application of essential oils and their isolates for blue mould decay control in Citrus reticulata Blanco. J. Food Sci. Technol. 14: 14-16.

1.8-23 Arsu, V. 1978. Garden sweet basil used in the treatment of spare combs to control the wax moth [in Romanian]. Apic. Rom. 53{1}: 9-10. AGRICOLA

1.8-24 Asari, P.A.R., and Thomas, M.J. 1974. On the use of lemongrass leaf infusion for the control of brinjal. Agric. Res. J. Kerala 12{1}: 77. Bib.Ag. 39: 234657.

1.8-25 Barbalic, L. 1973. Effect of some ethereal oils on the germination and seedling growth of garden cress [in German]. Sci. Pharm. 41: 18-28. CA 78: 155385.

1.8-26 Barbalic, L. 1973. Effect of some ethereal oils on the germination, growth and development of rye (Secale cereale) [in German]. Sci. Pharm. 41: 28-35. CA 78: 155386.

1.8-27 Barone, F.E., and Tansey, M.R. 1977. Isolation, purification, identification, synthesis, and kinetics of activity of the anticandidal component of Allium sativum and a hypothesis for its mode of action. Mycologia 69: 793-825.

1.8-28 Bekesi, P. 1979. The effect of the pollen of some weed species on germination of conidia of Botrytis cinerea. Acta Phytopathologica Academiae Scientiarum Hungaricae 14{3/4}: 379-382.

1.8-29 Bhatnagar-Thomas, P.L., and Pal, A.K. 1974. Studies on the insecticidal activity of garlic oil. I. Differential toxicity of the oil to Musca domestica nebulo Fabr and Trogoderma granarium Everts. J. Food Sci. Technol. 11: 110-113. RAE-B 63: 3467.

1.8-30 Bhatnagar-Thomas, P.L., and Pal, A.K. 1974. Studies on the insecticidal activity of garlic oil. II. Mode of action of the oil as a pesticide in Musca domestica nebulo Fabr and Trogoderma granarium Everts. J. Food Sci. Technol. 11: 153-158. RAE-B 63: 3468.

1.8-31 Bhatti, D.S., and Dhawan, S.C. 1980. Effect of crushed seeds of carrot and coriander on wheat plant growth and multiplication of Heterodera avenae. Haryana Agric. Univ. J. Res. 10{3}: 419-420.

1.8-32 Bhuyan, M., Saxena, B.N., and Rao, K.M. 1974. Repellant property of oil fraction of garlic, Allium sativum Linn. Indian J. Exp. Biol. 12: 575-576.

1.8-33 Bock, W., Dongowski, G., Goebel, H., and Krause, M. 1975. Detection of the inhibition of microbial pectin and pectate lyases using inhibitors of vegetable origin [in German]. Nahrung 19: 411-416.

1.8-34 Bogin, E., and Abrams, M. 1976. The effect of garlic extract on the activity of some enzymes. Food Cosmet. Toxicol. 14: 417-419. NAR-A 47: 4886.

1.8-35 Borukh, I.F., Kirbaba, V.I., Demkevnch, L.I., and Bapabash, O.Yu. 1975. On activity duration of garlic bactericidal properties [in Russian]. Izv. Vyssh. Ucheb. Zaved. Pishch. Tekhnol. 1975{1}: 21-23.

1.8-36 Bowers, W.S., and Nishida, R. 1980. Juvocimenes: potent juvenile hormone mimics from sweet basil. Science (USA) 209{4460}: 1030-1032.

1.8-37 Boyzdzhiev, Kh. 1972. Treatment of garden bean seeds with fungicides and antibiotics [in Bulgarian]. Rastit. Zasht. 20{8}: 26-30. HA 44: 388.

1.8-38 Burgett, M. 1980. The use of lemon balm (Melissa officinalis) for attracting honeybee swarms. Bee World 61: 44-46. AA 32: 180.

1.8-39 Chaturvedi, S.N., Siradhana, B.S., and Muralia, R.N. 1974. The influence of cumin seed exudates on fungal spore germination. Plant Soil 40: 49-56.

1.8-40 Chaurasia, S.C., and Kher, A. 1978. Activity of essential oils of three medicinal plants against various pathogenic and nonpathogenic fungi. Indian J. Hosp. Pharm. 15: 139-141. HA 50: 6524.

1.8-41 Cherevatyi, V.S., Vashchenko, T.N., and Shishkov, G.Z. 1980. Comparative evaluation of the antibacterial action of different extracts from Salvia officinalis [in Russian]. Rastit. Resur. 16: 137-139. HA 50: 9409.

1.8-42 Choe, R.S., Kims, S.J., Chung, P.R., and Lee, J.W. 1970. Effect of *Panax* *ginseng* extract on the development of various parasites. Annot. Zool. Jpn. 43: 28-33. Helm.A-A.

1.8-43 Crisan, A., and Hodisan, V. 1980. The possibility of preventing some mycoses of stored fruits and vegetables by using essential oil mixtures [in Romanian]. Stud. Univ. Babes-Bolyai [Ser.] Biol. 25{2}: 22-27. RPP 60: 5247.

1.8-44 Czajkowska, B. 1973. The influence of some active substances of medicinal herbs on stored product mites. Pages 365-369 in M. Daniel and B. Rosicky, eds. Proceedings of the 3rd international congress of acarology, Prague, Czechoslovakia, Aug. 31-Sept. 6, 1971. Dr. W. Junk Pub., The Hague, Neth.

1.8-45 Damjanic, A.F., Durakovic, S., and Juric, Z. 1977. Effect of rosmarine oil on some species of pathogenic yeasts [in Serbo-Croatian]. Acta Biol. Iugosl. Ser. B. 14: 21-25. RMVM 14: 309.

1.8-46 Dankert, J., Tromp, T.F.J., De Vries, H., and Klasen, H.J. 1979. Antimicrobial activity of crude juices of *Allium* *ascalonicum*, *Allium* *cepa* *and* *Allium* *sativum*. Zentralbl. Bakteriol. Parasitenkd. Infektionskr. Hyg. Abt. 1: Orig. Reihe A 245: 229-239.

1.8-47 Dao D., F. 1972. Influence of different crops on the population of nematodes [in Spanish]. Nematropica 2{2}: 30-32. HELM AB-B 42: 758.

1.8-48 Dayal, B., and Purohit, R.M. 1971. Screening of some Indian essential oils for their antifungal properties. Flavour Ind. 2: 484-485.

1.8-49 De Pasquale, A., and Costa, R. 1977. Effects of "*Lippia* *triphylla*" oil on the keeping away reactions conditioned in the rat [in Italian]. Essenze Deriv. Agrum. 47: 400-404. AGRICOLA.

1.8-50 Deb-Kirtaniya, S., Ghosh, M.R., Mitra, S.R., Adityachaudhury, N., and Chatterjee, A. 1980. Note on insecticidal properties of the fruits of chilli. Indian J. Agric. Sci. 50: 510-512. RAE-A 69: 6868.

1.8-51 Deb-Kirtaniya, S., Ghosh, M.R., Adityachaudhury, N., and Chatterjee, A. 1980. Extracts of garlic as possible source of insecticides. Indian J. Agric. Sci. 50{6}: 507-510. Bib.Ag. 45: 63280.

1.8-52 Deshpande, R.S., and Tipnis, H.P. 1977. Insecticidal activity of *Ocimum* *basilicum* Linn. Pesticides 11{5}: 11-12. CA 88: 17266.

1.8-53 Dhaliwal, A.S., and Dhaliwal, G.K. 1971. Inhibition of tobacco mosaic virus multiplication by extracts from *Allium* *cepa* and *Allium* *sativum*. Adv. Front. Plant Sci. 28: 305-310. RPP 52: 637.

1.8-54 Dikshit, A., Singh, A.K., and Dixit, S.N. 1980. Fungitoxic activity of some essential oils against *Helminthosporium* *oryzae*. Indian Perfum. 24{4}: 222-223.

1.8-55 Dobrochinskaya, I.B. 1975. How to be free of the gladiolus thrips [in Russian]. Zashch. Rast. 1975{7}: 61. RAE-A 64: 7408.

1.8-56 Dwivedi, R., and Dwivedi, R.S. 1972. Rhizosphere microflora of coriander with emphasis on fungistasis. Ann. Inst. Pasteur, Paris 122: 455-461.

1.8-57 Dwivedi, R. 1972. The effect of fungal metabolites and of coriander seeds on the growth of pathogenic bacteria. Ann. Inst. Pasteur, Paris 123: 311-314. AGRICOLA.

1.8-58 El-Malek, Y.A., El-Leithy, M.A., Reda, F.A., and Khalil, M. 1973. Antimicrobial principles in leaves of Lawsonia inermis L. Zentralbl. Bakteriol. Parasitenkd. Infektionsk. Hyg. Abt. 2 128: 61-67.

1.8-59 El-Sayed, S.A., and El-Wazeri, S.M. 1977. Application of an induced phytoalexin formed by pepper fruits to control rot incidence in irradiated potatoes. Egypt. J. Hortic. 4: 157-163.

1.8-60 Eom, C.K., and Joo, C.N. 1978. The effect of Korean ginseng tea on the early phase of plant growth. Hanguk Senghwa Hakhoe Chi 11: 227-238.

1.8-61 Fliermans, C.B. 1973. Inhibition of Histoplasma capsultum by garlic. Mycopathologia et Mycologia Applicata 50: 227-231.

1.8-62 Freedman, B., Nowak, L.J., Kwolek, W.F., Berry, E.C., and Guthrie, W.D. 1979. A bioassay for plant-derived pest control agents using the European corn borer. J. Econ. Entomol. 72: 541-545.

1.8-63 Gavrilov, K.I., Gromova, L.I., and Malyshev, A.A. 1972. On the stimulating and inhibiting (phytoncidal) properties of Teberde ginseng [in Russian]. Trudy Teberdinskogo Gosudarstvennogo Zapovednika 1972{8}: 198-203. HA 43: 6305.

1.8-64 Goulart, E.G., Jourdan, M.C., Brazil, R.P., Brazil, B.G., Cosendey, A.E., Barr, M., Do Carmo, E.C., and Gilbert, B. 1977. Ecological control of hookworm and strongyoidiasis. J. Helminthol. 51: 131-132.

1.8-65 Grospicova, A., and Curda, D. 1971. The study of antimicrobial effects of some substances of phytoncide character. Sb. Vys. Sk. Chem-Technol. Praze Potraviny 1971{E32}: 53-71. HA 44: 1905.

1.8-66 Gupta, V.K. 1974. Effect of seed of Trigonella foenum-graecum on the growth of its Rhizobium. Indian Phytopathol. 27: 403-404.

1.8-67 Hill, A.W., and Rivers, J.P.W. 1972. The antibacterial action of spices and its nutritional implications. J. Sci. Food Agric. 23: 545-546 (Abstr.)

1.8-68 Hoffman, G.R., and Hazlett, D.L. 1977. Effects of aqueous Artemisia extracts and volatile substances on germination of selected species. J. Range Manage. 30: 134-137.

1.8-69 Hovadik, A.,, and Chladek, M. 1974. The antimicrobial activity of the essential oils of some aromatic plants [in Czech]. Bulletin, Vyzkumny Ustav Zelinarsky Olomouc 1974{18}: 61-71. HA 46: 4933.

1.8-70 Ingham, J.L. 1977. An isoflavin phytoalexin from leaves of Glycyrrhiza glabra. Phytochemistry 16: 1457-1458.

1.8-71 Jain, S.R., and Jain, M.L. 1973. Investigations on the essential oil of Ocimum basilicum. Planta Med. 24: 286-289. HA 44: 4210.

1.8-72 Jain, S.R., and Jain, M.R. 1973. Effect of some common essential oils on pathogenic fungi. Planta Med. 24: 127-132. HA 44: 5985.

1.8-73 Jamal, A., and Ghouse, A.K.M. 1977. Influence of certain oil cakes on the germination process of Phaseolus aureus seeds. Acta Agron. Acad. Sci. Hung. 26: 273-274.

1.8-74 Jonas, H. 1975. Bleaching of chlorophyll by digitoxin. Z. Pflanzenphysiol. 77: 42-53.

1.8-75 Joshi, R.D., and Prakash, J. 1978. Inhibition of sugar cane mosaic virus by plant rhizome extracts. Int. Sugar J. 80{954}: 173-174. HA 48: 10164.

1.8-76 Kakabadze, E.V., and Turchinskaya, T.N. 1972. Phytoncidal properties of some sub-tropical plants [in Russian]. Tr. Sukhum. Bot. Sada 1972{18}: 92-98. HA 44: 3401.

1.8-77 Kashyap, N.P., Gupta, V.K., and Kaushal, A.N. 1974. Mentha spicata, a promising protectant to stored wheat against Sitophilus oryzae. Bull. Grain Technol. 12: 41-44. RAE-A 64: 1566.

1.8-78 Kaul, V.K., Nigam, S.S., and Dhar, K.L. 1976. Antimicrobial activities of the essential oils of Artemisia absinthium Linn., Artemisia vestita Wall, and Artemisia vulgaris Linn. Indian J. Pharm. 38: 21-22. HA 47: 1838.

1.8-79 Kaul, V.K., Nigam, S.S., and Banerjee, A.K. 1978. Insecticidal activity of some essential oils. Indian J. Pharm. 40: 22. HA 48: 10813.

1.8-80 Khanin, M.L., Prokopchuk, A.F., Nikolaeva, L.A., Krivonazova, L.V., and Smetanin, Iu. I. 1972. Antibacterial properties of extracts from roots of Valeriana officinalis extracted by compressed carbonic gas [in Russian]. Pages 101-103 in B.E. Aizenmann, ed. Fitonsidy; rezul'taty ierspektivy i zadachi issledovanii. Soveshchanie po probleme fitontisidov, 6th, Kiev, 1969. Naukova Dumka, Kiev, USSR. AGRICOLA.

1.8-81 Khanna, P., Mohan, S., and Nag, T.N. 1971. Antimicrobials from plant tissue cultures. Lloydia 34: 168-169.

1.8-82 Kharchenko, S.N., and Sytnik, N.I. 1973. Fungistatic action of Xanthium strumarium and Taraxacum officinale on phytopathogenic fungi [in Russian]. Pages 121-122 in B.E. Aizenmann, S.I. Zelepukha and A.K. Negrash, eds. Fitontsidy; eksperimental'nye issledovaniia, voprosy teorii i praktiki. Soveshchanie po probleme fitonsidov, 7th, Kiev, 1973. Naukova Dumka, Kiev, USSR. AGRICOLA.

1.8-83 Kim, N.G., and Cho, Y.D. 1978. Effects of the ginseng saponin fraction on growth of microorganisms (II). Hanguk Saenghwa Hakhoe Chi 11{4}: 16 (Abstr.).

1.8-84 Kokate, C.K., and Varma, K.C. 1971. A note on the antimicrobial activity of volatile oils of Cymbopogon nardus (Linn.) Rendle and Cymbopogon citratus Stapf. Sci. Cult. 37: 196-198.

1.8-85 Komala, Z., Oswiecimska, M., and Strzalka, M. 1979. The effect of extracts of Asperula odorata on Paramecium primaurelia and Lepidium sativum. Folia Biol. (Krakow) 27{1}: 17-23. AGRICOLA.

1.8-86 Lahariya, A.K., and Rao, J.T. 1979. In vitro antimicrobial studies of the essential oils of Cyperus scariosus and Ocimum basilicum. Indian Drugs 16: 150-152. AGRICOLA.

1.8-87 Lalonde, R.T., Wong, C.F., Hofstead, S.J., Morris, C.D., and Gardner, L.C. 1980. N-(2-methylpropyl)-(E,E)- 2,4-decadienamide: a mosquito larvicide from Achillea millefolium L. J. Chem. Ecol. 6: 35-48.

1.8-88 Latheef, M.A., and Irwin, R.D. 1979. The effect of companionate planting on lepidopteran pests of cabbage. Can. Entomol. 111: 863-864.

1.8-89 Lee-Stadelmann, O.Y. 1979. Cell permeability as affected by Panax ginseng root extracts. Plant Physiol. 63 (5 Suppl.): 125 (Abstr.).

1.8-90 Lichtenstein, E.P., Liang, T.T., Schulz, K.R., Schnoes, H.K., and Carter, G.T. 1974. Insecticidal and synergistic components isolated from dill plants. J. Agric. Food Chem. 22: 658-664.

1.8-91 Liszka, B., Sendra, J., and Starzyk, J. 1977. Fungistatic properties of chosen plant derived compounds. Acta Biol. Cracov. Ser. Bot. 20: 57-65.

1.8-92 Lorber, P., and Muller, W.H. 1980. Volatile growth inhibitors produced by Salvia leucophylla: effects on metabolic activity in mitochondrial suspensions. Comp. Physiol. Ecol. 5{2}: 68-75.

1.8-93 Lorber, P., and Muller, W.H. 1980. Volatile growth inhibitors produced by Salvia leucophylla: effects on cytological activity in Allium cepa. Comp. Physiol. Ecol. 5{2}: 60-67.

1.8-94 Lundgren, L. 1975. Natural plant chemicals acting as oviposition deterrents on cabbage butterflies (Pieris brassicae (L.), P. rapae (L.) and P. napi (L.). Zool. Scr. 4: 253-258.

1.8-95 Mabrouk, S.S., and El-Shayeb, N.M.A. 1980. Inhibition of aflatoxin formation by some spices. Z. Lebensm.-Unters. -Forsch. 171: 344-347. MVM 16: 2364.

1.8-96 MacGregor, J.T., Layton, L.L., and Buttery, R.G. 1974. California bay oil. II. Biological effects of constituents. J. Agric. Food Chem. 22: 777-780.

1.8-97 Malaka, S.L.O. 1972. Some measures applied in the control of termites in parts of Nigeria. Nigerian Entomol. Mag. 2: 137-141. RAE-A 63: 5059.

1.8-98 Mantis, A.J., Karaioannoglou, P.G., Spanos, G.P., and Panetsos, A.G. 1978. The effect of garlic extract on food poisoning bacteria in culture media. I. Staphylococcus aureus. Lebensm. Wiss. Technol. 11: 26-28.

1.8-99 Mantis, A.J., Koidis, P.A., Karaioannoglou, P.G., and Panetsos, A.G. 1979. Effect of garlic extract on food poisoning bacteria. II. Clostridium perfringens. Lebensm. Wiss. Technol. 12: 330-332.

1.8-100 Marcus, C., and Lichtenstein, E.P. 1979. Biologically active components of anise: toxicity and interactions with insecticides in insects. J. Agric. Food Chem. 27: 1217-1223.

1.8-101 Margineanu, C., Hintz, I., Cucu, V., Grecu, L., Cioaca, C., Rosca, M., Hodisan, V., and Tomas, M. 1978. Antimicrobial action of 12 triterpene saponins obtained from indigenous plants [in Rumanian]. Clujul Med. 51: 254-259. HA 50: 4575.

1.8-102 Misra, S.B., and Dixit, S.N. 1976. Fungicidal spectrum of the leaf extract of Allium sativum. Indian Phytopathol. 29: 448-449. RPP 58: 2113.

1.8-103 Misra, S.B., and Dixit, S.N. 1977. Antifungal spectrum of the leaf extract of Allium sativum Linn. Geobios 4: 176. RPP 57: 942.

1.8-104 Misra, S.B., and Dixit, S.N. 1977. Antifungal properties of Allium sativum Linn. Sci. Cult. 43: 487-488.

1.8-105 Mitscher, L., Park, Y.H., Omoto, S., Clark, G.W., III, and Clark, D. 1978. Antimicrobial agents from higher plants, Glycyrrhiza glabra L. (var. Spanish). I. Some antimicrobial isoflavans, isoflavenes, flavanones and isoflavones. Heterocycles 9{11}: 1533-1538. CA 90: 54859.

1.8-106 Mitscher, L.A., Park, Y.H., and Clark, D. 1980. Antimicrobial agents from higher plants. Antimicrobial isoflavanoids and related substances from Glycyrrhiza glabra L. var. typica. J. Nat. Prod. 43: 259-269. HA 51: 683.

1.8-107 Mitscher, L.A., Leu, R.-P., Bathala, M.S., Wu, W.-N., and Beal, J.L. 1972. Antimicrobial agents from higher plants. I. Introduction, rationale, and methodology. Lloydia 35: 157-166.

1.8-108 Moore, G.S., and Atkins, R.D. 1977. The fungicidal and fungistatic effects of an aqueous garlic extract on medically important yeast-like fungi. Mycologia 69: 341-348.

1.8-109 Murakashi, S., Kamikado, T., Chang, C.-F., Sakurai, A., and Tamura, S. 1976. Effects of several components from the leaves of four species of plants on the growth of silkworm larvae [in Japanese]. Jpn. J. Appl. Entomol. Zool. 20: 26-30. RAE-A 65: 1364.

1.8-110 Murthy, N.B.K., and Amonkar, S.V. 1974. Effect of a natural insecticide from garlic (Allium sativum L.) and its synthetic form (diallyl-disulphide) on plant pathogenic fungi. Indian J. Exp. Biol. 12: 208-209.

1.8-111 Nasirov, I.R., Kasumov, F.Yu., and Ibragimov, G.G. 1977. Study of the essential oil of Thymus kotschyamus and its antimicrobial activity [in Russian]. Azerb. Med. Zh. 54{9}: 24-29.

1.8-112 Novak, D. 1974. Note on the use of some plants, plant extracts and oils in insect control [in Czech]. Biologia (Bratislava) 29: 445-447. RAE-B 63: 1103.

1.8-113 Novak, D. 1974. Several experiences from the entomological laboratory OHS Hodonin [in German]. Folia Fac. Sci. Nat. Univ. Purkynianae Brun. 15{43}{1}: 27.

1.8-114 Novak, D. 1979. Mixture of mucilaginous seeds for mosquito larvae control. Biologia (Bratislava) 34: 983-985. RAE-B 68: 2120.

1.8-115 Nawamaki, T., Sakakibara, T., and Ohta, K. 1979. Isolation and identification of lachnophyllum lactone and osthol as repellants against a sea snail. Agric. Biol. Chem. 43{7}: 1603-1604.

1.8-116 Oeda, J., and Kato, J. 1980. Isolation and identification of a senescence-promoting substance from wormwood (Artemisia absinthium L.). Plant Physiol. 66: 246-249.

1.8-117 Osmani, Z., Sighamony, S., and Khan, M.A. 1978. Effect of Marjorana hortensis oil on metamorphosis of Aedes aegypti. Indian J. Exp. Biol. 16: 702-703.

1.8-118 Osmani, Z., Anees, I., and Naidu, M.B. 1972. Insect repellent creams from essential oils. Pesticides 6{3}: 19-21. RAE-B 62: 1905.

1.8-119 Osmani, Z., Anees, I., and Naidu, M.B. 1974. Effect of different temperatures on the repellency of certain essential oils against house flies and mosquitoes. Pesticides 8{9}: 45-47. RAE-B 64: 884.

1.8-120 Osmani, Z., and Sighamony, S. 1980. Effects of certain essential oils on mortality and metamorphosis of Aedes aegypti. Pesticides 14{9}: 15-16. RAE-B 69: 2879.

1.8-121 Pandey, N.D., Singh, S.R., and Tewari, G.C. 1976. Use of some plant powders, oils and extracts as protectants against pulse beetle, Callosobruchus chinensis Linn. Indian J. Entomol. 38: 110-113. RAE-A 67: 325

1.8-122 Papacostea, P., and Petre, N. 1977. The use of Valeriana officinalis root extracts in the studies of soil fungi [in Romanian]. An. Inst. Cercet. Pedol. Agrochim. 42: 109-112. AGRICOLA.

1.8-123 Polishchuk, P.L. 1975. Dill against (vine) mildew [in Russian]. Sadovodstvo (Moscow) 1975{9}: 29. HA 46: 4433.

1.8-124 Polyakov, D.K., Khaidarov, K.M., and Shreter, A.I. 1977. The acaricidal and repellent effect of plants of native flora of the USSR and introduced species on ixodid ticks [in Russian]. Rastit. Resur. 13: 267-275. RAE-B 68: 246.

1.8-125 Pontovich, V.E., Ivanova, O.B., and Marchenko, T.F. 1976. Effect of some phenolic compounds of the placenta of opium poppy on embryogenesis of isolated ovules. Dokl. Bot. Sci. (Engl. Transl.) 226/228: 74-76. Translation of Dokl. Akad. Nauk SSSR 228: 1489-1491, 1976.

1.8-126 Popovici, N. 1973. Effect of volatile herbicides from horseradish on the growth and mitotic activity of maize [in Romanian]. An. Stiint. Univ. 'Al. I. Cuza' Iasi Sect. 2a 19: 359-364. FCA 28: 8045.

1.8-127 Popovici, N. 1974. Herbicidal activity of volatiles from horseradish root on mitosis in meristems of maize at various ages [in Romanian]. An. Stiint. Univ. 'Al. I. Cuza' Iasi Sect. 2a 20: 35-40. FCA 30: 183

1.8-128 Prikhodko, V.A., Mishenkova, E.L., and Meshcheriakov, A.A. 1973. Study of antibiotic activity of Glycyrrhiza glabra L. [in Russian]. Pages 126-131 in B.E. Aizenmann, S.I. Zelepukha and A.K. Negrash, eds.

Fitontsidy; eksperimental'nye issledovaniia, voprosy teorii i praktiki. Soveshchanie po probleme fitontsidov, 7th, Kiev, 1973. Naukova Dumka, Kiev. AGRICOLA.

1.8-129 Prokhorova, Yu. M. 1977. Phytoncidal properties of ground cover plants [in Russian]. Byull. Gl. Bot. Sada 1977{103}: 87-91. HA 48: 3683.

1.8-130 Ramadan, F.M., El-Zanfaly, R.T., El-Wakeil, F.A., and Alian, A.M. 1972. Antibacterial effects of some essential oils. I. Use of agar diffusion method. Chem. Mikrobiol. Technol. Lebensm. 2: 51-55. CA 77: 122532.

1.8-131 Rao, B.G.V.N., and Rao, P.S. 1972. The efficacy of some essential oils on pathogenic fungi. II. Flavour Ind. 3: 368-370.

1.8-132 Rao, B.G.V.N., and Joseph, P.L. 1971. Activity of some essential oils toward phytopathogenic fungi [in German]. Riechst. Aromen Koerperpflegem. 21: 405-406, 408, 410. CA 76: 81621.

1.8-133 Rao, G.S., Sinsheimer, J.E., and Cochran, K.W. 1974. Antiviral activity of triterpenoid saponins containing acylated beta-amyrin aglycones J. Pharm. Sci. 63: 471-473. HA 44: 8935.

1.8-134 Ray, P.G., and Majumdar, S.K. 1976. Antimicrobial activity of some Indian plants. Econ. Bot. 30: 317-320.

1.8-135 Rhoades, H.L. 1976. Effect of Indigofera hirsuta on Belonolaimus longicaudatus, Meloidogyne incognita, and Meloidogyne javanica and subsequent crop yields. Plant Dis. Rep. 60: 384-386.

1.8-136 Roia, F.C., Jr., and Smith, R.A. 1977. The antibacterial screening of some common ornamental plants. Econ. Bot. 31: 28-37.

1.8-137 Rouquayrol, M.Z., Fonteles, M.C., Alencar, J.E., De Abreau Matos, F.J., and Aragao Craveiro, A. 1980. Molluscicidal activity of essential oils from the Brazilian northeast plants [in Portuguese]. Rev. Bras. Pesqui. Med. Biol. 13: 135-144.

1.8-138 Roussel, J.-L., Pellecuer, J., and Andary, C. 1973. Comparative antifungal properties of three Mediterranean Labiates rosemary, savory and thyme [in French]. Trav. Soc. Pharm. Montp. 33: 587-592.

1.8-139 Russell, P.E., and Mussa, A.E.A. 1977. The use of garlic (Allium sativum) extracts to control foot rot of Phaseolus vulgaris caused by Fusarium solani f.sp. phaseoli. Ann. Appl. Biol. 86: 369-372.

1.8-140 Sadykhov, I.A., and Ryabinin, A.K. 1979. The effect of an infusion of Artemisia absinthium on Dictyocaulus filaria larvae and adults [in Russian]. Izv. Akad. Nauk Az. SSR Ser. Biol. Nauk 1979{5}: 84-86. HELM -AB-A 49: 5922.

1.8-141 Sahdev, R.K., Banerjee, S.K., Handa, K.L., and Rao, P.R. 1975. Synthesis of possible pyrethrum synergists: some N-substituted amides of dillapiolic acid. J. Inst. Chem., Calcutta 47(pt. 6): 234-236. CA 84: 150546.

1.8-142 Sangappa, H.K. 1977. Effectiveness of oils as surface protectants against the bruchid, Callosobruchus chinensis Linnaeus infestation on redgram. Mysore J. Agric. Sci. 11: 391-397.   RAE-A 66: 6250.

1.8-143 Sarbhoy, A.K., Varshney, J.L., Maheshwari, M.L., and Saxena, D.B. 1978. Efficacy of some essential oils and their constituents on few ubiquitous molds. Zentralbl. Baketeriol. Parasitenkd. 133: 723-725.

1.8-144 Semenikhin, I.D., and Mush, N.N. 1972. Effect of moisture supply of common valerian on secretion of volatile organic substances into soil and their residual effect on oil-bearing poppy [in Russian]. Fiziol.-Biokhim. Osn. Vzaimodeistviia Rast. Fitotsenozakh 1972{3}: 52-55.

1.8-145 Sharma, O.P., and Kulkarni, S.N. 1975. Inhibitory property of Lawsonia alba Lam. against some plant pathogenic fungi. JNKVV Res. J. 9: 27-30.

1.8-146 Sharma, O.P., and Kulkarni, S.N. 1980. Inhibitory property of Lawsonia alba Lam. against plant pathogenic fungi - II. JNKVV Res. J. 10: 391-392.

1.8-147 Sharma, S.K., and Wattal, B.L. 1979. Efficacy of some mucilaginous seeds as biological control agents against mosquito larvae. J. Entomol. Res. 3: 172-176. RAE-B 69: 2601.

1.8-148 Sharma, V.D., Sethi, M.S., Kumar, A., and Rarotra, J.R. 1977. Antibacterial property of Allium sativum Linn.: in vivo and in vitro studies. Indian J. Exp. Biol. 15: 466-468.

1.8-149 Shcherbanovskii, L.R., Kapelev, I.G., Chirkina, N.N., and Kirmanova, N.F. 1973. Antimicrobial properties of essential oil of dill (Anethum graveolens L.) [in Russian]. Pages 150-152 in B.E. Aizenmann, S.I. Zelepukha and A.K. Negrash, eds. Fitonsidy; eksperimental'nye issledovaniia, voprosy teorii i praktiki. Soveshchanie po probleme fitontsidov, 7th, Kiev, 1973. Naukova Dumka, Kiev, USSR. AGRICOLA.

1.8-150 Shcherbanovskii, L.R., and Kapelev, I.G. 1975. Volatile oil of dill (Anethum graveolens L.) as an inhibitor of yeast and Lactobacillaceae. Appl. Biochem. Microbiol. (Engl. Transl.) 11: 426-427. Translation of Prikl. Biokhim. Mikrobiol. 11: 476-477, 1975.

1.8-151 Sidorov, N.G., Stolbov, N.M., and Platukhina, N.I. 1977. The effect of ethereal oils of higher plants on the agent of varroatosis of bees [in Russian]. Veterinariya (Moscow) USSR 1977{7}: 65-68. RAE-A 66: 436.

1.8-152 Simeon de Bouchberg, M., Allegrini, J., Bessiere, C., Attisso, M., Passet, J., and Granger, R. 1976. Microbiological properties of essential oils of Thymus vulgaris Linnaeus chemotypes [in French]. Riv. Ital. Essenze, Profumi, Piante Off., Aromi, Saponi, Cosmet., Aerosol 58{10}: 527-536 CA 86: 84201.

1.8-153 Singh, A.K., Dikshit, Anupam, Sharma, M.L., and Dixit, S.N. 1980. Fungitoxic activity of some essential oils. Econ. Bot. 34: 186-190.

1.8-154 Singh, D.B., Singh, S.P., and Gupta, R.C. 1979. Antifungal effect of volatiles from seeds of some Umbelliferae. Trans. Br. Mycol. Soc. 73: 349-350.

1.8-155 Singh, L., and Joshi, R. 1977. The inhibitory activity of some plant juices and chemicals on the infectivity of potato virus X (PVX). Geobios (Jodhpur) 4{3}: 116-117.

1.8-156 Stoessl, A., Unwin, C.H., and Ward, E.W.B. 1972. Postinfectional inhibitors from plants. I. Capsidiol, an antifungal compound from Capsicum frutescens. Phytopathol. Z. 74: 141-152.

1.8-157 Sukul, N.C., Das, P.K., and De, G.C. 1974. Nematicidal action of some edible crops. Nematologica 20: 187-191. HA 45: 3926.

1.8-158 Supavarn, P., Knapp, F.W., and Sigafus, R. 1974. Biologically active plant extracts for control of mosquito larvae. Mosq. News 34: 398-402.

1.8-159 Szalontai, M., Verzar-Petri, G., and Florian, E. 1977. Study of the antimycotic effects of biologically active components of Matricaria chamomilla L. [in German]. Parfuem. Kosmet. 58{5}: 121-127. CA 87: 96715.

1.8-160 Szalontai, M., Verzar-Petri, G., and Florian, E. 1976. Antifungal effect of the biologically active components of Matricaria chamomilla L. [in Hungarian]. Acta Pharm. Hung. 46{5-6}: 232-247. RMVM 13: 893.

1.8-161 Tansey, M.R., and Appleton, J.A. 1975. Inhibition of fungal growth by garlic extract. Mycologia 67: 409-413.

1.8-162 Tarnopol, J.H., and Ball, H.J. 1972. A survey of some common Midwestern plants for juvenile hormone activity. J. Econ. Entomol. 65: 980-982.

1.8-163 Tayal, M.S., Maheshwari, D.K., and Goel, A.K. 1980. Effect of the diseased and healthy plant tissue extract of coriander on germination and radicle growth of mungbean (Phaseolus aureus Roxb.). Indian J. Bot. 3: 194-196. AGRICOLA.

1.8-164 Thind, T.S., and Dahiya, M.S. 1977. Inhibitory effects of essential oils of four medicinal plants against some keratinophilic fungi. East. Pharm. 20: 147-148. HA 48: 8522.

1.8-165 Thorsell, W., Mikiver, A., Mikiver, M., and Malm, E. 1979. Plant extracts as protectants against disease-causing insects [in Swedish]. Entomol. Tidskr. 100{3/4}: 138-141. RAE-B 68: 2262.

1.8-166 Tomar, S.S., Maheshawari, M.L., and Mukerjee, S.K. 1979. Syntheses and synergistic activity of some pyrethrum synergists from dillapiole. Agric. Biol. Chem. 43: 1479-1483.

1.8-167 Towers, G.H.N., Wat, C.K., Graham, E.A., Bandoni, R.J., Chan, G.F.Q., Mitchell, J.C., and Lam, J. 1977. Ultraviolet-mediated antibiotic activity of species of Compositae caused by polyacetylenic compounds. Lloydia 40: 487-498.

1.8-168 Tripathi, R.D., Srivastava, H.S., and Dixit, S.N. 1980. Regulation of nitrate reductase, soluble and protein nitrogen by lawsone in Helminthosporium oryzae Breda de Haan. Experientia 36: 960-961.

1.8-169 Tripathi, R.D., Srivastava, H.S., and Dixit, S.N. 1978. A fungitoxic principle from the leaves of Lawsonia inermis Lam. Experientia 34: 51-52.

1.8-170 Tripathi, R.D., Tripathi, S.C., and Dixit, S.N. 1980. Structure activity relationship amongst some fungi toxic alpha-naphthquinones of angiosperm origin. Agric. Biol. Chem. 44: 2483-2485.

1.8-171 Trivedi, P.C., Bhatnagar, A., and Tiagi, B. 1978. Control of root-knot nematode on Capsicum annuum by application of oil-cakes. Indian Phytopathol. 31{1}: 75-76.

1.8-172 Trivedi, V.P., and Mann, A.S. 1972. Vegetable drugs regulating fat metabolism in Caraka (Lekhaniya dravyas). Q. J. Crude Drug Res. 12{4}: 1988-1999.

1.8-173 Tucker, A.O. 1979. A garden of feline delights. Herbarist 45: 34-42.

1.8-174 Tynecka, Z., and Gos, Z. 1975. The fungistatic activity of garlic (Allium sativum L.) in vitro. Ann. Univ. Mariae Curie-Sklodowska Sect. D 30: 5-13. RMVM 12: 1239.

1.8-175 Urs, N.V.R.R., and Dunleavy, J.M. 1974. Bactericidal activity of horseradish peroxidase on Xanthomonas phaseoli var. sojensis. Phytopathology 64: 542-545.

1.8-176 Verma, G.S., Verma, H.N., Srivastava, K.M., and Mukerji, K. 1975. Properties and mode of action of a tobacco mosaic virus inhibitor from seed extract of Lawsonia alba. New Bot. 2: 109-113.

1.8-177 Vichkanova, S.A., Rubinchik, M.A., Adgina, V.V., Izosimova, S.B., Makarova, L.V., Patudin, A.V., and Pakaln, D.A. 1974. Antimicrobial activity of root extracts of Salvia spp. [in Russian]. Rastit. Resur. 10: 389-395. HA 45: 2743

1.8-178 Ward, E.W.B., and Stoessl, A. 1972. Postinfectional inhibitors from plants. III. Detoxification of capsidiol, an antifungal compound from peppers. Phytopathology 62: 1186-1187.

1.8-179 West, L.G., Nonnamaker, B.J., and Greger, J.L. 1979. Effect of ammoniated glycyrrhizin on the mineral utilization of rats. J. Food Sci. 44: 1558-1559. NAR-B 50: 3545.

1.8-180 Wheeler, A.W. 1980. Auxin-like growth activity of 3-phenylpropionitrile from watercress (Nasturtium officinale R.Br.). Ann. Bot. (London) 46{1}: 1-5.

1.8-181 Witkowski, W. 1972. Investigations into the insecticidal effect of garlic (Allium sativum Linne) against the Colorado potato beetle (Leptinotarsa decemlineata Say) [in Polish]. Biul. Inst. Ochr. Rosl. 54: 365-372. RAE-A 64: 513.

1.8-182 Yajima, T., and Munakata, K. 1979. Phloroglucinol-type furocoumarins, a group of potent naturally-occurring insect antifeedants. Agric. Biol. Chem. 43: 1701-1706.

1.8-183 Zalkow, L.H., Gordon, M.M., and Lanir, N. 1979. Antifeedants from rayless goldenrod and oil of pennyroyal: toxic effects for the fall armyworm. J. Econ. Entomol. 72: 812-815.

1.8-184 Zuelsdorff, N.T., and Burkholder, W.E. 1978. Toxicity and repellency of Umbelliferae plant compounds to the granary weevil, Sitophilus granarius. Proc. North Cent. Branch Entomol. Soc. Am. 33: 28 (Abstr.). RAE- A 68: 6173.

BOTANY

2.1 Biology

2.1-1 Antoun, M.D., and Roberts, M.F. 1975. Phosphatases in the latex of Papaver somniferum. Phytochemistry 14: 1275-1278.

2.1-2 Antoun, M.D., and Roberts, M.F. 1974. Methylating and demethylating enzymes in Papaver somniferum latex. J. Pharm. Pharmacol. 26 (Suppl.): 114P-115P.

2.1-3 Antoun, M.D., and Roberts, M.F. 1973. Phosphomonoesterases in Papaver somniferum latex. J. Pharm. Pharmacol. 25 (Suppl.): 114 (Abstr.).

2.1-4 Arak, E., Mayaeorg, U., and Pehk, T. 1980. Changes in the composition of essential oil of chamomile [in Russian]. Tartu Riikliku Ulik. Toim. 1980{523}: 6-18. HA 51: 2975.

2.1-5 Arak, E.H., Tammeorg, J.K., and Myaeorg, U.J. 1980. Dynamics of some components of chamomile essential oil [in Russian]. Tartu Riikliku Ulik. Toim. 1980{523}: 19-32. HA 51: 4933.

2.1-6 Archakova, L.I. 1978. Biological and economic features of parsley on the Kola peninsula [in Russian]. Byull. Vses. Inst. Rasteniovod. 1978{82}: 46-50. PBA 50: 8933.

2.1-7 Asllani, U. 1974. Biochemical data on Origanum L. and its essential oil [in Albanian]. Bul. Univ. Shteteror Trianes, Ser. Shkencat. Nat. 28{2}: 61-82. AGRICOLA.

2.1-8 Asllani, U. 1973. Albanian thyme varieties and their essential oils [in Albanian]. Bul. Shkencave Natyr., Univ. Shtereror Tiranes 27: 111-129. CA 80: 149025.

2.1-9 Azcon, R., Azcon-G de Aguilar, C., and Barea, J.M. 1978. Effects of plant hormones present in bacterial cultures on the formation and responses to endomycorrhiza. New Phytol. 80: 359-364.

2.1-10 Barsegyan, S.G., Barsegian, S.G., Avakian, T.T., Barseghyan, S.G., and Avagyan, T.T. 1974. A study of species of essential oil bearing geranium - Pelargonium capitatum and P. radula [in Russian]. Biol. Zh. Arm. 27{5}: 111-112 (Abstr.). PBA 45: 559.

2.1-11 Bednarova, J., and Bednar, V. 1979. Calcium, magnesium and sodium levels in the above ground biomass of some plant populations from the Tatra National Park [in Czech]. Acta Univ. Palacki. Olomuc., Fac. Rerum Nat. 63(Biol. 19): 71-80. CA 93: 235164.

2.1-12 Beringer, H., and Dompert, W.U. 1976. Fatty acid- and tocopherol-pattern in oil seeds. Fette: Seifen: Anstrichm. 78: 228-231.

2.1-13 Bouniols, A., Delecolle, M.-T., Kronenberger, J., and Margara, J. 1973. Changes in the free amino acid composition of chicory roots under different conditions inducing the vegetative or reproductive development of the buds [in French]. C. R. Hebd. Seances Acad. Sci. Ser. D 276: 2797-2800.

2.1-14 Buchecker, R., Liaaen-Jensen, S., and Eugster, C.H. 1976. Reinvestigation of original taraxanthin samples. Helv. Chim. Acta 59: 1360-1364.

2.1-15 Champagnol, F. 1976. Carbonic anhydrase activity in the roots of some calcifuge plants [in French]. C.R. Hebd. Seances Acad. Sci. Ser. D 282: 1273-1275.

2.1-16 Cherezhanova, L.V., and Aleksakhin, R.M. 1975. The biological effect of an increased ionizing level of radiation and the processes of radioadaptation in populations of herbaceous plants [in Russian]. Zh. Obshch. Biol. 36: 303-311.

2.1-17 Chkhmaidze, D.Kh., Sardzhveladze, G.P., and Dzhugeli, R.I. 1976. Variability of essential oil content in the leaves of laurel for seed reproduction [in Russian]. Subtrop. Kul't. 1976{5/6}: 156-159.

2.1-18 Conklin, A.R., Jr., and Biswas, P.K. 1978. A survey of asymbiotic nitrogen fixation in the rhizosphere of weeds. Weed Sci. 26: 148-150.

2.1-19 Corbet, S.A. 1978. Bee visits and the nectar of Echium vulgare L. and Sinapis alba L. Ecol. Entomol. 3: 25-37.

2.1-20 Dagite, S.Yu., and Yuknyavichene, G.K. 1979. Biological and biochemical characteristics of Origanum vulgare L. cultivated in the Kaunas Botanical Garden. (1. Phenology of flowering and seed germination) [in Russian]. Liet. TSR Mokslu Akad. Darb. Ser. C 1979{2}: 21-26.

2.1-21 De Pasquale, A., and Silvestri, R. 1975. The active principle content of different parts of Matricaria chamomilla [in Italian]. Essenze Deriv. Agrum. 45: 292-298. HA 47: 6843.

2.1-22 Dhindsa, K.S., and Gupta, S.K. 1974. Variability in chemical composition of raya (Brassica juncea Coss.). Haryana Agric. Univ. J. Res. 4: 192-195. FCA 29: 6725.

2.1-23 Egler, F.E. 1973. The hybrid nature of Monarda media Willd. Castanea 38: 209-214.

2.1-24 Eksuzyan, A.A. 1972. Dynamics of the accumulation of essential oil and eugenol by basil [in Russian]. Maslo-Zhir. Prom. 38{1}: 25-26. CA 76: 117419.

2.1-25 Elgamal, M.H.A., El-Tawil, B.A.H., and Fayez, M.B.E. 1974. The C2 C3 glycol derivatives of glycyrrhetic acid. Tetrahedron 30: 4083-4088.

2.1-26 Ermakov, A.I., and Yarosh, N.P. 1976. Peculiarities and variability of oil in oilseed crops of the USSR [in Russian]. Tr. Prikl. Bot. Genet. Sel. 56{3}: 3-56. FCA 30: 4168.

2.1-27 Esilai, A. 1978. Variability in saffron (_Crocus_
Experientia 34: 725.

2.1-28 Farley, D.R., and Howland, V. 1980. The natural variation
pulegone content in various oils of peppermint. J. Sci. Food Ag.
31: 1143-1151.

2.1-29 Fehr, D. 1980. On the essential oil of _Levisticum officinale_. I.
Investigations on the oil from fruit, leaves, stems and roots [in
German]. Planta Med. 1980(Suppl.): 34-40.

2.1-30 Fikenscher, L.H., Hegnauer, R., and Ruijgrok, H.W.L. 1980.
Distribution of hydrocyanic acid in cormophytes. Part 14. New
observations on cyanogenic compounds in the Compositae [in German].
Planta Med. 40: 202-211.

2.1-31 Florya, V.N. 1971. Coumarin level in the fruit of some species of
Umbelliferae [in Russian]. Izv. Akad. Nauk Mold. SSR, Ser. Biol. Khim.
Nauk 1971{6}: 77-80. CA 76: 151014.

2.1-32 Fonin, V.S., and Sheberstov, V.V. 1972. Biological
characteristics of foxgloves and the role of external factors in their
glycoside accumulation. Farmatsiya (Moscow) 21{3}: 86-89.

2.1-33 Forsen, K. 1979. Aroma constituents of _Angelica archangelica_.
Variations in the composition of the essential root oil of strains of
var. _norvegica_ and var. _sativa_. Turun Yliopiston Julk., Sar. A2 62:
1-7. CA 93: 22624.

2.1-34 Franz, C., and Glasl, H. 1976. Information on the essential oils
of parsley. II. Comparative investigations of fruit- leaf- and
root-oils of some parsley varieties [in German]. Qual. Plant. Plant
Foods Hum. Nutr. 25: 253-262.

2.1-35 Fratiglioni, P., Giachetti, D., and Taddei, I. 1976. Qualitative
and quantitative variations in essential oil in relation to flower
colour: studies on _Lavandula officinalis_ var. _delphinensis_ [in
Italian]. Riv. Ital. Essenze Profumi Piante Off. Aromi Saponi Cosmet.
Aerosol 58: 609-611. HA 48: 1657.

2.1-36 Freeman, G.G., and Mossadeghi, N. 1972. Studies on sulphur
nutrition, flavour and allyl isothiocyanate formation in _Brassica
juncea_ (L.) Coss. and Czern. (brown mustard). J. Sci. Food Agric. 23:
1335-1345.

2.1-37 Fujita, S., Asami, Y., and Nozaki, K. 1980. The constituents of
the essential oils from _Foeniculum vulgare_ Miller. Miscellaneous
contributions to the essential oil of the plants from various
territories. Part XLVI [in Japanese]. Nippon Nogei Kagaku Kaishi 54:
765-767

2.1-38 Gawlowska, M., and Sendra, J. 1974. Research on bisabolol in
azulate and selected oleic raw materials [in Polish]. Farm. Pol.
30{2}: 131-135. CA 81: 96375.

2.1-39 Georgiev, E., Dimitrov, D., and Genov, N. 1973. Comparative study
of oils from the flowers and pedicels of _Lavandula vera_ [in
Bulgarian]. Nauchni Tr., Vissh Inst. Khranit. Vkusova Prom-st.,
Plovdiv 20{1}: 107-112. CA 83: 168313.

-40 Gliozheni, E. 1974. Biochemical considerations on coriander and its oil [in Albanian]. Bul. Shkencave Nat., Univ. Shteteror Tiranes 28{3}: 41-50. CA 83: 15477.

2.1-41 Gomez-Serranillos, M., and San Roman, L. 1975. Study of the biological evaluation of the genus Digitalis [in Spanish]. An. Inst. Bot. A.J. Cavinilles 32: 659-665.

2.1-42 Gorin, A.G., and Yakovlev, A.I. 1975. Products of the enzymic hydrolysis of Matricaria chamomilla polysaccharides [in Russian]. Sb. Nauchn. Tr., Ryazan Med. Inst. 50: 9-12. CA 84: 79626.

2.1-43 Grashchenkov, A.E. 1973. Study of Mentha piperita and Mentha sachalinensis in the Leningrad region [in Russian]. Pages 199-203 in K. Jankevicius, ed. Poleznye rasteniia Pribaltiiskikh respublik i Belorussii. Nauchnaia konferentisiia po issledovaniiu i obogashcheni, lu rastitel'nykh resurov pribaltiiskikh respublik i Belorussii, 2nd, Vilna, 1973. AGRICOLA.

2.1-44 Gray, E., McGehee, E.M., and Carlisle, D.F. 1973. Seasonal variation in flowering of common dandelion. Weed Sci. 21: 230-232.

2.1-45 Grigoryants, L.G. 1980. Changes in anthocyanins in leaves and shoots of laurel [in Russian]. Tr. Sukhum. Bot. Sada 1980{26}: 60-68. HA 51: 6479.

2.1-46 Grob, K., and Matile, P. 1980. Compartmentation of ascorbic acid in vacuoles of horseradish root cells. Note on vacuolar peroxidase. Z Pflanzenphysiol. 98: 235-243. CA 93: 128822.

2.1-47 Han, B.H., and Woo, L.K. 1975. Chemical and biochemical aspects of dammarane triterpene glycosides of Korean ginseng. Pages 32-46 in Terpenoids, proceedings of symposium on terpenoids, Seoul, October 5, 1974. Natural Products Research Institute, Seoul National University, Seoul, Korea. CA 84: 98995.

2.1-48 Harborne, J.B., and Saleh, N.A.M. 1971. Flavonol glycoside variation in fennel, Foeniculum vulgare. Phytochemistry 10: 399-400.

2.1-49 Hart, J.W., and Sabnis, D.D. 1976. Colchicine binding activity in extracts of higher plants. J. Exp. Bot. 27: 1353-1360.

2.1-50 Heinrich, G. 1977. Fine structure and the essential oil of a certain type of gland hair in Monarda fistulosa [in German]. Biochem. Physiol. Pflanz. (BPP) 171: 17-24.

2.1-51 Iaskonis, Iu.A. 1972. Biological and biochemical characteristics of Mentha piperita. 2. Biochemical characteristics [in Russian]. Liet TSR Mokslu Akad. Darb. Ser. C 1972{4}: 53-60. AGRICOLA.

2.1-52 Ilieva, S., Peneva, P., Mateeva, D., and Dimitova, S. 1976. The influence of grafting on the accumulation of santonin in the Artmesia genus. Dokl. Bolg. Akad. Nauk 29: 1661-1664. HA 47: 7779.

2.1-53 Ivanova, L.N., and Gogiya, V.T. 1973. Changes in essential oil accumulation in some geranium species [in Russian]. Subtrop. Kul't. 1973{1}: 160-164. HA 44: 663.

2.1-54 Jimenez Misas, C.A., Rojas Hernandez, N.M., and Lopez Abraham,

A.M. 1979. The biological assessment of Cuban plants. 5. [in Spanish]. Rev. Cubana Med. Trop. 31: 37-43.

2.1-55 Joergensen, L.B., Behnke, H.-D., and Mabry, T.J. 1977. Protein-accumulatin G cells and dilated cisternae of the endoplasmic reticulum in three glucosinolate-containing genera: Armoracia, Capparis, Drypetes. Planta 137: 215-224.

2.1-56 Josefsson, E. 1972. Variation of pattern and content of glucosinolates in seed of some cultivated Cruciferae. Z. Pflanzenzuecht. 68: 113-123.

2.1-57 Kapelev, I.G. 1974. Studies on catmint (Nepeta) as an essential oil plant [in Russian]. Byull. Gos. Nikitsk. Bot. Sada 1974{1}: 34-37. HA 45: 1888.

2.1-58 Kapyla, M. 1978. Amount and type of nectar sugar in some wild flowers in Finland. Ann. Bot. Fenn. 15{2}: 85-88. CA 89: 193862.

2.1-59 Kas'yanov, G.I., Shaftan, E.A., and Klimova, E.S. 1977. An investigation of CO2 extracts from the roots and rhizomes of Potentilla erecta and Archangelica officinalis. Chem. Nat. Compd. (Engl. Transl.) 13: 94-95. Translation of Khim. Prir. Soedin. 1977{1}: 108-109.

2.1-60 Kasumov, F.Yu. 1975. Study of the biology and dynamics of accumulation of essential oils in thyme species grown on Apsheron Peninsula [in Russian]. Izv. Akad. Nauk Az. SSR Ser. Biol. Nauk 1975{2}: 16-22.

2.1-61 Katoch, P.C., Bhardwaj, S.D., and Kaushal, A.N. 1980. Genetic evaluation for herbage yield and essential oil content in some collections of Ocimum basilicum Linn. Indian For. 106: 427-430. Bib.Ag. 46: 20323.

2.1-62 Katyuzhanskaya, A.N. 1977. The composition of organic acids of CO2 extracts of some spice-aromatic plants. Chem. Nat. Compd. (Engl. Transl.) 13: 643-646. Translation of Khim. Prir. Soedin. 1977{6}: 763-767.

2.1-63 Kaurov, I.A., Min'ko, I.F., and Budkevich, T.A. 1975. Studies on contents of amino acid in leaves, roots and root exudates of some crops [in Belorussian]. Vestsi Akad. Navuk BSSR Ser. Biyal. Navuk. 1975{1}: 25-29. FCA 28: 8463.

2.1-64 Kaushal, P.K., Shrivas, S.R., and Gangrade, S.K. 1973. A note on variation in oil and protein content in seeds of capsules borne at different nodes of Sesamum plant (Sesamum indicum Linn.). JNKVV Res. J. 7: 190-191. AGRICOLA.

2.1-65 Khan, M.I. 1972. Distribution of peroxidase in regenerating root segments of Taraxacum officinale Web. Pak. J. Bot. 4: 99-110.

2.1-66 Kharchenko, L.N. 1977. Lipids in the seeds of irradiated plants of mustard and sunflower in the first and second generations [in Russian]. Tsitol. Genet. 11: 419-422. PBA 48: 2605.

2.1-67 Khodzhimatov, K.Kh., Sagatov, S.S., and Khaidmukhamedov, L.P. 1971. Dynamics of the accumulation of essential oils in Origanum tutthanthum [in Russian]. Uzb. Biol. Zh. 1971{6}: 12-13. AGRICOLA.

2.1-68 Khodzhimatov, K.Kh., and Ramazanova, N. 1975. Certain biological characteristics and changes in the content and composition of the essential oil of Hyssopus officinalis grown in the Tashkent region [in Russian]. Rastit. Resur. 11: 238-242. HA 45: 9995.

2.1-69 Khrzhanovskii, V.G., Patudin, A.V., and Pyzhov, V. Kh. 1977. Protein and amino acid content of Salvia seeds [in Russian]. Byull. Gl. Bot. Sada 1977{103}: 74-78. HA 48: 3892.

2.1-70 Kiselev, V.P., and Voloshina, D.A. 1975. Biological characteristics and content of sapogenins in fenugreek grown in the Moscow region [in Russian]. Rastit. Resur. 11: 384-387.

2.1-71 Kocurik, S. 1979. Variability of essential oil and chamazulene content in chamomile (Matricaria chamomilla) [in Slovak]. Pol'nohospodarstvo 25: 67-75. HA 49: 6965.

2.1-72 Kotaeva, D.V., and Chkhubianishvili, E.I. 1978. The content of protein and nitrous compounds in the leaves of dioecious plants [in Russian]. Soobshch. Akad. Nauk Gruz. SSR 90: 677-680.

2.1-73 Kowal, T., and Pic, S. 1971. Dynamics of oil accumulation in Levisticum officinale [in Polish]. Pr. Kom. Farm. Poznan. Tow. Przyj. Nauk 9: 45-56. CA 76: 37337.

2.1-74 Kuiper, D., and Kuiper, P.J.C. 1978. Lipid composition of the roots of Plantago species: response to alteration of the level of mineral nutrition and ecological significance. Physiol. Plant. 44: 81-86.

2.1-75 Kulikova, N.T. 1975. Variability of the chemical composition of some herbs and flavoring vegetables from the region north of the Arctic Circle [in Russian]. Byull. Vses. Inst. Rastenievod. 52: 58-69. AGRICOLA.

2.1-76 Kulikov, G.V., and Ivantsova, Z.V. 1977. Changes in the leaf pigments of evergreen and deciduous woody plants in the Crimea [in Russian]. Bot Zh. (Leningrad) 62{7}: 1053-1062.

2.1-77 Kuzina, E.F. 1975. Some biological and biochemical characteristics of coriander grown in the Leningrad region [in Russian]. Byull. Vyses. Inst. Rastenievod. 1975{47}: 68-70. HA 46: 7942.

2.1-78 Ladygina, E.Va. 1972. Investigation of the localization of coumarins in plant tissues [in Russian]. Postep Dziedzinie Leku Rosl. Pr. Ref. Dosw. Wygloszone Symp. 1970: Herba Pol. Suppl. 1972: 94-97.

2.1-79 Logvinov, V.A., Volodicheva, L.F., Dedukh, A.Ya., Logvinova, A.P., and Sunkin, V.M. 1975. Changes in the essential oil content and quality of ripening coriander fruits [in Russian]. Tr. Vses. Nauchno-Issled. Inst. Efirnomaslichn. Kul't. 8: 18-24. HA 47: 7759.

2.1-80 Lombard, A., Cassone, M.C., Damonte, A., and Tourn, M.L. 1971. The soluble carbohydrates in the leaves of Artemisia absinthium L. at various stages of vegetative life, in plants grown on the plains and in the mountains [in Italian]. Atti Accad. Sci. Torino Cl. Sci. Fis. Mat. Nat. 105: 769-783.

2.1-81 MacKenzie, S.L. 1975. Subunit structure of the 12S protein from seeds of Brassica juncea. Can. J. Bot. 53: 2901-2907.

2.1-82 Mairapetyan, S.Kh. 1976. Quantitative and qualitative diurnal changes in the essential oil of rose geranium grown in outdoor hydroponics [in Armenian]. Soobshch. Inst. Agrokhim. Probl. Gidroponiki Akad. Nauk Arm. SSR 1976{15}: 85-89. HA 47: 11743.

2.1-83 Marczal, G., and Verzar-Petri, G. 1980. Essential oil production and composition during the ontogeny in Matricaria chamomilla L. Acta Hort. 96: 325-329.

2.1-84 Mathieu, R.F. 1978. Quaker or Russian comfrey. Herbarist 44: 16-25.

2.1-85 Mathur, G. 1974. Famous plants: peppermint. Botanica 24: 110-112. AGRICOLA.

2.1-86 Mazurova, T.A. 1978. Tartaric acid in the seeds and etiolated seedlings of chicory (Cichorium intybus) [in Russian]. Vestn. Leningr. Univ. Biol. 1978{2}: 112-119. HA 49: 380.

2.1-87 Minkov, S. 1975. Grecian laurel (Laurus nobilis) [in Bulgarian]. Priroda (Sofiia) 24{3}: 60-62. AGRICOLA.

2.1-88 Mishurova, S.S., and Abbasov, R.M. 1977. Dynamics of essential oil accumulation and its quality in MS-401 mint on the Apsheron Peninsula [in Russian]. Izv. Akad. Nauk Az. SSR Ser. Biol. Nauk 1977{4}: 9-11.

2.1-89 Mix, G.P., and Marschner, H. 1976. Calcium content in fruits of paprika, bean, quince, and Kamtchatka rugosa rose during fruit growth [in German]. Z. Pflanzenernaehr. Bodenkd. 1976{5}: 537-549. CA 86: 54337.

2.1-90 Moelgaard, P. 1976. Plantago major ssp. major and spp. pleiosperma. Morphology, biology and ecology in Denmark. Bot. Tidsskr. 71: 31-56.

2.1-91 Nano, G.M., Sacco, T., and Frattini, C. 1976. Botanical and chemical studies of Anthemis nobilis L. and some of its cultivars [in Italian]. Essenze Deriv. Agrum. 46: 171-175. CA 86: 177153.

2.1-92 Nano, G.M., Sacco, T., and Frattini, C. 1973. Genus Anthemis. I [in Italian]. Essenze Deriv. Agrum. 43{2}: 107-114. CA 80: 143045.

2.1-93 Narain, A. 1974. Rape and mustard. Pages 67-70 in J. Hutchinson, ed. Evolutionary studies of world crops. Cambridge University Press, New York, N.Y.

2.1-94 Natalucci de Demolis, C.L., and Caffini, N.O. 1980. Floral carotenoids from Argentine plants. Part II. [in Spanish]. Phyton (Buenos Aires) 39: 95-98. HA 51: 8683.

2.1-95 Nawaz, R., and Soerensen, H. 1977. Distribution of saccharopine and 2-aminoadipic acid in higher plants. Phytochemistry 16: 599-600.

2.1-96 Nayar, N.M. 1976. Sesame: Sesamum indicum (Pedaliaceae). Pages 231-233 in N.W. Simmonds, ed. Evolution of crop plants. Longman, London, G.B. AGRICOLA.

2.1-97 Ochimiya, H., and Wildman, S.G. 1978. Evolution of fraction I protein in relation to origin and amphidiploid Brassica species and other members of the Cruciferae. J. Hered. 69: 299-303.

2.1-98 Ornduff, R. 1974. Heterostyly in South African flowering plants: A conspectus. J. S. Afr. Bot. 40: 169-187.

2.1-99 Pakaln, D.A., Zakharov, A.M., and Zakharova, O.I. 1976. Search for flavonoid and iridoid compounds in the mint family of Caucasus flora [in Russian]. Farmatsiya 25{5}: 36-41.

2.1-100 Pfab, I., Heinrich, G., and Schultze, W. 1980. The essential oil occurring in glandular and non-glandular tissues of Monarda fistulosa [in German]. Biochem. Physiol. Pflanz. (BPP) 175: 29-44.

2.1-101 Poniedzialek, M. 1973. Botanical characteristics and utility value of horseradish (Armoracia rusticana Gaertn.) originating from various regions of cultivation in Poland [in Polish]. Acta Agrar. Silvestria Ser. Agrar. 8{2}: 67-83. AGRICOLA.

2.1-102 Popa, D.P., Pasechnik, G.S., and Orgiyan, T.M. 1974. Dynamics of diterpenoid accumulation in some Labiatae family plants [in Russian]. Rastit. Resur. 10: 365-367. CA 82: 28678.

2.1-103 Puchalski, J.T., Robinson, R.W., and Provvidenti, R. 1978. Peroxidase electrophoretic patterns of some species and cultivars of Cichorium. HortScience 11: 387 (Abstr.).

2.1-104 Raghuvanshi, S.S., and Singh, A.K. 1976. Effect of gamma rays on growth and karyokinetic activity in Trigonella foenum-graecum L. Cytologia 41: 177-186.

2.1-105 Ragimov, M.A., and Babaev, R.I. 1971. Biology and ecology of Mentha pulegium L. in Azerbaidzhan [in Russian]. Izv. Akad. Nauk Az. SSR Ser. Biol. Nauk 1971{4}: 7-11.

2.1-106 Raju, G.S.N., Feys, J.L., and Vlassak, K. 1976. Biological nitrogen fixation activity in the rhizosphere of Cichorium intybus L. treated with fungicides. Meded. Fac. Landbouwwet. Rijksuniv. Gent 41: 617-621. SF 41: 1102.

2.1-107 Repcak, M., Smajda, B., Cernaj, P., Honcariv, R., and Podhradsky, D., 1980. Diurnal rhythms of certain sesquiterpenes in wild camomile (Matricaria chamomilla L.). Biol. Plant. 22: 420-427.

2.1-108 Resh, F.M. 1974. Content of cardiac glycosides in leaves of Digitalis purpurea L. depending on geographic origin of the seeds and morphological characteristics of the plants [in Russian]. Rastit. Resur. 10: 558-563.

2.1-109 Rieder, J.B. 1973. Mineral content of dried green fodder in relation to the botanical composition of the plant stand [in German]. Landwirtsch. Forsch. Sonderh. 28{2}: 207-214. HERB AB 45: 1500.

2.1-110 Rivals, P. 1971. White-flowered borage: A vegetable from Aragon [in French]. J. Agr. Trop. Bot. Appl. 18: 575. AGRICOLA.

2.1-111 Roberts, M.F., and Antoun, M.D. 1978. The relationship between L-dopa decarboxylase in the latex of Papaver somniferum and alkaloid formation. Phytochemistry 17: 1083-1087.

2.1-112 Roberts, M.F. 1971. Polyphenolases in the 1000g fraction of Papaver somniferum latex. Phytochemistry 10: 3021-3027.

2.1-113 Roberts, M.F. 1973. The oxidation of tyrosine a precursor of morphine by polyphenolase in the 1000g organelles of Papaver somniferum. J. Pharm. Pharmacol. 25 (Suppl.) 115 (Abstr.).

2.1-114 Ruminska, A. 1976. Melissa officinalis [in Polish]. Wiad. Zielarskie 18{5}: 22-23. AGRICOLA.

2.1-115 Rutherford, P.P., and Deacon, A.C. 1972. The mode of action of dandelion root beta-fructo-furanosidases on inulin. Biochem. J. 129: 511-512.

2.1-116 Saad, M.M. 1978. Characteristics of coriander fruit from Egypt [in Russian]. Izv. Vyssh. Uchebn. Zaved Pishch. Tekhnol. 1978{4}: 48-51.

2.1-117 Sarkany, S., and Michels-nyomarkay, K. 1977. Alkaloid spectrum of seedlings and reproductive organs in some poppy (Papaver somniferum L.) varieties. Acta Agron. Acad. Sci. Hung. 26: 404-411.

2.1-118 Schintgen, C., and Mathis, C. 1975. Study of the vitamin B1 and B2 content of some medically used plants [in French]. Plant. Med. Phytother. 9: 107-117.

2.1-119 Schultz, J.E.R., and Hansen, H. 1971. Investigations on the variation and content of volatile oils in Danish-grown caraway [in Danish]. Tidsskr. Planteavl 75: 377-380. AGRICOLA.

2.1-120 Sellier, M., and Hannoteaux, J. 1978. Honey flora: rosemary, Rosmarinus officinalis, family of the Labiatae [in French]. Rev. Fr. Apic. 360: 18-19. AGRICOLA.

2.1-121 Shevchenko, S.V. 1973. Seasonal and diurnal changes in Salvia sclarea essential oil content [in Russian]. Rastit. Resur. 9: 566-570. HA 44: 4214.

2.1-122 Shimizu, S. 1974. Chemistry and biology of Mentha plants [in Japanese]. Kagaku To Seibutsu 12{10}: 659-666. CA 82: 135630.

2.1-123 Shlyapyatis, Yu.Yu. 1974. Biology and biochemistry of wormwood. {7. Dynamics and accumulation of chamazulene accumulation) [in Russian]. Liet. TSR Mokslu Akad. Darb. Ser. C 1974{4}: 29-34.

2.1-124 Shlyapyatis, Yu.Yu. 1975. Biology and biochemistry of the common wormwood. (8. Accumulation dynamics of tannic substances, ascorbic acid and carotene [in Russian]. Liet. TSR Mokslu Akad. Darb. Ser. C 1975{1}: 43-48.

2.1-125 Sirnik, V. 1980. Important components of parsley (Petroselinum hortense) of different origin [in Slovak]. Zb. Biotehn. Fak. Univ.ljublj Agric. 33: 409-416.

2.1-126 Smaikov, G. 1979. Biology and ecology of the sesame plant [in Bulgarian]. Priroda (Sofiia) 28{4}: 80-83. AGRICOLA.

2.1-127 Soldatovic, M. 1975. A contribution to the study of Origanum heracleoticum [in Serbo-Croatian]. Arh. Farm. 25: 435-438. HA 47: 5878.

2.1-128 Sommer, L., Palade, M., Draghici, I., and Constantinescu, C. 1974. Localization of azulenic precursors from Absinthii herba. VIII [in Romanian]. Farmacia (Bucharest) 22: 277-282. CA 81: 148527.

2.1-129 Srivastava, V.K., Hill, D.C., and Slinger, S.J. 1976. Comparison of some chemical characteristics of Indian and Canadian Brassica seeds. Indian J. Nutr. Diet. 13: 336-342. FCA 31: 5569.

2.1-130 Steiner, A.M. 1974. Anthocyanin accumulation and composition in seedings of different cultivars of Sinapis alba L. Z. Pflanzenphysiol. 71: 186-188.

2.1-131 Suprunov, N.I., Kurlyanchik, I.A., and Deren'ko, S.A. 1976. Dynamics of essential oil accumulation in dill from different geographical regions [in Ukranian]. Farm. Zh. (Kiev) 1976{6}: 52-54, 85. HA 48: 1651.

2.1-132 Szujko-Lacza, J., and Szocs, Z. 1975. The architecture and the quantitative investigation of some characteristics of anise, Pimpinella anisum L. Acta Bot. Acad. Sci. Hung. 21: 443-450.

2.1-133 Szujko-Lacza, J. 1978. Structural conditions of volatile oil production in the leaves of Pimpinella anisum L. [in Hungarian]. He rba Hung. 17{3}: 31-38. AGRICOLA.

2.1-134 Tamas, M., and Rosca, M. 1978. Studies on the essential oil from Origanum vulgare [in Rumanian]. Clujul Med. 51: 168-172. HA 49: 4440.

2.1-135 Topalides, Eu. 1973. A good honey plant: Taraxacum officinale, wild dandelion, endive or wild lettuce [in Greek]. Melissokomikhellas 23{275}: 321. AGRICOLA.

2.1-136 Toyoda, T., Muraki, S., and Yoshida, T. 1979. Pyridine and nicotinate derivatives in jasmine. Int. Congr. Essent. Oils, [Pap.], 7th, 1977. 7: 473-476. CA 92: 135100.

2.1-137 Tsertsvadze, T.A. 1972. Sugar content in the flowers of some winter blooming plants. Soobshch. Akad. Nauk Gruz. SSR 65: 145-148.

2.1-138 Vaichyunene, Y.A. 1975. Comparative study of the biology of Digitalis lanata, ambigua, purpurea and a purpurea inoculated population [in Russian]. Liet. TSR Mokslu Akad. Darb. Ser. C 1974{1}: 49-55.

2.1-139 Vas'kovskii, V.E., Gorovoi, P.G., and Suppes, Z.S. 1972. Phospholipase D in Far Eastern plants. Int. J. Biochem. 3{18}: 647-656. CA 78: 82054.

2.1-140 Verzar-Petri, G., and Then, M. 1975. The study of the localization of volatile oil in the different parts of Salvia sclarea and Salvia officinalis by applying 2 carbon-14 sodium-acetate. Acta Bot. Acad. Sci. Hung. 21: 189-205.

2.1-141 Verzar-Petri, G., and Shalaby, A.S. 1977. Volatile oil production and formation in Achillea millefolium spp. collina Becker (A. collina Becker). Acta Agron. (Budapest) 26: 337-342. HA 48: 3846.

2.1-142 Vlassak, K., and Jain, M.K. 1976. Biological nitrogen fixation studies in the rhizosphere of Cichorium intybus and Taraxacum officinale. Rev. Ecol. Biol. Sol. 13: 411-418. SF 40: 2959.

2.1-143 Wacquant, J.-P. 1978. Some properties of roots and their ecological consequences, demonstrated by a study of cationic adsorption as a function of pH [in French]. Physiol. Veg. 16: 67-79. HA 48: 7005.

2.1-144 Wassink, E.C. 1972. Some recent observations on Digitalis purpurea L. f. heptandra de Chamisso. Meded. Landbouwhogesch. Wageningen Pages 72-82.

2.1-145 Yakhontova, L.D., Sheichenko, V.I., and Tolkachev, O.N. 1971. A study of Rosmarinus officinalis: IV. Isorosmaricin. Chem. Nat. Compd. (Engl. Transl.) 7: 396-398. Translation of Khim. Prir. Soedin. 1971{4}: 416-420.

2.1-146 Yankulovich, I., Ivanov, I.N., and Alipur, Kh. 1975. Variability in the quantity and quality of mint (Mentha piperita) essential oil [in Bulgarian]. Rastenievud. Nauki 12{6}: 61-68. HA 46: 4938.

2.1-147 Yankulov, Y., and Alipur, H. 1974. Changes in the activity of essential oil glands in autopolyploids of Mentha piperita L. Dokl. S-kh. Akad. (Sofia) 7{3}: 13-16. HA 46: 579.

2.1-148 Yaskonis, Y.A. 1972. Biological and biochemical characteristics of peppermint (I. Biological characteristics) [in Russian]. Liet. TSR Mokslu Akad. Darb. Ser. C 1972{2}: 61-70. PBA 43: 4089.

2.1-149 Yuknyavichene, G.K., Dagite, S.Yu., and Stankyavichene, N.A. 1977. Biological properties and essential oil content of some spice plants grown at the Kaunas Botanical Garden. 2. Plant seeds used as raw materials for spices [in Russian]. Liet. TSR Mokslu Akad. Darb. Ser. C 1977{3}: 9-16.

2.1-150 Yuknyavichene, G.K., Stankyavichene, N.A., and Puzhene, G.A. 1976. Some biochemical characteristics of catmint [in Russian]. Page 225 in Okhrana sredy i ratsional'noe ispol'zovanie rastilel'nykh resursov. Izd Nauka, Moscow, USSR. HA 47: 7765.

2.1-151 Zauralov, O.A. 1978. Changes in the essential oil content and in the number of essential oil glands in plants of the Labiatae from different geographical zones [in Russian]. Rastit. Resur. 14: 412-418. HA 49: 2123.

2.1-152 Zauralov, O.A. 1975. The physiological importance of essential oils in plants [in Russian]. Rastit. Resur. 11: 289-304. HA 45: 9992.

2.1-153 Zlatev, S. 1977. Diurnal variations in the essential oil of dill [in Bulgarian]. Rastenievud. Nauki 14{3}: 45-49.

2.1-154 Zlatev, S. 1976. Dynamics of essential oil accumulation in dill (Anethum graveolens Linnaeus) during 24 hours. Riv. Ital. Essenze Profumi Piante Off. Aromi Saponi Cosmet. Aerosol 58: 553-555. HA 47: 11735.

2.2 Seed Physiology and Germination

2.2-1 Anjou, K., Lonnerdal, B., Uppstrom, B., and Aman, P. 1977.

Composition of seeds from some _Brassica_ cultivars. Swedish J. Agric. Res. 7: 169-178.

2.2-2 Arinshtein, A.I., and Mendel'son, L.S. 1975. Studies on the sensitivity of coriander and clary sage to chemical mutagens [in Russian]. Tr. Prikl. Bot. Genet. Sel. 54{2}: 223-226. HA 46: 10593.

2.2-3 Ashri, A., and Palevitch, D. 1979. Seed dormancy in sesame (S. indicum) and the effect of gibberellic acid. Exp. Agric. 15: 81-83.

2.2-4 Bare, C.E., Toole, V.K., and Gentner, W.A. 1978. Temperature and light effects on germination of _Papaver bracteatum_, _P. orientale_ L. and _P. somniferum_ L. Planta Med. 34{2}: 135-143.

2.2-5 Biddington, N.L., and Thomas, T.H. 1978. Thermodormancy in celery seeds and its removal by cytokinins and gibberellins. Physiol. Plant. 42: 401-405.

2.2-6 Biddington, N.L., Thomas, T.H., and Dearman, A.S. 1980. The effect of temperature on the germination-promoting activities of cytokinin and gibberellin applied to celery seeds (_Apium graveolens_). Physiol. Plant. 49: 68-70.

2.2-7 Biddington, N.L., and Thomas, T.H. 1979. Residual effects of high temperatures on pre-treatments on the germination of celery seeds (_Apium graveolens_). Physiol. Plant. 47: 211-214.

2.2-8 Blom, C.W.P.M. 1978. Germination seedling emergence and establishment of some _Plantago_ species under laboratory and field conditions. Acta Bot. Neerl. 27: 257-271.

2.2-9 Bohra, S.P., Vyas, S.P., Harsh, G.D., and Sankhla, N. 1973. Effect of substituted alkoxycarbonylmethoxy-2,1,3-benzo- thiadiazoles on seed germination of _Brassica juncea_. Biochem. Physiol. Pflanz. (BPP) 164: 98-102.

2.2-10 Bostock, S.J. 1978. Seed germintion strategies of five perennial weeds. Oecologia 36: 113-126.

2.2-11 Chaturvedi, S.N., and Muralia, R.N. 1975. Germination inhibitors in some umbellifer seeds. Ann. Bot. 39: 1125-1129.

2.2-12 Chavagnat, A. 1978. Lavender seed dormancy and germination. Acta Hortic. 83: 147-154.

2.2-13 Chavagnat, A. 1978. A laboratory study of _Lavandula angustifolia_ seed germination [in French]. Seed Sci. Technol. 6: 775-784.

2.2-14 Choi, K.G. 1977. Studies on seed germination in _Panax ginseng_. {2} The effect of growth regulators on dormancy breaking [in Japanese]. Bull. Inst. Agric. Res. Tohoku Univ. 28: 159-170. HA 48: 7598.

2.2-15 Choi, K.G., and Takahashi, N. 1977. Studies on seed germination in _Panax ginseng_. {1} The effect of germination inhibitors in fruits on dormancy breaking [in Japanese]. Bull. Inst. Agric. Res. Tohoku Univ. 28: 145-157. HA 48: 7597.

2.2-16 Clermont, S., Foglietti, M.-J., and Percheron, F. 1973. Presence of a pyrophosphatase nucleotide in the germinated seeds of fenugreek [in French]. C.R. Hebd. Seances Acad. Sci. Ser. D 276: 843-845.

2.2-17 Coonse, M. 1979. Don't wait so long for parsley. Org. Gard. 26{2}: 92-93.

2.2-18 Cowley, P.S., and Evans, F.J. 1972. Variation in the amounts of glucoside and lipid phytosterols in Digitalis purpurea during germination. Planta Med. 22: 88-92.

2.2-19 Cseresnyes, Z., and Baleanu, M. 1978. Improving the methods for germinating seed of Hypericum perfuratum, Atropa belladonna, Marjorana hortensis, Salvia sclarea and Solanum laciniatum [in Romanian]. An. Inst. Cercet. Cereale Plante Teh. Fundule Acad. Stiinte Agric. Silvice Ser. C 43: 111-116. HA 50: 5481.

2.2-20 Darby, R.J., Salter, P.J., and Whitlock, A.J. 1980. Effects of osmotic treatment and pre-germination of celery seeds on seedling emergence. Exp. Hortic. 1980{31}: 10-20.

2.2-21 Deschenes, J.-M., and Moineau, D. 1972. The germination conditions of 4 weeds of Quebec [in French]. Nat. Can. 99: 103-114.

2.2-22 Duranti, A., and Cuocolo, L. 1975. A contribution to the rapid recognition of seeds of species belonging to the genus Brassica [in Italian]. Sementi Elette 21{3}: 3-8. HA 46: 5676.

2.2-23 Esnin, S.A., Myakota, B.V., and Sokolova, L.F. 1978. A method for germinating coriander seeds [in Russian]. Sel. Semenovod. (Moscow) 1978{3}: 56. HA 49: 2113.

2.2-24 Foglietti, M.-J., and Percheron, F. 1972. Oligomannoside beta-1,4 orthophosphate mannosyl transferase (oligomannosyl beta-1,4 phosphorylase) in germinated grains of Trigonella foenum graecum L. [in French]. C.R. Hebd. Seances Acad. Sci. Ser. D 274: 130-132.

2.2-25 Formanowiczowa, H., and Kozlowski, J. 1975. Biology of germination of medical plants seeds. Part XIIIa. Seeds of Papaveraceae, Chelidonium and Papaver spp. [in Polish]. Herba Pol. 21: 284-300. HA 47: 3955.

2.2-26 Formanowiczowa, H., and Kozlowski, J. 1971. Germination biology and laboratory valuation of medicinal plant seeds used for seeding. VIC. The seeds of two Umbelliferae species: Archangelica officinalis Hoffm. and Levisticum officinale Koch. cultivated in Poland [in Polish]. Herba Pol. 17: 355-366.

2.2-27 Formanowiczowa, H., and Kozlowski, J. 1971. The germination biology and laboratory valuation of medicinal plant seeds used for seeding purposes. Part IXa. The seeds of species from the Scrophulariaceae family - the genus Digitalis L. [in Polish]. Herba Pol. 17: 209-225.

2.2-28 Formanowiczowa, H., and Kozlowski, J. 1980. Biology of germination of medicinal plants seeds. Part XII A. Seeds of species from Solanaceae [in Polish]. Herba Pol. 26: 21-38.

2.2-29 Glazurina, A.N., and Evmenenko, L.S. 1976. Comparative sensitivity to irradiation of seeds of Compositae flower crops [in Russian]. Byull. Gos. Nikitsk. Bot. Sada 1976{1}: 65-70.

2.2-30 Goldthwaite, J.J., Bristol, J.C., Gentile, A.C., and Klein, R.M. 1971. Light-suppressed germination of California poppy seed. Can. J. Bot. 49: 1655-1659.

2.2-31 Gorski, T. 1975. Germination of seeds in the shadow of plants. Physiol. Plant. 34: 342-346.

2.2-32 Grover, I.S., and Dhanju, M.S. 1979. Effect of gamma radiation on the germination of Papaver somniferum and P. rhoeas. Indian J. Plant Physiol. 22: 75-77.

2.2-33 Guy, R. 1978. Effect of pre-germination on the germination of 14 agricultural and vegetable species [in French]. Rev. Suisse Agric. 10: 185-188. HA 49: 3340.

2.2-34 Guy, R. 1979. Observations on the dormancy and germination of fennel seeds [in French]. Rev. Suisse Agric. 11: 131-133. HA 49: 8823.

2.2-35 Guy, R. 1980. Some examples of the effects of temperature on the germination of various vegetables [in French]. Rev. Suisse Vitic. Arboric. Hortic. 12: 35-37. HA 50: 7054.

2.2-36 Guy, R. 1979. New observations on the maturity, dormancy, germination and sprouting of fennel [in French]. Rev. Suisse Vitic. Arboric. Hortic. 11: 215-217. AGRICOLA.

2.2-37 Hari Singh, and Kkattra, G.S. 1977. Germination-inhibitor in chilli fruit and seed extract. Indian J. Agric. Sci. 47: 445-447. HA 48: 4634.

2.2-38 Heit, C.E. 1973. Germination testing of Mentha piperita (peppermint) seed in the laboratory. News Lett. Assoc. Off. Seed Anal. 47{2}: 27-29. AGRICOLA.

2.2-39 Hradilik, J., and Fiserova, H. 1980. Role of abscissic acid in dormancy of cummin (Carum carvi L.) seeds [in Czech]. Acta Univ. Agric. Fac. Agron. 28{2}: 39-64. AGRICOLA.

2.2-40 Hradilik, J., and Cisarova, H. 1975. The role of abscisic acid (ABA) in achenes of dormant cumin. Acta Univ. Agric. Brno. Fac. Agron. 23: 747-753. HA 48: 5855.

2.2-41 Hradilik, J., and Cisarova, H. 1975. Studies on the dormancy of caraway (Carum carvi) achenes [in Czech]. Rostl. Vyroba 21: 351-364. HA 46: 7026.

2.2-42 Ilieva, S., and Mateeva, D. 1971. Intensiveness of the germination process and growth at secondary sprouting of clary sage (Salvia sclarea L.) and garden sage (Salvia officinalis L.) seeds [in Bulgarian]. Rastenievud. Nauki 8{6}: 55-61. AGRICOLA.

2.2-43 Jacobsen, J.V., and Pressman, E. 1979. A structural study of germination in celery (Apium graveolens L.) seed with emphasis on endosperm breakdown. Planta 144: 241-248.

2.2-44 Kaoulla, N., MacLeod, A.J., and Gil, V. 1980. Investigation of Brassica oleracea and Nasturtium officinale seeds for the presence of epithiospecifier protein. Phytochemistry 19: 1053-1056.

2.2-45 Khudaibergenov, E.B., and Mikhailova, V.P. 1972. Laboratory and field germination of Glycyrrhiza uralensis seeds [in Russian]. Rastit. Resur. 8: 225-229. HA 43: 1457.

2.2-46 Kichanova, L.A. 1973. Radiosensibility of coriander seeds. Byull. Gos. Nikitsk. Bot. Sada 1973{1}: 58-61. AGRICOLA.

2.2-47 Kirk, J.T.O., and Pyliotis, N.A. 1976. Cruciferous oilseed proteins: the protein bodies of Sinapis alba seed. Aust. J. Plant Physiol. 3: 731-746

2.2-48 Kobakhidze, L.A. 1975. Studies on some processes influencing the formation of endosperm and endosperm haustoria in sweet basil (Ocimum basilicum) [in Russian]. Soobshch. Akad. Nauk Gruz. SSR 80{1}: 137-140. HA 46: 11647.

2.2-49 Komendar, V.I., Dubanych, N.V., and Berets, V.P. 1978. On storage of seeds in soil under some meadow cenoses of low-lying and mountain meadow zones of the Transcarpathian [in Ukrainian]. Ukr. Bot. Zh. 35: 375-378.

2.2-50 Kowal, T., Krupinska, A., Latowski, K., Pic, S., and Wojterska, H. 1977. Comparative study of the influence of vitamins, cytostatistics, and new chemical compounds of expected anti-irradiation effects on the germination of pea, dill and sunflower diaspores [in Polish]. Acta Agrobot. 30: 33-49. AGRICOLA.

2.2-51 Kryukova, L.M., and Abdrakhmanov, O.K. 1972. The effect of X-rays on licorice root growth and development [in Russian]. Tr. Inst. Bot. Akad. Nauk Kaz. SSR 31: 79-85. HA 43: 7109.

2.2-52 Kuribayashi, T., and Ohashi, H. 1975. Physiological and ecological studies in Panax ginseng. VII. Effects of kinetin treatment on germinating stimulation, especially on the threshold value [in Japanese]. Syoyakugaku Zasshi 29: 62-69. CA 84: 70225.

2.2-53 Labouriau, L.G. 1980. Effects of deuterium oxide on the lower temperature limit of sesame seed germination. J. Therm. Biol. 5: 113-117. AGRICOLA.

2.2-54 Lago, A.A. do, Banzatto, N.V., Savy Filho, A., and Goddy, I.J. de. 1979. Longevity of seeds of two sesame cultivars [in Portuguese]. Bragantia 38: 175-180. Bib.Ag. 46: 38860.

2.2-55 Lamba, L.C. 1975. Structure and development of seed in Brassica nigra Koch. J. Indian Bot. Soc. 54: 225-233. FCA 31: 1425.

2.2-56 Linhart, Y.B. 1976. Density-dependent seed germination strategies in colonizing versus non-colonizing plant species. J. Ecol. 64: 375-380

2.2-57 Menghini, A., and Venanzi, G. 1977/1978. The effect of growth regulators on the germination of seeds of various medicinal plants [in Italian]. Ann. Fac. Agrar. Univ. Studi Perugia 32: 771-783. HA 50: 4582.

2.2-58 Menghini, A., and Venanzi, G. 1978. Effects of phytohormones on seed germination in some officinalis species [in Italian]. Ann. Fac. Agrar. Univ. Studi Perugia 32: 773-783. CA 92: 1572.

2.2-59 Mezynski, P.R., and Cole, D.F. 1974. Germination of dandelion seed on a thermogradient plate. Weed Sci. 22: 506-507.

2.2-60 Miles, L.J., and Parker, G.R. 1980. Effect of soil Cd addition on germination of native plant species. Plant Soil 54: 243-247.

2.2-61 Mulligan, G.A., and Bailey, L.G. 1976. Seed coats of some Brassica and Sinapis weedy and cultivated in Canada. Econ. Bot. 30: 143-148.

2.2-62 Nettles, V.F., and Poe, L.N. 1973. Germination studies with celery seed. Proc. Fla. State Hortic. Soc. 86: 172-175. HA 45: 8565.

2.2-63 Ogawa, K. 1978. The germination pattern of a native dandelion (Taraxacum platycarpum) as compared with introduced dandelions. Nippon Seitaigau Kaishi 28(1): 9-15.

2.2-64 Olatoye, S.T., and Hall, M.A. 1973. Interaction of ethylene and light on dormant weed seeds. Pages 233-249 in W. Heydecker, ed. Seed ecology. Proceedindgs of the Nineteenth Easter School in Agricultural Science, University of Nottingham, 1972. Butterworths, London, UK.

2.2-65 Palevitch, D., Thomas, T.H., and Austin, R.B. 1971. Dormancy-release of celery seed by a growth retardant, n-dimethylaminosuccinamic acid (alar). Planta 100: 370-372.

2.2-66 Palevitch, D., and Thomas, T.H. 1976. Enhancement by low pH of gibberellin effects on dormant celery seeds and embryoless half-seeds of barley. Physiol. Plant. 37: 247-252.

2.2-67 Palevitch, D., and Thomas, T.H. 1978. Release of celery seed thermodormancy by gibberellins applied in low pH solution. Acta Hortic. 72: 27-37.

2.2-68 Palevitch, D., and Thomas, T.H. 1974. Thermodormancy release of celery seed by gibberellins, 6-benzylaminopurine, and ethephon applied in organic solvent to dry seeds. J. Exp. Bot. 25: 981-986.

2.2-69 Palevitch, D., Thomas, T.H., and Austin, R.B. 1971. Dormancy-release of celery seed by a growth retardant, N-dimethylaminosuccinamic acid (Alar). Planta 100: 370-372.

2.2-70 Pandya, R.B., Khan, M.I., and Yadava, T.P. 1973. Varietal response of raya (Brassica juncea Coss.) to different moisture regimes during germination. Indian J. Plant Physiol. 16: 79-83. FCA 29: 4152.

2.2-71 Patudin, A.V. 1975. On seed germination of species of the sage genus [in Russian]. Dokl. TSKhA. 209: 151-155. AGRICOLA.

2.2-72 Poncova, J., and Plskova, M. 1971. Effect of gibberellic acid on slightly germinating or nongerminating seeds of some vegetables [in Czech]. Acta Univ. Palacki. Olomuc., Rerum Natur. 34: 75-103. CA 76: 95636.

2.2-73 Pressman, E., Negbi, M., Sachs, M., and Jacobsen, J.V. 1977. Varietal differences in light requirements for germination of celery (Apium graveolens L.) seeds and the effects of thermal and solute stress. Aust. J. Plant Physiol. 4: 821-831.

2.2-74 Pressman, E., Negbi, M., Sachs, M., and Jacobsen, J.V. 1976. Germination characters in cultivated and wild celery (Apium graveolens L.). Israel J. Bot. 25{1/2}: 94-95.

2.2-75 Putievsky, E. 1977. Tests on caraway seed germination [in Hebrew]. Hassadeh 57: 1413-1415. HA 47: 11724.

2.2-76 Putievsky, E. 1980. Germination studies with seed of caraway, coriander and dill. Seed Sci. Technol. 8: 245-254.

2.2-77 Reid, J.S.G., and Meier, H. 1971. Carbohydrate metabolism in the germinating seeds of Trigonella foenum-graecum [in German]. Verh. Schweiz. Naturforsch. Ges. 151: 68-70 (Abstr.). CA 77: 85727.

2.2-78 Reid, J.S.G., Davies, C., and Meier, H. 1977. Endo-beta-mannanase, the leguminous aleurone layer and the storage galactomannan in germinating seeds of Trigonella foenum-graecum L. Planta 133: 219-222.

2.2-79 Reid, J.S.G., and Meier, H. 1972. The function of the aleurone layer during galactomannan mobilisation in germinating seeds of fenugreek (Trigonella foenum-graecum L.), crimson clover (Trifolium incarnatum L.) and lucerne (Medicago sativa L.): a correlative biochemical and ultrastructural study. Planta 106: 44-60.

2.2-80 Reid, J.S.G., and Meier, H. 1973. Enzymic activities and galactomannan mobilisation in germinating seeds of fenugreek (Trigonella foenum-graecum L. Leguminosae). Secretion of alpha-galactosidase and beta-mannosidase by the aleurone layer. Planta 112: 301-308.

2.2-81 Reid, J.S.G., and Bewley, J.D. 1979. A dual role for the endosperm and its galactomannan reserves in the germinative physiology of fenugreek (Trigonella foenum-graecum L.), and endospermic leguminous seed. Planta 147: 145-150.

2.2-82 Renard, H.A., and Clerc, P. 1978. Dormancy breaking with gibberellins in four species: Impatiens balsamina, Lavandula angustifolia, Brassica rapa and Viola odorata [in French]. Seed Sci. Technol. 6: 661-6677. HA 49: 5995.

2.2-83 Rest, J.A., and Vaughan, J.G. 1972. The development of protein and oil bodies in the seed of Sinapis alba L. Planta 105: 245-262.

2.2-84 Rijven, A.H.G.C. 1972. Control of the activity of the aleurone layer of fenugreek, Trigonella foenum-graecum L. Acta Bot. Neerl. 21: 381-386.

2.2-85 Roberts, H.A. 1979. Periodicity of seedling emergence and seed survival in some Umbelliferae. J. Appl. Ecol. 16: 195-201.

2.2-86 Robocker, W.C. 1977. Germination of seeds of common yarrow (Achillea millefolium) and its herbicidal control. Weed Sci 25: 456-459.

2.2-87 Rosenthal, G.A. 1974. Interrelation of canavanine and urease in seeds of the Lotoideae. J. Exp. Bot. 25{87}: 609-613. CA 82: 82940.

2.2-88 Roy, U., and Gupta, S.K.D. 1975. A note on the changes in some qualitative characters during the last phase of maturation of Indian mustard seed (Brassica junce Coss). Curr. Sci. 44: 18-19. FCA 28: 7649

2.2-89 Ruminska, A., Suchorska, K., and Weglarz, Z. 1976. Effect of gibberellin on germination of true lavender, Lavandula vera L. [in Polish]. Herba Pol. 22{2}: 132-137. AGRICOLA.

2.2-90 Ruminska, A., Suchorska, K., and Weglarz, Z. 1978. Effect of gibberellic acid on seeds germination of some vegetable and medicinal plants. Acta Hortic. 1978{73}: 131-136.

2.2-91 Russwurm, W., and Martin, B. 1977. Studies on the germination behaviour of dandelion (Taraxacum officinale Web.) under specific conditions [in German]. Nachrichtenbl. Pflanzenschutz DDR 31: 223-227. WA 27: 3037.

2.2-92 Salehuzzaman, M., and Pasha, M.K. 1979. Effects of high and low temperatures on the germination of the seeds of flax and sesame. Indian J. Agric. Sci. 49: 260-261.

2.2-93 Shaw, D.E. 1976. Germination of spores of Marasmiellus epochnous. Pa pua New Guinea Agric. J. 27{3}: 67-68.

2.2-94 Shchelokova, L.G. 1976. Studies on foxglove seed dormancy and germination as affected by different factors [in Russian]. Zap. Perm. Univ. 1976{336}: 122-124. HA 47: 8788.

2.2-95 Sheelavantar, M.N., and Ramanagowda, P. 1978. Physiological maturity and seed viability in Sesamum (Sesamum indicum L.). Mysore J. Agric. Sci. 12: 22-25. AGRICOLA.

2.2-96 Shukurullaev, P.Sh., and Khamdamov, I.Kh. 1976. Uniform germination of Glycyrrhiza glabra seeds [in Russian]. Uzb. Biol. Zh. 1976{2}: 64-65. HA 47: 5923.

2.2-97 Simon, E.W., Minchin, A., McMenamin, M.M., and Smith, J.M. 1976. The low temperature limit for seed germination. New Phytol. 77: 301-311.

2.2-98 Solomina, V.F. 1976. Changes in the activity of endogenous cytokinins during the relative dormancy of garlic bulbs [in Russian]. S-kh. Biol. 11: 571-574. HA 47: 4476.

2.2-99 Son, E.R., Park, W.M., and Pertzsch, C. 1979. Effects of plant growth regulators on physiology of germinating Panax ginseng seed. Hanguk Changmul Hakhoe Chi 24: 99-106.

2.2-100 Srivastava, A.K., Sirhoi, S.S., and Chaurasia, B.D. 1974. Improvement of seed germination in Cichorium intybus L. (chicory) with growth regulators. Labdev J. Part B. 12: 17-18. HA 47: 7387.

2.2-101 Steiner, A.M. 1975. The development of seedlings from graded mustard seed under water stress [in German]. Landwirtsch. Forsch. Sonderh. 31(II Kongressband 1974): 27-33. SF 39: 1631.

2.2-102 Steiner, A.M., and Werth, H. 1979. The influence of the pH on the tetrazolium viability value in seeds of agricultural and horticultural crops of woody plants [in German]. Landwirtsch. Forsch. Sonderh. 36: 209-218. CA 94: 2168.

2.2-103 Stritzke, J.F. 1975. Germination characteristics and chemical control of horehound. J. Range Manage. 28: 225-226.

2.2-104 Szynalska, M. 1972. Seeding value of root celery seeds of different size fractions after long-term storage [in Polish]. Biul. Inst. Hodowli Aklim. Rosl. 1972{1/2}: 21-25. AGRICOLA.

2.2-105 Szynalska, M. 1972. Effect of the period of seed attachment to the maternal plant on seeding value and the process of viability decline in celery seeds [in Polish]. Biul. Inst. Hodowli Aklim. Rosl. 1972{1/2}: 27-29. AGRICOLA.

2.2-106 Tayal, M.S., and Gopal, R. 1976. Synergistic and antagonistic behaviour of maleic hydrazide, morphactin and giberrellic [sic] acid with reference to the seed germination in fenugreek (Trigonella foenum graecum L.). Indian J. Plant Physiol. 19: 71-75.

2.2-107 Tewari, M.N., Balasimha, D., and Ram, C. 1976. Biochemical changes in the germinating seeds of Trigonella foenum-graceum L. in relation to s-triazine herbicides. Biol. Plant. 18: 268-272. HA 47: 3972.

2.2-108 Theimer, R.R., and Schuster, R. 1978. Light-dependent inhibition of germination and early seedling development of Borago officinalis. Z. Pflanzenphysiol. 90: 111-118.

2.2-109 Thind, T.S., Vyas, K.M., and Prakash, V. 1977. Effect of some antibiotics on the germination of coriander seeds. Indian J. Exp. Biol. 15: 247-248.

2.2-110 Thomas, T.H., Palevitch, O., and Austin, R.B. 1974. Hormonal involvement in the phytochrome-controlled dormancy-release of celery seeds (Apium graveolens). Plant Physiol. 53 (6 Suppl.): 41 (Abstr.).

2.2-111 Thomas, T.H., Biddington, N.L., and O'Toole, D.F. 1979. Relationship between position on the parent plant and dormancy characteristics of seeds of three cultivars of celery (Apium graveolens). Physiol. Plant. 45: 492-496.

2.2-112 Thomas, T.H. 1973. Growth regulatory effect of three benzimidazole fungicides on the germination of celery (Apium graveolens seeds. Ann. Appl. Biol. 74: 233-238.

2.2-113 Thomas, T.H., Palevitch, D., Biddington, N.L., and Austin, R.B. 1975. Growth regulators and the phytochrome-mediated dormancy of celery seeds. Physiol. Plant. 35: 101-106.

2.2-114 Thomas, T.H., Biddington, N.L., and O'Toole, D.F. 1979. Relationship between position on the parent plant and dormancy characteristics of seeds of three cultivars of celery (Apium graveolens). Physiol. Plant. 45: 492-496.

2.2-115 Toole, V.K. 1973. Effects of light, temperature and their interactions on the germination of seeds. Seed Sci. Technol. 1: 339-396

2.2-116 Trunina, N.P., Panov, N.V., Trunin, R.F., and German, V.N. 1974. Investigation of the dicotyledonous plant seed behaviour under the action of strong shock waves [in Russian]. Dokl. Akad. Nauk SSR 219: 1249-1250. AGRICOLA.

2.2-117 Trunina, N.P., Panov, N.V., Trunin, R.F., and German, V.N. 1974. Effect of strong shock waves on dicotyledon seeds. Dokl. Biosphys. (Engl. Transl.) 217/219: 130-131. Translation of Dokl. Akad. Nauk SSSR 219: 1249-1250.

2.2-118 Tsvetkov, R. 1977. Radiation mutagenesis in lavender. I. Dose and emissive power as affecting the radiosensibility of lavender seeds in gamma-ray treatment [in Bulgarian]. Rastenievud. Nauki 14{3}: 34-44.

2.2-119 Uebelmann, G. 1978. Germination of the fenugreek seed: Uptake by the embryo of sugars released on breakdown of the storage galactomannan in the endosperm [in German]. Z. Pflanzenphysiol. 88: 235-253.

2.2-120 Vaichyunene, Ya.A. 1973. Plantain of the Lithuanian SSR (1. Seed germination biology) [in Russian]. Liet. TSR Mokslu Akad. Darb. Ser. C 1973{3}: 37-46.

2.2-121 Vaichyunene, Ya.A. 1978. Bunting of the Lithuanian SSR. (2. Seed germination in relation to the duration of their storage and their localization in the spikelet) [in Russian]. Liet. TSR Mokslu Akad. Darb. Ser. C 1978{1}: 63-70.

2.2-122 Van Loon, J. 1973. Composition of seed fats of some Umbelliferae [in German]. Z. Lebensm.-Unters. Forsch. 153: 289-293. CA 80: 69375.

2.2-123 Vasiuta, G.G., Il'inskaia, L.R., and Timasheva, L.A. 1978. Germination of Coriandrum sativum seed in rolls of filter paper [in Russian]. Sel. Semenovod. (Moscow) 1978{4}: 73. Bib.Ag. 43: 104245.

2.2-124 Vasyuta, G.G., Il'inskaya, L.R., and Timasheva, L.A. 1978. Characteristics of germination of freshly harvested coriander seeds [in Russian]. T r. Vses. Nauchno-Issled. Inst. Efirnomaslichn. Kul't. 11: 41-44. HA 50: 7906.

2.2-125 Veluswamy, P., Thangaraj, T., and Muthuswamy, S. 1975. A study of germination of seeds of some Jasminum species and clones. South Indian Hortic. 23{1/2}: 71-72. HA 46: 10597.

2.2-126 Veluswamy, P., Thangaraj, T., and Muthuswamy, S. 1977. Studies on seed germination in jasmine (Jasminum auriculatum Vahl.). South Indian Hortic. 25: 20-25.

2.2-127 Vose, J.R. 1974. Chemical and physical studies of mustard and rapeseed coats. Cereal Chem. 51: 658-665.

2.2-128 Wanner, H., Stocker, S., and Stocker, H. 1977. Different effects of long chain fatty acids on seed germination. Biochem. Physiol. Pflanz. (BPP) 171: 391-399.

2.2-129 Weisaeth, G. 1978. Germination capacity of Carum carvi seed in relation to the life cycle of caraway plants [in German]. Seed Sci. Technol. 6: 685-693.

2.2-130 Werker, E., and Vaughan, J.G. 1974. Anatomical and ultrastructural changes in aleurone and myrosin cells of Sinapis alba during germination. Planta 116: 243-255.

2.2-131 Woodstock, L.W. 1975. Freeze-drying as an alternative method for lowering seed moisture. Proc. Assoc. Off. Seed Anal. 65: 159-163.

2.3 Plant Growth and Development

2.3-1 Abdrakhmanov, O.K., and Dzhakupova, N.U. 1974. The effect of ionizing radiation on the qualitative composition of the glycyrrhizic acid of liquorice [in Russian]. Biol. Nauki (Alma Atta) 1974{1}: 31-33. HA 47: 3946.

2.3-2 Abou-Zied, E.N. 1973. The seasonal variations of growth and volatile oil in the two introduced types of Majorana hortensis Mnch., grown in Egypt. Pharmazie 28: 55-56.

2.3-3 Albaa, S.I., Mahran, G.H., El-Hossary, G.A., and Selim, M.A. 1975. Effect of locality, age, season and collection on the glycyrrhizin content of roots and rhizomes of Glycyrrhiza glabra L. growing in Egypt. Bull. Fac. Pharm. Cairo univ. 14{2}: 41-51. CA 89: 87164.

2.3-4 Amrutavalli. 1979. Gibberellic acid (GA3) induced enhancement in flowering in Bulgarian coriander (Coriander sativum L.) in relation to changes in carbohydrate metabolism. Curr. Sci. 48: 5-6.

2.3-5 Amrutavalli, S.A. 1978. Sex expression in coriander (Coriander sativum L.) as affected by growth regulators. Curr. Sci. 47: 929-930.

2.3-6 Anderson, J.E., and Kreith, F. 1978. Effects of film-forming and silicone antitranspirants on four herbaceous plant species. Plant Soil 49: 161-173.

2.3-7 Andringa, R. 1973. Caraway seed: development and potential yield [in Dutch]. Bedrijfsontwikkeling 4: 911-916. AGRICOLA.

2.3-8 Arnozis, P.A., Caso, O.H., and Cagliatti, D.H. 1977. Effect of GA3 and light intensity on foliar morphogenesis in Taraxacum officinale [in Spanish]. Phyton (Buenos Aires) 35: 1-9.

2.3-9 Balasimha, D., and Tewari, M.N. 1979. Auxin-cytokinin interaction on growth and auxin metabolism in fenugreek (Trigonella foenum graecum L.). Indian J. Plant Physiol. 22: 207-218. HA 51: 7356.

2.3-10 Balasimha, D., and Tewari, M.N. 1978. Oxidation of glutathione by peroxidase isoenzymes in fenugreek. Biol. Plant. 20: 387-391.

2.3-11 Balatkova, V., and Tupy, J. 1972. The stimulatory effect of uracil and 5-bromouracil on the seed set in Papaver somniferum L. Biol. Plant. 14: 140-145.

2.3-12 Balbaa, S.I., Mahran, G.H., and El-Hossary, G.A. 1973. Study of the active constituents of the rhizomes and roots of Valeriana officinalis grown in Egypt in the different seasons of the year and a new method for their determination. Egypt. J. Pharm. Sci. 14{1}: 5-11.

2.3-13 Balogh, M., Marczal, G., and Lemberkovics, E. 1978. Development of active principles in Petroselinum hortense var. longum during ontogeny [in Hungarian]. Herba Hung. 17{3}: 39-48. HA 50: 4542.

2.3-14 Batal, K.D., and Granberry, D. 1980. Effects of some growth
regulators on ripening of pimiento and paprika peppers. HortScience
15: 278 (Abstr.).

2.3-15 Bernier, G., Raju, M.V.S., Jacqnard, A., Bodson, M., Kinet, J.M.,
and Havelange, A. 1974. Release in mitosis of the meristematic G2
cells as an early and essential effect of the floral stimulus in
mustard and cocklebur. Bull. R. Soc. N.Z. 1974{12}: 547-551. FCA 29:
3203.

2.3-16 Bhan, S., and Singh, A. 1973. Response of sesame (Sesamum
orientale L.) to succinic acid. Sci. Cult. 39: 94-95.

2.3-17 Bhan, S., Singh, A., and Singh, H.G. 1973. A note on preliminary
investigations on the effect of cycocel on the growth and yield of
sesame (Sesamum orientale L.). Indian J. Agron. 18: 232-233.

2.3-18 Bhatia, I.S., Mann, S.K., and Singh, R. 1974. Biochemical changes
in the water-soluble carbohydrates during the development of chicory
(Cichorium intybus Linn) roots. J. Sci. Food Agric. 25: 535-539.

2.3-19 Bhattacharya, N.K. 1974. Demonstration of the effect of chemicals
on a few genera yielding spices of commerce. Bull. Bot. Soc. Bengal
28(1-2): 19-24.

2.3-20 Bodson, M. 1977. Changes in the carbohydrate content of the leaf
and the apical bud of Sinapis during transition to flowering. Planta
135: 19-23.

2.3-21 Bopp, M., and Capesius, I. 1973. Regulation of the
differentiation of seedlings [in German]. Ber. Dtsch. Bot. Ges. 86:
257-270.

2.3-22 Bosela, Kh.A., and Smik, G.K. 1977. Biomorphological changes in
Mentha piperita and M. crispa caused by growth regulators [in
Ukrainian]. Ukr. Bot. Zh. 34: 95-99. HA 48: 2696.

2.3-23 Bourdot, G.W., and Field, R.J. 1979. Seasonality of growth and
development in yarrow. Proc. N.Z. Weed Pest Control Conf. 32: 49-54.
AGRICOLA.

2.3-24 Bravo M., A., and Duimovic M., A. 1978. Cropping conditions that
affect the incidence of lateral shoots in plants of white garlic [in
Spanish]. Cienc. Invest. Agrar. 5: 225-229. HA 49: 3349.

2.3-25 Bukhbinder, A.A. 1975. The effect of the age of the leaf on the
accumulation of certain plastic substances, pigments and essential
oils in geranium grown on alluvial soils of the Colchis Lowland [in
Russian]. Subtrop. Kul't. 1975{1}: 106-110.

2.3-26 Buyukli, M.V., and Kovarskii, A.E. 1971. The comparative
characteristics of Lavandula officinalis Ch. as affected by lasting
vegetative and sexual reproduction. S-kh. Biol. 6: 712-718.

2.3-27 Calabrese, E.J., and Howe, K.J. 1976. Stimulation of growth of
peppermint (Mentha piperita) by Phosfon, a growth retardant. Physiol.
Plant. 37: 163-165.

2.3-28 Cantoria, M., and Cuevas-Gacutan, M.V.T. 1974. Studies on the physiology of Philippine mint (Mentha cordifolia Opiz). II. Effect of two different light intensities on the vegetative growth and oil yield. Philipp. J. Sci. 103: 13-19.

2.3-29 Carbonnier, J., and Molho, D. 1978. Change of coumarin contents of inflorescences of Angelica sylvestris L. [in French]. Bull. Mus. Natl. Hist. Nat. Sci. Phys.-Chim. 19: 29-35. CA 90: 200417.

2.3-30 Chang, I.W., Chang, T.L., Chang, Y.C., and Tien, Y.M. 1980. Physiological changes of red pepper fruits during maturation and storage [in Chinese]. Yuan I Hsueh Pao 7{1}: 17-23. AGRICOLA.

2.3-31 Chapelle, J.-P. 1972. Seasonal changes of valeropotriates in native Valeriana procurrens Wallr [in French]. J. Pharm. Belg. 27: 570-576. CIM 14{8}: 9005.

2.3-32 Chaurasia, L.C., and Rathore, J.S. 1975. Inhibition of root elongation and root initiation by urea. Indian J. Exp. Biol. 13: 516-517.

2.3-33 Chaurasia, L.C., and Rathore, J.S. 1977. Repression of root elongation and root initiation in nutrient medium by the fertilizer urea. Sci Cult. 43: 444-445.

2.3-34 Chipiga, A.P., and Ryaboshapko, T.M. 1978. The effect of dill developmental phase on the content and composition of essential oil [in Russian]. Tr. Vses. Nauchno-Issled. Inst. Efirnomaslichn. Kul't. 11: 68-74. HA 50: 7909.

2.3-35 Chkhaidze, D.Kh., Zarkua, M.D., and Vadachkoriya, Ts.T. 1972. The growth and development of bay laurel seedlings obtained from selected seed trees [in Russian]. Subtrop. Kul't. 1972{3}: 95-100. HA 43: 3019.

2.3-36 Chladek, M. 1970/1971. The determination of the start of growth, apex differentiation in caraway grown under natural conditions [in Czech]. Bulletin, Vyzkumny Ustav Zelinarsky Olomouc 1970/71{14/15}: 33-40. HA 43: 6249.

2.3-37 Chladek, M. 1974. Requirements for vernalization in Carum carvi L. [in Czech]. Genet. Slechteni 10: 155-162. AGRICOLA.

2.3-38 Chladek, M. 1972. The control of the vegetation peak in Carum carvi [in German]. Postep Dziedzinie Leku Rosl. Pr. Ref. Dosw. Wygloszone Symp., 1970; Herba Pol. Suppl. 1972: 252-260.

2.3-39 Chloupek, O. 1976. Evaluation of the root system of mustard by means of dielectric characters with respect to yield [in German]. Biol. Plant. 18: 44-49. HA 46: 11260.

2.3-40 Cho, S.Y., and Lee, S.W. 1974. Studies on changes in the composition of garlic during growth. I. Changes in the alliin and amino acid contents in various parts [in Korean]. Hanguk Wonye Hakhoe Chi 15: 1-6. HA 45: 3923.

2.3-41 Cho, S.Y., and Lee, S.W. 1974. Studies on changes in the composition of garlic during growth. II. Changes in the mineral contents in various parts. Hanguk Wonye Hakhoe Chi 15: 7-10. HA 45: 3924.

2.3-42 Cho, S.Y., and Lee, S.W. 1974. Studies on changes in the composition of garlic during growth. III. Alliin and amino acids in the bulbil [in Korean]. Hanguk Wonye Hakhoe Chi 15: 11-13. HA 45: 3925.

2.3-43 Christov, C., and Petrova, L. 1973. Content of phosphorus compounds in Salvia sclarea seedlings treated with gibberellic acid. Pr. Inst. Sadow Ser. E Mater Zjazdow Konf. 3: 521-531.

2.3-44 Chung, H., Kim, J., and Lee, J. 1974. The effect of the time of maleic hydrazide application on the growth and chemical constituents of garlic plants [in Korean]. Hanguk Wonye Hakhoe Chi 15: 14-19. HA 45: 3121.

2.3-45 Chung, H.D., Lee, W.S., and Lee, J.P. 1973. Maleic hydrazide-growth regulator interactions in the growth of shoots and roots of garlic [in Korean]. Hanguk Wonye Hakoe Chi 14: 31-35. HA 44: 5732.

2.3-46 Chung, H.D. 1973. The effect of maleic hydrazide on alliinase activity in garlic [in Korean]. Hanguk Wonye Hakhoe Chi 14: 37-40. HA 44: 4761.

2.3-47 Codaccioni, M. 1973/1974. "In vitro" growth modalities of young buds of Mentha viridis during hardening with sudden thermal cooling [in French]. Botaniste 56: 215-230.

2.3-48 Croteau, R. 1980. Control of oil composition and yield in mint. Proc. Annu. Meet. Oreg. Essent. Oil Grow. League 31: 84-86.

2.3-49 Cumbus, I.P., and Robinson, L.W. 1977. The function of root systems in mineral nutrition of watercress (Rorippa nasturtium-aquaticum (L.) Hayek). Plant Soil 47: 395-406.

2.3-50 Czabajska, W., Jernas, B., Maciolowska-Ludowicz, E., and Kazmierczak, K. 1976. Essential oil content in summer savory (Satureja hortensis L.) herb during its annual vegetation [in Polish]. Herba Pol. 22: 45-50.

2.3-51 Dasgupta, S.K. 1974. Changes in chemical and fatty acid composition during the last phase of maturation of seeds of two Indian mustard cultivars (Brassica juncea Coss). Indian J. Biochem. Biophys. 11: 263-264. FCA 29: 7457.

2.3-52 Dasgupta, S.K., and Friend, J. 1973. Changes in the lipid and fatty acid composition during maturation of seeds of white mustard (Sinapis alba). J. Sci. Food Agric. 24: 463-470.

2.3-53 Delcourt, A., and Deysson, G. 1976. Effects of trifluralin on radicular meristems of Allium sativum L. [in French]. Cytologia 41: 75-84. WA 26: 3965.

2.3-54 Dikshit, U.N. 1976. Study on vernalization in sesame (Sesamum indicum L.). Sci. Cult. 42: 517-518.

2.3-55 Dimitrova-Ruseva, E., and Lilova, T. 1971. Effect of the absence of certain macroelements in the nutritive medium on the absorption of nitrogen and phosphorus and on the metabolism of nitrogen in M. piperita L. [in Bulgarian]. Rastenievud. Nauki 8{4}: 45-56.

2.3-56 Do Quy Hai, Kovacs, K., Matkovics, I., and Matkovics, B. 1975. Properties of enzymes. 10. Peroxidase and superoxide dismutase contents of plant seeds. Biochem. Physiol. Pflanz. (BPP) 167: 357-359.

2.3-57 Druzina, V.D. 1980. Seasonal and annual kinetics of accumulation and chemical composition of below-ground phytomass of meadow plant communities [in Russian]. Bot. Zh. (Leningrad) 65: 677-685. HERB AB 51: 5476.

2.3-58 Duhan, S.P.S., and Garg, S.N. 1975. Effect of age of plant on the quality and oil content of spearmint (Mentha spicata Linn.). Indian Drugs Pharm. Ind. 10{5}: 15-17. HA 47: 7764.

2.3-59 Duhan, S.P.S., Garg, S.N., and Roy, S.K. 1975. Effect of age of plant on the quality of essential oil of peppermint (Mentha piperita Linn.). Indian J. Pharm. 37: 41-42. HA 46: 3689.

2.3-60 Eggens, J.L., and Hilton, R.J. 1971. Growth responses of ground cover plants to varied pH in nutrient culture. J. Am. Soc. Hortic. Sci. 96: 474-476.

2.3-61 El-Labban, H.M. 1977. Growth and chemical changes in Pimpinella anisum after treatment with CCC. Sci. Biol. J. 3{3}: 335-340. AGRICOLA.

2.3-62 El-Antably, H.M.M., Ahmed, S.S., and Eid, M.N.A. 1975. Effects of some growth hormones on plant vigour and volatile oil of Origanum majorana L. Pharmazie 30: 400-401. HA 46: 3668.

2.3-63 El-Gengaihi, S., and Abou-Zied, E.N. 1975. The effect of CMH on growth, volatile oil, and carbohydrate content on Majorana hortensis Mnch., prior and after cutting. Pharmazie 30: 744-745. HA 46: 7944.

2.3-64 El-Gengaihi, S.E., and Hornok, L. 1978. The effect of plant age on content and composition of dill essential oil Anethum graveolens L. Acta Hortic. 1978{73}: 213-218.

2.3-65 El-Gharbawi, M.I. 1977. Development of capsaicin in the fruits of two ripening varieties of genus Capsicum during growth and ripening Libyan J. Agric. 6: 205-212.

2.3-66 El-Labban, H.M., and Abou-Zied, E.N. 1975. Stimulation effect of CCC on growth and chemical constituents of caraway and fennel plants. Ann. Agric. Sci. 20{2}: 187-192. AGRICOLA.

2.3-67 Endress, P.K. 1972. Comparative developmental morphology, embryology and taxonomy in the Laurales [in German]. Bot. Jahrb. Syst. Pflanzengesch. Pflanzengeogr. 92: 331-428.

2.3-68 Evstratova, R.I., Kabanov, V.S., Krylova, I.L., and Prokosheva, L.I. 1978. Level of essential oil and ledol in wild rosemary (Ledum palustre L.) leaves in different vegetation phases [in Russian]. Khim.-Farm. Zh. 12{11}: 71-77. CA 90: 51413.

2.3-69 Fairbairn, J.W., and Helliwell, K. 1977. Papaver bracteatum Lindley: Thebaine content in relation to plant development. J. Pharm. Pharmacol. 29: 65-69.

2.3-70 Felklova, M., Motl, O., Jasicova, M., and Lukes, V. 1978.

Analysis of the main components in the volatile oil of Matricaria chamomilla L. during the flowering period [in Czech]. Cesk. Farm. 27: 322-325. CIM 20{13}: 10018.

2.3-71 Foelster, E., and Krug, H. 1977. Influence of the environment on growth and development of chives (Allium schoenoprasum L.). II. Breaking of the rest period and forcing. Sci. Hortic. (Amsterdam) 7: 213-224.

2.3-72 Fonin, V.S., and Sheberstov, V.V. 1973. Effect of growth conditions on the content of glycosides in Digitalis leaves [in Russian]. Farmatsiya (Moscow) 22{3}: 83-86.

2.3-73 Franke, W. 1978. On the contents of vitamin C and thiamine during the vegetation period in leaves of three spice plants (Allium schoenoprasum L., Melissa officinalis L. and Petroselinum crispum (Mill.) nym. ssp. crispum). Acta Hortic. 1978{73}: 205-212.

2.3-74 Franz, C., Holzl, J., and Vomel, A. 1978. Variation in the essential oil of Matricaria chamomilla L. depending on plant age and stage of development. Acta Hortic. 1978{73}: 229-238. HA 49: 706.

2.3-75 Frommhold, I. 1976. The application of silicone-oil sprays as antitranspirants for ornamental plants [in German]. Arch. Gartenbau 24{5}: 319-326.

2.3-76 Ganich, L.Yu., and Aleksandrova, V.S. 1976. Content of phenol compounds in ontogenesis of Petroselinum sativum [in Russian]. Pages 187-188 in N.V. Tsitsin, et al., eds. Okhrana sredy i ratsional'noe ispol'zovanie rastitel'nykh resursov. Izd. Nauka, Moscow, USSR. CA 89: 176494.

2.3-77 Georgieva, S., and Koseva-Kovacheva, D. 1978. Effect of pH of the nutrient medium on the growth, development and essential oil content of lavender [in Bulgarian]. Rastenievud. Nauki 15{5}: 15-20. HA 49: 7850.

2.3-78 Ghildiyal, M.C., Pandey, M., and Sirohi, G.S. 1977. Proline accumulation under zinc deficiency in mustard. Curr. Sci. 46: 792-793.

2.3-79 Golcz, L., Kordana, S., and Zalecki, R. 1975. Nutritional requirements of Valeriana officinalis L. [in Polish]. Herba Pol. 21: 159-172. AGRICOLA.

2.3-80 Goldschmidt, E.E. 1979. The fate of chlorophyll protein complexes during senescence of detached parsley leaves. Plant Physiol. 3 (5 Suppl.): 73 (Abstr.).

2.3-81 Goliya, V.T., and Ivanova, L.N. 1974. Seasonal and age-induced changes in the content of geranium essential oil and its components [in Russian]. Page 255 in A.A. Baev et al., eds. Ref. nauchn. soobshch. vses. biokhim. s'ezd., 3rd. Akad. Nauk Latviiskoi SSR, Inst. Org. Sint., Riga, USSR.

2.3-82 Grashchenkov, A.E., and Kozlova, N.A. 1972. The effect of maleic hydrazide on peppermint (Mentha piperita) [in Russian]. Pages 39-40 in P.V. Naumenko et al., eds. Mezhdunarodnyi kongress po efirnym maslam, 4th, Tiflis, 1968, [Materialy], v. 2. Pishchevaya Promyshlennost', Moscow, USSR. HA 44: 4207.

2.3-83 Gupta, V.K. 1974. Effect of rhizosphere fungi on nodule number and shoot and root length of Trigonella foenum-graecum L. Indian Phytopathol. 27: 463-465. SF 39: 5488.

2.3-84 Gurny, L., Vuagnat, P., Gurny, R., and Kapetanidis, I. 1980. Culture of Digitalis purpurea L. calli. Part I. Study of growth by analysis of variance [in French]. Pharm. Acta. Helv. 55: 302-306.

2.3-85 Haapala, E. 1973. The growth of the primary roots and root hairs of Sinapis alba and Lepidium sativus in Triton X-100. Physiol. Plant. 28: 56-60.

2.3-86 Haccius, B. 1975. Leafless nodes experimentally induced by use of phenylboric-acid. A contribution to the definition of sprouting nodes [in German]. Bot. Jahrb. Syst. Pflanzengesch. Pflanzengeogr. 96{1-4}: 90-106.

2.3-87 Han, B.H., Song, B.J., and Ro, H.S. 1976. Time course change in the composition of ginseng polyacetylenes [in Korean]. Soul Taehakkyo Saengyak Yonguso Opjukjip 15: 128-130. CA 88: 47506.

2.3-88 Hawthorn, W.R., and Cavers, P.B. 1978. Resource allocation in young plants of two perennial species of Plantago. Can. J. Bot. 56: 2533-2537.

2.3-89 Hendriks, H., and Os, F.H.L. Van. 1976. Essential oil of two chemotypes of Mentha suaveolens during ontogenesis. Phytochemistry 15: 1127-1130

2.3-90 Herisset, A., Jolivet, J., Chaumont, J.-P., and Boussarie, M.-F. 1972. Development of the essential oil of peppermint (Mentha piperita L.) in the course of the day [in French]. Plant. Med. Phytother. 6: 20-24.

2.3-91 Hofman, P.J., and Menary, R.C. 1980. Variations in morphine, codeine and thebaine in the capsules of Papaver somniferum L. during maturation. Aust. J. Agric. Res. 31: 313-326.

2.3-92 Hofman, P.J., and Menary, R.C. 1980. Changes in the surface characteristics of capsules of Papaver somniferum L. during maturation. Aust. J. Plant Physiol. 7: 353-361.

2.3-93 Hore, B.K., and Bose, T.K. 1972. Effects of B-Nine on growth and flowering in some tropical ornamental plants. Indian J. Hortic. 29: 93-96. HA 45: 5202

2.3-94 Humphrey, W.A., Nyland, G., and Mock, T. 1973. Growth of heat-treated jasmine. Flower Nursery Rep. Commer. Grow. Univ. Calif. Agric. Ext. Nov., 1973: 11. AGRICOLA.

2.3-95 Ivanova, L.N. 1978. Quality of the essential oil from a hybrid No. 7 geranium with respect to gathering time and leaf age [in Russian]. Pages 136-140 in Sb. St. po Efiromaslich. Kul'turam i Efir. Maslam. CA 90: 209941.

2.3-96 Ivanova, R.M., and Levandovskii, G.S. 1980. Pattern of correlations of morphological and biological indices in fenugreek (Trigonella foenum-graecum) [in Russian]. Khim.-Farm. Zh. 14{3}: 71-74. HA 50: 8465.

2.3-97 Iwai, K., Suzuki, T., and Fujiwake, H. 1979. Formation and accumulation of pungent principle of hot pepper fruits, capsaicin and its analogues, in Capsicum annuum var. annuum cv. Karayatsubusa at different growth stages after flowering. Agric. Biol. Chem. 43: 2493-2498.

2.3-98 Iwasaki, F. 1975. Studies on bolting in Brassica. VII. Morphological and histochemical observations on internode elongation [in Japanese]. Engei Gakkai Zasshi 44{1}: 22-32. HA 46: 8407.

2.3-99 Jager, A. de, and Posno, M. 1979. A comparison of the reaction to a localized supply of phosphate in Plantago major, Plantago lanceolata and Plantago media. Acta Bot. Neerl. 28: 479-489.

2.3-100 Janardhan, K., and Hanmanth Rao, P. 1979. Estimation of leaf area in Capsicum frutescens L. by rapid method. Indian J. Bot. 2{1}: 76-79.

2.3-101 Jaskonis, J. 1976. Reproduction and growth of Spanish licorice Glycyrrhiza glabra and the content of active substances in its roots. 1. Reproduction and growth [in Russian]. Liet. TSR Mokslu Akad. Darb. Ser. C 1976{2}: 45-52. CAIN 77080723.

2.3-102 Jolivet, E., Lefevre, S., and Coninck, B. de. 1974. Determining the maturity of witloof chicory root by means of a simple biochemical test [in French]. Pepinier. Hortic. Maraichers 1974{149}: 97-100. HA 45: 7323.

2.3-103 Joseph, C., and Paulet, P. 1973. Variations in the endogenous cytokinin content of chicory roots in relation to vernalization by cold treatment [in French]. C. R. Hebd. Seances Acad. Sci. Ser. D. 277: 785-788.

2.3-104 Joseph, C., and Paulet, P. 1975. Study of the effects of cold vernalization on Cichorium intybus L. roots [in French]. Physiol. Veg. 13: 517-525.

2.3-105 Kabdal, P.B., and Joshi, P. 1978. Effect of 2,4-dichlorophenoxy acetic acid (2,4-D) on development and corm formation in Crocus sativus Linn. Indian J. Pharm. 40: 165-166.

2.3-106 Kamentseva, I.E. 1974. Thermostability of some cellular functions in leaves of various Allium species with ephemeroid and prolonged vegetation cycles [in Russian]. Bot. Zh. (Leningrad) 59 1669-1675.

2.3-107 Kato, T., Kobayashi, M., Sasaki, N., Kitahara, Y., and Takahashi, N. 1978. The coumarin heraclenol as a growth inhibitor in parsley seeds. Phytochemistry 17: 158-159. HA 48: 3820.

2.3-108 Kazakova, K., and Astadzov, N. 1971. Productivity of Salvia sclarea L. at different age of the plants [in Bulgarian]. Rastenievud. Nauki 8{4}: 63-70.

2.3-109 Khanna, R., and Sinha, S.K. 1974. Photosynthesis and photosynthetic enzymes in reproductive organs of some crop plants. Indian J. Genet. Plant Breed. 34A: 1041-1047. FCA 29: 7488.

2.3-110 Kharchenko, L.N. 1973. Changes in the steroid composition during the ripening of Indian mustard seeds [in Russian]. Fiziol. Biokhim. Kult. Rast. 5: 90-94. HA 43: 7970.

2.3-111 Kharchenko, L.N. 1973. Metabolism of lipids during the process of ripening of Indian mustard seeds. Sov. Plant Physiol. (Engl. Transl.) 20: 100-105. Translation of Fiziol. Rast. (Moscow) 20: 123-129, 1973.

2.3-112 Khidir, M.O., and Khattab, A.H. 1972. Oil, protein and dry matter development in sesame seed. Exp. Agric. 8: 61-65.

2.3-113 Khristov, Kh., and Petrova, L. 1976. Effect of gibberellic acid on the water state of Salvia seedlings grown in the dark and in the light [in Bulgarian]. Fiziol. Rast. (Sofia) 2{2}: 79-87. CA 86: 38508.

2.3-114 Khristov, Kh.D. 1978. Phosphorus compound content in salvia seedlings grown in light and darkness and treated with gibberellic acid [in Bulgarian]. Fiziol. Rast. (Sofia) 4{3}: 36-42. HA 50: 8430.

2.3-115 Kireeva, S.A., Pavlenko, V.A., and Krivtsova, N.V. 1975. Induction of dormancy condition in peppermint for increasing its frost resistance [in Russian]. Tr. Vses. Nauchno-Issled. Inst. Efirnomaslichn. Kul't. 8: 177-183. AGRICOLA.

2.3-116 Koblet, R. 1979. Development of seasonal course in dry weight increase and competitive behavior of meadow plants in the alpine area [in German]. Z. Acker- Pflanzenb. 148: 23-53.

2.3-117 Kodash, A.G., Zakharova, O.I., and Zakharova, A.M. 1974. The dynamic accumulation of essential oil and menthol in Menthol piperita of the "Polyhybrid-7" sort [in Russian]. Farmatsiya (Moscow) 23{4}: 66-67.

2.3-118 Kornievsk'ii, Iu.I., and Koreshchuk, K.E. 1971. Dynamics of the seasonal accumulation of the main groups of chemical compounds of Valeriana stolonifera Czern [in Ukrainian]. Farm. Zh. (Kiev) 26: 67-70. CIM 13{2}: 1948.

2.3-119 Kotaeva, D.V., and Chanishvili, S.S. 1971. Incorporation of phosphorus-32 into the RNA of the leaves of some dioecious plants [in Russian]. Soobshch. Akad. Nauk Gruz. SSR 63: 149-152.

2.3-120 Kotecha, A.-K., Yermanos, D.M., and Shropshire, F.M. 1975. Flowering in cultivars of sesame (Sesamum indicum) differing in photoperiodic sensitivity. Econ. Bot. 29: 185-191.

2.3-121 Kowal, T., and Pic, S. 1971. Dynamics of oil accumulation in Levisticum officinale [in Polish]. Ann. Pharm. (Poznan) 9: 45-56. CA 76: 37337.

2.3-122 Krastina, E.E., and Loseva, A.S. 1976. Developmental rate in white mustard and spring wheat under different lengths of the light:dark cycle [in Russian]. Izv. Timiryazevsk. S-kh. Akad. 1976{5}: 14-20. FCA 30: 5543.

2.3-123 Kravets, T.I., Tanasienko, F.S., Vasyuta, G.G., and Moskalenko, M.L. 1975. Changes in the essential oil content and composition of fresh and lightly dried peppermint plants during different phases of ontogeny [in Russian]. Tr. Vses. Nauchno-Issled. Inst. Efirnomaslichn. Kul't. 8: 239-246. HA 47: 7763.

2.3-124 Kreasky, J.B., and Bailey, J.C. 1977. Papaver somniferum L.:
Effect of gibberellins on flowering and growth. J. Miss. Acad. Sci.
22: 79-82. CA 88: 100265.

2.3-125 Krug, H., and Foelster, E. 1978. Influence of the environment on
growth and development of chives (Allium shoenoprasum L.). I.
Induction of the rest period. Sci. Hortic. (Amsterdam) 4: 211-220.

2.3-126 Kubicek, F. 1975. Contribution to measuring the leaf area in
Asperula odorata L. [in Slovak]. Biologia Ser. A (Bratislava) 30:
791-794. AGRICOLA.

2.3-127 Kubicek, F. 1976. Growth and development of Asperula odorata L.
in an oak-hornbeam Quercus, Carpinus ecosystem. Biologia Ser. A
(Bratislava) 31: 41-53.

2.3-128 Kuiper, P.J.C. 1979. Response of Plantago species from
nutrient-rich and nutrient-poor habitats: Growth response, ATPase and
lipids of the roots, as affected by mineral nutrition. Plant Physiol.
63 (5 Suppl.): 116 (Abstr.).

2.3-129 Kuperman, F.M., and Kuryanchik, I.A. 1973. The characteristics
of organogenesis in Anethum graveolens under different light regimes
[in Russian]. Doklady Vsesoyuznoi Ordena Lenina Akademii
Sel'skokhozyaistvennykh Nauk imeni V.I. Lenina 1973{3}: 21-23. HA 44:
3423.

2.3-130 Kuribayashi, T., Harima, M., and Ohashi, H. 1975. Physiological
and ecological studies in Panax ginseng. VI. Effects of gibberellin,
water and forced aeration on the dehiscence of seed [in Japanese].
Syoyakugaku Zasshi 29{1}: 52-61.

2.3-131 Kurlyanchik, I.A. 1973. Organogenesis of dill (Anethum
graveolens L.) [in Russian]. Biol. Nauki (Moscow) 1973{10}: 74-77.

2.3-132 Kuszlik-Jochym, K., and Mazur, B. 1973. A search for inhibitors
of anaerobic metabolism of carbohydrates among the triterpene saponin
glycosides. Preliminary screening of plant extracts. Acta Biol.
Cracov. Ser. Bot. 16: 203-213. CA 85: 189205.

2.3-133 Kuzina, E.F., Mikhailenko, M.A., Poliakova, N.I., Tiurina, E.V.,
and Sharygina, I.S. 1975. Characteristics of development of coriander
in relation to the place of testing [in Russian]. Byull. Vses. Inst.
Rastenievod. 1975{55}: 81-84.

2.3-134 Landsberg, E.-C. 1980. Fe-deficiency stress induced development
of transfer cells in the epidermis of red pepper roots. Plant Physiol.
65 (6 Suppl.): 17 (Abstr.).

2.3-135 Lee, C.L., and Kwei, Y.L. 1973. Studies on the morphological
differentiation of excised stems of Mentha haplocalyx. II. The effect
of maleic hydrazide on excised stem tips [in Chinese]. Chih Wu Hsueh
Pao 15: 147-154. HA 44: 9938.

2.3-136 Lee, W.S. 1974. Studies on dormancy of Korean local garlics [in
Korean] Hanguk Wonye Hakhoe Chi 15: 119-141. HA 45: 9471.

2.3-137 Lee, W.S. 1975. A study on storage leaf formation in Korean
garlic bulbs during storage [in Korean]. Hanguk Wonye Hakhoe Chi 16:
48-52. HA 47: 2497.

2.3-138 Lengauer, E., and Mullner, E. 1974. The reaction of some phosphate-fractions in plants upon increased superphosphate-doses [in German]. Land Forstwirtsch. Forsch. Osterr. 6: 199-211. AGRICOLA.

2.3-139 Lovell, P.H., Illsley, A., and Moore, K.G. 1973. The effect of sucrose on primordium development and on protein and RNA levels in detached cotyledons of Sinapis alba L. Ann. Bot. 37{152}: 805-816.

2.3-140 Love, J.E., Fontenot, J.F., and White, J.W. 1971. Ripening hot peppers with ethrel. La. Agric. 14{4}: 14-15. AGRICOLA.

2.3-141 Lukasik, S., and Hortynska, E. 1976. Ethephon speeds up the ripening of paprika [in Polish]. Ogrodnictwo 13: 150-151. AGRICOLA.

2.3-142 Maarse, H. 1974. Volatile oil of Origanum vulgare L. ssp. vulgare. III. Changes in composition during maturation. Flavour Ind. 5: 278-281.

2.3-143 Mantovani, E.C., and Conde, A.R. 1980. Development and physiological maturation of seeds of the bush red pepper (Capsicum annuum L.) [in Portuguese]. Rev. Ceres. 27{152}: 356-368. AGRICOLA.

2.3-144 Margara, J. 1974. Vernalization in vitro of Cichorium intybus buds having lost the ability to respond to photoperiodic flower induction [in French]. C. R. Hebd. Seances Acad. Sci. Ser. D 278: 2283-2286.

2.3-145 Margara, J. 1977. The effects of growth regulators in association with different photoperiodic cycles on flower induction in vitro in spontaneously formed buds of Cichorium intybus L. [in French]. C. R. Hebd. Seances Acad. Sci. Ser. D. 284: 1991-1994.

2.3-146 Matusevich, E.V. 1972. The photoperiodic reaction of peppermint [in Russian]. Pages 108-110 in P.V. Naumenko et al., eds. Mezhundarodnyi Kongress po Efirnym Maslam, 4th, Tiflis, 1968, [Materialy], v.2. Pishchevaya Promyshlennost', Moscow, USSR. HA 44: 4206.

2.3-147 Megha, B.M., and Laloraya, M.M. 1977. Effect of abscisic acid on growth, IAA oxidase, peroxidase and ascorbate oxidizing systems in Trigonella foenum-graecum L. seedlings. Biochem. Physiol. Pflanz. (BPP) 171: 269-277.

2.3-148 Mehta, S., Punj, M.L., Hundal, L.S., and Bhatia, I.S. 1972. Studies on the structural carbohydrates of raya (Brassica juncea L.) at different stages of maturity and their metabolism in the rumen. Indian J. Dairy Sci. 25: 276-283. HERB AB 43: 2893.

2.3-149 Mialoundama, F., and Paulet, P. 1975. Variations in chlorogenic and isochlorogenic acids during the cold treatment of Cichorium intybus roots in connection with their disposition to produce flowers in vitro [in French]. C. R. Hebd. Seances Acad. Sci. Ser. D 280: 1385-1387.

2.3-150 Mialoundama, F., and Paulet, P. 1975. Changes in the content of chlorogenic and "isochlorogenic" acids during the cold treatment of Cichorium intybus roots [in French]. Physiol. Plant. 35: 39-44.

2.3-151 Mikhailova, V.P., Kashkarova, N.F., and Kuz'min, E.V. 1976. The biological productivity of the principal liquorice plant associations in the valley of the river Syr-Dar'ya [in Russian]. Tr. Inst. Bot. Akad. Nauk Kaz. SSR 35: 88-105. HA 47: 4969.

2.3-152 Misra, G., and Padhee, D.K. 1975. The effect of age, petiole, light and chemicals on senescence of leaves. Proc. Indian Sci. Cong. 62: (pt. III Sect. VI): 110 (Abstr.).

2.3-153 Mlodzianowski, F., and Mlodzianowska, L. 1973. Chloroplast degeneration and its inhibition by kinetin in detached leaves of Cichorium intybus L. Acta Soc. Bot. Pol. 42: 649-656. HA 44: 9482.

2.3-154 Muchnik, Zh.S. 1974. Kinetics of accumulation of nutrients in plants of Glycyrrhiza glabra L. [in Russian]. Page 96 in Introduktsiya i akklimatizatsiya rastenii na Ukraine i v Moldavii. 'Naukova dumka', Kiev, USSR. HERB AB 46: 1687.

2.3-155 Mukhortova, T.G., and Mashanova, N.S. 1973. Lavandin flowering in relation to essential oil accumulation and composition [in Russian]. Byull. Gos. Nikitsk. Bot. Sada 1973{2}: 35-37. HA 45: 3428.

2.3-156 Muthuswami, S., and Rao, V.N.M. 1980. Heat units and flowering in jasmines. Pages 7-9 in National Seminar on Production Technology for Commercial Flower Crops. Tamil Nadu Agricultural University, Coimbatore, India. HA 51: 7229.

2.3-157 Narayana, H.S., and Jain, P.S. 1978. Effect of postemergence application of Lasso and nitrogen on growth and nodulation in Trigonella foenum-graecum L. Geobios 5: 193-196. WA 28: 3063.

2.3-158 Novak, V. 1974. The determination and use of a critical growth stage in caraway [in Czech]. Rostl. Vyroba 20: 117-128. HA 45: 2693.

2.3-159 Nover, L., Luckner, M., Tewes, A., Thommes, R., and Vogel, E. 1979. Cell specialization and cardiac glycoside formation in cell cultures of Digitalis spec. Planta Med. 36: 227-228 (Abstr.).

2.3-160 Olszewski, Z., Pluta, J., and Szymczak, J. 1974. Examination of essential oil of a mint (Mentha crispa) during different vegetation seasons [in Polish]. Herba Pol. 20: 247-252. AGRICOLA.

2.3-161 Paliwal, N., Barma, B., and Paliwal, G.S. 1975. A comparative study of the effect of morphactin and Niagra on the leaf epidermis. Biol. Plant. 17: 189-197. HA 46: 2771.

2.3-162 Pal, P., Maity, R.G., and Bose, T.K. 1980. Effects of growth regulators on Jasminum sambac var. Khoya and J. auriculatum var. Double. Pages 35-38 in National Seminar on Production Technology for Commercial Flower Crops. Tamil Nadu Agricultural University, Coimbatore, India. HA 51: 7182.

2.3-163 Pappiah, C.M., and Muthuswamy, S. 1977. Effect of growth regulants on growth and flowering in Jasminum grandiflorum L. clone Thimmapuram. South Indian Hortic. 25{2}: 68-74. HA 48: 10029.

2.3-164 Pappiah, C.M., and Muthuswamy, S. 1978. Effect of growth regulators on growth, flowering, flower quality and essential oil content of Jasminum auricultatum Vahl. var. pari-mullai. South Indian Hortic. 26: 66-71.

2.3-165 Park, H., Kim, K.S., and Bae, H.W. 1979. Effect of gibberellin and kinetin on bud dormancy breaking and growth of Korean ginseng root (Panax ginseng C.A. Mey.). Proc. Plant Growth Regul. Work. Group (6th): 210-217. Bib. Ag. 45: 866.

2.3-166 Park, H., Park-Lee, Q., and Lee, C.H. 1980. Saponin pattern of Panax ginseng root in relation to stem color. Hanguk Nonghwa Hakhoe Chi 23: 222-227.

2.3-167 Park, S.K., and Jeong, H.J. 1976. The effect of shading on blossom-dropping and fruit-dropping of the hot pepper plant (Capsicum annuum L.) [in Korean]. Res. Rep. Off. Rural Dev. (Hortic. Agri-Engin.) 18: 1-8. AGRICOLA.

2.3-168 Pavlov, P., and Ilieva, S. 1972. Certain biochemical changes in the initial developmental phases of Salvia sclarea plants grown in different light [in Bulgarian]. Rastenievud. Nauki 9{10}: 13-19. HA 43: 7085.

2.3-169 Pelyakh, E.M., Chobanu, V.I., Nikolaev, A.G., and Nguen Kuang Zung. 1976. Terpenoid composition of an interspecific mint hybrid and its variability in ontogeny [in Russian]. Izv. Akad. Nauk Mold. SSR Ser. Biol. Khim. Nauk 1975{6}: 16-23.

2.3-170 Penny, M.G., Moore, K.G., and Lovell, P.H. 1976. Some effects of potassium deficiency on seedling development. Ann. Bot. 40: 801-813.

2.3-171 Phundan Singh. 1975. Note on the study of manganese and zinc deficiencies in India mustard (Brassica juncea (L) Czern & Coss). Indian J. Agric. Res. 9: 225-226. FCA 30: 496.

2.3-172 Platt-Aloia, K.A., and Thomson, W.W. 1977. Chloroplast development in young sesame plants. New Phytol. 78: 599-605.

2.3-173 Pogorelova, O.V. 1978. Localization of essential oil in common valerian during ontogenesis. Pharm. Chem. J. (Engl. Transl.) 12: 242-247. Translation of Khim.-Farm. Zh. 12{2}: 107-113, 1978.

2.3-174 Rahimi, A., and Bussler, W. 1974. Diagnosis of copper deficiency by means of visible symptoms on higher plants [in German]. Z. Pflanzenernaehr. Bodenkd. 135: 267-283. CA 81: 12433.

2.3-175 Rakhimbaev, I.R. and Ol'shanskaya, R.V. 1976. Dynamics of endogenous gibberellins during the process of transition of garlic bulbs from the state of dormancy to active growth. Sov. Plant Physiol. (Engl. Transl.) 23: 59-62. Translation of Fiziol. Rast. (Moscow) 23: 76-79, 1976.

2.3-176 Rao, P.G., and Sriramulu, M. 1977. Physiological characterization of a spice (Coriandrum sativum) and a condiment (Trigonella foenum graecum) during vegetative and reproductive stages. Curr. Sci. 46: 615-616.

2.3-177 Rasmussen, K.E., Rasmussen, S., and Baerheim Svendsen, A. 1972. Terpenes and related substances. XVII. Quantitative fluctuation in the composition of essential oils in the leaves of Rosmarinus officinalis as a function of the development of the leaves. Experimental design [in German]. Sci. Pharm. 40: 24-27. CA 77: 2770.

2.3-178 Rasmussen, K.E., Rasmussen, S., and Baerheim Svendsen, A. 1972. Terpenes and related compounds. XIX. Quantitative variations of some components of the foliage volatile oil of Rosmarinus officinalis in the spring. Pharm. Weekbl. 107: 309-313. CA 77: 58757.

2.3-179 Raymakers, A. 1973. Carbohydrates in Digitalis purpurea at various stages of development. Phytochemistry 12: 2331-2334.

2.3-180 Razhinskaite, D. 1972. Changes of essential oil content in the organs of caraway and coriander during plant ontogeny [in Russian] Pages 147-150 in P.V. Naumenko et al., eds. Mezhdunarodnyi kongress po efirnym maslam, 4th, Tiflis, 1968, [Materialy], v. 2. Pishchevaya Promyshlennost', Moscow, USSR. HA 44: 6955.

2.3-181 Rijven, A.H.G.C., and Eckhardt, L. 1972. Potassium and ammonium in the kinetin-induced expansion of fenugreek cotyledons. Z. Pflanzenphysiol. 66: 372-374.

2.3-182 Rivas-Martinez, S., Garcia Vallejo, C., and Garcia Martin, D. 1974. On the essential oil of Thymus gypsicola (Labiatae) [in Spanish]. An. Inst. Bot. A.J. Cavanilles 31: 317-323. PBA 44: 8287.

2.3-183 Rozov, N.F. 1973. The characteristics of growing, and the chemical composition of head lettuce, borage and cress in the phytotron [in Russian]. Izv. Timiryazevsk. S-kh. Akad. 1973{5}: 141-147. HA 44: 7564.

2.3-184 Ruminska, A., Suchorska, K., and Weglarz, Z. 1976. Effect of Woxal on the yield of some medicinal plants and the content of active substances in them [in Polish]. Zesz. Probl. Postepow Nauk Roln. 184: 169-174.

2.3-185 Saga, K. 1979. A study on the pungency of red pepper fruit (Capsicum annuum L.): Changes of the capsaicin and sugar contents in fruit in relation to fruit growth [in Japanese]. Hirosaki Daigaku Gakujutsu Hokoku 1979{31}: 39-47. Bib. Ag. 44: 66133.

2.3-186 Saha, S.N., and Bhargava, S.C. 1980. Physiological analysis of the growth, development and yield of oil-seed sesame. J. Agric. Sci. 95: 733-736.

2.3-187 Saidov, D.K., and Shamsuvalieva, L. 1976. Adventitious root formation on horizontal rhizomes of liquorice in saline soils [in Russian]. Pages 48-53 in D.K. Saidov, ed. Biologicheskie i morfologicheskie osobennosti poleznykh rastenii Uzbekistana. Fan., Tashkent, Uzbek SSR. HA 47: 5924.

2.3-188 Sakata, I., and Koshimizo, K. 1980. Seasonal variations in levels of menthy glucoside, menthol, menthone and related monoterpenes in developing plants of Japanese peppermint [in Japanese]. Nippon Nogei Kagaku Kaishi 54: 1037-1043. HA 51: 7233.

2.3-189 Sankhla, N., and Vyas, S.P. 1973. Growth and sex expression in Sesamum indicum Linn. as affected by morphactin. Biochem. Physiol. Pflanz. (BPP) 164: 22-33.

2.3-190 Sarkany, S., Nyomarkay, K.M., and Gracza, P. 1974. Studies on the connection between alkaloid formation, tissue structure, and organ differentiation in Papaver somniferum. Part 3 and Part 4. Studies on the reproductive stem apex and developing flower [in Russian]. Ann. Univ. Sci. Budap. Rolando Eotvos Nominatae Sect. Biol. 16: 103–121.

2.3-191 Sekhon, K.S., and Bhatia, I.S. 1972. Fatty acid changes during ripening of sesame (Sesamum indicum L.). Oleagineux 27: 371–373. AGRICOLA.

2.3-192 Semenikhin, I.D. 1976. Features of the ontogenesis of common valerian in pure and mixed crops. Pharm. Chem. J. (Engl. Transl.) 10: 923–925. Translation of Khim.-Farm. Zh. 10{7}: 83–85, 1976.

2.3-193 Sen, D.N., Bhandari, D.C., and Bansal, R.P. 1976. Antholysis of Sesamum indicum L. (til). Curr. Sci. 45: 248–249.

2.3-194 Sergeeva, D.S., and Selezneva, V.A. 1979. Essential oil accumulation, and changes in its qualitative composition during peppermint ontogeny [in Russian]. Fiziol. Biokhim. Kult. Rast. 11: 268–270.

2.3-195 Sergeeva, D.S., and Pavlenko, V.A. 1974. Frost resistance of the rhizomes in peppermint [in Russian]. Tr. Vses. Nauchno-Issled. Inst. Efirnomaslichn. Kul't. 7: 33–39. PBA 47: 2855.

2.3-196 Shalaby, A.S., and Verzar-Petri, G. 1978. Essential oil production and formation of its constituents during ontogeny in Achillea millefolium L. spp. collina Becker. Acta Hortic. 1978{73}: 219–228.

2.3-197 Sharma, B.N., and Bhatia, I.S. 1972. Changes in lipid classes during the ripening of seeds of sarson (Brassica campestris) and raya (Brassica juncea). J. Res., Punjab Agric. Univ. 9: 321–326.

2.3-198 Shatilov, I.S., and Rozov, N.F. 1973. The biological characteristics of some leaf vegetables in the phytotron [in Russian]. Izv. Timiryazevsk. S-kh. Akad. 1973{2}: 111–121. HA 43: 8617.

2.3-199 Shevchenko, S.V., and Denisova, G.A. 1971. Development of glandular formations in the leaf of Salvia sclarea [in Russian]. Rastit. Resur. 7: 282–287.

2.3-200 Shlyapyatis, Yu.Yu. 1974. Biology and biochemistry of the common wormwood. (6. Growth and development biology) [in Russian]. Liet. TSR Mokslu Akad. Darb. Ser. C 1974{3}: 61–65.

2.3-201 Shoferistova, E.G. 1971. The development of the essential glands in Lavandula vera DC. and L. spica L. with special reference to the biological role of the essential oil [in Russian]. Bot. Zh. (Leningrad) 56: 882–891.

2.3-202 Shoferistova, E.G., Rabotyagov, V.D., and Mashanov, V.I. 1977. Organogenesis and flowering biology of lavender and lavandin [in Russian]. Bot Zh. (Leningrad) 62: 1479–1491.

2.3-203 Shutenko, E.P. 1980. Structure of middle storey organs of Anethum graveolens L. shoot as affected by nitrogen deficiency [in Russian]. Vestn. Leningr. Univ. Biol. 1980{3}: 55–62. AGRICOLA.

2.3-204 Singh, B.P., and Garg, O.K. 1976. Relative growth and development in Mentha arvensis L. during summer and winter seasons. Indian J. Agric. Res. 10: 91–96. HA 48: 2693.

2.3-205 Singh, D.P., and Singh, J.N. 1971. Uptake and accumulation of phosphorus by Japanese mint (Mentha arvensis L. var. piperascens Holmes) as affected by phosphorus deficiency. Indian J. Agric. Sci. 41: 265-270. AGRICOLA.

2.3-206 Sinha, R.P., and Singh, C.P. 1972. Study of water balance in Capsicum annuum L. and C. frutescens L. Proc. Indian Sci. Cong. 59 (pt. III): 382 (Abstr.).

2.3-207 Skrubis, B., and Markakis, P. 1976. The effect of photoperiodism on the growth and the essential oil of Ocimum basilicum (sweet basil). Econ. Bot. 30: 389-393.

2.3-208 Slepetys, J. 1974. Biology and biochemistry of wormwood, Artemisia absinthium. 6. Growth and development biology [in Russian]. Liet. TSR Mokslu Akad. Darb. Ser. C 1974{3}: 61-65. AGRICOLA.

2.3-209 Stankiavichene, N.A., Morkunas, A.V., and Aliukonite, A.A. 1973. Changes in quantitative composition of essential oil of Coriandrum sativum according to ripeness of fruits [in Russian]. Pages 269-272 in K. Jankevicius, ed. Poleznye rasteniia Pribaltiiskikh respublik i Belorussii. Nauchnaia konferentisiia po issledovaniiu i obogashcheni, lu rastitel'nykh resurov pribaltiiskikh respublik i Belorussii, 2nd, Vilna, 1973. AGRICOLA.

2.3-210 Steward, F.C. 1971. Interacting effects of nutrients, growth factors and environments on metabolism and growth. Pages 595-621 in R.M. Samish, ed. Proceedings of the 6th international colloquium on plant analysis and fertilizer problems, Recent advances in plant nutrition. Tel-Aviv, Israel, March 1970, vol. 2. Gordon and Breach Sci. Publ., New York, N.Y.

2.3-211 Stieber, G., Lassanyi, Z., and Tyihak, E. 1979. Investigations on the essential oil secretory system of the chamomile flower. II. Changes in the prochamazulene content in the glandular hairs of chamomile flowers during ontogeny [in Hungarian]. Herba Hung. 18{1}: 27-39. HA 50: 548.

2.3-212 Suchorska, K. 1977. Changes in the enzyme activity of the redox system of Coriandrum sativum during ontogenesis [in German]. Herba Hung. 16{1}: 61-65. H.x a 49: 1435.

2.3-213 Suraj Bhan, and Amar Singh. 1973. Preliminary investigation on the root development of some oleiferous Brassicae. Sci. Cult. 39: 41-43.

2.3-214 Szujko-Lacza, J., Szocs, Z., and Hornok, L. 1975. LAR, RGR and NAR parameters internodially, and crop volatile oil yield in Pimpinella anisum L. sown periodically. Acta Bot. Acad. Sci. Hung. 21: 175-188.

2.3-215 Takagi, H., and Aoba, T. 1975. Studies on bulb formation in garlic. IV. Effects of storage temperature and humidity on dormancy, sprouting and rooting of bulbs [in Japanese]. Yamagata Norin Gakkaiho 1975{32}: 71-79. HA 48: 6453.

2.3-216 Takagi, H., and Aoba, T. 1976. Studies on bulb formation in garlic. VI. The effect of growth regulators on shoot growth and bulb formation [in Japanese]. Yamagata Norin Gakkaiho 1976{33}: 39-50. HA 48: 6454.

2.3-217 Tavadze, P.G., and Gugunava, N.A. 1972. Photosynthetic intensity and productivity and essential oil content in bay laurel [in Russian]. Pages 181-184 in P.V. Naumenko et al., eds. Mezhdunarodnyi kongress po efirnym maslam, 4th, Tiflis, 1968, [Materialy], v 2. Pishchevaya Promyshlennost', Moscow, USSR. HA 44: 4958.

2.3-218 Tavberidze, A.I. 1971. Changes in the composition of the essential oil of the spike-bearing savory in different vegetation stages [in Russian]. Tr. Gruz. Nauchno Issled. Inst. Pishch. Prom. 5: 178-183. CA 78: 20108.

2.3-219 Tayal, M.S., Sharma, C.B., and Gopal, R. 1978. The effect of some growth regulators on phosphorus metabolism in germinating seeds of fenugreek. Indian J. Plant Physiol. 21: 17-22. HA 48: 10865.

2.3-220 Thieme, H., and Tam, N.T. 1972. Investigations on the accumulation and composition of the essential oils of Satureja hortensis L., Satureja montana L. and Artemisia dracunculus in the course of development (ontogenesis): 2. Changes in oil content and in oil composition [in German]. Pharmazie 27: 324-331.

2.3-221 Thieme, H., and Tam, N.T. 1972. Investigations on the accumulation and the composition of the essential oils of Satureja hortensis L., Satureja montana L. and Artemisia dracunculus L. in the course of ontogenesis: I. Literature review, thin layer, and gas chromatographic investigations [in German]. Pharmazie 27: 255-265.

2.3-222 Udalova, V.I. 1976. Changes in the content and composition of essential oil of lavender and lavandine in relation to conditions of growth [in Russian]. Pages 221-222 in N.V. Tsitsin, ed. Okhrana sredy i ratsional'noe ispol'zovanie rastitel'nykh resursov. Izd. Nauka, Moscow, USSR. CA 89: 193951.

2.3-223 Uematsu, J., and Tomita, H. 1975. Studies on the flowering of some potted ornamental trees and shrubs. I. Time of flower bud differentiation and flower bud development in 6 species of ornamental shrub [in Japanese]. Bulletin of the Saitama Horticultural Experiment Station 1975{5}: 1-10. HA 46: 11618.

2.3-224 Unnikrishnan, K., and Hariharan, M. 1975. Leaf variation due to 2,4-D influence in Trigonella foenum-graecum L. Proc. Indian Acad. Sci. Sect. B 82B: 167-174.

2.3-225 Vadachkoriya, Ts.T. 1977. The dynamics of shoot growth and development on a Laurus nobilis plantation [in Russian]. Subtrop. Kul't. 1977{1/2}: 136-138. HA 48: 7550.

2.3-226 Vardukadze, D.A., and Chaukvadze, S.A. 1971. Root system development of young seedlings of bay laurel in relation to the type of soil [in Russian]. Subtrop. Kul't. 1971{5}: 144-148.

2.3-227 Vardukadze, D.A. 1975. Dynamics of root dying-off and alteration of its average length (root coefficient) in the seedlings of bay laurel [in Russian]. Subtrop. Kul't. 1975{4}: 85-88.

2.3-228 Vaverkova, S., and Priehradny, S. 1976. Changes in the growth of the wild chamomile and in the morphogenesis of the calathidum after treatment with flurenol [in Slovak]. Agrochemia 16: 279-282. AGRICOLA.

2.3-229 Veber, K., and Simmer, J. 1971. Compensation intensity of lighting in the cultivation of cucumber, tomatoes, and paprika in greenhouses [in German]. Int. Z. Landwirtsch. 1971{3}: 314-318. AGRICOLA.

2.3-230 Veerannah, L., and Rao, J.S. 1974. Studies on the effect of manganese on the nitrogen fractions in gingelly (Sesamum indicum L.). Madras Agric. J. 61: 501-504. AGRICOLA.

2.3-231 Velev, B., Dimov, I., Popov, D., and Murzov, Zh. 1977. Application of physiologically active substances for accelerating red pepper ripening [in Bulgarian]. Gradinarstvo 58{4}: 21-23. AGRICOLA.

2.3-232 Vertrees, G.L., and Mahlberg, P.G. 1978. Structure and ontogeny of laticifers in Cichorium intybus (Compositae). Am. J. Bot. 65: 764-771.

2.3-233 Verzar-Petri, G., Marczal, G., Lemberkovics, E., and Rajki, E. 1978. Morphological and essential oil production phenomena in chamomile growing in phytotron. Acta Hortic. 1978{73}: 273-282.

2.3-234 Wally, Y.A., Nassar, A.R., and Bunduq, A.Z. 1977. Effect of N6-benzyladenine on the chlorophyll and amino acids in parsley leaves during senescence. Egypt. J. Hortic. 4: 83-89. AGRICOLA.

2.3-235 Wanjari, K.B. 1976. Effect of gamma irradiation in Trigonella foenum graecum LJ. J. Maharashtra Agric. Univ. 1: 222-224. AGRICOLA.

2.3-236 Whitaker, J.R. 1976. Development of flavor, odor, and pungency in onion and garlic. Adv. Food Res. 22: 73-133. HA 47: 2498.

2.3-237 Wils, M.C. 1979. Botany: lemon balm and rosemary [in Flemish]. Vlaams. Imkersblad. 9: 45-48. AGRICOLA.

2.3-238 Worku, Z., Herner, R.C., and Carolus, R.L. 1975. Effect of stage of ripening and ethephon treatment on color content of paprika pepper. Sci. Hortic. (Amsterdam) 3: 239-246.

2.3-239 Yaskonis, Yu.A. 1976. The propagation and growth of liquorice and the active substances accumulation in the roots. (II. Active principle accumulation) [in Russian]. Liet. TSR Mokslu Akad. Darb. Ser. C 1976{3}: 49-56.

2.3-240 Zderkiewicz, T. 1971. The oil content during different ripening stages of seeds of diploid and tetraploid Carum carvi [in Polish]. Acta Agrobot. 24: 121-127. HA 43: 8980.

2.3-241 Zderkiewicz, T., and Dyduch, J. 1972. Dynamics of the accumulation of L-ascorbic acid and essential oil in different stages of parsley growth [in Polish]. Acta Agrobot. 25{2}: 179-184. CA 78: 133477.

2.3-242 Zlatev, S., Iliev, L., Vassilev, G.N., and Zlateva, M. 1980. Influence of certain purine and urea cytokinins on the rootstock yields of peppermint. Dokl. Bolg. Akad. Nauk 33: 555-557. HA 51: 601.

2.3-243 Zlatev, S., Zlateva, M., and Iliev, L. 1977. Effect of indole-acetic acid and some cytokinins and carbamide type over the growth and development of mint. Perfum. Flavor. 2{5}: 56 (Abstr.). HA 48: 5880.

2.3-244 Zlatev, S., and Balinova-Tsvetkova, A. 1974. The rate of essential oil accumulation in dill (Anethum graveolens) [in Bulgarian]. Rastenievud. Nauki 11{3}: 69-76. HA 44: 7953.

2.3-245 Zukalova, H., and Bechyne, M. 1975. Changes in morphological characteristics of poppy capsules and seeds and in oil content and fatty acid composition in the course of ripening [in Czech]. Rost. Vyroba 21: 977-985. PBA 46: 4572.

2.4 Plant Physiology and Metabolism

2.4-1 Abad Farooqi, A.H., and Maheshwari, S.C. 1977. Does cAMP stimulate nitrate reductase level in fenugreek cotyledons?. Biochem. Physiol. Pflanz. (BPP) 171: 231-234.

2.4-2 Abdrakhmanov, O.K., Filippova, N.F., and Kryukova, L.M. 1974. Effects of ionizing radiations on certain physiological processes of licorice. Radiobiology 14{5}: 175-177 Translation of Radiobiologiia 14: 787-789, 1974.

2.4-3 Abdrakhmanov, O.K., and Dzhakupova, N.U. 1976. Effect of gamma-rays on the germination, productivity and glycyrrhizic acid content of Glycyrrhiza glabra [in Russian]. Tr. Inst. Bot. Akad. Nauk Kaz. SSR 35: 112-115. HA 47: 4970.

2.4-4 Abdrakhmanov, O.K., and Baimurzaeva, A. 1978. Gibberellin like substances from licorice seeds [in Russian]. Vestn. Akad. Nauk Kaz. SSR 1978{5}: 71-72. CA 89: 72961.

2.4-5 Abou-Zied, E.N. 1974. Increase in volatile oil and chemical composition in the seeds of caraway and fennel plants induced by succinic acid-2,2-dimethylhydrazide. Biol. Plant. 16: 123-126. HA 44: 9928.

2.4-6 Abutalybov, M.G., Agabeili, R.A., Alekperov, U.K., and Askerov, I.T. 1976. Effect of the growth regulator Ionol on the vegetative propagation of Crocus sativus [in Russian]. Byull. Gl. Bot. Sada 100: 112-113. AGRICOLA.

2.4-7 Ahmed, S.S., and Eid, M.N.A. 1975. Effect of gibberellic acid and Cycocel on yield of seeds and essential oil of some umbelliferous plants. Egypt. J. Hortic. 2: 227-232. HA 47: 760.

2.4-8 Akita, S., and Moss, D.N. 1972. Differential stomatal response between C3 and C4 species to atmospheric CO2 concentration and light. Crop Sci. 12: 789-793.

2.4-9 Antoun, M.D., and Roberts, M.F. 1975. Enzymic studies with Papaver somniferum. 5. Occurrence of methyltransferase enzymes in poppy latex. Planta Med. 28: 6-11. CA 83: 160832.

2.4-10 Antoun, M.D., and Roberts, M.F. 1975. Some enzymes of general metabolism in the latex of Papaver somniferum. Phytochemistry 14: 909-914.

2.4-11 Aulakh, M.S., Pasricha, N.S., and Sahota, N.S. 1977.

Nitrogen-sulphur relationship in brown-sarson and Indian mustard. Indian J. Agric. Sci. 47: 249-253. FCA 32: 428.

2.4-12 Azizbekova, N.Sh., Milyaeva, E.L., Lobova, N.V., and Chailakhyan, M.Kh. 1978 Effects of gibberellin and kinetin of formation of flower organs in saffron crocus. Sov. Plant Physiol. (Engl. Transl.) 25: 471-476. Translation of Fiziol. Rast. (Moscow) 25: 603-609, 1978.

2.4-13 Bai, N.J., Sreekumar, K., and Krishnamurthy, S. 1972. Solubilization and properties of lipase from Sesamum indicum (gingelly) seeds. Indian J. Physiol. Pharmacol. 16: 270-271 (Abstr.).

2.4-14 Balasimha, D., Ram, C., and Tewari, M.N. 1976. Effect of 2,4-dichlorophenoxy acetic acid on growth and some aspects of metabolism in Trigonella foenum graecum L. seedlings. Biochem. Physiol. Pflanz. (BPP) 169: 515-518.

2.4-15 Balasimha, D., Ram, C., and Tewari, M.N. 1978. Effect of morphactin on some enzymes and peroxidase isoenzymes in fenugreek seedlings. Plant Biochem. J. 5: 77-82. AGRICOLA.

2.4-16 Benesova, M., Kovacs, P., and Senkpiel, K. 1974. Aminopeptidase activity in poppy seedlings (Papaver somniferum L. cv. "Dubsky") [in German]. Biochem. Physiol. Pflanz. (BPP) 166: 173-179.

2.4-17 Bernath, J., and Tetenyi, P. 1979. Alteration in compositional character of poppy, Papaver somniferum, chemotaxa affected by different light and temperature conditions. Herba Hung. 18{3}: 91-99.

2.4-18 Bernier, G., Kinet, J.M., Jacqmard, A., Havelange, A., and Bodson, M. 1977. Cytokinin as a possible component of the floral stimulus in Sinapis alba. Plant Physiol. 60: 282-285.

2.4-19 Cachita-Cosma, D., Ionica, A., Radulescu, T., and Popovici, G. 1975. The influence of procaine upon the phosphorus-32 and calcium-45 absorption into the red pepper seeds. Rev. Roum. Biol. 20: 193-198.

2.4-20 Camacho-B, S.E., and Hall, A.E., and Kaufmann, M.R. 1974. Efficiency and regulation of water transport in some woody and herbaceous species. Plant Physiol. 54: 169-172.

2.4-21 Chemarin, N.G., Glazurina, A.N., and Kucherova, T.P. 1972. The effect of gamma irradiation on lavender productivity [in Russian]. Byull. Gos. Nikitsk. Bot. Sada 1972{3}: 67-69. HA 44: 4205.

2.4-22 Croteau, R., Burbott, A.J., and Loomis, W.D. 1972. Apparent energy deficiency in mono- and sesqui-terpene biosynthesis in peppermint. Phytochemistry 11: 2937-2948.

2.4-23 Croteau, R., and Hooper, C.L. 1978. Metabolism of monoterpenes. Acetylation of (-)-menthol by a soluble enzyme preparation from peppermint (Mentha piperita) leaves. Plant Physiol. 61: 737-742.

2.4-24 Croteau, R., and Martinkus, C. 1979. Metabolism of monoterpenes. Demonstration of (+)-neomenthyl-beta -D-glucoside as a major metabolite of (-)-menthone in peppermint (Mentha piperita). Plant Physiol. 64: 169-175.

2.4-25 Croteau, R., Burbott, A.J., and Loomis, W.D. 1971.

Compartmentation of lower terpenoid biosynthetic sites in peppermint. Plant Physiol. 47 (Suppl.): 21 (Abstr.).

2.4-26 Cumbus, I.P., Hornsey, D.J., and Robinson, L.W. 1977. The influence of phosphorus, zinc and manganese on absorption and translocation of iron in watercress. Plant Soil 48: 651-660.

2.4-27 Czerwisnki, W., Stachurska, A., and Wiulczkowski, S. 1973. Initial investigation of the effect of detergents on plant growth and germination of seeds [in Polish]. Zesz. Nauk. Akad. Roln. Wroclawiu Roln. 1973{30}: 9-20. FCA 30: 1813.

2.4-28 Deacon, A.C., and Rutherford, P.P. 1972. Response of dandelion root tissue to treatment with 2,4- and 3,5-dichlorophenoxyacetic acids. Phytochemistry 11: 3143-3148.

2.4-29 Dhindsa, K.S., Gupta, S.K., and Pandya, R.B. 1975. Nitrogen metabolism of raya (Brassica juncea Coss.) during germination under simulated drought. Agrochimica 19: 394-398. SF 39: 4393.

2.4-30 Dimitrova-Ruseva, E., and Chuldzhiian, Kh. 1973. Mineral composition of Mentha piperita L. grown without nitrogen, phosphorus, potassium, magnesium, sulfur or iron [in Bulgarian]. Pages 261-267 in K. Daskalov, ed. Nauchna sesiia na instituta po genetika i selektsiia na rasteniiata, Sofia, 1971. Izd. vo na B'lgarskata Akademiia na Naukite, Sofia, Bulgaria. AGRICOLA.

2.4-31 Downing, M.R., and Mitchell, E.D. 1974. Metabolism of mevalonic acid to phosphorylated intermediates in a cell-free extract from Nepeta cataria leaves. Phytochemistry 13: 1419-1421.

2.4-32 Durand, J. 1972. Some results about the effect of GA3 on nucleic acids metabolism in Sinapis alba L. seedlings. Z. Pflanzenphysiol. 66: 468-472.

2.4-33 Eid, M.N.A., and Ahmed, S.S. 1976. Preliminary studies on the effect of gibberellic acid and cycocel on the growth and essential oil content of Ocimum basilicum L. Egypt. J. Hortic. 3: 83-87. 47: 10752.

2.4-34 Ellabban, H.M. 1978. Effect of Cycocel and spacings on the growth and volatile oil of Cymbopogon citratus. Sci. Hortic. (Amsterdam) 8: 237-242.

2.4-35 Elstner, E.F., and Heupel, A. 1976. Formation of hydrogen peroxide by isolated cell walls from horseradish (Armoracia lapathifolia Gilib.). Planta 130: 175-180.

2.4-36 El-Shourbagy, M.N., and Kishk, H.T. 1975. Sodium chloride effects on the sugar metabolism of several plants. Phyton (Horn, Austria) 17{1-2}: 101-108.

2.4-37 Erkan, Z., and Bangerth, F. 1980. Investigations on the effect of phytohormones and growth regulators on transpiration, stomata aperture and photosynthesis of pepper (Capsicum annuum L.) and tomato (Lycopersicon esculentum Mill.) plants [in German]. Angew. Bot. 54: 207-220.

2.4-38 Fairbairn, J.W., Handa, S.S., Gurkan, E., and Phillipson, J.D. 1978. In-vitro conversion of morphine to its N-oxide in Papaver somniferum latex. Phytochemistry 17: 261-262.

2.4-39 Fairbairn, J.W., Hakim, F., and El-Kheir, Y. 1974. Alkaloidal storage, metabolism and translocation in the vesicles of Papaver somniferum latex. Phytochemistry 13: 1133-1139.

2.4-40 Flood, A.E., Price, R., and Rowe, H.F. 1973. Effect of 2,4-dichlorophenoxyacetic acid treatment on the soluble and cell wall bound protein in Cichorium intybus root tissue. Phytochemistry 12: 1005-1008.

2.4-41 Franz, C., and Wunsch, A. 1972. Variations in nitrogen metabolism and essential oil content in wilting peppermint leaves [in German]. Angew. Bot. 46: 223-226.

2.4-42 French, C.S., Takamiya, A., and Murata, T. 1973. Resolution of the low temperature absorption spectra of chlorophyll-protein complexes into their component bands. Carnegie Institution of Washington Year Book 1972: 335-351.

2.4-43 Fridriksson, S., and Jonsson, A. 1975. Energy measurements of five vascular species in Iceland Deschampsia [in Icelandic]. Isl. Landbunadarrannsoknir 7{1/2}: 63-66. AGRICOLA.

2.4-44 Gej, B. 1971. Changes in 14CO2 absorption rates by the successive leaves in buckwheat and white mustard plants of various ages. Acta Soc. Bot. Pol. 40: 599-614. FCA 26: 2401.

2.4-45 Gil, V., and MacLeod, A.J. 1980. Degradation of glucosinolates of Nasturtium officinale seeds. Phytochemistry 19: 1657-1660.

2.4-46 Goldschmidt, E.E. 1976. Differences between gibberellins and cytokinins in retardation of leaf senescence in parsley (Petroselinum sativum L.). Isr. J. Bot. 25: 92 (Abstr.).

2.4-47 Gracza, P., and Verzar-Petri, G. 1972. Effect of cytokinins on the morphological conditions and alkaloid content of Papaver somniferum L. [in German]. Postep Dziedzinie Leku Rosl. Pr. Dosw. Wygloszone Symp., 1970; Herba Pol. Suppl. 1972: 182-189.

2.4-48 Grahl, H., and Wild, A. 1972. The variability of the photosynthetic unit in sun and shade plants [in German]. Z. Pflanzenphysiol. 67: 443-453

2.4-49 Gugunava, N.A. 1971. Productivity of photosynthesis in Laurus nobilis in relation to periodic operation [in Russian]. Subtrop. Kul't. 1971{3}: 84-90.

2.4-50 Hack, H.R.B. 1978. Stomatal infiltration in irrigation experiments on cotton, grain sorghum, groundnuts, kenaf, sesame and wheat. Ann. Bot. (London) 42: 509-547.

2.4-51 Hahlbrock, K., Knobloch, K.H., Kreuzaler, F., Potts, J.R.M., and Wellmann, E. 1976. Coordinated induction and subsequent activity changes of two groups of metabolically interrelated enzymes. Light-induced synthesis of flavonoid glycosides in cell suspension cultures of Petroselinum hortense. Eur. J. Biochem. 61: 199-206.

2.4-52 Hall, A.E., and Yermanos, D.M. 1975. Leaf conductance and leaf water status of sesame strains in hot, dry climates. Crop Sci. 15: 789-793.

2.4-53 Hall, A.E., and Kaufmann, M.R. 1975. Stomatal response to environment with Sesamum indicum L. Plant Physiol. 55: 455-459.

2.4-54 Henderson, H.M., and McEwen, T.J. 1972. Effect of ascorbic acid on thioglucosidases from different crucifers. Phytochemistry 11: 3127-3133.

2.4-55 Herath, H.M.W., and Ormrod, D.P. 1977. Carbon dioxide compensation values in citronella and lemongrass. Plant Physiol. 59: 771-772.

2.4-56 Herath, H.M.W., and Ormrod, D.P. 1979. Photosynthetic rates of citronella and lemongrass. Plant Physiol. 63: 406-408.

2.4-57 Hoad, G.V. 1973. Hormones in the phloem of higher plants. Pr. Inst. Sadow Ser. E Mater Zjazdow Konf. 3: 17-30. CA 30: 143130.

2.4-58 Hoagland, R.E. 1975. Hydrolysis of 3',4'-dichloropropionanilide by an aryl acylamidase from Taraxacum officinale. Phytochemistry 14: 383-386.

2.4-59 Hoesel, W., Shaw, P.D., and Barz, W. 1972. Degradation of flavonols in plant suspension cultures [in German]. Z. Naturforsch. B: Anorg. Chem. Org. Chem. Biochem. Biophys. Biol. 27: 946-954.

2.4-60 Hook, I.L.I., O'Connor, C.S., and Timoney, R.F. 1973. Some effects of chlorocholine chloride on Mentha piperita. Planta Med. 24: 249-259. HA 44: 6975.

2.4-61 Hopf, H., and Kandler, O. 1976. Physiology of umbelliferose [in German] Biochem. Physiol. Pflanz. (BPP) 169: 5-36.

2.4-62 Iqbal, J. 1972. Effects of acute gamma radiation on the survival, growth and radiosensitivity of the apical meristems of Capsicum annuum L. at different stages of seedling development. Radiat. Bot. 12: 197-204.

2.4-63 Jorgensen, L.B., Behnke, H.-D., and Mabry, T.J. 1977. Protein-accumulating cells and dilated cisternae of the endoplasmic reticulum in three glucosinolate containing genera: Armoracia, Capparis, Drypetes. Planta (Berl.) 137: 215-224.

2.4-64 Kahnt, G. 1972. Effects of stereoisomers of derivatives of cinnamic acid on growth in length of germ roots of different cultivated plants [in German]. Z. Acker- Pflanzenbau 135: 43-56.

2.4-65 Kaiser, W.M., Paul, J.S., and Bassham, J.A. 1979. Release of photosynthates from mesophyll cells in vitro and in vivo. Z. Pflanzenphysiol. 94: 377-385.

2.4-66 Karpova, G.Ya., Sivtsev, M.V., and Khilik, L.A. 1973. The physiological characteristics of Nepeta transcaucasica under irrigated conditions [in Russian]. Rastit. Resur. 9: 242-250.

2.4-67 Kaskey, J.B., and Tindall, D.R. 1979. Physiological aspects of growth and heteroblastic development of Nasturtium officinale under natural conditions. Aquat. Bot. 7: 209-229. AGRICOLA.

2.4-68 Kaufmann, M.R., and Eckard, A.N. 1971. Evaluation of water stress control with polyethylene glycols by analysis of guttation. Plant Physiol. 47: 453–456.

2.4–69 Kent, S.S. 1977. On the metabolic relationship between the Calvin cycle and the tricarboxylic acid cycle. 4. A plant survey for anomalous acetyl coenzyme A. Plant Physiol. 60: 274–276.

2.4–70 Khan, M.I. 1980. Effect of indoleacetic acid on the metabolic activity of Taraxacum officinale root segments. Biol. Plant. 22: 86–90.

2.4–71 Khristov, K., and Petrova, L. 1973. Content of phosphorus compounds in Salvia sclarea seedlings treated with gibberellic acid. Pr. Inst. Sadow. Skierniewice, Ser. E 3: 521–531. CA 82: 69111.

2.4–72 Kindl, H. 1971. Aromatic amino acids in the metabolism of higher plants [in German]. Naturwissenschaften 58: 554–563.

2.4–73 Kjonaas, R., Martinkus-Taylor, C., and Croteau, R. 1980. Metabolism of levo-methone in peppermint. Plant Physiol. 65 (6 Suppl.): 96 (Abstr.).

2.4–74 Knox, R.L., and Loomis, W.D. 1972. Physiology of plant secretory glands transport and metabolism of carbon compounds in oil and resin glands. Plant Physiol. 49 (Suppl.): 26 (Abstr.).

2.4–75 Kolosova, N.A. 1973. Nutrient uptake by mustard plants in relation to nutrition conditions [in Russian]. Khim. Sel'sk. Khoz. 11{7}: 27–31. FCA 27: 4169.

2.4–76 Komissarov, V.A., and Andreeva, A.V. 1972. Winter hardiness of garlic cloves in relation to their carbohydrate content [in Russian]. Dokl TSKhA 1972{179}: 35–39. PBA 44: 6289.

2.4–77 Koseva-Kovacheva, D., and Stanev, D. 1978. Effect of some growth regulators and hydrogen peroxide on peppermint oil content and composition [in Bulgarian]. Rastenievud. Nauki 15{5}: 21–25. HA 49: 7852.

2.4–78 Koseva, D., and Stanev, D. 1972. The effect of maleic hydrazide on the development and quantity of essential oil constituents in mint [in Bulgarian]. Rastenievud. Nauki 9{9}: 3–10. HA 43: 5499.

2.4–79 Kovacs, P. 1976. Dipeptidase activity in Papaver somniferum L. cv. "Dubsky" seedlings. Biochem. Physiol. Pflanz. (BPP) 169: 273–279.

2.4–80 Kozlova, N.A., and Grashchenkov, A.E. 1973. The action of maleic hydrazide on Mentha piperita [in Russian]. Pages 190–196 in Iu.V. Rakitin, ed. Gidrazid maleinovoi kisloty kak reguliator rosta rastenii. "Nauka", Moscow, USSR.

2.4–81 Kryukova, L.M., and Abdrakhmanov, O.K. 1971. Effect of ionizing radiations and phytohormones on germination and growth in Ural licorice. Sov. Plant Physiol. (Engl. Transl.) 18: 887–889. Translation of Fiziol. Rast. 18: 1043–1045, 1971.

2.4–82 Kuiper, D., and Kuiper, P.J.C. 1979. Ca2+- and Mg2+-stimulated ATPases from roots of Plantago major and Plantago maritima: response to alterations of the level of mineral nutrition and ecological significance. Physiol. Plant. 45: 1–6.

2.4-83 Kurian, T., and Iyengar, E.R.R. 1971. Evaluation of sea water tolerance of crop plants. 1. Effect of sea water dilutions on the process of germination and seedling growth of some crop varieties. Indian J. Agric. Res. 5: 145-150. FCA 26: 2415.

2.4-84 Kvet, J. 1975. Transpiration in seven plant species colonizing a fishpond shore. Biol. Plant. 17: 434-442. HERB AB 46: 2246.

2.4-85 Laisne, G., and Codaccioni, M. 1978. The effects of temperature and mannitol upon osmotic pressure in epidermal cells [in French]. C.R. Hebd. Seances Acad. Sci. Ser. D 286: 1191-1194.

2.4-86 Lambers, H. 1979. Efficiency of root respiration in relation to growth rate, morphology and soil composition. Physiol. Plant. 46: 194-202.

2.4-87 Lambers, H., and Hofstra, R. 1980. Energy and nitrogen metabolism of Plantago species. Plant Physiol. 65 (6 Suppl.): 121 (Abstr.).

2.4-88 Legrand, B., Gaspar, T., Penel, C., and Greppin, H. 1976. Light and hormonal control of phenolic inhibitors of peroxidase in Cichorium intybus L. Plant Biochem. J. 3: 119-127.

2.4-89 Loomis, W.D., and Burbott, A.J. 1977. Physiology of essential oil production in mint. Proc. Annu. Meet. Oreg. Essent. Oil Grow. League 28: 37-51. AGRICOLA.

2.4-90 Mees, J. 1974. The nutrient uptake of red pepper [in Hungarian]. Bull. Zoldsegtermesztesi Kut. Intez. 9: 137-141. AGRICOLA.

2.4-91 Megha, B.M., and Laloraya, M.M. 1978. Effect of gallic acid on dark-growth, IAA oxidase and peroxidase activities in Trigonella foenum graecum L. Biochem. Physiol. Pflanz. (BPP) 172: 305-310.

2.4-92 Megha, B.M., and Laloraya, M.M. 1978. Effect of ethrel on dark-growth, IAA oxidase, peroxidase and ascorbate oxidising system in Trigonella foenum graecum L. seedlings. Biochem. Physiol. Pflanz. (BPP) 173: 229-237.

2.4-93 Mendez, J. 1978. Endogenous abscisic acid in umbelliferous fruits. Z Pflanzenphysiol. 86: 61-64.

2.4-94 Merino, J., Garcia Novo, F., and Sanchez Diaz, M. 1976. Annual fluctuation of water potential in the xerophytic shrub of the Donana Biological Reserve (Spain). Oecol. Plant. 11: 1-11.

2.4-95 Mihalyfi, J.P. 1976. The changes in internal potassium concentration in Sinapis seedlings with external nutrition [in Hungarian]. Bot. Kozl. 63: 143-147. FCA 32: 3326.

2.4-96 Miller, R.J., Jolles, C., and Rapoport, H. 1973. Morphine metabolism and normorphine in Papaver somniferum. Phytochemistry 12: 597-603.

2.4-97 Mitchell, E.D., Downing, M., and Griffith, G.R. 1972. 14CO2 incorporation into nepetalactone. Phytochemistry 11: 3193-3194.

2.4-98 Moelgaard, P., and Hardman, R. 1980. Boron requirement and deficiency symptoms of fenugreek (Trigonella foenum-graecum) as shown

in a water culture experiment with inoculation of Rhizobium. J. Agric.
Sci. 94: 455-460.

2.4-99 Moore, K.G., Bentley, K., and Lovell, P.H. 1972. A comparative
study of chlorophyll production in coytledons. J. Exp. Bot. 23:
432-439.

2.4-100 Mueller, H.L., and Kirchgessner, M. 1972. Major and trace
element contents of dandelions and their dependence on growth stage
[in German]. Wirtschaftseigene Futter 18: 213-221. HERB-AB 45: 483.

2.4-101 Muller, F., and Meinert, G. 1971. Studies on the translocation
of 14-carbon-labelled-4-chloro-2- methylphenoxyacetic acid in the
various stages of Mentha arvensis L. development [in German]. Z.
Pflanzenkr. 78: 477-488. AGRICOLA.

2.4-102 Muthuswamy, S., and Pappiah, C.M. 1977. Nutritional studies on
Jasminum grandiflorum L. Indian J. Hortic. 34: 289-293. AGRICOLA.

2.4-103 Nagawiecka, H., and Boron, K. 1974. Evapotranspiration and field
water consumption by crops at Chelm near Krakow. Zesz. Probl. Postepow
Nauk Roln. 1974{161}: 155-168. FCA 29: 2207.

2.4-104 Narendra Singh, and Mahendra Singh. 1978. Effect of cations and
anions on the absorption of sulphur (S35) by raya seedlings (Brassica
juncea Coss). Indian J. Plant Physiol. 21: 34-40.

2.4-105 Nozzolillo, C. 1971. The effect of imbibition of solutions on
aniline on germination, growth, and red pigmentation of seedlings Can.
J. Bot. 49: 2113-2117.

2.4-106 Ogawa, T., and Shibata, K. 1977. Two phases of carbon dioxide
absorption on leaves. Pages 183-195 in Akira Mitsui, ed. Biological
solar energy conversion, Academic Press, Inc. New York, N.Y., London,
England. CA 88: 34673.

2.4-107 Palevitch, D., and Thomas, T.H. 1975. Enhancement of gibberellin
activity by ethylenediaminetetraacetic acid in celery seeds and
embryoless barley seeds. Physiol. Plant 34: 134-137.

2.4-108 Pallas, J.E., Jr. 1973. Diurnal changes in transpiration and
daily photosynthetic rate of several crop plants. Crop Sci. 13{2}:
82-84.

2.4-109 Pandya, R.B., Khan, M.I., Gupta, S.K., and Arora, S.K. 1974.
Effect of cycocel on growth, yield and chemical composition of raya
(Brassica juncea Coss.). Biochem. Physiol. Pflanz. (BPP) 165: 283-289.

2.4-110 Parkash, V. 1972. Synergism between cytokinins and nitrate in
induction of nitrate reductase activity in fenugreek cotyledons.
Planta 102: 372-373.

2.4-111 Pasricha, N.S., and Randhawa, N.S. 1972. Interaction effect of
sulphur and molybdenum on the uptake and utilization of these elements
by raya (Brassica juncea L.). Plant Soil 37: 215-220.

2.4-112 Patterson, B.D., and Graham, D. 1977. Effect of chilling
temperatures on the protoplasmic streaming of plants from different
climates. J. Exp.Bot. 28: 736-743.

2.4-113 Paul, J.S., Cornwell, K.L., and Bassham, J.A. 1978. Effects of ammonia on carbon metabolism in photosynthesizing leaf-free mesophyll cells from Papaver sommniferum. Plant Physiol. 61 (4 Suppl.): 38 (Abstr.).

2.4-114 Paul, J.S., Krohne, S.D., and Bassham, J.A. 1978. Effects of 2,4-D on photosynthesis in mesophyll cells isolated from a C-3 plant, Papaver somniferum. Plant Physiol. 61 (4 Suppl.): 44 (Abstr.).

2.4-115 Pfaff, W., and Schopfer, P. 1974. Phytochrome-induced regeneration of adventitious roots in the mustard seedling [in German]. Planta 117: 269-278.

2.4-116 Phillips, D.E., and Rutherford, P.P. 1976. Some enzyme changes in chicory (Cichorium intybus) during forcing. Ann. Appl. Biol. 84: 251-257.

2.4-117 Pihakaski, K., and Pihakaski, S. 1978. Myrosinase in Brassicaceae (Cruciferae). II. Myrosinase activity in different organs of Sinapis alba L. J. Exp. Bot. 29: 335-345.

2.4-118 Prakash, V., and Nandi, P.K. 1977. Association-dissociation behavior of sesame alpha-globulin in electrolyte solutions. J. Biol. Chem. 252: 240-243.

2.4-119 Purohit, S.D., Shekhawat, N.S., Ramawat, K.G., and Arya, H.C. 1979. Role of some oxidative enzymes and metabolites in Sesamum phyllody. Indian J. Exp. Biol. 17: 714-716.

2.4-120 Rai, B., and Agarwal, K.P. 1976. Rhizosphere microflora of garlic in relation to pretreatment of roots. Acta Bot. Indica 4: 97-104. RPP 57: 886.

2.4-121 Rama Das, V.S., Raja Reddy, K., Krishna, C.M., Samba Murthy, S., and Rao, J.V.S. 1979. Transpirational rates in relation to quality of leaf epicuticular waxes. Indian J. Exp. Biol. 17: 158-163.

2.4-122 Rijven, A.H.G.C. 1974. Ethylene and carbon dioxide in the growth regulation of isolated cotyledons of fenugreek (Trigonella foenum graecum L.) in darkness. Plant Sci. Lett. 2: 55-61.

2.4-123 Rijven, A.H.G.C., and Parkash, V. 1971. Action of kinetin on cotyledons of fenugreek. Plant Physiol. 47: 59-64.

2.4-124 Rijven, A.H.G.C. 1979. Cytokinin ribosides as inhibitors of ribonuclease activity on ribosomes from fenugreek (Trigonella foenum-graecum L.). Aust. J. Plant Physiol. 6: 621-627.

2.4-125 Rijven, A.H.G.C. 1976. Effects of fusicoccin and kinetin in isolated cotyledons of fenugreek (Trigonella foenum-graecum L.). Aust. J. Plant Physiol. 3: 567-574.

2.4-126 Rijven, A.H.G.C. 1972. Inhibitors and the dependence of kinetin-induced expansion on RNA synthesis in fenugreek cotyledons. J. Exp. Bot. 23: 1039-1049.

2.4-127 Rishi, Y.V., and David, S.B. 1977. Studies on the nitrogen metabolism of leguminous plants - I. Nitrogen fixation and distribution in Indigofera and Trigonella. J. Univ. Poona Sci. Technol. 50: 111-118. CA 88: 117842.

2.4-128 Robbins, M.L., and Sherwood, C.H. (21) Interaction of 2,4-D, ethephon and morphactin on pepper and zinnia. 1973. Interaction of 2,4-D, ethephon and morphactin on pepper and zinnia. Proc. Iowa Acad. Sci. 80: 72-73.

2.4-129 Roberts, M.F. 1974. Oxidation of tyrosine by Papaver somniferum latex. Phytochemistry 13: 119-123.

2.4-130 Robinson, L.W., and Cumbus, I.P. 1977. Determination of critical levels of nutrients in watercress (Rorippa nasturtium-aquaticum (L.) Hayek) grown in different solution concentrations of N, P and K. J. Hortic. Sci. 52: 383-390.

2.4-131 Robinson, T. 1974. Metabolism and function of alkaloids in plants. Science 184{4135}: 430-435.

2.4-132 Rossi, C. 1980. Effect of the potassium-magnesium interrelationship on phosphorus-32 absorption and translocation in sesame (Sesamum indicum L.) [in Spanish]. Turrialba 30{1}: 77-79. CA 93: 941474.

2.4-133 Rutherford, P.P., and Phillips, D.E. 1975. Carbohydrate changes in chicory during forcing. J. Hortic. Sci. 50: 463-473.

2.4-134 Rutherford, P.P., and Deacon, A.C. 1974. Seasonal variation in dandelion roots of fructosan composition, metabolism, and response to treatment with 2,4-dichlorophenoxyacetic acid. Ann. Bot. (London) 38: 251-260.

2.4-135 Sacco, T. 1978. Studies on the behaviour of Mentha piperita cultivar Italo Mitcham in Rio Grande do Sul, Brazil [in Italian]. Riv. Ital. Essenze Profumi Piante Off. Aromat. Synadets Saponi Cosmet. Aerosols 60: 63-65. HA 49: 5258.

2.4-136 Sadykov, B.F., and Umarov, M.M. 1980. Detection of nitrogen-fixing activity in the plant phyllosphere. Microbiology (Engl. Transl.) 49: 125-128. Translation of Microbiologiya 49: 147-150, 1980.

2.4-137 Sankhla, N., Huber, W., and Eder, A. 1979. Effect of fusicoccin on chlorophyll biosynthesis. I. Biochem. Physiol. Pflanz. (BPP) 174: 296-304.

2.4-138 Sanzharova, N.I. 1978. Change in the strontium-90 and calcium proportion during their uptake by plants from the soil [in Russian]. Vestn. Mosk. Univ. Ser 17: Pochoved. 1978{3}: 59-61. CA 90: 53740.

2.4-139 Sell, Y. 1974. Accumulation of radioactive phosphorus by axillary buds of Sinapis alba L. Relationship to preliminary treatment with unlabelled phosphate [in French]. C. R. Hebd. Seances Acad. Sci. Ser. D 278: 2441-2444.

2.4-140 Senich, V.Ya., Shishkov, G.Z., and Polyakov, A.F. 1974. Composition of CO2-extract of peppermint [in Russian]. Izv. Vyssh. Uchebn. Zaved. Pishch. Tekhnol. 1974{4}: 85-87. FSTA 7: 5T240.

2.4-141 Shih, J.H.C., Shannon, L.M., Kay, E., and Lew, J.Y. 1971. Peroxidase isoenzymes from horseradish roots. IV. Structural relationships. J Biol. Chem. 246: 4546-4551.

2.4-142 Singh, D.P., and Singh, J.N. 1971. Nitrogen and carbohydrate metabolism of Japanese mint as affected by phosphorus deficiency and seasonal variations. Physiol. Plant 24: 126-129.

2.4-143 Singh, J.P. 1978. Effect of nitrate nitrogen on carbohydrate metabolism of Japanese mint. Geobios (Jodhpur) 5: 255-259.

2.4-144 Singh, J.P., and Singh, J.N. 1979. Nitrogen and carbohydrate metabolism of Japanese mint as affected by forms of nitrogen. Indian J. Hortic. 36: 301-304.

2.4-145 Singh, J.P., and Singh, J.N. 1978. Effect of nitrate on respiration of Mentha arvensis. Biol. Plant. 20: 403-408.

2.4-146 Singh, O. 1979. Sulphur deficiency and alkaloid contens in mustard (Brassica campestris L. var. sarson, Prain) plants. Indian J. Plant Physiol. 22{1}: 78-80.

2.4-147 Slepyan, E.I., and Kotin, A.M. 1971. Use of the water-soluble carcinogen auramine-OO to induce cell hypertrophy in seedlings of flowering plants and prevention of such hypertrophy with actinomycin D. Dokl Bot. Sci. (Engl. Transl.) 199-201: 161-164. Translation of Dokl. Akad. Nauk SSSR 201: 747-750, 1971.

2.4-148 Srivastava, V.K., and Hill, D.C. 1974. Glucosinolate hydrolytic products given by Sinapis alba, and Brassica napus thioglucosidases. Phytochemistry 13: 1043-1046.

2.4-149 Steer, B.T. 1972. Leaf-growth parameters associated with photosynthetic capacity in expanding leaves of Capsicum frutescens L. Ann. Bot. (London) 36{145}: 377-384.

2.4-150 Steer, B.T. 1971. The dynamics of leaf growth and photosynthetic capacity in Capsicum frutescens L. Ann. Bot. (London) 35{143}: 1003-1015.

2.4-151 Steer, B.T. 1973. Diurnal variations in photosynthetic products and nitrogen metabolism in expanding leaves. Plant Physiol. 51: 744-748.

2.4-152 Steer, B.T. 1973. Control of ribulose-1,5-diphosphate carboxylase activity during expansion of leaves of Capsicum frutescens L. An N. Bot. (London) 37: 823-829.

2.4-153 Stohs, S.J., and Haggerty, J.A. 1973. Metabolism of 4-cholesten-3-one to 5-alpha-cholestan-3-one by leaf homogenates. Phytochemistry 12: 2869-2872.

2.4-154 Stohs, S.J., and El-Olemy, M.M. 1972. Pregnenolone and progesterone metabolism by cardenolide producing plants. Phytochemistry 11: 2409-2413.

2.4-155 Stulen, I., Hofstra, R., and Kuiper, P.J.C. 1980. Some interactions between energy and nitrogen metabolism of Plantago species. Plant Physiol. 65 (6 Suppl.): 121 (Abstr.).

2.4-156 Subramanian, R., and Shanmugavelu, K.G. 1980. Ascorbic acid, nucleic acids, protein, amino acid and carbohydrate metabolism in the flowering of Jasminum grandiflorum L. Indian J. Hortic. 37{4}: 409-414. CA 95: 184038.

2.4-157 Sutter, A., Poulton, J., and Grisebach, H. 1975. Oxidation of flavanone with cell-free extracts from young parsley leaves. Arch. Biochem. Biophys. 170: 547-556.

2.4-158 Tychsen, K., and Andersen, A.S. 1973. Abscisic acid and dormancy of chives (Allium schoenoprasum L.). Arsskr. K. Vet. Landbohoejsk. Copenhagen 226: 39-48.

2.4-159 Vagabova, M.E. 1975. Respiration in cotyledons after gamma-irradiation of seeds with stimulating doses [in Russian]. Rad iobiologiya 15: 470-471. FCA 29: 556.

2.4-160 Vartanian, N. 1971. Morphogenetic effect of the hydric factor on the root system of Sinapis alba L. 1. Rhizogenesis and root water potential [in French]. Rev. Gen. Bot. 78: 171-183. FCA 26: 6837.

2.4-161 Vincent, W.F., and Downes, M.T. 1980. Variation in nutrient removal from a stream by watercress (Nasturtium officinale R.Br.). Aquat. Bot. 9: 221-235. AGRICOLA.

2.4-162 Wacquant, J.-P. 1972. Effect of some basic solutions on the cation adsorption of rootlets [in French]. C.R. Hebd. Seances Acad. Sci. Ser. D 274: 2057-2060.

2.4-163 Wagner, H., Schaette, R., Hoerhammer, L., and Hoelzl, J. 1972. Dependence of the valepotriate and ethereal oil content in Valeriana officinalis L. s.l. upon different exogenous and endogenous factors [in German]. Arzneim.-Forsch. 22: 1204-1209. CA 77: 123810.

2.4-164 Wild, A., and Zerbe, R. 1977. The effect of different light intensities on the nitrate reductase activity and the concentration of soluble proteins and soluble reducing sugars in Sinapis alba during development from germination to flowering [in German]. Biochem. Physiol. Pflanz. (BPP) 171: 201-209. HA 47: 11730.

2.4-165 Zeinalov, Yu.A. 1977. Calorimetric determination of energy accumulation by phytomass of different plant groups in Azerbaijan SSR [in Russian]. Izv. Akad. Nauk Az. SSR Ser. Biol. Nauk 1977{4}: 53-59. HERB AB 48: 2773.

2.4-166 Zholkevich, V.N., Volkov, D.I., Prudnikov, V.N., and Shidlovskaya, I.L. 1971 A new approach to the link between respiration and energy-requiring physiological processes. Dokl. Bot. Sci. (Engl. Transl.) 196-198: 66-68. Translation of Dokl. Akad. Nauk SSSR 197: 1210-1213, 1971.

2.4-167 Zlatev, S., Iliev, L., Zlateva, M., and Vasilev, G. 1978. Effect of some cytokinins on fresh plant material and essential oil yields in peppermint [in Bulgarian]. Rastenievud. Nauki 15{2}: 51-56. HA 49: 7851.

2.5 Reproduction and Regeneration

2.5-1 Amrutavalli, S.A. 1980. Interaction of gibberellic acid (GA3) and benzyladenine (BA) on flowering and sex expression in Bulgarian coriander (Coriandrum sativum L.). Indian J. Plant Physiol. 23: 14-20.

2.5-2 Andronova, N.N. 1978. The sporogenesis and the development of gametophytes in Asperula odorata L. (Rubiaceae Juss., Galieae Dumort.) [in Russian]. Bot. Zh. (Leningrad) 63: 404-410.

2.5-3 Antonova, L.A. 1979. Entomophilous pollination in oak forests of the forest-steppe [in Russian]. Zh. Obshch. Biol. 40: 290-294.

2.5-4 Arinshtein, A.I., and Zobenko, L.P. 1972. The biology of fertilization and fruit formation in clary sage [in Russian]. Sel. Semenovod. (Kiev) 1972{20}: 75-79. HA 43: 1411.

2.5-5 Arinshtein, A.I., Volkovskaya, N.S., and Lyalushkin, V.I. 1975. Characteristics of flowering in Salvia sclarea in Moldavia [in Russian]. Tr. Vses. Nauchno-Issled. Inst. Efirnamaslichn. Kul't. 8: 25-28. PBA 48: 12315.

2.5-6 Assouad, M.W., Dommee, B., Lumaret, R., and Valdeyron, G. 1978. Reproductive capacities in the sexual forms of the gynodioecious species of Thymus vulgaris L. Bot. J. Linn. Soc. 77: 29-39.

2.5-7 Assouad, W., and Valdeyron, G. 1975. Notes on the biology of the flower of Thymus vulgaris L. [in French]. Bull. Soc. Bot. Fr. 122: 21-34.

2.5-8 Babajev, R.A., and Rahimov, M. 1975. The biology of mint flowering in Azerbaijan [in Azerbaijani]. Pages 156-165 in Introduktsiya i akklimatizatisiya rastenii. Elm, Baku, Azerbaijan SSR. HA 47: 4900.

2.5-9 Bochkarev, N.I. 1973. Characteristics of pollen germination after crosses between the parental species of Indian mustard [in Russian]. Byul. nauch.-tekhn. inform. po maslich. kul'turam 1973{2}: 15-18. PBA 46: 3598.

2.5-10 Bodson, M., King, R.W., Evans, L.T., and Bernier, G. 1977. The role of photosynthesis in flowering of the long-day plant Sinapis alba. Aust. J. Plant Physiol. 4: 467-478. HA 48: 5858.

2.5-11 Bostock, S.J., and Benton, R.A. 1979. The reproductive strategies of five perennial Compositae. J. Ecol. 67: 91-107.

2.5-12 Brabant, Ph., Gouyon, P.H., Lefort, G., Valdeyron, G., and Vernet, Ph. 1980. Pollination studies in Thymus vulgaris L. (Labiatae). Acta Oecol. [Ser.]: Oecol. Plant. 1: 37-45.

2.5-13 Bryzgalova, N.V. 1974. Pollen viability of Jasminum sambac Ait. and Jasminum mesnyi Hanse [in Russian]. Zap. Leningr. S-kh. Inst. 226: 48-50. AGRICOLA.

2.5-14 Bryzgalova, N.V. 1974. Blossoming of several Jasminum species grown in sheltered ground [in Russian]. Zap. Leningr. S-kh. Inst. 226: 50-54. AGRICOLA.

2.5-15 Burgett, M. 1980. Pollination of parsley (Petroselinum crispum grown for seed. J. Apic. Res. 19: 79-82.

2.5-16 Buyukly, M.V. 1971. Flower morphogenesis and some peculiarities of micro- and macrosporogenesis in Lavandula vera DC [in Russian]. Bot. Zh. (Leningrad) 56: 1496-1498.

2.5-17 Caillas, A. 1972. Lavender and lavandins [in French]. Abeille Fr. Apic. 554: 338-339. AGRICOLA.

2.5-18 Chaudhari, P.N., and Zope, R.E. 1977. Studies on vicinism in Sesamum (Sesamum indicum L.). J. Maharashtra Agric. Univ. 2: 233-235. AGRICOLA.

2.5-19 Chauhan, S.V.S., and Singh, S.P. 1971. Induction of male sterility in sesame (Sesamum indicum L.). Indian J. Agric. Sci. 41: 725-729. AGRICOLA.

2.5-20 Colombo, P.M., Lucchin, F., and Colombo, B. 1977. On the control of the population effect on in vitro assays of pollen germination. J. Exp. Bot. 28: 425-438.

2.5-21 Corduan, G. 1976. Isozyme variation as an indicator for the generative of somatic origin of anther-derived plants of Digitalis purpurea L. Z. Pflanzenzuecht. 76: 47-55. PBA 47: 2599.

2.5-22 Crane, E. 1972. Bees in the pollination of seed crops. J. R. Agric. Soc. Eng. 133: 118-135. HA 43: 5899.

2.5-23 D'Albore Giancarlo, R., and D'Ambrosio, M. 1979. First observation on the pollinating activity of the honeybee (Apis mellifera ligustica Spin.) and other insects on coriander (Coriandrum sativum) [in Italian]. Apic. Mod. 70: 151-157. AGRICOLA.

2.5-24 Dabral, K.C., and Mandloi, K.C. 1974. A peculiar sterility in sesame, (Sesamum indicum L.). JNKVV Res. J. 8: 54-56. AGRICOLA.

2.5-25 Devi, H.M. 1975. Embryology of jasminums and its bearing on the composition of Oleaceae. Page 110 in V.S. Motial, ed. Seminar on recent advances in plant sciences. Abstracts of papers. Association for Advancement of Plant Sciences, Kalyani, India.

2.5-26 Dharamadhaj, P., and Prakash, N. 1978. Development of the anther and ovule in Capsicum L. Aust. J. Bot. 26: 433-439.

2.5-27 Diettrich, B., Neumann, D., and Luckner, M. 1980. Protoplast-derived clones from cell cultures of Digitalis purpurea. Planta Med. 39: 375-382.

2.5-28 Dommee, B., Assouad, M.W., and Valdeyron, G. 1978. Natural selection and gynodioecy in Thymus vulgaris L. Bot. J. Linn. Soc. 77: 17-28.

2.5-29 Dubey, R. 1972. Embutox (2,4-dichlorophenoxybutryic acid) - a new phytogametocide. Curr. Sci. 41: 297-298.

2.5-30 Duke, J.A. 1980. Pollinators of Panax. Castanea 45: 141.

2.5-31 Dzevaltovs'ky, A.K., and Polishchuk, V.S. 1974. Aspects of flower morphogenesis in certain representatives of the family Lamiaceae Lindl. [in Ukrainian]. Ukr. Bot. Zh. 31: 645-648.

2.5-32 Dzhurmanski, G. 1977. Study of diploids, tetraploids and chimeras of Allium sativum L. and A. fistulosum L. [in Bulgarian]. Gradinar. Lozar. Nauka 14{4}: 52-59. PBA 48: 4346.

2.5-33 Ebrahimzadeh, H., and Fotowati, A. 1980. Development of cytoplasmic and nuclear proteins in saffron (Crocus sativus L.) during flower formation [in French]. Physiol. Veg. 18: 411-417.

2.5-34 Eenink, A.H. 1975. Induction of flowering in witloof chicory (Cichorium intybus L. var. foliosum) and a wild lettuce species (Lactuca virosa L.) by cold treatment [in Dutch]. Zaadbelangen 29: 8-10. HA 46: 2118.

2.5-35 Eisner, T., Eisner, M., and Aneshansley, D. 1973. Ultraviolet patterns on rear of flowers: Basis of disparity of buds and blossoms. Proc. Natl. Acad. Sci. USA 70: 1002-1004.

2.5-36 El-Berry, A.A., Moustafa, M.A., Abdel-Gawaad, A.A., and El-Bialey, S. 1974. Pollinators other than honey bees visiting certain vegetable plants in Egypt. Z. Angew. Entomol. 77: 106-110.

2.5-37 El-Berry, A.R., Gawaad, A.A.A., Moustafa, M.A.K., and El-Gayar, F.H. 1974. Pollinators other than honey bees visiting certain medicinal plants in Egypt. Z. Angew. Entomol. 76: 113-119.

2.5-38 Estilai, A., and Aghamohammadi, Z. 1977. Pollen stainability and pollen germination in relation to sterility of saffron (Crocus sativus L.). Q. Bull. Fac. Sci. Tehran Univ. 9{1/2}: 10-15. AGRICOLA.

2.5-39 Ferrazzi, P. 1978. The common dandelion (Taraxacum officinale Web. family of Asteraceae) [in Italian]. Apic. Mod. 69: 57-58. AGRICOLA.

2.5-40 Free, J.B. 1975. Pollination of Capsicum frutescens L., Capsicum annuum L. and Solanum melongena L. (Solanaceae) in Jamaica. Trop. Agric. 52: 353-357.

2.5-41 Friden, F. 1972. Bumblebees and agricultural crops [in Swedish]. Svensk Frotidning 41: 77-82. HERB AB 45: 2070.

2.5-42 Gary, N.E., Witherell, P.C., and Lorenzen, K. 1980. Distribution of foraging honey bees to multiple, small floral plots of various species. Environ. Entomol. 9: 43-46.

2.5-43 Georgiev, St. 1972. A study on the biology of blooming and fertilization in sesame (Sesamum indicum L.) under temperate climate conditions concerning their use for selection and seed production purposes [in Bulgarian]. Rastenievud. Nauki 9{8}: 39-47.

2.5-44 Ghatnekar, S.D., and Kulkarni, A.R. 1978. Studies on pollen storage in Capsicum frutescens and Ricinus communis. J. Palynol. 14: 150-157.

2.5-45 Gogina, E.E. 1971. Some characteristics of the flowering of thyme [in Russian]. Byull. Gl. Bot. Sada 77: 64-71. AGRICOLA.

2.5-46 Gopal, J., and Singh, A. 1979. Meiotic behaviour and seed fertility in advanced generation autotetraploids of fenugreek. Indian J. Genet. Plant Breed. 39: 323-329.

2.5-47 Gopinath, P.M. 1974. A case of rare triploidy in excised root cultures of Trigonella foenum-graecum Linn. Curr. Sci. 43: 524-525.

2.5-48 Guh, J.O., and Lee, S.S. 1980. Comparative study with some sesame cultivars on ripening development [in Korean]. Hanguk Changmul Hakhoe Chi 25{2}: 58-63.

2.5-49 Hackett, W.P., Kister, J., and Tse, A.T.Y. 1974. Flower induction of Pelargonium domesticum Baily cv. Lavender Grand Slam with exposure to low temperature and low light intensity. HortScience 9: 63-65.

2.5-50 Hammer, K. 1978. Evolutionary trends concerning pollination ecology in Plantago [in German]. Flora (Jena) 167: 41-56.

2.5-51 Huang, H. 1973. Effect of ethrel on the ripening of hot pepper [in Chinese]. Kuo Li Taiwan Ta Hsueh Nung Hsueh Yuan Yen Chiu Pao Kao 14{8}: 1-11. AGRICOLA.

2.5-52 Ibrahim, S.H. 1976. A list of pollen plants visited by honeybees in Egypt. Agric. Res. Rev. 5{41}: 217-219. FCA 31: 2169.

2.5-53 Ilieva, S. 1972. Investigation of the biology of flowering and pollination of clary (Salvia sclarea L.) in connexion with its breeding [in Russian]. Pages 76-78 in P.V. Naumenko et al., eds. Mezhdunarodnyi kongress po efirnym maslam, 4th, Tiflis, 1968, [Materialy], v. 2. Pishchevaya Promyshlenost', Moscow, USSR. PBA 46: 1008.

2.5-54 Iwasaki, F. 1972. The characteristics of isozyme in male sterile rape (Brassica napus L.) [in Japanese]. Ikushugaku Zasshi 22: 274-276.

2.5-55 Kamal, S., and Akhtar, M. 1976. Role of insects in pollination of raya (Brassica juncea H.F. & T.) flowers. Pak. J. Agric. Sci. 13{1}: 65-72. AA 29: 700.

2.5-56 Kandelaki, G.V., and Kobakhidze, L.A. 1977. Studies on the embryo sac and double fertilization in Ocimum basilicum [in Russian]. Soobshch Akad. Nauk Gruz. SSR 86{1}: 177-180. HA 48: 738.

2.5-57 Kapil, R.P., and Kumar, S. 1974. Foraging activity of Apis dorsata Fab. on Brassica juncea Hook. and Thomas. J. Bombay Nat. Hist. Soc. 71: 327-332. FCA 30: 5541.

2.5-58 Karlova, A.A. 1973. Development of the anther wall microsporogenesis and formation of the male gametophyte in 4 species of the genus Digitalis L. [in Russian]. Biol. Nauki.16{8}: 55-57

2.5-59 Kennedy, H., and Ganders, F.R. 1979. The invisible patterns of flowers. Davidsonia 10: 1-6.

2.5-60 Khamidov, G.Kh. 1972. New data on the nectar productivity of Capparis spinosa L. in the southwestern Tien Shan [in Russian]. Dokl Akad. Nauk Uzb. SSR 9: 49-50. AGRICOLA.

2.5-61 Khan, M.I. 1976. Metabolic changes in the regenerating and non-regenerating Taraxacum root segments. Pak. J. Bot. 8: 53-62.

2.5-62 Kheyr-Pour, A. 1980. Nucleo-cytoplasmic polymorphism for male sterility in Origanum vulgare L. J. Hered. 71: 253-260.

2.5-63 Khoklov, S.S., and Zaitseva, M.I. 1975. Study of gynodiecy and the possibilities of apomixis in some species of the Labiatae [in

Russian]. Pages 316 in Apomiksis i tsitoembirol rastenii, 3. Saratov Univ., Saratov, USSR. PBA 47: 6942.

2.5-64 Kinet, J.M., Bodson, M., Jacquard, A., and Bernier, G. 1975. The inhibition of flowering by abscisic acid in Sinapis alba L. Z. Pflanzenphysiol. 77: 70-74.

2.5-65 Kiss, A. 1974. Order of the flowering process of some paprika varieties [in Hungarian]. Agrobotanika 16: 77-88. AGRICOLA.

2.5-66 Konon, N.T. 1978. Biology of flowering and pollination in Valeriana officinalis L. in the Moscow region [in Russian]. Rastit. Resur. 14: 73-77. AGRICOLA.

2.5-67 Konvicka, O., Nienhaus, F., and Fischbeck, G. 1978. Investigations on the causes of pollen sterility in Allium sativum L. [in German]. Z. Pflanzenzeucht. 80: 265-276.

2.5-68 Krejcik, V. 1974. Basil [in Czech]. Vcelarstvi 27{2}: 34. AGRICOLA.

2.5-69 Kucherov, E.V., and Siraeva, S.M. 1980. Nectar productivity and the composition of nectar sugars of certain wild nectariferous plants of Bashkiria [in Russian]. Rastit. Resur. 16{4}: 523-530. CA 94: 44065.

2.5-70 Kugler, H. 1972. Pollination of Salvia sclarea by carpenter bees, Xylocopa violacea [in German]. Oesterr. Bot. Z. 120{1/2}: 77-85.

2.5-71 Kukheva, L.V. 1976. Pollen variability of Glycyrrhiza glabra, Glycyrrhiza uralensis and Glycyrrhiza pallidiflora [in Russian]. Pages 136-141 in N.V. Smol'skii, ed. Introduktsiia rastenii. Nauka Tekhnika, Minsk, USSR.

2.5-72 Kurbanov, E.A. 1975. Biology of the flowering of introduced species of thyme on the Apsheron Peninsula (Thymus karamarjanicus Klok etshost; Thymus collinus M.B.) [in Russian]. Izv. Akad. Nauk Az. SSR Ser. Biol. Nauk 1975{3}: 17-21.

2.5-73 Kurennoy, N.M. 1971. Effect of bee population rates on yield and quality of coriander seeds. Pages 512-516 in International Apicultural Congress, 23d, Moscow, 1971. Apimondia, Bucharest, Romania.

2.5-74 Lachowska, H. 1971. A study of autotetraploid chicory [in Polish]. Howdowla Rosl. Aklim. Nasienn. 15: 229-273. PBA 43: 5502.

2.5-75 Lee, H.J., Yun, J.I., and Kwon, Y.W. 1980. Flowering and seed maturation of sesame cropped after winter barley [in Korean]. Hanguk Changmul Hakhoe Chi 25{1}: 66-71.

2.5-76 Levandovskii, G.S., Yurtseva, N.S., and Ivanova, R.M. 1979. The specificity of pollination of Trigonella foenum-graecum [in Russian]. S-kh. Biol. 14{1}: 118-119.

2.5-77 Lieux, M.H. 1978. Minor honeybee plants of Louisiana indicated by pollen analysis. Econ. Bot. 32{4}: 418-432.

2.5-78 Lloyd, D.G. 1976. The transmission of genes via pollen and ovules in gynodioecious angiosperms. Theor. Popul. Biol. 9: 299-316.

2.5-79 Margara, J. 1973. The interaction of nutritional factors on floral initiation in buds of Cichorium intybus formed in vitro [in French]. C. R. Hebd. Seances Acad. Sci. Ser. D 277: 2673-2676.

2.5-80 Margara, J. 1973. The effect of isolating chicory buds on their vegetative or floral development [in French]. C. R. Hebd. Seances Acad. Sci. Ser. D. 277: 497-500.

2.5-81 Mathur, S.C., Anwer, M., Mathur, P.K., and Chandola, R.P. 1973. Studies on fruit formation with controlled nitrogen supply in coriander (Coriandrum sativum L.). Sci. Cult. 39: 351-352.

2.5-82 Mercy, S.T., Nair, V.G., and Babu, L.C. 1979. Anthesis in Indian lemongrass, Cymbopagon flexuosus Stapf. Agric. Res. J. Kerala 17 (pt. 2): 200-203. AGRICOLA.

2.5-83 Mihalea, A. 1971. Some aspects of the biology of foxglove [in Romanian]. Comun. Bot. 1971{12}: 481-488. AA 26: 557.

2.5-84 Muchnik, Zh.S. 1979. Flowering and fruiting of liquorice grown in the Moldavian SSR [in Russian]. Rastit. Resur. 15: 376-380. HA 50: 538.

2.5-85 Munakata, M. 1971. Relative abundance, phenology and flower preference of Andrenid bees at Akagawa near Hakodate, northern Japan (Hymenoptera, Apoidea). Hokkaido Kyoiku Daigaku Kiyo, Dai-2-Bu,B 22{1}: 26-39. RAE-A 61: 351.

2.5-86 Muthuswami, S., and Rao, V.N.M. 1980. The concept of relative temperture disparity (RTD) in the flowering of Jasminum species. Pages 11-14 in National Seminar on Production Technology for Commercial Flower Crops. Tamil Nadu Agricultural University, Coimbatore, India. HA 51: 7230.

2.5-87 Normatov, B.A., and Ashurmetov, A.A. 1980. Peculiarities of the development of ovule and embryo sac in Glycyrrhiza aspera [in Russian]. Uzb. Biol. Zh. 1980{3}: 35-38. HERB AB 51: 4546.

2.5-88 Novak, F.J. 1972. Tapetal development in the anthers of Allium sativum L. and Allium longicuspis Regel. Experientia 28: 1380-1381.

2.5-89 Okada, M. 1973. On the flower bud control of medicinal Angelica "Obuka-Toki", Angelica acutiloba Kit. [in Japanese]. Shokubutsu Kenkyu Zasshi 48: 344.

2.5-90 Petkov, V. 1978. Studies on the nectar bearing capacity of some seed oil, essential oil and medicinal plants [in Bulgarian]. Rastenievud Nauki 15{3}: 63-70.

2.5-91 Pierard, D., Jacqmard, A., and Bernier, G. 1977. Changes in the protein composition of the shoot apical bud of Sinapis alba in transition to flowering. Physiol. Plant. 41: 254-258.

2.5-92 Pillai, S.S., and Srinivasan, K. 1976. Studies on the effect of F, W-450 and MH as male gametocides in chillies (Capsicum frutescens L.). I-Effect on growth flowers and pollen grains. Pages 252-261 in K.L. Chadha, ed. Proceedings of the third international symposium on sub-tropical and improvement of horticultural, plantation and medicinal plants, Bangalore, India, Feb. 8-14, 1972. Today and Tomorrow's Printers & Publishers, New Delhi, India. vol. I.

2.5-93 Ponamarev, A.N., and Dem'yanova, E.I. 1975. A study of gynodiecy in plants [in Russian]. Bot. Zh. (Leningrad) 60: 3-15. PBA 45: 5948.

2.5-94 Pryke, J.A., and Bernier, G. 1978. RNA synthesis in the apex of Sinapis alba in transition to flowering. J. Exp. Bot. 29: 953-961.

2.5-95 Rabotyagov, V.D. 1973. Microsporogenesis in diploid and tetraploid lavender [in Russian]. Byull. Gos. Nikitsk. Bot. Sada 1973{2}: 52-56. HA 45: 2707.

2.5-96 Rabotyagov, V.D. 1980. Flower and inflorescence anomalies in Lavandula vera (illustrated description) [in Russian]. Bot. Zh. (Leningrad) 65: 219-222. HA 50: 7913.

2.5-97 Reader, R.J. 1977. Bogericad flowers: self compatibility and relative attractiveness to bees. Can. J. Bot. 55: 2279-2287.

2.5-98 Rihar, J. 1977. Honeybee colonies foraging on winter savory [in Slovenian]. Slovenski Cebelar 77: 258-259. AGRICOLA.

2.5-99 Savenko, L.A. 1978. Nectar productivity of coriander. Pchelovodstvo 1978{9}: 24. Bib. Ag. 43: 112081.

2.5-100 Sheldon, J.C., and Burrows, F.M. 1973. The dispersal effectiveness of the achene-pappus units of selected Compositae in steady winds with convection. New Phytol. 72: 665-675.

2.5-101 Shilova, S.N. 1972. The flowering biology of dill and fennel [in Russian]. Nauchn. Tr. Maikopskoi Opytn. Stan. Vses. Nauchno-Issled. Inst. Rastenievod. im. V.I. Vavilova 1972{5}: 115-120. HA 44: 645.

2.5-102 Shivanna, K.R., Heslop-Harrison, Y., and Heslop-Harrison, J. 1978. The pollen-stigma interaction: bud pollination in the Cruciferae. Acta Bot. Neerl. 27: 107-119.

2.5-103 Shoferistova, E.G. 1973. The early stages of ovary and ovule formation in lavender [in Russian]. Byull. Gos. Nikitsk. Bot. Sada 1973{2}: 57-61. HA 45: 3429.

2.5-104 Shoferistova, E.G., and Reznikova, S.A. 1977. Localization and dynamics of stored nutrients in developing anthers of lavender and lavendine. Cytol. Genet. (Engl. Transl.) 11{5}: 11-16. Translation of Tsitol. Genet. 11{5}: 403-408, 1977. AGRICOLA.

2.5-105 Singh, V.P., and Ramanujam, S. 1973. Expression of andromonecy in coriander, Coriandrum sativum L. Euphytica 22: 181-188.

2.5-106 Stead, A.D., and Moore, K.G. 1979. Studies on flower longevity in Digitalis: pollination induced corolla abscission in Digitalis purpurea flowers. Planta 146: 409-414.

2.5-107 Stead, A.D., and Moore, K.G. 1977. Flower development and senescence in Digitalis purpurea L. ev. cultivar foxy. Ann. Bot. 41: 283-292.

2.5-108 Szabo, M., and Gulyas, S. 1973. Red pepper as nectar yielding plant [in Hungarian]. Meheszet 21: 205. AGRICOLA.

2.5-109 Szujko-Lacza, J. 1976. Fertilization and fusion of free endosperm nuclei in Pimpinella anisum L. Acta Biol. Acad. Sci. Hung. 27: 65-70.

2.5-110 Szujko-Lacza, J. 1975. Nectary gland development and functional duration in Pimpinella anisum L. Acta Biol. Acad. Sci. Hung. 26: 51-65.

2.5-111 Teittinen, P. 1980. Observations on the food plants of the honeybee. Ann. Agric. Fenn. 19{2}: 156-163. AGRICOLA.

2.5-112 Trehan, K.B., Chand, H., Mehta, S.K., and Baijal, S.K. 1974. Studies on floral biology in sesame (Sesamum indicum L.). Telhan Patrika Oilseeds J. 4{3}: 7-11.

2.5-113 Valdeyron, G., Dommee, B., and Vernet, P. 1977. Self-fertilisation in male-fertile plants of a gynodioecious species: Thymus vulgaris L. Heredity 39: 243-249.

2.5-114 Valdeyron, G., Dommee, B., and Valdeyron, A. 1973. Gynodioecy: Another computer simulation model. Am. Nat. 107: 454-459.

2.5-115 Veluswamy, P., Thangaraj, T., and Muthuswamy, S. 1976. Studies on anthesis and pollination in some Jasminum species and varieties. South Indian Hortic. 24: 45-49.

2.5-116 Vereshchagina, V.A., and Malanina, L.I. 1974. Gynodiecy in marjoram (Origanum vulgare L.) [in Russian]. Nauchn. Dokl. Shk. Biol. Nauki 1974{6}: 51-57. PBA 45: 4126.

2.5-117 Vereshchagina, V.A., and Malanina, L.I. 1974. Gynodioecy of Origanum vulgare [in Russian]. Biol. Nauki 1974{6}: 51-57.

2.5-118 Wassink, E.C. 1975. Different bumble bees visiting Digitalis purpurea and its forma heptandra. Meded. Landbouwhogesch. Wageningen 75{20}: 1-6. AA 30: 473.

2.5-119 Yang, H.-Y., and Chang, C. 1975. Effect of pollen-grain number on fertilization, embryo development and progeny's characteristics in Sesamum indicum L. [in Chinese]. Ch'uan Hseuh Pao 2: 322-332.

2.5-120 Zhmykhova, V.S. 1977. Data of flowering and fruitification of plants in the Kursk region [in Russian]. Rastit. Resur. 13: 622-627.

2.6 Anatomy and Morphology

2.6-1 Aloni, R., and Sachs, T. 1973. The three-dimensional structure of primary phloem systems. Planta 113: 345-353.

2.6-2 Arevshatyan, I.G. 1977. Anatomical study of achenes in Armenian representatives of Taraxacum Wigg [in Russian]. Biol. Zh. Arm. 30{8}: 60-65.

2.6-3 Asoeva, E.Z., and Efimova, F.V. 1977. Anatomical investigations of species of the Psuedoglycyrrhiza section. I. [in Russian]. Rastit. Resur. 13: 491-498. HA 48: 1599.

2.6-4 Baciu, E., and Marin, J. 1971. Studies on the fruiting of some Salvia species [in Romanian]. Lucr. Stiint. Inst. Agron. Bucuresti Ser. B. 14: 131-136. HA 45: 4378.

2.6-5 Baranov, M.P., and Rumyantseva, L.A. 1975. Anatomical structure of the adventitious roots of some herbaceous dicotyledons [in Russian]. Vestn. Leningr. Univ. Biol. 1975{2}: 61-67.

2.6-6 Benbasat, E., and Ilieva, S. 1972. Morphological-anatomical investigations on the inflorescence of Salvia sclarea [in Bulgarian]. Rastenievud. Nauki 9{7}: 21-35. HA 43: 3037.

2.6-7 Berko, I.M. 1979. Semantics and use of the terms "half rosette shoot" and "half rosette plants" [in Ukrainian]. Ukr. Bot. Zh. 36: 269-271.

2.6-8 Bishnoi, S. 1973. Morphological embryological and histochemical studies in some angiosperms. Botanica 23: 150 (Abstr.).

2.6-9 Bobak, M. 1974. Translosomes, their arising, differentiation and function in the cells of primary roots. Acta Fac. Rerum Nat. Univ. Comenianae Physiol. Plant. 1974{8}: 25-31.

2.6-10 Borisovskaia, G.M., and Sokolova, A.E. 1974. The structure of Digitalis grandiflora and Digitalis purpurea in relationship to their life cycle [in Russian]. Vestn. Leningr. Univ. Biol. 1974 {21}: 37-45.

2.6-11 Borisovskaya, G.M., and Trifonova, H.L. 1980. On the structure of the stem of some representatives of the family Lamiaceae in connection with the evolution of life forms [in Russian]. Bot. Zh. (Leningrad) 65: 531-538.

2.6-12 Cappelletti, E.M. 1979. Microscopic characteristics of the epicarp of achenes of Carum carvi and its adulterant Aegopodium podagraria [in French]. Plant. Med. Phytother. 13: 205-212. HA 50: 4538.

2.6-13 Chloupek, O. 1977. Evaluation of the size of a plant's root system using its electrical capacitance. Plant Soil 48: 525-532.

2.6-14 Corovic, M., Stjepanovic, L., Pavlovic, S., and Klajn, E. 1976. A contribution to the study of the characteristics of the anatomical structure of the organs of fennel, Peucedanum longifolium W. et K. from the mountain Orjen, with reference to the quantity of coumarin and essential oil [in Serbo-Croatian]. Glas Prir. Muz. Beogr. Ser. B Biol. Nauke 31: 43-54. AGRICOLA.

2.6-15 Dagite, S.Yu. 1977. The distribution of essential oil glands on peppermint leaves [in Russian]. Liet. TSR Mokslu Akad. Darb. Ser. C 1977{2}: 27-30. HA 48: 5877.

2.6-16 Dave, Y.S., Patel, N.D., and Rao, K.S. 1979. Developmental and anatomical studies in the pericarp of capsicums. Flora (Jena) 168: 263-275.

2.6-17 De Padua, L.S. 1978. Anatomy of Symphytum officinale L. Phillip. J. Sci. 107: 41-50.

2.6-18 Dranygina, L.M. 1977. Morphological characteristics of the aerial parts and underground parts of horseradish [in Russian]. Tr. Vses. S-kh. Inst. Zaochn. Obraz. 1977{132}: 114-117. HA 48: 7546.

2.6-19 Elias, P., and Kozinka, V. 1976. Stomata in the leaves of Asperula odorata L. and Pulmonaria officinalis L. subsp. maculosa (Hanye) Gams. Biologia Ser. A (Bratislava) 31: 33-40.

2.6-20 Endrodi, G., and David, A. 1976. Stomatal resistance in different plants. Acta Agron. Acad. Sci. Hung. 25: 382-390.

2.6-21 Fairbairn, J.W., and Williamson, E.M. 1978. Anatomical studies on Papaver bracteatum (Lindley). Planta Med. 33{1}: 34-45.

2.6-22 Fairbairn, J.W., Hakim, F., and Dickenson, P.B. 1973. The alkaloidal vesicles of Papaver somniferum. J. Pharm. Pharmacol. 25 (Suppl.): 113-114 (Abstr.).

2.6-23 Ferreira, A.G., and Purper, C. 1972. Pollen grains of Umbelliferae from Rio Grande do Sul. III. Rev. Bras. Biol. 32{1}: 15-19.

2.6-24 Fisher, D.A., and Bayer, D.E. 1972. Thin sections of plant cuticles demonstrating channels and wax platelets. Can. J. Bot. 50: 1509-1511.

2.6-25 Freeman, J., and Aboulela, M.M. 1974. Anatomical studies of leaves from gamma irradiated and washed fenugreek beans. Tex. J. Sci. 25{1/4}: 15-34. AGRICOLA.

2.6-26 Furst, G.G. 1976. Anatomical and histochemical properties of onion leaf mesophyll [in Russian]. Byull. Gl. Bot. Sada 1976{102}: 74-80. HA 47: 5478.

2.6-27 Gomez-Campo, C. 1979. Studies on Cruciferae: VII. A leaf shape mutant in Brassica nigra (L.) Koch. An. Jard. Bot. Madrid 36: 115-118. PBA 51: 5371.

2.6-28 Govindarajalu, E., and Karunakaran, D. 1978. Comparative study of foliar anatomy of South Indian species of Jasminum. 1. Coastal sclereids as a new type. Adansonia 17: 281-292.

2.6-29 Grushvitskii, I.V., Skvortsova, N.T., Vysotskaia, R.I., Glinina, L.V., and Tarasova, T.S. 1975. Comparative anatomical and morphological study of the leaf in the genus Panax L. (Araliaceae) [in Russian]. Pages 80-89 in L.Iu. Budantsev, ed. Voprosy sravnitel'noi morfologii semennykh rastenii. "Nauka" Lendingradskoe otd-nie, Leningrad, USSR. AGRICOLA.

2.6-30 Hagemann, W. 1973. The organization of shoot development. Rev. Biol. 9: 43-67.

2.6-31 Heinrich, G. 1973. The development, fine structure and oil content of the glandular scales of Monarda fistulosa [in German]. Planta Med. 23: 154-166. HA 43: 9001.

2.6-32 Heinrich, G. 1973. The fine structure of the trichome hydathodes of Monarda fistulosa [in German]. Protoplasma 77: 271-278.

2.6-33 Heinrich, G. 1973. Development, fine structure, and oil content

of the patelliform glands of <u>Monarda</u> <u>fistulosa</u> [in German]. Planta
Med. 23: 154-166. CA 79: 2820.

2.6-34 Inamdar, J.A., and Bhatt, D.C. 1972. Structure and development of
stomata in some Labiatae. Ann. Bot. 36: 335-344.

2.6-35 Inamdar, J.A., and Murthy, G.S.R. 1977. Vessels in some
Solanaceae. Flora (Jena) 166: 441-448.

2.6-36 Issar, R.K. 1978. <u>Achillea</u> <u>millefolium</u> Linn. - Floristic
variability of morphological characters. Indian For. 104: 90-93.
AGRICOLA.

2.6-37 Iwasaki, F. 1972. Morphological and histochemical features of
pistil of <u>Brassica</u> varieties at flowering stage [in Japanese].
Ikushugaku Zasshi 22{6}: 340-345. FCA 27: 522.

2.6-38 Kadry, A., Tewfic, H.A., and Habib, S.A. 1978. Morphology and
distribution of glandular structures in <u>Foeniculum</u> <u>vulgare</u>, Mill.
Egypt. J. Hortic. 5: 13-19. HA 49: 690.

2.6-39 Kapoor, L.D. 1973. Constitution of amphicribral vascular bundles
in capsule of <u>Papaver</u> <u>somniferum</u> Linn. Bot. Gaz. (Chicago) 134:
161-165.

2.6-40 Khan, M.I. 1973. Anatomy of regenerating root segments of
<u>Taraxacum</u> <u>officinale</u> Web. Pak. J. Bot. 5: 71-77.

2.6-41 Kondratyeva-Melville, H.A. 1974. Morphological and anatomical
structure of <u>Papaver</u> <u>somniferum</u> L. in ontogenesis [in Russian]. Bot.
Zh. (Leningrad) 59: 1493-1501.

2.6-42 Lamba, L.C. 1979. Vascular anatomy of fruit in <u>Brassica</u> <u>nigra</u>
Koch. Acta Bot. Indica 7: 93-100.

2.6-43 Landre, P. 1972. Origin and development of cotyledon and leaf
epidermis in mustard (<u>Sinapis</u> <u>alba</u> L.). Ultrastructural
differentiation of stomata [in French]. Ann. Sci. Nat. Bot. Biol. Veg.
13: 247-322. FCA 26: 5155.

2.6-44 Lassanyi, Z., and Stieber, G. 1976. The volatile oil secretory
system of the tarragon (<u>Artemisia</u> <u>dracunculus</u> L.) leaf. Acta. Agron.
(Budapest) 25: 269-280.

2.6-45 Li, C.L., and Kwei, Y.I. 1973. Studies on the morphological
differentiation of excised stems of <u>Mentha</u> <u>haplocalyx</u> Briq. II. The
effect of MH on excised stem tips. Acta Bot. Sin. (Engl. Transl.) 15:
129-135. Translation of Chih Wu Hsueh Pao 15: 147-155, 1973. Bib.Ag.
40: 46508.

2.6-46 Lumsden, A.G.S. 1979. A simple technic for orientation of small
specimens incorporating reference guides for microreconstruction.
Stain Technol. 54: 105-106.

2.6-47 Lyon, N.C., and Mueller, W.C. 1974. A freeze-etch study of plant
cell walls for <u>Ectodesmata</u>. Can. J. Bot. 52: 2033-2036.

2.6-48 Meier, H., and Reid, J.S.G. 1977. Morphological aspects of the
galactomannan formation in the endosperm of <u>Trigonella</u> <u>foenum-graecum</u>
L. (Leguminosae). Planta 133: 243-248.

2.6-49 Mukhortova, T.G. 1977. Anatomical structure of the aerial organs of the lavender hybrid, lavandin [in Russian]. Rastit. Resur. 13: 83-90. HA 47: 7755.

2.6-50 Mukhortova, T.G. 1980. The correlation between morphological characteristics and commercial indices of lavandin [in Russian]. Sel. Semenovod. (Kiev) 1980{44}: 79-82. HA 51: 2874.

2.6-51 Nessler, C.L., and Mahlberg, P.G. 1977. Cell wall perforation in laticifers of Papaver somniferum L. Bot. Gaz. (Chicago) 138: 402-408.

2.6-52 Nessler, C.L., and Mahlberg, P.G. 1976. Laticifers in stamens of Papaver somniferum L. Planta 129: 83-85.

2.6-53 Nessler, C.L., and Mahlberg, P.G. 1976. Laticifers in the stamens of the opium poppy Papaver somniferum L. Proc. Indiana Acad. Sci. 85: 110 (Abstr.).

2.6-54 Neubauer, H.F. 1977. Nodal anatomy and leaf buttress of Cordia myxa, Anchusa officinalis L. and Borago officinalis L. (Boraginaceae) [in German]. Bot. Jahrb. Syst. Pflanzengesch. Pflanzengeogr. 98: 362-371.

2.6-56 Niyazov, B.N., and Khodzhimatov, K.Kh. 1976. Morphological-anatomical characteristics of Salvia sclarea and S. virgata [in Russian]. Pages 53-58 in D.K. Saidov, ed. Biologicheskie i morfologicheskie osobennosti poleznykh rastenii Uzbekistana. Fan., Tashkent, Uzbek SSR. HA 47: 7770.

2.6-57 Niyazov, B.N., and Khodzhimatov, K.Kh. 1974. Morphological and anatomic characteristics of fruits of some sage species [in Russian]. Uzb. Biol. Zh. 18{3}: 34-37.

2.6-58 Norris, R.F. 1971. Comparative cuticle morphology between some xerophytic and crop or weed species. Am. J. Bot. 53(5 pt. 2): 455 (Abstr.).

2.6-59 Pohlheim, F. 1971. Spiraea bumalda 'Anthony Waterer' and Mentha arvensis 'Variegata' — two eversporting periclinal chimeras among the angiosperms [in German]. Biol. Zentralbl. 90: 295-319.

2.6-60 Prakash, N., Shen, T.C., Yap, K.C., and Yim, K.M. 1976. A survey of the leaf structure and its relationship to the photosynthetic pathways in certain Malaysian plants. Malays. J. Sci. 4: 67-73.

2.6-61 Rabotyagov, V.D. 1977. Comparative studies of the anatomical-morphological characteristics of diploid and tetraploid lavender plants [in Russian]. Byull. Gos. Nikitsk. Bot. Sada 1977{1}: 66-71. HA 48: 7562.

2.6-62 Rockenstein, E., and Volk, O.H. 1971. Contributions to the study of Digitalis purpurea L. of Sardinian origin [in German]. Planta Med. 19: 270-278.

2.6-63 Romanenko, L.G., and Visloukhova, N.P. 1978. Morphological anomalies in lavender, Lavandula officinalis [in Russian]. Bot. Zh. (Leningrad) 63: 74-79. HA 48: 10816.

2.6-64 Sarkany, S., Kovacs, A.Z., Nyomarkay, K.M., and Kerekes-Liszt, K.

1973. Fine structure and storage function of the radicle and seedling root of some dicotyledonous plants. Mikroskopie 29: 47 (Abstr.).

2.6-65 Shah, G.L., and Kothari, M.J. 1975. Observations on stomata and hairs on vegetative and floral organs in the tribe Trifolieae (family Papilionaceae). Aust. J. Bot. 23: 111-122.

2.6-66 Shah, J.J., and Patel, J.D. 1972. The shell zone its differentiation and probable function in some dicotyledons. Am. J. Bot. 59: 683-690.

2.6-67 Shevchenko, S.V. 1974. Morphological features of Salvia sclarea L. growing in the Crimea [in Russian]. Rastit. Resur. 10: 594-598. PBA 45: 8695.

2.6-68 Shutenko, E.P., and Vasilev, B.R. 1980. Some regularities in the morphological structure of Anethum graveolens L. shoot [in Russian]. Vestn. Leningr. Univ. Biol. 1980{4}: 60-65. AGRICOLA.

2.6-69 Singh, C.P., and Sinha, R.P. 1975. Anatomical changes in Capsicum frutescens in response to gibberellic acid. Indian Sci. Cong. Assoc. Proc. 62 (pt. III Sect. VI): 68 (Abstr.).

2.6-70 Slepyan, L.I. 1973. Anatomical-morphological description of emerged ginseng seedlings [in Russian]. Rastit. Resur. 9: 18-31.

2.6-71 Solodovnichenko, N.M. 1974. Morphological-anatomical characteristics of the fruit of Anethum graveolens L. and location of coumarins [in Ukrainian]. Farm. Zh. (Kiev) 29: 87-92.

2.6-72 Spaldon, E., and Gromova, Z. 1972. A study of the morphogenesis of red peppers (Capsicum annuum var. longum L.) [in Slovak]. Pol'nohospodarstvo 18: 445-457. AGRICOLA.

2.6-73 Srivastava, K. 1979. Epidermal studies in some members of Oleaceae. Curr. Sci. 48: 79-80.

2.6-74 Suzuki, T., Fujiwake, H., and Iwai, K. 1980. Intracellular localization of capsaicin and its analogues, capsaicinoid, in Capsicum fruit. I. Microscopic investigation of the structure of the placenta of Capsicum annuum var. annuum cv. Karayatsubusa. Plant Cell Physiol. 21: 839-853.

2.6-75 Szujko-Lacza, J. 1974. The relationship between essential oil ducts and epithelial cells and their localization in Pimpinella anisum [in Hungarian]. Herba Hung. 13{1/2}: 19-37. HA 45: 7739.

2.6-76 Szujko-Lacza, J. 1978. Structural aspects of essential oil production in Pimpinella anisum leaves [in Hungarian]. Herba Hung. 17{3}: 31-38. HA 50: 4554.

2.6-77 Szujko-Lacza, J. 1979. Hypostase, embryonic sac and endosperm in Anethum graveolens L. and in various families. Acta Biol. Acad. Sci. Hung. 29: 255-271.

2.6-78 Szujko-Lacza, J. 1971. The outer and inner morphological description of Anethum graveolens L. II. Acta Bot. Acad. Sci. Hung. 17: 189-215.

2.6-79 Szujko-Lacza, J. 1974. Do trends or significant differences prevail in the Zalensky' law? (Quantitative anatomical studies on the leaves of Pimpinella anisum L.). Stud. Bot. Hung. 9: 71-85.

2.6-80 Tarabaeva, B.I. 1975. Classification of the leaf epidermis features of the mint family, Labiatae Juss. [in Russian]. Pages 89-102 in G.Z. Biiashev, B.A. Bykov and B.P. Goloskokov, eds. Flora i rastitel'nye resursy Kazakhstana: Sbornik pamiati N.V. Pavlova. Nauka Kazakhskoi SSR, Alma-Ata, USSR. AGRICOLA.

2.6-81 Teplitskaia, L.M., and Mankova, E.N. 1975. Anatomic studies of anise in relation to the processing of whole plants [in Russian]. Tr. Vses. Nauchno-Issled. Inst. Efirnomaslichn. Kul't. 8: 72-77.

2.6-82 Tutaiuk, V.Kh., and Arazov, B.M. 1974. Morphological-anatomical structure of vegetable organs of Nasturtium officinale L. [in Azerbaijanian]. Izv. Akad. Nauk Az. SSR Ser. Biol. Nauk 1974{3}: 3-9. AGRICOLA.

2.6-83 Van Cotthem, W.R.J. 1977. Shoot apex structure in some Lamiaceae. Biol. Jaarb. 45: 181-197.

2.6-84 Vasilevskaya, V.K., Baranov, M.P., and Borisovskaya, G.M. 1973. Structure of rosette plant Plantago major L. during first year of its life [in Russian]. Bot. Zh. (Leningrad) 58: 33-42.

2.6-85 Viegi, L., Pagni, A.M., Corsi, G., and Renzoni, G.C. 1976. The embryo suspensors in Cruciferae. I. Morphology and structure [in Italian]. Giornale Botanico Italiano 111(4/5): 347-357.

2.6-86 Vysotskaya, R.I., Slepyan, L.I., and Grushvitskii, I.V. 1974. Morphological-anatomical and histochemical studies on certain Panax species [in Russian]. Rastit. Resur. 10: 53-62. HA 44: 6038.

2.6-87 Zhestyanikova, L.L., and Zykina, A.V. 1976. Anatomical structure of the fleshy scales of the most widely grown onion species [in Russian]. Byull. Vses. Inst. Rastenievod. 1976{64}: 35-40. HA 48: 349.

2.6-88 Ziesak, W. 1980. Laurel leaves microscopy of a leafy spice. Mikrokosmos 69: 104-106.

2.7 Cytology and Histology

2.7-1 Alekseeva, T.V., Matveenko, N.P., Il'ina, G.M., and Ermakov, I.P. 1976. Cytochemical study of the antipodal complex of Papaver somniferum L. [in Russian]. Biol. Nauki (Moscow) 19{6}: 97-102. CA 85: 174236.

2.7-2 Ammal, E.K.J., and Sreenivasan, T.V. 1971. Observations on the cytology of the Madras mint. Curr. Sci. 40: 544-545.

2.7-3 Androshchuk, A.F. 1978. Frequency of spontaneous chromosome aberrations in yarrow species. Cytol. Genet. (Engl. Transl.) 12{1}: 13-17. Translation of Tsitol. Genet. 12{1}: 15-20, 1978. AGRICOLA.

2.7-4 Aoba, T. 1972. Histological observations of seed coat in Brassica

<u>juncea</u> Coss. [in Japanese]. Ikushugaku Zasshi 22: 323-328. FCA 27: 547.

2.7-5 Bagnard, C., Bernier, G., and Arnal, C. 1972. Physiological and histological studies on inflorescence reversion in <u>Sinapis</u> <u>alba</u> [in French]. Physiol. Veg. 10: 237-254.

2.7-6 Bartels, D., and Kiper, M. 1979. DNA sequence representation in RNA of the higher plant <u>Petroselinum</u> <u>crispum</u>. Plant Syst. Evol. (Suppl. 2): 141-149.

2.7-7 Belyaeva, R.G. 1972. Instability of chromosome number in gametes and somatic cells of allopolyploid peppermint <u>Mentha</u> <u>piperita</u> L. Sov Genet. (Engl. Transl.) 8: 561-567. Translation of Genetika 8{5}: 5-14.

2.7-8 Benbadis, M.-C., Delage, M., and Deysson, G. 1975. Cytokinesis inhibition in root meristems; effects of dibutyryl cyclic AMPC and caffeine [in French]. C. R. Hebd. Seances Acad. Sci. Ser. D 280: 969-972.

2.7-9 Benbadis, M.C., and Deysson, G. 1975. The ultrastructural morphology of the Golgi bodies in meristematic root tip cells of <u>Allium</u> <u>sativum</u>: the effects of barbital [in French]. Planta 123: 283-290.

2.7-10 Bernier, G., Kinet, J.M., Bodson, M., Rouma, Y, and Jacqmard, A. 1974. Experimental studies on the mitotic activity of the shoot apical meristem and its relation to floral evocation and morphogenesis in <u>Sinapis</u> <u>alba</u>. Bot. Gaz. (Chicago) 135: 345-352.

2.7-11 Bocher, T.W. 1975. Experimental and cytological studies on plant species. XIII. <u>Clinopodium</u> <u>vulgare</u> L. Bot. Tidsskr. 70: 152-179.

2.7-12 Bonzi, L.M., Bigazzi, M., and Malquori, M.P. 1979. Ultrastructural observations on the nuclear paracrystals in some species of the genus <u>Lavandula</u>. Caryologia 32: 129 (Abstr.).

2.7-13 Bougourd, S.M., and Parker, J.S. 1975. The B-chromosome system of <u>Allium</u> <u>schoenoprasum</u>. I. B-distribution. Chromosoma (Berl.) 53{3}: 273-282.

2.7-14 Bougourd, S.M., and Parker, J.S. 1979. The B-chromosome system of <u>Allium</u> <u>schoenoprasum</u>. II. Stability, inheritance and phenotypic effects Chromosoma (Berl.) 75: 369-383.

2.7-15 Bougourd, S.M., and Parker, J.S. 1979. The B-chromosome system of <u>Allium</u> <u>schoenoprasum</u>. III. An abrupt change in B-frequency. Chromosoma (Berl.) 75: 385-392.

2.7-16 Bougourd, S.M., and Parker, J.S. 1976. Nucleolar-organiser polymorphism in natural populations of <u>Allium</u> <u>schoenoprasum</u>. Chromosoma (Berl.) 56: 301-307.

2.7-17 Bowes, B.G. 1975. Light and electron microscopic observations on tylosis development in the excised root of <u>Taraxacum</u> <u>officinale</u> Weber. Flora (Jena) 164: 27-36.

2.7-18 Bowes, B.G. 1976. Polar regeneration in excised roots of <u>Taraxacum</u> <u>officinale</u> Weber: A light and electron microscope study. Ann. Bot. 40: 423-432.

2.7-19 Brighton, C.A. 1977. Cytology of Crocus sativus and its allies (Iridaceae). Plant Syst. Evol. 128: 137-157.

2.7-20 Bugaenko, L.A., and Reznikova, S.A. 1980. Cytological study of interspecies hybrids of mint. Cytol. Genet. (Engl. Transl.) 14{2}: 24-27. Translation of Tsitol. Genet. 14{2}: 24-27, 1980. AGRICOLA.

2.7-21 Casadora, G., and Rascio, N. 1978. Chloroplast ontogenesis in Lippia citriodora L. Pages 416-417 in J.M. Sturgess, ed. Electron microscopy 1978. Volume II: Biology. Ninth international congress on electron microscopy, Aug. 1-9, 1979, Toronto. Microscopical Society of Canada, Toronto.

2.7-22 Cheshmedzhiev, I. 1975. Chromosome polymorphism in some Allium species [in Russian]. Genet. 1. 8: 184-191.

2.7-23 De Padua, L.S., and Pantastico, J.B. 1976. Histochemistry of comfrey, Symphytum officinale L. Kalikasan 5: 351-356. AGRICOLA.

2.7-24 De Pasquale, A., Tumino, G., and Costa, R. 1980. Study of Digitalis purpurea L. by scanning electron microscopy. Q.J. Crude Drug Res. 18: 97-103.

2.7-25 Devani, M.B., Shishoo, C.J., and Dadia B.K. 1975. Histochemical localisation of some thio compounds in plants. Planta Med. 27: 217-221. HA 46: 1790.

2.7-26 Dickenson, P.B., and Fairbairn, J.W. 1975. The ultrastructure of the alkaloidal vesicles of Papaver somniferum latex. Ann. Bot. (London) 39: 707-712.

2.7-27 Dubey, R.S. 1977. Histological studies on chemically induced male sterile lines of fennel. Genet. Agrar. 31: 309-314.

2.7-28 Dubrova, N.A., Malakhova, L.A., and Kartashova, N.N. 1976. Karyological characteristics of some species of Plantago L. (Plantaginaceae) [in Russian]. Biol. Nauki (Moscow) 1976{3}: 99-101.

2.7-29 Dudits, D., Fejer, O., Hadlaczky, G., Koncz, C., Lazar, G., and Horvath, G. 1980. Intergeneric gene transfer mediated by plant protoplast fusion. Mol. Gen. Genet. 179: 283-288.

2.7-30 Duhrssen, E., Saavedra, E., and Neumann, K.-H. 1980. DNA reassociation kinetics and hybridization in different angiosperms. Plant Syst. Evol. 136: 267-273. PBA 51: 6599.

2.7-31 El-Gadi, A., and Elkington, T.T. 1975. Comparison of the Giemsa C-band karyotypes and the relationships of Allium cepa, A. fistulosum and A. galanthum. Chromosoma 51: 19-23.

2.7-32 Ermakov, I.P., Morozova, E.M., and Karpova, L.V. 1980. DNA content in nuclei of male gametophytes of some flowering plants. Dokl. Bot. Sci. (Engl. Transl.) 250-252: 32-33. Translation of Dokl. Akad. Nauk SSSR 251: 1023-1024, 1980.

2.7-33 Favali, M.A., and Conti, G.G. 1971. Fine structure of healthy and virus-infected leaves following ultracentrifugation. Cytobiologie 3: 153-161.

2.7-34 Favarger, C., and Vasudevan, K.N. 1972. Cytological and morphological study of the Plantago major and Plantago lanceolata populations of the western Himalayas comparison with plants of Switzerland [in French]. Bull. Soc. Neuchatel Sci. Nat. 95: 63-74.

2.7-35 Gacek, W.F., Jr. 1980. An ultrastructural analysis of the lipid bodies of Trigonella foenum-graecum. Proc. Annu. Meet. Electron. Micros. Soc. Am. 38: 534-535. AGRICOLA.

2.7-36 Gaddipati, J.P., and Sen, S.K. 1977. Repair of genetic material in higher plants with varying genome size. Nucleus (Calcutta) 20: 178-180.

2.7-37 Ghosh, S., and Roy, S.C. 1976. Orientation of interphase chromosomes as detected by Giemsa C-bands. J. Cell Biol. 70(2 pt. 2): 418a (Abstr.).

2.7-38 Ghosh, S., and Roy, S.C. 1977. Orientation of interphase chromosomes as detected by Giemsa C-bands. Chromosoma 61{1}: 49-55.

2.7-39 Gill, B.S., and Gupta, R.C. 1980. Cytological investigations on the north west Himalayan Taraxacum officinale complex (Compositae). Pages 292-301 in S.S. Bir, ed. Recent researches in plant sciences. Kalyani Pub., New Delhi, India, 1980.

2.7-40 Golyshkin, L.V. 1977. Cytological study of microsporogenesis and pollen formation in five Allium species [in Russian]. Tr. Prikl. Bot. Genet. Sel. 60{2}: 39-81. PBA 49: 5238.

2.7-41 Grob, K., and Matile, P. 1979. Vacuolar location of glucosinolates in horseradish root cells. Plant Sci. Lett. 14: 327-335.

2.7-42 Grover, I.S. 1979. Meiosis in triploid opium poppy, Papaver somniferum L. CIS, Chromosome Inf. Serv. 26: 9-11. AGRICOLA.

2.7-43 Gupta, K.C. 1973. Cytology of fenugreek calli cultivated in vitro. Cytologia 38: 437-447.

2.7-44 Gupta, K.C. 1972. Histogenesis of fenugreek calli originating from hypocotyl explants. Can. J. Bot. 50: 2687-2588.

2.7-45 Gupta, K.C. 1972. Effects of some antimitotics on the cytology of fenugreek roots in vivo and in vitro. Cytobios 5: 179-187.

2.7-46 Gvaladze, G.E. 1973. The X bodies of species of the genus Allium. Soob shch. Akad. Nauk Gruz. SSR 71: 485-488.

2.7-47 Hatano, K., Nishioka, I., and Iwasa, S. 1977. Cytogenetical studies of Umbelliferous plants: IV. On the chromosome changes in cultivated "Toki" Angelica acutiloba var. acutiloba [in Japanese]. Shoyakugaku Zasshi 31: 1-6.

2.7-48 Hatano, K., Nishioka, I., and Iwasa, S. 1977. Cytogenetic studies of Umbelliferous plants. V. Intraspecific hybrids among original plants of Japanese "Toki" [in Japanese]. Shoyakugaku Zasshi 31: 7-25.

2.7-49 Havelange, A., Kinet, J.M., and Bernier, G. 1974/1976. Ultrastructural changes in the shoot apex of Sinapis alba during transition from the vegetative to the reproductive condition: descriptive and quantitative study. Port. Acta Biol. Ser. A 14: 397-412. FCA 31: 6393.

2.7-50 Havelange, A. 1977. Ultrastructure of foliar chloroplasts during vegetative development and floral initiation in Sinapis alba L. [in French]. Physiol. Veg. 15: 723-734.

2.7-51 Hesse, M. 1979. Development and ultrastructure of pollenkitt and exine in closely related entomophilous and anemophilous angiosperms in Oleaceae, Scrophulariaceae, Plantaginaceae, and Asteraceae [in German]. Plant Syst. Evol. 132: 107-140.

2.7-52 Hodisan, V. 1979. Studies on Anethum graveolens L. I. Histological and histochemical studies [in Romanian]. Contrib. Bot. Univ. Babes-Bolyai Cluj Gradina Bot. 1979: 51-53. AGRICOLA.

2.7-53 Hofsten, A.V. 1976. Ultrastructure and X-ray analysis of protein-rich seeds of oil poppy (Papaver somniferum). J. Ultrastruct. Res. 54: 493 (Abstr.).

2.7-54 Hussain, L.A.-S., and Elkington, T.T. 1978. Giemsa C-band karyotypes of diploid and triploid Allium caeruleum and their genomic relationship. Cytologia (Tokyo) 43: 405-410.

2.7-55 Jacqmard, A. 1978. Histochemical localization of enzyme activity during floral evocation in the shoot apical meristem of Sinapis alba. Protoplasma 94: 315-324.

2.7-56 Jahagirdar, H.A. 1974. The behavior of nucleolus in mitosis in Foeniculum vulgare, Mill. Botanique (Nagpur) 5: 125-132.

2.7-57 Jain, K.K. 1978. Cytology of the polymorphic Plantago major Linn. Cytologia 43: 345-349.

2.7-59 Jalas, J., and Uotila, M. 1976. Chromosome studies in Thymus L. (Labiatae). VI. Counts on Macedonian and Thracian taxa. Ann. Bot. Fenn. 13: 61-64. PBA 47: 12241.

2.7-60 Kashevarov, G.P. 1979. DNA nucleotide composition in some species of Achillea [in Ukrainian]. Ukr. Bot. Zh. 36: 235-237. CA 91: 137299.

2.7-61 Kim, J.H. 1974. The study of scattering of chromosomes in cells. Scattering of chromosomes by treatment with potassium ferricyanide solution under light [in Korean]. Singmal Hakhoe Chi 17: 113-117. PBA 46: 9782.

2.7-62 Kiper, M., Bartels, D., and Kochel, H. 1979. Gene number estimates in plant tissues and cells. Plant Syst. Evol. (Suppl. 2): 129-140. Bib.Ag. 45: 35006.

2.7-63 Kiper, M., and Herzfeld, F. 1978. DNA sequence organization in the genome of Petroselinum sativum (Umbelliferae). Chromosoma (Berl.) 65: 335-351.

2.7-64 Kothari, I.L., and Shah, J.J. 1974. Histogenesis of seed stalk and inflorescence in garlic. Phytomorphology 24: 42-48.

2.7-65 Kothari, I.L., and Shah, J.J. 1974. Structure and organization of shoot apex of Allium sativum L. Isr. J. Bot. 23: 216-222.

2.7-66 Koul, A.K., Wakhlu, A.K., and Karihaloo, J.L. 1980. A natural hexaploid of Jasminum humile L., Oleaceae. Cell Chromosome Newsl. 3{1}: 3-5.

2.7-67 Kubo, M., Tani, T., Katsuki, T., Ishizaki, K., and Arichi, S. 1980. Histochemistry. I. Ginsenosides in ginseng (Panax ginseng C.A. Meyer) root. J. Nat. Prod. 43: 278-284. HA 51: 1529.

2.7-68 Lang, E., Hoester, H., Freidrich, H., Themann, H., and Amelunxen, F. 1977. Electron microscope investigation of the origin and location of lamiaceous tannins in Ocimum basilicum cell suspension cultures [in German]. Cytobiologie 15: 372-381.

2.7-69 Lassanyi, Z., Stieber, G., and Tyihak, E. 1978. Investigations on the essential oil secretory system of the chamomile flower. I. Histochemical studies on glandular hairs [in Hungarian]. Herba Hung. 17{2}: 31-42. HA 49: 2860.

2.7-70 Lassanyi, Z. 1977. Histochemical study of pectin and hemicellulose of the glandular hair of chamomile [in Hungarian]. Acta Pharm. Hung. 47: 186-189. CIM 19{13}: 9664.

2.7-71 Levy, F. 1971. Antimitotic activity and inhibition of proteogenesis under the influence of cycloheximide in meristematic root cells of Allium sativum L. [in French]. C. R. Hebd. Seances Acad. Sci. Ser. D 272: 553-556.

2.7-72 Maggini, F., Barsanti, P., and Marazia, T. 1978. Individual variation of the nucleolus organizer regions in Allium cepa and A. sativum. Chromosoma 66: 173-183.

2.7-73 Maggini, F., and Garbari, F. 1977. Amounts of ribosomal DNA in Allium (Liliaceae). Plant Syst. Evol. 128: 201-208. PBA 48: 4845.

2.7-74 Maheswari Devi, H. 1975. Embryology of jasminums and its bearing on the composition of Oleaceae. Acta Bot. Indica 3: 52-61.

2.7-75 Malik, C.P., and Grover, I.S. 1979. Cytogenetic studies in Papaver. V. Cytogenetic studies on P. sominiferum X P. setigerum hybrids and amphiploids. Cytologia 44: 59-69.

2.7-76 Mandl, A. 1975. Ultrastructural and form variability of pollen grains 1. The pollen of anemophilous plants [in German]. Mikrokosmos 64: 186-189.

2.7-77 Markhova, M., and Ivanova, P. 1972. Karyological study of the Bulgarian species of the families Boraginaceae, Labiatae and Scrophulariaceae. III. [in German]. Izv. Bot. Inst. B"lg. Akad. Nauk Otd. Biol. Nauki 1972{22}: 149-157.

2.7-78 Maron, R., and Fahn, A. 1979. Ultrastructure and development of oil cells in Laurus nobilis L. leaves. Bot. J. Linn. Soc. 78: 31-40.

2.7-79 Martin, E.S., and Larbalestier, G. 1977. A membrane-bound plastid inclusion in the epidermis of leaves of Taraxacum officinale. Can. J. Bot. 55: 222-225.

2.7-80 Miege, J., and Greuter, W. 1973. Chromosome numbers of some plants collected in Crete [in French]. Ann. Mus. Goulandris 1: 105-111.

2.7-81 Mikeladze, R.M., Topuriia, O.I., and Gakheladze, K.L. 1977. Histochemical studies of _Rosmarinus officinalis_ and _Betonica officinalis_ for the content of some biologically active compounds [in Georgian]. Vopr. Introd. Rast. Zelenogo Stroit. 1977{10}: 83-88.

2.7-82 Milyaeva, E.L., and Azizbekova, N.Sh. 1978. Cytophysiological changes in the course of development of stem apices of saffron crocus. Sov. Plant Physiol. (Engl. Transl.) 25: 227-233. Translation of Fiziol. Rast. (Moscow) 25: 288-295, 1978.

2.7-83 Miroshnichenko, G.P., Antonov, A.S., and Val'ekho-Roman, K.M. 1973. Results of an investigation of the kinetics of the reassociation of denatured fragmented DNA of certain higher plants. Dokl. Biochem. (Engl. Transl.) 205{1-6}: 320-322. Translation of Dokl. Akad. Nauk SSSR 205: 1243-1245.

2.7-84 Mlodzianowski, F. 1971. Ultrastructure of mesophyll in senescent leaves of parsley (_Petroselinum sativum_ cv. Berlinska). Folia Histochem. Cytochem. 9: 405-406 (Abstr.).

2.7-85 Mlodzianowski, F., and Wieczorek, W. 1973. DNA configuration in chloroplasts of _Brassica oleracea_ var. _gonglodes_ and _Petroselinum sativum_. Biochem. Physiol. Pflanz. (BPP) 164: 429-437.

2.7-86 Morton, J.K. 1973. A cytological study of the British Labiatae (excluding _Mentha_). Watsonia 9: 239-246.

2.7-87 Mulligan, G.A. 1977. Seed coats under the scanning electron microscope. J. Seed Technol. 2{2}: 24-29. FCA 32: 5581.

2.7-88 Murin, A. 1976. Polyploidy and mitotic cycle. Nucleus (Calcutta) 19: 192-195.

2.7-89 Murty, A.S., and Khanna, K.R. 1971. A study of triploid _Jasminum grandiflorum_ L. Curr. Sci. 40: 555-556.

2.7-90 Nabli, M.A. 1975. Description of 2 ectexinic and endexinic primordial lamellae in the exine of some Labiatae [in French]. C.R. Hebd. Seances Acad. Sci. Ser. D 281: 251-254.

2.7-91 Nagl, W. 1974. Mitotic cycle time in perennial and annual plants with various amounts of DNA and heterochromatin. Dev. Biol. 39: 342-346.

2.7-92 Nagl, W. 1974. Role of heterochromatin in the control of cell cycle duration. Nature (London) 249: 53-54.

2.7-93 Nessler, C.L., and Mahlberg, P.G. 1978. Lacticifer ultrastructure and differentiation in seedlings of _Papaver bracteatum_ Lindl. in population Arya II Papaveraceae. Am. J. Bot. 65: 978-983.

2.7-94 Nessler, C.L., and Mahlberg, P.G. 1979. Plastids in laticifers of _Papaver_. I. Development and cytochemistry of laticifer plastids in _Papaver somniferum_ L. (Papaveraceae). Am. J. Bot. 66: 266-273.

2.7-95 Nessler, C.L., and Mahlberg, P.G. 1977. Ontogeny and cytochemistry of alkaloidal vesicles in laticifers of _Papaver somniferum_ L. (Papaveraceae). Am. J. Bot. 64: 541-551.

2.7-96 Novak, F.J., and Havranek, P. 1974. A cytological study on tissue cultures of Allium sativum L. in vitro. Acta Fac. Rerum Nat. Univ. Comenianae Genet. 197{45}: 143-147. PBA 48: 3866.

2.7-97 Pandey, K.N., Benner, J.F., and Sabharwal, P.S. 1978. Cytogenetic effects of the gaseous phase of cigarette smoke on root-tip cells of Allium sativum L. Env. Exp. Bot. 18: 67-75.

2.7-98 Platt-Aloia, K.A., and Thomson, W.W. 1979. Membrane bound inclusions in epidermal plastids of developing sesame leaves and cotyledons. New Phytol. 83: 793-799.

2.7-99 Pogliani, M., and Del Grosso, F. 1972. Karyological study of Crocus sativus L. [in Italian]. Inf. Bot. Ital. 4: 25-29.

2.7-100 Polishchuk, V.S. 1972. Embryological investigation of Salvia officinalis L. and Salvia sclarea L. [in Ukrainian]. Ukr. Bot. Zh. 29: 25-30.

2.7-101 Polishchuk, V.S., and Dzevaltovs'kyi, A.K. 1971. Embryology of Lavandula spica L. [in Ukrainian]. Ukr. Bot. Zh. 28: 778-781.

2.7-102 Rachele, L.D. 1974. Pollen morphology of the Papaveraceae of the northeastern United States and Canada. Bull. Torrey Bot. Club 101: 152-159

2.7-103 Sarkar, A. 1973. A preliminary report on cytohistogenetic effects of X-rays on shoot apices of Trigonella foenum-graecum L. Sci. Cult. 39: 222-224. HA 44: 3466.

2.7-104 Shah, J.J., and Kothari, I.L. 1973. Histogenesis of garlic clove. Phytomorphology 23: 162-170.

2.7-105 Sinha, B.M.B., and Sinha, A.K. 1977. Meiotic studies on some species of Umbelliferae. Cytologia 42: 465-471.

2.7-106 Sinha, B.M.B., and Sinha, A.K. 1977. Cyto-morphological studies in X-irradiated plants of Coriandrum sativum L. J. Indian Bot. Soc. 56: 107-115.

2.7-107 Skvarla, J.J., and Turner, B.L. 1971. Fine structure of the pollen of Anthemis nobilis L. (Anthemidae; Compositae). Proc. Okla. Acad. Sci. 51: 61-62.

2.7-108 Tacina, F. 1972. Ultrastructure of nectariferous cells in Borago officinalis [in Romanian]. Rev. Roum. Biol. Ser. Bot. 17: 227-234. AA 26: 222.

2.7-109 Thompson, E.W., Richardson, M., and Boulter, D. 1971. The amino acid sequence of sesame (Sesamum indicum L.) and castor (Ricinus communis L.) cytochrome c. Biochem. J. 121: 439-446.

2.7-110 Vaverkova, S., and Herichova, A. 1980. Histochemical proof of prochamazulene at different stages of flower development in Matricaria chamomilla [in Slovak]. Biologia (Bratislava) 35: 753-757. HA 51: 4872.

2.7-111 Voronkina, N.V. 1975. Histogenesis in root apices of angiospermous plants and possible ways of its evolution [in Russian]. Bot. Zh. (Leningrad) 60: 170-187.

2.7-112 Waller, G.R., Hamilton, B.K., Fairbairn, J.W., and Steel, M. 1978. Ultrastructural comparison of the vesicles of fresh latex of Papaver somniferum, P. bracteatum and P. soma. Lloydia 41: 656-657 (Abstr.).

2.7-113 Welinder, K.G., and Mazza, G. 1977. Amino-acid sequences of heme-linked, histidine-containing peptides of five peroxidases from horseradish and turnip. Eur. J. Biochem. 73: 353-358.

2.7-114 Welinder, K.G., and Mazza, G. 1975. Similarities and differences of five peroxidases from turnip and horseradish: peptide mapping studies on glycoproteins. Eur. J. Biochem. 57: 415-424.

2.8 Botanical Taxonomy

2.8-1 Accorsi, C.A., and Forlani, L. 1976. Cards for an Italian palynological flora: 4. Cards based on new guidelines [in Italian]. Arch. Bot. Biogeogr. Ital. 52: 58-111.

2.8-2 Adema, F. 1975. Thymus praecox Opiz in the Netherlands [in Dutch]. Gorteria (Leiden) 7: 122-123.

2.8-3 Ananda Rao, T., and Silpi Das. 1978. Idioblasts typology on the taxonomy of Capparis spinosa complex. Curr. Sci. 47: 917-919.

2.8-4 Ball, P.W. 1972. Flora Europaea Notulae Systematicae ad Floram Europeam spectantes No. 13; Labiatae Satureja L. Bot. J. Linn. Soc. 65: 356.

2.8-5 Banerjee, R.N. 1972. Generic delimitation in Indian Araliaceae. Bull. Bot. Soc. Bengal 26: 77-78.

2.8-6 Banerjee, S.K., Lall, V.K., and Verma, K. 1979. Use of scanning electron microscopy in seed identification. Seed Res. 7: 83-85.

2.8-7 Bassett, I.J. 1973. The plantains of Canada. Can. Dep. Agric. Res. Branch Monogr. 7. 47 pp.

2.8-8 Belkina, K.V. 1972. On the dimorphism of pollen in plants of the family Labiatae from Yakutia [in Russian]. Bot. Zh. (Leningrad) 57: 1286-1290.

2.8-9 Bokhari, M.H., and Hedge, I.C. 1975. Anatomical characters in Capparis spinosa and its allies. Notes R. Bot. Gard. Edinb. 34: 231-240.

2.8-10 Clarke, G.C.S. 1977. The northwest European pollen flora, 10: Boraginaceae. Rev. Palaeobot. Palynol. 24{2}: NEPF 59-101.

2.8-11 Clarke, G.C.S., and Jones, M.R. 1977. The northwest European pollen flora, 15: Plantaginaceae. Rev. Palaeobot. Palynol. 24{4}: NEPF 129-154.

2.8-12 Clarke, G.C.S., and Jones, M.R. 1977. The northwest European pollen flora, 16: Valerianaceae. Rev. Palaeobot. Palynol. 24{5}: NEPF 155-179.

2.8-13 Conolly, A. 1976. Use of the scanning electron microscope for the identification of seeds, with special reference to Saxifraga and Papaver. Folia Quat. 47: 29-32.

2.8-14 Dabrowska, J. 1971. The size of stomata guard cells and of pollen grains in four Achillea L. species [in Polish]. Herba Pol. 17: 13-30.

2.8-15 Darrah, H.H. 1974. Investigation of the cultivars of the basils (Ocimum). Econ. Bot. 28: 63-57.

2.8-16 Dorokhina, L.N. 1978. Some life forms of wormwoods of the subgenus Dracunculus (Bess.) Rydb. and the transition from herbs to sub-shrubs [in Russian]. Byull. Mosk. O-va. Ispyt. Prir. Otd. Biol. 83: 97-108.

2.8-17 Duvigneaud, J., and Lebeau, J. 1972. A new combination in the genus Mentha [in French]. Bull. Soc. R. Bot. Belg. 105{1}: 213.

2.8-18 Eifrig, H. 1975. A contribution to Brassica seed identification [in German]. Seed Sci. Technol. 3: 473-479. FCA 30: 2353.

2.8-19 El-Gadi, A., and Elkington, T.T. 1977. Numerical taxonomic studies on species in Allium subgenus rhizirideum. New Phytol. 79: 183-201.

2.8-20 Estilai, A., and Knowles, P.F. 1976. Cytogenetic studies of Carthamus divaricatus with eleven pairs of chromosomes and its relationship to other Carthamus species (Compositae). Am. J. Bot. 63: 771-782.

2.8-21 Everson, L.E. 1974. Classification of all empty fruits, florets and seeds into pure seed or inert on the same basis. Seed Sci. Technol. 2: 210-211.

2.8-22 Ferguson, D.K. 1974. On the taxonomy of recent and fossil species of Laurus (Lauraceae). Bot. J. Linn. Soc. 63: 51-72.

2.8-23 Fernandes, R. 1971. Note on the identification of Origanum majoricum Camb. [in French]. Bot. J. Linn. Soc. 64: 234-235.

2.8-24 Girenko, M.M. 1974. The variability of characters in coriander (Coriandrum sativum) [in Russian]. Tr. Prikl. Bot. Genet. Sel. 51{3}: 148-157. HA 45: 8783.

2.8-25 Gruas-Cavagnetto, C., and Bui, N.-S. 1976. Presence of Araliaceae pollen in the English and French Paleogene [in French]. Rev. Palaeobot. Palynol. 22: 61-72.

2.8-26 Guinea, E. 1972. Flora Europaea Notulae Systematicae ad Floram Europeam spectants No. 12; Labiatae, Lavandula L. Bot. J. Linn. Soc. 65: 263.

2.8-27 Gupta, M.L., and Bhambie, S. 1977. Studies on Lamiaceae. I. The node. Proc Indian Acad. Sci. Sect. B 86: 281-286.

2.8-28 Gupta, M.L., and Bhambie, S. 1978. Studies in Lamiaceae. IV. Foliar appendages in Ocimum L. and their taxonomic significance. Proc. Indian Natl. Sci. Acad. Part B 44: 154-160.

2.8-29 Hamalova, O. 1976. Morphology of pollen grains in species of the genus Achillea cited in the flora of the Czechoslovakia Socialist Republic [in Slovak]. Biologia (Bratislava) 31: 501-520.

2.8-30 Hardin, J.W. 1974. Studies of the southeastern United States flora. IV. Oleaceae. SIDA Contrib. Bot. 5: 274-285.

2.8-31 Heiser, C.B., Jr., and Pickersgill, B. 1975. Names for the bird peppers [Capsicum solanaceae]. Baileya 19: 151-156.

2.8-32 Herisset, A., Jolivet, J., Zoll, A., and Chaumont, J.-P. 1973. On the falsifications of the summer savory (Satureia horteniis L.) [in French]. Plant. Med. Phytother. 7: 121-134. AGRICOLA.

2.8-33 Herisset, A., Jolivet, J., Zoll, A., and Chaumont, J.-P. 1974. New observations concerning the falsifications of the garden savory (Satureia hortensis L.) [in French]. Plant. Med. Phytother. 8: 287-294. AGRICOLA.

2.8-34 Heywood, V.H. 1972. Flora Europaea Notulae Systematicae ad Floram Europaeam spectantes No. 13; Scrophulariaceae, Digitalis L. Bot. J. Linn. Soc. 65: 357.

2.8-35 Hinata, K., and Konno, N. 1975. Number of pollen grains in Brassica and allied genera. Tohoku J. Agric. Res. 26: 117-124. FCA 29: 9038.

2.8-36 Hore, A. 1975. Karyomorphological studies of the genus Carum L. Indian Agric. 19: 303-312.

2.8-37 Ietswaart, J.H. 1975. A new species of Origanum (Labiatae) from Libya. Acta Bot. Neerl. 24: 285-287.

2.8-38 Ietswaart, J.H. 1978. Some results of a taxonomic revision of the genus Origanum Labiatae. Acta Bot. Neerl. 27: 144-145 (Abstr.).

2.8-39 Inceoglu, O., and Karamustafa, F. 1977. The pollen morphology of plants in Ankara region. V. Plantaginaceae. Commun. Fac. Sci. Univ. Ankara Ser. C2 Bot. 21: 145-149.

2.8-40 Iosebidze, N.I. 1975. Identification of Digitalis spp. based on morphological characteristics of sprouts [in Russian]. Rastit Resur. 11: 124-130.

2.8-41 Jalas, J. 1973. Thymus subsect. Pseudomarinati in the Himalayas and adjoining western mountain ranges and in Caucasia. Ann. Bot. Fenn. 10: 104-122.

2.8-42 Jalas, J. 1974. Notes on Thymus L. (Labiatae) in Europe. III. Ann. Bot. Fenn. 11: 262-266. PBA 45: 9526.

2.8-43 Jalas, J. 1971. Notes on Thymus L. (Labiatae) in Europe. I. Supraspecific classification and nomenclature. Bot. J. Linn. Soc. 64: 199-215.

2.8-44 Jalas, J. 1980. Turkish taxa of Thymus (Labiatae) described as new or revised. Ann. Bot. Fenn. 17: 315-324.

2.8-45 Jurenitsch, J., Kubelka, W., and Jentzsch, K. 1979.

Identification of cultivated taxa of Capsicum: taxonomy, anatomy and composition of pungent principle. Planta Med. 35: 174-183.

2.8-46 Khan, M.S., and Khanam, M. 1975. Taxonomic studies in Labiatae of Dacca and its surroundings - 1 (Subfamilies Ajugoideae and Ocimoideae). Bangladesh J. Bot. 4: 37-47.

2.8-47 Kiger, R.W. 1975. Papaver in North America north of Mexico. Rhodora 77{811}: 410-422.

2.8-48 Kitagawa, M. 1971. On the syntype specimen of Angelica-koreana Maximowicz [in Japanese.] Shokubutsu Kenkyu Zasshi 46: 367-372. AGRICOLA.

2.8-49 Komissarov, V.A., and Tarasova, E.M. 1979. Morphometric study of the caryotypes of nine diploid Allium L. species [in Russian]. Izv. Timiryazevsk. S'kh. Akad. 1979{1}: 188-193. PBA 49: 7535.

2.8-50 Korovina, O.N. 1978. New combinations of infraspecific taxa in wild relatives of crop plants [in Russian]. Byull. Vses. Inst. Rastenievod. 1978{81}: 35-37. PBA 50: 9002.

2.8-51 Kotov, M.I. 1974. The problem of the number of species in the genus Thymus L. [in Ukrainian]. Ukr. Bot. Zh. 31: 359-361. PBA 44: 8288.

2.8-52 Kuperman, F.M., and Kurlyanchik, I.A. 1974. Trials on the morphological-physiological classification of dill (Anethum graveolens) [in Russian]. Tr. Prikl. Bot. Genet. Sel. 51{3}: 49-55. HA 45: 8781.

2.8-53 Lawrence, G.H.M. 1971. The horseradish. Herbarist 37: 17-19.

2.8-54 Lebeau, J. 1974. New names for Mentha hybrids and a proposal for a new rank of sub-hybrid [in French]. Bull. Jard. Bot. Nat. Belg. 44: 249-257. HA 45: 6796.

2.8-55 Lebeau, J. 1974. New data on the genus Mentha [in French]. Nat. Mosana 27: 109-141.

2.8-56 Lippert, W. 1979. Knowledge of the Salvia section Salvia in the western Mediterranean [in German]. Mitt. Bot. Staatssamml. Muench. 15: 397-423.

2.8-57 Maeki, G. 1978. Morphological observation of pollens of various species origin by scanning electron microscopy. J. Electron. Microscr. 27: 373 (Abstr.).

2.8-58 Makarov, V.V. 1974. A short summary of the genus Mentha in the USSR flora [in Russian]. Byull. Gl. Bot. Sada 91: 32-38.

2.8-59 Mangath, K.S., Pokhriyal, S.C., and Patil, R.R. 1974. Nature of divergence in some genotypes of Brassica juncea (Coss). Indian J. Hered. 6: 35-40. PBA 48: 6802.

2.8-60 Mathew, B. 1977. Crocus sativus and its allies (Iridaceae). Plant Syst. Evol. 128{1/2}: 89-103. AGRICOLA.

2.8-61 Menitskii, Yu. L. 1973. Supraspecific taxa in the genus Thymus L.

(Labiatae) I. [in Russian]. Bot. Zh. (Leningrad) 58: 794-805. PBA 44: 3660.

2.8-62 Menitskii, Yu. L. 1973. Supraspecific taxa in the genus Thymus L. (Labiatae) II. [in Russian]. Bot. Zh. (Leningrad) 58: 983-994. PBA 44: 3660.

2.8-63 Mobayen, S., and Gahraman, A. 1978. A new species of the genus Origanum from the Caspian Region of Iran [in French]. Bull. Soc. Bot. Fr. 125: 389-390.

2.8-64 Murin, A., and Ferakova, V. 1973. Caryotypes of some cultivated species of genus Allium L. [in Slovak]. Biologia (Bratislava) 28: 65-71. PBA 43: 4661.

2.8-65 Negre, R. 1972. A new taxon of thyme in the area of Luchon, Thymus vulgaris L. var. prostrata nov. var [in French]. Monde des Plantes 67{374}: 3-4. PBA 43: 4091.

2.8-66 Panigrahi, G. 1975. Taxonomic notes on certain taxa of Asiatic angiosperms. Phytologia 32: 473-479.

2.8-67 Perino, K.W. 1972. A contribution to the identification of seeds of economically important Brassica species [in German]. Landwirtsch Aft. Forsch. 25: 272-274. FCA 28: 2245.

2.8-68 Ponert, J. 1973. Thymus artvinicus Ponert - a new species from Turkey [in German]. Feddes Repertorium 84: 737-738. PBA 44: 5612.

2.8-69 Ponzi, R., Pizzolongo, P., and Caputo, G. 1978. Ultrastructural particularities in ovular tissues of some Rhoeadales taxa and their probable taxonomic value. J. Submicrosc. Cytol. 10: 31-38.

2.8-70 Ponzi, R., Pizzolongo, P., and Caputo, G. 1977. Ultrastructural particularities in ovular tissues of some Rhoeadales taxa and their probable taxonomic value. Caryologia 30: 497 (Abstr.).

2.8-71 Rabotiagov, V.D. 1977. Comparative study of anatomo-morphological characters of diploid and tetraploid lavender plants [in Russian]. Byull. Gos. Nikitsk. Bot. Sada 1977{1}: 66-71. AGRICOLA.

2.8-72 Rivas-Martinez, S. 1977. Plants of Spain taxonomic, chorologic and ecologic notes, III. [in Spanish]. An. Inst. Bot. A.J. Cavinilles 34: 539-552.

2.8-73 Sameth, E. 1971. The thymes. Herbarist 37: 47-50.

2.8-74 Schmidt, P. 1973. Conspectus of the Central European species of the genus Thymus L. [in German]. Feddes Repertorium 83: 663-671. PBA 43: 7523.

2.8-75 Schmidt, P., and Opiz, P.M. 1977. Revision of the Thymus species of P.M. Opiz [in German]. Folia Geobot. Phytotaxon. 12: 377-416. PBA 48: 6129.

2.8-76 Sebald, O. 1977. The drug plant (Valeriana officinalis Agg.) in Wurttemberg [in German]. Jahresh Ges Naturkd. Wurttemb. 132: 152-168. AGRICOLA.

2.8-77 Sharma, D. 1980. Pollen morphology of two cultivars of Papaver somniferum L. Curr. Sci. 49: 710-712.

2.8-78 Silvia, M.-F. 1974. The leave epidermis of some species in the genus Valeriana. Lucr. Gradinii Bot. Bucur. 1974: 65-76.

2.8-79 Singh, G., and Oza, G.M. 1977. Nomenclatural note on the Indian Archangelica. Bull. Bot. Surv. India 16: 167-169.

2.8-80 Singh, V., Sharma, M., and Jain, D.K. 1974. Trichomes in Salvia (Labiatae) and their taxonomic significance. Bull. Bot. Surv. India 16: 27-34.

2.8-81 Srivastava, K. 1975. Epidermal studies in some species of Jasminum Proc. Indian Acad. Sci. Sect. B 81: 111-117.

2.8-82 Taylor, R.L., and MacBryde, B. 1978. New taxa and nomenclatural changes with respect to vascular plants of British Columbia: A descriptive resource inventory. Can. J. Bot. 56: 184-195.

2.8-83 Tucker, A.O. 1974. Botanical aspects of oregano reconsidered. Herbarist 40: 11-13.

2.8-84 Tucker, A.O., Harley, R.M., and Fairbrothers, D.E. 1980. The Linnaean types of Mentha (Lamiaceae). Taxon 29: 233-255.

2.8-85 Vaczy, C. 1975. The correct grammatical gender of some generic names. Phytocoenologia 2: 442-450.

2.8-86 Vinogradova, V.M. 1977. What is Peucedanum crophyllum Schischk. (Apiaceae) [in Russian]. Bot. Zh. (Leningrad) 62: 532-533.

2.8-87 Ward, D.B., and Fantz, P.R. 1977. Keys to the flora of Florida--3, Boraginaceae. Phytologia 36: 309-323.

2.8-88 Weinert, E. 1973. The taxanomic position and range of Angelica archangelica L. and Angelica lucida [in German]. Feddes Repert. 84: 303-313.

2.9 Chemical Taxonomy

2.9-1 Adzet, T., and Passet, J. 1976. Chemotaxonomic studies on Thymus piperella L. [in Spanish]. Collect. Bot. (Barc.) 10{1}: 5-11. PBA 47: 9041.

2.9-2 Adzet, T., Granger, R., Passet, J., and San Martin, R. 1976. Chemotypes of Thymus hiemalis Lange [in French]. Plant Med. Phytother. 10: 6-15.

2.9-3 Adzet, T., and Martinez, F. 1978. Luteolin and 6-hydroxyluteolin: taxonomically important flavones in Thymus [in German]. Planta Med. 33: 266 (Abstr.).

2.9-4 Adzet, T., Granger, R., Passet, J., and Martin, R. San. 1977. Thymus mastichina chemotypes [in French]. Plant. Med. Phytother. 11: 275-280. HA 48: 9238.

2.9-5 Adzet, T., and Passet, J. 1972. Chemotaxonomy of the genre Satureia calamintha. Riv. Ital. Essenze Profumi Piante Off. Aromi Saponi Cosmet. Aerosol 54: 482-486.

2.9-6 Afzal-Rafii, Z. 1976. Cytotaxonomic and phylogenetic study of some Mediterranean Salvia: the Salvia officinalis group [in French]. B ull. Soc. Bot. Fr. 123: 515-531.

2.9-7 Afzal-Rafii, Z. 1972. Contribution to the cytotaxonomic study of Salvia of Turkey, Part II [in French]. Bull. Soc. Bot. Fr. 119: 157-175.

2.9-8 Afzal, Z. 1971. A cytotaxonomic study of some Salvia of Turkey [in French]. Bull. Soc. Bot. Fr. 118: 59-75.

2.9-9 Al-Mayah, A.-R.A., and Al-Shehbaz, I.A. 1977. Chromosome numbers for some Leguminosae from Iraq. Bot. Not. 130: 437-440.

2.9-10 Androshchuk, O.F., Kostynenko, L.D., and Khmel, N.V. 1978. Study of karyotypes in representatives of the genus Achillea L. of the flora of the Ukrainian SSR [in Ukrainian]. Ukr. Bot. Zh. 35: 273-278.

2.9-11 Anonymous. 1975. Triterpenoids from Panax Linn. and their relationship with taxonomy and geographical distribution [in Chinese]. Chih Wu Fen Lei Hsueh Pao 13{2}: 29-48.

2.9-12 Arano, H., and Saito, H. 1979. Cytological studies in family Umbelliferae. IV. Karyotypes in genus Angelica 2. Kromosomo (Tokyo) 1979{II-15/16}: 417-426.

2.9-13 Arano, H., and Saito, H. 1977. Cytological studies in family Umbelliferae. I. Karyotypes in Angelica [in Japanese]. Kromosomo (Tokyo) (II-5): 146-157.

2.9-14 Arevshatyan, I.G. 1973. Chromosome numbers and size of pollen grains of Taraxacum Weber in the Armenian SSR [in Russian]. Biol. Zh. Arm. 26{3}: 38-44.

2.9-15 Baijal, S.K., and Kaul, B.K. 1973. Karyomorphological studies in Coriandrum sativum L. and Cuminum cyminum L. Cytologia 38: 211-217.

2.9-16 Baslas, B.K., and Baslas, R.K. 1972. Biogenetic relation between terpenic and nonterpenic constituents in the volatile oils from Anethum graveolens and A. sowa [in German]. Riechst., Aromen, Koerperpflegem. 22{8}: 270-271. CA 77: 130489.

2.9-17 Basler, A. 1972. Cytotaxonomic study of the genus Symphytum L. of the Boraginaceae family. Studies on the predominantly north German plants of the species of Symphytum asperum Lepech., Symphytum officinale L. and Symphytum X uplandicum Nym. [in German]. Bot. Jahrb. Syst. Pflanzengesch. Pflanzengeogr. 92: 508-553.

2.9-18 Betts, T.J. 1976. Possible new Western Australian fennel chemovar. Aust. J. Pharm. Sci. 5: 78.

2.9-19 Bhalla, N.P., and Dakwale, R.N. 1978. Chemotaxonomy of Indigofera Linn. J. Indian Bot. Soc. 57{2}: 180-185. CA 93: 66178.

2.9-20 Bhattacharya, S. 1978. A cytotaxonomic study of some members of the tribe Ocimoideae (Labiatae). Rev. Roum. Biol. 23: 3-9.

2.9-21 Biste, C. 1977. Cytotaxonomic studies of the group Achillea millefolium (Asteraceae) in East Germany. Feddes Report 88: 533-613.

2.9-22 Blair, A. 1975. Karyotypes of 5 plant species with disjunct distributions in Virginia and the Carolinas. Am. J. Bot. 62: 833-337.

2.9-23 Bogonina, Z.S., and Nikolaev, A.G. 1972. On chemical races in plants of the genus Mentha [in Russian]. Pages 28-40 in A.G. Nikolaev, ed. Khimicheskaia izmenchivost' rastenii. Shtiintsa, Kishinev, USSR. AGRICOLA.

2.9-24 Bonzani da Silva, J., and Rocha, A.B. 1971. Chemical varieties of Artemisia absinthium L., Compositae [in Portuguese]. Rev. Farm. Bioquim. Univ. Sao Paulo 9{1}: 101-106.

2.9-25 Boulter, D., Gleaves, J.T., Haslett, B.G., Peacock, D., and Jensen, U. 1978. The relationships of 3 tribes of the Compositae as suggested by plastocyanin amino acid sequence data. Phytochemistry 17: 1585-1589.

2.9-26 Brieskorn, C.H., and Biechele, W. 1971. Distinction between Salvia officinalis and Salvia triloba [in German]. Dtsch. Apoth. Ztg. 111{5}: 141-142. CA 75: 40508.

2.9-27 Brieskorn, C.H., and Biechele, W. 1971. Distinction between Salvia officinalis and Salvia triloba. Q.J. Crude Drug Res. 11: 1784-1787.

2.9-28 Bubarova, M. 1973. A study of the essential oils in the leaves of celery, parsley and their hybrid and its taxonometric aspects [in Bulgarian]. Gradinar. Lozar. Nauka 10{1}: 23-32. PBA 43: 8370.

2.9-29 Bubarova, M., Hristova, I., and Madzharova, D. 1977. Comparative electrophoretic study of peroxidase in hybrids resulting from remote hybridization of Petroselinum hortense Hoffm. and Apium graveolens L. Z. Pflanzenzeucht. 78: 65-72.

2.9-30 Cheshmedzhiev, I. 1973. A cytotaxonomic investigation of the cultivated Allium species in Bulgaria [in Bulgarian]. Genet. Sel. 6: 283-294. PBA 44: 2811.

2.9-31 Constance, L., Chuang, T.-I., and Bell, C.R. 1976. Chromosome numbers in Umbelliferae. V. Am. J. Bot. 63: 608-625.

2.9-32 Crawford, D.J., and Hartman, R.L. 1972. Chromosome numbers and taxonomic notes for Rocky Mountain Umbelliferae. J. Am. Bot. 59: 386-392.

2.9-33 Dabrowska, J. 1972. Observations on the distribution in Silesia of forms of Achillea L. both with and without azulene, in relation to data on the distribution of taxa of the genus in that region [in Polish]. Herba Pol. 18: 40-69. PBA 43: 6177.

2.9-34 Dabrowska, J. 1977. Karyological observations of sixteen taxa of Achillea L. occurring in Poland and adjacent territories [in Polish]. Herba Pol. 23: 225-233.

2.9-35 Daniel, M., and Sabnis, S.D. 1979. Chemotaxonomy of Oleaceae. Indian J. Exp. Biol. 17: 995-997.

2.9-36 Dasgupta, A., and Sharma, A. 1975. Chromosome studies in Indian jasmines. Pages 43-51 in H.Y. Mohan Ram, J.J. Shah and C.K. Shah, eds. Form, structure and function in plants. Sarita Prakashan, Nauchandi, India.

2.9-37 Duhrssen, E., Schafer, A., and Neumann, K.H. 1979. Qualitative differences in the DNA of some higher plants, and aspects of selective DNA replication during differentiation. Plant Sys. Evol. (Suppl. 2): 95-103. Bib.Ag. 45: 35008.

2.9-38 Durkee, A.B., and Harborne, J.B. 1973. Flavonal glycosides in Brassica and Sinapis. Phytochemistry 12: 1085-1089.

2.9-39 Ehrendorfer, F. 1973. New chromosome numbers and remarks on the Achillea millefolium polyploid complex in North America. Oesterr. Bot. Z. 122: 133-143.

2.9-40 Elena-Rosello, J.-A. 1980. Karyological study of Spanish thymes [in Spanish]. An. Inst. Bot. A.J. Cavinilles 37: 113-115.

2.9-41 Fernandez Casas, J., Gonzalez Aguilera, J., and Ruiz Rejon, M. 1977. Notes on the karyology of Lamiaceae [in Spanish]. An. Inst. Bot. A.J. Cavinilles 34: 723-732.

2.9-42 Fernandez, G.C.J., and Herath, H.M.W. 1976. Characterization and identification of some West Indian (Cymbopogon citratus (L.) Stapf) and East Indian (Cymbopogon flexuosus (L.) Stapf) lemongrass strains. Journal of the National Agricultural Society of Ceylon 13: 101-114. HA 47: 9753.

2.9-43 Florya, V.N., and Kretsu, L.G. 1980. Characteristics of Umbelliferae of Moldavia according to the content of coumarins and extractive substances [in Russian]. Izv. Akad. Nauk Mold. SSR Ser. Biol. Khim. Nauk 1980{2}: 89-91.

2.9-44 Gadella, T.W.J., Kliphuis, E., and Perring, F.H. 1974. Cytotaxonomic studies in the genus Symphytum. VI. Some notes on Symphytum in Britain. Acta Bot. Neerl. 23: 433-437.

2.9-45 Gadella, T.W.J., and Kliphuis, E. 1972. Cytotaxonomic studies in the genus Symphytum. IV. Cytogeographic investigations in Symphytum officinale L. Acta Bot. Neerl. 21: 169-173.

2.9-46 Gadella, T.W.J., and Kliphuis, E. 1971. Cytotaxonomic studies in the genus Symphytum. III. Some Symphytum hybrids in Belgium and The Netherlands. Biol. Jaarb. 39: 97-107. AGRICOLA.

2.9-47 Gadella, T.W.J., and Kliphuis, E. 1973. Cytotaxonomic studies in the genus Symphytum. V. Some notes on European plants with the chromosome number 2N = 40. Bot. Jahrb. Syst. Pflanzengesch. Pflanzengeogr. 93: 530-538.

2.9-48 Gadella, T.W.J., and Kliphuis, E. 1975. Cytotaxonomic studies in the genus Symphytum. VIII. Some hybrids between S. asperum Lepech. and S. officinale L. in Denmark. Proc. K. Ned. Akad. Wet. Ser. C 78: 182-188.

2.9-49 Gadella, T.W.J., and Kliphuis, E. 1973. Chromosome numbers of flowering plants in The Netherlands. VI. Proc. K. Ned. Akad. Wet. Ser. C 76: 303-311.

2.9-50 Gadella, T.W.J., and Kliphuis, E. 1978. Cytotaxonomic studies in the genus Symphytum. VIII. Chromosome numbers and classification of ten European species. Proc. K. Ned. Akad. Wet. Ser. C 81: 162-172.

2.9-51 Galun, E., Aviv, D., Raveh, D., Vardi, A., and Zelcer, A. 1977. Protoplasts in studies of cell genetics and morphogenesis. Pages 302-312 in W. Barz, E. Reinhard and M.H. Zenk, eds. Plant tissue culture and its bio-technological application. Proceedings of the first international congress on medicinal plant research, Section B, Munich, Germany, Sept. 6-10, 1976. Springer-Verlag, New York.

2.9-52 Gervais, C. 1977. Cytological investigation of the Achillea millefolium complex (Compositae) in Quebec. Can. J. Bot. 55: 796-808. AGRICOLA.

2.9-53 Gill, L.S. 1977. A cytosystematics study of the genus Monarda L. (Labiatae) in Canada. Caryologia 30: 381-394.

2.9-54 Gill, L.S. 1979. Cytotaxonomic studies of the tribe Nepeteae (Labiatae) in Canada. Genetica (The Hague) 50: 111-117.

2.9-55 Gogina, E.E., and Svetozarova, V.V. 1972. Classification and caryology of some species of Thymus sect. Subbracteati Klok [in Russian]. Byull. Gl. Bot. Sada 1972{84}: 36-41. PBA 44: 6380.

2.9-56 Granger, R., and Passet, J. 1973. Thymus vulgaris native to France: chemical races and chemotaxonomy [in French]. Phytochemistry 12: 1683-1691.

2.9-57 Granger, R., and Passet, J. 1971. Chemical types (chemotypes) of the species Thymus vulgaris L. [in French]. C.R. Hebd. Seances Acad. Sci. Ser. D 273: 2350-2353.

2.9-58 Granger, R., Passet, J., and Teulade-Arbousset, G. 1973. On the Labiatae Lavandula stoechas [in French]. Trav. Soc. Pharm. Montp. 33: 355-360.

2.9-59 Greger, H. 1979. Polyacetylenes and sesamines as chemical characters in the Artemisia absinthium group [in German]. Planta Med. 35: 84-91.

2.9-60 Gulati, B.C. 1979. Ocimum basilicum Linn. - methyl chavicol type. Int Congr. Essent. Oils, [Pap.], 7th, 1977. 7: 148-152.

2.9-61 Gurvich, N.L. 1977. Some regularities of intraspecific chemoevolution in plants [in Russian]. Herba Hung. 16{1}: 17-37. HA 49: 1440.

2.9-62 Harborne, J.B., and Green, P.S. 1980. A chemotaxonomic survey of flavonoids in leaves of the Oleaceae. Bot. J. Linn. Soc. 81: 155-167.

2.9-63 Harborne, J.B., and Williams, C.A. 1972. Flavonoid patterns in the fruits of the Umbelliferae. Phytochemistry 11: 1741-1750.

2.9-64 Harley, R.M., and Brighton, C.A. 1977. Chromosome numbers in the genus Mentha L. Bot. J. Linn. Soc. 74: 71-96.

2.9-65 Hatano, K., Nishioka, I., and Iwasa, S. 1974. Cytogenetic studies of Umbelliferous plants. II. The karyotype on Angelica anomala and its cross-compatibility with original plants of Japanese "Toki" [in Japanese]. Shoyakugaku Zasshi 28: 65-71.

2.9-66 Hatano, K., Nishioka, I., and Iwasa, S. 1974. Cytogenetic studies of Umbelliferous plants. I. The karyotype and cross-compatibility on the original plants of Japanese "Toki" [in Japanese]. Shoyakugaku Zasshi 28: 51-64.

2.9-67 Hatano, K., Nishioka, I., and Iwasa, S. 1975. Cytogenetical studies of Umbelliferous plants. III. The karyotype analyses of Angelica species in Japan [in Japanese]. Syoyakugaku Zasshi 29{1}: 10-21.

2.9-68 Hefendehl, F.W., and Murray, M.J. 1973. Monoterpene composition of a chemotype of Mentha piperita having high limonene. Planta Med. 23: 101-109. HA 43: 9000.

2.9-69 Hefendehl, F.W., and Nagell, A. 1975. Differences in the composition of the essential oils of Mentha rotundifolia, Mentha longifolia and F1 hybrid of both species [in German]. Parfuem. Kosmet. 56: 189-193. AGRICOLA.

2.9-70 Hegnauer, R., and Kooiman, P. 1978. The taxonomic significance of iridoids of the Tubiflorae sensu Wettstein [in German]. Planta Med. 33: 1-33.

2.9-71 Hendriks, H. 1971. Chemotaxonomic research of Mentha rotundifolia (L.) Hudson [in Dutch]. Pharm. Weekbl. 106: 158-164. AGRICOLA.

2.9-72 Hentschel, G. 1977. Paprika: variations in form and color [in German] Gemuse 13: 11-12. AGRICOLA.

2.9-73 Honcariv, R., and Repcak, M. 1979. Chemotypes of Matricaria chamomilla L. Herba Pol. 25: 261-267. HA 51: 1480.

2.9-74 Hoo, G., and Tseng, C.-J. 1973. On the Chinese species of Panax Linn. [in Chinese]. Chih Wu Fen Lei Hsueh Pao 11: 431-438.

2.9-75 Hore, A., and Sharma, A.K. 1975. Structure and behavior of chromosomes in the evolution of certain taxa of Umbelliferae: I. Tribe Ammineae Pages 73-74 in V.S. Motial, ed. Seminar on recent advances in plant sciences. Abstracts of papers. Association for Advancement of Plant Sciences, Kalyani, India.

2.9-76 Humphries, C.J., Murray, B.G., Bocquet, G., and Vasudevan, K. 1978. Chromosome numbers of phanerogams from Morocco and Algeria. Bot. Not. 131: 391-406.

2.9-77 Iwasa, S., Inada, I., and Endo, M. 1978. Analysis of phylogenetic relationships of Brassica and its allied genera by paper chromatography [in Japanese]. Engei Gakkai Zasshi 47{1}: 45-56. FCA 32: 1173.

2.9-78 Jensen, R.J., McLeod, M.J., Eshbaugh, W.H., and Guttman, S.I. 1979. Numerical taxonomic analyses of allozymic variation in Capsicum (Solanaceae). Taxon 28: 315-327.

2.9-79 Kamala, T. 1978. Basic chromosome number and the probable origin of the genomes in Brassica. Curr. Sci. 47: 128-129.

2.9-80 Keller, L. 1973. On the cytogeography of Valeriana officinalis in Switzerland. Bull. Soc. Neuchatel Sci. Nat. 96: 67-79.

2.9-81 Khrimlyan, A.I., and Gambaryan, P.P. 1975. Statistical analysis of the classification of mint chemotaxa based on the essential oil components [in Russian]. Herba Hung. 14{1}: 29-35. HA 46: 3690.

2.9-82 Khrimlyan, A.I., and Tetenyi, P. 1977. Chemical differentiation within and between mint species in the USSR and Hungary [in Russian]. Herba Hung. 16{3}: 7-14. HA 49: 1483.

2.9-83 Khrimlyan, A.I., and Makarov, V.V. 1971. Chemotypes of wild species of mint in the flora of the USSR [in Russian]. Rastit. Resur. 7: 24-31. PBA 43: 7520.

2.9-84 Konvicka, O., and Levan, A. 1972. Chromosome studies in Allium sativum. Hereditas 72: 129-148.

2.9-85 Kremer, B.P. 1978. Experiment: Chemical races in plant kingdom [in German]. Biol. Unserer Ziet. 8: 92-94. AGRICOLA.

2.9-86 Kurosawa, S. 1979. Notes on chromosome numbers of spermatophytes {2}. Shokubutsu Kenkyu Zasshi 54: 155-160.

2.9-87 Lawrence, B.M., and Morton, J.K. 1972. Cytological and chemical variation in Mentha arvensis L. An. Acad. Bras. Cienc. 44(Suppl.): 38-41 CA 83: 128676.

2.9-88 Leshukova, N.B. 1971. Karyological characteristics of some specimens of the mint family (Tribe Stachydeae) [in Russian]. Nauchn. Dokl. Vyssh. S-hk. Biol. Nauki 1971{2}: 48-49. AGRICOLA.

2.9-89 Loeve, A. 1980. Chromosome number reports LXIX. Taxon 29: 703-730.

2.9-90 MacKenzie, S.L., and Blakely, J.A. 1972. Purification and characterization of seed globulins from Brassica juncea, B. nigra, and B. hirta. Can. J. Bot. 50: 1825-1834.

2.9-91 Magulaev, A. Yu. 1980. Chromosome numbers of some legumes of the northern Caucasus [in Russian]. Bot. Zh. (Leningrad) 65: 836-843. PBA 51: 9744.

2.9-92 Makarov, V.V., and Reznikova, S.A. 1972. Chromosome numbers in the genus Mentha L. [in Russian]. Byull. Mosk. O-va. Ispyt. Prir. Otd. Biol. 77: 133-141. PBA 43: 2400.

2.9-93 Malecka, J. 1971. Cytotaxonomical and embryological investigations on a natural hybrid between Taraxacum kok-saghyz Rodin and Taraxacum officinale Web. and their putative parent species. Acta Biol. Cracov. Ser. Bot. 14: 179-197.

2.9-94 Malingre, T.M. 1971. Chemotaxonomic research on Mentha arvensis L. [in Dutch]. Pharm. Weekbl. 106: 165-171. AGRICOLA.

2.9-95 Marchi, P. 1971. Chromosome numbers of the Italian flora. XLVI-LVI [in Italian]. Inf. Bot. Ital. 3: 82-94. PBA 43: 730.

2.9-96 Mikhailova, Iu. 1975. Chromosome numbers for three essential-oil bearing plants: Cephalophora aromatica Schrad., Origanum majorana L. and Origanum heracleoticum L. [in Bulgarian]. Genet. Sel. 8: 406-408. AGRICOLA.

2.9-97 Mikhailova, Yu. 1975. Chromosome numbers of three essential oil plants - Cephalophora aromatica Schrad., Origanum majorana L. and O. heracleoticum L. [in Bulgarian]. Genet. Sel. 8: 406-408. PBA 46: 5620.

2.9-98 Mizianty, M., and Frey, L. 1973. Chromosome numbers of some vascular plants in the Western Zieszczady Mts. (south-eastern Poland). Fragm. Florist. Geobot. (Krakow) 19: 265-270.

2.9-99 Morton, G.H. 1972. Documented plant chromosome numbers, 1972. Part 1. SIDA Contrib. Bot. 5: 50-51.

2.9-100 Mukherjee, P. 1975. Chromosome study as an aid in tracing the evolution in Cruciferae. Cytologia 40: 727-734.

2.9-101 Nakamura, S. 1977. Studies on the determination of species and cultivars on the basis of electrophoretic patterns of seed protein and seed enzymes. 1. Brassica spp., radish and Cucurbita spp. Engei Gakkai Zasshi 45{1}: 32-47.

2.9-102 Nano, G.M., Sacco, T., and Frattini, C. 1974. Botanical and chemical research on Anthemis nobilis and some of its cultivars [in French]. Int. Congr. Essent. Oils, [Pap.], 6th, 1974. 114, 4 pp. CA 84: 40768.

2.9-103 Nesom, G.L. 1978. Notes on the chromosome number of Gaultheria procumbens L. (Ericaceae). Rhodora 80{824}: 594-595.

2.9-104 Okada, H., and Tanaka, R. 1975. Karyological studies in some species of Lauraceae. Taxon 24: 271-280.

2.9-105 Ono, Y., Deki, M., and Tanaka, S. 1975. Discrimination of the species of peppermint oils by gas chromatography and GC-MS [gas chromatography-mass spectrometry] [in Japanese]. Bunseki Kagaku 24{9}: 589-593. CA 85: 204916.

2.9-106 Oswiecimska, M. 1973. Chemotaxonomic investigations on an azulene Achillea. Herba Pol. 19: 207-215.

2.9-107 Oswiecimska, M. 1974. Correlation between chromosome number and prochamazulene in East European Achillea [in German]. Planta Med. 25: 389-395.

2.9-108 Passet, J. 1971. Thymus vulgaris L., chemotaxonomy and biogenesis of monoterpenes [in French]. C. R. Seances Acad. Agric. Fr. 57: 1197-1200. PBA 43: 1648.

2.9-109 Pichitakul, N., and Sthapitanonda, K. 1977. The constituents of oil from different mint varieties [in Thai]. J. Nat. Res. Counc. Thailand 9{2}: 1-9. PBA 47: 12237.

2.9-110 Prakash, S. 1980. Taxonomy, cytogenetics and origin of crop brassicas, a review. Opera Botanica 55. 57 pp.

2.9-111 Pulatova, T.P. 1973. Phenolic compounds of some species of mint [in Russian]. Uzb. Biol. Zh. 17{6}: 17-19. CA 80: 130493.

2.9-112 Pushpangadan, P., Sobti, S.N., and Reayat Khan. 1975. Karyomorphological studies in the genus Ocimum I. Basilicum group. Nucleu (Calcutta) 18: 177-182. PBA 47: 901.

2.9-113 Racz, G., Racz-Kotilla, E., and Jozsa, J. 1980. Hypotensive activity of some species belonging to Labiatae on the central nervous system of mice. Acta Hort. 96: 49-53.

2.9-114 Remanadan, P., and Mehra, P.N. 1974. Cytological investigations on Indian Compositae. III. Tribe Cichorieae. Nucleus (Calcutta) 17: 87-96.

2.9-115 Resh, F.M. 1975. Correlations between chemical and anatomical characters of the leaves in Digitalis purpurea [in Russian]. Rastit. Resur. 11: 403-406. PBA 47: 4548.

2.9-116 Rhyu, H.Y. 1979. Gas chromatographic characterization of sages of various geographic origins. J. Food Sci. 44: 758-762.

2.9-117 Rostovtseva, T.S. 1974. The chromosome numbers in several species of the family Apiaceae Lindl. Dokl. Biol. Sci. (Engl. Transl.) 214{1-6}: 31-32. Translation of Dokl. Akad. Nauk SSSR 214: 449-450, 1974.

2.9-118 Rostovtseva, T.S. 1976. Chromosome numbers of some species from the family Apiaceae in South Siberia [in Russian]. Bot. Zh. (Leningrad) 61: 93-99.

2.9-119 Sacco, T., Nano, G.M., and Scannerini, S. 1972. Comparative analysis of caryological and chemotaxonomic characters of several mints of the Spicata section [in French]. An. Acad. Bras. Cienc. 44(Suppl.): 42-45.

2.9-120 Sacco, T., and Scannerini, S. 1972. Cytotaxonomy and chemotaxonomy of two mint producers of menthol; Mentha piperita Huds. var. officinalis Sole f. rubescens et f. pallescens Camus [in French]. An. Acad. Bras. Cienc. 44(Suppl.): 46-49.

2.9-121 Saleh, N.A.M. 1979. The biosynthesis of flavonoid glycosides and their importance in chemosystematics. Biochem. Syst. Ecol. 7: 37-45.

2.9-122 San Martin, R., Granger, R., Adzet, T., Passet, J., and Teulade-Arbousset, G. 1973. Chemical polymorphism in two Mediterranean Labiates: Satureia montana and Satureia obovata Lag (Spanish nature stations) [in French]. Plant. Med. Phytother. 7: 95-103.

2.9-123 Sen, A.R., Sengupta, P., Mondal, A., and Roy, B.R. 1974. Differentiation of caraway, coriander, and cumin by study of their volatile oils, using thin layer chromatography. J. Assoc. Off. Anal. Chem. 57: 763-764.

2.9-124 Sen, S. 1976. Cryptic structural changes in the evolution of cultivated alliums. Indian J. Hered. 8: 41-50.

2.9-125 Seo, B.B., and Kim, J.H. 1975. Karyotypic analysis based on heterochromatin distribution in Allium fistulosum and Allium ascalonicum. Singmul Hakhoe Chi 18: 92-100. PBA 47: 6829.

2.9-126 Shiu, Y.H., Ruedenberg, L., and Tredici, P. del. 1980. Studies of American ginsengs. Rhodora 82: 627-636.

2.9-127 Skrzypczak, L., and Skrzypczakowa, L. 1976. Flavonoid compounds in the chemical taxonomy of the Liliaceae. Herba Pol. 22: 336-349.

2.9-128 Stahl, E. 1972. Chemical races of pharmaceutical plants containing essential oils [in Russian]. Pages 245-246 in P.V. Naumenko, et al., eds. Mezhundarodnyi kongress po efirnym maslam, 4th, Tiflis, 1968, [Materialy]. v. 2. Pishchevaya Promyshlennost', Moscow, USSR. CA 81: 74886.

2.9-129 Tarasova, E.M. 1973. Investigation of the caryotypes of nine species of the genus Allium [in Russian]. Byull. Vses. Inst. Rastenievod. 1973{29}: 74-87. PBA 44: 224.

2.9-130 Tetenyi, P. 1974. Chemotaxonomic data on the Boraginaceae [in French] Acta Bot. Acad. Sci. Hung. 20: 159-167.

2.9-131 Tetenyi, P. 1976. Chemotaxonomy of the range of saponins in the vegetable kingdom [in Hungarian]. Herba Hung. 15{3}: 27-48.

2.9-132 Turkov, V.D., Shelepina, G.A., Kazakova, A.A., and Tarasova, E.M. 1979. Caryotiypic polymorphism in onion and garlic [in Russian]. Vestn. S-kh. Nauki (Moscow) 1979{5}: 49-54. PBA 50: 868.

2.9-133 Turner, B.L. 1977. Chemosystematics and its effect upon the traditionalist. Ann. Mo. Bot. Gard. 64: 235-242.

2.9-134 Valen, F. van. 1979. Contribution to the knowledge of cyanogenesis in angiosperms. 12. Cyanogenesis in Boraginaceae. Proc. K. Ned. Akad. Wet. Ser. C 82: 171-176.

2.9-135 Van Loon, J.C., and Oudemans, J.J.M.H. 1976. Chromosome numbers of some angiosperms of the southern USSR. Acta Bot. Neerl. 25: 329-336.

2.9-136 Vaughan, J.G., and Gordon, E.I. 1973. A taxonomic study of Brassica juncea using the techniques of electrophoresis, gas-liquid chromatography and serology. Ann. Bot. 37: 167-184.

2.9-137 Verzar-Petri, G., Cuong, B.N., Tamas, J., Radics, L., and Ujszaszi, K. 1979. The main azulenogenous sesquiterpene lactones of Achillea millefolium L.-ssp-collina as compounds in the plant kingdom. Planta Med. 36: 273-274 (Abstr.).

2.9-138 Vosa, C.G. 1976. Heterochromatic patterns in Allium. I. The relationship between the species of the cepa group and its allies. Heredity 36: 383-392. PBA 47: 791.

2.9-139 Voskanian, V.E. 1974. Ecology and number of chromosomes of some alpine plants of Aragatz [in Russian]. Biol. Zh. Arm. 27{6}: 64-69.

2.9-140 Wcislo, H. 1972. Karyological studies in Symphytum L. Acta Biol. Cracov. Ser. Bot. 15: 153-163.

2.9-141 Yadava, J.S., Chowdhury, J.B., Kakar, S.N., and Nainawatee, H.S. 1979. Comparative electrophoretic studies of proteins and enzymes of some Brassica species. Theor. Appl. Genet. 54: 89-91.

2.9-142 Yoshida, T., and Hasegawa, M. 1977. Distribution of stizolamine in some leguminous plants. Phytochemistry 16: 131-132. CA 86: 152631.

2.9-143 Zalzala, A., Talalaj, S., and Al-Shamma, A. 1977. Chemotaxonomic studies of the Mentha species of Iraq. Bull. Biol. Res. Cent. (Baghdad) 8: 105-113.

2.9-144 Zemskova, E.A. 1977. Karyologic study of certain Plantago L. species (Plantaginaceae) [in Russian]. Bot. Zh. (Leningrad) 62: 1301-1305.

2.9-145 Zonev, D., Markova, M., and Popova, D. 1971. Spectra of protein and globulin fractions of paprika (Capsicum annuum L.) seeds in heterotic varieties and their parents [in German]. Dokl. S-kh. Akad. (Sofia) 4: 223-227. AGRICOLA.

3.0 BIONOMICS

3.1 Geographic Distribution

3.1-1 Adam, J.-G. 1975. Description of the flora of the Nimba Mountains, 3rd part [in French]. Mem. Mus. Natl. Hist. Nat. Ser. B Bot. 24: 913-1374.

3.1-2 Aichele, D. 1976. The dandelion [in German]. Kosmos (Stockholm) 72: 158-161. AGRICOLA.

3.1-3 Androshchuk, A.F., Klokov, M.V., Kritskaya, L.I., and Kostinenko, L.D. 1979. Achillea millefolium L. (Asteraceae) in the Ukraine [in Russian]. Bot. Zh. (Leningrad) 64: 378-386.

3.1-4 Avetisian, V.E., and Barsegian, A.M. 1975. Some new and rare species of flora in Armenia and the Caucasus [in Russian]. Biol. Zh. Arm. 28{2}: 80-83.

3.1-5 Babaev, R.I., and Ragimov, M.A. 1975. Distribution and resources of mint in the Azerbaijan SSR. Izv. Akad. Nauk Az. SSR Ser. Biol. Nauk 1975{4}: 3-7.

3.1-6 Bangerter, E.B. 1975. New and interesting records of adventive plants from the Auckland Institute and Museum Herbarium 1. Rec. Auckland Inst. Mus. 12: 91-94.

3.1-7 Biondi, E. 1972. Sites of Laurus nobilis in the Marche region (Italy) [in Italian]. Arch. Bot. 48: 74-79. BBB 380: 1226.

3.1-8 Bortnyak, M.M. 1975. Contribution to the flora of the Kiev region [in Ukrainian]. Ukr. Bot. Zh. 32: 445-448.

3.1-9 Boufford, D.E. 1973. New or noteworthy New Hampshire plants. Rhodora 75{801}: 158-161.

3.1-10 Bradley, T.R. 1973. Plant records for the northern Virginia fall belt counties. Castanea 38: 175-182.

3.1-11 Ceska, A. 1975. Additions to the adventive flora of Vancouver Island, British Columbia. Can. Field-Nat. 89: 451-453.

3.1-12 Cheshmedzhiev, I. 1977. Floristic materials and critical notes on Bulgarian flora [in Bulgarian]. Fitologiya 1977{7}: 75-83.

3.1-13 Coste, I. 1979. Contribution to the study of a _Molinio_
arrhenatheretea Tx. {1937} 1970 in the Locva Mountains (southwestern
Romania) [in German]. Rev. Roum. Biol. Ser. Biol. Veg. 24{1}: 17-26.
HERB-AB 50: 5235.

3.1-14 D'Arcy, W.G., Woodson, R.E., Jr., Schery, R.W., and
Collaborators. 1971. Flora of Panama. Part IX. Family 178.
Plantaginaceae. Ann. Mo. Bot. Gard. 58: 363-369.

3.1-15 D'Arcy, W.G., Woodson, R.E., Jr., Schery, R.W., and
Collaborators. 1976. Flora of Panama. Part VIII. Family 158. Oleaceae.
Ann. Mo. Bot. Gard. 63: 553-564.

3.1-16 Da Silva, R.A.P., ed. 1971. Thirteen new species and subspecies
to the flora of Portugal [in Portuguese]. Agron. Lusit. 33(1-4): 1-24.

3.1-17 Dabrowska, A. 1973. The occurrence of some vascular plant species
in the Male Pieniny range [in Polish]. Fragm. Florist. Geobot.
(Krakow) 19: 309-321.

3.1-18 De Penafort Malagarriga Heras, R. 1976. Catalog of the higher
plants of the Alt Emporda [in Spanish]. Acta Phytotaxon Barcinonensia
1976{18}: 1-146.

3.1-19 Dulepova, B.I. 1974. Floristic finds in the Chita District [in
Russian] Bot. Zh. (Leningrad) 59: 540-542.

3.1-20 Duppstadt, W.H. 1980. New plant records for West Virginia.
Castanea 45: 71-72.

3.1-21 Duppstadt, W.H. 1977. Some new state records and other plant
finds in West Virginia. Castanea 42: 257-258.

3.1-22 Filipello, S., Sartori, F., and Tomaselli, R. 1979. Presentation
of physionomic and structural map of the vegetation on the island of
Montecristo (Tuscan Archipelago) [in Italian]. Atti Ist. Bot. Univ.
Lab. Crittogam. Pavia Ser. 6, 12: 181-182.

3.1-23 Gladun, Ya.D. 1980. Resources of some wild growing medicinal
plants in Eastern regions of Chernovtsy Oblast Ukrainian-SSR, USSR [in
Ukrainian]. Farm. Zh. (Kiev) 1980{1}: 75-76.

3.1-24 Gouyon, P.H. 1975. Note on the provisional map of the
distribution of different chemical forms of _Thymus vulgaris_ L. in the
Saint-Martin-de-Londres basin (Herault, France) [in French]. Oecol.
Plant. 10: 187-194.

3.1-25 Hansen, A. 1975. Contributions to the flora of the Azores,
Portugal - V. Anu. Soc. Broteriana 41: 45-61.

3.1-26 Harms, V.L., and Hudson, J.H. 1978. Some vascular plants new to
the flora of Saskatchewan. Can. Field-Nat. 92: 389-391.

3.1-27 Hensen, K.J.W. 1974. The range of lavender varieties. 1. [in
Dutch]. Vakbl. Bloemisterij 29{17}: 40-41. HA 45: 3406.

3.1-28 Hensen, K.J.W. 1974. The range of lavender varieties. 2. [in
Dutch]. Vakbl. Bloemisterij 29{18}: 31. HA 45: 3407.

3.1-29 Huang, T.-C., and Cheng, W.-T. 1978. Labiatae. Pages 439-529 in Hui-Lin Li, ed. Flora of Taiwan, vol. 4. Angiospermae. Epoch Publishing Co. Ltd., Taipei, Taiwan.

3.1-30 Jalas, J., Kukkonen, I., and Uotila, P. 1976. Notes on the flora of European Turkey. Notes R. Bot. Gard. Edinb. 35: 69-76.

3.1-31 Jehlik, V., and Rostanski, K. 1975. Angelica archangelica subspecies litoralis now found also in Czechoslovakia [in German]. Preslia 47: 145-157. AGRICOLA.

3.1-32 Johnson, F.D., and Steele, R. 1978. New plant records for Idaho from Pacific coastal refugia. Northwest Sci. 52: 205-211.

3.1-33 Jones, S.B., Jr. 1976. Mississippi flora. V. The mint family. Castanea 41: 41-58.

3.1-34 Karlsson, L. 1977. Floristic observations in northern Lapland [in Swedish]. Sven. Bot. Tidskr. 71: 161-163.

3.1-35 Karlsson, T. 1978. Floristic notes [in Swedish]. Sven. Bot. Tidskr. 72: 149-150.

3.1-36 Kent, D.H. 1972. Notes on the Scottish flora. Observations in West Ross (v.c. 105). Trans. Bot. Soc. Edinb. 41: 547-554.

3.1-37 Kerrigan, W.J., Jr., and Blackwell, W.H., Jr. 1973. The distribution of Ohio Araliaceae. Castanea 38: 168-170.

3.1-38 Kholmuminov, A., and Dubovskii, G.K. 1979. On the fauna of Cicadina of the Golodnostep plain [in Russian]. Uzb. Biol. Zh. 1979{4}: 61-63. RAE-A 68: 2346

3.1-39 Kornas, J. 1975. Vascular plants of the Gorce mountains (Polish Western Carpathians). Supplement III. Fragm. Florist. Geobot. (Cracow) 21: 467-490.

3.1-40 Kozma, A., and Tolgyesi, Gy. 1979. Plant associations of flood plains along the middle Tisza and their agricultural utilization. Tiscia 14: 105-122. CA 94: 99782.

3.1-41 Kuijt, J. 1973. New plant records in Waterton Lakes National Park, Alberta. Can. Field-Nat. 87: 67-69.

3.1-42 Lahham, J. 1974. Distribution and use of licorice in Syria. Rastit. Resur. 10: 144-149.

3.1-43 Li, H.-L. 1978. Plantaginaceae. Pages 701-703 in Hiu-Lin Li, ed. Flora of Taiwan, vol. 4. Angiospermae. Epoch Publishing Co. Ltd., Taipei, Taiwan

3.1-44 Li, H.-L. 1978. Oleaceae. Pages 133-150 in Hui-Lin Li, ed. Flora of Taiwan, vol. 4. Angiospermae. Epoch Publishing Co. Ltd., Taipei, Taiwan.

3.1-45 Lorenzoni, G.G. 1974. Main phytosociological groupings on Tavolara Island (northeastern Sardinia) [in Italian]. Arch. Bot. Biogeogr. Ital. 50: 61-83.

3.1-46 Mamluk, O.F., and Weltzien, H.C. 1978. Distribution and host range of some Cuscuta strains in the Near and Middle East [in German]. Z. Pflanzenkr. Pflanzenschutz 85: 102-107. WA 28: 1644.

3.1-47 Michalak, S. 1971. Some interesting synanthropic plants in Opol (Silesia). Part II. [in Polish]. Fragm. Florist. Geobot. (Krakow) 17: 11-16.

3.1-48 Mikheeva, N.N. 1977. New data on the flora of the Aktyubinsk Oblast [in Russian]. Izv. Akad. Nauk Kaz. SSR Ser. Biol. 1977{2}: 5-9.

3.1-49 Musaev, I.F. 1978. On the methods of mapping of plant areas [in Russian]. Bot. Zh. (Leningrad) 63: 36-50.

3.1-50 Nadezhina, T.P., and Dashzhamts, Ya. 1980. Glycyrrhiza uralensis in the Mongolian People's Republic. Part 1. Distribution and phytocoenotic characteristics [in Russian]. Rastit. Resur. 16: 293-302. HA 51: 1518.

3.1-51 Nair, S.S.C., Nair, P.V., Sharatchandra, H.C., and Gadgil, M. 1977. An ecological reconnaissance of the proposed Jawahar National Park. J. Bombay Nat. Hist. Soc. 74: 401-435.

3.1-52 Nakagawa, K., and Enomoto, T. 1975. The distribution of tall goldenrod (Solidago altissima L.) in Japan [in Japanese]. Nogaku Kenkyu 55{2}: 67-77. AGRICOLA.

3.1-53 Nechaeva, T.I. 1980. Floristic findings in Vladivostok [in Russian]. Bo t. Zh. (Leningrad) 65: 421-422.

3.1-54 Nilsson, O., and Gustafsson, L.-A. 1978. Report from Project Linnaeus. Part 80-92 [in Swedish]. Sven. Bot. Tidskr. 72: 189-204.

3.1-55 Ormonde, J., and Paiva, J.A.R. 1973. Additions and annotations to the flora of the Azores - Part 1 [in Spanish]. Anu. Soc. Broteriana 39: 39-52.

3.1-56 Ormonde, J. 1973. Additions and annotations to the flora of the Azores - III. Anu. Soc. Broteriana 39: 65-73.

3.1-57 Parr, P.D., and Taylor, F.G., Jr. 1979. Plant species on the Department of Energy-Oak Ridge Reservation that are rare, threatened or of special concern. J. Tenn. Acad. Sci. 54: 100-102.

3.1-58 Peng, C.I. 1978. Some new records for the flora of Taiwan. Bot. Bull. Acad. Sin. 19{1}: 83-86. WA 28: 1332.

3.1-59 Pereira, C., and Pereira, E. 1973. Flora of the state of Parana family Labiatae [in Portuguese]. Arq. Jard. Bot. Rio de Janeiro 19: 79-104.

3.1-60 Pietsch, W., and Mueller-Stoll, W. 1974. Survey of the dwarf rush associations occurring in the Brandenburg District (Isoeto-Nanojuncetea) [in German]. Verh. Bot. Ver. Prov. Brandenb. 109-111: 56-95.

3.1-61 Pireh, W., and Tyrl, R.J. 1980. Cytogeography of Achillea mmillefolium in Oklahoma and adjacent states. Rhodora 82{830}: 361-367.

3.1-62 Powell, A.C. 1977. Radnor. Nat. Wales 15: 143-144.

3.1-63 Resmerita, I. 1971. New and rare taxa of the Apuseni Mountains and the Vladeasa Massif [in Italian]. Commun. Bot. 12: 247-251.

3.1-64 Saxena, H.O. 1972. The flora of Amarkantak (Madhya Pradesh). Bull. Bot. Surv. India 12: 37-66.

3.1-65 Skrubis, B.G. 1972. Seven wild aromatic plants growing in Greece and their essential oils. Flavour Ind. 3: 566-568, 571.

3.1-66 Sobolevskaya, K.A., Tyurina, E.V., and Gus'kova, I.N. 1973. The umbelliferous essential-oil bearing plants in the flora of Western Siberia [in Russian]. Rastit. Resur. 9: 68-72.

3.1-67 Sokolov, S.I. 1974. Complexity in the southern chernozem subzone of the Kustanai Oblast [in Russian]. Izv. Akad. Nauk Kaz. SSR Ser. Biol. Nauk 1974{4}: 45-51.

3.1-68 Standley, P.C., and Williams, L.O. 1973. Flora of Guatemala. IX. 3. Labiatae: Mint family. Fieldiana Bot. 24 Part IX{3/4}: 237-317.

3.1-69 Stenstorp, S., and Nelin, G. 1976. The vascular plants of the Virserum area southeast Sweden [in Swedish]. Sven. Bot. Tidskr. 70: 275-291.

3.1-70 Strid, A. 1978. Contribution to the flora of Mount Kajmakcalan (Vorasoros) Northern Greece. Ann. Mus. Goulandris 4: 211-248.

3.1-71 Strid, A. 1976. Floristic notes from Mt. Olympos and Mt. Falakron (Boz-dagh), Northern Greece. Bot. Not. 129: 251-256.

3.1-72 Sugar, I., Trinajstic, I., and Martinis, Z. 1972. Contribution to knowledge about the area of distribution of Salvia officinalis in Croatia [in Serbo-Croatian]. Farm Glas. 28{2}: 35-42.

3.1-73 Synnott, D. 1977. Additions to the flora of Louth. Ir. Nat. J. 19{4}: 131.

3.1-74 Todorov, T.D. 1979. Distribution of Spanish licorice (Glycyrrhiza glabra L.) in Bulgaria [in Bulgarian]. Fitologiya 1979{11}: 68-70.

3.1-75 Tyrl, R.J. 1975. Origin and distribution of polyploid Achillea millefolium (Compositae) in western North America. Brittonia 27: 187-196.

3.1-76 Van der Werff, H. 1977. Vascular plants from the Galapagos Islands: New records and taxonomic notes. Bot. Not. 130: 89-100.

3.1-77 Vasudevan, K.N. 1976. Contribution to the cytotaxonomy and cytogeography of the flora of the western Himalayas (with an attempt to compare it with the flora of the Alps). Part 3. Ber. Schweiz. Bot. Ges. 86: 152-203.

3.1-78 Vernet, Ph., Guillerm, J.L., and Gouyon, P.H. 1977. Chemical polymorphism of Thymus vulgaris L. (Labiatae). II. Map, scale 1:25000,of chemical forms in the region Saint-Martin-de-Londres (Herault, France) [in French]. Oecol. Plant. 12: 181-194.

3.1-79 Vernet, P., Guillerm, J.L., and Gouyon, P.H. 1977. Chemical polymorphism of Thymus vulgaris L. (Labiatae). I. Distribution of chemical forms in relation to some ecological factors [in French]. Oecol. Plant. 12: 159-179.

3.1-80 Virot, R., and Besancon, H. 1975. Contributions to the knowledge of the flora of central Guyenne Part 2. Cah. Nat. 31: 73-102.

3.1-81 Voliotis, D. 1973. Contribution to the knowledge of the Greek flora: New taxa of the mountainous region Cholomon Greek Macedonia. Feddes Repert. 84: 327-328.

3.1-82 Wayner, G.A., Landers, K.E., and Cochis, T. 1976. Lamiaceae of northeast Alabama. J. Ala. Acad. Sci. 47{3}: 119 (Abstr.).

3.2 Area Introduction

3.2-1 Abbasov, R.M., Mashanov, V.I., and Mamedov, F.M. 1976. Henna as a prospective culture for cultivation in the Azerbaijan [in Russian] Izv. Akad. Nauk Az. SSR Ser. Biol. Nauk 1976{3}: 25-29.

3.2-2 Adam, C.S. 1977. Vegetable cultivars recommended for Seychelles. Vegetables for the Hot, Humid Tropics 1977{2}: 53-58. HA 48: 1330.

3.2-3 Archakova, L.I. 1975. Prospects of cultivating salad and perennial vegetable crops in the Murmansk Region [in Russian]. Byull. Vses. Inst. Rastenievod. 1975{49}: 63-68. HA 46: 9230.

3.2-4 Arinshtein, A.I., and Radchenko, N.M. 1978. New promising essential oil plants for introduction into cultivation in the Crimea [in Russian]. Rastit. Resur. 14: 20-30. HA 48: 6781.

3.2-5 Aschenazi, D., Lifshitz, A., and Putievsky, E. 1979. Content and composition of essential oils in Mentha piperita L. and Origanum vulgare and their influence on the feasibility of growing these plants in Israel. Isr. J. Med. Sci. 15: 97-98 (Abstr.).

3.2-6 Ashirova, A.A. 1979. Experiments on cultivation of ethereal oil plants (Seriphidium balchanorum (Krasch.) Poljak, Mentha asiatica Boriss and Mentha kopetdagensis Boriss.) under the conditions of Turkmenistan. Int. Congr. Essent. Oils, [Pap.], 7th, 1977. 7: 163-164. CA 92: 99424.

3.2-7 Bachthaler, G., Franz, C., Fritz, D., Holzl, J., and Vomel, A. 1976. Comparative investigations of different provenances and varieties of Mentha piperita L. Part 2. Suitability for cultivation (growth, yield and chemical composition) at different localities in the German Federal Republic [in German]. Bayer. Landwirtsch. Jahrb. 53{1}: 35-47. PBA 47: 2853.

3.2-8 Balakrishnan, R., Raman, K.R., Veerannah, L., and Vasudevan, P. 1977. Potentialities of geranium (Pelargonium graveolens L'Herit) in South India. Pages 314-316 in C.K. Atal and B.M. Kapur, eds. Cultivation & utilization of medicinal and aromatic plants. Regional Research Laboratory, Jammu-Tawi, India.

3.2-9 Beech, D.F. 1977. Growth and oil production of lemongrass (Cymbopogon citratus in the Ord Irrigation Area, Western Australia. Aust. J. Exp. Agric. Anim. Husb. 17: 301-307. HA 47: 11738.

3.2-10 Bellinghen, A. van. 1975. Note on a cultivation and distribution test of Capsicum frutescens L. (Pilipili) in Bugesera [in French]. Bull. Agric. Rwanda 8{1}: 33-35. AGRICOLA.

3.2-11 Bernardi, J.B., and Igue, T. 1972. Performance of short and medium- cycle garlic varieties in the Campinas area [in Portuguese]. Bragantia 31{1}: 9-15. PBA 44: 5517.

3.2-12 Black, R.P., and Piyapongse, S. 1979. Thailand: the introduction of mint agriculture and processing. Pages 307-328 in D.D. Evans and L.N. Adler, eds. Appropriate technology for development: A discussion and case histories. Westview Press, Boulder, Colo.

3.2-13 Bodrug, M.V. 1978. Trials on introducing catmint into Moldavia [in Russian]. Izv. Akad. Nauk Mold. SSR Ser. Biol. Khim. Nauk 1978{1}: 83-84. HA 49: 2829.

3.2-14 Bodrug, M.V. 1980. Essential oil bearing plants new for cultivation in Moldavia. Izv. Akad. Nauk Mold. SSR Ser. Biol. Khim. Nauk 1980{1}: 77-79.

3.2-15 Brain, B.B., and Smith, R.C.G. 1980. Potential for mint production in Australia: A preliminary study. J. Aust. Inst. Agric. Sci. 46: 207-213. AGRICOLA.

3.2-16 Busch, W. 1974. New cultivars often require different cultural conditions [in German]. Dtsch. Gaertnerboerse 74: 653-654. HA 45: 5127.

3.2-17 Cantoria, M. 1972. Research on mint in the Philippines. An. Acad. Bras. Cienc. 44(Suppl.): 64-67.

3.2-18 Chaudhury, R.R., and Kochar, P.S. 1972. Mentha arvensis crop: a cash-earner for farmers. Agric. Agro-Ind. J. 5{1}: 13-15. AGRICOLA.

3.2-19 Chen, L.S., and Sze, T.C. 1977. Introduction of Crocus sativus L. in Peking area and observations of its biological characteristics. Chih Wu Hsueh Pao 19: 313-314.

3.2-20 Chopra, M.M., and Handa, K.L. 1972. Menthol from Japanese mint introduced in Jammu and Kashmir. Indian Perfum. 16(pt. 2): 15-18. CA 80: 100104

3.2-21 Chubey, B.B., and Dorrell, D.G. 1976. Quality and yield of dill oil produced in Manitoba. Can. J. Plant Sci. 56: 215-216.

3.2-22 Chubey, B.B., and Dorrell, D.G. 1976. Quality and yield of dill oil in Manitoba. Can. J. Plant Sci. 56: 427 (Abstr.).

3.2-23 Dimitroff, D. 1971. Research on sesame (Sesamum indicum L.) cultivated in Bulgaria and on sesame oil [in German]. Nahrung 15: 521-525 AGRICOLA.

3.2-24 Dimri, B.P., Khan, M.N.A., and Rasool, G. 1976. Prospects of cultivation of jasmine (Jasminum grandiflorum Linn.) in South India -

a study of flowering and yield. Indian Perfum. 20{1A}: 23-27. HA 48: 9282.

3.2-25 Dutta, P.K. 1971. Introduction of medicinal and aromatic plants in Orissa region. Indian J. Pharm. 33: 92-94.

3.2-26 Fontes, P.C.R., Marinato, R., Carvalho, V., Alves, H.M., and Menezes Sobrinho, J.A. 1976. Study of the possibility of cultivating mint (Mentha arvensis L. and Mentha spicata) in the Jaiba area [in Portuguese]. Bol. Assoc. Bras. Pesqui. Plant. Aromat. Oleos. Essenc. 19: 120-128. AGRICOLA.

3.2-27 Fontes, P.C.R., Marinato, R., Carbalho, V., Alves, H.M., and Menezes Sobrinho, J.A. 1976. Preliminary study of the possibility of cultivating mint (Mentha arvensis L. and Mentha spicata) in the Jaiba area, Minas Gerais State [in Portuguese]. Bol. Assoc. Bras. Pesqui. Plant. Aromat. Oleos. Essenc. 19: 63-73. AGRICOLA.

3.2-28 Gergelyi, O. 1972. Origin and development of paprika culture in Slovakia [in Slovak]. Agrikultura 11: 111-121. AGRICOLA.

3.2-29 Ghosh, J., and Gupta, S.K.D. 1974. Varuna pays after jute and rice. Indian Farming 24{2}: 17. FCA 28: 5956.

3.2-30 Ghosh, M.L., and Chatterjee, S.K. 1976. Cultivation of Mentha spp. in Burdwan district, West Bengal and its prospects. Indian Perfum. 20{1A}: 79-84. HA 48: 8508.

3.2-31 Giulakhmedov, A.N., Mashanov, V.I., Bukin, V.P., and Mamedov, D.Sh. 1978. Results of the first testing of Lawsonia inermis L. in the Shirvan Natural-Economic Area of Azerbaidzhan [in Russian]. Izv. Akad. Nauk Az. SSR Ser. Biol. Nauk 1978{4}: 56-61.

3.2-32 Gomez-Campo, C. 1977. Studies on Cruciferae: IV. Chorological notes. An Inst. Bot. A.J. Cavanilles 34: 485-496. PBA 49: 9420.

3.2-33 Gulati, B.C., and Garg, S.N. 1980. Introduction of Salvia sclarea L. (clary sage) in Kashmir. Indian Perfum. 24: 204-206.

3.2-34 Gulati, B.C., Duhan, S.P.S., Gupta, R., and Bhagat, S.D. 1972. Introduction of French basil (Ocimum basilicum) in Tarai of Nainital, Uttar Pradesh. Proc. Indian Sci. Cong. 59 (pt. III): 317-318 (Abstr.).

3.2-35 Gulati, B.C., Duhan, S.P.S., Gupta, R., and Bhattacharya, A.K. 1977. Introduction of French basil oil (Ocimum basilicum L.) in Tarai of Nainital (Uttar Pradesh) [in German]. Parfuem. Kosmet. 58: 165-169. CA 87: 122628.

3.2-36 Gupta, R., Gulati, B.C., Duhan, S.P.S., and Bhattacharya, A.K. 1971. Quality of oil of peppermint & spearmint crops introduced in Tarai region of Up. Agric. Agro-Ind. J. 4{5}: 33-40. AGRICOLA.

3.2-37 Gupta, S., Thapa, R.K., Vashisht, V.N., Madan, C.L., and Atal, C.K. 1971. Introduction of French basil, Ocimum basilicum, in Jammu, cultural practices and chemical constituents. Flavour Ind. 2: 707-708.

3.2-38 Haro-Guzman, L. 1974. Possibilities of producing other essential oils in Mexico. Flavour Ind. 5: 277, 281.

3.2-39 Hemmerly, T.E. 1977. A ginseng farm in Lawrence County, Tennessee. Econ. Bot. 31: 160-162.

3.2-40 Hilik, L.A., Bondarenko, T.I., Shlyapnikov, V.A., Fedorovich, A.N., Drevyanikov, I.M., and Raihman, D.V. 1977. Introduction of a new essential oil-bearing plant (Nepeta transcaucasica Grossh.). Perfum. Flavor. 2{5}: 57-58 (Abstr.). HA 48: 5885.

3.2-41 Hindich, O.V. 1971. Perspectives of culture of Grecian laurel in the Carpathians [in Ukrainian]. Visnyk. Sil's'kohospod. Nauk 1971{5}: 78-80. AGRICOLA.

3.2-42 Javier Acuna, G. 1974. Carum carvi (Kuemmel) a new cultivated plant in Azapa [in Spanish]. Idesia 1974{3}: 219.

3.2-43 Kapelev, I.G. 1973. Introduction of aromatic plants [in Russian]. Byull. Gos. Nikitsk. Bot. Sada 1973{2}: 16-23. HA 45: 2702.

3.2-44 Kapelev, I.G. 1980. Some results of introducing fennel in the Nikitskii Botanic Garden [in Russian]. Rastit. Resur. 16: 541-546. HA 51: 5708.

3.2-45 Kapelev, I.G. 1976. Results of introducing Monarda as an essential oil crop [in Russian]. Byull. Gos. Nikitsk. Bot. Sada 1976{2}: 35-39. AGRICOLA.

3.2-46 Kapitany, J. 1974. Economic evaluation of red pepper seedling raising and production [in Hungarian]. Bull. Zoldsegtermesztesi Kut. Intez. 9: 143-146. AGRICOLA.

3.2-47 Khodzhaev, K.Kh., and Dzhuraev, I.N. 1977. The possibility of cultivating henna in the Uzbek SSR [in Russian]. Med. Zh. Uzb. 1977{2}: 75-79.

3.2-48 Khrushkova, N.G., and Odegova, A.A. 1971. Comfrey on Sakhalin [in Russian]. Tr. Akad. Nauk SSSR Sakhalin- Kompleksn. 1971{23}: 175-179.

3.2-49 Kirk, J.T.O., and Oram, R.N. 1978. Mustards as possible oil and protein crops for Australia. J. Aust. Inst. Agric. Sci. 44: 143-156. FCA 33: 3748.

3.2-50 Kuzina, E.F. 1973. Possibilities of shifting crops of Coriandrum sativum to regions farther north [in Russian]. Byull. Vses. Inst. Rastenievod. 1973{32}: 60-64.

3.2-51 Lammerink, J., and Manning, T.D.R. 1971. Yields and composition of oil from peppermint grown at Lincoln, New Zealand. N.Z. J. Agric. Res. 14: 745-751.

3.2-52 Leffingwell, J.C., Stallings, J.W., Seller, F.O., Lloyd, R.A., and Kane, F.C., Jr. 1974. Clary sage production in the southeastern United States. Int. Congr. Essent. Oils, [Pap.], 6th, 1974. 3, 11 pp. CA 84: 49723.

3.2-53 Lenches, O. 1973. The importance of introducing Hungarian medicinal plants into cultivation [in Hungarian]. Herba Hung. 12{2/3}: 17-21. HA 45: 6096.

3.2-54 Lewis, Y.S., Krishnamurthy, N., Nambudiri, E.S., and Mathew, A.G.

1972. Paprika for India. Arecanut and Spices Bulletin 4{2}: 6-9. AGRICOLA.

3.2-55 Machanov, V.I., and Kapelev, I.G. 1972. Aromatic plant introduction in the south of U.S.S.R. An. Acad. Bras. Cienc. 44(Suppl.): 69 (Abstr.).

3.2-56 Mairapetian, S.Kh. 1979. Some results of experiments on growing henna and basma in Armenia [in Russian]. Biol. Zh. Arm. 32: 1243-1245.

3.2-58 Manning, S.H., Mortlock, C.T., and Young, H.T. 1974. Investigations into the development of oil seed crops in New Zealand. Proc. Agron. Soc. N.Z. 4: 19-23. FCA 29: 3207.

3.2-59 Martynov, A.M., and Murav'eva, D.A. 1975. Some results of horse-mint introduction in Pyatigorsk [in Russian]. Biol. Nauki (Moscow) 1975{2}: 82-84.

3.2-60 Mashanov, V.I., Bukin, V.P., Abbasov, R.M., and Mamedov, F.M. 1977. Introduction of henna into the dry subtropics of Azerbaijan [in Russian]. Byull. Gos. Nikitsk. Bot. Sada 1977{3}: 54-59. HA 50: 7311.

3.2-61 Mashanov, V.I. 1978. Some results and problems of essential oil plant introduction and selection [in Russian]. Tr. Gos. Nikitsk. Bot. Sad. 75: 5-28. HA 51: 2867.

3.2-62 Mashkunova, V.A., and Oleinikova, E.F. 1978. Results of studies on a lavandin collection under conditions of north Caucasus foothills [in Russian]. Tr. Vses. Nauchno-Issled. Inst. Efirnomaslichn. Kul't. 1978{11:} 27-32. HA 50: 7912.

3.2-63 Mukhortova, T.G., and Mashanov, V.I. 1977. Introduction and breeding of essential oil plants in the steppe branch of the Nikita Botanic Gardens [in Russian]. Tr. Gos. Nikitsk. Bot. Sad. 72: 98-113. HA 49: 9558.

3.2-64 Murav'ev, I.A., and Durdyev, D.D. 1974. Lower Amu Darya River as a new region for preparation of licorice root [in Russian]. Aktual. Vopr. Farm. 2: 57-61. CA 84: 95561.

3.2-65 Nath, R. 1978. Japanese mint (Mentha arvensis --a potential medicinal crop for northern plains. Agric. Agro-ind. J. 11{11}: 15-17. AGRICOLA.

3.2-66 Neborak, E.I. 1980. The Ukrainian steppes must produce high yields [in Russian]. Kormoproizvodstvo 1980{5}: 23. HERB AB 51: 3945.

3.2-67 Petrova, V.P., Burachyns'kaya, N.S., and Pobirchenko, G.A. 1974. Content of essential oil and polyphenols in some species of sage introduced into the forest steppe of the Ukr.aine [in Ukr.ainian]. Ukr. Bot. Zh. 31{1}: 13-17.

3.2-68 Pichitakul, N., and Chomchalow, N. 1978. Basil oil production in Thailand. Thai J. Agric. Sci. 11: 67-74. WAERSA 21: 1031.

3.2-69 Piergentili, D., and Pettoruti, C.A. 1971. Lavandula dentata, a new aromatic plant grown in Argentina: possible uses for its essential oil [in Spanish]. Rev. Fac. Agron. Univ. Nac. La Plata 47: 307-312 HA 43: 6258.

3.2-70 Ribeiro dos Santos, S. 1972. Production of essential oils in Brazil. An. Acad. Bras. Cienc. 44(Suppl.): 5-7.

3.2-71 Sarrazyn, R., and Pollet, E. 1980. An alternative vegetable: Florence fennel [in Flemish]. Boer en de Tuinder 86{43}: 18. HA 51: 2689.

3.2-72 Saxena, A.K., Saxena, A.L., and Sarkar, K.P. 1976. Experimental cultivation and chemical composition of oil of Mentha piperita Linn. at Kashipur. Indian Perfum. 20{1-B}: 1-3. CA 88: 141484.

3.2-73 Sharma, B.K., Verma, V.P.S., and Jain, P.P. 1979. Introduction of an exotic strain of Valeriana officinalis Linn. (from U.S.S.R.) for its cultivation and exploitation in Chakrata Hills, Distt. Dehr Dun, India. Indian For. 105: 211-216.

3.2-74 Shein, I.V. 1978. Economic efficiency of growing caraway in the Ukraine [in Ukrainian]. Visn. Sil's'kohospod. Nauky 1978{4}: 94-95.

3.2-75 Singh, A.S., Bhagat, S.D., Mathur, R.K., Gopinath, K.W., and Ganguly, D. 1971. Cultivation of basil (Ocimum basilicum L.) at Jorhat, Assam, and chemical composition of its oil. Flavour Ind. 2: 481-483.

3.2-76 Singh, R.A., and Singh, M. 1976. It pays to select a suitable variety for drylands. Indian Farming 26{3}: 27, 29. FCA 30: 3687.

3.2-77 Sinitsin, G.S. 1973. Introduction of Panax ginseng in the south of the Alma-Ata region [in Russian]. Vestn. Akad. Nauk Kaz. SSR 1973{9}: 43-47. AGRICOLA.

3.2-78 Sokolov, V.S., Buiko, R.A., and Grasschenkov, A.E. 1972. Trials on introducing aromatic plants in the Soviet Union [in Russian]. Herba Hung. 11{3}: 9-16. HA 44: 7922.

3.2-79 Stanev, D. 1974. Studies on Thymus vulgaris in Bulgaria [in Bulgarian]. Rastenievud. Nauki 11{2}: 29-33. HA 44: 8920.

3.2-80 Stauffer, M.D., and Chubey, B.B. 1979. Spice crops: production potential in the prairies. Can. Agric. 24{3}: 26-28. HA 50: 6513.

3.2-81 Stojanov, B. 1971. Sesame in Macedonia [in Macedonian]. Sovremenozemjod. 18{6}: 7. AGRICOLA.

3.2-82 Tashmatova, N. 1975. Experience in introduction of Hyssopus officinalis L. to the Botanical Garden of the Uzbek SSR Academy of Sciences [in Russian]. Introd. Akklim. Rast. 12: 76-77.

3.2-83 Taysi, V., Vomel, A., and Ceylan, A. 1977. New cultivation experiments with anise in the Ege region of Turkey [in German]. Z. Acker- Pflanzenbau 145: 8-21. HA 43: 3835.

3.2-84 Thimmegowda, S., and Krishnamurthy, K. 1975. Wealth of oil crops in Karnataka. Current Research 4: 109-110. PBA 46: 3593.

3.2-85 Tyurina, E.V. 1973. Mint under western Siberian conditions [in Russian]. Tr. Vses. Nauchno-Issled. Inst. Efirnomaslichn. Kul't. 6: 71-75 PBA 46: 8570.

3.2-86 Vershchako, F.A., and Gevko, V.A. 1973. Prospects for the cultivation of interspecific high-menthol hybrids of mint in Podol'e [in Russian]. Tr. Kishinev. Skh. Inst. im. M.V. Frunze 104: 57-61. PBA 46: 3944.

3.2-87 Walker, W.F. 1972. Mint oil production prospects in Tasmania. Tasmanian J. Agric. 43: 162-167. HA 43: 4744.

3.3 Economic Biology

3.3-1 Akman, Y. 1974. Phytoecological study of the region of Beypazari Karasar and Nallihan [in French]. Commun. Fac. Sci. Univ. Ankara Ser. C Nat. 18{3}: 1-113.

3.3-2 Akman, Y., and Ketenoglu, O. 1976. The phytosociological and phytoecological investigation on the Ayas Mountains. Commun. Fac. Sci. Univ. Ankara Ser. 2(Suppl. 1): 1-44.

3.3-3 Alpande de Morais, A., Correa Mourao, J., Gottlieb, O.R., Leao da Silva, M., Marx, M.C., Soares Maia, J.G., and Taveira Magalhass, M. 1972. Essential oils of Amazonia containing thymol [in Portuguese]. An. Acad. Bras. Cienc. 44(Suppl.): 315-316. CA 83: 120651.

3.3-4 Ametova, E.F., Nikonov, G.K., and Gorovoi, P.G. 1976. Coumarins of Angelica sachalinensis. Chem. Nat. Compd. (Engl. Transl.) 12: 335. Translation of Khim. Prir. Soedin. 1976{3}: 385-386.

3.3-6 Atal, C.K., and Bradu, B.L. 1976. Search for aroma chemicals of industrial value from genus Cymbopogon. Part II. Cymbopogon pendulus (Nees ex Steud.) Wats. (Jammu lemongrass) - a new superior source of citral. Indian J. Pharm. 38{2}: 61-63. CA 85: 74912.

3.3-7 Avramenko, L.G., and Nikonov, G.K. 1971. Saxalin - A new furocoumarin from the roots of Angelica saxatilis. Chem. Nat. Compd. (Engl. Transl.) 7: 804-805. Translation of Khim. Prir. Soedin. 1971{6}: 830-831.

3.3-8 Ayyad, M.A., and Ammar, M.Y. 1974. Vegetation and environment of the western Mediterranean coastal land of Egypt. 2. The habitat of inland ridges. J. Ecol. 62: 439-456.

3.3-10 Banerjee, S.K., Gupta, B.D., Sheldrick, W.S., and Hofle, G. 1980. Dimeric ligusticum lactone from Angelica glauca. Planta Med. 39: 261-262 (Abstr.).

3.3-11 Bang, T.B., and Nikolaev, A.G. 1974. The composition of the essential oil of Mentha lavanduliodora. Chem. Nat. Compd. (Engl. Transl.) 10: 537. Translation of Khim. Prir. Soedin. 1974{4}: 525.

3.3-12 Basker, D., and Putievsky, E. 1976. Caraway seeds or caraway oil [in Hebrew]. Hassadeh 57: 209, 211-212. HA 47: 7748.

3.3-13 Baudouin, G., and Paris, R. 1975. Polyphenols of Digitalis. Part 5. The polyphenols of the flowers of the Canary Island foxglove (Digitalis canariensis = Isoplexis canariensis = Callianassa canariensis) [in French]. Plant. Med. Phytother. 9: 278-288.

3.3-14 Bourwieg, D., and Pohl, R. 1973. The flavonoids of Mentha longifolia [in German]. Planta Med. 24: 304-314. HA 44: 6972.

3.3-15 Brasil e Silva, G.A. de A., and Bauer, L. 1973. Essential oil of Foeniculum vulgare collected in Rio Grande do sul [in Portuguese]. Rev. Bras. Farm. 54: 143-145. CA 84: 21978.

3.3-16 Brieskorn, C.H., and Poehlmann, R. 1976. The occurrence of isomeric catalponol and tectol dimethyl ether in the root of Lippia origanoides H.B.K. Arch. Pharm. (Weinheim) 309: 829-836.

3.3-17 Brockie, W.B. 1973. Botanical notes. N.Z. J. Bot. 11: 581-584.

3.3-18 Buchanan, R.A., Cull, I.M., Otey, F.H., and Russell, C.R. 1978. Hydrocarbon- and rubber-producing crops. Econ. Bot. 32{2}: 131-145.

3.3-19 Buchanan, R.A., Cull, I.M., Otey, F.H., and Russell, C.R. 1978. Hydrocarbon- and rubber-producing crops. Evaluation of 100 U.S. plant species. Econ. Bot. 32{2}: 146-153.

3.3-20 Bui Tkhi Bang , and Nikolaev, A.G. 1975. Composition of the essential oil of Mentha longifolia L. [in Russian]. Izv. Akad. Nauk Mold. SSR Ser. Biol. Khim. Nauk 1975{3}: 89.

3.3-21 Burduja, C., and Horeanu, C. 1976. Studies of herbaceous vegetation of the Casimcea plateau (Dobrogea) [in French]. Rev. Roum. Biol. Ser. Biol. Veg. 21{1}: 11-18. HERB AB 48: 3407.

3.3-22 Calvarano, I., and Codignola, A. 1974. Chemical research on Mentha longifolia var. mollissima, gathered from Stura di Demonte Valley in the Cuneo region [in Italian]. Essenze Deriv. Agrum. 44{3}: 236-240. CA 83: 65314.

3.3-23 Cantoria, M. 1974. Studies on the physiology of Philippine mint (Mentha cordifolia Opiz). III. Variation in oil yield. Philipp. J. Sci. 103: 67-71.

3.3-24 Catalan, C.A.N., Merep, D.J., and Retamar, J.A. 1977. The essential oil of Lippia alba (Miller) N.E. Brown from the Tucuman province [in Spanish]. Riv. Ital. Essenze, Profumi, Piante Off., Aromi, Saponi, Cosmet., Aerosol 59{10}: 513-518. CA 88: 78947.

3.3-25 Chatterjee, S.K. 1977. Availability of medicinal and aromatic plants in north-eastern India with special reference to West Bengal. Pages 485-492 in C.K. Atal and B.M. Kapur, eds. Cultivation & utilization of medicinal and aromatic plants. Regional Research Laboratory, Jammu-Tawi, India.

3.3-26 Chawla, J.S. 1977. Utilization of ligno-cellulosic waste of essential oil industry. Pages 398-402 in C.K. Atal and B.M. Kapur, eds. Cultivation & utilizaton of medicinal and aromatic plants. Regional Research Laboratory, Jammu-Tawi, India.

3.3-27 China. First Institute of Light Industry, Research Group of Perfumery. 1978. Study on the essential oils of the Thymus quinquecostatus Celak. Chih Wu Hsueh Pao 20{1}: 31-36.

3.3-28 Chobanu, V.I., and Nikolaev, A.G. 1974. Composition of the essential oil of the Caucasian mint [in Russian]. Izv. Akad. Nauk Mold. SSR Ser. Biol. Khim. Nauk 1974{4}: 87-89.

3.3-29 Chubey, B.B., and Dorrell, D.G. 1977. Chicory, another potential fructose crop. Can. Inst. Food Sci. Technol. J. 10: 331-332.

3.3-30 Chubey, B.B. 1975. Commercial mint?. Prairie Gard. 32: 120-121. AGRICOLA.

3.3-31 Ciaramello, D., Azzini, A., Andrea Pinto, A.J. de , Guilherme, M., and Donalisio, R. 1972. Preliminary studies on the distillation of the leaves of citronella, lemongrass, palmarosa and vetiver in the production of cellulose and paper [in Portuguese]. An. Acad. Bras. Cienc. 44(Suppl.): 430-441.

3.3-32 Clancy, M.J. 1980. Production of pharmaceutical crops in Ireland. Pages 1-12 in Kernan, R.P., Mooney, O.V. and Went, A.E.J., eds. The introduction of exotic species advantages and problems: proceedings of a symposium, Jan. 4-5, 1979, Dublin. Royal Irish Academy, Dublin.

3.3-33 Cochrane, H.S.C. 1972. Parsley for profit. Agriculture North. Ire. 47: 250-252. HA 43: 4733.

3.3-34 Cody, W.J., and MacLaren, R.B. 1976. Additions and rediscoveries of five plant species in Prince Edward Island. Can. Field-Nat. 90: 53-54.

3.3-35 Danin, A. 1971. Influence of edaphic factors on distribution of plant communities in the Rakhme Mountains of the northern Negev. Isr. J. Bot. 20: 338-339.

3.3-36 Darrah, H. 1978. The clove scented basil: Ocimum gratissimum L. Herbarist 44: 31-37.

3.3-37 Darrah, H.H. 1972. The basils in folklore and biological science. Herbarist 38: 3-10.

3.3-38 Davies, G.W. 1980. Fiber measurements of some aquatic species with a view to new sources of papermaking fiber. Aquat. Bot. 8: 381-383.

3.3-39 Deikalo, T.A., Kaganskaya, K.A., and Zavorkhina, N.A. 1974. Drilling fluid stabilization by alkali-treated licorice root pulp [in Russian]. Tr Inst. Khim. Nefti Prir. Solei Akad. Nauk Kaz. SSSR 7: 35-43. CA 83: 166554.

3.3-40 Delfini, A.A., and Retamar, J.A. 1974. The essential oil of Lippia fissicalyx [in Italian]. Essenze Deriv. Agrum. 44: 23-33. AGRICOLA.

3.3-41 Didukh, Ya.P. 1974. Steppe vegetation of the Vishneva Mountain near Rovno [in Ukrainian]. Ukr. Bot. Zh. 31: 361-364.

3.3-42 Duncan, W.H. 1971. Angelica triquinata (Umbelliferae) southward and Lotus helleri (Leguminosae) westward into Georgia. Castanea 36: 163-164.

3.3-43 Embong, M.B., Haziyev, D., and Molnar, S. 1977. Essential oils from herb and spices grown in Alberta. Sage oil, Salvia officinalis, L. (Labiatae). Can. Inst. Food Sci. Technol. J. 10: 201-207.

3.3-44 Embong, M.B., Hadziyev, D., and Molnar, S. 1977. Essential oils from spices grown in Alberta. Dill seed oil, Anethum graveolens, L. (Umbelliferae). Can. Inst. Food Sci. Technol. J. 10: 208-214.

3.3-45 Esvandzhiya, G.A. 1976. Some valuable essential oil plants from the Sukhimi Experimental Station [in Russian]. Dokl. TSKhA 224(pt. 2): 72-77. CA 87: 19016.

3.3-46 Favre, R. 1972. Native essential oils of Latin America [in Spanish]. An. Acad. Bras. Cienc. 44(Suppl.): 417-422.

3.3-47 Fleischer, A., and Putievsky, E. 1978. Evaluation of essential oil from sweet basil (Ocimum basilicum L.) growing in Israel. Spec. Publ. Agric. Res. Organ. Volcani Cent. (Bet Dagan, Isr.). 146-E: 240.

3.3-48 Fountain, M.S., and Willett, R.L. 1980. Status of wild American ginseng in Arkansas. Arkansas Farm Res. 29{1}: 4. AGRICOLA.

3.3-49 Frantskevich, N.A. 1978. Wild relatives of crop plants and their conservation in the basin of the river Ai-dere (Kara-Kala region of the Turkmen SSR) [in Russian]. Byull. Vses. Inst. Rastenievod. 1978{81}: 86-91. PBA 50: 7692.

3.3-50 Fujita, S., Taka, K., and Fujita, Y. 1978. Studies on the essential oils of the genus Mentha. XI. Components of the essential oils of Mentha gentilis var. lanata [in Japanese]. Nippon Nogei Kagaku Kaishi 52: 277-280. HA 49: 3712.

3.3-51 Fujita, S., Nakano, T., and Fujita, Y. 1972. Essential oils of the genus Mentha. VIII. Biochemical study of the essential oils of Mentha gattefossei [in Japanese]. Nippon Nogei Kagaku Kaishi 46: 393-397. CA 78: 40494.

3.3-52 Fujiwara, H., Yokoi, T., Tani, S., Saiki, Y., and Kato, A. 1980. Studies on constituents of Angelicae dahuricae Radix. I. On a new furocoumarin derivative [in Japanese]. Yakugaku Zasshi 100{12}: 1258-1261. CA 94: 136088.

3.3-53 Galt, A.H., and Galt, J.W. 1978. Peasant use of some wild plants on the island of Pantelleria, Sicily. Econ. Bot. 32{1}: 20-26.

3.3-54 Gerhardt, U. 1980. Sweet woodruff (Asperula odorata L.), a typical forest plant. Fleischwirtschaft 60: 1796-1797. AGRICOLA.

3.3-55 Glazek, T. 1976. Some rare species of vascular plants from the calciferous hills of the Checiny District [in Polish]. Fragm. Florist. Geobot. (Cracow) 22: 291-293.

3.3-56 Goodwillie, R.N. 1975. Plant notes from County Westmeath. Ir. Nat. J. 18: 157-159.

3.3-57 Gorokhov, G.F. 1975. Ginseng and its role in the hunting and industrial areas of the Maritime Territory [in Russian]. Lesn. Khoz. 1975{12}: 80-82. Bib. Ag. 40: 38553.

3.3-58 Guillen, R.F., and Batlle, E.V. 1975. Cistus populifolius L. in the mountains of Prades and in the Sierra del Pradell, a new species for Catalonia [in Catalan]. Acta Phytotaxon. Barcinonensia 1975{17}: 5-13.

3.3-59 Gulati, B.C., and Duhan, S.P.S. 1973. Sweet basil for handsome profit. Indian Farming 22{11}: 24-26.

3.3-60 Gusakova, S.D., Kholmatov, Kh.K., and Umarov, A.U. 1976. Composition of the seed oils of Origanum tyttanthum and Mentha asiatica. Chem. Nat. Compd. (Engl. Transl.) 12: 134-139. Translation of Khim. Prir. Soedin. 1976{2}: 149-145.

3.3-61 Gusakova, S.D., and Umarov, A.U. 1976. Dibromo- and tetrabromostearic acids in the seed oil of Eremostachys moluccelloides. Chem. Pharm. Bull. (Engl. Transl.) 12: 645-650. Translation of Khim. Prir. Soedin. 1976{6}: 717-723.

3.3-62 Harriman, N.A. 1971. Records on the flora of Wisconsin. Rhodora 73{793}: 60-61.

3.3-63 Hart, R.H. 1976. Comfrey miracle or mirage?. Crops Soils 29{1}: 12-14.

3.3-64 Hata, K., Kozawa, M., Baba, K., Yen, K.Y., and Yang, L.L. 1974. Coumarins from the roots of Angelica morii Hayata. Chem. Pharm. Bull. (Tokyo) 22: 957-961.

3.3-65 Hata, K., Kozawa, M., Baba, K., and Yen, K.Y. 1971. Coumarins from the roots of Angelica laxiflora Diels. Chem. Pharm. Bull. (Tokyo) 19: 640-642.

3.3-66 Hata, K., Kozawa, M., Baba, K., and Mitsui, M. 1973. New ester coumarins, angeladin and isoedultin from Angelica longeradiata. Chem. Pharm. Bull. (Tokyo) 21{3}: 518-522. CA 79: 2772.

3.3-67 Hata, K., Kozawa, M., Baba, K., and Mitsui, M. 1973. Chemical components of the roots of Ligusticum hultenii and Angelica shikokiana [in Japanese]. Yakugaku Zasshi 93{2}: 248-251. CA 78: 133334.

3.3-68 Hecht, H. 1978. Trace elements in herbs and spices. Levels of transition elements chromium, iron, copper, manganese and zinc [in German]. Fleischwirtschaft 78: 1351-1357. HA 49: 8819.

3.3-69 Hill, M. 1973. Parsley. Potomac Herb J. 9{2}: 7-9. AGRICOLA.

3.3-70 Hodge, W.H. 1974. Wasabi - native condiment plant of Japan. Econ. Bot. 28: 118-129.

3.3-71 Hogg, J.W., and Lawrence, B.M. 1972. Essential oils and their constituents. VIII. A new bicyclic monoterpene from Mentha x cardiaca Ger. Flavour Ind. 3: 321-323.

3.3-72 Hong, M.W. 1974. History of Korean ginseng [in Korean]. Pages 9-23 in Y.C. Lee. Korean ginseng science symposium. Korean Society of Pharmacognosy. Natural Products Research Institute, : Seoul National University, Seoul, Korea.

3.3-73 Horvath, P. 1975. On the history of saffron culture in the Upper Nitra region [in Slovak]. Agrikultura 13: 5-19. AGRICOLA.

3.3-74 Hruska, K. 1972. On Thymus L. species in Hrvatsko Zagorje [in Serbo-Croatian]. Acta Bot. Croat. 31: 207-209.

3.3-75 Hruska, K., and Segulja, N. 1971. A new location of the species
Thymus illyricus Ronn. in Yugoslavia [in Serbo-Croatian]. Acta Bot.
Croat. 30: 127-130.

3.3-76 Hruska, K. 1971. Thymus praecox in the Croatian flora [in
Serbo-Croatian]. Acta Bot. Croat. 30: 123-125.

3.3-77 Huet, R. 1972. Mint essential oil in Brazil [in Portuguese].
Fruits 27: 469-472. HA 43: 2328.

3.3-78 Huffman, M., and Huffman, E. 1980. Catnip. Herb Q. 1: 30-31.

3.3-79 Hussey, J.S. 1974. Some useful plants of early New England. Econ.
Bot. 28: 311-337.

3.3-80 Iakubovich, V.B. 1972. Acetates of isomer menthols in essential
oil of Mentha [in Russian]. Pages 104-109 in A.G. Nikolaev, ed.
Khimicheskaia izmenchivost' rastenii. Shtiintsa, Kishinev, USSR.
AGRICOLA.

3.3-81 Ietswaart, J.H., Fokkinga, A., and Vroman, M. 1972. Delimitation
of Origanum scabrum Boiss. et Heldr. (Labiatae) by means of
morphological criteria. Acta Bot. Neerl. 21: 439-447.

3.3-82 Ilyas, M. 1980. Spices in India: III. Econ. Bot. 34: 236-259.

3.3-84 Ilyas, M. 1978. The spices of India - II. Econ. Bot. 32{3}:
238-263.

3.3-85 Ilyas, M. 1976. Spices in India. Econ. Bot. 30: 273-280.

3.3-86 Institute of Botany Terpenoid Research Group, Academia Sinica,
China. 1978. Studies on the essential oils of Thymus quinquecostatus
[in Chinese]. Chih Wu Hsueh Pao 20: 31-36.

3.3-87 Isaac Sepulveda, J. 1976. Lippia palmeri in the peninsula on
lower California [in Spanish]. Cienc. For. 1{4}: 50-52. AGRICOLA.

3.3-88 Ivanic, R., and Savin, K. 1975. A comparative analysis of
essential oils from several wild species of Salvia with special
reference to Salvia officinalis. Lloydia 38: 533 (Abstr.).

3.3-89 Ivanova, V.M., and Gvozdeva, L.V. 1977. Use of glazes,
surfactants and pigments for glazing hardened articles [in Russian].
Steklo Keram. 1977{4}: 14-15. CA 87: 27646.

3.3-90 Kaicker, U.S., Singh, B., Singh, H.P., and Choudhury, B. 1975.
Try your hand at black gold - opium poppy. Indian Hortic. 20{3}: 7, 9,
28.

3.3-91 Kakuliia, A.V., and Esvandzhiia, G.A. 1975. Sage, Salvia garedzii
N.A. Troitzky, as an essential oil plant [in Russian]. Dokl. TSKhA
211: 203-204. AGRICOLA.

3.3-92 Kapil, V.B., and Sinha, G.K. 1977. Essential oil of Mentha
sylvestris var. incana of Kumaon Hills (India). Perfum. Flavor. 2{5}:
60 (Abstr.). HA 48: 5883.

3.3-93 Kapil, V.B., and Sinha, G.K. 1979. Essential oil of Mentha sylvestris var. incana of Kumaon Hills (India). Int. Congr. Essent. Oils, [Pap.], 7th, 1977. 7: 190-192. CA 92: 99426.

3.3-94 Kapoor, S.K., Sharma, Y.N., and Zaman, A. 1972. Extractives of Angelica glauca. Phytochemistry 11: 475-476.

3.3-95 Karryev, M.O. 1971. Phytochemical and anatomical studies of Ziziphora turcomanica Juz. sp. N. and Thymus transcapsicus Klok [in Russian]. Izv. Akad. Nauk Turkm. SSR Ser. Biol. Nauk 1971{1}: 35-41.

3.3-96 Kasumov, F.Yu. 1979. Essential oil of Thymus rariflorus. Chem. Nat. Compd. (Engl. Transl.) 15: 770. Translation of Khim. Prir. Soedin. 1979{6}: 863.

3.3-97 Kerbabaev, B.B. 1976. Prospects of utilizing the plant resources of the Turkmen SSR [in Russian]. Izv. Akad. Nauk Turkm. SSR Ser. Biol. Nauk 1976{6}: 3-7.

3.3-98 Khodzhimatov, K.Kh., and Ramazanova, N.Kh. 1980. Some essential oil plants growing wild in Uzbekistan are promising for use by the food industry [in Russian]. Rastit. Resur. 16: 104-107. HA 51: 596.

3.3-99 Khort, T.P. 1972. On some new wild essential oil-bearing plants of the Crimea [in Russian]. Pages 206-209 in P.V. Naumenko et al., eds. Mezhdunarodnyi kongress po efirnym maslam, 4th, Tiflis, 1968, [Materialy], v. 2. Pishchevaya Promyshlennost', Moscow, USSR. HA 44: 6968.

3.3-100 Khort, T.P., and Mashanova, N.S. 1975. The Crimean wild mint species as essential oil plants [in Russian]. Byull. Gos. Nikits. Bot. Sada 1975{1}: 58-61. HA 47: 3915.

3.3-101 Kir'yalov, N.P., Bogatkina, V.F., and Nadezhina, T.P. 1973. Glabrolide from the roots of Glycyrrhiza aspera. Chem. Nat. Compd. (Engl. Transl.) 9: 268. Translation of Khim. Prir. Soedin. 1973{2}: 277.

3.3-102 Kir'yalov, N.P., Bogatkina, V.F., and Nadezina, T.P. 1972. 24-Hydroxyglycyrrhetic acid from roots of Glycyrrhiza korshinskyi. Chem. Nat. Compd. (Engl. Transl.) 8: 393. Translation of Khim. Prir. Soedin. 1972{3}: 395-396.

3.3-103 Kitagawa, M. 1971. Brief notes on East Asian flora {27}. Shokubutsu Kenkyu Zasshi 46: 283-288.

3.3-104 Kitagawa, M. 1973. Notulae fractae ob floram Asiae Orientalis [Notes on East Asian flora] {30}. Shokubutsu Kenkyu Zasshi 48: 235-237.

3.3-105 Kobylyanskaya, K.A., Denislov, N.I., and Bochkarnikova, N.M. 1978. Plant resources of the Primor'e and north-western spurs of the Sikhote-Alin' mountains [in Russian]. Byull. Vses. Inst. Rastenievod. 1978{81}: 42-47. PBA 50: 7691.

3.3-106 Koch, H. 1976. Peppermint misguided [in German]. Gartenpraxis 1976{6}: 283-284. AGRICOLA.

3.3-107 Komendar, V.I., Dubanych, M.V., Cherneki, I.M., Bedei, M.I., Manivchuk, Yu.V. , and Tovt, E.S. 1975. Distribution reserves and rational use of certain drug plants in the Ciscarpathian region [in Ukrainian]. Ukr. Bot. Zh. 32: 307-311.

3.3-108 Kozawa, M., Morita, N., Baba, K., and Kiyoshi, H. 1978. Chemical components of the roots of Angelica keiskei Koidzumi. II. The structure of the chalcone derivatives [in Japanese]. Yakugaku Zasshi 98: 210-214. HA 48: 10838.

3.3-109 Kubrak, M.N., and Popa, D.P. 1980. Lactones of the essential oil of Nepeta transcaucasica and N. sibirica [in Russian]. Khim. Prir. Soedin. 1980{3}: 420-421. HA 51: 2083.

3.3-110 Kurbanov, E.A., and Kasumov, F.Yu. 1974. Ontogenesis and essential oil accumulation in Thymus karamarianicus in Apsheron [in Russian]. Izv. Akad. Nauk Az. SSR Ser. Biol. Nauk 1974{5-6}: 3-8. HA 46: 4945.

3.3-111 Kuvaev, V.B. 1975. Novelties for the flora of the southern part of the Putorana Mountains. 3. [in Russian]. Bot. Zh. (Leningrad) 60: 522-527.

3.3-112 Kuwahara, Y., Kishino, K., Kayama, K., and Ito, K. 1979. A study on Mentha candicens. Int. Congr. Essent. Oils, [Pap.], 7th, 1977. 7: 237-239. CA 92: 82201.

3.3-113 Ladygina, E.Ya., and Zorin, E.B. 1971. Luminescence of root tissues of Angelica anomala and localization of coumarins in them [in Russian]. Farmatsiya (Moscow) 20{5}: 32-37. CA 76: 70067.

3.3-114 Latorre, D.L., and Latorre, F.A. 1977. Plants used by the Mexican Kickapoo Indians. Econ. Bot. 31{3}: 340-357.

3.3-115 Lawrence, B.M., Bromstein, A.C., and Langeheim, J.H. 1974. Terpenoids in Satureja douglasii. Phytochemistry 13: 1014.

3.3-116 Lawrence, B.M., and Morton, J.K. 1974. Acorenone-B in Angelica lucida oil. Phytochemistry 13: 528.

3.3-117 Leao da Silva, M., Maia, J.G. Soares , Mourao, J. Correa , Pedreira, G., Marx, M.C., Gottlieb, O.R., and Magalhaes, M. Taveira. 1973. Essential oils from Amazonia. VI. [in Portuguese]. Acta Amazonica 3{3}: 41-42. CA 82: 135732.

3.3-118 Lees, P. 1978. Norfolk grows a miracle crop. Esso Farmer 30{1}: 7-11.

3.3-119 Lincoln, D.E., and Langenheim, J.H. 1976. Geographic patterns of monoterpenoid composition in Satureja douglasii. Biochem. Syst. Ecol. 4: 237-248. AGRICOLA.

3.3-120 Lu, R.M., Ho, L.I., and Lo, S.Y. 1980. Determination of ferulic acid in danggui (Angelica sinensis) [in Chinese]. Chung Ts'ao Yao 11: 395-398. CA 94: 109411.

3.3-121 Lynov, Yu.S. 1980. Weather anomalies and seasonal plant development in midmountain and highmountain belts of southeastern Fergana, Kirgiz SSR, USSR [in Russian]. Byull. Mosk. O-va. Ispyt. Prir. Otd. Biol. 85: 79-85.

3.3-122 Malingre, T.M., and Maarse, H. 1974. Composition of the essential oil of Mentha aquatica. Phytochemistry 13: 1531-1535.

3.3-123 Mann, H.S., and Singh, P. 1977. Oilseeds in India with special reference to arid zone. Ann. Arid Zone 16: 240-256. FCA 31: 5567.

3.3-124 Margaris, N.S., and Papadogianni, P. 1978. Cambial activity in some plants dominating phryganic formations in Greece. Phyton 36: 1-5.

3.3-125 Marshall, H.H., and Chubey, B.B. 1975. What is Monarda? Prairie Gard. 32: 52-53. AGRICOLA.

3.3-126 Marticorena, C., and Quezada, M. 1977. Synopsis of the genus Satureja L. (Labiatae) in Chile [in Spanish]. Bol. Soc. Biol. Concepcion 51{1}: 141-147.

3.3-127 Mashanov, V.I. 1973. The contribution of the Nikita Botanic Gardens to the development of essential oil plant production in the south of the USSR [in Russian]. Byull. Gos. Nikitsk. Bot. Sada 1973{2}: 9-15. HA 45: 2701.

3.3-128 Matveev, V.I., Biryukova, E.G., Simakova, N.S., and Zotov, A.M. 1976. On the plant species new for the Kuibyshev and Orenburg regions [in Russian]. Bot. Zh. (Leningrad) 61: 980-981.

3.3-129 Mehra, B.K. 1977. Mentha oil and menthol production in India - in past, present and future. Pages 173-191 in C.K. Atal and B.M. Kapur, eds. Cultivation & utilization of medicinal and aromatic plants. Regional Research Laboratory, Jammu-Tawi, India.

3.3-130 Mendez, J., Rubido, J., and Mato, M.C. 1973. Coumarins of Angelica pachycarpa. Experientia 29: 371-372.

3.3-131 Mendez, J., and Rubido, J. 1979. Coumarins of Angelica pachycarpa fruits. Planta Med. 36: 219-220.

3.3-132 Mijatovic, K. 1973. A contribution to the study of distribution and ecology of Mediterranean sage (Salvia aethiopis L.) [in Croatian]. Zast. Bilja 24{123}: 131-146. AGRICOLA.

3.3-133 Miquel, J.D., Richard, H.M.J., and Sandret, F.G. 1976. Volatile constituents of Moroccan thyme oil. J. Agric. Food Chem. 24: 833-835.

3.3-135 Mirkin, B.M., Kashapov, R.Sh. 1975. Analysis of altitudinal topoclines [in Russian]. Biol. Nauki (Moscow) 1975{2}: 136-141.

3.3-136 Mishurova, S.S., and Shikhiev, A.Sh. 1977. The monoterpenic fraction of the essential oil of Nepeta transcaucasica. Chem. Nat. Compd. (Engl. Transl.) 13: 733. Translation of Khim. Prir. Soedin. 1977{6}: 865-866. HA 48: 6786.

3.3-137 Moldenke, H.N. 1978. Additional notes on the genus Lippia. XII. Phytologia 40: 58-85.

3.3-138 Moldenke, H.N. 1978. Additional notes on the genus Lippia. VIII. Phytologia 39: 162-182.

3.3-139 Moldenke, H.N. 1978. Additional notes on the genus Lippia. IX. Phytologia 39: 252-267.

3.3-140 Moldenke, H.N. 1975. Notes on new and noteworthy plants. LXXVIII. Phytologia 31: 229-234.

3.3-141 Montes, M.G., Valenzuela, L.R., Wilkomisrsky, T.F., and Arrive, M.V. 1975. Some constituents in the fragrant oil of Satureja gilliesii (Grah.) Briq. [in French]. Ann. Pharm. Fr. 33: 707-709. AGRICOLA.

3.3-142 Moon, C.K., and Yoon, M.H. 1976. The screening of polyacetylene compounds in Korean plants. I. [in Korean]. Yakhak Hoe Chi 20{1}: 44-46. CA 85: 119630.

3.3-143 Morais, A.A. de , Mourao, J.C., Silva, M.L. da , Maia, J.G.S., Gottlieb, O.R., Marx, M.C., and Magalhaes, M.T. 1976. Essential oils containing thymol from the Amazon region [in Portuguese]. Ser. Conf. Cursos Reun. Interam. Inst. Agric. Sci. 93: 145-146. AGRICOLA.

3.3-144 Morais, A.A.D., Mourao, J.C., Gottlieb, O.R., Da Silva, M.L., Marx, M.C., Maia, J.G.S., and Magalhaes, E.M.T. 1972. Essential oils of Amanzonia containing thymol [in Portuguese]. Acta Amazonica 2{1}: 45-46.

3.3-145 Morton, J.K. 1979. Observations on Houghton's goldenrod (Solidago Houghtonii). Mich. Bot. 18{1}: 31-35. AGRICOLA.

3.3-146 Motial, V.S. 1974. Why not grow saffron. Farmer Parliament 9{3}: 13-14, 26.

3.3-147 Mozo, M.T. 1972. Lemongrass [in Spanish]. Rev. Esso Agr. 18{3}: 28-31.

3.3-148 Murata, G. 1977. New or interesting plants from Southeast Asia. 2. Shokubutsu Bunrui Chiri (Acta Phytotaxon. Geobot.) 28: 26-30.

3.3-149 Nagasawa, T., Umemoto, K., Tsuneya, T., and Shiga, M. 1976. Studies on the wild mints of Tokai districts. Part VII. The essential oil of wild mints containing (+)-menthofuran as a major constituent [in Japanese]. Nippon Nogei Kagaku Kaishi 50: 291-293. HA 47: 4897.

3.3-150 Nagasawa, T., and Umemoto, K. 1976. Studies on the chemical constituents of wild mints. VIII. The essential oil of Mentha gentilis containing (+)-pipertone as a major component [in Japanese]. Nippon Nogei Kagaku Kaishi 50: 381-383. HA 47: 7762.

3.3-151 Nagasawa, T., Umemoto, K., and Hirao, N. 1977. Studies on chemical constituents of wild mints. IX. Isolation and configuration of (+)-1-acetoxy-p- menth-3-one from essential oil of Mentha gentilis [in Japanese]. Nippon Nogei Kagaku Kaishi 51: 81-85. HA 47: 10750.

3.3-152 Nagasawa, T., Umemoto, K., Tsuneya, T., and Shiga, M. 1975. Studies on the wild mints of Tokai districts. IV. New terpenic alcohols in essential oil of Mentha gentilis L. containing (+)-pulegone as a main component [in Japanese]. Nippon Nogei Kagaku Kaishi 49{4}: 31-35. AGRICOLA.

3.3-153 Nagasawa, T., Umemoto, K., Tsuneya, T., and Shiga, M. 1975. Studies on the wild mints of the Tokai district. V. The essential oil of Mentha gentilis containing (+)-neomenthol as a major constituent [in Japanese]. Nippon Nogei Kagaku Kaishi 49: 491-493. HA 46: 7943.

3.3-154 Nagasawa, T., Umemoto, K., Tsuneya, T., and Shiga, M. 1975. (-)-1.u R-8-Hydroxy- 4- p-menthen-3-one isolated from essential oil of Mentha gentilis L. Agricultural and Biological Chemistry 39: 553-554. HA 45: 9997.

3.3-155 Nagasawa, T., Umemoto, K., Tsuneya, T., and Shiga, M. 1974. Wild mints of Tokai district. I. Identification of d-1,2-epoxymenthol from the essential oil of Mentha gentilis [in Japanese]. Nippon Nogei Kagaku Kaishi 48{1}: 39-42. CA 81: 54288.

3.3-156 Nechaev, A.P., and Nechaev, A.A. 1976. Flora of lower Amur River area. 2. [in Russian]. Byull. Gl. Bot. Sada 1976{101}: 55-58. HERB AB 48: 2054.

3.3-157 Neidlein, R., and Stahle, R. 1973. Substances in Lippia javanica (Spreng). II. [in German]. Dtsch. Apoth. Ztg. 113: 1219-1222. AGRICOLA.

3.3-158 Neidlein, R., and Daldrup, V. 1979. Isolation and structure of substances in Lippia americana. I. Essential oil [in German]. Arch. Pharm. (Weinheim, Ger.) 312: 914-922. CA 92: 164099.

3.3-159 Neidlein, R., and Daldrup, V. 1980. Studies on substances in Lippia americana. II. [in German]. Arch. Pharm. (Weinheim, Ger.) 313: 97-108. CA 92: 125003.

3.3-160 Ognyanov, I., and Botcheva, D. 1971. Pangeline and angeloylpangeline, two new furocoumarines in the roots of Angelica pancici Vandas. Dokl. Bolg. Akad. Nauk 24: 315-318. AGRICOLA.

3.3-161 Paredes, C. 1973. Aromatic plant species of Ecuador [in Spanish]. Politecnica 3: 163-170. CA 84: 102302.

3.3-162 Park, D.S., Moon, C.Y., and Park, N.S. 1976. The screening of polyacetylenic compounds in Korean plants [in Korean]. Soul Taehakkyo Yakhak Nonmunjip 1: 132-135. CA 87: 114583.

3.3-163 Pimenov, M.G., and Pimenova, M.E. 1973. Some new and rare plants in the flora of the Amur region [in Russian]. Byull. Gl. Bot. Sada 1973{88}: 52-53.

3.3-164 Plarre, W. 1971. Plant production. IV. Economic plants. B. Fat and protein plants. 4. Sesame [in German]. Pages 349-355 in P. von Blanckenburg and H.-D. Cremer, eds. Handbuch der Landwirtschaft und Ernahrung in den Entwicklungslandern. Verlag Eugen Ulmer, Stuttgart, v. 2.

3.3-165 Prodan, G., Mihalache, M., Florescu, E., Baciu, E., Visarion, M., Dorobantu, N., and Tudor, T. 1973. Information on aromatic herbs from the biological and usefulness viewpoint [in Hungarian]. Lucr. Stiint., Inst. Agron. Bucuresti Ser. B 16: 23-30. CA 85: 75175.

3.3-166 Pryde, E.H. 1977. Nonfood uses for commercial vegetable oil crops. Pages 25-45 in D.S. Seigler, ed. Crop resources. Academic Press Inc., New York, USA. FCA 32: 1955.

3.3-167 Raclaru, P. 1973. Floristic contributions. II. An. Univ. Bucuresti Biol. Veg. 22: 125-127.

3.3-168 Rahman, M.S., and Alam, A.K.M.S. 1980. Ecotypic and ecophenic
variations in Lippia nodiflora Rich. Bangladesh J. Bot. 9: 60-66.

3.3-169 Ramachandran Nair, A.G., Ramesh, P., Nagarajan, S., and Sankara
Subramanian, S. 1973. New flavone glycosides from Lippia nodiflora.
Indian J. Chem. 11: 1316-1317.

3.3-170 Razdan, T.K., and Koul, G.L. 1975. Composition of wild thyme oil
[in German]. Riechst. Aromen Koerperpflegum. 25: 166, 168. CA 83:
168307.

3.3-171 Rea, M.-A.F. 1975. Early introduction of economic plants into
New England. Econ. Bot. 29: 333-356.

3.3-172 Rechinger, K.H. 1979. New Iranian Labiatae. Plant Syst. Evol.
133: 105-108.

3.3-173 Retamar, J.A., Talenti, E.C.J., and Delfini, A.A. 1975.
Essential oil of Lippia fissicalyx (2nd communication) [in Spanish].
Essenze Deriv. Agrum. 45{1}: 31-33. AGRICOLA.

3.3-174 Rhoades, D.G., Lincoln, D.E., and Langenheim, J.H. 1976.
Preliminary studies of monoterpenoid variability in Satureja
douglasii. Biochem. Syst. Ecol. 4: 5-12. AGRICOLA.

3.3-175 Rovesti, P. 1972. Ecological influence on the composition of
essential oils. Note IX - The essences of Lippia adoensis Hochst. et
de Lippia schimperi Hochst. [in French]. An. Acad. Bras. Cienc.
44(Suppl.): 91-93.

3.3-176 Saidkhodzhaev, A.I., and Nikonov, G.K. 1976. Coumarins of the
roots of Archangelica tschimganica. Chem. Nat. Compd. (Engl. Transl.)
12: 84-85. Translation of Khim. Prir. Soedin. 1976{1}: 96.

3.3-177 Saif, S.R. 1975. The occurrence of mycorrhizas and endogone
spores in the rhizospheres of plants growing around university campus
Islamabad. Pak. J. Bot. 7: 175-182.

3.3-178 Saiki, Y., Morinaga, K., Okegawa, O., Sakai, S., Amaya, Y.,
Uneo, A., and Fukushima, S. 1971. Coumarins of the roots of Angelica
dahurica [in Japanese]. Yakugaku Zasshi 91: 1313-1316. CA 76: 56621.

3.3-179 Sainsbury, M., and Sofowora, E.A. 1971. Essential oil from the
leaves and inflorescence of Ocimum gratissimum. Phytochemistry 10:
3309-3310

3.3-180 Samoilov, Yu.I. 1973. Some results of comparison of the
ecological scales of Ramensky Ellenberg, Hundt and Klapp [in Russian].
Bot. Zh. (Leningrad) 58: 646-655.

3.3-181 Sandercock, T.A. 1974. Dill oil production in Manitoba 1974.
Pages 117-120 in Proc. Annu. Conf. Manit. Agron. AGRICOLA.

3.3-182 Schmidt, A. 1971. Plant production. IV. Economic plants. C.
Vegetables. 3. Paprika [in German]. Pages 396-401 in P. von
Blanckenburg and H.-D. Cremer, eds. Handbuch der Landwirtschaft und
Ernahrung in den Entwicklungslandern. Verlag Eugen Ulmer, Stuttgart,,
v. 2.

3.3-183 Seabra, A.N. 1976. Mint and its importance for the Brazilian economy [in Portuguese]. Bol. Assoc. Bras. Pesqui. Plant. Aromat. Oleos Essenc. 19: 9-62. AGRICOLA.

3.3-184 Seigler, D.S. 1976. Plants of the northeastern United States that produce cyanogenic compounds. Econ. Bot. 30: 395-407.

3.3-185 Semenchenko, V.F., and Murav'ev, I.A. 1974. Study of saponins in the roots of Glycyrrhiza macedonica Boiss. et Orph. [in Russian]. Aktual. Vopr. Farm. 2: 70-71. CA 84: 132598.

3.3-186 Sendra, J.M., and Cunat, P. 1980. Volatile constituents of Spanish Origanum coridothymus-capitatus essential oil. Phytochemistry 19: 89-92.

3.3-187 Seoane, E., Rene, E., and Ribo, J.M. 1974. Thymus chamaedris. I. Volatile components [in Spanish]. An. Quim. 70: 1023-1027. CA 83: 168328.

3.3-188 Seoane, E., Francia, E., and Rene, E. 1972. Study of "Thymus caespitittius". II. Volatile components [in Spanish]. An. Quim. 68: 951-954.

3.3-189 Shah, N.C., and Joshi, M.C. 1971. An ethnobotanical study of the Kumaon Region of India. 25{4}: 414-422.

3.3-190 Shavarda, A.L., Markova, L.P., Nadezhina, T.P., Sinitskii, V.S., Belenovskaya, L.M., Fokina, G.A., Ligaa, U., and Tumbaa, Kh. 1980. Essential oil plants of Mongolia. Terpenoid composition of the essential oils of some species of Labiatae [in Russian]. Rastit. Resur. 16: 286-292. HA 51: 1476.

3.3-191 Shimizu, S., Karasawa, D., and Ikeda, N. 1974. Essential oils of various mints growing wild in Japan. Int. Congr. Essent. Oils [Pap.], 6th, 1974. 13, 7 pp. CA 84: 49724.

3.3-192 Shimkus, G.T. 1978. Life forms of Bothriochloa ischaemum plant communities of the Crimea forest belt [in Ukrainian]. Ukr. Bot. Zh. 35: 19-21. HERB AB 48: 4511.

3.3-193 Shlyun'ko, E.K., Shagova, L.I., Tikhomirova, L.I., and Nadezhina, T.P. 1977. Coumarins of the roots of Angelica dahurica. Chem. Nat. Compd. (Engl. Transl.) 13: 241. Translation of Khim. Prir. Soedin. 1977{2}: 280.

3.3-194 Simkin, B.E. 1977. Glycyrrhiza glabra root from Soviet Central Asian jungles [in Russian]. Khim. Zhizn. 12: 85-86. AGRICOLA.

3.3-195 Simonyan, A.V. 1972. Flavone glycosides of some species of the genus Thymus. Chem. Nat. Compd. (Engl. Transl.) 8: 783. Translation of Khim. Prir. Soedin. 1972{6}: 801.

3.3-196 Sinnadurai, S. 1973. Shallot farming in Ghana. Econ. Bot. 27: 438-441.

3.3-197 Sinnadurai, S., and Abu, J.F. 1977. Onion farming in Ghana. Econ. Bot. 31: 312-314.

3.3-198 Smith, C.E., Jr., and Cameron, M.L. 1977. Ethnobotany in the Puuc, Yucatan. Econ. Bot. 31{2}: 93-110.

3.3-199 Solomko, O.V., Dzhumrko, V.A., and Kompantsev, V.A. 1978. Flavonoids from Achillea nobilis [in Russian]. Khim. Prir. Soedin. 1978{2}: 266-267.

3.3-200 Stepanenko, G.A., Umarov, A.U., and Markman, A.L. 1975. Oils of the family Umbelliferae. Chem. Nat. Compd. (Engl. Transl.) 11: 86-87. Translation of Khim. Prir. Soedin. 1975{1}: 86-87.

3.3-201 Sumida, M. 1978. Watercress of Hawaii, Inc. Misc. Publ. Hawaii Univ. Coop. Ext. Serv. 154: 11-13.

3.3-202 Talalaj, S., and Talalaj, D. 1976. A preliminary investigation of volatile oil yielding plants of Iraq. Bull. Biol. Res. Cent. (Baghdad) 7: 32-42.

3.3-203 Tewari, M.N. 1979. The distribution of medicinal plants in the arid and semi-arid regions of Rajasthan - Thar Desert. Pages 186-194 in J.R. Goodin and D.K. Northington, eds. Arid lands plant resources: proceedings of the international arid lands conference on plant resources, Texas Tech University. International Center for Arid and Semi-Arid Land Studies (ICASALS), Texas Tech University, Lubbock, Texas. ALA 1: 3179.

3.3-204 Tischler, W. 1973. On structural patterns in the ecosystem, exemplified by structural units of the Umbelliferous plant Angelica sylvestris L. [in German]. Biol. Zentralbl. 92: 337-355.

3.3-205 Tiwari, K.C., Majumder, R., and Bhattacharjee, S. 1978. Some medicinal plants from District Tirap of Arunachal Pradesh. Indian J. Pharm. Sci. 40: 206-208. HA 51: 1490.

3.3-206 Trabaud, L. 1976. Flammability and combustibility of the main species of the garrigues in the Mediterranean region [in French]. Oecol. Plant. 11: 117-136.

3.3-207 Traxl, V. 1975. Mentha crispa [in Czech]. Nase Liecive Rastliny 12: 97-98. HA 46: 3685.

3.3-208 Trela-Sawicka, Z. 1972. Further cytological studies in the genus Thymus from Poland. Acta Biol. Cracov. Ser. Bot. 15: 61-68.

3.3-209 Tsibanova, N.A. 1977. Life cycle and age structure of coenopopulations of Thymus marschallianus Willd. (Lamiaceae) in the northern steppe (Kursk region) [in Russian]. Bot. Zh. (Leningrad) 62: 101-105.

3.3-210 Tucakov, J. 1976. Biological, pharmaco-economical and pharmaco-medicinal importance of protecting medicinal and similar plants in Yugoslavia [in French]. Riv. Ital. Essenze Profumi Piante Off. Aromi Saponi Cosmet. Aerosol 58: 238-242. HA 47: 8770.

3.3-211 Turner, N.C., and Bell, M.A.M. 1971. The ethnobotany of the Coast Salish Indians of Vancouver Island. Econ. Bot. 25: 63-104.

3.3-212 Turner, N.C., and Bell, M.A.M. 1973. The ethnobotany of the southern Kwakiutl Indians of British Columbia. Econ. Bot. 27: 257-310.

3.3-213 Tyner, G.E. 1975. The geography of California's culinary herb industry. Herbarist 41: 42-47.

3.3-214 Ulubelen, A., and Brieskorn, C.H. 1977. Chemical study of the herba of Salvia amplexicaulis. Planta Med. 31: 80-82. CIM 18{13}: 10225.

3.3-215 Ulubelen, A., and Uygur, I. 1976. Flavonoidal and other compounds of Salvia aethiopis. Planta Med. 29: 318-320. CIM 17{3}: 4590.

3.3-216 Ulubelen, A., Miski, M., Neuman, P., and Mabry, T.J. 1979. Flavonoids of Salvia tomentosa (Labiatae). J. Nat. Prod. 42{3}: 261-263.

3.3-217 Umemoto, K., and Nagasawa, T. 1977. Studies on chemical constituents of wild mints. X. Absolute configuration of a new monoterpene diol isolated from the essential oil of Mentha gentilis L. [in Japanese]. Nippon Nogei Kagaku Kaishi 51: 245-251. HA 48: 1659.

3.3-218 Umemoto, K., and Nagasawa, T. 1979. Studies on the chemical constituents of wild mints. XIII. Essential oil of Mentha gentilis L. containing pulegone-8-hydroxy-3- p-menthene as a major component [in Japanese]. Nippon Nogei Kagaku Kaishi 53: 269-271. HA 50: 5464.

3.3-219 Umemoto, K., and Nagasawa, T. 1977. Studies on the chemical constituents of wild mints. XI. The essential oil of Mentha gentilis containing 1-acetoxymenthone [in Japanese]. Nippon Nogei Kagaku Kaishi 51: 659-661. HA 48: 7565.

3.3-220 Uttal, L.J. 1973. Floristic notes from Virginia. Castanea 38: 194-195.

3.3-221 Van Den Broucke, C.O., and Lemli, J.A. 1980. Chemical investigation of the essential oil of Origanum compactum. Planta Med. 38: 264-266.

3.3-222 Voronina, E.P. 1977. Introduction of coriander in the Main Botanic Garden of the Academy of Sciences of the USSR (Moscow) [in Russian]. Byull. Gl. Bot. Sada 1977{106}: 17-22. HA 48: 7547.

3.3-223 Voroshilov, V.P., and Sidel'nikov, A.N. 1978. Features of vegetation distribution in the area of solphataric field of Mendeleev Volcano. Sov. J. Ecol. (Engl. Transl.) 9: 515-519. Translation of Ekologiya 1978{6}: 30-35.

3.3-224 Walker, M.R. 1977. Poppy crop increasing. Tasmanian J. Agric. 48: 87-88.

3.3-225 Yoshihara, K., and Hirose, Y. 1973. Terpenes from Aralia species. Phytochemistry 12: 468.

3.3-226 Younos, C., Lorrain, M., and Pelt, J.M. 1972. Contribution to the chemical and pharmacological study of essences of Labiatae from Afghanistan. III. The essences of two endemic species of Stachyoidea (Thyminae) from Afghanistan: Ziziphora afghanica Rech. Fil. and Origanum glaucum Rech. Fil. and Edelb. [in French]. Plant. Med. Phytother. 6: 251-258. AGRICOLA.

3.3-227 Zeinalova, S.A., and Aleshina, L.A. 1972. Palynomorphology of the Azerbaidzhan species of Satureja L. [in Russian]. Dokl. Akad. Nauk Az. SSR 28{4}: 78-82.

3.3-228 Zhadan, A., and Kripun, V.I. 1975. Use of wastes from processing of plants containing essential oils for preparing monorations [in Ukrainian]. Korma Korml. S-kh. Zhivotn. 35: 7-12. CA 84: 104027.

3.3-229 Zhang, H.-Q., Yuan, C.-Q., Chen, G.-Y., and Deng, Y.-M. 1980. Study on the chemical constituents of the root of Angelica dahurica var. formosana [in Chinese]. Yao Hsueh T'ung Pao 15{9}: 2-4. CA 95: 67848.

3.4 Ecological Relations

3.4-1 Abd El-Rahman, A.A., Batanouny, K.H., and Zayed, K.M. 1974. Water relations of Glycyrrhiza glabra under desert conditions. Flora (Jena) 163: 143-155.

3.4-2 Allayarov, I. 1974. The main types of vegetation on sands in North-West Uzbekistan [in Russian]. Uzb. Biol. Zh. 1974{5}: 33-35. HERB AB 45: 3100

3.4-3 Arevshatian, I.G. 1971. Taraxacum officinale Web. in the flora of Armenia [in Russian]. Izv. Biol. Zh. Arm. 24{3}: 118-119.

3.4-4 Arora, D.K., Singh, D.B., and Tandon, R.N. 1977. Studies on rhizosphere mycoflora of mustard varieties with emphasis on mycostasis. Fert. Technol. 14: 62-65. SF 41: 4824.

3.4-5 Assouad, M.W., and Dommee, B. 1974. Research on the ecological genetics of Thymus vulgaris L. Experimental study of sexual polymorphism. Genetic determinism and ecological distribution of sexual forms [in French]. C. R. Seances Acad. Agric. Fr. 60: 57-62. PBA 45: 1719.

3.4-6 Ataev, E.A., Kerbabaev, B.B., and Gladyshev, A.I. 1974. Indicative value of licorice associations in the Amudarya flood-lands [in Russian]. Izv. Akad. Nauk Turkm. SSR Ser. Biol. Nauk 1974{3}: 3-6.

3.4-7 Ataev, E.A. 1977. Tamarix meyeri associations and their relationship with the saline soils of the piedmont plain of central Kopet-Dag [in Russian]. Izv. Akad. Nauk Turkm. SSR Ser. Biol. Nauk 1977{6}: 64-66.

3.4-8 Atkinson, D. 1973. Observations on the phosphorus nutrition of two sand dune communities at Ross Links. J. Ecol. 61: 117-133.

3.4-9 Ayyad, M.A., and Ammar, M.Y. 1973. Relationship between local physiographic variations and the distribution of common Mediterranean desert species. Vegetatio 27: 163-176.

3.4-10 Azcon, R., Azcon-G. de Aguilar, C., and Barea, J.M. 1978. Effects of plant hormones present in bacterial cultures on the formation and responses to VA endomycorrhiza. New Phytol. 80: 359-364.

3.4-11 Azcon, R., Barea, J.M., and Hayman, D.S. 1976. Utilization of rock phosphate in alkaline soils by plants inoculated with mycorrhizal fungi and phosphate-solubilizing bacteria. Soil Biol. Biochem. 8: 135-138. HA 46: 10601.

3.4-12 Bakhiev, A. 1979. Glycyrrhiza glabra L. communities as indicators of soil salinization in the Amu-Darya delta [in Russian]. Probl. Osvo. Pustyn'. 3: 69-70.

3.4-13 Bakhtavar, F. 1979. Comparison of Glycyrrhiza glabra collected in Azerbaijan (Iran) [in Persian]. Pazhoohandeh (Tehran) 23: 9-19. CA 92: 143254.

3.4-14 Bell, D.T. 1974. The influence of osmotic pressure in tests for allelopathy. Trans. Ill. State Acad. Sci. 67: 312-317.

3.4-15 Bell, D.T., and Muller, C.H. 1973. Dominance of California annual grasslands by Brassica nigra. Am. Midl. Nat. 90: 277-299.

3.4-16 Blom, C.W.P.M. 1977. Effects of trampling and soil compaction on the occurrence of some Plantago species in coastal sand dunes. II. Trampling and seedling establishment. Oecol. Plant. 12: 363-382.

3.4-17 Blom, C.W.P.M. 1976. Effects of trampling and soil compaction on the occurrence of some Plantago species in coastal sand dunes. 1. Soil compaction, soil moisture and seedling emergence. Oecol. Plant. 11: 225-241.

3.4-18 Bokhari, M.H., and Khan, R.A. 1976. Preliminary observations on plant-rock type relationships in the Shiraz-Dashte Arjan area, south-west Iran. Vegetatio 31: 193-199.

3.4-19 Bonnemaison, F., and Jacquard, P. 1979. Experimental study of competition between sexual forms of Thymus vulgaris L. [in French]. Oecol. Plant. 14: 85-101.

3.4-20 Budryunene, D.K. 1978. Estimation of nonarboreal plant resources in the forests of the Lithuanian SSR on the course of forest exploitation [in Russian]. Rastit. Resur. 14: 477-482.

3.4-21 Bunce, J.A. 1980. Growth and physiological characteristics of disturbance ecotypes of Taraxacum officinale. Bull. Ecol. Soc. Am. 61: 139 (Abstr.). AGRICOLA.

3.4-22 Cadbury, C.J. 1976. Botanical implications of bracken control. Bot. J. Linn. Soc. 73: 285-294.

3.4-23 Caputa, J., and Sustar, F. 1975. Observations on the phenological stages of pasture plants at different altitudes [in German]. Schweiz. Landwirtsch. Forsch. 14{1}: 15-33. HERB AB 45: 4744.

3.4-24 Cirtu, D. 1973. The vegetation of sandy soils between the Jiu and Desantui rivers [in Romanian]. An. Univ. Craiova, Ser. 3 5: 36-43. HERB AB 45: 4157.

3.4-25 Crawford, A.K., and Liddle, M.J. 1977. The effect of trampling on neutral grassland. Biol. Conserv. 12: 135-142.

3.4-26 Damman, A.W.H. 1978. Geographical changes in the vegetation pattern of raised bogs in the Bay of Fundy region of Maine and New Brunswick. Pages 91-106 in Maarel, E. van der and M.J.A. Werger, eds. Plant species and plant communities: proceedings of the international symposium, Nijmegen, Netherlands, Nov. 11-12, 1976. Dr. W. Junk BV Pub., Boston, Mass.

3.4-27 Darwent, A.L., and Elliott, C.R. 1979. Effect of grass species and row spacing on dandelion establishment and growth. Can. J. Plant Sci. 59: 1031-1036.

3.4-28 Delcourt, H.R., and Delcourt, P.A. 1975. The blufflands: Pleistocene pathway into the Tunica Hills. Am. Midl. Nat. 94: 385-400.

3.4-29 Deschenes, J.-M. 1974. Intraspecific competition in experimental populations of weeds. Can. J. Bot. 52: 1415-1421.

3.4-30 Dobereiner, J., Day, J.M., and Dart, P.J. 1972. Nitrogenase activity in the rhizosphere of sugar cane and some other tropical grasses. Plant Soil 37: 191-196. HERB AB 43: 1054.

3.4-31 Duke, J.A., and Hurst, S.J. 1975. Ecological amplitudes of herbs, spices and medicinal plants. Lloydia 38: 404-410.

3.4-32 Duke, J.A. 1979. Ecosystematic data on economic plants. Q. J. Crude Drug Res. 17{3-4}: 91-110.

3.4-33 Eichenberger, M.D., and Parker, G.R. 1976. Goldenseal(Hydrastis canadensis L.) distribution, phenology and biomass in an oak-hickory forest. Ohio J. Sci. 76: 204-210.

3.4-34 Elias, P. 1975. A contribution to the study of water relations of forest herbs. Biologia (Bratislava) 30: 771-779.

3.4-35 Endler, Z. 1971. Higher fungi in beech forests of Katy forestry [in Polish]. Acta Mycol. 7: 279-298.

3.4-36 Fekete, G., Precsenyi, I., Molnar, E., and Melko, E. 1976. Niche studies on some plant species of a grassland community. Part I. Comparison of various measurements. Acta Bot. Acad. Sci. Hung. 22: 321-354.

3.4-37 Felklova, M., Motl, O., Jasicova, M., and Lukes, V. 1977. The effect of acclimitization on the properties of Matricaria chamomilla L. of foreign origin [in Czech]. Cesk. Farm. 26: 446-451. CIM 19{13}: 446-451.

3.4-38 Fisher, R.F., Woods, R.A., and Glavicic, M.R. 1978. Allelopathic effects of goldenrod and aster on young sugar maple. Can. J. For. Res. 8: 1-9.

3.4-39 Franchi, G. 1971. Composition of the essential oil of Lavandula latifolia [lavender] growing spontaneously in the hills of Siena [Italy] [in Italian]. Riv. Ital. Essenze, Profumi, Piante Off., Aromi, Saponi, Cosmet., Aerosol 53{5}: 245-248. CA 75: 121286.

3.4-40 Franz, V.C., Fritz, D., and Schroeder, F.J. 1975. Influence of ecological factors on the essential oils and flavonoids of two chamomile cultivars. 2.: Effect of light and temperature [in German]. Planta Med. 27: 46-52. CIM 17{7}: 10554.

3.4-41 Friedman, K.A. 1978. American ginseng under review as possible endangered species. Light Gard. 15: 26-27.

3.4-42 Giraud, M., and Negre, R. 1974. Variations in chemical composition in the Pyrenean Campanulo-Violetum [in French]. Phyton (Horn, Austria) 15: 203-214. HERB AB 46: 1843.

3.4-43 Gladyshev, A.I., and Kazakov, I.F. 1972. Structure and productivity of the phytomass of gigantic bunch forming grasses in the Amudarya floodplain [in Russian]. Izv. Akad. Nauk Turkm. SSR Ser. Biol. Nauk 1972{3}: 33-39.

3.4-44 Gorshenin, M.M., Krynyts'kyi, H.T., and Savych, I.P. 1972. Dynamics of fell area grass cover in Carpathian beech forests [in Ukrainian]. Ukr. Bot. Zh. 29: 185-190.

3.4-45 Goryshina, T.K., Zabotina, L.N., and Pruzhina, E.G. 1975. Plastid apparatus of herbaceous plants of a forest-steppe oak forest under different light conditions. Sov. J. Ecol. (Engl. Transl.) 6: 401-406. Translation of Ekologiya 1975{5}: 15-22.

3.4-46 Goryshina, T.K. 1971. Seasonal dynamics of the photosynthesis and productivity in certain summer-green herbage plants of an oakwood in the forest-steppe zone [in Russian]. Bot. Zh. (Leningrad) 56: 62-75.

3.4-47 Goryshina, T.K. 1976. Research of biological productivity of the herbaceous cover in the oak wood of the forest-steppe zone. Pol. Ecol. Stud.2: 135-145.

3.4-48 Granger, R., Passet, J., and Arbousset, G. 1973. Essential oil of Rosmarinus officinalis L. II. Influence of ecological and individual factors [in French]. Parfums Cosmet. Savons Fr. 3: 307-312. CA 79: 57559.

3.4-49 Grinkevich, N.I., Gribovskaya, I.F., and Garbuzova, V.M. 1973. Effect of geochemical environment on the chemical composition and pharmacological properties of certain representatives of the genus Digitalis [in Russian]. Rastit. Resur. 9: 183-191.

3.4-50 Grube, H.-J. 1975. The macrophytic vegetation of running waters in Sud-Niedersachsen and their relations to water pollution [in German]. Arch. Hydrobiol. Suppl. 45: 376-456.

3.4-51 Guillemin, M., Rouiller, J., and Bruckert, S. 1978. Relationships between plant associations and physicochemical characteristics of soils in a catena of crystalline mountains (Vosges, France) [in French]. Ann. Sci. For. 35: 139-150.

3.4-52 Gupta, V.K. 1974. Effect of subamycin on nodulation in Trigonella foenum-graecum. Indian Phytopathol. 27: 262. SF 38: 5791.

3.4-53 Gupta, V.K. 1974. Effect of foliar application of subamycin on rhizosphere and rhizoplane mycoflora. Indian Phytopathol. 27: 267. SF 38: 5772.

3.4-54 Guzikowa, M., Latocha, E., Pancer-Kotejowa, E., and Zarzycki, K. 1976. The effect of fertilization on a pine forest ecosystem in an industrial region. III. Herbs. Ecol. Pol. 24: 307-318. WA 27: 4188.

3.4-55 Halasova, J., and Busova, D. 1974. Ecological factors and their influence on the essential oil content of chamomile in eastern Slovakia [in Slovak]. Nase Liecive Rastliny 11: 99-103. HA 45: 2708.

3.4-56 Hallisey, D.M., and Wood, G.W. 1976. Prescribed fire in scrub oak habitat in central Pennsylvania. J. Wildl. Manage. 40: 507-516.

3.4-57 Hansen, K., and Jensen, J. 1972. The vegetation on roadsides in Denmark. Qualitative and quantitative composition. Dan. Bot. Ark. 28{2}: 1-61.

3.4-58 Hartmann, F.K. 1974. On the ecological characterization of subalpine mountains and their montane forest communities according to climactic factors. II. The climactic conditions on the montane level of the natural beach pine forests sometimes with valuable broadleaf trees [in German]. Acta. Bot. Acad. Sci. Hung. 20: 55-62.

3.4-59 Hawthorn, W.R., and Cavers, P.B. 1976. Population dynamics of the perennial herbs Plantago major L. and P. rugelli Decne. J. Ecol. 64: 511-527.

3.4-60 Heredia, J., Bellinfante, N., and Paneque, G. 1980. Weathering of rocks and pedogenesis in the Riotinto area (Huelva). I. Ecological factors [in Spanish]. An. Edafol. Agrobiol. 39: 1253-1261.

3.4-61 Higgins, P.D., and Spomer, G.G. 1976. Soil temperature effects on root respiration and the ecology of alpine and subalpine plants. Bot. Gaz. (Chicago) 137: 110-120.

3.4-62 Hirrel, M.C., Mehravaran, H., and Gerdemann, J.W. 1973. Vesicular-arbuscular mycorrhizae in the Chenopodiaceae and Cruciferae: Do they occur?. Can. J. Bot. 56: 2813-2817.

3.4-63 Hoelzi, V.J., and Demuth, G. 1975. Influence of ecological factors on the composition of the essential oil and the flavones in Matricaria chamomilla of different origin [in German]. Planta Med. 27: 37-45. CIM 17{7}: 10554.

3.4-64 Horsley, S.B. 1977. Allelopathic inhibition of black cherry by fern, grass, goldenrod and aster. Can. J. For. Res. 7: 205-216.

3.4-65 Hufstader, R.W. 1976. Precipitation, temperature and the standing crop of some southern California grassland species. J. Range Manage. 29: 433-435.

3.4-66 Iqbal, S.H., Sultana, K., and Perveen, B. 1975. Endogone spore numbers in the rhizosphere and the occurrence of vesicular arbuscular mycorrhizas in plants of economic importance. Biologia (Lahore) 21: 227-237.

3.4-67 Ivanova, R.G., Kazantseva, A.S., and Tuganaev, V.V. 1975. The adaptation of weed plants to certain crops [in Russian]. Biol. Nauki (Alma Ata) 18{1}: 71-75. WA 25: 277.

3.4-68 Izdebski, K., Baszynski, T., Kozak, K., Malicki, J., and Uziak, S. 1974. Investigations on the beech wood production in the Obrocz Forest Reservation in the central Roztocze [in Polish]. Ann. Univ. Mariae Curie-Sklodowska Sect. C 29: 281-332.

3.4-69 Khripunova, E.F. 1977. Specific composition of the fungus flora of clary [in Russian]. Izv. Akad. Nauk Mold. SSR Ser. Biol. Khim. Nauk 1977{6}: 28-33. RPP 58: 833.

3.4-70 Kitamoto, T. 1972. The spatial pattern in a natural population of goldenrod (Solidago altissima L.) with particular reference to its change during the shoot growth. Res. Population Ecol. 14{1}: 129-136. AGRICOLA.

3.4-71 Kornilievs'kyi, Iu.I., Fursa, M.S., Rybal'chenko, A.S., and Koreshchuk, K.Ie. 1979. Flavonoid makeup of Valeriana officinalis from the southern and central provinces of the Ukraine [in Ukrainian]. Farm. Zh. (Kiev) 1979{4}: 71-72. CIM 21{4}: 3083.

3.4-72 Kostyna, A.E., and Portianko, L.V. 1972. Ecological peculiarities of Taraxacum officinale Web. ex Wigg [in Ukrainian]. Ukr. Bot. Zh. 29: 38-41. AGRICOLA.

3.4-73 Kowal, T., and Krupinska, A. 1979. Productivity of the species Thymus pulegioides L. in natural habitats [in Polish]. Acta Agrobot. 32: 81-90

3.4-74 Kowal, T., and Pic, S. 1979. Productivity of the species Achillea millefolium L. in natural habitats [in Polish]. Acta Agrobot. 32: 91-100.

3.4-75 Kubicek, F. 1977. Energy values of selected species of the herbaceous layer and organic litter in the forest ecosystem. Biologia (Bratislava) 32: 505-516.

3.4-76 Kullberg, R.G. 1974. Distribution of aquatic macrophytes related to paper mill effluents in a southern Michigan stream. Am. Midl. Nat. 91: 271-281.

3.4-77 Lejoly-Gabriel, M. 1973. Phytosociologic studies on the leafy forests of the valley of the Our [in French]. Bull. Jar. Bot. Natl. Belg. 43: 101-185.

3.4-78 Lye, K.A. 1973. The vascular plants on alpine peaks at Fillefjell, South Norway. Norw. J. Bot. 20: 51-55.

3.4-79 Mall, O.P. 1975. Root-region mycoflora of coriander. Proc. Nat. Acad. Sci. India Sect. B. 45: 13-21. RPP 58: 4964.

3.4-80 Meagher, T.R., Antonovics, J., and Primack, R. 1978. Experimental ecological genetics in Plantago. III. Genetic variation and demography in relation to survival of Plantago cordata, a rare species. Biol. Conserv. 14: 243-258.

3.4-81 Merino, J., and Garcia Novo, F. 1975. Ordination of populations of Rosmarinus officinalis L. by mineral composition, using factorial analysis techniques [in Spanish]. An. Inst. Bot. A.J. Cavanilles 32: 521-536.

3.4-82 Michaelis, F.B. 1976. Watercress (Nasturtium microphyllum (Boenn.) Rchb. and Naturtium officinale) in New Zealand cold springs. Aquat. Bot. 2: 317-325. AGRICOLA.

3.4-83 Mishra, R.R., and Srivastava, V.B. 1977. Comparison of mycoflora associated with certain crop and weed seeds. Acta Mycol. 13: 145-149.

3.4-84 Moelgaard, P. 1977. Competitive effect of grass on establishment and performance of Taraxacum officinale. Oikos 29: 376-382.

3.4-85 Montenegro, G., Hoffmann, A.J., Aljard, M.E., and Hoffmann, A.E. 1979. Satureja gilliesii, a poikilohydric shrub from the Chilean Mediterranean vegetation. Can. J. Bot. 57: 1206-1213.

3.4-86 Morozov, V.L. 1978. Reserves of the above-ground and below-ground phytomass of tall-herb vegetation and its dominants on Sakhalin [in Russian]. Bot. Zh. (Leningrad) 63: 381-387. HERB AB 49: 2491.

3.4-87 Mosquin, T. 1971. Competition for pollinators as a stimulus for the evolution of flowering time. Oikus 22: 398-402.

3.4-88 Musaev, M.A., and Ibadov, R.R. 1979. Specific composition and the population of soil protozoa in the rhizosphere of some subtropical plants (tangerines, feijoa, laurel) in the Lenkoran Natural Area [in Russian]. Izv. Akad. Az. SSR Ser. Biol. Nauk 1979{2}: 76-82.

3.4-89 Nagy, I. 1972. Effect of rhizospheric microorganisms on the growth and development of paprika plants. Symp. Biol. Hung. 11: 325-328.

3.4-90 Neshataev, Yu.N., and Shaposhnikov, E.S. 1976. Significance of interspecific contingencies for distinguishing forest associations [in Russian]. Vestn. Leningr. Univ. Biol. 1976{3}: 48-57.

3.4-91 Neshataev, Yu.N., and Sobakinskikh, V.D. 1976. The lowered Alps and thyme communities in the Reservation Region Barkalovka (Kursk District) [in Russian]. Bot. Zh. (Leningrad) 61: 480-487.

3.4-92 Neshataev, Yu.N. 1976. The simplest algorithms for calculating the Brave interspecific correlation coefficient for the purpose of vegetation classification [in Russian]. Bot. Zh. (Leningrad) 61: 653-662.

3.4-93 Nitsenko, A.A. 1971. Attempted study of a time continuum in the course of succession in pine plantations [in Russian]. Vestn. Leningr. Univ. Biol. 1971{1}: 59-67.

3.4-94 Ocampo, J.A. 1980. Effect of crop rotations involving host and non-host plants on vesicular-arbuscular mycorrhizal infection of host plants. Plant Soil 56: 283-291.

3.4-95 Ocampo, J.A., Barea, J.M., and Montoya, E. 1977. Root extracts as a possible factor affecting the establishment of azobacter and phosphobacteria in the rhizosphere. Pol. J. Soil Sci. 10: 123-130.

3.4-96 Parpiev, Yu.P. 1977. The moisture regime of some wild plants on theadyry of the Fergana Meadow. Uzb. Biol. Zh. 3: 37-39.

3.4-97 Patterson, B.D., Wahba Khalil, S.K., Schermeister, L.J., and Quraishi, M.S. 1975. Plant insect interactions. I. Biological and phytochemical evaluation of selected plants. Lloydia 38: 391-403.

3.4-98 Paul, P. 1971. Demonstration of the inhibiting effect on germination of Thymus serpyllum ssp. serpyllum (L.) [in French]. Bull. Soc. Bot. Fr. 117: 325-334.

3.4-99 Picci, V., and Manunta, A. 1973. Environmental factors and essential oil content. Preliminary observations in Lavandula vera based on culture tests made in different Sardinian territories [in Italian]. Riv. Ital. Essenze, Profumi, Piante Off., Aromi, Saponi, Cosmet., Aerosol 55{8}: 489-493. CA 81: 1261.

3.4-100 Ponomarev, A.N., and Kolesnik, L.Ya. 1974. Anthecology of some steppe plantains [in Russian]. Biol. Nauki (Moscow) 1974{3}: 50-56.

3.4-101 Precsenyi, I., Fekete, G., Melko, E., and Molnar, E. 1977. Niche studies on some plant species of a grassland community. Part II. Seasonal niche dynamic. Acta Bot. Acad. Sci. Hung. 23: 193-218.

3.4-102 Prin, R. 1978. The Crown Forest of Perthe (Aube) and its botanical preserve [in French]. Cah. Nat. 33: 57-65.

3.4-103 Rabotnov, T.A., and Demin, A.P. 1971. Number of adventitious roots in the structure of meadow phytocenosis. Dokl. Bot. Sci. (Engl. Transl.) 199-201: 169-172. Translation of Dokl. Akad. Nauk SSSR 201: 246-249, 1971.

3.4-104 Rao, V.M., Kant, S., Ratnam, B.V., and Narayana, H.S. 1978. Effect of indole acetic acid (IAA) on the rhizosphere micropopulation of Trigonella foenum-graecum Linn. J. Indian Bot. Soc. 57{1}: 83-86. SF 43: 5444.

3.4-105 Riter-Studnicka, H. 1971. Ecological observations on winter savory Satureja montana L. var. serpeninica Janchen [in German]. Bull. Sci. Sect. A Sci. Natur. Tech. Med. (Zagreb) 16{5/6}: 142-144.

3.4-106 Roberts, C.R. 1979. American ginseng. Herba Hung. 18{3}: 85-90. AGRICOLA.

3.4-107 Rozenberg, G.S. 1979. Nonlinear ordination of biological objects exemplified by ordination of plant communities [in Russian]. Zh. Obshch. Biol. 40: 75-82.

3.4-108 Ryabov, V.A. 1978. Experience of the fitofenological prognosis in the Central Black Earth Reserve [in Russian]. Bot. Zh. (Leningrad) 63: 1656-1663.

3.4-109 Saif, S.R. 1977. The influence of stage of host development on vesicular arbuscular mycorrhizae and endogonaceous spores in field-grown vegetable crops. II. Winter-grown crops. Pak. J. Bot. 9: 119-128.

3.4-110 Seroczynska, M. 1976. Geobotanic relations of thyme (Thymus L.) species in the Lublin region [in Polish]. Herba Pol. 22: 63-71.

3.4-111 Sharashova, V.S., Kononenko, L.A., and Rubina, E.P. 1975. The causes of the wide distribution of Artemisia dracunculus in pastures [in Russian]. Izv. Akad. Nauk Kirgizskoi SSR 1975{1}: 38-39. WA 28: 2424.

3.4-112 Shelyag-Sosonko, Yu.R., Didukh, Ya.P. 1978. Stipa steppes of Crimean Yaila [in Ukrainian]. Ukr. Bot. Zh. 35: 9-14. HERB AB 48: 4525.

3.4-113 Sidorenko, G. 1977. Halophilous shrub-type and halophilous grass-type winter grasslands [in Russian]. Pages 200-204 in P.N. Ovchinnikov, ed. Pastbishcha i senokosy Tadzhikstana. 'Donish', Dushanbe, Tajik SSR. HERB-AB 49: 1636.

3.4-114 Simonovic, V. 1973. Study of the root biomass in the herb layer of an oak-hornbeam forest. Biologia (Bratislava) 28: 11-22.

3.4-115 Slade, N.A., Horton, J.S., and Mooney, H.A. 1975. Yearly variation in the phenology of California annuals. Am. Midl. Nat. 94: 209-214.

3.4-116 Solbrig, O.T., and Simpson, B.B. 1974. Components of regulation of a population of dandelions in Michigan. J. Ecol. 62: 473-486.

3.4-117 Solbrig, O.T., and Simpson, B.B. 1977. A garden experiment on competition between biotypes of the common dandelion (Taraxacum officinale). J. Ecol. 65: 427-430.

3.4-118 Solbrig, O.T. 1971. The population biology of dandelions. Am. Sci. 59: 686-694.

3.4-119 Stocker, O. 1974. Water- and photosynthesis-relations of desert plants in the South-Algerian Sahara. I. Habitats and investigated plants [in German]. Flora (Jena) 163: 46-88.

3.4-120 Strzemska, J. 1973. Mycorrhiza of cultivated plants of the Papilionaceae family. Part IV. Fenugreek (Trigonella foenum-graecum) and soybean (Glycine hispida). Pol. J. Soil Sci. 6: 57-62. SF 38: 584.

3.4-121 Tanghe, M. 1975. 1st Outline on the semi-natural marshy meadows of the Woluwe Valley in Woluwe St. Lambert [in French]. Bull. Soc. R. Bot. Belg. 108: 79-92.

3.4-122 Terzo, V., and Valcuvia Passadore, M.G. 1979. Flora of the "Giuseppe Negri" woods of the commune of Pavia [in Italian]. Atti. Ist. Bot. Univ. Lab. Crittogam. Pavia 12{6}: 3-29.

3.4-123 Todorov, T. 1977. A rare plant [in Bulgarian]. Gorsko Stopanstvo 33{7}: 46-49. Bib. Ag. 42: 29862.

3.4-124 Tuganaev, V.V., Efimova, T.P., and Tychinin, V.A. 1978. Plant immigrants of the Udmurt ASSR (1974-1977 studies) [in Russian]. Bot. Zh. (Leningrad) 63: 1510-1513. HERB AB 50: 1496.

3.4-125 Uslu, T. 1974. A plant ecological and sociological research on the dune and maguis vegetation between Mersin and Silifke [in French]. Commun. Fac. Sci. Univ. Ankara Ser. C2 Bot. 21 (1 Suppl. 1): 1-60.

3.4-126 Valdeyron, G., Dommee, B., and Pour Kheyr, A. 1975. On some cases of ecotypic diversification of the genetic system in species of the Mediterranean flora [in French]. Pages 353-357 in M. Guinochet, ed. La flore du bassin Mediterraneen; Essci de systematique synthetique, 4-8 June, Montpelier, France, 1974. (Colloques internationaux du Centre National de la Recherche Scientifique; no. 235). Editions du CNRS, Paris, France.

3.4-127 Vernet, P., Guillerm, J.L., and Gouyon, P.H. 1977. Chemical polymorphism in Thymus vulgaris L. (Labiatae). I. Distribution of chemical forms in relation to certain ecological factors [in French]. Oecol. Plant. 12: 159-179.

3.4-128 Vostokova, E.A. 1975. Ecology and hydrogeologic role of feathergrass communitites in the sand deserts of the northern Aral region. Sov. J. Ecol. (Engl. Transl.) 6: 62-67. Translation of Ekologiya 1975{1}: 83-89.

3.4-129 Walter, H. 1973. Ecological considerations on the vegetation conditions in the Ebro Basin (Northeastern Spain) [in German]. Acta Bot. Acad. Sci. Hung. 19: 393-402.

3.4-130 Walton, D.W.H., and Smith, R.I.L. 1973. Status of the alien vascular flora of South Georgia. Br. Antarct. Surv. Bull. 1973{36}: 79-97. WA 24: 1895.

3.4-131 Ward, D.B. 1976. Gaultheria procumbens at Pine Hills, Indiana--its measured decline. Proc. Indiana Acad. Sci. 86: 131-139.

3.4-132 Warwick, S.I., and Briggs, D. 1979. The genecology of lawn weeds. III. Cultivation experiments with Achillea millefolium L., Bellis perennis L., Plantago lanceolata L., Plantago major L. and Prunella vulgaris L. collected from lawns and constrasting grassland habitats. New Phytol. 83: 509-536.

3.4-133 Warwick, S.I., and Briggs, D. 1980. The genecology of lawn weeds. VI. The adaptive significance of variation in Achillea millefolium L. as investigated by transplant experiments. New Phytol. 85: 451-460.

3.4-134 Warwick, S.I., and Briggs, D. 1980. The genecology of lawn weeds. V. The adaptive significance of different growth habit in lawn and roadside populations of Plantago major L. New Phytol. 85: 289-300.

3.4-135 Whitford, P.C., and Whitford, P.B. 1978. Effects of trees on ground cover in old-field succession. Am. Midl. Nat. 99: 435-443.

3.4-136 Williams, W.T. 1974. Species dynamism in the coastal strand plant community at Morro Bay, California. Bull. Torrey Bot. Club 101: 83-89.

3.4-137 Williams, W.T., and Potter, J.R. 1972. The coastal strand community at Morro Bay State Park, California. Bull. Torrey Bot. Club 99: 163-171.

3.4-138 Zarzycki, K. 1976. Small populations of relict and endemic plant species of the Pieniny Range Poland (West Carpathians Mountains) their endangerment and conservation [in Polish]. Ochr. Przyr. 41: 7-76.

3.4-139 Zarzycki, K. 1976. Ecodiagrams of common vascular plants in the Pieniny Mountains (the Polish West Carpathians). Part II. Ecodiagrams of selected grassland species. Fragm. Florist. Geobot. (Cracow) 22: 499-528.

3.5 Environmental Pollution and Plant Growth

3.5-1 Arvik, J.H., and Zimdahl, R.L. 1974. Barriers to the foliar uptake of lead. J. Environ. Qual. 3: 369-373.

3.5-2 Assche, C. van, and Mey, I.W. de. 1977. Plant diseases caused by heavy metals and their phytiatry with cation exchangers. Acta Agrobot. 30: 167-179. HA 49: 2505.

3.5-3 Beauford, W., Barber, J., and Barringer, A.R. 1977. Uptake and distribution of mercury within higher plants. Physiol. Plant 39: 261-265.

3.5-4 Bora, K.K., Sankhla, D., and Sankhla, N. 1979. Pollutants and growth of Indian desert plants. I. Role of fluoride in early seedling growth and enzyme activity. Trans. Indian Soc. Desert Technol. Univ. Cent. Desert Stud. 4{1}: 42-46. Bib.Ag. 45: 58979.

3.5-5 Bromfield, A.R. 1972. Absorption of atmospheric sulphur by mustard (Sinapis alba) grown in a glasshouse. J. Agric. Sci. 78: 343-344.

3.5-6 Chrenekova, E. 1975. Uptake and distribution of arsenate ions by mustard under conditions of varying phosphorus nutrition [in Slovak]. Pol'nohospodarstvo 21: 752-758.

3.5-7 Chrenekova, E., and Hornak, J. 1972. Phytotoxic effects of arsenic on various plant species [in Slovak]. Pol'nohospodarstvo 18: 962-972. FCA 26: 5899.

3.5-8 Chrenekova, E., and Holobrady, K. 1972. The resorption and distribution of arsenic at the vegetative growth stage [in Russian]. Sci. Agric. Bohemoslov. 4: 87-96. FCA 27: 4170.

3.5-9 Clain, E., and Deysson, G. 1976. Cytotoxicity of cadmium: study on Allium sativum root meristems [in French]. C. R. Seances Soc. Biol. Fil. 170: 1151-1155.

3.5-10 Cronin, J.A. 1977. A study of pollution by some lead-emitting industries in the Dublin area. Proc. R. Ir. Acad. Sect. B 77B{19-47}: 403-410. CA 89: 64280.

3.5-11 De Santo, A.V., Bartoli, G., Alfani, A., and Ianni, M. 1979. Responses of Mentha piperita L. and Arabidopsis thaliana L. to fumigation with SO2 sulfur dioxide at different concentrations. J. Environ. Sci. Health Part A A14: 313-332. AGRICOLA.

3.5-12 Elsokkary, I.H. 1980. Contamination of edible parts of seven plant crops and soils by heavy metals in urban area by air pollution in Alexandria district, Egypt. Stud. Environ. Sci. 8: 433-438. CA 93: 162111.

3.5-13 Elsokkary, I.H. 1978. Contamination of roadside soils and plants near highway traffic with Cd, Ni, Pb and Zn in Alexandria District, Egypt. Pages 25-28 in M.M. Benarie, ed. Atmospheric Pollution 1978. Studies in Environmental Science. 1. Elsevier Pub., New York, N.Y.

3.5-14 Ernst, W.H.O., and Bast-Cramer, W.B. 1980. The effect of lead contamination of soils and air on its accumulation in pollen. Plant Soil 57: 491-496.

3.5-15 Flueckiger, W., and Flueckiger-Keller, H. 1978. Changes in content of B-carotene and vitamin C in parsley plants in the vicinity of a highway [in German]. Qual. Plant. Plant Foods Hum. Nutr. 28: 1-9.

3.5-16 Gardner, W.S., Redman, K., and Safford, J. 1972. Sensitive medicinal and poisonous plants monitor ozone and 2,4-D air pollution in South Dakota. Proc. S.D. Acad. Sci. 51: 268 (Abstr.).

3.5-17 Grodzinska, K., and Kazmierczakowa, R. 1977. Heavy metal content in the plants of Cracow parks. Bull. Acad. Pol. Sci. Ser. Sci. Biol. 25: 227-234. HERB AB 48: 984.

3.5-18 Haghiri, F. 1973. Cadmium-uptake by plants. J. Environ. Qual. 2: 93-96.

3.5-19 Haney, A., Carlson, J.A., and Rolfe, G.L. 1974. Lead contamination of soils and plants along highway gradients in east central Illinois. Trans. Ill. State Acad. Sci. 67: 323-335.

3.5-20 Hodgson, R.H., and Hoffer, B.L. 1977. Diphenamid metabolism in pepper and an ozone effect. I. Absorption, translocation, and the extent of metabolism. Weed Sci. 25: 324-330.

3.5-21 Hodgson, R.H., and Hoffer, B.L. 1977. Diphenamid metabolism, in pepper and an ozone effect. II. Herbicide metabolite characterization. Weed Sci. 25: 331-337.

3.5-22 Kazmierczakowa, R., and Rams, B. 1974. The effect of industrial air pollution on the lead and zinc content of some medicinal plants in the Olkusz area [in Polish]. Herba Pol. 20: 373-378. HA 46: 4959.

3.5-23 Kazmierczakowa, R. 1975. Correlation between the amount of industrial dust fall and the lead and zinc accumulation in some plant species. Bull. Acad. Pol. Sci. Ser. Sci. Biol. 23: 611-621.

3.5-24 Krivolutskii, D.A., Smurov, A.V., and Snetkov, M.A. 1972. The effect of the radioactive pollution of the soil with strontium-90 on variability in some organisms [in Russian]. Zh. Obshch. Biol. 33: 587-591.

3.5-25 Lag, J., and Elsokkary, I.H. 1978. A comparison of chemical methods for estimating Cd, Pb, and Zn availability to six food crops grown in industrially polluted soils at Odda, Norway. Acta Agriculturae Scandinavica 28{1}: 76-80. HA 48: 5425.

3.5-26 Lezhneva, N.D., and Akzhigitova, N.I. 1977. Lead and zinc in plants in the central part of the Almalyk ore region [in Russian]. Uzb. Biol. Zh. 1977{1}: 73-75. CA 86: 136346.

3.5-27 Miles, L.J., and Parker, G.R. 1980. Effects of cadmium and a one-time drought stress on survival, growth, and yield of native plant species. J. Environ. Qual. 9: 278-283.

3.5-28 Miles, L.J., and Parker, G.R. 1979. The effect of soil-added cadmium on several plant species. J. Environ. Qual. 8: 229-232.

3.5-29 Miles, L.J., and Parker, G.R. 1979. DTPA soil extractable and plant heavy metal concentrations with soil-added Cd treatments. Plant Soil 51: 59-68.

3.5-30 Nassery, H., Ogata, G., Nieman, R.H., and Maas, E.V. 1978. Growth, phosphate pools, and phosphate mobilization of salt-stressed sesame and pepper. Plant Physiol. 62: 229-231.

3.5-31 Nassery, H., Ogata, G., and Maas, E.V. 1979. Sensitivity of sesame to various salts. Agron. J. 71: 595-597.

3.5-32 Oshima, R.J., Bennett, J.P., and Braegelmann, P.K. 1978. Effect of ozone on growth and assimilate partitioning in parsley. J. Am. Soc. Hortic. Sci. 103: 348-350.

3.5-33 Pais, I., Somos, A., and Tarjanyi, F. 1975. Chemically objective experiments on trace element toxicity and deficiency with tomato and red pepper plants. Pages 405-410 in P. Kozma, D. Polyak and E. Hervay, eds. Le controle de l'alimentation des plants cultivees. 3rd Colloque Europeen et Mediterraneen, Budapest, Hungary, Sept. 4-7, 1972. Akademiai Kiado, Budapest, Hungary. vol. I.

3.5-34 Pettersson, O. 1977. Differences in cadmium uptake between plant species and cultivars. Swedish J. Agric. Res. 7: 21-24. FCA 30: 6436.

3.5-35 Poletschny, H., and Kick, H. 1973. Nitrogen availability and uptake of copper, lead and zinc by mustard, barley and oats with high rates of differently treated sewage sludge [in German]. Landwirtsch. Forsch. Sonderh. 28{1}: 376-385. FCA 28: 2342.

3.5-36 Quinche, J.-P. 1971. Pollution of crops by lead from vehicle exhaust gases [in French]. Problemes de l'environment et agriculture, Berne 1971: 13-14.

3.5-37 Runeckles, V.C., and Rosen, P.M. 1974. Effects of pretreatment with low ozone concentrations on ozone injury to bean and mint. Can. J. Bot. 52: 2607-2610.

3.5-38 Szinten, C. 1978. Effect of sulfur dioxide on the main biochemical processes and yield of tomato and paprika. Proc. Hung. Annu. Meet. Biochem. 18: 59-60 (Abstr.). CA 90: 17197.

3.5-39 Taylor, R.J. 1978. Industrial impact in northwestern Whatcom County, Washington. Water, Air Soil Pollut. 10: 199-213.

3.5-40 Tripathi, N., and Misra, S.G. 1974. Uptake of applied selenium by plants. Indian J. Agric. Sci. 44: 804-807. FCA 30: 7985.

3.5-41 Tumova, E. 1973. The effect of chlorine on the yield of mustard [in Czech]. Agrochemia 13: 333-335. FCA 27: 6461.

3.5-42 Von Willert, D.J. 1974. Effect of sodium chloride on respiration and the activity of malate dehydrogenase in some halophytes and glycophytes [in German]. Oecologia 14: 127-137.

3.5-43 Webber, J. 1972. Effect of toxic metals in sewage on crops. Water Pollut. Control (Maidstone, Engl.) 71: 404-413.

3.5-44 Yousif, Y.H., Bingham, F.T., and Yermanos, D.M. 1972. Growth, mineral composition, and seed oil of sesame (Sesamum indicum L.) as affected by NaCl. Proc. Soil Sci. Soc. Am. 36: 450-453.

3.5-45 Zamfir, G., Apostol, S., Melinte, C., and Gava, V. 1971. The toxicity of residual waters from a wood industry combine shown by seedling tests [in Romanian]. Cercetari Agronomic in Moldova 1971{4}: 29-38. FCA 26: 6904.

3.6 Land Reclamation

3.6-1 Bhatia, K.S., and Srivastava, K.K. 1976. Effect of erosion-resisting crops in kharif and their effect on the yield of rai (Brassica juncea Coss.) under rainfed conditions. Soil Conservation Digest 4{1}: 4-9. SF 41: 6597.

3.6-2 Craig, R.M., and Smith, D.C. 1979. Vegetation in areas stripmined for limestone. Proc. Soil Crop. Sci. Fla. 38: 8-12.

3.6-3 Debano, L.F., and Conrad, C.E. 1974. Effect of a wetting agent and nitrogen fertilizer on establishment of ryegrass and mustard on a burned watershed. J. Range Manage. 27: 57-60.

3.6-4 Dunbar, G.A. 1971. The effectiveness of some herbaceous species for montane and subalpine revegetation. N.Z. Ecol. Soc. Proc. 18: 48-57.

3.6-5 Gemmell, R.P. 1973. Revegetation of derelict land polluted by a chromate smelter, part 1: chemical factors causing substrate toxicity in chromate smelter waste. Environ. Pollut. 5: 181-197.

3.6-6 Golcz, L., Czabajski, T., Kordana, S., Zorawska, B., and Polkowski, M. 1975. Experiments in the cultivation of peppermint (Mentha piperita L.) woolly foxglove (Digitalis lanata Ehrh.) and medicinal poppies (Papaver somniferum L.) on deforested grounds in the Pulawy region [in Polish]. Herba Pol. 21: 70-78. HA 46: 9654.

3.6-8 Gorbachev, B.N., and Lutsenko, A.I. 1978. The experience of phytoindication of sand terrace landscapes in river valleys of the steppe zone (exemplified by the terraces of the middle and lower reaches of the Don River) [in Russian]. Bot. Zh. (Leningrad) 63: 389-394.

3.6-9 Hundt, R. 1978. Studies on the development of new forest lands on former strip mining sites in the Duebner Heide DDR [in German]. Vegetatio 38: 1-12.

3.6-10 Juhren, M.C., and Montgomery, K.R. 1977. Long-term responses of Cistus and certain other introduced shrubs on disturbed wildland sites in Southern California. Ecology 58: 129-138.

3.6-11 Simon, E. 1975. Vegetation dynamics in some metalliferous areas in the neighborhood of Eupen and Aachen in relation to edaphic factors [in French]. Bull. Soc. R. Bot. Belg. 108: 273-286.

3.6-12 Slavonovsky, F. 1972. Comparison of quality of roots of four Psammophile species [in Czech]. Scr. Fac. Sci. Nat. Univ. Purkynianae Brun. 2{3}: 121-147.

3.6-13 Swieboda, M., and Dabrowska, L. 1976. The occurrence of some chosen plants on sites with differing degrees of soil degradation induced by man's industrial activity [in Polish]. Fragm. Florist. Geobot. (Kracow) 22: 545-551.

3.7 Germplasm Collections

3.7-1 Khoroshailov, N.G., and Zhukova, N.V. 1973. Long term storage of seed samples in collections [in Russian]. Tr. Prikl. Bot. Genet. Sel. 49: 269-279. HA 44: 7533.

3.7-2 Martinek, V., and Liska, O. 1972. The evaluation of the world collection of poppy [in Czech]. Rostl. Vyroba 18: 677-686. FCA 27: 6465.

3.7-3 Miakota, B.V. 1977. Study of the world collection of coriander as initial breeding material [in Russian]. Byull. Vses. Inst. Rastenievod. 69: 82-84. AGRICOLA.

3.7-4 Moravec, J., and Kvasnicka, S. 1975. An evaluation of world collection of garlic cultivars [in Czech]. Sb. UVTI Zahradnictvi 2(V): 117-123. HA 47: 1378.

3.7-5 Nechiporenko, N.A., Prikhod'ko, T.N., Yudaeva, V.E., and Korchemnaya, N.A. 1977. Study of a collection of culinary and fodder root crops in the Moscow area [in Russian]. Tr. Prikl. Bot. Genet. Sel. 60{3}: 141-152. PBA 49: 5212.

3.7-6 Nechiporenko, N.A., Emmerikh, N.S., and Korchemnaya, N.A. 1977. Results of studies on horseradish and asparagus collections [in Russian]. Tr. Prikl. Bot. Genet. Sel. 60{3}: 153-160. HA 49: 3704.

3.7-7 Okoniewska, J. 1974. Evaluation of a collection of caraway [in Polish]. Herba Pol. 20: 138-141. HA 45: 9974.

3.7-8 Pravikovskaia, K.N. 1972. New samples of peanut and sesame in VIR collection [in Russian]. Tr. Prikl. Bot. Genet. Sel. 48: 234-239.

3.7-9 Sazonova, L.V., Kazakova, A.A., and Boos, G.V. 1977. The world collection of vegetables and cucurbits and its role in the development of the Soviet vegetable industry [in Russian]. Tr. Prikl. Bot. Genet. Sel. 60{1}: 91-95. PBA 48: 10166.

3.7-10 Shestopalova, R.E., Berestovaia, M.M., and Moskalenko, L.M. 1975. World collection of Coriandrum sativum as initial material for breeding [in Russian]. Sel. Semenovod. (Kiev) 31: 48-53. AGRICOLA.

3.7-11 Singh, H. 1977. Introduction, maintenance and utilization of germplasm of medicinal and allied plants. Pages 472-478 in C.K. Atal and B.M. Kapur, eds. Cultivation & utilization of medicinal and aromatic plants. Regional Research Laboratory, Jammu-Tawi, India.

3.7-12 Yermanos, D.M., Hemstreet, S., Saleeb, W., and Huszar, C.K. 1972. Oil content and composition of the seed in the world collection of sesame introductions. J. Am. Oil Chem. Soc. 49: 20-23.

3.7-13 Yuknyavichene, G.K., and Dagite, S.Y. 1973. Biological properties and essential oil content of some spice plants grown at the Kaunas Botanical Garden. 1. Plants whose herbage is used as raw material for spices. Liet. TSR Mokslu Akad. Darb. Ser. C 1973{4}: 57-63.

4.0 HORTICULTURE

4.1 Plant Selection

4.1-1 Anais, G. 1977. Improved varieties of shallot (Allium cepa var. aggregatum) for cultivation in the West Indies [in French]. Nouv. Agron. Antilles Guyane 3{2}: 45-48. PBA 51: 3657.

4.1-2 Anikeenko, V.S. 1980. Hybrids of hot pepper [in Russian]. Kartofel. Ovoshchi 1980{5}: 25-26. AGRICOLA.

4.1-3 Anonymous. 1980. List of varieties. Mutation Breeding Newsl. 1980{15}: 12-17. PBA 51: 3860.

4.1-4 Anonymous. 1972. Trial of curled parsley stocks [in Danish]. Gartner Tidende 88{47}: 693-694. HA 43: 7071.

4.1-5 Anonymous. 1973. Notice of the new varieties of summer crops bred by the Ministry of Agriculture and Forestry in 1973 [in Japanese]. Nogyo Oyobi Engei 48: 1139. PBA 46: 2126.

4.1-6 Anonymous. 1974. P.F.35 - a new variety of fennel (Foeniculum vulgare Mill). Arecanut and Spices Bulletin 6: 10-11. HA 46: 4918.

4.1-7 Anonymous. 1974. Choosing caraway varieties: Bleija, a good crop, provided that it is harvested at the right time and in the right way [in Dutch]. Zaadbelangen 28: 209-210. HA 45: 9973.

4.1-8 Anonymous. 1979. Some other oilcrops [in French]. Cultivar 119: 97-99, 101. AGRICOLA.

4.1-9 Aprikyan, S.V. 1979. Angelica tatianae Bordz as a valuable feed-silage and vegetable plant [in Armenian]. Izv. S-kh. Nauk 22{4}: 24-32. CA 92: 20782.

4.1-10 Asthana, K.S., and Narain, B. 1977. Evaluation of sesame varieties in Bihar for summer. Indian J. Agric. Sci. 611-613.

4.1-11 Bannerot, H., and Coninck, B. de. 1976. Witloof chicory [in French]. Bull. Tech. Inf. 1976{311}: 455-462. PBA 47: 7889.

4.1-12 Benoit, F., and Ceustermans, N. 1980. Comparisons of fennel selections for culture from June to November [in Flemish]. Boer en de Tuinder 86{23}: 19. HA 50: 9385.

4.1-13 Bhupal Rao, J.V.R., and Krishnan, R. 1980. A spontaneous variant with larger flowers in Jasminum auriculatum Vahl. Curr. Sci. 49: 323.

4.1-14 Bogatirenko, A.K. 1976. New promising garlic cultivar Boguslavskii-10 [in Ukrainian]. Visn. Sil's'kogospod Nauki 1976{7}: 31-37. HA 47: 7354.

4.1-15 Bogatyrenko, A. 1975. The garlic variety Boguslav 10 [in Russian]. Kartofel Ovoshchi 1975{9}: 26. PBA 46: 2898.

4.1-16 Boyadzhieva, V., and Staikov, V. 1972. Report on the study of the content and quality of the essential oils in certain lavender varieties [in French]. An. Acad. Bras. Cienc. 44(Suppl.): 268-272.

4.1-17 Bradu, B.L., and Atal, C.K. 1974. Comparative yield trials on new geraniol-rich Cymbopogon species. Indian Perfum. 18: 7-16. HA 47: 7760.

4.1-18 Bugaenko, L.A., and Reznikova, S.A. 1980. Selection of highly productive frost-resistant forms in the first generation of interspecies hybrids of mint. Cytol. Genet. (Engl. Transl.) 14{1}: 41-45.

4.1-19 Buishand, T. 1979. Growing interest in the expansion of the range of vegetables [in Dutch]. Bedrijfsontwikkeling 10: 407-412. HA 49: 7491.

4.1-20 Ceapoiu, N. 1976. New varieties and hybrids of agricultural plants bred in Romania [in Romanian]. Probleme di Genetica Teoretica si Aplicata 8: 93-121. PBA 48: 3081.

4.1-21 Chaudhari, P.N., and Patil, N.Y. 1980. Phule Til No. 1 - A promising Sesamum variety for central and western Maharashtra. J. Maharashtra Agric. Univ. 5: 26-29.

4.1-22 Chingova-Boyadzhieva, B., and Staikov, V. 1973. Results of comparative variety trials with lavandin [in Bulgarian]. Rastenievud. Nauki 10{1}: 35-43. HA 43: 7986.

4.1-23 Chladek, M., and Dvorak, S. 1972. Chamomile varieties and flower quality [in Czech]. Nase Liecive Rastliny 9: 104-106. HA 43: 2352.

4.1-24 Collura, A.M., and Marzocca, I.M. y A. 1972. Selection and performance in Argentina of clone 626 of Mentha piperita L. introduced from England [in Spanish]. An. Acad. Bras. Cienc. 44(Suppl.): 31-37.

4.1-25 Croon, F. 1972. Varietal trials of witloof chicory [in Flemish]. Tuinbouwberichten 36: 100-102. PBA 43: 4679.

4.1-26 Devarathinam, A.A., and Subramanian, M. 1976. A new variety of Sesamum Linn. from Madurai, South India. Madras Agric. J. 63: 169-171.

4.1-27 Devetak, Z. 1971/1972. Lavender and lavandin selection [in Serbo-Croatian]. Rad. Poljopr. Fak. Univ. Sarajevu 20/21,22/23: 165-180. HA 43: 8996.

4.1-28 Dimri, B.P., Khan, M.N.A., and Narayana, M.R. 1976. Some promising selections of Bulgarian coriander (Coriandrum sativum Linn) for seed and essential oil with a note on cultivation and distillation of oil. Indian Perfum. 20{1A}: 13-21. HA 48: 8507.

4.1-29 Dimri, D.P., Khan, M.N.A., and Narayana, M.R. 1977. Introduction and improvement of Bulgarian coriander (Coriandrum sativum Linn.) by selection for higher yield and essential oil content. Pages 353-358 in C.K. Atal and B.M. Kapur, eds. Cultivation & utilization of medicinal and aromatic plants. Regional Research Laboratory, Jammu-Tawi, India.

4.1-30 Donalisio, N.G.R., De Souza, C.J., and D'Andrea Pinto, A.J. 1974. New cultivar of Mentha arvensis containing methofuran [in Spanish]. Int. Congr. Essent. Oils [Pap.], 6th, 1974. 10, 2 pp. CA 84: 126634.

4.1-31 Duke, J.A. 1978. The quest for tolerant germplasm. Pages 1-61 in Crop tolerance to suboptimal land conditions. ASA, CSSA, SSSA, Madison, Wisc.

4.1-32 Eenink, A.H. 1978. Sugar-loaf chicory. A new vegetable for growing in the open [in Flemish]. Groenten Fruit 33: 46-47. PBA 48: 12179.

4.1-33 Erdei, I., and Somogyi, Gy. 1977. The adaptability of red pepper cultivars according to studies on water utilization [in Hungarian]. Kertgazdasag 9{4}: 25-30. AGRICOLA.

4.1-34 Eremenko, L.L., Komissarov, V.A., and Starikova, D.A. 1977. Garlic varieties in Novosibirsk province [in Russian]. Kartofel Ovoshchi 1977{3}: 28-30. PBA 47: 8898.

4.1-35 Garcia, A., and Oliveira, J.J. 1973. Preliminary studies on the performance of garlic cultivars (<u>Allium sativum</u>) in Pelotas, Rio Grande do Sul [in Portuguese]. Pesquis. Agropecu. Bras. Ser. Agron. 8: 277-285.

4.1-36 Gidnavar, V.S., and Krishnamurthy, K. 1979. I. S-711 variety fennel has a possibility as a pure crop. Current Research 8: 111. HA 50: 3661.

4.1-37 Gretsinger, V.Kh., and Gortanova, L.N. 1974. Trials on geranium cultivars in Tadzhikistan [in Russian]. Subtrop. Kul't. 1974{4}: 82-85. HA 45: 10003.

4.1-38 Gulati, B.C., Duhan, S.P.S., Garg, S.N., and Roy, S.K. 1975. Performance of peppermint (<u>Mentha piperita</u> Linn) varieties in Tarai of Uttar Pradesh. Indian Perfum. 19{2}: 24-27. HA 47: 11740.

4.1-39 Gulati, B.C. 1977. <u>Ocimum basilicum</u> Linn. (methyl chavicol type). Perfum Flavor. 2{5}: 58 (Abstr.). PBA 48: 10354.

4.1-40 Ham, Y.S., Lee, J.I., Kim, K.C., and Cho, J.H. 1978. New sesame variety, "Suweon 21" [in Korean]. Res. Rep. Off. Rural Dev. (Crop) 20: 169-171. AGRICOLA.

4.1-41 Hansen, L., Stokholm, E., and Gregersen, A. 1975. A cultural trial with vegetables at Hoejer and Jyndevad 1964-73 [in Danish]. Tidsskr. Planteavl 79: 239-242. HA 45: 9457.

4.1-42 Hari Om, and Srivastava, R.P. 1976. Performance of different locally selected garlic clones. Prog. Hortic. 7{4}: 69-76. PBA 47: 6828.

4.1-43 Heltmann, H., and Arslan, O. 1978. Comparative trials of different cultivars and sources of <u>Papaver somniferum</u> [in German]. Acta Hortic. 1978{73}: 27-34.

4.1-44 Hoang, V.P., Thach, K., and La, D.M. 1980. Mint and the chemical composition of clone NV74 [in Vietnamese]. Tap Chi Hoa Hoc 18{1}: 25-29. CA 94: 52678.

4.1-45 Hoelzl, J., Fritz, D., Franz, C., and Garte, L. 1974. Comparative tests on <u>Mentha piperita</u> L. of different varieties and origins. I. Characterization from morphological-anatomical features and from the nature of the essential oil [in German]. Dtsch. Apothztg. 114: 513-517. HA 45: 4376.

4.1-46 Ilieva, S. 1979. New <u>Salvia sclarea</u> L. cultivars developed by hybridization. Herba Hung. 18{3}: 197-203. PBA 51: 10190.

4.1-47 Ilieva, S., Nicolov, N., Dragostinov, P., Lesseva, I., and Ivanov, I. 1972. The Bulgarian types of <u>Salvia sclarea</u> L. and the quality of the essential oils obtained from them [in French]. An. Acad. Bras. Cienc. 44(Suppl.): 256-261.

4.1-48 Joubert, G., Marrou, J., and Vergniaud, P. 1976. Garlic [in French]. Bull. Tech. Inf. 1976{311}: 433-439. PBA 47: 7871.

4.1-49 Kanters, F.M.L. 1976. Fifteen chicory selections recommended for forcing without soil cover [in Flemish]. Groenten Fruit 31: 1787. HA 46: 10208.

4.1-50 Kaushik, L.S., Singh, R.P., and Yadava, T.P. 1977. A uniformity trial with mustard. Indian J. Agric. Sci. 47: 515-518. FCA 32: 1889.

4.1-51 Khalafov, L.Kh. 1976. Varietal trial of garlic in the Kuba-Khachmas area of Azerbaijan [in Russian]. Tr. Vses. S-kh. Inst. Zaochn. Obraz. 1976{116}: 104-108. PBA 48: 12162.

4.1-52 Khanna, K.R. 1975. Note on the performance of European varieties and cultivars of opium poppy. Indian J. Agric. Res. 9{4}: 211-213.

4.1-53 Khvatysh, G.A. 1973. Local cultivars of vegetables and cucurbits in Transcaucasia [in Russian]. Tr. Prikl. Bot. Genet. Sel. 50{3}: 92-102. PBA 44: 6275.

4.1-54 Knyazeva, A.S. 1975. Root-parsley cultivar trials [in Russian]. Nauchn. Tr.-Voronezh. S-kh. Inst. im. K.D. Glinki 74: 99-103.

4.1-55 Kovineva, V.M., and Kodash, A.G. 1976. A promising interspecific mint hybrid [in Russian]. Herba Pol. 22: 281-283. HA 48: 4875.

4.1-56 Kvasnikov, B.V., and Belik, T.A. 1978. Varieties of vegetable crops [in Russian]. Kartofel Ovoshchi 1978{1}: 36-38. PBA 48: 5983.

4.1-57 Lee, J.I., Oh, S.G., Lee, S.T., Kang, C.H., Lee, H.S., and Ham, Y.S. 1980. New sesame variety "Suweon 26" [in Korean]. Res. Rep. Off. Rur. Dev. (Crop) 22: 134-137. AGRICOLA.

4.1-58 Lee, W.S. 1974. Studies on bulb and clove characteristics of local Korean strains of garlic [in Korean]. Hanguk Wonye Hakhoe Chi 15: 20-29.

4.1-59 Madjarova, D., Madzharova, D., and Bigeva, Kh. 1979. New yielding species "Svejen" - Mentha spicata L. (Mentha viridis Huds.). Herba Hung. 18{3}: 205-210.

4.1-60 Madjarova, D., Bidjeva, N., and Bubarova, M. 1979. New high yielding varieties of Mentha viridis L. Planta Med. 36: 243 (Abstr.).

4.1-61 Madzharova, D., Petrova, V., and Bubarova, M. 1973. Studies on dills of different origin [in Bulgarian]. Gradinar. Lozar. Nauka 10{2}: 63-67. HA 43: 8978.

4.1-62 Malinina, V.M., and Ivanova, R.M. 1975. Cultivars of oilseed poppy with high contents of alkaloids [in Russian]. Sel. Semenovod. (Moscow) 1975{6}: 39-40. FCA 29: 7461.

4.1-63 Mandy, Gy. 1975. Red pepper kalocsai, Determinate 601. Acta Agron. Acad. Sci. Hung. 24: 143-145.

4.1-64 Manucharyan, M.A. 1977. Mutant 14 in stands of Pelargonium roseum in Armenia [in Russian]. Biol. Zh. Arm. 30{12}: 83 (Abstr.). PBA 48: 7896.

4.1-65 Marshall, H.H., and Scora, R.W. 1972. A new chemical race of Monarda fistulosa (Labiatae). Can. J. Bot. 50: 1845-1849.

4.1-66 Mistruzzi, M. 1977. Chicory cultivar Rosso di Verona can lead to better returns and lower production costs [in Italian]. Informatore Agrario 33: 26507-26517. HA 48: 8101.

4.1-67 Mital, S.P., Singh, R.P., and Bhagat, N.R. 1972. A synchronous flowering mutant in celery (Apium graveolens L.). Curr. Sci. 41: 856. PBA 43: 8286.

4.1-68 Moravec, J., Kvasnicka, S., and Jelinek, J. 1973. Creation of a new shallot variety "Milka" (Allium cepa var. ascalonicum (L.) Backer 1951) [in Czech]. Genet. Slechteni 9: 141-148. AGRICOLA.

4.1-69 Moutet, L. 1980. Lavandin Abrialis, lavandin Grosso: what is their future?. Perfum. Flavor. 4{6}: 27, 29. HA 50: 7319.

4.1-70 Nadezhina, T.P. 1972. A trial on growing Glycyrrhiza spp. in the Leningrad region [in Russian]. Tr. Bot. Inst. Akad. Nauk SSSR Ser. 5 1972{16}: 65-79. HA 43: 4768.

4.1-71 Nair, E.V.G., Chinnamma, N.P., and Kumari, R.P. 1980. A new lemongrass. Intensive Agric. 18{8}: 13.

4.1-72 Nair, N.R., Santhakumari, S., and Gopalakrishnan, R. 1975. A note on a natural multicapsuled mutant of Sesamum and its yielding ability. Sci. Cult. 41: 38-39.

4.1-73 Nakagawa, J., Toledo, F.F. de, and Machado, J.R. 1975. Competition of sesame varieties (Sesamum indicum L.). I. First year [in Portuguese] Rev. Agric. (Piracicaba, Braz.) 50: 183-190. AGRICOLA.

4.1-74 Nakagawa, J., Toledo, F.F. de, and Machado, J.R. 1976. Competition between sesame (Sesamum indicum L.) varieties. II. Second year [in Portuguese]. Rev. Agric. (Piracicaba, Braz.) 51: 243-250. AGRICOLA.

4.1-75 Nassar, S.H., Moustafa, S., Fouda, S., Gheita, M., and Ghebrial, S. 1972. A better garlic variety for export. Agric. Res. Rev. 50{4}: 47-58. PBA 43: 7390

4.1-76 Nyman, U., and Hall, O. 1976. Some varieties of Papaver somniferum L. with changed morphinane alkaloid content. Hereditas 84: 69-76.

4.1-77 Nyman, U. 1978. Selection for low morphine content in Papaver somniferum L. [in Swedish]. Tidskr. Sver. Utsadesforen. 88{1/2}: 27-34. AGRICOLA.

4.1-78 Oliva, M. 1977. Koral, a new variety of spice paprika [in Czech]. Zahradnictvo 2: 269. AGRICOLA.

4.1-79 Pareek, S.K., Maheshwari, M.L., and Gupta, R. 1980. Domestication studies on Ocimum sanctum for high oil and eugenol content. Indian Perfum. 24: 93-100.

4.1-80 Peneva, P. 1975. Studies on local and introduced chamomile [in Bulgarian]. Rastenievud. Nauki 12{5}: 27-33. HA 46: 3751.

4.1-81 Perceali, G. 1975. New varieties of winter garlic [in Romanian]. Prod.Veg. Hortic. 24{9}: 16. PBA 46: 1870.

4.1-82 Petkov, L., and Simeonova, I. 1977. Salad mustard, a new vegetable in Bulgaria [in Bulgarian]. Priroda (Sofia) 26{6}: 73-75. HA 49: 4301.

4.1-83 Pichitakul, N., and Sthapitanonda, K. 1977. The constituents of oil from different mint varieties [in Thai]. J. Natl. Res. Counc. Thailand 9{2}: 1-9. PBA 47: 12237.

4.1-84 Pisklova, A., and Sustikova, E. 1977. Evaluation of an assortment of paprika [in Slovak]. Zahradnictvo 2: 560. AGRICOLA.

4.1-85 Pisklova, A. 1977. New varieties of thermophilic vegetables [in Slovak]. Zahradnictvo 2: 308. AGRICOLA.

4.1-86 Popovich, A.L., and Vorobiova, G.V. 1979. New winter-hardy mint cultivars in the Ukrainian SSR [in Ukrainian]. Visn. Sil's'kogospod. Nauki 1979{7}: 26-27, 89-90. HA 50: 3627.

4.1-87 Popov, P., Dimitrov, Y., Georgiev, S., and Iliev, L.S. 1973. Indigenous and foreign poppy varieties characterized by the morphine content of their dry capsules. Bull. Narc. 25{3}: 51-56.

4.1-88 Reckin, J. 1972. Hybrids within the genus Papaver. 2. Artificial hybrids of Papaver somniferum L. and Papaver pilosum Sibth et Smith [in German]. Herba Hung. 11{1}: 39-45. AGRICOLA.

4.1-89 Riepma, P., and Schaap, C. 1973. Choice of chicory cultivar for forcing without soil cover [in Flemish]. Groenten Fruit 28: 1644. HA 43: 7621.

4.1-90 Riepma, P., and Schaap, C. 1973. Choice of chicory cultivars forcing without ground cover [in Flemish]. Groenten Fruit 28: 2263. HA 44: 329.

4.1-91 Ritz, J. 1971. Quantity and quality of domestic varieties of chicory in comparison with some foreign varieties [in Croatian]. Poljopr. Znan. Smotra 27: 167-180. PBA 43: 8287.

4.1-92 Saha, B.N., Baruah, A.K.S., Singh, K.K., and Bordoloi, D.N. 1980. Performance of SD-68 lemongrass strain at Sepahijala, Tripura. Indian Perfum. 24: 85-87.

4.1-93 Satikov, V., and Boyadzhieva, B. 1976. Hemus, a new highly productive lavender variety [in Bulgarian]. Rastenievud. Nauki 13{7}: 39-43. CA 86: 195052.

4.1-94 Shah, C.S. 1977. Varieties of Indian dill and their importance. Pages 335-337 in C.K. Atal and B.M. Kapur, eds. Cultivation & utilization of medicinal and aromatic plants. Regional Research Laboratory, Jammu-Tawi, India.

4.1-95 Sharapov, N.I., Kuzina, E.F., and Tiurina, E.V. 1974. About some results of testing essential oil plants in the USSR [in Russian]. Tr. Vses. Nauchno-Issled. Inst. Efirnomaslichn. Kul't. 7: 46-51.

4.1-96 Sharma, Y.K., Deodhar, A.D., and Gangrade, S.K. 1975. Chemical composition of sesame varieties of Madhya Pradesh, India. Iran J. Agric. Res. 3{2}: 59-64. AGRICOLA.

4.1-97 Shelud'ko, L.A., and Korneva, E.I. 1980. Seed productivity of peppermint and the use of fertile forms in practical selection [in Russian]. Khim.-Farm. Zh. 14{5}: 53-56. HA 50: 9402.

4.1-98 Shpota, V.I., Konovalov, N.G., Podkolzina, V.E., and Safiullina, N.A. 1978. Brassica juncea 'Yubileinaya' and 'Skorospelka 2' [in Russian]. Sel. Semenovod. (Moscow) 1978{6}: 39-40. PBA 49: 5007.

4.1-99 Shrivas, S.R., and Kaushal, P.K. 1972. Phenotypic variability in sesamum (Sesamum indicum Linn.) grown in Madhya Pradesh. JNKVV Res. J. 6: 140-144. AGRICOLA

4.1-100 Sinha, S.K. 1972. Crop selection for water use efficiency. Indian Farming 22{2}: 62-63. FCA 26: 4421.

4.1-101 Staikov, V., and Boyadzhieva, B. 1976. Khemus, a new highly productive lavender cultivar [in Bulgarian]. Rastenievud. Nauki 13{7}: 39-43. HA 47: 6813.

4.1-102 Stieber, G., Tetenyi, P., and Nyaradi, J. 1975. A new trial variety of tarragon (Artemisia dracunculus L.) Zoldzamat [in Hungarian]. Herba Hung. 14{2-3}: 25-36. PBA 47: 5727.

4.1-103 Tateo, F., and Lionetto, M.A. 1980. Selectivity in the production of vegetable food-flavoring extracts [in Italian]. Riv. Soc. Ital. Sci. Aliment. 9{3}: 205-210. CA 93: 202650.

4.1-104 Thuesen, A. 1974. Trials with horseradish types [in Danish]. Gartner Tidende 90{18}: 278. HA 45: 3413.

4.1-105 Topalova, V. 1974. New essential oil plants from the People's Republic of Bulgaria [in German]. Int. Z. Landwirtsch. 1974{1}: 110-112. PBA 45: 6645.

4.1-106 Topalova, V. 1974. Results of studies on Bulgarian and Soviet lavender cultivars [in Bulgarian]. Rastenievud. Nauki 11{2}: 21-27. HA 44: 8915.

4.1-107 Topalov, V., and Chodzhukov, M. 1972. The biological and economic properties of cumin varieties grown in Bulgaria [in Bulgarian]. Rastenievud. Nauki 9{5}: 43-49.

4.1-108 Trehan, K.B., Mehta, S.K., and Chand, H. 1976. A new sesame for western Rajasthan. Intensive Agric. 14{4}: 15.

4.1-109 Tsangas, F.T. 1971. Local varieties of vegetables in central Asia [in Russian]. Tr. Prikl. Bot. Genet. Sel. 45{2}: 113-117. HA 43: 1942.

4.1-110 Tsangas, F.T. 1979. Yield and chemical composition of varieties of celery, parsley, and parsnips [in Russian]. Mirov. Rastitel'n. Resursy v Srednei Azii, (Tashkent) 1979{5}: 63-69. CA 93: 66085.

4.1-111 Uncini, L. 1977. Vulcan 145-73: New hybrid of hot pepper. Acta Hortic. 58: 29-34.

4.1-112 Vereshchako, F.A., and Gevko, V.A. 1973. The prospects of growing inter-specific highly productive peppermint hybrids in Podol'e [in Russian]. Tr. Kishinev. S-kh. Inst. 104: 57-61. HA 44: 7923.

4.1-113 White, G.A., Willingham, B.C., Skrdla, W.H., Massey, J.H., Higgins, J.J., Calhoun, W., Davis, A.M., Dolan, D.D., and Earle, F.R. 1971. Agronomic evaluation of prospective new crop species. Econ. Bot. 25: 22-43.

4.1-114 Yankulov, I., Ivanov, I., and Leseva, I. 1975. Comparative trials with Bulgarian and foreign peppermint cultivars [in Bulgarian]. Rastenievud. Nauki 12{8}: 64-70. HA 46: 7040.

4.1-115 Yankulov, J.K., Stoeva, T.D., Ivanov, I.N., and Zuzulova, A.N. 1979. Production of peppermint oils with new aroma components [in German]. Dokl. Bolg. Akad. Nauk 32: 981-983. HA 50: 3628.

4.1-116 Zelenova, K.P. 1973. Some results of national variety trials with essential oil crops [in Russian]. Byull. Gos. Nikitsk. Bot. Sada 1973{2}: 28-30. HA 45: 4370.

4.1-117 Zobenko, L.P. 1975. S1122, a new early variety of Salvia sclarea [in Russian]. Tr. Vses. Nauchno-Issled. Inst. Efirnomaslichn. Kul't. 8: 33-34. PBA 48: 7193.

4.2 Plant Breeding

4.2-1 Abdrakhmanov, O.K., Baimurzaeva, A.N., and Isambaev, A.I. 1980. Effect of pre-sowing gamma irradiation on the growth, productivity, and food value of licorice [in Russian]. Izv. Akad. Nauk. Kaz. SSR Ser. Biol. 1980{2}: 19-21. CA 93: 108799.

4.2-2 Adema, F., and Rauchert, S. 1979. {464} Proposal to conserve 8485 Asperula L. {1753} with a conserved type species, A. arvensis L. against Asperula L. {1753} with the lectotype species A. odorata L. (Rubiaceae). Taxon 28: 422-423.

4.2-3 Agaev, Iu.M., Muzaferova, R.Sh., and Savchenko, S.P. 1975. Results of experiments in treating the corms of saffron with colchicine [in Russian]. Vestn. S-kh. Nauki Kaz. 10: 121-123. AGRICOLA.

4.2-4 Akhundtzade, I.M., and Muzaferova, R.Sh. 1975. Study of the effectiveness of gamma irradiation of the saffron. Radiobiology 15{2}: 168-171 Translation of Radiobiologiia 15: 319-322, 1975.

4.2-5 Akhundtzade, I.M., and Muzaferova, R.Sh. 1976. Irradiation effect observed during the first, second and third years of vegetation of saffron [in Russian]. Tr. Inst. Genet. Sel. Akad. Nauk Az. SSR 8: 149-153. Bib. Ag. 41: 68834.

4.2-6 Al-Hamidi, A., El-Gengaihi, S.E., and Shalaby, A.S. 1977. Variability and heritability studies on the major agronomic characters of Capsicum frutescens red peppers grown in Egypt. Acta Agron. Acad. Sci. Hung. 26: 412-419.

4.2-7 Anand, I.J., and Rawat, D.S. 1978. Combining ability studies on Indian mustard (Brassica juncea Coss.). Z. Pflanzenzeucht. 81: 241-247.

4.2-8 Andringa, R. 1973. Poppy seed. Progress and yield prospects [in Dutch]. Bedrijfsontwikkeling 4: 369-373. FCA 27: 5290.

4.2-9 Arinshtein, A.I., Chemarin, N.G., and Kichanova, L.A. 1973. Determination of stimulating doses of gamma rays for irradiating coriander seeds [in Russian]. Tr. Vses. Nauchno-Issled. Inst. Efirnomaslichn. Kul't. 1973{6}: 4-9. HA 46: 3661.

4.2-10 Arinshtein, A.I., Romanenko, L.G., Nazrenko, L.G., and Zobenko, L.P. 1973. The results of breeding perennial essential oil plants (rose, lavender and sage) [in Russian]. Pages 363-373 in V.S. Pustovoit, ed. Selektsiya i Semenovodstvo Tekhnicheskikh Kul'tur, Kolos, Moscow, USSR. HA 44: 9935.

4.2-11 Arinshtein, A.N., Radchenko, N.M., and Chursa, M.E. 1972. Problems and prospects of breeding minor and new crops producing essential oils [in Russian]. Tr. Prikl. Bot. Genet. Sel. 47{2}: 165-170. PBA 43: 9017.

4.2-12 Arumugam, R., and Muthukhrishnan, C.R. 1979. Studies on the variability and association of characters in coriander. Prog. Hortic. 11{3}: 29-35. AGRICOLA.

4.2-13 Badwal, S.S., Singh, M., Labana, K.S., and Chaurasia, B.D. 1976. General versus specific combining ability in raya (Brassica juncea L. Czern and Coss). J. Res., Punjab Agric. Univ. 13: 319-323. PBA 48: 2607.

4.2-14 Barrios, E.P., and Mosokar, H.I. 1972. The inheritance of pod color and bearing habit in Capsicum frutescens L. J. Am. Soc. Hortic. Sci. 97: 65-66.

4.2-15 Barry, J.R., Davis, G.J., and Jeffries, G. 1980. Yield comparison of mechanically harvested red peppers for tabasco and for two selections of this cultivar. HortScience 15: 277 (Abstr.).

4.2-16 Bayai, L. 1973. Botanical and qualitative studies on ecotypes of fenugreek (Trigonella foenum-graecum L.) [in Hungarian]. Agrobotanika 15: 175-187.

4.2-17 Belyaeva, R.G., and Kovineva, V.M. 1972. A study of first-generation mint hybrids [in Russian]. Genetika 8{1}: 46-53. PBA 43: 1642.

4.2-18 Belyaeva, R.G., and Kovineva, V.M. 1972. A study of interspecies hybrids of mint in the first generation. Sov. Genet. (Engl. Transl.) 8: 34-39. Translation of Genetika 8{1}: 46-53.

4.2-19 Belyaeva, R.G., and Kovineva, V.M. 1974. Second generation of interspecies hybrids of Mentha L. Cytol. Genet. (Engl. Transl.) 8{4}: 27-30. Translation of Tsitol. Genet. 8{4}: 320-324, 1974. AGRICOLA.

4.2-20 Bergh, B.O., and Lippert, L.F. 1975. Inheritance of axillary shooting in Capsicum. Bot. Gaz. (Chicago) 136: 141-145.

4.2-21 Betlach, J. 1973. Combining capacity of vegetable paprika, as well as the heredity of cytoplasmic male sterility and its use in the production of hybrid seeds [in Hungarian]. Kert. Kut. Intez. Kozl. 3: 67-85. AGRICOLA.

4.2-22 Bezuneh, T. 1973. The collection and evaluation of Ethiopian pepper cultivars for use in the development of improved commercial types. Acta Hortic. 33: 143-147.

4.2-23 Bhowmik, G., and Devee, A. 1978. Induced polyploidy in coriander and fennel. Broteria, Ser. Trimest. Cienc. Nat. 48{3/4}: 75-81.

4.2-24 Biswas, A.K., and Chatterji, A.K. 1971. Studies on the induction of ploidy in some spices. Bull. Bot. Soc. Bengal 25: 19-21.

4.2-25 Biswas, A.K., and Bhattacharyya, N.K. 1975. Effects of some radiomimetic chemicals on plant chromosomes. Sci. Cult. 41: 129-130.

4.2-26 Bradu, B.L., Agarval, S.G., Vashist, V.N., and Atal, C.K. 1971. Comparative performance of diploid and tetraploid Mentha arvensis and evaluation of their oils. Planta Med. 20: 219-222.

4.2-27 Broertjes, C. 1978. Commercialized mutants of vegetatively propagated crops. Mutation Breeding Newsl. 1978{12}: 9. PBA 49: 7397.

4.2-28 Bugaenko, L.A., Reznikova, S.A., and Popovich, A.L. 1975. The method of interspecific hybridization in breeding peppermint [in Russian]. Tr. Prikl. Bot. Genet. Sel. 54{2}: 267-272. PBA 46: 4899.

4.2-29 Bugaenko, L.A., and Reznikova, S.A. 1974. Study of some economically useful characters in interspecific mint hybrids in breeding for frost resistance [in Russian]. Tr. Vses. Nauchno-Issled. Inst. Efirnomaslichn. Kul't. 7: 17-25. PBA 47: 6944.

4.2-30 Bugaenko, L.A., and Reznikova, S.A. 1974. Variation in chemical characters following self pollination of mint [in Russian]. Tr. Vses. Nauchno-Issled. Inst. Efirnomaslichn. Kul't. 7: 25-31. PBA 47: 6947.

4.2-31 Chaudhari, P.N., Zope, R.E., and Patil, N.Y. 1979. Inheritance of some qualitative characters in sesame (Sesamum indicum L.). J. Maharashtra Agric. Univ. 4: 137-139. AGRICOLA.

4.2-32 Chaudhari, P.N., Zope, R.E., Deokar, A.B., and Patil, N.Y. 1979. Heterosis in sesame. J. Maharashtra Agric. Univ. 4: 125-126. Bib.Ag. 44: 50149.

4.2-33 Chaudhary, P.N., Patil, G.D., and Zope, R.E. 1977. Genetic variability and correlation studies in sesame (Sesamum indicum L.). J. Maharashtra Agric. Univ. 2: 30-33. AGRICOLA.

4.2-34 Chauhan, S.V.S. 1977. Dual role of the tapetum. Curr. Sci. 46: 674-675.

4.2-35 Chaurasia, L.C., and Rathore, J.S. 1976. A preliminary report on radiation protective effects of 'rakta chandan' (Pterocarpus santalinus Linn.). Sci. Cult. 42: 484-485.

4.2-36 Chkhaidze, D.Kh., Tsikvadze, A.P., and Tabagari, R.D. 1974. Winter hardiness, yield and quality of plants established with local and Italian seeds of Grecian laurel [in Russian]. Subtrop. Kul't. 1974{3}: 133-135.

4.2-37 Chladek, M., and Patakova, D. 1972. New thyme hybrids (Thymus vulgaris L.) [in German]. Pharmazie 27: 113-115.

4.2-38 Clemente, G., and Caldera, P.G. 1975. Radiostimulation of seeds. The results of five years of study [in Italian]. Ital. Agric. 112: 103-115. HA 46: 2080.

4.2-39 Conti, S., and Ferraresi, A. 1974. Biometrical analysis of garlic clones and local cultivars in relation to plant breeding [in Italian]. Riv. Agron. 8: 47-57. HA 45: 3117.

4.2-40 Crowe, L.K. 1971. The polygenic control of outbreeding in Borago officinalis. Heredity 27: 111-118.

4.2-41 Czabajska, W., and Maciolowska-Ludowicz, E. 1976. Growth of the foxglove (Digitalis lanata Ehrh.). Part IV: Selection work to improve the value of the raw material [in Polish]. Herba Pol. 22: 38-44.

4.2-42 Dabral, K.C., and Holker, A.S. 1971. Variability in sesame with special reference to capsule characters. JNKVV Res. J. 5: 49-50. AGRICOLA.

4.2-43 Delwiche, P.A., and Williams, P.H. 1977. Genetic studies in Brassica nigra (L.) Koch. Cruciferae Newsletter 1977{2}: 39. PBA 51: 633.

4.2-44 Delwiche, P.A., and Williams, P.H. 1976. Identification of marker genes in Brassica nigra. Proc. Am. Phytopathol. Soc. 3: 234 (Abstr.). PBA 48: 11919

4.2-45 Deneva, T. 1975. Correlations between capsule number and morphine content in hybrids of Papaver somniferum L. [in Bulgarian]. Genet. Sel. 8: 419-423. AGRICOLA.

4.2-46 Denton, O.A., and Whittington, W.J. 1976. Varietal responses to temperature in swedes. Ann. Bot. (London) 40: 129-136.

4.2-47 Diachenko, I.P. 1974. Varietal purity and productivity of spearmint in the northern zone of the Ukrainian SSR [in Russian]. Tr. Vses. Nauchno-Issled. Inst. Efirnomaslichn. Kul't. 7: 32-33. AGRICOLA.

4.2-48 Dijkstra, H., and Speckmann, G.J. 1980. Autotetraploidy in caraway (Carum carvi L.) for the increase of the aetheric oil content of the seed. Euphytica 29: 89-96.

4.2-49 Divakar, N.G., and Rao, J.V.R.B. 1980. Screening of flowers of Jasminum species for indole. Indian Perfum. 24{1}: 46-47. CA 93: 245247.

4.2-50 Dixit, R.K. 1978. Combining ability analysis in sesame. Indian J. Agric. Sci. 48: 362-364.

4.2-51 Dixit, R.K. 1976. Heterosis and inbreeding depression in sesame. Indian J. Agric. Sci. 46: 514-517.

4.2-52 Dixit, R.K. 1976. Inheritance of yield and its components in sesame. Indian J. Agric. Sci. 46: 187-191.

4.2-53 Dnyansagar, V.R., and Jahagirdar, H.A. 1975. The effect of combination treatment of gamma rays and ethyl methane sulfonate on M-1 parameters in Foeniculum vulgare Mill. Proc. Indian Sci. Cong. 62 (pt. III Sect. VI): 120 (Abstr.).

4.2-54 Dnyansagar, V.R., and Jahagirdar, H.A. 1980. Induced mutants of Foeniculum vulgare in relation to seed and essential oil content. Pages 286-291 in S.S. Bir, ed. Recent researches in plant sciences. Kalyani Pub., New Delhi, India, 1980.

4.2-55 Dommee, B. 1976. Male sterility in Thymus vulgaris L.: ecological distribution in the French Mediterranean region [in French]. C.R. Hebd. Seances Acad. Sci. Ser. D 282: 65-68. SF 39: 4443.

4.2-56 Dommee, B. 1980. Allozymatic polymorphism, breeding system and degree of disturbance of environmental conditions in the gynodioecious species Thymus vulgaris L. Page 184 in Second international congress of systematic and evolutionary biology, July 17-24, Vancouver, B.C., 1980. University of British Columbia, Vancouver, B.C., Canada.

4.2-57 Dubey, R.N. 1976. Genetic divergence in Indian rai (Brassica juncea (L.) Czern and Coss). Indian J. Hered. 8{1/2}: 33-40. PBA 48: 3650.

4.2-58 Dudits, D., Hadlaczky, Gy., Fejer, O., Koncz, Cs., Lazar, G., Szabados, L., and Horvath, G. 1980. Approaches to parasexual gene transfer in higher plants. Eur. J. Cell Biol. 22{1}: 32 (Abstr.).

4.2-59 Eenink, A.H., and Dam, R. van. 1973. A rapid method of testing witloof crosses for (in)compatibility [in Dutch]. Zaadbelangen 27: 275-276. PBA 44: 4079.

4.2-60 Eenink, A.H. 1973. Breeding witloof chicory [in Dutch]. Zaadbelangen 27: 295-298. PBA 44: 5532.

4.2-61 Ekbote, A.P., and Tayyab, M.A. 1974. A correlation and path coefficient analysis of yield components in sesame (Sesamum indicum L.). PKV Res. J. 2: 116-121. AGRICOLA.

4.2-62 Elena-Rossello, J.A., Kheyr-Pour, A., and Valdeyron, G. 1976. Genetic structure and fecundation regime in Origanum vulgare L. Distribution of an enzymatic marker in two natural populations [in French]. C.R. Hebd. Seances Acad. Sci. Ser. D 283: 1587-1589.

4.2-63 Elena-Rossello, J.A. 1979. Identification of a species-specific enzyme marker in Thymus L. J. Hered. 70: 147-149.

4.2-64 El-Ballal, A.S. 1978. Stability of selection response for high essential oil yield in local caraway (Carum carvi L.). Acta Hortic. 1978{73}: 59-64.

4.2-65 El-Ballal, A.S.I. 1979. Genotype-environmental interaction in essential oil yield in the selected caraway type 1.4.36. Herba Hung. 18{3}: 155-166.

4.2-66 Erdei, I. 1974. Red pepper breeding at Szeged [in Hungarian]. Bull. Zoldsegtermesztesi Kut. Intez. 9: 123-128. AGRICOLA.

4.2-67 Ermakov, A.I., Yarosh, N.P., Kuznetsova, R.Ya., and Megorskaya, O.M. 1975. Genotypical characteristics of species and cultivars of Brassicaceae in relation to contents and quality of oil in seeds [in Russian]. Tr. Prikl. Bot. Genet. Sel. 55{1}: 159-174. FCA 30: 503.

4.2-68 Ezevaltovs'ky, A.K., and Polishchuk, V.S. 1975. Experiments on artificial hybridization of Majorana hortensis Moench. with Origanum vulgare L. [in Ukrainian]. Ukr. Bot. Zh. 32: 89-93. AGRICOLA.

4.2-69 Fedin, P., Zlatev, S., and Zlateva, M. 1976. The effect of pre-sowing treatment of dill seeds with gamma rays on the dynamics, quantity and quality of essential oil [in Bulgarian]. Rastenievud. Nauki 13{5}: 19-25. HA 47: 4885.

4.2-70 Franz, C., Holzl, J., and Vomel, A. 1978. Preliminary morphological and chemical characterization of some populations and varieties of Matricaria chamomilla L. Acta Hortic. 1978{73}: 109-114.

4.2-71 Futehally, S., and Vahidy, A.A. 1974. Variation among five varieties of coriander, Coriandrum sativum L. Pak. J. Bot. 6: 109-115.

4.2-72 Gallino, M., and Codignola, A. 1980. A mentha of the group "viridis": Mentha crispata Schrader. Botanical and chemical research [in Italian]. Essenze Deriv. Agrum. 50: 79-85. AGRICOLA.

4.2-73 Gertsuskiy, D.F., and Alekseyenko, L.V. 1971. Biological effect of protons and gamma-rays on watercress seeds. Radiobiologiya (Engl. Transl.) 11: 121-126. Translation of Radiobiologiia 11: 575-579, 1971.

4.2-74 Ghai, B.S., Gill, K.S., and Singh, J.R. 1972. Inheritance of some qualitative characters in chillies (Capsicum frutescens L.). J. Res. Punjab Agric. Univ. 9{1}: 7-11.

4.2-75 Ghisleni, P.L., and Quagliotti, L. 1971. Genetic improvement of peppers [in Italian]. Riv. Agron. 5: 193-199.

4.2-76 Gilly, G. 1978. Vegetative propagation and plant breeding for condiment plants grown in Provence. Acta Hortic. 1978{73}: 81-84.

4.2-77 Gill, K.S., Ghai, B.S., and Singh, J.R. 1973. Inheritance of amount of capsaicin in chilli (Capsicum frutescens L. and Capsicum annuum L.). Indian J. Agric. Sci. 43: 839-841. AGRICOLA.

4.2-78 Gill, L.S., Lawrence, B.M., and Morton, J.K. 1973. Variation in Mentha arvensis L. (Labiatae). I. The North American populations. Bot. J. Linn. Soc. 67: 213-232.

4.2-79 Glushchenko, N.N. 1972. Breeding methods and varieties of essential oil plants (Umbelliferae) [in Russian]. Pages 36-38 in P.V. Naumenko et al., eds. Mezhdunarodnyi kongress po efirnym maslam, 4th, Tiflis, 1968, [Materialy], v.2. Pishchevaya Promyshlennost', Moscow, USSR. PBA 44: 9160.

4.2-80 Gogina, E.E. 1974. The hybrid origin of the Moscow race of Thymus loevyanus [in Russian]. Byull. Gl. Bot. Sada 1974{92}: 20-27. PBA 45: 2438.

4.2-81 Gogina, E.E. 1973. Inherited female diecy in Thymus loevyanus Opiz [in Russian]. Byull. Gl. Bot. Sada 1973{88}: 54-59. PBA 45: 801.

4.2-82 Gogol, O.N., Bogonina, Z.S., and Kubrak, M.N. 1972. Chemical variability in seed descendants of Mentha species under self-pollination [in Russian]. Pages 40-55 in A.G. Nikolaev, ed. Khimicheskaia izmenchivost' rastenii. Shtiintsa, Kishinev, USSR. AGRICOLA.

4.2-83 Gostev, A.A., Kovalenko, N.P., Romanenko, L.G., and Zherebtsova, V.G. 1976. Utilization of cytoplasmic male sterility in clary (Salvia sclarea L.) and lavender (Lavandula officinalis Ch.) breeding. Cytol. Genet. (Engl. Transl.) 10{5}: 75-77. Translation of Tsitol. Genet. 10{5}: 462-464, 1976.

4.2-84 Gostev, A.A. 1975. Prospects of using induced autopolyploidy as a method of breeding agricultural plants of the Labiatae family [in Russian]. Tr. Prikl. Bot. Genet. Sel. 54{2}: 247-250. HA 46: 10655.

4.2-85 Gouyon, P.H., and Vernet, Ph. 1980. Study of the genetic variation in a population of Thymus vulgaris L. observations on the sexual and chemical polymorphisms, effects of a breeding regime [in French]. Acta Oecol. [Ser.]: Oecol. Plant. 1: 165-178.

4.2-86 Grinberg, E.G., and Klimova, A.I. 1980. Results of breeding work with shallot [in Russian]. Nauchno-Tekh. Byull. Sib. Nauchno-Issled. Inst. Rastenievod. i Selektsii 1980{4}: 24-29. PBA 51: 9236.

4.2-87 Grover, I.S., and Virk, G.S. 1979. Some observations on F2 and backcross plants derived from hybrids between Papaver somniferm L. and P. setigerum DC. Broteria, Ser. Trimest. Cienc. Nat. 48{1/4}: 7-11.

4.2-88 Grover, I.S., Mangat, G.S., and Malik, C.P. 1974. Cytogenetical evolution within some Papaver species. Pages 244-248 in P. Kachroo, ed. Advancing frontiers in cytogenetics in evolution and improvement of plants. Proceedings of national seminar. Kashmir, India, Oct. 14-19, 1972. Hindustan Publishing Corp., Delhi, India.

4.2-89 Grover, I.S. 1979. Possibilities of exchange of genes in opium poppy via triploid hybrids. Planta Med. 36: 229 (Abstr.).

4.2-90 Gupta, R. 1971. Isolation of a new cultivar of European dill (Anethum graveolens Linn.) in India. Curr. Sci. 40: 141-142.

4.2-91 Habib, A.F., and Mensinkai, S.W. 1971. Inheritance of stem colour at seedling stage in an intervarietal cross of Capsicum frutescens L. Mysore J. Agric. Sci. 5: 340. AGRICOLA.

4.2-92 Hack, H.R.B. 1976. Components of error in field experiments with cotton, groundnuts, kenaf and sesame in the central Sudan rainlands. I. Field and statistical methods; increasing precision by replication and its cost. Exp. Agric. 12: 209-224.

4.2-93 Hack, H.R.B. 1976. Components of error in field experiments with cotton, groundnuts, kenaf and sesame in the central Sudan rainlands. II. Variation in plant measurements through the season and a discussion of surface drainage as a source of variation. Exp. Agric. 12: 225-240.

4.2-94 Hall, O., and Nyman, U. 1975. An interesting line of opium poppy [in Swedish]. Svensk Frotidning 44{10}: 131-132. AGRICOLA.

4.2-95 Hanelt, P., and Hammer, K. 1977. Report of an expedition to Poland in 1976 to collect local strains of cultivated plants [in German]. Kulturpflanze 25: 33-44. PBA 48: 5097.

4.2-96 Hanumanthappa, H.S., and Seetharam, A. 1974. Colchicine induced mixoploid in coriander. Curr. Sci. 43: 496.

4.2-97 Harn, C. 1978. Surveys on the possibilities of ginseng breeding [in Korean]. Yuk Jong Hak Hoi Ji 1{1}: 66-74. PBA 51: 4495.

4.2-98 Hefendehl, F.W., and Murray, M.J. 1976. Genetic aspects of the biosynthesis of natural odors. Lloydia 39: 39-52.

4.2-99 Hefendehl, F.W. 1975. Genetic aspects of the biosynthesis of natural odors. Lloydia 38: 532 (Abstr.).

4.2-100   Hefendehl,   F.W.   1977.   Monoterpene   composition   of   a
carvone-containing polyploid strain of Mentha longifolia (L.) Huds.
Herba Hung. 16{1}: 39-43. HA 49: 1450.

4.2-101 Hefendehl, F.W., and Murray, M.J. 1976. Genetic aspects of the
biosynthesis of natural odors. Lloydia 39: 39-52.

4.2-102 Hefendehl, F.W. 1973. The use of genetic experiments to
elucidate the biosynthesis of essential oils [in German]. Planta Med.
23: 301-307. HA 44: 1801.

4.2-103 Hefendehl, F.W., and Murray, M.J. 1972. Changes in monoterpene
composition in Mentha aquatica produced by gene substitution.
Phytochemistry 11: 189-195.

4.2-104 Heiser, C.B., Jr. 1974. A spontaneous hybrid of Capsicum annuum
var. minimum and Capsicum frutescens. Proc. Indiana Acad. Sci. 83:
397-398 (Abstr.).

4.2-105 Hendriks, H. 1975. Crossing experiments between some chemotypes
of Mentha longifolia (L.) Hudson and Mentha suaveolens Ehrh. Lloydia
38: 533 (Abstr.).

4.2-106 Hendriks, H., Os, F.H.L. van, and Feenstra, W.J. 1976. Crossing
experiments between some chemotypes of Mentha longifolia and Mentha
suaveolens. Planta Med. 30: 154-162. PBA 48: 3970.

4.2-107 Hendriks, H., and Os, F.H.L. van. 1972. The heredity of the
essential oil composition in artificial hybrids between Mentha
rotundifolia and Mentha longifolia. Planta Med. 21: 421-425. HA 43:
3033.

4.2-108 Heyne, F.W. 1977. Analysis of unreduced gametes in the
Brassiceae by crosses between species and ploidy levels. Z.
Pflanzenzucht. 78: 13-30.

4.2-109 Hinata, K., Konno, N., and Mizushima, U. 1974. Interspecific
crossability in the tribe Brassiceae with special reference to the
self-incompatibility. Tohoku J. Agric. Res. 25{2}: 58-66.

4.2-110 Hlavackova, Z. 1978. Application of the three and six-parameter
test to the genetical analysis of seed weight per plant and plant
height in seed poppy [in Czech]. Sb. UVTIZ Genet. Slechteni 14:
153-160. PBA 48: 10865.

4.2-111 Hlavackova, Z. 1972. A study of the inheritance of plant height
and seed weight in poppy (Papaver somniferum L.) [in Czech]. Sb. UVTIZ
Genet. Slechteni 8: 87-94.

4.2-112 Hlavackova, Z. 1972. Investigation of the inheritance of plant
height and seed weight in poppy (Papaver somniferum L.) [in Czech].
Sb. UVTIZ Genet. Slechteni 8: 87-93. AGRICOLA.

4.2-113 Hlavackova, Z. 1973. An investigation of the inheritance of
morphine content and oil content in seed of Papaver somniferum [in
Czech]. Sb. UVTIZ Genet. Slechteni 9: 39-44. PBA 44: 1919.

4.2-114 Honma, S., and Lacy, M.L. 1980. Hybridization between pascal
celery and parsley. Euphytica 29: 801-805.

4.2-115 Hore, A. 1979. Improvement of minor (Umbelliferous) spices in India. Econ. Bot. 33: 290-297.

4.2-116 Hore, A. 1977. Study of the structure and behaviour of chromosomes of different agricultural strains of Coriandrum sativum (coriander). Caryologia 30: 445-459.

4.2-117 Hore, A. 1979. Improvement of minor (Umbelliferous) spices in India. Econ. Bot. 33{3}: 290-297.

4.2-118 Horner, C.E., and Melouk, H.A. 1975. Proposal for mutation breeding for improved oil yield in wilt-resistant Mitcham-type peppermints. Pro c. Annu. Meet. Oreg. Essent. Oil Grow. League 26: 4-8.

4.2-119 Huyskes, J.A. 1972. A new method of breeding witloof chicory [in French]. Ann. Amelior. Plant. 22: 301-309. HA 43: 5907.

4.2-120 Ilieva, St. 1979. New Salvia sclarea L. obtained by hybridization. Planta Med. 36: 243 (Abstr.).

4.2-121 Ilieva, S., Krusheva, R., and Mateeva, D. 1977. Morphological nature of some flower modifications in the opium poppy (Papaver somniferum L.) mutant form [in Bulgarian]. Rastenievud. Nauki 14{9}: 60-66. AGRICOLA.

4.2-122 Ilieva, S., Mekhandzhiev, A., Moinova, K., and Mateeva, D. 1972. Biological and biochemical changes in Salvia sclarea caused by ionizing radiation [in Russian]. Dokl. Sel'skokhoz. Akad. Sofia 5{2}: 127-134. CA 78: 25841.

4.2-123 Ivanova, R.M., and Brykin, A.I. 1975. Results of breeding and seed-production work with oil-bearing poppy in Moscow province [in Russian]. Sb. Nauchn. Rab. Vses. Nauchno-Issled. Inst. Lek. Rast. 1975{7}: 184-189. PBA 47: 4504.

4.2-124 Ivanova, R.M. 1975. Development of induced mutations in opium poppy [in Russian]. S-kh. Biol. 10: 828-831.

4.2-125 Jatasra, D.S., and Lodhi, G.P. 1980. Crossing technique in fenugreek (Trigonella foenum graecum). Forage Res. 6: 231-233.

4.2-126 Jonsson, R., and Loof, B. 1973. Interspecific hybridization between Papaver somniferum L. and Papaver orientale L. [in Swedish]. Sver. Utsadesfoeren. Tidskr. 83: 248-251. AGRICOLA.

4.2-127 Kaicker, U.S., and Saini, H.C. 1980. Genotypic and phenotypic variability in opium poppy. Indian J. Agric. Sci. 50: 331-333.

4.2-128 Kaicker, U.S., Singh, B., Balakrishnan, K.A., Singh, H.P., and Choudhury, B. 1975. Correlation and path coefficient analysis of opium poppy. Genet. Agrar. 29: 357-370. AGRICOLA.

4.2-129 Kak, S.N., and Kaul, B.L. 1977. X-ray induced creeper mutant in Mentha citrata Ehrh. Indian J. Exp. Biol. 15: 394-395.

4.2-130 Kak, S.N., and Kaul, B.L. 1977. Mutation breeding of some novel chemotypes in Japanese mint, Mentha arvensis L. Mutation Breeding Newsl. 1977{10}: 10-11. PBA 48: 6126.

4.2-131 Kak, S.N., and Kaul, B.L. 1980. Radiation induced useful mutants of Japanese mint (Mentha arvensis L.). Z. Pflanzenzeucht. 85: 170-174.

4.2-132 Kang, Y.H., and Lee, J.S. 1977. Plant nutritional and physiological studies of Korean ginseng. The preliminary experiments of the obstacle factor of ginseng consecutive cultivation, on the view of growth inhibitor exudated from ginseng roots [in Korean] Hakurwon Nonmunjip Cha'yon Kwahak P'yon 16: 27-61. AGRICOLA.

4.2-133 Kapelev, I.G., and Akimov, Yu.A. 1980. Intraspecific chemical variability of Mentha longifolia [in Russian]. Rastit. Resur. 16: 436-441. HA 51: 4873.

4.2-134 Karasawa, D., and Shimizu, S. 1978. Mentha candicans, a new chemical strain of section Spicatae, containing trans-sabinene hydrate as the principal component of essential oil. Agric. Biol. Chem. 42: 433-437.

4.2-135 Kasahara, J., Nakamura, T., and Yoneyama, Y. 1973. Grafting induced mutation in cayenne peppers [in Japanese]. Ikushugaku Saikin No Shinpo (Latest Adv. Breed) Nihon Ikushu Gakkai 13: 73-89. AGRICOLA.

4.2-136 Kasano, H., Furuyama, S., Kimura, M., and Inagaki, H. 1976. Breeding the new mint variety Wasenami [in Japanese]. Hokkaido Nogyo Shikenjo Kenkyu Hokoku 1976{113}: 45-66. PBA 47: 4865.

4.2-137 Kaul, B.L., and Kak, S.N. 1974. Improvement of Mentha arvensis through induced mutations. Pages 189-195 in P. Kachroo, ed. Advancing frontiers in cytogenetics in evolution and improvement of plants. Proceedings of national seminar. Kashmir, India, Oct. 14-19, 1972. Hindustan Publishing Corp., Delhi, India.

4.2-138 Kaul, B.L., Tandon, V., and Choudhary, D.K. 1979. Cytogenetic studies in Papaver somniferum L. Proc. Indian Acad. Sci. Sect. B 88: 321-325.

4.2-139 Kaushal, P.K., Shrivas, S.R., and Goswami, U. 1980. Correlation and path analysis of yield components in branched types of sesame (Sesamum indicum Linn.). JNKVV Res. J. 11: 44-47.

4.2-140 Keshav Ram, and Saini, S.S. 1971. Compatibility studies in some Capsicum species. Himachal J. Agric. Res. 1{1}: 34-39.

4.2-141 Khan, A.A., and Ahmad, A. 1973. Comparative studies on morphological characters, yield of opium and seeds in different varieties of Papaver somniferum cultivated at Peshawar. Pak. J. For. 23: 187-201.

4.2-142 Khidir, M.O. 1972. Natural cross-fertilization in sesame under Sudan conditions. Exp. Agric. 8: 55-59.

4.2-143 Khidir, M.O., and Ali, M.A. 1974. Induced autopolyploidy in sesame (Sesamum orientale L.). Acta Agron. Acad. Sci. Hung. 23: 459-468.

4.2-144 Khidir, M.O., and Ali, M.A. 1971. Genetic studies in sesame. I. Inheritance of seed coat colour. Acta Agron. Acad. Sci. Hung. 20: 79-84.

4.2-145 Kim, Y.-C., and Lee, W.-S. 1977. Agronomic characteristics and correlations in ecotypes of garlic [in Korean]. Hanguk Wonye Hakhoe Chi 18: 36-39. HA 48: 10455.

4.2-146 Kiper, M., Herzfeld, F., and Richter, G. 1979. The expression of a plant genome of the Petroselinum sativum, parsley, in hnRNA and mRNA. Nucleic Acids Res. 6: 1961-1978.

4.2-147 Kiskeri, Mrs. R., Morasz, S., and Bocsa, I. 1977. Experiments to produce tetraploid poppy (Papaver somniferum L.) [in Hungarian]. Novenytermeles 26: 347-354. AGRICOLA.

4.2-148 Kobayashi, T. 1977. Breeding for high yield sesame by induced mutations. Pages 9-32 - 9-35 in Plant breeding papers; 3rd international congress of the Society for the Advancement of Breeding Researches in Asia and Oceania (SABRAO), in association with Australian Plant Breeding Conference, Canberra, Australia, February, 1977, v.2. AGRICOLA.

4.2-149 Konvicka, O. 1973. Causes of sterility in Allium sativum L. [in German]. Biol. Plant. 15: 144-149.

4.2-150 Korneva, E.I. 1971. Improvement of medicinal plants by hybridization [in Russian]. S-kh. Biol. 6: 616-618.

4.2-151 Kotukov, G.N. 1973. Interspecific hybridization in the genus Digitalis [in Russian]. Tsitol. Genet. 7: 361-364.

4.2-152 Koul, A.K., and Gohil, R.N. 1970. Causes averting sexual reproduction in Allium sativum Linn. Cytologia 35: 197-202.

4.2-153 Koul, A.K., Gohil, R.N., Sharma, M.C., and Kapoor, H.K. 1972. Genetic stocks of Kashmir Papavers, I. Plant morphology, chromosome numbers and meiosis. Nucleus (Calcutta) 15: 117-123.

4.2-154 Kovalenko, N.P. 1975. The problem of breeding sterility-maintaining forms of Salvia sclarea and their sterile analogues [in Russian]. Tr. Vses. Nauchno-Issled. Inst. Efirnomaslichn. Kul't. 1975{8}: 37-40. PBA 48: 7195.

4.2-155 Kravchenko, Yu.S., and Bronshtein, B.D. 1971. Variability of lavender seed-progeny plants [in Russian]. Tr. Vses. Nauchno-Issled. Inst. Efirnomaslichn. Kul't. {3}: 7-11. CA 80: 30589.

4.2-156 Kravets, T.I., and Tanasienko, F.S. 1975. Changes in the essential oil yield and composition by leaf tiers in the peppermint cultivar Prilukskaya-6 [in Russian]. Tr. Vses. Nauchno-Issled. Inst. Efirnomaslichn. Kul't. 1975{8}: 77-81. HA 47: 8759.

4.2-157 Kryukova, L.M., and Abdrakhmanov, O.K. 1973. X-rays during the cultivation of licorice [in Russian]. Vestn. Sel'skhkhoz. Nauki (Moscow) 1973{8}: 28-32. CA 79: 123124.

4.2-158 Kuchuloriya, T.L. 1972. The results of (essential-oil) geranium breeding [in Russian]. Pages 88-90 in P.V. Naumenko et al., eds. Mezhdunarodnyi kongress po efirnym maslam, 4th, Tiflis, 1968, [Materialy], v. 2. Pishchevaya Promyshlennost', Moscow, USSR. HA 44: 3437.

4.2-159 Kulina, E.N. 1973. Breeding Indian mustard [in Russian]. Nauchn. Tr. Nauchno-Issled. Inst. Sel'sk. Khoz. Yugo-Vostoka 1973{33}: 76-78. PBA 45: 9223.

4.2-160 Kumar, C.R. 1977. Floral biology and breeding systems in Bulgarian coriander (Coriandrum sativum L.). New Bot. 4{1/4}: 131-135. AGRICOLA.

4.2-161 Kvachadze, M.B. 1973. The genetics of some traits of the cayenne pepper, Capsicum annuum [in Russian]. Soobshch. Akad. Nauk Gruz. SSR 70: 697-699.

4.2-162 Lammerink, J., and Manning, T.D.R. 1973. Peppermint oil composition and yield, flowering time, and morphological characters of four naturalized South Island clones and the Mitcham strain of Mentha piperita. N.Z. J. Agric. Res. 16: 181-184.

4.2-163 Lawrence, B.M., Hogg, J.W., Terhune, S.J., Morton, J.K., and Gill, L.S. 1972. Terpenoids of some Mentha hybrids from Canada. Phytochemistry 11: 2638-2639.

4.2-164 Lee, J.I., Min, K.S., and Kwon, B.S. 1976. Breeding for improvement of fatty acid composition in rape seed, Brassica napus L. VIII. Specific and varietal differences in oil content and fatty acid composition of cruciferous crops [in Korean]. Res. Rep. Off. Rural Dev. (Crops) 18: 209-217.

4.2-165 Lee, J.I., and Kang, C.W. 1980. Breeding of sesame (Sesamum indicum L.) for oil quality improvement. 1. Study on the evaluation of oil quality and the differences of fatty acid composition between varieties in sesame. Hanguk Changmul Hakhoe Chi 25{1}: 54-65.

4.2-166 Levandovskaya, L.I. 1979. Collection of condiment root crops as initial material for different breeding objectives [in Russian]. Byull. Vses. Inst. Rastenievod. 1979{90}: 29-32. PBA 51: 9209.

4.2-167 Lichter, R. 1973. Population genetics. Fortschr. Bot. 35: 233-244.

4.2-168 Lincoln, D.E., and Murray, M.J. 1978. Monogenic basis for reduction of (+)-pulegone to (-)-menthone in Mentha oil biogenesis. Phytochemistry 17: 1727-1730.

4.2-169 Lincoln, D.E., Marble, P.M., Cramer, F.J., and Murray, M.J. 1971. Genetic basis for high limonene-cineole content of exceptional Mentha citrata hybrids. Theor. Appl. Genet. 41: 365-370.

4.2-170 Logachev, S.A. 1973. Development of coriander as a raw material in the central chernozem zone and in the Volga area [in Russian]. Maslo. -Zhir. Prom-st. 1973{3}: 29-31.

4.2-171 Lorincz, Gy. 1978. Some results of breeding in poppy and other drug plants in the Soviet Union [in Hungarian]. Herba Hung. 17{1}: 109-111. PBA 49: 7392.

4.2-172 Lorincz, K. 1976. Some results in poppy (Papaver somniferum L.) breeding [in Russian]. Herba Hung. 15{1}: 63-68.

4.2-173 Louant, B.-P., Bochkoltz-Maufroid, C., and Plumier, W. 1978. New outlook for breeding witloof chicory (Cichorium intybus L.) [in French]. Rev Agric. (Brussels) 31: 5-19. PBA 48: 11054.

4.2-174 Lutkov, A.N., Belyaeva, R.G., Shugaeva, E.V., Bulgakov, S.V., and Kovineva, V.M. 1972. Allopolyploidy and interspecific hybridization in breeding mint for menthol [in Russian]. Pages 94-97 in P.V. Naumenko et al., eds. Mezhdunarodnyi kongress po efirnym maslam, 4th, Tiflis, 1968, [Materialy], v. 2. Pischevaya Promyshlennost', Moscow, USSR. PBA 46: 5903.

4.2-175 Mackenzie, S.L. 1973. Cultivar differences in proteins of Oriental mustard (Brassica juncea (L.) Coss.). J. Am. Oil Chem. Soc. 50: 411-414.

4.2-176 Madjarova, D., Georgiev, G., Benbassat, E., Boubarova, M., and Chavdarov, I. 1971. New plant forms, obtained by parsley (Petroselinum hortense Hoffm.) and celery (Apium graveolens L.) hybridization. Dokl. S-kh. Akad. (Sofia) 4: 261-267. AGRICOLA.

4.2-177 Madjarova, D., Bubarova, M., and Hristova, I. 1979. The biochemical nature of forms obtained by the remote hybridization between genera Apium L. and Petroselinum L. Planta Med. 36: 242 (Abstr.).

4.2-178 Madjarova, D., and Hristova, I. 1979. The biochemical nature of forms obtained by the remote hybridization between genera - Apium, Petroselinum. II. Essential oils. Herba Hung. 18{3}: 185-195.

4.2-179 Madjarova, D.J., and Bubarova, M.G. 1978. New forms obtained by hybridization of Apium graveolens and Petroselinum hortense. Acta Hortic. 1978{73}: 65-72.

4.2-180 Madzharova, D., Georgiev, G., Benbasat, E., Bubarova, M., and Chavdarov, I. 1971. New plant forms, obtained by parsley (Petroselinum hortense) and celery (Apium graveolens) hybridization. Dokl. Akad. Sel'skokhz. Nauk Bolg. 4: 261-267. CA 77: 58982.

4.2-181 Madzharova, D., Bubarova, M., and Genchev, S. 1978. Some anatomical-morphological and biochemical aspects of Apium x Petroselinum hybrids [in Bulgarian]. Gradinar. Lozar. Nauka 15{1}: 59-65. CA 90: 83716.

4.2-182 Malik, C.P., and Grover, I.S. 1971. Failure of chromosome pairing in opium poppy (Papaver somniferum). Z. Biol. 116: 472-480.

4.2-183 Markus, F. 1974. Red pepper breeding at Kalocsa [in Hungarian]. Bull. Zoldsegtermesztesi Kut. Intez. 9: 115-121. AGRICOLA.

4.2-184 Mashanova, N.S. 1972. Changeability of chemical characters in lavender and their inheritance by distan [sic] hybrids. An. Acad. Bras. Cienc. 44(Suppl.): 219 (Abstr.).

4.2-185 Mashanov, V.I. 1972. New varieties of essential oil crops bred in the Nikita Botanical Gardens and methods of their obtaining. An. Acad. Bras. Cienc. 44(Suppl.): 22-23.

4.2-186 Maskunova, V.A., and Romanenko, L.G. 1978. Studies on winter hardiness of lavender clones on the northern foothills of the Caucasus [in Russian]. Tr. Vses. Nauchno-Issled. Inst. Efirnomaslichn. Kul't. 1978{11}: 22-27. HA 50: 7911.

4.2-187 Mathur, S.C., Mathur, P.K., and Chandola, R.P. 1971. Genetic variability in cumin (Cuminum cyminum L.). Indian J. Agric. Sci. 41: 513-515. AGRICOLA.

4.2-188 Mathur, S.C., Answer, M., and Bhargava, P.D. 1971. Studies on splitting of phenotypic and genotypic complexes and their correlations in coriander (Coriandrum sativum L.). Rajasthan J. Agric. Sci. 2: 63-71.

4.2-189 May, D.S. 1975. Genetic and physiological adaptation of the Hill reaction in altitudinally-diverse populations of Taraxacum. Photosynthetica 9: 293-298.

4.2-190 Mazhar, H. Nadvi, and Wahid, M. 1979. Studies on the varietal suitability of garlic (Allium sativum L.) for irradiation preservation. Page 26C in Proceedings of XXVI/XXVII Pakistan science conference, Lahore, 1979. Part III. Abstracts of papers. Pakistan Association for the Advancement of Science, Lahore, Pakistan. PBA 51: 6612.

4.2-191 Mazzani, B., Gonzalez, V., and Martinez, A. 1971. Gameticidal effects of chemical preparations on sesame plants [in Spanish]. Agron. Trop. (Maracay, Venez.) 21: 39-47. AGRICOLA.

4.2-192 Medvedev, P.F. 1974. Duration of economic utilization and the yielding capacity of five Symphytum L. species [in Russian]. Rastit. Resur. 10: 598-605.

4.2-193 Michellon, R. 1978. Rose geranium in Reunion: intensifying growing and the possibilities of genetic improvement [in French]. Agron. Trop. 33: 80-89. HA 48: 9287.

4.2-194 Michna, M. 1971. A breeding research on red pepper (Capsicum annuum L.) [in Polish]. Hodowla Rosl. Aklim. Nasienn. 15: 275-299. AGRICOLA.

4.2-195 Mihalea, A., and Silva, F. 1972. Trials on crossing Digitalis species [in Hungarian]. Herba Hung. 11: 29-37. HA 43: 6294.

4.2-196 Mihalea, A. 1971. Breeding foxgloves (Digitalis purpurea L.) [in Romanian]. Probleme di Genetica si Aplicata 3: 191-237. PBA 43: 8124.

4.2-197 Mihalea, A. 1975. Results and considerations on the improvement of the lavender (Lavandula angustifolia Mill.) [in Romanian]. An. Inst. Cercet. Cereale Plante Teh. Fundulea Acad. Stiinte Agric. Silvice Ser. C 40: 369-376. AGRICOLA.

4.2-198 Mital, S.P., Bhagat, N.R., and Maheshwari, M.L. 1976. Improvement of celery (Apium graveolens L.). Indian Perfum. 20{1B}: 9-13. PBA 50: 3334.

4.2-199 Mital, S.P., Issar, S.C., Kidwai, M.A., and Saxena, D.B. 1972. Improvement in Japanese mint (Mentha arvensis L. var. piperascens Holmes) through gamma-irradiation. Indian J. Agric. Sci. 42: 550-553.

4.2-200 Miyazawa, Y., and Hagiwara, H. 1972. Studies on the interspecific hybrid of ginseng plant (Panax L.). 1. Characters of hybrid F1 [in Japanese]. Bull. Nagano Hort. Exp. Stn. 10: 32-42. AGRICOLA.

4.2-201 Moelgaard, P., Skjoth, L., and Kaufmann, U. 1980. A genetic investigation of the esters of caffeic acid with rhamnose or glucose in leaves of Plantago major. Biochem. Syst. Ecol. 8: 277-278. AGRICOLA.

4.2-202 Moravec, J., Kvasnicka, S., and Velicka, O. 1974. Correlations between bulb weight and other characters in cultivars of bolting garlic (Allium sativum ssp. sagittatum) [in Czech]. Bulletin, Vyzkumny Ustav Zelinarsky Olomouc 1974{18}: 15-23. HA 46: 4464.

4.2-203 Moravec, J., Kvasnicka, S., and Jelinek, J. 1973. Breeding the shallot variety Milka (Allium cepa var. ascalonicum (L) Backer 1951) [in Czech]. Genet. Slechteni 9: 141-148. PBA 44: 1144.

4.2-204 Morkunas, A.V., Stankiavichene, N.A., Dagite, S.Iu., Aliukonite, A.A., and Morkunene, M.P. 1973. Investigation of the quantitative composition of essential oils of some varieties of Mentha piperita [in Russian]. Pages 225-228 in K. Jankevicius, ed. Poleznye rasteniia Pribaltiishikh respublick i Belorussii. Nauchnaia konferentsiia po issledovaniiu i obogashcheni, lu rastitel'nykh resurov pribaltiiskikh respublik i Belorussii, 2nd, Vilna, 1973. AGRICOLA.

4.2-205 Muhammad, V., Chandrasekharan, N.R., Sivasubramanian, P., Sundaram, N., Rangaswamy, M., and Sundaresan, N. 1973. KRR 2, a white seeded Sesamum strain. Farm Fact. 7{6}: 13-14. AGRICOLA.

4.2-206 Muralidharan, V., Ramachandran, T.K., and Palaniswami, M.S. 1977. Varietal tolerance in Gingelly sesame to shoot webber (Antigasytra catalunalis D.) and aphid (Aphis gossypii G.). Agric. Agro-Ind. J. 10{12}: 17-18. AGRICOLA.

4.2-207 Murray, M.J., Marble, P.M., and Lincoln, D.E. 1971. Inter-subgeneric hybrids in the genus Mentha. J. Hered. 62: 363-366.

4.2-208 Murray, M.J., and Lincoln, D.E. 1972. Oil composition of Mentha aquatica-M. longifolia F1 hybrids and M. dumetorum. Euphytic 21: 337-343.

4.2-209 Murray, M.J., Lincoln, D.E., and Marble, P.M. 1972. Oil composition of Mentha aquatica X M. spicata F1 hybrids in relation to the origin of X M. piperita. Can. J. Genet. Cytol. 14: 13-29.

4.2-210 Murray, M.J., and Hefendehl, F.W. 1972. Changes in monoterpene composition of Mentha aquatica produced by gene substition from M. arvensis. Phytochemistry 11: 2469-2474.

4.2-211 Murray, M.J., and Hefendehl, F.W. 1973. Changes in monoterpene composition of Mentha aquatica produced by gene substitution from a high limonene strain of M. citrata. Phytochemistry 12: 1875-1880.

4.2-212 Murray, M.J., Lincoln, D.E., and Hefendehl, F.W. 1980. Chemogenetic evidence supporting multiple allele control of the biosynthesis of (-)-menthone and (+)-isomenthone stereoisomers in Mentha species. Phytochemistry 19: 2103-2110.

4.2-213 Murray, M.J. 1971. Additional observations on mutation breeding to obtain Verticillium-resistant strains of peppermint. Pages 171-195 in Mutation Breeding for Disease Resistance (IAEA Panel Proceedings Series). Unipub, Inc., New York, NY.

4.2-214 Murray, M.J. 1972. Mutation breeding for disease resistance in vegetatively propagated essential oil crops. An. Acad. Bras. Cienc. 44(Suppl.): 73-75.

4.2-215 Murray, M.J. 1972. Genetic observation on Mentha oil biogenesis. An. Acad. Bras. Cienc. 44(Suppl.): 24-30.

4.2-216 Murty, D.S. 1975. Heterosis, combining ability and reciprocal effects for agronomic and chemical characters in sesame. Theor. Appl. Genet. 45: 294-299.

4.2-217 Murty, D.S., and Hashim, M. 1974. Diallel analysis in sesame. Indian J. Genet. Plant Breed. 34A: 703-712. AGRICOLA.

4.2-218 Murty, D.S., and Hashim, M. 1973. Inheritance of oil and protein content in a diallel cross of sesame (Sesamum indicum L.). Can. J. Genet. Cytol. 15: 177-184.

4.2-219 Murty, G.S.S. 1979. Heterosis in inter-mutant hybrids of Sesamum indicum L. Curr. Sci. 48: 825-827.

4.2-220 Murty, G.S.S. 1980. Radiation induced small capsule mutant in sesame (Sesamum indicum L.). Curr. Sci. 49: 717-719.

4.2-221 Murugesan, M., Dhamu, K.P., and Raj, A.A. 1979. Genetic variability in some quantitative characters of Sesamum. Madras Agric. J. 66: 366-369.

4.2-223 Murugesan, M., Dhamu, K.P., and Raj, A.A. 1979. Genotypic, phenotypic correlations and path analysis of some quantitative characters in Sesamum. Madras Agric. J. 66: 631-634.

4.2-222 Mustiatse, G.I. 1972. Production tests of Mentha with high-menthol content. I. [in Russian]. Pages 124-128 in A.G. Nikolaev, ed. Khimicheskaia izmenchivost rastenii. Shtiintsa, Kishinev, USSR. AGRICOLA

4.2-224 Nano, G.M., Sacco, T., Calvino, R., Frattini, C., Fundaro, A., and Martelli, A. 1972. Research on the minor elements of the essential oils from Mentha viridis (L) L. cultivar X Lavanduliodora sacco new cultivar produced in Brazil [in Italian]. Essenze Deriv. Agrum. 42: 333-339. AGRICOLA.

4.2-225 Naphade, D.S., and Kolte, N.N. 1974/1975. Interrelationship and path analysis for some characters contributing to yield of sesame (Sesamum indicum L.). Mag. Univ. Nagpur Coll. Agric. 47: 32-35. AGRICOLA.

4.2-226 Naragund, V.R., Krishnan, R., and Vasantha Kumar, T. 1979. Inheritance of pigmentation in Ocimum basilicum Linn. Curr. Sci. 48: 822-823.

4.2-227 Narain, A., and Prakash, S. 1972. Investigations on the artificial synthesis of amphidiploids of Brassica tournefortii Gouan with the other elementary species of Brassica. I. Genomic relationships. Genetica (The Hague) 43: 90-97.

4.2-228 Natarajan, S.T., Sathiamoorthy, M.R., and Ramachandran, T.K. 1977. A note on character association in sesame (Sesamum indicum Linn). Agric. Agro-ind. J. 10{9}: 13-14.

4.2-229 Nayar, G.G. 1977. Induced mutations in mustard (Brassica juncea). Mutation Breeding Newsletter 1977{10}: 9-10. PBA 48: 5278.

4.2-230 Nikolaev, A.G., Dizdar', A.V., Peplyakh, E.M., Popov, Yu.S., and Chelovskaya, L.N. 1977. Inheritance of monoterpenoid composition in interspecific crosses of mint and carrot [in Russian]. Izv. Akad. Nauk Mold. SSR Ser. Biol. Khim. Nauk 1977{6}: 16-21.

4.2-231 Novak, F.J., and Havranek, P. 1975. Attempts to overcome the sterility of common garlic (Allium sativum L.). Biol. Plant. 17: 376-379.

4.2-232 Nyman, U. 1980. Alkaloid content in the F1 and F2 generations obtained from crosses between different chemoprovarieties in Papaver somniferum L. Hereditas 93: 115-119.

4.2-233 Nyman, U., and Hall, O. 1974. Breeding oil poppy (Papaver somniferum) for low content of morphine. Hereditas 76: 49-54.

4.2-234 Nyman, U., and Hansson, B. 1978. Morphine content variation in Papaver somniferum L. as affected by the presence of some isoquinoline alkaloids. Hereditas 88: 17-26.

4.2-235 Nyman, U. 1978. Selection for high thebaine/low morphine content in Papaver somniferum L. Hereditas 89: 43-50.

4.2-236 Nyman, U. 1980. Papaver somniferum L. - Breeding for a modified morphinane alkaloid pattern. Acta Pharm. Suec. 17: 166.

4.2-237 Ohno, T., Kinoshita, K., and Komine, T. 1977. On the productivity of the disease resistant strains in opium poppy (Papaver somniferum L.) [in Japanese]. Eisei Shikenjo Hokoku 95: 30-33. RPP 57: 3555.

4.2-238 Ohta, Y. 1973. Identification of cytoplasms of independent origin causing male sterility in red peppers (Capsicum annuum L.). Rep. Kihara Inst. Biol. Res. 24: 105-106. AGRICOLA.

4.2-239 Olivieri, A.M. 1972. Identifying some genetic parameters in a cross of Cichorium intybus L. [in Italian]. Riv. Agron. 6: 171-174. PBA 43: 8288.

4.2-240 Olivieri, A.M. 1972. Considerations on crossing frequency in populations of Cichorium [in Italian]. Riv. Agron. 6: 235-241. PBA 44: 2074.

4.2-241 Olivieri, A.M., and Parrini, P. 1974. Diallel analysis of four Cichorium intybus L. populations [in Italian]. Riv. Agron. 8: 39-46. PBA 45: 1631.

4.2-242 Olsson, G. 1974. Continuous selection for seed number per pod and oil content in white mustard. Hereditas 77: 197-204.

4.2-243 Ono, S. 1972. Studies on the radiation breeding in the genus Mentha. XII. The mutations of Japanese mint induced by X-rays. Ikushugaku Zasshi 22: 269-273. PBA 43: 3253.

4.2-244 Ono, S. 1975. Studies on radiation breeding in the genus Mentha. XVI. Radiosensitivity of physiological and morphological characters [in Japanese]. Ikushugaku Zasshi 25: 24-30. PBA 46: 1007.

4.2-245 Ono, S. 1979. Studies on the improvement of the components of essential oil of genus Mentha by radiation. Gamma Field Symp. 1979{18}: 97-113. CA 93: 235304.

4.2-246 Ono, S. 1971. Studies on the radiation breeding in the genus Mentha. XII. Variation in quantitative characters of X2 plant after hybridization and irradiation in mint. Okayama Daigaku Nogakubu Gakujutsu Hokoku 38: 1-7. AGRICOLA.

4.2-247 Ono, S. 1972. Studies on the radiation breeding in the genus Mentha. XIII. Effects of irradiation on pollen. Okayama Daigaku Nogakubu Gakujutsu Hokoku 39: 1-8.

4.2-248 Ono, S. 1972. Studies on the radiation breeding in the genus Mentha. (XV). A comparison of biological effects between gamma-rays and X-rays on mint seeds. Okayama Daigaku Nogakubu Gakujutsu Hokoku 40: 1-7. PBA 44: 8283.

4.2-249 Osman, H. El G., and Khidir, M.O. 1974. Estimates of genetic and environmental variability in sesame. Exp. Agric. 10: 105-112.

4.2-250 Oulton, K., Williams, G.J., III, and May, D.S. 1979. Ribulose-1,5-bisphosphate carboxylase from altitudinal populations of Taraxacum officinale. Photosynthetica 13: 15-20.

4.2-251 Palaniswamy, K.M., Govinda Dass, G., and Subramanian, A.S. 1978. Correlations and path analysis of yield and yield components in sesame. Indian J. Agric. Sci. 48: 681-683.

4.2-252 Paul, N.K., Joarder, O.I., and Eunus, A.M. 1976. Genotypic and phenotypic variability and correlation studies in Brassica juncea L. Z. Pflanzenzuecht. 77: 145-154.

4.2-253 Paun, E., and Popescu, R. 1976. Somatic mutations in mint (Mentha piperita L.), an important source of initial material [in Romanian] An. Inst. Cercet. Cereale Plante Teh. Fundulea Acad. Stiinte Agric. Silvice Ser. C 41: 661-665. PBA 47: 6945.

4.2-254 Paun, E., Dumitrescu, A., Silva, F., Verzea, M., Mihalea, A., Cosocariu, O., and Braga, A. 1975. The wild flora of medicinal and aromatic plants and their importance in breeding [in Romanian]. Probleme di Genetica Teoretica si Aplicata 7: 112-123. PBA 45: 9260.

4.2-255 Paun, E., and Popescu, R. 1972. Results of peppermint breeding [in Romanian]. An. Inst. Cercet. Cereale Plante Teh. Fundulea Acad. Stiinte Agric. Silvice Ser. C 38: 357-366. HA 44: 2703.

4.2-256 Paun, E., and Popescu, R. 1976. Achievements in breeding mint (Mentha crispa L.) [in Romanian]. An. Inst. Cercet. Cereale Plante Teh. Fundulea Acad. Stiinte Agric. Silvice Ser. C 41: 667-674. PBA 47: 8041.

4.2-257 Paun, E., Mihalea, A., and Silva, F. 1974. Genetical characteristics of quality reflected in the breeding of various medicinal and aromatic plants [in Romanian]. Probleme di Genetica Teoretica si Aplicata 6: 561-581. PBA 46: 665.

4.2-258 Pearson, O.H. 1972. Cytoplasmically inherited male sterility characters and flavor components from the species Brassica nigra (L.) Koch X B. oleracea L. J. Am. Soc. Hortic. Sci. 97: 397-402.

4.2-259 Pelyakh, E.M. 1978. Mint hybrids, synthesizing carvone [in Russian]. Izv. Akad. Nauk Mold. SSR Ser. Biol. Khim. Nauk 1978{3}: 5-8.

4.2-260 Peneva, P. 1976. Correlations between some characters of coriander [in Bulgarian]. Genet. Sel. 9: 439-450. AGRICOLA.

4.2-261 Persson, A.R., and Rod, H.K. 1977. Paprika: importation, culture, varieties [in Norwegian]. Gartneryrket 67: 198, 200, 202, 204. AGRICOLA.

4.2-262 Pieribattesti, J.C., Conan, J.Y., and Guerre, M. 1979. Study of certain anomalies observed in geranium Bourbon essential oil [in French]. Riv. Ital. Essenze Profumi, Piante Off. Aromat., Syndets, Saponi, Cosmet., Aerosols 61{3}: 119-122. CA 91: 78750.

4.2-263 Plumier, W. 1972. Chicory improvement [in French]. Rev. Agric. (Brussels) 25: 567-585. HA 43: 132.

4.2-264 Polishchuk, V.S. 1973. Cytoembryological studies of sweet marjoram (Majorana hortensis Moench) in connection with its introduction and acclimatization in the Ukraine [in Russian]. Izv. Akad. Nauk Mold. SSR Ser. Biol. Khim. Nauk 1973{1}: 81-82.

4.2-265 Popova, D. 1972. A study of the influence of reciprocal crossbreeding on heterosis effect in F1 generation in red peppers (Capsicum annuum L.) [in Slovak]. Pol'nohospodarstvo 18: 471-475. AGRICOLA.

4.2-266 Popovich, A.L., Bugaenko, L.A., and Reznikova, S.A. 1978. Breeding a new winter-hardy variety of mint by means of interspecific hybridization [in Russian]. Tr. Vses. Nauchno-Issled. Inst. Efirnomaslichn. Kul't. 1978{11}: 11-17. PBA 51: 5715.

4.2-267 Popov, P., Dimitrov, I., Georgiev, S., and Deneva, T. 1974. The effect of irradiation with gamma rays from 137Cs on the radiosensitivity of opium poppy (Papaver somniferum) and the morphine content in the dry capsules of M1 plants [in Bulgarian]. Genet. Sel. 7: 251-257. HA 45: 4409.

4.2-268 Popov, P., Dimitrov, I., and Deneva, T. 1975. Study on the morphine content of dry capsules of some introduced poppy varieties (Papaver somniferum L.) of the Eurasian ecological group [in Bulgarian]. Rastenievud. Nauki 12{5}: 34-39. AGRICOLA.

4.2-269 Popov, P., Dimitrov, I., and Deneva, T. 1976. Study on the morphine content of dry capsules of intervarietal poppy (Papaver somniferum L.) hybrids [in Bulgarian]. Rastenievud. Nauki 13{3}: 9-15. AGRICOLA.

4.2-270 Prakash, S. 1973. Non-homologous meiotic pairing in the A and B genomes of Brassica; its breeding significance in the production of variable amphidiploids. Genet. Res. 21: 133-137.

4.2-271 Prakash, S. 1973. Artificial synthesis of Brassica juncea Coss. Genetica (The Hague) 44: 249-263.

4.2-272 Prakash, S. 1974. Haploid meiosis and origin of Brassica tournefortii Gouan. Euphytica 23: 591-595.

4.2-273 Prochazka, F., and Urbanova, J. 1972. Relations between various quantitative characters in caraway [in Czech]. Sb. UVTI (Ustav. Vedeckotech. Inf.) Genet. Slecteni 8: 123-126. AGRICOLA.

4.2-274 Pushpangadan, P., Sobti, S.N., and Khan, R. 1975. Inheritance of major essential oil constituents in Ocimum basilicum var. glabratum Benth. (French basil). Indian J. Exp. Biol. 13: 520-521.

4.2-275 Rabotyagov, V.D., and Yakovlev, L.K. 1980. Study of the variability of the content of essential oil in lavender. Cytol. Genet. (Engl. Transl.) 14{2}: 33-35. Translation of Tsitol. Genet. 14{2}: 32-34, 1980.

4.2-276 Rabotyagov, V.D. 1975. Overcoming sterility in lavandines (Lavandula angustifolia Mill. X Lavandula latifolia Medic.). Cytol. Genet. (Engl. Transl.) 9{5}: 57-60. Translation of Tsitol. Genet. 9{5}: 443-446, 1975.

4.2-277 Rabotyagov, V.D. 1975. Biological and economical properties of tetraploid lavenders in relation to breeding [in Russian]. Tr. Prikl. Bot. Genet. Sel. 54{2}: 257-262. HA 46: 10600.

4.2-278 Radhakrishnan, K.P., Mercy, S.T., and George, M.K. 1977. Crossability studies and analysis of incompatibility in three species of Capsicum. Agric. Res. J. Kerala 15{2}: 124-127.

4.2-279 Ramachandran, M., Ramanathan, T., and Sridharan, C.S. 1972. Association of certain morphological characters with yield in Sesamum indicum. Madras Agric. J. 59: 567-568. AGRICOLA.

4.2-280 Ram, K., Singh, D., Verma, V.S., and Katiyar, R.P. 1976. Inter-relationships between some metric traits in segregating population of Indian mustard (Brassica juncea (L.) Czern and Coss.). J. Maharashtra Agric. Univ. 1: 21-22. FCA 30: 7188.

4.2-281 Rao, T.S., Babu, M.K., Dasarathi, T.B., and Rao, S.N. 1979. C.S. 2(Lam selection) a promising coriander type for Andhra Pradesh. Indian Cocoa, Arecanut & Spices Journal 3{2}: 44-45. HA 50: 5441.

4.2-282 Reddy, G.P., Reddy, P.S., and Raghunatham, G. 1971. Inheritance studies in Sesamum indicum L. Andhra Agric. J. 18{1}: 35-37. AGRICOLA.

4.2-283 Reznikova, S.A. 1972. The use of natural and experimental polyploidy in peppermint breeding [in Russian]. Pages 150-154 in P.V. Naumenko et al., eds. Mezhdunarodnyi kongress po efirnym maslam, 4th, Tiflis, 1968, [Materialy], v. 2. Pishchevaya, Promyshlennost', Moscow, USSR. PBA 46: 2005.

4.2-284 Reznikova, S.A., and Vorobeva, G.V. 1973. Breeding Mentha piperita and problems of improving varietal qualities [in Russian]. Pages 352-362 in P.S. Pustovoit, ed. Selektsiia i semenovodstvo tekhnicheskikh kul'tur. "Kolos", Moscow, USSR. AGRICOLA.

4.2-285 Reznikova, S.A., Gostev, A.A., and Semenova, V.M. 1972. Experimental polyploidy in breeding essential-oil plants [in Russian]. Tr. Prikl. Bot. Genet. Sel. 47{2}: 151-159. PBA 43: 9018.

4.2-286 Romanenko, L.G. 1973. Evaluation of the combining ability of clones of true lavender (Lavandula vera D.C.) [in Russian]. Dokl. Vses. Akad. S-kh. Nauk. Im V.I. Lenina 1973{6}: 17-18.

4.2-287 Romanenko, L.G. 1975. Breeding lavender for economically valuable characters [in Russian]. Tr. Prikl. Bot. Genet. Sel. 54{2}: 235-247. HA 46: 11656.

4.2-288 Romanenko, L.G. 1974. Inheritance of the major morphologic and economically useful characters of lavender [in Russian]. Tr. Vses. Nauchno-Issled. Inst. Efirnomaslichn. Kul't. 7: 4-6. AGRICOLA.

4.2-289 Rossello, J.E., Kheyr-Pour, A., and Valdeyron, G. 1976. Genetics structure and breeding system in Origanum vulgare distribution of an enzymatic marker in 2 natural populations [in French]. C. R. Hebd. Seances Acad. Sci. Ser. D Sci. Nat. 283: 1587-1589.

4.2-290 Rouanet, G. 1972. A program of variety improvement for bush red pepper cultivation of awasa (Ethiopia) [in French]. Agron. Trop. (Paris) 27: 1032-1035. AGRICOLA.

4.2-291 Royal Botanic Gardens, Kew, UK. 1977. Review of the work of the Royal Botanic Gardens, Kew, in 1975. Kew Bull. 31: 859-914.

4.2-292 Roy, N.N. 1978. A study on disease variation in the populations of an interspecific cross of Brassica juncea L. X B. napus L. Euphytica 27: 145-149. RPP 58: 425.

4.2-293 Ruzicka, R., and Novy, J. 1979. Studies on the effect of gamma irradiation of poppy seed on increasing crop yield and quality [in Slovak]. Rostl. Vyroba 25: 529-536. HA 50: 556.

4.2-294 Ryauzova, N. 1973. At the Exhibition of National Economic Achievements of the USSR [in Russian]. Sel. Semenovod. (Moscow) 1973{6}: 12-14. PBA 44: 4212.

4.2-295 Rykunova, V.N., and Zhivotova, L.V. 1972. Obtaining distant hybrids of mustard (1967-1970) [in Russian]. Tr. Volgogr. S-kh. Inst. 44: 120-128. PBA 45: 7590.

4.2-296 Sadowska, A. 1973. Selected problems in mint breeding [in Polish]. Biul. Inst. Hodowli Aklim. Rosl. 1973{3/4}: 123-127. PBA 44: 4848.

4.2-298 Sadowska, A. 1979. Quantitative and qualitative changes in peppermint (Mentha piperita L.) essential oil induced by irradiation. Planta Med. 36: 285 (Abstr.).

4.2-299 Sadowska, A. 1979. Studies on the influence of irradiation upon the quantity and quality of essential oil of peppermint. Herba Hung. 18{3}: 331-336.

4.2-300 Salazar R., D., and Onoro C., P. 1975. Heritability studies of plant height, number of capsules and seed yield in sesame species [in Spanish]. Rev. Inst. Colomb. Agropecu. 10: 109-114. AGRICOLA.

4.2-301 Sarafi, A., and Zali, A. 1977. Utilization of gamma rays in the improvement of sesame, Sesamum indicum L. [in French]. Bull. Soc. Hist. Nat. Toulouse 113{1/2}: 164-169. AGRICOLA.

4.2-302 Sarafi, A., and Fayze, A.M. 1976. Study of some characters of five varieties of sesame and comparison of the effects of three harvesting methods on their yield and percentage in oil [in French].

Inf. Tech. Cent. Tech. Interprof. Ol. Metrop. 52: 18-22. Bib. Ag. 41:
122357.

4.2-303 Sarkany, S., Danos, B., and Sarkanykiss, I. 1971. New results of
Papaver somniferum breeding: "Hybrid BC-2" [in German]. Herba Pol. 17:
410-421. AGRICOLA.

4.2-304 Sarozhveladze, T.P. 1978. Results of studies on quality indices
of bred varieties and clones of Soviet Georgian tea and Laurus noblis
[in Russian]. Subtrop. Kul't. 1978{1}: 13-19. AGRICOLA.

4.2-305 Sastri, D.C., and Shivanna, K.R. 1976. Attempts to overcome
interspecific incompatibility in Sesamum by using recognition pollen.
Ann. Bot. (London) 40: 891-893.

4.2-306 Sathiamoorthy, M.R., Natarajan, S.T., and Ramachandran, T.K.
1977. Heritability estimates in sesame (Sesamum indicum Linn.).
Botanique (Nagpur) 8: 141-144.

4.2-307 Savchenko, L.F., and Reznikova, S.A. 1975. Some features of
cytoplasmic male sterility (CMS) in Salvia sclarea [in Russian]. Tr.
Prikl. Bot. Genet. Sel. 54{2}: 250-254. PBA 46: 4902.

4.2-308 Sawant, A.R. 1971. Genetic variation and heritability of
quantitative characters in some improved varieties of sesame. Mysore
J. Agric. Sci. 5: 88-95. AGRICOLA.

4.2-309 Sawant, A.R. 1971. Preliminary study in natural
cross-pollination in sesame in Bundelkhand region of Madhya Pradesh.
Allahabad Farmer 45{1}: 75-76. AGRICOLA.

4.2-310 Sazonova, L.V., Burenin, V.I., and Levandovskaya, L.I. 1978.
Collection of culinary root crops and its role in the development of
breeding [in Russian]. Byull. Vses. Inst. Rastenievod. 1978{85}:
24-33. PBA 50: 9374.

4.2-311 Schoneveld, J.A. 1974. Some costs aspects with regard to chicory
improvement [in Dutch]. Zaadbelangen 28: 11, 13. WAERSA 17: 1024.

4.2-312 Schuster, W., Alawi, A., and El-Seidy, R.G. 1978. Investigations
on inbreeding and heterosis in black mustard (Brassica nigra L.) [in
German]. Angew. Bot. 52: 215-232.

4.2-313 Schuster, W., El-Seidy, R.G., and Alavi, A. 1978. Investigations
on inbreeding depression in the 10 to 16 and heterosis effects in
Sinapis alba (white mustard) [in German]. Z. Pflanzenzeucht. 80:
277-298

4.2-314 Sehgal, C.B. 1972. Experimental induction of zygotic multiple
embryos in Coriandrum sativum L. Indian J. Exp. Biol. 10: 457-459.

4.2-315 Selenina, L.V., and Stepanenko, O.G. 1979. Effect of pre-sowing
gamma irradiation on the productivity and active principle content of
Matricaria-recutita [in Russian]. Rastit. Resur. 15: 91-98. HA 49:
7893.

4.2-316 Selim, A.K.A., and el-Ahmar, B.A. 1976. Genetic behaviour of oil
content in sesame Sesamum indicum seed and its relation to some
economic characters. Egypt. J. Genet. Cytol. 5: 456-459. AGRICOLA.

4.2-317 Shah, C.S., Qadry, J.S., and Chauhan, M.G. 1971. Intraspecific variability in Indian dill. Curr. Sci. 40: 328-329.

4.2-318 Shankaranarayana, M.L., Raghavan, B., and Natarjan, C.P. 1972. Mustard - varieties, chemistry and analysis. Lebensmm.-Wiss. Technol. 5: 191-197. HA 43: 6247.

4.2-319 Shelyd'ko, L.O. 1973. The improvement of inherited qualities in medicinal plants: chamomile, restharrow and ripple-seed plantain [in Ukranian]. Farm. Zh. (Kiev) 1973{6}: 70-72. HA 45: 1229.

4.2-320 Shevchenko, V.V., Protopopova, E.M., Grigoriyeva, G.A., and Bolotova, T.Kh. 1971. Interaction between chemical mutagens with a delayed effect and metabolites of seeds. Communication 2: Changes in mutagenic activity. Theor. Appl. Genet. 41: 52-56.

4.2-321 Shifriss, C., and Sacks, J.M. 1980. The effect of distance between parents on the yield of sweet pepper X hot pepper hybrids, Capsicum annuum L. in a single harvest. Theor. Appl. Genet. 58: 253-256.

4.2-322 Shimizu, S., Karasawa, D., and Ikeda, N. 1972. Studies on the essential oils of interspecific hybrids in the genus Mentha. Part VI. On a new chemical strain in the hybrids involving Mentha spicata var. crispa Benth. [in Japanese]. Shinshu Daigaku Nogakubu Kiyo Nogakubu 9{2}: 73-81. PBA 44: 263.

4.2-323 Shpota, V.I., and Podkolzina, V.E. 1975. The cross compatibility of Brassica juncea with swede rape containing no erucic acid and the inheritance of erucic acid content in the hybrids [in Russian]. Byul. nauch.-techn. inform. po maslich. kul'turam 1975{3}: 14-17. PBA 48: 11922.

4.2-324 Shpota, V.I., and Bochkarev, N.I. 1974. Initial material for the resynthesis of winter mustard [in Russian]. Byul. nauch.-tekhn. inform. po maslich. kul'turam 1974{3}: 3-5. PBA 47: 1501.

4.2-325 Shpota, V.I., and Konovalov, N.G. 1978. Resynthesis of Indian mustard from primary species by breeding [in Russian]. S-kh. Biol. 13: 617-619. PBA 48: 11918.

4.2-326 Shpota, V.I., and Bochkarev, N.I. 1972. A breeding and commercial evaluation of tetraploid forms of winter rape and Brassica nigra [in Russian]. Byul. nauch.-yekhn. inform. po maslich. kul'turam 1974{3}: 9-12. PBA 46: 2691.

4.2-327 Shugaeva, E.V. 1979. Male sterility of Valeriana officinalis L.S.L. [in Russian]. Genetika (Moscow) 15: 138-143.

4.2-328 Shukla, G.P., and Sharma, R.K. 1978. Genetic variability, correlation and path analysis in fenugreek. Indian J. Agric. Sci. 48: 518-521.

4.2-329 Shukla, G.P., and Verma, G. 1976. Correlations and heritability in sesame. Indian J. Agric. Sci. 46: 283-285.

4.2-330 Shyam Prakash. 1973. Haploidy in Brassica nigra Koch. Euphytica 22: 613-614.

4.2-331 Simon, U. 1976. Improvement of the protein content in forage plants by plant cultural and breeding measures. Plant Res. Dev. 3: 90-100. HERB AB 48: 1551.

4.2-332 Singh, R.N. 1976. A note on the crossability relationship of some species of oleiferous Brassicae. Oilseeds J. 6{1}: 36-37. PBA 50: 2239.

4.2-333 Singh, U.P., and Khanna, K.R. 1975. Heterosis and combining ability in opium poppy. Indian J. Genet. Plant Breed. 35: 8-12.

4.2-334 Sip, V., Martinek, V., and Skorpik, M. 1975. Diallel analysis of plant height in seed poppy [in Czech]. Sb. UVTIZ Genet. Slechteni 11: 289-296. PBA 46: 6453.

4.2-335 Sip, V., Martinek, V., and Skorpik, M. 1975. The additive-dominant model of analysis of plant height in seed poppy [in Czech]. Sb. UVTIZ Genet. Slechteni 11: 297-305.

4.2-336 Sirikulvadhana, S., Jennings, W.G., and Derafols, W. 1976. Lemongrass oil from mutant clones of Cymbopogon flexuosus. Chem. Mikrobiol. Technol. Lebensm. 4: 129-131. AGRICOLA.

4.2-337 Sobti, S.N., Pushpangadan, P., Thapa, R.K., Aggarwal, S.G., Vashist, V.N., and Atal, C.K. 1978. Chemical and genetic investigations in essential oils of some Ocimum species their F-1 hybrids and synthesized allopolyploids. Lloydia 41: 50-55.

4.2-338 Sobti, S.N., and Pushpangadan, P. 1977. Studies in the genus Ocimum: cytogenetics, breeding and production of new strains of economic importance. Pages 273-286 in C.K. Atal and B.M. Kapur, eds. Cultivation & utilization of medicinal and aromatic plants. Regional Research Laboratory, Jammu-Tawi, India.

4.2-339 Sobti, S.N. 1975. Interspecific hybrids in the genus Mentha. III. Mentha arvensis Linn. X M. spicata Linn. Cytologia 40: 263-267. PBA 46: 11678.

4.2-340 Sobti, S.N., Pushpangadan, P., Thapa, R.K., Aggarwal, S.G., Vashist, V.N., an d Atal, C.K. 1978. Chemical and genetic investigations in essential oils of some Ocimum species, their F1 hybrids and synthesized allopolyploids. Lloydia 41: 50-55.

4.2-341 Sobti, S.N. 1971. Interspecific hybrids in the genus Mentha. I. Mentha longifolia (Linn.) Huds X rotundifolia Linn. Cytologia 36: 121-125.

4.2-342 Sobti, S.N. 1971. Interspecific hybrid in the genus Mentha. II. Mentha arvensis Linn. X M. longifolia (Linn.) Huds. Cytologia 36: 304-308.

4.2-343 Sobti, S.N. 1974. Origin of Mentha piperita Linn. in relation to peppermint oils. Pages 224-230 in P. Kachroo, ed. Advancing frontiers in cytogenetics in evolution and improvement of plants. Proceedings of national seminar. Kashmir, India, Oct. 14-19, 1972. Hindustan Publshing Corp., Delhi, India.

4.2-344 Sobti, S.N., Pushpangadan, P., Bradu, B.L., and Jain, B.B. 1979. Development of an eugenol-containing Ocimum species. Indian Perfum. 23{1}: 16-20. CA 92: 135103.

4.2-345 Stambera, J. 1978/1979. Possibilities of using intervariety hybridization in the red pepper Capsicum annuum L. [in Czech]. Sb. UVTI (Ustav Vedeckotech Inf.) Zahradnictivi 5/6{1/2}: 93-98. AGRICOLA.

4.2-346 Staneff, D. 1972. Spontaneous mutations in mint [in French]. An. Acad. Bras. Cienc. 44(Suppl.): 80-84.

4.2-347 Stringam, G.R. 1973. Inheritance and allelic relationships of seven chlorophyll-deficient mutants in Brassica campestris L. Can. J. of Genet. Cytol. 15{2}: 335-339. PBA 44: 1924.

4.2-348 Subramanian, M. 1977. Pollen germination and growth studies in Sesamum indicum (cv. TMV 2). Madras Agric. J. 64: 630.

4.2-349 Subramanian, M. 1977. A natural triploid in Sesamum indicum Linn. Madras Agric. J. 64: 134-135.

4.2-350 Subramanian, M. 1977. A trisomic in Sesamum indicum L. Madras Agric. J. 64: 338-339.

4.2-351 Suthanthirapandian, I.R., Shaw, H.A., and Muthuswami, S. 1980. Genetic variability in coriander (Coriandrum sativum L.). Madras Agric. J. 67: 450-452.

4.2-352 Tatlioglu, T., and Wricke, G. 1980. Genetical and breeding studies of chives (Allium schoenoprsum L.) [in German]. Gartenbauwissenschaft 45: 278-282.

4.2-353 Teplitskaya, L.M., and Reznikova, S.A. 1975. Studies on the glandular apparatus of mint in relation to breeding problems [in Russian]. Tr. Prikl. Bot. Genet. Sel. 54{2}: 262-267. HA 46: 10604.

4.2-354 Thangraj, T., Muthukrishnan, C.R., and Muthuswami, S. 1980. Correlation studies in open pollinated seedlings of Jasminum ariculatum Vahl. Madras Agric. J. 67: 391-393.

4.2-355 Todd, W.A., Green, R.J., Jr., and Horner, C.E. 1977. Registration of Murray Mitcham peppermint (Reg. No. 2). Crop Sci. 17: 188.

4.2-356 Tokarska, B., and Karwowska, K. 1977. Comparative studies on extracts obtained from selected horseradish types [in Polish]. Pr. Inst. Lab. Badaw. Przem. Spozyw. 27: 285-292. HA 51: 3885.

4.2-357 Tokarska, B., and Karwowska, K. 1977. Qualitative evaluation of the horseradish types cultivated in Poland [in Polish]. Pr. Inst. Lab. Badaw. Przem. Spozyw. 27{1}: 13-18. CA 88: 103423.

4.2-358 Tokumasu, S., and Kato, M. 1979. Variation of chromosome numbers and essential oil components of plants derived from anther culture of the diploid and the tetraploid in Pelargonium roseum. Euphytica 28: 329-338.

4.2-359 Trippel' V.V., and Chubrikova, L.P. 1976. Variability of the main commercial characteristics and productivity of the garlic cultivar Dushanbinskii [in Russian]. Temat. Sb. Nauchn. Tr. Tadzh. Nauchno-Issled. Inst. Zemledeliya 8: 257-271. HA 48: 7194.

4.2-360 Tsvetkov, R. 1973. Induced polyploidy in Salvia sclarea L. [in Bulgarian]. Genet. Sel. 6: 129-138. PBA 44: 264.

4.2-361 Tsvetkov, R. 1972. Induced polyploidy on <u>Salvia</u> <u>sclarea</u>. An. Acad. Bras. Cienc. 44(Suppl.): 76-79.

4.2-362 Tucker, A.O., and Fairbrothers, D.E. 1974. Evaluation of the <u>Mentha</u> X <u>gentilis</u> L. hybrid complex utilizing morphology, monoterpenes, and chromosome numbers. Am. J. Bot. 61{5 Suppl.}: 51 (Abstr.).

4.2-363 Turkov, V.D., Nushikyan, V.A., and Drozdova, N.S. 1973. Spontaneous mutations in the caryotypes of vegetable crops [in Russian]. Dokl. Vses. Akad. S-kh. Nauk im. V.I. Lenina 1973{12}: 15-16. PBA 44: 4754.

4.2-364 Uncini, L., Sozzi, A., and Gorini, F. 1977. Yield, fruit quality and storage of new hot pepper varieties and hybrids. Acta Hortic. 58: 497-501.

4.2-365 Valdivia B., V.A., and Badilla M., M.E. 1977. Artificial and natural crosses between rape or colza (<u>Brassica</u> <u>napus</u> L.) and wild and cultivated crucifers [in Spanish]. Agric. Tec. Santiago 37{1}: 25-30. PBA 48: 618.

4.2-366 Van Rheehan, H.A. 1980. Aspects of natural cross-fertilization in sesame (<u>Sesamum</u> <u>indicum</u> L.). Trop. Agric. (Guildford) 57{1}: 53-59. AGRICOLA.

4.2-367 Vereshchagin, A.G. 1976. Effect of the phenotype and genotype of oil-producing plants on fatty acid composition of the oil. Sov. Plant Physiol. (Engl. Transl.) 23: 507-518. Translation of Fiziol. Rast. (Moscow) 23: 600-614, 1976. FCA 32: 1163.

4.2-368 Vereshchako, F.A., and Gevko, V.A. 1973. The prospects of growing inter-specific highly productive peppermint hybrids in Podol'e [in Russian]. Tr. Kishinev. S-kh. Inst. 104: 57-61. HA 44: 7923.

4.2-369 Vernet, P. 1977. Variations in the composition of the essential oil of <u>Thymus</u> <u>vulgaris</u> L.: method of hereditary transmission of three terpenes (thymol, carvacrol and linalool) [in French]. C. R. Hebd. Seances Acad. Sci. Ser. D. 284: 1289-1292.

4.2-370 Verzar-Petri, G., Marczal, G., and Lemberkovics, E. 1973. Comparative studies on the alpha-bisabolol content of Hungarian chamomile cultivars [in Hungarian]. Herba Hung. 12{2/3}: 119-128. HA 46: 3750.

4.2-371 Veselovskaya, M.A. 1975. The poppy (variability, classification, evolution) [in Russian]. Tr. Prikl. Bot. Genet. Sel. 55{1}: 175-223. FCA 30: 502.

4.2-372 Vinot, M., and Bouscary, A. 1971. Studies on lavender. (VI). The hybrids. Recherches 1971{18}: 29-44.

4.2-373 Vodyanova, O.S. 1980. Production of high-yielding shallot forms by means of colchicine treatment and their use in breeding [in Russian . S-kh. Biol. 15: 145-146. PBA 50: 6800.

4.2-374 Voskresenskaya, G.S., and Lygina, L.M. 1973. Outcrossing in Indian mustard [in Russian]. Doklady Vsesoyuznoi Ordena Lenina Akademii Sel'skokhozyaistvennykh Nauk Imeni V.I. Lenina 1973{6}: 16-17. PBA 44: 1926.

4.2-375 Wahhab, M.A., and Bechyne, M. 1977. Heritability estimates for some yield-contributing characters in Indian mustard. Indian J. Agric. Sci. 47: 556-559. PBA 48: 8836.

4.2-376 Wallace, A., Romney, E.M., Kinnear, J.E., and Mueller, R.T. 1980. Metal ratios as an index of plant species differences on uptake characteristics of different trace metals. J. Plant Nutr. 2: 25-34. HA 51: 3306.

4.2-377 Weimarck, G. 1974. Population structures in higher plants as revealed by thin-layer chromatographic patterns. Bot. Not. 127: 224-244

4.2-378 Widen, K.-G., Alanko, P., and Uotila, M. 1977. Thymus serpyllum L. X vulgaris L., morphology, chromosome number and chemical composition. Ann. Bot. Fenn. 14: 29-34. HA 47: 11746.

4.2-379 Widholm, J.M. 1977. Selection and characterization of biochemical mutants. Pages 112-122 in W. Barz, E. Reinhard and M.H. Zenk, eds. Plant tissue culture and its bio-technological application. Proceedings of the first international congress on medicinal plant research, Section B, Munich, Germany, Sept. 6-10, 1976. Springer-Verlag, New York, N.Y.

4.2-380 Yadava, T.P., Kumar, P., and Yadav, A.K. 1980. Association of yield and its components in sesame. Indian J. Agric. Sci. 50: 317-319.

4.2-381 Yadav, T.P., Hari Singh, and Yadav, A.K. 1976. Inheritance of leaf colour in Indian mustard. Crop Improv. 3{1/2}: 134. PBA 48: 617.

4.2-382 Yankoulov, Y., Yankulov, I., and Alipur, Kh. 1974. Analysis of experimentally produced autopentaploids of Mentha piperita L. [in German]. Dokl. S-kh. Akad. (Sofia) 7{4}: 23-36. PBA 45: 6952.

4.2-383 Yankoulov, Y., and Alipur, H. 1974. Determining the ploidy of Mentha piperita L. by the frequency of essential oil glands. Dokl. S-kh. Akad. (Sofia) 7{2}: 55-58. HA 45: 2711.

4.2-384 Yankulov, I., Alipur, Kh., and Ivanov, I.N. 1974. A study of experimentally produced autopolyploids of Mentha piperita L. [in Bulgarian]. Rastenievud. Nauki 11{10}: 23-29. PBA 45: 5946.

4.2-385 Yankulov, I., Stoeva, T., Ivanov, I., and Zuzulova, A. 1979. Production of mint oil with new odor components [in German]. Dokl. Bolg. Akad. Nauk 32{7}: 981-983. CA 92: 135097.

4.2-386 Yaskonis, Yu.A. 1972. The biochemical characteristics and yield of the mint MS-41 and a series of peppermint varieties in the Lithuanian SSR [in Russian]. Pages 259-261 in P.V. Naumenko et al., eds. Mezhdunarodnyi kongress po efirnym maslam, 4th, Tiflis, 1968, [Materialy], v. 2. Pishchevaya Promyshlennost', Moscow, USSR. PBA 45: 6954.

4.2-387 Yoganarasimhan, S.N., Togunashi, V.S., Nayar, R.C., and Mary, Z. 1978. Studies on additional source for the Indian valerian from South India. Agric. Agro-ind. J. 11{11}: 7-11. Bib. Ag. 43: 77626.

4.2-388 Zaostrovskaya, E.N., and Emmerikh, N.S. 1973. Initial material for breeding green fennel [in Russian]. Tr. Prikl. Bot. Genet. Sel. 49: 108-121. HA 44: 4957.

4.2-389 Zhila, E.D. 1975. The radiosensitivity of aerial bulbils of garlic [in Russian]. Tsitol. Genet. 9: 501-504. PBA 46: 8471.

4.2-390 Zitter, T.A., and Guzman, V.L. 1977. Evaluation of cos lettuce crosses, endive cultivars, and Cichorium introductions for resistance to Bidens mottle virus. Plant Dis. Rep. 61: 767-770.

4.2-391 Zobenko, L.P. 1972. The question of breeding Salvia sclarea [in Russian]. Tr. Prikl. Bot. Genet. Sel. 47{2}: 178-182. PBA 43: 9923.

4.2-392 Zobenko, L.P. 1973. The biological composition of varietal populations of Salvia sclarea in relation to problems of breeding [in Russian]. Tr. Vses. Nauchno-Issled. Inst. Efirnomaslichn. Kul't. 5: 6-9. PBA 46: 3037.

4.2-393 Zobenko, L.P. 1975. Use of varieties as initial material for breeding Salvia sclarea [in Russian]. Tr. Vses. Nauchno-Issled. Inst. Efirnomaslichn. Kul't. 8: 40-45. PBA 48: 7194.

4.2-394 Zolotovich, G., and Stanev, D. 1971. Studies on certain varieties and clones of Mentha spicata in Bulgaria [in Bulgarian]. Rastenievud. Nauki 8{8}: 47-54. AGRICOLA.

4.3 Field Production and Cultural Methodology

4.3-1 Abdel-Al, Z.E. 1973. Experimental investigations on the yield and quality of garlic. Acta Hortic. 1973{33}: 43-49. SF 38: 2565.

4.3-2 Ahmad, R.U., and Srivastava, P.C. 1977. About the utilization and cultivation of medicinal flora of J+K State. Pages 150-153 in C.K. Atal and B.M. Kapur, eds. Cultivation & utilisation of medicinal and aromatic plants. Regional Research Laboratory, Jammu-Tawi, India, 1977.

4.3-3 Ahuja, K.L., Saini, J.S., Sekhon, K.S., and Gupta, T.R. 1971. Effect of some cultural treatments on the yield and chemical composition of sesame (Sesamum indicum L.). Indian J. Agron. 16: 445-448. AGRICOLA.

4.3-4 Andoskina, L.T., Muinova, S.S., and Pauzner, L.E. 1979. Effect of the time of mowing on the productivity and quality of liquorice roots [in Russian]. Uzb. Biol. Zh. 1979{3}: 44-47. HA 50: 539.

4.3-5 Anonymous. 1977/1978. Get higher yields from fennel. Intensive Agric. 15{10/11}: 35-36.

4.3-6 Anonymous. 1980. Perennial crops: uncommon species of onions, Artemisia dracunculus, cultivation recommendations [in Russian]. Kartofel Ovoshchi. {1980} 2: 35-36.

4.3-7 Anonymous. 1974. Peppermint [in Spanish]. Tierra 29{1}: 16-17. AGRICOLA.

4.3-8 Anonymous. 1975. Lighting of young paprika and experiment with their varieties in 1973 and 1974 [in German]. Gartenbaul. Versuchsber. Landwirtsch. Rheinl. Abt. Gemuse Obst. Gartenbau 14: 85-93. AGRICOLA.

4.3-9 Anonymous. 1976. Increased interest in the cultivation of paprika [in Norwegian]. Gartneryrket 66: 568. AGRICOLA.

4.3-10 Baer, E.G., Tanasienko, F.S., and Ponomarev, E.D. 1975. Losses of essential oil from lavender under field conditions [in Russian]. Maslo-Zhir. Prom-st. 1975{1}: 36-37. CA 83: 65309.

4.3-11 Bahl, B.K., Vashist, V.N., and Atal, C.K. 1977. Cultivation of celery seed in India. Pages 330-334 in C.K. Atal and B.M. Kapur, eds. Cultivation & utilization of medicinal and aromatic plants. Regional Research Laboratory Jammu-Tawi, India.

4.3-12 Bains, D.S., Mahajan, V.P., and Randhawa, J.S. 1977. Agronomic investigations on the seed crop of celery. Pages 324-330 in C.K. Atal and B.M. Kapur, eds. Cultivation & utilization of medicinal and aromatic plants. Regional Research Laboratory, Jammu-Tawi, India.

4.3-13 Bains, D.S., Sarma, J.S., and Saini, S.S. 1977. Salient findings on Mentha arvensis cultivation under Punjab conditions. Pages 191-194 in C.K. Atal and B.M. Kapur, eds. Cultivation & utilization of medicinal and aromatic plants. Regional Research Laboratory, Jammu-Tawi, India.

4.3-14 Bardroma, M. 1976. Is there a chance to grow Carum carvi commercially [in Hebrew]. Hassadeh 56: 1707. AGRICOLA.

4.3-15 Basker, D., and Putievsky, E. 1978. Seasonal variation in the yields of herb and essential oil in some Labiatae species. J. Hortic. Sci. 53: 179-183.

4.3-16 Beliaev, V.V. 1973. Some experience in growing lavender seedlings at the Nikita Botanical Gardens [in Russian]. Byull. Gos. Nikitsk. Bot. Sada 1973{2}: 65-67. AGRICOLA.

4.3-17 Benoit, F., and Cuestermans, N. 1978. Possibilities of low-energy requiring vegetables. Acta Hortic. 76: 127-130.

4.3-18 Berenyi, M. 1974. Recent results of red pepper growing methods at Kalocsa [in Hungarian]. Bull. Zoldsegtermesztesi Kut. Intez. 9: 129-136. AGRICOLA.

4.3-19 Berger, F. 1971. Angelica root, its culture and use [in German]. Acta Phytotherap. 18{5}: 86-93. AGRICOLA.

4.3-20 Bhan, S. 1979. Get better returns from sesame. Indian Farming 29{2}: 9-10

4.3-21 Bijl, J. 1977. Not all alliums are easy to grow. The capricious Allium schubertii is first rate for drying [in Dutch]. Bloembollencultuur 87{49}: 1040. HA 48: 1598.

4.3-22 Brasil, G. de A., Bauer, L., Grim, S.S., Cauduro, F.A., and Barradas, C.I. 1976. Final report on research work with Mentha piperita L. [in Portuguese]. Bol. Assoc. Bras. Pesqui. Plant. Aromat. Oleos. Essenc. 19: 75-94. AGRICOLA.

4.3-23 Calambosi, B. 1979. Results of cultivation of some wild flower medicinal plants in the "Szilasmenti" Cooperative. Planta Med. 36: 297 (Abstr.).

4.3-24 Ceylan, A. 1976. A study of Salvia officinalis [in Turkish]. Ege
Universitesi Ziraat Fakultesi Dergisi 13: 283-288. HA 48: 740.

4.3-25 Chan Castaneda, J.L. 1973. Determination of the size and optimal
form of the experimental plot in Mirasol chili red peppers [in
Spanish]. Proc. Trop. Reg. Am. Soc. Hortic. Sci. 17: 271-276.
AGRICOLA.

4.3-26 Chandra, V., and Kapoor, L.D. 1972. Cultivation of Matricaria
chamomilla L. in India. An. Acad. Bras. Cienc. 44(Suppl.): 114-116.

4.3-27 Chikov, P.S., Lovyannikov, P.T., and Vaginskii, O.V. 1975.
Economic efficiency of cultivating medicinal plants and ways to
improve it [in Russian]. Rastit. Resur. 11: 328-333.

4.3-28 Chomchalow, N. 1976. Hill tribe mint production and processing.
Thai J. Agric. Sci. 9: 127-144. WAERSA 19: 4291.

4.3-29 Choudhary, D.K., Kaul, B.L., Kak, S.N., Singh, C., and Ram, G.
1977. Cultivation and utilisation of opium poppy in India--a review.
Indian Drugs 15: 2-8. AGRICOLA.

4.3-30 Cirnu, I. 1976. Cultivation of lavender and its hybrids [in
Romanian] Apic. Rom. 51{9}: 8-9. AGRICOLA.

4.3-31 Cuenot, G. 1974. Notes on cress [in French]. Bull. Tech. Inf.
Minist. Agric. (Paris) 286: 15-22. AGRICOLA.

4.3-32 Czabajska, W., Jaruzelski, M., and Ubysz, D. 1976. New methods in
the cultivation of Valeriana officinalis. Planta Med. 30: 9-13.

4.3-33 Dabral, K.C., and Patel, O.P. 1975. Poppy cultivation in
Chhindwara District - preliminary studies on opium, seed and capsule
yield. JNKVV Res. J. 9: 73-74. PBA 47: 572.

4.3-34 Dabral, K.G., and Patel, O.P. 1976. Cultivation of opium poppy in
Chhindwara. Indian Farming 26{7}: 15-18. FCA 30: 5544.

4.3-35 Dabrowska, B., and Chroboczek, E. 1976. Influence of different
methods of cultivation on the quantity and quality of horseradish
yield [in Polish]. Ogrodnictwo 9: 77-99.

4.3-36 Delaveau, P., and Tessier, A.-M. 1977. Quality of medicinal
plants. Results of the cutting [in French]. Ann. Pharm. Fr. 35:
343-349. CIM 19{3}: 1878.

4.3-37 Deshmukh, M.G., Gore, S.B., Mungikar, A.M., and Joshi, R.N. 1974.
The yields of leaf protein from various short-duration crops. J. Sci.
Food Agric. 25: 717-724.

4.3-38 Desmarest, P. 1978. New aspects of fennel cultivation in France.
Acta Hortic. 1978{73}: 289-295.

4.3-39 Dikshit, U.N. 1975. Towards successful cultivation of Sesamum.
Telhan Patrika Oilseeds J. 5{2}: 17-18.

4.3-40 Dutta, P.K. 1971. Cultivation of Mentha arvensis in India.
Flavour Ind. 2: 233-240.

4.3-41 Dworecki, E. 1977. The goals in increasing of buckwheat, pea, bean, poppy seed and mustard production [in Polish]. Nowe Roln. 26{7}: 10-11. AGRICOLA.

4.3-42 El Motaz, M.B., Omar, F.A., El Shiaty, M.A., Arafa, A.I., Gheta, M.A., Shahin, A.H., and Zein, A. 1971. The effect of some treatments yield and quality of Egyptian garlic. III. Breaking rest period for early crop production. Agric. Res. Rev. 49{5}: 157-172. HA 45: 8318.

4.3-43 Fijalkowski, D., and Seroczynska, M. 1977. Investigation on cultivation and on the content of allantoin in comfrey (Symphytum officinale L.) [in Polish]. Herba Pol. 23: 47-53. AGRICOLA.

4.3-44 Fijalkowski, D., and Seroczynska, M. 1976. Studies on the culture of comfrey as drug plant [in Polish]. Wiad. Zielarskie 18{6}: 9-10.

4.3-45 Floria, V. 1975. Experience of growing foxglove Digitalis species as drug plants [in Russian]. Sel'sk. Khoz. Mold. 10: 25. AGRICOLA.

4.3-46 Foldesi, D., and Nagy, J. 1977. Catnip (Valeriana officinalis L.) culture in USSR [in Hungarian]. Herba Hung. 16{3}: 107-113. AGRICOLA.

4.3-47 Galambosi, B. 1979. Common wormwood (Artemisa absinthium L.) cultivation trials. I. Propagation, spacing and chemical weed control experiments [in Hungarian]. Herba Hung. 18{2}: 53-62. WA 30: 3138.

4.3-48 Galambosi, B. 1979. Results of cultivation of some wildflower medicinal plants in the "Szilasmenti" cooperative. Herba Hung. 18{3}: 343-352. WA 30: 2422.

4.3-49 Gaur, B.L., and Snigh, H.G. 1975. Sesame cultivation in Rajasthan. Farmer Parliament 10{6}: 21-22. AGRICOLA.

4.3-50 Ghosh, M.L., and Chatterjee, S.K. 1978. Cultivation of Mentha citrata Ehrh in Burdwan District, West Bengal. Proc. Indian Acad. Sci. Sect. B 87B: 157-160.

4.3-51 Giannakou, G. 1975. Crocus sativus cultivation [in Greek]. Agrotike 1975{7}: 10-14.

4.3-52 Gladyshev, A.I. 1971. Productivity of plant matter of Glycyrrhiza glabra L.-Imperata cylindrica (L.) P.B. formation in flood plain of the Amudar'ya River [in Russian]. Izv. Akad. Nauk Turkm. SSR Ser. Biol. Nauk 1971{4}: 33-39.

4.3-53 Gliozheni, E. 1972. Culture and distillation of aromatic plants in Albania [in Albanian]. Bul. Univ. Shteteror Tiranes Ser. Shkencat Nat. 26{102}: 101-113. AGRICOLA.

4.3-54 Gorini, F. 1976. Vegetable list. 3. Bulb vegetables. 3.1. Garlic [in Italian]. Inf. Orto-fruttic. 17{5}: 3-6. HA 47: 11340.

4.3-55 Gorini, F. 1976. Vegetable notes. 2. Leafy vegetables. 2.4. Dill (vegetables of secondary importance) [in Italian]. Inf. Orto-fruttic. 17{7}: 3-5. HA 48: 727.

4.3-56 Gorini, F. 1976. 5. Leafy condiment vegetables. 5.1. Basil [in Italian]. Inf. Orto-fruttic. 17{9}: 3-5. HA 47: 6806.

4.3-57 Gorini, F. 1977. Vegetable list. 2. Leafy vegetables. 2.9. Fennel [in Italian]. Inf. Orto-fruttic. 18{10}: 3-6. HA 48: 4863.

4.3-58 Gorini, F. 1977. Vegetable list. 8. Aromatic leafy vegetables 8.1. Spearmint (Mentha spicata) [in Italian]. Inf. Orto-fruttic. 18{12}: 3-5. HA 48: 5882.

4.3-59 Gorini, F. 1978. Vegetable list. 2. Leafy vegetables. 2.13. Parsley [in Italian]. Inf. Orto-fruttic. 19{6}: 3-6. HA 49: 692.

4.3-60 Gorini, F. 1978. Vegetable list. 4. Root vegetables. 4.6. Turnip-rooted parsley [in Italian]. Inf. Orto-fruttic. 19{6}: 6. HA 49: 693.

4.3-61 Gorini, F. 1978. Vegetable list. 9. Seed vegetables. 9.2. Anise (a vegetable of secondary importance) [in Italian]. Inf. Orto-fruttic. 19{10}: 3-5. HA 50: 1329.

4.3-62 Gorini, F. 1979. Vegetable list. 2. Leafy vegetables. 2.23. Hyssop (vegetable of secondary importance) [in Italian]. Inf. Orto-fruttic. 20{4}: 6-8. HA 50: 5444.

4.3-63 Gorini, F. 1979. Vegetable list. 11. Seed or root vegetables. 11.1. Lovage (vegetable of secondary importance) [in Italian]. Inf. Orto-fruttic. 20{5}: 7. HA 50: 5287.

4.3-64 Gorini, F. 1979. Vegetable notes. 4. Root vegetables. 4.9. Horseradish [in Italian]. Inf. Orto-fruttic. 20{8}: 3-5. HA 50: 9381.

4.3-65 Gorini, F. 1979. Vegetable notes. 9. Seed vegetables. 9.6. Coriander [in Italian]. Inf. Orto-fruttic. 20{8}: 5-7. HA 50: 9382.

4.3-66 Gorini, F. 1979. Vegetable schedules. 3. Vegetables with bulbs. 3.3. Shallot [in Italian]. Inf. Orto-fruttic. 20{11}: 3-4. HA 51: 7756.

4.3-67 Gorini, F. 1980. Vegetable schedules. 2. Leafy vegetables. 2.32. Wild marjoram (Origanum vulgare) [in Italian]. Inf. Orto-fruttic. 21{9}: 5-6. HA 51: 5710.

4.3-68 Gorini, F. 1979. Vegetable list. 2. Leafy vegetables. 2.21. Tarragon (vegetable of secondary importance) [in Italian]. Inf. Orto-fruttic. 20{4}: 3-4. HA 50: 5439.

4.3-69 Gorini, F. 1980. Vegetable schedules. 2. Leafy vegetables. 2.31. Rosemary [in Italian]. Inf. Ortoflorofruttic. 21{9}: 3-5. HA 51: 5711.

4.3-70 Granda, E., San Roman, L., Rivas Goday, S., and Gomez Serranillas, M. 1975. Growing Digitalis purpurea L. in soils originating from the disintegration of cretaceous sediments [in Spanish]. An. R. Acad. Farm. 41: 341-348.

4.3-71 Green, R.J., Jr. 1975. Peppermint and spearmint - production in the United States - progress and problems. Int. Flavours Food Addit. 6: 246-247.

4.3-72 Gulati, B.C., Duhan, S.P.S., Thappa, R.K., Agarwal, S.G., Dhar, K.L., and Atal, C.K. 1977. Cultivation of Pelargonium graveolens as annual crop. Pages 303-309 in C.K. Atal and B.M. Kapur, eds.

Cultivation & utilization of medicinal and aromatic plants. Regional Research Laboratory, Jammu-Tawi, India.

4.3-73 Gulati, B.C., and Duhan, S.P.S. 1972. Cultivation of sweet basil. Indian Farmers' Dig. 5{8}: 33-35. AGRICOLA.

4.3-74 Gungaadorzh, Sh., and Kononkov, P.F. 1975. Shallot culture in the Mongolian People's Republic [in Russian]. Sib. Vestn. S-kh. Nauki 2: 53-55. AGRICOLA.

4.3-75 Gupta, R. 1972. Cultivation and distillation of Japanese mint in India. Indian Farming 22{3}: 18-23. HA 43: 5500.

4.3-76 Gupta, R. 1977. Studies in cultivation and improvement of dill (Anethum graveolens) in India. Pages 337-349 in C.K. Atal and B.M. Kapur, eds. Cultivation & utilization of medicinal and aromatic plants. Regional Research Laboratory, Jammu-Tawi, India.

4.3-77 Gupta, R., and Sharma, V.S. 1972. Grow jasmine for flowers and perfume. Indian Hortic. 16{4}: 23, 25-27. AGRICOLA.

4.3-78 Guttormsen, G. 1974. Growing paprika and cucumber on peat beds of different shape and volume, and different levels of water supply [in Norwegian]. Res. Norw. Agric. 25: 307-315. AGRICOLA.

4.3-79 Guttormsen, G. 1976. Cultivation of paprika and snake cucumber on sod beds [in Norwegian]. Gartneryrket 66: 13. AGRICOLA.

4.3-80 Hajas, M. 1973. Large-scale parsley production [in Hungarian]. Kertes Zet es Szoleszet 22(49 Supplement): 6-8. HA 44: 4960.

4.3-81 Hamon, N.W., and Zuck, D.A. 1972. Peppermint as a cash crop in Saskatchewan. Can. J. Plant Sci. 52: 837-839.

4.3-82 Hanawa, J. 1972. Bud induction in Sesamum indicum by splitting shoot apices followed by treatment with Amo-1618. Bot. Mag. 85: 17-27. AGRICOLA.

4.3-83 Heinen, B. 1972. Special cultivation of chives [in German]. Landwirtschaftskammer Rheinl. Gartenbauliche Versuchsber 11: 117-121. AGRICOLA.

4.3-84 Homma, N., and Horikoshi, T. 1978. Studies on the cultivation of medicinal plants. X. Standard cultivation method of Papaver somniferum L. in northern Hokkaido. Eisei Shikenjo Hokoku 1978{96}: 158-161.

4.3-85 Hoque, M.M. 1974. A study on the cultivation of Cuminum cyminum in Bangladesh. Bangladesh Hortic. 2{1}: 37. HA 45: 9977.

4.3-86 Hore, B.K., and Bose, T.K. 1971. Effect of growth retarding chemicals on tropical ornamental shrubs. Indian Agr. 15{1-2}: 115-125. CA 77: 160955.

4.3-87 Hornok, L., Foldesi, D., and Szasz, K. 1975. Trials on modernizing thyme (Thymus vulgaris) cultivation [in Hungarian]. Herba Hung. 14{2/3}: 47-64 HA 46: 6071.

4.3-88 Isambaev, A.I., and Kuz'min, E.V. 1978. Cultivation of Glycyrrhiza uralensis and G. glabra on the flood-plain of the Syrdarya

river [in Russian]. Tr. Inst. Bot. Akad. Nauk Kaz. SSR 38: 114-121. HA
49: 2852.

4.3-89 Ivanchenko, N.Ya., and Ksendz, A.T. 1974. About the productivity
of sage at different cultural practices [in Russian]. Tr. Vses.
Nauchno-Issled. Inst. Efirnomaslichn. Kul't. 7: 69-74.

4.3-90 Ivashchenko, A.A. 1972. Ways of improving production of Mentha
piperita products [in Russian]. Pages 115-124 in A.G. Nikolaev, ed.
Khimicheskaia izmenchivost' rastenii. Shtiintsa, Kishinev, USSR.
AGRICOLA.

4.3-91 Ivashenko, A. 1973. Raising cultural technique [in Russian].
Zemledelie 5: 49-50. AGRICOLA.

4.3-92 Jackson, D. 1979. How to grow and enjoy the common basil. Flower
Gard. West Ed. 23{5}: 17. AGRICOLA.

4.3-93 Jaruzelski, M., and Uszynska, U. 1976. Planting and harvesting
lovage roots in Legnica region [in Polish]. Wiad. Zielarski 18{3}:
7-9. AGRICOLA.

4.3-94 Jaruzelski, M. 1977. Yields of caraway [in Polish]. Wiad.
Zielarskie 19{9}: 4-7. AGRICOLA.

4.3-95 Kapoor, L.D. 1977. Availability of medicinal and aromatic plants
in north-west India. Pages 439-448 in C.K. Atal and B.M. Kapur, eds.
Cultivation & utilization of medicinal and aromatic plants. Regional
Research Laboratory, Jammu-Tawi, India.

4.3-96 Karnick, C.R. 1976. Cultivation of Indian medicinal drug plants:
Glycyrrhiza glabra Linn. Agric. Agro-ind. J. 9{5}: 19-21.

4.3-97 Kasano, H. 1975. Characteristics of the high- yielding mint
variety Wasenami and cultural and processing techniques [in Japanese].
Nogyo Oyobi Engei 50: 123-127. PBA 46: 10757.

4.3-98 Kaushik, S.N., and Sing, D. 1977. Mint cultivation in India.
Kurukshetra 25{19}: 16-17. HA 48: 5876.

4.3-99 Khan, M.N.A., and Sarwar, M. 1977. On the production of plant
based raw materials for aromatic and pharmaceutical industries. Pages
492-494 in C.K. Atal and B.M. Kapur, eds. Cultivation & utilization of
medicinal and aromatic plants. Regional Research Laboratory,
Jammu-Tawi, India.

4.3-100 Khan, M.N.A. 1977. Cultivation of geranium. Pages 316-318 in
C.K. Atal and B.M. Kapur, eds. Cultivation & utilization of medicinal
and aromatic plants. Regional Research Laboratory, Jammu-Tawi, India.

4.3-101 Khilik, L.A., Bondarenko, T.I., Drevyatnikov, I.M., and
Raikhman, D.B. 1976. Methods of cultivating the new essential oil crop
plant Nepeta transcaucasica [in Russian]. Rastit. Resur. 12: 281-287.
HA 46: 1160.

4.3-102 Khotin, A. 1972. Methods of growing of Papaver somniferum and
the value of the obtained raw material. Postep Dziedzinie Leku Rosl.
Pr. Ref. Dosw. Wygloszone Symp., 1970; Herba Pol. Suppl. 1972:
196-202.

4.3-103 Khristov, S., Dimov, I., and Belev, B. 1977. Nontransplanted crops of red pepper [in German]. Int. Z. Landwirtsch. 1977{1}: 31-33.

4.3-104 Khudaibergenov, E.B., Isambaev, A.I., and Demidovskaya, L.F. 1976. The productivity of Glycyrrhiza uralensis in the delta of the river Ili [in Russian]. Tr. Inst. Bot. Akad. Nauk Kaz. SSR 35: 106-111. HA 47: 3947.

4.3-105 Klassen, A.J., and Downey, R.K. 1979. Rapeseed today. Can. Agric. 24{1}: 3-4. PBA 50: 2242.

4.3-106 Kneissl, P. 1976. Paprika culture experiments 1972 to 1974 [in German]. Gemuse 12: 194-196. AGRICOLA.

4.3-107 Kokate, C.K., and Varma, K.C. 1971. Cultivation of lemon-grass (Cymbopogon citratus (DC) Stapf) and citronella-grass (C. nardus Rendle) at Sagar, Madhya Pradesh. Indian J. Agric. Sci. 41: 382-385.

4.3-108 Kolev, E. 1972. Investigations on the aerodynamic properties of vegetable seeds and their impurities [in Bulgarian]. Gradinar. Lozar. Nauk 9{6}: 81-89. HA 43: 4373.

4.3-109 Koto, T. 1971. Growth of Spanish paprika and its production stability [in Japanese]. Nogyo Oyobi Engei 46: 1323-1326. AGRICOLA.

4.3-110 Kozhanov, N.T. 1973. Increasing the effectiveness of coriander production [in Russian]. Zernovye Maslichn. Kul't. 1973{11}; 37-38.

4.3-111 Krejcik, V. 1973. Where are the flowers borne on chamomile [in Czech]. Nase Liecive Rastliny 10: 44-46. HA 43: 8030.

4.3-112 Krejcik, V. 1977. Agricultural practices (for medicinal plants) [in Czech]. Nase Liecive Rastliny 14: 137-147. HA 48: 3845.

4.3-113 Krikorian, A.D., and Ledbetter, M.C. 1975. Some observations on the cultivation of opium poppy (Papaver somniferum L.) for its latex. Bot. Rev. 41: 30-103.

4.3-114 Kuribayashi, T., and Ohashi, H. 1977. Physiological and ecological studies on the stage of development of Panax ginseng. Approach to cultivation [in Japanese]. Michurin Seibutsugaku Kenkyu 13{1}: 16-24.

4.3-115 Kuz'min, E.V., Isambaev, A.I., Dzhakupova, N.U., and Saurambaev, B.N. 1977. Trials on cultivation of Glycyrrhiza glabra and fodder crops in Kzyl-Ordyn province [in Russian]. Izv. Akad. Nauk Kaz. SSR Ser. Biol. 1977{4}: 10-13. HERB AB 49: 472.

4.3-116 Kuz'min, E.V. 1972. The effect of the depth of ploughing of licorice meadows and methods of root harvesting on licorice regeneration in the Ural region [in Russian]. Tr. Inst. Bot. Akad. Nauk Kaz. SSR 31: 69-78. HA 43: 5524.

4.3-117 Kuz'min, E.V., and Mikhailova, V.P. 1978. Seed propagation of cultivated Glycyrrhiza uralensis and G. glabra in the Ural river valley [in Russian]. Tr. Inst. Bot. Akad. Nauk Kaz. SSR 38: 122-128. HA 49: 2853.

4.3-118 Laczko, T. 1976. Culture of pimento peppers is in danger [in Hungarian]. Kertgazdasag 8{1}: 78-82. AGRICOLA.

4.3-119 Larkcom, J. 1978. Basil. Garden (London) 103: 236-237.

4.3-120 Larkcom, J. 1978. Inside the french lavender scene. GC HTJ 183{2}: 36-37.

4.3-121 Lawrence, B.M. 1979. Commercial production of non-citrus essential oils in North America. Perfum. Flavor. 3{6}: 21-33. HA 49: 6963.

4.3-122 Laza, A., Mihalea, A., and Silva, F. 1972. Methods and results of growing Digitalis lanata and Digitalis purpurea in Romania [in Polish]. Herba Pol. Suppl. 1972: 212-228.

4.3-123 Lee, R.B. 1980. Thymes. Herb Q. 2{6}: 11-13. Bib. Ag. 44: 74141.

4.3-124 Lenkiewicz, W., and Wisniewski, A. 1976. Comparison of different methods of growing horseradish [in Polish]. Biul. Warzywniczy 19: 89-104. HA 48: 1645.

4.3-125 Lukianov, I.A. 1973. Seed culture of Coriandrum aand Pimpinella anisum and problems of improvement [in Russian]. Pages 373-380 in P.S. Pustovoit, ed. Selektsiia i semenovodstvo tekhnicheskikh kul'tur. "Kolos", Moscow, USSR. AGRICOLA.

4.3-126 Maccioni, G. 1972. Cultivation of dill in Liguria [in Italian]. Not. Ortofruttic. 24: 2463-2466. AGRICOLA.

4.3-127 Maiti, R.G. 1978. Grow cumin, it pays. Intensive Agric. 15{8}: 22-23.

4.3-128 Malik, S., Iftikhar, S., Shah, H., and Malik, N.A. 1972. Cultivation of Melissa officinalis L. at Peshawar. Pak. J. Sci. 24{1/2}: 96-99. HA 44: 3432.

4.3-129 Mandal, B.K., and Rao, M.V. 1976. Improving the yield of Sesamum in Orissa. Indian Farming 27, i.e. 26{6}: 25.

4.3-130 Martindale, W.L. 1973. Vegetables, parsley and mint. J. Agric. (Victoria, Aust.) 71: 142-143.

4.3-131 Martindale, W.L. 1973. Vegetables: marjoram, sage and thyme. J. Agric. (Victoria, Aust.) 71: 185-186.

4.3-132 Marzi, V. 1976. Salad crops: improving growing methods to recapture the market [in Italian]. Informatore Agrario 32: 23283-23286. HA 47: 5496.

4.3-133 Mathur, N.K. 1972. Grow mint this way. Agric. Agro-Ind. J. 5{8}: 7-8. AGRICOLA.

4.3-134 Mathur, S.C. 1973. Saffron cultivation in Himachal Pradesh. Indian Farming 23{5}: 29, 31. AGRICOLA.

4.3-135 Meeker, J. 1979. Fennel: A good late-season vegetable. Org. Gard. 26{7}: 63-65.

4.3-136 Mehta, K.G. 1977. Fenugreek cultivation in Gujarat. Indian Arecanut, Spices and Cocoa Journal 1{1}: 5-6. HA 48: 6851.

4.3-137 Meshcheriuk, G., and Sergeeva, E. 1977. Foeniculum vulgare as an essential oil crop [in Russian]. Sel'sk. Khoz. Mold. 9: 25. AGRICOLA.

4.3-138 Messiaen, C.M. 1971. Garlic growing in Guadelope [in French]. Nouvelles Maraicheres et Vivrieres de l'INRA aux Antilles 1971{1}: 1-4. HA 43: 5294.

4.3-139 Metcalf, H.N., and Burnham, M. 1977. Miscellany, including celeriac, horseradish, artichoke, peanuts, vegetable soybeans. U.S. Dep. Agric., Yearb. Agric. 1977: 228-244. Bib. Ag. 44: 38848.

4.3-140 Mills, W.D. 1975. Garlic growing in the Lockyer Valley. Queensl. Agric. J. 101: 529-549.

4.3-141 Mital, S.P., Kazim, M., Bhagat, N.R., Maheshwari, M.L., and Saxena, D.B. 1977. Russian peppermints for high oil. Indian Hortic. 21{4}: 13-14, 24.

4.3-142 Miyazawa, Y. 1976. Studies on the culture of Panax quinquefolium L. and Panax japonicum C.A. Meyer [in Japanese]. Bull. Nagano Hortic. Exp. Stn. 13: 32-36. AGRICOLA.

4.3-143 Miyazawa, Y. 1975. Techniques for the culture of ginseng, Panax ginseng, for medical use [in Japanese]. Nogyo Oyobi Engei 50{1}: 117-122. AGRICOLA.

4.3-144 Molyneux, F. 1975. Licorice production and processing. Food Technology in Australia 27: 231-234. HA 46: 7082.

4.3-145 Mullenberg, M., and Rogoll, H. 1976. The growing and plant protection of medicinal and spice plants [in German]. Nachrichtenbl. Pflanzenschutz DDR 30: 172-174. HA 47: 5865.

4.3-146 Muller-Haslach, W., and Hirschfeld, D. 1980. Raising herbs for sale as young plants. An additional source of income for retailers [in German]. Dtsch. Gartenbau 35: 2042-2044. HA 51: 7217.

4.3-147 Munoz de Con, L. 1973. Increased productivity in garlic [in Spanish]. Rev. Agric. (Havana) 6{2}: 12-51. PBA 46: 2987.

4.3-148 Nerum, K. van. 1976. Scientific studies of and for chicory production in Belgium [in Flemish]. Agricultura (Heverlee, Belg.) 24{2}: 1-84. WAERSA 19: 4290.

4.3-149 Nieweglowski, A. 1974. Some problems involved in poppy culture. Nowe Roln. 23{3}: 11. AGRICOLA.

4.3-150 Nikitina, A.Ya. 1975. Results of studies on cress and coriander sown on different dates at the Dagestan experiment station of VIR [in Russian]. Tr. Prikl. Bot. Genet. Sel. 55{2}: 185-192. HA 46: 10249.

4.3-151 Nikitushkin, M.F. 1976. Cultivation of German chamomile in Czechoslovakia. Pharm. Chem. J. (Engl. Transl.) 10: 208-211. Translation of Khim.-Farm. Zh. 10{2}: 75-80, 1976.

4.3-152 Ota, K., and Miyawaki, K. 1975. Cultivation and forcing methods in chicory [in Japanese]. Nogyo Oyobi Engei 50: 551-554. PBA 47: 819.

4.3-153 Padula, L.Z., Collura, A.M., Rondina, R.V.D., Mizrahi, I.,

Coussio, J.D., and Juarez, M.A. 1977. Experimental cultivation of *Elyonurus* *muticus* in Argentina. Qualitative and quantitative analysis of the essential oil [in Spanish]. Riv. Ital. Essenze Profumi Piante Off. Aromi Saponi Cosmet. Aerosol 59: 58–63. HA 48: 4897.

4.3-154 Palevitch, D. 1978. Cultural practices and cultivars for once-over harvested sweet paprika. Acta Hortic. 73: 255–262.

4.3-155 Pank, F. 1974. The influence of different types of plant material on the production of peppermint (*Mentha* *piperita* L.) in the 1st year of cultivation. Pharmazie 29: 344–346.

4.3-156 Pantielev, Ia.Kh., Agafonova, I.P., and Smirnov, I.M. 1976. Effective method of growing parsley and celery greens [in Russian]. Kartofel. Ovoshchi 1975{8}: 29–30. AGRICOLA.

4.3-157 Pappiah, C.M., Sambandamurthi, S., and Jayapal, R. 1980. Agrotechniques in jasmines – a resume. Pages 21–24 *in* National seminar on production technology for commercial flower crops. Tamil Nadu Agricultural University, Coimbatore, India. HA 51: 7987.

4.3-158 Pareek, S.K., Trivedi, K.C., Maheshwari, S.K., Gangarade, S.K., Masheshwari, M.L., and Gupta, R. 1980. Studies on cultivation of anise in India. Indian Perfum. 24: 88–92.

4.3-159 Pattanaik, S. 1974. Til in Orissa. Intensive Agric. 11{11}: 14.

4.3-160 Peterka, V. 1972. Experience in growing cumin in eastern Bohemia [in Czech]. Uroda 20: 185–186. AGRICOLA.

4.3-161 Pimpini, F. 1978. Red leaved chicory. Types, cultural techniques and breeding [in Italian]. Informatore Agrario 34: 2201–2222. HA 49: 1168.

4.3-162 Prasad, S., and Saxena, M.C. 1979. Grow *Mentha* in right way. Farmer Parliament 14{1}: 13–14.

4.3-163 Putievsky, E., and Basker, D. 1977. Experimental cultivation of marjoram, oregano and basil. J. Hortic. Sci. 52: 181–188.

4.3-164 Putievsky, E., and Kuris, A. 1976. Spices of the family Labiatae (A) [in Hebrew]. Hassadeh 56: 1899–1903. HA 47: 3916.

4.3-165 Putievsky, E., and Kuris, A. 1976. Spices of the family Labiatae (C) *Marjoran* *hortensis* M. Hassadeh 57: 36–38. HA 47: 7766.

4.3-166 Putievsky, E. 1978. Growing mint for essential oil and leaves [in Hebrew]. Hassadeh 58: 1743–1746. HA 49: 9563.

4.3-167 Putievsky, E. 1978. *Laurus* *nobilis* as a cultivated crop [in Hebrew]. Hassadeh 58: 2026–2028. HA 49: 2115.

4.3-168 Putievsky, E., Kuris, A., and Ron, R. 1978. Spices of the family Labiatae: sage, balm and thyme [in Hebrew]. Hassadeh 58: 2222–2225. HA 49: 2832.

4.3-169 Putievsky, E., and Kuris, A. 1979. Spices of the family Labiatae: growing *Origanum* and *Majorana* for more than three years [in Hebrew]. Hassadeh 60: 452–454. HA 50: 7916.

4.3-170 Putievsky, E., Sanderowich, D., and Ron, R. 1980. Growing spice plants from seeds or cuttings [in Hebrew]. Hassadeh 60: 1262-1265. HA 51: 598.

4.3-171 Putievsky, E., and Kuris, A. 1977. A method for growing caraway as an annual crop [in Hebrew]. Hassadeh 57: 1776-1778. AGRICOLA.

4.3-172 Ramanathan, V.S., and Ramachandran, C. 1977. Opium poppy: cultivation, collection of opium, improvement and utilization for medicinal purposes. Pages 68-74 in C.K. Atal and B.M. Kapur, eds. Cultivation & utilization of medicinal and aromatic plants. Regional Research Laboratory, Jammu-Tawi, India.

4.3-173 Rhodes, A.M. 1977. Horseradish--Problems and research in Illinois. Pages 137-148 in D.S. Seigler, ed. Crop resources. Proceedings of the 17th annual meeting of the Society for Economic Botany, Urbana, Ill., June, 1976. Academic Press, New York, N.Y.

4.3-174 Rod, H.K. 1979. Paprika: pruning, varieties, labor [in Norwegian]. Gartneryrket 69: 36-38. AGRICOLA.

4.3-175 Ruminska, A. 1978. Exotic condiments: saffron [in Polish]. Wiad. Zielarskie 20{3}: 13-14. AGRICOLA.

4.3-176 Ruminska, A., Suchorska, K., and Weglarz, Z. 1977. Growing mint in an annual or several years' cycle [in Polish]. Wiad. Zielarskie 19{3}: 1-3. AGRICOLA.

4.3-177 Ruminska, A. 1976. Paprika, Capsicum annuum [in Polish]. Wiad. Zielarskie 18{6}: 14-16. AGRICOLA.

4.3-178 Rynkowski, H. 1978. Cultivation of caraway on the Zulawy lowlands [in Polish]. Wiad. Zielarskie 20{7}: 12-13. AGRICOLA.

4.3-179 Savenko, L.A. 1977. Effectiveness of coriander seed production [in Russian]. Zernovoe Khoz. 1977{6}: 43-44. AGRICOLA.

4.3-180 Savenko, L.A. 1978. Coriander crops on the fields of the Zhdanov Collective Farm [in Russian]. Zernovoe Khoz. 1978{10}: 42-43. AGRICOLA.

4.3-181 Sawhney, J.S., Mahajan, V.P., and Sidhu, M.S. 1980. Harvest a good crop of coriander. Prog. Farming 17{4}: 10. AGRICOLA.

4.3-182 Scherer, H. 1976. Hints for parsley cultivation [in German]. Leben. Erde 5 (Suppl. 106): 34-35. AGRICOLA.

4.3-183 Scherer, J. 1980. Sweet woodruff. Herb Q. 2{7}: 20-21. AGRICOLA.

4.3-184 Sharma, R.K., and Agarwal, H.R. 1978. Package of practices for cumin cultivation. Farmer Parliament 13{12}: 6, 29-30.

4.3-185 Sharma, S.N., and Singh, A. 1979. Studies on agro-technology for the cultivation of peppermint: row spacing and stolen rate. Indian J. Agron. 24: 370-371.

4.3-186 Sharma, T.R. 1978. Grow Sesamum this way. Intensive Agric. 15{5}: 14-15.

4.3-187 Silva, V. de P.S. da. 1976. Considerations on comfrey culture [in Portuguese]. Anu. Tec. Inst. Pesqui. Zootec. 3: 609-615. AGRICOLA.

4.3-188 Singh, A., Balyan, S.S., and Shahi, A.K. 1977. Cultivation of Mentha piperita in Jammu. Pges 199-203 in C.K. Atal and B.M. Kapur, eds. Cultivation & utilization of medicinal and aromatic plants. Regional Research Laboratory, Jammu-Tawi, India.

4.3-189 Singh, A. 1977. Cultivation of Matricaria chamomilla. Pages 350-352 in C.K. Atal and B.M. Kapur, eds. Cultivation & utilization of medicinal and aromatic plants. Regional Research Laboratory, Jammu-Tawi, India.

4.3-190 Singh, B.S., and Singh, S.P. 1980. How to make Mentha cultivation profitable. Farmer Parliament 15{5}: 11-12, 29.

4.3-191 Singh, C. 1972. Toward high yields of til. Indian Farmers' Dig. 5{7}: 55-56. AGRICOLA.

4.3-192 Singh, H.S., Bhagat, S.D., Mathur, R.K., Gopinath, K.W., and Ganguly, D. 1971. Cultivation of basil (Ocimum basilicum L. at Jorhat, Assam, and the chemical composition of its oil. Flavour Ind. 2: 481-483.

4.3-193 Singh, J.P., Singh, J.N., Gulati, B.C., and Singh, D.P. 1977. The effects of growth conditions on the yield and quality of essential oil of Mentha arvensis L. New Bot. 4{1/4}: 19-22. Bib.Ag. 43: 112976.

4.3-194 Singh, L. 1977. Commercial cultivation of Mentha arvensis in Tarai area. Pages 195-198 in C.K. Atal and B.M. Kapur, eds. Cultivation & utilization of medicinal and aromatic plants. Regional Research Laboratory, Jammu-Tawi, India.

4.3-195 Singh, P. 1977. Cultivation of Digitalis spp. Pages 80-85 in C.K. Atal and B.M. Kapur, eds. Cultivation & utilization of medicinal and aromatic plants. Regional Research Laboratory, Jammu-Tawi, India.

4.3-196 Sinnadurai, S. 1973. Hot pepper production. Ghana Farmer 17{1}: 9-12. AGRICOLA.

4.3-197 Sinnadurai, S. 1973. Vegetable production in Ghana. Acta Hortic. 1973{33}: 25-27.

4.3-198 Skroumites, V. 1975. Aromatic plants: the culture of Mentha [in Greek]. Agrotika Niata 6{3}: 18-19. AGRICOLA.

4.3-199 Skrubis, B. 1979. Origanum dictamus L., a Greek native plant. J. Ethnopharmacol. 1: 411-415. HA 50: 6532.

4.3-200 Sreedharan, A., and Chandrasekharan Nair, K. 1975. Lemon grass cultivation. Indian Farming 25{9}: 27. PBA 47: 596.

4.3-201 Sundararajan, S., and Polappan, S. 1972. Cultivation of saffron. Farm Fact. 5{12}: 27-28. AGRICOLA.

4.3-202 Suzuki, H. 1974. Horseradish culture [in Japanese]. Ringyo Gijitsu 3: 17-20. AGRICOLA.

4.3-203 Svab, J. 1979. New aspects of chamomile cultivation [in German]. Herba Pol. 25: 35-39. HA 50: 550.

4.3-204 Svab, J. 1978. Problems and results of Foeniculum vulgare cultivation in large scale production in Hungary. Acta Hortic. 1978{73}: 297-302.

4.3-205 Szucs, K. 1974. The part of science in promoting red pepper growing [in Hungarian]. Bull. Zoldsegtermesztesi Kut. Intez. 9: 99-105. AGRICOLA.

4.3-206 Takahashi, K., and Senba, M. 1971. Culture of short-root ginseng [in Japanese]. Nogyo Oyobi Engei 46: 1725-1730. AGRICOLA.

4.3-207 Tikka, S.B.S., and Patel, V.J. 1977. Grow cumin for higher profits. Intensive Agric. 15{7}: 22-23.

4.3-208 Toba, K. 1975. Changes in the culture and production of dye plants [in Japanese]. Nogyo Oyobi Engei 50: 199-204.

4.3-209 Tursin, G.S., Zinchenko, V.K., and Sologub, F.I. 1975. Results of introducing a new method for producing garden sage seed [in Russian]. Tr. Prikl. Bot. Genet. Sel. 54{2}: 254-256. HA 46: 10670.

4.3-210 Tyuleneva, N.A. 1975. Growing garlic from aerial bulbils in Central Ural conditions [in Russian]. Tr. Ural. Nauchno-Issled. Inst. Sel'sk. Khoz. 15: 172-178. HA 46: 11212.

4.3-211 Uhlig, S.K. 1976. Indian production of essential oils - the situation, problems and trends in development [in German]. Pharm. Prax. 31: 188-192. HA 47: 3910.

4.3-212 Vandemark, J.S., and Splittstoesser, W.E. 1979. Growing herbs in the home garden. Ill. Res. 21{2}: 12-13.

4.3-213 Vanossi, L. 1975. Commercial notes on the spices: pepper and paprika [in Italian]. Ind. Aliment. (Pinerdo, Italy) 14{4}: 103-105. AGRICOLA.

4.3-214 Vaudois, J. 1975. Vegetable production, technical progress and economic organization of producers: chicory in the northern region [in French]. Hommes et Terres du Nord 1: 29-69. WAERSA 18: 6503.

4.3-215 Veeranna, V.S., Shanthamallaiah, N.R., and Patil, N.M. 1976. Growing safflower, castor and sunflower in rabi is profitable. Current Research 5: 202-203. FCA 30: 6397.

4.3-216 Walker, M.R., and Beattie, B.M. 1980. Peppermint oil production in Tasmania. Journal of Agriculture, Tasmania 51{1}: 5-8. HA 50: 9386.

4.3-217 Weisaeth, G. 1979. Investigations involving production of young caraway sprouts and of Carum carvi L. [in Norwegian]. Gartneryrket 69: 312, 314, 316-318. AGRICOLA.

4.3-218 Yermanos, D.M. 1971. Success with sesame [in Spanish]. Agric. Am. 20{5}: 12-14, 48. AGRICOLA.

4.3-219 Yokota, M. 1973. An experiment on the growth of Russian comfrey [in Japanese]. Nippon Sochi Gakkai-shi 19: 399-402. AGRICOLA.

4.3-220 Zalecki, R. 1972. The cultivation and manuring of tetraploid chamomile. Part II. Row width and sowing density [in Polish]. Herba Pol. 18: 70-78. HA 44: 3455.

4.3-221 Zaostrovskaya, E.N., and Emmerikh, N.S. 1974. Resources of less popular vegetables [in Russian]. Byull. Vses. Inst. Rastenievod. 1974{39}: 58-63. HA 45: 239.

4.3-222 Zlamev, S. 1975. Ascertainment of the seeding date of dill (Anethum graveolens L.) grown for essential oil [in Bulgarian]. Gradinar. Lozar. Nauka 12: 104-112. AGRICOLA.

4.3-223 Zwaving, J.H., and Smith, D. 1971. Composition of the essential oil of Austrian Mentha pulegium. Phytochemistry 10: 1951-1953.

4.4 Planting, Propagation, and Transplanting

4.4-1 Adjei-Twum, D.C. 1980. The influence of bulb size and bulb cutting on the growth and yield of shallots (Allium cepa var. aggregatum G. Don.) in Ghana. J. Hortic. Sci. 55: 139-143.

4.4-2 Alborishvili, Ch.A. 1971. The variability of economic and biological characters in lettuce and coriander varieties in relation to the time of sowing [in Russian]. Tr. Prikl. Bot. Genet. Sel. 45{1}: 216-227. HA 43: 4407.

4.4-3 Anonymous. 1973. Disposable containers: no quality reduction. Gdnrs. Chron. 174{23}: 28-29.

4.4-4 Anonymous. 1979. Mechnical horseradish planting [in German]. Gemuse 15: 22. HA 49: 6094.

4.4-5 Arumugam, R., and Kumar, N. 1980. Effect of leaves on rooting of stem cuttings of bergamot mint (Mentha citrata Ehrh). Indian Perfum. 24: 166-167.

4.4-6 Babichev, V.A. 1971. On planting ratio of coriander in seed growing plantations [in Russian]. Pages 414-417 in I.I. Siniagin, ed. Normy vyseva, sposoby poseva i ploshchadi pitaniia sel'skohoziaistvennykh kul'tur. "Kolos", Moscow, USSR. AGRICOLA.

4.4-7 Balyan, S.S., and Singh, A. 1975. Studies on optimum time of planting Mentha. Indian J. Agron. 20: 192-193. HA 47: 768.

4.4-8 Beauchesne, G., Albouy, J., Morand, J.C., and Daquenet, J. 1977. Clonal propagation of Pelargonium X hortorum and Pelargonium X peltatum from meristem culture for disease free cuttings [in French]. Acta Hortic. 1977{78}: 397-402.

4.4-9 Belyaev, V.V. 1973. Experiments on growing lavender transplants at the Nikita Botanic Gardens [in Russian]. Byull. Gos. Nikitsk. Bot. Sada 1973{2}: 65-67. HA 45: 3430.

4.4-10 Bobrova, R.A., and Mukminova, F.Z. 1976. Effect of the size of planting material on the yield of horseradish roots [in Russian]. Vestn. S-kh. Nauki Kaz. 1976{7}: 115-119. AGRICOLA.

4.4-11 Bobrova, R.A., and Mukminova, F.Z. 1976. Methods of planting horseradish [in Russian]. Vestn. S-kh. Nauki Kaz. 1976{5}: 37-39. 47: 5868.

4.4-12 Booth, A., and Satchuthananthavale, R. 1974. Regeneration in root cuttings of Taraxacum officinale. I. The nature and levels of endogenous hormones. New Phytol. 73: 445-452.

4.4-13 Bose, T.K., Mondal, D.P., and Pramanik, D.K. 1973. Propagation of Ixora, Hibiscus and Jasminum from cutting under mist. Prog. Hortic. 5{3}: 43-50. HA 46: 1454.

4.4-14 Bose, T.K., and Mondal, D.P. 1972. Propagation of ornamental plants under mist. Punjab Hortic. J. 12: 223-234. HA 44: 4064.

4.4-15 Boyadzhieva, B., Zlatev, S., Koseva, D., and Decheva, R. 1977. Studies on the vegetative propagation of lavender [in Bulgarian]. Rastenievud Nauki 14{6}: 77-85. HA 48: 6783.

4.4-16 Bukhbinder, A.A. 1973. The effect of planting density on the biological characteristics of geranium development in the Kolkhida lowland [in Russian]. Subtrop. Kul't. 1973{2}: 120-123. HA 44: 3438.

4.4-17 Buyukli, M.V., and Shagieva, Z.A. 1974. Lavender propagation by hardwood cuttings [in Russian]. Tr. Kishinev. S-kh. Inst. im. M.V. Frunze 121: 114-118. HA 45: 8797.

4.4-18 Cappelle, W., and Lips, J. 1977. Planting witloof chicory roots in beds [in French]. Rev. Agric. (Brussels) 30: 417-436. HA 48: 2281.

4.4-19 Cesar, G. 1974. Some notes on the effect of seed size on germination in witloof chicory and carrot [in French]. Pepinier. Hortic. Maraichers 1974{144}: 53, 55-56. HA 45: 260.

4.4-20 Chen, J.-B., Kwong, K.-H., and Chiu, Y.-M. 1976. Studies on the feasibility of mechanical planting for garlic (Allium sativum L.) [in Chinese]. T'ai-wan T'ang Yeh Yen Chiu So Yen Chiu Hui Pao 73: 31-41. HA 47: 8359.

4.4-21 Chingova-Boyadzhieva, B. 1974. Vegetative and seed propagation of lavender [in Bulgarian]. Rastenievud. Nauki 11{10}: 84-92. HA 45: 7737.

4.4-22 Christov, S., Dimov, I., and Velev, B. 1977. Direct sowing of paprika [in German]. Int. Z. Landwirtsch. 1977{1}: 31-33. AGRICOLA.

4.4-23 Darby, R.J., and Salter, P.J. 1976. A technique for osmotically pre-treating and germinating quantities of small seeds. Ann. Appl. Biol. 83: 313-315.

4.4-24 Darby, R.J. 1980. Effects of seed carriers on seedling establishments after fluid drilling. Exp. Agric. 16: 153-160. CA 93: 127099.

4.4-25 Debergh, P., and Maene, L. 1977. Rapid clonal propagation of pathogen-free Pelargonium plants starting from shoot tips and apical meristems. Acta Hortic. 1977{78}: 449-454.

4.4-26 Diachenko, I.P. 1975. Reproduction of planting material, yield and raw product quality of peppermint [in Russian]. Tr. Vses. Nauchno-Issled. Inst. Efirnomaslichn. Kul't. 8: 45-47.

4.4-27 Dranygina, L.M. 1978. The shoot forming capacity of horseradish in relation to the diameter of the planting material [in Russian]. Tr. Vses. S–kh. Inst. Zaochn. Obraz. 1978{148}: 95. HA 49: 8820.

4.4-28 Duhan, S.P.S., Bhattacharya, A.K., and Gulati, B.C. 1974. Effect of date of sowing and nitrogen on the yield of seed and quality of oil of Anethum graveolens. Indian J. Pharm. 36: 5-7. HA 45: 1218.

4.4-29 Fawusi, M.O.A. 1978. Emergence and seedling growth of pepper as influenced by soil compaction nutrient status and moisture regime. Sci. Hortic. (Amsterdam) 9: 329-336.

4.4-30 Foldesi, D., and Havas, I. 1979. Peppermint (Mentha piperita) propagation by rooted stolon shoots [in Hungarian]. Herba Hung. 18{1}: 63-73. HA 50: 499.

4.4-31 Franken, A.A. 1975. Forcing witloof chicory in containers [in Dutch]. Bedrijfsontwikkeling 6: 865-867. HA 46: 7566.

4.4-32 Garland, P., and Stoltz, L.P. 1980. In-vitro propagation of tarragon Artemisia dracunculus var. sativa. HortScience 15: 739.

4.4-33 Griffin, R.H. 1977. Direct seeding in Northern forest types. U.S. For. Serv. Gen. Tech. Rep. NE 29: 111-125.

4.4-34 Gunay, A.L., and Rao, P.S. 1978. In vitro plant regeneration from hypocotyl and cotyledon explants of red pepper (Capsicum). Plant Sci. Lett. 11: 365-372.

4.4-35 Hagiladi, A., and Ben-Jaacov, J. 1977. The use of "Speedling Trays" for rooting ornamental cuttings [in Hebrew]. Hassadeh 57: 1086, 1088-1089. HA 47: 10585.

4.4-36 Hardman, R., and Petropoulos, G.A. 1975. The response of Trigonella foenum-graecum (fenugreek) to field inoculation with Rhizobium meliloti 2012. Planta Med. 27: 53-57.

4.4-37 Hartmann, H.D., and Waldhor, O. 1979. Planting distances with winter parsley [in German]. Gemuse 15: 282-284. HA 50: 3614.

4.4-38 Heydecker, W., and Hendy, A. 1975. Pre-treating bedding plant seed for 'instant' germination. Commer. Grow. 1975{4163}: 613-615. HA 46: 4755.

4.4-39 Horikoshi, T., Homma, N., and Furuki, M. 1975. Studies on the cultivation of medicinal plants. IV. On the raising of seedlings of Angelica acutiloba Kitagawa var. sugiyamae Hikino [in Japanese]. Bull. Natl. Inst. Hyg. Sci. (Tokyo) 93: 145-147. CIM 17{2}: 2672.

4.4-40 Hornok, L. 1976. The effect of sowing date on the yield and essential oil content of coriander (Coriandrum sativum) [in Hungarian]. Herba Hung. 15{1}: 55-62. HA 47: 1824.

4.4-41 Hor, Y.L. 1973. A survey of the quality of some vegetable, spice and cover crop seeds on sale in Kuala Lumpur. Malaysian Agric. Res. 2{2}: 23-29. FCA 28: 4985.

4.4-42 Ivanov, V.V. 1975. Growing sweet basil with pelleted seeds [in Russian]. Subtrop. Kul't. 1975{6}: 71-72. HA 47: 2905.

4.4-43 Jaruzelski, M., and Zdziechowski, J. 1976. Evaluation of two methods of planting lovage [in Polish]. Wiad. Zielarskie 18{2}: 5-6. AGRICOLA.

4.4-44 Jayapal, R., Sambandamurthi, S., and Vedamuthu, P.G.B. 1980. A rapid method of propagation of jasmines. Pages 15-16 in National seminar on production technology for commercial flower crops. Tamil Nadu Agricultural University, Coimbatore, India. HA 51: 7175.

4.4-45 Kazakova, K. 1971. Study of planting method and seeding rate of annual fennel [in Russian]. Rastenievud. Nauki 8{2}: 97-103. AGRICOLA.

4.4-46 Khoder, M., Villemur, P., and Jonard, R. 1979. In vitro micropropagation and stem cuttings of Jasminum officinale [in French]. C. R. Hebd. Seances Acad. Sci. Ser. D 228: 323-326.

4.4-47 Kireeva, S.A., and Bylda, A.Z. 1973. The physiology of root formation in lavender softwood cuttings [in Russian]. Tr. Vses. Nauchno-Issled. Inst. Efirnomaslichn. Kul't. 5: 35-40. HA 44: 5987.

4.4-48 Kohder, M., Villemur, P., and Jonard, R. 1979. Micropropagation and stem cutting in vitro of jasmine (Jasminum officinale L.) [in French]. C.R. Hebd. Seances Acad. Sci. Ser. D 288: 323-326.

4.4-49 Koseva, D., and Decheva, R. 1972. The effect of endogenous factors on rooting of two varieties of lavender. Sov. Plant Physiol. (Engl. Transl.) 19: 628-631. Translation of Fiziol. Rast. (Moscow) 19: 748-751, 1972.

4.4-50 Kuris, A., Altman, A., and Putievsky, E. 1980. Rooting and initial establishment of stem cuttings of oregano, peppermint and balm. Sci. Hortic. (Amsterdam) 13: 53-59.

4.4-51 Kusumo, S., and Widjajanto, D.D. 1973. The effect of large bulblets used as seed on the yield and quality of garlic [in Indonesian]. Bul. Hortik. 'Tjahort' 1973{10}: 16-20. HA 46: 1063.

4.4-52 Ku, Y.S., Nho, S.P., Lee, G.J., Chung, D.S., and Kang, J.C. 1974. Studies on garlic cultivation from bulbils [in Korean]. Res. Rep. Off. Rural Dev. (Hortic. Agri-Eng.) 16: 99-106. PBA 45: 6837.

4.4-53 Laroche, M., and Verhoyen, M. 1980. Trials on rapid multiplication in vitro of shallot (Allium ascalonicum) [in French]. Meded. Fac. Landbouwwet. Rijksuniv. Gent 45: 323-333. HA 51: 5436.

4.4-54 Maiti, R.G. 1975. Propagation of Jasminum sambac by short piece stem cuttings under auto humid chamber. Indian Sci. Cong. Assoc. Proc. 62 (pt. III Sect. X): 64 (Abstr.).

4.4-55 Mamedov, F.M. 1973. Propagation of some trees and shrubs by cuttings in open ground [in Russian]. Izv. Akad. Nauk Az. SSR Ser. Biol. Nauk 1973{2}: 7-10.

4.4-56 Mann, H., and Cavers, P.B. 1979. The regenerative capacity of root cuttings of Taraxacum officinale under natural conditions. Can. J. Bot. 57: 1783-1791.

4.4-57 Margara, J. 1977. Scheme of development with in vitro culture of Cichorium intybus, an example of a biennial long day plant needing vernalization [in French]. Bull. Soc. Bot. Fr. 124: 491-501.

4.4-58 Matai, S., Bagghi, D.K., and Chanda, S. 1973. Optimal seed rate and fertilizer dose for maximum yield of extracted protein from the leaves of mustard (Brassica rapa L.). Indian J. Agric. Sci. 43: 165-169. SF 39: 1507.

4.4-59 Mazzani, B., Martinez, A., and Allievi, J. 1971. Plant emergence and hypocotil [sic] length in four varieties of sesame sowed at different depths [in Spanish]. Agron. Trop. (Maracay, Venez.) 21: 11-15. AGRICOLA.

4.4-60 Meijer, E.N.C. 1978. Temporary covering of drilled lines of vegetable crops with transparent polythene film. Acta Hortic. 1978{72}: 251-253. HA 49: 1150.

4.4-61 Mendt, R.D., and Monaco, T.J. 1979. Prickly sida and cocklebur interference in transplanted peppers. Proc. South. Weed Sci. Soc. 32: 149 (Abstr.). WA 29: 3741.

4.4-62 Meyer, M.M., Jr., and Milbrath, G.M. 1977. In vitro propagation of horseradish with leaf pieces. HortScience 12: 544-545.

4.4-63 Mikailov, M.A., and Ragimova, Z.G. 1979. The biology of vegetative propagation of henna [in Russian]. Dokl. Akad. Nauk Az. SSR 35{2}: 65-69. HA 50: 3621.

4.4-64 Moskalenko, V.S. 1972. Autumn sowing of coriander (Coriandrum sativum) [in Russian]. Pages 120-122 in P.V. Naumenko et al., eds. Mezhdunarodnyi kongress po efirnym maslam, 4th, Tiflis, 1968, [Materialy], v. 2. Pishchevaya Promyshlennost', Moscow, USSR. HA 44: 4193.

4.4-65 Mustiatse, G. 1976. The requirement of high quality planting material. Sel'sk. Khoz. Mold. 1976{10}: 24-25. Bib. Ag. 42: 54841.

4.4-66 Nambisan, K.M.P., and Krishnan, B.M. 1980. Interspecies grafting in Jasminum. Pages 19-20 in National seminar on production technology for commercial flower crops. Tamil Nadu Agricultural University, Coimbatore, India. HA 51: 7177.

4.4-67 Norman, J.C. 1977. Effects of age of transplants on hot pepper (Capsicum sinense). Acta Hortic. 53: 43-48.

4.4-68 Om, H., and Srivastava, R.P. 1977. Influence of the planting material and spacing on the growth and yield of garlic. Indian J. Hortic. 34: 152-156. HA 48: 3358.

4.4-69 Om, H., and Srivastava, R.P. 1974. Influence of the time of planting on the growth and yield of garlic. Prog. Hortic. 6{2/3}: 71-76. HA 46: 2095.

4.4-70 Opsteeg, L.M. 1972. Annual bedding plants sown direct in the pot? [in Dutch]. Vakbl. Bloemisterij 27{6}: 21, 23. HA 43: 2165.

4.4-71 Osina, N.I. 1978. Pre-planting treatment of horseradish [in Russian]. Kartofel Ovoshchi 1978{7}: 33. HA 49: 6093.

4.4-72 Pandya, R.B., and Khan, M.I. 1973. Enhancement of raya (Brassica juncea Coss.) germination under simulated drought, by seed treatment with Cycocel (2-chloroethyl) trimethyl ammonium chloride. Biochem. Physiol. Pflanz. (BPP) 164: 112-115.

4.4-73 Pank, F. 1974. The influence of different planting material on the yield potential of the peppermint (Mentha piperita) in the first growing year [in German]. Pharmazie 29: 344-346. HA 44: 8917.

4.4-74 Pappiah, C.M., and Muthuswamy, S. 1976. A note on the effect of growth regulators on rooting of stem cuttings of Jasminum sambac Ait. var. gundumalli. South Indian Hortic. 24: 30-32.

4.4-75 Paulas, D. 1980. A new method of rapid multiplication of plants of Jasminum sambac Ait. cv. Gundumalli. Pages 17-18 in National seminar on production technology for commercial flower crops. Tamil Nadu Agricultural University, Coimbatore, India. HA 51: 7176.

4.4-76 Paupardin, C., Garcia-Rodriguez, M.J., and Bricout, M.J. 1980. Vegetative propagation of some aromatic plants: problems posed by essential oil production [in French]. C. R. Seances Acad. Agric. Fr. 66: 658-666. HA 51: 1478.

4.4-77 Pierik, R.L.M., Bragt, J. van, and Gelder, H. van. 1975. The rooting of cuttings. Immersion in a growth substance solution [in Dutch]. Vakbl. Bloemisterij 30{50}: 18-19. HA 46: 7791.

4.4-78 Putievsky, E. 1978. The optimal date for planting of Origanum vulgare [in Hebrew]. Hassadeh 58: 1269-1271. HA 48: 8510.

4.4-79 Ramakrishnan, V., Nagarajan, M., Thangaraj, M., and Giridharan, S. 1976. A study on the response of fenugreek (Trigonella foenum-graecum L.) to seed inoculation with Rhizobium. South Indian Hortic. 24: 60-61.

4.4-80 Raman, K.R., Veerannah, L., Balakrishnan, R., and Vasudevan, P. 1977. Effect of certain growth regulators on the rooting of geranium (Pelargonium graveolens L'Herit) (. Pages 310-313 in C.K. Atal and B.M. Kapur, eds. Cultivation & utilization of medicinal and aromatic plants. Regional Research Laboratory, Jammu-Tawi, India.

4.4-81 Roy, B.N., Roychoudhury, N., Bose, T.K., and Basu, R.N. 1972. Endogenous phenolic compounds as regulators of rooting in cuttings. Phyton 30{1-2}: 147-151.

4.4-82 Ruminska, A., and Suchorska, K. 1976. Attempts to improve field germination of the Grecian foxglove [in Polish]. Wiad. Zielarskie 18{10}: 5.

4.4-83 Ruminska, A., Lewkowicz-Mosiej, T., and Suchorska, K. 1976. Influence of soil conditions on germination and development of the Grecian foxglove seedlings [in Polish]. Wiad. Zielarskie 18{9}: 4-5.

4.4-84 Rutherford, P.P., and Thoday, P.R. 1976. Clonal production of tap-rooted plants of chicory. J. Hortic. Sci. 51: 167-168.

4.4-85 Sadowska, A. 1974. The effect of Wuxal on the rooting of Mentha piperita cuttings [in Polish]. Zesz. Probl. Postepow Nauk Roln. 1974{143}: 209-213. HA 45: 9998.

4.4-86 Saraswathamma, D.M., and Jayachandra. 1979. The influence of pre-sowing soaking with mineral solutions on the seedling growth in methi (Trigonella foenum-graecum L.) var. "Pusa Early Bunching". Curr. Sci. 48: 786-787.

4.4-87 Schreier, J. 1979. The optimal stand structure in oilseed poppy seed sown with pelleted seed [in Czech]. Rostl. Vyroba 25: 515-520. FCA 34: 3655.

4.4-88 Schroder, F.-J. 1978. Vegetative propagation and variability of Matricaria chamomilla L. Acta Hortic. 1978{73}: 73-80.

4.4-89 Serbina, N.M., and Demidov, L.V. 1975. The effect of planting material quality on the productivity of rose and lavender plantations [in Russian]. Tr. Vses. Nauchno-Issled. Inst. Efirnomaslichn. Kul't. 8: 82-85 HA 47: 8762.

4.4-90 Sheldon, J.C. 1974. The behavior of seeds in soil. 3. The influence of seed morphology and the behaviour of seedlings on the establishment of plants from surface-lying seeds. J. Ecol. 62: 47-66.

4.4-91 Shtonda, N.I. 1975. Vegetative propagation of the ginseng family Araliaceae [in Russian]. Introd. Akklim. Rast. 12: 29-33.

4.4-92 Singh, R.D. 1975. Effect of seed dressing fungicides on the germination, vigour and yield of cumin. Indian J. Mycol. Plant Pathol. 5: 44 (Abstr.). HA 47: 2896.

4.4-93 Singh, S.P. 1979. Speed up propagation of Jasminum. Indian Farmers Digest 12{3}: 37-38. HA 50: 9330.

4.4-94 Singh, S.P. 1976. Rooting of Jasminum sambac by semi-hardwood cuttings under intermittent mist. Haryana J. Hortic. Sci. 5: 111-114. HA 48: 2647.

4.4-95 Singh, S.P. 1979. Effect of rooting media and indole-3-butyric acid on root formation in Jasminum sambac cv. 'Motia' semi-hardwood cuttings under intermittent mist. Prog. Hortic. 11{2}: 49-52. HA 50: 6478.

4.4-96 Singh, S.P. 1980. Regeneration of Jasminum sambac under intermittent mist. Punjab Hortic. J. 20: 218-221. HA 51: 7988.

4.4-97 Sinkovics, M. 1974. A method of seed treatment with vitamin solutions for eating paprika. Acta Agron. Acad. Sci. Hung. 23: 410-413.

4.4-98 Srivastava, G.S., Shukla, D.S., and Awasthi, D.N. 1973. Comparative study on in situ and transplanting methods on growth and yield of Pimpinella anisum at Lucknow. Indian Perfum. 17{1}: 35-36. HA 46: 9610.

4.4-99 Staikov, V., Chingova, B., and Koseva, D. 1971. Possibilities of vegetative propagation of some lavender varieties with the aid of growth substances [in Russian]. Rastenievud. Nauki 8{2}: 89-95. AGRICOLA.

4.4-100 Stanley, J., and Williams, S. 1977. Direct rooting. GC & HTJ 182: 31-33. HA 48: 3641

4.4-101 Szepesy, K. 1974. Optimum spacing of the Szegedi red pepper varieties [in Hungarian]. Bull. Zoldsegtermesztesi Kut. Intez. 9: 151-154. AGRICOLA.

4.4-102 Thomas, T.H., Biddington, N.L., and Palevitch, D. 1978. Improving the performance of pelleted celery seeds with growth regulator treatments. Acta Hortic. 83: 235-243.

4.4-103 Tyl, M. 1972. New methods of sowing chamomile [in Czech]. Nase Liecive Rastliny 9: 132-134. HA 43: 3082.

4.4-104 Vadiel, B., Arumugam, R., and Kumar, N. 1980. Influence of row spacing on the yield and oil content of bergamot mint (Mentha citrata Ehrh.). Indian Perfum. 24{4}: 207-209.

4.4-105 Valovich, E.M., and Grif, V.G. 1974. Minimal temperatures for seed germination [in Russian]. Fiziol. Rast. 21: 1258-1264. HA 45: 6514.

4.4-106 Van Bragt, J., Van Gelder, H., and Pierik, R.L.M. 1976. Rooting of shoot cuttings of ornamental shrubs after immersion in auxin-containing solutions. Sci. Hortic. (Amsterdam) 4{1}: 91-94. CA 86: 101803.

4.4-107 Vasseur, J., and Bouriquet, R. 1973. The interaction of maleic hydrazide and purine and pyrimidine bases on bud initiation in vitro by chicory leaf pieces [in French]. C. R. Hebd. Seances Acad. Sci. Ser. D. 277: 641-644. HA 44: 5590.

4.4-108 Veluswamy, P., Vijayakumar, M., and Muthuswamy, S. 1980. Grafting in jasmines. South Indian Hortic. 28{4}: 156-157. HA 51: 3829.

4.4-109 Volosky, Y.,E. 1972. The size of the garlic clove and the type of bulb harvested [in Spanish]. Agric. Tec. (Santiago) 32: 32-37. HA 43: 3756.

4.4-110 Wieser, F. 1976. Possibilities and drawbacks of pelleting seeds [in German]. Bodenkultur 27: 385-397. HA 47: 10362.

4.4-111 Yaskonis, Yu.A. 1976. The propagation and growth of liquorice and the active principle content in the roots. (I. Propagation and growth) [in Russian]. Liet. TSR Mokslu Akad. Darb. Ser. C 1976{2}: 45-52. HA 47: 7794.

4.4-112 Zlatev, S. 1975. Determining the sowing date for dill (Anethum graveolens) grown for essential oil [in Bulgarian]. Gradinar. Lozar. Nauka 12{4}: 104-112. HA 46: 4934.

4.4-113 Zlatev, S., Atanasov, Zh., Zlateva, M., and Stoyanov, M. 1977. Interrow spacing of dill grown for essential oil [in Bulgarian]. Rastenievud Nauki 14{3}: 83-93.

4.4-114 Zlatev, S. 1977. Sowing rates of dill grown for essential oil production [in Bulgarian]. Rastenievud. Nauki 14{5}: 57-63. HA 48: 5865.

4.4-115 Zobenko, L.P., Romanenko, L.G., and Karpacheva, A.N. 1975. Comparative studies on the clonal and seed propagation of lavender [in Russian]. Tr. Vses. Nauchno-Issled. Inst. Efirnomaslichn. Kul't. 8: 29-32 HA 47: 8755.

4.5 Crop Maintenance

4.5-1 Abdallah, N., El-Gengaihi, S., and Sedrak, E. 1978. The effect of fertilizer treatments on yield of seed and volatile oil of fennel (Foeniculum vulgare Mill.). Pharmazie 33: 607-608. HA 49: 1447.

4.5-2 Alekseev, A.P., and Melent'eva, K.M. 1975. The effect of mineral nutrition on the productivity and nutrient consumption by plants of brown mustard [in Russian]. Agrokhimiya 1975{1}: 114-121. SF 39: 652.

4.5-3 Aliudin, and Suminto Tj. 1978. Utilization of compound fertilizers on garlic [in Indonesian]. Bull. Penelitian Hortik. 6{3}: 3-10. HA 49: 350.

4.5-4 Anonymous. 1974. Fertilization of red pepper [in Spanish]. Not. Agric. 7{11}: 43-44. AGRICOLA.

4.5-5 Anthonissen, J.J., Plumier, W., and Tilkin, V.E. 1975. Reflections on the fertilization of some vegetables [in French]. Rev. Agric. (Brussels) 28: 1243-1265. SF 39: 3154.

4.5-6 Antonov, V.I. 1972. Fertilization of Sinapis alba on grey forest soils in the Moscow Province [in Russian]. Doklady Moskovskoi Sel'skokhozyaistvennoi Akademii im. K.A. Timiryazeva 1972{181}: 150-151. HERB AB 43: 1460.

4.5-7 Arazyan, S.M. 1976. The effect of mineral fertilizers on the yield of geranium fresh herbage on ameliorated saline sodic soils [in Russian]. Tr. Nauchno-Issled. Inst. Pochvoved. Agrokhim. (Yerevan) 1976{11}: 231-241. HA 48: 2697.

4.5-8 Arora, S.K., Gupta, S.K., Khan, M.I., and Yadava, T.P. 1971. Chemical composition and yield of raya (Brassica juncea L.) (Czern and Coss) as affected by chemical treatment. Haryana Agric. Univ. J. Res. 1{3}: 24-27. FCA 27: 545.

4.5-9 Atanasov, Zh., Zlatev, S., Zlateva, M., and Stoyanov, M. 1976. Green mass yield and ethereal oil content of dill (Anethum graveolens) as influenced by mineral fertilization [in Bulgarian]. Rastenievud. Nauki 13{1}: 138-143.

4.5-10 Atanasov, Zh. 1976. The fertilizer requirements of lavender on a podzolized cinnamon soil [in Bulgarian]. Rastenievud. Nauki 13{6}: 119-126. SF 40: 2702.

4.5-11 Atanasov, Zh. 1976. The effect of different nitrogen fertilizers on lavender productivity and oil quality [in Bulgarian]. Rastenievud. Nauki 13{10}: 113-118. HA 47: 8754.

4.5-12 Atanasov, Zh., Slavov, S.I., Koseva, D., Decheva, R., and Gargova, N. 1979. Application of single and compound mineral fertilizers to peppermint [in Bulgarian]. Rastenievud. Nauki 16{1}: 61-65. HA 50: 6530.

4.5-13 Azcon, R., Barea, J.M., and Montoya, E. 1978. Biological fertilization with vesicular-arbuscular mycorrhiza and phosphobacteria. I. The effect of phosphorus on the growth and nutrition of Lavendula spica and establishment of vesicular-arbuscular symbiosis [in Spanish]. An. Edafol. Agrobiol. 37: 91-98. HA 50: 1336.

4.5-14 Azcon, R., Barea, J.M., and Montoya, E. 1978. Biological fertilization with vesicular-arbuscular mycorrhiza and phosphobacteria. II. The effect of manuring and time of phosphorus application on mycorrhiza establishment in Lavendula spica in seed bed [in Spanish]. An. Edafol. Agrobiol. 37: 99-104. HA 50: 1337.

4.5-15 Badry, D. El, and Hilal, M. 1975. Effect of N fertilization on yield and quality of peppermint oil. Egypt. J. Soil Sci. 1975 Special Issue): 319-326.

4.5-16 Badr, M., and Abu-Zaid, M. 1975. Effect of nitrogenous fertilizer on the herb yield and oil production in Mentha spp. L. Alexandria J. Agric. Res. 23: 275-279. Bib.Ag. 40: 82959.

4.5-17 Berenyi, M. 1978. Effect of mineral fertilizer doses and ratios on the yield of red pepper [in Hungarian]. Bull. Zoldsegtermeszetesi Kut. Intez. 13: 37-48. AGRICOLA.

4.5-18 Berenyi, M. 1976. Results with foliar nutrient sprays in the treatment of red pepper [in Hungarian]. Bull. Zoldsegtermesztesi Kut. Intez. 10: 85-93. AGRICOLA.

4.5-19 Berenyi, M. 1973. Effect of fertilizers applied separately and in combination on the yield of red pepper [in Hungarian]. Bull. Duna. Tisza. Kozi. Mezogazd. Kiserl. Intez. Kecsk. 8: 69-79. AGRICOLA.

4.5-20 Bernath, J., Foldesi, D., Lassanyi, Zs., and Zambo, I. 1975. Effect of state of nutrient supply and soil type on the common valerian (Valeriana officinalis L. spp. collina (Wallr.)). II. Changes in volatile oil and valepotriate content [in Hungarian]. Herba Hung. 14{2/3}: 37-46.

4.5-21 Bessis, M.C., and Olivain, C. 1974. A test for the biologically active concentration of a herbicide [in French]. C. R. Seances Acad. Agric. Fr. 60: 896-905. WA 24: 3102.

4.5-22 Bezdolnyi, N. 1971. Mentha piperita under irrigation [in Russian]. Zernovye Maslichn. Kul't. 2: 29-30. AGRICOLA.

4.5-23 Bhan, S., and Singh, A. 1974. Studies on the optimum dose of fertilizer for rai (Brassica juncea Coss.) in Agra Tract in Uttar Pradesh. Indian J. Agric. Res. 8: 69-70. SF 39: 3699.

4.5-24 Bhan, S., and Singh, A. 1976. Note on the response of mustard (Brassica juncea L. Czern and Coss) to NPK fertilizers in central tract of Uttar Pradesh. Indian J. Agric. Res. 10: 207-208. FCA 31: 4884.

4.5-25 Bhan, S., and Dhama, C.S. 1977. Relative response of wheat, barley and mustard to different frequencies and timings of irrigation in light-textured alluvium of central Uttar Pradesh. Indian J. Agric. Sci. 47: 568-573.

4.5-26 Bhardwaj, S.D., Katoch, P.C., and Kaushal, A.N. 1979. Effect of different levels of nitrogen on herb yield and essential oil content of Mentha species. Indian J. For. 2{1}: 27-30. SF 43: 8789.

4.5-27 Blanc, D., Bellenand-Mayeur, P., Moulinier, H., and Gras, H. 1975. Lavandin requirements in major and minor elements [in French]. C. R. Seances Acad. Agric. Fr. 61: 128-136. HA 46: 3684.

4.5-28 Bogatirenko, A.K., and Timchenko, V.I. 1976. Application of fertilizers to a garlic crop [in Ukrainian]. Visn. Sil's'kogospod Nauki 1976{1}: 27-30. HA 47: 11341.

4.5-29 Bogatyrenko, A.K. 1976. Fertilization of seed garlic in the forest steppe of the Ukrainian SSR [in Russian]. Khim. Sel'sk. Khoz. 14{5}: 36-39. HA 47: 1381.

4.5-30 Borkovskaia, S.E. 1971. Seed yields of the sage in relation to the nutrition area of plants [in Russian]. Pages 418-421 in I.I. Siniagin, ed. Normy vyseva, sposoby poseva i ploshchadi pitaniia sel'skokhoziaistvennykh kul'tur. "Kolos", Moscow, USSR. AGRICOLA.

4.5-31 Bziava, M.L. 1978. Organic fertilizers in humid subtropics [in Russian]. Subtrop. Kul't. 1978{4}: 109-115.

4.5-32 Casalichio, G., and Ciafardini, G. 1977. Sulphur and agriculture [in Italian]. Ital. Agric. 114: 81-106. HA 48: 4154.

4.5-33 Cerda, A., and Bingham, F.T. 1979. Interactive effect of sodium chloride-phosphorus on foliar iron, manganese, zinc, copper, and boron in plants. An. Edafol. Agrobiol. 38{1/2}: 233-243. CA 91: 139610.

4.5-34 Ceylan, A., Yurtseven, M., and Ozansoy, Y. 1979. The effect of nitrogen fertilizing on the agronomic and technical properties of Salvia officinalis [in Turkish]. Ege Universitesi Ziraat Fakultesi Dergisi 16: 83-96. HA 51: 7238.

4.5-35 Clark, R.J., and Menary, R.C. 1980. The effect of irrigation and nitrogen on the yield and composition of peppermint oil (Mentha piperita L.). Aust. J. Agric. Res. 31: 489-498.

4.5-36 Coic, Y., Cook, C., and LeSaint, C. 1972. Preliminary tests on growing watercress (Nasturtium officinale) using very little water [in French]. C.R. Hebd. Seances Acad. Agric. 58: 101-106. AGRICOLA.

4.5-37 Costes, C., Milhet, Y., Candillon, C., and Magnier, G. 1976. Mineral nutrition and morphine production in Papaver somniferum. Physiol. Plant. 36: 201-207.

4.5-38 Croteau, R. 1977. Effect of irrigation method on essential oil yield and rate of oil evaporation in mint grown under controlled conditions. HortScience 12: 563-565.

4.5-39 Cumbus, I.P., Robinson, L.W., and Clare, R.G. 1980. Mineral nutrient availability in watercress. Aquat. Bot. 9: 343-349.

4.5-40 Czapla, J., and Nowak, G. 1979. The effect of different rates of mineral fertilizers on the yield and chemical composition of some grasses and herbage species. 2. Dandelion [in Polish]. Zesz. Nauk. Akad. Roln.-Tech. Olsztynie Roln. 1979{26}: 87-94. SF 43: 8580.

4.5-41 Dabrowska, B., and Skapski, H. 1976. Some factors influence the spiciness of horseradish [in Polish]. Ogrodnictwo 9: 101-118.

4.5-42 Dagite, S.Yu., Yuknyavichene, G.K., and Morkunas, A.V. 1980. Biological and biochemical characteristics of the wild marjoram Origanum vulgare grown in the Kaunas Botanical Garden Lithuanian SSR. 2. Effect of nitrogen fertilizers on the wild marjoram yield and on

accumulation of essential oil in it [in Russian]. Liet. TSR Mokslu
Akad. Darb. Ser. C 1980{2}: 11-16.

4.5-43 Dastane, N.G., Yusuf, M., and Singh, N.P. 1971. Performance of
different rabi crops under varying frequencies and timings of
irrigation. Indian J. Agron. 16: 483-486. FCA 27: 650.

4.5-44 Dempsey, A.H., and Boswell, F.C. 1979. Effects of soil
applications of magnesium sulfate and dolomitic limestone on pimiento
pepper. Hor tScience 14: 537-539.

4.5-45 Dhakshinamoorthy, M., Arumugam, R., and Mani, A.K. 1980. Effect
of copper and molybdenum on the herbage yield and oil of geranium
(Pelargonium graveolens L'Herit). Indian Perfum. 24: 214-215.

4.5-46 Dimitrova-Ruseva, E. 1972. The effect of vitamins B1, B6 and PP
on the growth and essential oil synthesis in peppermint (Mentha
piperita) [in Russian]. Pages 59-61 in P.V. Naumenko et al., eds.
Mezhdunarodnyi kongress po efirnym maslam, 4th, Tiflis, 1968,
[Materialy], v. 2. Pishchevaya Promyshlennost', Moscow, USSR. HA 44:
5990.

4.5-47 Duhan, S.P.S., Singh, V.P., Bhattacharya, A.K., and Husain, A.
1977. Response of Japanese mint (Mentha arvensis Linn.) to different
irrigation schedules. Perfum. Flavor. 2{5}: 57 (Abstr.). HA 48: 5875.

4.5-48 Dwivedi, R.S., and Randhawa, N.S. 1974. Evaluation of a rapid
test for the hidden hunger of zinc in plants. Plant Soil 40: 445-451.

4.5-49 El-Sahhar, K., Fahamy, G.E., and El-Zanati, M. 1977. Effect of
different rates of nitrogen, phosphorus and potassium fertilizers on
Mentha piperita L. Agric. Res. Rev. 55{5}: 119-130. HA 50: 5465.

4.5-50 Eryusheva, E.M., and Ivanchenko, N.Ya. 1971. Effect of forms of
nitrogenous fertilizers on the productivity of clary sage [in
Russian]. Tr. Vses. Nauchno-Issled. Inst. Efirnomaslichn. Kul't. 3:
79-84 CA 79: 145226.

4.5-51 Fageria, N.K., Bajpai, M.R., and Parihar, R.L. 1972. Effect of
nitrogen, phosphorus and potassium fertilization on yield and yield
contributing characters of cumin crop (Cuminum cyminum L.
Kreuz-Kummel). Z. Pflanzenernahr. Bodenkd. 132: 30-34.

4.5-52 Fernandez Caldas, E., and Garcia, V. 1972. Study on the nutrition
of the plantain in the Canary Islands. I. Effect of nitrogenous
nutrition on the circumference of the pseudostem [in Spanish]. An.
Edafol. Agrobiol. 31(11/12): 917-925. AGRICOLA.

4.5-53 Fernandez Fabregas, S., and Martin Ramirez, E. 1978. Cultivation
of lavender: mineral nutrition. I. Preliminary results [in Spanish].
An. Edafol. Agrobiol. 37: 683-688. HA 50: 496.

4.5-54 Ferrari, V.A., and Churata Masca, M.G.C. 1975. Effects of
increasing rates of nitrogen and borax on yield of garlic (Allium
sativum L.) [in Portuguese]. Cientifica 3: 254-262. SF 39: 5558.

4.5-55 Fomin, P.I., Fomina, O.G., and Lazareva, R.P. 1976. Application
of phosphogypsum as a sulphur fertilizer in the Moscow region [in
Russian]. Khim. Sel'sk. Khoz. 14{9}: 43-48. FCA 30: 3766.

4.5-56 Franz, C. 1972. The effect of various N and K fertilizer regimes on the growth and nutrient uptake of Mentha piperita [in German]. Gartenbauwissenschaft 37: 495-509. HA 44: 4968.

4.5-57 Franz, C., and Kirsch, C. 1974. Growth and flower formation by Matricaria chamomilla in relation to varied nitrogen and potassium nutrition [in German]. Gartenbauwissenschaft 39: 9-19. HA 45: 2737.

4.5-58 Franz, C. 1972. The effect of the nutrients potassium and nitrogen on the formation of the essential oil of Mentha piperita [in German]. Planta Med. 22: 160-183. HA 43: 6263.

4.5-59 Freeman, G.G., and Mossadeghi, N. 1972. Studies on sulphur nutrition and flavour production in watercress (Rorippa nasturtium-aquaticum (L.) Hayek). J. Hortic. Sci. 47: 375-387.

4.5-60 Fritz, J. 1976. Effect of nitrogenous fertilization on the essential oil production of the rose geranium [in French]. Agron. Trop. (Paris) 31: 369-374. AGRICOLA.

4.5-61 Gabal, M. 1979. Effects of nitrogen forms on the growth and yield of paprika [in Hungarian]. Hajtatas Korai Termesztes Kert. Egy. Zoldsegtermesztesi Intez. S.L., Intezet. 10{3}: 21-22. AGRICOLA.

4.5-62 Gadiwewasam, B.D.K. de S., and Aturupana, U.T. 1975. Fertilizer experiment with shallot (red onion) at Kundasale. Trop. Agric. (Ceylon) 131{3/4}: 140-146.

4.5-63 Gaur, B.L., and Trehan, K.B. 1973. A note on the effect of nitrogen levels, time of application and forms of nitrogen on rainfed sesamum (Sesamum indicum Linn.). Indian J. Agron. 18: 94-95.

4.5-64 Gerasimova, L.K., and Barelko, I.B. 1980. Minor elements in food plants with medicinal properties in Kirgizia [in Russian]. Fiziol. Biokhim. Kult. Rast. 12: 186-188. HA 51: 8260.

4.5-65 Ghosh, M.L., and Chatterjee, S.K. 1976. Effects of N:P:K fertilizers on growth, development and essential oil content of Mentha spp. Indian J. Exp. Biol. 14: 366-368.

4.5-66 Gindich, N.N., and Kuznetsova, I.G. 1977. The principle of determining the requirement of Valeriana officinalis in nutrients on the basis of results of chemical analysis of plants [in Russian]. Agrokhimiya 1977{7}: 129-135. AGRICOLA.

4.5-67 Gindich, N.N., Sheberstov, V.V., and Erokhina, L.T. 1974. On the problem of mineral nutrition of Valeriana officinalis [in Russian]. Agrokhimiya 1974{12}: 106-111. AGRICOLA.

4.5-68 Gindich, N.N., and Sheberstov, V.V. 1971. Some aspects of the mineral nutrition of wild chamomile [in Russian]. Sb. Nauchn. Rab. Vses. Nauchno-Issled. Inst. Lek. Rast. 1971{3}: 122-128. HA 43: 3972.

4.5-69 Giulakhmedov, A.N., Mamedov, D.Sh., and Agaev, N.A. 1978. The influence of mineral fertilizers to growth, development and crop capacity of henna plants in different norms and correlations under condition of Absheron's grey-brown soils (Azerbaijan SSR) [in Russian]. Dokl. Akad. Nauk Az. SSR 34{4}: 85-89.

4.5-70 Golcz, L., Kordana, S., Nowak, A., and Zalecki, R. 1977. Effect of nitrogen and calcium fertilization on herbage yield and nutrient uptake by marjoram (Origanum majorana) [in Polish]. Herba Pol. 23: 313-324. HA 49: 1436.

4.5-71 Golcz, L., and Kordana, S. 1979. The effect of differential NPK rates and Mg and Ca fertilization on plant yield and uptake of mineral elements by Trigonella foenum-graecum [in Polish]. Herba Pol. 25: 121-131. HA 50: 3675.

4.5-72 Gretskaia, R.L., and Oleinikova, E.F. 1972. Fertilizing peppermint in Krasnodar Territory [in Russian]. Khim. Sel'sk. Khoz. 10{1}: 17-18. AGRICOLA.

4.5-73 Grzesiuk, W., Chodan, J., Zawartka, L., and Kucharski, J. 1977. Preliminary evaluation of agramid and agroform as fertilizers. Pol. J. Soil Sci. 10: 79-85. FCA 32: 3441.

4.5-74 Guimbard, C., Jeune, B. le, and Pennors, J. 1979. Use of plastics films for mulching shallots. Plasticulture 1979{42}: 13-26. SF 43: 6079.

4.5-75 Gulati, B.C., Duhan, S.P.S., and Garg, S.N. 1978. Effect of nitrogen on the yield of herbage and oil and on the quality of essential oil of Ocimum basilicum (methyl cinnamate type). Indian Perfum. 22{1}: 53-54. CA 90: 85827.

4.5-76 Gupta, S.B., Dhar, N.R., and Ghildyal, B.P. 1974. Effect of rock phosphate in conjunction with organic matter in increasing the essential oil contents of Mentha arvensis. Pages 149-152 in N.R. Dhar, ed. Symposium on green revolution. National Academy of Sciences, Allahabad, India. AGRICOLA.

4.5-77 Gupta, S.K.D., and Friend, J. 1975. Effect of major plant nutrients on the fatty acid composition of seed oil of white mustard (Sinapis alba). Indian Agric. 19: 275-281. SF 40: 5888.

4.5-78 Gupta, V.K., and Agarwal, S.B. 1973. Effect of foliar sprays of manganese sulphate and copper sulphate on nodule development, shoot and root length. Indian Phytopathol. 26: 726-727. SF 38: 4305.

4.5-79 Gupta, V.K., and Raj, H. 1980. A note on effect of zinc application on the yield and phosphorus nutrition of coriander. Haryana J. Hortic. Sci. 9: 82-83.

4.5-80 Guttormsen, G. 1973. Results of irrigation experiments with greenhouse vegetables. I. [in Norwegian]. Gartneryket 63: 798-800. AGRICOLA.

4.5-81 Hansen, H. 1978. The influence of nitrogen fertilization on the chemical composition of vegetables. Qual. Plant. Plant Foods Hum. Nutr. 28: 45-63.

4.5-82 Hardh, J.E. 1972. Comparison of peat and bark-humus in greenhouse and outdoor vegetable culture. Acta Hortic. 1972{26}: 69-73. HA 43: 7605.

4.5-83 Hornok, L. 1974. The effect of nutrient supply on peppermint yields and essential oil content [in Hungarian]. Kerteszetiegy. Kozl. 38{6}: 73-82. HA 45: 9999.

4.5-84 Hornok, L. 1978. Effect of the major nutrients (NPK) at different rates on the yield of some essential oil bearing plants [in Hungarian]. Kerteszetiegy. Kozl. 42{10}: 235-244. HA 50: 7908.

4.5-85 Hornok, L. 1979. Effect of nutrition supply on yield of dill (Anethum graveolens L.) and the essential oil content. Herba Hung. 18{3}: 337-342.

4.5-86 Iruthayaraj, M.R., and Kulandaivelu, R. 1973. NPK requirements of K1 chillies (Capsicum annuum Linn.). Indian J. Agron. 18: 22-24. SF 39: 3173.

4.5-87 Islam, M.A., and Rashid, M.M. 1973. Tolerance of different winter vegetables to the foliar application of urea. Bangladesh Hortic. 1{2}: 12-15. HA 45: 2321.

4.5-88 Ivanchenko, N.Ya. 1975. The effect of magnesium fertilizers on the productivity of Salvia sclarea [in Russian]. Tr. Vses. Nauchno-Issled. Inst. Efirnomaslichn. Kul't. 8: 113-117. HA 47: 9763.

4.5-89 Ivanchenko, N.Ya., Eriusheva, E.M., and Mustiatse, G.I. 1974. The problem of the effect of inorganic fertilizers on the quality of the yield of clary sage [in Russian]. Tr. Vses. Nauchno-Issled. Inst. Efirnomaslichn. Kul't. 7: 74-78. AGRICOLA.

4.5-90 Ivankova, J. 1977. Effect of mineral and organic fertilizers on the qualitative composition of phosphorus compounds in brown soil. II. Transformations of phosphorus bound to organic matter [in Slovak]. Acta Fytotech. 32: 27-38. CA 88: 135404.

4.5-91 Jasa, B., Koutnik, V., and Reznicek, V. 1972. Possibilities of utilizing the urea-metaphosphate systems in the nutrition of vegetables. I. Bush red peppers [in Czech]. Rostl. Vyroba 18: 769-776. AGRICOLA.

4.5-92 Jaworski, C.A., and Webb, R.E. 1971. Pepper performance after transplant clipping. HortScience 6: 480-482.

4.5-93 Jaworski, C.A., Kays, S.J., and Smittle, D.A. 1978. Effects of nitrogen and potassium fertilization in trickle irrigation on yield of pepper and polebean. HortScience 13: 477-478.

4.5-94 Jaworski, C.A., and Williamson, R.E. 1976. Supplemental nitrogen and potassium fertilization in sprinkler irrigation for field production of southern pepper transplants. HortScience 11: 226 (Abstr.).

4.5-95 Jessen, T. 1973. Lime and fertilizer on drained peat soil [in Danish]. Tidsskr. Planteavl 77: 547-567. FCA 28: 5076.

4.5-96 Jessen, T. 1975. Lime and superphosphate on low-lying land [in Danish]. Tiddskr. Planteavl 79: 517-535. FCA 30: 253.

4.5-97 Jolivet, J. 1977. Importance of mineral nutrition in the production of capitula and essential oil of Anthemis nobilis [in French]. Plant. Med. Phytother. 11: 119-123. HA 48: 763.

4.5-98 Joshi, D.C., Seth, S.P., and Pareek, B.L. 1973. Studies on sulphur and phosphorus uptake by mustard. J. Indian Soc. Soil Sci. 21: 167-172. FCA 27: 4168.

4.5-99 Karaeva, M.M., and Liatifov, D.Kh. 1975. Effect of different
levels and combinations of inorganic elements on the growth and
development of the cultivated mint in the conditions of the
Sheki-Zakataly zone [in Russian]. Izv. Akad. Nauk Az. SSR Ser. Biol.
Nauk 1975{6}: 20-25.

4.5-100 Kasper, J. 1976. Effect of fertilization rates on the
development and chemical composition of the commonest species of herbs
in permanent pastures [in Slovak]. Rostl. Vyroba 22: 639-650. SF 43:
1431.

4.5-101 Kerekes, J., and Hornok, L. 1972. Data on the irrigation and
nutrition of peppermint [in Hungarian]. Herba Hung. 11{3}: 39-44. HA
44: 7925.

4.5-102 Khanna, K.R., Murty, A.S., and Prabha, C. 1974. Effect of
different timings of fertilizer application on opium poppy, Papaver
somniferum L. Indian J. Agric. Res. 8: 53-56. AGRICOLA.

4.5-103 Khan, M.A.R., and Suryanarayana, V. 1978. Effect of N, P and K
on growth of chilli var. N.P. 46 A. Orissa J. Hortic. 6{1/2}: 34-42.
HA 50: 8290.

4.5-104 Khilik, L.A., Zal'tsfas, A.A., and Bondarenko, T.I. 1979.
Phosphorus uptake by Transcaucasian catmint (Nepeta transcaucasica)
from superphosphate applied by different methods [in Russian].
Agrokhimiya 1979{6}: 40-41. HA 50: 5467.

4.5-105 Khilik, L.A., and Bondarenko, T.I. 1975. Catnip under irrigation.
[in Russian]. Tr. Vses. Nauchno-Issled. Inst. Efirnomaslichn. Kul't.
8: 110-113.

4.5-106 Kim, H.K., and Ho, Q.S. 1978. Effect of MH-30 and ethrel on the
yield of red pepper varieties [in Korean]. Hanguk Wonye Hakhoe Chi 19:
110-116.

4.5-107 Kinra, K.L., Saran, G., and Rao, S.B.P. 1972. Note on the
response of appressed mutant of Indian mustard (Brassic junea (L.)
Czern. and Coss) to varying levels of nitrogen and plant density.
Indian J. Agron. 17: 234-235. FCA 39: 3136.

4.5-108 Kodatskii, I.V. 1978. Application of fertilizers in the crops of
Plantago major on low humus chernozem [in Russian]. Khim. Sel'sk.
Khoz. 16{5}: 72-74. Bib. Ag. 43: 92941.

4.5-109 Komarova, E.N. 1974. The effect of boron, zinc and copper on the
growth and development of winter garlic planted in spring [in
Russian]. Tr. Vses. S-kh. Inst. Zaochn. Obraz. 1974{90}: 152-158. HA
46: 4465.

4.5-110 Konsler, T.R., and Shelton, J.E. 1980. Some early influences of
N, P, and pH on cultivated ginseng (Panax quinquifolium). HortScience
15: 281 (Abstr.).

4.5-111 Ksendz, A.P. 1974. The response of lavender to phosphates of
different solubility [in Russian]. Tr. Vses. Nauchno-Issled. Inst.
Efirnomaslichn. Kul't. 1974{7}: 64-68. HA 46: 8640.

4.5-112 Kuduk, C. 1975. Effect of straw fertilization on light soils and

its content of basic nutrients [in Polish]. Rocz. Nauk Roln. Ser. A.
101: 73–82. FCA 30: 3764.

4.5–113 Kujira, Y., and Kanda, M. 1976. Competition among the individual
plants within a crop. II. Absorption of nitrogen and competition in
<u>Allium</u> spp. [in Japanese]. Tohoku Branch Crop Science Society, Japan
1976{19}: 109–110. SF 44: 5241.

4.5–114 Kuribayashi, T., Sato, S., and Ohashi, H. 1972. Physiological
and ecological studies on the saffron (<u>Crocus sativus</u>). V. Fertilizer
experiment of the three essential nutrients [in Japanese]. Shoyakugaku
Zasshi 26: 137–140. CA 79: 52240.

4.5–115 Kusomo, S., and Widjajanto, D.D. 1973. Fertilizer use in garlic
[in Indonesian]. Bul. Hortik. 'Tjahort' 1973{11}: 2–7. HA 46: 2096.

4.5–116 Kusumainderawati, E.P., Dasi, D.W., Suminto, T., and Widodo, R.
1976. The effects of nitrogen and phosphorus fertilizers on bulb
production of shallot [in Indonesian]. Bull. Penelitian Hortik. 4{2}:
53–63. AGRICOLA.

4.5–117 Kusumo, S., and Indrawati, E.P.K. 1976. Fertilizer experiment on
shallot [in Indonesian]. Bull. Penelitian Hortik. 4{4}: 27–36.
AGRICOLA.

4.5–118 Kuszelewski, L., and Garscia, A. 1973. Estimation of fertilizing
value of slurry from large-scale pig fattening farms [in Polish].
Rocz. Nauk Roln. Ser. A. 99: 93–113. FCA 28: 7154.

4.5–119 Kuzminska, K. 1973. Effect of NPK fertilizing on the content of
some principal alkaloids in the capsules of <u>Papaver somniferum</u> [in
Polish]. Herba Pol. 19: 256–261. AGRICOLA.

4.5–120 Kwiaton, D. 1973. Effect of magnesium fertilizer on coriander
(<u>Coriandrum sativum</u> L.) at different potassium levels [in Polish].
Biul. Inst. Hodowli Aklim. Rosl. 1973{3/4}: 129–134. AGRICOLA.

4.5–121 Lahiri, J.R., and De, R. 1971. Increase mustard yields by
supplying a part of nitrogen through foliage. Indian Farming 20{10}:
20–22. FCA 26: 1905.

4.5–122 Laszlo, H. 1979. Effect of nutrition supply on yield of dill
(<u>Anethum graveolens</u> L.) and its essential oil content. Planta Med. 36:
295–296 (Abstr.).

4.5–123 Laughlin, J.C. 1979. The boron nutrition of poppies (<u>Papaver
somniferum</u> L.) on chernozem and alluvial soils of Tasmania. Planta
Med. 36: 245 (Abstr.).

4.5–124 Laughlin, J.C. 1978. The effect of band placed nitrogen and
phosphorus fertiliser on the yield of poppies (<u>Papaver somniferum</u> L.)
grown on krasnozem soil. Acta Hortic. 1978{73}: 165–172.

4.5–125 Laughlin, J.C. 1979. The boron nutrition of poppies (<u>Papaver
somniferum</u> L.) on krasnozem and alluvial soils of Tasmania [in
Russian]. Herba Hung. 18{3}: 227–234. AGRICOLA.

4.5–126 Lawande, K.E., Bhore, D.P., and Patil, A.V. 1977. A note on the
foliar application of urea in fenugreek (<u>Trigonella foenum-graecum</u>
L.). Haryana J. Hortic. Sci. 6: 196–197. HA 48: 8577.

4.5-127 Lazic, B., Durovka, M., and Markovic, V. 1976. Effect of foliar renutrition on the characterisitics of seedlings and yield of paprika [in Serbo-Croatian]. Savrem. Poljopr. 24(1/2): 29-38. AGRICOLA.

4.5-128 Lehmann, K. 1973. Effect of magnesium supply on occurrence of some nitrogen forms in plants [in Polish]. Zesz. Probl. Postepow Nauk Roln. 1973{149}: 181-187. FCA 28: 4106.

4.5-129 Liloyan, O.Ts., and Manukyan, A.T. 1978. The yield and quality of fertilized rose geranium [in Russian]. Khim. Sel'sk. Khoz. 16{6}: 48-50. HA 49: 709.

4.5-130 Lin, C.H. 1973. Optimum rates of NPK for Chinese leek [in Chinese]. T'ai-wa n Nung Yeh Chi K'an 9{1}: 68-161. SF 37: 1056.

4.5-131 Lobl, F., Kuldova, M., and Petrikova, V. 1971. Agronomical aspects of the use of power station fly ash. 5. Effect of high rates of fly ash on the yields of some crops and biochemical changes in the soil [in Czech]. Rostl. Vyroba 17: 1165-1178. FCA 26: 4050.

4.5-132 Luk'yanova, E.I., and Semenikhina, N.G. 1974. Fertilization of aniseed [in Russian]. Tr. Vses. Nauchno-Issled. Inst. Efirnomaslichn. Kul't. 1974{7}: 62-64. HA 46: 10606.

4.5-133 Mahajan, V.P., Randhawa, G.S., Bains, D.S., and Sawhney, J.S. 1978. Effect of sewage irrigation on the seed yield of celery. Indian J. Agric. Sci. 48: 270-273. HA 49: 1970.

4.5-134 Mahajan, V.P., Sawhney, J.S., and Randhawa, G.S. 1973. Response of celery (Apium graveolens L.) to different levels of nitrogen and phosphorus application. Indian J. Agric. Sci. 43: 1006-1008. HA 46: 462.

4.5-135 Mahendra Singh, and Narendra Singh. 1977. Effect of sulphur and selenium on sulphur containing amino acids and quality of oil in raya (Brassica juncea Coss.) in normal and sodic soil. Indian J. Plant Physiol. 20: 56-62. FCA 32: 429.

4.5-136 Mathur, O.P., and Tomar, P.S. 1972. Irrigation requirement of raya (Brassica juncea) crop in Western Rajasthan. Indian J. Agron. 17: 306-308. SF 39: 3703.

4.5-137 Matusiewicz, E., and Madziar, Z. 1971. Effect of nitrogen forms and liming on the growth, oil content and yields of peppermint [in Polish]. Poznan. Tow. Przyj. Nauk, Wydz. Nauk Roln. Les., Pr. Kom. Nauk Roln. Kom. Nauk Les 31: 395-402. CA 76: 45069.

4.5-138 McHugh, J.J., Jr., and Nishimoto, R.K. 1980. Effect of overhead sprinkler irrigation on watercress yield, quality and leaf temperature. Hortscience 15: 801-802.

4.5-139 Mecs, J. 1971. Influence of ration of nutrients on yield and nutrient uptake of spice paprika [in Hungarian]. Kiserl. Kozl. A 64A{1/3}: 83-91. AGRICOLA.

4.5-140 Mehrotra, O.N., Sinha, N.S., Srivastava, R.D.L., and R. Kumar. 1972. Effect of fertilizers on uptake of nutrients, yield and oil content of Indian mustard (Brassica juncea L. Czern Coss.). Indian Agric. 16: 49-55. FCA 28: 2702.

4.5-141 Mel'nik, T.K. 1973. The effect of minor elements on chlorophyll content in garlic leaves [in Russian]. Tr. Vses. S-kh. Inst. Zaochn. Obraz. 1973{58}: 17-20. HA 45: 2325.

4.5-142 Mitchell, G.A., Bingham, F.T., and Yermanos, D.M. 1974. Growth, mineral composition and seed characteristics of sesame as affected by nitrogen, phosphorus, and potassium nutrition. Soil Sci. Soc. Am. Proc. 38: 925-931.

4.5-143 Mitchell, G.A., Bingham, F.T., Labanauskas, C.K., and Yermanos, D.M. 1976. Protein and free amino acid composition of sesame meal as affected by nitrogen, phosphorus, and potassium nutrition. Soil Sci. Soc. Am. Proc. 40: 64-68.

4.5-144 Mohandass, S., Arumugam, R., and Srinivasan, P.S. 1980. Efficacy of foliar application of nitrogen on foliage and oil yield in geranium (Pelargonium graveolens L'Herit). Indian Perfum. 24{4}: 216-218.

4.5-145 Mohan, R., Mohamed Mustaq Ahmed, N., Doraiswamy, S., and Thenammai, V. 1977. Influence of potash nutriment on phenol and soluble carbohydrates in chilli leaves. Curr. Sci. 46: 616. SF 41: 2235.

4.5-146 Mungikar, A.M., Batra, U.R., Tekale, N.S., and Joshi, R.N. 1976. Effects of nitrogen fertilizers on yields of proteins extracted from seven crops. Exp. Agric. 12: 353-359.

4.5-147 Mustyatse, G.I., and Makovskii, M.I. 1978. Application of fertilizers for clary sage under Moldavian conditions [in Russian]. Khim. Sel'sk. Khoz. 16{6}: 50-53. HA 49: 710.

4.5-148 Muthuswami, S., and Rao, V.N.M. 1980. Effect of pinching of shoots in jasmines. Pages 25-26 in National Seminar on Production Technology for Commercial Flower Crops. Tamil Nadu Agricultural University, Coimbatore, India. HA 51: 7179.

4.5-149 Muthuswamy, S., and Pappiah, C.M. 1977. Nutritional studies on Jasminum grandiflorum L. Indian J. Hortic. 34: 289-293. HA 48: 7511.

4.5-150 Muthuswamy, S., and Pappiah, C.M. 1980. Effect of foliar application on nitrogen in Jasminum auriculatum Vahl. Indian J. Hortic. 37: 92-96. AGRICOLA.

4.5-151 Muthuswamy, S., and Pappiah, C.M. 1976. Studies on the response of Jasminum auriculatum Vahl. to NPK fertilisation. South Indian Hortic. 24{3}: 88-93. HA 49: 9534.

4.5-152 Natarajan, S., and Rao, V.N.M. 1980. Effect of frequency of fertilizer application in Jathimalli (Jasminum grandiflorum L.). Madras Agric. J. 67: 207-210.

4.5-153 Natarajan, S., and Rao, V.N.M. 1980. Response of jathimalli (Jasminum grandiflorum L.) to nitrogen and phosphorus. Madras Agric. J. 67: 252-255.

4.5-154 Naumova, G.E., and Sheberstov, V.V. 1972. On the effect of P on poppy seed yields and alkaloid contents in the capsule [in Russian]. Agrokhimiya 1972{5}: 36-39. FCA 26: 419.

4.5-155 Nesterov, N.N., Baginskii, O.V., and Sheberstov, V.V. 1972. Economic effectiveness of applying mineral and organic fertilizers to Papaver somniferum in Khmel'nitskii region of the Ukraine [in Russian]. Khim. Sel'sk. Khoz. 10{1}: 56-59. Bib. Ag. 36: 76776.

4.5-156 Niazi, M.H.K., and Raja, M.R. 1971. Effect of NPK on the yield of white zeera (cumin-cyminum). J. Agric. Res. (Lahore) 9: 124-127. HA 43: 3938.

4.5-157 Novais, R.F. de, and Menezes Sobrinho, J.A. De. 1972. The effect of soil application of boron, molybdenum and zinc on garlic production and storage [in Portuguese]. Rev. Ceres 19{101}: 1-6. HA 43: 227.

4.5-158 Oliveira, G.D. de, Fernandes, P.D., Sarruge, J.R., and Haag, H.P. 1971. Mineral nutrition of vegetable crops. XIII. Major nutrient extraction by vegetable crops [in Portuguese]. Solo 63{1}: 7-12. HA 43: 4381.

4.5-159 Opitz von Boberfeld, W. 1980. Effects of various K salts on some properties of crop growth and soils in relation to K and N input in hay pastures [in German]. Z. Acker- Pflanzenbau 149: 58-74.

4.5-160 Paliwal, S.K., and Singh, U.B. 1979. Response of kingscumin (Foeniculum sp.) to nitrogen and phosphorus application. J. Maharashtra Agric. Univ. 4: 308. HA 51: 1471.

4.5-161 Pal, P., Maity, R.G., and Bose, T.K. 1980. Effect of time and height of pruning on growth and yield of flowers in Jasminum auriculatum vars. Single and Double. Pages 180-190 in National seminar on production technology for commercial flower crops. Tamil Nadu Agricultural University, Coimbatore, India. HA 51: 7181.

4.5-162 Pal, P., Maity, R.G., and Bose, T.K. 1980. Effect of different time and height of pruning on growth and yield of flowers in Jasminum sambac var. Khoya. Pages 27-29 in National Seminar on Production Technology for Commercial Flower Crops. Tamil Nadu Agricultural University, Coimbatore, India. HA 51: 7180.

4.5-163 Parsa, A.A., Wallace, A., and Martin, J.P. 1979. Enhancement of iron availability by some organic materials. J. Agric. Sci. 93: 115-120.

4.5-164 Pasricha, N.S., and Randhawa, N.S. 1973. Sulphur nutrition of crops from native and applied sources. Indian J. Agric. Sci. 43: 270-274. FCA 27: 5933.

4.5-165 Pavlenko, V.A. 1971. On the rational application of mineral fertilizers in mint [in Russian]. Tr. Vses. Nauchno-Issled. Inst. Efirnomaslichn. Kul't. 1971{4,1}: 48-53. HA 43: 6262.

4.5-166 Penkauskiene, E. 1971. Effect of nitrogen fertilizers on growth, yields and accumulation of essential oils in the common balm [in Russian]. Pages 433-439 in V.K. Ozolin'sh, ed. Botanicheskie sady Pribaltiki. Zinatne, Riga, USSR. AGRICOLA.

4.5-167 Penka, M. 1978. Influence of irrigation on the contents of effective substances in officinal plants. Acta Hortic. 1978{73}: 181-198.

4.5-168 Peters, E.J., and Lowance, S.A. 1978. Effects of multiple mowing on western ironweed (Veronia baldwinii and gray goldenrod (Solidago nemoralis). Weed Sci. 26: 190-192.

4.5-169 Pillai, O.R., and Boominathan, H. 1975. Effect of NPK fertilisers on the yield of coriander. Arecanut and Spices Bulletin 6: 82-83. HA 46: 10583.

4.5-170 Platash, I.T., and Artemchenko, S.S. 1974. Effect of microelements on the accumulation of cardiac glycosides in Digitalis lanata [in Russian]. Farm Zh. (Kiev) 29{1}: 81-84.

4.5-171 Ploszynski, M., and Pantera, B. 1973. Influence of aqueous ammonia on growth and qualitative changes of some cultivated plants [in Polish]. Pamiet. Pulawski 1973{56}: 179-194. FCA 28: 3143.

4.5-172 Poniedzialek, M. 1977. The effect of various nitrogen treatments on the yield and quality of horseradish roots [in Polish]. Zesz. Nauk. Ogrod. Akad. Roln. Krakow. 1977{5}: 131-145.

4.5-173 Popov, P., Dimitrov, I., and Georgiev, S. 1976. Study on nitrogen rates and time of their application to sesame [in Bulgarian]. Rastenievud Nauki 13{4}: 134-139. AGRICOLA.

4.5-174 Prasad, L.K. 1978. Effect of nitrogen, phosphorus and potassium on the yield of lemon grass (Cymbopogon citratus). Sci. Cult. 44: 167-168.

4.5-175 Prasad, L.K., and Mukherji, S.K. 1980. Effect of nitrogen, phosphorus and potassium on lemon grass. Indian J. Agron. 25: 42-44.

4.5-176 Putievsky, E. 1978. Spices of the family Labiatae: 10. Fertilization of oregano [in Hebrew]. Hassadeh 59: 44-46. HA 49: 5259.

4.5-177 Ramanathan, V.S., and Ramachandran, C. 1973. Effect of organic manure and chemical fertilizers on opium poppy. Part I. A study on the yield of opium, morphine and poppy seeds. Indian J. Agron. 18: 372-375.

4.5-178 Ramanathan, V.S. 1979. Effect of micronutrients on the yield of opium and its morphine content in opium poppy. Indian J. Agric. Res. 13: 85-89. AGRICOLA.

4.5-179 Ramirez H., V.E., Lopez G., C.A., and Loria M., W. 1973. Response of garlic, Allium sativum, to phosphorus fertilizer [in Spanish]. Boletin Tecnico Facultad da Agronoma. Universidad de Costa Rica 6{6}: 1-14. HA 45: 7294.

4.5-180 Ramirez H., V.E., Lopez, G., C.A., and Loria, M., W. 1973. The response of garlic to phosphorus nutrition [in Spanish]. Proc. Trop. Reg. Amer. Soc. Hortic. Sci. 17: 247-254. HA 45: 9469.

4.5-181 Ramteke, J.R., Badhe, N.T., and Bathkal, B.G. 1975. Effect of nitrogen fertilisation on yield of herb and yield of oil of mint (Mentha sp.) varieties. Agric. Agro-Ind. 8{1}: 30-32. HA 47: 6815.

4.5-182 Rasp, H. 1973. A pot experiment with hyperphos magnesia [in German]. Landwirtsch. Forsch. 26: 247-254. FCA 28: 3306.

4.5-183 Reissbrodt, R., and Fiedler, H.J. 1973. Trial in fertilizing Digitalis purpurea L. with nitrogen and phosphorus [in German]. Wiss. Z. Tech. Univ. Dresden 22: 917-919. Bib. Ag. 38: 67682.

4.5-184 Resh, F.M. 1974. The effect of mineral fertilizers on pigment and glycoside biosynthesis in digitalis leaves [in Russian]. Fiziol. Biokhim. Kult. Rast. 6: 198-200. HA 44: 8946.

4.5-185 Rieder, J.B., and Reiner, L. 1972. High fertilizer rates for subalpine areas in combination with many-cut utilization and hot-air drying [in German]. Bayer. Landwirtsch. Jahrb. 49: 425-453. HERB AB 45: 32.

4.5-186 Ruminska, A., Suchorska, K., and Weglarz, Z. 1976. The effect of Wuxal on the yield and biologically active substance content of some medicinal plants [in Polish]. Zesz. Probl. Postepow Nauk Roln. 1976{184}: 169-174. HA 47: 11753.

4.5-187 Ruminska, A. 1978. The influence of fertilizers on the content and yield of active compounds in spice and medicinal crop plants [in German]. Acta Hortic. 1978{73}: 143-164.

4.5-188 Ruminska, A., Suchorska, K., and Lesisz, L. 1976. Effect of the form and date of application of nitrogen fertilizers on the yield of seeds, poppyheads and alkaloids of the opium poppy [in Polish]. Wiad. Zielarskie 18{5}: 17-18.

4.5-189 Ruminska, A. 1974. The effect of foliar treatment of medicinal plants with chemical substances on the productivity and the content of active substances [in Polish]. Zesz. Probl. Postepow Nauk Roln. 143: 197-208. HA 45: 4392.

4.5-190 Sadowska, A. 1974. The effect of foliar nutrition of peppermint on plant health and yield and on essential oil quantity and quality [in Polish]. Zesz. Probl. Postepow Nauk Roln. 1974{143}: 215-219. HA 46: 3686.

4.5-191 Sadowska, A. 1974. Foliar nutrition of peppermint in greenhouses [in Polish]. Zesz. Probl. Postepow Nauk Roln. 1974{143}: 221-227. HA 46: 3687.

4.5-192 Sagyte, S., and Morkunas, A. 1971. Effect of methods of planting and mineral fertilizers on yields and quality of Valeriana officinalis [in Russian]. Pages 425-432 in V.K. Ozolin'sh, ed. Botanicheskie sady Pribaltiki. Zinatne, Riga, USSR. AGRICOLA.

4.5-193 Samra, J.S., Saini, S.S., and Bains, D.S. 1977. Effect of nitrogen levels and height of cutting on the fresh herb and oil yield of Mentha arvensis L. Food Farming and Agriculture 8{11}: 13-15. SF 42: 2035.

4.5-194 Satsiyati, Said, A., and Dahro. 1974. The effects of liming and fertilizer on yields of shallot and Brassica juncea [in Indonesian]. Bull. Penelitian Hortik. 2{1}: 26-40. HA 46: 4480.

4.5-195 Scalopi, E.J., Klar, A.E., and Vasconcellos, E.F.C. 1971. Irrigation and nitrogen fertilization in garlic growing [in Portuguese]. Solo 63{1}: 63-66. HA 43: 5296.

4.5-196 Schickluna, J.C. 1972. New way to probe plant nutrient needs. Better Crops with Plant Food 56{2}: 24-28.

4.5-197 Schreier, J. 1972. The effect of the time of supplementary nitrogen fertilization on seed yield in poppy [in Czech]. Rostl. Vyroba 18: 671-676. FCA 27: 6464.

4.5-198 Sennaiyan, P., and Arunachalam, L. 1977. The influence of micronutrients on gingelly (Sesamum indicum L.). Oils Oilseeds J. 30{2}: 22.

4.5-199 Sen, H., Jana, P.K., and Dasgupta, S.K. 1977. Response of mustard variety Varuna (Brassica juncea Coss.) to high doses of nitrogen. Indian Agric. 19: 347-350. FCA 30: 4903.

4.5-200 Sharma, S.N., Singh, A., and Tripathi, R.S. 1980. Effect of NPK and micronutrients on herb, oil and menthol yield of Japanese mint. Indian J. Agron. 25: 279-281.

4.5-201 Shebierstov, V.V., Fomienko, K.P., Zhuravlev, J.P., Arsyuchina, L.J., Gnidich, N.N., Poludiennyi, L.V., Niesterov, N.N., Naumovwa, G.Z., and Fonin, W.S. 1972. Fertilizing, crops and the content of active substances in medicinal plants [in Russian]. Postep Dziedzinie Leku Rosl. Pr. Ref. Dosw. Wygloszone Symp. 1970; Herba Pol. Suppl. 1972: 268-275.

4.5-202 Shedeed, M.R., Mostafa, M.B., Elgendy, S.A., and Othman, M.A. 1974. Effect of different fertilization treatments on the volatile oil content and its qualities of fennel (Foeniculum capillaceum). Ann. Agric. Sci. 910{2}: 183-189. AGRICOLA.

4.5-203 Shelke, D.K., and Morey, D.K. 1978. Growth, yield and quality of Japanese mint (Mentha arvensis) as influenced by various levels of nitrogen and topping. J. Maharashtra Agric. Univ. 3: 28-30. SF 43: 5171.

4.5-204 Singh, A., Balyan, S.S., and Shahi, A.K. 1978. Effect of nitrogen on the volatile oil content of Mentha piperita L. Indian J. Agron. 23{1}: 67-68. Bib.Ag. 43: 92890.

4.5-205 Singh, A., and Balyan, S.S. 1975. Effect of nitrogenous fertilizers on the fresh herb, oil yield and oil content of Mentha. Indian J. Agron. 20: 311-313.

4.5-206 Singh, D.P., and Singh, J.N. 1971. Dry-matter accumulation and mineral composition of Japanese mint as affected by phosphorus deficiency. Indian J. Agric. Sci. 41: 830-839. HA 43: 337.

4.5-207 Singh, J.P., and Singh, J.N. 1978. Nitrate and ammonium as sources of nitrogen for Japanese mint and their influence on the uptake of other ions. Indian J. Agric. Sci. 48: 274-278. HA 49: 2124.

4.5-208 Singh, J.P., and Singh, J.N. 1979. Effect of varying levels of nitrate on the growth and nitrogen metabolism of Japanese mint (Mentha arvensis L. var. piperascens). Indian J. Plant Physiol. 22: 14-17. HA 50: 6531.

4.5-209 Singh, K., Singh, B.P., Bhola, A.L., and Yadava, T.P. 1972. Effect of sowing and nitrogen application in varieties of Indian mustard (Brassica juncea (L.) Czern & Coss.) under irrigated condition in Haryana. Indian J. Agric. Sci. 42: 601-603. SF 36: 2456.

4.5-210 Singh, K.P., Sandhu, A.S., and Husain, A. 1973. Effect of N, P and K fertilization on the yield of green herb oil and oil content of Mentha piperita L. Indian J. Agron. 18: 47-50. SF 39: 3172.

4.5-211 Singh, R.N., and Singh, J.R. 1974. Studies on the influence of boron nutrition on the growth characteristics of garlic (Allium sativum L.). Indian J. Hortic. 31: 255-258. HA 46: 3188.

4.5-212 Singh, R.S., Singh, L.B., and Singh, C.P. 1971. Response of N and P yield and essential oil content of dill in non-saline alkali soils. Fert. News 15{2}: 48-49.

4.5-213 Singh, U.B., Tomar, S.P., and Tomar, P.S. 1974. Comparative performance of different oil seed crops and their response to irrigation and fertilizer application. Indian J. Agron. 19: 1-5. SF 39: 3129.

4.5-214 Singh, U.B., and Tomar, S.P. 1971. Response of mustard to varying irrigation levels, spacing and fertilizer application. Indian J. Agron. 16: 465-467. FCA 27: 544.

4.5-215 Singh, U.P., Tomar, S.P., and Rathi, R.S. 1971. Effect of application of NPK and varying irrigation levels on the production of small seeded coriander. Indian J. Agron. 16: 313-315. SF 36: 3470.

4.5-216 Singh, V.P., and Duhan, S.P.S. 1979. Response of spearmint (Mentha spicata Linn.) to nitrogen in Tarai region of Nainital. Indian J. Pharm. Sci. 41: 87-88. HA 50: 1339.

4.5-217 Singh, V.P. 1979. Response of Japanese mint (Mentha arvensis Linn.) to phosphatic fertilizers. Indian J. Pharm. Sci. 41: 202-203. HA 50: 7321.

4.5-218 Slepetys, J. 1973. The biology and biochemistry of wormwood. 4. Effect of different norms of mineral fertilizers on the harvest [in Russian]. Liet. TSR Mokslu Akad. Darb. Ser. C 1973{2}: 51-56. AGRICOLA.

4.5-219 Slepetys, J. 1973. The biology and biochemistry of wormwood. 5. Effect of different norms of mineral fertilizers on the yield and amount of essential oil [in Russian]. Liet. TSR Mokslu. Akad. Darb. Ser. C 1973{3}: 29-35. AGRICOLA.

4.5-220 Slepetys, J. 1973. Effect of different rates of mineral fertilizers on the production of chamazulene in common wormwood [in Russian]. Page 294 in K. Jankevicius, ed. Poleznye rasteniia Pribaltiishikh respublik i Belorussii, Nauchnaia konferentsiia po issledovaniiu i obogashcheni, lu rastitel'nykh resurov Pribaltiiskikh respublik i Belorussii, 2nd, Vilna, 1973. CA 81: 62501.

4.5-221 Somogyi, Gy. 1974. Water demand and irrigation of red pepper [in Hungarian]. Bull. Zoldsegtermesztesi Kut. Intez. 9: 147-150. AGRICOLA.

4.5-222 Somos, A., Tarjanyi, F., Terbe, I., and Juhasz, K. 1975. Investigations into the effect of nutrient element supply on the paprika plant. Pages 437-447 in P. Kozma, D. Polyak and E. Hervay, eds. Le controle de l'alimentation des plantes cultivees. 3rd Colloque Europeen et Mediterraneen, Budapest, Hungary, Sept. 4-7, 1972. Akademiai Kiado, Budapest, Hungary. vol. I.

4.5-223 Sotomayor, R.I. 1975. Effect of nitrogen fertilization and plant density on yield of garlic [in Spanish]. Agric. Tec. (Santiago) 35: 175-178. SF 39: 6674.

4.5-224 Sotomayor, R.I. 1975. Garlic fertilization [in Spanish]. Invest. Prog. Agric. 7{1}: 34. HA 47: 370.

4.5-225 Steen, T.N. 1971. Fertilizer experiments in horseradish 1963-1969 [in Danish]. Tidsskr. Planteavl. 75: 758-765. AGRICOLA.

4.5-226 Strelec, V. 1974. Red pepper productivity in relation to irrigation [in Czech]. Pages 87-94 in Agronomicko-Biologicke Problemy Zavlah. Domtechniky Svts., Bratislava, Czechoslovakia.

4.5-227 Stroehlein, J.L., and Oebker, N.F. 1979. Effects of nitrogen and phosphorus on yields and tissue analyses of chili peppers. Commun. Soil Plant Anal. 10: 551-563. SF 42: 8423.

4.5-228 Subbiah, K., Helkiah, J., and Rajagopal, C.K. 1980. Effect of nitrogen, phosphorus and potassium on capsaicin content of MDU-1 chilli. South Indian Hortic. 28{3}: 103-104. HA 51: 6995.

4.5-229 Szyrmer, J. 1976. The effect of NPK fertilizer and environment on seed yield and quantity and quality of oil and white mustard, safflower and sunflower [in Polish]. Hodowla Rosl. Aklim. Nasienn. 18: 389-405. SF 40: 1462.

4.5-230 Takkar, P.N., Mann, M.S., and Randhawa, N.S. 1973. Major rabi (winter) and kharif (summer monsoon) crops respond to zinc. Indian Farming 23{8}: 5-8. FCA 28: 2341.

4.5-231 Talha, M., Aziz, M.A., and El-Toni, E.M. 1980. The combined effect of irrigation intervals and cycocel treatments on Pelargonium graveolens L. II. Evapotranspiration and water economy. Egypt. J. Soil Sci. 20: 121-136. SF 44: 7159.

4.5-232 Talha, M., Reda, F., and El-Toni, E.M. 1980. The combined effect of irrigation frequencies and cycocel treatments on Pelargonium graveolens L. I. Vegetative growth and yield of oil. Egypt. J. Soil Sci. 20: 111-120. SF 44: 7158.

4.5-233 Terbe, I. 1978. Effect of nutrient phosphorus, potassium and nitrogen supply on growth and development of forced sweet pepper (paprika) [in Hungarian]. Kert. Egy. Kozl. 10{2}: 47-54. AGRICOLA.

4.5-234 Terbe, I. 1979. The effect of fertilization on the growth and development of forced paprika [in Hungarian]. Agrartud. Kozl. 38: 427-432. AGRICOLA.

4.5-235 Terbe, I. 1977. Symptoms of nutritional deficiency and toxicity of vegetable paprika [in Hungarian]. Hajtatas Korai Termesztes Kert. Egy. Zoldsegtermesztesi Tansz. 8{3}: 12-13. AGRICOLA.

4.5-236 Terelak, H. 1975. The influence of polyhalite fertilization on the potassium and magnesium content in soil and plants [in Polish]. Pamiet. Pulawski 1975{63}: 67-84. FCA 31: 5630.

4.5-237 Tomar, S.P., Parihar, N.S., and Singh, U.B. 1971. Response of bold seeded coriander to levels of fertilizers and irrigation. Indian J. Agron. 16: 468-470. SF 36: 3469.

4.5-238 Uchida, Y., Takahashi, T., Danbara, H., and Nagase, T. 1976. Nutrient uptake by garlic [in Japanese]. Nippon Dojo-Hiryogaku Zasshi 47{1}: 1-5. SF 40: 850.

4.5-239 Uribe, A.A., and Gacitua, M.E. 1976. Effect of nitrogen fertilizers and plant population on garlic (Allium sativum L.) [in Spanish]. Agric. Tec. (Santiago) 36: 63-68. SF 40: 2732.

4.5-240 Valette, R. 1972. A study on water requirements during chicory forcing. An experimental irrigation apparatus with constant water tension [in French]. Rev. Agric. (Brussels) 25: 435-452.

4.5-241 Vasconcellos, E.F.C., Scalopi, E.J., and Klar, A.E. 1971. The influence of irrigation and nitrogen fertilization on precocity and premature sprouting in garlic [in Portuguese]. Solo 63: 15-19. HA 43: 5297.

4.5-242 Veerannah, L., and Rao, J.S. 1973. Effect of manganese on the uptake of major elements in gingelly (Sesamum indicum L.). Madras Agric. J. 60: 242-245. AGRICOLA.

4.5-243 Veerannah, L., and Rao, J.S. 1973. Interrelationship of manganese with macronutrients in Sesamum indicum L. Madras Agric. J. 60: 393-395. AGRICOLA

4.5-244 Vrzalova, J., and Nespor, L. 1971. Variations in the yield and quality of chamomile (Matricaria chamomilla L.) caused by different application rates of calcium nitrate and some growth substances [in German]. Acta Univ. Agric. Fac. Agron. (Brno) 19: 257-266. HA 43: 3054.

4.5-245 Yanazawa, T., and Fujii, S. 1972. Studies on leaf chlorosis in Baker's garlic grown on sandy soils. IV. Foliar sprays for correcting zinc deficiencies in garlic plants [in Japanese]. Engei Gakkai Zasshi 41{1}: 61-65. HA 43: 6022.

4.5-246 Zal'tsfas, A.A. 1975. The uptake of phosphorus by coriander from different phosphorus fertilizers [in Russian]. Tr. Vses. Nauchno-Issled. Inst. Efirnomaslichn. Kul't. 8: 144-149. HA 47: 9744.

4.5-247 Zatyko, F. 1973. Six to eight days earlier yield, income higher 10-12% when paprika fertilized with carbon dioxide [in Hungarian]. Kert. Szolesz. 22{21}: 3-6. AGRICOLA.

4.5-248 Zlatev, S. 1974. The effect of pruning the roots and tops of lavender on the take and development of the bushes [in Bulgarian]. Rastenievud. Nauki 11{4}: 49-55. HA 45: 1884.

4.6 Harvesting and Post-Harvest Handling

4.6-1 Akamine, E.K. 1976. Postharvest handling of tropical ornamental cut crops in Hawaii. HortScience 11: 125-127.

4.6-2 Alimov, F.A., and Chumakova, N.V. 1971. Timely harvesting of geraniums as a guarantee of a high yield of essential oil [in Russian]. Maslo-Zhir. Prom. 37{12}: 22-23. CA 76: 89936.

4.6-3 Baer, E.G., and Tanasienko, F.S. 1973. Change in content and quality of the essential oil when storing lavender inflorescences [in Russian]. Tr. Vses. Nauchno-Issled. Inst. Efirnomaslichn. Kul't. 6: 190-194. CA 83: 65319.

4.6-4 Balbaa, S.I., Hilal, S.H., and Haggag, M.Y. 1974. Effect of the use of different methods of drying of Digitalis lanata leaves on their quality and glycosidal content. Planta Med. 26{1}: 20-25. CA 81: 111421.

4.6-5 Bayer, J. 1973. Hungarian red pepper [in Hungarian]. Termeszet Vilaga 1973{8}: 358-360.

4.6-6 Behrend, G. 1973. Harvesting chicory with the root crop harvester EM 11 [in German]. Gartenbau 20: 322-323. HA 45: 5815.

4.6-7 Benoit, F., and Ceustermans, N. 1974. Quick comparison of ethrel application on autumn paprika [in Dutch]. Tuinbouwberichten 38: 250-254 AGRICOLA.

4.6-8 Benoit, F., and Ceustermans, N. 1980. Fennel from June to November [in Flemish]. Boer en de Tuinder 86{8}: 41. HA 50: 7213.

4.6-9 Bolotin, V.M., and Reznikov, A.R. 1971. Study of factors causing the bruising of coriander fruit during the threshing [in Ukrainian]. Visnyk Sil's'kohospod. Nauk 1971{2}: 20-23.

4.6-10 Carrington, R.G. 1976. Commercial processing of mint oils. Proc. Annu. Meet. Oreg. Essent. Oil Grow. League 27: 38-46. AGRICOLA.

4.6-11 Chandramani, R., Krishnamoorthy, K.K., Balasundaram, C.S., and Balakrishnan, T. 1975. Optimum time of cutting for obtaining maximum yield of extractable protein from fenugreek (Trigonella foenumgraecum) varieties. Madras Agric. J. 62: 230-231.

4.6-12 Chandrasekharan Nair, K., and Nair, E.V.G. 1975. Effect of salt water treatment on the extraction of soil from lemongrass (Cymbopogon flexuousus). Agric. Res. J. Kerala 13: 205-206. AGRICOLA.

4.6-13 Chaurasia, B.D., Sirohi, S.S., and Chohan, J.S. 1972. Effect of harvesting period on the growth and yield of chicory (Cichorium intybus L.). Indian J. Agric. Sci. 42: 1132-1134. HA 44: 3170.

4.6-14 Chinnamma, N.P., and Menon, P.K.G. 1973. Effect of harvest at different intervals on the grass and oil yield and citral content in lemongrass (Cymbopogon flexuosus Stapf.). Agric. Res. J. Kerala 11: 119-121. HA 45: 9994.

4.6-15 Chladek, M., and Patakova, D. 1972. The effect of maleic hydrazide on the shattering of flower heads in chamomile [in Czech]. Nase Liecive Rastliny 9: 136-137. HA 43: 3083.

4.6-16 Chladek, M. 1973. Suitable dates for harvesting thyme [in Czech]. Nase Liecive Rastliny 10: 105-107. HA 44: 2711.

4.6-17 Chudoba, Z. 1972. Effect of storage conditions on the germination ability of crambe (Crambe abyssinica Hochst et Fries), hemp (Cannabis sativa L.) and white mustard (Sinapis alba L.) seeds [in Polish]. Biul. Inst. Hodowli Aklim. Rosl. 1972: 85-87. FCA 26: 1975.

4.6-18 Chudoba, Z. 1972. Laboratory attempts at determining losses of dry matter in seeds during storage [in Polish]. Biul. Inst. Hodowli Aklim. Rosl. 1972: 11-14. FCA 26: 1972.

4.6-19 Dainello, F.J., and Heinemann, R.R. 1980. Postharvest ripening of Jalapeno peppers as influenced by preharvest application of ethephon and storage duration. Prog. Rep. - Tex. Agric. Exp. Stn. 3756. 7 pp. Bib.Ag. 46: 27209.

4.6-20 Davila Cardenas, R.E. 1979. Analysis of mechanized systems for harvesting sesame (Sesamum indicum) [in Spanish]. Rev. Fac. Agron. Univ. Cent. Venez. 10{1/4}: 287-343. AGRICOLA.

4.6-21 Deneva, T. 1975. Raw stuff bulk and morphine content of soporific poppy (Papaver somniferum L.) as affected by the fruit stalk length [in Bulgarian]. Rastenievud. Nauki 12{6}: 49-53. AGRICOLA.

4.6-22 Donalisio, M.G.R., Andrea Pinto, A. J. de, Souza, C.J. de, and Grid-Papp, E.I. 1972. Experiment on the timing and frequency of harvests of lemon-grass (Cymbopogon citratus D.C. Stapf.) [in Portuguese]. An. Acad. Bras. Cienc. 44(Suppl.): 117-122.

4.6-23 Evans, J. 1978. Some notes on ginseng harvest in West Virginia - Panax quinquefolius L.; American ginseng. Castanea 43: 262.

4.6-24 Franken, A.A. 1972. Some aspects of harvest planning in vegetable growing in the open [in Dutch]. Bedryfsontwikkeling 3: 831-838. HA 43: 5886.

4.6-25 Franz, C., and Wunsch, A. 1973. Post-harvest physiology of peppermint [in German]. Planta Med. 24: 1-7. HA 44: 4208.

4.6-26 Gatzke, E., and Lekve, O. 1978. Storage of chicory roots in large clamps [in German]. Gartenbau 25: 360-361. HA 50: 3270.

4.6-27 Georgiev, E., and Van Hong Tam. 1973. Changes of essential and glyceride oils during storage of raw material. Changes of the essential oil during short-term storage of ground cumin fruits [in Bulgarian]. Nauchni Tr., Vissh Inst. Khranit. Vkusova Prom-st., Plovdiv 20:99-106. CA 83: 168312.

4.6-28 Gruidze, V.G., and Tukvadze, S.G. 1975. Catechin of leaves of Laurus nobilis L. and their change during leaf drying and storage [in Russian]. Prikl. Biokhim. Mikrobiol. 11: 589-592. AGRICOLA.

4.6-29 Gulati, B.C., Garg, S.N., and Duhan, S.P.S. 1978. Effect of period of harvest on the yield and quality of oil of Mentha piperita Linn. Indian J. Pharm. Sci. 40: 88-90. HA 49: 2828.

4.6-30 Hartmann, H.D., and Waldhor, O. 1979. Picking dates with winter parsley [in German]. Gemuse 15: 316-318. HA 50: 4543.

4.6-31 Henriksen, K. 1975. Effects of time and method of harvesting and of weather conditions during windrowing on seed yield and quality in white mustard (Sinapis alba) [in Danish]. Tidsskr. Planteavl 79: 337-356. FCA 29: 9997.

4.6-32 Herisset, A., Jolivet, J., and Chaumont, J.-P. 1975. Efforts at industrial extraction of the essential oil of Roman chamomile from the total aerial parts of the plants [in French]. Plant. Med. Phytother. 9: 140-147.

4.6-33 Herisset, A., Jolivet, J., and Boussarie, M.F. 1971. Determination of the optimum time for harvesting some medicinal plants. III. Plants with essential oils [in French]. Plant. Med. Phytother. 5: 118-125.

4.6-34 Il'inykh, Z.G. 1975. The yield and quality of garlic in relation to the harvest date and the length of after-ripening in Central Ural conditions [in Russian]. Tr. Ural. Nauchno-Issled. Inst. Sel'sk. Khoz. 15: 167-171. HA 46: 10180.

4.6-35 Ilieva, S., Mateeva, D., and Dimitrova, S. 1976. Santonin content of santonin wormwood in dependence on the mode of drying [in Bulgarian]. Rastenievud. Nauki 13{1}: 79-84. AGRICOLA.

4.6-36 Iordanov, D. 1978. Problems of application of a technological complex of machines for commercial production of red pepper for grinding [in Bulgarian]. Gradinarstvo 1978{6}: 12-16. Bib. Ag. 43: 72303.

4.6-37 Janzso, J. 1980. Mechanization of the harvest and processing of green beans and of paprika [in Hungarian]. Elelmez. Ip. 34: 139-143. AGRICOLA.

4.6-38 Jerko, S. 1973. Achievements in the mechanization of harvesting string beans and spice paprika, and the future agrotechnical and engineering tasks [in Hungarian]. Jarmuvek, Mezogazd. Gepek 20: 401-406. AGRICOLA.

4.6-39 Jolivet, J. 1976. Influence of the time of harvest on the composition and essential oil content of "Hungarian" mint grown in Anjou [in French]. Plant. Med. Phytother. 10: 217-220. HA 47: 9756.

4.6-40 Kalmbacher, R.S., Hodges, E.M., and Martin, F.G. 1980. Effect of plant height and cutting height on yield and quality of Indigofera hirsuta. Trop. Grassl. 14: 14-18.

4.6-41 Kapeller, K., and Kapitany, J. 1977. Results in machine harvest trials of red pepper [in Hungarian]. Bull. Zoldsegtermesztesi Kut. Intez. 12: 107-154. AGRICOLA.

4.6-42 Karim, A., Ashraf, M., Pervez, M., and Bhatty, M.K. 1977. Studies on the essential oils of the Pakistani species of the family Umbelliferae. Part VIII. Carum carvi Linn. (caraway, kala zira) oil of the mature and the immature seeds and the whole immature plant. Pak. J. Sci. Ind. Res. 20: 100-102.

4.6-43 Kaur, B., and Manjrekar, S.P. 1975. Effect of dehydration on the stability of chlorophyll and beta-carotene content of green leafy vegetables available in northern India. J. Food Sci. Technol. 12: 321-323.

4.6-44 Kodash, A.G., Zakharova, O.I., and Zakharov, A.M. 1976.
Harvesting times for "Kubanskaia-6" peppermint [in Russian].
Farmatsiya (Moscow) 25{2}: 54-56. CIM 17{7}: 10551.

4.6-45 Kruistum, G. van, and Schouten, S.P. 1978. Are there
possibilities for storing witloof chicory roots at below freezing
point [in Dutch]. Bedrijfsontwikkeling 9: 1115-1117. HA 49: 3364.

4.6-46 Kunev, K., and Tsachev, S. 1975. Improvement of the mechanization
of the main harvesting processes in lavender [in Bulgarian]. Farm
Mach. 12{3}: 60-66. AGRICOLA.

4.6-47 Laszlo, K. 1975. Role of stem-fruit relation in the
after-ripening process of red peppers. Acta Agron. Acad. Sci. Hung.
24: 380-385.

4.6-48 Laughlin, J.C. 1980. The effect of time of harvest on the yield
components of poppies (Papaver somniferum L.). J. Agric. Sci. 95:
667-676.

4.6-49 Lee, B.Y., Hwang, J.M., and Chun, J.K. 1977. The effects of
dipping and field treatment of ethephon on the coloring and major
components of the red pepper [in Korean]. Seoul Taeghakkyo Nonghak
Yonku Coll. Agric. Bull. 2{2}: 43-50.

4.6-50 Lenches, O., Svab, J., and Foldesi, D. 1978. Drying medicinal
plants with TSZP equipment [in Hungarian]. Kertgazdasag 10{5}: 69-78.
HA 49: 5262.

4.6-51 Lips, J., and Cappelle, W. 1976. Storage of witloof chicory roots
- a concise summary of experimental results 1968-1975 [in French].
Rev. Agric. (Brussels) 29: 1139-1170. HA 47: 6486.

4.6-52 Loewer, O.J., Jr., White, G.M., and Ross, I.J. 1976. Evaluation
of flotation process for separating garlic from wheat. Trans. ASAE 19:
1158-1162.

4.6-53 Lordkipanidze, I.N., Tavadze, F.N., Mandzhgaladze, S.N.,
Gigolashvili, M.V., Akhvlediani, L.A., and Margiani, E.A. 1971.
Selection of corrosion-resistant alloys for equipment of plants
producing galenicals [in Russian]. Vop. Metalloved. Korroz. Metal.
1971{2}: 186-190. CA 77: 91944.

4.6-54 Lukianov, I.A., Logachev, S.A., and Shevchenko, P.I. 1972.
Harvesting schedule for Coriandrum sativum [in Russian]. Maslo.-Zhir.
Prom-st. 1977{1}: 19-20. AGRICOLA.

4.6-55 Madzharova, D., and Bubarova, M. 1972. Some biochemical features
of celery, parsley and parsnip related to the root storage [in
Bulgarian]. Gradinar. Lozar. Nauka 9{4}: 53-58. AGRICOLA.

4.6-56 Manachov, S. 1972. Harvesting lavender by use of a curved
uninertial cut instead of a passive one [in French]. An. Acad. Bras.
Cienc. 44(Suppl.): 139-141.

4.6-57 Masters, K. 1972. Continuous extraction for liquorice. Process
Biochem. 7{3}: 18-19. CA 77: 18139.

4.6-58 Mikailov, M.A., Mirzaliev, D.D., and Ragimova, Z.G. 1980. Effect

of the method of plucking fruit organs from Lawsonia inermis bushes on
the increase of leaf yields [in Russian]. Dokl. Akad. Nauk Az. SSR
36{8}: 68-71. Bib. Ag. 46: 3038.

4.6-59 Mukhopadhyay, T.P., Bose, T.K., Maity, R.G., Mitra, S.K., and
Biswas, J. 1980. Effect of chemicals on the post-harvest life of
jasmine flowers. Pages 47-50 in National Seminar on Production
Technology for Commercial Flower Crops. Tamil Nadu Agricultural
University, Coimbatore, India. HA 51: 7183.

4.6-60 Murray, M.J., Faas, W., and Marble, P. 1972. Chemical composition
of Mentha arvensis var. piperascens and four hybrids with Mentha
crispa harvested at different times in Indiana and Michigan. Crop Sci.
12: 742-745.

4.6-61 Murray, M.J., Faas, W., and Marble, P. 1972. Effects of plant
maturity on oil composition of several spearmint species grown in
Indiana and Michigan. Crop Sci. 12: 723-728.

4.6-62 Muthuswamy, S., Khan, W.M.A., Sayed, S., and Pappiah, C.M. 1973.
Chemical defoliation studies in Jasminum auriculatum Vahl. South
Indian Hortic. 21{1}: 10-14. HA 44: 7895.

4.6-63 Nagy, J., and Murany, E. 1977. Study of the possibilities
concerning the storage and post ripening of machine harvested spice
paprika [in Hungarian]. Konzerv. Paprikaip 1977{6}: 223-225.

4.6-64 Novobranova, T.I., and Telegina, R.F. 1979. Development of
measures for controlling fruit fungal diseases during storage [in
Russian]. Pages 284-291 in P.F. Sokol and Zh.A. Ter-Ovakimyan, eds.
Khranenie i pererabotka kartofelia, Ovoshchei, plodov i vinograda.
Izd. Kolos, Moscow, USSR. CA 91: 191657.

4.6-65 Nowosielska, B. 1978. The quality of differently ripened seeds of
vegetable crops [in Polish]. Post. Nauk Roln. 25{4}: 23-34. HA 50:
264.

4.6-66 Palevitch, D., Managem, E., Harel, S., Kanner, J., and Bengera,
I. 1975. Once-over harvesting of sweet paprika for industrial
processing [in Hebrew]. Hassadeh 55: 1472-1475. AGRICOLA.

4.6-67 Palevitch, D., Harel, S., Kanner, J., and Ben-Gera, I. 1975. The
effects of pre-harvest dehyration on the composition of once-over
harvested sweet paprika. Sci. Hortic. (Amsterdam) 3: 143-148.

4.6-68 Patil, V.R., Kulkarni, D.N., and Kulkarni, K., and Ingle, U.M.
1978. Effect of blanching factors on quality and durability of sun
dried and dehydrated fenugreek (Methi). Indian Food Packer 32{1}:
43-49. AGRICOLA.

4.6-69 Pavlenko, V.A., and Sergeeva, D.S. 1975. The effect of the
harvesting date on the frost resistance of mint rhizomes [in Russian].
Tr. Vses. Nauchno-Issled. Inst. Efirnomaslichn. Kul't. 1975{8}:
97-104. HA 47: 7761.

4.6-70 Pogorelova, O.V. 1978. Study of mechanically harvested valerian
raw material. Pharm. Chem. J. (Engl. Transl.) 12: 1174-1177.
Translation of Khim.-Farm. Zh. 12{9}: 69-72, 1978.

4.6-71 Pogorelova, O.V. 1978. Washing and curing of valerian rhizomes with roots. Pharm. Chem. J. (Engl. Transl.) 12: 1170-1173. Translation of Khim.-Farm. Zh. 12{9}: 65-69, 1978.

4.6-72 Putievsky, E., and Chizer, D. 1978. Spices of the family Labiatae (F). Harvesting frequency for three spice plants [in Hebrew]. Hassadeh 58: 1974-1976. HA 49: 2126.

4.6-73 Pyo, H.K., and Lee, B.Y. 1973. A physiological and ecological study on post-harvest garlic [in Korean]. Hanguk Wonye Hakhoe Chi 14: 25-30. HA 44: 7698.

4.6-74 Raev, R.Ts., Balinova-Tsvetkova, A., Atanasov, Zh., and Zlatev, S. 1980. High quality essential oil production from the aerial parts of annual fennel [in Bulgarian]. Rastenievud. Nauki 17{2}: 8-12. HA 51: 3903.

4.6-75 Ragheb, M.S., Atwa, A.A., Hamouda, M.A., Risk, N.A.M., and Oraby, S.G. 1972. Seasonal changes in garlic and its effect on bulbs during storage. Agric. Res. Rev. 50{5}: 157-165. HA 44: 1608.

4.6-76 Raikhman, L.B., and Reznikov, A.R. 1974. Mechanization of experimental plots of lavender [in Russian]. Tr. Vses. Nauchno-Issled. Inst. Efirnomaslichn. Kul't. 7: 124-126. AGRICOLA.

4.6-77 Saini, S.S. 1975. Effect of cuttings on the seed yield of methi (Trigonella foenumgraecum). Haryana J. Hortic. Sci. 4: 82-85. HA 47: 2985.

4.6-78 Sharma, M.L., Chandra, V., and Singh, A. 1973. Determination of optimum harvesting time for essential oil bearing crops raised at Lucknow. Mentha spicata Linn. (Spearmint). Indian Perfum. 17{1}: 26-29. HA 46: 9625.

4.6-79 Simeonova, V. 1973. Changes in the composition of some vegetable plants used as seasonings during their withering and drying [in Bulgarian]. Izv. Inst. Khranene, Bulg. Akad. Nauk. 11: 35-43. CA 79: 77167.

4.6-80 Simo, D. 1977. On some problems and directions of rationalization of hop harvesting [in Slovak]. Acta Operativo-oecononica Universitatis Agriculture Nitra Czechoslovakia 1977{32}: 125-135. AEA 4: 1068

4.6-81 Singh, R.P., Singh, B.P., and Yadava, T.P. 1975. Effect of harvesting time on the grain and oil yield of raya (Brassica juncea (L.) Czern and Coss). Haryana Agric. Univ. J. Res. 5: 354-357. FCA 32: 1168.

4.6-82 Skorikova, Yu.G., Grushevskaya, L.N., Vetokhina, R.F., Drozd, A.M., and Oleshko, L.N. 1973. Optimum harvesting time for green vegetable spices [in Russian]. Tr. Krasnodar. Nauchno-Issled. Inst. Pishch. Prom.-sti. 6: 186-194. CA 82: 110465.

4.6-83 Solomakhin, A. 1976. Machine harvesting of true lavender [in Ukrainian]. Mek. Sil's'k. Hospod. 1976{9}: 16-17.

4.6-84 Solomakhin, A.P. 1975. Effectiveness of machine harvesting of true lavender [in Russian]. Tr. Vses. Nauchno-Issled. Inst. Efirnomaslichn. Kul't. 8: 203-207. AGRICOLA.

4.6-85 Sosnowski, A., and Grabowski, I. 1977. Drying of Valeriana officinalis [in Polish]. Wiad. Zielarskie 19{7/8}: 1-2. AGRICOLA.

4.6-86 Stevlikova, M. 1977. Reducing the postharvest losses of paprika [in Slovak]. Zahradnictvo 2: 413-414. AGRICOLA.

4.6-87 Tavberidze, A.I., Chelishvili, R.B., and Zeituridze, Ts.G. 1971. Stability of the essential oil of spike-bearing savory [in Russian]. Tr. Gruz. Nauch.-Issled. Inst. Pishch. Prom. 5: 183-186. CA 78: 47639.

4.6-88 Tavberidze, A.I. 1971. Storage conditions for the spike-bearing savory [in Russian]. Tr. Gruz. Nauch.-Issled. Inst. Pishch. Prom. 5: 187-190. CA 78: 20109.

4.6-89 Tsvetkov, R., Kamburova, K., and Lucheva, M. 1975. Studies on retaining the sowing qualities of some essential oil plant seeds [in Bulgarian]. Rastenievud. Nauki 12{5}: 46-56. HA 46: 6060.

4.6-90 Turysheva, N.A., Perestova, T.A., and Saad, M.M. 1978. Reasons for losses of coriander volatile oil, connected with fruit structure [in Russian]. Izv. Vyssh. Ucheb. Zaved Pishch. Tekhnol. 1978{6}: 33-36.

4.6-91 Tyl, M. 1975. Mechanized harvesting of chamomile in Czechoslovakia in 1973 [in Czech]. Nase Liecive Rastliny 12: 33-35. HA 45: 9996.

4.6-92 Tyl, M. 1979. Mechanized harvesting of chamomile in Czechoslovakia in 1977 [in Czech]. Nase Liecive Rastliny 16: 2-4. HA 49: 4438.

4.6-93 Velichko, R.N., Sergeeva, D.S., and Selezneva, V.A. 1978. Characteristics of the formation and growth rate of herbage in mint cultivars after a double harvest [in Russian]. Tr. Vses Nauchno-Issled. Inst. Efirnomaslichn. Kul't. 11: 88-92. HA 50: 7914.

4.6-94 Woodstock, L.W., Simkin, J., and Schroeder, E. 1975. Freeze-drying to improve seed storability. Seed Sci. Technol. 4: 301-311. AGRICOLA.

4.6-95 Yamauchi, N., Hamaguchi, S., and Ogata, K. 1980. Physiological and chemical studies on ascorbic acid of fruits and vegetables. VII. Mechanism of chlorophyll degradation and action of ascorbic acid in the inhibition of yellowing in harvested parsley leaves [in Japanese]. Engei Gakkai Zasshi 49: 414-420. CA 94: 138091.

4.6-96 Zdun, K., Waszkiewicz, C., Elbanowska, A., and Gorecki, P. 1975. Investigations of the process of Valerian officinalis rhizome drying in a screen chamber drying oven. I. Established parameters of drying process [in Polish]. Herba Pol. 21: 39-49. AGRICOLA.

4.6-97 Zlatev, S., Balinova, A., and Zlateva, M. 1976. Changes in the essential oil of dill plants during post-harvest storage [in Bulgarian]. Rastenievud. Nauki 13{9}: 51-57. HA 47: 7758.

4.7 Agricultural Machinery

4.7-1 Doggendorf, N. 1972. Machine for the planting of chives [in Romanian] Mec. Electrif. Agric. 6: 65-66. AGRICOLA.

4.7-2 Dreviatnikov, I.M., and Khilik, L.A. 1975. Mechanization of planting of catnip [Nepeta transcaucasica] [in Russian]. Tr. Vses. Nauchno-Issled. Inst. Efirnomaslichn. Kul't. 8: 118-120.

4.7-3 Gabarashvili, A.E. 1971. Selecting optimum values for cutting speed in a machine for trimming and stacking branches of laurel [in Russian]. Subtrop. Kul't. 1971{1}: 128-134.

4.7-4 Gentry, J.P., Miles, J.A., and Hinz, W.W. 1978. Development of a chili pepper harvester. Trans. ASAE 21: 52-54.

4.7-5 Ivanov, V.V. 1977. Machine for producing cuttings of essential oil geranium [in Russian]. Subtrop. Kul't. 1977{1/2}: 166-168.

4.7-6 Ivanov, V.V., and Shvets, A.V. 1974. Design base for the type of a section for cutting basil and geranium [in Russian]. Tr. Vses. Nauchno-Issled. Inst. Efirnomaslichn. Kul't. 7: 138-146. AGRICOLA.

4.7-7 Ivanov, V.V., and Shvets, A.V. 1974. The problem of a basis for technical scheme of machines for harvesting East Indies basil [in Russian]. Tr. Vses. Nauchno-Issled. Inst. Efirnomaslichn. Kul't. 7: 133-138. AGRICOLA.

4.7-8 Kostov, D., Karaivanov, V., Kumanov, B., Stanev, G., Karapachov, P., Popov, D.,vulchev, S., and Nikolova, Ts. 1977. Optimization of the size of area and the number of machines in technological flow lines for middle-early tomatoes, red pepper for grinding and kidney beans [in Bulgarian]. Farm Mach. 14{2}: 3-9. AGRICOLA.

4.7-9 Lyon, M. 1975. The mechanization of garlic harvesting and drying [in French]. Pepinier. Hortic. Maraichiers 1975{154}: 35-39. HA 45: 7297.

4.7-10 Miles, J.A., Hinz, W.W., and Pike, W.H. 1978. Development of a mechanism for picking chilli peppers. Trans. ASAE 21: 419-421.

4.7-11 Popov, D., and Petkov, Ch. 1977. Studies of front-mounted combing operating device for mechanized harvesting of red peppers for grinding [in Bulgarian]. Farm Mach. 14{1}: 14-21. AGRICOLA.

4.7-12 Popov, D. 1980. Interrow soil loosening in red pepper crops with a rototilling bed former [in Bulgarian]. Gradinarstvo 61{3}: 27-29. AGRICOLA.

4.7-13 Smolianov, A.M. 1972. The news in the field of mechanical cultivation and extraction of essential oils of mint, lavender, rose and some other aromatic plants in the USSR. An. Acad. Bras. Cienc. 44(Suppl.): 134-137.

4.7-14 Vakarelski, I. 1974. Study of machines for the mechanized preparation and planting of peppermint roots [in Bulgarian]. Farm Mach. 11{1}: 81-89. AGRICOLA.

4.7-15 Varga, I., and Trefas, L. 1975. The state and characteristics of mechanization in medicinal plant production [in Hungarian]. Herba Hung. 14{2/3}: 135-149. HA 46: 4962.

4.8 Alternative Systems of Cultivation

4.8-1 Abe, Y., and Kito, S. 1975. Early cultivation of garlic under vinyl [in Japanese]. Nogyo Oyobi Engei 50: 898-902. PBA 47: 9903.

4.8-2 Alam, M.M., Ahmad, M., and Khan, A.M. 1980. Effect of organic amendments on the growth and chemical composition of tomato, eggplant and chilli and their susceptibility to attack by Meloidogyne incognita. Plant Soil 57: 231-236.

4.8-3 Bannerot, H., Lesaint, C., and Coninck, B. de. 1976. Forcing techniques for witloof chicory roots continue to develop [in French]. Pepinier Hortic. Maraichers 1976{170}: 21-27. HA 47: 7388.

4.8-4 Bell, S.M., and Coorts, G.D. 1979. The effects of growth mediums on three selected herb species. Florists Rev. 163{4232}: 48-49.

4.8-5 Benoit, F., and Ceusterman, N. 1974. Cultivation of paprika during the winter [in Dutch]. Tuinbouwberichten 38: 402-405. AGRICOLA.

4.8-6 Benoit, F., and Linden, F. Van. 1980. Plastic applications in the culture of fennel [in Flemish]. Boer en de Tuinder 86{2}: 16. HA 50: 6529.

4.8-7 Benoit, F., and Ceustermans, N. 1979. Glasshouse vegetables with low energy requirements [in Flemish]. Boer en de Tuinder 85{41}: 13-14. HA 50: 3286.

4.8-8 Bianco, V.V. 1975. The use of composted solid town refuse in seedbeds of vegetable crops [in Italian]. Riv. Agron. 9: 61-66. HA 46: 2088.

4.8-9 B"chvarov, S. 1978. Possibilities of using shallots (Allium cepa var. aescalonicum) for green onion and bulb production [in Bulgarian]. Gradinar. Lozar. Nauka 15{2}: 56-64. HA 50: 277.

4.8-10 Cappelle, W. 1977. Growing witloof chicory roots in double rows on ridges [in French]. Pepinier. Hortic. Maraichers 1977{174}: 27-39. HA 47: 8372.

4.8-11 Coninck, M. de. 1974. Perfecting chicory root forcing methods in a controlled atmosphere [in French]. Pepinier. Hortic. Maraichers 1974{146}: 47-59. HA 44: 8493.

4.8-12 Dancette, J.-P. 1976. The present position regarding chicory forcing [in French]. Pepinier. Hortic. Maraichers 1976{165}: 11-18. HA 46: 10209.

4.8-13 Davtyan, G.S., and Mairapetyan, S.Kh. 1972. Growing rose geraniums in open hydroponics [in Russian]. Pages 48-51 in P.V. Naumenko et al., eds. Mezhdunarodnyi kongress po efirnym maslam, 4th, Pishchevaya Promyshlennost', Moscow, USSR. HA 44: 4972.

4.8-14 Davtyan, G.S., and Mairapetyan, S.Kh. 1979. Results of long-term trials on the production of rose geraniums grown hydroponically in the open. Short communication [in Russian]. Soobshch. Inst. Agrokhim. Probl. Gidroponiki Akad. Nauk Arm. SSR 1979{18}: 3-14. HA 50: 3629.

4.8-15 Deibert, E.J., French, E., Hoag, B., and Nowatzki, R. 1978. No-till: North Dakota research emphasis. N.D. Farm Res. 35{4}: 3-6. FCA 32: 1917.

4.8-16 Denamany, G., Ahmad, M.S. bin, and Hamid, N. bin B. 1979. Coconut intercropping systems in peninsular Malaysia. Oleagineux 34{1}: 7-15. HA 49: 7127.

4.8-17 Desai, N.D., and Goyal, S.N. 1980. Intercropping of sesame with other oilseed crops. Indian J. Agric. Sci. 50: 603-605.

4.8-18 De, R. 1974. Development of agronomic practices for unfavourable rainfed conditions. Information Bulletin, Cereal Improvement and Production, Near East Project 11{3}: 9-14. FCA 29: 10106.

4.8-19 Dronova, T. 1976. Best cover crops for lucerne [in Russian]. Zemledelie 1976{9}: 59-61. HERB AB 47: 684.

4.8-20 Duke, J.A. 1974. Notes on Meo and Yao poppy cultivation. Phytologia 28: 5-8.

4.8-21 Filimonova, L.N. 1974. Root development of a pea and its productivity in mixed stands [in Russian]. Izv. Timiryazevsk. S-kh. Akad. 1974{3}: 41-48. HERB AB 45: 117.

4.8-22 Franken, A.A., and Hamersma, J. 1974. The low-temperature treatment of chicory roots for extra-early forcing [in Dutch]. Bedrijfsontwikkeling 5: 267-270. HA 44: 7556.

4.8-23 Franken, A.A., and Hamersma, J. 1974. The influence of ground and air temperatures during forcing on the yield and quality of chicory grown without a soil covering [in Dutch]. Bedrijfsontwikkeling 5: 1007-1011. HA 45: 6494.

4.8-24 Fulara, A. 1977. On mixed sowing of poppy and other farm crops [in Polish]. Nowe Roln. 26{2}: 12-16. AGRICOLA.

4.8-25 Gonetowa, I., Sienkiewicz, J., and Zurawski, H. 1974. Influence of an inserted asphalt layer on plant yield on a light soil [in Polish]. Pamiet. Pulawski 1974{60}: 7-17. FCA 30: 2376.

4.8-26 Harris, J. 1977. In mint condition. Greenhouse 2{2}: 23.

4.8-27 Hazarika, J.N., Bora, A.C., and Kanjilal, P.B. 1976. Cultivation of Japanese mint as an intercrop of citronella Java. Indian Drugs Pharm. Ind. 11{6}: 35-40. HA 48: 7564.

4.8-28 Hazarika, J.N., Bora, A.C., and Adhikary, R.K. 1976. Black peppermint (Mentha piperita L. var. vulgaris Sole) as intercrop. Agric. Agro-ind. J. 9{12}: 18-20.

4.8-29 Heinze, W., and Werner, H. 1971. Early forcing of chives [in German]. Gemuse 7: 245-246. AGRICOLA.

4.8-30 Hendriks, J.P., and Schoneveld, J.A. 1972. New ways of forcing chicory [in Flemish]. Groenten Fruit 28: 697. HA 43: 3639.

4.8-31 Herklots, G.A.C. 1974. Jasminum maingayi C.B. Clarke. J. Royal Hortic. Soc. 99: 215-216.

4.8-32 Jacot, D. 1972. Forcing witloof chicory in hydroponic culture without soil cover [in French]. Rev. Hortic. Suisse 45: 157-161. HA 43: 5177.

4.8-33 Jaruzelski, M., and Mazurkiewicz, M. 1977. Evaluation of various crops for interplanting with caraway [in Polish]. Wiad. Zielarskie 19{6}: 2-4.

4.8-34 Jayatillake, K.S.E., and Tennakoon, M.U.A. 1975. Competitiveness of chilli and paddy cultivation. An examination of data from Anuradhapura district. Staff Studies, Central Bank of Ceylon 5{1}: 191-200. WAERSA 19: 1524.

4.8-35 Karaman, M.M., Rieznikov, A.R., and Dreviatnykov, I.M. 1971. Economic efficiency of film hotbed of new type during growing of lavender seedlings [in Ukrainian]. Visnyk. Sil's'kohospod. Nauk 1971{4}: 14-16. AGRICOLA.

4.8-36 Kathi, K.S., Tripathi, H.N., and Singh, D. 1974. Studies on inter-cropping of rabi crops in autumn planted sugarcane. Indian Sugar 24: 701-705. FCA 29: 6778.

4.8-37 Khan, M.M., Aswathiah, B., Krishna, K.S., Reddy, C., and Hanumappa, P. 1976. Adoption pattern of improved agronomic practices of chilly cultivation in Kolar district. Mysore J. Agric. Sci. 10: 705-713. SF 40: 6671.

4.8-38 Kim, J.H., Yim, M.S., and Park, D.M. 1979. Experiment of intercropping on apple trees in the hilly orchard [in Korean]. Res. Rep. Off. Rural Dev. (Hortic. Agric. Eng.) 21: 29-36.

4.8-39 Kim, K.C., Lee, H.S., and Lee, J.I. 1979. Effects of accelerated initial growth by vinyl mulching on important agronomic characters of sesame (Sesamum indicum L.) [in Korean]. Res. Rep. Off. Rural Dev. (Crop) 21: 161-166.

4.8-40 Kneissl, P., and Sollner, V. 1978. Forcing of cut flowers from perennials under plastic [in German]. Dtsch. Gartenbau 32: 1946-1947. HA 49: 7729.

4.8-41 Kocurik, S., and Dovjak, V. 1977. Cultivation of true chamomile below the Tatra mountains [in Slovak]. Nase Liecive Rastliny 14: 3-6. HA 47: 8796.

4.8-42 Komarova, R.A. 1975. Problems of increasing the number of vegetable varieties grown under cover [in Russian]. Byull. Vses. Inst. Rastenievod. 1975{49}: 31-37. PBA 46: 6606.

4.8-43 Kozhukhar, V.S. 1976. Agrotechnics of parsley seed crops [in Russian]. Sel'sk. Khoz. Mold. 1976{2}: 18.

4.8-44 Kruistum, G. van. 1978. Chicon production in three forcing systems for witloff chicory over the whole forcing season [in Dutch]. Bedrijfsontwikkeling 9: 1013-1018. HA 49: 4154.

4.8-45 Kurinec, V. 1977. Our experiences in growing paprika under film covering [in Slovak]. Zahradnictvo 2: 119-120. AGRICOLA.

4.8-46 Lazic, B., Plavsic, V., and Durovka, M. 1975. Experience in paprika production in plastic greenhouses [in Serbo-Croatian]. Savrem. Poljopr. 23{5/6}: 11-18. AGRICOLA.

4.8-47 Lekve, O. 1972. Possibilities and preliminary results of forcing chicory on industrial lines [in German]. Gartenbau 19: 227-228. HA 44: 6600.

4.8-48 Lekve, O. 1973. Forcing chicory in dark rooms [in German]. Gartenbau 20: 326-328. HA 45: 4862.

4.8-49 Lesel, R., Ifergan, C., and Blanc, D. 1975. Test of integrated aquicultural productions: utilization of wastewaters of a circuit experimental fish culture farm for the cultivation of watercress [in French]. Bull. Fr. Piscic. 48{259}: 41-52. AGRICOLA.

4.8-50 Maher, M.J., and Bannon, J.J. 1972. Experiments on sweet pepper production under glass. Ir. J. Agric. Res. 11: 287-294. AGRICOLA.

4.8-51 Maier, I., Echim, T., and Enachescu, G. 1971. Results of forcing trials with witloof chicory [in Romanian]. Lucr. Stiint. Inst. Agron. Bucuresti Ser. B. 41: 21-23. HA 45: 3149.

4.8-52 Mairapetyan, S.Kh. 1972. Studies on the essential oil production of sweet basil (Ocimum basilicum) in open-air hydroponics [in Armenian]. Soobshch. Inst. Agrokhim. Probl. Gidroponiki Akad. Nauk Arm. SSR 1972{12}: 14-18. HA 44: 1803.

4.8-53 Mairapetyan, S.Kh. 1979. The effectiveness of cultivating lemongrass hydroponically in the open [in Russian]. Soobshch. Inst. Agrokhim. Probl. Gidroponiki Akad. Nauk SSR 1979{18}: 15-21. HA 50: 3623.

4.8-54 Malachowski, A. 1974. The effect of a plastic cover on cropping in cabbage, dill and dwarf beans [in Polish]. Rocz. Akad. Roln. Poznaniu 69: 109-121. HA 45: 4931.

4.8-55 Mandal, B.K., and Vamadevan, V.K. 1975. Effect of mulches on the growth and yield of rabi (winter) crops in the Mahandi delta. Indian J. Agron. 20: 190-192. FCA 29: 10121.

4.8-56 Meshcheriakova, R. 1971. Preparing parsley for forcing [in Russian]. Kartofel. Ovoshchi 1971{11}: 22-24. AGRICOLA.

4.8-57 Mikaelyan, L.N., Gasparyan, O.B., and Aleksanyan, D.S. 1972. The productivity and quality of some spice and salad crops in open-air hydroponic culture [in Russian]. Soobshch. Inst. Agrokhim. Probl. Gidroponiki Akad. Nauk Arm. SSR 1972{12}: 44-49. HA 43: 5487.

4.8-58 Mol, C. 1980. The advance of minor crops under glass is continuing [in Flemish]. Groenten Fruit 36: 41-43, 45. HA 51: 4472.

4.8-59 Novak, V. 1971. A contribution to the method of growing caraway (Carum carvi L.) by sowing in June after the harvest of an early preceding crop [in Czech]. Bulletin, Vyzkumny Ustav Zelinarsky Olomouc 1970/71{14/15}: 41-49. HA 43: 4730.

4.8-60 Nowaczyk, P. 1975. Growing paprika in the ground and in hot beds [in Polish]. Owoce Warz. Kwiaty 14{7}: 15-16. AGRICOLA.

4.8-61 Osumi, T. 1973. On improving the volume of sunlight and shade for the culture of medicinal Panax ginseng [in Japanese]. Nogyo Oyobi Engei 48{9}: 83-86. AGRICOLA.

4.8-62 Oswal, M.C., and Dakshinamurti, C. 1976. Effect of different tillage practices on water-use efficiency of pearl-millet and mustard under dry-farming conditions. Indian J. Agric. Sci. 45: 264-269. FCA 31: 1122.

4.8-63 Patel, P.M., Wallace, A., Romney, E.M., and Alexander, G.V. 1980. A Collander-type experiment in large tanks of solution culture (with plant species including bush beans and mint). J. Plant Nutr. 2: 127-133. HA 51: 3320.

4.8-64 Persson, A.R. 1973. Can paprika remain a greenhouse cultivar in Norway [in Norwegian]. Aktuelt. Landbruksdep. Opplysningstjeneste Norw. 1: 83-88. AGRICOLA.

4.8-65 Persson, A.R. 1973. Can paprika remain a greenhouse cultivar in Norway [in Norwegian]. Gartneryket 63: 730-731. AGRICOLA.

4.8-66 Pimpini, F. 1972. The use plastic films and the effect of nitrogen and phosphorus fertilizers on yield and quality of the chicory cv. Variegato di Castelfranco [in Italian]. Riv. Agron. 6: 105-117. HA 43: 5176.

4.8-67 Pimpini, F. 1975. A further experimental contribution to the use of plastic films for blanching and mulching chicory (Cichorium intybus) cv. Variegato di Castelfranco [in Italian]. Riv. Ortoflorofruttic. Ital. 59: 149-161. HA 46: 6684.

4.8-68 Pimpini, F. 1977. The effect of tap root diameter, time of lifting and temperture during blanching, on the yield of chicory (Cichorium intybus) cv. Variegato di Castelfranco [in Italian]. Riv. Ortoflorofruttic. 61: 55-64. HA 48: 368.

4.8-69 Plomacher, H. 1974. Chicory cultivation in a new form [in German]. Dtsch. Gaertnerboerse 74: 58-59. HA 44: 9481.

4.8-70 Popescu, V., Ridiche, N., and Amza, M. 1977. Improved technology of paprika cultivation in greenhouses [in Romanian]. Prod. Veg. Hortic. 26{1}: 13-17. AGRICOLA.

4.8-71 Riedel, H. 1973. The present situation and future requirements of vegetable production in greenhouses [in German]. Gartenbau 20: 285-287. HA 45: 1624.

4.8-72 Sans, L.M.A., Menezes Sobrinho, J.A. de, Novais, R.F. de, and Santos, H.L. dos. 1974. The effect of mulching on soil humidity and other characteristics under a crop of garlic [in Portuguese]. Rev. Ceres 21{114}: 91-104. HA 45: 2324.

4.8-73 Saurambaev, B.N. 1977. Glycyrrhizic acid content of liquorice from mixed sowings with fodder grains [in Russian]. Izv. Akad. Nauk Kaz. SSR Ser. Biol. 1977{6}: 15-18. HA 48: 10868.

4.8-74 Schmidt, S. 1973. Preliminary results with new methods of forcing chicory [in German]. Gartenbau 20: 328-329. HA 45: 4863.

4.8-75 Semenikhin, I.D., and Mush, N.N. 1974. Combined cultures of Valeriana L. and certain annual medicinal plants [in Russian]. Rastit. Resur. 10: 229-233.

4.8-76 Sheikh, A.S., and Mall, L.P. 1978. Effect of antitranspirants on transpiration and water-use-efficiency of chillies. J. Indian Bot. Soc. 57{1}: 6-8. SF 43: 6090.

4.8-77 Sheryshov, V.E. 1975. The effect of shading, mulching and irrigation on the growth of laurel seedlings in Lenkoran' [in Russian]. Izv. Akad. Nauk Az. SSR Ser. Biol. Nauk 1975{3}: 47-50. HA 46: 9609.

4.8-78 Sheryshov, V.E. 1973. Significance of spray irrigation and mulching of the Laurus nobilis nursery in the Lenkoran District of Azerbaijan SSR [in Russian]. Subtrop. Kul't. 1973{3}: 82-85.

4.8-79 Simon, J. 1974. Dry-matter production by white mustard (Sinapis alba L.) in a zero-tillage system [in Czech]. Rostl. Vyroba 20: 1039-1051. SF 38: 6484.

4.8-80 Singh, R.P., Singh, A., and Ramakrishna, Y.S. 1974. Cropping patterns for dry lands of India - an agro-climatic approach. Ann. Arid Zone 13: 145-164 FCA 28: 8506.

4.8-81 Siposova, M. 1977. Possibilities of using polyethylene film in growing paprika transplantings [in Slovak]. Zahradnictvo 2: 460.

4.8-82 Sondern, J.A. 1975. Seed protection with narrow plastic film [in Flemish]. Groenten Fruit 31: 1128-1129. HA 46: 8177.

4.8-83 Spaldon, E., and Vargova, E. 1971. Studies on some new agrotechnical factors of red pepper (Capsicum annuum L.) acceleration [in German] Acta Fytotech. 22: 117-142.

4.8-84 Sprague, M.A., Anderson, H.L., Motto, H.L., and Lopez Diaz, J.M. 1979. Alternatives to a monoculture of henequen in Yucatan. II. Studies with maize, sorghum and sesame. Interciencia 4: 84-91.

4.8-85 Stehlik, K. 1974. Irrigation with brewery waste water from the point of view of yield and soil effects [in German]. Sci. Agric. Bohemoslov. 6: 67-74. FCA 28: 8515.

4.8-86 Trauner, M. 1971. Austrian experiences with growing paprika in greenhouses [in German]. Gemuse 7: 64-68. AGRICOLA.

4.8-87 Tripathi, R.L., and Ajit Singh. 1977. Observations on the assessment of the scope of inter-cropping in autumn planted sugarcane in Dhuri Mill area. Indian Sugar 26: 753-757. HA 48: 4084.

4.8-88 Tsachev, S., Tanev, I., and Stanev, D. 1975. A contribution to the cultural practices for peppermint grown as a bienniel crop [in Bulgarian]. Rastenievud. Nauki 12{7}: 104-110. HA 46: 6067.

4.8-89 Tsachev, S., Zlatev, S., and Neshev, M. 1976. Studies on reconstructing close spaced lavender plantations for mechanized cultivation and harvesting [in Bulgarian]. Rastenievud. Nauki 13{9}: 105-111. HA 47: 8757.

4.8-90 Vaigl, M., and Graf, V. 1971. Chamomile as an undercrop in apple orchards [in Czech]. Zahradnicke Listy 64: 297-298. HA 44: 7963.

4.8-91 Valette, R. 1975. The influence of cultural conditions on the yield of witloof chicory roots [in French]. Pepinier. Hortic. Maraichers 1975{162}: 37-40. HA 46: 7567.

4.8-92 Vardaniya, K.Kh., and Vardaniya, L.Ya. 1976. The effect of soya and soya mulch on the growth and development of some sub tropical crops [in Russian]. Subtrop. Kul't. 1976{2}: 121-124. HA 47: 5973.

4.8-93 Velde, H.A. te. 1977. Yields of stubble catch crops as affected by sowing date and weather [in Dutch]. Bedrijfsontwikkeling 8: 587-590. HERB AB 48: 2305.

4.8-94 Vente, J.M. 1978. Chicory growing in water [in Flemish]. Groenten Fruit 33: 62-64. HA 48: 7212.

4.8-95 Verma, H.N., Prihar, S.S., Ranjodh Singh, and Nathu Singh. 1978. Yields of sub-humid rainfed crops in relation to soil water retention and cropping sequence. Exp. Agric. 14: 253-259.

4.8-96 Viall, S. 1979. The finishing touch. Greenhouse 3{9}: 35.

4.8-97 Vos, J. de, and Liekens, F. 1972. Views on the cultivation of paprika under glass [in Dutch]. Tuinbouwberichten 36: 240-241. AGRICOLA.

4.8-98 Wacker, H.D. 1976. Growing fennel in clusters, recommended for summer cultivation [in German]. Gartenpraxis 1976{7}: 338-339. AGRICOLA.

4.8-99 Waele, N. De. 1976. The effect of an asphalt emulsion treatment on some properties of non saline soils and plant growth in Tunisia. Meded. Fac. Landbouwwet. Rijksuniv. Gent 41: 175-186. HA 47: 5455.

4.8-100 Zatyko, L., Moor, Mrs. J. 1973. Forcing Hungarian paprika hybrids [in Hungarian]. Kert. Kut. Intez. Kozl. 3: 194-210. AGRICOLA.

4.8-101 Zitukawa, S. 1973. Tunnel culture of short-root Panax in Chiba Prefecture [in Japanese]. Nogyo Oyobi Engei 48{1}: 74-78. AGRICOLA.

4.9 Tissue Culture

4.9-1 Abo el-Nil, M.M. 1977. Organogenesis and embryogenesis in callus cultures of garlic (Allium sativum L.). Plant Sci. Lett. 9: 259-264. PBA 47: 12066.

4.9-2 Aleksandrova, I.V., Danilina, A.N., Gruzdev, L.G., Streletz, N.I., and Pastushenko, T.M. 1979. Ginseng tissue culture, a promising plant raw material [in Russian]. Rastit. Resur. 15: 361-367. HA 50: 554.

4.9-3 Alfermann, A.W., Boy, H.M., Doeller, P.C., Hagedorn, W., Heins,

M., Wahl, J., and Reinhard, E. 1977. Biotransformation of cardiac glycosides by plant cell cultures. Pages 125-141 in W.E.R. Barz, E. Reinhard and M.H. Zenk, eds. Plant tissue culture and its bio-technological application. Proceedings of the first international congress on medicinal plant research, Section B, Munich, Sept. 6-10, 1976. Springer-Verlag, New York, N.Y.

4.9-4 Ammirato, P.V. 1980. Regulation of development of somatic embryos in vitro. In Vitro 16: 221 (Abstr.).

4.9-5 Ammirato, P.V. 1978. The effects of 8-azaguanine on the development of somatic embryos from cultured caraway cells. Plant Physiol. 61 (4 Suppl.): 46 (Abstr.).

4.9-6 Ammirato, P.V. 1977. Hormonal control of somatic embryo development from cultured cells of caraway. Interactions of abscisic acid, zeatin, and gibberellic acid. Plant Physiol. 59: 579-586.

4.9-7 Ammirato, P.V. 1974. The effects of abscisic acid on the development of somatic embryos from cells of caraway (Carum carvi L.). Bot. Gaz. (Chicago) 135: 328-337.

4.9-8 Antony, A., Gopinathan, K.P., and Vaidyanathan, C.S. 1975. Biosynthesis of trigonelline in root callus cultures of fenugreek (Trigonella foenum-graecum L.). Indian J. Exp. Biol. 13: 39-41.

4.9-9 Ayabe, S.-I., Kobayashi, M., Hikichi, M., Matsumoto, K., and Furuya, T. 1980. Flavonoids from the cultured cells of Glycyrrhiza echinata. Phytochemistry 19: 2179-2183.

4.9-10 Azizbekova, N.Sh., and Milyaeva, E.L. 1978. Ontogenesis of saffron crocus (Crocus sativus) plants and changes in stem apices. Sov. J. Dev. Biol. (Engl. Transl.) 9: 266-271. Translation of Ontogenez 9: 309-314, 1978. AGRICOLA.

4.9-11 Ballade, P. 1972. Experimental study of axillary organogenesis in Nasturtium officinale behavior of isolated axils or axillary parts cultivated in vitro [in French]. C.R. Hebd. Seances Acad. Sci. Ser. 274: 1282-1285.

4.9-12 Ballade, P. 1971. Experimental study of auxiliar organogenesis in Nasturtium officinale R.Br. Behavior of isolated nodes cultivated in vitro [in French]. C.R. Hebd. Seances Acad. Sci. Ser. D 273: 2079-2082.

4.9-13 Barz, W. 1977. Degradation of polyphenols in plants and plant cell suspension cultures. Physiol. Veg. 15: 261-277.

4.9-14 Barz, W., Mohr, F., and Teufel, E. 1974. Catabolism of 4',6-dihydroxyaurone in vegetable cell suspension cultures [in German]. Phytochemistry 13: 1785-1787.

4.9-15 Becker, H., and Schrall, R. 1979. Callus and suspension cultures of different Valerianaceae species, their ability to accumulate valepotriates. Planta Med. 36: 228-229 (Abstr.).

4.9-16 Becker, H., Schrall, R., and Hartmann, W. 1977. Callus cultures of a valerian species. 1. Installation of a callus culture of Valeriana wallichii DC and 1st analytical studies [in German]. Arch. Pharm. (Weinheim) 310{6}: 481-484. CIM 18{2}: 1508.

4.9-17 Bekker, A.M., Gurevich, L.S., Mikhailova, N.V., and Slepyan, L.I.
1977. Dynamics of endogenous IAA in auxin-dependent strains of tissue
cultures from Panax ginseng and Polyscias filicifolia. Sov. Plant
Physiol. (Engl. Transl.) 24: 687-689. Translation of Fiziol. Rast.
(Moscow) 24: 841-844, 1977.

4.9-18 Bilkey, P.C., and Cocking, E.C. 1980. Isolation and properties of
plant microplasts: newly identified subcellular units capable of wall
synthesis and division into separate microcells. Eur. J. Cell Biol.
22{1}: 502 (Abstr.).

4.9-19 Booth, A., and Satchuthananthavale, R. 1974. Regeneration in root
cuttings in Taraxacum officinale. II. Effects of exogenous hormones on
root segments and root callus cultures. New Phytol. 73: 453-460.

4.9-20 Bouniols, A. 1974. In vitro neoformation of inflorescence buds
from Cichorium intybus root fragments: the influence of tissue
hydration and its consequences for amino acid composition [in French].
Plant Sci. Lett. 2: 363-371.

4.9-21 Bouriquet, R., and Vasseur, J. 1973. Effect of the origin of
explants on bud formation in leaf tissues of Cichorium intybus [in
French]. Bull. Soc. Bot. Fr. 120{1/2}: 27-32.

4.9-22 Bowes, B.G. 1971. The occurrence of shoot teratomata in tissue
cultures of Taraxacum officinale. Planta 100: 272-276.

4.9-23 Bowes, B.G. 1979. Fine structure of established callus cultures
of Taraxacum officinale Weber. Ann. Bot. 43: 649-656.

4.9-24 Bowes, B.G. 1975. The morphology of teratomatous organs in tissue
cultures of Taraxacum officinale Weber. Cellule 71: 19-29.

4.9-25 Brain, K.R., and Lockwood, G.B. 1976. Hormonal control of steroid
levels in tissue cultures from Trigonella foenumgraecum.
Phytochemistry 15: 1651-1654.

4.9-26 Bricout, J., Garcia-Rodriguez, M.-J., and Paupardin, C. 1978.
Effect of colchicine on essential oil synthesis in Mentha piperita
tissues grown in vitro [in French]. C. R. Hebd. Seances Acad. Sci.
Ser. D. 286: 1585-1588.

4.9-27 Bricout, J., Garcia-Rodriguez, M.-J., Paupardin, C., and Saussay,
R. 1978. The biosynthesis of monoterpene compounds by the tissues of
various mint species cultured in vitro [in French]. C. R. Hebd.
Seances Acad. Sci. Ser. D. 287: 611-613.

4.9-28 Bricout, J., and Paupardin, C. 1975. The essential oil
composition of Mentha piperita: cultured in vitro: influence of some
factors on its synthesis [in French]. C. R. Hebd. Seances Acad. Sci.
Ser. D. 281: 383-386.

4.9-29 Butenko, R.G., Slepyan, L.I., Khretonova, T.I., Mikhailova, N.V.,
and Vysotskaya, R.I. 1979. Studies on some tissue culture strains of
three Panax species as possible sources of stimulants [in Russian].
Rastit. Resur. 15: 265-270. HA 49: 9589.

4.9-30 Butenko, R.G., Khretnova, T.I., Slepyan, L.I., Mikhailova, N.V.,
and Vysotskaya, R.I. 1979. Phytochemical analysis of a suspension

strain of ginseng root tissue culture and standardization of its preparations [in Russian]. Rastit. Resur. 15: 356-360. HA 50: 1381.

4.9-31 Butenko, R.G. 1977. The cultivation of higher plant cells in suspension culture [in Russian]. Izv. Akad. Nauk SSSR Ser. Biol. 1977{5}: 697-709.

4.9-32 Bychkova, G.S. 1976. Synchronization of cell divisions achieved with the aid of 5-aminouracil in a suspension culture of ginseng. Sov. Plant Physiol. (Engl. Transl.) 23: 296-300. Translation of Fiziol. Rast. (Moscow) 23: 347-352, 1976.

4.9-33 Bychkova, G.S., and Butenko, R.G. 1974. Effects of auxin and kinetin on the mitotic cycle in partially synchronized population of ginseng (Panax ginseng C.A. Mey) cells in vitro. Dokl. Bot. Sci. (Engl. Transl.) 217/219: 59-62. Translation of Dokl. Akad. Nauk SSSR 217: 489-492, 1974. AGRICOLA.

4.9-34 Caldas, L.S., Sharp, W.R., and Crocomo, O.J. 1979. Callus cultures from seeds and anthers of Sesamum indicum L. An. Esc. Super. Agric. 'Luiz de Queiroz', Univ. Sao Paulo 36: 403-411. Bib.Ag. 46: 38842.

4.9-35 Chang, W.C., and Hsing, Y.I. 1978. Studies on the cell culture of ginseng. I. Callus induction, growth and rhizogenesis from roots of Panax ginseng, C.A. Meyer. Nat. Sci. Counc. Mon. (Taipei) 6: 76-79. HA 51: 1530.

4.9-36 Chang, W.C., and Hsing, Y.I. 1978. Studies on the cell culture of ginseng. II. Somatic embryogenesis of root callus of Panax ginseng, C.A. Meyer on a defined medium. Nat. Sci. Counc. Mon. (Taipei) 6: 770-772. HA 51: 1531.

4.9-37 Chang, W.C., and Hsing, Y.I. 1978. Studies on the cell culture of ginseng. III. Shoot formation on root callus of Panax ginseng, C.A. Meyer in vitro. Nat. Sci. Counc. Mon. (Taipei) 6: 1171-1173. HA 51: 1532.

4.9-38 Chang, W.C., and Hsing, Y.I. 1979. Studies on the cell culture of ginseng. IV. Suspension culture of root callus of Panax ginseng, C.A. Meyer. Nat. Sci. Counc. Mon. (Taipei) 7: 147-155. HA 51: 1533.

4.9-39 Chang, W.C., and Hsing, Y.I. 1980. In vitro flowering of embryoids derived from mature root callus of ginseng (Panax ginseng). Nature 284: 341-342.

4.9-40 Chang, W.C., and Hsing, Y.I. 1980. Plant regeneration through somatic embryogenesis in root-derived callus of ginseng (Panax ginseng C.A. Meyer). Theor. Appl. Genet. 57: 133-135.

4.9-41 Chang, W.C., and Hsing, Y.I. 1980. In vitro flowering of embryoids derived from mature root callus of ginseng (Panax ginseng). Nature (London) 284: 341-342.

4.9-42 Codaccioni, M., and Laisne, G. 1978. Influence of the composition of the culture medium on the morphology of Mentha viridis cultivated in vitro [in French]. C. R. Hebd. Seances Acad. Sci. Ser. D. 286: 29-32.

4.9-43 Codaccioni, M., and Laisne, G. 1980. The mannitol and cold reciprocal interaction of the growth in vitro of Mentha viridis [in French] Rev. Gen. Bot. 87{1031/1033}: 123-132. AGRICOLA.

4.9-44 Codaccioni, M., and Laisne, G. 1979. Effects of the presence of mannitol on the growth in vitro of Mentha viridis [in French]. Bull. Soc. Bot. Fr. 126: 15-29.

4.9-45 Corduan, G., and Spix, C. 1975. Haploid callus and regeneration of plants from anthers of Digitalis purpurea L. Planta 124: 1-11.

4.9-46 Dhandapani, M., Antony, A., and Rao, P.V.S. 1977. Biosynthesis of phenolic compounds in hypocotyl callus cultures of fenugreek (Trigonella foenum-graecum L.). Indian J. Exp. Biol. 15: 204-207.

4.9-47 Doeller, P.C., Alfermann, A.W., and Reinhard, E. 1977. Biotransformation of cardenolides by cell suspension cultures of Digitalis lanata and Thevetia neriifolia [in German]. Planta Med. 31: 1-6. CIM 18{13}: 10226.

4.9-48 Dougall, D.K., and Block, J. 1976. A survey of the presence of glutamate synthase in plant cell suspension cultures. Can. J. Bot. 54: 2924-2927. CA 86: 68374.

4.9-49 Downing, M.R., and Mitchell, E.D. 1975. Mevalonate-activating enzymes in callus culture cells from Nepeta cataria. Phytochemistry 14: 369-371.

4.9-50 Ellenbracht, F., Barz, W., and Mangold, H.K. 1980. Unusual fatty acids in the lipids from organs and cell cultures of Petroselinum crispum. Planta 150: 114-119.

4.9-51 Elze, H., Pilgrim, H., and Teuscher, E. 1974. The biotransformation of cholesterol-26-14C by tissue cultures of Euonymus europaea and Digitalis purpurea [in German]. Pharmazie 29: 727-728. HA 45: 3456.

4.9-52 El-Nil, M.M.A. 1977. Organogenesis and embryogenesis in callus cultures of garlic (Allium sativum L.). Plant Sci. Lett. 9: 259-264.

4.9-53 Erdelsky, K. 1971. Growth characteristics of a callus tissue culture of Papaver somniferum L. [in German]. Acta Fac. Rerum Nat. Univ. Comenianae Physiol. Plant. 1971{3}: 1-10.

4.9-54 Frey-Schroeder,G., and Barz, W. 1979. Isolation and characterization of flavonol converting enzymes from Mentha piperita plants and from Mentha arvensis cell suspension cultures. Z. Naturforsch. C. Biosci. 34: 200-209.

4.9-55 Fujiwake, H., Suzuki, T., Oka, S., and Iwai, K. 1980. Enzymatic formation of capsaicinoid from vanillylamine and iso-type acids by cell-free extracts of Capsicum annuum var. annuum cv. Karayatsubusa hot pepper. Agric. Biol. Chem. 44: 2907-2912.

4.9-56 Furmanowa, M., and Olszowska, O. 1980. Thymus vulgaris L. propagation through tissue culture. Acta Pol. Pharm. 37: 243-247.

4.9-57 Furuya, T., Kawaguchi, K., and Hirotani, M. 1973. Biotransformation of progesterone by suspension cultures of Digitalis purpurea cultured cells. Phytochemistry 12: 1621-1626.

4.9-58 Furuya, T., Nakano, M., and Yoshikawa, T. 1978. Biotransformation of (RS)-reticuline and morphinan alkaloids by cell cultures of Papaver somniferum. Phytochemistry 17: 891-893.

4.9-59 Garcia-Rodriguez, M.-J., Paupardin, C., and Saussay, R. 1978. The formation of secretory tissue and the synthesis of anethole by fennel tissue cultures [in French]. C. R. Hebd. Seances Acad. Sci. Ser. D. 287: 693-696.

4.9-60 Gorecka, K., Srzednicka, W., and Jankiewicz, L.S. 1978. Tissue culture of horse-radish (Cochlearia armoracia L.) meristems: sterilization of buds and comparision of media. Acta Agrobot. 31: 195-203. HA 50: 2765.

4.9-61 Grill, R., Frauenkron, I., and Schraudolf, H. 1979. Phytochrome in callus tissue cultures of Cruciferae. Z. Pflanzenphysiol. 94: 195-200.

4.9-62 Gupta, K.C. 1974. Influence of auxins on growth and cytohistology of fenugreek (Trigonella foenum-graecum L.) calli. Cytobios 9: 103-107.

4.9-63 Gusev, M.V., Butenko, R.G., Korzhenevskaya, T.G., Lobakova, E.S., and Baulina, O.I. 1980. Intercellular symbiosis of suspension ginseng culture cells and cyanobacteria. Eur. J. Cell Biol. 22{1}: 503 (Abstr.).

4.9-64 Gwozdz, E. 1973. Effect of IAA on growth, organogenesis and RNA metabolism during the development of Cichorium intybus root explants cultured "in vitro". Acta Soc. Bot. Pol. 42: 493-506. HA 44: 8496.

4.9-65 Gwozdz, E., Wozny, A., and Szweykowska, A. 1974. Induction by auxin of polyribosomes and granular endoplasmic reticulum in the callus tissue of Cichorium intybus. Biochem. Physiol. Pflanz. (BPP) 165: 82-92.

4.9-66 Hagimori, M., Matsumoto, T., and Kisaki, T. 1980. Studies on the production of Digitalis cardenolides by plant tissue culture. I. Determination of digitoxin and digoxin contents in first and second passage calli and organ redifferentiating calli of several Digitalis species by radioimmunoassay. Plant. Cell Physiol. 21: 1391-1404.

4.9-67 Hahlbrock, K., and Kuhlen, E. 1972. Relationship between growth of parsley and soybean cells in suspension cultures and changes in the conductivity of the culture medium. Planta 108: 271-278.

4.9-68 Hahlbrock, K. 1977. Regulatory aspects of phenylpropanoid biosynthesis in cell cultures. Pages 95-111 in W. Barz, E. Reinhard, and M.H. Zenk, eds. Plant tissue culture and its bio-technological application. Proceedings of the first international congress on medicinal plant research, Section B, Munich, Germany, Sept. 6-10, 1976. Springer-Verlag, New York, N.Y.

4.9-69 Hahlbrock, K., Ebel, J., Ortmann, R., Sutter, A., Wellmann, E., and Grisebach, H. 1971. Regulation of enzyme activities related to the biosynthesis of flavone glycosides in cell suspension cultures of parsley (Petroselinum hortense). Biochim. Biophys. Acta 244{1}: 7-15.

4.9-70 Hahlbrock, K. 1975. Further studies on the relationship between

the rates of nitrate uptake, growth and conductivity changes in the
medium of plant cell suspension cultures. Planta 124: 311-318.

4.9-71 Hahlbrock, K., and Schroeder, J. 1975. Specific effects on enzyme
activities upon dilution of Petroselinum hortense cell cultures into
water. Arch. Biochem. Biophys. 171: 500-506.

4.9-72 Hahlbrock, K. 1976. Regulation of the enzymes of phenylpropanoid
metabolism in relation to specific growth stages of plant cell
suspension cultures. Physiol. Veg. 14: 207-213.

4.9-73 Hardman, R., and Stevens, R.G. 1978. The influence of NAA and
2,4-D on the steroidal fractions of Trigonella foenum graecum static
cultures. Planta Med. 34: 414-419.

4.9-74 Heller, W., Egin-Buhler, B., Gardiner, S.E., Knobloch, K.-H.,
Matern, U., Ebel, J., and Hahlbrock, K. 1979. Enzymes of general
phenylpropanoid metabolism and of flavonoid glycoside biosynthesis in
parsley. Differential inducibility by light during the growth of cell
suspension cultures. Plant Physiol. 64: 371-373.

4.9-75 Hirotani, M., and Furnya, T. 1975. Metabolism of
5-betapregnane-3, 20-dione and 3-betahydroxy 5-betapregnan-20-one by
Digitalis suspension cultures. Phytochemistry 14: 2601-2606.

4.9-76 Hirotani, M., and Furuya, T. 1980. Biotransformation of
digitoxigenin by cell suspension cultures of Digitalis purpurea.
Phytochemistry 19: 531-534.

4.9-77 Hodges, C.C., and Rapoport, H. 1980. Enzymic reduction of
codeinone in vitro cell-free systems from Papaver somniferum and P.
bracteatum. Phytochemistry 19: 1681-1684.

4.9-78 Hoesel, W., Burmeister, G., Kreysing, P., and Surholt, E. 1977.
Enzymological aspects of flavonoid catabolism in plant cell cultures.
Pages 172-177 in W. Barz, E. Reinhard and M.H. Zenk, eds. Plant tissue
culture and its bio-technological application. Proceedings of the
first international congress on medicinal plant research, Section B,
Munich, Germany, Sept. 6-10, 1976. Springer-Verlag, New York.

4.9-79 Hrazdina, G., Kreuzaler, F., Hahlbrock, K., and Grisebach, H.
1976. Substrate specificity of flavanone synthase from cell suspension
cultures of parsley and structure of release products in vitro. Arch.
Biochem. Biophys. 175: 392-399.

4.9-80 Hsu, A.-F. 1980. Effect of protein synthesis inhibitors on cell
growth and alkaloid accumulation in cell cultures of Papaver
somniferum. Plant Physiol. 65 (6 Suppl): 91 (Abstr.).

4.9-81 Huber, J., Constabel, F., and Gamborg, O.L. 1978. A cell counting
procedure applied to embryogenesis in cell suspension cultures of
anise (Pimpinella anisum L.). Plant Sci. Lett. 12: 209-215.

4.9-82 Hui, L.H., and Zee, S.-Y. 1980. The effect of ginseng on the
plantlet regeneration % of cotyledon and hypocotyl explants of
broccoli. Z. Pflanzenphysiol. 96: 297-302.

4.9-83 Hui, L.H., and Zee, S.-Y. 1978. In vitro plant formation from
hypocotyls and cotyledons of leaf-mustard cabbage (Brassica juncea
Coss). Z. Pflanzenphysiol. 89: 77-80.

4.9-84 Jain, S.C., and Khanna, P. 1973. Incorporation of DL-tyrosine-1-14C in the biosynthesis of sesamin in suspension cultures of Sesamum indicum L. sesame. Indian J. Exp. Biol. 11: 578.

4.9-85 Jain, S.C., and Khanna, P. 1973. Production of sterols from Sesamum indicum Linn. Indian J. Pharm. 35: 163-164. AGRICOLA.

4.9-86 Jain, S.C., Nag, T.N., Mohan, S., and Khanna, P. 1975. Effect of ascorbic acid on and its estimation in plant tissue cultures. Sci. Cult. 41: 292-293.

4.9-87 Jhang, J.J., Staba, E.J., and Kim, J.Y. 1972. American and Korean ginseng tissue culture growth and examination for saponins. Lloydia 35: 473.

4.9-88 Jhang, J.J., Staba, E.J., and Kim, J.Y. 1974. American and Korean ginseng tissue cultures: Growth, chemical anlysis, and plantlet production. In Vitro 9: 253-259.

4.9-89 Karasawa, D., and Shimizu, S. 1980. Triterpene acids in callus tissues from Mentha arvensis var. piperascens Mal. Agric. Biol. Chem. 44: 1203-1205.

4.9-90 Kartnig, T., Russheim, U., Trousil, G., and Maunz, B. 1979. Cardenolides in callus cultures of Digitalis purpurea and Digitalis lanata. III. Callus cultures derived from roots [in German]. Planta Med. 35: 275-278.

4.9-91 Kartnig, T., Russheim, U., and Maunz, B. 1976. Observations on the occurrence and formation of cardenolides in tissue cultures of Digitalis purpurea and Digitalis lanata. 1. Cardenolides in surface area cultures of cotyledons and leaves of Digitalis purpurea [in German]. Planta Med. 29: 275-282. CA 85: 59609.

4.9-92 Kartnig, T., and Kobosil, P. 1977. Observations on the occurrence and the formation of cardenolides in tissue cultures of Digitalis purpurea and Digitalis lanata. 2. Cardenolides in submerse cultures of the leaves of Digitalis purpurea [in German]. Planta Med. 31: 221-227. CA 87: 36075.

4.9-93 Kartnig, T. 1977. Cardiac glycosides in cell cultures of Digitalis Pages 44-51 in W.E.R. Barz, E. Reinhard and M.H. Zenk, eds. Plant tissue culture and its bio-technological application. Proceedings of the first international congress on medicinal plant research, Section B, Munich, Sept. 6-10, 1976. Springer-Verlag, Berlin.

4.9-94 Kartnig, T., Moeckel, H., and Maunz, B. 1975. The occurrence of coumarins and sterols in tissue cultures of roots of Anethum graveolens and Pimpinella anisum [in German]. Planta Med. 27: 1-13. CIM 17{7}: 10552.

4.9-95 Kehr, A.E., and Schaeffer, G.W. 1976. Tissue culture and differentiation of garlic. HortScience 11: 422-423.

4.9-96 Keller, E., Eberspacher, J., and Lingens, F. 1979. Metabolism of chloridazon and antipyrin in plant cell suspension cultures [in German]. Z. Naturforsch. C: Biosci. 34: 914-922. WA 29: 4236.

4.9-97 Khanna, P., and Jain, S.C. 1972. Effect of nicotinic acid on growth and production of trigonelline by Trigonella foenum-graecum L. tissue cultures. Indian J. Exp. Biol. 10: 248-249.

4.9-98 Khanna, P., Mohan, S., Nag, T.N., and Jain, S.C. 1971. Tissue differentiation in ten plant species in vitro. Indian J. Plant Physiol. 14: 35-43. HA 46: 3709.

4.9-99 Khanna, P., and Khanna, R. 1976. Production of major alkaloids from in vitro tissue cultures of Papaver somniferum Linn. Indian J. Exp. Biol. 14: 628-630.

4.9-100 Khanna, P., Khanna, R., and Sharma, M. 1978. Production of free ascorbic acid and effect of exogenous ascorbic acid and tryosine on production of major opium alkaloids from in vitro tissue culture of Papaver somniferum Linn. Indian J. Exp. Biol. 16: 110-112.

4.9-101 Khanna, P. 1977. Tissue culture and useful drugs – a review on twenty plant species grown in vitro. Pages 495-500 in C.K. Atal and B.M. Kapur, eds. Cultivation & utilization of medicinal and aromatic plants. Regional Research Laboratory, Jammu-Tawi, India.

4.9-102 Khanna, P., and Jain, S.C. 1973. Diosgenin, gitogenin and tigogenin from Trigonella foenum-graecum tissue cultures. Lloydia 36: 96-98.

4.9-103 Khanna, P., and Jain, S.C. 1973. Production of sapogenins from Trigonella foenumgraecum L. tissue cultures. Proc. Indian Sci. Cong. 60 (Sect. VI): 385 (Abstr.).

4.9-104 Khan, M.I. 1975. Regeneration of Taraxacum roots in relation to carbon and nitrogen supply. Pak. J. Bot. 7{2}: 161-167.

4.9-105 Kireeva, S.A., Mel'nikov, V.N., Reznikova, S.A., and Meshcheryakova, N.I. 1978. Essential oil accumulation in a peppermint callus culture. Sov. Plant Physiol. (Engl. Transl.) 25: 438-443. Translation of Fiziol. Rast. (Moscow) 25: 564-570, 1978.

4.9-106 Kirkland, D.F., Matsuo, M., and Underhill, E.W. 1971. Detection of glucosinolates and myrosinase in plant tissue cultures. Lloydia 34: 195-198.

4.9-107 Kiss, A., and Paal, H. 1974. In vivo investigations on pollen-tube growth with paprika (Capsicum annuum L.) [in Hungarian]. Agrobotanika 16: 89-95. AGRICOLA.

4.9-108 Kohl, H.C. 1977. Biosynthesis of secondary metabolites in plant tissue cultures. In Vitro 13: 169 (Abstr.).

4.9-109 Kokate, C.K., and Radwan, S.S. 1979. Mucilage in callus cultures of higher plants. Phytochemistry 18: 662-663.

4.9-110 Kreuzaler, F., and Hahlbrock, K. 1973. Flavonoid glycosides from illuminated cell suspension cultures of Petroselinum hortense. Phytochemistry 12: 1149-1152.

4.9-111 Kudielka, R.A., and Theimer, R.R. 1980. Induction of glyoxysomes in suspension cultures of anise (Pimpinella anisum L.). Plant Physiol. 65 (6 Suppl.): 92 (Abstr.).

4.9-112 Kuo, C.C., Wang, Y.Y., Chien, N.F., Ku, S.J., Kung, M.L., and Hsu, H.C. 1973. Investigations on the anther culture in vitro of Nicotiana tabacum L. and Capsicum annuum L. Acta Bot. Sin. (Engl. Transl.) 15: 33-46. Translation of Chih-Wu Hsueh Pao 15{1}: 37-52, 1973. AGRICOLA.

4.9-113 Kuzovkina, I.N., Kuznetsova, G.A., and Smirnov, A.M. 1975. Essential oils in the culture of isolated plant tissues [in Russian]. Izv. Akad. Nauk SSSR Ser. Biol. 377-381.

4.9-114 Laisne, G., and Codaccioni, M. 1977. Osmotic pressure in the epidermic cells of Mentha viridis L. cultivated in vitro according to the culture temperature and the glucose concentration in the culture medium [in French]. C.R. Hebd. Seances Acad. Sci. Ser. D 284: 539-541. AGRICOLA.

4.9-115 Lang, E., and Horster, H. 1977. Sugar-bound regular monoterpenes. Part II. Production and accumulation of essential oils in Ocimum basilicum callus and suspension cultures [in German]. Planta Med. 31: 112-118. HA 47: 9759.

4.9-116 Lee, K.H., and Kim, Y.K. 1975. Studies on the tissue culture of garlic [in Korean]. Hanguk Wonye Hakhoe Chi 16: 64-69. HA 47: 2496.

4.9-117 Legrand, B. 1975. The effect of iron and EDTA on bud formation by leaf explants of witloof chicory growin in vitro [in French]. C. R. Hebd. Seances Acad. Sci. Ser. D 280: 2215-2218. HA 46: 5662.

4.9-118 Legrand, B. 1974. The effect of light conditions on bud regeneration by chicory leaf tissues grown in vitro and on the peroxidase activity these tissues [in French]. C. R. Hebd. Seances Acad. Sci. Ser. D. 278: 2425-2428.

4.9-119 Leienbach, K.-W., and Barz, W. 1976. Metabolism of nicotinic acid in plant cell suspension cultures. II. Isolation, characterization and enzymology of nicotinic acid N-alpha-arabinoside isolated [in German]. Hoppe Seylers Z. Physiol. Chem. 357: 1069-1080.

4.9-120 Liebert, J., and Tran Thanh Van, M. 1972. Progress in intensive clonal propagation of cultivated plants: chicory. Studies on the capacity for the renewed formation of thin layers of cells such as the epidermis of Cichorium intybus [in French]. C.R. Seances Acad. Agric. Fr. 58: 472-477. HA 43: 3638.

4.9-121 Light, R.J., and Hahlbrock, K. 1980. Randomization of the flavonoid A ring during biosynthesis of kaempferol from {1,2-13C2}acetate in cell suspension cultures of parsley. Z. Naturforsch. C. Biosci. 35: 717-721.

4.9-122 Lockwood, G.B., and Brain, K.R. 1976. Influence of hormonal supplementation on steroid levels during callus induction from seeds of Trigonella foenumgraecum. Phytochemistry 15: 1655-1660.

4.9-123 Lockwood, G.B. 1976. Hormonal control of steroid levels during callus induction from seeds of Trigonella foenumgraecum. Indian J. Pharm. 38: 159 (Abstr.).

4.9-124 Majid, R., Sharma, N.D., and Mathur, J.M.S. 1974. Studies on the Capsicum frutescens anther culture and nature of callus pigment. Indian Soc. Nuclear Tech. Agric. Biol. Newsl. 3{1}: 10-11.

4.9-125 Mangold, H.K. 1977. The common and unusual lipids of plant cell cultures. Pages 55-65 in W. Barz, E. Reinhard and M.H. Zenk, eds. Plant tissue culture and its bio-technological application. Proceedings of the first international congress on medicinal plant research, Section B, Munich, Germany, Sept. 6-10, 1976. Springer-Verlag, Berlin.

4.9-126 Margara, J. 1974. Conditions for the vegetative or reproductive development of buds regenerated on pieces of the flower stalk of Cichorium intybus [in French]. C. R. Hebd. Seances Acad. Sci. Ser. D 278: 1195-1198.

4.9-127 Margara, J. 1973. Experimental analysis by in vitro culture of vernalization requirements in Cichorium intybus [in French]. C. R. Hebd. Seances Acad. Sci. Ser. D 276: 2373-2376.

4.9-128 Margara, J. 1978. Perfection of a range of mineral media for in vitro culture conditions [in French]. C.R. Seances Acad. Agric. Fr. 64: 654-661. HA 49: 2324.

4.9-129 Masuda, K., Kikuta, Y., and Okazawa, Y. 1979. Significance of sugars on callus induction of parsley endosperm. J. Fac. Agric. Hokkaido Univ. 59: 249-253.

4.9-130 Masuda, K., Koda, Y., and Okazawa, Y. 1977. Callus formation and embryogenesis of endosperm tissues of parsley seed cultured on hormone-free medium. Physiol. Plant. 41: 135-138.

4.9-131 Misawa, M. 1977. Production of natural substances by plant cell cultures described in Japanese patents. Pages 17-26 in W. Barz, E. Reinhard and M.H. Zenk, eds. Plant tissue culture and its bio-technological application. Proceedings of the first international congress on medicinal plant research, Section B, Munich, Germany, Sept. 6-10, 1976. Springer-Verlag, Berlin.

4.9-132 Mitchell, E.D., and Arebalo, R.E. 1976. Mevalonate metabolism in cell-free extracts from Nepeta cataria leaf and callus tissues. Plant Physiol. 57 (5 Suppl.): 41 (Abstr.).

4.9-133 Modos, K., and Maroti, M. 1979. Experiment for establishment of geranium callus culture. Bot. Kozl. 66: 313-317.

4.9-134 Nickel, S., and Staba, E.J. 1977. RIA - test of Digitalis plants and tissue cultures. Pages 278-284 in W.E.R. Barz, E. Reinhard and M.H. Zenk, eds. Plant tissue culture and its bio-technological application. Proceedings of the first international congress on medicinal plant research, Section B, Munich, Sept. 6-10, 1976. Springer-Verlag, New York, N.Y.

4.9-135 Nikitina, I.V., and Aleksandrova, I.V. 1977. Growth and metabolism of nitrogenous substances in a culture of callus tissue of Panax ginseng. Sov. Plant Physiol. (Engl. Transl.) 24: 441-446. Translation of Fiziol. Rast. (Moscow) 24: 549-554, 1977.

4.9-136 Noma, M., Huber, J., and Pharis, R.P. 1979. Occurrence of delta 1{10} gibberellin A1 counterpart, GA1, GA4 and GA7 in somatic cell embryo cultures of carrot and anise. Agric. Biol. Chem. 43: 1793-1794.

4.9-137 Novak, F.J. 1974. The changes of karyotype in callus cultures of Allium sativum L. Caryologia 27: 45-54.

4.9-138 Novak, F.J. 1974. Induction of a haploid callus in anther cultures of Capsicum sp. Z. Pflanzenzuecht. 72: 46-54.

4.9-139 Overton, K.H., and Picken, D.J. 1977. Studies in secondary metabolism with plant tissue culture. Fortschr. Chem. Org. Naturst. 34: 249-298.

4.9-140 Paulet, P. 1977. An approach to the regulation of the in vitro flowering of root explants of Cichorium intybus L. Acta Hortic. 1977{68}: 179-184.

4.9-141 Paul, J.S., and Bassham, J.A. 1977. Maintenance of high photosynthetic rates in mesophyll cells isolated from Papaver somniferum. Plant Physiol. 60: 775-778.

4.9-142 Paul, J.S., and Bassham, J.A. 1978. Effects of sulfite on metabolism in isolated mesophyll cells from Papaver somniferum. Plant Physiol. 62: 210-214.

4.9-143 Petiard, V., Demarly, Y., and Paris, R.-R. 1972. Physiological evidence of cardiotonic substances in vitro culture of Digitalis purpurea L. tissue [in French]. C.R. Hebd. Seances Acad. Sci. Ser. D. 274: 846-847.

4.9-144 Petiard, V., Demarly, Y., and Paris, R.-R. 1971. Manifestation of cardiotonic heterosides in the tissue cultures of Digitalis purpurea [in French]. C.R. Hebd. Seances Acad. Sci. Ser. D. 272: 1365-1367.

4.9-145 Petiard, V., and Demarly, Y. 1972. Presence of glucosides and alkaloids in plant tissue cultures [in French]. Ann. Amelior. Plant. 22: 361-374.

4.9-146 Pfruener, H., and Bentrup, F.W. 1978. Fluxes and compartmentation of K+, Na+ and Cl- and action of auxins in suspension-cultured Petroselinum cells. Planta 143: 213-223.

4.9-147 Pilgrim, H., Elze, H., and Teuscher, E. 1974. Formation and transformation of steroids by vegetable tissue cultures [in German]. Pharmazie 29: 78 (Abstr.).

4.9-148 Pilgrim, H. 1977. The suspension culture of Digitalis purpurea tissues [in German]. Pharmazie 32: 130-131. HA 47: 9787.

4.9-149 Pilgrim, H. 1977. Sapogenin growth in suspension cultures of Digitalis purpurea [in German]. Phytochemistry 16: 1311-1312. HA 48: 782.

4.9-150 Porcelli-Armenise, V., Scaramuzzi, F., and DeGaetano, A. 1976. In vitro associations of cambium tissues of some plant species belonging to the family Oleaceae [in French]. C.R. Hebd. Seances Acad. Sci. Ser. D 282: 851-854.

4.9-151 Radwan, S.S., and Kokate, C.K. 1980. Production of higher levels of trigonelline by cell cultures of Trigonella foenum-graecum than by the differentiated plant. Planta 147: 340-344.

4.9-152 Ratnamba, S.P., and Chopra, R.N. 1974. In vitro inductin of embryoids from hypocotyls and cotyledons of Anethum graveolens seedlings. Z. Pflanzenphysiol. 73: 452-455.

4.9-153 Ratnamba, S.P. 1973. In vitro flowering in Anethum graveolens. Botanica 23: 155-156 (Abstr.).

4.9-154 Reichling, J., and Becker, H. 1976. Tissue culture of Matricaria chamomilla L. I. Isolation and maintenance of the tissue culture and preliminary phytochemical investigations [in German]. Planta Med. 30: 258-268. HA 47: 5934.

4.9-155 Reinhard, E. 1975. Possibilities for using cell cultures in medicinal plant research [in German]. Planta Med. Suppl. 1975: 1-4.

4.9-156 Ruecker, W., Jentzsch, K., and Wichtl, M. 1976. Root differentiation and glycoside formation in tissues of Digitalis purpurea L. cultured in vitro [in German]. Z. Pflanzenphysiol. 80: 323-335.

4.9-157 Schenck, H.R., and Hoffmann, F. 1979. Callus and root regeneration from mesophyll protoplasts of basic Brassica species: B. campestris, B. oleracea and B. nigra. Z. Pflanzenzuecht. 82: 354-360

4.9-158 Schrall, R., and Becker, H. 1980. Valepotriate in callus and suspension cultures of different Valerianaceae. Acta Hort. 96: 75-83.

4.9-159 Sehgal, C.B. 1978. Differentiation of shoot-buds and embryoids from inflorescence of Anethum graveolens in cultures. Phytomorphology 28: 291-297.

4.9-160 Sen, B., and Gupta, S. 1979. Differentiation in callus cultures of leaf of two species of Trigonella. Physiol. Plant. 45: 425-428.

4.9-161 Shah, R.R., and Dalal, K.C. 1980. In vitro multiplication of Glycyrrhiza. Curr. Sci. 49: 69-71.

4.9-162 Shchigel'skii, O.A., Yashchenko, V.K., Butenko, R.G., and Vollosovich, A.G. 1974. Emission spectral analysis of the content of certain trace elements in cultures of isolated tissues and intact medicinal plants. Sov. Plant Physiol. (Engl. Transl.) 21: 74-77. Translation of Fiziol. Rast. (Moscow) 21: 93-97, 1974. HA 44: 6996.

4.9-163 Shchigel'skii, O.A., Butenko, R.G., Vollosovich, A.G., and Yashchenko, V.K. 1979. Aluminum content in cultures of isolated tissues intact medicinal plants. Sov. Plant Physiol. (Engl. Transl.) 26: 511-517. Translation of Fiziol. Rast. (Moscow) 26: 635-638, 1979.

4.9-164 Shivanna, K.R., Jaiswl, V.S., and Mohan Ram, H.Y. 1974. Effect of cycloheximide on cultured pollen grains of Trigonella foenum-graecum. Plant Sci. Lett. 3: 335-339.

4.9-165 Slepyan, L.I. 1971. Callus development in an isolated ginseng root tissue culture [in Russian]. Rastit. Resur. 7: 175-186.

4.9-166 Spiess, E., and Seitz, U. 1975. Quantitative determination of growth-dependant changes in the ultrastructure of freely suspended callus cells of parsley (Petroselinum crispum (Mill.) A.W. Hill) [in German]. Ber. Dtsch. Bot. Ges. 88: 319-328.

4.9-167 Stohs, S.J. 1977. Metabolism of steroids in plant tissue culture. Pages 142-150 in W. Barz, E. Reinhard and M.H. Zenk, eds. Plant tissue culture and its bio-technological application.

Proceedings of the first international congress on medicinal plant
research, Section B, Munich, Germany, Sept. 6-10, 1976.
Springer-Verlag, New York, N.Y.

4.9-168 Suga, T., Hirata, T., and Yamamoto, Y. 1980. Lipid constituents
of callus tissues of Mentha spicata. Agric. Biol. Chem. 44: 1817-1820.

4.9-169 Sung Cho Yoo, and Sung Soon Kim. 1976. Studies on tissue culture
of medicinal plants. {2} Tissue cultures of Glycyrrhiza glabra var.
glandulifera [in Korean]. Korean Journal of Pharmacognosy 7{1}: 55-57.
HA 47: 10801.

4.9-170 Szoeke, E., Kuzovkina, I.N., Verzar-Petri, G., and Smirnov, A.M.
1977. Cultivation of wild chamomile tissues. Sov. Plant Physiol.
(Engl. Transl.) 24: 679-686. Translation of Fiziol. Rast. (Moscow) 24:
832-840, 1977.

4.9-171 Szoeke, E., Verzar-Petri, G., Kuzovkina, I.N., Lemberkovics, E.,
and Keri, A. 1978. Synthesis of essential oils in callus cultures of
wild chamomile. Sov. Plant Physiol. (Engl. Transl.) 25: 144-147.
Translation of Fiziol. Rast. (Moscow) 25: 178-181, 1978.

4.9-172 Szoke, E., Kuzovkina, I.N., Verzar-Petri, G., and Szmirnov, A.M.
1979. Effect of growth regulators on biomass formation in callus
culture of chamomile (Matricaria chamomilla) [in Hungarian]. Herba
Hung. 18{1}: 41-57. HA 50: 549.

4.9-173 Szoke, E., Shavarda, A.L., and Kuzovkina, I.N. 1978. Effect of
culturing conditions on essential oil formation in callus tissue of
wild chamomile inflorescences. Sov. Plant Physiol. (Engl. Transl.) 25:
579-584. Translation of Fiziol. Rast. (Moscow) 25: 743-750, 1978.

4.9-174 Tabata, M. 1977. Recent advances in the production of medicinal
substances by plant cell cultures. Pages 3-16 in W. Barz, E. Reinhard
and M.H. Zenk, eds. Plant tissue culture and its bio-technological
application. Proceedings of the first international congress on
medicinal plant research, Section B, Munich, Germany, Sept. 6-10,
1976. Springer-Verlag, New York, N.Y.

4.9-175 Tanaka, H., Machida, Y., Tanaka, H., Mukai, N., and Misawa, M.
1974. Accumulation of glutamine by suspension cultures of Symphytum
officinale. Agric. Biol. Chem. 38: 987-992.

4.9-176 Teuscher, E. 1973. Problems in the production of secondary
active principles by means of plant cell cultures [in German].
Pharmazie 28: 6-18. HA 43: 8001.

4.9-177 Theiler, R. 1977. In vitro culture of shoot tips of Pelargonium
species. Acta Hortic. 1977{73}: 403-414.

4.9-178 Tomoda, G., Matsuyama, J., and Iikubo, H. 1976. Tissue culture
of fragrant plants. Tamagawa Daigaku Nogakubu Kenkyu Hokoku 1976{16}:
16-22. HA 48: 6760.

4.9-179 Turner, T.D., and Williams, M.H. 1978. Techniques in plant cell
and dispersion culture. J. Pharm. Pharmacol. 30 (Suppl.): 94P
(Abstr.).

4.9-180 Uddin, A., Sharma, G.L., and Khanna, P. 1977. Flavonoids from in vitro seedling callus culture of Trigonella foenum-graecum Linn. Indian J. Pharm. 39: 142-143. HA 48: 7619.

4.9-181 Vasseur, J. 1972. Incorporation of orotic acid-14C and uracil-14C into the ribonucleotides of chicory leaf fragments cultured in vitro [in French]. C. R. Hebd. Seances Acad. Sci. Ser. D. 275: 2865-2868.

4.9-182 Verger, A., Joseph, C., and Paulet, P. 1976. Comparative effects on some quaternary trimethylammonium compounds on the growth and development of Cichorium intybus root tissue cultured in vitro [in French]. C. R. Hebd. Seances Acad. Sci. Ser. D 282: 49-52. HA 46: 10211.

4.9-183 Vysotskaya, R.I., and Slepyan, L.I. 1980. Tissue culture of ginseng. I. Chemical composition of the biomass of ginseng tissue culture [in Russian]. Rastit. Resur. 16: 123-129. HA 50: 9491.

4.9-184 Waris, H., Kaarina Simola, L., and Grano, A. 1972. Aseptic cultures of seed plants at various sucrose concentrations with and without gibberellin. Ann. Acad. Sci. Fenn. Ser. A4 1972{188}: 1-12.

4.9-185 Wichtl, M., Jentzsch, K., and Ruecker, W. 1978. Growth and glycoside formation in callus cultures and tissues of various Digitalis purpurea organs [in German]. Pharmazie 33: 229-233. HA 48: 9328.

4.9-186 Wink, M., Hartmann, T., and Witte, L. 1980. Biotransformation of cadaverine and potential biogenetic intermediates of lupanine biosynthesis by plant cell suspension cultures. Planta Med. 40: 31-39.

4.9-187 Withers, L.A., and Street, H.E. 1977. The freeze-preservation of plant cell cultures. Pages 226-244 in W. Barz, E. Reinhard and M.H. Zenk, eds. Plant tissue culture and its bio-technological application. Proceedings of the first international congress on medicinal plant research, Section B, Munich, Germany, Sept. 6-10, 1976. Springer-Verlag, New York, N.Y.

4.9-188 Wu, C.-H., Zabawa, E.M., and Townsley, P.M. 1974. The single cell suspension culture of the licorice plant, Glycyrrhiza glabra. Can. Inst. Food Sci. Technol. J. 7: 105-109.

4.9-189 Yoneda, K., and Imahori, Y. 1978. Seed biology of medicinal plants. (IV) The characters of fennel after ovary culture [in Japanese]. Shoyakugaku Zasshi 32: 158-161.

4.9-190 Zargarian, O.P., Marshavina, Z.V., Gevorkian, A.G., and Aslaniantz, L.K. 1976. Biochemical characteristics of sterile cell tissue culture of some essential oil plants [in Russian]. Biol. Zh. Arm. 29{1}: 52-55.

4.9-191 Zholkevich, V.N., Butenko, R.G., and Pisetskaya, N.F. 1971. Relationships between heat emission, oxygen consumption, and mitotic activity in a culture of isolated tissue of Panax ginseng. Sov. Plant Physiol. (Engl. Transl.) 18: 650-653. Translation of Fiziol. Rast. 18: 767-771, 1971.

4.9-192 Zilkah, S., and Gressel, J. 1977. Cell cultures vs. whole plants for measuring phytotoxicity. 1. The establishment and growth of callus and suspension cultures; definition of factors affecting toxicity on calli. Plant Cell Physiol. 18: 641-655.

5.0 PRODUCTION ECOLOGY

5.1 Crop Dynamics

5.1-1 Agaev, M.G. 1974. Population density as the regulating factor in plant development [in Russian]. Dokl. Akad. Nauk SSSR Ser. Biol. 217: 705-708

5.1-2 Arunachalam, L., and Sennaiyan, P. 1977. Spacing and fertilizer response studies with TMV 3 sesame. Madras Agric. J. 64: 758-759.

5.1-3 Arunachalam, L., and Sennaiyan, P. 1977. Effect of spacing row distance and nitrogen on the growth attributes of Sesamum indicum L. Oils Oilseeds J. 30{2}: 14-18.

5.1-4 Arunachalam, L., and Sennaiyan, P. 1978. Effect of spacing, row distance and nitrogen application on the yield attributes of summer sesame. Oils Oilseeds J. 31{1}: 18-22.

5.1-5 Bazzaz, F.A., and Harper, J.L. 1976. Relationship between plant weight and numbers in mixed populations of Sinapis alba (L.) Rabenh. and Lepidium sativum L. J. Appl. Ecol. 13: 211-216.

5.1-6 Berenyi, M. 1976. The effect of planting methods and irrigation on yield, quality and ripening of a determinate red pepper variety [in Hungarian]. Bull. Zoldsegtermesztesi Kut. Intez. 11: 65-76. AGRICOLA.

5.1-7 Bhan, S., Singh, H.G., and Amar Singh. 1975. Note on the effect of variety, spacing and fertility levels on the yield of ancillary characters of mustard (Brasica juncea (L.) Czern. and Coss.). Indian J. Agric. Res. 9: 208-210. FCA 30: 497.

5.1-8 Bhardwaj, S.D., Katoch, P.C., Kaushal, A.N., and Raina, V. 1978. Effects of times of planting and spacings in relation to herbage yield and oil content in Mentha piperita Linn. in Himachal Pradesh. Indian J. Agric. Sci. 48: 463-466.

5.1-9 Bukhbinder, A.A. 1973. Spacing in relation to the yield of herbage and essential oil of geranium grown on the alluvial soils of the Kolkhida lowland [in Russian]. Subtrop. Kul't. 1973{5}: 84-86. HA 44: 6977.

5.1-10 Chubey, B.B., and Dorrell, D.G. 1978. Total reducing sugar, fructose and glucose concentrations and root yield of two chicory cultivars as affected by irrigation, fertilizer and harvest dates. Can. J. Plant Sci. 58: 789-793.

5.1-11 Clark, R.J., and Menary, R.C. 1979. The importance of harvest date and plant density on the yield and quality of Tasmanian peppermint oil. J. Am. Soc. Hortic. Sci. 104: 702-706.

5.1-12 Davletov, Sh. 1974. Seed production in mustard and rape [in Russian]. Zemledelie 1974{10}: 27. FCA 29: 498.

5.1-13 Dayanand, and Mahapatra, I.C. 1974. A note on effect of different
row spacings and doses of nitrogen on the grain yield of raya
(Brassica juncea). Indian J. Agron. 19: 234-235. SF 39: 3700.

5.1-14 Delgado, M., and Yermanos, D.M. 1975. Yield components of sesame
(Sesamum indicum L.) under different population densities. Econ. Bot.
29: 69-78.

5.1-15 Domokos, J. 1977. Investigations on the correlation between
seedling size and root yield in Angelica archangelica crops [in
Hungarian]. Herba Hung. 16{2}: 49-53. HA 49: 1443.

5.1-16 Domokos, J. 1979. Studies on correlations between plant density
and seedling size between root size and root weight in Angelica
archangelica [in Hungarian]. Herba Hung. 18{1}: 81-86. HA 50: 517.

5.1-17 Duhan, S.P.S., Bhattacharya, A.K., and Husain, A. 1977. Effect of
weeds on the yield of herb, oil and quality of oil of peppermint
(Mentha piperita Linn.). Perfum. Flavor. 2{5}: 54 (Abstr.). WA 28:
719.

5.1-18 Duhan, S.P.S., Gulati, B.C., and Bhattacharya, A.K. 1975. Effects
of nitrogen and row spacing on the yield and quality of essential oil
in Japanese mint. Indian J. Agron. 20: 14-16.

5.1-19 El Nadi, A.H., and Lazim, M.H. 1974. Growth and yield of
irrigated sesame. II. Effects of population and variety on
reproductive growth and seed yield. Exp. Agric. 10: 71-76.

5.1-20 El-Gengaihi, S., and Abdallah, N. 1978. The effect of date of
sowing and plant spacing on yield of seed and volatile oil of fennel
(Foeniculum vulgare Mill.). Pharmazie 33: 605-606.

5.1-21 Gaur, B.L., and Trehan, K.B. 1974. Effect of spacing and
fertilization on the yield of rainfed sesame (Sesamum indicum Linn.).
Indian J. Agron. 19: 217-219.

5.1-22 Ghosh, D.C., and Sen, J.R. 1980. Management practices for
increasing seed yield of sesame in dry season. Farmer Parliament
15{2}: 23-25. AGRICOLA.

5.1-23 Gowda, K.T.K., and Krishnamurthy, K. 1977. Response of Sesamum
varieties to spacings and fertilizer levels. Mysore J. Agric. Sci. 11:
351-355. AGRICOLA.

5.1-24 Gupta, R.R. 1972. Interrelationship studies among some yield
contributing attributes in rai (Brassica juncea (L.) Czern and Coss.).
Madras Agric. J. 59: 421-425. FCA 26: 3415.

5.1-25 Gutnikova, Z.I. 1971. The seed productivity of Panax ginseng C.A.
Mey on experimental industrial plantations of maritime territory [in
Russian]. Rastit. Resur. 7: 110-114.

5.1-26 Haizel, K.A. 1972. The canopy relationship of pure and mixed
populations of barley (Hordeum vulgare L.), white mustard (Sinapis
alba L.) and wild oats (Avena fatua L.). J. Appl. Ecol. 9: 589-600.

5.1-27 Haizel, K.A. 1972. The productivity of mixtures of two and three
species. J. Appl. Ecol. 9: 601-608.

5.1-28 Haizel, K.A., and Harper, J.L. 1973. The effects of density and the timing of removal on interference between barley, white mustard and wild oats. J. Appl. Ecol. 10: 23-31.

5.1-29 Hornok, L. 1972. The effect of sowing time on the yield and essential oil content of dill [in Hungarian]. Kerteszetiegy. Kozl. 36{4}: 175-181. HA 44: 4964.

5.1-30 Jain, K.K., and Dubey, C.S. 1972. Study of yield attributes and heritability in some varieties of coriander (Coriandrum sativum L.). Madras Agric. J. 59: 193-194. HA 43: 1405.

5.1-31 Kapitany, J. 1978. Comparison of plant population in planted and direct seeded red pepper [in Hungarian]. Bull. Zoldsegtermeszetesi Kut. Intez. 13: 25-35. AGRICOLA.

5.1-32 Karlin, V.R. 1973. The yielding capacity of Valeriana officinalis L. in the floodplain forests of the Don and its tributaries [in Russian]. Rastit. Resur. 9: 82-86.

5.1-33 Katiyar, R.P., and Singh, B. 1974. Interrelationships among yield and its components in Indian mustard. Indian J. Agric. Sci. 44: 287-290. FCA 30: 3655.

5.1-34 Katoch, P.C., and Bhardwaj, S.D. 1978. Optimum time of planting and row spacings for cultivation of Mentha citrata Ehrh. at Solan in Himachal Pradesh. Indian J. For. 1: 199-202. AGRICOLA.

5.1-35 Katsumata, H. 1975. Ecology and cultivation of garlic [in Japanese]. Nogyo Oyobi Engei 50: 177-180. PBA 46: 10619.

5.1-36 Katsumata, H. 1975. Ecology and cultivation of garlic [in Japanese]. Nogyo Oyobi Engei 50: 281-283. PBA 46: 10618.

5.1-37 Kazakova, Kl. 1971. Investigations on the density of lavender (Lavandula vera) planting [in Bulgarian]. Rastenievud. Nauki 8{8}: 121-127. AGRICOLA.

5.1-38 Khanna, K.R., and Singh, U.P. 1975. Correlation studies in Papaver sominiferum and their bearing on yield improvement. Planta Med. 28: 92-96. HA 46: 4996.

5.1-39 Kigelman, M., and Orinshtein, Z. 1976. Dense planting of lavender [in Russian]. Sel'sk. Khoz. Mold. 1977{2}: 28.

5.1-40 Kim, H.K., and Ho, Q.S. 1980. Effect of dense planting and pinching of axillary buds by treatment of MH on yield of red pepper [in Korean]. Hanguk Wonye Hakhoe Chi 21: 135-142.

5.1-41 Klein, H., Schuster, W., and Marquard, R. 1980. Influence of variety, locality and sulphur fertilizers on the properties of different varieties of mustard as raw materials for the production of condiments [in German]. Fette Seifen Anstrichm. 82: 5-10. HA 51: 7218.

5.1-42 Krarup, H.C., and Trobok, V.S. 1975. The effect of planting systems on yield, bulb quality and efficiency of N-fertilizer use in garlic (Allium sativum) [in Spanish]. Fitotec. Latinoam. 11{1}: 39-42. HA 47: 2495.

5.1-43 Krylova, I.L. 1973. Number of sample plots and model specimens needed for determining the yield of medicinal plants [in Russian]. Rastit. Resur. 9: 457-466.

5.1-44 Kuzminska, K. 1972. Effect of magnesium fertilization at two calcium levels and soil moisture on yields and morphine content in opium poppy (Papaver somniferum L.) [in Polish]. Herba Pol. 18: 266-274 AGRICOLA.

5.1-45 Lazic, B., Markovic, V., and Gavric, M. 1975. The effect of variety and mode of production on paprika yield [in Serbo-Croatian]. Savrem. Poljopr. 23{7/8}: 41-50. AGRICOLA.

5.1-46 Lazim, M.H., and El Nadi, A.H. 1974. Growth and yield of irrigated sesame. I. Effects of population and variety on vegetative growth. Exp. Agric. 10: 65-69.

5.1-47 Lund, E.W., and Dorph-Petersen, K. 1973. Yield relationships of agricultural crops. 2. Oil crops and legumes [in Danish]. Tidsskr. Planteavl 77: 206-211. FCA 28: 2764.

5.1-48 Mahajan, V.P., Randhawa, G.S., and Bains, D.S. 1977. Effect of row-spacing and nitrogen levels on the seed yield of celery (Apium graveolens L.). J. Res., Punjab Agric. Univ. 14: 15-17. SF 41: 2978.

5.1-49 Marquard, R., Schuster, W., and Klein, H. 1979. Yield, contents and composition of fats and proteins in several varieties and types of mustard at distinctly different ecological locations [in German]. Fette Seifen Anstrichm. 81: 381-389. NAR-B 50: 2569.

5.1-50 Matai, S., Bagchi, D., and Chanda, S. 1976. Effect of seed rate, nitrogen level and leaf age on the yield of extracted protein from five different crops in West Bengal. J. Sci. Food Agric. 27: 736-742.

5.1-51 Mehrotra, O.N., Saxena, H.K., and Moosa, M. 1976. Physiological analysis of varietal differences in seed yield of Indian mustard (Brassica juncea, L. Czern and Coss). Indian J. Plant Physiol. 19: 139-146. FCA 31: 755.

5.1-52 Menezes Sobrinho, J.A. de, Novais, R.F. de, Santos, H.L. dos, and Sans, L.M.A. 1974. The effect of nitrogen fertilization, plant spacing and mulching on the yield of garlic cultivar Amarante [in Portuguese]. Rev. Ceres 21{115}: 203-212. HA 45: 6470.

5.1-53 Menezes Sobrinho, J.A. de, Couto, F.A.A., Medina, P.V.L., and Regina, S.M. 1974 The effect of the planting density of small cloves and the type of soil cover on the yield of cloves for planting in three garlic cultivars [in Portuguese]. Rev. Ceres 21{117}: 349-357. HA 45: 3922.

5.1-54 Menezes Sobrinho, J.A. de, Novais, R.F. de, Santos, H.L. dos, and Sans, L.M.A. 1974. The effect of nitrogen rates and mulching on the production of three garlic cultivars [in Portuguese]. Rev. Ceres 21{118}: 458-469. HA 46: 290.

5.1-55 Minard, H.R.G. 1978. Effect of clove size, spacing, fertilisers, and lime on yield and nutrient content of garlic (Allium sativum). N.Z. J. Exp. Agric. 6: 139-143. HA 49: 1160.

5.1-56 Munoz Burgos, M.S. 1978. Varieties and sowing date, density and methods of seeding [in Spanish]. Circ. Ciano (Cent. Invest. Agric. Noroeste) 96: 1-7. AGRICOLA.

5.1-57 Nambisan, K.M.P., Nanjan, K., Veeraragavathatham, D., and Krishnan, B.M. 1979. A note on the density of planting in relation to yield of flower in Jasminum sambac Ait. cv. 'Gundumalli'. Prog. Hortic. 10{4}: 19-20. HA 50: 4489.

5.1-58 Neubauer, S., Kral, J., and Klimes, K. 1974. New methods for increasing peppermint yields [in Czech]. Nase Liecive Rastliny 11: 36-38. HA 44: 6976.

5.1-59 Novais, R.F. de, Menezes Sobrinho, J.A. de, Santos, H.L. dos, and Sans, L.M.A. 1974. The effect of nitrogen fertilization and mulching on the N, P, K, Ca and Mg leaf contents of three garlic cultivars [in Portuguese]. Rev. Ceres 21{114}: 125-141. HA 45: 4846.

5.1-60 Novais, R.F. de, Menezes Sobrinho, J.A. de, Santos, H.L. dos, and Sans, L.M.A. 1974. The effect of nitrogen fertilization, mulching and three planting distances on the leaf N, P, K, Ca and Mg levels in the garlic cultivar Amarante [in Portuguese]. Rev. Ceres 21{118}: 486-499. HA 46: 1064.

5.1-61 Ocampo, J.A., Barea, J.M., and Montoya, E. 1975. Interactions between Azobacter and "phosphobacteria" and their establishment in the rhizosphere as affected by soil fertility. Can. J. Microbiol. 21: 1160-1165.

5.1-62 Ogg, A.G. 1972. Effects of certain weeds on peppermint oil quality. Page 4 in Abstracts, 1972 Meeting of the Weed Science Society of America. The Society, Champaign, Ill. WA 23: 950.

5.1-63 Osei Bonsu, K. 1977. The effect of spacing and fertilizer application on the growth, yield and yield components of sesame (Sesamum indicum L.). Acta Hortic. 53: 355-373.

5.1-64 Osman, H. El G., and Khidir, M.O. 1974. Relations of yield components in sesame. Exp. Agric. 10: 97-103.

5.1-65 Palevitch, D. 1973. The effect of variety plant spacing and sowing date on the yield and fruit development of red pepper in single harvest. Acta Hortic. 1973{27}: 150-159.

5.1-66 Pal, S.R., Nath, D.K., and Saha, G.N. 1976. Effect of time of sowing and aphid infestation on rai (Brassica juncea Coss.). Indian Agric. 20: 27-34. FCA 30: 7187.

5.1-67 Pirtskhalaishvili, S.Kh., Chkanidze, D.Kh., and Vadachkoriya, Ts.T. 1975 The effect of spacing laurel trees on leaf yield [in Russian]. Subtrop. Kul't. 1975{5}: 67-70. HA 47: 1828.

5.1-68 Prasad, S., and Saxena, M.C. 1980. Effect of date of planting and row spacing on the growth and development of peppermint (Mentha piperita L.) in Tarai. Indian J. Plant Physiol. 23: 119-126. AGRICOLA.

5.1-69 Prasad, S., and Saxena, M.C. 1978. Effect of dates of planting and row spacings on the concentration and uptake of nitrogen phosphorus and potassium by Mentha piperita in Tarai. Indian J. Agron. 23: 389-392.

5.1-70 Putievsky, E. 1976. Yield component in Carum carvi [in Hebrew]. Hassadeh 56: 1702-1706. HA 47: 3898.

5.1-71 Putievsky, E. 1978. Yield components of annual Carum carvi L. growing in Israel. Acta Hortic. 1978{73}: 283-287.

5.1-72 Rawat, D.S., and Arand, I.J. 1977. Association of seed yield and oil content with yield components in Indian mustard. Crop Improv. 4{1}: 95-102. FCA 32: 3324.

5.1-73 Razgon, L., Tovbin, I., and Gelis, A. 1976. Increasing the seed oil content - an important reserve for increasing oil production [in Russian]. Maslo-zhir. 1976{3}: 13-17. FCA 31: 1472.

5.1-74 Rice, E.L. 1980. Roles of allelopathy in pasture and forage crops. Proc. South. Pasture Forage Crop Improv. Conf. 37: 56-63.

5.1-75 Rice, E.L. 1979. Allelopathy - an update. Bot. Rev. 45{1}: 15-109.

5.1-76 Rudny, R. 1976. The effect of sowing time, methods of cultivation and protective measures on the health and yield of poppy (Papaver somniferum L.) variety Mak niebieski KM [in Polish]. Pr. Nauk. Inst. Ochr. Rosl. 18: 167-182. RPP 58: 3399.

5.1-77 Sambandamurthi, S., Jeyapal, R., and Vedamuthu, P.G.B. 1980. Effect of density of planting on yield of flowers in J. grandiflorum. Pages 39-40 in National Seminar on Production Technology for Commercial Flower Crops. Tamil Nadu Agricultural University, Coimbatore, India. HA 51: 7178.

5.1-78 Shalaby, Y.Y., and Mohamed, L.K. 1976. Effect of seeding rate, inoculation and nitrogen fertilization on yield of fenugreek. Annals of Agricultural Science of Moshtohor 6: 71-78. HA 48: 823.

5.1-79 Shivahare, M.D., Singh, A.B., Chauhan, Y.S., and Singh, P. 1975. Path-coefficient analysis of yield components in Indian mustard. Indian J. Agric. Sci. 45: 422-425. PBA 48: 3644.

5.1-80 Sims, R.E.H. 1976. Effects of planting pattern and sowing method on the seed yield of safflower, oilseed rape, and lupin. N.Z. J. Exp. Agric. 4: 185-189. FCA 30: 578.

5.1-81 Singh, P.P., and Kaushal, P.K. 1975. Response of rainfed sesame (Sesamum indicum L.) to row and plant spacings and fertilizer levels. JNKVV Res. J. 9: 61-62.

5.1-82 Singh, R., Singh, J., and Bains, D.S. 1977. Note on the influence of planting dates, rates of nitrogen and row spacings on the seed yield of celery. Indian J. Agric. Sci. 47: 423-425. HA 48: 2482.

5.1-83 Sip, V., Skorpik, M., and Martinek, V. 1980. Correlation analysis of the yield components in poppy [in Czech]. Sb. UVTIZ Genet. Slechteni 16: 233-239 FCA 34: 4845.

5.1-84 Szujko-Lacza, J. 1977. The current space demand and its variability during development of Pimpinella anisum L. Acta Bot. Acad. Sci. Hung. 22: 463-474.

5.1-85 Tabin, S., Berbeck, S., and Bobrzynski, T. 1973. The yields of several ecotypes of Symphytum officinale [in Polish]. Hodowla Rosl. Aklim. Nasienn. 17: 505-511.

5.1-86 Tanaka, H., Aruga, F., Kadota, J., and Watanabe, M. 1974. Effects of spacing and nitrogen level on growth and yield of pimento [in Japanese]. Tamagawa Daigaku Nogakubu Kenkyu Hokoku 14: 71-80. AGRICOLA.

5.1-87 Tashmukhamedov, R.I. 1973. Some data on seed productivity of Glycyrrhiza glabra plants [in Russian]. Uzb. Biol. Zh. 1973{1}: 31-33. AGRICOLA.

5.1-88 Terpo, A., and Kotori, E. 1974. Allelopathic effects on germinating seeds of cultivated plants [in Hungarian]. Kerteszetiegy. Kozl. 38{6}: 273-282. HA 46: 1792.

5.1-89 Tookey, H.L., Spencer, G.F., Grove, M.D., and Duke, J.A. 1975. Effects of maturity and plant spacing on the morphine content of two varieties of Papaver somniferum L. Bull. Narc. 27{4}: 49-57.

5.1-90 Vadachkoriia, Ts.T. 1980. Effect of planting density of Laurus nobilis on development of the root system [in Russian]. Subtrop. Kul't. 1980{2}: 97-102. AGRICOLA.

5.1-91 Valette, R., and Laruelle, R. 1974. Witloof chicory: the effect of planting density and row spacing on the yield of heads [in French]. Rev. Agric. (Brussels) 27: 1421-1437. HA 46: 1091.

5.1-92 Valette, R., and Laruelle, R. 1973. The effect of row distance and plant number on chicory production [in Dutch]. Tuinbouwberichten 57: 411-413. HA 44: 1506.

5.1-93 William, R.D. 1974. Competition of purple nutsedge in vegetable crops. Pages 75-76 in Abstracts, 1974 Meeting Weed Science Society of America. The Society, Champaign, Ill. WA 26: 724.

5.1-94 Woltz, S.S., and Waters, W.E. 1975. Chives production as affected by fertilizer practices, soil mixes and methyl bromide soil residues. Proc. Fla. State Hortic. Soc. 88: 133-137. AGRICOLA.

5.1-95 Yadava, T.P. 1973. Variability and correlation studies in Brassica juncea (L.) Czern and Coss. Madras Agric. J. 60: 1508-1511. FCA 29: 2135.

5.2 Agrometeorology

5.2-1 Akimov, Yu.A., Ponurova, N.P., and Chipiga, A.P. 1973. The essential oil content of some garlic cultivars growing in different regions of the USSR [in Russian]. Tr. Vses. Nauchno-Issled. Inst. Efirnomaslichn. Kul't. 1973{6}: 197-199. HA 45: 7298.

5.2-2 Ataev, E.A., Gladyshev, A.I., Kerbabaev, B.B., and Bakholdin, A.A. 1971. Geobotanical study of Ishakrabat lands related to licorice cultivation [in Russian]. Izv. Akad. Nauk Turkm. SSR Ser. Biol. Nauk 1971{6}: 30-34.

5.2-3 Balazs, S. 1971. Studies on influence climatic factors and on the nutrient requirement of paprika [in German]. Tagungsber. Dtsch. Akad. Landwirtschaftswiss. Berlin 114: 55-66. AGRICOLA.

5.2-4 Bernath, J., and Tetenyi, P. 1979. The effect of environmental factors on growth. Development and alkaloid production of poppy (Papaver somniferum L.). I. Responses to day-length and light intensity. Biochem. Physiol. Pflanz. (BPP) 174: 468-478.

5.2-5 Bezdolnyi, N. 1973. In the zone of insufficient moisture [in Russian] Zemledelie 5: 46-48. AGRICOLA.

5.2-6 Bose, T.K. 1973. Effect of temperature and photoperiod on growth, flowering and seed formation in mustard (Brassica juncea Coss.). Indian Agric. 17: 75-80. FCA 29: 2137.

5.2-7 Bouniols, A., Delecolle, M.-T., and Kronenberger, J. 1973. The effect of photoperiod on the free and protein amino acid composition of chicory root tissues during the development of vegetative or flower buds [in French]. C. R. Hebd. Seances Acad. Sci. Ser. D 277: 161-164.

5.2-8 Brar, G.S. 1980. Effects of temperature on fatty acid composition of sesame (Sesamum indicum L.) seed. Plant Biochem. J. 7: 133-137. AGRICOLA.

5.2-9 Brewster, J.L. 1979. The response of growth rate to temperature in seedlings of several Allium crop species. Ann. Appl. Biol. 93: 351-358.

5.2-10 Chandola, R.P., Dixit, P.K., Sharma, K.N., and Saxena, D.K. 1974. Variability in Brassica juncea under three environments. Indian J. Genet. Plant Breed. 34A: 680-683. FCA 29: 5942.

5.2-11 Clark, R.J., and Menary, R.C. 1979. Effects of photoperiod on the yield and composition of peppermint oil. J. Am. Soc. Hortic. Sci. 104: 699-702.

5.2-12 Clark, R.J., and Menary, R.C. 1980. Environmental effects on peppermint (Mentha piperita L.). I. Effect of daylength, photon flux density, night temperature and day temperature on the yield and composition of peppermint oil. Aust. J. Plant Physiol. 7: 685-692.

5.2-13 Clark, R.J., and Menary, R.C. 1980. Environmental effects on peppermint (Mentha piperita L.). II. Effects of temperature on photosynthesis, photorespiration and dark respiration in peppermint with reference to oil composition. Aust. J. Plant Physiol. 7: 693-697.

5.2-14 Codaccioni, M., and Laisne, G. 1977. The development of frost resistance: a comparison of the growth of shoots formed before and during cold hardening [in French]. Bull. Soc. Bot. Fr. 124: 5-14.

5.2-15 Codaccioni, M. 1975. Effects of the temperature and the glucose nutrition upon the ponderal growth relationship with hardening to frost [in French]. C.R. Hebd. Seances Acad. Sci. Ser. D 280: 287-290.

5.2-16 Dragutin, M., and Zlatko, B. 1977. The influence of climatic factors and elevation on the tannin content of Salvia officinalis leaves [in Serbo-Croatian]. Arh. Farm. 27: 99-102. HA 48: 5938.

5.2-17 Durdyev, D.D., and Shcherbatenko, T.P. 1974. Effect of low temperatures on the content of glycyrrhizinc acid and extractives in licorice root [in Russian]. Aktual. Vopr. Farm. 2: 65-67. CA 84: 132597.

5.2-18 Edmiston, J. 1972. The effect of the field of a permanent magnet on the germination and growth of white mustard (Brassica alba L.) seeds. Int. J. Biometeorol. 16: 13-24. FCA 26: 5852.

5.2-19 Edmiston, J. 1975. Effect of exclusion of the earth's magnetic field on the germination of seeds of white mustard (Sinapis alba L.). Biochem. Physiol. Pflanz. (BPP) 167: 97-100.

5.2-20 Erickson, V.L., Armitage, A., Carlson, W.H., and Miranda, R.M. 1980. The effect of cumulative photosynthetically active radiation on the growth and flowering of the seedling geranium, Pelargonium x hortorum Bailey. HortScience 15: 815-817.

5.2-21 Girenko, M.M., and Emmerikh, N.S. 1975. The effect of low temperature on the development of chicory (Cichorium intybus) and endive (C. endivia) [in Russian]. Tr. Prikl. Bot. Genet. Sel. 55{2}: 225-235. HA 46: 11230.

5.2-22 Gras, R. 1975. Climate, yield and longevity of lavandin [in French]. C. R. Seances Acad. Agric. Fr. 61: 865-869. HA 46: 10599.

5.2-23 Gras, R., Chiaverini, J., Montanaro, C., and Tournier, J.P. 1980. Effects of the environment and cultivation techniques on the life expectancy of the Abrial lavandin [in French]. Ann. Agron. 31: 191-218. HA 51: 2873.

5.2-24 Guttormsen, G. 1974. Effects of root medium and watering on transpiration, growth and development of glasshouse crops. II. The relationship between evaporation pan measurements and transpiration in glasshouse crops. Plant Soil 40: 461-478.

5.2-25 Gyurova, M., Tsvetkov, R., and Chingova-Boyadzhieva, B. 1975. Agroclimatic conditions for coriander growing in the Sub-Balkan valley [in Bulgarian]. Rastenievud. Nauki 12{1}: 56-64. HA 45: 8784.

5.2-26 Habovstiak, J., and Javorkova, A. 1977. The rate of development of some species with increasing altitude [in Slovak]. Ved. Pr. Vysk. Ustavu Luk Pasienkov Banskej Bystrici 12: 73-82. HERB AB 50: 2816.

5.2-27 Hack, H.R.B. 1980. Effects of pre-sowing flooding, rainfall, irrigation and surface drainage on sesame in central Sudan rainlands. Exp. Agric. 16: 137-148.

5.2-28 Hall, A.E., Thomson, W.W., Asbell, C.W., Platt-Aloia, K., and Leonard, R.T. 1977 Stomatal response to humidity and lanthanum. Physiol. Plant 41: 89-94

5.2-29 Hardh, J.E., Persson, A.R., and Ottosson, L. 1977. Quality of vegetables cultivated at different latitudes in Scandinavia. Acta Agric. Scand. 27: 81-96.

5.2-30 Hardh, J.E. 1975. The influence of the environment of the nordic latitudes on the quality of vegetables [in German]. Qual. Plant. Plant Foods Hum. Nutr. 25: 43-56.

5.2-31 Horvath, I., Mihalik, E., and Takacs, E. 1978. The effect of the sodium vapor lamp upon the dry-substance production of the plants [in Hungarian]. Bot. Kozl. 65: 115-121.

5.2-32 Ileva, S., Mekhandzhiev, A., Mateeva, D., and Dimitrova, S. 1975. Biological and biochemical changes in Papaver somniferum L. under effect of ionizing radiation [in Russian]. Herba Pol. 21{4}: 412-419.

5.2-33 Jacobsohn, M.K., Orkwiszewski, J.A.J., and Jacobsohn, G.M. 1978. Annual variation in the effect of red light on sterol biosynthesis in Digitalis purpurea L. Plant Physiol. 62: 1000-1004.

5.2-34 Jodha, N.S., and Purohit, S.D. 1971. Weather and crop instability in the dry region of Rajasthan. Indian J. Agr. Econ. 26: 286-295. AGRICOLA.

5.2-35 Kaicker, U.S., Saini, H.C., Singh, H.P., and Choudhury, B. 1978. Environmental effects on morphine content in opium poppy (Papaver somniferum L.). Bull. Narc. 30{3}: 69-74.

5.2-36 Kamino, Y. 1971. Temperature control in Spanish paprika cultivation [in Japanese]. Nogyo Oyobi Engei 46: 762-766. AGRICOLA.

5.2-37 Kemp, P.R., Williams, G.J., III, and May, D.S. 1977. Temperature relations of gas exchange in altitudinal populations of Taraxacum officinale. Can. J. Bot. 55: 2496-2502.

5.2-38 Koren', N.F. 1971. Characteristics of the growth cycle of dill in relation to the zone of cultivation [in Russian]. Tr. Prikl. Bot. Genet. Sel. 45{1}: 122-130. HA 43: 4729.

5.2-39 Kuhbauch, W., Voigtlander, G., and Spatz, G. 1978. Contents of nonstructural carbohydrates in forage plants from different altitudes in the northern Alpine region and their dependence on climatic conditions [in German]. Wirtschaftseigene Futter 24: 177-186.

5.2-40 Kuperman, F.M., Rjanova, E.I., and Akhoundova, V.A. 1978. The effect of the action of the spectrum and of light intensity in terms of the length of the photoperiod. Phytotronic Newsletter 1978{17}: 37-42. HA 50: 3942.

5.2-41 Laouar, S., Vartanian, N., and Silva, J.V. da. 1973. Effects of interactions between atmospheric humidity and the osmotic potential of the culture solution on the water relations of Sinapis alba L. Relative water content and leaf diffusion resistance to water vapour [in French]. C. R. Hebd. Seances Acad. Sci. Ser. D 277: 713-716.

5.2-42 Laouar, S., Vartanian, N., and Silva, J.V. da. 1973. The effects of interaction between atmospheric relative humidity and the osmotic potential of the culture solution on the water relations of Sinapis alba: water and osmotic potentials in the plant [in French]. C. R. Hebd. Seances Acad. Sci. Ser. D 276: 41-44.

5.2-43 Lavigne, C., Cosson, L., Jacques, R., and Miginiac, E. 1979. The effect of daylength and temperature on growth, flowering and essential oil composition in Jasminum grandiflorum L. [in French]. Physiol. Veg. 17: 363-373. HA 49: 8833.

5.2-44 Lincoln, D.E., and Langenheim, J.H. 1978. Effect of light and temperature on monoterpenoid yield and composition in Satureja douglasii. Biochem. Syst. Ecol. 6: 21-32. AGRICOLA.

5.2-45 Lincoln, D.E., and Langenheim, J.H. 1979. Variation of Satureja douglasii monoterpenoids in relation to light intensity and herbivory. Biochem. Syst. Ecol. 7: 289-298. AGRICOLA.

5.2-46 Lisovskii, G.M., Parshina, O.V., Ushakova, S.A., Bayanova, Yu.I., and Sirotinina, L.A. 1979. Productivity and chemical composition of some vegetable crops grown under a "lunar" photoperiod [in Russian]. Izv. Sib. Otd. Akad. Nauk SSSR Ser. Biol. Nauk 1979{5/1}: 104-108. HA 50: 3415.

5.2-47 Looper, J.A., and Aboul-Ela, M. 1971. Influence of light intensity and temperature on growth of fenugreek (Trigonella foenum-graecum L.) bean seedlings, from gamma-irradiated seed. Radiat. Bot. 11: 355-361.

5.2-48 Lutomski, J., and Turowska, M. 1973. Effect of relative humidity on the content of valepotrianes and volatile oil in Valeriana officinalis [in Polish]. Herba Pol. 19: 333-341. AGRICOLA.

5.2-49 Lyahyenchanka, B.I., Luk'yanava, N.M., and Smirnow, A.V. 1980. Light curves of photosynthesis of some species of evergreen plants. Vyestsi Akad. Navuk BSSR Syer. Biyal. Navuk O{4}: 22-28.

5.2-50 Mann, H.S., and Singh, R.P. 1975. Crop production in the arid zone with special reference to western Rajasthan. Ann. Arid Zone 14: 347-357. FCA 30: 4228.

5.2-51 May, D.S. 1976. Temperature response of succinate dehydrogenase in altitudinally diverse populations of Taraxacum officinale. Am. Midl. Nat. 95: 204-208.

5.2-52 Melcarek, P.K., and Brown, G.N. 1977. The effects of chilling stress on the chlorophyll fluorescence of leaves. Plant Cell Physiol. 18: 1099-1107.

5.2-53 Murko, D., and Baldasar, Z. 1977. Effect of climatic factors and height above sea level on the content of tannic acid in the leaves of Salvia officinalis [in Serbo-Croatian]. Arh. Farm. 27: 99-103. CA 87: 130506.

5.2-54 Nicastro, C. 1977. Relation between climatic conditions and crop production. Relation between precipitations and sesame productions in the Maracay area, Venezuela [in Italian]. Riv. Agric. Subtrop. Trop. 71{1/6}: 59-67. AGRICOLA.

5.2-55 Ohno, T., Kinoshita, K., and Komine, T. 1977. Effects of climatic factors upon the productivity of opium poppy (Papaver somniferum). I. Correlation between the productivity of 'Ikkanshu' a variety of opium poppy and various climatic factors [in Japanese]. Shoyakugaku Zasshi 31: 44-56.

5.2-56 Ohno, T., Kinoshita, K., and Komine, T. 1979. Effects of climatic factors upon productivity of opium poppy Papaver somniferum. 2. Correlation between productivity of the early maturity strain of opium poppy bred at the station and various climatic factors [in Japanese]. Shoyakugaku Zasshi 33: 11-15.

5.2-57 Paroda, R.S., and Karwasra, R.R. 1975. Prediction through genotype-environment interactions in fenugreek (Trigonella foenum-graecum L.). Forage Res. 1: 31-39. AGRICOLA.

5.2-58 Peneva, P., and Krilov, A. 1977. The influence of ecological conditions on the productivity of some Russian coriander cultivars [in Bulgarian]. Rastenievud. Nauki 14{1}: 67-76. HA 47: 11725.

5.2-59 Peneva, P., Krilov, Al., Dimitrova, S., and Petrakov, B. 1977. Effect of ecological conditions on the productivity of fennel [in Bulgarian]. Rastenievud. Nauki 14{8}: 87-95. HA 48: 7561.

5.2-60 Peneva, P. Is., Dimitrova, S., and Kelchev, G. 1977. Comparative trials of German chamomile (Matricaria chamomilla L.) climatic conditions [in Bulgarian]. Rastenievud. Nauki 14{3}: 94-103.

5.2-61 Puri, H.S., and Hardman, R. 1976. Effect of different light periods on the seed surface of fenugreek during the maturation phase. Proc. Indian Acad. Sci. Sect. B 83: 221-224.

5.2-62 Puziene, G., and Gudanavicius, S. 1978. Data on the phenological investigations of common horehound [in Lithuanian]. Liet. TSR Aukst. Mokyklu Mokslo Darb. Med. 1978{16}: 130-136. HA 49: 7042.

5.2-63 Richardson, S.G., and Salisbury, F.B. 1977. Plant responses to the light penetrating snow. Ecology 58: 1152-1158.

5.2-64 Rosenfeld, H.J. 1975. The effect of temperature on the ascorbic acid content of parsley (Petroselinum crispum var. crispum forma crispum [in Norwegian]. Meld. Norg. Landbrukshoegsk. 54{20}: 2-12. HA 46: 10586.

5.2-65 Rosenfeld, H.J. 1975. Temperature effects with forcing parsley [in Norwegian]. Gartneryrket 65{22/23}: 417. HA 46: 4923.

5.2-66 Rovesti, P. 1972. Ecological incidence in the composition of essential oils. IX. The essence of Lippia adoensis Hochst. and Lippia schimperi Hochst. [in Italian]. Riv. Ital. Essenze Profumi Piante Off. Aromi Saponi Cosmet. Aerosol 54: 254-258. AGRICOLA.

5.2-67 Ruminska, A. 1971. Variations in the content and composition of peppermint oil under the influence of different light intensity and wind strength [in Polish]. Poznan. Inst. Przemyslu Zielarskiego Biul. 17: 140-154. CA 75: 137611.

5.2-68 Sadowska, A. 1979. Effect of irradiation upon the essential oil content of peppermint (Mentha piperita L.) and its composition. Gamma Field Symp. 1979{18}: 115-118. CA 93: 234052.

5.2-69 Saleh, M. 1973. Effects of light upon quantity and quality of Matricaria chamomilla oil. III. Preliminary study of light intensity effects under controlled conditions. Planta Med. 24: 337-340 HA 44: 6035.

5.2-70 Saleh, M. 1972. Effects of light upon quantity and quality of Matricaria chamomilla L. oil. Part 2. Preliminary study of supplementary coloured light effects under controlled conditions. Pharmazie 27: 608-611. HA 43: 3081.

5.2-71 Savchuk, L.P. 1976. Influence of weather conditions on the amounts of essential oils in lavender and coriander. Sov. Meteorol. Hydrol. (Engl. Transl.) 1976{7}: 74-78. Translation of Meteorol. Gidrol. 1976{7}: 94-99.

5.2-72 Savchuk, L.P. 1975. Agrometeorological indices of overwintering conditions and yield in clary sage [in Russian]. Tr. Vses. Nauchno-Issled. Inst. Efirnomaslichn. Kul't. 8: 189-196. HA 47: 7769.

5.2-73 Savchuk, L.P. 1975. The effect of weather on coriander yield [in Russian]. Tr. Vses. Nauchno-Issled. Inst. Efirnomaslichn. Kul't. 8: 196-202. HA 47: 9746.

5.2-74 Schafer, E. 1976. The 'high irradiance reaction'. Pages 45-59 in H. Smith, ed. Light and plant development. Butterworth & Co., London, U.K. FCA 30: 4166.

5.2-75 Schoch, P.G. 1972. Effects of shading on structural characteristics of the leaf and yield of fruit in Capsicum annuum. 1. Red peppers. J. Am. Soc. Hortic. Sci. 97: 461-464. AGRICOLA 72082541.

5.2-76 Schuster, W., and Klein, H. 1978. Ecological influences on seed performance and quality in some cultivars of Sinapis alba, Brassica juncea and Brassica nigra [in German]. Z. Acker- Pflanzenbau 147: 204-227. FCA 33: 566.

5.2-77 Seidel, K. 1973. Production of higher water plants under todays extreme environmental conditions [in German]. Verh.-Int. Ver. Theor. Angew. Limnol. 18: 1395-1405.

5.2-78 Shpota, V.I., and Bochkareva, E.V. 1974. Conditions of hardening and frost resistance in winter cruciferous crops. Sov. Plant Physiol. (Engl. Transl.) 21: 690-692. Translation of Fiziol. Rast. (Moscow) 21: 833-836, 1974.

5.2-79 Sinnadurai, S., Abu, J.F., and Amuti, S.K. 1971. The effect of day-length on some tropical crops. J. West Afr. Sci. Assoc. 16{1}: 1-4. HA 43: 602.

5.2-80 Sip, V., and Skorpik, M. 1980. The effect of environment on the variability and average value of yield components in poppy [in Czech]. Sb. UVTIZ Genet. Slecteni 16: 225-232. FCA 34: 4844.

5.2-81 Sirnik, V., and Kulcar, V. 1980. Influence of weather on the quality of red pepper [in Slovak]. Zb. Biotehn. Fak. Univ. Ljublj Agric. 33: 399-408.

5.2-82 Steiner, A.M. 1975. The influence of light on growth under water stress as depending on the molecular weight of the osmoticum (hypocotyl of Sinapis alba L.). Plant Sci. Lett. 4: 395-399.

5.2-83 St. Margaris, N. 1975. Effect of photoperiod on seasonal dimorphism of some Mediterranean plants. Ber. Schweiz. Bot. Ges. 85: 96-102.

5.2-84 Szujko-Lacza, J., Sen, S., and Horvath, I. 1979. Effect of different light intensities of the anatomical characteristics of the leaves of Pimpinella anisum L. Acta Agron. (Budapest) 28: 120-131.

5.2-85 Takagi, H., and Aoba, T. 1977. Studies on bulb formation in garlic. VII. Effect of temperature and day length on the induction, formation and swelling of storage leaves [in Japanese]. Yamagata Daigaku Kiyo 7{4}: 423-438. PBA 48: 3864.

5.2-86 Terabun, M. 1978. Bulb formation of onion, Allium fistulosum and garlic under a combination of red and far-red light [in Japanese]. Kobe Daigaku Nogakubu Kenkyu Hokoku 13{1}: 1-6. PBA 48: 12155.

5.2-87 Tomar, D.P.S., and Bhargava, S.C. 1980. A comparative study of the effects of photoperiod on the growth, flowering, yield attributes and oil content of ten sesame genotypes. Indian J. Plant Physiol. 23: 65-72.

5.2-88 Udalova, V.I. 1975. The effect of altitude on the essential oil content and composition of lavandin inflorescences [in Russian]. Byull. Gos. Nikitsk. Bot. Sada 1975{1}: 62-65. HA 47: 3914.

5.2-89 Verheij, E.W.M., and Verwer, F.L.J.A.W. 1973. Light interception and yield of peppers grown under glass in relation to plant spacing. Acta Hortic. 1973{32}: 149-159. HA 44: 2506.

5.2-90 Virzo de Santo, A. 1973. Ecological studies on Mentha piperita L. II. - Effect of different light intensities on water relations. Oecol. Plant. 8: 25-40.

5.2-91 Virzo de Santo, A., and Alfani, A. 1980. Adaptability of Mentha piperita L. to irradiance. Growth, specific leaf area and levels of chlorophyll, protein and mineral nutrients as affected by shading. Biol. Plant. 22: 117-123.

5.2-92 Virzo De Santo, A., and Algani, A. 1976. Ecological studies on Mentha piperita. The effect of light intensity on the chemical composition of the leaves [in Italian]. G. Bot. Ital. 110: 456 (Abstr.). HA 48: 10819.

5.2-93 Zhila, E.D. 1978. Response of garlic to daylength. Fiziol. Biokhim. Kult. Rast. [in Russian] 10: 190-193.

5.2-94 Zlatev, S. 1977. Influence of meteorological factors on the quantity and quality of essential oil in dill [in Bulgarian]. Rastenievud. Nauki 14{4}: 23-32. HA 48: 4871.

5.2-95 Zlatev, S.K. 1976. Influence of meteorologic factor on quantity and quality of the essential oil synthesized in dill. Riv. Ital. Essenze Profumi Piante Off. Aromi Saponi Cosmet. Aerosol 58: 541-547. HA 48: 1652.

5.3 Soil and Water Relations

5.3-1 Abdrakhmanov, O.K., Isambaev, A.I., Baimurzaeva, A.N., and Dzhakupova, N.U. 1977. Effect of ionizing radiation and growth substances on the below-ground parts of licorice [in Russian]. Izv. Akad. Nauk Kaz. SSR, Ser. Biol. 15{4}: 8-10. CA 87: 195362.

5.3-2 Abrol, I.P., Gaul, B.L., and Acharya, C.L. 1975. Efficient water management key to success in alkali soils. Indian Farming 25{4}: 15-17. FCA 29: 5226.

5.3-3 Aho, N., Daudet, F.A., and Vartanian, N. 1977. Transitory pattern of respiration during increasing water stress [in French]. C.R. Hebd. Seances Acad. Sci. Ser. D 285: 159-162. SF 41: 1561.

5.3-4 Anderson, J.E., and McNaughton, S.J. 1973. Effects of low soil temperature on transpiration, photosynthesis, leaf relative water content, and growth among elevationally diverse plant populations. Ecology 54: 1220-1233.

5.3-5 Balasubramanian, V., Rajagopal, V., and Sinha, S.K. 1974. Stability of nitrate reductase under moisture and salt stress in some crops. Indian J. Genet. Plant Breed. 34A: 1055-1061. FCA 29: 7493.

5.3-6 Bandyopadhaya, A.K., and Sen, H.S. 1976. Winter crops in saturated soils of Sunderbans. Indian Farming 26{3}: 15-17. FCA 30: 3682.

5.3-7 Bernstein, L., and Francois, L.E. 1975. Effects of frequency of sprinkling with saline waters compared with daily drip irrigation. Agron. J. 67: 185-190.

5.3-8 Bhan, S. 1976. Water management problems in Uttar Pradesh. Indian Farming 26{2}: 11-13, 20. FCA 30: 3770.

5.3-9 Blom, C.W.P.M., Husson, L.M.F., and Westhoff, V. 1979. Effects of trampling and soil compaction on the occurrence of some Plantago species in coastal sand dunes. IVa. Vegetation of two dune grasslands in relation to physical soil factors. Proc. K. Ned. Akad. Wet. Ser. C 82: 245-259.

5.3-10 Buchanan, G.A., Hoveland, C.S., and Harris, M.C. 1975. Response of weeds to soil pH. Weed Sci. 23: 473-477.

5.3-11 Cerda, A., Bingham, F.T., and Hoffman, G.J. 1977. Interactive effect of salinity of phosphorus on sesame. J. Soil Sci. Soc. Am. 41: 915-918.

5.3-12 Dabrowska, J. 1977. Effect of soil moisture on some morphological characters of Achillea collina Becker, A. millefolium L. ssp. millefolium and A. pannonica Scheele. Ekol. Pol. 25: 275-288. SF 44: 5307.

5.3-13 Dhir, R.P., and Bhatia, O.P. 1975. Use of saline water in agriculture. 1.Description of the system. Ann. Arid Zone 14: 206-211. FCA 29: 6799.

5.3-14 Doerffling, K., Streich, J., Kruse, W., and Muxfeldt, B. 1977. Abscisic acid and the after-effect of water stress on stomatal opening potential. Z. Pflanzenphysiol. 81: 43-56.

5.3-15 Durdyev, D.D. 1974. Effect of the content of glycyrrhizic acid and extractives in flooded licorice root [in Russian]. Aktual. Vopr. Farm. 2: 62-64. CA 84: 95562.

5.3-16 El-Badry, D., and Hilal, M.H. 1975. A preliminary study of the effect of pH of irrigation water on the production of chamomile flower-heads. Annals of Agricultural Science of Moshtohor 3: 183-188. HA 46: 594.

5.3-17 Freeman, G.G., and Mossadeghi, N. 1973. Studies on relationship between water regime and flavour strength in watercress (Rorippa nasturtium-aquaticum (L.) Hayek), cabbage (Brassica oleracea capitata) and onion (Allium cepa). J. Hortic. Sci. 48: 365-378.

5.3-18 Garcia, B.J., Mazzani, B., and Sainz, J.M. 1971. Relationship between the water balance in soil and the yield of sesame plant (Sesamum indicum) [in Spanish]. Agron. Trop. (Maracay, Venez.) 21: 49-57. AGRICOLA.

5.3-19 Georgieva, S., Koseva, D., and Atanasov, Zh. 1976. Effect of the pH of the nutrient solution on the development of lavender, and on the content of essential oil, free amino acids, and sugars [in Bulgarian]. Fiziol. Rast. (Sofia) 2{1}: 83-92. CA 85: 106722.

5.3-20 Gershenzon, J., Lincoln, D.E., and Langenheim, J.H. 1978. The effect of moisture stress on monoterpenoid yield and composition in Satureja douglasii. Biochem. Syst. Ecol. 6: 33-43. AGRICOLA.

5.3-21 Gerson, R., and Honma, S. 1978. Emergence response of the pepper at low soil temperature. Euphytica 27: 151-156.

5.3-22 Higazy, M.K., Shanan, S.A., Billah, M. El-M., and Ramadan, H.M. 1974. Effect of soil moisture levels on postharvest changes in garlic. Egypt. J. Hortic. 1{1}: 13-22. HA 44: 9637.

5.3-23 Ilieva, S.D., Mekhandzhiev, A.D., Moinova, E.G., and Mateeva, D.P. 1972. Studies on biological and biochemical changes in Salvia sclarea caused by ionising radiation [in Russian]. Dokl. S-kh. Akad. (Sofia) 5{2}: 127-134. HA 43: 3026.

5.3-24 Iyanaga, K., and Tajino, N. 1977. Studies of improved property of underdrainage. V. Hydrodynamic balance of heichi-shiki cultivated land of Wasabi, or horseradish fields [in Japanese]. Kagawa Daigaku Engeigakubu Gakujutsu Hokoku 29: 141-165.

5.3-25 Karawya, M.S., El Badry, D. El-D., and Awaad, K.E. 1972. Effect of pH of soil on yield of flower heads and oil content of chamomile. Bull. Fac. Pharm. Cairo Univ. 11{1}: 329-338. CA 81: 103839.

5.3-26 Kochkin, M.A., and Shubina, L.S. 1971. The rational utilization of soils for essential oil-bearing rose and lavander growing in the Crimea [in Russian]. Tr. Gos. Nikitsk. Bot. Sad. 53: 15-25. HA 43: 764.

5.3-27 Kocurik, S., Busova, D., and Spalek, J. 1976. Problems of mineral nutrition in true chamomile on saline soils [in Slovak]. Nase Liecive Rastliny 13: 40-43. HA 47: 796.

5.3-28 Kocurik, S., and Dovjak, V. 1979. Effect of molybdenum and boron on dry matter production and drug yield in chamomile (Matricaria chamomilla) [in Slovak]. Nase Liecive Rastliny 16: 69-74. HA 49: 9588.

5.3-29 Konarzewski, Z., and Guminski, S. 1975. The chemotropic effect of some metal cations on Sinapis alba L. roots as affected by several factors [in German]. Biol. Plant. 17: 458-467.

5.3-30 Krikava, J., Petrikova, K., and Kucerova, M. 1974. The possibility of using land with a high water table for cultivating

selected medicinal plant species [in Slovak]. Nase Liecive Rastliny
11: 123-128. HA 45: 4390.

5.3-31 Kruzela, J. 1978. Root system formation in poppy (Papaver
somniferum L.) at different soil moisture content [in Czech]. Rostl.
Vyroba 24: 193-200. AGRICOLA.

5.3-32 Kuiper, D., and Kuiper, P.J.C. 1979. Comparison of Plantago
species from nutrient-rich and nutrient-poor conditions: growth
response. ATPases and lipids of the roots as affected by the level of
mineral nutrition. Physiol. Plant. 45: 489-491.

5.3-33 MacBryde, B., Jefferies, R.L., Alderfer, R., and Gates, D.M.
1971. Water and energy relations of plant leaves during period of heat
stress. Oecol. Plant. 6: 151-162.

5.3-34 Mashanova, N.S., Mukhortova, T.G., and Udalova, V.I. 1973. The
effect of soil conditions on the chemical composition of lavandin
essential oil [in Russian]. Byull. Gos. Nikitsk. Bot. Sada
1973{2}{21}: 31-34. HA 45: 3427.

5.3-36 Matusiewicz, E. 1972. Reponse of Mentha piperita (peppermint) to
soil reaction [in Polish]. Poznan. Tow. Przyj. Nauk, Wydz. Nauk Roln.
Les., Pr. Kom. Nauk Roln. Kom. Nauk Les. 33: 211-220. CA 77: 138845.

5.3-37 Mazza, C.A., Vallejos, W.E., Lopez, C., and Grazen, A.M. 1971.
Soil fertility and irrigation water quality in the garlic-growing
zone, Medanos-Villarino, Buenos Aires Province [in Spanish]. Rev. Fac.
Agron. Univ. Nac. La Plata 47: 123-130. HA 43: 4518.

5.3-38 Melke, J. 1978. The influence of soils and moisture levels on the
content and accumulation of alkaloids in plants of opium poppy
(Papaver somniferum L.) and deadly nightshade (Atropa belladonna L.)
[in Polish]. Ann. Univ. Mariae Cure-Sklodowska Sect. C. 33: 55-74.
AGRICOLA.

5.3-39 Mirkin, B.M., Antipov, E.A., and Sagitov, S.I. 1971. The salt
tolerance of Glycyrrhiza glabra [in Russian]. Rastit. Resur. 7:
417-420. HA 44: 1836.

5.3-40 Muchnik, Zh.S. 1973. Some biological characteristics of liquorice
cultivated in Moldavia [in Russian]. Rastit. Resur. 9: 176-183.

5.3-41 Nairizi, S., and Rydzewski, J.R. 1977. Effects of dated soil
moisture stress on crop yield. Exp. Agric. 13: 51-59.

5.3-42 Oomes, M.J.M., and Elberse, W.T. 1976. Germination of six
grassland herbs in microsites with different water contents. J. Ecol.
64{2}: 745-755.

5.3-43 Pandya, R.B., Khan, M.I., Gupta, S.K., and Dhindsa, K.S. 1975.
Germination, seedling growth and sugar metabolism of two species of
Brassica under polyethylene glycol (PEG) induced water stress.
Biochem. Physiol. Pflanz. (BPP) 167: 439-445.

5.3-44 Patarroyo, F., Lopez, V., and Camacho-B, S.E. 1977. Sesame growth
and production under two conditions of water provision [in Spanish].
Pages 205-215 in S.B. Camacho-B., S.B., ed. Informe de progreso 1976
del programa nacional de fisiologia vegetal. Instituto Colombiana
Agropecuario, Bogota, Colombia.

5.3-45 Purushothaman, D., Kasirajan, C., Rethinam, P., and Sankaran, S. 1976. Studies on the influence of nitrofen on the microbial activity of soil under ragi crop. Madras Agric. J. 63: 523-526. WA 27: 2414.

5.3-46 Rai, M. 1977. Salinity tolerance in Indian mustard and safflower. Indian J. Agric. Sci. 47: 70-73. FCA 32: 430.

5.3-47 Rheenen, H.A. van. 1979. Soil moisture and growth of sesame. Plant Soil 53: 277-285.

5.3-48 Sharma, M.L., Pandey, M.B., Khanna, R.K., and Kapoor, L.D. 1972. Essential oils from plants raised on alkaline soils. Indian Perfum. 16(pt. 2): 27-30. CA 80: 100105.

5.3-49 Shewry, P.R., and Peterson, P.J. 1976. Distribution of chromium and nickel in plants and soil from serpentine and other sites. J. Ecol. 64: 195-212.

5.3-50 Singh, H.G., and Singh, B.P. 1978. Mustard on vertisols in Rajasthan. Indian Farming 27{10}: 21-22. FCA 32: 3323.

5.3-51 Singh, K.N., Joshi, Y.C., and Singh, T.N. 1974. In saline sodic soils raya is better than other oilseed crops. Indian Farming 24{2}: 9, 23. FCA 28: 5958.

5.3-52 Singh, R.S. 1971. Influence of soil salinity on production of seed and essential oil content of dill (Anethum graveolens L.). Indian Oil Soap J. 36: 243-245.

5.3-53 Sivtsev, M.V., Karpova, G.Ya., and Vasyuta, G.G. 1972. The state of plastid pigments in the leaves of essential oil plants under varying water supply [in Russian]. Fiziol. Biokhim. Kult. Rast. 4: 390-395. HA 43: 6269.

5.3-54 Sonneveld, C., and Beusekom, J. van. 1975. Influence of salt water on the cultivation of pepper and paprika under glass [in Dutch]. Landbouwkd. Tijdschr. 86: 241-245. AGRICOLA.

5.3-55 Srivastava, H.P., and Sharma, M.L. 1974. Cultivation of Jasminum grandiflorum L. on saline alkali soils. Indian Perfum. 18{1}: 25-26. HA 47: 8752.

5.3-56 Steglik, K. 1978. Trace elements and irrigation water [in Russian]. Sci. Agric. Bohemoslov. 10: 87-97. SF 42: 1020.

5.3-57 Suchorska, K. 1972. The influence of a seasonal drought and of the level of NPK on the development and on the crop yield of Coriandrum sativum [in Polish]. Postep Dziedzinie Leku Rosl. Pr. Ref. Dosw. Wygloszone Symp. 1970 Herba Pol. Suppl. 1972: 283-292.

5.3-58 Taha, S.M., Zayed, M.N., Saber, M.S.M., and Badr El-Din, S.M.S. 1973. Nitrogen transformation in soils. II. In sandy soil under horse-bean and sesame in a two years' rotation. Zentralb. Bakteriol. Parasitenkd. Infektionskr. Hyg. Abt. 2 Naturwiss. Allg. Landwirtsch. Tech. Mikrobiol. 128: 126-134.

5.3-59 Tajino, N., and Iyanaga, K. 1975. Studies of property of underdrainage. III. The underdrainage works in a gravel culture land of Wasabi, or horseradish fields [in Japanese]. Kagawa Daigaku Engeigakubu Gakujutsu Hokoku 26: 108-135.

5.3-60 Tajino, N., and Iyanaga, K. 1977. Studies of improved property of underdrainage. IV. Study on hydrodynamic balance of jisawa-shiki culture land of Wasabi, or horseradish fields [in Japanese]. Kagawa Daigaku Engeigakubu Gakujutsu Hokoku 28: 111-127.

5.3-61 Tan, H.-M., and Fedorova, L.V. 1974. Level of nitrogen nutrition in habitats of gigantic herbs in Sakhalin [in Russian]. Pochvovedenie 1974{4}: 94-98. CA 81: 12407.

5.3-62 Vartanian, N. 1973. Adaptive characteristic of white mustard, Sinapis alba L., to drought [in French]. Pages 277-288 in Plant response to climatic factors. Proceedings of the Uppsala symposium. UNESCO, Paris, France. FCA 27: 2351.

5.3-63 Yousif, Y.H., Bingham, F.T., and Yermanos, D.M. 1972. Growth, mineral composition, and seed oil of sesame (Sesamum indicum L.) as affected by boron and exchangeable sodium. Proc. Soil Sci. Soc. Am. 36: 923-926.

5.3-64 Zlatev, S. 1973. The effect of drought on the survival of lavender [in Bulgarian]. Rastenievud. Nauki 10{10}: 49-55. HA 44: 5988.

5.4 Pests

5.4-1 Ali, A.D., Donia, A.R., and El-Sawaf, S.K. 1974. The influence of natural food on the development and reproductive rate of Lasioderma serricorne Fab. (Coleoptera: Anobiidae). Bull. Soc. Entomol. Egypte 58: 45-53. RAE-A 64: 4096.

5.4-2 Alleyne, E.H., and Morrison, F.O. 1977. The lettuce root aphid, Pemphigus bursarius (L.) (Homoptera: Aphidoidea) in Quebec, Canada. Ann. Soc. Entomol. Que. 22: 171-180. RAE-A 67: 1126.

5.4-3 Bailey, C.G., and Mukerji, M.K. 1976. Feeding habits and food preferences of Melanoplus bivittatus and M. femurrubrum (Orthoptera: Acrididae). Can. Entomol. 108: 1207-1212.

5.4-4 Bajoi, A.H., and Knutson, H. 1977. Effects when restricting an acridid species to a specific plant species. Acrida 6: 219-229. RAE-A 66: 1887.

5.4-5 Beddiny, E.A.M. 1977. Biological effects of some types of food on the snails of Helisoma duryi and Physa acuta. Bull. Fac. Sci., Assiut Univ. 6: 35-46.

5.4-6 Berry, R.E. 1975. Redbacked cutworm: flight period and egg development under field conditions. Environ. Entomol. 4: 603-605.

5.4-7 Bochen, K. 1980. Bionomy of three species of the genus Macrosiphoniella del Guercio, 1911 (Homoptera, Aphididae) [in Polish]. Annales Universitatis Marie Curie-Sklodowska C (Biologia) 33: 429-442.

5.4-8 Bogarada, A.P., and Spiridonova, V.P. 1978. Pests of peppermint [in Russian]. Byull. Gl. Bot. Sada 1978{108}: 88-91. HA 49: 1453.

5.4-9 Bonfils, J., and Lauriaut, F. 1975. Presence of Synophropsis lauri new record in Languedoc France Homoptera Cicadellidae [in French]. Entomologiste (Paris) 31: 69-71.

5.4-10 Bougeard, M., and Vegh, I. 1980. Preliminary study on Cercosporidium punctum (Lacroix) Deighton, the agent of Cercosporidium disease of fennel (Foeniculum vulgare Mill.) [in French]. Cryptogram. Mycol. 1: 205-221. AGRICOLA.

5.4-11 Bouseman, J.K., Irwin, B., Eastman, C., and Sherrod, D. 1978. A bibliography of the imported crucifer weevil, Baris lepidii (Coleoptera: Curculionidae). Bull. Entomol. Soc. Am. 24: 409-411.

5.4-12 Bouseman, J.K., Sherrod, D., Eastman, C., Luckmann, W., Randell, R., and White, C. 1978. Note on the establishment in Illinois of Baris lepidii, a destructive European weevil. Bull. Entomol. Soc. Am. 24: 407-408.

5.4-13 Bouyjou, B., and Nguyen, T.X. 1974. Observations on the morphogenesis and structure of the gall of Trioza alacris Flor (Homoptera-Psyllidae) on Laurus nobilis L. [in French]. Marcellia 38: 49-55. RAE-A 64: 2764.

5.4-14 Brar, K.S., Ratual, H.S., and Lobana, K.S. 1976. Differential reaction of mustard aphid, Lipaphis erysimi Kalt. to different rapeseed and mustard varieties under natural and artificial infestation. J. Res., Punjab Agric. Univ. 13: 14-18. RAE-A 65: 4992.

5.4-15 Brovdii, V.M. 1976. Data on the ecology of the rape leaf-eater (Entomoscelis adonidis Pall.) in the Ukraine [in Russian]. Vestn. Zool. 1976{4}: 38-42. RAE-A 65: 2069.

5.4-16 Brovdii, V.M. 1978. Leaf-beetles of the genus Chrysolina Motsch. - pests of medicinal plants in the Ukraine [in Russian]. Vestn. Zool. 1978{1}: 43-48. RAE-A 66: 3904.

5.4-17 Caresche, L.A., Hasan, S., and Wapshere, A.J. 1974. Biology and host specificity of two aphids Dactynotus chondrillae (Nevsk.) and Chondrillobium blattnyi (Pintera) (Hemiptera) living on Chondrilla juncea. Bull. Entomol. Res. 64: 277-288.

5.4-18 Carmona, M.M. 1971. Diptacus camarae n.sp. (Acarina Eriophyoidea Rhyncaphytoptidae). Agron. Lusit. 33(1-4): 71-74.

5.4-19 Chand, P. 1975. Host preference in Diacrisia obliqua Walker (Lepidoptera-Arctiidae) in the field. Sci. Cult. 41: 604-606.

5.4-20 Chevin, H., and Choppin de Janvry, G. 1980. A pest of poppy in France [in French]. Phytoma 1980{317}: 20-21. AGRICOLA.

5.4-21 Chumak, V.A. 1975. Pests of Salvia sclarea [in Russian]. Zashch. Rast. 1975{12}: 35-36. RAE-A 65: 2104.

5.4-22 Chumak, V.A. 1975. Spittlebug, Lepyronia coleoptrata--a new pest of lavender in Crimea [in Russian]. Tr. Vses. Nauchno-Issled. Inst. Efirnomaslichn. Kul't. 8: 149-153. AGRICOLA.

5.4-23 Cohn, E. 1973. Histology of the feeding site of Rotylenchulus reniformis. Nematologica 19: 455-458.

5.4-24 Connell, W.A. 1975. Hosts of Carpophilus dimidiatus. J. Econ. Entomol. 68: 279-280.

5.4-25 Danielson, S.D., and Berry, R.E. 1978. Redbacked cutworm: sequential sampling plans in peppermint. J. Econ. Entomol. 71: 323-328.

5.4-26 Dayal, R., and Ram, A. 1973. Physiological studies of Cercospora jasminicola Muller and Chupp. III. Effect of environmental factors. Proc. Nat. Acad. Sci. India Sect. B. 43: 140-146. RPP 55: 5546.

5.4-27 Easwaramoorthy, S., Sivagami Vadivelu, R., and Muthukrishnan, T.S. 1980 Sycophila sp. (Eurytomidae: Hymenoptera), a new pest of Jasminum grandiflorum. Entomon. 5: 246.

5.4-28 Elnagar, S., and Murant, A.F. 1978. Aphid-injection experiments with carrot mottle virus and its helper virus, carrot red leaf. Ann. Appl. Biol. 89: 245-250.

5.4-29 Emenegger, D.B., and Berry, R.E. 1978. Biology of strawberry root weevil on peppermint in western Oregon. Environ. Entomol. 7: 495-498.

5.4-30 Finch, S., and Ackley, C.M. 1977. Cultivated and wild host plants supporting populations of the cabbage root fly. Ann. Appl. Biol. 85: 13-22.

5.4-31 Flint, J.H. 1975. Eupteryx origani Zakh. (Hemiptera: Cicadellidae) in Yorkshire England. Entomol. Mon. Mag. 111{1337-1339}: 204.

5.4-32 Fursova, M.F. 1972. A study of the food relationships and distribution of root aphids in Turkmenia [in Russian]. Izv. Akad. Nauk Turkm. SSR Ser. Biol. Nauk 1972{3}: 69-72. RAE-A 62: 1110.

5.4-33 Gainsford, P. 1975. Mellicta athalia in East Cornwall, 1974. Entomol. Res. J. Var. 87: 172-175.

5.4-34 Gaylor, M.J., and Sterling, W.L. 1976. Development, survival, and fecundity of the cotton fleahopper, Pseudatomoscelis seriatus (Reuter), on several host plants. Environ. Entomol. 5: 55-58.

5.4-35 Gerdes, C. 1979. Thysanoptera associated with horseradish in Illinois. Entomol. News 90: 236-238.

5.4-36 Giesemann, K.J. 1975. Onion thrips in the Lockyer. Queensl. Agric. J. 101: 71-72.

5.4-37 Gokulpure, R.S. 1975. Record of new host-plants of four Agromyzids. J. Bombay Nat. Hist. Soc. 72: 223-225. RAE-A 64: 3519.

5.4-38 Gould, F. 1979. Rapid host range evolution in a population of the phytophagous mite Tetranychus urticae Koch. Evolution 33: 791-802.
5.4-39 Govindarajan, R., David, B.V., Srinivasan, P.M., and Subramaniannn, T.R. 1974. Aleurotrachelos sp. - a new whitefly pest of Jasminum auriculatum and its control. South Indian Hortic. 22{3/4}: 84-85. RAE-A 65: 356.

5.4-40 Graniti, A. 1975. Centre for the study of toxins and systemic parasites of vegetables, Bari. Report of scientific activity for 1974 [in Italian]. Ric. Sci. 45{1}: 201-205. HELM AB-B 46: 722.

5.4-41 Griffiths, D.C. 1974. Susceptibility of plants to attack by wireworms (Agriotes spp.). Ann. Appl. Biol. 78: 7-13.

5.4-42 Griffiths, G.C.D. 1973. Studies on boreal Agromyzidae (Diptera). IV. Phytomyza miners on Angelica, Heracleum, Laserpitium a Pastinaca (Umbelliferae). Quaest. Entomol. 9: 219-253.

5.4-43 Gyorffy, G. 1976. Data on seasonal dynamics and environmental claims of Empoasca fabae Harris (Homoptera: Cicadellidae) on condiment paprika. Acta Biol. (Szeged) 22: 87-95.

5.4-44 Halstead, A. 1976. From Wisley. Three common pests of bay trees. Garden (U.K.) 101: 380-381.

5.4-45 Hamid, S., Shah, M.A., and Anwar, A.M. 1974. Investigations on Acyrthosiphon pisum Harris with special reference to its parasite Aphidius smithi Sharma and Subba Rao. Tech. Bull. Common. Inst. Biol. Control 1974{7}: 69-85. RAE-A 65: 2081.

5.4-46 Harakly, F.A., and Assem, M.A.H. 1978. Ecological studies on the truely pests of leguminous plants in Egypt. I. Biting and chewing pests. Pages 233-236 in Proceedings of the fourth conference of pest control, September 30 - October 3, 1978 (Part I). Academy of Scientific Research and Technology and National Research Centre, Cairo, Egypt. RAE-A 68: 4357.

5.4-47 Harris, K.M. 1975. The taxonomic status of the carob gall midge, Asphondylia gennadii (Marchal) comb. (Diptera, Cecidomyiidae), and of other Asphondylia species recorded from Cyprus. Bull. Entomol. Res. 65: 377-380.

5.4-48 Hasan, S. 1978. Biology of a Buprestid beetle, Sphenoptera clarescens (Col.: Buprestidae), from skeleton weed, Chondrilla juncea. Entomophaga 23: 19-23.

5.4-49 Hasan, S. 1978. Biology of the root coccid, Neomargarodes chondrillae (Hem.: Margarodidae), living on Chondrilla juncea and related plants. Entomophaga 23: 25-30.

5.4-50 Hauss, R. 1975. Methods and first results on the determination of the food-plants of cockchafer grubs (Melolontha melolontha L.) [in German]. Mitt. Biol. Bundesanst. Land- Forstwirtsch. Berlin-Dahlem 1975{163}: 72-77. RAE-A 64: 1759.

5.4-51 Hauss, R., and Schuette, F. 1978. Studies on the oviposition of the cockchafer (Melolontha melolontha L.) in relation to the larval food-plants [in German]. Z. Angew. Entomol. 86: 167-174.

5.4-52 Hauss, R., and Schuette, F. 1977. Experiments on polyphagous habits of white grubs (Melolontha melolontha L.) on plants of grassland [in German]. Z. Angew. Entomol. 82: 275.

5.4-53 Haus, R., and Schutte, F. 1976. On the polyphagous habits of the grubs of Melolontha melolontha L. on meadow and wasteland plants [in German]. Anz. Schadlingsk. Pflanz. Umweltschutz. 49: 129-132. RAE-A 65: 2368.

5.4-54 Hawthorn, W.R. 1978. Some effects of different Plantago species on feeding preference and egg laying in the flea beetle Dibolia borealis (Chrysomelidae). Can. J. Zool. 56: 1507-1513.

5.4-55 Hicks, K.L., and Tahvanainen, J.O. 1974. Niche differentiation by crucifer-feeding flea beetles (Coleoptera:Chyrsomelidae). Am. Midl. Nat. 91: 406-423.

5.4-56 Holman, J., and Szelegiewicz, H. 1978. Further aphids of the genus macrosiphoniella (Homptera aphididae) from Mongolia. Acta. Entomol. Bohemoslov. 75: 178-193. BIOL 66: 071581.

5.4-57 Hooper, D.J., and Doncaster, C.C. 1972. Stem and inflorescence galls on yarrow (Achillea millefolium L.) caused by the nematode Anguina millefolii (Loew, 1874) Filipjev, 1936. Plant Pathol. 21: 46.

5.4-58 Itamies, J. 1977. Amphipoea lucens (Frr.) (Lepidoptera, Noctuidae) found on Eriophorum vaginatum and Hydraecia nordstroemi Horke (Lepidoptera, Noctuidae) on Allium schoenoprasum. Ann. Entomol. Fenn. 43: 95-96. AGRICOLA.

5.4-59 Ivanovskaya, O.I. 1979. A new species of aphid (Homoptera, Aphididae) from the Kamchatka Peninsula [in Russian]. Tr. Vses. Entomol. O-va. 61: 39-41. RAE-A 69: 614.

5.4-60 I-Shying Tjying. 1971. A new Ascid mite (Laseioseius martini n.sp.) recovered from shallots in Taiwan (Acarina:Ascidae). Chih Wu Pao Hu Hsueh Hui Hui K'an 13{1}: 1-5. RAE-A 62: 207.

5.4-61 Jai Rao, K., and Thirumalachar, D.K. 1977. New record of alternate host plants of groundnut leaf miner Stomopteryx subsecivella Zeller (syn.: S. nerteria Meyrick) (Lepidoptera: Gelechiidae). Curr. Sci. 46: 91-92.

5.4-62 Jakhmola, S.S., and Yadav, H.S. 1973. Some observations on Mermis sp. as a parasite of til leaf roller (Antigastra catalaunalis Dup.). Indian J. Entomol. 35: 170-172. AGRICOLA.

5.4-63 Jakhmola, S.S., and Kaushik, U.K. 1974. Occurrence of Monomorium destructor Jard on til (Sesamum indicum L.). Indian J. Entomol. 36: 164-165. AGRICOLA.

5.4-64 Joshi, G. 1975. Ephestia cautella (Lepidoptera: Pyralidae) infesting a new host, red hand-ground dry chillies, Capsicum frutescens in India with some notes on the habits of its larvae. Z. Angew. Zool. 62: 243-248. RAE-A 64: 3092.

5.4-65 Karabag, T., and Tutkun, E. 1976. Investigations in Central Anatolia on the existence or nonexistence of parthenogenetic reproduction and on the establishment of fecundity in Calliptamus barbarus (Costa) [in Turkish]. Bitki Koruma Bul. 16: 80-91. RAE-A 65: 2367.

5.4-66 Kareem, A.A., Nachiappan, R.M., and Sadakathulla, S. 1972. Note on a new pest, Cacoecia epicyrta Meyr. (Tortricidae: Lepidoptera) of the Japanese peppermint, Mentha arvensis L. in South India. South Indian Hortic. 20{1/4}: 100-101. HA 44: 2702.

5.4-67 Kareem, A.A., Subramanian, K.N., Sadakathulla, S., and Subramaniam, T.R. 1974. A note on a few sucking pests on Indian lavender tree in Tamil Nadu. South Indian Hortic. 22{1/2}: 70.

5.4-68 Katiyar, O.P., Lakshaman Lal, and Mukharji, S.P. 1975. Response of newly hatched caterpillars of Diacrisia obliqua Walker to certain host plants. Indian J. Entomol. 37: 57-59. RAE-A 66: 4002.

5.4-69 Keyder, S., and Atak, U. 1972. Studies on vegetable flies (Hylemya spp.). Page 136 in Tarim Bakanligi Zirai Mucadele ve Zirai Karantina Genel Mudurlugu Arastirma Subesi. Plant protection research annual. Zirai Mucadele Arastirma Yilligi. Ankara, Turkey. RAE-A 62: 4444.

5.4-70 Khalifa, A., Isa, A.L., and Awadallah, W.H. 1972. Studies on Cnephasia in Egypt. II – Symptoms of infestation. (Lepidoptera:Tortricidae). Bull. Soc. Entomol. Egypte 56: 323-331. RAE-A 63: 1600.

5.4-71 Khristova, E., and Loginova, E. 1978. Study of the black cutworm Agrostis ypsilon Rott. in glasshouse conditions [in Bulgarian]. Gradinar. Lozar. Nauka 15{7/8}: 137-141. RAE-A 68: 68.

5.4-72 Khurana, A.D. 1975. Alternative host plants of 'ak' grasshopper Poekilocerus pictus (Fabricius). Entomologists' Newsletter 5{6/7}: 34. RAE-A 64: 7169.

5.4-73 Klindic, O., and Petrovic, D. 1974. Contribution to study of Heterodera achilleae G.-K. I. The knowledge of the host plants and the distribution of the parasite [in Serbian]. Zast. Bilja 25(128-129): 141-150.

5.4-74 Korcz, A. 1972. Incidence of plant bugs of the genus Lygus on carrot, parsley and dill seed [in Polish]. Ochr. Rosl. 16{11}: 17-19.

5.4-75 Korcz, A. 1976. The intensity of the occurrence of phytophagous bugs of the order Heteroptera on some seed crops of umbelliferous plants [in Polish]. Pr. Nauk. Inst. Ochr. Rosl. 18: 125-155. RAE-A 67: 717.

5.4-76 Korcz, A. 1977. Biology, morphology and occurrence of Lygus campestris (L.) - and other bugs of the genus Lygus (Heteroptera, Miridae) in Poland [in Polish]. Pr. Nauk. Inst. Ochr. Rosl. 19: 209-240. RAE-A 67: 718.

5.4-77 Kraft, J. 1979. The genus Orobanche in Sweden [in Swedish]. Sven. Bot. Tidskr. 73: 27-37.

5.4-78 Lazorko, W. 1977. Eurrhypara hortulata L. (urticata L.) on the Pacific coast (Lepidoptera: Pyralidae). J. Entomol. Soc. B.C. 74: 31. RAE-A 66: 3518.

5.4-79 Lewartowski, R. 1974. Depressaria nerosa Haw. a dangerous insect pest of caraway, and its control [in Polish]. Ochr. Rosl. 17{6}: 17-19.

5.4-80 Lin, T. 1976. Studies on life cycle and control of coffee bean weevil, Araecerus fasciculatus (De Geer) (Coleoptera: Anthribidae) [in Chinese]. Chung-Lua Nung Yeh Yen Chiu 25: 44-52. RAE-A 65: 1520.

5.4-81 Lisbao, R.S., Bernardi, J.B., Lordello, R.R.A., and Flectmann, C.H.W. 1976. Observations on the performance of bush redpeppers (Capsicum annuum L.) and paprika (Capsicum sp.) in relation to attacks by the two-spotted spider mite (Tetranychus urticae Kock) [in Portuguese]. Ecossistema 1{1}: 3-5. AGRICOLA.

5.4-82 Lockyer, W. 1978. An unusual food plant of the eyed hawkmoth:
Smerinthus ocellata. Entomol. Rec. J. Var. 90: 278.

5.4-83 Loginova, M.M., and Baeva, V.G. 1972. A review of Psyllids of the
genus Psylla Geoffr. (Homoptera, Psylloidea) associated with species
of Glycyrrhiza [in Russian]. Tr. Vses. Entomol. O-va. 55: 4-13. RAE-A
61: 4768.

5.4-84 Mahar, M.M.M., and Batra, H.W. 1973. Carry over and host plants
of painted bug, Bagarada picta Fabr., (Pentatomidae: Heteroptera): a
pest of rabi oilseed crops. Agric. Pak. 24: 9-10. RAE-A 64: 2048.

5.4-85 Mallea, A.R., Macola, G.S., Garcia S., J.G., Bahamondes, L.A.,
Suarez, J.H., and Lanati, S.J. 1974. Population study on coccinellids
of Mendoza, Argentine Republic [in Spanish]. Rev. Facult. Cienc.
Agrar. 20: 153-155. RAE- A 69: 3524.

5.4-86 Menezes, M. de. 1978. Notes on the oviposition habits and the
host plants of Apogonalia grossa (Signoret, 1854) (Homoptera,
Cicadellidae, Cicadellinae). Rev. Bras. Entomol. 22: 61-64. RAE-A 67:
4412.

5.4-87 Mier Durante, M.P., and Nieto Nafria, J.M. 1979. New data on
aphids for the Province of Salamanca (Hom. Aphidoidea) [in Spanish].
Boletin de la Associacion Espanola de Entomologia 3: 153-162.

5.4-88 Mohanasundaram, M. 1972. On the new host records for some South
Indian crop pests. Indian J. Entomol. 34: 259-261. RAE-A 64: 1847.

5.4-89 Moreau, J.P., and Leclant, F. 1973. Contribution to the study of
two insects on hybrid lavender, Hyalesthes obsoletus Sign. and
Cechenotettix martini Leth. (Hom. Auchenorrh.) [in French]. Ann. Zool.
Ecol. Anim. 5: 361-364. RAE-A 64: 217.

5.4-90 Muller, F.P., and Hubert-Dahl, M.L. 1979. Host change, generation
sequence and reproductive isolation of Ovatus crataegarius (Walker,
1850) and O. insitus (Walker, 1849) (Homoptera: Aphididae) [in
German]. Dtsch. Entomol. Z. 26: 241-253. RAE-A 69: 616.

5.4-91 Munshi, G.H., and Mecci, A.K. 1972. A new record of host plant
Terias hecabe Lin., Pieridae at Tandojam. Agric. Pak. 23: 283. RAE-A
64: 1334.

5.4-92 Murant, A.F., Roberts, I.M., and Elnagar, S. 1976. Association of
virus-like particles with the foregut of the aphid Cavariella
aegopodii transmitting the semi-persistent viruses anthriscus yellows
and parsnip yellow fleck. J. Gen. Virol. 31: 47-57.

5.4-93 Myartseva, S.N. 1977. A new species of encyrtid Anathrix
acanthococci Myartseva, sp. n. (Hymenoptera, Chalcidoidea) - a
parasite of the coccid Acanthococcus sp. (Homoptera, Coccoidea) on
wormwood in southern Turkmenistan [in Russian]. Izv. Akad. Nauk Turkm.
SSR Ser. Biol. Nauk 1977{4}: 41-46. RAE-A 66: 2637.

5.4-94 Nagy, F., and Szalay-Marzso, L. 1976. New pests (Systole
albipennis and S. coriandri) damaging angelica, lovage and coriander
crops in Hungary [in Hungarian]. Herba Hung. 15{3}: 71-78. HA 47:
8773.

5.4-95 Nair, C.P.R., and Nair, M.R.G.K. 1974. Studies on the biology of the lace-wing Corythauma ayyari Drake a pest of jasmine. Agric. Res. Kerala 12: 172-173. RAE-E 64: 3029.

5.4-96 Nath, D.K., and Sen, B. 1976. Some observations on aphidophagus coccinellid beetles in mustard cultivation. Sci. Cult. 42: 288-290.

5.4-97 Nath, V.R., and Indira, S. 1975. Cuscuta reflexa Roxb. - a rival to Dendrophthoe falcata (L.F.) Ettingish in home gardens. J. Bombay Nat. Hist. Soc. 72: 607-608.

5.4-98 Nel, J. 1979. A new food plant for Charaxes jasius (Lepidoptera, Nymphalidae) [in French]. Alexanor 11: 157-158. AGRICOLA.

5.4-99 Neubauer, S., Kral, J., and Klimes, K. 1973. Aphids on chamomile [in Czech]. Nase Liecive Rastliny 10: 72-74. HA 44: 1148.

5.4-100 Neubauer, S., Kral, J., and Klimes, K. 1974. Insect pests of peppermint [in Czech]. Nase Liecive Rastliny 11: 38-41. HA 44: 8916.

5.4-101 Nielsen, J.K. 1978. Host plant selection of monophagous and oligophagous flea beetles feeding on crucifers. Entomol. Exp. Appl. 24: 562-569.

5.4-102 Nielsen, J.K., Dalgaard, L., Larsen, L.M., and Sorensen, H. 1979. Host plant selection of the horse-radish flea beetle Phyllotreta armoraciae (Coleoptera: Chrysomelidae): feeding responses to glucosinolates from several crucifers. Entomol. Exp. Appl. 25: 227-239.

5.4-103 Nielsen, J.K. 1977. Host plant relationships of Phyllotreta nemorum L. (Coleoptera: Chrysomelidae). I. Field studies. Z. Angew. Entomol. 84: 396-407.

5.4-104 Nielson, J.K., Larsen, L.M., and Sorensen, H. 1979. Host plant selection of the horseradish flea beetle Phyllotreta armoraciae (Coleoptera: Chyrsomelidae): identification of two flavonol glycosides stimulating feeding in combination with glucosinolates. Entomol. Exp. Appl. 26: 40-48.

5.4-105 Nijveldt, W. 1973. Gall-midges new for the fauna of the Netherlands (VI) [in Flemish]. Entomologische Berichten 33: 97-100. RAE-A 64: 1248.

5.4-106 Nikolaishvili, A.A. 1972. Results of studying Hemiberlesia rapax [in Russian]. Subtrop. Kul't. 1972{6}: 165-171. AGRICOLA.

5.4-107 Nowacka, W., and Adamska-Wilczek, J. 1974. Leafhoppers (Homoptera, Cicadodea) as pests of medicinal plants [in Polish]. Pol. Pismo Entomol. 44: 393-404. RAE-A 64: 1335.

5.4-108 Nuzzaci, G., and Vovlas, N. 1977. Eriophyid mites (Acarina: Eriophyoidea) of laurel, with the description of three new species [in Italian]. Entomologica (Bari) 13: 247-264. RAE-A 67: 304.

5.4-109 Ong, C.A., Ling, W.P., and Varghese, G. 1978. Role of aphid vectors in the spread of chilli veinal mottle virus. Pages 53-60 in L.L. Amin, A.A.S.A. Kadir, Lim Guan Soon, K.G. Singh, Tan Ah Moy, and G. Varghese, eds. Proceedings of the plant protection conference,

Kuala Lumpur, March, 1978. Rubber Research Institute of Malaysia, Kuala Lumpur, Malaysia. RAE-A 67: 3223.

5.4-110 Orphanides, G.M. 1975. Biology of the carob midge complex, Asphondylia spp. (Diptera, Cecidomyiidae), in Cyprus. Bull. Entomol. Res. 65: 381-390.

5.4-111 Osman, A.A., and Soliman, Z.R. 1974. Population studies of mites infesting some oil crops in Tahreer Province, Egypt with some reference to control. Bull. Soc. Entomol. Egypte 58: 415-421.

5.4-112 Ossiannilsson, F. 1979. The host plants of three Swedish Psayllids [in Swedish]. Entomol. Tidskr. 100{2}: 83-84. AGRICOLA.

5.4-113 Pacheco M. F., and Leon Lopez, R.L. 1978. Pests [in Spanish]. Circ. Ciano (Cent. Invest. Agric. Noroeste) 96: 21-26. AGRICOLA.

5.4-114 Pajni, H.R., and Virk, N. 1978. Comparative dietary efficiency of common spices and oilseeds for the larval growth of Trilobium castaneum Herbst (Coleoptera:Tenebrionidae). Entomon. 3: 135-134.

5.4-115 Perumal, R.S., Lakshmanan, P., Subramaniam, T.R., and Santhanaraman, T. 1971. Occurrence of the white grub Holotrichia sp. as a new pest of jasmine and Nerium. Madras Agric. J. 58: 519. RAE-A 63: 975.

5.4-116 Piekarczyk, K. 1974. Characteristics of development, appearance and injuriousness of the main pests of industrial plants in Poland in 1973 [in Polish]. Biul. Inst. Ochr. Rosl. 58: 169-210. RAE-A 64: 6648.

5.4-117 Popova, L.G. 1971. Typhaea stercorea - a pest of maize grain [in Russian]. Zashch. Rast. (Moscow) 16{6}: 45-46.

5.4-118 Popov, C. 1971. Studies on the colonisation and continuous rearing of the species Graphosoma semipunctata F. [in Romanian]. An. Inst. Cercet. Prot. Plant. Acad. Stiinte Agric. Silvice 9: 401-408. RAE-A 63: 3938.

5.4-119 Popov, P. 1979. A new pest of fennel [in Bulgarian]. Rastit. Zasht. 27{10}: 26. RAE-A 68: 2504.

5.4-120 Popov, P. 1972. Insect pests to the medicinal plants in Bulgaria. III. Coleoptera [in Bulgarian. Rastenievud. Nauki 9: 167-175.

5.4-121 Prasad, Y.K., and Phadke, K.G. 1980. Population dynamics of Lipaphis erysimi (Kalt.) on different varieties of Brassica species. Indian J. Entomol. 42: 54-63. RAE-A 69: 5361.

5.4-122 Puppin, O., and Duffy, E.A.J. 1972/1973. Observations on Penichroa fasciata Steph. (Coleoptera Cerambycidae) [in Italian]. Boll. Zool. Agrar. Bach. 11: 83-87. RAE-A 64: 2179.

5.4-123 Quiroz Escoba, C. 1975. Winter pests of some vegetables [in Spanish]. Invest. Prog. Agric. 7{1}: 29-30. RAE-A 64: 4329.

5.4-124 Raich, K.V. 1975. Thymus vulgaris aureus (Family: Labiatae), a new host plant of the cabbage web-worm, Crocidolomia binotalis Zell. (Pyralididae: Lepidoptera). Indian J. Entomol. 37: 313-314. RAE-A 66: 3227.

5.4-125 Reddy, D.B., comp. 1977. Pests, diseases and nematodes of major spices and condiments in Asia and the Pacific. Technical Document, Plant Protection Committee for the South East Asia and Pacific Region 108. 18 pp. HA 48: 5853.

5.4-126 Rice, R.L., Lincoln, D.E., and Langenheim, J.H. 1978. Palatability of monoterpenoid compositional types of Satureja douglasii to a generalist molluscan herbivore, Ariolimax dolichophallus. Biochem. Syst. Ecol. 6: 45-53. AGRICOLA.

5.4-127 Rizza, A., and Pecora, P. 1980. Biology and host specificity of Chrysomela rossia, a candidate for the biological control of Dalmatian toadflax, Linaria dalmatica. Ann. Entomol. Soc. Am. 73: 95-99.

5.4-128 Rosvall, T. 1979. Orobanche alba on Gotland Sweden [in Swedish]. Sven. Bot. Tidskr. 73: 1-6.

5.4-129 Ruter, G. 1978. Note on Phyllotreta armoraciae Coleoptera Chyrsomelidae. Entomologiste (Paris) 34: 150.

5.4-130 Sabatino, A. 1976. On the appearance of Psila rosae F. (Dipt. Psilidae) in fennel crops in Apulia [in Italian]. Entomologica (Bari) 12: 131-134. RAE-A 65: 6798.

5.4-131 Sagar, P. 1978. A new record of thrips, Thrip flavus Schrank as a pest of fennel, Phoenicum vugare and its control. Food Farming Agric. 9{7}: 183-184.

5.4-132 Sandhu, G.S., Balkarn, S., and Bhalla, J.S. 1975. Insect-pests of the Japanese mint (Mentha arvensis Linn) in India. Indian Perfum. 19{1}: 13-18. HA 47: 10749.

5.4-133 Scheibelreiter, G.K. 1979. Contributions to the knowledge of the poppy-sawfly (Corynis similis (Mocs.) (Hym., Cimbicida) [in German]. Z. Angew. Entomol. 87: 393-398.

5.4-134 Scheibelreiter, G.K. 1978. The poppy-cephid Pachycephus smyrnensis Stein (Hymenoptera: Cephidae). Z. Angew. Entomol. 86: 19-25.

5.4-135 Schette, F. 1976. Motivation for investigations on the population dynamics of the cockchafers (Melolontha melolontha L. and M. hippocastani F.). Z. Pflanzenkr. Pflanzenschutz. 83: 146-158.

5.4-136 Scholze, P. 1979. Brief exposition of existing knowledge and views of the course and causes of the variations in the population density of the cockchafer (Col., Scarabaeidae) [in German]. Entomolog Ische Nachrichten 23: 145-150. RAE-A 68: 5452.

5.4-137 Schroder, D. 1979. Investigations on Euzophera cinerosella Zeller (Lep.:Pyralidae), a possible agent for the biological control of the weed Artemisia absinthium L. Compositae in Canada. Mitt. Schweiz. Entomol. Ges. 52: 91-101. WA 30: 2560.

5.4-138 Seenappa, M., Stobbs, L.W., and Kempton, A.G. 1979. The role of insects in the biodeterioration of Indian red peppers by fungi. Int. Biodeterior. Bull. 15: 96-102. RAE-A 68: 4655.

5.4-139 Sehgal, V.K., Bhattacharya, A.K., and Singh, K.N. 1975. Food preferences of mustard sawfly grubs Athalia proxima Klug (Hymenoptera: Tenthredinidae). Sci. Cult. 41: 430-433.

5.4-140 Sharma, B.D., and Sharma, T. 1974. Occurrence of Gibbium psylloides (Czenp.) in stored foods in Jammu and Kashmir State. Indian J. Entomol. 36: 365. RAE-A 66: 2294.

5.4-141 Sharma, V.K., and Srivastava, A.K. 1973. Anatomical studies on root gall of chicory (Cichorium intybus L.). Acta Agron. (Budapest) 22: 131-136. HA 44: 2350.

5.4-142 Singh, S.M. 1971. A new species of Tripospermum. Sydowia 25: 147-148.

5.4-143 Sip, V., Martinek, V., and Skorpik, M. 1977. Study of the inheritance of economically important traits of the poppy [in Czech]. Genet. Slechteni 13: 207-218. AGRICOLA.

5.4-144 Staedler, E. 1972. The orientation and food plant selection of the carrot fly, Psila rosae F. (Diptera: Psilidae). II. Adults [in German] Z. Angew. Entomol. 70: 29-61.

5.4-145 Stiling, P.D. 1980. Host plant specificity, oviposition behavior and egg parasitismin some leafhoppers of the genus Eupteryx (Hemiptera: Cicadellidae). Ecol. Entomol. 5: 79-85.

5.4-146 Stoeva, R.I. 1976. A pest Otiorrhynchus ovalipennis of laurel [in Bulgarian]. Priroda (Sofiia) 25{2}: 55-57. AGRICOLA.

5.4-147 Sundararaju, D., and Jayaraj, S. 1977. The biology and the host range of Orosius albicinctus Dist. (Homoptera: Cicadellidae), the vector of sesame phyllody disease. Madras Agric. J. 64: 442-446.

5.4-148 Swailem, S.M. 1974. On the bionomics of Lindingaspis ferrisi McKenzie (Hemiptera- Homoptera:Diaspididae). Bull. Soc. Entomol. Egypte 58: 17-24. RAE-A 64: 3511.

5.4-149 Swatonek, F. 1973. The development of the Indian meal moth (Plodia interpunctella Hb) in different commercial qualities of paprika spice [in German]. Anz. Schadlingsk. Pflanz. Umweltschutz. 46: 107-109. RAE -A 64: 1546.

5.4-150 Syme, P.D. 1977. Observations on the longevity and fecundity of Orgilus obscurator (Hymenoptera:Braconidae) and the effects of certain foods on longevity. Can. Entomol. 109: 995-1000.

5.4-151 Teriaki, A., and Verner, P.H. 1975. List of stored product mites and insects in Syria. Sb. Vys. Sk. Zemed. Praze Fak. Agron. Rada A 1975{1}: 307-320. RAE-A 65: 3399.

5.4-152 Thangavelu, K. 1979. The pest status and biology of Spilostethus panduras (Scopoli) (Lygaeidae: Heteroptera). Entomon. 4{2}: 137-141.

5.4-153 Thirumurthi, S., and Abraham, E.V. 1975. Occurrence of the wingless grasshopper, Orthacris simulans B., on Sesamum. Madras Agric. J. 62: 61.

5.4-154 Tsalboukov, P.R. 1972. Insect kinetics in annual and biennial peppermint. An. Acad. Bras. Cienc. 44(Suppl.): 85-88.

5.4-155 Tuatay, N., Gur, O., and Dogan, N. 1972. Studies on anise pests in the Burdur district. Page 154 in Plant protecton research annual. Zirai Mucadele Arastirma Yilligi [Plant Protection Research Institutes of Turkey], Ankara, Turkey. RAE-A 62: 4458.

5.4-156 United States Department of Agriculture. 1980. Western black flea beetle (Phyllotreta pusilla) - Illinois - new state record. Cooperative Plant Pest Report 5: 196. RAE-A 69: 1693.

5.4-157 United States Department of Agriculture. 1978. Kirkaldy whitefly (Dialeurodes kirkaldyi) - Texas - new state record. Cooperative Plant Pest Report 3: 618. RAE-A 67: 2913.

5.4-158 United States Department of Agriculture. 1978. Strawberry root weevil (Otiorhynchus ovatus) - Oregon. Cooperative Plant Pest Report 3: 164. RAE-A 67: 581.

5.4-159 United States Department of Agriculture. 1977. Pests not known to occur in the United States or of limited distribution. A weevil (Baris lepidii Germar (Coleoptera: Curculionidae). Cooperative Plant Pest Report 2: 680-685. RAE-A 66: 1253.

5.4-160 United States Department of Agriculture. 1977. A weevil (Baris lepidii Germar) - Illinois. Cooperative Plant Pest Report 2: 490. RAE-A 66: 1252.

5.4-161 United States Department of Agriculture. 1977. A weevil (Pseudobaris nigrina) - Idaho. Cooperative Plant Pest Report 2: 468. RAE-A 66: 1942.

5.4-162 Venturini, V. 1972/1973. Donus salviae Schrank (Coleoptera Curculionidae), a new pest of strawberry [in Italian]. Boll. Zool. Agrar. Bach. 11: 211-215. RAE-A 64: 1995.

5.4-163 Verma, J.P., and Mathur, Y.K. 1973. Observations on the incidence and seasonal abundance of white grub Lachnosterna consanquinea Blanch. infesting Sesamum in Rajasthan. Ann. Arid Zone 11: 219-224. AGRICOLA

5.4-164 Viggiani, G. 1977. New findings on some root-inhabiting Coleoptera (Haplidia etrusca Kr., Otiorrhynchus armatus Boh., O. trophonius Reitt.) [in Italian]. Boll. Lab. Entomol. Agraria 'Filippo Silvestri' 34: 11-15. RAE-A 67: 205.

5.4-165 Vlk, F., and Holubcova, M. 1972. An investigation into the host range of the garlic race of stem-eelworm, Ditylenchus dipsaci Kuhn [in Czech]. Sb. Vys. Sk. Zemed. Prage Fak. Agron. Rada A 1972{Part 1}: 175-181. HELM AB-B 42: 302.

5.4-166 Walkowski, W. 1973. Aceria carvi, a dangerous insect pest of caraway [in Polish]. Ochr. Rosl. 17{6}: 19-21.

5.4-167 Wiklund, C. 1974. The concept of oligophagy and the natural habitats and host plants of Papilio machaon in Fennoscandia. Entomol. Scand. 5: 151-160.

5.4-168 Wiklund, C. 1973. Host plant suitability and the mechanism of host selection in larvae of Papilio machaon. Entomol. Exp. Appl. 16: 232-242.

5.4-169 Winder, J.A. 1976. Some observations on a Hylesia species probably fulviventris Berg (Lepidoptera, Saturniidae) which attacks Lantana tiliaefolia in Parana State. Dusenia 9{1}: 29-30. RAE-A 66: 1932.

5.4-170 Wolfson, J.L. 1980. Oviposition response of Pieris rapae to environmentally induced variation in Brassica nigra. Entomol. Exp. Appl. 27: 223-232.

5.4-171 Yang, C.K. 1979. Studies on Margarodidae (Homoptera: Coccoidea) [in Chinese]. Entomotaxonomia 1{1}: 35-48. RAE-A 69: 2186.

5.4-172 Yilmaz, M., and Varney, E.H. 1972. Effect of source and test plants, feeding time, and aphid numbers on transmission of tobacco etch virus. Phytopathology 62: 502 (Abstr.).

5.4-173 Yokoi, S., and Tsuji, H. 1975. Experimental studies on the movement behavior of the final instar noctuid larvae of the cabbage armyworm and the tobacco cutworm [in Japanese]. Nippon Oyo Dobutsu Konchu Gakkaishi 19: 157-161. RAE-A 65: 94.

5.4-174 Zaazou, M.H., Fahmy, H.S.M., Kamel, A.A.M., and El-Hamaesy, A.H. 1973. Effect of food on the development of the greasy cutworm, Agrotis ipsilon (Hufn.). Bull. Soc. Entomol. Egypte 57: 379-386. RAE-A 63: 699.

5.5 Diseases

5.5-1 Adilova, N.B. 1975. Comparative analysis of the nematode fauna of some medicinal plants [in Russian]. Uzb. Biol. Zh. 19{3}: 47-49.

5.5-2 Adilova, N.B. 1976. Nematodes of medicinal plants [in Russian]. Uzb. Biol. Zh. 1976{1}: 80-81.

5.5-3 Agrawat, J.M. 1979. Sclerotium rot of Glycyrrhiza glabra - a new host record from Rajasthan. Sci. Cult. 45: 366.

5.5-4 Ahlawat, Y.S. 1974. A mosaic disease of garlic in Darjeeling hills. Sci. Cult. 40: 466-467.

5.5-5 Ahmad, M., Jamil Khan, S.A. 1974. Fungus flora of til seeds (Sesamum indicum) of Sind. Pak. Sci. Conf. Proc. 25{3}: D-56 (Abstr.).

5.5-6 Alam, M., Janardhanan, K.K., Singh, H.N., and Husain, A. 1980. A new leaf blight of French basil caused by Colletotrichum capsici in India. Indian J. Mycol. Plant Pathol. 10: 99.

5.5-7 Alhassan, K.K., Alhassan, S.A., and Radhy, H.A. 1973. Study on Sclerotium bataticola the cause of charcoal rot disease of sesame. Iraqi J. Agric. Sci. 8: 93-103. AGRICOLA.

5.5-8 Amin, P.W. 1979. Leaf curl disease of chilli peppers in Maharashtra, India. PANS 25: 131-134. RAE 67: 5087.

5.5-9 Andreeva, L.T. 1980. The features of conidial germination and the development of Ramularia coriandri Moesz & Smarods in the Krasnodar region [in Russian]. Mikol. Fitopatol. 14{1}: 45-51. RPP 59: 5858.

5.5-10 Aquino, M. de L.N. de. 1973. Coriander (Coriandrum sativum L.) new disease produced by Glomerella cingulata (Ston.) in Pernambuco [in Portuguese]. Instituto de Pesquisas Agronomicas, Recife. 11 pp. AGRICOLA.

5.5-11 Arutyunyan, A.G. 1980. The effect of hydroponic conditions on microsporogenesis and accumulation of some substances in rose geranium leaves [in Russian]. Soobshch. Inst. Agrokhim. Probl. Gidroponiki Akad. Nauk Arm. SSR 1980{20}: 151-155. HA 51: 2881.

5.5-12 Avgelis, A., and Quacquarelli, A. 1973. Virus diseases of vegetable crops in Apulia. XII. A mosaic of Sinapis nigra L. Phytopathol. Mediterr. 12: 48-53.

5.5-13 Avgelis, A., and Quacquarelli, A. 1974. Virus diseases of vegetable crops in Apulia. XVI. Chlorotic mottle and bushy stunt of parsley [in Italian]. Phytopathol. Mediterr. 13: 1-9.

5.5-14 Avgelis, A., and Quacquarelli, A. 1974. Studies on parsley carrot-leaf virus. 1. Serological relation with Chicory yellow mottle virus [in Italian]. Phytopathol. Mediterr. 13: 97-100.

5.5-15 Avgelis, A., Piazzolla, P., Vovlas, C., and Quacquarelli, A. 1977. Studies on parsley carrot-leaf virus (PCLV). III.some factors affecting the production of virus-specific components [in Italian]. Phytopathol. Mediterr. 16: 5-10. AGRICOLA.

5.5-16 Awasthi, P.B., Mishra, U.S., and Pande, B.N. 1978. A new record of Protomyces macrosporus Ung. on Foeniculum vulgare L. Curr. Sci. 47: 823-824.

5.5-17 Balasubramanian, M., and Sita Rama Rao, D. 1975. A new host record for the grapevine girdler, Sthenias grisator F. (Cerambycidae: Coleoptera). Madras Agric. J. 62: 82-83.

5.5-18 Bandyopadhyay, B., Chakravarti, S., Chaudhuri, A.K., and Mukhopadhyay, S. 1980. Incidence of blight disease of cumin (Cuminum cyminum Linn.). Sci. Cult. 46: 341-342.

5.5-19 Barr, D.J.S. 1973. Rhizophydium graminis (Chytridiales): Morphology, host range, and temperature effect. Can. Plant Dis. Surv. 53: 191-193.

5.5-20 Beczner, L., Vassanyi, R., Salamon, P., and Dezseri, M. 1976. Virus diseases of Solanum dulcamara in Hungary. Part 1. Dulcamara mottle virus. Acta Phytopathol. Acad. Sci. Hung. 11: 245-257.

5.5-21 Benigno, D.A., Favali-Hedayat, M.A., and Retuerma, M.L. 1975. Sampaguita yellow ringspot mosaic. Philipp. Phytopathol. 11{1/2}: 91-92. RPP 57: 1230.

5.5-22 Berry, R.E. 1974. Biology of Pyrausta fumalis on peppermint in Oregon. Ann. Entomol. Soc. Am. 67: 580-582.

5.5-23 Bevan, R.J. 1980. Proceedings of B.M.S. meetings, Coelomycete Workshop Foray Group Meetings. Bull. Br. Mycol. Soc. 14: 75-76.

5.5-24 Bhargava, L.P., Handa, D.K., and Mathur, B.N. 1976. Occurrence of Orobanche indica on Trigonella foenum-graecum and Physalis minima. Plant Dis. Rep. 60: 871-872.

5.5-25 Bhargava, S.N., and Shukla, D.N. 1979. A new root rot of sesame (Sesamum indicum). Indian J. Mycol. Plant Pathol. 9: 244.

5.5-26 Blaszczak, W., Fiedorow, Z., and Golebniak, B. 1977. Virus diseases and blackening of horseradish roots [in Polish]. Biul. Warzywniczy 20: 259-274. HA 49: 2110.

5.5-27 Blaszczak, W., Fiedorow, Z., Gleczynski, E., and Lenkiewicz, W. 1977. Studies on the etiology of blackening of horseradish roots [in Polish]. Biul. Warzywniczy 20: 241-288. HA 49: 2109.

5.5-25 Blaszczak, W. 1976. Identification of some plant virus diseases in Poland [in Polish]. Rocz. Nauk Roln. Ser. E. Ochr. Rosl. 6: 69-88. RPP 58: 1660.

5.5-29 Blaszczak, W. 1976. Plantain (Plantago major L.) mosaic [in Polish]. Rocz. Nauk Roln. Ser. E. Ochr. Rosl. 6: 89-95. RPP 58: 2625.

5.5-30 Blotnicka, K. 1976. Harmfulness of Helminthosporium papaveris Sawada (perfect state of Pleospora calvescens (Fries) Tulasne) for poppy cultivation [in Polish]. Hodowla Rosl. Aklim. Nasienn. 20: 59-80. RPP 56: 1223

5.5-31 Boerema, G.H., and Verhoeven, A.A. 1976. Checklist for scientific names in common parasitic fungi. Series 2A: Fungi on field crops: Beet and potato; caraway, flax and oilseed poppy. Neth. J. Plant Pathol. 82: 193-214.

5.5-32 Bose, S.K., and Lal, B. 1976. Diseases of medicinal plants in Kumaon. I. Prog. Hortic. 8{2}: 23-29. HA 47: 8775.

5.5-33 Bos, L., and Maat, D.Z. 1979. Parsley latent virus, a new and prevalent seed-transmitted, but possibly harmless virus of Petroselinum crispum. Neth. J. Plant Pathol. 85: 125-136.

5.5-34 Bos, L., Huttinga, H., and Maat, D.Z. 1978. Shallot latent virus, a new carlavirus. Neth. J. Plant Pathol. 84: 227-237.

5.5-35 Boyles, D.T. 1976. The loss of electrolytes from leaves treated with hydrocarbons and their derivatives. Ann. Appl. Biol. 83: 103-113.

5.5-36 Bozai, J., and Gal, S. 1976. The role of Tetranychus telarius L. and T. atlanticus McGregor (Acarina: Tetranychidae) in the transmission of paprika viruses. Acta Phytopathol. 11: 291-293.

5.5-37 Brcak, J. 1975. Garlic mosaic virus particles and virus infections of some wild Allium species. Sb. UVTI (Ustav Vedeckotechnickych Informaci) Ochrana Rostlin 11: 237-242. RPP 55: 4405.

5.5-38 Brcak, J., and Prochazkova, Z. 1976. Differences between strains of the cabbage black ring virus from horse-radish and garlic mustard Sb. UVTI (Ustav Vedeckotechnickych Informaci) Ochrana Rostlin 12: 243-253.

5.5-39 Bruckner, K. 1972. Studies on the problem of physiological specialization of mint rust Puccinia menthae Persoon [in German]. Arch. Pflanzenschutz 8: 15-27.

5.5-40 Brunt, A.A., and Kenten, R.H. 1971. Pepper veinal mottle virus--a
new member of the potato virus Y group from peppers (Capsicum annuum
L. and C. frutescens L.) in Ghana. Ann. Appl. Bot. 69: 235-243.

5.5-41 Buldeo, A.N., Shukla, V.N., and Patil, B.G. 1979. A new
sclerotial disease of sesame. Indian Phytopathol. 32: 124-126.

5.5-42 Buturac, I. 1979. Contribution to the knowledge of virus diseases
of cultivated wild Umbelliferae [in Serbo-Croatian]. Agron. Glasn.
41{1}: 47-54. RPP 59: 2961.

5.5-43 Butzonitch, I.P. 1978. Identification of alfalfa mosaic on potato
(Solanum tuberosum L.) in the south-east of Buenos Aires province [in
Spanish]. Fitopatologia 13: 82-89. RPP 58: 4996.

5.5-44 Cadilhac, B., Marchoux, G., and Coulomb, P. 1972. Preliminary
study of a plant-virus interaction in an umbellifer: parsley
(Petroselinum sativum). Ultrastructural observations [in French]. Ann.
Phytopathol. 4: 345-352. HA 44: 4961.

5.5-45 Cadilhac, B., Quiot, J.B., Marrou, J., and Leroux, J.P. 1976.
Electron microscope demonstration of two viruses attacking garlic
(Allium sativum L.) and shallot (Allium cepa L. var. ascalonicum) [in
French]. Ann. Phytopathol. 8: 65-72. RPP 56: 3359.

5.5-46 Campbell, R.N., and Melugin, S.A. 1971. Alfalfa mosaic virus
strains from carrot and parsley. Plant Dis. Rep. 55: 322-325.

5.5-47 Chaudhary, K.C.B., and Singh, A.K. 1974. Foot rot disease of
sesame. Sci. Cult. 40: 115-116.

5.5-48 Chenlulu, V.V., and Vir, D. 1979. Seed mycoflora, its role in
grain spoilage and production of mycotoxins. Bull. Grain Technol. 17:
148-157 RMVM 16: 1506.

5.5-49 Choopanya, D. 1973. Mycoplasma-like bodies associated with sesame
phyllody in Thailand. Phytopathology 63: 1536-1537.

5.5-50 Chung, H.S. 1975. Studies on Cylindrocarpon destructans (Zins.)
Scholten causing root rot of ginseng. Rep. Tottori Mycol. Inst. 12:
127-138.

5.5-51 Cirulli, M. 1975. The powdery mildew of parsley caused by
Leveillula lanuginosa (Fuck.) Golovin. Phytopathol. Mediterr. 14:
94-99.

5.5-52 Cook, A.A., and Milbrath, G.M. 1971. Virus diseases of papaya on
Oahu (Hawaii) and identification of additional diagnostic host plants.
Plant Dis. Rep. 55: 785-788.

5.5-53 Cooper, J.I., and Sweet, J.B. 1976. The detection of viruses with
nematode vectors in six woody hosts. Forestry 49{1}: 73-78.

5.5-54 Cousin, M.-T., Moreau, J.-P., Kartha, K.K., Staron, T., and
Faivre-Amiot, A. 1971. Polymorphism in mycoplasma-type microorganisms
found in sieve tubes of Abrial lavandin suffering from "yellow
dieback" [in French]. C. R. Hebd. Seances Acad. Sci. Ser. D. 272:
2082-2085.

5.5-55 Cousin, M.-T., Moreau, J.-P., Kartha, K.-K., Staron, T., and Fivre-Amiot, A. 1971. Ultrastructural study on mycoplasmas infecting the sieve tubes of yellows- affected Abrial lavandin [in French]. Ann. Phytopathol. 3: 243-250. HA 43: 762.

5.5-56 D'Ercole, N. 1972. Garlic rot due to Penicillium corymbiferum [in Italian]. Inf. Fitopatol. 22{2}: 5-7. HA 43: 1244.

5.5-57 Dale, J.L. 1972. Yellows in dandelion. Plant Dis. Rep. 56: 270-271.

5.5-58 Das, V.M., and Sultana, S. 1979. Five new species of the genus Pratylenchus from vegetable crops of Hyderabad (Andhra Pradesh). Indian J. Nematol. 9: 5-14.

5.5-59 Decker, H., Dowe, A. 1974. The occurrence of species belonging to the genera Pratylenchus, Pratylenchoides and Hirschmanniella (Nematoda: Pratylenchidae) in the German Democratic Republic [in German]. Helminthologia Bratislava 15: 829-834. HELM AB-A 47: 1042.

5.5-60 Dekanoidze, G.I. 1971. The Japanese wax scale on mulberry [in Russian]. Zashch. Rast. (Moscow) 16{12}: 43-44.

5.5-61 Dennis, C., and Davis, R.P. 1978. Storage rots of chicory roots caused by Phoma and Botrytis. Plant Pathol. 27: 49.

5.5-62 Desmidts, M., and Laboucheix, J. 1974. Relationship betwen cotton phyllody and a similar disease of sesame. FAO Plant Prot. Bull. (Rome) 22: 19-20.

5.5-63 Devi, L.R., Menon, M.R., and Nair, M.C. 1979. Corynespora leaf spot of sweet basil. Indian Phytopathol. 32: 150-151.

5.5-64 Dirimanov, M. 1974. Some morphologo-biological peculiarities of Plusia gutta Gn. Rastenievud. Nauki 11{6}: 137-147. RAE-A 64: 4246.

5.5-65 Dodds, J.A., and Taylor, G.S. 1980. Cucumber mosaic virus infection of tobacco transplants and purslane (Portulaca oleracea). Plant Dis. 64{3}: 294-296.

5.5-66 Dry, P.R. 1976. A list of fungal plant diseases previously unrecorded in South Australia. Agric. Rec. 3{4}: 20-22. RPP 55: 5643.

5.5-67 Duan, Y.J., Wang, Y.X., and Lu, X.D. 1979. Studies on the weed carriers of bacterial leaf blight of rice [in Chinese]. Chih Wu Pao Hu Hsueh Pao 6{3}: 19-23.

5.5-68 Dube, H.C., and Gour, H.N. 1975. Extra-cellular pectic enzymes of Macrophomina phaseolina--the incitant of root-rot of Sesamum indicum. Proc. Indian Natl. Sci. Acad. Part B 41: 576-579.

5.5-69 Durgapal, J.C. 1977. Albinism in Xanthomonas sesami. Curr. Sci. 46: 274.

5.5-70 Ellis, M.B., and Holliday, P. 1971. Drechslera sacchari. Commonw. Mycol. Inst. Descr. Pathog. Fungi Bact. 31: no. 305.

5.5-71 Elnagar, S., and Murant, A.F. 1976. Relations of the semi-persistent viruses, parsnip yellow fleck and Anthriscus yellows, with their vector, Cavariella aegopodii. Ann. Appl. Biol. 84: 153-167.

5.5-72 Elnagar, S., and Murant, A.F. 1976. The role of the helper virus, Anthriscus yellows in the transmission of parsnip yellow fleck virus by the aphid Cavariella aegopodii. Ann. Appl. Biol. 84: 169-181.

5.5-73 Elnagar, S., and Murant, A.F. 1978. Relations of carrot red leaf virus and carrot mottle virus with their aphid vector, Cavariella aegopodii. Ann. Appl. Biol. 89: 237-244.

5.5-74 El-Sherif, M., and Embabi, M. 1975. The reniform nematode on jasmine in Egypt. Plant Dis. Rep. 59: 65.

5.5-75 Erfurth, P. 1976. Observations on the occurrence of diseases of caraway [in German]. Nachrichtenbl. Pflanzenschutz DDR 30: 186. HA 47: 5869.

5.5-76 Eskarous, J.K. 1971. Leaf curling of pepper. J. Indian Bot. Soc. 50: 258-264.

5.5-77 Eskarous, J.K. 1971. Leaf curling of pepper. Acta Agron. Acad. Sci. Hung. 20: 35-41.

5.5-78 Feldman, J.M., and Oremianer, S. 1972. An unusual strain of tobacco mosaic virus from pepper. Phytopathol. Z. 75: 250-267.

5.5-79 Feldman, J.M., and Gracia, O. 1977. Studies of weed plants as sources of viruses. V. Occurrence of alfalfa mosaic virus on Origanum crops and on some weeds in Argentina. Phytopathol. Z. 90: 87-90.

5.5-80 Fernandez, F.T. 1979. Incidence of tobacco etch virus (TEV) in several pepper and tomato producing regions in Cuba [in Spanish]. Agrotec. Cuba 11{2}: 109-114. RPP 60: 5825.

5.5-81 Filatova, I.T., and Mustiatse, G.I. 1976. White rot of clary sage [in Russian]. Zashch. Rast. (Moscow) 1976{1}: 53-54. AGRICOLA.

5.5-82 Fischer, H.U., and Lockhart, B.E.L. 1976. A Moroccan isolate of turnip mosaic virus infections to garden pea and other legumes. Plant Dis. Rep. 60: 398-401.

5.5-83 Fletcher, J.T., and Hims, M.J. 1980. A new disease of watercress. Plant Pathol. 29: 200-201.

5.5-84 Frenhani, A.A., Bernardi, J.B., Bastos Cruz, B.P., and Da Silveira, S.G.P. 1972 Behavior of green pepper (Capsicum annuum L.) and paprika (Capsicum sp.) cultivars to bacterial leaf spot (Xanthomonas vesicatoria (Doidge) Dowson) [in Portuguese]. Arq. Inst. Biol. Sao Paulo 39: 35-41.

5.5-85 Frezzi, M.J., Giorda, L.M., and March, G.J. 1974. Garlic "black head" (Helminthosporium allii Campanile) in Cordoba, Argentina [in Spanish]. IDIA 1974{321/324}: 1-5. RPP 57: 3209.

5.5-86 Frowd, J.A., and Tomlinson, J.A. 1972. The isolation and identification of parsley viruses occurring in Britain. Ann. Appl. Biol. 72: 177-188.

5.5-87 Frowd, J.A., and Tomlinson, J.A. 1972. Relationships between a parsley virus, nasturtium ringspot virus and broad bean wilt virus. Ann. Appl. Biol. 72: 189-195.

5.5-88 Fujikawa, T., Tomirai, T., Sato, S., and Ando, S. 1973. Spanish paprika epidemic [in Japanese]. Nippon Shokubutsu Byori Gakkaiho 39{2}: 145 (Abstr.). 5.5-89 Fushtey, S.G., and Kelly, C.B. 1975. A new record of stem and bulb nematode in Ontario. Can. Plant Dis. Surv. 55: 27-28.

5.5-90 Gaborjanyi, R., and Nagy, F. 1972. Virus and mycoplasma diseases of cultivated medicinal plants in Hungary [in Hungarian]. Herba Hung. 11{2}: 39-51. HA 44: 6010.

5.5-91 Gailhofer, M., Thaler, I., and Ruecker, W. 1977. Virus inclusions in the cell wall and in the protoplast from in vitro cultivated Armoracia tissues [in German]. Protoplasma 93: 71-88. 5.5-92 Gallo D., P. 1974. Nematodes associated with the cultivation of oregano, Origanum vulgare L. in the Department of Arica [in Spanish]. Idesia 1974{3}: 211-214. HELM AB-B 45: 1317.

5.5-93 Gandhi, S.K., and Prashar, R.D. 1977. Bacterial rot of raya (Brassica juncea). Indian Phytopathol. 30: 24-27. RPP 58: 2005.

5.5-94 Gay, J.D. 1972. Isolation and identification of a new lima bean virus. Phytopathology 62: 803 (Abstr.).

5.5-95 Gemawat, P.D., and Prasad, N. 1972. Epidemiological studies on Alternaria blight of Cuminum cyminum. Indian J. Mycol. Plant Pathol. 2: 65-75. HA 44: 9929.

5.5-96 Gemawat, P.D., and Verma, O.P. 1972. A new powdery mildew of Sesamum indicum by Sphaerotheca fuliginea. Indian J. Mycol. Plant Pathol. 2: 94. AGRICOLA.

5.5-97 Georgieva, M., and Kotev, S. 1977. Penicillium decay of garlic [in Bulgarian]. Gradinar. Lozar. Nauka 14{8}: 44-51. HA 49: 3350.

5.5-98 Gerlach, W., and Franz, W. 1973. Verticillium wilt and Theilaviopsis root rot--two previously unknown diseases of valerian (Valeriana officinalis L.) [in German]. Phytopathol. Z. 76: 172-178.

5.5-99 Giannotti, J., Sassine, J., and Czarnecky, D. 1972. Serological and biological characterization of three plant mycoplasmas corresponding to three different diseases [in French]. Parasitica 28: 78-88.

5.5-100 Giannotti, J., Vago, C., Leclant, F., Marchoux, G., and Czarnecky, D. 1972. Mycoplasma cultures obtained from Lavandula hybrida Reverchon attacked by "decline" and Hyalesthes obsoletus Sign., a probable vector of the diseases [in French]. C.R. Hebd. Seances Acad. Sci. Ser. D 274: 394-397.

5.5-101 Giunchedi, L., and Ferrer, M.M. de. 1972. A strain of alfalfa mosaic virus isolated from Lavandula latifolia X L. officinalis [in Italian]. Phytopathol. Mediterr. 11: 74-76.

5.5-102 Gjaerum, H.B. 1972. Additional Norwegian finds of Uredinales and Ustilaginales. III. Norw. J. Bot. 19: 17-24.

5.5-103 Glaeser, G. 1976. Studies on the problem of seed transmission of paprika viruses (Cucumber mosaic virus and tobacco mosaic virus) [in German]. Land. Forstwirtsch. Forsch. Osterr. 7: 111-124. AGRICOLA.

5.5-104 Glaeser, G. 1971. White-rust disease of horseradish must be taken seriously [in German]. Pflanzenarzt 24{7}: 77-79. AGRICOLA.

5.5-105 Golden, A.M., and Klindic, O. 1973. Heterodera achilleae n.sp. (Nematoda: Heteroderidae) from yarrow in Yugoslavia. J. Nematol. 5: 196-201.

5.5-106 Gourley, C.O. 1979. Verticillium dahliae from stunted plants of summer savory. Can. Plant Dis. Surv. 59: 18.

5.5-107 Goyal, J.P. 1977. Diseases of mint and their control. Farmer Parliament 12{12}: 4, 10.

5.5-108 Graichen, K. 1978. Investigations on the host range of leek yellow dwarf virus [in German]. Archiv Phytopathol. Pflanzenschutz 14: 1-6. RPP 57: 5795.

5.5-109 Graichen, K. 1978. Virus diseases of onions, leek and garlic and their control [in German]. Nachrichtenbl. Pflanzenschutz DDR 32: 245-247. RPP 58: 3042.

5.5-110 Graichen, K. 1975. Allium species as natural hosts of nematode transmissable viruses [in German]. Archiv Phytopathol. Pflanzenschutz 11: 399-403.

5.5-111 Granett, A.L. 1972. An unidentified isometric virus from Plantago. Phytopathology 62: 761 (Abstr.).

5.5-112 Grasso, S. 1975. Wilting of basil caused by Fusarium oxysporum [in Italian]. Inf. Fitopatol. 25{5}: 5-7. HA 46: 3667.

5.5-113 Green, R.J., Jr. 1977. Alteration of pathogenicity of Verticillium dahliae from Mentha sp. under field conditions. Plant Dis. Rep. 61: 373-374.

5.5-114 Grzybowska, T. 1976. The pathogenicity of isolates of Septoria digitalis Pass. and the susceptibility of foxglove species to these isolates [in Polish]. Rocz. Nauk Roln. Ser. E. Ochr. Rosl. 6: 165-182. RPP 58: 1882.

5.5-115 Grzybowska, T., Kapala, H., and Kwasna, H. 1976. More important fungus and virus diseases of the Grecian foxglove and ways of preventing them [in Polish]. Wiad. Zielarskie 18{5}: 6-8.

5.5-116 Grzybowska, T., Kwasna, H., and Kapala, H. 1977. Diseases of caraway [in Polish]. Wiad. Zielarskie 19{4}: 4-6. AGRICOLA.

5.5-117 Grzybowska, T., Kapala, H., and Kwasna, H. 1977. Diseases of drug poppy Papaver somniferum occurring in spring [in Polish]. Choroby Maku Lekarskiego Wystepujace Wiosna 19{5}: 5-7. AGRICOLA.

5.5-118 Grzybowska, T., Kapala, H., and Kwasna, H. 1977. Diseases of the drug poppy occurring in summer [in Polish]. Wiad. Zielarskie 19{6}: 4-6. AGRICOLA.

5.5-119 Grzybowska, T., Kapala, H., and Kwasna, H. 1976. Fungus diseases of the peppermint [in Polish]. Wiad. Zielarskie 18{7/8}: 1-3. AGRICOLA.

5.5-120 Gupta, J.H., and Srivastava, V.P. 1978. A new root rot of fennel caused by Fusarium solani. Indian J. Mycol. Plant Pathol. 8: 206.

5.5-121 Gupta, J.H. 1980. Damping-off of fenugreek Trigonella foenum-graecum caused by Rhizoctonia solani in India. Indian J. Mycol. Plant Pathol. 10: 103.

5.5-122 Gupta, R.N. 1973. Longevity of chlamydospores of coriander-gall fungus. Indian Phytopathol. 26: 581-582. RPP 54: 949.

5.5-123 Gupta, R.N., and Naqvi, S.A.M.H. 1979. Changes in amino acid content of coriander plant parts infected with Protomyces macrosporus Unger. Acta Bot. Indica 7: 171-172. HA 50: 9383.

5.5-124 Gupta, Y.K., Agarwal, V.K., Roy, A.N., and Gupta, M.N. 1977. Fungi associated with rai (Brassica juncea Hook. f. & Thomas) seeds. Curr. Sci. 46: 319-320.

5.5-125 Haeni, A. 1971. Epidemiological studies of cucumber mosaic virus in tobacco fields of southern Switzerland [in German]. Phytopathol. Z. 72: 115-144.

5.5-126 Hansen, A.J., Nyland, G., McElroy, F.D., and Stace-Smith, R. 1974. Origin, cause, host range and spread of cherry rasp leaf disease in North America. Phytopathology 64: 721-727.

5.5-127 Hanson, C.M., and Campbell, R.N. 1979. Strawberry latent ringspot virus from 'plain' parsley in California. Plant Dis. Rep. 63: 142-146.

5.5-128 Herbas, R. 1971. Mosaic of pepper Capsicum frutescens var. grossum in Boliva and some physical properties of its causal agent [in Spanish]. Turrialba 21: 28-33.

5.5-129 Hiremath, P.C., Anilkumar, T.B., and Sulladmath, V.V. 1976. Occurrence of collar rot of fenugreek in Karnataka. Curr. Sci. 45: 465. HA 47: 2984.

5.5-130 Holliday, P., and Ellis, M.B. 1972. Alternaria radicina. Commonw. Mycol. Inst. Descr. Fungi Bact. 35(341-350): 346.

5.5-131 Horvath, J. 1979. New data on the susceptibility of Labiatae (Lamiaceae) to plant viruses. 1. Ocimum basilicum L. and Ocimum canum Sims [in Hungarian]. Novenytermeles 28: 331-334. RPP 59: 3146.

5.5-132 Horvath, J., and Besada, W.H. 1975. Opium poppy (Papaver somniferum L.), a new natural host of turnip mosaic virus in Hungary. Z. Pflanzenkr. Pflanzenschutz. 82: 162-167.

5.5-133 Imoto, M. 1973. Broad bean wilt virus isolated from Spanish paprika [in Japanese]. Nippon Shokubutsu Byori Gakkaiho 39: 164-165 (Abstr.).

5.5-134 Imoto, M. 1975. Studies on mosaic disease of sweet pepper (Capsicum frutescens L.) varieties. 2. Occurrence of mosaic disease of sweet pepper and types of causal viruses in Hiroshima Prefecture [in Japanese]. Hiroshima-kenritsu Nogyo Shikenjo Hokoku 36: 57-66. AGRICOLA.

5.5-135 Inagaki, H., Furuyama, S., Kasano, H., and Sakusai, K. 1972. Studies on mint nematodes. I. The incidence of nematodes in mint fields, the damage caused and their ecology [in Japanese]. Hokkaido Nogyo Shikenjo Iho 1972{100}: 48-57. PBA 43: 5597.

5.5-136 Jimenez Roco, M. 1972. On the nematodes of Arica Department (Part Two) [in Spanish]. Idesia 1972{2}: 53-58. HELM AB-B 42: 779.

5.5-137 Jimenez Roco, M. 1979. Nematodes of Coquimbo Province Region IV (Part 2) [in Spanish]. Idesia 1979{5}: 25-32. HELM AB-B 50: 517.

5.5-138 Kamal, and Singh, R.P. 1978. Fungi of Gorakhpur. VI - Some new host records from India. Acta Bot. Indica 6 (Suppl.): 188-189.

5.5-139 Kamal, and Singh, S. 1976. Wet rot of sesame seedlings in India. Sci. Cult. 42: 269-270.

5.5-140 Kanaujia, R.S., Kishore, R., and Singh, C.S. 1978. Three new fungal diseases from India. Acta Bot. Indica 6: 92-93. RPP 58: 1157.

5.5-141 Kandaswamy, T.K., Usman, K.M., Ranganathan, K., and Ramakrishnan, C. 1973. Phyllody, a disease of jasmine. South Indian Hortic. 21{1}: 35-37.

5.5-142 Kandaswamy, T.K., and Subramanian, C.L. 1974. An additional host for Cercospora jasminicola Mueller and Chupp. Curr. Sci. 43: 701.

5.5-143 Karahan, O., and Maden, S. 1978. Research on root collar rot (Dendryphion papaveris [Saw.] Sawada) of opium poppy, its seed transmission and effectiveness of seed treatment [in Turkish]. Bitki Koruma Bul.18{1/4}: 1-9. RPP 58: 5453.

5.5-144 Kemp, W.G., and Frowd, J.A. 1975. The isolation and identification of celery mosaic virus in Ontario. Plant Dis. Rep. 59: 50-53.

5.5-145 Khadr, A.S., and Abdel-Kader, N.E. 1974. Alternaria leaf spot of basil and licorice-first report. Agric. Res. Rev. 52{2}: 85-88.

5.5-146 Khandelwal, G.L. 1971. Cumin and pepper diseases and their control. Indian Farmers' Dig. 4{4}: 11-12. AGRICOLA.

5.5-147 Khatri, H.L., and Sekhon, I.S. 1974. Studies on a virus causing mosaic disease of chilli. Indian J. Mycol. Plant Pathol. 4: 121-125. HA 46: 11365.

5.5-148 Khripunova, E.F. 1977. Mycoflora of mint in Moldavia [in Russian]. Pages 9-16 in I.S. Popushoi, Sh.M. Grinberg and M.F. Kulik, eds. Girbnye i virusnye bolezni sel'skokhozlaistevnnykh kul'tur Moldavii. "Shtiintsa", Kishinev, USSR. AGRICOLA.

5.5-149 Kitajima, E.W., and Costa, A.S. 1978. The fine structure of the intranuclear, fibrous inclusions associated with the infection by celery mosaic virus. Fitopatol. Bras. 3: 287-293. RPP 58: 4731.

5.5-150 Klein, M. 1977. Sesame phyllody in Israel. Phytopathol. Z. 88: 165-171.

5.5-151 Klinkowski, M., Muhle, E., Reinmuth, E., and Bochow, H., eds.

1976. Phytopathology and plant protection. Volume III. Diseases and pests of vegetables and fruit-crops [in German]. Akademie-Verlag, Berlin, German Democratic Republic, 2nd ed. 914 pp. RAE-A 66: 4329.

5.5-152 Koenning, S.R., and McClure, M.A. 1979. "Pinwheel" inclusions and virus particles of two potyviruses in syncytia of Meloidogyne incognita. J. Nematol. 11: 305 (Abstr.).

5.5-153 Kohn, S. 1977. Dill (Anethum graveolens), a new host plant for Pseudomonas viridiflava (Burkholder) Clara [in German]. Nachrichtenbl. Dtsch. Pflanzenschutzdienstes (Braunschweig) 29{6}: 91-92. RPP 57: 739.

5.5-154 Kotev, S., and Georgieva, M. 1971. New diseases in parsley and leeks in Bulgaria [in Bulgarian]. Rastit. Zashch. 19{3}: 24-26. AGRICOLA.

5.5-155 Kothari, K.L., and Verma, A.C. 1972. Germination of Conidia of poppy powdery mildew (Erysiphe polygoni DC). Mycopathol. Mycol. Appl. 47: 253-260.

5.5-156 Kovacs, J. 1974. Virus diseases of paprika [in Hungarian]. Kert. Szolesz. 23{21}: 3. AGRICOLA.

5.5-157 Kral, J., Neubauer, S., and Klimes, K. 1974. The principal diseases of foxglove caused by fungal parasites [in Czech]. Nase Liecive Rastliny 11: 77-81. RPP 56: 5747.

5.5-158 Kratchanova, B., and Ivanova, A. 1979. Identification of some potato viruses on two Capsicum species. Acta Phytopathol. Acad. Sci. Hung. 14: 103-114.

5.5-159 Krober, H., Plate, H.P., and Prillwitz, H.G. 1971. Downy mildew on summer savory (Satureja hortensis L.) (Peronospora lamii A. Braun) [in German]. Nachrichtenbl. Dtsch. Pflanzenschutzdienstes (Braunschweig) 23: 24-25. AGRICOLA.

5.5-160 Ksiazek, D. 1976. Investigation on an alfalfa mosaic strain isolated from weeds [in Polish]. Zesz. Probl. Postepow Nauk Roln. 1976{182}: 173-179. RPP 57: 3371.

5.5-161 Kucmierz, J. 1973. The parasitic fungi in the associations of vascular plants in the Ojcow National Park [in Polish]. Ochr. Przyr. 38: 155-211.

5.5-162 Kucmierz, J. 1976. Flora of parasitic fungi of the Pieniny Mountains (Western Carpathians). Part I. Plasmodiophoromycetes, Oomycetes, Chytridiomycetes, Ascomycetes [in Polish]. Fragm. Florist. Geobot. (Cracow) 22: 377-393.

5.5-163 Kuhne, H. 1973. Diseases of Lobelia cardinalis [in German]. Gartenwelt 73: 287-289. HA 44: 2616.

5.5-164 Kuroli, G. 1973. Study of significant virus and mycoplasma diseases of tomato and vegetable paprika, the biology of insect vectors, and the possible ways of control [in Hungarian]. Agrartud. Kozl.32: 485-496. AGRICOLA.

5.5-165 Kushi, K.K., and Khare, M.N. 1979. Comparative efficacy of five methods to detect Macrophomina phaseolina associated with Sesamum seeds. Indian Phytopathol. 31: 258-259.

5.5-166 La, Y.-J. 1973. Studies on garlic mosaic virus, its isolation, symptom expression in test plants, physical properties, purification, serology and electron microscopy [in Korean]. Hanguk Sikmul Poho Hakhoe Chi 12{3}: 93-107. RPP 54: 5175.

5.5-167 Lai, M., and Watson, T. 1973. Bacterial spots of tomato and pepper in California. Plant Dis. Rep. 57: 258-259.

5.5-168 Lal, B., Ghildiyal, P.C., and Singh, R.N. 1980. Seed mycoflora of some medicinal plants. Prog. Hortic. 12{2}: 47-49. 5.5-169 Lamberti, F., and Garibaldi, A. 1977. Leaf nematodes on basil [in Italian]. Nematol. Mediterr. 5: 335-338. HELM AB-B 47: 1229.

5.5-170 Lana, A.O., Gilmer, R.M., Wilson, G.F., and Shoyinka, S.A. 1975. Identification and characterisation of a severe strain of pepper veinal mottle virus isolated from pepper (Capsicum annuum and C. frutescens) in Nigeria. Niger. J. Plant Prot. 1{1}: 76-81.

5.5-171 Lana, A.O., Gilmer, R.M., Wilson, G.F., and Shoyinka, S.A. 1975. An unusual new virus, possibly of the potyvirus group, from pepper in Nigeria. Phytopathology 65: 1329-1332.

5.5-172 Layton, W.A. 1976. Marasmiellus collar rot of Japanese mint. Papua New Guinea Agric. J. 27{3}: 59-65.

5.5-173 Lee, R.F., Niblett, C.L., and Johnson, L.B. 1975. Properties of a Kansas strain of belladonna mottle virus isolated from pepper. Proc. Am. Phytopathol. Soc. 2: 70-71 (Abstr.).

5.5-174 Lee, R.F., Niblett, C.L., Hubbard, J.D., and Johnson, L.B. 1979. Characterization of belladonnna mottle virus isolates from Kansas and Iowa. Phytopathology 69: 985-989.

5.5-175 Leguizamon, C.J. and Barriga, O.R. 1976. Garlic (Allium sativum L.) diseases in Cundinamarca and Boyaca [in Spanish]. Not. Fitopatol. 5{1}: 4-19. RPP 56: 5300.

5.5-176 Lewartowski, R., and Piekarcyzk, K. 1978. Characteristic of development, appearance intensity and noxiousness of more important diseases and pests of industrial crops in Poland in 1976 [in Polish]. Biul. Inst. Ochr. Rosl. 62: 151-221. AGRICOLA.

5.5-177 Lindquist, J.C. 1979. Puccinia menthae and its varieties in Argentina [in Spanish]. Sydowia Beih. 8: 255-257.

5.5-178 Lindsey, D.L. 1979. Influence of initial inoculum densities of Meloidogyne incognita on three cultivars of chile. Abs. No. 546 in Thor Kommedahl, ed. International congress (IX) of plant protection: Abstracts of papers presented at the IX international congress of plant protection, 5-11 August, 1979, Washington, D.C. Burgess Pub., St. Paul, Minnesota. HELM AB-B 49: 1345.

5.5-179 Lisetskaya, L.F. 1971. Four nematode species from ethereal oil plant crops, new for the USSR [in Russian]. Parazity Zhivotn. Rast. 1971{7}: 144-150. HELM AB-B 42: 920.

5.5-180 Lisetskaya, L.F. 1971. Principal plant-parasitic nematodes of ethereal oil crops in Moldavia [in Russian]. Parazity Zhivotn. Rast. 1971{7}: 142-144. HELM AB-B 42: 788.

5.5-181 Lisetskaya, L.F., and Mel'nik, M.V. 1975. Ditylenchus dipsaci infection on garlic in Moldavia [in Russian]. Parazity Zhivotn. Rast. 1975{11}: 142-152. HELM AB-B 46: 346.

5.5-182 Lockhart, B.E.L., and Fischer, H.U. 1976. Cucumber mosaic virus infections of pepper in Morocco. Plant Dis. Rep. 60: 262-264.

5.5-183 Lundqvist, A. 1974. Notions on two Oland Orobanchaceae [in Swedish]. Sv en. Bot. Tidskr. 68: 94-105.

5.5-184 Lu, J., and Beaulieu, J. 1978. Observation of some viruses of plants cultivated among weeds [in French]. Phytoprotection 59: 187-188 (Abstr.).

5.5-185 MacDonald, J.D., and Leach, L.D. 1976. Evidence for an expanded host range of Fusarium oxysporum f. sp. betae. Phytopathology 66: 822-827.

5.5-186 Majewski, T. 1972. Species of Erysiphaceae, Uredinales and Ustilaginales rare or new in Poland. Acta Mycol. 8: 219-227.

5.5-187 Malaguti, G. 1973. Foliar diseases of sesame (Sesamum indicum L.) in Venezuela [in Spanish]. Rev. Fac. Agron. Univ. Cent. Venez. Fac. Agron. 7{2}: 109-125. AGRICOLA.

5.5-188 Malaguti, G., Subero, L.J., and Gomez, N. 1972. Alternaria sesamicola on sesame (Sesamum indicum) [in Spanish]. Agron. Trop. (Maracay, Venez.) 22: 75-80. AGRICOLA.

5.5-189 Mali, V.R. 1979. Tagar (Tabernaemontena coronaria)-A new host of jasmine chlorotic ringspot virus. Indian J. Mycol. Plant Pathol. 9: 242-243.

5.5-190 Mall, O.P. 1977. Root-region actinomyete flora of coriander. Acta Phytopathol. Acad. Sci. Hung. 12: 315-321. RPP 57: 3050.

5.5-191 Manoharachary, C., and Padmavathy, K. 1976. Fungi associated with chilli seeds. Geobios (Jodhpur) 3: 99-100.

5.5-192 Marchoux, G., and Rougier, J. 1974. Alfalfa mosaic virus isolated from lavendin and eggplant [in French]. Ann. Phytopathol. 6: 191-195. HA 45: 5269.

5.5-193 Mariappan, V., Govindaswamy, C.V., and Ramakrishnan, K. 1973. Studies on the role of weed plants in the spread of virus diseases. II. Role of Solanum nigrum in spreading chilli mosaic virus, a strain of potato virus Y. Madras Agric. J. 60: 120-121. HA 44: 4001.

5.5-194 Mariappan, V., and Ramanujam, K. 1975. Yellow ring mosaic of Jasminum spp. with particular reference to its transmission by an aleurodid. South Indian Hortic. 23{1/2}: 77-78. RAE-A 65: 4617.

5.5-195 Mathur, R.L. 1971. Nonspecific toxin production by Fusarium oxysporum f. corianderii Kul. Nik and Joshi. Rajasthan J. Agric. Sci. 2: 7-8.

5.5-196 Mathur, S.B., and Kabeere, F. 1975. Seed-borne fungi of sesame in Uganda. Seed Sci. Technol. 3: 655-660. AGRICOLA.

5.5-197 Matta, A. 1978. Fusarium tabacinum (Beyma) W. Gams, pathogen on basil and tomato in nature [in Italian]. Riv. Patol. Veg. 14: 119-125. RPP 58: 3753.

5.5-198 Matuo, T., and Snyder, W.C. 1972. Host virulence and the Hypomyces stage of Fusarium solani f. sp. pisi. Phytopathology 62: 731-735.

5.5-199 Mazzucchi, U., and Dalli, A. 1974. Bacterial soft rot of Fennel (Foeniculum vulgare var. dulce Mill.). Phytopathol. Mediterr. 13: 113-116.

5.5-200 McLeod, R.W., and Khair, G.T. 1971. Xiphinema australiae n. sp., its host range, observations on X radicicola Goodey, 1936 and X monohysterum Brown, 1968 and a key to monodelphic Xiphinema spp. (Nematoda: Longidoridae). Nematologica 17: 58-68.

5.5-201 Melouk, H.A., and Horner, C.E. 1976. Recovery of Verticillium dahliae pathogenic to mints from castings of earthworms. Proc. Am. Phytopathol. Soc. 3: 265 (Abstr.). HA 47: 9757.

5.5-202 Melouk, H.A., and Horner, C.E. 1972. Growth in culture and pathogenicity of Phoma strasseri to peppermint. Phytopathology 62: 576-578.

5.5-203 Melouk, H.A., and Horner, C.E. 1973. beta-Glucosidase from Phoma strasseri and its possible role in a disease of peppermint. Phytopathology 63: 973-975.

5.5-204 Melouk, H.A., and Horner, C.E. 1974. Verticillium nigrescens from peppermint. Phytopathology 64: 1267-1268.

5.5-205 Melouk, H.A., Horner, C.E., and Perkins, V.Q. 1973. Effect of light on uptake of Verticillium dahliae spores by mints. Phytopathology 63: 1217 (Abstr.).

5.5-206 Mention, M., and Bouhot, D. 1977. Role of Fusarium roseum in the symptom of pink roots of leek [in French]. Rev. Hortic. 1977{179}: 37-40. RPP 57: 371.

5.5-207 Meredith, J.A., and Perez, G. 1975. Plant parasitic nematode genera associated with sesame (Sesamum indicum L.) in Venezuala [in Spanish]. Nematropica 5{2}: 44-46. AGRICOLA.

5.5-208 Mijuskovic, M., and Vucinic, Z. 1976. Phytophthora capsici Leonian, a new parasite of paprika in Montenegro [in Serbo-Croatian]. Poljopr. Sumar. 22{3}: 23-44. AGRICOLA.

5.5-209 Milicic, D., and Plakolli, M. 1974. Spontaneous infection of some Labiates with alfalfa mosaic virus. Acta Bot. Croat. 33: 9-15.

5.5-210 Mishra, A.K., and Singh, T.K.S. 1973. Pathological anatomy of virus infected chilli plants. Indian Phytopathol. 26: 111-114. RPP 53: 4220.

5.5-211 Misra, A., Jha, A., and Singh, T.K.S. 1972. Note on morbid anatomy of the chilli (Capsicum frutescens L.) plants infected with mosaic virus Indian J. Agric. Sci. 42: 178-179. RPP 52: 547.

5.5-212 Misra, A., and Singh, T.K.S. 1971. Morbid anatomy of mosaic virus infected chilli plants. Bull. Bot. Soc. Bengal 25{1/2}: 79-80. RPP 52: 2440.

5.5-213 Misra, A., and Jha, A. 1973. Transmission of chilli-mosaic-virus through pollen and root-contact. Phyton (Horn, Austria) 15: 103-106. HA 44: 6726.

5.5-214 Mitchell, D.J., Strandberg, J.O., and Kannwischer, M.E. 1978. Root and stem rot of watercress (Nasturtium officinale) caused by Phytophthora cryptogea. Plant Dis. Rep. 62: 599-600.

5.5-215 Mitchell, D.J. 1978. Relationships of inoculum levels of several soilborne species of Phytophthora and Pythium to infection of several hosts. Phytopathology 68: 1754-1759.

5.5-216 Mitidieri, I.Z.M. de. 1973. The anthracnose of basil (Ocimum basilicum L.) by Colletotrichum gloeosporioides Penz. and its sexual state Glomerella cingulata (Stonem.) Spauld. et V. Schrenk [in Spanish]. Rev. Invest. Agropecu. Ser. 5 10{2}: 99-108. AGRICOLA.

5.5-217 Miyazawa, Y., and Hagihara, H. 1976. Ginseng root rot on the paddy field changed from ginseng field. Bull. Nagano Hortic. Exp. Stn. 13: 37-42.

5.5-218 Miyazawa, Y., and Hagiwara, H. 1972. Studies on the causal factors of Panax ginseng root rot and its control [in Japanese]. Bull. Nagano Hort. Exp. Stn. 9: 109-124. AGRICOLA.

5.5-235 Mohanraj, D., Samuel, G.S., and Vidhyasekaran, P. 1972. Occurrence of Alternaria blight of chicory in India. Curr. Sci. 41: 464.

5.5-220 Mont, R.M. 1972. Puccinia menthae recorded on mint (Mentha sp.) in Peru [in Spanish]. Fitopatologia 7: 35-36. RPP 52: 3019.

5.5-221 Moore, J.F. 1971. Studies on the persistence of Ditylenchus destructor in the potato tuber nematode with different cropping treatments. Ir. J. Agric. Res. 10: 207-211.

5.5-222 Movsesyan, L.I. 1978. Rust of flowering plants [in Russian]. Zashch. Rast. 1978{8}: 61. RPP 58: 3867.

5.5-223 Mukhopadhyay, A.N., and Pavgi, M.S. 1971. Environment in relation to infection of coriander by Protomyces macrosporus Unger. Nippon Shokubutsu Byori Gakkaiho 37: 215-219. AGRICOLA.

5.5-224 Muller, H.M., Hartleb, H., Opel, H., Proll, E., and Schmidt, H.B. 1976. Electron microscope determination of beet mild yellowing virus in the host plant Sinapis alba L. [in German]. Arch. Phytopathol. Pflanzenschutz 12: 293-295. RPP 56: 2707.

5.5-225 Nadazdin, M. 1972. Pyrenochaeta terrestris, a new onion disease in Yugoslavia [in Serbo-Croatian]. Zast. Bilja 23{121}: 311-316. HA 44: 2494.

5.5-226 Nagy, F., Voros, J., Barsony, A., and Leranth, J. 1972. Cercospora traversiana, a new pathogen of fenugreek in Hungary and possibilities of control [in Hungarian]. Herba Hung. 11{3}: 53-60. HA 44: 6046.

5.5-227 Nagy, G.S. 1977. Erysiphe monardae sp. nov. Phytopathol. Z. 88: 285-286.

5.5-228 Nakov, B., Kotetsov, P., and Angelov, D. 1974. A new disease of garlic [in Bulgarian]. Rastit. Zasht. 22{5}: 33. HA 45: 6471.

5.5-229 Narayanaswamy, P., Ranganathan, K., Jaganathan, T., and Palaniswami, A. 1972. An epiphytotic of jasmine rust at Coimbatore. South Indian Hortic. 20{1/4}: 104-107. RPP 54: 475.

5.5-230 Nelson, M.R., and Wheeler, R.E. 1978. Biological and serological characterization and separation of potyviruses that infect peppers. Phytopathology 68: 979-984.

5.5-231 Nemoto, M., Goto, T., and Yoshida, K. 1974. Studies on yellows disease of parsley and celery [in Japanese]. Hokkaido Nogyo Shikenjo Knekyu Hokoku 109: 107-113.

5.5-232 Novak, J.B., and Lanzova, J. 1977. Identification of some viruses occurring in celery and horseradish in Czechoslovakia [in Czech]. Sb. Fac. Agron. Vys. Sk. Zemed. Prague Rada A Rostl. Vyroba 1977{1}: 177-192.

5.5-233 Noviello, C., Marziano, F., Aloj, B., and Garibaldi, A. 1975/1976. Observations over three years on fennel diseases in Campania [in Italian]. Ann. Fac. Sci. Agar. Univ. Studi Napli, Portici 9/10: 259-271. HA 48: 7389.

5.5-234 Nuzzaci, G. 1977. Lygus (Orthops) kalmi L. injurious to fennel [in Italian]. Inf. Fitopatol. 27{3}: 3-5. RAE-A 66: 2094.

5.5-235 Ozaki, T., Arai, S., and Takahashi, J. 1973. Biological properties of tobacco mosaic virus isolated from red pepper [in Japanese]. Nippon Shokubutsu Byori Gakkaiho 39: 163-164 (Abstr.).

5.5-236 Paizs, L., and Nagy, F. 1975. Phoma strasseri, a new pathogen of mints (Mentha piperita and M. sachalinensis in Hungary [in Hungarian]. Herba Hung. 14{2/3}: 65-73. HA 46: 6068.

5.5-237 Paludan, N. 1973. Turnip mosaic virus in horseradish (Armoracia lapathifolia Gilib) [in Danish]. Tidsskr. Planteavl 77: 161-169. AGRICOLA.

5.5-238 Paludan, N. 1980. Virus attack on leeks: diagnosis, varietal tolerance, and overwintering [in Danish]. Tidsskr. Planteavl 84: 371-385 RPP 60: 2316.

5.5-239 Pandey, R., Shukla, P., Dwivedi, R.P., and Singh, R.P. 1977. Damping-off of fenugreek caused by Humicola fuscoatra. Indian J. Mycol. Plant Pathol. 7: 91-92. HA 48: 7618.

5.5-240 Parmelee, J.A. 1973. Puccinia allii on garlic, an interception. Can. Plant Dis. Sur. 53: 147-149.

5.5-241 Pasynkov, V. 1975. Broomrape parasitization on caraway [in Russian]. Byull. Vses. Inst. Rastenievod. 1975{51}: 77. WA 26: 3898.

5.5-242 Pauvert, P., and Jacqua, G. 1974. Critical study of some Helminthosporium isolates from Panicum, Pennisetum and sugar cane in the French West Indies [in French]. Ann. Phytopathol. 6: 285-296. PBA 45: 8294.

5.5-243 Pavlyuk, L.V. 1972. Analysis of nematode fauna of Valeriana officinalis L., cultivated in the Moscow region. Vestn. Zool. 6: 30-34.

5.5-244 Perez, J.E., Irizarry, H., and Cortes-Monlorr, A. 1974. Present status of virus infections of peppers in Puerto Rico. J. Agric. Univ. P.R. 58: 137-139.

5.5-245 Perveen, S., and Zakaullah. 1979. Diseases of cumin. A review. Pak. J. For. 29: 195-198.

5.5-246 Petersen, J., and Rowhani, A. 1977. Research into a virus of plantain (Plantago major) which may infect tomatoes [in French]. Phytoprotection 58: 125-126.

5.5-247 Piazzolla, P., Guantieri, V., Vovlas, C., and Tamburro, A.M. 1977. Circular dichroism studies of chicory yellow mottle virus. J. Gen. Virol. 37: 359-372.

5.5-248 Plese, N., and Milicic, D. 1974. Virus isolations from yellow-netted Forsythia suspensa and from Lycium halimifolium [in German]. Acta Bot. Croat. 33: 31-36.

5.5-249 Ploaie, P.G., Petre, Z., and Ionica, M. 1978. Identification of a virus infecting garlic cultivars in Romania [in Romanian]. Stud. Cercet. Biol. Ser. Biol. Veg. 30{1}: 65-71. RPP 58: 2054.

5.5-250 Polak, J., and Chod, J. 1975. The occurrence of beet mild yellowing virus in Czechoslovakia. Biol. Plant. 17: 304-308.

5.5-251 Polak, Z., and Chlumska, J. 1980. Further detection of spontaneous occurrence of tobacco mosaic virus in ruderal vegetation [in Czech]. Sb. UVTI (Ustav Vedeckotechnickych Informaci) Ochrana Rostlin 16: 101-104. RPP 59: 5540.

5.5-252 Prakasa Rao, C.G. 1972. Anatomical studies on abnormal growth caused by Protomyces macrosporus on Coriandrum sativum. Indian Phytopathol. 25: 483-496.

5.5-253 Prakash, O.M., and Misra, A.P. 1976. Collateral hosts for Helminthosporium sacchari and H. stenospilum. Indian Phytopathol. 29: 330-332.

5.5-254 Prasad, B.K. 1979. Enzymic studies of seed-borne fungi of coriander. Indian Phytopathol. 32: 92-94.

5.5-255 Pratt, B.H., Heather, W.A., and Shepherd, C.J. 1974. Pathogenicity to three agricultural plant species of Phytophthora drechsleri isolates from Australian forest communities. Aust. J. Bot. 22: 9-12. RPP 53: 3875.

5.5-256 Prochazkova, Z. 1977. Presumed role of mucilage of plantain seeds in spread of tobacco mosaic virus. Biol. Plant. 19: 259-263.

5.5-257 Prochazkova, Z. 1977. Host range and complex character of tobacco mosaic virus strain from Plantago major found in Southern Bohemia [in Czech]. Sb. UVTI (Ustav Vedeckotechnickych Informaci) Ochrana Rostlin 13: 189-195. RPP 58: 115.

5.5-258 Provvidenti, R., and Granett, A.L. 1976. Occurrence of Plantago mottle virus in pea, Pisum sativum, in New York state. Ann. Appl. Biol. 82: 85-89.

5.5-259 Quacquarelli, A., Vovlas, C., Piazzolla, P., Russo, M., and Martelli, G.P. 1972. Some characteristics of Chicory yellow mottle virus. Phytopathol. Mediterr. 11: 180-188.

5.5-260 Quacquarelli, A., Avgelis, A., and Piazzolla, P. 1974. Studies of carrot leaf virus of parsley. II. Determination of some of physiochemical characteristics [in Italian]. Phytopathol. Mediterr. 13: 155-159.

5.5-261 Ragozzino, A., and Stefanis, D. 1976. Urospermum picroides natural host of cucumber mosaic virus and alfalfa mosaic virus [in Italian]. Phytopathol. Z. 86: 27-36.

5.5-262 Rai, J.N., and Srivastava, S.K. 1975. Production of endo-polygalacturonase and cellulase by isolates of Macrophomina phaseoli causing stem and root rot disease of Brassica juncea. Indian J. Mycol. Plant Pathol. 5: 169-173. PBA 48: 6803.

5.5-263 Ramaiah, K.S., and Sastry, M.N.L. 1980. Seed mycoflora of Sesamum (Sesamum indicum L.). Mysore J. Agric. Sci. 14: 341-344.

5.5-264 Ramsdell, D.C., and Myers, R.L. 1978. Epidemiology of peach rosette mosaic virus in a Concord grape vineyard. Phytopathology 68: 447-450.

5.5-265 Ram, S., and Shukla, D.D. 1975. Studies on virus disease of chillies (Capsicum annuum and C. frutescens) in Rajasthan. Indian J. Mycol. Plant Pathol. 5: 29 (Abstr.).

5.5-266 Rana, G.L., and Vovlas, C. 1971. Virus diseases of vegetable crops in Apulia. Part V. A mosaic of eggplant [in Italian]. Phytopathol. Mediterr. 10: 273-277.

5.5-267 Ranganathan, K., Shanmugan, N., Ramakrishnan, V., and Ramalingam, C. 1974. Reaction of varieties of garlic (Allium sativum) to a new root rot caused by Macrosphomina phaseoli. Indian J. Mycol. Plant Pathol. 4: 93. PBA 47: 5919.

5.5-268 Rao, C.G.P. 1973. Anatomical studies on abnormal growth caused by Uromyces hobsoni on Jasminum grandiflorum. Indian Phytopathol. 26: 32-40. RPP 53: 3999.

5.5-269 Rao, N.N.R., and Pavgi, M.S. 1975. Stemphylium leaf blight of onion. Mycopathologia 56: 113-118. RPP 55: 2445.

5.5-270 Rast, A.T.B. 1977. Tobacco mosaic virus on paprika [in Dutch]. Gewasbescherming 8: 170-171. AGRICOLA.

5.5-271 Rathaiah, Y., and Pavgi, M.S. 1973. Perpetuation of species of
Cercospora and Ramularia parasitic on oil-seed crops. Ann.
Phytopathol. Soc. Jpn. 39: 103-108. RPP 53: 641.

5.5-272 Renuka Rao, B. 1977. Species of Alternaria on some Cruciferae.
Geobios (Jodhpur) 4: 163-166.

5.5-273 Roca, F., Conti, M., and Lamberti, F. 1977. Trichodorus
viruliferus (Nematoda, Trichodoridae), vector of tobacco rattle virus
in the province of Asti [in Italian]. Nematol. Mediterr. 5: 185-194.
HELM AB-B 47: 1315.

5.5-274 Romascu, E., and Lemeni, V. 1972. The nematode Ditylenchus
dipsaci Kuhn - a dangerous pest of garlic and onion crops [in
Romanian]. Rev. Hortic. Vitic. 21{5}: 73-78. PBA 43: 6357.

5.5-275 Rondomanski, W. 1974. White rot of onion (Sclerotium cepivorum
Berk.) in Poland [in Polish]. Biul. Inst. Ochr. Rosl. 57: 187-190. RPP
57: 1931.

5.5-276 Rowhani, A., and Peterson, J.F. 1980. Characterization of a
flexuous rod-shaped virus from Plantago. Can. J. Plant Pathol. 2{1}:
12-18. RPP 59: 5663.

5.5-277 Roy, A.N., Sharma, R.B., and Gupta, K.C. 1977. Occurrence of
three new rot diseases of stored garlic (Allium sativum L.). Curr.
Sci. 46: 716-717.

5.5-278 Russo, M., Martelli, G.P., Cresti, M., and Ciampolini, F. 1979.
Bean yellow mosaic virus in saffron. Phytopathol. Mediterr. 18:
189-191.

5.5-279 Russo, M., Martelli, G.P., and Vovlas, C. 1973. Virus diseases
of vegetable crops in Apulia. XIV. Broadbean wilt virus in broadbean
and bush red pepper [in Italian]. Phytopathol. Mediterr. 12: 61-66.

5.5-280 Sakamoto, A., and Matsuo, N. 1975. A virus isolated from Spanish
paprika [in Japanese]. Nippon Shokubutsu Byori Gakkaiho 41{1}: 95
(Abstr.).

5.5-281 Sakamoto, I., and Matsuo, M. 1973. Seed contagion of tobacco
mosaic virus in Spanish paprika. Nippon Shokubutsu Byori Gakkaiho 39:
164 (Abstr.).

5.5-282 Saksena, H.K., and Singh, D.V. 1975. Corynespora blight of
sesame in India. Indian J. Farm Sci. 3: 95-99. AGRICOLA.

5.5-283 Sanz B-M., H. 1978. Identification and pathogenecity of
Helminthosporium allii (Campanile) on pink garlic (Allium sativum L.).
Agric. Tec. (Santiago) 38: 122-123. RPP 58: 2502.

5.5-284 Sarwar, M. 1977. Two new Sphaeropsidaceous fungi on Salvia
sclarea L. Indian J. Microbiol. 17: 148-149. RPP 59: 404.

5.5-285 Sarwar, M., and Dimri, B.P. 1971. A new species of Cercospora on
Artemisia dracunculus L. Proc. Indian Acad. Sci. Sect. B 73: 51-52.
AGRICOLA

5.5-286 Sarwar, M. 1974. A new anthracnose disease of Salvia sclarea L.
Ceska Mykol. 28: 156-158. RPP 54: 955.

5.5-287 Sarwar, M., and Khan, M.N.A. 1971. Diseases and pests of aromatic plants from South India. Angew. Bot. 45: 211-216.

5.5-288 Sattar, A., and Husain, A. 1976. Stolon and root rot of Japanese mint in Uttar Pradesh. Indian Phytopathol. 29: 442-444. RPP 57: 4581.

5.5-289 Sattar, A., and Husain, A. 1978. Fusarium wilt of Japanese mint. New Bot. 5: 9-10. RPP 60: 5517.

5.5-290 Schmidt, H.E., and Schmelzer, K. 1976. Investigations on the ring mosaic of lemon balm (Melissa officinalis L.) [in German]. Archiv fur Gartenbau 24: 209-216. RPP 55: 5871.

5.5-291 Schultz, M.G., Harrap, K.A., and Land, J.B. 1975. A probable rhabdovirus infection of lemon-scented thyme. Ann. Appl. Biol. 80: 251-254.

5.5-292 Sehgal, S.P., Gupta, I.J., and Agrawat, J.M. 1971. Capsule rot of opium poppy (Papaver somniferum L.). Rajasthan J. Agric. Sci. 2: 61-62.

5.5-293 Shah, H.M., and Patel, D.J. 1979. Occurrence of root-knot disease in cumin. Indian J. Nematol. 9: 179-183.

5.5-294 Sharma, A.D., and Munjal, R.L. 1978. Blight of some commercial species of Mentha in Himachal Pradesh. Indian For. 104: 238-239. RPP 58: 324.

5.5-295 Sharma, A.D., and Jandaik, C.L. 1979. Rhizoctonia disease of Atropa and Salvia - new to India. Indian J. Mycol. Plant Pathol. 9: 86-87. RPP 60; 2717.

5.5-296 Sharma, A.D. 1996. Studies on seed mycoflora of some medicinal plants. Indian J. Mycol. Plant Pathol. 7: 171-172.

5.5-297 Sharma, K.R., and Mukerji, K.G. 1974. Incidence of pathogenic fungi on leaves. Indian Phytopathol. 27: 558-566.

5.5-298 Sharma, R.D., and Loof, P.A.A. 1972. Nematodes associated with different plants at the Centro de Pesquisas do Cacau, Bahia. Rev. Theobroma 2{4}: 38-43. HELM AB-B 43: 584.

5.5-299 Sharma, S.L., Nayar, S.K., and Shayam, K. 1973. Diseases of Thuja and Allium. FAO Plant Prot. Bull. 21: 18-19.

5.5-300 Sharma, V.K., and Singh, O.S. 1971. A new record of root galls in chicory (Cichorium intybus L.). Sci. Cult. 37: 578-579.

5.5-301 Shekhawat, P.S., and Chakravarti, B.P. 1979. Comparison of agar plate and cotyledon methods for the detection of Xanthomonas vesicatoria in chilli seeds. Phytopathol. Z. 94: 80-83.

5.5-302 Shreemali, J.L. 1979. Two new species of phoma from India. Indian J. Mycol. Plant Pathol. 8: 220-221.

5.5-303 Shukla, D.D., and Schmelzer, K. 1972. Studies on viruses and virus diseases of cruciferous plants. V. Viruses in horseradish. Acta Phytopathol. Acad. Sci. Hung. 7: 305-313. RPP 53: 306.

5.5-304 Shukla, D.D., and Ram, S. 1977. Natural occurrence of three different viruses in chilies in Rajasthan. Indian J. Mycol. Plant Pathol. 7: 122-126.

5.5-305 Shukla, D.D.,, and Schmelzer, K. 1972. Studies on viruses and virus diseases of cruciferous plants III.Nasturtium ringspot virus in Sinapis alba L. Acta Phytopathol. Acad. Sci. Hung. 7: 147-156. RPP 52: 2869.

5.5-306 Shukla, D.N., and Bhargava, S.N. 1977. Fungi isolated from seeds of pulses and oil crops stored for different intervals of time [in Hindi]. Vijnana Parishad Anusandhan Patrika 20: 363-368.

5.5-307 Singh, B.M., and Sharma, Y.R. 1977. Occurrence of leaf blight of garlic caused by Stemphylium botryosum in India. Indian Phytopathol. 30: 272-273. RPP 58: 2056.

5.5-308 Singh, B.M., and Sharma, Y.R. 1977. Rust on garlic. FAO Plant Prot. Bull. 25: 41-42.

5.5-309 Singh, R.D. 1974. Histopathology of fennel infected by Ramularia foeniculi. Indian J. Mycol. Plant Pathol. 4: 166-170. HA 46: 11645.

5.5-310 Singh, R.P., and Lopez-Abella, D. 1971. Natural infection of coriander plants by a strain of clover yellow vein virus. Phytopathology 61: 333-334.

5.5-311 Singh, N., Gill, J.S., and Krishnanada, N. 1979. Prevalence of root-knot nematode in Nilgiri hills. Indian Phytopathol. 32: 499-501. HELM AB-B 50: 960.

5.5-312 Skotland, C.B. 1979. A rhizome rot of Scotch spearmint, Mentha cardiaca caused by a sclerotium-forming basidiomycete. Phytopathology 69{8}: 920 (Abstr.).

5.5-313 Southards, C.J., and Priest, M.F. 1971. Physiologic variation of seventeen isolates of Meloidogyne incognita. J. Nematol. 3: 330 (Abstr.).

5.5-314 Southards, C.J., and Priest, M.F. 1973. Variation in pathogenicity of seventeen isolates of Meloidogyne incognita. J. Nematol. 5: 63-67.

5.5-315 Sparrow, F.K. 1975. Observations on chytridiaceous parasites of phanerogams. XXIII. Notes on Physoderma. Mycologia 67: 552-568.

5.5-316 Sridhar, T.S., and Ullasa, B.A. 1979. Scab of Ocimum basilicum - a new disease caused by Elsinoe arxii sp. nov from Bangalore. Curr. Sci. 48: 868-869.

5.5-317 Srivastava, H.P., and Mathur, P.K. 1979. Two new leaf spot diseases of Jasminum sambac. Indian Phytopathol. 32: 616-618. RPP 60: 3811.

5.5-318 Srivastava, U.S. 1972. Effect of interaction of factors on wilt of coriander caused by Fusarium oxysporum Schlecht ex. Fr. f. corianderii Kulkarni, Nikam & Joshi. Indian J. Agric. Sci. 42: 618-621. HA 43: 8981.

5.5-319 Srivastava, U.S. 1971. Edaphic factors and wilt of coriander. Indian Phytopathol. 24: 679-683. HA 44: 4948.

5.5-320 Srivastava, U.S., and Sinha, S. 1971. Effect of various soil amendments on the wilt of coriander (Coriandrum sativum L.). Indian J. Agric. Sci. 41: 779-782.

5.5-321 Staib, F. 1971. Plants as a substratum for growth of Cryptococcus nedformans [in German]. Zentralb. Bakteriol. Parasitenkd. Infektionskr. Hyg. Abt. I. Orig. 218{4}: 486-495.

5.5-322 Stefanac, Z. 1977. Onion yellow dwarf virus in Yugoslavia [in Serbo-Croatian]. Acta Bot. Croat. 36: 39-45. RPP 58: 987.

5.5-323 Stoyanov, D., Gandoy, P., and Ortega, J. 1980. Xiphinema basiri, a parasite of Capsicum frutescens in Cuba [in Spanish]. Ciencias de la Agricultura 1980{5}: 163-164. HELM AB-B 50: 549.

5.5-324 Subero, L.J. 1975. Corynespora cassiicola (Berk and Curt) Wei, a new pathogen of sesame (Sesamum indicum) in Venezuela [in Spanish]. Rev. Fac. Agron. Univ. Cent. Venez. 8: 141-144. AGRICOLA.

5.5-325 Sultana, S. 1978. Hirschmanniella orycrena n.sp. and H. oryzae (Nematoda: Tylenchida) from Hyderabad, India. Indian J. Nematol. 8: 174-176. HELM AB-A 49: 971.

5.5-326 Surgucheva, N.A. 1976. Etiology of yellows disease in plants of wild flora. Dokl. Bot. Sci. (Engl. Transl.) 226-228: 3-5. Translation of Dokl. Akad. Nauk SSR 226: 225-226, 1976.

5.5-327 Surgucheva, N.A., and Protsenko, A.E. 1971. Mycoplasma-like corpuscles in cells of mint affected by misgrowing [in Russian]. Dokl. Akad. Nauk SSR 200: 1447-1448. AGRICOLA.

5.5-328 Surico, G., and Iacobellis, N.S. 1978. Pectolytic strains of Pseudomonas fluorescens, Migula biotype C, causing a soft rot of fennel [in Italian]. Phytopathol. Mediterr. 17: 65-68. HA 49: 5250.

5.5-329 Sutabutra, T., and Campbell, R.N. 1971. Strains of celery mosaic virus from parsley and poison hemlock in California. Plant Dis. Rep. 55: 328-332.

5.5-330 Swarup, J., and Mathur, R.S. 1972. Seed microflora of some umbelliferous spices. Indian Phytopathol. 25: 125. RPP 52: 2705.

5.5-331 Tahvonen, R. 1978. Seed-borne fungi on parsley and carrot [in Finnish]. J. Sci. Agric. Soc. Finl. 50: 91-102. AGRICOLA.

5.5-332 Tanaka, S. 1971. Retransmission of Satsuma dwarf virus by means of the approach-graft inoculation. Tamagawa Daigaku Kogakubu Kiyo 11: 99-104. AGRICOLA.

5.5-333 Tarte, R. 1971. Studies on the distribution and populations of nematodes in intensive vegetable orchards [in Spanish]. Turrialba 21: 34-37.

5.5-334 Taylor, J.D., and Dudley, C.L. 1980. Bacterial disease of coriander. Plant Pathol. 29: 117-121. HA 51: 4857.

5.5-335 Taylor, M.B., and Hendry, D.A. 1973. A study of sap-transmissible virus diseases of chicory, Cichorium intybus L., in South Africa. Phytophylactica 5: 143-148. RPP 55: 997.

5.5-336 Teppner, H. 1978. Downy mildew Peronospora stigmaticola - a new for Austria [in German]. Mitt. Naturwiss. Ver. Steiermark 108: 177-178. RPP 58: 1885

5.5-337 Tewari, I. 1974. Ascus cytology in Elsinoe kamatii. Beihefte zur Nova Hedwigia 1974{47}: 607-615. RPP 54: 2925.

5.5-338 Thakur, R.N., Singh, K.P., and Husain, A. 1974. Curvularia leaf spot of Japanese mint in India. Indian J. Mycol. Plant Pathol. 4: 199. HA 46: 11658.

5.5-339 Thakur, R.N. 1973. A new leaf disease of Ocimum basilicum var. purpurescens. Indian J. Mycol. Plant Pathol. 3: 198. AGRICOLA.

5.5-340 Thite, A.N., and Patil, M.S. 1975. Some parasitic fungi from Kolhapur (Maharashtra). Botanique (Nagpur) 6: 109-116.

5.5-341 Thomas, W., and Procter, C.H. 1973. Tobacco ringspot virus in horseradish. N.Z. J. Agric. Res. 16: 233-237.

5.5-342 Timina, O.O., Treskin, N.G., and Samovol, A.P. 1979. Distribution of tobacco mosaic virus and certain other potato viruses in populations of Capsicum L. [in Russian]. Izv. Akad. Nauk Mold. SSR Ser. Biol. Khim. Nauk 1979{1}: 42-45.

5.5-343 Tomlinson, J.A., Webb, M.J.W., and Faithfull, E.M. 1972. Studies on broccoli necrotic yellows virus. Ann. Appl. Biol. 71: 127-134.

5.5-344 Tsalboukov, P.R. 1972. Early prognosis of calamity outbursts of Chloridea (Heliotis) peltigera Schif. in peppermint. An. Acad. Bras. Cienc. 44(Suppl.): 89-90.

5.5-345 Tulegenov, T.A. 1972. Virus disease of onion and garlic in the Alma-Ata region [in Russian]. Izv. Akad. Nauk Kaz. SSR Ser. Biol. 10{3}: 33-38 RPP 52: 944.

5.5-346 Turkoglu, T. 1979. Mosaic virus of opium poppy in Turkey. Journal of Turkish Phytopathology 8: 77-79. RPP 59: 5306.

5.5-347 Twardowicz-Jakusz, A., Kaniewski, W., and Dunajska-Zielinska, L. 1977. Diagnostic studies of horseradish viruses [in Polish]. Zesz. Probl. Postepow Nauk Roln. 195: 173-193.

5.5-348 Upadhyay, D.N., and Bordoloi, D.N. 1975. New records of diseases on cultivated essential oil bearing plants from North-East India. Indian Phytopathol. 28: 532-534. RPP 57: 3553.

5.5-349 Upadhyay, D.N., Bordoloi, D.N., Bhagat, S.D., and Ganguly, D. 1976. Studies on blight disease of Ocimum basilicum L. caused by Cercospora ocimicola Petrak et Ciferri. Herba Hung. 15{1}: 81-86. HA 47: 1846.

5.5-350 Valdivia, M.G. and Oshita, S.N. 1974. Root-knot nematode recorded on garlic in Tacna and Arequipa [in Spanish]. Advances en Investigacion, Peru 3{2/3}: 37. HELM AB 45: 1344.

5.5-351 Van Etten, H.D. 1977. Identification of additional habitats of Nectria haematococca (Fusarium solani) mating population. VI. Proc. Am. Phytopathol. Soc. 4: 96 (Abstr.).

5.5-352 Variar, M., and Pavgi, M.S. 1979. Resistance of germinating zoosporangia of Synchytrium sesamicola to heat and desiccation. Phytopathol. Mediterr. 18: 201-202.

5.5-353 Vasil'eva, T.Ya., and Mozhaeva, K.A. 1977. Properties of a strain of TMV isolated from Allium plants [in Russian]. Tr. Akad. Nauk SSSR, Dal'nevost. Nauchn. Tsentr, Biol.-Pochv. Inst. 1977{46/149}: 75-77. RPP 58: 2052.

5.5-354 Vegh, I., and Benoit, M.A. 1974. On a new species of Curvularia [in French]. Acta Phytopathol. Acad. Sci. Hung. 9: 47-53.

5.5-355 Vegh, I., Bourgeois, M., and Bousquet, J.F. 1973. A rot of witloof chicory roots caused by Phoma exigua var. exigua [in French]. Rev Hortic. 144{2313}: 43-46. HA 43: 8601.

5.5-356 Verhoyen, M. 1973. Chlorotic streak of leeks. II. Note concerning the epidemiology of the virus [in French]. Parasitica 29{1}: 35-40. RAE-A 62: 4868

5.5-357 Verma, V.L. 1979. Effect of sucrose concentration on growth and sporulation of three species of colletotrichum pathogenic on chilies. Indian J. Mycol. Plant Pathol. 9{1}: 130-131.

5.5-358 Vlasov, Iu.I., Larina, E.I., Mkervali, V.G., Babilodze, Ts.I., and Glonti, G.G. 1974. Virus and virus-like diseases and subtropical plants in West Georgia [in Russian]. Subtrop. Kul't. 1974{3}: 144-149.

5.5-359 Voros, J., and Nagy, F. 1972. Cercospora traversiana Sacc., a new destructive pathogen of fenugreek in Hungary. Acta Phytopathol. Acad. Sci. Hung. 7: 71-76.

5.5-360 Vovlas, C., and Roca, F. 1975. Nematode transmission of the agent of chicory chlorotic ringspot virus, a strain of artichoke Italian latent virus [in Italian]. Nematol. Mediterr. 3: 83-90. HA 47: 4493.

5.5-361 Vovlas, C., Martelli, G.P., and Quacquarelli, A. 1971. Virus diseases of market garden plants in Apulia. VI. The chicory ringspot complex [in Italian]. Phytopathol. Mediterr. 10: 244-254.

5.5-362 Vovlas, C. 1973. Seed transmission of Chicory yellow mottle virus [in Italian]. Phytopathol. Mediterr. 12: 104-105.

5.5-363 Vovlas, C., Martelli, G.P., and Quacquarelli, A. 1974. A natural variant of Chicory yellow mottle virus [in Italian]. Phytopathol. Mediterr. 13: 179-181.

5.5-364 Vovlas, C., and Quacquarelli, A. 1975. Virus diseases of vegetable crops in Apulia. XVII. A yellow mosaic of Lettuce induced by Chicory yellow mottle virus [in Italian]. Phytopathol. Mediterr. 14: 144-146.

5.5-365 Walker, J., and McLeod, R.W. 1972. New records of plant diseases in New South Wales, 1970-71. Agric. Gaz. NSW 83: 176-179. RPP 52: 663.

5.5-366 Wani, D.D., and Thirumalachar, M.J. 1975. Studies on Elsinoe and Sphaceloma diseases of plants from Maharashtra State (India) Nova Hedwigia 26: 309-315. RPP 55: 3074.

5.5-367 Was, M., and Chrzanowska, M. 1971. Short communication about tobacco mosaic virus detection in plantain (Plantago maior L.) [in Polish]. Biul. Inst. Ziemniaka 8: 49-54. AGRICOLA.

5.5-368 Waterworth, H.E. 1975. Purification of arabis mosaic virus isolated from a jasmine plant introduction. Phytopathology 65: 927-928.

5.5-369 Waterworth, H.E. 1971. Physical properties and host ranges of viruses latent in and mechanically transmitted from jasmine. Phytopathology 61: 228-230.

5.5-370 Werner, A., and Krzan, Z. 1979. Etiology of Puccinia porri (Sow.) winter and behaviour of its urediniospores on poplar leaves. Arbor. Kornickie 24: 201-207. AGRICOLA.

5.5-371 Wheeler, J.E., and Boyle, A.M. 1971. Identificaiton of four Phytophthora isolates previously unreported from Arizona. Phytopathology 61: 1293-1296.

5.5-372 Whipps, J.M., and Cooke, R.C. 1978. Interactions of species of Compositae with Albugo tragopogonis from Senecio squalidus. Trans. Br. Mycol. Soc. 70: 389-392.

5.5-373 Wijs, J.J. de. 1973. Pepper veinal mottle virus in Ivory Coast. Neth. J. Plant Pathol. 79: 189-193.

5.5-374 Wilkie, J.P., Dye, D.W., and Watson, D.R.W. 1973. Further hosts of Pseudomonas viridiflava. N.Z. J. Agric. Res. 16: 315-323.

5.5-375 Wolf, P. 1972. Virus diseases of dill, Anethum graveolens [in German]. Acta Phytopathol. Acad. Sci. Hung. 7: 209-211. HA 43: 8976.

5.5-376 Wolf, P., and Schmelzer, K. 1972. Investigations on virus diseases of umbelliferous plants [in German]. Zentralbl. Bakteriol. Parasitenkd. Infektionskr. Hyg. Abt. 2 127: 665-672. HA 43: 6781.

5.5-377 Wu, W.-S. 1977. Sclerotial disease of garlic in Taiwan. Chih Wu Pao Hu Hsueh Hui Hui K'an 19: 47-54. RPP 57: 889.

5.5-378 Yang, I.L. 1972. The occurrence of sesame witches broom in Taiwan [in Chinese]. Chung-Hua Chih Wu Pao Hu Hsueh Huui 14{2}: 58-64. AGRICOLA.

5.5-379 Zakaullah, and Perveen, S. 1979. Diseases of sesame. Pak. J. For. 29: 35-46.

5.5-380 Zhivkov, D., and Baicheva, O. 1973. On the nematode fauna of Mentha piperita and Lavandula vera in the Karlovo area [in Bulgarian]. Izv. Tsentr. Khelmintol. Lab. Bulg. Akad. Nauk 16: 73-79. HELM AB-B 43: 603.

5.5-381 Zinkernagel, V., and Krober, H. 1978. Stem rot caused in Gaultheria procumbens L. by Phytophthora cinnamomi Rands [in German]. Nachrichtenbl. Dtsch. Pflanzenschutzdienstes (Braunschweig) 30: 181-183.

5.6 Plant Injury and Crop Losses

5.6-1 Abraham, E.V., Natarajan, K., and Murugesan, M. 1977. Damage by pests and phyllody to Sesamum indicum in relation to the time of sowing. Madras Agric. J. 64: 298-301.

5.6-2 Abul-Nasr, S.E., Assem, M.A., and El-Sherif, A.R.A. 1974. Rates of infestation of the main insects attacking stored garlic bulbs. Bull. Soc. Entomol. Egypte 58: 31-34. RAE-A 64: 3780.

5.6-3 Ambika, S.R., and Jayachandra. 1980. Suppression of plantation crops by Eupatorium weed. Curr. Sci. 49: 874-875.

5.6-4 Baker, F.C., Brooks, C.J.W., and Hutchinson, S.A. 1975. Biosynthesis of capsidiol in sweet peppers (Capsicum frutescens) infected with fungi: evidence for methyl group migration from 13C nuclear magnetic resonance spectroscopy. Chem. Commun. 1975{8}: 293-294.

5.6-5 Bakhetia, D.R.C., and Sandhu, R.S. 1973. Differential response of Brassica species/varieties to the aphid (Lipaphis erysimi Kalt.) infestation. J. Res., Punjab Agric. Univ. 10: 272-279. RAE-A 64: 348.

5.6-6 Bergeson, G.B., and Green, R.J., Jr. 1979. Damage to cultivars of peppermint, Mentha piperita, by the lesion nematode Pratylenchus penetrans in Indiana. Plant Dis. Rep. 63: 91-94.

5.6-7 Bergquist, R.R., and Lorbeer, J.W. 1971. Reaction of Allium spp. and Allium cepa to botryotinia (Botrytis squamosa). Plant Dis. Rep. 55: 394-398.

5.6-8 Berry, R.E., and Shields, E.J. 1980. Variegated cutworm: leaf consumption and economic loss in peppermint. J. Econ. Entomol. 73: 607-608.

5.6-9 Bhardwaj, A.K., and Thakus, J.R. 1974. Ephestia cautella (Walker) (Phycitidae: Lepidotera) infesting stored garlic (Allium sativum) Curr. Sci. 43: 419-420. HA 45: 3927.

5.6-10 Bhardwaj, S.D., Katoch, P.C., Kaushal, A.N., and Gupta, R. 1980. Effect of blight caused by Rhizoctonia solani Kuhn. on herb yield and oil content of some important collection of Mentha species. Indian J. For. 3: 272-274.

5.6-11 Bleve Zacheo, T., Zacheo, G., and Lamberti, F. 1977. Histological and histochemical reactions induced by Longidorus apulus in celery and chicory roots [in Italian]. Nematol. Mediterr. 5: 85-92. HELM AB-B 47: 608.

5.6-12 Budai, C. 1977. Damage of the nematode Ditylenchus dipsaci (Kuhn) Filipjev in the onion producing area of Hungary (Mako) [in Hungarian] Novenyvedelem (Budapest) 13: 1-4. HELM AB-B 48: 678.

5.6-13 Budai, C.S. 1979. Spread of, and damage caused by the root knot nematode, Meloidogyne hapla Chitwood in the red pepper growing area of Szeged. Acta Phytopathol. Acad. Sci. Hung. 14: 543-548.

5.6-14 Camargo, I.J.B., Kitajima, E.W., and Costa, A.S. 1971. Electron microscopy of cytoplasmic inclusion and cell modification associated with carrot mosaic virus [in Portuguese]. Bragantia 30: 31-37.

5.6-15 Cardoso do Vale, J., and Proenca da Cunha, A. 1974. Chemical constitution of an essential oil of peppermint parasitized by Eriophyes menthes [in Portuguese]. Bol. Fac. Farm. Univ. Coimbra Ed. Cient. 34: 62-78. CA 83: 120641.

5.6-16 Ciampolini, M. 1978. Severe damage to market-garden crops in Puglia by Otiorrhynchus cribricollis Gyll. [in Italian]. Entomologica (Bari) 14: 55-62. RAE-A 68: 992.

5.6-17 Cimino, A., Brigati, S., and Bertolini, P. 1979. Susceptibility of fennel to bacterial infections in relation to methods of preservation [in Italian]. Fruitticoltura 41: 71-73. Bib.Ag. 44: 67731.

5.6-18 Cohn, E. 1976. Cellular changes induced in roots by two species of the genus Rotylenchulus. Nematologica 22: 169-172.

5.6-19 Cordrey, T.D., and Bergman, E.L. 1979. Influence of cucumber mosaic virus on growth and elemental composition of susceptible (Capsicum annuum L.) and resistant (Capsicum frutescens L.) peppers. J. Am. Soc. Hortic. Sci. 104: 505-510.

5.6-20 Dotsenko, V.D., and Sharonova, M.V. 1972. Effect of insecticides on the quantity and quality of essential oil [in Russian]. Maslo-Zhir. Prom. 1972{6}: 28-29. CA 77: 122975.

5.6-21 Dube, H.C., and Gour, H.N. 1975. The nature of pectic enzymes produced by Phytophithora parasitica var. sesami in two culture media. Curr. Sci. 44: 134-135.

5.6-22 Dzhashi, V.S., Nikolaishvili, A.A., and Bakanidze, M.Sh. 1977. The results of studies on some physiological and biochemical processes in laurel leaves damaged by Ceroplastes japonicus and treated with pesticides [in Russian]. Subtrop. Kul't. 1977{1/2}: 121-123. HA 48: 8501.

5.6-23 Eijsinga, J.P.N.L.R. van. 1973. Bitter pit, a new quality problem in red peppers [in Dutch]. Bedrijfsontwikkeling 4: 733-734. AGRICOLA.

5.6-24 Elliott, W.M., McClanahan, R.J., and Founk, J. 1978. A method of detecting oviposition in European corn borer moths, Ostrinia nubilalis (Lepidoptera: Pyralidae), and its relation to subsequent larval damage to peppers. Can. Entomol. 110: 487-493.

5.6-25 Felklova, M., and Plackova, V. 1976. Anatomic-physiological studies on Mentha piperita L. after an attack of Puccinia menthae Pers. Acta Fac. Pharm. Univ. Comenianae 29: 117-144.

5.6-26 Ferenc, N. 1971. Results of phytophylacological investigations related to the injury of coriander [in Hungarian]. Herba Hung. 10{1}: 37-46.

5.6-27 Francesconi, A. 1973. The rotting of bulbs of Crocus sativus L. by Penicillium cyclopium Westling. Ann. Bot. (Rome) 32: 63-70. AGRICOLA.

5.6-28 Gaikwad, S.J., Sabley, J.E., and Buldeo, A.N. 1977. Reaction of some sesame (Sesamum indicum L.) varieties to powdery mildew disease at Nagpur resistance. J. Maharashtra Agric. Univ. 2: 170-171. AGRICOLA.

5.6-29 Gemawat, P.D., and Prasad, N. 1972. Alternaria blight of Cuminum cyminum L. Physiology of pathogenesis. Proc. Indian Nat. Sci. Acad. Part B. 38: 38-43.

5.6-30 Giannotti, J., Giannotti, D., and Vago, C. 1980. Intracellular growth and pathogenicity of plant mollicutes in nonvector insects [in French]. C.R. Hebd. Seances Acad. Sci. Ser. D 290: 417-419.

5.6-31 Giunchedi, L. 1972. Pitting of red pepper caused by nasturtium ringspot virus (NRSV) [in Italian]. Inf. Fitopatol. 22{4}: 3-8. AGRICOLA.

5.6-32 Grewal, A.S., and Grower, R.K. 1973. Reaction of red pepper (Capsicum frutescens) varieties to Colletotrichum peperatum. Indian J. Mycol. Plant Pathol. 3: 100-101. AGRICOLA.

5.6-33 Gupta, R.N. 1975. Mineral matter content in coriander leaves and fruits as influenced by stem-gall disease. Indian Phytopathol. 28{1}: 136-137.

5.6-34 Guseinova, B.F. 1974. Septoria infection of bundles of vegetable greens in Azerbaijan [in Russian]. Izv. Akad. Nauk. Az. SSR Ser. Biol. Nauk 1974{1}: 48-50. AGRICOLA.

5.6-35 Havranek, P. 1974. Effect of virus diseases on garlic yield [in Czech]. Sb. UVTI (Ustav Vedeckotechnickych Informaci) Ochrana Rostlin 10: 251-256. RPP 54: 5176.

5.6-36 Horner, C.E. 1971. Rhizome and stem rot of peppermint caused by Phoma strasseri. Plant Dis. Rep. 55: 814-816.

5.6-37 Imoto, M. 1975. Studies on mosaic disease of sweet pepper (Capsicum frutescens L.). 3. The relationships between reduction in crop yield and infection period caused by mosaic virus [in Japanese]. Hiroshima-kenritsu Nogyo Shikenjo Hokoku 36: 67-72. AGRICOLA.

5.6-38 Joergensen, J. 1976. Occurrence and causes of seed discoloration in commercial seed lots of white mustard (Sinapis alba). Acta Agric. Scand. 26: 109-115.

5.6-39 Jones, D.R., Graham, W.G., and Ward, E.W.B. 1974. Ultrastructural changes in pepper cells in a compatible interaction with Phytophthora capsici. Phytopathology 64: 1084-1090.

5.6-40 Jones, D.R., Graham, W.G., and Ward, E.W.B. 1975. Ultrastructural changes in pepper cells in an incompatible interaction with Phytophthora infestans. Phytopathology 65: 1274-1285.

5.6-41 Jones, D.R., Graham, W.G., and Ward, E.W.B. 1975. Ultrastructural changes in pepper cells in interactions with Phytophthora capsici (isolate 18) and Monilinia fructicola. Phytopathology 65: 1409-1417.

5.6-42 Kannwischer, M.E., Mitchell, D.J., and Strandberg, J.O. 1977. The quantitative relationship of Phytophthora cryptogea zoospores to infection and mortality of watercress. Proc. Am. Phytopathol. Soc. 4: 99 (Abstr.).

5.6-43 Knaub, V. Ya', Mel'nik, M.V., and Lisetskaya, L.F. 1974. The distribution and pathogenicity of Ditylenchus dipsaci on garlic in Moldavia [in Russian]. Parazity Zhivotn. Rast. 1974{10}: 133-138. HELM AB 46: 777.

5.6-44 Kowalski, J., and Strzelecka, H. 1971. Investigation on changes in complex of cardiac glycosides under the influence of fungi parasitizing on foxgloves. Part I. Phyllosticta digitalis--preliminary investigations. Acta. Pol. Pharm. (Engl. Transl.) 28: 405-412.

5.6-45 Kowalski, J., and Strzelecka, H. 1971. Investigation on changes in complex of cardiac glycosides under the influence of fungi parasitizing on foxgloves. II. Phyllosticta digitalis - transformation of lanatoside C. Acta Pol. Pharm. (Engl. Transl.) 28: 635-641.

5.6-46 Kranz, J. 1975. Relationships between leaf mass and disease progress in foliar diseases [in German]. Z. Pflanzenkr. Pflanzenschutz 82: 641-654.

5.6-47 Lamptey, P.N.L., and Bonsi, C. 1977. The effects of pepper veinal mosaic virus in relation to time of inoculation of the symptom expression, flower initiation and yield of pepper (Capsicum frutescens L.). Acta Hortic. 53: 227-234.

5.6-48 Lecomte, C. 1976. First observations on the biology and damage caused by the leek tineid Acrolepiopsis (Acrolepia) assectella Zeller (Microlepidoptera Plutellidae) on the coast of Algeria [in French]. Bull. Soc. Hist. Nat. Afr. Nord 67{3/4}: 49-56. RAE-A 67: 2353.

5.6-49 Leiber, E. 1977. Entyloma infection of Borago officinalis, an economic problem [in German]. Gemuse 13: 105-106. AGRICOLA.

5.6-50 Malaguti, G. 1971. Severe bacterial leaf spot incidence in sesame of Venezuela [in Spanish]. Agron. Trop. (Maracay, Venez.) 21: 333-336. AGRICOLA.

5.6-51 Mel'nik, M.V. 1976. Decreases in carbohydrate content of garlic and onion tissue caused by Ditylenchus dipsaci [in Russian]. Izv. Akad. Nauk Mold. SSR Ser. Biol. Nauk 1976{6}: 66-68. HELM AB-B 48: 225.

5.6-52 Melouk, H.A., and Horner, C.E. 1972. Production of pectolytic and macerating enzyme by Phoma strasseri. Can. J. Microbiol. 18: 1065-1072.

5.6-53 Melouk, H.A., and Horner, C.E. 1972. Beta-glucosidase from Phoma strasseri. Phytopathology 62: 1104 (Abstr.).

5.6-54 Misra, A., and Jha, A. 1972. Changes in protein and carbohydrate content of mosaic virus infected chilli plants. Indian J. Plant Physiol. 15: 56-58. HA 45: 3248.

5.6-55 Mitchell, D.J., Kannwischer, M.E., and Moore, E.S. 1978. Relationship of numbers of zoospores of Phytophthora cryptogea to infection and mortality of watercress. Phytopathology 68: 1446-1448.

5.6-56 Miura-Nozu, M., and Yamamoto, M. 1971. Ultrastructure of rust tissue of Plantago major caused by Puccinia miscanthia. Shimane Daigaku Nogakubu Kenkyu Hokoku 1971{5}: 23-27.

5.6-57 Mlodzianowski, F. 1975. Cytoplasmic inclusions in yellowing parsley leaves. Acta Soc. Bot. Pol. 44: 449-450. HA 46: 10587.

5.6-58 Mraz, F. 1979. The dynamics of flowering in poppy (Papaver somniferum L.) in relation to capsule infection by Helminthosporium papaveris Hennig and weather conditions [in Czech]. Rostl. Vyroba 25: 545-550. FCA 34: 2249.

5.6-59 Murant, A.F., and Roberts, I.M. 1971. Cylindrical inclusions in coriander leaf cells infected with parsnip mosaic virus. J. Gen. Virol. 10: 65-70.

5.6-60 Murant, A.F., Roberts, I.M., and Hutcheson, A.M. 1975. Effects of parsnip yellow fleck virus on plant cells. J. Gen. Virol. 26: 277-285.

5.6-61 Murant, A.F., and Roberts, I.M. 1977. Virus-like particles in phloem tissue of chervil (Anthriscus cerefolium) infected with Anthriscus yellows virus. Ann. Appl. Biol. 85: 403-406.

5.6-62 Murant, A.F., and Roberts, I.M. 1979. Virus-like particles in phloem tissue of chervil (Anthriscus cerefolium) infected with carrot red leaf virus. Ann. Appl. Biol. 92: 343-346.

5.6-63 Nagy, F. 1971. Results of phytophylacological investigations related to the injury of coriander (Coriandrum sativum L.) [in Hungarian]. Herba Hung. 10{1}: 37-46. AGRICOLA.

5.6-64 Naqvi, S.A.M.H., and Gupta, R.N. 1980. Changes in the phenolic contents of coriander infected with Protomyces macrosporus Unger. Acta Bot. Indica 8: 268-269.

5.6-65 Nath, D.K., and Saha, G.N. 1974. Effect of infestation of Lipaphis erysimi (Kaltb.) (Aphididae, Homoptera) on qualitative and quantitative characters of seeds of mustard (Brassica juncea Coss.). Curr.Sci. 43: 448-449. RAE-A 64: 3080.

5.6-66 Neubauer, S., Klimes, K., and Kral, J. 1975. The harmfulness of Eupteryx atropunctata on Roman chamomile [in Czech]. Nase Liecive Rastliny 12: 108-109. HA 46: 2529.

5.6-67 Ohta, Y., and Chuong, P. Van. 1975. Hereditary changes in Capsicum annuum L. II. Induced by virus-inoculated grafting. Euphytica 24: 605-611.

5.6-68 Passama, L., Hamze, M., and Wacquant, J.-P. 1973. Compared behavior of two calcicolous and two calcifugous species on humus rich acid soil with or without liming. Oecol. Plant. 8: 1-16.

5.6-69 Pavgi, M.S., and Mukhopadhyay, A.N. 1972. Development of coriander fruit infected by Protomyces macrosporus Unger. Cytologia 37: 619-627 RPP 52: 2706.

5.6-70 Putnam, L.G. 1977. Response of four brassica seed crop species to attack by the crucifer flea beetle, Phyllotreta cruciferae. Can. J. Plant Sci. 57: 987-989.

5.6-71 Rabbani, G.M., and Mehrotra, B.S. 1978. Fungal infestation of marketed spices in India I. Coriander. Nat. Acad. Sci. Lett. (India) 1: 317-318. RPP 60: 426.

5.6-72 Radewald, J.D., Shibuya, F., Nelson, J., Brendler, R.A., and Vilchez, M. 1972 The influence of the root-knot nematode, Meloidogyne incognita, on parsley yields under controlled greenhouse conditions. Calif. Agric. 26{8}: 6-8. AGRICOLA.

5.6-73 Rai, J.N., and Dhawan, S. 1976. Studies on purification and identification of toxic metabolite produced by Sclerotinia sclerotiorum causing white rot disease of crucifers. Indian Phytopathol. 29: 407-411. RPP 57: 4672.

5.6-74 Rao, R.D.V.J.P., Yaraguntaiah, R.C., and Govindu, H.C. 1980. Reaction of chilli (Capsicum spp.) cultures (hybrids), varieties and species to six chilli mosaic viruses. Mysore J. Agric. Sci. 14: 11-14. HA 50: 7802.

5.6-75 Rathaiah, Y., and Pavgi, M.S. 1977. Development of sclerotia and spermogonia in Cercospora sesamicola and Ramularia catharmi. Sydowia 30: 148-153.

5.6-76 Sarwar, M. 1973. Impact of fusarium wilt on the production of geranium oil. Indian Perfum. 17{2}: 52-53. HA 46: 9622.

5.6-77 Savenko, L.O. 1978. Effect of favourable conditions on diseases and yield of coriander [in Ukrainian]. Zakhist Rosl. 1978{25}: 81-85. RPP 58: 1880.

5.6-78 Scalopi, E.J., Vasconcellos, E.F.C., and Nakano, O. 1971. The symptoms of mite attack on garlic varieties [in Portuguese]. Solo 63{1}: 37-38. HA 43: 3757.

5.6-79 Sehgal, S.P., and Agrawat, J.M. 1971. Drooping of fennel (Foeniculum vulgare) due to Sclerotinia sclerotiiorum. Indian Phytopathol. 24: 608-609. AGRICOLA.

5.6-80 Sekhawat, P.S., and Kothuri, K.L. 1971. Amino acid composition of healthy and downy mildewed plants of opium poppy (Papaver somniferum). Indian Phytopathol. 24: 403-405. AGRICOLA.

5.6-81 Shukla, B.N., Chand, J.N., and Kulkarni, S.N. 1975. Effect of leaf age on the bacterial blight of Sesamum. Indian Phytopathol. 28: 304-305.

5.6-82 Singhvi, S.M., Verma, N.D., and Yadava, T.P. 1973. Estimation of losses in rapeseed (Brassica campestris L. var. toria) and mustard (Brassica juncea Coss.) due to mustard aphid (Lipaphis erysimi Kalt.). Haryana Agric. Univ. J. Res. 3: 5-7. RAE-A 63: 4799.

5.6-83 Singh, B.P., Shukla, B.N., Kaushal, P.K., and Shrivas, S.R. 1980. Reaction of sesame germ plasm to Cercospora leaf spot. JNKVV Res. J. 10: 372-373.

5.6-84 Singh, D., Mathur, S.B., and Neergaard, P. 1980. Histological studies of Alternaria sesamicola penetration in sesame seed. Seed Sci. Technol. 8: 85-93. AGRICOLA.

5.6-85 Singh, J., and Thakur, M.R. 1979. Reaction of some hot pepper (Capsicum annuum) lines to cucumber mosaic virus. Indian J. Mycol. Plant Pathol. 9: 276.

5.6-86 Singh, T., and Singh, D. 1980. Anatomy of penetration of Macrophomina phaseoli in seeds of sesame. Pages 603-606 in S.S. Bir, ed. Recent researches in plant sciences. Kalyani Pub., New Delhi, India, 1980.

5.6-87 Srivastava, J.N., and Chauhan, S.V.S. 1980. Developmental changes in Coriandrum sativum L. anthers of plants infected by Protomyces macrosporous Ung. Curr. Sci. 49: 909-911.

5.6-88 Swarup, J., and Tandon, I.N. 1971. Effect of microorganisms on the germination of seed of Umbeliiferous species stored at different temperatures and relative humidities. Indian Phytopathol. 24: 615-616.

5.6-89 Tarabeih, A.M., and Abou-el-Fadl, I.A. 1979. Effect of Sclerotinia sclerotiorum on the volatile oil content of some medicinal plants. Acta Phytopathol. Acad. Sci. Hung. 14: 31-35. HA 50: 8429.

5.6-90 Toit, J.J. du, and Ingamells, C.J. 1972. Stubby root of chicory induced by Fusarium oxysporum. Photophylactica 4: 101-104.

5.6-91 Vajavat, R., and Chakravarti, B.P. 1977. Yield losses due to bacterial leaf spot of Sesamum orientale in Rajasthan. Indian J. Mycol. Plant Pathol. 7: 97-98.

5.6-92 Verma, A.C., and Yadav, B.S. 1975. Occurrence of Heterodera cajani in Rajasthan and susceptibility of certain sesame varieties. Indian J. Nematol. 5: 235-237.

5.6-93 Vito, M. di, and Saccardo, F. 1978. Response of lines and varieties of Capsicum spp. to Meloidogyne incognita in the glasshouse [in Italian]. Nematol. Mediterr. 6: 83-88. HELM AB-B 48: 673.

5.6-94 Wightman, J.A., and Morrison, G. 1978. Wireworms (Coleoptera: Elateridae) associated with damaged onions and garlic crops near Blenhein. N.Z. Entomol. 6: 438-441. RAE-A 67: 1981.

5.7 Plant Protection and Disease Control

5.7-1 Abd El-Ghany, A.K., Mahmoud, B.K., Seoud, M.B., El Alfy, K.A., Azab, M.W., and Abd El Gawwad, M.A. 1974. Tests with different varieties and strains of sesame for resistance to root rot wilt disease. Agric. Res. Rev. 52{2}: 75-84.

5.7-2 Abraham, E.V., Natarajan, K., and Jayaraj, S. 1977. Investigations on the insecticidal control of the phyllody disease of Sesamum. Madras Agric. J. 64: 379-383.

5.7-3 Alan, M.N., and Katsitadze, M.G. 1974. The effectiveness of Amiphos and Cyanox against pests of sub-tropical crops [in Russian]. Khim. Sel'sk. Khoz. 12{2}: 42. HA 45: 12166.

5.7-4 Al-Beldawi, A.S., Shaik Raddy, H.M., and Al-Hashimi, M.H. 1973.

Studies on the control of charcoal rot of sesame with benomyl. Phytopathol. Mediterr. 12: 83-86.

5.7-5 Anahosur, K.H., Fazalnoor, K., and Narayanaswamy, B.C. 1972. Control of seed mycoflora of fennel (Foeniculum vulgare Mill.). Indian J. Agric. Sci. 42: 990-992. HA 44: 2691.

5.7-6 Anonymous. 1972. The control of garlic and onion mites [in Spanish]. Not. Agric. 6{13}: 51. HA 43: 228.

5.7-7 Anonymous. 1972. The control of garlic and onion leaf borer [in Spanish]. Not. Agric. 6{14}: 53. HA 43: 5298.

5.7-8 Anonymous. 1974. Summer control of onion thrips [in Spanish]. Not. Agric. 7{1}: 1-2. HA 44: 8658.

5.7-9 Asthana, K.S., and Das, S.R. 1976. Varietal evaluation of rape-mustard to aphids (Lipaphis erysimi Kalt.). Proc. Bihar Acad. Agric. Sci. 24: 184-186. PBA 48: 11923.

5.7-10 Avdyshev, Sh.E., and Popov, P.F. 1974. Phylloxera and root parsley [in Russian]. Sadovod. Vinograd. Vinodel. Mold. 29: 56-57. HA 45: 5766.

5.7-11 Azam, M.F., Khan, A.M., and Saxena, S.K. 1978. Efficacy of certain nematicides for the control of plant parasitic nematodes around chilli and okra. Indian J. Mycol. Plant Pathol. 8: 65. HELM AB-B 49: 1836.

5.7-12 Baresi, F. 1976. A short guide for the control of pests of crops grown under glass [in Italian]. Informatore Agrario 32: 23637-23646. HA 47: 5460.

5.7-13 Barrios, E.P., Mosokar, H.I., and Black, L.L. 1971. Inheritance of resistance to tobacco etch and cucumber mosaic viruses in Capsicum frutescens. Phytopathology 61: 1318.

5.7-15 Basha, A.A., and Balasubramanian, M. 1980. New chemicals for the control of green peach aphid, Myzus persicae Sulz. on chillies. Pesticides 14{5}: 12-13, 20. RAE-A 69: 3203.

5.7-14 Bassino, J.P., and Blanc, M. 1975. Control of lavender and lavandin leaf midge [in French]. Def. Veg. 29{175}: 172, 174-182. HA 46: 7038.

5.7-16 Bazarbekov, K.U. 1971. The use of nematicides for the control of the onion stem nematode in the irrigation areas of south-eastern Kazakhstan [in Russian]. Vestn. S-kh. Nauki (Alma-Ata) 1971{6}: 100-103. HELM AB-B 45: 734.

5.7-17 Beglyarov, G.A., and Ushchekov, A.T. 1977. Biological control of aphids on green crops [in Russian]. Zashch. Rast. 1977{2}: 25-27. RAE-A 65: 6941.

5.7-18 Berry, R. 1980. Biology and management of insects on mint. Proc. Annu. Meet. Oreg. Essent. Oil Grow. League 31: 36-41.

5.7-19 Berry, R.E. 1973. Control of insect pests on peppermint. Proc. Oreg. Essent. Oil Growers League 24: 43-66.

5.7-20 Berry, R.E. 1975. Redbacked cutworm control on peppermint with leptophos. J. Econ. Entomol. 68: 411-412.

5.7-21 Berry, R.E. 1975. Biology and control of insect pests on peppermint in Oregon, 1973-1974. Proc. Annu. Meet. Oreg. Essent. Oil Grow. League 26: 16-35.

5.7-22 Bhargava, P.D., Mathur, S.C., Vyas, H.K., and Anwer, M. 1971. Note on screening fennel (Foeniculum vulgare L.) varieties against aphid (Hyadaphis coriandri (Das) Vagrants) infestation. Indian J. Agric. Sci. 41: 90-92. RAE-A 62: 3148.

5.7-23 Bindra, O.S., and Singh, J. 1971. Biological observations on the white-grub, Lachnosterna (Holotrichia) consanguina Blanchard (Coleoptera: Scarabeidae) and the relative efficacy of different insecticides against the adults. Indian J. Entomol. 33: 225-227. RAE-A 62: 4189.

5.7-24 Bogarada, A.P. 1973. Chemicals for the control of powdery mildew on new medicinal crop plants [in Russian]. Khim. Sel'sk. Khoz. 11{11}: 35-36. HA 44: 6011.

5.7-25 Boize, L., Gudin, C., and Purdue, G. 1976. The influence of leaf surface roughness on the spreading of oil spray drops. Ann. Appl. Biol. 84: 205-211.

5.7-26 Borisoglebskaya, M.S. 1979. Necessity of protecting decorative plants as well [in Russian]. Zashch. Rast. 1979{7}: 61. RAE-A 68: 1556.

5.7-27 Boxtel, W. van, and Lenteren, J.C. van. 1978. Determination of host-plant quality of eggplant (Solanum melongena L.), cucumber (Cucumis sativus L.), tomato (Lycopersicon esculentum L.), and paprika (Capsicum annuum L.) for the greenhouse whitefly (Trialeurodes vaporariorum (Westwood) (Homoptera: Aleyrodidae). Meded. Fac. Rijks. Univ. Landbouwet. 43{1}: 397-408. AGRICOLA.

5.7-28 Brar, K.S., and Sandhu, G.S. 1974. Control of mustard aphid, Lipaphis erysimi (Kalt). Pesticides 8{10}: 30. FCA 30: 2349.

5.7-29 Brar, K.S., and Sandhu, G.S. 1975. Comparison of methods of application for soil systemic granulates for the control of mustard aphid. Sci. Cult. 41: 229-230.

5.7-30 Bravenboer, L. 1975. Problems in biological control of pests in glasshouses [in German]. Z. Angew. Entomol. 77: 390-391.

5.7-31 Bridge, J. 1975. Hot water treatment to control plant parasitic nematodes of tropical crops. Meded. Fac. Landbouwwet. Rijksuniv. Gent 40: 249-259. HA 46: 10973.

5.7-32 Brzeski, M.W., and Kotlinski, S. 1975. Control of stem nematode (Ditylenchus dipsaci) on garlic [in Polish]. Rocz. Nauk Roln. Ser. E. Ochr. Rosl. 5: 17-21. HELM AB-B 45: 306.

5.7-33 Butani, D.K., and Verma, S. 1976. Insect pests of vegetables and their control: onion and garlic. Pesticides 10{11}: 33-35. HA 48: 4484.

5.7-34 Butcher, D.N., Searle, L.M., and Monsdale, D.M.A. 1976. The role of glucosinolates in the club root disease of the Cruciferae. Meded. Fac. Landbouwwet. Rijksuniv. Gent 41: 525-532. HA 47: 5461.

5.7-35 Cassini, R., Cassini, R., Alabouvette, C., Rouxel, F., Bonnel, L., Bremeersch, P., and Casenave, J.G. 1971. Soil disinfection with methyl bromide. Effect on plant losses in parsley, celery, cucumber and melon [in French]. Phytiatr. Phytopharm. 20: 215-231. HA 44: 2567.

5.7-36 Caveness, F.E., and Badra, T. 1980. Control of Helicotylenchus multicinctus and Meloidogyne javanica in established plantain and nematode survival as influenced by rainfall. Nematropica 10: 10-14. AGRICOLA.

5.7-37 Chadha, S.S. 1977. Use of neem (Azadirachta indica A. Juss.) seed as a feeding inhibitor against Antigastra catalaunalis Dupon. (Lepidoptera: Pyralidae) a sesame (Sesamum indicum L.) pest in Nigeria. East Afr. Agric. For. J. 42: 257-262.

5.7-38 Chadha, S.S. 1976. Some observations on the control of sesame gall midge (Asphondylia sesami Felt; Diptera; Cecidomyiidae) by cultural and chemical means. Samaru Res. Bull. 1976{262}: 83-97.

5.7-39 Chakravarti, B.P., Shekhawat, P.S., and Anilkumar, T.B. 1973. Control of damping off and root rot of sesame (Sesamum orientale) caused by Thielavia terricola var. minor by soil drenching with fungicides and antibiotics and their efficacy in treatment of seeds. Indian Phytopathol. 26: 646-649.

5.7-40 Chandra, K.J., Sastry, K.S., and Rao, J.V.R.B. 1979. Screening of Jasminum species against yellow ring mosaic virus. Curr. Sci. 48: 77-78.

5.7-41 Chang, L.C. 1972. Soil treatment with granular insecticides against stone leek leafminer, Phytobia cepae Hering [in Chinese]. Nung Yeh Yen Chiu 21: 203-208. RAE-A 64: 379.

5.7-42 Chaudhary, R., and Roy, C.S. 1975. Evaluation and economics of some insecticides for the control of mustard aphid Lipaphis erysimi Kalt. on rai (Brassica juncea Linn.). Indian J. Entomol. 37: 264-268. RAE-A 66: 3200.

5.7-43 Chauhan, M.S., and Duhan, J.C. 1977. Efficacy of some systemic and non-systemic fungicidal compounds to control anthracnose and ripe fruit rot of chillies. Pesticides 11{12}: 17-18.

5.7-44 Choi, H.J., and Chung, H.S. 1971. Effects of fungicidal drenches on damping-off organisms in ginseng seed bed and yield of seedling root. Hanguk Sikmul Poho Hakhoe Chi 10{1}: 7-12. HA 43: 3052.

5.7-45 Chumak, V.A. 1975. Leafhoppers on catnip and measures of controlling them [in Russian]. Tr. Vses. Nauchno-Issled. Inst. Efirnomaslichn. Kul't. 8: 161-164.

5.7-46 Cinar, A., and Bicici, M. 1977. Control of Phytophthora capsici Leonian on red peppers. J. Turk. Phytopathol. 6: 119-124.

5.7-47 Coninck, B., Bourdin, J., Vegh, I., and Bourgeois, M. 1975. Preliminary observations on a new disease of heads of witloof chicory

(Cichorium intybus). Symptoms, role of Rhizoctonia solani and fungicide trials [in French]. Pepinier. Hortic. Maraichers 1975{154}: 17-21. HA 45: 7322.

5.7-48 Cruz, B.P.B., Teranishi, J., Bernardi, J.B., and Silveira, S.G.P. da. 1973. White rot of garlic: behaviour of varieties [in Portuguese]. Biologico 39: 151-157. HA 44: 3984.

5.7-49 Daftari, L.N., and Verma, O.P. 1973. Effect of aurefoungin on seedling mortality and growth of two varieties of sesame with seed-borne infection of Fusarium solvani. Hind. Antibiot. Bull. 15: 91-92.

5.7-50 Daftari, L.N., and Verma, O.P. 1972. Control of seed borne infection of Macrophomina phaseoli (Sclerotium bataticola) on Sesamum seeds. Bull. Grain Technol. 10{1}: 44-46. AGRICOLA.

5.7-51 Daniel, G.H. 1972. Pest control trials in commercial crops of brown mustard. Int. Pest Control 14{3}: 6-10.

5.7-52 Delwiche, P.A., and Williams, P.H. 1974. Resistance to Albugo candida race 2 in Brassica sp. Proc. Am. Phytopathol. Soc. 1974{1}: 66 (Abstr.). PBA 46: 3843.

5.7-53 Doraswamy, K., and Sundaram, M. 1978. A new disease resistant variety of geranium. Indian Perfum. 22: 43-45. CA 90: 92240.

5.7-54 Drozdovskaya, L.S., and Nosyrev, V.I. 1978. Use of seed disinfectants in medicinal plant growing. Pharm. Chem. J. (Engl. Transl.) 12: 500-503. Translation of Khim.-Farm. Zh. 12{4}: 87-91, 1978.

5.7-55 Durbin, R.D., and Uchytil, T.F. 1971. The role of allicin in the resistance of garlic to Penicillium spp. Phytopathol. Mediterr. 10: 227-230.

5.7-56 Dueck, J., and Degenhardt, K. 1975. Effect of leaf age and inoculum concentration on reaction of oilseed Brassica spp. to Alternaria brassicae. Proc. Am. Phytopathol. Soc. 2: 59 (Abstr.). PBA 48: 9934.

5.7-57 Dzhashi, V., and Dzhashi, V. 1971. Measures for controlling pests of roots and root necks of laurel [in Russian]. Subtrop. Kul't. 1971{6}: 117-121.

5.7-58 Dzhashi, V.S. 1978. Results of testing ultracide, fenitrothion and trichlorfon for the control of Ceroplastes japonica on Laurus nobilis [in Russian]. Subtrop. Kul't. 1978{1}: 52-54. AGRICOLA.

5.7-59 Dzhashi, V.V. 1973. Results of testing ammiphos and cyanox against Ceroplastes japonica [in Russian]. Subtrop. Kul't. 1973{4}: 160-162.

5.7-60 Ebrahimi, A.G., Delwich, P.A., and Williams, P.H. 1976. Resistance in Brassica juncea to Peronospora parasitica and Albugo candida race 2. Proc. Am. Phytopathol. Soc. 3: 273 (Abstr.). PBA 48: 10874.

5.7-61 Easwaramoorthy, S., and Jayaraj, S. 1977. Control of guava scale,

Pulvinaria psidii Mask. and chilli aphid, Myzus persicae (Sulz.), with Cephalosporium lecanii Zimm. and insecticides. Indian J. Agric. Sci. 47: 136-139. RAE-A 66: 1559.

5.7-62 Feys, J.L., and Assche, C. Van. 1977. Field disinfestation in witloof chicory cultures. Meded. Fac. Landbouwwet. Rijksuniv. Gent 42: 1099-1104. HA 48: 5457.

5.7-63 Fischer, H., and Nienhaus, F. 1973. Virus inhibitors in bush red peppers (Capsicum annuum L.) [in German]. Phytopathol. Z. 78: 25-41.

5.7-64 Flanderkova, V. 1972. Effect of fungicides on infection of poppy with the fungus Helminthosporium papaveris Hennig [in Czech]. Sb. UVTI (Ustav Vedeckotechnickych Informaci) Ochrana Rostlin 8: 19-22. FCA 26: 3417.

5.7-65 Foster, R.E., Sherrod, D.W., Eastman, C.E., and Randell, R. 1979. Treatment of horseradish propagative stocks for control of the imported crucifer weevil. J. Econ. Entomol. 72: 555-556.

5.7-66 Gennari, M., Abbattista Gentile, I., and Matta, A. 1979. Antifungal substances in pepper plants infected by virulent or avirulent strains of Verticillium dahliae. Riv. Patol. Veg. 15: 127-132.

5.7-67 Gennatas, J. 1977. On the subject of an unusual infestation by galerucids in Alsace [in French]. Phytoma 29{286}: 9. RAE-A 65: 5573.

5.7-68 Greathead, A.S. 1978. Control of Penicillium decay of garlic. Calif. Agric. 32{6}: 18. HA 49: 351.

5.7-69 Green, R.J., Jr. 1975. Rust resistance in Mentha spp. by irradiation-induced mutation. Proc. Am. Phytopathol. Soc. 2: 85 (Abstr.).

5.7-70 Grinstein, A., Katan, J., and Eshel, Y. 1976. Effect of dinotroaniline herbicides on plant resistance to soilborne pathogens. Phytopathology 66: 517-522.

5.7-71 Grzybowska, T. 1976. The control of Septoria digitalis Pass. on foxglove [in Polish]. Rocz. Nauk Roln. Ser. E. Ochr. Rosl. 6: 183-200. RPP 58: 1883.

5.7-72 Grzybowska, T., and Mikolajewicz, M. 1975. Investigation of the efficacy of of some domestic preparations used in the control of (Lygus sp.) bugs on the Umbelleriferae plants [in Polish]. Herba Pol. 21: 50-52. AGRICOLA.

5.7-73 Grzybowska, T. 1974. Effect of chemical treating of mint (Mentha piperita L.) seedlings on their develoment and infection by rust (Puccinia menthae Pers.) [in Polish]. Herba Pol. 20: 192-198. AGRICOLA.

5.7-74 Grzybowska, T. 1974. Control of rust of mint (Puccinia menthae Pers.) [in Polish]. Herba Pol. 20: 11-19. AGRICOLA.

5.7-75 Grzybowska, T., and Mikolajewicz, M. 1974. Estimation of the efficacy of some insecticides in the control of mint-beetle (Chrysomela menthastri Sufr.) [in Polish]. Herba Pol. 20: 298-300. AGRICOLA.

5.7-76 Gupta, R.N., and Sinha, S. 1973. Varietal field trials in the control of stem-gall disease of coriander. Indian Phytopathol. 26: 337-340. RPP 53: 4540.

5.7-77 Gupta, R.N. 1976. Impact of nitrogen, phosphorus and manganese on the stem-gall disease of coriander. Acta Bot. Indica 4: 30-35. HA 47: 6802.

5.7-79 Harper, J.D. 1971. Preliminary testing of a nuclear polyhedrosis virus to control the variegated cutworm on peppermint. J. Econ. Entomol. 64: 1573-1574.

5.7-80 Hartmann, R.O. 1974. Fumigation: a possible fertilizer substitute. Proc. Annu. Meet. Oreg. Essent. Oil Grow. League 25: 15-17.

5.7-81 Hassan, S.A. 1977. The use of the lacewing Chrysopa carnea Steph. (Neuroptera, Chrysopidae) to control the green peach aphid Myzus persicae (Sulzer) on glasshouse red pepper [in German]. Z. Angew Entomol. 82: 234-239.

5.7-82 Havranek, P. 1972. Virus-free garlic clones obtained from meristem cultures [in Czech]. Sb. UVTI (Ustav Vedeckotechnickych Informaci) Ochrana Rostlin 8: 291-298. RPP 52: 3142.

5.7-83 Heimes, R., and Locher, F. 1977. Results of trials with Ronilan for the control of Botrytis spp. and Sclerotinia spp. in vegetables and ornamentals [in German]. Meded. Fac. Landbouwwetenschappen Rijksuniv. Gent 42: 1169-1180. HA 48: 5428.

5.7-84 Hiremath, P.C., Ponnappa, K.M., Janardhan, A., and Sundaresh, H.N. 1978. Chemical control of collar rot of fenugreek. Pesticides 12{1}: 30-31.

5.7-85 Hirosawa, T., Ozoe, S., and Takuda, T. 1973. The effects of several fungicides on alternaria blight of ginseng by Alternaria panax [in Japanese]. Bull. Shimane Agric. Exp. Stn. 1973{11}: 41-51. HA 45: 6108.

5.7-86 Hofsvang, T., and Hagvar, E.B. 1979. Different introduction methods of Ephedrus cerasicola Stary to control Myzus persicae (Sulzer) in small paprika glasshouses. Z. Angew. Entomol. 88: 16-23.

5.7-87 Hofsvang, T., and Hagvar, E.B. 1978. Biological control of the green peach aphid (Myzus persicae) (Sulzer) on greenhouse paprika: two methods of parasite introduction (Ephedrus cerasicola Stary) [in Norwegian]. Forsk. Fors. Landbruket. 29: 565-572. AGRICOLA.

5.7-88 Hofsvang, T., and Hagvar, E.B. 1978. Effect of parasitism by Ephedrus cerasicola Stary on Myzus persicae (Sulzer) in small glasshouses Z. Angew Entomol. 85: 1-15.

5.7-89 Horner, C.E. 1980. Mint disease control research report. Proc. Annu. Meet. Oreg. Essent. Oil Grow. League 31: 3-6.

5.7-90 Horner, C.E., and Melouk, H.A. 1975. Mint disease control research report, 1973-1974. Proc. Annu. Meet. Oreg. Essent. Oil Grow. League 26: 9-12.

5.7-91 Horner, C.E., and Melouk, H.A. 1974. Progress in wilt control. Proc. Annu. Meet. Oreg. Essent. Oil Grow. League 25: 4-6.

5.7-92 Horner, C.E., and Melouk, H.A. 1977. Screening, selection and evaluation of irradiation-induced mutants of spearmint dahliae for resistance to Verticillium mentha cardiaca wilt in induced mutations against plant diseases. Pages 253-262 in Proceedings of a symposium on the use of induced mutations for improved disease resistance in crop plants, Vienna, 1977. International Atomic Energy Agency, Vienna.

5.7-93 Imoto, M. 1976. Studies of mosaic disease of sweet pepper (Capsicum frutescens L.) transmitted by aphids. 4. The effects of soil mulching with polyethylene plastic strips on the control of mosaic disease and their economical use [in Japanese]. Hiroshima-ke nritsu Nogyo Shikenjo Hokoku 37: 51-56. AGRICOLA.

5.7-94 Inagaki, H., Sakurai, K., Furuyama, S., and Kasano, H. 1973. Studies on mint nematodes and their control. Part 2. Control of mint nematodes and black rot disease of rhizomes [in Japanese]. Hokkaido Nogyo Shikenjo Kenkyu Hokoku 1973{104}: 131-148.

5.7-95 Jain, K.L., and Agrawat, J.M. 1978. Control of Fusarium wilt of coriander by systemic fungicides. Indian J. Mycol. Plant Pathol. 8: 30. HA 50: 2233.

5.7-96 Jatala, P., and Jensen, H.J. 1974. Oxamyl controls Longidorus elongatus peppermint in greenhouse experiments. Plant Dis. Rep. 58: 591-593.

5.7-97 Jones, D.R., Unwin, C.H., and Ward, E.W.B. 1975. The significance of capsidiol induction in pepper fruit during an incompatible interaction with Phytophthora infestans. Phytopathology 65: 1286-1288.

5.7-98 Jones, D.R., Unwin, C.H., and Ward, E.W.B. 1975. Capsidiol induction in pepper fruit during interactions with Phytophthora capsici and Monilinia fructicola. Phytopathology 65: 1417-1419.

5.7-99 Joshi, R.D., and Dubey, L.N. 1976. Efficiency of certain insecticides in controlling leaf curl disease in chillies. Sci. Cult. 42: 273-275.

5.7-100 Kacharmazov, V., and Tanev, I. 1977. Curing the peppermint cv. Maritsa affected by filiform virus by combined thermotherapy and tissue culture [in Bulgarian]. Rastenievud. Nauki 14{5}: 114-118. HA 48: 5881.

5.7-101 Kakar, K.L., and Dogra, G.S. 1977. Comparative efficiency of soil and foliar applications of some systemic insecticides against Phytomyza atricornis Meign., infesting mustard. Indian J. Agric. Sci. 47: 405-407. RAE-A 66: 2111.

5.7-102 Kalchschmid, W., and Krause, C. 1976. The control of white blister in horseradish [in German]. Gesunde Pflanz. 28: 39-41. HA 47: 761.

5.7-103 Kaszonyi, S. 1974. Resistance of cruciferous weeds occurring in Hungary against Fusarium oxysporum f. conglutinans (Wr.) Sr. et Hn. [in Hungarian]. Kerteszetiegy. Kozl. 37: 48-57. HA 24: 2350.

5.7-104 Katan, J., and Eshel, Y. 1974. Effect of the herbicide diphenamid on damping-off disease of pepper and tomato. Phytopathology 64: 1186-1192.

5.7-105 Kebadze, N.A. 1979. Effect of chelate supplements on the resistance of geraniums to fusarial wilting [in Georgian]. Tr. NII Zashchity Rast. Gruz SSR 1979{30}: 19-23. CA 94: 29343.

5.7-106 Kekelidze, N.A., and Beradze, L.V. 1975. About the nonphenolic part of the essential oil from basil [in Russian]. Subtrop. Kul't. 1972{3}: 103-104.

5.7-107 Keshwal, R.L., Choubey, P.C., and Singh, K. 1979. Effect of different date of sowing and fungicidal spray on the incidence of "powdery mildew" of coriander. Pesticides 13{10}: 25. RPP 60: 2128.

5.7-108 Keshwal, R.L., Choubey, P.C., and Singh, K. 1979. Effect of date of sowing and fungicidal sprays on powdery mildew of coriander. Vegetable Sci. 6: 135-136. HA 51: 8023.

5.7-109 Keshwal, R.L., Choubey, P.C., and Singh, K. 1979. Note on the chemical control of cumin blight. Pesticides 13{12}: 36-37.

5.7-110 Khan, A.M., Siddiqui, Z.A., Alam, M.M., and Saxena, S.K. 1976. Note on the effect of different cropping sequences on the population of plant-parasitic nematodes. Indian J. Agric. Sci. 46: 439-441. HA 47: 8501.

5.7-111 Khatri, H.L., and Sekhon, I.S. 1973. Effect of oil spray on aphid transmission of chilli-mosaic virus. Indian J. Agric. Sci. 43: 667-669. RPP 54: 1528.

5.7-112 Khosla, S.N., Ajit Singh, and Singh, P. 1977. Chemical weed control in medicinal and aromatic plants - a review. Pages 539-551 in C.K. Atal and B.M. Kapur, eds. Cultivation & utilization of medicinal and aromatic plants. Regional Research Laboratory, Jammu-Tawi, India.

5.7-113 Koepsell, P.A. 1975. Fumigation in peppermint. Proc. Annu. Meet. Oreg. Essent. Oil Grow. League 26: 69-73.

5.7-114 Koltypina, S.B., Marenko, V.G., and Khalik, L.A. 1979. The microbial activity of the soil beneath muscatel sage treated with fluometuron [in Russian]. Izv. Timiryazevsk. S-kh. Akad. 1979{3}: 183-187. WA 29: 1226.

5.7-115 Kral, J., Neubauer, S., and Klimes, K. 1975. Results of experiments with foxglove seed disinfected against Septoria digitalis and other parasitic fungi [in Czech]. Nase Liecive Rastliny 12: 109-111. HA 46: 3734.

5.7-116 Kral, J. 1977. The protection of peppermint against mint rust [in Czech]. Nase Liecive Rastliny 14: 67-73. HA 48: 2695.

5.7-117 Krishnan, R., Vasantha Kumar, T., and Naragund, V.R. 1980. Inheritance of field reaction to Cercospora disease in Ocimum basilicum. Indian Perfum. 234{4}: 224-225.

5.7-118 Kuhne, H. 1975. The control of lobelia rust, Coleosporium campanulae [in German]. Nachrichtenbl. Dtsch. Pflanzenschutzdienstes (Braunschweig) 27{6}: 92-93. HA 46: 3498.

5.7-119 Kusumo, S., et al. 1971. Studies on the use of fungicides and insecticides on garlic [in Indonesian]. Bul. Hortik. 'Tjahort' 1971{2}: 1-19. HA 43: 6023.

5.7-120 Lakhtaria, R.P., and Pillai, S.N. 1978. Evaluation of fungicides against blight of cumin. Indian J. Mycol. Plant Pathol. 8:44. HA 50: 22434.

5.7-121 Lallan Singh, and Pavgi, M.S. 1979. Fungicidal control of a blight disease of fenugreek. Indian J. Agric. Sci. 49: 731-734. HA 50: 4547.

5.7-122 Ljubenov, J.A., and Kostadinov, K. 1972. Experiments for the chemical control of Echinochloa crus galli and Setaria spp. in the stands of sesame (Sesamum indicum L.) in Bulgaria [in French]. Not. Mal. Piante (Ser. 3, No. 13) 86: 79-88. AGRICOLA.

5.7-123 MacDonald, D.H. 1972. Effect of variations in the mineral nutrition of mint on the number of Pratylenchus penetrans in the roots. J. Nematol. 4: 229-230 (Abstr.).

5.7-124 Maia, E., Bettachini, B., Beck, D., Venard, P., and Maia, N. 1973. A contribution to improving the state of health of Abrial lavandin [in French]. Ann. Phytopathol. 5: 115-124. HA 44: 8914.

5.7-125 Mancini, G., Moretti, F., and Cotroneo, A. 1976. Trials on the control of rust infection of mint [in Italian]. Inf. Fitopatol. 26{5}: 9-11. HA 47: 2904.

5.7-126 Marien, W. 1975. The control of parasites in grapevine glasshouses [in Dutch]. Tuinbouwberichten 39: 154-159. HA 45: 9407.

5.7-127 Mathur, R.L., Mathur, B.N., and Sharma, B.S. 1972. Efficacy of fungicides in controlling powdery mildew of fenugreek. Indian J. Mycol. Plant Pathol. 2: 82-83. HA 45: 550.

5.7-128 Mathur, R.L., Masih, B., and Sankhla, H.C. 1971. Evaluation of fungicides against powdery mildew disease of cumin (Cumin cyminum) caused by Erysiphe polygoni. Indian Phytopathol. 24: 796-798. HA 44: 4949.

5.7-129 Mathur, R.L., Sankhla, H.C., and Masih, B. 1971. In vitro toxicity of oxathiin formulated compounds towards three soil fungi. Indian Phytopathol. 24: 617-619. AGRICOLA.

5.7-130 McIntyre, J.L., and Horner, C.E. 1973. Inactivation of Verticillium dahliae in peppermint stems by propane gas flaming. Phytopathology 63: 172-175.

5.7-131 Melouk, H.A., and Horner, C.E. 1975. Cross protection in mints by Verticillium nigrescens against V. dahliae. Phytopathology 65: 767-769.

5.7-132 Melouk, H.A., and Horner, C.E. 1976. Sources of resistance in mints to Verticillium wilt. Proc. Am. Phytopathol. Soc. 3: 273 (Abstr.). PBA 48: 11155.

5.7-133 Melouk, H.A., Perkins, V.Q., and Horner, C.E. 1975. Control of Phoma stem and rhizome rot on mints with benomyl. Plant Dis. Rep. 59: 88-90.

5.7-134 Merendonk, S. van de, and Lenteren, J.V. van. 1978. Determination of mortality of greenhouse whitefly _Trialeurodes vaporariorum_ (Westwood) (Homoptera: Aleyrodidae) eggs, larvae and pupae on four host-plant species: eggplant (_Solanum melongena_ L.), cucumber (_Cucumis sativus_ L.), tomato (_Lycopersicon esculentum_ L.), and paprika (_Capsicum annuum_ L.). Meded. Fac. Rijks. Univ. Landbouwet. Gent. 43{1}: 421-429. AGRICOLA.

5.7-135 Mirkova, E. 1978. Leaf scorch of parsley [in Bulgarian]. Rastit. Zasht. 26{3}: 33-34. HA 49: 2116.

5.7-136 Misra, A. 1976. Control of chilli mosaic in India. Meded. Fac. Landbouwwet. Rijksuniv. Gent 41: 1323-1329. HA 47: 8491.

5.7-137 Mkervali, V.G. 1977. Results of studies of problems of controlling fungus diseases of _Laurus nobilis_ [in Russian]. Subtrop. Kul't. 1977{3}: 93-96. AGRICOLA.

5.7-138 Mkervali, V.G., and Kechakmadze, L.A. 1972. System of measures for controlling diseases of laurel [in Russian]. Subtrop. Kul't. 1972{3}: 105-108.

5.7-139 Mkervali, V.G. 1977. Studies on the problems of artificial immunization of laurel and persimmon [in Russian]. Subtrop. Kul't. 1977{4}: 93-95. HA 48: 9430.

5.7-140 Murray, M.J., and Todd, W.A. 1973. The role of mutation breeding in genetic control of plant diseases. Pages 172-176 _in_ G.W. Bruehl, ed. Biology and control of soil-borne plant pathogens: International symposium on factors determining the behavior of plant pathogens in soil, 3rd, Minneapolis, Sept. 1973. American Phyopathological Society, St. Paul, Minn.

5.7-141 Murusidze, G.E., and Khintibidze, N.I. 1977. The effectiveness of some organophosphorus preparations in controlling _Trioza alacris_ and _Heliothrips haemorrhoidalis_ [in Russian]. Subtrop. Kul't. 1977{1/2}: 183-185. HA 48: 8502.

5.7-142 Nadejde, M. 1975. The control of the green peach aphid (_Myzus persicae_) in greenhouse crops with ULV insecticides [in Romanian]. An. Inst. Cercet. Prot. Plant. Acad. Stiinte Agric. Silvice 13: 257-267. HA 49: 1831.

5.7-143 Nagy, F., and Foldesi, D. 1972. Problems of plant protection in large-scale cultures of peppermint [in Hungarian]. Herba Hung. 11{2}: 81-83. AGRICOLA.

5.7-144 Nagy, F., and Csucs, M. 1976. Results of pest control experiments in poppy (_Papaver somniferum_ L.) with special regard to aphids (_Aphis fabae_ Scop.) [in Hungarian]. Herba Hung. 15{2}: 45-55. AGRICOLA.

5.7-145 Nath, D.K., and Pal, S.R. 1975. Control of insect pests of til (_Sesamum indicum_ L.). Sci. Cult. 41: 598-599.

5.7-146 Nath, D.K. 1975. Control of mustard aphid, _Lipaphis erysimi_ (Kaltb.) by soil application of insecticides. Sci. Cult. 41: 428-429.

5.7-147 Neel, P.L., and Reinert, J.A. 1976. Phytotoxicity evaluations of ten insecticides on twenty-three species of ornamental plants under slat shed conditions. Proc. Fla. State Hortic. Soc. 88: 586-590. CA 85: 15307.

5.7-148 Nelson, Z.A., Appleby, A.P., and Berry, R.E. 1974. Terbacil-insecticide interactions in peppermint. Page 86 in Abstracts, 1974 Meeting Weed Science Society of America. The Society, Champaign, Ill. WA 26: 3196.

5.7-149 Nerum, K. Van, and Scheys, G. 1976. The nutrient status of the soil and the appearance of symptoms of microbial disease. Pages 133-140 in Fertilizer use and plant health. Proceedings of the 12th colloquium of the International Potash Institute, Izmir, Turkey, 1976. International Potash Institute, Bern, Switzerland. SF 41: 5904.

5.7-150 Nikolaishvili, A.A. 1980. Importance of parasite Signiphora merceti in the reduction of the number of diaspididae pests [in Russian]. Subtrop. Kul't. 1980{1}: 88-92. AGRICOLA.

5.7-151 Nosyrev, V.I. 1978. The meadow moth- a pest of medicinal plants [in Russian]. Zashch. Rast. 1978{7}: 37-38. RAE-A 67: 1046.

5.7-152 Orphanides, G.M. 1976. Damage assessment and natural control of the carob midge complex, Asphondylia spp. (Dipt., Cecidomyidae) in Cyprus. Boll. Lab. Entomol. Agraria 'Filippo Silvestri' 33: 80-98. RAE-A 66: 276.

5.7-153 Osoe, S. 1971. Injuries of leaf spot disease to horseradish plants and the treatments [in Japanese]. Nogyo Oyobi Engei 46: 637-640. AGRICOLA.

5.7-154 Overman, A.J. 1978. Nematode control with foliar sprays of oxamyl at insecticidal rates. Nematropica 8: 19-20 (Abstr.). HELM AB-B 49: 1225.

5.7-155 Overman, A.J., and Poe, S.L. 1971. Suppression of aphids, mites, and nematodes with foliar applications of chemicals. Proc. Fla. State Hortic. Soc. 84: 419-422. HELM AB-B 42: 437.

5.7-156 Palaniswamy, A., Ranganathan, K., Jaganathan, T., and Narayanasamy, P. 1973. Control of Cercospora jasminicola leaf spot disease of jasmine. South Indian Hortic. 21{1}: 33-34.

5.7-157 Pal, S.K., Agarwal, S.C., and Sharma, P.L. 1971. Evolution of control schedule for mustard aphid Lipaphis erysimi Kalt. (Homoptera: Aphididae) in variety BSG 1. Indian J. Agric. Res. 5: 261-264. HA 43: 7971.

5.7-158 Pank, F., Hannig, H.J., Hauschild, J., and Zygmunt, B. 1980. Chemical weed control in the cropping of medicinal plants. Part 1: Valerian (Valeriana officinalis L.) [in German]. Pharmazie 35{2}: 115-119. CIM 21{5}: 3851.

5.7-159 Patel, R.M., and Desai, M.V. 1971. Alternaria burnsii blight of Cuminum cyminum and its control. Indian Phytopathol. 24{1}: 16-22. AGRICOLA.

5.7-160 Patil, B.G., and Rane, M.S. 1972/1973. White rot of garlic. Mag. Univ. Nagpur Coll. Agric. 45: 86-89. HA 44: 8646.

5.7-161 Petrov, A.S. 1974. Microflora of coriander seeds and the effects of thermal disinfection [in Russian]. Tr. Vses. Nauchno-Issled. Inst. Efirnomaslichn. Kul't. 1974{7}: 59-62. RPP 55: 4229.

5.7-162 Pinkerton, J.N., and Jensen, H.J. 1980. Systemic nematicides for control of root lesion and mint nematodes in peppermint. Proc. Annu. Meet. Oreg. Essent. Oil Grow. League 31: 30-35.

5.7-163 Pinkerton, J.N., and Jensen, H.J. 1979. Effects of carbamate nematicides on nematode populations and yield of peppermint. J. Nematol. 11: 311 (Abstr.).

5.7-164 Pucci, A., Avila, E.R., Zabala, A.J., and Silvetti, M.E. 1974. Use of biocides in the control of nematodes causing damage to garlic [in Spanish]. Revista de Agronomia y de Veterinaria 3{1}: 4-6. HELM AB-B 44: 849.

5.7-165 Rai, B., and Sehgal, V.K. 1975. Field resistance of Brassica germplasm to mustard aphid, Lipaphis erysimi (Kalt.). Sci. Cult. 41: 444-445.

5.7-166 Rai, J.N., and Srivastava, S.K. 1977. Studies on the chemical control of root and stem rot of Brassica juncea caused by Macrophomina phaseolina. Indian J. Mycol. Plant Pathol. 7: 47-51. RPP 57: 4185.

5.7-167 Ramallo, J.C., and Garcia, A.E. 1971. Influence of the vegetal barriers and insecticides in the control of insects which are virus vectors on yield of peppers [in Spanish]. Rev. Agron. Noroeste Argent. 8: 275-294.

5.7-168 Rangarajan, A.V., Mahadevan, N.R., and Iyemperumal, S. 1973. Incidence and control of the mite Amblyseius ovalis Evans on chilli (Capsicum annuum L.). Madras Agric. J. 60: 616-617. RAE-A 63: 4697.

5.7-169 Ravise, A., El Khatib, A., and Kirkiacharian, B.S. 1976. Relations between the structure of phenolic compounds and the in vitro inhibition of Phytophthora parasitica Dastur as well as the lytic enzyme activity [in French]. Poljopr. Znan. Smotra 39: 107-112. CA 87: 63369.

5.7-170 Reddy, A.S., Rao, G.S., Rao, B.H.K.M., and Lakshminarayana, K. 1980. Insecticidal control of the red spider mite, Tetranychus telarius L. on coriander. Indian Cocoa, Arecanut & Spices Journal 4{1}: 9-11. HA 51: 4856.

5.7-171 Reddy, A.S., Krishnamurthy Rao, B.H., and Wilson, Y. 1978. Chemical control of jasmine pests. South Indian Hortic. 26: 25-27.

5.7-172 Riaz Kirmani, M., Alam, M.M., Khan, A.M., and Saxena, S.K. 1975. Comparative efficacy of nematicides for the control of parasitic nematodes infesting certain vegetable and oil crops. Acta Bot. Indica 3: 39-42.

5.7-173 Rizza, A., Buckingham, G., and Pecora, P. 1980. Host specificity studies on Ceutorhynchus maculaalba, a potential candidate for the biological control of opium poppy. Environ. Entomol. 9: 681-688.

5.7-174 Romanenko, L.G., and Zhokova, L.M. 1975. Heritability of resistance to leaf spot in intervarietal hybrids of lavender [in

Russian]. Tr. Vses. Nauchno-Issled. Inst. Efirnomaslichn. Kul't. 8: 35-37.

5.7-175 Romascu, E., Lemeni, V., Popescu, I., Vasile, I., and Ciobanu, E. 1974. Experimental data on the control of Ditylenchus dipsaci Kuhn in garlic crops. I. Treatments applied to the planting material [in Romanian]. An. Inst. Cercet. Prot. Plant. Acad. Stiinte Agric. Silvice 12: 399-406. HA 48: 10457.

5.7-176 Romascu, E. 1975. Control of Ditylenchus dipsaci in garlic with soil-applied chemicals [in Romanian]. An. Inst. Cercet. Prot. Plant. Acad. Stiinte Agric. Silvice 13: 157-162. HA 49: 352.

5.7-177 Roth, H., and Kennedy, J.W. 1973. Helicella snails infesting rosemary seeds: Methyl bromide and other fumigants for quarantine control. J. Econ. Entomol. 66: 935-936.

5.7-178 Roy, A.K., and Saikia, U.N. 1976. White-blight of mustard and its control. Indian J. Agric. Sci. 46: 274-277. FCA 31: 756.

5.7-179 Saccardo, F. 1974. Resistance to CMV in Capsicum species. Genet. Agrar. 28: 97-104.

5.7-180 Saccardo, F. 1978. Wild species of Capsicum as sources of resistance to pathogens. Genet. Agrar. 31: 162-163 (Abstr.).

5.7-181 Sachan, J.N., and Pal, S.K. 1976. Insecticides and cakes for the control of white grub Holotrichia insularis Brenske in western Rajasthan Pesticides 10{6}: 37-38. RAE-A 66: 2766.

5.7-182 Sachan, J.N., and Pal, S.K. 1974. Control of white grub Holotrichia insularis in chillies (Capsicum frutescens). Pesticides 8{10}: 43-45. CA 82: 150462.

5.7-183 Saini, S.S., and Rattan, R.S. 1971. Induction of resistance against fruit rot (Phytophthora capsici) in bell pepper (Capsicum annuum L.). Himachal J. Agric. Res. 1{1}: 1-2.

5.7-184 Sankhla, B., Sankhla, H.C., and Mathur, R.L. 1973. Evaluation of fungicides against Alternaria blight disease of cumin (Cumin cyminum). Indian Phytopathol. 26{1}: 154-155.

5.7-185 Sastry, K.S.M., Thakur, R.N., and Pandotra, V.R. 1977. Diseases of medicinal and aromatic plants and their control. Pages 519-539 in C.K. Atal and B.M. Kapur, eds. Cultivation & utilization of medicinal and aromatic plants. Regional Research Laboratory, Jammu-Tawi, India.

5.7-186 Saxena, S.K., Alam, M.M., and Khan, A.M. 1974. Chemotheropeutic control of nematodes with Vydate oxamyl, VC-13 and Dazomet on chilli plants. Indian J. Nematol. 4: 235-238. HELM AB-B 45: 804.

5.7-187 Sehgal, S.P., and Prasad, N. 1972. Note on testing of different varieties, strains and species of Sesamum for resistance to Phytophthora prasitica blight. Indian J. Agric. Sci. 42: 122. AGRICOLA.

5.7-188 Shanmugam, N., Natarajan, S., and Ramakrishnan, G. 1976. Fungicidal control of powdery mildew of Sesamum indicum L. Madras Agric. J. 63: 420-421.

5.7-189 Shields, E.J. 1980. Summary of Oregon pest management project. Proc. Annu. Meet. Oreg. Essent. Oil Grow. League 31: 42-49.

5.7-190 Shukla, B.N., and Singh, B.P. 1973. Effect of fungicidal seed treatment on Macrophomina root rot of sesame (Sesamum indicum). Indian J. Mycol. Plant Pathol. 3: 208-209.

5.7-191 Shukla, D.D., Schmelzer, K., Wolf, P., and Gippert, R. 1974. Results of virological studies on cruciferous crop species in the German Democratic Republic [in German]. Nachrichtenbl. Pflanzenschutz DDR 28{4}: 69-72. HA 45: 278.

5.7-192 Singhvi, S.M., Verma, A.N., and Singh, R. 1975. Note on the chemical control of Bihar hairy-caterpillar. Indian J. Agric. Sci. 45: 74-75.

5.7-193 Singh, B.P., and Shukla, B.N. 1974. Efficacy of fungicides in controlling the seed borne fungi on Sesamum indicum. PKV Res. J. 3: 77-78. AGRICOLA.

5.7-194 Singh, G., and Gupta, R.B.L. 1976. Chemical control of powdery mildew (Erysiphe polygoni) of Cuminum cyminum. Indian J. Mycol. Plant Pathol. 6: 73-74. HA 48: 1646.

5.7-195 Singh, J., and Thakur, M.R. 1977. Genetics of resistance to tobacco mosaic virus cucumber mosaic virus and leaf-curl virus in hot pepper (Capsicum annuum L.). Pages 119-126 in E. Pochard, ed. Capsicum 77. Comptes rendus du 3 degre Congres EUCARPIA sur la genetique et la selection du piment. Institut National de la Recherche Agronomique, Montfavet-Avignon, France. AGRICOLA.

5.7-196 Singh, R.D. 1977. Evaluation of seed dressing fungicides for their effect on the stand, growth and yield of cumin in field. Indian Phytopathol. 30: 198-201. RPP 58: 1339.

5.7-197 Singh, R.D., Choudhary, S.L., and Patel, K.G. 1972. Seed transmission and control of Fusarium wilt of Cumin. Phytopathol. Mediterr. 11: 19-24.

5.7-198 Sivaprakasam, K., Pillayarsamy, K., Rangarajan, A.V., Mahadevan, N.R., and Iyemperumal, S. 1976. Efficacy of certain insecticides in the control of chilli mosaic. Madras Agric. J. 63: 236-237. RAE-A 66: 3614.

5.7-199 Skoropad, W.P., and Tewari, J.P. 1977. Field evaluation of the role of epicuticular wax in rapeseed and mustard in resistance to Alternaria black spot. Can. J. Plant Sci. 57: 1001-1003.

5.7-200 Sneep, J., and Dieleman, F.L. 1973. Breeding plant varieties resistant to pests. Bull. OEPP 3{3}: 89-93.

5.7-201 Solanki, J.S., Singh, R.R., and Dalela, G.G. 1973. Field evaluation of fungicides in controlling Alternaria blight of Cuminum cyminum. Indian J. Mycol. Plant Pathol. 3: 196-197. RPP 54: 2924.

5.7-202 Sooch, B.S., Thakur, M.R., and Mayee, C.D. 1976. Stability of some chilli (Capsicum annuum L.) genotypes against virus diseases. Z. Pflanzenkr. Pflanzenshutz 83: 514-518. RPP 56: 2798.

5.7-203 Spasskii, A.A., Mel'nik, M.V., Knaub, V.Ya., Bumbu, I.V., and Buslaeva, L.A. 1976. Control of Ditylenchus dipsaci infection on garlic [in Russian]. Pages 74-78 in A.A. Spasskii, P.I. Nesterov, and S.P. Dement'eva, eds. Fitoparaziticheskie i svobodnozhivushchie nematody. Izdatel'stvo "Shtiintsa", Kishinev, USSR. HELM AB-B 46: 1677.

5.7-204 Srinivasan, P.M., Govindarajan, R., Ali, K.A., Regupathy, A., and Subramaniam, T.R. 1974. Evaluation of certain acaricides in the control of red spider mite Tetranychus telarius L. on jasmine. South Indian Hortic. 22{1/2}: 68-69.

5.7-205 Srivastava, J.B. 1977. Insect pests of medicinal and aromatic plants and their control - a review. Pages 515-519 in C.K. Atal and B.M. Kapur, eds. Cultivation & utilization of medicinal and aromatic plants. Regional Research Laboratory, Jammu-Tawi, India.

5.7-206 Srivastava, J.L., and Dixit, R.V. 1978. Insecticidal control of Antigastra catalaunalis (Duponchel) (Lepidoptera: Pyraustidae) on sesame (Sesamum indicum L.). Pesticides 12{6}: 39-40. CA 89: 141880.

5.7-207 Srivastava, U.S., Rai, R.A., and Agrawat, J.M. 1971. Powdery mildew of coriander and its control. Indian Phytopathol. 24: 437-440. RPP 52: 810.

5.7-208 Stenseth, C. 1976. Biological/integrative control of pests in the greenhouse [in Norwegian]. Gartneryrket 66: 525-526. AGRICOLA.

5.7-209 Stoessl, A., Robinson, J.R., Rock, G.L., and Ward, E.W.B. 1977. Metabolism of capsidiol by sweet pepper tissue: some possible implications for phytoalexin studies. Phytopathology 67: 64-66.

5.7-210 Studzinski, A., and Mikolajewicz, M. 1976. Studies on the suitability of Acetellic 50 EC, Phosdrin 24 EC and Polfos for Lygus bug control on fennel [in Polish]. Herba Pol. 22: 307-311. HA 48: 4862.

5.7-211 Studzinski, A. 1976. More important insect pests occurring in plantings of poppy and caraway in 1975 [in Polish]. Wiad. Zielarskie 18{3}: 4-6. AGRICOLA

5.7-212 Suetomi, K., Tokawa, T., Miyake, H., Kanei, M., and Nakajima, K. 1973. Effect of validamycin on Panax ginseng blight. Nippon Shokubutsu Byori Gakkaiho 39: 168-169 (Abstr.).

5.7-213 Suss, L. 1970. Ophimyia pinguis Fall. (Diptera Agromyzidae) in Lombardy. Biological and morphological observations [in Italian]. Boll. Zool. Agrar. Bach. 10: 43-84. RAE-A 63: 1360.

5.7-214 Svab, J., and Nagy, F. 1972. Results of mint rust (Puccinia menthae Pers.) control experiments [in Hungarian]. Herba Hung. 11{1}: 67-77. AGRICOLA.

5.7-215 Szith, R., and Furlan, H. 1979. New experiences with the chemical treatment of the white rust on horseradish [in German]. Pflanzenarzt 32: 70-72. HA 50: 3606.

5.7-216 Tarabeih, A.-H.M. 1977. Studies on the rust of Majorana hortensis Mnch. in Egypt. Acta Phytopathol. Acad. Sci. Hung. 12: 307-310. RPP 57: 3561.

5.7-217 Terriere, L.C. 1975. Developing new pesticides for peppermint pests. Proc. Annu. Meet. Oreg. Essent. Oil Grow. League 26: 46-62.

5.7-218 Tolpa, S., Kukla, S., and Noga, H. 1976. The control of downy mildew of onion (Peronospora destructor (Berk.) Casp.) with preparations from peat [in Polish]. Rocz. Nauk Roln. Ser. E. Ochr. Rosl. 6: 239-252. RPP 53: 1973.

5.7-219 Tsalbukov, P. 1973. Integrated plant protection for peppermint and lavender [in Bulgarian]. Rastit. Zasht. 21{10}: 11-13. HA 45: 2709.

5.7-220 Tulisalo, U., Tuovinen, T., and Kurppa, S. 1977. Biological control of aphids with Chrysopa carnea on parsley and green pepper in the greenhouse. Ann. Entomol. Fenn. 43: 97-100. AGRICOLA.

5.7-221 Vergniaud, P., Leroux, J.-P., and Coirier, J.-M. 1972. Trials on plant protection in the grey shallot [in French]. Pepinier. Hortic. Maraichers 1972{127}: 43, 45-48. HA 43: 1258.

5.7-222 Virk, K.S., and Grover, R.K. 1975. Fungitoxic studies with thiophanate-methyl in vitro and in vivo. Indian J. Mycol. Plant Pathol. 5: 79-85.

5.7-223 Vomel, A., Reichling, J., Becker, H., and Drager, P.-D. 1977. Herbicides in the cultivation of Matricaria chamomilla. I. Communication: Influence of herbicides on flower production and weed [in German]. Planta Med. 31: 378-389.

5.7-224 Wangikar, P.D., and Kodmelwar, R.V. 1977. Screening of various fungicides against Aspergillus niger (seedling blight of groundnut) and Fusarium oxysporum f. sesami (wilt of sesame). Pesticides 11{2}: 41-42. CA 86: 166261.

5.7-225 Ward, E.W.B., and Stoessl, A. 1972. Studies on post infectional inhibitors in peppers. Proc. Can. Phytopathol. Soc. 1972{39}: 44 (Abstr.)

5.7-226 Ward, E.W.B., Unwin, C.H., and Stoessl, A. 1973. Postinfectional inhibitors from plants. VI. Capsidiol production in pepper fruit infected with bacteria. Phytopathology 63: 1537-1538.

5.7-227 Ward, E.W.B. 1976. Capsidiol production in pepper leaves in incompatible interactions with fungi. Phytopathology 66: 175-176.

5.7-228 Ward, E.W.B., Unwin, C.H., and Stoessl, A. 1973. Postinfectional inhibitors from plants, VII. Tolerance of capsidiol by fungal pathogens of pepper fruit. Can. J. Bot. 51: 2327-2332.

5.7-229 Wijs, J.J. de, and Schwinn, F.J. 1979. The viscosity of mineral oils in relation to their ability to inhibit the transmission of stylet-borne viruses. Neth. J. Plant Pathol. 85: 19-22.

5.7-230 Wohlmuth, N. 1978. Plant protection tests. 3. Aphids on paprika [in German]. Gartenbauwirtschaft 33: 229-230. AGRICOLA.

5.7-231 Yadava, C.P.S., Saxena, R.C., Mishra, R.K., and Dadheech, L.N. 1977. Evaluation of some granular insecticides for control of grubs of Holotrichia consanguinea Blanch. Indian J. Agric. Sci. 47: 139-142. RAE-A 66: 962.

5.7-232 Yadav, R.P., and Lal, B.S. 1978. Studies on the comparative
efficacy of some popular insecticides against sesamum pod borer
(Antigastra catalaunalis Dup.). Pesticides 12{10}: 25-26. CA 90:
93536.

5.7-233 Yarris, L.C. 1977. Spearmint mutations resist wilt. Agric. Res.
26{2}: 5.

5.7-234 York, A.C. 1977. Organic insect "control" in Indiana vegetables.
Proc. Indiana Acad. Sci. 87: 243 (Abstr.).

5.7-235 Zaleski, K., Jaruzelski, M., and Zdziechowski, J. 1977. Attempts
to control inflorescence rot and fruit decay in Coriandrum sativum [in
Polish]. Wiad. Zielarskie 19{3}: 4-5. AGRICOLA.

5.7-236 Zekovic, P. 1975. Red pepper blight (Phytophtora capsici
Leonian) in the region of Kosovu and the suggested measures for its
control [in Serbo-Croatian]. Agron. Glasn. 37: 459-463. AGRICOLA.

5.7-237 Zhukova, L.M. 1974. Remedies for lavender septoriosis [in
Russian]. Zashch. Rast. 1974{7}: 27.

5.7-238 Zhukova, L.M. 1975. The resistance of different lavender
cultivars to Septoria disease [in Russian]. Tr. Vses. Nauchno-Issled.
Inst. Efirnomaslichn. Kul't. 1975{8}: 67-68. HA 47: 8753.

5.7-239 Zitter, T.A., and Ozaki, H.Y. 1973. Reaction of susceptible and
tolerant pepper varieties to the pepper virus complex in South
Florida. Proc. Fla. State Hortic. Soc. 86: 146-152. RPP 54: 5670.

5.8 Weeds and Weed Control

5.8-1 Aamisepp, A. 1972. Chemical control of Agropyron repens,
1968-1971. Swed. Weed Conf. [Proc.] 13 (Pt. 1): E29-E39. WA 22: 1495.

5.8-2 Agamalian, H.S. 1975. Weed control in garlic. Proc. Ann. Calif.
Weed Conf. 27: 113-114. WA 25: 2953.

5.8-3 Ahmed, M., and Samad, K. 1980. Erythroneurine leafhoppers of fruit
and vegetable plants in Pakistan. Pak. J. Zool. 12{1}: 93-98. RAE-A
69: 6349.

5.8-4 Alfaro Garcia, A., and Garcia Baudin, J.M. 1972. Preliminary
herbicide trials in garlic [in Spanish]. An. Inst. Nac. Invest. Agrar.
Ser. Prot. Veg. (Spain) 1972{2}: 295-311. HA 44: 2486.

5.8-5 Anonymous. 1973. Rx for witchweed: soil-layering machine. Agric.
Res. 22{4}: 8-11. WA 23: 2928.

5.8-6 Appleby, A.P. 1974. Weed control in mint. Proc. Annu. Meet. Oreg.
Essent. Oil Grow. League 25: 45-47.

5.8-7 Appleby, A.P. 1976. Weed control in peppermint. Proc. Annu. Meet.
Oreg. Essent. Oil Grow. League 27: 33-35.

5.8-8 Appleby, A.P., and Brewster, B.D. 1980. Weed control in mint.
Proc. Annu. Meet. Oreg. Essent. Oil Grow. League 31: 50-52.

5.8-9 Arkharova, L.A. 1973. The residual phytotoxicity of herbicides in soil [in Russian]. Byull. Vses. Nauchno-Issled. Inst. Zashch. Rast. 1973{25}: 13-18.

5.8-10 Bain, C., Labit, B., Mimaud, J., and Tanguy, M. 1976. Results of the 1975 experimental work of the Plant Protection Service. 1. Weed control [in French]. Phytoma 28{281}: 7-13. WA 26: 2212.

5.8-11 Baldwin, B.J. 1977. Chemical weed control in oil-seed poppy (Papaver somniferum). Aust. J. Exp. Agric. Anim. Husb. 17: 837-841. WA 27: 1794.

5.8-12 Balicka, N., Lubczynska, J., and Wegrzyn, T. 1976. The effect of microorganisms on phytotoxicity of herbicides 3. Interaction of Bacillus sp. 72 with Venzar. Acta Microbiol. Pol. Ser. B 7{3}: 151-156. WA 25: 2147.

5.8-13 Banki, L. 1973. Synergism in some herbicide mixtures and a physiological and biochemical explanation [in French]. Acta Phytopathol. Acad. Sci. Hung. 8: 247-254. WA 23: 2870.

5.8-14 Bassino, J.P., and Blanc, M. 1980. Weed control in young lavender and lavandin plantations [in French]. Def. Veg. 34{201}: 11-15. WA 30: 169.

5.8-15 Bekshin, B.S., Bukina, N.V., Pushkina, G.P., and Efimova, V.N. 1974. Application of herbicides on plantations of peppermint [in Russian]. Agrokhimiya 1974{7}: 134-138. AGRICOLA.

5.8-16 Beshanov, A.V., and Aspidova, Zh. V. 1979. The use of herbicides in vegetable crops and potatoes [in Russian]. Byull. Vses. Nauchno-Issled. Inst. Zashch. Rast. 1979{45}: 57-61. WA 30: 1742.

5.8-17 Bianco, V.V. 1972. Weed control in salad crops. Informatore Agrario 28: 11147-11151. WA 23: 1818.

5.8-18 Blumenfeld, T., Kleifeld, Y., and Herzlinger, G. 1973. Experiments with a new herbicide: U-27267. Phytoparasitica 1{1}: 82-83. WA 24: 327.

5.8-19 Blumenfeld, T., Kleifeld, Y., and Herzlinger, G. 1973. Experiments with a new herbicide: pronamide. Phytoparasitica 1{1}: 83. WA 23: 2682.

5.8-20 Bouron, H., and Mimaud, J. 1972. Results of experiments carried out in 1971 by the Plant Protection Service. I. Weed control [in French]. Phytoma 24{242}: 5-13. HA 43: 5680.

5.8-21 Brewster, B.D. 1977. Weed control. Proc. Annu. Meet. Oreg. Oil Grow. League 28: 20-21. AGRICOLA.

5.8-22 Brewster, B.D., and Stanger, C.E. 1980. Bentazon for Canada thistle control in peppemint. Weed Sci. 28: 36-39. WA 29: 4077

5.8-23 Brown, J.F., and Swingle, H.D. 1977. Herbicide evaluation in vegetable crops. Proc. South. Weed Sci. Soc. 30: 168-175. WA 27: 179.

5.8-24 Bukina, N.V., Vekshin, B.S., Pushkina, G.P., and Dodotchenko, M.V. 1977. Herbicides in crops of greater plantain. Pharm. Chem. J. (Engl. Transl.) 10: 1659-1661. Translation of Khim.-Farm. Zh. 10{12}: 82-85, 1976.

5.8-25 Burgis, D.S. 1974. In-the-row weed control for peppers on full bed mulch. Proc. South. Weed Sci. Soc. 27: 194-198. WA 24: 2627.

5.8-26 Caramete, A., Bucur, E., and Rughinis, D. 1979. The effects of atrazine on weed species and vegetables [in Russian]. Pages 340-346 in H.R. Schutte, ed. Bericht zum Symposium der 12. Wissenschaftlichen Koordinierungskonferenz zum RGW-Thema "Wirkungsmechanismen von Herbidiziden und Synthetischen Wachstumsregulatoren". Muhlhausen, DDR, 1979. VEB Gustav Fischer Verlag, Jena, German Democratic Republic. WA 30: 3107.

5.8-27 Chandra, V., and Srivastava, K. 1972. Chemical control of weeds in Mentha arvensis sub sp. haplocalyx var. piperascens Holmes (Japanese mint). Indian Perfum. 15{2}: 60a-60d. HA 45: 4375.

5.8-28 Chiapparini, L. 1972. Weed control in tomatoes, peppers and eggplants [in Italian]. Informatore Agrario 28: 11092-11093. WA 23: 1815.

5.8-29 Csizi, J. 1976. Chemical weed control in paprika stands with Rideon 80 WPA [in Hungarian]. Novenyvedelem 12{2}: 79-81. AGRICOLA.

5.8-30 Daniau, P., and Beraud, J.M. 1976. Benfluralin and its use for weed control in chicory [in French]. Meded. Fac. Landbouwwet. Rijksuniv. Gent 41: 1165-1178. HA 47: 8373.

5.8-31 Daniel, G.H. 1976. Weed control in mustard. Proc. Br. Crop Prot. Conf.-Weeds 1976: 503-508, Vol. 2. WA 26: 1597.

5.8-32 Daniel, G.H. 1976. Terbacil as a residual herbicide for Mentha spicata. Proc. Br. Crop Prot. Conf.-Weeds 1976: 549-555, Vol. 2. WA 26: 1966.

5.8-33 Deysson, G., Thizy, A., and Negulesco-Rubingher, I. 1974. Comparative ultrastructural study of the cytotoxicity of various urea herbicides and related compounds [in French]. C. R. Hebd. Seances Acad. Sci. Ser. D. 278: 1723-1726.

5.8-34 Dobrzanski, A., and Daszewski, J. 1971. Weed control with herbicides in one-year plantings of horseradish [in Polish]. Biul. Warzywniczy 12: 171-184. AGRICOLA.

5.8-35 Elenkov, E., Velev, B., and Rankov, V. 1975. Use of herbicides for tomatoes and paprika [in German]. Int. Z. Landwirtsch. 1975{6}: 661-664. AGRICOLA.

5.8-36 Ellal, G., Koren, E., and Mermelstein, M. 1973. Activation of napropamid by irrigation or by incorporation for the control of weeds in peppers. Phytoparasitica 1{1}: 74. WA 23: 2541.

5.8-37 El-Labban, H.M., Ashry, M.A., and El-Nawawy, A.S. 1977. The effect of weed control treatments on both weeds and Cymbopogon citratus. Curr. Sci. 46: 532-533.

5.8-38 Ernst, J. 1971. Studies on the influence of soil on herbicide activity in mustard and sugar-beet [in German]. Feldwirtschaft 1971{11}: 526-527. WA 22: 701.

5.8-39 Eshel, Y., and Katan, J. 1973. Effect of time of application of diphenamid on pepper, weeds, and soil diseases. Phytoparasitica 1{1}: 73. WA 23: 2540.

5.8-40 Eshel, Y., Katan, J., Palevitch, D., and Sitti, E. 1974. Biocidic action of diphenamid and napropamid on direct-seeded pepper, weeds, and soil fungi. Phytoparasitica 1{1}: 65. WA 23: 2539.

5.8-41 Eshel, Y., Katan, J., and Palevitch, D. 1973. Selective action of diphenamid and napropamide in pepper (Capsicum annuum L.) and weeds. Weed Res. 13: 379-384.

5.8-42 Filippov, G.A., and Inshakova, K.P. 1979. The use of herbicides in crops of pepper and eggplants [in Russian]. Khim. Sel'sk. Khoz. 17{10}: 38-40. WA 29: 3232.

5.8-43 Filippov, G.A. 1975. The effectiveness of using herbicides under irrigated conditions [in Russian]. Tr. Vses. Nauchno-Issled. Inst. Zashch. Rast. 1975{43}: 162-170. WA 27: 5.

5.8-44 Fischer, B.B. 1975. Vegetation management in tomato and pepper production. Proc. Ann. Calif. Weed Conf. 27: 100-102. WA 25: 3591.

5.8-45 Foldesi, D., and Vasarhelyi, G. 1974. Weed control experiments in chicory (Cichorium intybus L.) [in Hungarian]. Novenyvedelem (Budapest) 10: 65-68. WA 24: 97.

5.8-46 Foldesi, D., and Bernath, J. 1979. Effective method for control of tolerant weeds in poppy cultivation (Papaver somniferum L.). Planta Med. 36: 248 (Abstr.).

5.8-47 Formigoni, A., and Castagna, G. 1972. 2,4,6-trichlorophenyl-4'-nitrophenylether (MO338), a new selective herbicide [in Italian]. Not. Mal. Piante 1972{86}: 163-178. WA 22: 1854.

5.8-48 Frye, D.M., Ilnicki, R.D., and Michieka, R.W. 1978. Weed control in southern greens. Proc. Annu. Meet. Northeast. Weed Sci. Soc. 32: 239-245. WA 28: 965.

5.8-49 Gad, A.M., and El-Mahde, M.A.M. 1972. Effect of the local herbicide M 15 and its residues on darnel and some vegetable and field crops. Desert Inst. Bull. A.R.E. 22: 407-419. HA 47: 1363.

5.8-50 Gawronski, W., Palamarczyk, G., Rudas, J., and Skapski, H. 1973. Evaluation of the suitability of Gesagard (50% prometryne) for weed control in dill in relation to herbicide residues in the crop [in Polish]. Biul. Warzywniczy 14: 149-160. HA 45: 2692.

5.8-51 Ghosh, D.C., and Mukhopadhyay, S.K. 1980. Weeds and weed control in sesame. Pesticides 14{11}: 24-29. CA 94: 78331.

5.8-52 Glaze, N.C., and Phatak, S.C. 1980. Herbicide evaluation in direct-seeded peppers for transplant production. Proc. South. Weed Sci. Soc. 33: 96 (Abstr.). WA 30: 2773.

5.8-53 Golcz, L., Ruminska, A., Czabajski, T., Zalecki, R. and Weglarz, Z. 1975. Control of weeds with the product Sinbar in the cultivation of Mentha piperita L. [in Polish]. Herba Pol. 21: 173-183. WA 25: 2974.

5.8-54 Guar, B.L., and Tomar, D.S. 1978. Chemical weed control in sesame. Indian J. Agron. 23: 71. AGRICOLA.

5.8-55 Gulati, B.C., and Bhan, V.M. 1971. Effect of post-emergence application of terbacil on the control of weeds in Japanese mint. Indian Perfum. 15{2}: 49-51. WA 23: 2165.

5.8-56 Gulati, B.C., and Bhan, V.M. 1971. Effect of pre-emergence application of terbacil on control of weeds in Japanese mint. Indian Perfum. 15{2}: 53-59. WA 23: 2166.

5.8-57 Hajdu, K., and Foldesi, D. 1972. Chemical weed control in caraway [in Hungarian]. Herba Hung. 11{3}: 45-51. HA 44: 7916.

5.8-58 Hammerton, J.L. 1974. Weed control work in progress at the University of the West Indies. Part 4. PANS 20: 429-436. WA 24: 2626.

5.8-59 Haramaki, C., Kuhns, L., and Grenoble, D. 1980. Preemergent weed control in ornamental liner beds. Proc. Annu. Meet. Northeast. Weed Sci. Soc. 34: 320-323.

5.8-60 Harper, D. 1975. Peppermint weed control. Proc. Annu. Meet. Oreg. Essent. Oil Grow. League 26: 65-68.

5.8-61 Harper, D.R., Burr, R.J., and Colbert, D.R. 1974. An evaluation of potential uses of asulam in Western Oregon. Proc. West. Soc. Weed Sci. 27: 42. WA 25: 3.

5.8-62 Hogue, E.J. 1976. Effects of soil surface drying on linuron activity in organic soils. Can. J. Soil Science 56: 175-180.

5.8-63 Horowitz, M. 1973. Competitive effects of Cynodon dactylon, Sorghum halepense and Cyperus rotundus on cotton and mustard. Exp. Agric. 9: 263-273.

5.8-64 Ignatov, B. 1972. The effect of some herbicides on different capsicum varieties grown on calcareous chernozem soil [in Bulgarian]. Gradinar. Lozar. Nauka 9{2}: 61-68. WA 23: 593.

5.8-65 Jaruzelski, M., Turowski, W., and Gnusowski, B. 1976. Studies on the suitability of Kerb 50 W and Kerb Mix B for weed control in medicinal plants [in Polish]. Herba Pol. 22: 291-300. HA 48: 4880.

5.8-66 Jaruzelski, M., and Zdziechowski, J. 1976. Investigating the use of trifluralin in red pepper (Capsicum annuum) crops [in Polish]. Herba Pol. 22: 301-306. WA 27: 970.

5.8-67 Jaruzelski, M. 1971. The influence of crop rotation and of mechanical and chemical stubble treatments on weed control in crops of foxglove [in Polish]. Herba Pol. 17: 273-286. WA 23: 2128.

5.8-68 Jaruzelski, M., Turowski, W., and Zdziechowski, J. 1976. Chemical control of weeds in fennel plantings [in Polish]. Wiad. Zielarskie 18{11}: 4-5. AGRICOLA.

5.8-69 Jaworski, C.A., McCarter, S.M., and Glaze, N.C. 1980. Effect of soil fumigation and alternate year seeding on weed control, bacterial spot incidence and yield of pepper transplants. HortScience 15: 650-652.

5.8-70 Kameneva, E.A., and Pen'kov, L.A. 1973. The application of promotryne and linuron in dill, celery and parsley [in Russian]. Khim. Sel'sk. Khoz. 11{2}: 46-49. HA 43: 8977.

5.8-71 Kameneva, E.A., and Pen'kov, L.A. 1973. Use of prometryne and linuron on dill, celery, and parsley sowings [in Russian]. Khim. Sel. Khoz. 11{2}: 126-129. CA 78: 132624.

5.8-72 Karpova, G.Ya., Semak, V.I., Koltypina, S.B., and Yakubovich, A.D. 1980. Long term use of simazine in lavender plantations [in Russian]. Khim. Sel'sk. Khoz. 18{1}: 53-57. HA 50: 4551.

5.8-73 Katan, J., and Eshel, Y. 1973. Interactions between herbicides and plant pathogens. Residue Rev. 45: 145-177. HA 44: 2011.

5.8-74 Kazakova, K. 1977. The weed control efficiency of terbacil in mint plots [in Bulgarian]. Rastit. Zasht. 25{12}: 18-20.

5.8-75 Kazakova, K., Stanev, D., and Neshev, M. 1976. Two years of growing Mentha with the use of herbicides [in Bulgarian]. Rastit. Zasht. 24{8}: 18-21. AGRICOLA.

5.8-76 Kazakova, K., and Tanev, I. 1972. Use of herbicides during cultivation of essential oil crops [in Russian]. Pages 78-81 in P.V. Naumenko et al., eds. Mezhdunarodnyi kongress po efirnym maslam, 4th, Tiflis, 1968, [Materialy], v.2. Pishchevaya Promyshlennost', Moscow, USSR. CA 81: 22183.

5.8-77 Khosla, S.N. 1978. Suitability of some more herbicides for chemical weed control in Japanese mint. Indian Perfum. 22: 110-114. WA 29: 3663.

5.8-78 Khosla, S.N., and Singh, P. 1978. Chemical weed control in Mentha arvensis L. with Amiben and Gramoxone. Herba Hung. 17{2}: 61-65. HA 49: 1451.

5.8-79 Kiss, E. 1978. Chemical weed control experiments in paprika stands established by direct seeding [in Hungarian]. Novenyvedelem 14: 170-173 AGRICOLA.

5.8-80 Kolb, W., Schwarz, T., and Trunk, R. 1980. The development of weeds in ground cover plantings with differing soil management [in German]. Zeitschrift fur Vegetationstechnik im Landschafts- und Sportstattenbau 3: 120-125. HA 51: 6428.

5.8-81 Koltypina, S.B., Khilik, L.A., and Gul'ko, N.B. 1979. The influence of herbicide combinations on the soil microflora under muscatel sage [in Russian]. Byull. Vses. Nauchno-Issled. Inst. Sel'skokhozyaistvennoi Mikrobiologii 1979{32}: 86-88. WA 29: 3477.

5.8-82 Koren, E., Ellal, G., and Mermelstein, M. 1973. A comparison between early and late pre-emergence application of napropamid in direct-seeded pepper. Phytoparasitica 1{1}: 74. WA 23: 2542.

5.8-83 Korosmezei, C. 1979. Post-em. weed control in non-transplanted red pepper [in Hungarian]. Novenyvedelem (Budapest) 15: 460-462. WA 30: 3505.

5.8-84 Kosinkiewicz, B., and Stankiewicz, M. 1975. The effect of micro-organisms on phytotoxicity of herbicides. 2. Increase of phytotoxicity of Venzar in the presence of phenolic compounds produced by Psuedomonas sp. 22. Acta Microbiol. Pol. B. 7: 15-23. WA 25: 1110.

5.8-85 Kostov, T. 1976. Effectiveness of trifluralin and chloramben herbicides in the weed control of paprika crops [in Serbo-Croatian]. Agrohemija 3/4: 131-136. AGRICOLA.

5.8-86 Kostov, T. 1975. The influence of trifluralin and chloramben on the chemical composition of pepper fruits [in Serbo-Croatian]. Agrohemija 18: 305-309. WA 26: 220.

5.8-87 Kostov, T. 1976. The efficacy of the herbicides trifluralin and chloramben for weed control in pepper crops [in Serbo-Croatian]. Agrohemija 18: 131-136. WA 26: 971.

5.8-88 Labrada, R., and Paredes, E. 1979. Herbicide evaluation in tomato, pepper and cabbage seedbeds [in Spanish]. Agrotec. Cuba 11{1}: 63-68. WA 30: 4277.

5.8-89 Labrada, R., and Paredes, E. 1979. Effectiveness of diphenamid in seedbeds of pepper (Capsicum annuum) [in Spanish]. Arotec. Cuba 11{1}: 63-68. WA 30: 3876.

5.8-90 Lackovic, A. 1975. Experiences with the use of the herbicide Gramoxone for the renovation of grass stands [in Slovak]. Agrochemia 15: 339-341. HERB AB 49: 1380.

5.8-91 Lehman, S.K., and Dickson, T.K. 1976. Hercules 26905, a phosphate herbicide. Proc. South. Weed Sci. Soc. 29: 438 (Abstr.). WA 26: 1120.

5.8-92 Liefstingh, G., Pande, P.N., and Sijtsma, R. 1971. Asulam for weed control in opium poppies [in Dutch]. Meded. Fac. Landbouwwet. Rijksuniv. Gent 36: 1257-1269. WA 22: 42.

5.8-93 Lovyanikov, P.T., Puchin, V.M., Baginskii, O.V., Vekshin, B.S., and Sheverdinov, V.T. 1980. Economic effectiveness of using herbicides in medicinal plant production [in Russian]. Rastit. Resur. 16: 451-455. HA 51: 4892.

5.8-94 Maas, G. 1979. Herbicide residues in some medicinal plants. Planta Med. 36: 251 (Abstr.).

5.8-95 Maddens, K., Sarrazyn, R., and Himme, M. Van. 1975. Chemical weed control in coffee chicory and witloof chicory [in Flemish]. Tuinbouwberichten 39: 253-255. HA 46: 313.

5.8-96 Magnifico, V. 1974. A comparison between herbicides used in peppers [in Italian]. Riv. Agron. 8: 305-309. WA 25: 164.

5.8-97 Mahay, S.C., Hundal, J.S., Pande, P.N., and Mittra, M.K. 1974. Paraquat for interrow weed control in sugarcane, maize and Japanese mint (Mentha) grown in Tarai. Indian J. Weed Sci. 5: 120-128. WA 24: 556.

5.8-98 Marinkovic, N., and Zivkovic, N. 1977. New possibilities for weed control in direct seeded tomato and pepper using the herbicide napropamide (Devrinol 50 WP) [in Serbo-Croatian]. Zast. Bilja 28{142}: 455-467 WA 29: 1620.

5.3-99 Marlow, H. 1980. Possible methods of controlling couch grass in horticultural crops [in German]. Nachrichtenbl. Pflanzenschutz DDR 34: 118-121. HA 51: 5417.

5.8-100 Martynyuk, V.I., and Martynyuk, A.A. 1974. Comparative effectiveness of herbicides in coriander crops [in Russian]. Tr. Vses. Nauchno-Issled. Inst. Efirnomaslichn. Kul't. 7: 53-58. WA 25: 2916.

5.8-101 Martynyuk, V.I. 1974. Test results of the application of 3,4-D (propanil) herbicides in coriander crops [in Russian]. Tr. Vses. Nauchno-Issled. Inst. Efirnomaslichn. Kul't. 7: 116-123. WA 25: 3304.

5.8-102 Martynyuk, V.I., and Martynyuk, A.A. 1975. Chemical weed control in basil plantings [in Russian]. Tr. Vses. Nauchno-Issled. Inst. Efirnomaslichn. Kul't. 8: 131-139. WA 28: 974.

5.8-103 McIntyre, G. 1978. Herbicide trials in garlic and onion crops [in French]. Rev. Agric. Sucr. Ile Maurice 57{1}: 21-22. HA 49: 1161.

5.8-104 Mehrotra, O.N., Garg, R.C., and Sharma, A.P. 1972. Chemical control of weeds in mustard (Brassica juncea L.). Indian J. Agron. 17: 194-198. WA 22: 2267.

5.8-105 Meier, F. 1976. Weed control in marjoram [in German]. Nachrichtenbl. Pflanzenschutz DDR 30: 177-178. HA 47: 5879.

5.8-106 Mikhailova, A., and Genov, G. 1978. Paarlan for dodder control on capsicum seedlings [in Bulgarian]. Rastit. Zasht. 26{3}: 30-32. WA 29: 2449

5.8-107 Misra, L.P., Kapoor, L.D., and Choudhri, R.S. 1973. Studies on the efficacy of some herbicides on the control of weeds in Japanese mint. Proc. Indian Acad. Sci. Sect. B 79: 110-119.

5.8-108 Moens, M., Jami, T., Himme, M. van, and Stryckers, J. 1980. Chemical weed control in capsicum crops in Tunisia [in French]. Meded. Fac. Landbouwwet. Rijksuniv. Gent 45: 1135-1152. WA 30: 2387.

5.8-109 Mollejas, J.F., and Mata, R.H. 1973. Chemical control of weeds in garlic (Allium sativum) [in Spanish]. Boletin Tecnico, Estacion Experimental Agricola Fabio Baudrit Moreno 6{4}: 1-13. WA 25: 986.

5.8-110 Monaco, T.J. 1975. Dinitroaniline herbicides in vegetable crops. Proc. South. Weed Sci. Soc. 28: 179 (Abstr.). WA 25: 982.

5.8-111 Monaco, T.J., and Sanders, D.C. 1976. Promising new herbicides for vegetable crops. Proc. South. Weed Sci. Soc. 29: 210-218. WA 26: 354.

5.8-112 Morales T., L. 1977. Demonstrative parcels for weed control in sesame and soybeans [in Spanish]. Pages 20-30 in S.B. Camacho-B., S.B., ed. Informe de progreso 1976 del programa nacional de fisiologia vegetal. Instituto Colombiana Agropecuario, Bogota, Columbia.

5.8-113 Muhlethaler, P. 1978. Weed control with Stomp in potatoes and vegetables [in German]. Mitt. Schweiz. Landwirtsch. 26{1}: 39-40. WA 27: 2530

5.8-114 Naber, H. 1977. Herbicide injury [in Flemish]. Gewasbescherming 1977{8}: 1-7. WA 26: 3535.

5.8-115 Nagaich, B.B., Chaubey, I.P., Singh, S.J., Upreti, G.C., and Kaley, D.M. 1972. Effect of herbicides on infection, concentration and spread of potato virus X. Indian J. Hortic. 29: 105-108. WA 24: 2184.

5.8-116 Nagy, F., and Szalay, P. 1978. Elaboration of an up-to-date chemical weed control method for tarragon grown on the farm scale [in Hungarian]. Herba Hung. 17{3}: 49-63. WA 29: 3627.

5.8-117 Nagy, F. 1977. Up to date weed control system in the large scale production of lavender, peppermint, tarragon and chamomile [in Hungarian]. Novenyvedelem (Budapest) 13: 399-408. Wd. Ab. 27: 4081.

5.8-118 Nagy, F., and Szalay, P. 1976. The possibilities of chemical weed control in cultivated angelica (Angelica archangelica) and lovage (Levisticum officinale) [in Hungarian]. Herba Hung. 15{1}: 69-79 HA 47: 1863.

5.8-119 Nagy, F., and Szalay, P. 1977. Development of modern chemical weed control technology in lavender [in Hungarian]. Herba Hung. 16{3}: 59-75. HA 49: 1448.

5.8-120 Nagy, F., Foldesi, D., and Szalay, P. 1978. Recent results of chemical weed control in peppermint (Mentha piperita) [in Hungarian]. Herba Hung. 17{1}: 65-81. HA 49: 1452.

5.8-121 Nagy, F., Szalay, P., and Foldesi, D. 1978. Development of chemical weed control technology in Roman chamomile (Anthemis nobilis) based on herbicide rotation [in Hungarian]. Herba Hung. 17{2}: 67-81. HA 49: 1444.

5.8-122 Nagy, F., Foldesi, D., and Szalay, P. 1980. Recent results of preemergent chemical weed control in combined plantings of dill and clary sage [in Hungarian]. Herba Hung. 19{2}: 37-55. CA 93: 162584.

5.8-123 Nastev, N. 1972. Herbicides for weed control on medicinal plants [in Bulgarian]. Priroda (Sofia) 21{6}: 30-32. HA 44: 4229.

5.8-124 Neel, P.L. 1976. Comparisons of phytotoxicity between soil-applied dicamba and two rates of an experimental dicamba analogue on twenty-three containerized species of environmental plants. Proc. Fla. State Hortic. Soc. 89: 341-343. HA 48: 3645.

5.8-125 Neubauer, S., Stary, F., and Klimes, K. 1972. Potablan, a suitable herbicide for chamomile culture [in Czech]. Nase Liecive Rastliny 9: 114-115. HA 23: 789.

5.8-126 Neururer, H. 1972. Recent results of weed control in chicory [in German]. Pflanzenarzt 25: 4-6. WA 22: 2829.

5.8-127 Neururer, H. 1975. Weed control in chicory [in German]. Pflanzenarzt 28: 123-125. HA 46: 10210.

5.8-128 Neururer, H. 1977. Weed control in chicory [in German]. Pflanzenarzt 30: 7-8. WA 27: 1827.

5.8-129 Neururer, H. 1978. There is no fully effective herbicide for chicory [in German]. Pflanzenarzt 31: 5-6. HA 48: 10476.

5.8-130 Nishi, S. 1972. 1971 Evaluation of candidate pesticides. (C-4)

Herbicides: vegetable fields. Jpn. Pestic. Inf. 1972{12}: 33-37. WA 23: 57.

5.8-131 Nishi, S. 1977. 1976 Evaluation of candidate pesticides. (C-IV). Herbicides: vegetable fields. Jpn. Pestic. Inf. 1977{32}: 25-28. WA 27: 2942.

5.8-132 Noeddegaard, E., and Hansen, K.E. 1972. Experiments with fungicides and insecticides in agricultural and other field crops in 1970 [in Danish]. Tidsskr. Planteavl 76: 63-76. RAE-A 61: 5065.

5.8-133 Ogg, A.G., Jr. 1980. Weed control research in mint. Proc. Annu. Meet. Oreg. Essent. Oil Grow. League 31: 82-83.

5.8-134 Pandey, R.K., and Singh, R.P. 1977. Chemical control of weeds in coriander (Coriandrum sativum L.) and spinach (Spinacia oleracea L.). Current Agriculture 1{1/2}: 45-49. WA 30: 1710.

5.8-135 Pank, F., Eichholz, E., Grubner, P., and Hauschild, J. 1980. Results of several years' trials on chemical weed control in marjoram (Majorana hortensis Moench) [in German]. Arch. Phytopathol. Pflanzenschutz 16: 135-147. WA 30: 910.

5.8-136 Pank, F., Hanitzch, J., and Zeuner, E. 1976. Weed control in poppies [in German]. Nachrichtenbl. Pflanzenschutz DDR 30: 174-176.

5.8-137 Pank, F., and Marlow, H. 1980. Chemical weed control in medicinal and culinary herbs [in German]. Nachrichtenbl. Pflanzenschutz DDR 34: 36-42. WA 30: 909.

5.8-138 Pank, F., Eichholz, E., and Hauschild, J. 1978. Chemical weed control in thyme (Thymus vulgaris) [in German]. Pharmazie 33: 369-371.

5.8-139 Pank, F., Marlow, H., Eichholz, E., Hauschild, J., and Zygmunt, B. 1979. Chemical control of weeds on Satureja hortensis L. plantations [in German]. Herba Pol. 25: 247-260. AGRICOLA.

5.8-140 Pank, F., and Neczypor, W. 1978. Studies on chemical weed control in row crop plantings of wooly foxglove (Digitalis lanata Ehrh.) [in German]. Pharmazie 33: 677-683.

5.8-141 Perugini, A. 1976. New possibilities for weed control in garlic [in Italian]. Not. Mal. Piante 1976{94-95}: 133-139. WA 27: 3301.

5.8-142 Peschken, D.P. 1977. Host specificity of Tingis ampliata (Tingidae: Heteroptera): a candidate for the biological control of Canada thistle (Cirsium arvense). Can. Entomol. 109: 669-674.

5.8-143 Picco, D., and Ottolini, P.L. 1972. Weed control in garlic [in Italian]. Informatore Agrario 28: 11110-11111. HA 43: 1256.

5.8-144 Pimpini, F. 1978. Weed control in various industrial crops [in Italian]. Inf. Fitopatol. 28{8}: 46-48. HA 49: 7162.

5.8-145 Pimpini, F. 1974. Weed control in a delayed pepper crop under a tunnel [in Italian]. Riv. Agron. 8: 298-304. WA 25: 163.

5.8-146 Pospichal, M.T., Burgis, D.S., and Locascio, S.J. 1976. Evaluation of napropamide for weed control in tomatoes and peppers. Proc. South. Weed Sci. Soc. 29: 196-202. WA 26: 106.

5.8-147 Raj Singh, Turkhede, B.B., and Singh, R.K. 1980. Use of farmyard manure as a crop protectant in chemical weed control in opium poppy. Indian J. Agron. 25: 308-310. WA 30: 3076.

5.8-148 Rajagopal, A., Muthukrishnan, C.R., and Asokmetha, V. 1976. Weed control studies in chilli. Madras Agric. J. 63: 470-472. WA 27: 2222.

5.8-149 Ramirez de Vallejo, A. 1973. The use of herbicides applied in garlic at different stages of growth [in Spanish]. Agric. Tec. (Santiago) 33: 87-90. HA 44: 2487.

5.8-150 Rapparini, G., and Bencivelli, A. 1974. Chemical weed control trials in transplanted tomatoes, peppers and egg-plant [in Italian]. Riv. Agron. 8: 293-297. WA 24: 2625.

5.8-151 Reichling, J., Becker, H., and Drager, P.-D. 1978. Herbicides in camomile cultivation. Acta Hortic. 1978{73}: 331-338.

5.8-152 Riggleman, J.D. 1971. Leaf crops-cole crops, spinach, lettuce, parsley. Proc. Northeast Weed Control Conf. 25 (Suppl.): 3. AGRICOLA.

5.8-153 Roberts, H.A., Bond, W., and Potter, M.E. 1980. Evaluation of R-40244 for weed control in drilled vegetable crops. Ann. Appl. Biol. 94(Suppl: Tests of Agrochemicals and Cultivars 1): 48-49.

5.8-154 Roberts, H.A., and Ricketts, M.E. 1973. Comparative tolerance of some dicotyledons to pronamide and chlorpropham. Pestic. Sci. 4: 83-87. FCA 26: 5218.

5.8-155 Roberts, H.A., and Bond, W. 1974. Evaluation of AC 92 553 for weed control in vegetable crops. Proc. Brit. Weed Cont. Conf. 12: 387-394. WA 24: 2607.

5.8-156 Romanowski, R.R. 1977. Weed control methodology with vegetable crops in the People's Republic of China. Proc. North Cent. Weed Control Conf. 1977. 32: 91 (Abstr.). WA 28: 1856.

5.8-157 Romanowski, R.R., and Warren, G.F. 1978. Research results with diclofop in vegetable crops. Proc. North Cent. Weed Control Conf. 1978. 33: 170 (Abstr.). WA 29: 2808.

5.8-158 Saimbhi, M.S., and Randhawa, K.S. 1976. Herbicidal control of weeds in transplanted chilli. Punjab Hortic. J. 16: 146-148. WA 30: 123.

5.8-159 Samoladas, T.Kh. 1971. The effects of repeated and combination herbicide treatments on the soil [in Russian]. Pochvovedenie 1971{7}: 148-149. WA 22: 2701.

5.8-160 Sanok, W.J., Selleck, G.W., and Kline, W.L. 1977. Herbicides for weed control in onions and shallots. Proc. Annu. Meet. Northeast. Weed Sci. Soc. Baltimore, 1977. 31: 261-265. WA 27: 961.

5.8-161 Semak, V. 1971. Effectiveness of simazine on fruit-producing fields of lavender [in Russian]. Khim. Sel. Khoz. 9{10}: 779-780. CA 76: 55174.

5.8-162 Shcheglov, Yu. V., Vladimirtsev, I.F., Cherkasov, V.M., Khripko, S.S., Boldyrev, I.V., Spiridonov, Yu. Ya., Kozina, L.S., and Savenko,

N.F. 1972. The herbicidal activity of some derivatives of tricholoroacetaldehyde (chloral). Report No. 1. 1-Hydroxy(alkoxy)-2-trichloroethyl amides and amines [in Russian]. Khim. Sel'sk. Khoz. 10: 780-783. WA 22: 1419.

5.8-163 Sheinbaum, Y. 1976. Sensitivity of solanaceous seedlings to dipping treatments of oxadiazon. Phytoparasitica 4{2}: 154. WA 27: 199.

5.8-164 Sijtsma, R., Baart, E.A.D., and Vreeke, S. 1975. Chemical weed control in caraway [in Dutch]. Meded. Fac. Landbouwwet. Rijksuniv. Gent 40: 961-973. WA 26: 575.

5.8-165 Singh, Ajit, and Balyan, S.S. 1973. New herbicides for controlling weeds in Mentha piperita L. Indian J. Weed Sci. 5: 38-41. WA 23: 1520.

5.8-166 Singh, A., and Balyan, S.S. 1975. Herbicidal control of weeds in Mentha citrata Ehrh. Indian J. Weed Sci. 7: 115-118. AGRICOLA.

5.8-167 Skrubis, B. 1971. Effect of weed control on the yield of herb and the yield and oil composition of Mentha piperita L. Flavour Ind. 2: 367-369.

5.8-168 Smirnov, B.A., and Zotov, L.I. 1972. The mutual interrelationships of plants in mixed associations as a factor influencing the phytotoxicity of herbicides [in Russian]. Izv. Timiryazevsk. S-kh. Akad. 1972{5}: 132-141. WA 22: 2924.

5.8-169 Stalder, L., Potter, C.A., and Barben, E. 1974. The state of chemical weed control and some results of research activity in 1973 with herbicides in Swiss vegetable growing [in German]. Gemusebau 36{1}: 1, 3-12. HA 44: 8475.

5.8-170 Stanger, C.E., and Rudd, O. 1979. Weed control in mint. Spec. Rep. Oreg. Agric. Exp. Stn. 1979{554}: 3-18. AGRICOLA.

5.8-171 Stonov, L.D. 1975. New organophosphorus herbicides and desiccants. Pages 141-147 in 8th International congress of plant protection, Papers at sessions. vol. 2, USSR Organizing Committee, Moscow, USSR. WA 25: 3486.

5.8-172 Stoyanov, P., Stoev, G., and Velev, B. 1973. Weed control in summer garlic [in Bulgarian]. Gradinarstvo 15{4}: 27-28. HA 45: 3120.

5.8-173 Sweet, R.D., Bonanno, A.R., Warholic, D.T., and Minotti, P.L. 1980. Alachlor for transplanted vegetables. Proc. Annu. Meet. Northeast. Weed Sci. Soc. 34: 170 (Abstr.). WA 29: 4029.

5.8-174 Synak, J., and Priehradny, S. 1972. On the interaction of nitrogen with pyrazone [in Slovak]. Agrochemia 12: 268-269. WA 22: 2458.

5.8-175 Temmerman, L. De, and Hofmans, E. 1978. Topical (weed) control problems in chicory [in Flemish]. Boer en de Tuinder 8{417}: 13. HA 48: 8102.

5.8-176 Timoshenko, M.A. 1972. Prometryne in dill culture [in Russian]. Zashch. Rast. 17{5}: 28.

5.8-177 Tkachenko, A.L. 1979. Efficacy of Propanid (propanil) in coriander crops [in Russian]. Khim. Sel'sk. Khoz. 17{10}: 41-42. WA 29: 1304.

5.8-178 Todua, N.A., and Khubitiya, R.A. 1972. The effectiveness of herbicides against Solanum carolinense [in Russian]. Khim. Sel'sk. Khoz. 10: 530-532. HA 43: 2495.

5.8-179 Trunkenboltz, M., and Prin, M. 1977. A contribution to the study of weed control in garlic (Allium sativum L.), shallot (A. ascalonium L.) and onion (A. cepa L.) crops [in French]. Pages 722-732 in Compte Rendu de la 9e Conference du COLUMA. Maison de l'UNESCO, Paris. WA 27: 1812.

5.8-180 Trunkenboltz, M. 1975. Chemical weed control in garlic [in French]. Pepinier. Hortic. Maraichers 1975{155}: 49-51.

5.8-181 Vekshin, B.S. 1976. Herbicides and the optimization of methods of cultivation of medicinal crops. Pharm. Chem. J. (Engl. Transl.) 10: 1655-1659. Translation of Khim.-Farm. Zh. 10{12}: 78-82, 1976. WA 2228.

5.8-182 Vekshin, B.S., Bukina, N.V., Pushkina, G.P., and Efimova, V.N. 1974. The use of herbicides in peppermint plantations [in Russian]. Agrokhimiya 11: 134-138. WA 24: 2085.

5.8-183 Vekshin, B.S., Bukina, N.V., and Pushkina, V.P. 1976. Herbicides in chamomile crops [in Russian]. Agrokhimiya 13: 119-123. WA 26: 979.

5.8-184 Vekshin, B.S., and Bukina, N.V. 1973. Herbicide application to stands of valerian [in Russian]. Khim. Sel'sk. Khoz. 11{1}: 46-51. AGRICOLA.

5.8-185 Vercesi, B. 1972. Chemical weed control in garlic. Results from a year's trials [in Italian]. Inf. Fitopatol. 22{1/2}: 11-15. HA 43: 660.

5.8-186 Voevodin, A.V., and Beshanov, A.V. 1977. Weed control in vegetable crops [in Russian]. Tr. Vses. Nauchno-Issled. Inst. Zashch. Rast. 1977{53}: 104-106. WA 29: 2436.

5.8-187 Vostral, H.J., Bowers, R.C., Hogan, W.H., and Holifield, E.L. 1972. U-27267 - A selective herbicide in vegetable crops. Page 1 in Abstracts, 1972 Meeting Weed Science Society of America. The Society, Champaign, Ill. WA 23: 776.

5.8-188 Whitesides, R.E., and Appleby, A.P. 1978. Canada thistle (Cirsium arvense (L.) Scop.) control in peppermint. Pages 29-30 in T.J. Monaco, ed. Abstracts, 1977 Meeting of the Weed Science Society of America. The Society, Champaign, Ill. WA 28: 1865.

5.8-189 Whitesides, R.E., and Appleby, A.P. 1979. DOWCO 290 herbicide for selective control of Canada thistle in peppermint. Down Earth 35{2}: 14-18.

5.8-190 Wilfret, G.J., and Burgis, D.S. 1976. Nutsedge (Cyperus rotundus L.) control using herbicides under fallow conditions. Proc. South. Weed Sci. Soc. 29: 237-243. WA 26: 31.

5.8-191 William, R.D., and Warren, G.F. 1975. Competition between purple nutsedge and vegetables. Weed Sci. 23: 317-323.

5.8-192 Wilson, G.J. 1977. Weed control post-emergence in garlic. N.Z. Commer. Grow. 33{9}: 20. HA 48: 7195.

5.8-193 Zemanek, J. 1971. Small-plot field experiments on chemical control of weeds in poppy. Sb. UVTI (Ustav Vedeckotech. Inform.) Ochr. Rostl. 7: 179-185. AGRICOLA.

5.9 Chemical Contaminants and Plant Growth

5.9-1 Ajit Singh, and Balyan, S.S. 1974. A note on the effect of herbicides on the oil content, herb and oil yield of Mentha arvensis. Indian J. Agron. 19: 231-232. WA 25: 3596.

5.9-2 Beitz, H., Seefeld, F., Hartisch, J., and Heinisch, E. 1971. The uptake of DDT by cultivated plants from DDT-contaminated soils and the factors influencing it [in German]. Nachrichtenbl. Pflanzenschutz. DDR 25: 229-234. RAE-A 63: 3778.

5.9-3 Blagonravova, L.N., and Nilov, G.I. 1976. Effect of pesticides on the activity of peroxidase in horseradish [in Russian]. Khim. Sel'sk. Khoz. 14{11}: 41-42. AGRICOLA.

5.9-4 Briggs, C.J. 1973. Effects of polybutene emulsion sprays on the composition of peppermint oils. Planta Med. 24: 120-126. HA 44: 6974.

5.9-5 Bulinski, R., and Kot, A. 1976. Effect of dinocap on catalase and peroxidase activities in watercress and peas [in Polish]. Bromatol. Chem. Toksykol. 9: 235-239. AGRICOLA.

5.9-6 Burth, U., and Zastrow, J. 1973. Fungicidal effect and several side-effects in benomyl use [in German]. Nachrichtenbl. Pflanzenschutzdienst DDR 27: 161-165. CA 80: 44622.

5.9-7 Caramete, A., Bucur, E., and Rughinis, D. 1979. The mode of action of atrazine in some species of weeds and vegetables [in Romanian]. An. Inst. Cercet. Prot. Plant. Acad. Stiinte Agric. Silvice 15: 359-366. WA 30: 3288.

5.9-8 Catizone, P., and Toderi, G. 1974. Residual effects on Sinapis alba L. of the treatment of wheat with herbicides. Riv. Agron. 8: 173-179. FCA 29: 5126.

5.9-9 Chang, F.-Y., Smith, L.W., and Stephenson, G.R. 1971. Insecticide inhibition of herbicide metabolism in leaf tissues. J. Agric. Food Chem. 19: 1183-1186. RAE-A 62: 1218.

5.9-10 Chauhan, S.V.S., and Singh, S.P. 1972. Effect of maleic hydrazide, FW-450 and dalapon on growth, flowering and pollen viability of Capsicum annuum L. and Datura alba. Indian J. Plant Physiol. 15: 138-147. WA 25: 844.

5.9-11 Chodova, D., and Zemanek, J. 1976. The effect of the herbicide simazine on the respiration rate of scentless mayweed, silky apera, white mustard, wheat and maize. Sb. UVTI (Ustav Vedeckotechnickych Informaci) Ochrana Rostlin 12: 293-298. WA 28: 1074.

5.9-12 Chodova, D., and Zemanek, J. 1977. The effect of simazine on sugar and nitrogen content in scentless mayweed (Tripleurospermum maritimum), silky apera (Apera spica-venti), white mustard (Sinapis alba), wheat and maize [in Czech]. Sb. UVTI (Ustav Vedeckotechnickych Informaci) Ochrana Rostlin 13: 71-75. WA 27: 2705.

5.9-13 Cooke, J.A. 1976. The uptake of sodium monofluoroacetate by plants and its physiological effects. Fluoride 9: 204-212.

5.9-14 Deli, J., and Warren, G.F. 1971. Relative sensitivity of several plants to diphenamid. Weed Sci. 19: 70-72.

5.9-15 Dunsing, M., and Windschild, J. 1976. Quintozene, hexachlorbenzol and pentachloraniline residues in lettuce and soil [in German]. Nachrichtenbl. Pflanzenschutz DDR 30: 106-108. HA 47: 5506.

5.9-16 Everett, P.H., Kalmbacher, R.S., Chambliss, C., and Teem, D.H. 1979. The effect of herbicides applied to corn on subsequent tomato, pepper and cucumber crops. Proc. Soil Crop Sci. Soc. Fl. 39: 122-125. WA 30: 2770.

5.9-17 Fedtke, C. 1977. Formation of nitrite in plants treated with herbicides that inhibit photosynthesis. Pestic. Sci. 8: 152-156.

5.9-18 Hinojo, J.M., and Ramallo, N.E.V. de. 1972. Contamination of irrigation water with hormonal herbicides [in Spanish]. Rev. Ind. Agric. Tucuman 49{2}: 1-8. WA 23: 1649.

5.9-19 Hodgson, R.H., and Hoffer, B.L. 1974. Diphenamid metabolism in pepper. Page 17 in Abstracts, 1974 Meeting Weed Science Society of America. The Society, Champaign, Ill. WA 25: 3106.

5.9-20 Hogue, E.J. 1978. Absorption and translocation of metobromuron and chlorbromuron. J. Environ. Sci. Health. Part B. 13: 323-339.

5.9-21 Janssen, O. 1974. Phylloquinone (Vitamin K1) levels in leaves of plant species differing in susceptibility to 2,4-dichlorophenoxyacetic acid. Physiol. Plant. 31: 323-325.

5.9-22 Karley, S.L.M. 1972. Plantago major L. - spray induced abnormalities. Watsonia 9: 44.

5.9-23 Kavanagh, T. 1974. The influence of herbicides on plant diseases. 2. Vegetables, root crops and potatoes. Sci. Proc. R. Dublin Soc. Ser. B. 3: 251-265.

5.9-24 Khilik, L.A., Bondarenko, T.I., and Karpova, G.Ya. 1979. The effects of 3-years' use of prometryne on the productivity of Nepeta transcaucasica and the soil microflora [in Russian]. Khim. Sel'sk. Khoz. 17{2}: 43-46. WA 28: 3154.

5.9-25 Kostov, T. 1975. Effect of trifluralin and chloramben on the chemical composition of paprika fruits [in Serbo-Croatian]. Agrohemija 7/8: 305-309. AGRICOLA.

5.9-26 Kozaczenko, H., Polak, K., and Przezdziecki, Z. 1974. Effect of urea herbicides on the mineral content of the test plant, Sinapis alba [in Polish]. Zesz. Nauk. Akad. Roln. Techn. Olsztynie Roln. 1974{9}: 155–163. SF 39: 653.

5.9–27 Lee, H.J., and Kwon, Y.W. 1980. Determination of harvesting time and effect of Diquat treatment on sesame cropping after winter barley [in Korean]. Hanguk Changmul Hakhoe Chi 25{2}: 64–67.

5.9–28 Lee, S.A. 1978. Phytotoxic effects of herbicides. Pages 357–366 in L.L. Amin, A.A.S.A. Kadir, Lim Guan Soon, K.G. Singh, Tan Ah Moy, and G. Varghese, eds. Proceedings of the plant protection conference, Kuala Lumpur, March, 1978. Rubber Research Institute of Malaysia, Kuala Lumpur, Malaysia. WA 29: 3113.

5.9–29 Moens, P., Lehmann-Baerts, M., and Boitquin, N. 1974. Action of 2,4-Dichlorophenoxyacetic acid genesis and tracheogenesis of Digitalis-purpurea L. [in French]. Cellule 70: 107–134.

5.9–30 Mohandas, T., and Grant, W.F. 1972. Cytogenetic effects of 2,4-D and amitrole in relation to nuclear volume and DNA content in some higher plants. Can. J. Genet. Cytol. 14: 773–783.

5.9–31 Murthy, P.K., and Rao, D. 1980. Effect of two fungicides on the germination and growth in Brassica nigra Koch. Geobios 7: 160–161. RPP 60: 3392.

5.9–32 Obarski, J. 1972. The influence of thiodan applied against Orthops sp. and Lygus sp. on yields and germination of carrot and parsley seeds [in Polish]. Rocz. Nauk Roln. Ser. E 2{2}: 69–81. AGRICOLA.

5.9–33 Osinskaya, T.V. 1973. Herbicide phytotoxicity and activity in relation to the nutrient level of plants [in Russian]. Khim. Sel'sk. Khoz. 11{1}: 39–42. WA 23: 926.

5.9–34 Ostrowski, J. 1972. Investigating the adsorption of monolinuron and its availability to plants [in Polish]. Rocz. Glebozn. 23: 51–75. WA 22: 1442.

5.9–35 Panchabhavi, K.S., and Thimmaiah, G. 1972. Note on the effect of insecticides on the yield of chilli (Capsicum frutescens L.). Indian J. Agric. Sci. 42: 1067.

5.9–36 Reichling, J., Becker, H., and Vomel, A. 1977. Herbicides in cultivation of Matricaria chamomilla L. II. Communication: Influence of herbicides on the composition of the essential oil [in German]. Planta Med. 32: 235–243.

5.9–37 Ruzicka, R., and Kralovic, J. 1979. Side-effects of insecticides on poppy plants (Papaver somniferum L.) toxicity [in Slovak]. Rostl. Vyroba 25: 537–544. AGRICOLA.

5.9–38 Salam, M.A., and Downey, R.K. 1973. Selectivity of benazolin in Cruciferae. Can. J. Plant Sci. 53: 891–896.

5.9–39 Schilcher, H. 1978. Influence of herbicides and some heavy metals on growth of Matricaria chamomilla L. and the biosynthesis of the essential oils. Acta Hortic. 1978{73}: 339–341.

5.9-40 Schilcher, H. 1977. Influence of herbicides on growth of Matricaria chamomilla and the biosynthesis of the essential oils [in German] Biochem. Physiol. Pflanz. (BPP) 171: 385-390.

5.9-41 Shikhotov, V.M., and Kuchin, V.V. 1975. The effect of herbicides on the carbohydrate content of alpine pasture plants [in Russian]. Khim. Sel'sk. Khoz. 13: 448-451. WA 25: 555.

5.9-42 Shikhotov, V.M., and Kuchin, V.V. 1975. Changes in ascorbic acid, carotene and chlorophyll contents of leaves of alpine plants under the influence of herbicides [in Russian]. Agrokhimiya 12: 107-112. WA 25: 554.

5.9-43 Singh, A. 1977. Effect of herbicide on Mentha. Indian J. Agron. 22: 63-65 WA 29: 1644.

5.9-44 Sperling, D., and Jakob, F. 1973. Herbicidal effect on phosphate uptake and transport [in German]. Wiss. Beitr. Martin-Luther-Univ. Halle-Wittenberg 1973{10 P1}: 115-126. FCA 29: 9998.

5.9-45 Szymczak, J., and Ciaciura, M. 1980. Effect of fungicides on ascorbinase and peroxidase activity in poppy seedlings [in Polish]. Herba Pol. 26: 73-76.

5.9-46 Takematsu, T., Takeuchi, Y., and Hojo, S. 1979. Studies on the behaviour of maleic hydrazide in plants. 1. Distribution and residues in perennial plants [in Japanese]. Zasso Kenkyu 24: 7-11. WA 29: 851.

5.9-47 Tewari, M.N., and Balasimha, D. 1976. The influence of substituted ureas and uracils on growth, sugar content and peroxidase activity in fenugreek (Trigonella foenum graecum L.) seedlings. Indian J. Plant Physiol. 19: 2217-219. HA 48: 2735.

5.9-48 Tomkins, D.J., and Grant, W.F. 1976. Monitoring natural vegetation for herbicide-induced chromosomal aberrations. Mutat. Res. 36: 73-83.

5.9-49 Vahidy, A.A. 1973. Differential tolerance within certain cruciferous crops to Vegaclex, CIPC, Dymid and Teflan. Pak. J. Bot. 5: 79-85.

5.9-50 Vassiliou, G., and Müller, F. 1978. Metabolism of metoxuron in umbelliferous crops of varying degrees of sensitivity [in German]. Meded. Fac. Landbouwwet. Rijksuniv. Gent 43: 1181-1191. WA 28: 3716.

5.9-51 Vekshin, B.S., Bukina, N.V., Pushkina, G.P., Kochetkov, V.P., Novikova, P.I., and Efimova, V.N. 1976. Action of herbicides on seeds (planting) of Tangutsk rhubarb, five lobed water dropwort, wooly foxglove, flea plantain, and leuzea. Pharm. Chem. J. (Engl. Transl.) 10: 926-929. Translation of Khim.-Farm. Zh. 10{7}: 86-90, 1976.

5.9-52 Watkin, E.M., and Sagar, G.R. 1972. Effect of paraquat on seed germination. Weed Res. 12: 195-198.

5.9-53 Weierich, A.J., Nelson, Z.A., and Appleby, A.P. 1977. Influence of Fonofos on the distribution and metabolism of 14C-terbacil in peppermint. Weed Sci. 25: 27-29.

5.9-54 Zemanek, J., and Kovar, J. 1975. The effect of herbicides on the carbohydrate content of sensitive and resistant plants [in Czech]. Sb. UVTI (Ustav Vedeckotech. Inform.) Ochr. Rostl. 11: 227–232.

5.9–55 Zhmurko, L.I., and Bobyr', A.D. 1975. Physiological and biochemical characteristics of the selectivity of triazines in the presence of viral infection [in Ukrainian]. Mikrobiol. Zh. 37: 197–201.

6.0 CULINARY STUDIES

6.1 Colorants, Condiments, and Flavorings

6.1-1 American Spice Trade Association. 1975. What you should know about paprika. Arecanut Spices Bull. 7: 7–9. AGRICOLA.

6.1-2 Andre, L. and Varga, Zs. 1976. Comparative color test of spice paprika characteristics from two successive years [in Hungarian]. Konzerv. Paprikaip. 1976{5}: 171–174.

6.1-3 Anonymous. 1974. Rosemary: a beloved southern spice [in German]. Fleischwirtschaft 54{7}: 1126–1127.

6.1-4 Balla, F. 1976. History of the production of red pepper pulp in Hungary [in Hungarian]. Konzerv. Paprikaip. 6: 201–205. AGRICOLA.

6.1-5 Bannar, R. 1978. Light oil-free dressings that never need shaking. Food Eng. 50{6}: EF–22 – EF–23.

6.1-6 Becker, H. 1971. Comparative studies on the composition of essential oils of various commercial products from Pimpinella anisum [in German]. Dtsch. Apoth. Ztg. 111{2}: 41–43. CA 74: 130269.

6.1-7 Belafi-Rethy, K., Iglewski, S., Kerenyi, E. and Kolta, R. 1973. Composition of domestic and foreign volatile oils. II. Analysis of Hungarian peppermint oils [in German]. Acta Chim. (Budapest) 76: 167–177. CA 80: 19365.

6.1-8 Benedek, L. and Mecs, J. 1971. Determination of the pigment content in paprika [in Hungarian]. Konserv-Paprikaipar 1971{2}: 61–64. CA 76: 32989.

6.1-9 Bennasar Bibiloni, C. and Farre Rovira, R. 1976. Analytical study of paprika oleoresins [in Spanish]. An. Bromatol. 28: 45–56. AGRICOLA.

6.1-10 Bizheva, N. 1976. Tarragon [in Bulgarian]. Gradinarstvo 57{7}: 40–41. Bib.Ag. 42: 51532.

6.1-11 Bizheva, N., Madzharova, D. and Rainova, L. 1977. Garden cress, tarragon and costmary, valuable condiment plants [in Bulgarian]. Gr adinar. Lozar. Nauka 14{6}: 78–83. HA 48: 9275.

6.1-12 Brasil, E., Silva, G.A. de A., Bauer, L., Saraiva de Sigueira, N.C., Bacha, C.T.M. and Santana, B.M.S. 1979. Essential oil of Lippia citriodora Kunth (Rio Grande do Sul) [in Portuguese]. Trib. Farm. (Curitiba) 47{1}: 96–98. AGRICOLA.

6.1-13 Bryant, T.G. 1977. Thyme honey - liquid gold. N.Z. J. Agric. 135{2}: 19, 20.

6.1-14 Charazka, Z., Karwowska, K. and Tokarska, B. 1975. Caraway extract. Its flavoring value [in Polish]. Pr. Inst. Lab. Badaw. Przem. Spozyw. 25{2}: 235-240. CA 84: 149405.

6.1-15 Chubey, B.B., Dorrell, D.G. and Marshall, H.H. 1976. Essential oil research. Can. Agric. 21{4}: 15-16. HA 47: 4883.

6.1-16 Cook, M.K. and Gominger, B.H. 1974. Glycyrrhizin. Pages 211-215 in G.E. Inglett, ed. Symposium: sweeteners. AVI Pub. Co., Westport, Conn. AGRICOLA.

6.1-17 Cornell, J. 1975. Herbs in vermouth. Herbarist 41: 35-36.

6.1-18 Dellaglio, F. 1973. Garlic-mustard odour in Grana cheese [in Italian]. Latte 47{1}: 31. DSA 35: 5273.

6.1-19 Demianowicz, Z. 1979. Nectar secretion and honey yield of Taraxacum officinale Web. [in Polish]. Pszczelnicze Zesz. Nauk 23: 97-103. AGRICOLA.

6.1-20 Domenech Montagut, M., Farre Rovira, R. and Torre Boronat, M.C. de la. 1971. Color stability of the oleoresin of the paprika [in Spanish]. An. Bromatol. 29: 461-482. AGRICOLA.

6.1-21 Duke, J.A. and Reed, C.F. 1978. Caraway--an economic plant. Q.J. Crude Drug Res. 16: 116-118. AGRICOLA.

6.1-22 Dwyer, J.E. 1977. What's in a name? Dandelion. Garden (N.Y.) 1{2}: 10-11.

6.1-23 Esaki, S., Konishi, F. and Kamiya, S. 1978. Synthesis and taste of some glycosides of glycyrrhetic acid. Agric. Biol. Chem. 42: 1599-1600.

6.1-24 Farnsworth, N.R. 1973. Current status of sugar substitutes. Cosmet. Perfum. 88{7}: 27-35.

6.1-25 Fassati, C. 1971. Saffron-vegetable gold [in Italian]. Rilancio Agric. Vet. Zootec. 3{1}: 8-9. AGRICOLA.

6.1-26 Ferrazzi, P. 1974. "Dandelion" honeys from Piedmont and Lombardy. I. Melisso-palynological analysis [in Italian]. Apic. Mod. 65: 21-26. AGRICOLA.

6.1-27 Ferrazzi, P. 1974. Investigations on the Taraxacum officinale pollen shortage in "dandelion" honeys from Piedmont and, Lombardy [in Italian]. Apic. Mod. 65: 58-64. AGRICOLA.

6.1-28 Ferrazzi, P. 1978. Sage [in Italian]. Apic. Mod. 69: 97-98. AGRICOLA.

6.1-29 Frattini, C., Bicchi, C., Barettini, C. and Nano, G.M. 1977. Volatile flavor components of licorice. J. Agric. Food Chem. 25: 1238-1241.

6.1-30 Gardner, R. 1978. Florence fennel: a touch of aniseed in salads and soups. J. Agric. (Victoria, Aust.) 76: 275-276.

6.1-31 Gerhardt, U. 1978. A spice whose smell is reminiscent of lovage and celery: fenugreek (Trigonella foenum-graecum) [in German]. Fleischwirtschaft 58: 1398-1399.

6.1-32 Gerhardt, U. 1976. Garlic: both a spice and a medicinal plant [in German]. Fleischwirtschaft 56: 910-911.

6.1-33 Gerhardt, U. 1976. Chives: a vitamin rich kitchen spice [in German]. Fleischwirtschaft 56: 1190-1191.

6.1-34 Gerhardt, U. 1979. Oregano: a piquant spice [in German]. Fleischwirtschaft 59: 1456-1457.

6.1-35 Gerhardt, U. 1980. Savory - a spice for soups, vegetables and salads [in German]. Fleischwirtschaft 60: 442-443.

6.1-36 Gerhardt, U. 1975. White and black mustard: spicy and preserving [in German]. Fleischwirtschaft 55: 1130-1131.

6.1-37 Gerhardt, U. 1974. Thyme: an aromatic spice plant [in German]. Fleischwirtschaft 54: 652-653.

6.1-38 Gerhardt, U. 1975. Laurel: a spice with dominant taste [in German]. Fleischwirtschaft 55: 594-595.

6.1-39 Gerhardt, U. 1974. Sage: a strong spicy herb [in German]. Fleischwirtschaft 54: 1402-1403.

6.1-40 Gerhardt, U. 1977. French tarragon: an aristocrat among kitchen herbs [in German]. Fleischwirtschaft 57: 828-829.

6.1-41 Gerhardt, U. 1975. Horseradish, a terribly sharp spice [in German]. Fleischwirtschaft 55: 1490-1491. AGRICOLA.

6.1-42 Gerhardt, U. 1974. Rosemary, a beloved southern spice [in German]. Fleischwirtschaft 54: 1126-1127.

6.1-43 Gerhardt, U. and Pladt, J. 1973. Is paprika a spice or a colour [in German]. Fleischwirtschaft 53: 1557, 1560-1563. AGRICOLA.

6.1-44 Gerhardt, U. 1979. Basil - a king among spice plants [in German]. Fleischwirtschaft 59: 1823-1829.

6.1-45 Gonzalez Soler, S. 1973. The caper: characteristics and commercialization [in Spanish]. Agricultura (Madrid) 42{495}: 422-425. AGRICOLA.

6.1-46 Govindarajan, V.S. 1973. Evaluation of spices and oleoresins. Pages 195-199 in N.M. Nayar, ed. Proceedings of the first national symposium on plantation crops, Dec. 8-9, 1972, Trivandrum, India. J. Plant. Crops 1(Suppl.).

6.1-47 Gunston, David. 1979. Saffron adds zest and colour to our food. Nutr. Food Sci. 1979{56}: 14. AGRICOLA.

6.1-48 Gunston, David. 1979. Paprika. Nutr. Food Sci. 1979{57}: 18. AGRICOLA.

6.1-49 Hills, L.D. 1973. Cooking and curing with comfrey. Soil Health 8: 38-39. AGRICOLA.

6.1-50 Hodge, W.H. 1975. Survey of flavour producing plants. Int. Flavours Food Addit. 6: 244-245.

6.1-51 Hook, E.B. 1978. Dietary cravings and aversions during pregnancy. Am. J. Clin. Nutr. 31: 1355-1362.

6.1-52 Howard, H.W. 1976. Watercress: Rorippa nasturtium-aquaticum (Cruciferae). Pages 62-64 in N.W. Simmonds, ed. Evolution of crop plants. Longman, London, G.B. AGRICOLA.

6.1-53 Ilyas, M. 1973. Famous plants: sesame. Botanica 23: 64-66. AGRICOLA.

6.1-54 Kamneva, Z.P., Galkina, S.N. and Yavorskaya, L.M. 1978. Use of spices in salads [in Russian]. Konservnaya i Ovoshchesushil'naya Promyshlennost' 1978{1}: 24-25. FSTA 13: 2T52.

6.1-55 Kojima, K. 1980. Natural sweeteners [in Japanese]. Shoku no Kaguku 56: 40-43. CA 95: 22970.

6.1-56 Kojima, M., Uchida, M. and Akahori, Y. 1973. Studies on the volatile components of Wasabia japonica, Brassica juncea, Cocholearia armoracia by gas chromatography- mass spectrometry. I. Determination of low mass volatile components [in Japanese]. Yakugaku Zasshi 93: 453-459. CA 80: 130475.

6.1-57 Kojima, M. and Nakano, V. 1979. Quality of Japanese horseradish ("Wasabi") gas chromatography. IX. Characteristics of volatile components in the hydrolysates of Wasabia japonica, horseradish and mustard [in Japanese]. Nippon Shokuhin Kogyo Gakkaishi 26: 209-214. CA 91: 191450.

6.1-58 Kojima, M. 1973. Volatile components of Wasabia japonica. 2. Volatile components, other than isothiocyanates, of Wasabia japonica [in Japanese]. Hakho Kogaku Zasshi 51: 670-676. CA 80: 1428.

6.1-59 Krishnamurthy, N., Mathew, A.G., Nambudiri, E.S. and Lewis, Y.S. 1973. Essential oils and oleoresins from major spices of India. Pages 171-174 in N.M. Nayar, ed. Proceedings of the first national symposium on plantation crops, Dec. 8-9, 1972, Trivandrum, India. J. Plant. Crops 1(Suppl.).

6.1-60 Latif, A. and Erian, F.A. 1973. Search for new fixed oils. Part 1. Fixed oils of high iodine value from seeds of marjoram (Marjorana hortensis Moench.) and of thyme (Thymus vulgaris L.). Agric. Res. Rev. 51{5}: 115-121. HA 45: 10000.

6.1-61 Lavie, P. 1976. Rosmary, Rosmarinus officinalis L. [in French]. Bull. Tech. Apic. 3{1}: 15-26. AA 29: 516.

6.1-62 Lawrence, B.M. 1979. Chemical evaluation of various bay oils. Int. Congr. Essent. Oils, [Pap.], 7th, 1977. 7: 172-179. CA 92: 64511.

6.1-63 Lengyel, A. 1976. Chamomile [in Hungarian]. Termeszet Vilaga 7: 328-331. AGRICOLA.

6.1-64 Liefstingh, G. and Kuizenga, J. 1972. Caraway [in Dutch]. Bedrijfsontwikkeling 3: 191-195. AGRICOLA.

6.1-65 Maga, J.A. 1975. Capsicum. CRC Crit. Rev. Food Sci. Nutr. 6: 177-199.

6.1-66 Martindale, W.L. 1972. Horseradish. J. Agric. (Victoria, Aust.) 70: 288-289. AGRICOLA.

6.1-67 Mathew, A.G., Nambudiri, E., Ananthakrishna, S.M., Krishnamurthy, N., and Lewis, Y.S. 1971. An important method for estimation of capsaicin in Capsicum oleoresin. Lab. Pract. 20: 856-858.

6.1-68 Mathew, A.G., Lewis, Y.S., Jagadishan, R., Nambudiri, E.S. and Krishnamurthy, N. 1971. Oleoresin capsicum. Flavour Ind. 2: 23-26.

6.1-69 Morales, Y. and Fraile, E. 1977. Saffron, a productive crop [in Spanish]. Agricultura (Madrid) 45{546}: 761-764. AGRICOLA.

6.1-70 Muller, P.A. 1971. Rosemary and rosemary oil. Flavour Ind. 2: 633-634.

6.1-71 Mupawose, R.M. 1971. Sesame (Sesamum indicum L.). Rhod. Agric. J. 68: 121-124, 127.

6.1-72 Nauriyal, J.P., Gupta, R. and George, C.K. 1977. Saffron in India. Arecanut Spices Bull. 8: 59-72.

6.1-73 Neuvel, J.J. 1979. More interest in fennel [in Flemish]. Groenten Fruit 34: 75, 77. HA 49: 6864.

6.1-74 Ohloff, G. and Flament, I. 1979. The role of heteroatomic substances in the aroma compounds of foodstuffs. Fortschr. Chem. Org. Naturst. 36: 231-283.

6.1-75 Paulet, M. and Felisaz, D. 1971.u Satureia montana essential oil [in Italian]. Riv. Ital. Essenze, Profumi, Piante Off., Aromi, Saponi, Cosmet., Aerosol 53: 618-619. CA 76: 131366.

6.1-76 Risnes, E. 1978. Common borage [in Norwegian]. Birokteren. 94: 117-118.

6.1-77 Ruminska, A. 1976. Garden sage, Salvia officinalis L. [in Polish]. Wiad. Zielarskie 18{10}: 13-14. AGRICOLA.

6.1-78 Ruminska, A. 1976. Common thyme, Thymus vulgaris L. [in Polish]. Wiad. Zielarskie 8{11}: 12-13. AGRICOLA.

6.1-79 Ruminska, A. 1976. Lovage, Levisticum officinale Koch [in Polish]. Wiad. Zielarskie 18{2}: 14-15. AGRICOLA.

6.1-80 Ruminska, A. 1976. Sweet marjoram, Origanum majorana [in Polish]. Wiad. Zielarskie 18{3}: 15-16. AGRICOLA.

6.1-81 Ruminska, A. 1976. The mint [in Polish]. Wiad. Zielarskie 18{4}: 21-22. AGRICOLA.

6.1-82 Ruminska, A. 1976. Fennel, Foeniculum vulgare Mill [in Polish]. Wiad. Zielarskie 18{1}: 11-12. AGRICOLA.

6.1-83 Ruminska, A. 1976. Dill, Anethum graveolens L. [in Polish]. Wiad. Zielarskie 18{1}: 12-13. AGRICOLA.

6.1-84 Ruminska, A. 1977. Bay leaf [in Polish]. Wiad. Zielarskie 19{12}: 3-4. AGRICOLA

6.1-85 Saga, K. 1972. Studies on the pungency of red pepper fruit. The effect of mineral nutrition, with special reference to phosphorus nutrition [in Japanese]. Hirosaki Daigaku Nogakubu Gakujutsu Hokoku 1972{18}: 96-106.

6.1-86 Salehiana, A. and Netien, G. 1973. Essential oil of marjoram from Provence. Comparison with foreign samples [in French]. Trav. Soc. Pharm. Montpellier 33: 329-334. CA 80: 124567.

6.1-87 Salzer, U.-J. 1975. Analytical evaluation of seasoning extracts (oleoresins) and essential oils from seasonings. I. Int. Flavours Food Addit. 6: 151-157.

6.1-88 Salzer, U.-J. 1975. Analytical evaluation of seasoning extracts (oleoresins) and essential oils from seasonings. II. Int. Flavours Food Addit. 6: 206-210.

6.1-89 Salzer, U.-J. 1975. Analytical evaluation of seasoning extracts (oleoresins) and essential oils from seasonings. III. Int. Flavours Food Addit. 6: 253-258.

6.1-90 Salzer, U.J. and Furia, T.E. 1977. The analysis of essential oils and extracts (oleoresins) from seasonings - a critical review. CRC Crit. Rev. Food Sci. Nutr. 9: 345-373. CIM 19{6}: 3905.

6.1-91 Scherer, H. 1977. Comfrey, a plant with health, cooking and garden value [in German]. Leben. Erde I (Suppl. 108): 2-3. AGRICOLA.

6.1-92 Schilcher, H. 1973. Recent data on the assessment of the quality of chamomile flowers or chamomile oil. Part 2: Qualitative assessment of the essential oil in "Flores Chamomillae" [in German]. Planta Med. 23: 132-144. HA 44: 1147.

6.1-93 Schollhorn, J. 1977. Is the common dandelion a weed [in German]. Bienenpflege 4: 77-79. AGRICOLA.

6.1-94 Shlyapnikova, A.P., Ponomarev, E.D., Shlyapnikov, V.A. and Kopeikovskii, V.M. 1974. Quantitative and qualitative changes in essential oils when drying coriander fruit [in Russian]. Tr. Vses. Nauchno-Issled. Inst. Efirnomaslich. Kul'tur 7: 151-156. CA 84: 155500.

6.1-95 Soliman, M.M., Kinoshita, S. and Yamanishi, T. 1975. Aroma of roasted sesame seeds. Agric. Biol. Chem. 39: 973-977.

6.1-96 Stevens, C.P. 1972. Watercress. Agriculture (London) 79: 1-5.

6.1-97 Tasmania. Dept. of Agriculture Agronomy Division. 1971. Horehound (Marrubium vulgare L.). Tasmanian J. Agric. 42{1}: 39-40. AGRICOLA.

6.1-98 Vanossi, L. 1974. The saffron [in Italian]. Ind. Aliment. (Pinerolo, Italy) 13{102}: 102-104. AGRICOLA.

6.1-99 Velappan, E. 1976. Fennel. Arecanut Spices Bull. 8: 11-12.

6.1-100 Wallon, D. and Whallon, R. 1977. The herbal teas of Crete: thryba (Satureja thymbra L.). Herbarist 43: 43-45.

6.1-101 Woodbury, J.E. 1977. Extractable color of capsicums and oleoresin paprika. J. Assoc. Off. Anal. Chem. 60: 1-4.

6.1-102 Yamanishi, T., Kosuge, M., Tokitomo, Y. and Maeda, R. 1930. Flavor constituents of pouchong tea and a comparison of the aroma pattern with jasmine tea. Agric. Biol. Chm. 44: 2139-2142.

6.2 Nutritional Aspects

6.2-1 Abd El-Karim, H.A., and Bamheer, A.M.S. 1979. Vitamin C content of vegetables and fruits available in Saudi Arabia. Z. Ernaehrungswiss. 18: 213-216. CA 92: 20794.

6.2-2 Akila, S.H., Abdella, M.M., Labib, A.I., Hilali, E., and Abdella, H.M. 1977. Evaluation of the protein quality of Egyptian sesame meal. Ann. Agric. Sci. (Moshtohor) 8: 195-203. AGRICOLA.

6.2-3 Anonymous. 1980. Fenugreek, latest multi-purpose protein source. Milling Feed Fert. 163{11}: 20-21.

6.2-4 Aprikyan, S.V., Adunts, G.T., and Akopyan, G.O. 1973. Vitamin composition of the most common edible wild herbs in Armenia [in Russian]. Biol. Zh. Arm. 26{6}: 52-56.

6.2-5 Ashur, S.S., Clark, H.E., Moon, W.H., and Malzer, J.L. 1973. Nitrogen retention of adult human subjects who consumed wheat and rice supplemented with chickpea, sesame, milk, or whey. Am. J. Clin. Nutr. 26: 1195-1201.

6.2-6 Awadalla, M.Z., Hudson, G.J., and Southgate, D.A.T. 1978. The composition of some native Egyptian foodstuffs. Plant Foods Man. 2: 147-151.

6.2-7 Awadalla, M.Z., El-Gedaily, A.M., El-Shamy, A.E., and El-Aziz, K.A. 1980. Studies on some Egyptian foods. 1. Biochemical and biological evaluation. Z. Ernaehrungswiss 19: 244-247. NAR-A 51: 7008.

6.2-8 Barakat, M.Z., Bassiouni, M., and El-Wakil, M. 1972. Evaluation of iodine content of certain vegetables. Bull. Acad. Pol. Sci., Ser. Sci. Biol. 20: 531-533. CA 77: 163212.

6.2-9 Beare-Rogers, J.L., Gray, L., Nera, E.A., and Levin, O.L. 1979. Nutritional properties of poppyseed oil relative to some other oils. Nutr. Metab. 23: 335-346.

6.2-10 Boloorforooshan, M., and Markakis, P. 1979. Protein supplementation of navy beans with sesame. J. Food Sci. 44: 390-391.

6.2-11 Caldwell, M.J. 1972. Ascorbic acid content of Malaysian leaf vegetables. Ecol. Food Nutr. 1: 313-317. FCA 26: 4415.

6.2-12 Caldwell, M.J., and Enoch, I.C. 1972. Riboflavin content of Malaysian leaf vegetables. Ecol. Food Nutr. 1: 309-312. FCA 26: 4414.

6.2-13 Casalichio, G., Rastelli, R., and Lerici, C.R. 1973. Chemical composition of the edible part of some vegetables from the market. I. [in Italian]. Sci. Technol. Alimenti 3: 311-314. FSTA 7: 6J829.

6.2-14 Chladek, M. 1970/1971. The vitamin C and beta-carotene content of cultivated aromatic and spice plants [in Czech]. Bulletin, Vyzkumny Ustav Zelinarsky Olomouc 1970/71{14/15}: 61-71. HA 43: 4728.

6.2-15 Clyde, D.D., Bertini, J., Dmochowski, R., and Koop, H. 1979. The vitamin A and C content of Coriandrum sativum and the variations in the loss of the latter with various methods of food preparation and preservation. Qual. Plant. Plant Foods Hum. Nutr. 28: 317-322.

6.2-16 De, S.K., and Laloraya, D. 1980. Effect of inorganic fertilizers on the contents of vitamin B1, C and E in chilli (Capsicum annuum) at seedling stage. Plant Biochem. J. 7: 116-119. HA 51: 8618.

6.2-17 Didry, N. 1977. Comparative chemical composition of some buds and adult organs [in French]. Bull. Soc. Pharm. Lille 33: 51-57. CA 87: 50251.

6.2-18 Eklund, A., and Agren, G. 1975. Nutritive value of poppy seed protein. J. Am. Oil Chem. Soc. 52: 188-190.

6.2-19 Ekpenyong, T.E., Fetuga, B.L., and Oyenuga, V.A. 1977. Fortification of maize flour based diets with blends of cashewnut meal, African locust bean meal and sesame oil meal. J. Sci. Food Agric. 28: 710-716.

6.2-20 Elmadfa, I. 1975. Fenugreek (Trigonella foenum graecum) protein [in German]. Nahrung 19: 683-686. HA 46: 7033.

6.2-21 Elmadfa, I., and Kuhl, B.E. 1976. The quality of fenugreek seed protein tested alone and in a mixture with corn flour. Nutr. Rep. Int. 14: 165-172.

6.2-22 El-Hawary, Z., El-Shobaki, F.A., Saleh, N., and Morcos, S.R. 1976. Intestinal absorption of iron alone and in combination with authentic or natural vitamin C and carotene. Z. Ernaehrungswiss. 15: 327-332. CA 86: 83489

6.2-23 Falkowski, M., and Kukulka, I. 1977. Carotene content as a characteristic feature of meadow plants [in Polish]. Rocz. Nauk Roln. Ser. F. 79: 97-104. HERB AB 49: 1509.

6.2-24 Franke, W., and Lawrenz, M. 1979. Proteins in leaves of some medicinal and spice plants. Planta Med. 36: 265 (Abstr.).

6.2-25 Gasparyan, O.B., and Aivazyan, S.M. 1974. Mineral composition of condiment herbs in open air hydroponic cultivation [in Russian]. Soobshch. Inst. Agrokhim. Probl. Gidroponiki Akad. Nauk Arm. SSR 1974{14}: 124-136. HA 45: 5253.

6.2-26 Gasparyan, O.B. 1976. Protein content in the herbage produced by plants grown in hydroponically in the open [in Armenian]. Soobshch. Inst. Agrokhim. Probl. Gidroponiki Akad. Nauk Arm. SSR 1976{15}: 136-142. HA 48: 725.

6.2-27 Gasparyan, O.B., and Khachatryan, N.A. 1972. Level of ascorbic acid and B-carotene in some spicy greens grown under open-air hydroponic conditions [in Armenian]. Soobshch. Inst. Agrokhim. Probl. Gidroponiki, Akad. Nauk. Arm. SSR 12: 132-139. CA 78: 121376.

6.2-28 Govedarica, P., and Veljkovic, S. 1976. Sesame and its proteins [in Serbo-Croatian]. Hrana Ishrana 17: 619-622. AGRICOLA.

6.2-29 Hamano, M., and Kawamina, T. 1973. A study on simultaneous assay of nitrate and nitrite in vegetables [in Japanese]. Shokuhin Eiseigaku Zasshi 14: 657 (Abstr.).

6.2-30 Herrera E., H., Gil P., A., and Tovar P., J. 1975. Influence of industrial processing on the nutritive value of sesame, cotton and soybean meals in Colombia [in Spanish]. Rev. Inst. Colomb. Agropecu. 10: 139-150. AGRICOLA.

6.2-31 Ifon, E.T., and Bassir, O. 1979. The nutritive value of some Nigerian leafy green vegetables - Part I: vitamin and mineral contents. Food Chem. 4: 263-267. HA 50: 5284.

6.2-32 Ismail, A.A., Shawki, W.M., and Hamza, A.S. 1978. Cholesterol in fruits, vegetables and edible oils. Egypt J. Hortic. 5: 83-91. CA 90: 102159.

6.2-33 Jain, A.K., and Bokadia, M.M. 1977. Nutritive contents of the seeds of some leguminous and non-leguminous plants. Acta Cienc. Indica 3{2}: 99-103. CA 88: 150850.

6.2-34 Johnson, L.A., Suleiman, T.M., and Lusas, E.W. 1979. Sesame protein: A review and prospectus. J. Am. Oil Chem. Soc. 56: 463-468.

6.2-35 Johnston, B.V. 1979. Alternate foods - a hope in the coming crisis. Agenda U.S. Agency Int. Dev. 2{3}: 3-12. AGRICOLA.

6.2-36 Jurics, E.W., Telegdy-Kovats, M., and Dworschak, E. 1971. Effect of treatment by cellulase on the nutrient contents of some vegetables [in Hungarian]. Elelmiszervizsgalati Kozlem 17: 199-208. CA 77: 3890.

6.2-37 Kabirullah, M., Khan, S.A., and Faruque, O. 1976. Studies on the nutritive value and properties of oil seed cakes. 2. Evaluation (in vivo) of nutritional quality of proteins of screw pressed, completely defatted and steam treated mustard oil cakes. Bangladesh J. Sci. Ind. Res. 11{1/4}: 8-13. NAR-A 48: 140.

6.2-38 Kaushal, J.R., Gill, R.S., and Negi, S.S. 1973. Comfrey, a forage rich in protein and phosphorus. Indian Farming 22{11}: 37, 41.

6.2-39 Koivistoinen, P., Ahlstroem, A., Varo, P., and Nissinen, H. 1974. Mineral element composition of Finnish vegetables, fruits, and berries. Acta Agric. Scand. 24 131-134. CA: 83 145935.

6.2-40 Lindner, K. 1973. Nutritional importance of free amino acids in plant products [in German]. Qual. Plant.-Plant Foods Hum. Nutr. 23: 251-262. CA 80: 35962.

6.2-41 Lobana, K.S., Garcha, J.S., Gupta, M.L., and Sharma, B.N. 1973. Chemical composition of tender shoots and leaves of Raya (Brassica juncea) mutants. J. Food Sci. Technol. 10: 125-126. NAR 44: 6193.

6.2-42 Lupea, V., and Vranceanu, C. 1972. Determination of the molybdenum content of certain foods from areas with endemic nephritis [in German]. Nahrung 16: 637-641. CA 78: 123012.

6.2-43 Matsuki, H., and Chiga, M. 1977. Changes of inorganic components in vegetables by cooking. I. Changes in the content of inorganic components (iron, copper, zinc, sodium, and calcium) in parsley, celery, and leek by immersion in water [in Japanese]. Miyagi Gakuin Joshi Daigaku Seikatsu Kagaku Kenkyusho Kenkyu Hokoku 11: 15-17. CA 89: 213831

6.2-44 Mattil, K.F. 1973. Considerations for choosing the right plant protein. Food Prod. Dev. 7{6}: 40, 42, 44.

6.2-45 Murphy, E.W., Marsh, A.C., and Willis, B.W. 1978. Nutrient content of spices and herbs. J. Am. Diet. Assoc. 72: 174-176.

6.2-46 Prodan, G., Florescu, E., Mihalache, M., Visarion, M., Baciu, E., Dorobantu, N., and Tudor, T. 1974. Biological characteristics and food value of bulb vegetables used for green leaves [in Romanian]. Lucr. Stiint. Inst. Agron. Bucuresti Ser. B. 17: 7-15. HA 50: 3251.

6.2-47 Rao, P.G., and Sreeramulu, M. 1978. Some nutritional factors in Coriandrum sativum (spice) and Trigonella foenum-graecum (condiment). Indian J. Nutr. Diet. 15: 377-380. NAR-A 50: 1768.

6.2-48 Saimbhi, M.S., Kaur, G., and Nandpuri, K.S. 1977. Chemical constituents in mature green and red fruits of some varieties of chilli (Capsicum annuum L.). Qual. Plant. Plant Foods Hum. Nutr. 27: 171-175. NAR-A 48: 1048.

6.2-49 Saimbhi, M.S., Padda, D.S., and Gurdalbir Singh. 1972. Ascorbic acid content of chilli varieties, as affected by fruit maturity. J. Res., Punjab Agric. Univ., Ludhiana 9{2}: 248-250. PBA 43: 6174.

6.2-50 Saleh, N., El-Hawary, Z., El-Shobaki, F.A., Abbassy, M., and Morcos, S.R. 1977. Vitamin content of fruits and vegetables in common use in Egypt. Z. Ernaehrungswiss. 16: 158-162. CA 88: 4998.

6.2-51 Sauvaire, Y., Baccou, J.C., and Besancon, P. 1976. Nutritional value of the proteins of leguminous seed: fenugreek (Trigonella foenum-graecum L.). Nutr. Rep. Int. 14: 527-537.

6.2-52 Schaeffer, E. 1976. Parsley, its life and times. Am. Hortic. 55: 34-35, 41.

6.2-53 Schmidt, M. 1979. The delightful dandelion. Org. Gard. 26{3}: 112-117.

6.2-54 Sehgal, K.K., Kawatra, B.L., and Bajaj, S. 1975. Studies on the nutritive value of sundried green leafy vegetables. J. Food Sci. Technol. 12: 303-305. NAR-A 47: 206.

6.2-55 Sengupta, A., and Roychoudhury, S.K. 1976. Triglyceride composition of Sesamum indicum seed oil. J. Sci. Food Agric. 27: 165-169.

6.2-56 Shehab, S.K., Afify, N., and El-Zoheiry, A. 1976. A study on the vitamin "C" content of vegetable salad constituents. Ain Shams Med. J. 27: 295-305. CA 86: 87857.

6.2-57 Shukla, P.C., and Talpada, P.M. 1977. Nutritive value of chicory leaves (Cichorium intybus L.). Gujarat Agric. Univ. Res. J. 3{1}: 15-17. NAR-B 48: 3781.

6.2-58 Sood, R., and Bhat, C.M. 1974. Changes in ascorbic acid and carotene content of green leafy vegetables in cooking. J. Food Sci. Technol. 11: 131-133. NAR 45: 5776.

6.2-59 Sosulski, F.W., and Sarwar, G. 1973. Amino acid composition of oilseed meals and protein isolates. Can. Inst. Food Sci. Technol. J. 6: 1-5.

6.2-60 Srinivasan, M.R., Sambaiah, K., Satyanarayana, M.N., and Rao, M.V.L. 1980. Influence of red pepper and capsaicin on growth, blood constituents and nitrogen balance in rats. Nutr. Rep. Int. 21: 455-467. NAR-B 50: 8003.

6.2-61 Sultanov, M.N., and Ragimov, A.V. 1972. Chemical composition of green and condiment plants used in nutrition [in Russian]. Vop. Pitan. 30{2}: 92-93. CA 77: 18366.

6.2-62 Tabekhia, M.M., and Mohamed, H.S. 1971. Effect of processing and cooking operations on thiamine, riboflavin and nicotinic acid content of some Egyptian national foods. II. Broad beans and sesame products. Alexandria J. Agric. Res. 19: 285-292. AGRICOLA.

6.2-63 Teodoru, V., and Rizescu, S. 1977. Iodine contents of some plant and animal products from goiter and nongoiter areas [in Romanian]. Rev. Ig. Bacteriol. Virusol. Parazitol. Epidemiol. Pneumoftiziol. 25{1}: 47-50. CA 92: 127251.

6.2-64 Toghrol, F., and Daneshpejouh, H. 1974. Estimation of free amino acids, protein and amino acid compositions of cumin seed (Cuminum cyninum [sic]) of Iran. J. Trop. Pediatr. Environ. Child Health 20: 109-111 NAR 45: 7901.

6.2-65 Toghrol, F., and Pourebrahimi, M. 1976. Estimation of vitamin C in fenugreek, coriander and ribes in Iran. Plant Foods Man. 2: 1-5. AGRICOLA.

6.2-66 Tomasevic, Z., and Naumovic, M. 1974. Composition and biological value of our foodstuffs. 1. Total vitamin C in fresh and frozen vegetables [in Serbo-Croatian]. Hrana Ishrana 15: 9-20. NAR 45: 3089.

6.2-67 Toma, R.B., Tabekhia, M.M., and Williams, J.D. 1979. Phytate and oxalate contents in sesame seed (Sesamum indicum L.). Nutr. Rep.Int. 20: 25-31.

6.2-68 Trehan, K.B., Dhawan, S., Mehta, S.K., Baijal, S.K., and Chand, H. 1974. Evaluation of indigenous and exotic varieties of sesame (Sesamum indicum L.) for oil and protein content. Telhan Patrika Oilseeds J. 4{3}: 20-23.

6.2-69 Trofimova, E.P. 1977. Some wild food plants of Tadzhikistan as sources of vitamins [in Russian]. Izv. Akad. Nauk Tadzh. SSR, Otd. Biol. Nauk 1977{1}: 43-48. CA 87: 65365.

6.2-70 and Van Veen, A.G., and Van Veen, Scott M.L. 1973. Pioneer work on protein foods. Nutr. Newslett. 11{4}: 22-25. AGRICOLA.

6.2-71 Vlasyuk, P.A. 1978. Characteristics of the trace elements manganese, zinc, molybdenum, boron, and lithium in the metabolism and productivity of plants [in Russian]. Nauch. Tr. Ukr. S.-kh. Akad. 1978{205}: 110-120. CA 91: 174034.

6.2-72 Watson, J.D.,, Dako, D.Y., and Amoakwa-Adu, M. 1975. Available carbohydrates in Ghanaian foodstuffs. Part 2. Sugars and starch in staples and other foodstuffs. Plant Foods Man 1{3/4}: 169-175. HA 47: 1374.

6.2-73 Whang, W.I., and Ju, J.S. 1977. A study on the improvement of dietary protein-efficiency by supplement of the Panax ginseng byproducts. Korean J. Biochem. 9{2}: 68-69 (Abstr.).

6.2-74 Yermanos, D.M., Saleeb, W., Labanuskas, C.K., and Cavanagh, G.C. 1971. The sesame plant as a source of protein and other nutrients. J. Am. Oil Chem. Soc. 48: 831-834.

6.2-75 Yermanos, D.M., and Saleeb, W. 1972. Leaf proteins from sesame. Calif. Agric. 26{2}: 10-11. AGRICOLA.

6.2-76 Zalewski, S., Kucharczyk, J., and Osypiuk, K. 1972. Technological usefulness and nutritive value of fresh and frozen parsley [in Polish]. Przem. Spozyw. 26: 544-546. AGRICOLA.

6.2-77 Zennie, T.M., and Ogzewalla, C.D. 1977. Ascorbic acid and vitamin A content of edible wild plants of Ohio and Kentucky. Econ. Bot. 31: 76-79

6.3 Drying, Processing, and Storing

6.3-1 Aniskin, V.I., Rybaruk, V.A., and Sapozhnikov, G.M. 1975. A method for calculating the duration of drying of coriander fruit by forced ventilation [in Russian]. Tr. Vses. Nauchno-Issled. Inst. Efirnomaslichn. Kul't. 8: 184-188. HA 47: 9745.

6.3-2 Anonymous. 1977. The storage of witloof chicory [in Flemish]. Boer en de Tuinder 83{1}: 13. HA 47: 7389.

6.3-3 Anonymous. 1975. Longer life for stored seeds. Agric. Res. 23{11}: 8-9.

6.3-4 Aponte, E., and Landaeta, C. 1972. Artificial drying of sesame seed [in Spanish]. Agron. Trop. (Maracay, Venez.) 22: 19-28. AGRICOLA.

6.3-5 Arkcoll, D.B. 1973. The preservation and storage of leaf protein preparations. J. Sci. Food Agric. 24: 437-445.

6.3-6 Bains, D.S., Mahajan, V.P., and Samra, J.S. 1973. Distil mentha for yourself for higher returns. Prog. Farming 10{3}: 15. AGRICOLA.

6.3-7 Balla, F. 1973. Inhibition of vitamin C decomposition with modern methods of preservation of fruits and vegetables [in Russian]. Vopr. Pitan. {32}{3}: 60-68.

6.3-8 Bass, L.N. 1973. Controlled atmosphere and seed storage. Seed Sci. Technol. 1: 463-492.

6.3-9 Beaud, P., and Ramuz, A. 1975. Influence of storage conditions on the cis-anethole content of anise flavored candies [in French]. Mitt. Geb. Lebensmittelunters. Hyg. 66: 384-389. AGRICOLA.

6.3-10 Berestovaia, M.M., and Esenin, S.A. 1976. The advisability of processing anise as whole plants [in Russian]. Maslo. Zhir. Prom-St. 1976{1}: 32-33. Bib. Ag. 42: 57309.

6.3-11 Biliczky, L., and Csiszar,F. 1975. Stabilizing effectof some antioxidants on the pigments of powdered red paprika (Capsicum annuum var. L.). Elelmiszervisgalati Kozl. 21{1/2}: 47-52. AGRICOLA.

6.3-12 Burtea, O., Paraschiv, A., and Popasecreteanu, E. 1975. Contributions to the improvement of dehydration technique for celery, parsley and parsnip [in Romanian]. Lucr. Stiint. Inst. Cercet. Pentru. Valor. Legum. Fruct. 6: 371-378. AGRICOLA.

6.3-13 Chaudhary, A.T., and Rao, B.Y. 1979. Retention of chlorophyll and ascorbic acid in dried fenugreek (Trigonella foenumgraecum). Indian Food Packer 33{1}: 35-36. AGRICOLA.

6.3-14 Chogovadze, Sh.K., and Bakhtadze, D.M. 1977. Analysis of the changes of the aromatic components of coriander by heat and sublimation drying [in German]. Lebensm. Ind. 24: 513-515. AGRICOLA.

6.3-15 Diatlev, V.A. 1975. Basis for the selection of optimal technological schemes and conditions of machine cleaning of coriander seed [in Russian]. Tr. Vses. Nauchno-Issled. Inst. Efirnomaslichn. Kul't. 8: 125-131.

6.3-16 Diatlev, V.A. 1975. Substantiation of the criterion of effectiveness of the process of machine cleaning the seed material of coriander [in Russian]. Tr. Vses. Nauchno-Issled. Inst. Efirnomaslichn. Kul't. 8: 172-176. AGRICOLA.

6.3-17 Farkas, J., Beczner, J., and Incze, K. 1973. Feasibility of irradiation of spices with special reference to paprika. Pages 389-402 in Radiation preservation of food; Proceedings of a symposium, Bombay, November, 1972. International Atomic Energy Agency, Vienna, Aust.

6.3-18 Feldman, A.L., Gusar, Z.D., Girkhovskaia, E.B., and Pozniakova, G.P. 1977. Alteration of physiologically active substances of vegetables in chamber storage [in Russian]. Izv. Vyssh. Ucheb. Zaved Pishch. Tekhnol. 1977{4}: 96-99.

6.3-19 Gatzke, E. 1973. Ideas on the storage of chicory roots [in German]. Gartenbau 20: 323-325. HA 45: 5813.

6.3-20 Georgiev, E., Genov, N., and Zlatev, S. 1978. On the changes of dill oil during storage [in Italian]. Riv. Ital. Essenze, Profumi, Piante Off., Aromat., Syndets, Saponi, Cosmet., Aerosols 60{5}: 307-313. CA 89: 135664.

6.3-21 Habibunnisa, Mathur, P.B., and Bano, Z. 1971. Effect of cobalt-60 gamma rays on the storage behavior of garlic bulbs at room temperature and in cold storage. Indian Food Packer 25{6}: 10-13. HA 44: 3986.

6.3-22 Hansen, H., and Bohling, H. 1980. Long term storage of horseradish roots [in German]. Gemuse 16: 262-264. HA 51: 4855.

6.3-23 Hardman, R., and Brain, K.R. 1972. Variations in the yield of total and individual 25 alpha- and 25 beta-sapogenins on storage of whole seed of Trigonella foenumgraecum L. Planta Med. 21: 426-430. HA 43: 3088.

6.3-24 Herregods, M. 1974. Determination of the storage ability of witloof chicory (Cichorium intybus) by biological aspects. Acta Hortic. 197{438}: 227-236. HA 45: 2335.

6.3-25 Ignat'ev, M.A. 1972. The effect of storage temperature on garlic growth and productivity [in Russian]. Tr. Chuv. S-kh. Inst. 9: 95-99. HA 44: 3985.

6.3-26 Iordachescu, C., Marin, I., Bucur, E., and Mihailescu, N. 1976. Performance of some garlic varieties in cold storage [in Romanian]. Lucr. Stiint. Inst. Cercet. pentru Valorificar. Legumelor Fructelor 7: 39-43 PBA 47: 800.

6.3-27 Iordachescu, C., Mihailescu, N., and Marin, I. 1978. Developing technology for keeping garlic in cold storage [in Romanian]. Lucr. Stiint. Inst. Cercet. pentru Valorificar. Legumelor Fructelor 9: 21-26 HA 48: 10458.

6.3-28 Jarczyk, A., and Zadrozna, M. 1973. Preservation of herbs by freeze-drying and changes during storage [in Polish]. Zesz. Nauk. Akad. Roln. Warszawie Technol. Rolno-Spozyw. 8: 25-35. NAR 44: 7813.

6.3-29 Johansson, A., and Appelqvist, L.A. 1979. The sterol composition of freshly harvested compared to stored seeds of rape, sunflower and poppy. J. Am. Oil Chem. Soc. 56: 995-997.

6.3-30 Kaczmarek, F., and Elbanowska, A. 1971. Influence of packing and storage conditions on the quality of the Digitalis lanata Ehrh. leaves [in Polish]. Herba Pol. 17: 171-184.

6.3-31 Kafedjiev, J.T., and Gentschev, L.N. 1971. Peeling paprika [in German]. Ind. Obst.- & Gemuseverwert. 56: 667-669. AGRICOLA.

6.3-32 Kanner, J., Harel, S., Palevitch, D., and Ben-Gera, I. 1977. Colour retention in sweet red paprika (Capsicum annuum L.) powder as affected by moisture contents and ripening stage. J. Food Technol. 12: 59-64.

6.3-33 Kazakova, A.A., and Starokozhev, S.I. 1973. The keeping quality of garlic cultivars in relation to their origin [in Russian]. Tr. Prikl. Bot. Genet. Sel. 49{2}: 156-161. HA 44: 7697.

6.3-34 Kim, K.S., Roh, S.M., and Park, J.R. 1979. Effect of light treatment (red, blue) on the major components of hot pepper fruit [in Korean]. Hanguk Sikp'unkwahakhoe Chi 11: 162-165.

6.3-35 Koiso, S., and Ogata, K. 1971. Samples of low temperature damaging to Spanish paprika in storage [in Japanese]. Nogyo Oyobi Engei 46: 799-800. AGRICOLA.

6.3-36 Kojima, M., and Nakano, V. 1980. The change of pungent components during the storage of horseradish, mustard and "wasabi" powder [in Japanese]. Nippon Shokuhin Kogyo Gakkaishi 27: 86-88. CA 93: 44137.

6.3-37 Kojima, M., and Nakano, Y.. 1978. Studies on the changes of volatile components, particularly allyl isothiocyanate, during storage of Wasabia japonica [in Japanese]. Hakho Kogaku Kaishi 56: 298-303. CA 89: 145315

6.3-38 Komissarov, V.A., and Andreeva, A.V. 1972. Changes in the phytoncidal properties of garlic in relation to variety and temperature during storage [in Russian]. Izv. Timiryazevsk. S-kh. Akad. 1972{3}: 209-212. PBA 44: 7269.

6.3-39 Kruistum, G. van, and Schouten, S.P. 1978. Storage of chicory roots below the freezing point? Results of the season 1977-1978 [in Flemish]. Boer en de Tuinder 3{439}: 13. HA 49: 1349.

6.3-40 Lakshmi, T.S., and Nandi, P.K. 1979. Studies on the effect of heat on the dissociation, denaturation, and aggregation of sesame alpha-globulin. J. Agric. Food Chem. 27: 818-821.

6.3-41 Lamy, J. 1973. 1st tests of marjoram from the Drome Department, Majorana hortensis [in French]. Trav. Soc. Pharm. Montp. 33: 335-343.

6.3-42 Lee, W.S. 1973. Physiological and ecological studies on Korean local strains of garlic. 1. On the process of sprouting in stored garlic [in Korean]. Hanguk Wonye Hakhoe Chi 14: 15-23. HA 44: 5733.

6.3-43 Luhadiya, A.P., and Kulkarni, P.R. 1978. Dehydration of green chillies (Capsicum frutescens). J. Food Sci. Technol. 15: 139-142.

6.3-44 Luk'yanov, I.A., and Berestovaya, M.M. 1973. Changes in the essential oil content of coriander seeds during storage [in Russian]. Tr. Vses. Nauchno-Issled. Inst. Efirnomaslichn. Kul't. 6: 166-170. HA 45: 9976.

6.3-45 Magnus, K.E. 1972. Drying pimento. Caribb. Farming 4{1}: 8-10. AGRICOLA.

6.3-46 Man'kova, E.N., and Chipiga, A.P. 1975. Development of condition parameters for the processing of anise as whole plants. Tr. Vses. Nauchno-Issled Inst. Efirnomaslichn. Kul't. 8: 227-230. AGRICOLA.

6.3-47 Maruyama, E., Kobayashi, M., Momosaki, S., and Kajita, T. 1976. Changes in lipids and pigments in parsley during storage [in Japanese]. Kaseigaku Zasshi 27: 428-433. CA 86: 154215.

6.3-48 Mazza, G. 1980. Thermodynamic considerations of water vapor sorption by horseradish roots. Lebensm.-Wiss. Technol. 13: 13-17.

6.3-49 Miuccio, C.F. 1974. Variations in content of some vitamins in vegetables during preservation [in Italian]. Acta Vitaminol. Enzymol. 28: 23-34. NAR-A 46: 2032.

6.3-50 Om, H., and Awasthi, D.N. 1978. Effect of maleic hydrazide sprays on the storage of garlic. Prog. Hortic. 9{4}: 63-67. HA 49: 355.

6.3-51 Pluzhnikov, I.I., Krotov, E.G., and Kareva, L.G. 1973. Destruction of ascorbic acid while freezing red peppers [in Russian]. Izv. Vyssh. Uchebn. Zaved. Pishch. Tekhnol. 1973{3}: 76-78. AGRICOLA.

6.3-52 Ponomarev, E.D., and Shliapnikova, A.P. 1978. Drying of coriander fruit used for seed [in Russian]. Nachno-Tekh. Byul. Vses. Nauchno-Issled. Inst. Mekh. Sel'sk. Khoz. 1978{35}: 33-34.

6.3-53 Porsdal Poutsen, K., and Nielsen, P. 1979. Freeze-drying of chives and parsley-optimization attempts. Pages 275-280 in Progress in refrigeration science and technology; Proceedings of the XVth international congress of refrigeration, 1979, Venice. Segretaria Generale del XV Congresso Internazionale del Freddo, Padova, Italy. v. III.

6.3-54 Pruidze, V.G., Alkhanashvili, N.G., Khakhaleishvili, N.T., Zautashvili, D.I., and Varnazova, N.G. 1977. Technology of production of dried spicy greens of Coriandrum sativum and Ocimum basilicum [in Russian]. Konservn. Ovoshchesush. Prom-St. 1977{9}: 14-16. AGRICOLA.

6.3-55 Pruidze, V.G., and Tukvadze, S.G. 1975. Catechins in leaves of Laurus nobilis and the changes they undergo during the drying and storage of the leaves. Appl. Biochem. Microbiol. (Engl. Transl.) 11: 530-532. Translation of Prikl. Biokhim. Mikrobiol. 11: 589-592, 1975.

6.3-56 Ramachandra, B.S., Subba Rao, L.S., Ramesh, A., and Ramanathan, P.K. 1971. Drying studies on the dehulled wet sesame seed. J. Food Sci. Technol. 8: 17-19.

6.3-57 Ravindran, P.N. 1978. Effect of post-irradiation storage and storage temperature on Sesamum indicum L. Madras Agric. J. 65: 59-61.

6.3-58 Rognerud, G., and Roennevig, A.S. 1977. Retention of ascorbic acid in some vegetables during storage [in Norwegian]. Forsk. Fors. Landbruket. 28: 639-649. CA 88: 133286.

6.3-59 Rutherford, P.P. 1977. Changes during prolonged cold storage in the reducing sugars in chicory roots and their effects on the chicons produced after forcing. J. Hortic. Sci. 52: 99-103.

6.3-60 Sagdullaev, Kh. 1977. The keeping quality of cold-stored garlic of different provenance [in Russian]. Byull. Vses. Inst. Rastenievod. 1977{74}: 60-63. HA 49: 4140.

6.3-61 Saito, Y., and Yoshihara, T. 1980. The changes of pH, acids, vitamin C, chlorophyll and colors of vegetables during storage. Tokyo Kasei Daigaku Kenkyu Kiyo 20{2}: 37-41. CA 94: 119663.

6.3-62 Saito, Y., Hosoda, H., and Hatayama, T. 1975. Changes in amino acids and sugars of vegetables during storage [in Japanese]. Tokyo Kasei Daigaku Kenkyu Kiyo 15: 33-41. CA 84: 42127.

6.3-63 Sapozhnikov, G.M., and Reznikov, A.R. 1975. Aerodynamic resistance of a layer of coriander [in Russian]. Tr. Vses. Nauchno-Issled. Inst. Efirnomaslichn. Kul't. 8: 218-222. AGRICOLA.

6.3-64 Saray, T., and Almasi, E. 1979. Ca storage stability of tomato-shaped paprika Capsicum annuum. Pages 713-722 in Progress in refrigeration science and technology; Proceedings of the XVth international congress of refrigeration, 1979, Venice. Segretaria Generale del XV Congresso Internazionale del Freddo, Padova, Italy. v. III.

6.3-65 Singh, H.G., and Sinha, S. 1978. Mould counts and biochemical changes in stored seeds of Indian mustard, taramira and safflower. Indian J. Agric. Sci. 48: 67-71. RPP 58: 1338.

6.3-66 Skorikova, Yu.G., and Gavrilishina, L.I. 1972. Preparation and storage of herbs in the frozen state [in Russian]. Konserv. Ovoshchesush. Prom. 27{1}: 8-10. CA 76: 111810.

6.3-67 Starcheus, P.A., and Sirotin, A.M. 1976. Influence of moisture, frequency of vibrations and heating temperature on the coefficient of dielectric losses of coriander seeds [in Russian]. Izv. Vyssh. Ucheb. Zaved Pishch. Tekhnol. 1976{2}: 111-113.

6.3-68 Steinbuch, E. 1980. Technical note: Quality retention of unblanched frozen vegetables by vacuum packing. II. Asparagus, parsley and celery. J. Food Technol. 15: 351-352.

6.3-69 Stork, H.W., and Schouten, S.P. 1977. Chicory storage [in Flemish]. Groent en Fruit 32: 1597. HA 47: 7390.

6.3-70 Takama, F., and Saito, S. 1974. Studies on the storage of vegetables and fruits. 2. Total carotene content of sweet pepper, carrot, leek and parsley during storage [in Japanese]. J. Agric. Sci. 19{1}: 11-15. AGRICOLA.

6.3-71 Toruk, S., and Szenes, Mrs. E. 1976. Activities and tasks of the Research Institute for Canning Industry and Paprika Manufacture [in Hungarian]. Elelmez. Ip. 30: 404-408. AGRICOLA.

6.3-72 Truszkowska, W., and Urban, M. 1978. Investigations of state of stored poppy seeds and sprouts obtained from them [in Polish]. Zesz. Probl. Postepow Nauk Roln. 202: 121-129.

6.3-73 Umiecka, L. 1973. Studies on the natural losses and marketable value of dill, parsley and chive tops in relation to storage conditions and type of packing [in Polish]. Biul. Warzywniczy 14: 231-257. HA 44: 7915.

6.3-74 Uncini, L., Sozzi, S., and Gorini, F. 1977. Evaluation of production quality and fitness of new Constitution Hot Peppers for conservation. Acta Hortic. 58: 491-494.

6.3-75 Wally, Y.A., Sharaf, M.A., and Maksoud, M.A. 1978. Effect of harvesting date and storage temperature on the storability of leafy vegetables. Egypt. J. Hortic. 5: 65-74. HA 49: 410.

6.3-76 Waszkiewicz, C. 1978. Effect of methods and technological parameters of drying on time of drying and quality of dried material [in Polish]. Rocz. Nauk Roln. Ser. C 73{4}: 49-60.

6.3-77 Zaussinger, A. 1975. Drying of parsley, chive and dill with high frequency energy [in German]. Pages 62-71 in Engineering & food quality; proceedings of the European Symposium − food, 6th, Cambridge, Sept. 8-10, 1975. Society of Chemical Industry, London, G.B.

6.4 Applications in Food and Flavor Industry

6.4-1 Agboola, S.D. 1973. Changes in the bacterial flora of fresh pulped Capsicum frutescens under various storage treatments. Trop. Sci. 15: 279-286.

6.4-2 Andre, L. 1973. Determining total color content of paprika [in German]. Gordian 73: 466, 468-469. AGRICOLA.

6.4-3 Anonymous. 1975. Dutch licorice products, healthful and medicinal [in Spanish]. Mex. Agric. 22{258/259}: 35-37. AGRICOLA.

6.4-4 Balinova-Tsvetkova, A., Zlatev, S., and Dimitrova, L. 1976. Changes in the essential oil during dill (Anethum graveolens) distillation [in Bulgarian]. Rastenievud. Nauki 13{5}: 12-18. HA 47: 4884.

6.4-5 Benedek, L. 1972. Carotenoid synthesis in seasoning paprika. Acta Aliment. Acad. Sci. Hung. 1{2}: 187-203. CA 78: 146479.

6.4-6 Blanc, M. 1978. The chicory root. The fructose changes during technological treatments [in French]. Lebensm.-Wiss. Technol. 11: 19-22. CA 88: 150900.

6.4-7 Brodnitz, M.H., Pascale, J.V., and Van Derslice, L. 1971. Flavor components of garlic extract. J. Agric. Food Chem. 19: 273-275.

6.4-8 Bucko, A., Obonova, L., and Ambrova, A. 1972. Effect of culinary technology on the vitamin C losses from potatoes and other vegetables [in Russian]. Vop. Pitan. 31: 86-89. CA 77: 60229.

6.4-9 Carnevale, J., Cole, E.R., and Crank, G. 1980. Photocatalyzed oxidation of paprika pigments. J. Agric. Food Chem. 28: 953-956.

6.4-10 Cash, D.B., Hrutfiord, B.F., and McKean, W.T., Jr. 1971. Effect of individual components on peppermint oil flavor. Food Technol. 25{11}: 53-54, 58.

6.4-11 Chandra, S., Netke, S.P., and Gupta, B.S. 1978. Studies on comparative utilization of xanthophylls from various natural sources for egg-yolk pigmentation. Indian J. Anim. Sci. 48: 456-460. FSTA 11: 3Q30.

6.4-12 Chang, S.S., Ostric-Matijasevic, B., Hsieh, O.A.L., and Huang, C.-L. 1977. Natural antioxidants from rosemary and sage. J. Food Sci. 42: 1102-1106.

6.4-13 Charazka, Z. 1980. Evaluation of quality and stability of taste and flavor obtained by the extraction method [in Polish]. Zesz. Probl. Postepow Nauk Roln. 1980{243}: 205-215.

6.4-14 Chun, J.K., and Park, S.K. 1979. Color measurement of red pepper powder and its relationship with the quality [in Korean]. Hanguk Nonghwa Hakhoe Chi 22: 18-23.

6.4-15 Chun, J.K., and Suh, C.S. 1980. The effect of sun light on color bleaching of red pepper powder [in Korean]. Hanguk Sikp'un Kwahakhoe Chi 12: 82-87.

6.4-16 Chun, J.K., Chun, J.K., Mok, C.K., and Chang, K.S. 1979. Studies on the measurement of thermal properties of kochujang [in Korean]. Hanguk Sikp'un Kwahakhoe Chi 11: 157-161.

6.4-17 Ciric, D., Vujicic, B., and Curcic, S. 1972. New products from paprika [in Croatian]. Hrana Ishrana 13: 427-435. AGRICOLA.

6.4-18 D'Souza Cletus, J.M., and Ramaiah, T.R. 1978. Polymerisation of sesame oil. Curr. Sci. 47: 17.

6.4-19 Dellaglio, F., and Bottazzi, V. 1971. Odour defect in Grana cheese caused by corynebacteria [in Italian]. Ann. Fac. Agrar. Univ. Cattol. Sacro Cuore 11: 412-428. DSA 35: 5275.

6.4-20 Devetak, Z., and Chenchi, A. 1972. The Dalmatian sage and sage oil [in Russian]. Pages 51-52 in P.V. Naumenko et al., eds. Mezhdunarodnyi kongress po efirnym maslam, 4th, Tiflis, 1968, [Materialy], v. 3. Pishchevaya Promyshlennost', Moscow, USSR. HA 44: 4213.

6.4-22 Ejsmond, J. 1979. Comparison of aromatic value in root parsley varieties [in Polish]. Biul. Warzywniczy 23: 405-417. PBA 51: 8655.

6.4-23 El-Wakeil, F., Morsi, S., Farag, R.S., and Hallabo, S.A.S. 1978. The antioxidant effect of naturally occurring unsaponifiable matter in linoleic acid and some vegetable oils. Grasas Aceites (Seville) 29: 9-15.

6.4-24 Ermolaev, V.N., and Blau, V.Yu. 1975. Studies on the physical and mechanical properties of garlic [in Russian]. Tr. Gor'k. Golovn. S-kh. Inst. 76: 72-75. HA 47: 5466.

6.4-25 Farbood, M.I., MacNeil, J.H., and Ostovar, K. 1976. Effect of rosemary spice extractive on growth of microorganisms in meats. J. Milk Food Technol. 39: 675-679.

6.4-26 Faruga, A., Majewska, T., and Ceglowski, J. 1975. Effect of paprika as feed supplement on egg production and colour of yolk in quail [in Polish]. Postep. Drobiarstwa Cent. Osrodek Badaw.-Rozwojowy Drobiarstwa 17{1}: 47-51. AGRICOLA.

6.4-27 Ferrando, R. 1977. Dairy products enriched with unsaturated fatty acids [in French]. Aliment. Vie 65: 328-335. DSA 41: 45.

6.4-28 Fletcher, D.L., and Halloran, H.R. 1980. An evaluation of commercially available marigold extract and paprika oleoresin of egg yolk pigmentation. Poult. Sci. 59: 1608 (Abstr.).

6.4-29 Freeman, G.G., and Whenham, R.J. 1976. Thiopropanal S-oxide; alk(en)yl thiosulphinates and thiosulphonates: simulation of flavor components of Allium species. Phytochemistry 15: 187-190.

6.4-30 Gafel, A. 1972. Evaluation of the present state of distribution, specialization and concentration of Capsicum for red pepper production [in Slovak]. Acta Oper-Oecon. 22: 15-27. AGRICOLA.

6.4-31 Gafel, A. 1972. Proposition to production layout and concentration of spice paprika in Czechoslovakia [in Czech]. Acta Oper-Oecon. 24: 63-82 AGRICOLA.

6.4-32 Gentschev, L.N. 1974. Heating of tomatoes and paprika during vacuum peeling [in German]. Ind. Obst. Gemuseverwert. 60: 10-11. AGRICOLA.

6.4-33 Gerhardt, U. 1977. Wormwood: a very bitter spice [in German]. Fleischwirtschaft 57: 1230-1231.

6.4-34 Gerhardt, U., and Wolff, M. 1976. Examining the essential oil content of new species of thyme for their suitability in meat product manufacture [in German]. Fleischwirtschaft 56: 1305-1308. AGRICOLA.

6.4-35 Gerhardt, U., and Boehm, Th. 1980. The redox behaviour of spices in meat products [in German]. Fleischwirtschaft 60: 1523-1526.

6.4-36 Gerhardt, U. 1972. Changes in spice constituents due to the influence of various factors [in German]. Fleischwirtschaft 52{1}: 77-80. CA 76: 125610.

6.4-37 Gilbert, J., and Nursten, H.E. 1972. Volatile constituents of horseradish roots. J. Sci. Food Agric. 23: 527-539.

6.4-38 Gonzalez-Cancho, F., Minguez-Mosquera, M.I., and Fernandez-Diez, M.J. 1972 Fermentation of red pepper used for stuffing green olives. Microbiol. Esp. 25: 81-90. FSTA 5{2}: 2J320.

6.4-39 Grandi, A., Venanzi, G., and Cagiotti, M.R. 1978. Red pepper for pigmenting egg yolks [in Italian]. Avicoltura 47{1}: 37-42. NAR-B 48: 3141.

6.4-40 Gyane, D.O. 1976. Preservation of shea butter. Drug Cosmet. Ind. 118{5}: 36-38, 138-140. CA 88: 158392.

6.4-41 Han, P.J., and Shin, D.H. 1978. Studies on the utilization of protein oil seed meals [in Korean]. Res. Rep. Off. Rural Dev. (Hortic. Agric. Eng.) 20: 59-65.

6.4-42 Hasegawa, K., Maeda, K., Fujino, Y. ', Wakinaga, T., and Fujino, S. 1978. Gelation characteristics of sesame seed protein [in Japanese]. Nippon Nogei Kagaku Kaishi 52: 341-346. AGRICOLA.

6.4-43 Hasegawa, K., Owaki, K., Tomita, A., and Fujino, S. 1979. Gelation characteristics and turbidities of sesame protein and soybean proteins [in Japanese]. Nippon Nogei Kagaku Kaishi 53: 375-384.

6.4-44 Haymon, L.W., and Aurand, L.W. 1971. Volatile constituents of tabasco peppers. J. Agric. Food Chem. 19: 1131-1134.

6.4-45 Heath, H.B. 1973. Herbs and spices for food manufacture. Trop. Sci. 14: 245-259.

6.4-46 Holasova, M., and Blattna, J. 1980. Lipolytic activity of poppy seed. Nahrung 24{7}: 607-613. AGRICOLA.

6.4-47 Huffman, F.L., Schadle, E.R., Villalon, B., and Burns, E.E. 1978. Volatile components and pungency in fresh and processed Jalapeno peppers. J Food Sci. 43: 1809-1811.

6.4-48 Huhtanen, C.N. 1980. Inhibition of Clostridium botulinum by spice extracts and aliphatic alcohols. J. Food Prot. 43: 195-196.

6.4-49 Ivanova, L.G., Sandulov, D.B., and Doktorevich, V.A. 1978. Investigation of the physicochemical properties of essential oils in aqueous solutions. J. Appl. Chem. USSR (Engl. Transl.) 51: 2585-2589. Translation of Zh. Prikl. Khim. (Leningrad) 51{12}: 2709-2713.

6.4-50 Ivanov, St. A., Seher, A., and Schiller, H. 1979. Natural antioxidants IV. Antioxidants in the fatty oil of Foeniculum vulgare, part 2 [in German]. Fette Seifen Anstrichm. 81: 105-107. HA 49: 8832.

6.4-51 Jaffe, W.G., and Chavez, J.F. 1971. The possible use of sesame flour for edible purposes [in Spanish]. Arch. Latinoamer. Nutr. 21{1}: 31-48. AGRICOLA.

6.4-52 Jasik, K., Matulis, Z., Ossowski, G., and Ambroziak, Z. 1979. Rheology-based identification of confectionery materials. Curd cheese and poppy seed [in Polish]. Zagadnienia Piekarstwa ZBPP 24{2}: 19-25. DSA 42: 8313.

6.4-53 Kacharava, I.A. 1977. Experience in the production of appetizing sauce at the V.I. Lenin Experimental Canning Combine in Sochi [in Russian]. Konservn. Ovoshchesush. Prom-st. 1977{9}: 9-10.

6.4-54 Kanner, J., and Budowski, P. 1978. Carotene oxidizing factors in red pepper fruits (Capsicum annuum L.): Effect of ascorbic acid and copper in a beta-carotene-linoleic acid solid model. J. Food Sci. 43: 524-526.

6.4-55 Kanner, J., Mendel, H., and Budowski, P. 1978. Carotene oxidizing factors in red pepper fruits (Capsicum annuum L.): oleoresin-cellulose solid model. J. Food Sci. 43: 709-712.

6.4-56 Kanner, J., Mendel, H., and Budowski, P. 1977. Carotene oxidizing factors in red pepper fruits (Capsicum annuum L.): peroxidase activity. J. Food Sci. 42: 1549-1551.

6.4-57 Katyuzhanskaya, A.N., Meerov, Ya.S., and Pekhov, A.V. 1972. Carbonic acid extract of horseradish [in Russian]. Maslo Zhir. Prom. 1972{7}: 15-16. CA 78: 41699.

6.4-58 Kawabata, S., and Deki, M. 1977. Flavor components of roasted chicory [in Japanese]. Kanzei Chuo Bunsekishoho 17: 63-71. CA 87: 66760.

6.4-59 Kenmochi, K., and Katayama, O. 1975. Studies on the utilization of plant pigments. I. Anthocyanin pigments of red garlic (Allium sativum) and red onion (Allium cepa) [in Japanese]. Nippon Shokuhin Kogyo Gakkaishi 22: 598-605. HA 46: 11214.

6.4-60 Kierstan, M.P.J. 1978. Production of fructose syrups from inulin-containing plants. Biotechnol. Bioeng. 20: 447-450.

6.4-61 Kim, C., Shimada, A., and Yoshimatsu, F. 1978. Studies on the cooking of sesame oil. 1. Flavor and stability of Korean home-made sesame oil [in Japanese]. Kaseigaku Zasshi 29: 290-296. CA 90: 21035.

6.4-62 Kinoshita, S., and Yamanishi, T. 1973. Identification of basic aroma components of roasted sesame seeds [in Japanese]. Nippon Nogei Kagaku Kaishi 47{11}: 737-739. CA 80: 106964.

6.4-63 Knoch, H. 1976. Processing of confectionary: licorice. Continuous "flow line" plant deals with all types. Confect. Prod. 42{10}: 461-467. BiB. Ag. 41: 106478.

6.4-64 Kostal, J. 1972. Aromatization of fermentation vinegar [in Czech]. Kvasny Prum. 18{10}: 226-227. CA 78: 95254.

6.4-65 Kurechi, T., and Kato, T. 1979. C-nitrosation of sesamol amonophenolic antioxidant present in sesame oil and its effects on N-nitrosamine formation in vitro. Chem. Pharm. Bull. (Tokyo) 27: 2442-2449.

6.4-66 Labana, K.S., Sekhon, K.S., Ahujua, K.L., and Gupta, M.L. 1976. Effect of gamma radiation on oil quality of raya (Brassica juncea). Indian J. Agric. Res. 10: 57-59. FCA 31: 1424. ·

6.4-67 Lapshin, A.A., Vorob'eva, N.I., and Kuz'min, V.I. 1974. Increasing the extraction efficiency of a coffee-chicory mixture during the production of a coffee-flavoured canned milk product. XIX International Dairy Congress, Delhi, India, 1974. XIX International Diary Congress Secretariat, New Delhi. 1E: 756-758. DSA 37: 2433.

6.4-68 Larry, D. 1974. Report on flavors and nonalcoholic beverages. J. Assoc. Off. Anal. Chem. 57: 287-288.

6.4-69 Larry, D. 1976. Report on flavors and nonalcoholic beverages. J. Assoc. Off. Anal. Chem. 59: 330-331.

6.4-70 Latrasse, A., and Vangheesdaele, G. 1972. Determination of allyl cyanide in mustard paste [in French]. Ann. Falsif. Expert. Chim. 65{697}: 29-36. CA 77: 18254.

6.4-71 Lee, T.-S., Yang, K.-J., Park, Y.-J., and Yu, J.-H. 1980. Studies on the brewing of kochujang (red pepper paste) with the addition of mixed cultures of yeast strains. Hanguk Sikp'un Kwahakhoe Chi 12: 313-323.

6.4-72 Lee, T.S., Shin, B.K., Lee, S.K., and Yu, J.H. 1971. Microbiological studies of red pepper paste fermentation. II. Physiological characteristics of the selected excellent yeasts [in Korean]. Misa Engmul Hakhoe Chi 9{2}: 55-60. AGRICOLA.

6.4-73 Lee, T.S., Cho, H.-O., Kim, C.-S., and Kim, J.G. 1980. The brewing of kochujang (red pepper paste) from different starch sources. I. Proximate component and enzyme activity during koji preparation [in Korean]. Hanguk Nonghwa Hakhoe Chi 23: 157-165.

6.4-74 Lee, T.S. 1979. Studies on the brewing of kochuzang (red pepper paste) by the addition of yeasts [in Korean]. Hanguk Nonghwa Hakhoe Chi 22: 65-90.

6.4-75 Lichman, M. 1980. The effect of mint on bourbon. Garden (N.Y.) 4{4}: 10-11.

6.4-76 Livingston, A.L., Knowles, R.E., Edwards, R.H., and Kohler, G.O. 1974. Processing of pimento waste to provide a pigment source for poultry feed. J. Sci. Food Agric. 25: 483-490.

6.4-77 Loof, B. 1974. Current questions concerning oil crops [in Danish]. Tolvmandsbladet 46: 573-578. FCA 29: 5934.

6.4-78 Lukianov, I.A., and Berestovaia, M.M. 1975. The quality of coriander essential oil affected by methods of its extraction. Maslo.-Zhir. Prom-st. 1975{10}: 30-31.

6.4-79 Lyon, C.K. 1972. Sesame: Current knowledge of composition and use. J. Am. Oil Chem. Soc. 49: 245-249.

6.4-80 MacNeil, J.H., Dimick, P.S., and Mast, M.G. 1973. Use of chemical compounds and a rosemary spice extract in quality maintenance of deboned poultry meat. J. Food Sci. 38: 1080-1081.

6.4-81 Mameishvili, M.G., and Sardzhveladze, G.P. 1973. Ground leaf of Laurus nobilis [in Russian]. Subtrop. Kul't. 1973{5}: 122-123.

6.4-82 Manley, C.H., Vallon, P.P., and Erickson, R.E. 1974. Some aroma components of roasted sesame seed (Sesanum indicum L.). J. Food Sci. 39: 73-76.

6.4-83 Manuelian, Kh. 1980. Evaluation and procurement of red peppers according to ASTA units [in Bulgarian]. Gradinarstvo. 1980{12}: 29-33. Bib. Ag. 45: 27741.

6.4-84 Masada, Y., Hashimoto, K., Inoue, T., and Suzuki, M. 1971. Analysis of the pungent principles of Capsicum annuum by combined gas chromatography-mass spectrometry. J. Food Sci. 36: 858-860.

6.4-85 Mathew, A.G., Lewis, Y.S., Krishnamurthy, N., and Nambudiri, E.S. 1971. Capsaicin. Flavour Ind. 2: 691, 693-695.

6.4-86 McGowan, C.L., Bethea, R.M., and Tock, R.W. 1979. Feasibility of controlling onion and garlic dehydration odors with ozone. Trans. ASAE 22: 899-905, 911.

6.4-87 Mihaly, V., and Zukal, E. 1976. Flavour dilution profile of spices. Acta Aliment. Pol. 2: 157-161. Bib. Ag. 41: 54780.

6.4-88 Miller, R.W., and Smith, C.R., Jr. 1973. Seeds of Indigofera species. Their content of amino acid that may be deleterious. J. Agr. Food Chem. 21{5}: 909-912. CA 79: 113233.

6.4-89 Milostic, I., and Lisak, J. 1971. Prevention of oxidative processes in oil by the use of antioxidants during preservation of sardines [in Croatian]. Prehrambeno-Technol. Rev. 9{3-4}: 6-8. CA 76: 152148.

6.4-90 Mori, K., Sawada, H., Nabetani, O., and Maruo, S. 1974. The effects of essential oils and spice extracts on prevention of slimy spoilage of wieners [in Japanese]. Nippon Shokuhin Kogyo Gakkai-Shi 21: 285-287. FSTA 7: 3S420.

6.4-91 Murav'ev, I.A., and Durdyev, D.D. 1974. Data for chemical evaluation of licorice root from industrial regions of Turkmenia [in Russian]. Aktual. Vopr. Farm. 2: 51-56. CA 84: 95560.

6.4-92 Nour El-Din, H., Osman, A.E., Higazy, S., and Mahmoud, H. 1979. Studies on the factors affecting the physicochemical properties of geranium oil. I. Mixing with fixed, mineral oils and aromatic chemicals. Egypt. J. Food Sci. 5{1/2}: 67-77. AGRICOLA.

6.4-93 Ohloff, G. 1978. Recent developments in the field of naturally-occurring aroma components. Fortschr. Chem. Org. Naturst. 35: 431-527.

6.4-94 Okuni, H., and Okubo, S. 1974. Response of rat taste sense receptor units to spices [in Japanese]. Shikwa Gakuho 74{1}: 208 (Abstr.).

6.4-95 Olkku, J., and Rha, C.K. 1975. Textural parameters of candy licorice. J. Food Sci. 40: 1050-1054.

6.4-96 Paris, M., and Clair, G. 1972. Contribution to the study of a savory from Persia [in French]. Plant. Med. Phytother. 6: 160-165. AGRICOLA.

6.4-97 Paulet, G., Mestres, G., and Cronenberger, L. 1974. Enzymic lipolysis of copra in media with low water content [in French]. Rev. Fr. Corps Gras 21{7}: 415-422. CA 82: 2691.

6.4-98 Philip, T., and Francis, F.J. 1971. Oxidation of capsanthin. J. Food Sci. 36: 96-97.

6.4-99 Pollock, C. 1974. Tools of the flavorist - essential oils and oleoresins. Flavour Ind. 5: 244-246.

6.4-100 Promayon, J., Barel, M., Fourny, G., and Vincent, J.-C. 1976. Chicory content determination tests in soluble mixtures of coffee and chicory [in French]. Cafe, Cacao, The 20{3}: 209-218. CA 86: 41883.

6.4-101 Rhyu, H.Y. 1979. Gas chromatographic characterization of oregano and other selected spices of the Labiatae family. J. Food Sci. 44: 1373-1378.

6.4-102 Rzepecka, M.A. 1973. A cavity peturbation method for routine permittivity measurement. J. Microwave Power 8: 3-11.

6.4-103 Sahasrabudhe, M.R., and Mullin, W.J. 1980. Dehydration of horseradish roots. J. Food Sci. 45{5}: 1440-1441,1443.

6.4-104 Saito, Y., and Sakamoto, T. 1976. Studies on the antioxidative properties of spices. III. The antioxidative effects of petroleum ether soluble and insoluble fractions from spices [in Japanese]. Eiyo To Shokuryo 29: 505-510. CA 87: 150314.

6.4-105 Sambaiah, K., Satyanarayana, M.N., and Rao, M.V.L. 1978. Effect of red pepper (chillies) and capsaicin on fat absorption and liver fat in rats. Nutr. Rep. Int. 18: 521-529.

6.4-106 Schwimmer, S., and Austin, S.J. 1971. Enhancement of pyruvic acid release and flavor in dehydrated Allium powders by gamma glutamyl transpeptidases. J. Food Sci. 36: 1081-1085.

6.4-107 Seher, A., and Ivanov, A. 1976. Natural antioxidants. II. Antioxidants in the fatty oil of Foeniculum vulgare Miller. 1. 6-Oxychroman derivatives [in German]. Fette Seifen Anstrichm. 78: 224-228. AGRICOLA.

6.4-108 Shankaracharya, N.B., Anandaraman, S., and Natarajan, C.P. 1973. Chemical composition of coriander varieties and changes on roasting. Pages 184-189 in N.M. Nayar, ed. Proceedings of the first national symposium on plantation crops, Dec. 8-9, 1972, Trivandrum, India. J. Plant. Crops 1(Suppl.).

6.4-109 Shelef, L.A., Naglik, O.A., and Bogen, D.W. 1980. Sensitivity of some common food-borne bacteria to the spices sage, rosemary, and allspice. J. Food Sci. 45: 1042-1044.

6.4-110 Sholto-Douglas, J. 1971. Choosing chillies. Flavour Ind. 2: 27.

6.4-111 Sienkiewicz, Z., Borawska, Z., Kazimierczak, W., and Wajnert, T.

1978. Development of production procedures for new types of flavored cheeses [in Polish]. Rocz. Inst. Przem. Mlecz. 20{2}: 19-36. DSA 42: 4184.

6.4-112 Surendranath, M.R., Lakshminarayana, T., Viswanadham, R.K., and Rao, S.D.T. 1971. A method of decuticling sesame seed. Trop. Sci. 13: 143-145.

6.4-113 Susheelamma, N.S., and Rao, M.V.L. 1980. Potentialities of peanut and sesame oilseed flours and proteins for replacing black gram components in the texture of leavened foods. J. Am. Oil Chem. Soc. 57: 212-215.

6.4-114 Tassan, C.G., and Russell, G.F. 1975. Chemical and sensory studies on cumin. J. Food Sci. 40: 1185-1188.

6.4-115 Toors, F.A., and Herczog, J.I.B. 1978. Acid production from a nonsugar licorice and different sugar substitutes in Streptococcus mutans monoculture and pooled plaque-saliva mixtures. Caries Res. 12{1}: 60-68. CA 88: 101498.

6.4-116 Tortuero, F. 1972. Comparative study of the effect of different levels of dehydrated alfalfa meal and oleoresin paprika residues on egg yolk pigmentation [in Spanish]. RNA Rev. Nutr. Anim. 10{2}: 79-84. AGRICOLA.

6.4-117 Watanabe, Y., and Oyana, Y. 1974. Antioxidative activities of distilled water-soluble and ethanol-soluble fractions from spices [in Japanese]. Eiyo To Shokuryo 27: 181-183. CA 81: 150686.

6.4-118 Weber, F.E., Taillie, S.A., and Stauffer, K.R. 1974. Functional characteristics of mustard mucilage. J. Food Sci. 39: 461-466.

6.4-119 Wilson, C.R., and Andrews, W.H. 1976. Sulfite compounds as neutralizers of spice toxicity for Salmonella. J. Milk Food Technol. 39: 464-466.

6.4-120 Yakobashvili, N.Z., Shvangiradze, O.E., and Arabidze, N.G. 1977. Improved technology for the extraction of the essential oil of eugenol from basil [in Russian]. Maslo-Zhir. Prom-st. 1977{5}: 21-22. CA 87: 44133.

6.4-121 Yamada, T., and Kiyama, K. 1977. Studies on drying, roasting and salt-coating of sesame seeds in the fluidized bed [in Japanese]. Nippon Nogei Kagaku Kaishi 51: 327-329. AGRICOLA.

6.4-122 Yamanishi, T., Kawatsu, M., Yokoyama, T., and Nakatani, Y. 1973. Methyl jasmonate and lactones including jasmine lactone in Ceylon tea. Agric. Biol. Chem. 37: 1075-1078.

6.4-123 Yatsko, M.A., Balan, G.M., and Korinetskaya, L.L. 1975. Use of the electrohydraulic effect for producing a vitamin-protein paste from spice green [in Russian]. Elektron. Obrab. Mater. 4: 62-63. CA 83: 176917

6.4-124 Zaika, L.L., and Kissinger, J.C. 1979. Effects of some spices on acid production by starter cultures. J. Food Prot. 42{7}: 572-576.

6.5 Quality Control

6.5-1 Abdalhafez, F.A., Ibrahim, S.S., and el Hindawy, S. 1975. The use of gas chromatography in detecting adulteration of geranium, peppermint and petitgrain bigrade oils with methanol and ethanol. Ann. Agric. Sci. (Moshtohor) 3: 119-130. AGRICOLA.

6.5-2 Al-Hakim, S., and Solaka, A. 1976. Stability evaluation of some Iraqi seed oils and commercial fate. Mesopotamia J. Agric. 11: 45-54. FCA 31: 2699.

6.5-3 Andre, L. 1973. Critical evaluation of Benedek's method for the determination of total pigment content in paprika [in German]. Z. Lebensm.-Unters.-Forsch. 151: 320-325. CA 79: 3897.

6.5-4 Arikawa, A., and Shiga, M. 1980. Determination of trace acrylamide in the crops by gas chromatography [in Japanese]. Bunseki Kagaku 29{7}: T33-T39. CA 93: 202742.

6.5-5 Babonove, C. 1973. Research on the fraudulent aromatization of natural sweet wines (French fortified wines) and mistelle wines by coriander (Coriandrum sativum L.) and elder (Sambucus nigra L.) [in French]. Ann. Technol. Agric. 22: 153-163. AGRICOLA.

6.5-6 Barakat, M.Z., Bassiouni, M., and El-Wakil, M. 1972. Ascorbimetry, the determination of ferric iron and cupric copper content of certain vegetables. J. Sci. Food Agric. 23: 685-686.

6.5-7 Baranov, Yu.S., Khilik, L.A., and Klisenko, M.A. 1979. Determining sym-triazine herbicides in essential oils and plants [in Russian]. Khim. Sel'sk. Khoz. 17{6}: 57-59. WA 29: 860.

6.5-8 Baranov, Yu.S., Khilik, L.A., and Bondarenko, T.I. 1979. Redistribution of herbicide residues from peppermint raw materials during distillation of an essential oil [in Russian]. Maslo-Zhir. Prom-st. 1979{12}: 23-24. CA 92: 99433.

6.5-9 Barudi, W., and Bielig, H.J. 1980. Heavy metal content (arsenic, lead, cadmium, mercury) of vegetables which grow above ground and fruits [in German]. Z. Lebensm.-Unters. Forsch. 170: 254-257. CA 93: 44261.

6.5-10 Beacs, P.A., and Katalin, G. 1980. The effect of gamma-irradiation on the lipid composition of spices: sweet noble paprika, black pepper and nutmeg. Acta Hortic. 96{II}: 133-137.

6.5-11 Becker, G. 1979. Multimethod for simultaneous detection of 75 plant treatment preparations on plant material [in German]. Dtsch. Lebensm.-Rundsch. 75: 148-152. CA 91: 54679.

6.5-12 Beitz, H., Pank, F., and Ehrt, M. 1972. Residues of plant protection materials on medicinal and spice plants - dimethoate residues on caraway and fennel [in German]. Pharmazie 27: 265-268. HA 43: 326.

6.5-13 Beitz, H., and Pank, F. 1972. Residues of plant protection materials in medicinal and spice plants. Methyl parathion residues in fennel and peppermint [in German]. Pharmazie 27: 532-534. HA 43: 2320.

6.5-14 Beitz, H., Seefield, F., and Pank, F. 1973. Residues of plant protection chemicals on medicinal plants - DDT and lindane residues in peppermint [in German]. Pharmazie 28: 270-271. HA 43: 7988.

6.5-15 Beuchat, L.R. 1976. Sensitivity of Vibrio parahaemolytiocus to spices and organic acids. J. Food Sci. 41: 899-902.

6.5-16 Braun, G., and Hiecke, E. 1976. Detection of oil and extracts from coriander (Coriandrum sativum L.) in wine and champagne [in German] Dtsch. Lebensm.-Rundsch. 72: 273-275. AGRICOLA.

6.5-17 Bulinski, R., and Kot, A. 1972. Residues and degradation dynamics of malathion on vegetables grown in greenhouses [in Polish]. Bromatol. Chem. Toksykol. 5: 167-173. CA 77: 99780.

6.5-18 Casanova, M., and Dubroca, J. 1972. Residues of pentachloronitrobenzene and its impurity hexachlorobenzene in soil and lettuces [in French]. C. R. Seances Acad. Agric. Fr. 58: 990-996. HA 44: 1027.

6.5-19 Chand, S., Srinivasulu, C., Vijayalakshmi, Mrs. K., and Mahapatra, S.N. 1974. Colorimetric estimation of sesame oil in adulterated samples. Curr. Sci. 43: 790.

6.5-20 Colliflower, E.J., and Thrasher, J.J. 1979. Mineral oil extraction of light filth from rubbed sage: Collaborative study. J. Assoc. Off. Anal. Chem. 62: 597-599.

6.5-21 Conacher, H.B.S. 1973. Gas chromatographic determination of brominated sesame oil in orange drinks: Collaborative study. J. Assoc. Off. Anal. Chem. 56: 602-606.

6.5-22 Copin, A., Kettman, R., Closset, J.-L., Duculot, C., and Martens, P.H. 1973. The application of total reflection infrared spectrometry to the study of pesticide residues [in French]. Bull. Rech. Agron. Gembloux 8: 135-146. RPP 54: 4774.

6.5-23 Corvi, C., and Vogel, J. 1976. Chlorinated pesticide residues in aromatic plants [in French]. Mitt. Geb. Lebensmittelunters Hyg. 67: 262-268.

6.5-24 Damiani, P. 1972. The determination of lead in vegetables by means of atomic absorption spectrophotometry [in Italian]. Industrie Alimentari 11: 106-110. HA 43: 6784.

6.5-25 Debelyi, A.S., and Troshko, E.V. 1972. Residues of pyrazone in medicinal plant tissue [in Russian]. Khim. Sel'sk. Khoz. 10: 542-543. WA 22: 2422.

6.5-26 Debska, W., and Domeracki, S. 1973. Determination of residual pesticides and their degradation products in vegetable drugs and crude drugs. I. Content of organochlorine pesticides in Matricaria chamomilla flowerheads [in Polish]. Herba Pol. 19: 15-22. HA 44: 7965.

6.5-27 Dejonckheere, W., Steurbant, W., and Kips, R.H. 1975. The problems posed by quintozene and hexachlorobenzene residues in lettuce and witloof chicory crops [in French]. Rev. Agric. (Brussels) 28: 581-591.

6.5-28 Dejonckheere, W., Steurbaut, W., and Kips, R.H. 1974. Quintozene (PCNB) residues in witloof chicory. Parasitica 30{1}: 28-36. RPP 54: 2651.

6.5-29 Dent, R.G. 1977. Collaborative study of a modified method for the extraction of light filth from ground white pepper, cardamom, celery seed, coriander, and ginger. J. Assoc. Off. Anal. Chem. 60: 117-121

6.5-30 El-Halfawy, M.A. 1977. Entomofauna of dried medical and aromatical plants with a short note on their occurrence and populations. Agric. Res. Rev. 55{1}: 103-160.

6.5-31 El-Halfawy, M.A. 1977. Biology of Lasioderma serricorne F. on certain medical and aromatical dried plants (Coleoptera:Anobiidae). Agric. Res. Rev. 55{1}: 107-110. RAE-A 68: 2608.

6.5-32 Ennet, D., and Pank, F. 1980. Residues of triazine herbicides in vegetable drugs. Acta Hortic. 1980{96} (II): 211-216.

6.5-33 En, A.R., Sardar, P.K., Sil, S., and Mathew, T.V. 1973. Suggested modification of PFA specification in case of coriander (dhania). J. Food Sci. Technol. 10: 126-127. Bib. Ag. 38: 9459.

6.5-34 Ercolani, G.L. 1976. Bacteriological quality assessment of fresh marketed lettuce and fennel. Applied and Environmental Microbiology 31: 847-852. HA 47: 4502.

6.5-35 Ferreira, L.A.B., Oliveira, E.F., Vilar, H.D., and Aguiar, M.C. 1973. Contributions to the determination of coffee purity [in Portuguese]. Garcia de Orta Ser. Estud. Agron. 1{1}: 35-40. HA 46: 3958.

6.5-36 Frank, H.K., Orth, R., and Figge, A. 1977. Patulin in foods of vegetable origin. II. Several kinds of fruit and vegetables and their prepared products [in German]. Z. Lebensm.-Unters. Forsch. 163: 111-114. CA 86: 138217.

6.5-37 Freeman, C.C. 1979. New brine saturation technique for the extraction of light filth from rubbed sage, paprika, and corn meal: Intralaboratory study. J. Assoc. Off. Anal. Chem. 62: 602-603.

6.5-38 Gecan, J.S., and Brickey, P.M., Jr. 1973. Collaborative study of a method for the extraction of light filth from prepared horseradish. J. Assoc. Off. Anal. Chem. 56: 629-630.

6.5-39 Georgieva, S., Lucheva, M., Kazakova, K., Sengalevich, G., and Kostadinova, P. 1978. Determination of Herbazin (simazine) residues in the soil and in lavender leaves [in Bulgarian]. Rastenievud. Nauki 15{9/10}: 212-218. HA 50: 2773.

6.5-40 Girgis, A.N., El-Sherif, S., Rofael, N., and Nesheim, S. 1977. Aflatoxins in Egyptian foodstuffs. J. Assoc. Off. Anal. Chem. 60: 746-747.

6.5-41 Glaze, L.E. 1975. Collaborative study of a method for the extraction of light filth from whole, cracked or flaked, and ground spices. J. Assoc. Off. Anal. Chem. 58: 447-450.

6.5-42 Golacka, J. 1971. Toxicological evaluation of some vegetables contaminated with fenitrothion, an insecticide used in plant cultivation. II. Dynamics of fenitrothion decline during the growth period. Bromatol. Chem. Toksykol. 4{1}: 77-85. CA 76: 11051.

6.5-43 Gruiz, K., and Biacs, P.A. 1978. Changes in the hydrocarbon composition of decontaminated spices after gamma-irradiation. Proc. Hung. Annu. Meet. Biochem. 18: 209-210. CA 90: 4604.

6.5-44 Haefner, M. 1978. Pentachloronitrobenzene, pentachloraniline and methylopentachlorobenzene residues in vegetables and in horticultural soils [in German]. Anz. Schaedlingskd. Pflanz.-Umweltschutz 51{4}: 49-57. CA 89: 85535.

6.5-45 Hall, R.L. 1973. Toxicants occurring naturally in spices and flavors. Pages 448-463 in Toxicants occurring naturally in foods, 2nd ed. National Academy of Sciences, Washington, D.C.

6.5-46 Hamano, M. 1976. Nitrite content and nitrosomamine formation with special reference to the storage and cooking of vegetables with fish and shellfish [in Japanese]. Tokyo Ika Daigaku Zasshi 34: 635-657. CA 86: 138295.

6.5-47 Heinisch, E. 1972. Herbicide residues in foods from plants [in German]. Nahrung 16: 132. WA 23: 1987.

6.5-48 Hellqvist, H., Renvall, S., Clementz, E., Lindskog, E., and Akerblom, M. 1974. Residues of some organophosphorous pesticides in horseradish after treatment against the cabbage root fly, Hylemya brassicae (Bouche) and the turnip root fly, H. floralis (Fallen) (Diptera, Muscidae) [in Swedish]. Medd. Statens Vaxtskyddanst. (Stockh.) 16{158/159}: 15-26.

6.5-49 Henneberg, M., and Lutomski, J. 1972. Investigation on residues of chlorinated insecticides in leaves of Mentha and flowers of Matricaria chamomilla [in German]. Herba Hung. 11{1}: 79-85. AGRICOLA.

6.5-50 Holtgreve, N.D. 1978. Mineral oil extraction of light filth from rubbed sage: Collaborative study. J. Assoc. Off. Anal. Chem. 61: 906-907.

6.5-51 Husain, S.S., and Ahmed, M.A. 1971. Studies on stored food grain fungi. Part II.- Fungi from oilseeds and Plantago ovata. Pak. J. Sci. Ind. Res. 14: 137-141.

6.5-52 Inal, T., Keskin, S., Tolgay, Z., and Tezcan, I. 1975. Sterilization of spices by means of gamma rays [in German]. Fleischwirtschaft 55: 675-677 CA 83: 74783.

6.5-53 James, T. 1973. Fluorometric determination of estradiol valerate in sesame oil or ethyl oleate injectables. II. Collaborative study J. Assoc. Off. Anal. Chem. 56: 86-87.

6.5-54 Josimovic, L., and Premovic, P. 1978. Study on some chemical changes in irradiated spices: I. Ground paprika. Bull.-Acad. Serbe Sci. Arts, Cl. Sci. Nat. Math., Sci. Nat. 1978{17}: 103-116.

6.5-55 Josimovic, L., and Premovic, P. 1978. Study on some chemical changes in irradiated spices. I. Ground paprika. Bull.-Acad. Serbe Sci. Arts, Cl. Sci. Nat. Math. Sci. Nat. 61{17}: 103-115. CA 90: 202327.

6.5-56 Julseth, R.M., and Deibel, R.H. 1974. Microbial profile of selected spices and herbs at import. J. Milk Food Technol. 37: 414-419.

6.5-57 Kadas, L. 1976. Nitrate contents of vegetables grown in Hungary [in Hungarian]. Elelmiszervizsgalati Kozl. 22: 346-349. CA 87: 100822.

6.5-58 Kadas, L. 1978. Amount of nitrate in different parts of some vegetables [in Hungarian]. Bot. Kozl. 65: 81-84. CA 90: 148449.

6.5-59 Kaferstein, F.K. 1976. The microflora of parsley. J. Milk Food Technol. 39: 837-840.

6.5-60 Kartnig, T., Mueller, E., Pelzmann, H., Still, F., and Werani, J. 1979. Analysis of residues of phosphorothioic acid esters on medicinal plants. 1. Mitteilung [in German]. Sci. Pharm. 47: 232-240.

6.5-61 Kasidas, G.P., and Rose, G.A. 1980. Oxalate content of some common foods: determination by an enzymic method. J. Hum. Nutr. 34: 255-266. CA 93: 184400.

6.5-62 Kiigemagi, U., and Deinzer, M.L. 1979. Dislodgeable and total residues of methomyl on mint foliage. Bull. Environ. Contam. Toxicol. 22: 517-521

6.5-63 Kiigemagi, U., Wellman, D., Cooley, E.J., and Terriere, L.C. 1973. Residues of the insecticides phorate and methomyl in mint hay and oil. Pestic. Sci. 4: 89-99. CA 79: 3919.

6.5-64 Kiss, I., Farkas, J., Ferenczi, S., Kalman, B., and Beczner, J. 1974. Effects of irradiation on the technological and hygienic qualities of several food products. Pages 157-177 in Improvement of food quality by irradiation; Proceedings, Vienna, 1973. Unipub, New York, N.Y. CA 83: 146022

6.5-65 Klein, D. 1978. The problem of declaring the presence of paprika in bruhwurst products [in German]. Fleischwirtschaft 58: 227-228. AGRICOLA.

6.5-66 Kojima, M. 1975. Studies on determination of the quality of Japanese horseradish ('Wasabi') powder by gas chromatography. V. An attempt for the practical use of simple checking method by headspace gas chromatography [in Japanese]. Nippon Shokuhin Kogyo Gakkai-shi 22: 13-18 AGRICOLA.

6.5-67 Kojima, M. 1976. A simple checking method for quality of the Japanese horseradish ('Wasabi') powder by head space gas chromatography [in Japanese]. Nippon Shokuhin Kogyo Gakkai-shi 23: 322-324. AGRICOLA.

6.5-68 Kojima, M. 1971. Studies on the check of quality of Japanese horseradish ("Wasabi") powder by gas chromatography. III. Investigation of the recovery [in Japanese]. Nippon Shokuhin Kogyo Gakkai-shi 18: 198-201. AGRICOLA.

6.5-69 Kojima, M. 1973. Evaluation of the quality of Japanese horseradish powder by gas chromatography. IV. Simple quality control method using head-space gas chromatography [in Japanese]. Nippon Shokuhin Kogyo Gakkai-Shi 20: 316-320. CA 84: 57452.

6.5-70 Kojima, M., and Yoshiaki, N. 1978. Studies on methods to check the quality of Japanese horseradish (wasabi) powder by gas chromatography. VIII. Comparison of analytical methods for the determination of allyl isothiocyanate in mustard, horseradish, and wasabi powder [in Japanese]. Nippon Shokuhin Kogyo Gakkaishi 25: 581-583. CA 91: 106705.

6.5-71 Kojima, M. 1977. Quality of Japanese horseradish (wasabi) powder measured by gas chromatography. VII. A simple quantitative method for determination of allyl isothiocyanate in the hydrolyzates from mustard, horseradish, and Japanese horseradish (wasabi) by head-space gas chromatography [in Japanese]. Nippon Shokuhin Kogyo Gakkaishi 24: 637-642. CA 91: 209468.

6.5-72 Komives, T., Katona, Mrs. A., Marton, A.F., and Dutka, F. 1977. Identification of organophosphorus pesticide residues in spice paprika [in Hungarian]. Elelmiszervizgalati Kozl. 23: 244-248. AGRICOLA.

6.5-73 Konecsni, I., and Lendvai, I. 1976. Study of methods for the determination of ash and sand content of spice paprika [in Hungarian]. Konzerv. Paprikaip 1976{4}: 121-125.

6.5-74 Krishnaswamy, M.A., Patel, J.D., Parthasarathy, N., and Nair, K.K.S. 1973. Some of the types of coliforms, aerobic mesophilic spore formers, yeasts, and moulds present in spices. Pages 200-203 in N.M. Nayar, ed. Proceedings of the first national symposium on plantation crops, Dec. 8-9, 1972, Trivandrum, India. J. Plant. Crops 1(Suppl.).

6.5-75 Langerak, D.I. 1975. The influence of irradiation and packaging on the keeping quality of prepacked cut endive, chicory and onions. Acta Aliment. Acad. Sci. Hung. 4: 123-138. HA 46: 314.

6.5-76 Lemieszek-Chodorowska, K., Michalak, I., Pukorska, W., Lisowska, W., Kotlarek, J., Cywinska, M., Kula, H., Mazurkiewicz, K., Jarysz, M., et al. 1972. Determination of nitrites and nitrates in some Polish vegetables [in Polish]. Rocz. Panstw. Zakl. Hig. 23: 549-555. CA 78: 41631.

6.5-77 Loof, B. 1972. The quality of Swedish oilseeds [in Swedish]. Svensk Frotidning 41: 138-143. FCA 28: 2706.

6.5-78 Loof, B. 1972. The quality of Swedish oilseeds [in Swedish]. Svensk Frotidning 41: 115-121. FCA 28: 2705.

6.5-79 Loof, B. 1972. The quality of Swedish oilseeds [in Swedish]. Svensk Frotidning 41: 146-149. FCA 28: 2707.

6.5-80 Loof, B. 1973. The quality of Swedish oilseeds [in Swedish]. Svensk Frotidning 42: 2-13. FCA 28: 2708.

6.5-81 Loof, B. 1973. The quality of Swedish oilseeds [in Swedish]. Svensk Frotidning 42: 121-126. FCA 28: 2709.

6.5-82 Loof, B. 1973. The quality of Swedish oilseeds [in Swedish]. Svensk Frotidning 42: 138-143. FCA 28: 2710.

6.5-83 Lorenz, O.A., and Weir, B.L. 1974. Nitrate accumulation in vegetables. Pages 93-103 in Environmental quality and food supply. Futura Pub., Mount Kisco, N.Y. CA 82: 85295.

6.5-84 Martens, P.H., and Cus, M. 1972. The determination of residues in vegetables [in French]. Meded. Fac. Landbouwwet. Rijksuniv. Gent 37: 882-888. HA 43: 7609.

6.5-85 Martens, P.H., and Cus, M. 1972. Oscillopolarographic method for the determination of thiophanate residues in vegetables [in French]. Meded. Fac. Landbouwwet. Rijksuniv. Gent 37: 891-896. HA 43: 7610.

6.5-86 McNeal, J.E. 1976. Qualitative tests for added coloring matter in meat products. J. Assoc. Off. Anal. Chem. 59: 570-577.

6.5-87 Merck-Luengo, J.G. 1972. Residues of methyl bromide in almonds, hazelnuts, groundnuts, copra, royal palm, garlic, beans and Citrus peel during the 1971 national phytosanitary campaign [in Spanish]. Boletin Informativo de Plagas 1972{100}: 29-80. RAE-A 62: 4016.

6.5-88 Mitteilung, K. 1976. Residues of chlorinated pesticides in aromatic plants [in French]. Trav. Chim. Aliment. Hyg. 67: 262-268.

6.5-89 Munjal, K., Rai, J., and Verma, M.R. 1971. Evaluation of purity of saffron. Res. Ind. 16: 294-298. AGRICOLA.

6.5-90 Muranyi, E., Nagy, J., and Kormendy, I. 1977. Results in decreasing the bacterial count with ethylene oxide in differently packaged ground spice paprika [in Hungarian]. Konzerv. Paprikaip 1977{5}: 184-186.

6.5-91 Murko, D., Ramic, S., and Kekic, M. 1974. Tannins of Salvia officinalis and their change during storage [in German]. Planta Med. 25: 295-300. CA 81: 23085.

6.5-92 Myron, D.R., Givand, S.H., and Nielsen, F.H. 1977. Vanadium content of selected foods as determined by flameless atomic absorption spectroscopy. J. Agric. Food Chem. 25: 297-300.

6.5-93 Nagle, B.J., Villalon, B., and Burns, E.E. 1979. Color evaluation of selected capsicums. J. Food Sci. 44: 416-418.

6.5-94 Nakamura, K., Matsuoka, M., and Kaneda, Y. 1973. Gas chromatographic analysis of pesticide residues in food. Screening method for organochlorine pesticide residues in fragrant vegetables [in Japanese]. Shokuhin Eiseigaku Zasshi 14: 474-477.

6.5-95 Ninomiya, T., Okada, T., and Hosogai, Y. 1976. Germanium contents in foods [in Japanese]. Shokuhin Eiseigaku Zasshi 17: 481-482. HA 47: 11090.

6.5-96 Ogbadu, G. 1979. Effect of low dose gamma irradiation on the production of aflatoxin B1 by Aspergillus flavus growing on Capsicum annuum. Microbios. Lett. 10{39/40}: 139-142. CA 92: 196619.

6.5-97 Oishi, K., Mori, K., and Nishiura, Y. 1974. Food hygienic studies on Anisakinae larvae. V. Effect of some spice essential oils and food preservatives on the mortality of Anisakinae larvae [in Japanese]. Nippon Suisan Gakkaishi 40{12}: 1241-1250. CA 82: 84722.

6.5-98 Palumbo, S.A., Rivenburgh, A.I., Smith, J.L., and Kissinger, J.C. 1975. Identification of Bacillus subtilis from sausage products and spices. J. Appl. Bacteriol. 38: 99-105.

6.5-99 Parvaneh, V. 1972. A note on the assessment of the purity of saffron colour. J. Assoc. Public Anal. 10{2}: 31-32. AGRICOLA 72083690.

6.5-100 Pathak, R.K., Sharma, M.K., Singh, R.N., and Tripathi, R.D. 1973. Quality studies of some cruciferous oilseeds. Indian J. Agric. Res. 7: 99-103. FCA 28: 448.

6.5-101 Pestemer, W., and Mann, W. 1980. Herbicide residues in some cooking herbs [in German]. Z. Lebensm.-Unters. -Forsch. 171: 272-277. WA 30: 2630.

6.5-102 Plouvier, V. 1976. Cyanogenetic glycosides and enzymes: detection and estimation of hydrocyanic acid in several species, distribution of linamarase [in French]. C.R. Hebd. Seances Acad. Sci. Ser. D 282{8}: 723-726. CA 85: 2508.

6.5-103 Powers, E.M., Latt, T.G., and Brown, T. 1976. Incidence and levels of Bacillus cereus in processed spices. J. Milk Food Technol. 39: 668-670.

6.5-104 Powers, E.M., Lawyer, R., and Masuoka, Y. 1975. Microbiology of processed spices. J. Milk Food Technol. 38: 683-687.

6.5-105 Quinche, J.-P., and Dvorak, V. 1980. Nitrate determination in vegetables, herbs and soils with a specific ion electrode and by gas liquid chromatography [in French]. Rev. Suisse Vitic. Arboric. Hortic. 12: 7-20. HA 50: 7056.

6.5-106 Rajukkannu, K., Salivaraj, K., Vasudevan, P., and Balasubramanian, M. 1978. Carbofuran and aldicarb residues in green chillies (Correspondence). Curr. Sci. 47: 784. HELM AB-B 48: 833.

6.5-107 Ramakrishnan, T.V., and Francis, F.J. 1973. Color and carotenoid changes in heated paprika. J. Food Sci. 38: 25-28.

6.5-108 Regula, E., and Wassermann, L. 1979. Pesticide residues in poppy seed [in German]. Z. Lebensm.-Unters. -Forsch. 169: 444-446. NAR-B 50: 3335.

6.5-109 Reifenstein, H., and Pank, F. 1975. Triazine residues in medicinal plants [in German]. Pharmazie 30: 391-393. WA 25: 2131.

6.5-110 Renvall, S., and Ekstrom, G. 1976. Residues of chlorfenvinphos and trichloronate in soil and horseradish after treatment against cabbage root fly and turnip root fly [in Swedish]. Vaxtskyddsnotiser 40: 98-101, 112. HA 47: 6801.

6.5-111 Robin, A., Guillot, B., Ferry, S., and Collombel, C. 1978. A study of the content of organochlorine insecticides in medicinal plants [in French]. Plant. Med. Phytother. 12: 130-136. HA 49: 4444.

6.5-112 Rodriguez-Rebollo, M. 1974. Coliforms and Escherichia coli on market fruits and vegetables [in Spanish]. Microbiol. Esp. 27: 225-234.

6.5-113 Sakai, T., Ageishi, K., Mikage, M., Namba, T., and Yanagita, T. 1977. Microbiological studies on drugs and their raw materials. Part 3. Growth and aflatoxin production by Aspergillus parasiticus in ginseng root. J. Gen. Appl. Microbiol. 23{5}: 279-283. CA 88: 126254.

6.5-114 Santoprete, G. 1978. Variability of the contents of oligoelements (chromium, manganese, cobalt, copper, zinc, cadmium, mercury, and lead) in vegetables in Italy coming from the principal zone of production [in Italian]. Riv. Merceol. 17: 431-450. CA 91: 89847.

6.5-115 Sapetti, C., and Arduino, E. 1973. Pollution with lead near the Torino—Milano motorway [in Italian]. Agrochimica 17: 540-545. HERB AB 44: 3878.

6.5-116 Schoer, J., and Nagel, U. 1980. Thallium in plants and soils. Studies in the southern Rhine-Neckar region [in German]. Naturwissenschaften 67: 261-262. CA 93: 62934.

6.5-117 Schulze, A.E. 1975. Report on analytical mycology of foods and drugs. J. Assoc. Off. Anal. Chem. 58: 244 (Abstr.).

6.5-118 Schuszter, F., and Kulcsar, A. 1975. Rapid method for the determination of paprika and black pepper in quick-frozen foods [in Hungarian]. Hutoipar 22{1}: 26-29. AGRICOLA.

6.5-119 Scott, P.M., and Kennedy, B.P.C. 1975. The analysis of spices and herbs for aflatoxins. Can. Inst. Food Sci. Technol. J. 8: 124-125.

6.5-120 Sengupta, P., Sil, S., and Sen, A.R. 1977. Detection of tobacco seed oil in sesame and other oils by thin layer chromatography. J. Food Sci. Technol. 14: 56-57.

6.5-121 Shah, C.S., Qadry, J.S., and Chauhan, M.G. 1972. Indian dill as substitute for European dill. Indian J. Pharm. 34: 69-70.

6.5-122 Shiliapnikova, A.P., Kopeikovskii, V.M., Ponomarev, E.D., and Shliapnikov, V.A. 1972. Hygroscopic properties of coriander fruit [in Russian]. Izv. Vyssh. Ucheb. Zaved. Pishch. Tekhnol. 1972{4}: 26-29. AGRICOLA.

6.5-123 Shin, K.S., and Namkung, S. 1977. Studies on the accumulation of nitrite and nitrite [sic] in vegetables and fruits [in Korean]. Hanguk Yongyang Hakhoe Chi 10: 299-303. CA 90: 53358.

6.5-124 Shliapnikova, A.P., Ponomarev, E.D., Kopeikovskii, V.M., and Shliapnikov, V.A. 1972. Heat resistance of coriander fruits [in Russian]. Izv. Vyssh. Ucheb. Zaved. Pishch. Tekhnol. 1972{3}: 17-19. AGRICOLA.

6.5-125 Skorikova, Yu.G., and Isagulyan, E.A. 1974. Biochemical changes in root crops of parsley, parsnips, and celery during vegetation and storage [in Russian]. Fiziol. Biokhim. Kul't. Rast. 6: 621-626. CA 82: 71793.

6.5-126 Sobotka-Wierzbowicz, J. 1971. Assays of residual pesticides in anise oil. Acta Pol. Pharm. (Engl. Transl.) 28: 182-186. Translation of Acta Pol. Pharm. 28: 181-184.

6.5-127 Sommer, L., Tulbedgian, A., Forstner, S., and Constantinescu, C. 1972. Contributions to purity testing in chamomile [in German]. Herba Hung. 11{3}: 21-30.

6.5-128 Stoffelsma, J., and De Roos, K.B. 1973. Identification of

2,4,6-trichloroanisol in several essential oils. J. Agr. Food Chem. 21: 738-739. CA 79: 83377.

6.5-129 Szabad, Mrs. J., Halasz, K., Kendvai, I., and Fabri, I. 1977. Micbrobiological analysis in spice paprika manufacturing [in Hungarian]. Konzer v. Paprikaip. 5: 187-188. AGRICOLA.

6.5-130 Szabo, F., and Tokes, B. 1978. Radioactivity of some agricultural and vegetal products in Bistrita-Nasaud, Mures and Harghita Counties [in Romanian]. Rev. Ig. Bacteriol. Virusol. Prazitol. Epidemiol. Pneumoftiziol. Ig. 27: 361-366. CA 91: 86548.

6.5-131 Szymczak, J. 1979. Effect of fungicides used in poppy plantings on the content and composition of seed oil [in Polish]. Bromatol. Chem. Tokysykol. 12: 357-361. AGRICOLA.

6.5-132 Tanaka, Y., and Langerak, D.I.S. 1975. Effects of gamma-irradiation on quality and enzyme activities of prepacked cut chicory. J. Food Technol. 10: 415-425.

6.5-133 Technical Committee ISO/TC 54. 1972. The international standardization of essential oils [in French]. An. Acad. Bras. Cienc. 44(Suppl.): 149-156.

6.5-134 Teisseire, P., and Galfre, A. 1974. Essential oil of ylang-ylang. Adulteration of the oil of exotic basil [in French]. Recherches 19: 269-274. CA 83: 84694.

6.5-135 Thrasher, J.J. 1975. Collaborative study of a method for the extraction of light filth from crushed red peppers. J. Assoc. Off. Anal. Chem. 58: 445-446.

6.5-136 Thrasher, J.J., and Gentry, R. 1977. Collaborative study of a mineral oil method for the extraction of light filth from ground paprika. J. Assoc. Off. Anal. Chem. 60: 114-116.

6.5-137 Thrasher, J.J., and Colliflower, E.J. 1978. Oil flotation extraction of light filth from ground capsicums excluding paprika: Collaborative study. J. Assoc. Off. Anal. Chem. 61: 900-902.

6.5-138 Thrasher, J.J. 1976. Collaborative study of a method for the extraction of light filth from ground mace and ground caraway seed. J. Assoc. Off. Anal. Chem. 59: 827-829.

6.5-139 Tkachuk, R., and Kuzina, F.D. 1972. Mercury levels in wheat and other cereals, oilseed and biological samples. J. Sci. Food Agric. 23: 1183-1195.

6.5-140 Tucker, A.O., Maciarello, M.J., and Howell, J.T. 1980. Botanical aspects of commercial sage. Econ. Bot. 34: 16-19.

6.5-141 Udagawa, S.-I., and Muroi, T. 1979. Some interesting species of Ascomycetes from imported spices. Nippon Kingakkai Kaiho 20{1}: 13-22 RPP 59: 2285.

6.5-142 U.S. Environmental Protection Agency. 1980. 0,0-Dimethyl S-[(4-oxo-1,2,3- benzotriazin-3(4H)-yl)methyl] phosphorodithioate; tolerances for residues. Fed. Regist. 45{224}: 76146. CA 94: 63914.

6.5-143 Vajdi, M., and Pereira, R.R. 1973. Comparative effects of ethylene oxide, gamma irradiation and microwave treatments on selected spices. J. Food Sci. 38: 893-895.

6.5-144 Vasundhara, T.S., and Parihar, D.B. 1980. Studies in pyrazines in roasted spices: Coriandrum sativum, Cuminum cyminum and Trigonella foenum-graecum. Nahrung 24: 645-651.

6.5-145 Venter, H.A. van de. 1978. An index for wilting in roots of chicory (Cichorium intybus L.). Agroplantae 10: 9-11. HA 49: 382.

6.5-147 Vilar, H.D., and Ferreira, L.A.B. 1973. Chlorogenic acid in coffee - how chlorogenic acid can contribute to the evaluation of the coffee contents of soluble coffees containing substitutes [in Portuguese]. Garcia de Orta Ser. Estud. Agron. 1{1}: 41-48. HA 46: 3959.

6.5-148 Walker, R. 1975. Naturally occurring nitrate/nitrite in foods. J. Sci. Food Agric. 26: 1735-1742.

6.5-149 Wallace, A., and Cha, J.W. 1977. Trace metals in two garden products derived from sewage sludge. Commun. Soil Sci. Plant Anal. 8: 819-821.

6.5-150 Wambeke, E. van, Vanachter, A., Temmerman, L. de, and Assche, C. van. 1973. Problems concerning Sclerotinia rot in chicory forcing beds and pentachloronitrobenzene residues in the marketable crop [in Dutch]. Meded. Fac. Landbouwwet. Rijksuniv. Gent 38: 899-910. HA 44: 5588.

6.5-151 Welch, R.M., and Cary, E.E. 1975. Concentration of chromium, nickel and vanadium in plant materials. J. Agric. Food Chem. 23: 479-482.

6.5-152 Wiederholt, E., Overberg, U., and Plempel, M. 1974. Paper chromatographic determination of artificial food coloring in licorice [in German]. Prax. Naturwiss., Teil 3. 23{1}: 8-11. CA 80: 132176.

6.5-153 Wojtal, R., Urbanowicz, M., and Zielinski, A. 1979. Evaluation of freshness of fruit and vegetable salads on the basis of changes of enzyme activity. Rocz. Akad. Roln. Poznaniu 107: 101-106. CA 91: 156266.

6.5-154 Wulf, L.W., Nagel, C.W., and Branen, A.L. 1978. High-pressure liquid chromatographic separation of the naturally occurring toxicants myrristicin, related aromatic ethers and falcarinol. J. Chromatogr. 161: 271-278.

6.5-155 Yanagita, T., Sakai, T., Ageishi, K., Uesora, H., and Moriya, S. 1977. Microbiological studies on drugs and their raw materials. Part 2. Growth and aflatoxin production in fungi developing on cereal and crude drug samples. J. Gen. Appl. Microbiol. 23{5}: 261-274. CA 88: 84332.

6.5-156 Yannai, S., and Haas, A. 1973. Occurrence of lead in sesame paste and factors responsible for it. Cereal Chem. 50: 613-616.

7.0 PHARMACOLOGY

7.1 Medicinal Plants

7.1-1 Aikman, L. 1974. Nature's gifts to medicine. Natl. Geogr. Mag. 146: 420-440.

7.1-2 Aizenman, B.E. 1978. Higher plants as the source of new antibiotics [in Russian]. Mikrobiol. Zh. 40: 233-241.

7.1-3 Albert-Puleo, M. 1978. Mythobotany, pharmacology, and chemistry of thujone-containing plants and derivatives. Econ. Bot. 32: 65-74.

7.1-4 Aplin, T.E.H., and Cannon, J.R. 1971. Distribution of alkaloids in some Western Australian plants. Econ. Bot. 25{4}: 366-380.

7.1-5 Astadzhov, N. 1972. Investigation on medicinal plants in the Institute of Kazanlyk [in Russian]. Postep Dziedzinie Leku Rosl. Pr. Ref. Dosw. Wygloszone Symp. 1970 Herba Pol. Suppl. 1972: 30-38.

7.1-6 Attisso, M.A. 1979. Medicinal plants make a comeback. Unesco Courier 32{7}: 6-8.

7.1-7 Balbaa, S.I., Mahran, G.H., El-Hossary, G.A., and Selim, M.A. 1975. A phytochemical study of Glycyrrhiza glabra L. growing in Egypt. Bull. Fac. Pharm., Cairo Univ. 14{1}: 213-229. CA 87: 206410.

7.1-8 Baldwin, C. 1971. Green gold from the forest. Am. For. 77: 40-43. AGRICOLA.

7.1-9 Bhavsar, G.C., Kapadia, N.S., and Patel, N.M. 1980. Studies on Trigonella foenum-graecum (Linn.). Indian J. Pharm. Sci. 42: 39-40. HA 51: 2997.

7.1-10 Bohm, H. 1974. Papaver bracteatum Lindl., a potentially medicinal plant. Pharmazie 29: 70-71 (Abstr.).

7.1-11 Chandra, V., and Srivastava, K. 1973. Genus Cymbopogon, its botany and pharmacognosy. Indian J. Pharm. 35{6}: 209 (Abstr.).

7.1-12 Chichiricco, G., Cifani, M.P., Frizzi, G., and Tammaro, F. 1980. Phytotherapy in the Subequana valley, Abruzzo, Central Italy. J. Ethnopharmacol. 2: 247-257. HA 51: 2091.

7.1-13 Collins, P. 1975. Turkey's flower powers. Nature (London) 253: 488-489.

7.1-14 Cuenot, G. 1971. Notes on medicinal plants [in French]. Bull. Tech. Inf. 1971{260}: 549-551.

7.1-15 Czabajska, W., and Okoniewska, J. 1971. Evaluation of development of Valeriana officinalis L. and the analysis of the oil content in the drug [in Polish]. Herba Pol. 17: 367-387. AGRICOLA.

7.1-16 Deneva, T. 1978. Opium poppy: a valuable drug plant [in Bulgarian]. Priroda (Sofiia) 27{6}: 63-66. Bib. Ag. 43: 100578.

7.1-17 Dominguez, X.A., Gonzalez, H., Aragon, R. and others. 1976. Mexican medicinal plants. XXIX. Three new diterpene quinones from Salvia ballotaeflora. Planta Med. 30: 237-241. CIM 18{3}: 2041.

7.1-18 Dominquez, X.A., Martinez, C., Calero, A., Dominquez, X.A., Jr., Hinojosa, M., Zamudio, A., Watson, W.H., and Zabel, V. 1978. Mexican medicinal plants. XXXI. Chemical components from "jiguelite", Indigofera suffruticosa, Mill. Planta Med. 34{2}: 172-175. CA 90: 36306.

7.1-19 Duke, J.A. 1973. Utilization of Papaver. Econ. Bot. 27: 390-400.

7.1-20 Euler, K.L. 1979. A survey of current medicinal and other uses of herbs. Herbarist 45: 59-69.

7.1-21 Farnsworth, N.R., and Segelman, A.B. 1971. Hypoglycemic plants. Tile and Till 57{3}: 52-56.

7.1-22 Foye, W.O. 1977. Medicinals of plant origin: past and present. Herbarist 43: 13-20.

7.1-23 Fulder, S. 1977. Ginseng: useless root or subtle medicine?. New Scientist 73{1035}: 138-139.

7.1-24 Gerbaud, O. 1980. Foxglove, Digitalis purpurea [in French]. Notes de Toxicologie Veterinaire {1980} 8: 450-452. IV 49: 77647.

7.1-25 Hnatyszyn, O., Rondina, R.V.D., and Coussio, J.D. 1976. Phytochemical screening of Argentine plants with potential pharmacological activity (Part VI). Planta Med. 29: 234-240. HA 47: 1859.

7.1-26 Hoelzl, J. 1975. Role of chemical races, sources, cultivars, and species for the in vivo preparation of radioactively labeled natural compounds described using Valeriana as an example [in German]. Planta Med. 28{3}: 301-304. CA 84: 102380.

7.1-27 Holod, A. 1976. Yarrow [in Slovak]. Nase Liecive Rastliny 13: 14-16. HA 46: 11675

7.1-28 Hu, S.Y. 1976. The genus Panax (ginseng) in Chinese medicine. Econ. Bot. 30: 11-28.

7.1-29 Hu, S.Y. 1977. A contribution to our knowledge of ginseng. Am. J. Chin. Med. 5: 1-23. CIM 18{4}: 2648.

7.1-30 Ikram, M., and Zirvi, K.A. 1976. Chemistry and pharmacology of liquorice (genus Glycyrrhiza). Herba Pol. 22: 312-320. HA 48: 4881.

7.1-31 Johansson, A. 1979. The content and composition of sterols and sterol esters in sunflower and poppy seed oils. Lipids 14: 285-291.

7.1-32 Kalinkina, G.I., and Berezovskaya, T.P. 1975. Achillea asiatica as a possible source of chamazulene [in Russian]. Rastit. Resur. 11: 220-227. CA 83: 1975.

7.1-33 Khaitov, I.Kh. 1974. Prospecting chemical studies of several medicinal plants of the flora in Tadzhikistan [in Russian]. Actual. Vopr. Farm. 2: 7-11. CA 84: 86768.

7.1-34 Kozlowski, J. 1977. Utilization of domestic resources of medicinal plants by the Polish drug plant industry. VI. A. [in Polish]. Wiad. Zielarskie 19{2}: 11-12. AGRICOLA.

7.1-35 Krochmal, A., Wilken, L., and Chien, M. 1972. Plant and lobeline harvest of Lobelia inflata L. Econ. Bot. 26: 216-220.

7.1-36 Krochmal, A., and Krochmal, C. 1978. Ginseng, panacea of five leaves. Garden (N.Y.) 2{5}: 25-28.

7.1-37 Kurlyanchik, I.A., and Lebedyuk, V.G. 1974. The productivity of certain wild medicinal plants in the Ryazanj region [in Russian]. Rastit. Resur. 10: 212-216.

7.1-38 Li, C.P., and Li, R.C. 1973. An introductory note to ginseng. Am. J. Chin. Med. 1: 249-261. CIM 15{2}: 2104.

7.1-39 Medina, J.F., Rondina, R.V.D., and Coussio, J.D. 1977. Phytochemical screening of Argentine plants with potential pharmacological activity. Part VII. Planta Med. 31: 136-140. HA 47: 9771.

7.1-40 Merkes, K. 1979. Medicinal plants with essential oil. III. Mentha piperita L. - peppermint [in German]. PTA Repetitorium 1979{5}: 17-20. CA 91: 128883.

7.1-41 Morelli, I. 1977. Constituents and uses of Melissa officinalis [in Italian]. Boll. Chim.-Farm. 116: 334-340. AGRICOLA.

7.1-42 Mulevich, V.M., Bogacheva, N.G., Volovel'skii, L.N., Kogan, L.M., Kiselev, V.P., and Levandovskii, G.S. 1977. Economic justification of the use of fenugreek Trigonella as a raw material for the production of steroid drugs. Pharm. Chem. J. (Engl. Transl.) 11: 282-284. Translation of Khim.-Farm. Zh. 11{2}: 138-140, 1976.

7.1-43 Nyman, U., and Bruhn, J.G. 1979. Papaver bracteatum - A summary of current knowledge. Planta Med. 35: 97-117. CA 91: 9363.

7.1-44 Ovodova, R.G., Mikheiskaya, L.V., and Ovodov, Yu.S. 1975. A phytochemical investigation of plantation ginseng. Chem. Nat. Compd. (Engl. Transl.) 11: 447. Translation of Khim. Prir. Soedin. 1975{3}: 430-431.

7.1-45 Palevitch, D. 1978. Medicinal plants and their value. I. Modern medicine [in Hebrew]. Science 6: 264-270.

7.1-46 Papatzikos, G. 1975. Mentha: an important medicinal and aromatic plant [in Greek]. Agrotike 1975{1}: 9-11. AGRICOLA.

7.1-47 Pecorari, P., Vampa, G., Melegari, M., and Bianchi, A. 1976. Studies on medicinal plants cultivated in the Modena High Appenines. I. Comparative investigations of Salvia sclarea [in Italian]. Atti Soc. Nat. Mat. Modena 107: 25-32. HA 48: 10822.

7.1-48 Petiard, V., Demarly, Y., and Paris, R.R. 1972. Proof of heterosides and alkaloids in tissue cultures of medicinal plants [in French]. Plant Med. Phytother. 6: 41-49.

7.1-49 Proserpio, G. 1976. Ginseng (Panax ginseng). Recent results of chemical and pharmacological studies. Prospects for the practical use of extracts in cosmetics and dermatology [in Italian]. Riv. Ital. Essenze Profumi Piante Off. Aromi Saponi Cosmet. Aerosol 58: 570-578. HA 48: 1716.

7.1-50 Raman, K.R., and Vasudevan, P. 1977. Wild plants of medicinal value in the south. Pages 447-454 in C.K. Atal and B.M. Kapur, eds. Cultivation & utilization of medicinal and aromatic plants. Regional Research Laboratory, Jammu-Tawi, India.

7.1-51 Ruminska, A. 1976. Common wormwood, Artemisia absinthium L. [in Polish]. Wiad. Zielarskie 18{7/8}: 15-16. AGRICOLA.

7.1-52 Sandberg, F. 1973. Two glycoside-containing genera of the Araliaceae family Panax and Eleutherococcus. Planta Med. 24: 392-396. CA 80: 115843.

7.1-53 Sanyal, P.K. 1977. Homoeopathic [sic] pharmacy in India. Pages 141-144 in C.K. Atal and B.M. Kapur, eds. Cultivation & utilisation of medicinal and aromatic plants. Regional Research Laboratory, Jammu-Tawi, India, 1977.

7.1-54 Sarkany, S., Michels-Nyomarkay, C., and Sarkany-Kiss, I. 1976. Accumulation of alkaloids in Papaver somniferum L. Nova Acta Leopoldina Suppl. 7: 83-88.

7.1-55 Scholz, H. 1972. Medicine from foxglove [in German]. Kosmos. 68: 355-358. AGRICOLA.

7.1-56 Silva, F. 1973. Several chemical studies of medicinal plants cultivated in Romania in the field of experimental agriculture during the last 10 years [in French]. Fitoterapia 44{2}: 51-60.

7.1-57 Specchia, V. 1976. Licorice: extraction and uses [in Italian]. Rass.chim. 28{6}: 227-232. CA 88: 197468.

7.1-58 Srepel, B., Vitaic, D., and Besic, J. 1974. Herba satureiae montanae. Drug and essential oils [in Croatian]. Acta Pharm. Jugosl. 4: 167-171. CA 82: 47673.

7.1-59 Teteny, P. 1979. Medicinal and aromatic plants in present and future. Chron. Hortic. 19: 3-5.

7.1-60 Tokareva, V.D. 1977. Specialization of different districts of the Kursk region with respect to the purveyance of medicinal-plant materials [in Russian]. Rastit. Resur. 13: 42-46.

7.1-61 Tyler, V.E. 1979. Plight of plant-drug research in the United States today. Econ. Bot. 33: 377-383.

7.1-62 Uke, G. 1974. Medicinal plants of Samoa. A preliminary survey of the use of plants for medicinal purposes in the Samoan Islands. Econ. Bot. 28: 1-30.

7.1-63 Ulubelen, A. 1979. Medicinal plants of Turkey. Shoyakugaku Zasshi 33: 125-129.

7.1-64 Vohora, S.B., Rizwan, M., and Khan, J.A. 1973. Medicinal uses of common Indian vegetables. Planta Med. 23: 381-393. HA 44: 2326.

7.1-65 Watanabe, K. 1973. Pharmacology of licorice root [in Japanese]. Taisha 10: 626-631. CA 82: 10902.

7.2 Compounds of Medicinal Value

7.2-1 Ahn, Y.P., and Chung, C.C. 1970. A study on the chemical components of Korean Panax ginseng [in Korean]. Academical Theses Kon Kuk University 11: 661-667. HA 43: 1445.

7.2-2 Albulescu, D., Palade, M., and Dafincescu, M. 1975. Coumarin derivatives from Levisticum officinale [in Romanian]. Farmacia (Bucharest) 23: 159-166. CA 84: 147632.

7.2-3 Bhale, R., and Bokadia, M.M. 1979. Sterol from the seeds of Indigofera linifolia (Retz.). Oils Oilseeds J. 31{3}: 21. CA 92: 90904.

7.2-4 Bird, G.W.G., and Wingham, J. 1973. Anti-TN agglutinins from clary seeds. Transfusion (Phila.) 13: 348 (Abstr.).

7.2-5 Bird, G.W.G., and Wingham, J. 1974. Haemaagglutinins from Salvia. Vox Sang. 26: 163-166.

7.2-6 Bird, G.W.G., and Wingham, J. 1976. More Salvia agglutinins. Vox. Sang. 30: 217-219.

7.2-7 Blunden, G., Culling, C., and Jewers, K. 1975. Steroidal sapogenins: a review of actual and potential plant sources. Trop. Sci. 17: 139-154. HA 46: 10645.

7.2-8 Brochmann-Hanssen, E., Fu, C.-C., Leung, A.Y., and Zanati, G. 1971. Opium alkaloids. X: Biosynthesis of 1-benzylisoquinolines. J. Pharm. Sci. 60: 1672-1676.

7.2-9 Buckova, A., Grznar, K., Haladova, M., and Eisenreichova, E. 1977. Active principles in Valeriana officinalis L. [in Slovak]. Cesk. Farm. 26{7}: 308-309. CA 88: 86063.

7.2-10 Creasey, W.A. 1979. Biochemical effects of berberine. Biochem. Pharmacol. 28: 1081-1084.

7.2-11 Culvenor, C.C.J., Edgar, J.A., Frahn, J.L., and Smith, L.W. 1980. The alkaloids of Symphytum X uplandicum (Russian comfrey). Aust. J. Chem. 33: 1105-1113.

7.2-12 Dauksha, A.D. 1974. Study of chemical composition of coumarin derivatives in Levisticum officinale [in Russian]. Aktual. Vopr. Farm. 2: 77-78. CA 84: 132599.

7.2-13 Dawidar, A.M., Saleh, A.A., and Elmotei, S.L. 1973. Steroid sapogenin constituents of fenugreek seeds. Planta Med. 24: 367-370. CA 80: 57459.

7.2-14 Duquenois, P.A. 1977. Review of hydrolates of linden, daffodil, borage and primrose [in French]. Q.J. Crude Drug Res. 15: 203-211.

7.2-15 El Kheir, Y.M. 1975. The alkaloids of the stamens of Papaver somniferum. Planta Med. 27: 275-280.

7.2-16 Elgamal, M.H.A., El-Tawil, B.A.H., and Fayez, M.B.E. 1973. Glycyrrhetic acid derivatives with modified ring A. J. Pharm. Sci. 62: 1557-1558.

7.2-17 Elyakov, G.B., and Ovodov, Y.S. 1972. Glycosides of Araliaceae. Chem. Nat. Compd. (Engl. Transl.) 8: 683-693. Translation of Khim. Prir. Soedin. 1972{6}: 697-709.

7.2-18 Fairbairn, J.W., and Steele, M.J. 1980. Bound forms of alkaloids in Papaver somniferum and Papaver bracteatum. Phytochemistry 19: 2317-2321.

7.2-19 Farnsworth, N.R., and Cordell, G.A. 1976. A review of some biologically active compounds isolated from plants as reported in the 1974-1975 literature. Lloydia 39: 420-455.

7.2-20 Funke, E.D., and Friedrich, H. 1974. Valepotriates in the superterranean organs of several species of Valerianaceae [in German]. Phytochemistry 13: 2023-2024.

7.2-21 Funke, E.D., and Friedrich, H. 1975. Valepotriates in the aerial parts of some more Valerianaceae species [in German]. Planta Med. 28: 215-224. CIM 17{8}: 12261.

7.2-22 Furuya, T., and Hikichi, M. 1971. Alkaloids and triterpenoids of Symphytum officinale-D. Phytochemistry 10: 2217-2220.

7.2-23 Ghosal, S., Srivastava, R.S., Chatterjee, D.C., Dutta, S.K. 1974. Fenugreekine, a new steroidal sapogenin-peptide ester of Trigonella foenum-graecum. Phytochemistry 13: 2247-2251.

7.2-24 Gleye, J., and Stanislas, E. 1972. Alkaloids of the underground parts of Hydrastis canadensis L. The presence of 1-alpha-hydrastine [in French]. Plant. Med. Phytother. 6: 306-310. HA 43: 8027.

7.2-25 Gleye, J., Ahond, A., and Stanislas, E. 1974. Canadaline: a new alkaloid from Hydrastis canadensis [in French]. Phytochemistry 13: 675-676.

7.2-26 Gross, D., Edner, G., and Schuette, H.R. 1971. Monoterpenoid Valeriana alkaloids [in German]. Arch. Pharm. (Weinheim, Ger.) 304: 19-27. CA 74: 84040.

7.2-27 Grove, M.D., Spencer, G.F., Wakeman, M.V., and Tookey, H.L. 1976. Morphine and codeine in poppy seed. J. Agric. Food Chem. 24: 896-897.

7.2-28 Handa, S.S., and Phillipson, J.D. 1976. Morphine N-oxide in Papaver somniferum L. Indian J. Pharm. 38: 158 (Abstr.).

7.2-29 Han, B.H., and Woo, L.K. 1976. Chemical and biochemical studies of Korean ginseng in Korea [in Korean]. Haksurwon Nonmunjip Cha'yon Kwahak P'yon 15: 77-109. AGRICOLA.

7.2-30 Herisset, A., Chaumont, J.-P., and Paris, R. 1974. The acid phenols and coumarins of Roman chamomile (Anthemis nobilis), simple variety [in French]. Plant. Med. Phytother. 8: 306-313. HA 46: 2502.

7.2-31 Hikino, H., Ono, M., and Takemoto, T. 1972. Constituents of wild Japanese valerian valerian root. 2. Valerianaceae [in Japanese]. Yakugaku Zasshi 92: 479-481.

7.2-32 Hikino, H., Hikino, Y., Nakamara, R., Ono, M., and Takemoto, T. 1972. Constituents of wild Japanese root. 3. Valerianaceae [in Japanese]. Yakugaku Zasshi 92: 498-502. AGRICOLA.

7.2-33 Hiller, K. 1971. Old drugs - new active substances [in German]. Wiss. Fortschr. 21{1}: 14-18.

7.2-34 Hillestad, A. 1980. Glycoproteins of the opium poppy. Phytochemistry 19: 1711-1715.

7.2-35 Hoelzl, J., and Jurcic, K. 1975. Valepotriate in the leaves of Valerian jatamansii [in German]. Planta Med. 27: 133-139. AGRICOLA.

7.2-36 Hou, J.P. 1977. The chemical constituents of ginseng plants. Comp. Med. East West 5: 123-146.

7.2-37 Ikuta, A., Syono, K., and Furuya, T. 1974. Alkaloids of callus tissues and redifferentiated plantlets in the Papaveraceae. Phytochemistry 13: 2175-2179.

7.2-38 Jain, S.C., Kamal, R., and Rathore, A.K. 1980. A note on phytosterols in some species. Indian Drugs 17{5}: 145. CA 93: 66139.

7.2-39 Janot, M.M., Guilhem, J., Contz, O., Venera, G., and Cionga, E. 1979. Contribution to the study of valerian alkaloids (Valeriana officinalis L.): actinidine and naphtyridylmethylketone, a new alkaloid [in French]. Ann. Pharm. Fr. 37: 413-420. Bib.Ag. 45: 35530.

7.2-40 Jaskonis, J. 1976. Multiplication and growth of licorice and the accumulation of active substances in roots. (2. Accumulation of active substances) [in Russian]. Liet. TSR Mokslu Akad. Darb. Ser. C 1976{3}: 49-56. CA 86: 52688.

7.2-41 Jones, J.L. 1974. Morphine direct from the opium poppy. World Crops 26: 92-93.

7.2-42 Joshi, V., Merchant, J.R., Nadkarny, V.V., and Vaghani, D.D. 1974. Chemical components of some Indian medicinal plants. Indian J. Chem. 12: 226.

7.2-43 Jukneviciene, G., Dagyte, S., and Stankeviciene, N. 1977. Biological properties and essential oils of some spice plants grown at the Kaunas Botanical Garden. (2. Plants, the seeds of which are used as raw material for spicery) [in Russian]. Liet. TSR Mokslu Akad. Darb., Ser. C 1977{3}: 9-16. CA 88: 3090.

7.2-44 Karimov, A., Telezhenetskaya, M.V., Lutfullin, K.L., and Yunusov, S.Yu. 1978. Alkaloids of Berberis integerrima. Chem. Nat. Compd. (Engl. Transl.) 14: 360-361. Translation of Khim. Prir. Soedin. 1978{3}: 419.

7.2-45 Khanna, P., Jain, S.C., and Bansal, R. 1975. Effect of cholesterol on growth and production of diosgenin, gitogenin, tigogenin and sterols in suspension cultures. Indian J. Exp. Biol. 13: 211-213.

7.2-46 Khanna, P., Bansal, R., and Jain, S.C. 1975. Effect of various hormones on production of sapogenins and sterols in Trigonella foenum-graecum L. suspension cultures. Indian J. Exp. Biol. 13: 582-583.

7.2-47 Kim, J.Y., Staba, E.J., and Abul-Hajj, Y. 1972. Saponins from American ginseng plants. Lloydia 35: 472-473 (Abstr.).

7.2-48 Kinoshita, T., Saitoh, T., and Shibata, S. 1978. Chemical studies on the oriental plant drugs. XLII. A new 3-arylcoumarin from licorice root. Chem. Pharm. Bull. 26{1}: 141-143. CA 88: 133257.

7.2-49 Kornievs'kii, Iu.I., D'ogot', A.V., and Litvinenko, V.I. 1972. Qualitative characteristics of iridoids of Valeriana stolonifera Czern [in Ukrainian]. Farm. Zh. 27: 75-76. CIM 14{2}: 1884.

7.2-50 Krochmal, A., Wilken, L., and Chien, M. 1972. Lobeline content of four Appalachian lobelias. Lloydia 35: 303-304.

7.2-51 Kupchan, S.M., Eakin, M.A., and Thomas, A.M. 1971. Tumor inhibitors. 69. Structure-cytotoxicity relationships among the sesquiterpene lactones. J. Med. Chem. 14: 1147-1152.

7.2-52 Kurmukov, A.G., Akhmedkhodzhaeva, Kh.S., Sidyakin, V.G., and Syrov, V.N. 1976. Phytoestrogens from plants of central Asia [in Russian]. Rastit. Resur. 12: 515-525. CA 86: 13826.

7.2-53 Kurucz, I., and Hornok, L. 1978. Phytoncides (antimicrobial agents) in medicinal plants [in Hungarian]. Kert. Egy. Kozl. 42: 291-299. CA 92: 191892.

7.2-54 Lin, T.T., and Lin, M.C. 1976. Chemical studies on the Orient plant drugs. II. Structure of glycoside-P1, a steryl glucoside of Panax ginseng rhizoma. J. Chin. Chem. Soc. (Ser. 2) 23{2}: 107-110. AGRICOLA.

7.2-55 Li, X.-G., and Teng, F.-T. 1979. Studies on the triterpenoids in Panax ginseng. Chih Wu Hsueh Pao 21: 181-185.

7.2-56 Lopez Abraham, A.M., Rojas Hernandez, N.M., and Jimenez Misas, C.A. 1979. Extracts from plants with cytostatic properties growing in Cuba. Part II. [in Spanish]. Rev. Cubana Med. Trop. 31: 105-111.

7.2-57 Lugt, C.B. 1976. Variability in the occurrence of formylated digitalose glycosides in Digitalis purpurea L. III. The cardiac-glycoside composition of different Digitalis purpurea L. populations. Pharm. Weekbl. 111: 441-455.

7.2-58 Lugt, C.B. 1976. Variability in the occurrence of formylated digitalose glycosides in Digitalis purpurea L. Pharm. Weekbl. 111: 405-417.

7.2-59 Lui, J.H.-C., and Staba, E.J. 1980. The ginsenosides of various ginseng plants and selected products. J. Nat. Prod. 43: 340-346. HA 51: 1528.

7.2-60 Makarov, V.A. 1971. Rutin from Laurus nobilis. Chem. Nat. Compd. (Engl. Transl.) 7: 196. Translation of Khim. Prir. Soedin. 1971{2}: 203.

7.2-61 Mamochkina, L.F., Gaevskii, A.V., and Ban'kovskii, A.I. 1976. Alkaloids of the capsules of the opium poppy. Chem. Nat. Compd. (Engl. Transl.) 12: 750-751. Translation of Khim. Prir. Soedin. 1976{6}: 829-830.

7.2-62 Marczal, G., Balogh, M., and Verzar-Petri, G. 1977. Phenol-ether components of diuretic effect in parsley, I. Acta Agron. (Budapest) 26: 7-13. HA 48: 1647.

7.2-63 Marekov, N., Khandzhieva, N., Popov, S., and Yankulov, I. 1975. Study of the valepotriate content of the roots of some Valeriana species in Bulgaria [in Bulgarian]. Izv. Khim. 8{4}: 672-680. CA 85: 74960.

7.2-64 Megges, R., Portius, H.J., and Repke, K.R.H. 1976. Pengitoxin – the prototype of a pro-drug in the cardiac glycoside series. Acta. Pharm. Suec. 13 (Suppl.): 15 (Abstr.).

7.2-65 Messana, I., and Galeffi, C. 1980. The alkaloids of Hydrastis canadensis L. (Ranunculaceae). Two new alkaloids: hydrastidine and isohydrastidine. Gazz. Chim. Ital. 110: 539-543.

7.2-66 Miyoshi, H. 1972. Licorice root product [in Japanese]. Kagawa-Ken Hakho Shokuhin Shikenjo Hokoku 63: 50-54. CA 78: 158019.

7.2-67 Murach, M., Hiller, K., Franke P., and Hintsche, R. 1975. Bayogenin – a sapogenin in Solidago canadensis L. 2. The saponins of the species Solidago [in German]. Pharmazie 30: 619-620. CIM 17{7}: 10551.

7.2-68 O'Donovan, D.G., Long, D.J., Forde, E., and Geary, P. 1975. The biosynthesis of Lobelia alkaloids. Part III. Intermediates in the biosynthesis of lobeline; biosynthesis of 8,10-diethyl- lobelidione. J. Chem. Soc. Perkin Trans. I. 1975{5}: 415-419.

7.2-69 Olechnowicz-Stepien, W., and Lamer-Zarawska, E. 1975. Investigation of flavonoid fraction of some crude drugs from the family Labiatae (Serpyllum L. plant, thyme plant, marjoram plant, oregano plant [in Polish]. Herba Pol. 21: 347-356.

7.2-70 Panosyan, A.G., Barikyan, M.L., Lebedeva, M.N., Amroyan, E.A., and Gabrielyan, E.S. 1980. Search for substances with prostaglandin-like activity in plants [in Russian]. Khim. Prir. Soedin. 1980{6}:825-826. HA 51: 7274.

7.2-71 Pellecuer, J., Allegrini, J., Simeon de Bouchberg, M., and Passet, J. 1975. The place of essential oil of Satureia montana L. (Labiates) in the therapeutic armamentarium. Plant. Med. Phytother. 9: 99-106.

7.2-72 Pethes, E., Verzar-Petri, G., Mikita, K., and Lemberkovics, E. 1975. Essential oils of Valeriana officinalis, with special consideration of the ester ccomponents [in German]. Sci. Pharm. 43{3}: 173-182. CA 84: 21981.

7.2-73 Phillipson, J.D., Handa, S.S., and El-Dabbas, S.W. 1976. N-oxides of morphine, codeine and thebaine and their occurrence in Papaver species. Phytochemistry 15: 1297-1301.

7.2-74 Phillipson, J.D., Handa, S.S., and El-Dabbas, S. 1976. Morphine, codeine and thebaine N-oxides. J. Pharm. Pharmacol. 28 (Suppl.): 70P (Abstr.).

7.2-75 Pleinard, J.F. 1979. Saponins of Panax ginseng [in French]. Plant. Med. Phytother. 13: 4-12. HA 50: 555.

7.2-76 Pontovich, V.E., Volynets, A.P., and Golenko, I.L. 1978. Phenolic compounds in ovules of opium poppy. Sov. Plant Physiol. (Engl.

Transl.) 25: 556-561. Translation of Fiziol. Rast. (Moscow) 25: 713-719.

7.2-77 Popov, S., Handjieva, N., and Marekov, N. 1974. A new valepotriate: 7-.x epi-deacetylisovaltrate from Valeriana officinalis. Phytochemistry 13: 2815-2818.

7.2-78 Prokopienko, A.P. 1972. Search for coumarins in some Umbelliferae species [in Russian]. Postep Dziedzinie Leku Rosl. Pr. Ref. Dosw. Wygloszone Symp. 1970 Herba Pol. Suppl. 1972: 90-93.

7.2-79 Puri, H.S., Jefferies, T.M., and Hardman, R. 1976. Diosgenin and yamogenin levels in some Indian plant samples. Planta Med. 30: 118-121. HA 47: 4990.

7.2-80 Ruecker, G. 1979. The active substance of Valeriana [in German]. Pharm. Unserer Zeit 8{3}: 78-86. CIM 20{13}: 10018.

7.2-81 Saitoh, T., Noguchi, H., and Shibata, S. 1978. Chemical studies on the oriental plant drugs. XLIV. A new isoflavone and the corresponding isoflavanone of licorice root. Chem. Pharm. Bull. 26{1}: 144-147. CA 88: 133258

7.2-82 Scheemaeker, H. de, Rousseau, J., and Pousset, J.-L. 1977. Study of the traditional pharmacopeia of the Pitou-Charente Region [in French]. Plant. Med. Phytother. 11: 310-314.

7.2-83 Semenchenko, V.F., and Murav'ev, I.A. 1975. Studies on the saponins of certain species of Glycyrrhiza L. section Pseudoglycyrrhiza Krug. [in Russian]. Rastit. Resur. 11: 381-384.

7.2-84 Shafiee, A., Lalezari, I., Nasseri-Nouri, P., and Asgharian, R. 1975. Alkaloids of Papaver orientale and Papaver psuedo-orientale. J. Pharm. Sci. 64: 1570-1572. HA 46: 6103.

7.2-85 Shah, C.S., Quadry, J.S., and Bhatt, M.G. 1972. Lobeline from Lobelia nicotianaefolia. Phytochemistry 11: 2884-2885.

7.2-86 Slepetys, J. 1979. Biology and biochemistry of wormwood. 7. Localization and dynamics of chamazulene accumulation [in Russian]. Liet. TSR Mokslu Akad. Darb. Ser. C 1974{4}: 29-34. CA 83: 111201.

7.2-87 Sun, H.-D., Lin, Z.-W., and Niu, F.-T. 1978. The study of Chinese drugs of the Umbelliferae. I. The chemical consitutents of Angelica apaensis Shan et Yuan., Heracleum rapula Fr. and Heracleum scabridum Fr. roots [in Chinese]. Chi Wu Hsueh Po 20: 244-253.

7.2-88 Tanaka, O., and Yahara, S. 1978. Dammarane saponins of leaves of Panax pseudo-ginseng subsp. himalaicus. Phytochemistry 17: 1353-1358.

7.2-89 Tomoda, M., and Uno, M. 1972. Plant mucilages. III. Smith degradation products of plantasan. Chem. Pharm. Bull. (Tokyo) 20: 778-782.

7.2-90 Tomoda, M., and Tanaka, M. 1973. Plant mucilages. VI. Three disaccharides obtained from plantasan by partial acid hydrolysis. Chem. Pharm. Bull. (Tokyo) 21: 989-994.

7.2-91 Tookey, H.L., Spencer, G.F., Grove, M.D., and Kwolek, W.F. 1976.

Codein and morphine in Papaver somniferum grown in a controlled environment. Planta Med. 30: 340-348. CA 86: 86215.

7.2-92 Tschesche, R., and Wulff, G. 1973. Chemistry and biology of saponins [in German]. Fortschr. Chem. Org. Naturst. 30: 461-606.

7.2-93 Voloshina, D.A., Kiselev, V.P., and Rumyantzeva, G.N. 1977. Sapogenin content and yield of fenugreek seeds [in Russian]. Rastit. Resur. 13: 655-657. HA 48: 3908.

7.2-94 Wold, J.K. 1978. Bound morphine and codeine in the capsule of Papaver somniferum. Phytochemistry 17: 832-833.

7.2-95 Yahara, S., Tanaka, O., and Komori, T. 1976. Saponins of the leaves of Panax ginseng C.A. Meyer. Chem. Pharm. Bull. (Tokyo) 24: 2204-2208.

7.2-96 Yahara, S., Kasi, K., and Tanaka, O. 1979. Further study on dammarane-type saponins of roots, leaves, flower-buds, and fruits of Panax ginseng C.A. Meyer. Chem. Pharm. Bull. (Tokyo) 27: 88-92. Bib. Ag. 43: 78489.

7.2-97 Yahara, S., Kasai, R., and Tanaka, O. 1977. New dammarane type saponins of leaves of Panax japonicus C.A. Meyer. 1. Chikusetsusaponins-L5, -L9A and L10. Chem. Pharm. Bull. (Tokyo) 25: 2041-2047.

7.2-98 Yahara, S., Tanaka, O., and Nishioka, I. 1978. Dammarane type saponins of leaves of Panax japonicus C.A. Meyer. 2. Saponins of the specimens collected in Tottoriken, Kyoto-shi, and Nigata-ken. Chem. Pharm. Bull. (Tokyo) 26: 3010-3016. AGRICOLA.

7.2-99 Zapotyl'ko, F.T. 1974. Comparative investigation of Radix ginseng and roots of P. quinquefolium L. cultivated in Korea, China, and Japan [in Ukrainian]. Farm. Zh. (Kiev) 29: 54-59.

7.3 Extraction, Isolation, Analysis, and Identification

7.3-1 Akada, Y., and Tanase, Y. 1976. High-speed liquid chromatographic determination of glycyrrhizin in liquorice roots and extracts [in Japanese]. Yakugaku Zasshi 96{8}: 1035-1037. CA 85: 149175.

7.3-2 Andreev, L.V., Slepyan, L.I., and Nikitina, I.K. 1974. Micro-thin-layer chromatography of panaxosides [in Russian]. Rastit. Resur. 10: 126-129. HA 44: 7026.

7.3-3 Bakshi, V.M., and Hamied, Y.K. 1971. Isolation of diosgenin from fenugreek seeds. Indian J. Pharm. 33: 55-56. AGRICOLA.

7.3-4 Bancher, E., Prey, T., and Wurst, P. 1976. A new method for the quantitative determination of some important glycosides in drug extracts of Digitalis lanata [in German]. Planta Med. 29: 393-399. CIM 17{5}: 6972.

7.3-5 Beasley, T.H., Sr., Ziegler, H.W., and Bell, A.D. 1979. Separation of major components in licorice using high-performance liquid chromatography. J. Chromatogr. 175: 350-355.

7.3-6 Benzar, T.P. 1975. Photoelectrocolorimetric determination of codeine and ethylmorphine in drug mixtures [in Ukrainian]. Farm. Zh. (Kiev) 30{1}: 59-61. CA 83: 65505.

7.3-7 Besso, H., Saruwatari, Y., Futamura, K., Kunihiro, K., Fuwa, T., and Tanaka, O. 1979. High performance liquid chromatographic determination of ginseng saponin by ultraviolet derivatisation. Planta Med. 37: 226-233.

7.3-8 Bhardwaj, D.K., Jain, R.K., and Mehta, C.K. 1979. Constitution of laxanthone-III synthetic studies. Curr. Sci. 48: 614-615.

7.3-9 Bilogurova, V.A., Kovalenko, L.I., and Kondrat'eva, T.S. 1974. Quantitative determination of the sorbic acid in a liquid valerian extract [in Ukrainian]. Farm. Zh. 1974{4}: 72-74. CIM 16{2}: 201.

7.3-10 Bo Sup Chung. 1976. Studies on the components of Korean ginseng. {2}. The composition of ginseng essential oils [in Korean]. Korean Journal of Pharmacognosy 7{1}: 41-45. HA 47: 10809.

7.3-11 Bochorishvili, B.S., Zhvania, L.I., and Goncharenko, G.K. 1973. Extraction of foxglove (Digitalis) under conditions of stirring [in Russian]. Soobshch. Akad. Nauk Gruz. SSSR 69: 361-364.

7.3-12 Bogacheva, N.G., Kiselev, V.P., and Kogan, L.M. 1976. Isolation of 3,26-bisglycoside of yamogenin from Trigonella foenum-graecum. Chem. Nat. Compd. (Engl. Transl.) 12: 242-243. Translation of Khim. Prir. Soedin. 1976{2}: 268-269.

7.3-13 Bombardelli, E., Bonati, A., Gabetta, B., and Martinelli, E.M. 1980. Gas-liquid chromatographic method for determination of ginsenosides in Panax ginseng. J. Chromatogr. 196: 121-132.

7.3-14 Bombardelli, E., Bonati, A., Gabetta, B., Martinelli, E.M., and Mustich, G. 1976. Gas-liquid chromatographic and mass spectrometric investigation on saponins in Panax ginseng extract. Fitoterapia 47: 99-106. HA 47: 11813.

7.3-15 Bombardelli, E., Gabetta, B., Martinelli, E.M., and Mustich, G. 1979. Gas chromatograph-mass spectrometric (GC-MS) analysis of medicinal plants. Part III. Quantitative evaluation of glycyrrhetic acid and GC-MS investigation on licorice triterpenoids. Fitoterapia 50{1}: 11-24 CA 92: 28457.

7.3-16 Bridges, C.D.B. 1977. A method for preparing stable digitonin solutions for visual pigment extraction. Vision Res. 17: 301-302.

7.3-17 Brochmann-Hanssen, E., Fu, C.-C., and Zanati, G. 1971. Opium alkaloids. IX: Detection of coreximine in Papaver somniferum L. based on its biosynthesis from reticuline. J. Pharm. Sci. 60: 873-878.

7.3-18 Chapelle, J.-P., and Denoel, A. 1972. Contribution to the study of valepotriates in the roots of Valeriana officinalis [in French]. Plant. Med. Phytother. 6: 91-105.

7.3-19 Chen, S.E., and Staba, E.J. 1980. American ginseng. II. Analysis of ginsenosides and their sapogenins in biological fluids. J. Nat. Prod. 43: 463-466. HA 51: 2980.

7.3-20 Chen, S.E., and Staba, E.J. 1978. American ginseng. I. Large scale isolation of ginsenosides from leaves and stems. Lloydia 41: 361-366.

7.3-21 Chirva, V.Ya., Cherno, N.K., and Maznichenko, S.A. 1977. Isolation and characteristics of the pectin of Mentha piperitae utilization of wastes. Chem. Nat. Compd. (Engl. Transl.) 13: 578. Translation of Khim. Prir. Soedin. 1977{5}: 695-696.

7.3-22 Cho, H.O., Lee, J.-H., Cho, S.-H., and Choi, Y.-H. 1976. Approach to the extraction method of minerals of ginseng extract [in Korean]. Hanguk Sikp'um Kwahakhoe Chi 8{2}: 95-106. CA 86: 21736.

7.3-23 Choi, J.H., Kim, W.J., Hong, S.K., Oh, S.K., and Oura, H. 1980. High performance liquid chromatographic isolation of ginsenoside -RF, -Rg2, -Rh1. Hanguk Nonghwa Hakhoe Chi 23: 206-210.

7.3-24 Choi, J.H., Kim, W.-J., Bae, H.W., Oh, S.K., and Oura, H. 1980. Large quantity isolation of ginsenoside -Rb1, -Rb2, -Rc, -Rd, -Re, -Rg1 in Panax ginseng C.A. Meyer by high performance liquid chromatography. Hanguk Nonghwa Hakhoe Chi 23: 199-205.

7.3-25 Chu, C., and Yi, S. 1975. Determination of critical micellar concentration of the saponin of Korean ginseng [in Korean]. Hanguk Saenghwa Hakhoe Chi 8: 238 (Abstr.).

7.3-26 Cionga, E., Popesco, V., Contz, O., and Boniforti, L. 1976. The alkaloids from Valeriana officinalis: identification of actinidine. Adv. Mass Spectrom. Biochem. Med. 1: 299-302. CA 85: 74964.

7.3-27 Cowley, P.S., Evans, F.J., and Ginman, R.F.A. 1971. Simultaneous spectrometric determination of 5-ene and 7-ene sterols from the leaves and seeds of Digitalis purpurea L. Planta Med. 19: 249-257.

7.3-28 Dawidar, A.M., and Fayez, M.B.E. 1972. Thin layer chromotographic detection and estimation of steroid sapogenins in fenugreek. Steroid sapogenins. XIV. Fresenius' Z. Anal. Chem. 259: 283-285.

7.3-29 De Orellana Segovia, M. 1972. Determination of 18 beta-glycyrrhetinic acid content in root and extract of Glycyrrhiza glabra [in Spanish]. An. Real Acad. Farm. 38{1}: 167-179/. CA 77: 92897.

7.3-30 Derbentseva, N.A., Zelepukha, S.I., and Pavlenko, L.V. 1978. Determination of salvin concentration in drug solutions by means of spectra [in Russian]. Mikrobiol. Zh. (Kiev) 40: 479-500. CA 90: 29083.

7.3-31 Desage, M., Becchi, M., Trouilloud, M., and Raynaud, J. 1980. Chemical ionization mass spectrometry of 20-S-protopanaxadiol and 20-S-protopanaxatriol. Planta Med. 39: 189-191.

7.3-32 Dixit, B.S., and Srivastava, S.N. 1977. Detection of (0.38%) diosgenin in the seeds of Trigonella foenumgraecum Linn. by GLC method. Indian J. Pharm. 39: 62. HA 48: 4917.

7.3-33 Duquenois, P. 1972. Saffron in the modern pharmacy. Identification and purity analyses [in French]. Bull. Soc. Pharm. Strasbourg 15: 149-159. CA 79: 45885.

7.3-34 Dziuba, N.P., Vorob'ev, N.E., Kazarinov, N.A., Puchkova, E.I., and Sokolova, A.I. 1972. Chromatographic and spectrophotometric determination of cardiac glycosides in preparations and in crude drugs [in Polish]. Postep Dziedzinie Leku Rosl. Pr. Ref. Dosw. Wygloszone Symp., 1970. Herba Pol. Suppl. 1972: 53-56.

7.3-35 Dzyuba, N.P., Vorob'ev, N.E., and Sokolova, A.I. 1971. Quantitative determination of digitoxin and gitoxin in the purple foxglove. Pharm. Chem. J. (Engl. Transl.) 5: 699-702. Translation of Khim.-Farm. Zh. 5{11}: 51-55, 1971.

7.3-36 Eiden, F., and Khammash, G. 1973. Analysis of liquid cough remedies [in German]. Pharm. Ztg. 118{17}: 638-645. CA 79: 97034.

7.3-37 Eiden, F., and Kammash, G. 1972. Analysis of cough remedy [in German]. Pharm. Ztg. 117{51-52}: 1994-1998. CA 78: 102071.

7.3-38 Eiden, F., and Kammash, G. 1972. Analysis of cough remedy [in German]. Pharm. Ztg. 117{41}: 1503-1508. CA 78: 102071.

7.3-39 Elbanowska, A., Gorecki, P., Zdun, K., and Waszkiewicz, C. 1975. Investigations of the process of valerian rhizome Radix valerianae drying in a screen chamber drying oven. II. Analytical evaluation of the crude drug and determination of drying [in Polish]. Herba Pol. 21: 301-316. AGRICOLA.

7.3-40 Ellnain-Wojtaszek, M., Kowalewski, Z., Lutomski,J., and Skrzypezakowa, L. 1975. Quantitative determination of digitonin in Digitalis purpurea L. seeds [in Polish]. Herba Pol. 21: 377-384.

7.3-41 Ellnain-Wojtaszek, M., Kowalewski, Z., Lutomski, J., and Skrzypczakowa, L. 1976. Comparison of different methods for isolation of digitonin from Digitalis purpurea L. seeds [in Polish]. Herba Pol. 22: 28-32.

7.3-42 Felklova, M., Riessnerova, E., Rychnovska, M., and Stefek, S. 1976. The content of morphine in opium poppy (Papaver somniferum L.) [in Czech]. Rostl. Vyroba 22: 383-398. AGRICOLA.

7.3-43 Foldesi, D. 1975. Experiments on producing medicinal plant drugs by microwave energy [in Hungarian]. Herba Hung. 14{2/3}: 75-83. HA 46: 6081.

7.3-44 Francois, M.T. 1974. Examination of a few plant species with anthelmintic properties by thin layer chromatography in conjunction with the T.A.S. micro-oven [in French]. Plant. Med. Phytother. 8: 109-112. HELM AB-A 44: 4460.

7.3-45 Furuya, T., Kojima, H., Syono, K., Ishii, T., Uotani, K., and Nishio, M. 1973. Isolation of saponins and sapogenins from callus tissue of Panax ginseng. Chem. Pharm. Bull. (Tokyo) 21: 98-101.

7.3-46 Furuya, T., Ikuta, A., and Syono, K. 1972. Alkaloids from callus tissue of Papaver somniferum. Phytochemistry 11: 3041-3044.

7.3-47 Gal, I.E. 1972. Extraction of antibiotic capsicidin from mature Capsicum annuum seeds by a simple method [in German]. Z. Lebensm.-Unters.-Forsch. 148: 286-289. CA 77: 72319.

7.3-48 Glasl, H., and Wagner, H. 1974. Gas chromatographic investigation of pharmacopeia drugs. 3. Standard method for gas chromatographic evaluation of essential oils and essential oil drugs of DAB 7 (spike oil to cinnamon oil) [in German]. Dtsch. Apoth.-Ztg. 114: 363-369. CA 80: 137159.

7.3-49 Glowniak, K., Gawron, A., and Kwietniewskia, B. 1976. Investigations on coumarins of Archangelica officinalis Hoffm. fruits [in Polish]. Ann. Univ. Mariae Curie Sklodowska Sect. D. Med. 31: 349-354. CIM 19{13}: 9665.

7.3-50 Habib, A.A.M., El-Sebakhy, N.A., and Kadry, H.A. 1979. New and simple methylene blue colorimetric assay for glycyrrhizin in pharmaceuticals. J. Pharm. Sci. 68: 1221-1223. CIM 21{4}: 2570.

7.3-51 Hardman, R., and Fazli, F.R.Y. 1972. Studies in the steroidal sapogenin yield from Trigonella foenumgraecum seed. Planta Med. 21: 322-328. HA 43: 5537.

7.3-52 Hardman, R., and Elujoba, A.A. 1980. Endogenous enzymic yield of monohydroxysapogenins from fenugreek seed. Planta Med. 39: 225-226 (Abstr.).

7.3-53 Hardman, R., and Jefferies, T.M. 1972. A combined column-chromatographic and infrared spectrophotometric determination of diosgenin and yamogenin in fenugreek seed. Analyst (London) 97{1155}: 437-441.

7.3-54 Hardman, R., and Jeffries, T.M. 1971. The determination of diosgenin and yamogenin in fenugreek seed by combined column chromatography and infrared spectrometry. J. Pharm. Pharmacol. 23 (Suppl.): 231S-232S (Abstr.).

7.3-55 Hata, K., Kozawa, M., Baba, K., Chi, H.-J., and Konoshima, M. 1971. Coumarins and a sesquiterpene from the crude drug "Korean oianghuo", the roots of Angelica spp. Chem. Pharm. Bull. (Tokyo) 19: 1963-1967.

7.3-56 Helliwell, K., and Fairbairn, J.W. 1976. Isolation of meconic acid from Papaver, section macrantha (Oxytona). J. Pharm. Pharmac 28: 940.

7.3-57 Hethelyi, I., and Tetenyi, P. 1979. Pyrolysis gas chromatography in medicinal plant research [in Hungarian]. Herba Hung. 18{1}: 87-96. HA 50: 537.

7.3-58 Hiai, S., Oura, H., Odaka, Y., and Nakajima, T. 1975. A colorimetric estimation of ginseng saponins. Planta Med. 28: 363-369. HA 46: 8678.

7.3-59 Hiyama, C., Miyai, S., Yoshida, H., Yamasaki, K., and Tanaka, O. 1978. Application of high-speed liquid chromatography and dual wave-length thin-layer chromatograph-densitrometry to analysis of crude drugs: Nucleosides and free bases of nucleic acids in ginseng roots [in Japanese]. Yakugaku Zasshi 98: 1132-1137. CA 89: 169157.

7.3-60 Hlavackova, Z. 1975. The use of a three-parameter and six-parameter test in the genetic analysis of morphine and oil contents in poppy [in Czech]. Sb. UVTI-Genet. Slecht. 11: 113-124.

7.3-61 Honda, G., Tosirisuk, V., and Tabata, M. 1980. Isolation of an antidermatophytic, tryptanthrin, from indigo plants, Polygonum tinctorium and Isatis tinctoria. Planta Med. 38: 275-276.

7.3-62 Horster, H., Rucker, G., and Tautges, J. 1977. Valeranone content in the underground parts of Nardostachys jatamansi and Valeriana officinalis [in German]. Phytochemistry 16: 1070-1071.

7.3-63 Hoton-Dorge, M. 1974. Identification of some flavonoid aglycone extracts from Glycyrrhiza glabra roots [in French]. J. Pharm. Belg. 29: 560-572. CA 83: 111099.

7.3-64 Isaev, I., Bozadjieva, M., Totev, T., Mitev, D., and Dimov, H. 1971. The possibility of using the electrohydraulic effect for extraction of natural substances from medicinal plants [in French]. Arch. Union Med. Balk. 9: 745-747.

7.3-65 Jain, G.C., and Dahiya, M.S. 1974. Separation and identification of opium alkaloids by thin layer chromatography. Curr. Sci. 43: 444-445.

7.3-66 Janssen, A., and Sopczak, D. 1980. Optimisation of the TLC separation of Digitalis purpurea extracts [in German]. Chromatographia 13: 479-484.

7.3-67 Jefferies, T.M., and Hardman, R. 1972. The infra-red spectrometric estimation of diosgenin and yamogenin individually and as their mixtures. Planta Med. 22: 78-87. HA 43: 3087.

7.3-68 Jeffries, T.M., and Hardman, R. 1976. An improved column-chromatographic quantitative isolation of diosgenin and yamogenin from plant crude extracts prior to their determination by infrared spectrophotometry. Analyst 101{1199}: 122-124.

7.3-69 Jellema, R., Elema, E.T., and Malingre, T.M. 1979. Optical brighteners as thin-layer chromatography detection reagents for glycoalkaloids and steroid alkaloids in Solanum species. I. Calcofluor M2R New. J. Chromatogr. 176: 435-439.

7.3-70 Jellema, R., Elema, E.T., and Malingre, T.M. 1980. Optical brighteners as thin-layer chromatographic detection reagents for glycoalkaloids and steroid alkaloids in Solanum species. II. Blankophor BA 267%, BBU neu and KU, and Tinopal CBS-X and 5 BMS-X. J. Chromatogr. 189: 406-409.

7.3-71 Johnson, R.D., and Waller, G.R. 1971. Isolation of actinidine from Valeriana officinalis. Phytochemistry 10: 3334-3335.

7.3-72 Jonas, H., and De Planas, G.M. 1974. Extraction and chromatographic purification of Digitalis cardiac glycosides and their binding to plant pigments. Prep. Biochem. 4: 411-434.

7.3-73 Kapoor, S.K., and Zaman, A. 1972. Extractives of Angelica glauca. Proc. Indian Sci. Cong. 59 (pt. III): 142 (Abstr.).

7.3-74 Karawya, M.S., Abdel-Wahab, S.M., and Zaki, A.Y. 1971. Colorimetric method for the estimation of alkaloids in Lobelia and its pharmaceutical preparations. J. Assoc. Off. Anal. Chem. 54{6}: 1423-1425. CA 76: 27965.

7.3-75 Kartnig, T., and Kobosil, P. 1977. The separation of digitalis cardenolides by means of high efficiency thin layer chromatography [in German]. J. Chromatogr. 138: 238-242.

7.3-76 Khafagy, S.M., and Girgis, A.N. 1974. A micro method for the estimation of the individual glycosides in Digitalis leaves and pharmaceutical preparations. Planta Med. 25: 350-360.

7.3-77 Khorrami, J.S. 1979. Determination of lawsone in henna by the colorimetric method [in French]. Q.J. Crude Drug Res. 17: 131-134. AGRICOLA.

7.3-78 Kiryanov, A.A., Krivut, B.A., and Perelson, M.E. 1976. Chromatospectrophotometric method of determining acetylpectolinarin in plant raw material, the finished product, and the medicinal form. Pharm. Chem. J. (Engl. Transl.) 10: 348-351. Translation of Khim.-Farm. Zh. 10{3}: 75-79, 1976.

7.3-79 Knight, J.C. 1977. Analysis of fenugreek sapogenins by gas-liquid chromatography. J. Chromatogr. 133: 222-225.

7.3-80 Komori, T., Tanaka, O., and Nagai, Yumiko. 1974. Saponins from medicinal ginseng root. Mass spectra of ginsenoside Rg1 decaacetate and related compounds [in German]. Org. Mass Spectrom. 9: 744-752. CA 82: 156159.

7.3-81 Kornievs'skii, Iu.I., Nikolaeva, A.G., and Koroshchuk, K.E. 1972. Chemistry of Valeriana stolonifera [in Ukrainian]. Farm. Zh. (Kiev) 27: 81-82. CIM 13{2}: 1948.

7.3-82 Linley, P.A. 1973. The evaluation of Digitalis purpurea by direct densitometry from paper chromatograms. Planta Med. 23: 272-280. HA 44: 687.

7.3-83 Linley, P.A., and Rowson, J.M. 1973. The evaluation of Digitalis purpurea. A comparison of colorimetric and chromatographic methods. Planta Med. 24: 211-218.

7.3-84 Liptak, J., Verzar-Petri, G., and Boldvai, J. 1980. Use of the 'TAS' method for the examination of drugs and volatile oils. Pharmazie 35: 545-546.

7.3-85 Litvinenko, V.I., and Nadezhina, T.P. 1971. Chemical study of the above-ground parts of Glycyrrhiza enchinata [in Russian]. Rastit. Resur. 7{4}: 576-580. CA 76: 70073.

7.3-86 Lugt, C.B., and Noordhoek-Ananias, L. 1974. Quantitative fluorimetric determination of the main cardiac glycosides in Digitalis purpurea leaves. Planta Med. 25: 267-273.

7.3-87 Lugt, C.B. 1973. Quantitative determination of digitoxin, gitaloxin, gitoxin, verodoxin and strospesid in the leaves of Digitalis purpurea by means of fluorescence. Planta Med. 23: 176-181.

7.3-88 Lunder, T.L., and Nielsen, C. 1980. Determination of glycyrrhizin in licorice roots and extracts by high-performance liquid chromatography. Mitt. Geb. Lebensmittelunters. Hyg. 71{2}: 236-241. CA 93: 192086.

7.3-89 Lutomski, J., and Nguyen Thoi Nham. 1976. Chemical study on a species of Panax growing in Viet Nam "Panax K5VN". Part I: Comparative study of the saponins from Panax K5VN and Panax ginseng by thin layer chromatography [in Polish]. Herba Pol. 22: 23-27. HA 47: 4976.

7.3-90 Lutomski, J., Debska, W., and Okulicz-Kozarynowa, B. 1976. Examination of the valepotriates of Valeriana officinalis roots from Poland [in German]. Herba Hung. 15{2}: 13-21. AGRICOLA.

7.3-91 Mahran, G.H., Balbaa, S.I., El-Hossary, G.A., and Selim, M.A. 1973. Isolation, identification and estimation of glycyrrhizin from Glycyrrhiza glabra L. growing in Egypt. Bull. Fac. Pharm., Cairo Univ. 12{1}: 71-81. CA 85: 25439.

7.3-92 Makarevich, I.F., Kislichenko, S.G., Kolesnikov, D.G., and Klimenko, O.I. 1972. On a new technology for obtaining digitoxin. Pharm. Chem. J. (Engl. Transl.) 6: 590-591. Translation of Khim.-Farm. Zh. 6{9}: 31-32.

7.3-93 Mechler, E. 1978. Comparative determinations of volatile oils in drugs following the European and German pharmacopeias [in German]. Dtsch. Apoth.-Ztg. 118{10}: 364-366. CA 88: 197695.

7.3-94 Mincsovics, E., Tyichak, E., Nagy, J., and Kalasz, H. 1980. Thin-layer chromatographic investigation of components in essential oil of Matricaria chamomilla L. by means of classical and pressurized chamber systems. Acta Hortic. 96{II}: 181-188.

7.3-95 Minina, S.A., Gromova, N.A., Filipin, N.A., Kotovskii, B.K., and Tyukina, T.N. 1976. Study of extraction from plant raw material in a press-extractor (experimental model 2) [in Russian]. Khim.-Farm. Zh. 10{3}: 135-138. CA 85: 112692.

7.3-96 Mitsuhashi, H., Yamagishi, T., Inoue, K., and Homma, N. 1975. Studies on the cultivation of medicinal plants. Isolation and purification procedures of morphine and codeine from poppy [in Japanese]. Syoyak ugaku Zasshi 29: 45-51.

7.3-97 Mueller-Stock, A., Joshi, R.K., and Buechi, J. 1973. Thin-layer and column chromatographic separation of capsaicinoids from drugs. 5. Study on the constituents of capsicum [in German]. J. Chromatogr. 79: 229-241.

7.3-98 Munshi, G.K. 1976. Detection of glycyrrhizic acid by T.L.C. Indian J. Pharm. 38: 105-106.

7.3-99 Murav'ev, I.A., and Zyubr, T.P. 1972. Repercolation during the extraction of roots and rhizomes of Glycyrrhiza uralensis [in Russian]. Khim.-Farm. Zh. 6{12}: 47-52. CA 78: 88553.

7.3-100 Muraviev, I.A., and Pshukov, Y.G. 1975. Extraction of Glycyrrhiza glabra roots by rolling [in Russian]. Farmatsiya (Moscow) 24: 20-22.

7.3-101 Mushynskaya, S.H., Danieliants, V.A., and Sych, A.M. 1972. Chromatographic analysis of the composition of poppy heads grown in the USSR and a chromato-spectrophotometric method of alkaloid determination [in Russian]. Postep Dziedzinie Leku Rosl. Pr. Ref. Dosw. Wygloszone Symp., 1970; Herba Pol. Suppl. 1972: 203-211.

7.3-102 Nagasawa, T., Choi, J.H., Nishino, Y., and Oura, H. 1980. Application of high-performance liquid chromatography to the isolation of ginsenoside-Rf, -Rg2, and -Rh1 from a crude saponin mixture of ginseng. Chem. Pharm. Bull. (Tokyo) 28: 3701-3707.

7.3-103 Namba, T., Yoshizaki, M., Tomimori, T., Tsuboi, M., and Kato, K. 1975. Evaluation of crude drugs. IV. Quantitative analysis of constituents in crude drugs by rod thin-layer chromatography with an FID [flame ionization detector]. 1. Determination of glycyrrhizin in liquorice roots [in Japanese]. Yakugaku Zasshi 95: 809-814. CA 83: 120949.

7.3-104 Neczypor, W., Poetter, H., Thren, R., and Dauth, C. 1980. Studies concerning the obtaining of a high-class Digitalis lanata drug. Acta Hortic. 96{II}: 207-209.

7.3-105 Nishimura, S., and Takeyama, K. 1976. Studies on the biological active component of garlic (Allium scorodoprasm L. or Allium sativum). 1. Isolation and bacteriostatic effect of scordinin A1 and its decomposition production [in Japanese]. Oyo Yakuri 11{6}: 941-944. CA 88: 99210.

7.3-106 Nowak, A., Krajewska, A., and Dedio, I. 1980. Quantitative method for determination of diosgenin in crude drugs [in Polish]. Herba Pol. 26: 39-45.

7.3-107 Nowak, A., Krajewska, A., and Dedio, I. 1980. Method for quantitative determination of diosgenin in plant raw materials [in Polish]. Herba Pol. 26{1}: 39-45. CA 93: 217448.

7.3-108 Ogawa, S., Yoshida, A., and Mitani, Y. 1976. Analytical studies on the active constituents of crude drugs. II. Determination of glycyrrhizin in pharmaceutical preparations including glycyrrhiza radix by high-speed liquid chromatography [in Japanese]. Yakugaku Zasshi 96{12}: 1488-1491. CA 86: 96056.

7.3-109 Ogawa, S., Yoshida, A., and Mitani, Y. 1976. Analytical studies on the active constituents in crude drugs. I. Determination of glycyrrhizin in Glycyrrhizae radix by high speed liquid chromatography [in Japanese]. Yakugaku Zasshi 96{1}: 122-124. CA 84: 126813.

7.3-110 Otsuka, H., Morita, Y., Ogihara, Y., and Shibata, S. 1977. The evaluation of ginseng and its congeners by droplet counter-current chromatography (DCC). Planta Med. 32: 9-17. HA 48: 1715.

7.3-111 Oura, H., Hiai, S., Odaka, Y., and Yokozawa, T. 1975. Studies on the biochemical action of Ginseng saponin. I. Purification from Ginseng extract of the active component stimulating serum protein biosynthesis. J. Biochem. 77: 1057-1065.

7.3-112 Patudin, A.V., Voloshina, D.A., and Rumyantseva, G.N. 1975. The use of enzymes for sapogenin extraction from Trigonella foenum-graecum seeds [in Russian]. Izv. Timiryazevsk. S-kh. Akad. 1975{5}: 226-229. HA 46: 6115.

7.3-113 Pleinard, J.F., Delaveau, P., and Guernet, M. 1977. Testing of Panax ginseng C.A. Meyer [in French]. Ann. Pharm. Fr. 35: 465-473. CA 89: 12034.

7.3-114 Pohl, P., and Haedrich, W. 1976. A new method for the quantitative determination of glycyrrhizinic acid in Radix Liquiritiae [in German]. Dtsch. Apoth.-Ztg. 116{18}: 625-627. CA 85: 37296.

7.3-115 Proske, G. 1975. Assay of Succus liquiritiae in drugs. Analysis of bisuc [in German]. Arch. Pharm. (Weinheim, Ger.) 308: 832-839. CA 84: 49873.

7.3-116 Reichelt, J., and Cizek, J. 1978. Steroid sapogenins. II. Determination of disogenin in Trigonella foenum-graecum L. by gas chromatography and photometry [in Czech]. Cesk. Farm. 27: 221-224. HA 49: 7912.

7.3-117 Resh, F.M. 1973. Quantitative determination of digitoxin and gitoxin in the leaves of Digitalis purpurea. Chem. Nat. Compd. (Engl. Transl.) 9: 654. Translation of Khim. Prir. Soedin. 1973{5}: 679-680.

7.3-118 Ronsch, H., and Schade, W. 1979. Thebaine methochloride from Papaver bracteatum. Phytochemistry 18: 1089-1090.

7.3-119 Rybal'chenko, A.S., and Fursa, M.S. 1978. Analysis of the essential oils of brilliant valerian and tall valerian by gas-liquid chromatography [in Ukrainian]. Farm. Zh. 1978{5}: 82-83. CIM 20{5}: 3959.

7.3-120 Sakamoto, I., Morimoto, K., and Tanaka, O. 1975. Quantitative analysis of dammarane type saponins of ginseng and its application to the evaluation of the commercial ginseng tea and ginseng extract [in Japanese]. Yakugaku Zasshi 95: 1456-1461. CA 84: 95665.

7.3-121 Saruwatari, Y., Besso, H., Futamura, K., Fuwa, T., and Tanaka, O. 1979. Thin- layer chromatographic determination of panaxadiol and panaxatriol derivatization. Chem. Pharm. Bull. (Tokyo) 27: 147-151. Bib. Ag. 43: 78502.

7.3-122 Sauvaire, Y., and Baccou, J.C. 1978. Improvements in the extraction of steroidal sapogenins. Making use of by-products [in French]. Lloydia 41: 588-596.

7.3-123 Schneider, M. 1978. Determination of morphine content in capsules and stems of the opium poppy (Papaver somniferum L.) [in Polish]. Rocz. Akad. Roln. Poznaniu 1978{108}: 105-108. AGRICOLA.

7.3-124 Shostenko, Yu.V., Vysotskaya, E.S., Mushinskaya, S.Kh., Bozhko, N.G., and Sedova, S.G. 1975. Isolation of natural codeine from the bolls of oil-bearing poppies [in Ukrainian]. Farm. Zh. (Kiev) 30{6}: 58-63. CA 84: 155559

7.3-125 Sita, F., Chmelova-Hlavata, V., and Chmel, K. 1974. Identification of certain essential compounds in drugs by a modified thermofractography method [in German]. J. Chromatogr. 91: 441-450. CA 81: 29583.

7.3-126 Sofowora, E.A., and Hardman, R. 1974. Chromatographic detection and spectrophotometric determination of diosgenin and other delta 5-sapogenins in crude plant extracts. Planta Med. 26: 385-390.

7.3-127 Soldati, F., and Sticher, O. 1980. HPLC Separation and quantitative determination of ginsenosides from Panax ginseng, Panax quinquefolium and from ginseng drug preparations. 2nd communication. Planta Med. 39: 348-357.

7.3-128 Srivastava, V.K., Mukerjee, S.K., and Maheshwari, M.L. 1977. Estimation of glycyrrhizic acid in glycyrrhiza roots. Indian Drugs 14{14}: 80-82. CA 86: 177375.

7.3-129 Stabrowska-Ostrowska, E. 1974. Comparison of methods for determining glycyrrhizic acid in a dried Glycyrrhiza extract [in Polish]. Farm. Pol. 30{10}: 941-943. CA 82: 160295.

7.3-130 Stankeviciene, N., Morkunas, A., and Alinkonite, A. 1973. Gas-liquid chromatographic study of the essential oils of the medicinal Melissa [in Russian]. Pages 264 in K. Jankevicius, ed. Polezny rasteniia Priblatiishikh respublik Belorussii Nauchnaia konferentissia po issledovaniiu i obogascheni, lu rastitel'nykh resurov Pribaltiiskikh respublik i Belorussii, 2nd, Vilna, 1973. CA 81: 111399.

7.3-131 Sticher, O., Soldati, F., Joshi, R.K., and Lehmann, D. 1978. Mass spectrometric investigation of ginsenoside Rg2. Fitoterapia 49: 147-152. CA 91: 20977.

7.3-132 Sticher, O., and Soldati, F. 1979. HPLC Separation and quantitative determination of ginsenosides from Panax ginseng, Panax quinquefolium and from ginseng drug preparations. 1. Communication [in German]. Planta Med. 36: 30-42.

7.3-133 Sticher, O., and Soldati, F. 1978. Glycyrrhizic acid determination in Radix liquiritiae using high-performance liquid chromatography [in German]. Pharm. Acta Helv. 53{2}: 46-52. CA 89: 117936.

7.3-134 Strigina, L.I., Remennikova, T.M., El'kin, Yu.N., Dzizenko, A.K., Isakov, V.V. , and Elyakov, G.B. 1973. On obtaining the naturally occurring aglycone panaxoside A from Panax ginseng C.A. Meyer by means of enzymatic hydrolysis [in Russian]. Doklady Akademii Nauk SSSR 210: 727-730. HA 44: 1842.

7.3-135 Suska, M., Olszewski, Z., Wendt, L., Lukaszewicz, J., and Stefanczuk, H. 1979. Preliminary mathematical formulation of the progress of extracting leaves of woolly foxglove using centrifugal force [in Polish]. Herba Pol. 25: 29-33.

7.3-136 Suska, M., Olszewski, Z., Wendt, L., Glinka, J., and Heryszck, E. 1978. Elaboration of optimum extraction conditions of cardenolide raw materials by use of centrifugal force. Herba Pol. 24: 27-34.

7.3-137 Suss, W. 1972. The extraction of foxglove leaves with ultrasonics [in German]. Pharmazie 27: 615-616. HA 43: 5521.

7.3-138 Takino, Y., Koshioka, M., Shiokawa, M., Ishii, Y., Maruyama, S., Higashino, M., and Hayashi, T. 1979. Quantitative determination of glycyrrhizic acid in liquorice roots and extracts by TLC-densitometry: Studies on the evaluation of crude drugs. VI. Planta Med. 36: 74-78.

7.3-139 Tam, W.H.J., Constabel, F., and Kurz, W.G.W. 1980. Codeine from cell suspension cultures of Papaver somniferum. Phytochemistry 19: 486-487.

7.3-140 Tattje, D.H.E., and Bos, R. 1979. Valeranone, valeranal and vitispirane in the leaf oil of Liquidambar styraciflua. Phytochemistry 18: 876.

7.3-141 Thieme, H., and Hartmann, U. 1974. Comparison of various methods for the spectrophotometric determination of glycyrrhizinic acid in Radix liquiritiae (licorice root) DAB7-DDR [in German]. Pharmazie 29{1}: 50-53. CA 80: 149120.

7.3-142 Tin-Wa, M., Crane, F.A., Baines, R., and Farnsworth, N.R. 1975. Germination and morphine content of Papaver somniferum plants produced from commercially available poppy seed. J. Pharm. Sci. 64: 2024-2025. CIM 17{3}: 4523.

7.3-143 Tittel, G., Hinz, H., and Wagner, H. 1979. Quantitative estimation of the pyrrolizidinalkaloids of Radix symphyti by HPLC [in German]. Planta Med. 37: 1-8.

7.3-144 Tittel, G., and Wagner, H. 1978. High-performance liquid chromatographic separation and quantitative determination of valepotriates in Valeriana drugs and preparations [in German]. J. Chromatogr. 148: 459-468.

7.3-145 Tomoda, M., and Uno, M.I. 1971. Plant mucilages. I. Isolation and property of a mucous polysaccharide "plantasan" from Plantago major var. asiatica seeds. Chem. Pharm. Bull. (Tokyo) 19: 1214-1217.

7.3-146 Vaidya, P.V., Punklik, M.D., and Meghal, S.K. 1980. Rapid method for extraction and colorimetric estimation of morphine in Indian opium. J. Assoc. Off. Anal. Chem. 63: 685-688.

7.3-147 Ventura, P., Visconti, M., and Piffer, G. 1978. A simple GLC analysis of ammonium glycyrrhizinate. Boll. Chim. Farm. 117{4}: 217-221. CA 89: 204283.

7.3-148 Verzar-Petri, G., Bahn Nhu Cuong, Radics, L., and Ujszaszi, K. 1979. Isolation of azulene from yarrow oil (Achillea millefolium L. species complex) and its identification. Herba Hung. 18{2}: 83-95.

7.3-149 Verzar-Petri, G., Marczal, G., and Lemberkovics, E. 1976. Determination of the composition of chamomile oil [in German]. Pharmazie 31: 256-257. CIM 17{7}: 10552.

7.3-150 Verzar-Petri, G., and Marczal, G. 1976. A method for the determination of the camazulene content of chamomile oil [in Hungarian]. Acta Pharm. Hung. 46: 282-288. CA 86: 127343.

7.3-151 Vincent, P.G., and Engelke, B.F. 1979. High pressure liquid chromatographic determination of the five major alkaloids in Papaver somniferum L. and thebaine in Papaver bracteatum Lindl. Capsular tissue. J. Assoc. Off. Anal. Chem. 62: 310-314.

7.3-152 Voloshina, D.A., Rumyantseva, G.N., Shain, S.S., Kalunyants, K.A., and Grebeshova, R.N. 1975. Effect of fermentation on the yield of sapogenins from seeds of Trigonella foenum graecum L. Appl. Biochem. Microbiol. (Engl. Transl.) 11: 774-777. Translation of Prikl. Biokhim. Mikrobiol. 11: 896-900, 1975.

7.3-153 Wagner, H., and Wurmboeck, A. 1978. Determination of the ginseng root components and their preparation through combined thin-layer chromatography-fluorometry [in German]. Dtsch. Apoth.-Ztg. 118{33}: 1209-1213. CA 89: 169153.

7.3-154 Wagner, H., and Wurmboeck, A. 1977. Chemistry, pharmacology and thin-layer chromatography of ginseng and Eleutherococcus drugs [in German]. Dtsch. Apoth.-Ztg. 117: 743-748. CA 87: 58551.

7.3-155 Weber, J.M., and Ma, T.S. 1975. Microchemical investigation of medicinal plants. XI. Identification of morphine and codeine in opium using GS/MS [gas chromatography/ mass spectrometry]. Mikrochim. Acta 2: 401-405. CA 84: 22134.

7.3-156 Wernick, K.R. 1974. Problems in the analysis of gas-liquid chromatography of volatile substances used in medicaments. Proc. Soc. Anal. Chem. 11: 297-299. CA 82: 145026.

7.3-157 Wittwer, J.D., Jr. 1973. Liquid chromatographic determination of morphine in opium. J. Forensic Sci. 18: 138-142. CIM 15{3}: 3198.

7.3-158 Woo, L.K., Han, B.H., Baik, D.W., and Park, D.S. 1973. Characterization of ginseng extracts. Yakhak Hoe Chi 17: 129-136. CA 81: 148472.

7.3-159 Yahara, S., Matsuura, K., Kasai, R., and Tanaka, O. 1976. Saponins of buds and flowers of Panax ginseng C.A. Meyer. {1}. Isolation of ginsenosides-Rd, -Re and -Rg. Chem. Pharm. Bull. (Tokyo) 24: 3212-3213.

7.3-160 Yakubova, M.R., Genkina, G.L., and Sharikov, T.T. 1977. UV-spectrophotometric determination of glycyrrhizic acid in Glycyrrhiza glabra. Chem. Nat. Compd. (Engl. Transl.) 13: 676-679. Translation of Khim. Prir. Soedin. 1977{6}: 802-806.

7.3-161 Yim, K.Y. 1977. Identification of sugar from Korean ginseng saponins by acid hydrolysis [in Korean]. Hakhoe Chi 10: 26-33. CA 87: 90643.

7.3-162 Zwaving, J.H., and De Jong-Havenga, E.H.J. 1972. Determination of hydrastine in Hydrastis fluid extract. Pharm. Weekbl. 107{8}: 137-146. CA 76: 158399.

7.3-163 Zwaving, J.H. 1975. Comparative investigation of some methods for the determination of glycyrrhizin in liquorice root and its preparations. Pharm. Weekbl. 110{39}: 873-879. CA 83: 209448.

7.4 Pharmaceutical Preparations

7.4-1 Ando, T., Muraoka, T., Yamasaki, N., and Okuda, H. 1980. Preparation of anti-lipolytic substance from Panax ginseng. Planta Med. 38: 18-23.

7.4-2 Barber, R.B., and Rapoport, H. 1975. Synthesis of thebaine and oripavine from codeine and morphine. J. Med. Chem. 18: 1074-1077.

7.4-3 Battersby, A.R., Jones, R.C.F., and Kazlauskas, R. 1975.

Experiments on the early steps of morphine biosynthesis (3)
Tetrahedron Lett. 1975{22/23}: 1873-1876.

7.4-4 Blazejewska, B., Ellnain-Wojtaszek, M., Kowalewski, Z., Lutomski,
J., and Skrzypczakowa, L. 1974. Estimation of the utilization of
domestic digitonin for the quantitative determination of the
esterified cholesterol in the blood serum [in Polish]. Herba Pol. 20:
344-348.

7.4-5 Cappelletti, E.M. 1980. Botanical identification of anise and
hemlock fruits in powdered drug samples. Planta Med. 39: 88-94.

7.4-6 Chystyakova, L.M. 1978. Technology of manufacturing concentrates
of Aqua menthae and rosae [in Ukrainian]. Farm. Zh. (Kiev) 1978{3}:
39-40.

7.4-7 Danielak, R., Popowska, E., and Borkowski, B. 1973. The
preparation of vegetable products containing isofraxidin, silibin, and
Glaucium alkaloids and evaluation of their choleretic action. Pol. J.
Pharmacol. Pharm. 25: 271-283.

7.4-8 Debska, W., and Gnusowski, B. 1980. Propyzamide residues in
medicinal plants. Planta Med. 39: 292 (Abstr.).

7.4-9 Duquenois, P., Anton, R., and Dupin, M. 1977. Standardization of
natural drugs. Problems related with fennel fruits [in French]. Ann.
Pharm. Fr. 35: 497-502. CA 89: 12025.

7.4-10 Dyke, S.F., and Tiley, E.P. 1975. The synthesis of berberastine.
Tetrahedron 31: 561-568.

7.4-11 Elbanowska, A., Kaczmarek, F., and Zurawski, P. 1975. Sorption of
moisture by crude drugs. III. Leaf of Mentha piperita, thyme plant,
fruit of Foeinculus, anthodium of chamomile [in Polish]. Herba Pol.
21: 392-401.

7.4-12 Elbanowska, A., Malek, B., and Zurawski, P. 1973. Studies on the
sorption of moisture by dry plant extracts. Part I. Extracts of
Taraxacum, Chelidonium, Stoechados, Carum, Calam Chamomile, Mentha,
Cardus benedictus, Belladonna, and the "gastrochol" preparation [in
Polish]. Herba Pol. 19: 34-47.

7.4-13 Elmadfa, I., and Koken, M. 1980. Effect of vitamin E and protein
quality on the haemolytic action of Trigonella sapogenins in rats [in
German]. Z. Ernaehrungswiss 19: 280-289. NAR-A 51: 7134.

7.4-14 Fu, K.C. 1974. Root qualities of the cultivated Chinese liquorice
(Glycyrrhiza uralensis) [in Chinese]. Chih Wu Hsueh Pao 16{4}:
304-312. CA 83: 32946.

7.4-15 Gaal, G., Kerekes, P., Gorecki, P., and Bognar, R. 1971.
Morphine-associated alkaloids: 5. Synthesis and structure of
narcotoline ethers [in German]. Pharmazie 26: 431-434.

7.4-16 Gaevskii, A.V., Ivanova, R.M., Loshkarev, P.M., and Matveev, N.D.
1976. Quality of raw materials used in the preparation of morphine.
Pharm. Chem. J. (Engl. Transl.) 10: 627-629. Translation of
Khim.-Farm. Zh. 10{5}: 75-77, 1976.

7.4-17 Gorodnichev, V.I., and Borisov, G.N. 1976. Study of the recovery of drug granules after their treatment in apparatus with a fluidized bed [in Russian]. Khim.-Farm. Zh. 10{12}: 107-110. CA 86: 145872.

7.4-18 Gorodnichev, V.I., Borisov, G.N., and Egorova, V.I. 1975. Parameters of drying of medicinal granulates in apparatus with a fluidized bed [in Russian]. Khim.-Farm. Zh. 9{10}: 33-38. CA 84: 22075.

7.4-19 Gorodnichev, V.I., Egorova, V.I., and Borisov, G.N. 1973. Selection and substantiation of the optimum moisture content for drug granulates during tableting [in Russian]. Khim.-Farm. Zh. 7{7}: 38-42. CA 80: 6830.

7.4-20 Gorodnichev, V.I., and Borisov, G.N. 1977. Effect of the temperature on water content equilibrium in drug granulates [in Russian]. Khim.-Far m. Zh. 11{10}: 113-116. CA 87: 206439.

7.4-21 Issar, R.K. 1977. Comparative chemico-morphological studies of the imported Unani drug 'zufah-yabis' and indigenous herb 'dyanku'. Indian J. Pharm. 39: 167 (Abstr.).

7.4-22 Karryiew, M.O. 1972. Medical preparations produced from different species of volatile oil plants found in Turkmenian flora [in Russian]. Postep Dziedzinie Leku Rosl. Pr. Ref. Dosw. Wygloszone Symp., 1970; Herba Pol. Suppl. 1972: 149-152.

7.4-23 Karwowska, K., and Geca, Z. 1972. Production of red pepper extracts for the pharmaceutical industry [in Polish]. Pr. Inst. Lab. Badaw. Przem. Spozyw. 22: 503-508. CA 80: 30731.

7.4-24 Kasai, R., Shinzo, K., and Tanaka, O. 1976. Syntheses of betulafolienetriol and the ginseng sapogenin, 20(s)-protopanaxadiol. Chem. Pharm. Bull. (Tokyo) 24: 400-406.

7.4-25 Kassem, A.A., and Abd El-Bary, A. 1972. Stability of fluid extract of licorice. Bull. Fac. Pharm., Cairo Univ. 11{1}: 219-232. CA 81: 68430.

7.4-26 Khreshchenyuk, S.I., Goncharenko, G.K., Prokopenko, O.P., and Lytvynenko, V. 1974. Effect of grinding on the process of extraction of medicinal vegetal raw material [in Ukrainian]. Farm. Zh. (Kiev) 29: 61-63.

7.4-27 Kowalewska, K., and Kaczmarek, F. 1972. Evaluation of processing offals of Radix valerianae [in Polish]. Herba Pol. 18: 18-27. AGRICOLA.

7.4-28 Kudryavtseva, G.M., Borisov, G.N., and Egorova, V.I. 1977. Thermodynamic parameters of drug granules [in Russian]. Khim.-Farm. Zh. 11{4}: 95-97. CA 87: 28921.

7.4-29 Kudryavtseva, G.M., and Egorova, V.I. 1978. Experimental determination of the mass transfer potential for medicinal granules [in Russian] Khim.-Farm. Zh. 12{8}: 101-104. CA 89: 185989.

7.4-30 Kustrak, D., and Benzinger, F. 1977. Studies on chamomile, flos chamomillae in relation to criteria of drug quality [in Serbo-Croatian]. Farm. Glas. 33: 331-353. HA 48: 10087.

7.4-31 Liberti, L.E., and Der Marderosian, A. 1978. Evaluation of commercial ginseng products. J. Pharm. Sci. 67: 1487-1489.

7.4-32 Martinelli, E.M. 1980. Gas chromatography in the control of extracts Fitoterapia 5{1}: 35-57. CA 94: 20477.

7.4-33 Martin, J., and Garcia Rumbao, M.C. 1980. New method for the determination of the levels of glycyrrhizinic acid in extracts of licorice root [in Spanish]. An. R. Acad. Farm. 46{2}: 183-201. CA 94: 53030.

7.4-34 McMurry, J.E., and Choy, W. 1980. Total synthesis of alpha and beta panasinsene. Tetrahedron Lett. 1980{21}: 2477-2480.

7.4-35 Murav'ev, I.A., and Savchenko, L.N. 1979. Preparation of glycyrrhetinic acid from licorice root extracts [in Russian]. Khim.-Farm. Zh. 13{5}: 97-102. CA 91: 71699.

7.4-36 Murav'ev, I.A., Mor'yasis, E.D., Starokozhko, L.E., Chebotarev, V.V., and Krasova, T.G. 1977. Determination of the bioavailability of some preparations for topical use by experimental dermatological methods [in Russian]. Farmatsiya (Moscow) 26{4}: 15-19. CA 87: 145782.

7.4-37 Murav'ev, I.A., and Semenchenko, V.F. 1978. Study of the solubilization of antineoplastic drugs [in Russian]. Farmatsiya (Moscow) 27{2}: 13-15. CA 189: 12066.

7.4-38 Murav'ev, I.A., Bashura, G.S., and Krasova, T.G. 1974. Production of some licorice root preparations and a study of their surface-active properties [in Russian]. Farmatsiya (Moscow) 23{4}: 14-18. CA 82: 64385.

7.4-39 Muraviev, I.A., Bashura, G.S., and Krasova, T.G. 1974. The production of some liquorice root preparations and a study of their surface active properties. Farmatsiya 23{4}: 14-18.

7.4-40 Nour, M.G., El-Taie, N.H., and Shabara, M. 1976. Preparation and evaluation of commercial ammoniated glycyrrhizin. Egypt. J. Pharm. Sci. 17{3}: 283-289. CA 90: 127443.

7.4-41 Os, F.H.L. van, and Elema, E.T. 1977. Assessment of thyme and its pharmaceutical preparations. I. [in Dutch]. Pharm. Weekbl. 112: 557-562. HA 48: 5890.

7.4-42 Paik, N.H., Lee, W.K., Park, M.K., and Jung, I. 1979. Determination of geranium in botanical drugs by flameless atomic absorption spectrophotometry [in Korean]. Yakhak Hoe Chi 23{3-4}: 141-146. CA 93: 163812.

7.4-43 Petricic, J., and Petricic, V. 1975. Evaluation of the drug and liquid extract from licorice root (Glycyrrhizae radix) [in Croatian]. Farm. Glas. 31{12}: 453-459. CA 84: 155558.

7.4-44 Puri, S.C., Dhar, K.L., and Atal, C.K. 1977. Synthesis of 3,11-dioxo-3a-aza-A-homo-12-oleanen- 30-oic acid. Indian J. Chem. Sect. B 15B: 917-918.

7.4-45 Raftery, M.M. 1975. Explosibility tests for industrial dusts. Fire Res. Tech. Pap. (U.K. Jt. Fire Res. Org.) 21. 14 pp. CA 88: 140915.

7.4-46 Raj, K.P.S., Agrawal, Y.K., and Patel, M.R. 1978/1979. Metal analyses of some subterranean crude drugs. J. Soc. Sci. Number. Maharaja Sayajirao Univ. Baroda 27/28{3}: 45-48. AGRICOLA.

7.4-47 Ramanathan, V.S. 1980. Study on the deterioriation of morphine and its preservation by chemicals in the fresh latex of opium poppy (Papaver somniferum L.). Part II. Indian J. Agric. Res. 14: 6-12. CA 95: 30272.

7.4-48 Ramanathan, V.S. 1980. A study on the deterioration of morphine and its preservation by chemicals in the fresh latex of opium poppy (Papaver somniferum L.). Part III. Indian J. Agric. Res. 14: 82-90. CA 94: 197457.

7.4-49 Ramanathan, V.S. 1979. A study on the deterioration of morphine and its preservation by chemicals in the fresh latex of opium poppy (Papaver somniferum Linn.). Part I. Indian J. Agric. Res. 13: 229-237. CA 93: 210150.

7.4-50 Rybal'chenko, A.S., and Fursa, N.S. 1978. Comparative study of the medical quality of the raw materials from Valeriana nitida and Valeriana exaltata [in Ukrainian]. Farm. Zh. (Kiev) 1978{2}: 67-71. CIM 19{5}: 3877.

7.4-51 Sauvaire, Y., and Baccou, J.C. 1978. The production of diosgenin, (25R)-spirost-5-ene-3 beta -ol; problems of acid hydrolysis of the saponins [in French]. Lloydia 41: 247-256.

7.4-52 Tomimori, T., and Yoshimoto, M. 1980. Quantitative variation of glycyrrhizin in the decoction of glycyrrhizae radix mixed with other crude drugs [in Japanese]. Shoyakugaku Zasshi 34{2}: 138-144. CA 94: 36184.

7.4-53 Vondenhof, Th., Glombitza, K.W., and Steiner, M. 1973. Determination of glycyrrhizinic acid in crude licorice, licorice products, and medical preparations [in German]. Sci. Pharm. 41: 155-161. CA 79: 70251.

7.4-54 Yamagishi, T., Kaneshima, H., Kinoshita, Y., and Honma, S. 1975. The standardization of crude drugs produced in Hokkaido. VII. The ether soluble components of Angelica radix (Touki). I. [in Japanese]. Hokkaidoritsu Eisei Kenkyusho Ho 25: 20-24. CA 84: 132662.

7.4-55 Yamagishi, T., Kaneshima, H., Kinoshita, Y., and Honma, S. 1975. The standardization of crude drugs produced in Hokkaido. VIII. The comparison quality and components of Touki cultivated in different places [in Japanese]. Hokkaidoritsu Eisei Kenkyusho Ho 25: 25-29. CA 84: 132663.

7.4-56 Zatula, E.I., Konev, F.A., Bugrim, N.A., and Timoshenko, N.V. 1977. The stability and formulation of solutions of cardenolides of Digitalis lanata Ehrh. for injections [in Russian]. Farmatasiya (Mosc.) 26{2}: 23-26.

7.5 Pharmacognosy

7.5-1 Abd-el-Malek, Y., El-Leithy, M.A., Reda, F.A., and Khalil, M. 1973. Antimicrobial principles in leaves of Lawsonia inermis. Zentralbl. Bakteriol., Parasitenk., Infektionskr. Hyg., Abt. 128{1-2}: 61-67. CA 79: 62033.

7.5-2 Afaq, S.H., Dutt, A.K., and Atal, C.K. 1974. Pharmacognosy of the commercial caraways. III. Pharmacognostical study of the fruits of Bunium cylindricum (Boiss & Hoh.) Drude. Indian J. Pharm. 36: 140-142.

7.5-3 Albert-Puleo, M. 1980. Fennel and anise as estrogenic agents. J. Ethnopharmacol. 2: 337-344. HA 51: 3886.

7.5-4 Albert-Puleo, M. 1978. Mythobotany, pharmacology, and chemistry of thujone-containing plants and derivatives. Econ. Bot. 32{1}: 65-74.

7.5-5 Baas, E.U., Holtermueller, K.H., Sinterhauf, K., and Walter, U. 1976. The behavior of gastrin, renin, aldosterone and electrolytes following administration on deglycyrrhizinized succus liquiritiae and carbonoxolone in healthy subjects [in German]. Z. Gastroenterol. 14{2}: 273-276. CA 90: 66845.

7.5-6 Balbaa, S.I., Zaki, A.Y., Abdel-Waheb, S.M., El-Denshary, E.S.M., and Motazz-Bellah, M. 1973. Preliminary phytochemical and pharmacological investigations of the roots of different varieties of Cichorium intybus. Planta Med. 24: 133-144. HA 44: 5589.

7.5-7 Barnaulov, O.D., Bukreyeva, T.V., Kokarev, A.A., and Shevchenko, A.I. 1978. Primary evaluation of the spasmolytic properties of some natural compounds and galenic preparations [in Russian]. Rastit. Resur. 14: 573-579.

7.5-8 Benoit, P.S., Fong, H.H.S., Svoboda, G.H., and Farnsworth, N.R. 1976. Biological and phytochemical evaluation of plants. XIV. Antiinflammatory evaluation of 163 species of plants. Lloydia 39: 160-171.

7.5-9 Bergmann, F. 1975. On the mechanism of morphine action. Pahlavi. Med. J. 6: 473-478.

7.5-10 Brochmann-Hanssen, E., Chen, C.H., Chiang, H.-C., Fu, C.-C., and Nemoto, H. 1973. Opium alkaloids. XIV: Biosynthesis of aporphines – detection of orientaline in opium poppy. J. Pharm. Sci. 62: 1291-1293.

7.5-11 Bulhoes, G.C., and Da Mota e Silva, A. 1977. Phytochemical screening of plants native to northeastern Brazil. II [in Portuguese]. An. Fac. Farm., Univ. Fed Pernambuco 15: 51-54. CA 91: 16730.

7.5-12 Caldes, G., and Prescott, B. 1973. A potential antileukemic substance present in Allium ascalonicum. Planta Med. 23: 99-100. HA 43: 6035.

7.5-13 Caldes, G., Prescott, B., and King, J.R. 1975. Potential antileukemic substance present in Globularia alypum. Planta Med. 27: 72-76. CA 82: 164725.

7.5-14 Caldwell, J., and Sever, P.S. 1974. The biochemical pharmacology of abused drugs. III. Cannabis, opiates, and synthetic narcotics. Clin. Pharmacol. Ther. 16: 989-1013. CA 82: 80204.

7.5-15 Charya, M.A.S., Reddy, S.M., Kumar, B.P., and Reddy, S.R. 1979. Laboratory evaluation of some medicinal plants extracts against two pathogenic fungi. New Bot. 6: 171-174. RPP 60: 4232.

7.5-16 Chaurasia, S.C., and Jain, P.C. 1978. Antibacterial activity of essential oils of four medicinal plants. Indian J. Hosp. Pharm. 15: 166-168. HA 50: 6523.

7.5-17 Dardymov, I.V. 1976. Adaptogens, drugs for stress [in Russian]. Khim. Zhizn. 1976{3}: 66-72. CA 85: 15.

7.5-18 De Pasquale, A., and Ragusa, S. 1979. Applications of scanning electron microscopy in pharmacognasy [in French]. Plant. Med. Phytother.13: 46-65.

7.5-19 Der Marderosian, A.H. 1980. Controversies concerning herbal remedies. Am. Drugg. 182{2}: 35-39.

7.5-20 Dobrynin, V.N., Kolosov, M.N., Chernov, B.K., and Derbentseva, N.A. 1976. Antimicrobial substances from Salvia officinalis. Chem. Nat. Compd. (Engl. Transl.) 12: 623-624. Translation of Khim. Prir. Soedin. 1976{5}: 686-687

7.5-21 Duquenois, P. 1971. Study of a method for the evaluation of therapeutic activity and industrial value of Digitalis purpurea leaves [in French]. Plant. Med. Phytother. 5: 240-251.

7.5-22 Dutt, A.K., Afaq, S.H., and Atal, C.K. 1972. Pharmacognosy of the commercial caraways. Part I. Pharmacognostical study of the fruits of Carum gracile Lindl. Indian J. Pharm. 34: 147-150. HA 43: 7973.

7.5-23 Dutt, A.K., Afaq, S.H., and Atal, C.K. 1973. Pharmacognosy of the commercial caraways: Part II – pharmacognostical study of the fruits of Bupleurum falcatum Linn. Indian J. Pharm. 35: 52-54. HA 44: 1789.

7.5-24 El-Merzabani, M.M., El-Aaser, A.A., Attia, M.A., El-Duweini, A.K., and Ghazal, A.M. 1979. Screening system for Egyptian plants with potential anti-tumor activity. Planta Med. 36: 150-155.

7.5-25 Farnsworth, N.R., Bingel, A.S., Cordell, G.A., Crane, F.A., and Fong, H.H.S. 1975. Potential value of plants as sources of new antifertility agents. II. J. Pharm. Sci. 64{5}: 717-754.

7.5-26 Farnsworth, N.R., Bingel, A.S., Cordell, G.A., Crane, F.A., and Fong, 4.H.S. 1975. Potential value of plants as sources of new antifertility agents. I. J. Pharm. Sci. 64{4}: 535-598.

7.5-27 Fong, H.H.S., Trojankova, M., Trojanek, J., and Farnsworth, N.R. 1972. Alkaloid screening. II. Lloydia 35: 117-149.

7.5-28 Fong, H.H.S., Farnsworth, N.R., Henry, L.K., Svoboda, G.H., and Yates, M.J. 1972. Biological and phytochemical evaluation of plants. X. Test results from a third two-hundred accessions. Lloydia 35: 35-48.

7.5-29 Garg, S.K., Mathur, V.S., and Chaudhury, R.R. 1978. Screening of Indian plants for antifertility activity. Indian J. Exp. Biol. 16: 1077-1079.

7.5-30 Garg, S.K. 1976. Antifertility screening of plants--effect of four indigenous plants. Early pregnancy in female albino rats. Indian J. Med. Res. 64: 1133-1135.

7.5-31 Goncalves de Lima, O., Coelho, J.S. de B., Leoncio d'Albuquerque, I., Francisco de Mello, J., Martino, D.G., Lacerda, A.L., and De Moraes e Souza, M.A. 1971. Antimicrobial compounds from higher plants. XXXV. Antimicrobial and antitumor activity of lawsone (2-hydroxy-1,4-napthoquinone) compared with that of lapachol [2-hydroxy-3-(3-methyl-2-butenyl)-1,4 naphthoquinone] [in Portuguese]. Rev. Inst. Antibiot., Univ. Fed. Pernambuco, Recife 11: 21-26. CA 77: 29629.

7.5-32 Grabrczyk, H., Drozdz, B., Hladon, B., and Wojciechowska, J. 1977. Sesquiterpene lactions. Part XV. New cytostatic active sesquiterpene lactone from herb of Anthemis nobilis. Pol. J. Pharmacol. Pharm. 29: 419-423.

7.5-33 Grahame-Smith, D.G. 1978. Some aspects of the clinical pharmacology of digoxin. Pages 235-245 in C.J. Dickinson and J. Marks, eds. Developments in cardiovascular medicine. University Park Press, Baltimore, Md.

7.5-34 Granda, E., San Roman, L., Rivas Goday, S., and Serranillos, M. 1975. Pharmacognostic study of Digitalis-purpurea grown in soils derived from the disintegration of cretaceous sediments. An. R. Acad. Farm. 41: 415-422.

7.5-35 Guillot, J.P., Saboya, C., Blanc, G., Guyot, J.Y., Petit, J.P., and San-Jose, A. 1977. Adaptation of a method for evaluating the possible phototoxic and photoallergenic characteristics of topical applications in the albino guinea pig. Results obtained with psoralen, isopsoralen, 3,3',4',5-tetrachlorosalicylanilide, absolute of jasmin, and a sun cream [in French]. Parfums, Cosmet., Aromes 18: 61-62, 65-69. CA 88: 145869.

7.5-36 Guz, A. 1978. The clinical value of digoxin in patients with heart failure and sinus rhythm. Pages 255-261 in C.J. Dickinson and J. Marks, eds. Developments in cardiovascular medicine. University Park Press, Baltimore, Md.

7.5-37 Harney, J.W., Barofsky, I.B., and Leary, J.D. 1977. Studies of Nepeta cataria L. for behaviorally-active substances. Lloydia 40: 619 (Abstr.).

7.5-38 Hartley, T.G., Dunstone, E.A., Fitzgerald, J.S., Johns, S.R., and Lamberton, J.A. 1973. A survey of New Guinea plants for alkaloids. Lloydia 36: 217-319.

7.5-39 Hayashi, E., and Nagao, J. 1976. Pharmacological study on the SAIKO-ZAI. Jpn J. Pharmacol. 26 (Suppl.): 138P (Abstr.).

7.5-40 Hayashi, M. 1977. Pharmacological studies on crude plant drugs, Shikon and Tooki. (I). Ether and water extracts [in Japanese]. Nippon Yakurigaku Zasshi 73{2}: 177-191. CA 88: 44862.

7.5-41 Hiraga, Y., Hosoyama, K., Takahashi, K., and Shibata, S. 1979. TCL-profile analysis of Chinese medicinal preparations [in Japanese]. Shoyakag Aku Zasshi 33{1}: 38-42. CA 92: 116486.

7.5-42 Hirosue, T., Kawai, H., and Hosogai, Y. 1978. The antioxidative activities of crude drugs [in Japanese]. Nippon Shokuhino Kogyo Gakkaishi 25{12}: 291-293. CA 91: 44437.

7.5-43 Ieven, M., Vanden Berghe, D.A., Mertens, F., Vlietinck, A., and Lammens, E. 1979. Screening of higher plants for biological activities. I. Antimicrobial activity. Planta Med. 36{4}: 311-321. HA 50: 5479.

7.5-44 Israili, A.H., and Issar, R.K. 1973. Pharmacognostical studies of the Unani drug 'afsanteen' (Artemisia absinthium L.). Indian J. Pharm. 35: 208 (Abstr.).

7.5-45 Jain, M.L., and Jain, S.R. 1972. Therapeutic utility of Ocimum basilicum var. album. Planta Med. 22: 66-70. CIM 14{2}: 1734.

7.5-46 Jain, R.C. 1976. Onion and garlic in experimental cholesterol induced atherosclerosis. Indian J. Med. Res. 64: 1509-1515. NAR-A 47: 6451.

7.5-47 Joo, C.N., Choi, R.S., Lee, S.J., Cho, S.H., and Son, M.H. 1973. Biochemical studies on ginseng saponins. II. Surface activity of ginseng saponin and its effect on lipid dispersion [in Korean]. Han'guk Saenghwahakhoe Chi 6: 185-194. CA 81: 45820.

7.5-48 Joo, C.N., and Lee, S.J. 1977. Biochemical studies on ginseng saponins. IX. Determination of critical micellar concentration of the saponin of Korean ginseng roots and its effect on lipid dispersion and enzyme reactions. Hanguk Saenghwa Hakhoe Chi 10{2}: 59-69. CA 88: 100647.

7.5-49 Kaminski, B., Glowniak, K., Majewska, A., Petkowicz, J., and Szaniawska-DeKurdy, D. 1978. Search for coumarin compounds in fruit and seeds. I. Fruits of the family Umbelliferae-Apiaceae [in Polish]. Farm. Pol. 34{1}: 25-28. CA 89: 3161.

7.5-50 Kapoor, L.D., Srivastava, S.N., Singh, A., Kapoor, S.L., and Shah, N.C. 1972. Survey of Indian plants for saponins, alkaloids and flavonoids. III. Lloydia 35: 288-295.

7.5-51 Kapoor, L.D., Kapoor, S.L., Srivastava, S.N., Singh, A., and Sharma, P.C. 1971. Survey of Indian plants for saponins, alkaloids and flavonoids. II. Lloydia 34: 94-102.

7.5-52 Karryev, M.O., Bairyev, Ch.B., and Ataeva, A.S. 1976. Some therapeutic properties and phytochemistry of Marrubium vulgare [in Russian]. Izv. Akad. Nauk Turkm. SSR Ser. Biol. Nauk 1976{3}: 86-88.

7.5-53 Kar, A., and Jain, S.R. 1971. Investigations on the antibacterial activity of some Indian indigenous aromatic plants. Flavour Ind. 2: 111-113.

7.5-54 Kholkute, S.D., Mudgal, V., Deshpande, P.J., and Udupa, K.N. 1975. Preliminary antifertility screening of indigenous plants. Proc. Indian Sci. Cong. 62: (pt. III Sect. IX): 43-44 (Abstr.).

7.5-55 Kholkute, S.D., Mudgal, V., and Deshpande, P.J. 1976. Screening of indigenous medicinal plants for antifertility potentiality. Planta Med. 29: 150-155. CIM 17{2}: 2911.

7.5-56 Kim, H.-S., Park, J.-S., Park, H.-J., and Chi, H.-J. 1980. A study of the effects of the root components of Angelica gigas Nakai on voluntary activity in mice [in Korean]. Soul Taehakkyo Saengyak Yonguso Opjukjip 19: 65-68. CA 95: 143966.

7.5-58 Konowal, A., Snatzke, G., and Thies, P.W. 1978. Circular dichroism--LXVIII. Compounds from valerian- XII. On the chiroptical properties of valepotriates and related compounds. Tetrahedron 34: 253-258.

7.5-59 Kumagai, A. 1973. Hormone-like action of licorice and glycyrrhizin [in Japanese]. Taisha 10: 632-645. CA 81: 130969.

7.5-60 Kvirkveliya-Petriashvili, A.A. 1977. Some problems of the mechanism of action of a new supetin preparation [in Russian]. Pages 46-48 in Mater. Resp. Rasshir. Konf. Farmacol. Gruz. 2nd, 1977. CA 91: 13650.

7.5-61 Kyi, K.K., Bwin, M., Gwan, S., Maung, C., Than, A., Tya-tu, M., and Tha, S.J. 1971. Hypotensive property of Plantago major Linn. Union Burma Life Sci. J. 4{1}: 167-169. AGRICOLA.

7.5-62 Lahiri, K., Raju, D.S.N., and Rao, P.R. 1980. Influence of deglycyrrhizinated licorice on the bioavailability of nitrofurantoin. East. Pharm. 23{268}: 191-193. CA 94: 52816.

7.5-63 Lahon, L.C., and Singh, N. 1978. Pharmacological study of Lawsonia inermis Linn. Indian J. Physiol. Pharmacol. 22: 235-236 (Abstr.).

7.5-64 Lavrenov, V.K. 1971. Use of colibacterin and submerged intestinal lavage in the treatment of patients with chronic colitis [in Russian]. Vrach. Delo. 7: 17-20. CIM 13{2}: 2032.

7.5-65 Lee, Y.M., Saito, H., Takagi, K., Shibata, S., Shoji, J., and Kondo, N. 1977. Pharmacological studies of Panacis japonici rhizoma II. Chem. Pharm. Bull. (Tokyo) 25: 1391-1398.

7.5-66 Lemmi, C.T., and Rovesti, P. 1979. Studies on the cosmetic effect of capers [in Italian]. Riv. Ital. Essenze Profumi Piante Off. Aromat. Syndets Saponi Cosmet Aerosols 61: 2-9. HA 50: 1357.

7.5-67 Lin, Y.-C., Yang, T.-I., Chen, J.-Y., and Yang, C.-S. 1972. Search for biologically active substances in Taiwan medicinal plants 1. Screening for anti-tumor and anti-microbial substances. Chin. J. Microbiol. 5: 76-81.

7.5-68 Liszka, B., and Sendra, J. 1978. The bacteriostatic properties of chosen extracts and substances derived from plants. Acta Biol. Cracov. Ser. Bot. 21: 23-30.

7.5-69 Maksyutina, N.P., Nikitina, N.I., Lipkan, G.M., Gorin, A.G., and Voitenko, I.M. 1978. Chemical composition and hypochloesterolemic action of some drugs from Plantago major leaves. Part I. Polyphenolic compounds [in Ukranian]. Farm. Zh. (Kiev) 1978{4}: 56-61. CA 90: 48400.

7.5-70 Malekzadeh, L.F., and Shabestari, P.P. 1975. Therapeutic effects of Lawsonia inermis. Abstr. Annu. Meet. Am. Soc. Microbiol. 75: 11 (Abstr.).

7.5-71 Man'ko, I.V., Poskalenko, O.N., Korkhov, V.V., and Baikova, V.V. 1977. Isolation and study of 'ces' series preparations with contraceptive activity from plants of the borage family (Boraginaceae Don.). I. [in Ukrainian]. Farm. Zh. 1977{3}: 60-65. CIM 18{13}: 10224.

7.5-72 Meshcherskaya, K.A., Kropotov, A.V., Kruglov, S.K., Moiseeva, R.K., and Sedykh, T.N. 1975. The biological activity of preparations obtained from plants of the Araliaceae, Ranunculaceae, Labiatae, Papaveraceae and Fumariaceae growing in the Soviet Far East [in Russian]. Rastit. Resur. 11: 279-289. HA 45: 10014.

7.5-73 Moon, C.K., and Yoon, M.H. 1976. Screening of polyacetylenic compounds in Korean plants. I. [in Korean]. Soul Taehakkyo Saengyak Yonguso Opjukjip 15: 83-85. CA 88: 47502.

7.5-74 Morris, J.A., Khettry, A., and Seitz, E.W. 1979. Antimicrobial activity of aroma chemicals and essential oils. J. Am. Oil Chem. Soc. 56: 595-603.

7.5-75 Mueller-Limmroth, W., and Froehlich, H. 1980. Mode of action of some phytotherapeutic expectorants on the mucociliar transport [in German]. Fortschr. Med. 98{3}: 95-101. CA 92: 174244.

7.5-76 Munshi, S.R., Shetye, T.A., and Nair, R.K. 1977. Antifertility activity of three indigenous plant preparations. Planta Med. 31: 73-75. HA 47: 9795.

7.5-77 Murav'ev, I.A., and Konokhina, N.F. 1972. The oestrogenic properties of Glycyrrhiza glabra herbage [in Russian]. Rastit. Resur. 8: 490-497. HA 43: 6299.

7.5-78 Nabata, H., Saito, H., and Takagi, K. 1973. Pharmacological studies of neutral saponins (GNS) of Panax ginseng root. Jpn. J. Pharmacol. 23{1}: 29-41. CA 78: 143761.

7.5-79 Namba, T., Yoshizaki, M., Tomimori, T., Kobashi, K., Mitsui, K., and Hase, J. 1974. Fundamental studies on the evaluation of the crude drugs. (I) Hemolytic and its protective activity of ginseng saponins. Planta Med. 25: 28-38.

7.5-80 Namba, T., Yoshizaki, M., Tomimori, T., Kobashi, K., Mitsui, K., and Hase, J. 1974. Fundamental studies on the evaluation of the crude drugs. III. Chemical and biochemical evaluation of ginseng and related crude drugs [in Japanese]. Yakugaku Zasshi 94: 252-260. CA 80: 112556.

7.5-81 Noamesi, B.K. 1977. Power tea (Lippian multiflora)- A potent hypertensive therapy. West Afr. J. Pharmacol. Drug Res. 4: 33-36.

7.5-82 Odebiyi, O.O., and Sofowora, E.A. 1978. Phytochemical screening of Nigerian medicinal plants. II. Lloydia 41: 234-246.

7.5-83 Olaniyi, A.A., Sofowora, E.A., and Oguntimehin, B.O. 1975. Phytochemical investigations of some Nigerian plants used against fevers. II. Cymbopogon citratus. Planta Med. 28: 186-189. HA 46: 6063.

7.5-84 Patakova, D., and Chladek, M. 1974. The antibacterial activity of the oils of thyme and wild thyme [in German]. Pharmazie 29: 140, 142. HA 44: 7934.

7.5-85 Petkov, V., and Manolov, P. 1975. To the pharmacology of iridoids. Agressologie 16{B}: 25-29.

7.5-86 Petrovski, S. 1972. The causative agents of glanders and melioidosis as affected directly and at a distance by rose, savory, spearmint, lavender, dill and geranium essential oils [in Bulgarian]. Vet. Med. Nauki 9{2}: 27-35.

7.5-87 Pizsolitto, A.C., Mancini, B., Longo Fracalanzza, S.E., and Donini Mancini, M.A. 1975. Determination of antibacterial activity of essential oils officialized by the Brazilian Pharmocopeia, 2nd edition [in Portuguese]. Rev. Fac. Farm. Odontol. Araraquara 9{1}: 55-61. CA 86: 12226.

7.5-88 Prakash, A.O., and Mathur, R. 1976. Screening of Indian plants for antifertility activity. Indian J. Exp. Biol. 14: 623-626.

7.5-89 Racz, G., Racz-Kotilla, E., and Jozsa, J. 1979. Activity of some species belonging to Labiatae on the central nervous system of mice. Planta Med. 36: 259-260 (Abstr.).

7.5-90 Racz-Kotilla, E., Racz, G., and Jozsa, J. 1980. Activity of some species belonging to the Labiatae on the central nervous system of mice. Acta Hort. 96: 49-53.

7.5-91 Rice, K.C., and Wilson, R.S. 1976. Isothujone, a small nonnitrogenous molecule with antinociceptive activity in mice. J. Med. Chem. 19: 1054-1057. CA 85: 56669.

7.5-92 Ross, S.A., Megalla, S.E., Bishay, D.W., and Awad, A.H. 1980. Studies for determining antibiotic substances in some Egyptian plants. Part I. Screening for antimicrobial activity. Fitoterapia 51: 303-308. CA 95: 93339.

7.5-93 Saito, H., Morita, M., and Takagi, K. 1973. Pharmacological studies of Panax ginseng leaves. Jpn. J. Pharmacol. 23: 43-56. CA 78: 143762.

7.5-94 Saito, H., Lee, Y.-M., Takagi, K., Shibata, S., Shoji, J., and Kondo, N. 1977. Pharmacological studies of Panacis japonici rhizoma. I. Chem. Pharm. Bull. (Tokyo) 25: 1017-1025.

7.5-95 Sanada, S., and Shoji, J. 1978. Comparative studies on the saponins of ginseng and related crude drugs (I). Shoyakugaku Zasshi 32: 96-99.

7.5-96 Saxena, H.O. 1975. A survey of the plants of Orissa (India) for tannins, saponins, flavonoids and alkaloids. Lloydia 38: 346-351.

7.5-97 Seki, Y., Aizawa, A., Uchiyama, T., and Tanihata, Y. 1979. Experimental and clinical studies on lecithin-bound iodine and lecithin-bound iodine with licorice as remedies for bronchial asthma [in Japanese]. Toho Igakkoi Zasshi 26{3}: 304-326. CA 92: 15825.

7.5-98 Setty, B.S., Kamboj, V.P., Garg, H.S., and Khanna, N.M. 1976. Spermicidal potential of saponins isolated from Indian medicinal plants. Contraception 14: 571-578. CA 86: 47243.

7.5-99 Shah, N.C., Mitra, R., and Kapoor, L.D. 1972. Pharmacognostic studies of Angelica glauca Edgew. Indian J. Pharm. 34{6}: 171 (Abstr.).

7.5-100 Shah, N.C., Mitra, R., and Kapoor, L.D. 1974. Pharmacognostical studies of Angelica glauca Edgew. Bull. Bot. Surv. India 16: 40-47.

7.5-101 Shani, J., Goldshmied, A., Joseph, B., Ahronson, Z., and Sulman, F.G. 1974. Hypoglycemic effect of Trigonella foneum-graecum and Lupinis terminis (Leguminosae) seeds and their major alkaloids in alloxan-diabetic and normal rats. Arch. Int. Pharmacodyn. Ther. 210: 27-37. CA 83: 90765.

7.5-102 Sharaf, A., and Gomaa, N. 1971. Oestrogenic activity of different plants. Qual. Plant. Mater. Veg. 20: 271-277.

7.5-103 Sherry, C.J., and Koontz, J.A. 1979. Pharmacologic studies of "catnip tea": the hot water extract of Nepeta cataria. Q.J. Crude Drug Res. 17: 68-72.

7.5-104 Shibata, S. 1977. Saponins with biological and pharmacological activity. Pages 177-196 in H. Wagner and P. Wolff, eds. Proceedings in Life Sciences. New natural products and plant drugs with pharmacological, biological or therapeutical activity. Proceedings of the first international congress on medicinal plant research, Munich, West Germany, Sept. 6-10, 1976. Springer-Verlag, New York, NY.

7.5-105 Smolenski, S.J., Silinis, H., and Farnsworth, N.R. 1972. Alkaloid screening. I. Lloydia 35: 1-34.

7.5-106 Smolenski, S.J., Silinis, H., and Farnsworth, N.R. 1974. Alkaloid screening. V. Lloydia 37: 506-536.

7.5-107 Smolenski, S.J., Silinis, H., and Farnsworth, N.R. 1974. Alkaloid screening. IV. Lloydia 37: 30-61.

7.5-108 Smolenski, S.J., Silinis, H., and Farnsworth, N.R. 1973. Alkaloid screening. III. Lloydia 36: 359-389.

7.5-109 Smolenski, S.J., Silinis, H., and Farnsworth, N.R. 1975. Alkaloid screening. VIII. Lloydia 38: 497-528.

7.5-110 Smolenski, S.J., Silinis, H., and Farnsworth, N.R. 1975. Alkaloid screening. VII. Lloydia 38: 411-441.

7.5-111 Sobotka-Wierzbowicz, J. 1972. Evaluation of rhizomes and roots of Valeriana officinalis. Pharmacognostic investigations [in Polish]. Herba Pol. 18: 3-10.

7.5-112 Sokolova, L.N., and Kurten, M.V. 1971. The pharmacology of the alkaloid rosmaricin [in Russian]. Tr. Vses. Nauchno-Issled. Inst. Lik. Rast. 14: 129-140.

7.5-113 Suk, K.-K., Nitta, A., and Konoshima, M. 1974. Studies on origin of Japanese chuanziong. I. Angelica spp. Yakugaku Zasshi 94: 865-871.

7.5-114 Szafran, H., Szmal, Z., and Sobotka-Iwerzbowicz, J. 1972. Evaluation of rhizomes and roots of Valeriana officinalis: pharmacological investigations [in Polish]. Herba Pol. 18: 11-17.

7.5-115 Takagi, K., Saito, H., and Tsuchiya, M. 1972. Pharmacological studies of Panax ginseng root: Pharmacological properties of a crude saponin fraction. Jpn. J. Pharmacol. 22: 339-346. CIM 14{3}: 2826.

7.5-116 Tanaka, S., Hoshino, C., Ikeshiro, Y., Tabata, M., and Konoshima, M. 1977. Studies on antinociceptive activities of aqeous extracts from different varieties of Toki [in Japanese]. Yakugaku Zasshi 97{1}: 14-17. CA 86: 150457.

7.5-117 Tanker, M., and Ozkal, N. 1978. Pharmacognostic comparisons on the varieties of Glycyrrhiza glabra growing in Turkey [in Turkish]. Ank. Univ. Ecza. Fac. Mecm. 8{1}: 69-79. CA 94: 12811.

7.5-118 Todorov, V., and Genov, G. 1973. Helminthograph studies of some Bulgarian medicinal plants and other substances [in Bulgarian]. Epidemiol. Mikrobiol. Infekts. Boles. 10{1}: 37-91. HELM AB-B 44: 337.

7.5-119 Tucakov, J., and Mikhajlov, M. 1977. Comparative pharmacognostic studies of garden sage (Salvia officinalis L.) from Pastrovici [in Serbo-Croatian]. Glas. Srp. Akad. Nauk. Umet. Od. Med. Nauka 298{27}: 47-60. CIM 18{6}: 4476.

7.5-120 Valnet, J., Duraffourd, C., Duraffourd, P., and Lapraz, J.C. 1978. The aromagram: new results and an attempt at interpretation of 268 clinical cases [in French]. Plant Med. Phytother. 12: 43-52.

7.5-121 Villar, A., and Paya, M. 1979. Study of the hyperglycemia antagonizing activity of ten popularly used plants [in Spanish]. Arc h. Farmacol. Toxicol. 5: 301-302.

7.5-122 Virus, R.M., and Gebhart, G.F. 1979. Pharmacologic actions of capsaicin: apparent involvement of substance P and serotonin. Life Sci. 25: 1273-1284.

7.5-123 Waldeck, F., and Jennewein, H.M. 1975. Methodological aspects and initial experience with the acetic ulcer in rat. Pages 171-174 in T. Gheorghiu, ed. Experimental ulcer: models, methods and clinical validity. International conference on experimental ulcer, Cologne, 1972. Gerhard Witzstrock, Baden-Baden, Ger. CA 85: 61022.

7.5-124 Wollman, H., Habicht, G., Lau, I., and Schultz, I. 1973. Some properties of the essential oil of Pelargonium roseum cultivated locally [in German]. Pharmazie 28: 56-58. HA 43: 7989.

7.5-125 Woo, W.S., Shin, K.H., and Ryu, K.S. 1980. Studies on crude drugs acting on drug metabolizing enzymes. Part 3. A survey of the action of Korean Angelica plants on drug metabolism. Arch. Pharmacol. Res. 3{2}: 79-84 CA 95: 192270.

7.5-126 Yasuda, I., Seto, T., Okusawa, A., Shimohira, A., and Takubo, E. 1979. The evaluation of crude drugs. V. Quality of licorice roots and its oriental medicinal preparations [in Japanese]. Eisei-Toritsu Eisei Kenkyusho Kenkyu Nempo {30-1}: 93-97. CA 93: 79930.

7.6 Pharmodynamics

7.6-1 Abe, H., Archi, S., and Hayshi, T. 1979. Ultrastructural studies of Moris hepatoma cells reversely transformed by ginsenosides. Experientia 35: 1647-1649.

7.6-2 Abe, H., Odashima, S., Konishi, H., and Arichi, S. 1980. The phenotypic reverse transformation in cultured cancer cells. 1. Characteristics of cells reversely transformed by ginsenosides. Eur. J. Cell Biol. 22{1}: 396 (Abstr.).

7.6-3 Abraham, M., Sarada Devi, N., and Sheela, R. 1979. Inhibiting effect of jasmine flowers on lactation. Indian J. Med. Res. 69: 88-92.

7.6-4 Adzet, T., Iglesias, J., San Martin, R., and Torrent, M.T. 1976. Activity of tincture of Centranthus ruber by the oral route. Planta Med. 29: 305-309.

7.6-5 Ahmad, P., and Muztav, A.J. 1971. Effect of allyl-isothiocyanate on the thyroid glands of rat. Pak. J. Biochem. 4: 72-77. CA 77: 160858.

7.6-6 Alekseeva, L.V., Bykhovtsova, T.L., Bezlepkin, V.G., Motlokh, N.N., and Strizhov, N.I. 1975. Influence of liquid extracts of ginseng and Eleuterococcus roots on some systems of the cell metabolism [in Russian]. Izv. Akad. Nauk SSSR Ser. Biol. 1975{4}: 609-612.

7.6-7 Anand, K.K., Chand, D., and Ray Ghatak, B.J. 1979. Protective effect of alcoholic extract of Indigofera tinctoria Linn. in experimental liver injury. Indian J. Exp. Biol. 17: 685-687.

7.6-8 Anisimov, M.M., Suprunov, N.I., and Prokof'eva, N.G. 1972. The effect of some compounds isolated from plants of the Araliaceae on protein biosynthesis in vitro [in Russian]. Rastit. Resur. 8: 378-380. HA 43: 3961.

7.6-9 Anisimov, M.M., Prokofieva, N.G., Kuznetsova, T.A., and Peretolchin, N.V. 1971. Influence of some triterpene glycosides on protein synthesis in tissue cultures of the bone marrow of rats [in Russian]. Izv. Akad. Nauk SSSR Ser. Biol. 137-140.

7.6-10 Atanasova-Shopova, S., Rusinov, K.S., and Biocheva, I. 1973. Central neurotropic effects of lavender essential oil. II. Effects of linalooel and of terpinenol. Izv. Inst. Fiziol., Bulg. Akad. Nauk. 15: 149-156. CA 81: 53356.

7.6-11 Augusti, K.T., and Mathew, P.T. 1973. Effect of long-term feeding of the aqueous extracts of onion (Allium cepa Linn.) and garlic (Allium sativum Linn.) on normal rats. Indian J. Exp. Biol. 11: 239-241.

7.6-12 Augusti, K.T. 1977. Hypocholesterolaemic effect of garlic Allium sativum Linn. Indian J. Exp. Biol. 15: 489-490.

7.6-13 Avakian, E.V., and Sugimoto, B.R. 1980. Effect of Panax ginseng extract on blood energy substrates during exercise. Fed. Proc. 39: 287 (Abstr.).

7.6-14 Avakian, E.V., Jr., and Evonuk, E. 1979. Effect of Panax-ginseng extract on tissue glycogen and adrenal cholesterol depletion during prolonged exercise. Planta Med. 36: 43-48. CA 91: 151240.

7.6-15 Baas, E.U., Sinterhauf, K., Holtermueller, K.H., Noe, G., and Lommer, D. 1975. The effect of carbenoxolone and deglycyrrhizinated licorice root extract on the plasma cortisol of healthy test persons [in German]. Verh. Dtsch. Ges. Inn. Med. 81: 1239-1241. CA 84: 145011.

7.6-16 Baltassat-Millet, F., and Ferry, S. 1976. Pharmacology of Glycyrrhiza glabra L. liquorice [in French]. Lyon Pharm. 27{1}: 7-13. CA 84: 144362.

7.6-17 Banerjee, A.K. 1976. Effect of aqueous extract of garlic on arterial blood pressure of normotensive and hypertensive rats. Artery (Fulton, Mich.) 2: 369-373. VB 47: 8195.

7.6-18 Bardhan, K.D., Cumberland, D.C., Dixon, R.A., and Holdsworth, C.D. 1978. Clinical trial of deglycyrrhizinised liquorice in gastric ulcer. Gut 19: 779-782. NAR-A 49: 4611.

7.6-19 Bennet, A., Clark-Wibberley, T., Stamford, I.F., and Wright, J.E. 1980. Aspirin-induced gastric mucosal damage in rats: cimetidine and deglycyrrhizinated licorice together give greater protection than low doses of either drug alone. J. Pharm. Pharmacol. 32{2}: 151. CA 93: 19117.

7.6-20 Bird, G.W.G. 1978. The application of lectins to some problems in blood group serology. Rev. Fr. Transfus. Immuno-Hematol. 21{1}: 103-118.

7.6-21 Bodhankar, S.L., Garg, S.K., and Mathur, V.S. 1974. Antifertility screening of plants Part IX. Effect of five indigenous plants on early pregnancy in female albino rats. Indian J. Med. Res. 62: 831-837.

7.6-22 Bordia, A., Bansal, H.C., Arora, S.K., and Singh, S.V. 1975. Effect of the essential oils of garlic and onion on alimentary hyperlipemia. Atherosclerosis 21: 15-19.

7.6-23 Bordia, A., Arora, S.K., Kothari, L.K., Jain, K.C., Rathore, B.S., Rathore, A.S., Dube, M.K., and Bhu, N. 1975. The protective action of essential oil of onion and garlic in cholesterol-fed rabbits. Atherosclerosis 22: 103-109.

7.6-24 Bordia, A., Verma, S.K., Vyas, A.K., Khabya, B.L., Rathore, A.S., Bhu, N., and Bedi, H.K. 1977. Effect of essential oil of onion and garlic on experimental atherosclerosis in rabbits. Atherosclerosis 26: 379-386.

7.6-25 Bordia, A.K., Joshi, H.K., Sanadhya, Y.K., and Bhu, N. 1977. Effect of essential oil of garlic on serum fibrinolytic activity in patients with coronary artery disease. Atherosclerosis 28: 155-159.

7.6-26 Brekhman, I.I., Bierdishev, G.D., and Golotin, V.G. 1971. The influence of Eleuterococcus and ginseng extracts on the activity and the adaptive synthesis of TP-ase in rats [in Russian]. Izv. Akad. Nauk SSSR Ser. Biol. 1971: 31-37.

7.6-27 Buck, S.H., Galligan, J.J., Miller, M.S., Peterson, A.M., and Burks, T.F. 1980. Intestinal stimulation and selective mesenteric artery vasoconstriction by capsaicin in dogs. Dig. Dis. Sci. 25: 727 (Abstr.).

7.6-28 Bykhovtseva, T.L., and Dzadzijeva, M.F. 1973. Influence of the liquid extract of ginseng roots on some indices of fat metabolism [in Russian]. Izv. Akad. Nauk SSSR Ser. Biol. 442-443.

7.6-29 Chandhoke, N., and Ghatak, B.J. 1975. Pharmacological investigations of angelicin--a tranquillosedative and anticonvulsant agent. Indian J. Med. Res. 63{6}: 833-841. CIM 17{2}: 1801.

7.6-30 Chang, M.-W., Tasaka, H., Kuwabara, M., Watanabe, T., and Matsuo, Y. 1979. Effects of Panax ginseng extracts on the growth of Mycobacterium tuberculosis H-37RV. Hiroshima J. Med. Sci. 28: 115-118. CIM 21{3}: 1834.

7.6-31 Cha, S., and Hwang, W.I. 1975. A cytotoxic compound from Panax ginseng Fed. Proc. 34: 806 (Abstr.).

7.6-32 Chin, H.W. 1975. Effect of ginseng on the patterns of open-field behavior in mice [in Korean]. Soul Vitae Chapchi 15{3}: 147-152. CA 84: 144947.

7.6-33 Choi, S.N., and Kim, C. 1973. Influence of Panax ginseng upon splenic DNA cycle in mice [in Korean]. Kalullik Taehak Uihakpu Nonmunjip 25: 143-151.

7.6-34 Chow, S.Y., Chen, S.M., and Yang, C.M. 1976. Pharmacological studies on Chinese herb medicines. III. Analgesic effect of 27 Chinese herb medicines [in Chinese]. T'ai-wan I Hsueh Hui Tsa Chih 75: 349-357. CIM 18{3}: 1831.

7.6-35 Chow, S.Y., Chen, S.M., and Yang, C.M. 1977. Pharmacological studies on Chinese herbs. {4} Effect of 40 Chinese drugs on arterial blood pressure [in Chinese]. T'ai-wan I Hsueh Hui Tsa Chih 76: 47-53. CIM 18{3}: 1831.

7.6-36 Chow, S.Y., Chen, S.M., and Yang, J.C. 1977. Pharmacological studies on Chinese herbs. {5} Antipyretic effects of 12 Chinese herbs [in Chinese]. T'ai-wan I Hsueh Hui Tsa Chih 76: 338-343. CIM 18{3}: 1831.

7.6-37 Chow, S.Y., Liu, K.C., and Chen, S.M. 1976. Protection effects of glycyrrhetic acid derivatives on the exogenous gastric ulcer in rats [in Chinese]. Chung-Hua I Hsueh Tsa Chih (Taipei) 23{4}: 217-223. CA 86: 177203

7.6-38 Chu, C., and Han, C. 1975. Effect of ginseng saponin on liver mitochondrial tricarboxylic acid cycle [in Korean]. Hanguk Saenghwa Hakhoe Chi 8: 238 (Abstr.).

7.6-39 Clifford, D.H., Lee, D.C., Kim, C.Y., and Lee, M.O. 1979. Effects of the third (aqeous) extract of ginseng on the cardiovascular dynamics of dogs during halothane anesthesia. Comp. Med. East West 6: 253-259. CIM 21{3}: 1896.

7.6-40 Das, P.N., and Thakuria, B.N. 1974. Anthelmintic effect of garlic (Allium sativum) against Ascaridia galli. Vetcol 14: 47-52. HELM AB-A 46: 5018.

7.6-41 Dei, S., Das, B.N., and Devi, I. 1976. Cholinomimetic effect of Foeniculum vulgare. Indian J. Pharm. 38: 165 (Abstr.).

7.6-42 Del Castillo, J., Anderson, M., and Rubottom, G.M. 1975. Marijuana, absinthe and the central nervous system. Nature (London) 253: 365-366.

7.6-43 Desai, H.G., Venugopalan, K., and Antia, F.P. 1973. Effect of red chilli powder on DNA content of gastric aspirates. Gut 14: 974-976. NAR 45: 3327.

7.6-44 Dittmann, J. 1973. Effect of extracts from Solidago virgaurea on the metabolism of rabbit brain slices. Planta Med. 24: 329-336.

7.6-45 Drozdov, D.D. 1975. Use of aminazine with valerian in hypertensive disease [in Russian]. Vrach Delo 1975{1}: 48-50. CIM 16{8}: 6750.

7.6-46 Dumnova, A.G. 1971. Treatment of primary arterial hypertension in children and adolescents. Pediatriya (Moscow) 50: 79-81.

7.6-47 Edgar, W.M. 1978. Reduction in enamel dissolution by licorice and glycyrrhizinic acid. J. Dent. Res. 57{1}: 59-64. CA 89: 141063.

7.6-48 El-Mahdy, S.A., Ali, H.I., Helmi, R., and Moustafa, M. 1973. Studies on the effect of licorice on the circulation. J. Egypt. Med. Ass. 55{11/12}: 925-933. CA 81: 130938.

7.6-49 Engqvist, A., Feilitzen, F. Von, Pyk, E., and Reichard, H. 1973. Double-blind trial of deglycyrrhizinated liquorice in gastric ulcer. Gut 14: 711-715. NAR 44: 6686.

7.6-50 Epstein, M.T., Espiner, E.A., Donald, R.A., Hughes, H., Cowles, R.J., and Lun, S. 1978. Licorice raises urinary cortisol in man. J. Clin. Endocrinol. Metab. 47: 397-400. NAR-A 49: 6112.

7.6-51 Eui, S., Kim, B.Y., Paik, T.H., and Joo, C.N. 1978. The effect of ginseng on alcohol metabolism. A histochemical study of alcohol fed rat liver. Hanguk Saenghwa Hakhoe Chi 11{1}: 1-15. CA 91: 84768.

7.6-52 Forster, H.B., Niklas, H., and Lutz, S. 1980. Antispasmodic effects of some medicinal plants. Planta Med. 40: 309-319.

7.6-53 Fromtling, R.A., and Bulmer, G.S. 1978. In vitro effect of aqueous extract of garlic (Allium sativum) on the growth and viability of Cryptococcus neoformans. Mycologia 70: 397-405.

7.6-54 Fulder, S.J. 1977. The growth of cultured human fibroblasts treated with hydrocortisone and extracts of the medicinal plant Panax ginseng. Exp. Gerontol. 12: 125-131.

7.6-55 Furnadzhiev, G., Vutov, M., and Lambev, I. 1976. A contribution to the study of the antiinflammatory effect of furin-m [in Bulgarian]. Stomatologiya (Sofia) 58: 37-40. CA 85: 13897.

7.6-56 Gaion, R.M., Dorigo, P., Prosdocimi, M., and Fassina, G. 1976. Influence of tetrahydropapaveroline on adipose tissue metabolism in comparison with that of noradrenaline theophylline and papaverine. Pharmacol. Res. Commun. 8: 525-538.

7.6-57 Gershbein, L.L. 1977. Regeneration of rat liver in the presence of essential oils aand their components. Food Cosmet. Toxicol. 15: 173-181

7.6-58 Goulart, E.G., Jourdan, M.C., Brazil, R.P., Brazil, B.G., Cosendey, A.E., Bar, M., Carmo, E.C. do, and Gilbert, B. 1976. Environmental prophylaxis of hookworm and stronglyoidiasis using plant extracts [in Portuguese]. Rev. Soc. Bras. Med. Trop. 10: 195-203. HELM AB-B 50: 5069.

7.6-59 Goutam, M.P., Jain, P.C., and Singh, K.V. 1980. Activity of some essential oils against dermatophytes. Indian Drugs 17{9}: 269-270. CA 93: 89359.

7.6-60 Grochulski, A., and Borkowski, B. 1972. Influence of chamomile oil on experimental glomerulonephritis in rabbits [in German]. Planta Med. 21: 289-292. CIM 13{7}: 8196.

7.6-61 Gupta, O.P., Singh, B., and Atal, C.K. 1977. Pharmacological investigations of Withania somnifera (Ashwagandha) as an adaptogen. Indian J. Pharm. 39: 163 (Abstr.).

7.6-62 Gupta, S., Agarwal, S.S., Epstein, L.B., Fernandes, G., and Good, R.A. 1980. Panax-A new mitogen and interferon inducer. Clin. Res. 28: 504A (Abstr.).

7.6-63 Habermehl, G. 1977. Pharmaceutical aspects of low molecular venoms from amphibia and echinoderms. Toxicon 15: 269 (Abstr.).

7.6-64 Hakanson, R., Liedberg, G., Oscarson, J., Rehfeld, J.F., and Stadil, F. 1973. Effect of deglycyrrhizinized liquorice on gastric acid secretion, histidine decarboxylase activity and serum gastrin level in the rat. Experientia 29: 570-571.

7.6-65 Han, B.H., Lee, E.B., Yoon, U.C., and Woo, L.K. 1976. Metabolism of dammarane glycosides of Korean ginseng. (I). Absorption and excretion of Panax saponin A [in Korean]. Hanguk Saenghwa Hakhoe Chi 9{1}: 21-27. CA 85: 186438.

7.6-66 Hart, B.L. 1974. The catnip response. Feline Pract. 4{6}: 8, 12. AGRICOLA.

7.6-67 Hatch, R.C. 1972. Effects of drugs on catnip (Nepeta cataria)-induced pleasure behavior in cats. Am. J. Vet. Res. 33: 143-155

7.6-68 Hiaia, S., Yokoyama, H., Oura, H., and Yano, S. 1979. Stimulation of pituitary-adrenocortical system ginseng saponin. Endocrinol. Jpn. 26{6}: 661-665. CA 92: 174456.

7.6-69 Hiai, S., and Oura, H. 1973. Essay on biochemical and physiological action of Panax ginseng roots. Tampakushitsu Kakusan Koso 18{5}: 13-24. AGRICOLA.

7.6-70 Hiai, S., Yokoyama, H., Oura, H., and Yano, S. 1979. Stimulation of pituitary adreno-cortical system by ginseng, Panax ginseng, saponin. Endocrinol. Jpn. 26: 661-666.

7.6-71 Hiai, S., Sasaki, S., and Oura, H. 1979. Effect of ginseng saponin on rat adrenal cyclic AMP. Planta Med. 37: 15-19.

7.6-72 Hiai, S., Oura, H., Tsukada, K., and Hirai, Y. 1971. Stimulating effect of Panax ginseng extract on RNA polymerase activity in rat liver nuclei. Chem. Pharm. Bull. (Tokyo) 19: 1656-1663.

7.6-73 Hill, J.O., Pavlik, E.J., Smith, G.L., III, Burghardt, G.M., and Coulson, P.B. 1976. Species-characteristic reponses to catnip by undomesticated felids. J. Chem. Ecol. 2: 239-253.

7.6-74 Holm, E., Kowollik, H., Reinecke, A., von Henning, G.E., Behne, F., and Scherer, H.D. 1980. Comparative neurophysiologic studies using valtratum/isovaltratum and valerian extract in cats [in German]. Med. Welt. 31{26}: 982-990. CIM 22{4}: 2909.

7.6-75 Hong, B.J., Kim, C.I., Kim, U.H., and Rhee, Y.C. 1976. Effect of feeding ginseng crude saponin on body weight gain and reproductive function of chicken [in Korean]. Hanguk Ch'uksan Hakhoe Chi 18: 355-361. CA 86: 70589.

7.6-76 Hong, S.A., and Park, C.W. 1976. Effect of ginseng on the acquisition of conditioned avoidance response in rats [in Korean]. Taehan Yakrihak Chapchi 12{1}: 63-67.

7.6-77 Hwang, W.I. 1976. A study on the cytotoxic activity of extract of Panax ginseng root against some cancer cells. Korean J. Biochem. 8: 1-6.

7.6-78 Hwang, W.I. 1978. A study on the cytotoxic activity of Panax ginseng extract against some cancer cells in vitro and in vivo. Korean J. Biochem. 10: 58 (Abstr.).

7.6-79 Iijima, M., Higashi, T., Sanada, S., and Shoji, J. 1976. Effect of ginseng saponins on nuclear ribonucleic acid (RNA) metabolism. I. RNA synthesis in rats treated with ginsenosides. Chem. Pharm. Bull. (Tokyo) 24: 2400-2405.

7.6-80 Ikehara, M., Shibata, Y., Higashi, T., Sanada, S., and Shoji, J. 1978. Effect of ginseng saponins on cholesterol metabolism. III. Effect of ginsenoside-Rb1 on cholesterol synthesis in rats fed on high-fat diet. Chem. Pharm. Bull. (Tokyo) 26: 2844-2349.

7.6-81 Isaac, O., and Thiemer, K. 1975. Biochemical studies on chamomile components. III. In vitro studies of the antipeptic activity of (-)-alpha-bisabolol [in German]. Arzneim.-Forsch. 25: 1352-1354. CA 83: 172515.

7.6-82 Isaac, O. 1979. Pharmacological investigations with compounds of chamomile. i. on the pharmacology of (-)-alpha-bisabolol and bisabolol oxides (Review) [in German]. Planta Med. 35: 118-124. CIM 20{13}: 10018

7.6-83 Ishii, Y., and Sugawara, N. 1973. Pharmacological studies of Fm 100, an antiulcer fraction of licorice root [in Japanese]. Oyo Yakuri 7{6}: 871-880. CA 80: 66677.

7.6-84 Ishii, Y., and Fujii, Y. 1974. Effects of several mild antiulcer agents on pylorus ligated rats (Shay rats) [in Japanese]. Nippon Yakurigaku Zasshi 70{6}: 863-869. CA 83: 188283.

7.6-85 Jain, R.C. 1975. Onion and garlic in experimental atherosclerosis. Lancet 1975{7918}: 1240.

7.6-86 Jain, R.C., and Konar, D.B. 1976. Garlic oil in experimental atherosclerosis. Lancet 1976{7965}: 918.

7.6-87 Jain, R.C. 1977. Effect of garlic on serium lipids, coagulability and fibrinolytic activity of blood. Am. J. Clin. Nutr. 30: 1380-1381.

7.6-88 Jain, R.C., and Vyas, C.R. 1975. Garlic in alloxan-induced diabetic rabbits. Am. J. Clin. Nutr. 28: 684-685.

7.6-89 Jain, R.C., and Konar, D.B. 1976. Onion and garlic in experimental cholesterol atherosclerosis in rabbits 2. Effect on serum proteins and development of atherosclerosis. Artery (Fulton, Mich.) 2: 531-539. NAR-A 48: 1289.

7.6-90 Jain, R.C., and Konar, D.B. 1978. Effect of garlic oil in experimental cholesterol atherosclerosis. Atherosclerosis 29: 125-129.

7.6-91 Jain, R.C., and Vyas, C.R. 1977. Onion and garlic in atheroslerotic heart disease. Medikon 6{5}: 12-14, 17-18. CA 87: 116795.

7.6-92 Jakovlev, V., Isaac, O., Thiemer, K., and Kunde, R. 1979. Pharmacological investigations with compounds of chamomile. ii. new investigations on the antiphlogistic effects of (-)-alpha-bisabolol and bisbolol oxides [in German]. Planta Med. 35: 125-140. CIM 20{13}: 10018.

7.6-93 Johnson, L.P., Girma, B., Zenabe, H.L., Wondemu, M., and Worku, S. 1978. The effect of red pepper on gastric secretion in Ethiopia. Ethiop. Med. J. 16: 111-113. NAR-A 49: 5802.

7.6-94 Joo, C.N., and Han, J.H. 1976. Biochemical studies on ginseng saponins. (V). The effect of ginseng saponins on chicken's hepatic mitochondrial succinate dehydrogenase, malate dehydrogenase and alpha-ketoglutarate dehydrogenase [in Korean]. Hanguk Saenghwa Hakhoe Chi 9{1}: 43-51. CA 85: 171619.

7.6-95 Joo, C.N., Oh, J.W., and No, S.J. 1976. Biochemical studies on ginseng saponins. (VI). The effect of ginseng saponins on L-glutamate dehydrogenase and transaminase [in Korean]. Hanguk Saenghwa Hakhoe Chi 9{1}: 53-59. CA 85: 171260.

7.6-96 Joo, C.N., and Han, J.H. 1976. Biochemical studies on ginseng saponins. VII. The effect of ginseng saponins on pig cardiac isocitrate dehydrogenase. Hanguk Saenghwa Hakhoe Chi 9{4}: 237-245. CA 88: 100340.

7.6-97 Joo, C.N., Yoo, H.S., Lee, S.J., and Lee, H.S. 1973. Biochemical studies on ginseng saponins. I. Effect of ginseng saponin on several dehydrogenases in vitro [in Korean]. Han'guk Saenghwahakhoe Chi 6: 177-184. CA 81: 45819.

7.6-98 Kagramanov, K.M., Kulieva, Z.T., Eferdieva, L.G., and Seidova, K.G. 1977. The effect of the essential oils of some thyme growing in Azerbaidzhan on cardiovascular activity and respiration [in Russian]. Azerb. Med. Zh. 54{5}: 49-51. CA 87: 145903.

7.6-99 Kang, H.S., Cho, Y.H., and Shinn, S.J. 1975. Effect of dietary Panax ginseng on the ethanol metabolism in rat. Korean J. Biochem. 7: 78 (Abstr.).

7.6-100 Kang, H.S., Cho, Y.H., and Shinn, S.J. 1975. Effect of dietary ginseng on certain components of blood and hepatic vitamin A in alcoholic rat. Hanguk Saenghwa Hakhoe Chi 8: 236-237 (Abstr.).

7.6-101 Kang, J.H., and Hwang, W.I. 1980. The changes on some components in rat treated with carbon tetrachloride and Panax ginseng. Korean J. Biochem. 12{2}: 98-99 (Abstr.).

7.6-102 Kapoor, M., Garg, S.K., and Mathur, V.S. 1974. Antiovulatory activity of five indigenous plants in rabbits. Indian J. Med. Res. 62: 1225-1227.

7.6-103 Kim, B.H., and Kim, C. 1973. Influence of Panax ginseng upon DNA cycle of colonic epithelium in mice [in Korean]. Kalullik Taehak Uihakpu Nonmunjip 25: 105-113.

7.6-104 Kim, C., Choi, H., Kim, C.C., Kim, J.K., Kim, M.S., Ahn, B.T., and Park, H.J. 1976. Influence of ginseng on mating behavior of male rats. Am. J. Chin. Med. 4: 163-168.

7.6-105 Kim, E.S. 1974. The effect on serum cholesterol levels of experimental rats of vit. E, garlic and different levels of proteins in their diet [in Korean]. Hanguk Yongyang Hakhoe Chi 7{1}: 45-50. NAR 45: 7128.

7.6-106 Kim, H.J., Lee, J.W., and Kang, D.H. 1977. Effect of Panax ginseng alcohol extract on activities of sodium ion-potassium ion activated ATPase and calcium ion activated ATPase in several biological membranes [in Korean]. Yonse Uidae Nonmunjip 10{1}: 116-124. CA 90: 80809.

7.6-107 Kim, H.S., Choi, H.J., and Lee, H.J. 1980. Effects [of] diets containing some red ginseng extracts in rats. Hanguk Sikp'un Kwahakhoe Chi 12: 103-108.

7.6-108 Kim, S.J., and Soh, C.T. 1975. Effect of Panax ginseng on productivity of antibodies in the host [in Korean]. Kisaengch'ung Hak Chopchi 13: 179 (Abstr.). HELM AB-A 45: 6238.

7.6-109 Kim, T., Yi, H., and Kim, H. 1975. A biochemical study on the active ingredients of Panax ginseng. (X) Effects of ginseng extracts on serum L-isocitrate dehydrogenase and L-malate dehydrogenase activities. Korean Biochem. J. 8: 242-243.

7.6-110 Kim, T.B., Lee, H.S., and Kim, H. 1975. Biochemical studies on the active principles in Panax ginseng. X. The effect of ginseng extracts on the activity of human serum L-isocitrate and L-malate dehydrogenase [in Korean]. Hanguk Saenghwa Hakhoe Chi 8{3}: 155-160. CA 85: 74127.

7.6-111 Kim, T.B., Lee, H.S., Lee, K.B., and Kim, H. 1975. Biochemical studies on the active principles in Panax ginseng. IX. The effect of ginseng extracts on the activity of L-glutamate dehydrogenase [in Korean]. Hanguk Saenghwa Hakhoe Chi 8: 149-153.

7.6-112 Kim, T.B., Lee, H.S., Lee, K.B., and Bang, J.S. 1975. Biochemical studies on the active principles in Panax ginseng. VII. The effect of ginseng extracts on the aerobic metabolism of Bakers' yeast [in Korean]. Hanguk Saenghwa Hakhoe Chi 8: 141-148.

7.6-113 Kim, T.B., Lee, H.S., and Lee, K.B. 1977. Biochemical studies on the active principles in Panax ginseng. XI. The effect of ginseng extracts on the activity of L-glutamate hydrogenase. 2. [in Korean]. Hanguk Saenghwa Hakhoe Chi 10{3}: 219-223. CA 90: 50491.

7.6-114 Kim, T.B., Lee, H.S., and Lee, K.B. 1977. Biochemical studies on the active principles in Panax ginseng. XII. The effect of ginseng extracts on the activity of human serum glutamate-oxaloacetate transaminase and glutamate-pyruvate transaminase [in Korean]. Hanguk Saenghwa Hakhoe Chi 10{4}: 253-257. CA 90: 50492.

7.6-115 Klement, A.A., Fedorova, Z.D., Volkova, S.D., Egorova, L.V., Shul'kina, N.M., Shitikova, A.S., Khrolova, P.V., and Papayan, L.P. 1978. Use of Origanum infusion in patients with hemophilia in dental extractions [in Russian]. Probl. Gematol. Pereliv. Krovi. 23: 25-28.

7.6-116 Kourteva, B.T., Manolova, V.R., and Mitova, D.K. 1977. TN-polyagglutinability of red blood cells and acquired A-like specificity. Transfusion (Philadelphia) 17: 272-276. CIM 13{4}: 2958.

7.6-117 Kowal, T., and Krupinska, A. 1979. Antibacterial activity of essential oil from Thymus pulegioides L. [in Polish]. Herba Pol. 25{4}: 303-310.

7.6-118 Ko, T-S., and Chun, S.Y. 1978. Effect of Korean ginseng on cell surface membranes in relation to its various pharmacological effects. Hanguk Saenghwa Hakhoe Chi 11{1}: 17-28. CA 91: 68357.

7.6-119 Kritchevsky, D. 1975. Effect of garlic oil on experimental atheroslerosis in rabbits. Artery (Leonidas, Mich.) 1{4}: 319-323. CA 84: 41631.

7.6-120 Kulieva, Z.T., and Seidova, K.G. 1976. An experimental study of the effect of essential oils of various species of thyme on the state of the visual organ. Azerb. Med. Zh. 3: 59-60.

7.6-121 Kulieva, Z.T., Kagramanov, K.M., Seidova, K.G., and Efendieva, L.G. 1977. The effect of essential oils of some thyme species growing in Azerbaijan on the electroencephalogram, electroretinogram and opthalmotonus [in Russian]. Dokl. Akad. Nauk Az. SSR 33{7}: 71-75.

7.6-122 Kun-jen, W., Ya-li, Z., Dai-shu, W., Meng-lian, Z., Shong-niang, M., Yau, G., Giu-zhi, L., Ya-yan, L., and Rui-yu, L. 1980. In vivo effect of Chinese medical compositions and adenosine 3'5' on Erlich ascites tumor cells and changes of the levels of cAMP and 3'5' cAMP-PDE activity in these tumor cells. Eur. J. Cell Biol. 22{1}: 548 (Abstr.).

7.6-123 Kurechi, T., Kikugawa, K., and Nishizawa, A. 1980. Transformation of hemoglobin A into methemoglobin by sesamol. Life Sci. 26: 1675-1681.

7.6-124 Kushwah, A., Amma, M.K.P., and Sareen, K.N. 1978. Effect of some anti-inflammatory agents on lysosomal and testicular hyaluronidases. Indian J. Exp. Biol. 16{2}: 222-224. CA 89: 344.

7.6-125 Lahiri, K. 1979. Recent approach to peptic ulcer therapy. East. Pharm. 22{260}: 103-106. CA 92: 103889.

7.6-126 Lee, D.C., Kim, C.Y., Lee, M.O., and Clifford, D.H. 1979. Effects of the second (ethanol) extract of ginseng on the cardiovascular dynamics of dogs during halothane aneshesia. Comp. Med. East West 6: 247-252. CIM 21{4}: 3221.

7.6-127 Lee, J. 1978. A decrease in ammonia content in portal blood of rabbits administered with ginseng powder. Jpn. J. Vet. Sci. 40: 727-731. AGRICOLA.

7.6-128 Lee, J.-H., Woun, B.-R. 1980. Electron microscopic study of fat-storing cells in the liver of rabbits given ginseng [in Korean]. Taehan Su'ui Hakhoe Chi 20: 143-150. IV 49: 80779.

7.6-129 Lee, K.-D., and Huemer, R.P. 1971. Antitumoral activity of Panax ginseng extracts. Jpn. J. Pharmacol. 21: 299-302. CIM 12: 1855.

7.6-130 Lee, Y.-M., Saito, H., and Kasuya, Y. 1979. Potentiation of the NGF-mediated neurite outgrowth by ginsenoside Rb-1 in organ cultures of chick embryonic ganglia. Jpn. J. Pharmacol. 29 (Suppl.): 191P.

7.6-131 Lim, J.K., Kim, M.S., and Chung, M.H. 1976. The effect of ginseng saponin on the activity of hepatic microsomal drug metabolizing enzyme system in mouse [in Korean]. Soul Uitae Chapchi 17{1}: 56-61. CA 85: 87285.

7.6-132 Liu, C.K. 1974. Immunosuppressive effects of platycodi radix and glycyrhizae radix [in Chinese]. Memoirs of the College of Agriculture National Taiwan University 15{1}: 52-55. IV 43: 9852.

7.6-133 Lysenko, L.V., and Sila, V.I. 1972. Antiallergic effect of peppermint oil azulene [in Ukrainian]. Farm. Zh. (Kiev) 27{6}: 65-68. CA 78: 79771.

7.6-134 Malinow, M.R., McLaughlin, P., and Stafford, C. 1978. Prevention of hypercholesterolemia in monkeys (Macaca fascicularis) by digitonin. Am. J. Clin. Nutr. 31: 814-818.

7.6-135 Mansurov, M.M. 1972. Effect of the stachydrine on the blood clotting system [in Russian]. Farmakol. Toksikol. (Moscow) 35{6}: 715-717. CA 78: 52725.

7.6-136 Mathew, P.T., and Augusti, K.T. 1973. Effect of allicin (diallyl disulfide oxide) on alloxan diabeties. I. Hypoglycemic action and enhancement of serum insulin effect and glycogen synthesis. Indian J. Biochem. Biophys. 10{3}: 209-212. CA 81: 45370.

7.6-137 Matuashvili, S.I., Tsilosani, G.A., Lomsadze, R.N., and Berozashvili, T.I. 1973. Action of volatile phytoncides of Satureja (C. Koch) Boiss on Dendroctonus micans Kugel [in Russian]. Biol. Zh. Arm. 26: 88-90.

7.6-138 Mueller-Limroth, W., and Ehrenstein, W. 1977. Experimental studies of the effects of Seda-Kneipp on the sleep of sleep disturbed subjects: implications for the treatment of different sleep disturbances [in German]. Med. Klin. 72{25}: 1119-1125. CIM 18{5}: 3458.

7.6-139 Musim, M.N., Khadzhai, Ia.I., and Litvinenko, V.I. 1976. Anti-inflammatory activity of a polyphenolic preparation obtained from peppermint [in Ukrainian]. Farm. Zh. 1976{2}: 76-79. CIM 17{7}: 10551.

7.6-140 Nagasawa, T., Oura, H., Hiai, S., and Nishinaga, K. 1977. Effect of ginseng extract on ribonucleic acid and protein synthesis in rat kidney. Chem. Pharm. Bull. (Tokyo) 25: 1665-1670.

7.6-141 Nagasawa, T., Shibutani, S., Oura, H. 1979. Effects of kampo-prescriptions on rat serum constituents after the administration. I. [in Japanese]. Yakugaku Zasshi 92{12}: 1642-1650. CA 90: 132819.

7.6-142 Narayana, K., Subba Rao, H., and Setty, D.R.L. 1975. Successful treatment of demodectic mange with a combination of Erythrina indica, Ocimum basilicum and Leucas aspera. Indian Vet. J. 52: 494-495. RAE-B 64: 3510.

7.6-143 Nickel, S.L., and Staba, E.J. 1977. Suitability of antidigoxin anti-serum for digoxin in plant extracts. Lloydia 40: 230-235.

7.6-144 Niiho, Y., Takayanagi, I., and Takagi, K. 1977. Effects of a combined stomachic and its ingredients on rabbit stomach motility in situ. Jpn. J. Pharmacol. 27{1}: 177-179. CA 87: 15851.

7.6-145 Nopanitaya, W., and Nye, S.W. 1974. Duodenal mucosal response to the pungent principle of hot pepper (Capsaicin) in the rat: light and electron microscopic study. Toxicology and Applied Pharmacology 30: 149-161.

7.6-146 Nopanitaya, W. 1973. Long term effects of capsaicin on fat absorption and the growth of the rat. Growth 37: 269-279.

7.6-147 Nopanitaya, W., and Nye, S.W. 1971. Effects of the pungent principle of red pepper (capsaicin) on the duodenal epithelial absorptive cells of the rat. Fed. Proc. 30: 543 (Abstr.).

7.6-148 Odashima, S., Nakayabu, Y., Honjo, N., Abe, H., and Arichi, S. 1979. Induction of phenotypic reverse transformation by ginsenosides in cultured Morris hepatoma cells. Eur. J. Cancer 15: 885-892.

7.6-149 Oh, S.K., and Hong, S.A. 1976. The effects of long-term administration of Panax ginseng and Acanthopanax on the metabolism of hens [in Korean]. Taehan Yakrihak Chapchi 12: 103-114.

7.6-150 Olah, L.V., and Bozzola, J.J. 1972. Effect of digitonin on cellular division, IV. Interrelation between nucleus and phragmoplast. Cytologia 37: 365-376. PBA 46: 5918.

7.6-151 Olah, L.V., and Hanzely, L. 1973. Effect of digitonin on cellular division. V. The distribution of microtubules. Cytologia 38: 55-72. PBA 46: 6736.

7.6-152 Oscarson, J., Hakanson, R., and Liedberg, G. 1974. Effect of secretagogues and antisecretagogues on histidine decarboxylase activity in rat gastric mucosa. Agents Actions 4{3}: 183-184. CA 81: 131164.

7.6-153 Oura, H., Hiai, S., Nabetani, S., Nakagawa, H., Kurata, Y., and Sasaki, N. 1975. Effect of ginseng extract on endoplasmic reticulum and ribosome. Planta Med. 28: 76-88.

7.6-154 Oura, H., Nakashima, S., Tsukada, K., and Ohta, Y. 1972. Effect

of Radix ginseng extract on serum protein synthesis. Chem. Pharm.
Bull. (Tokyo) 20: 980-986.

7.6-155 Oura, H., Hiai, S., Nakashima, S., and Tsukada, K. 1971.
Stimulating effect of the roots of Panax ginseng C.A. Meyer on the
incorporation of labeled precursors into rat liver RNA. Chem. Pharm.
Bull. (Tokyo) 19: 453-459.

7.6-156 Oura, H., Tsukada, K., and Nakagawa, H. 1972. Effect of Radix
ginseng extract on cytoplasmic polysome in rat liver. Chem. Pharm.
Bull. (Tokyo) 20: 219-225.

7.6-157 Oura, H., Nakashima, S., Kumagai, A., and Takata, M. 1973.
Immunosuppressive effects of licorice root extracts [in Japanese].
Taisha 10: 651-658. CA 81: 76115.

7.6-158 Park, J.J., Koo, J.H., and Joo, C.N. 1978. Biochemical studies
on ginseng saponins. XII. The effect of ginseng saponin on human serum
glutamate-pyruvate transaminase in vitro. Hanguk Saenghwa Hakhoe Chi
11{3}: 161-168. CA 92: 52808.

7.6-159 Petkov, V., and Manolov, P. 1978. Pharmacological studies on
substances of plant origin with coronary dilatating and antiarrhythmic
action. Comp. Med. East West 6: 123-130. CIM 20{5}: 3694.

7.6-160 Petkov, V., Koushev, V., and Panova, Y. 1977. Accelerated
ethanol elimination under the effect of ginseng (experiments on rats).
Acta Physiol. Pharmacol. Bulg. 3{1}: 46-50.

7.6-161 Petkov, V.D., Manolov, P.N., Marekov, N.L., Popov, S.S., and
Khandzhieva, N.B. 1974. Pharmacological studies on a mixture of
valepotriates isolated from Valeriana officinalis. Dokl. Bolg. Akad.
Nauk 27: 1007-1010. CA 82: 51636.

7.6-162 Petrovski, Sv.N. 1971. Effect of some essential oils on cholera
and paracholera vibrios [in Bulgarian]. Suvrem. Med. 22{6}: 51-56. CA
76: 54759.

7.6-163 Pompei, R., Flore, O., Marccialis, M.A., Pani, A., and Loddo, B.
1979. Glycyrrhizic acid inhibits virus growth and inactivates virus
particles. Nature (London) 281: 689-690.

7.6-164 Pompei, R. 1979. Activity of Glycyrrhiza glabra extracts and
glycyrrhizic acid on virus growth and infectivity [in Italian]. Riv.
Farmacol. Ter. 10{3}: 281-284. CA 92: 104967.

7.6-165 Popov, I.M., and Goldwag, W.J. 1973. A review of the properties
and clinical effects of ginseng. Am. J. Chin. Med. 1: 263-270 CIM
15{3}: 2549.

7.6-166 Provincial Institute of Traditional Chinese Medicine, Coronary
Care Unit. 1974. Effect of shengmaisan on cardiac arrest due to acute
hemorrhage [in Chinese]. Chin. Med. J. (Peking) 1974{4}: 249-250.
English translation 1974{4}: 68.

7.6-167 Racz-Kotilla, E., Racz, G., and Solomon, A. 1974. The action of
Taraxacum officinale extracts on the body weight and diuresis of
laboratory animals. Planta Med. 26: 212-217.

7.6-168 Ramadan, F.M., El-Zanfaly, H.T., Alian, A.M., and El-Wakeil, F.A. 1972. Antibacterial effects of some essential oils. II. Semisolid agar phase. Chem. Mikrobiol. Technol. Lebensm. 1: 96-102. CA 77: 122533.

7.6-169 Rao, B.G.V.N., and Joseph, P.L. 1971. Activity of some essential oils toward phytopathogenic fungi [in German]. Riechst., Aromen, Koerperpflegem. 21: 405-406, 408, 410. CA 76: 81621.

7.6-170 Rees, W.D.W., Evans, B.K., and Rhodes, J. 1979. Treating irritable bowel syndrome with peppermint oil. Br. Med. J. 2{6194}: 835-836.

7.6-171 Rees, W.D.W., Rhodes, J., Wright, J.E., Stamford, I.F., and Bennett, A. 1979. Effect of deglycyrrhizinated liquorice on gastric mucosal damage by aspirin. Scand. J. Gastroenterol. 14{5}: 605-607. CA 92: 584.

7.6-172 Rovesti, P. 1971. Therapeutic effect of the aroma of lavender essence [in Italian]. Riv. Ital. Essenze Profumi Piante Off. Aromi Saponi Cosmet. Aerosol 53: 251-269. AGRICOLA.

7.6-173 Rovesti, P., and Gallefosse, H.M. 1973. Pharmacology and tolerance of lavender essence [in French]. Labo-Pharma-Probl. Tech. 21{223}: 32-38. CA 79: 132756.

7.6-174 Rovesti, P., and Gattefosse, H.M. 1974. Tolerance and pharmacology of lavender essential oil [in French]. Riv. Ital. Essenze, Profumi, Piante Off., Aromi, Saponi, Cosmet., Aerosol 56{2}: 71-77. CA 81: 85835.

7.6-175 Rybal'chenko, A.S., Fursa, N.S., and Litvinenko, V.I. 1980. Recent data of chemical-pharmacological studies on valerian [in Ukrainian]. Farm. Zh. (Kiev) 1980{4}: 28-33. CA 93: 225554.

7.6-176 Sainani, G.S., Desai, D.B., and More, K.N. 1976. Onion, garlic, and atherosclerosis. Lancet 1976{7985}: 575-576.

7.6-177 Saito, H., Yoshida, Y., and Takagi, K. 1974. Effect of Panax ginseng root on exhaustive exercise in mice. Jpn. J. Pharmacol. 24: 119-127. CIM 15{3}: 2705.

7.6-178 Saito, H., Tsuchiya, M., Naka, S., and Takagi, K. 1977. Effects of Panax ginseng root on conditioned avoidance response in rats. Jpn. J. Pharmacol. 27: 509-516. CIM 19{6}: 3892.

7.6-179 Saito, H., Tsuchiya, M., Naka, S., and Takagi, K. 1979. Effects of Panax ginseng root on acquisition of sound discrimination behavior in rats. Jpn. J. Pharmacol. 29: 319-324. CA 91: 102095.

7.6-180 Saito, H., and Takagi, K. 1973. Effect of ginsenoside Rg-1, a saponin of Panax ginseng root on learning and memory in rats. Jap. J. Pharmacol. 23 (Suppl.): 65 (Abstr.).

7.6-181 Saito, H., Lee, Y.-M., and Kasuya, Y. 1977. Potentiation of the NGF-mediated nerve fiber outgrowth by saponins in organ cultures of chicken embryonic dorsal root and sympathetic ganglia. Jpn. J. Pharmacol. 27 (Suppl.): 114P (Abstr.).

7.6-182 Sakakibara, K., Shibata, Y., Higashi, T., Janada, S., and Shoji, J. 1975. Effect of ginseng saponins on cholesterol metabolism. I. The level and the synthesis of serum and liver cholesterol in rats treated with ginsenosides. Chem. Pharm. Bull. 23: 1009-1016.

7.6-183 Sambaiah, K., and Satyanarayana, M.N. 1980. Hypocholesterolemic effect of red pepper and capsaicin. Indian J. Exp. Biol. 18: 898-899. NAR-A 51: 6454.

7.6-184 Scherbauer, I. 1977. Efficacy of Rutacholan (extracts from several plants plus vitamin B) for the treatment of metabolic disorders in dogs and cats [in German]. Tierarztl. Umsch. 32: 588-590. IV 46: 11689.

7.6-185 Sethi, O.P., Desai, D.G., Bhatia, O.S., and Darasari, H.R. 1977. An investigation on the effect of xanthotoxol (XT) - A crystalline substance obtained from plant origin. Indian J. Physiol. Pharmacol. 21: 247-248 (Abstr.).

7.6-186 Sethi, O.P., and Nair, K. 1979. Xanthotoxol (XT) - A potent 5-HT[Hydroxytryptamine] antagnonist. Indian J. Physiol. Pharmacol. 23: 142-143.

7.6-187 Seth, G., Kokate, C.K., and Varma, K.C. 1976. Effect of essential oil of Cymbopogon citratus Stapf. on central nervous system. Indian J. Exp. Biol. 14: 370-371.

7.6-188 Sharma, K.K., Sharma, A.L., Dwivedi, K.K., and Sharma, P.K. 1976. Effect of raw and boiled garlic on blood cholesterol in butter fat lipaemia. Indian J. Nutr. Diet. 13: 7-10. NAR-A 47: 7030.

7.6-189 Sherry, C.J., and Hunter, P.S. 1979. The effect of an ethanol extract of catnip (Nepeta cataria) on the behavior of the young chick. Experientia 35: 237-238.

7.6-190 Shibata, Y., and Higashi, T. 1978. Stimulated incorporation of carbon-14 amino acids and carbon-14 fatty acids in various tissues of ginsenoside-treated rats of Panax ginseng-treated rats. Chem. Pharm. Bull. (Tokyo) 26: 3832-3835. CA 90: 115338.

7.6-191 Shibata, Y., Nozaki, T., Higashi, T., Sanada, S., and Shoji, J. 1976. Stimulation of serum protein synthesis in ginsenoside treated rat. Chem. Pharm. Bull. (Tokyo) 24: 2818-2824.

7.6-192 Shihata, I.M., Hassan, A.B., and Mayah, G.Y. 1978. Pharmacological effects of Lawsonia inermis leaves (el-henna). Egypt. J. Vet. Sci. 15: 31-35. IV 49: 83171.

7.6-193 Shin, H.S., Kim, H.S., Chi, H.J., and Kim, J.W. 1979. A study of the effects of the root components of Angelica koreana Max. on voluntary activity in mice [in Korean]. Soul Taehakkyo Saengyak Yonguso Opjukjip 18: 99-103. CA 94: 222.

7.6-194 Silvera, R.S., and Muehlemann, H.R. 1973. Interdental plaque pH and sweet root chewing. Helv. Odontol. Acta 17{2}: 96-98. HA 80: 46386.

7.6-195 Sobocky, L., Cernacek, J., and Wagnerova, M. 1971. Effect of Valman (complex of 3 alkaloids from Valeriana root) on the vegetative tonus and excitability in vegetative dysfunction of neurotic origin [in Slovak]. Cesk. Neurol. 34: 240-244. CIM 13{3}: 2867.

7.6-196 Sourgens, H., Winterhoff, H., Gumbinger, H.G., Mendes, R., and Kemper, F.H. 1980. Antihormonal effects of plant extracts of hypophyseal hormones in the rat. Acta Endocrinol. (Copenhagen) Suppl. 234: 49 (Abstr.).

7.6-197 Stets, V.R., Linenko, V.I., Koreshchuk, K.E., and Korniyevsky, Y.I. 1975. On the pharmacology of Valeriana stolonifera Czern. [in Ukrainian]. Farm. Zh. (Kiev) 30: 51-54.

7.6-198 Suh, C.M., and Kim, C. 1973. Influence of Korean Panax ginseng upon sexual behavior of male rats [in Korean]. Kalullik Taehak Uihakpu Nonmunjip 25: 303-307.

7.6-199 Suzuki, Y., Nagamatsu, T., and Ito, M. 1979. Pharmacological studies on experimental nephritic rats..PP 7. Changes of serum complement levels in modified Masugi nephritic rats and effects of drugs on it. Oyo Yakuri 18{3}: 461-467. CA 92: 140576.

7.6-200 Szalontai, M., Verzar-Petri, G., and Florian, E. 1976. Data on the antifungal effect of the biologically active components of Matricaria chamomilla L. [in Hungarian]. Acta Pharm. Hung. 46: 232-247. CA 86: 101395.

7.6-201 Takagi, K., Saito, H., and Tsuchiya, M. 1974. Effect of Panax ginseng root on spontaneous movement and exercise in mice. Jpn. J. Pharmacol. 24: 41-48. CIM 15{3}: 2970.

7.6-202 Takagi, K., Saito, H., and Nabata, H. 1972. Pharmacological studies of Panax ginseng root: Estimation of pharmacological actions of Panax ginseng root. Jpn. J. Pharmacol. 22{2}: 245-249. CIM 14{3}: 2826.

7.6-203 Takagi, K., Okabe, S., Kawashima, K., and Hirai, T. 1971. Therapeutic effect of FM100, a fraction of licorice root on acetic acid ulcer in rats. Jpn. J. Pharmacol. 21{6}: 832-833. CA 77: 544.

7.6-204 Takagi, K., and Fukao, T. 1971. Effects of some drugs on capillary permeability in the anaphylaxis of the mouse. Jpn. J. Pharmacol. 21{4}: 455-465. CA 76: 81279.

7.6-205 Takamura, K., Kakimoto, M., Kawaguchi, M., and Iwasaki, T. 1973. Pharmacological studies on the constituents of crude drugs and plants. I. Pharmacological actions of Valeriana officinalis var. latifolia [in Japanese]. Yakugaku Zasshi 93: 599-606. CA 79: 61706.

7.6-206 Tanaka, S., Kano, Y., Tabata, M., and Konoshima, M. 1971. Effects of "Toki" (Angelica acutiloba Kitagawa) extracts on writhing and capillary permeability in mice (analgesic and antiinflammatory effects) [in Japanese]. Yakugaku Zasshi 91: 1098-1104.

7.6-207 Tanaka, S., Ikeshiro, Y., Tabata, M., and Konoshima, M. 1977. Anti-nociceptive substances from the roots of Angelica acutiloba. Arzneim.-Forsch. 27{11}: 2039-2045. CIM 19{6}: 4287.

7.6-208 Ueno, N., Suzuki, H., and Okabe, S. 1977. Effects of meta-magnesium aluminosilicate, extracts of licorice root and their

combination on various experimental gastric ulcers [in Japanese]. Oyo
Yakuri 13{4}: 519-523. CA 88: 83588.

7.6-209 Van Den Broucke, C.O., and Lemli, J.A. 1980. Antispasmodic
activity of Origanum compactum. Planta Med. 38: 317-331.

7.6-210 Vasilenko, Y.K., Oganesyan, E.T., Lisevitskaya, L.I.,
Aleksanyan, R.A., Shinkarenko, A.L., Simonyan, A.V., Golovina, T.N.,
Milenina, N.G., Frolova, L.M., Asatryan, T.O., and Tokarenko, L.F.
1978. Isolation and physiological activity of triterpene compounds
found in residues of industrial thyme extraction. Pharm. Chem. J.
(Engl. Transl.) 12: 1165-1169. Translation of Khim.-Farm. Zh. 12{9}:
61-65, 1978.

7.6-211 Vichkanova, S.A., and Goryunova, L.V. 1971. Antiviral activity
of some saponins [in Russian]. Tr. Vses. Nauch.-Issled. Inst. Tek.
Rast. 14: 204-212 CA 78: 155107.

7.6-212 Wagner, H., and Sprinkmeyer, L. 1973. Pharmacological effect of
balm spirit [in German]. Dtsch. Apoth.-Ztg. 113: 1159-1166. CA 80:
244.

7.6-213 Wagner, H., and Jurcic, K. 1979. On the spasmolytic activity of
Valeriana extracts [in German]. Planta Med. 37{1}: 34-86. CIM 21{6}:
4873.

7.6-214 Wang, Y.-T., Su, C.-Y., Ko, W.-C., Hsu, S.-Y., and Tsai, C.-S.
1972. Antiulcer biopharmaceuticals produced in Taiwan [in Chinese].
T'ai-Wan I Hsueh Hui Tsa Chih 71{4}: 256-259. CA 77: 96972.

7.6-215 Wang, Y.L., Hsu, S.G., and Fan, S.F. 1979. Electrophysiological
studies on the antiarrhythmic effect of the water extract of valerian
[in Chinese]. Chung Hua Hsin Hsueh Kuan Ping Tsa Chih 7{4}: 275-282.
CIM 22{6}: 5296.

7.6-216 Yamaura, T., Baba, Y., Numoto, T., and Tosaka, K. 1977. Effects
of pipethanate hydrochloride, meta-magnesium aluminosilicate, extract
of licorice root and their combination on various experimental ulcers
[in Japanese]. Oyo Yakuri 14{3}: 347-355. CA 88: 32101.

7.6-217 Yen, K.-Y. 1973. Chinese crude drugs in Taiwan. 1. Glycyrrhizae
radix. 5. Pharmacology of Kan-ts'ao (Glycyrrhizae radix) [in Chinese].
Pei I Hsueh Pao 1973{5}: 23-25. CA 81: 85799.

7.6-218 Yokozawa, T., Kitahara, N., Okuda, S., and Oura, H. 1979. Effect
of Panax ginseng principle on pyruvate kinase activity in rat liver
diet. Chem. Pharm. Bull. (Tokyo) 27: 419-423.

7.6-219 Yokozawa, T., Kanai, K., Takefuji, M., and Oura, H. 1976. Effect
of ginseng saponin on liver glycogen content. Chem. Pharm. Bull.
(Tokyo) 24: 3202-3204.

7.6-220 Yokozawa, T., Seno, H., and Oura, H. 1975. Effect of ginseng
extract on lipid and sugar metabolism. I. Metabolic correlation
between liver and adipose tissue in rats. Chem. Pharm. Bull. (Tokyo)
23: 3095-3100.

7.6-221 Yokozawa, T., and Oura, H. 1976. Effect of ginseng extract on
lipid and sugar metabolism. II. Nutritional states in rats. Chem.
Pharm. Bull. (Tokyo) 24: 987-990.

7.6-222 Yoneda, F., Furusawa, Y., Kurosawa, Y., and Chuman, I. 1974. Trypsin inhibitory action of glycyrrhetinic acid derivatives [in Japanese]. Nippon Nogei Kagaku Kaishi 48: 147-149.

7.6-223 Yoon, H.S., and Kim, C. 1971. Influence of Panax ginseng upon rectal temperature of rats exposed to cold [in Korean]. Kalullik Taehak Uihakpu Nonmunjip 21: 25-35.

7.6-224 Zelepukha, S.I., Derbentseva, N.A., and Pavlenko, L.V. 1978. Effect of drugs on the antibacterial activity of salvin [in Russian]. Mikrobiol. Zh. (Kiev) 40: 641-644.

7.7 Ethno-Pharmacology

7.7-1 Anonymous. 1973. Back to folk medicine: the pros and cons. Medical World News 14{45}: 65-66, 68.

7.7-2 Anonymous. 1975. The many-faceted mint. Givaudian Flavor. 2: 5-6, 8. AGRICOLA.

7.7-3 Arenas, P., and Moreno Azorero, R. 1977. Plants of common use in Paraguayan folk medicine for regulating fertility. Econ. Bot. 31{3}: 298-301.

7.7-4 Bardanyan, S.A. 1978. Phytotherapy for bronchial asthma in medieval Armenian medicine. Ter. Arkh. 50: 133-136.

7.7-5 Cecy, C., and Yassumoto, Y. 1973. Observations about popular phytotherapy in the surroundings of Curitiba. III. [in Spanish]. Trib Farm (Curitiba) 41: 14-22.

7.7-6 Chang, C.-L., Huang, C.-Y., Yao, Y.-C., Ch'ien, W.-Y., Ch'in, H.-K., and Chao, P.-N. 1974. 200 Cases of psoriasis treated with traditional Chinese medicine [in Chinese]. Chin. Med. J. (Peking) 1974{4}: 205-207 [English abstract 1974{4}: 57].

7.7-7 Dukes, M.N.G. 1980. Remedies used in non-orthodox medicine. Side Eff. Drugs Annu. 4: 341-347.

7.7-8 Duquenois, P. 1972. Salvia officinalis L., an ancient panacea and condiment of choice [in French]. Q.J. Crude Drug Res. 12: 1841-1849.

7.7-9 Duquenois, P. 1973. On gathering medicinal plants, of yore, to their cultivation today [in French]. Plant. Med. Phytother. 7: 267-278.

7.7-10 El'yashevich, D.G., and Choliy, R. 1972. On some kinds of treatment in popular medicine in Lvov region [in Ukrainian]. Farm. Zh. (Kiev) 27: 78-79

7.7-11 Gibson, M.R. 1978. Glycyrrhiza in old and new perspectives. Lloydia 41: 348-354.

7.7-12 Goldring, D. 1973. Withering's account of foxglove and its use in children. Pediatrics 51: 549-550.

7.7-13 Goldstein, B. 1975. Ginseng: its history, dispersion, and folk tradition. Am. J. Chinese Med. 3: 223-234. CIM 17{2}: 2407.

7.7-14 Grinevich, M.A., Brekhman, I.I., and Kim, B.K. 1977. The investigation of complex recipes of oriental medicine and of their components with the use of an electronic computer. 5. The medicinal plants used most frequently in the traditional medicine of Japan and China [in Russian]. Rastit. Resur. 13: 261-267.

7.7-15 Hartwell, J.L. 1971. Plants used against cancer. Table of contents. Lloydia 34: 427-438.

7.7-16 Hartwell, J.L. 1971. Plants used against cancer. A survey. Lloydia 34: 386-425.

7.7-17 Hartwell, J.L. 1971. Plants used against cancer. A survey. Lloydia 34: 310-361.

7.7-18 Hartwell, J.L. 1971. Plants used against cancer. A survey. Lloydia 34: 204-255.

7.7-19 Hartwell, J.L. 1971. Plants used against cancer. A survey. Lloydia 34: 103-160.

7.7-20 Jones, D.B. 1973. The great dittany of Crete - Then and now. Herbarist 39: 13-18.

7.7-21 Kerharo, J., and Paccioni, J.P. 1974. An old Senegalese remedy fallen into oblivion: the remedy of Joal Garab Diafan. J. Agric. Trop. Bot. Appl. 21{10-12}: 345-350.

7.7-22 Lal, S.D., and Lata, K. 1980. Plants used by the Bhat community for regulating fertility. Econ. Bot. 34{3}: 273-275.

7.7-23 Leifertova, I. 1973. Let us pay attention to creeping thyme [in Czech]. Nase Liecive Rastliny 10: 132-133. PBA 46: 3038.

7.7-24 Mandl, A. 1977. Examination of common medicinal tea mixtures 1. Cough and chest teas. Mikrokosmos 66: 309-314.

7.7-25 Mitsuhashi, H. 1976. Medicinal plants of the Ainu. Econ. Bot. 30: 209-217.

7.7-26 Nikolaeva, V.G. 1979. Certain plants used in folk medicine in the USSR for symptoms of bronchial asthma [in Russian]. Rastit. Resur. 15: 298-307. HA 50: 508.

7.7-27 Nikolaeva, V.T. 1977. Plants used by some nations of the USSR for diseases of the liver and biliary ducts [in Russian]. Rastit. Resur. 13: 396-403.

7.7-28 Nikolaeva, V.G., and Khokhlova, A.A. 1978. Antimicrobial effect of some plants used as antiseptics in folk medicine in the USSR [in Russian]. Rastit. Resur. 14: 234-237.

7.7-29 Said, H.M. 1979. Avicenna: hearts and flowers. Unesco Courier 32{7}: 4-6.

7.7-30 Sayed, M.D. 1980. Traditional medicine in health care. J. Ethnopharmacol. 2{1}: 19-22. CIM 22{6}: 1200.

7.7-31 Singh, M.P., Malla, S.B., Rajbhandari, S.B., and Manandhar, A. 1979. Medicinal plants of Nepal- retrospects and prospects. Econ. Bot. 33{2}: 185-189.

7.7-32 Smith, K.H. 1971. Some Argentine herbs. Herbarist 37: 35-38.

7.7-33 Stimson, W.R. 1971. Ethnobotanical notes from Puerto Rico. Lloydia 34: 165-167.

7.7-34 Szecsody, V. 1975. Rosemary and peppermint are household remedies. Org. Gard. Farming 22{12}: 122-124.

7.7-35 Takagi, K. 1973. Pharmacological studies of some oriental medicines [in Korean]. Yakhak Hoe Chi 17: 1-8. CA 82: 261.

7.7-36 Wen, W. 1979. China: a new medicine born of tradition. Unesco Courier 32{7}: 25-27.

7.7-37 Wilson, R.T., and Mariam, W.G. 1979. Medicine and magic in central Tigre: a contribution to the ethnobotany of the Ethiopian plateau. Econ. Bot. 33{1}: 29-34.

7.7-38 Wohlfart, R. 1974. Radix valerianae. History of an old medical drug, its active substances and their importance in modern therapy [in German]. Z. Allgemeinmed. 50{17}: 787-800. CIM 16{8}: 6750.

7.7-39 Wong, W. 1976. Some folk medicinal plants from Trinidad. Econ. Bot. 30{2}: 103-142.

7.8 Toxicology

7.8-1 Addo, H.A., Johnson, B.E., and Frain-Bell, W. 1980. A study of the relationship between contact allergic sensitivity and persistent light reaction. Br. J. Dermatol. 103{18}: 20-21.

7.8-2 Anonymous. 1978. Herbal teas often nice, sometimes noxious. Nutrition & M.D. 4{14}: 4. AGRICOLA.

7.8-3 Anonymous. 1979. Ginseng abuse syndrome. Nutr. & M.D. 5{9}: 4. AGRICOLA.

7.8-4 Anonymous. 1977. Licorice, Glycyrrhiza and ammoniated glycyrrhizin. Proposed affirmation of GRAS status with special limitations as direct human food ingredients. Fed. Regist. 42{148}: 39117-39120. CA 87: 182738.

7.8-5 Asakawa, Y., Benezra, C., Ducombs, G., Foussereau, J., Muller, J.C., and Ourisson, G. 1974. Cross-sensitization between Frullania and Laurus nobilis: the allergen laurel. Arch. Dermatol. 110: 957. CIM 15{2}: 80.

7.8-6 Barna, J. 1976. Liver function of animals fed with irradiated ground paprika. Acta Physiol. Acad. Sci. Hung. 47: 150 (Abstr.).

7.8-7 Baumann, J.C. 1975. Effect of chelidonium, absinth and Carduus marianus on the bile and pancreatic secretion in liver diseases [in German]. Med. Monatsschr. 29: 173-180. CIM 17{7}: 10551.

7.8-8 Bazhenova, E.D., Ashrafova, R.A., Aliev, Kh.V., and Tulyaganov, P.D. 1977. Effect of arsumin and absynthin on the regeneration of experimentally-induced stomach ulcer [in Russian]. Med. Zh. Uzb. 1977{7}: 47-52. CA 87: 193909.

7.8-9 Bitter, J. 1977. Uncommon case of dysphagia caused by a foreign body. Cesk. Gastroenterol. VYZ 31: 47-48.

7.8-10 Blachley, J.D., and Knochel, J.P. 1980. Tobacco chewer's hypokalemia: licorice revisited. New Engl. J. Med. 302: 784-785.

7.8-11 Brun, R. 1976. Photosensitization of the skin and fluorescence spectra [in French]. Dermatologica 152: 295-303. CA 86: 366.

7.8-12 Buchanan, R.L. 1978. Toxicity of spices containing methylenedioxybenzene derivatives: a review. J. Fd. Safety 1: 275-293.

7.8-13 Chudapongse, P., and Janthasoot, W. 1976. Studies on the effect of capsaicin on metabolic reactions of isolated rat liver mitochondria. Toxicol. Appl. Pharmacol. 37: 263-270. CA 85: 17281.

7.8-14 Corrigall, W., Moody, R.R., and Forbes, J.C. 1978. Foxglove (Digitalis purpurea) poisoning in farmed red deer (Cervus elaphus). Vet. Rec. 102: 119-122.

7.8-15 Cronin, E. 1979. Immediate-type hypersensitivity to henna. Contact Dermatitis 5: 198-199. CIM 20{3}: 1841.

7.8-16 Culvenor, C.C.J., Clarke, M., Edgar, J.A., Frahn, J.L., Jago, M.V., Peterson, J.E., and Smith, L.W. 1980. Structure and toxicity of the alkaloids of Russian comfrey (Symphytum X uplandicum Nyman), a medicinal herb and item of human diet. Experientia 36: 377-379.

7.8-17 Dickstein, E.S., and Kunkel, F.W. 1980. Foxglove Digitalis purpurea tea poisoning. Am. J. Med. 69: 167-169.

7.8-18 Dorange, J.L., Delaforge, M., Janiaud, P., and Padieu, P. 1977. Mutogenicity of the metabolites of the epoxide-diol pathway of safrole and its analogs. Study on Salmonella typhmurium [in French]. C.R. Seances Soc. Biol. Ses. Fil. 171: 1041-1048. CIM 19{9}: 6548.

7.8-19 Drinkwater, N.R., Miller, E.C., Miller, J.A., and Pitot, H.C. 1976. Hepatocarcinogenicity of estragole (1-allyl-4-methoxybenzene) and 1'-hydroxyestragole in the mouse and mutagenicity of 1'acetoxyestragole in bacteria. J. Natl. Cancer Inst. 57: 1323-1331. CIM 13{3}: 2062.

7.8-20 Epstein, M.T., Espiner, E.A., Donald, R.A., and Hughes, H. 1977. Effect of eating liquorice on the renin-angiotensin aldosterone axis in normal subjects. Br. Med. J. 1{6059}: 488-490.

7.8-21 Ermekova, R.K. 1978. Formation of allergic reactivity to wormwood pollen in combined sensitization to pollen and bacteria. Bull. Exp. Biol. Med. (Engl. Transl.) 86: 1082-1084. Translation of Byull. Eksp. Biol. Med. 86{8}: 221-223.

7.8-22 Farber, T.M., Ritter, D.L., Weinberger, M.A., Bierbower, G., Tanner, J.T., Friedmann, M.H., Carter, C.J., Earl, F.L., and Van Loon, E.J. 1976. The toxicity of brominated sesame oil and brominated soybean oil in miniature swine. Toxicology 5: 319-335. CA 84: 178365.

7.8-23 Farnsworth, N.R., and Morgan, B.M. 1972. Herb drinks: camomile tea. J. Am. Med. Assoc. 221: 410. CIM 13{2}: 1384.

7.8-24 Glinsukon, T., Stitmunnaithum, V., Toskulkao, C., Burawanuti, T., and Tangkrisanavinont, V. 1980. Acute toxicity of capsaicin in several animal species. Toxicon 18: 215-220. CA 93: 38912.

7.8-25 Goodpasture, C.E., and Arrighi, F.E. 1976. Effects of food seasonings on the cell cycle and chromosome morphology of mammalian cells in vitro with special reference to turmeric. Food Cosmet. Toxicol. 14: 9-14.

7.8-26 Gubankova, S.G. 1977. Study of allergenic pollen grains with the aid of a scanning electron microscope. Dokl. Bot. Sci. (Engl. Transl.) 232-234: 3-6. Translation of Dokl. Nauk SSR 232: 1222-1224, 1976.

7.8-27 Halbach, H., Harris, L.S., Knoll, J., Ogunremi, O.O., Garem, O., Schuster, C.R., Willette, R., Yanagita, T., Ling, G.M., Braenden, O., Chrusciel, T.L., Kha n, I., and Jasinski, D.R. 1980. The dependence potential of thebaine report of a WHO Advisory Group. Bull. Narc. 32: 45-54.

7.8-28 Hinsch, O.M. 1976. The goldenrod plant poisonous for sheep [in Spanish]. Din. Rural. 8{89}: 66-70. AGRICOLA.

7.8-29 Hirono, I., Mori, H., and Haga, M. 1978. Carcinogenic activity of Symphytum officinale. J. Natl. Cancer Inst. 61: 865-869.

7.8-30 Hirono, I., Haga, M., Fujii, M., Matsuura, S., Matsubara, N., Nakayama, M., Furuya, T., Hikichi, M., Takanashi, H., Uchida, E., Hosaka, S., and Ueno, I. 1979. Induction of hepatic tumors in rats by senkirkine and symphytine. J. Natl. Cancer Inst. 63: 469-472.

7.8-31 Hirono, I., Mori, H., Haga, M., Fujii, M., Yamada, K., Hirata, Y., Takanashi, H., Uchida, E., Hosaka, S., et al. 1979. Edible plants containing carcinogenic pyrrolizidine alkaloids in Japan. Pages 79-87 in E.C. Miller et al., eds. Proceedings of the international symposium of the Princess Takamatsu Cancer Research Fund 9. Naturally occurring carcinogens-mutagens and modulators of carcinogenesis, Tokyo, Japan, 1979. CA 93: 180283.

7.8-32 Jamwal, K.S., and C.K. Atal. 1977. Photosensitizing agents. Pages 101-111 in C.K. Atal and B.M. Kapur, eds. Cultivation & utilization of medicinal and aromatic plants. Regional Research Laboratory, Jammu-Tawi, India.

7.8-33 Komiyama, K., Kawakubo, Y., Fukushima, T., Sugimoto, K., Takeshima, H., Ko, Y., Sato, T., Okamoto, M., Umezawa, I., and Nishiyama, Y. 1977. Acute and subacute toxicity test on the extract from Glycyrrhiza [in Japanese]. Oyo Yukuri 14{4}: 535-548. CA 88: 69205.

7.8-34 Krauskopf, J., and Adamkova, D. 1975. Three cases of simultaneous contact hypersensitivity to wild chamomile (Matricaria chamomilla) and Frullania tamarisci [in Czech]. Cesk. Dermatol. 50: 299-302. CIM 17{7}: 10551.

7.8-35 Krishnaswamy, M.A., Nair, K.K.S., Patel, J.D., and Parthasarathy, N. 1975. Preliminary observations on the survival of Salmonella in curry, sambar, coriander and red-chilly powders. J. Food Sci. Technol. 12{4}: 195-196. FSTA 8{8}: 8T373.

7.8-36 Lampe, K.F. 1974. Systemic plant poisoning in children. Pediatrics 54: 347-351.

7.8-37 Lee, K.-H., Huang, E.-S., Piantadosi, C., Pagano, J.S., and Geissman, T.A. 1971. Cytotoxicity of sesquiterpene lactones. Cancer Res. 31: 1649-1654.

7.8-38 Lewis, E.A., and Aderoju, E.A. 1978. Factors in the aetiology of chronic duodenal ulcer in Ibadan. Trop. Geogr. Med. 30{1}: 75-79. NAR-A 49: 7335.

7.8-39 Meneghini, C.L., and Angelini, G. 1979. Contact allergy to antirheumatic drugs. Contact Dermatitis 5: 197-198. CIM 20{5}: 3311.

7.8-40 Mitchell, J.C. 1975. Contact allergy from plants. Recent Advances in Phytochemistry 9: 119-138.

7.8-41 Monsereenusorn, Y. 1980. In vitro intestinal absorption of capsaicin. Toxicol. Appl. Pharmacol. 53: 134-139. CA 93: 38690.

7.8-42 Monsereenusorn, Y. 1979. Effect of capsaicin on intestinal glucose metabolism in vitro. Toxicol. Lett. 3: 279-283. CA 91: 50504.

7.8-43 Monsereenusorn, Y., and Glinsukon, T. 1979. The inhibitory effect of capsaicin on intestinal glucose absorption in vitro. II. Effect of capsaicin upon intestinal (sodium-potassium ion)-dependent ATPase activities. Toxicol. Lett. 4: 399-406. CA 92: 39973.

7.8-44 Monsereenusorn, Y., and Glinsukon, T. 1979. The inhibitory effect of capsaicin on intestinal glucose absorption in vitro. I. Effects of capsaicin on the serosal side of everted intestinal sacs. Toxicol. Lett. 4: 393-397. CA 92: 39972.

7.8-45 Morton, J.F. 1975. Is there a safer tea?. Morris Arboretum Bull. 26: 24-30.

7.8-46 Mourad, G., Gallay, P., Oules, R., Mimran, A., and Mion, C. 1978. Hypokalemic myopathy with rhabdomyolysis and acute renal failure in the course of chronic licorice ingestion. Kidney Int. 14: 543 (Abstr.). NAR-A 49: 8705.

7.8-47 Nagao, M., Sugimura, T., and Matsushima, T. 1978. Environmental mutagens and carcinogens. Annu. Rev. Genet. 12: 117-159.

7.8-48 Panconesi, E., Sertoli, A., Fabbri, P., Giorgini, S., and Spallanzani, P. 1980. Anaphylactic shock from mustard after ingestion of pizza. Contact Dermatitis 6: 294-295. CIM 21{5}: 3849.

7.8-49 Pascual, H.C., Reddy, P.M., Nagaya, H., Lee, S.K., Lauridsen, J., Gupta, S., and Jerome, D. 1977. Agreement between radioallergosorbent test and skin test. Ann. Allergy 39: 325-327.

7.8-50 Rao, G.S.C.R. 1972. Common poisonous plants found in India and the effect of their toxins on the health of animals. J. Remount Veterinary Corps 11{2}: 9-19. VB 43: 5784.

7.8-51 Rockwell, P., and Raw, I. 1979. A mutagenic screening of various herbs, spices, and food additives. Nutr. Cancer 1{4}: 10-15.

7.8-52 Schimmer, O., Beck, R., and Dietz, U. 1980. Phototoxicity and photomutagenicity of furocoumarins and furocoumarin drugs in Chlamydomonas rheinhardii. Comparison of biological activities as a basis of risk evaluation [in German]. Planta Med. 40{1}: 68-76. CA 94: 798.

7.8-53 Siegel, R.K. 1979. Ginseng abuse syndrome. Problems with the panacea. J. Am. Med. Assoc. 241: 1614-1615.

7.8-54 Siegel, R.K. 1976. Herbal intoxication, psychoactive effects from herbal cigarettes, tea, and capsules. J. Am. Med. Assoc. 236: 473-476.

7.8-55 Solanke, T.F. 1973. The effect of red pepper (Capsicum frutescens) on gastric acid secretion. J. Surg. Res. 15: 385-390.

7.8-56 Steentoft, A. 1973. Fatal Digitalis poisoning. Acta. Pharmacol. Toxicol. 32: 353-357.

7.8-57 Steinmetz, M.D., Tognetti, P., Mourgue, M., Jouglard, J., and Millet, Y. 1980. The toxicity of some commercial essential oils: The essential oil from hyssop and sage [in French]. Plant Med. Phytother. 14: 34-35. Bib. Ag. 45: 61504.

7.8-58 Stransky, L., and Tsankov, N. 1980. Contact dermatitis from parsley (Petroselinum). Contact Dermatitis 6: 233-234. CIM 21{6}: 4557.

7.8-59 Sullivan, J.B., Jr., Rumack, B.H., Thomas, H., Jr., Peterson, R.G., and Bryson, P. 1979. Pennyroyal oil poisoning and hepatotoxicity. J. Am. Med. Assoc. 242: 2873-2874.

7.8-60 Summers, R.S. 1979. Cardiotoxic principle in comfrey [letter]. S. Afr. Med. J. 55{2}: 37. CIM 20{13}: 10017.

7.8-61 Taylor, A.A., and Bartter, F.C. 1977. Hypertension in licorice intoxication, acromegaly, and Cushing's syndrome. Pages 755-767 in J. Genest, E. Koiw, and O. Kuchel, eds. Hypertension: Physiology and treatment. McGraw-Hill, New York, N.Y. CA 88: 35289.

7.8-62 Tsurumi, K., and Fujimura, H. 1975. Change of purgative activity and subacute toxicity by successive administration of cathartic preparation (DK-ext) made from water extract of rhubarb and licorice [in Japanese]. Oyo Yakuri 10{2}: 329-341. CA 88: 115375.

7.8-63 Ueho, N., Suzuki, H., Okabe, S., Tauchi, K., and Igarashi, A. 1978. Effect of meta-magnesium aluminosilicate, extracts of licorice root and their combination on experimental ulcer and toxicity test [in Japanese]. Oyo Yakuri 15{1}: 21-29. CA 89: 562.

7.8-64 Watanabe, C., and Kawada, A. 1977. Exfoliative dermatitis from Chinese herbs (decoction), an example of purely epidermal contact-type hypersensitivity to ingested medicines. J. Dermatol. (Tokyo) 4: 109-114.

7.8-65 Wilson, B.J., Garst, J.E., Linnabary, R.D., and Channell, R.B. 1977. Perilla ketone: a potent lung toxin from the mint plant, Perilla frutescens Britton. Science (Washington, D.C.) 197: 573-574.

7.8-66 Zavarzin, G.M., and Chudnova, I.M. 1971. Determination of the toxicity of lavender oil in an experiment [in Russian]. Vop. Med. Teor. Klin. Prakt. Kurortnogo Lech. 1971{4}: 300-302. CA 79: 101300.

7.8-67 Zimowski, A. 1973. Intoxication of mink with Digitalis purpurea [in Polish]. Med. Weter. 29: 226. Bib.Ag. 37: 85788.

8.0 PERFUMERY

8.1 Perfume Plants

8.1-1 Bhattacharjee, S.K. 1980. Native jasmines of India. Indian Perfum. 24{3}: 126-133. AGRICOLA.

8.1-2 Bisgrove, R. 1979. Jasmine house. Garden (London) 104: 97-100.

8.1-3 Chladek, M., and Stompfova, H. 1975/1976. Quality evaluation of selected Lavandula vera clones [in Czech]. Bulletin, Vyzkumny Ustav Zelinarsky Olomouc 1975/76{19/20}: 73-80. HA 49: 5257.

8.1-4 Chorbadzhiev, S., Ivanov, D., and Vlakhov, R. 1971. Chemical composition of Bulgarian Salvia sclarea (clary sage) oil - sesquiterpene hydrocarbons [in Russian]. Pages 435-437 in P.V. Naumenko et al., eds. Mezhdunarodnyi kongress po eifrnym maslam, 4th, 1968, [Materialy], v. 1. Pishchevaya Promyshlennost', Moscow, USSR. CA 78: 128344.

8.1-5 Esvandzhiya, G.A. 1976. Some valuable essential oil plants from the Sukhumi experimental station [in Russian]. Dokl. TSKhA 224(Pt. 2): 72-77. CA 87: 19016.

8.1-6 Gambee, E.B. 1972. Lavender and thyme. Plants Gard. (New Ser.) 28{1}: 76-78. AGRICOLA.

8.1-7 Gambee, E.B. 1976. A dash of sage. Gard. J. 26: 174-175.

8.1-8 Garlick, B.K. 1977. Quality factors in lavandin. Perfum. Flavor. 2{4}: 25-26. HA 48: 4874.

8.1-9 Garnero, J., Joulain, D., and Burl, P. 1980. Differentiation of the geographic origins of jasmine flower absolutes and some unpublished constituents of jasmine solids and absolutes [in French]. Riv. Ital. Essenze, Profumi, Piante Off., Aromat., Syndets, Saponi, Cosmet., Aerosols 62{1}: 8-18. CA 92: 185710.

8.1-10 Giusti, G. 1971. Italian lavandin. Naarden News 22{230}: 7-9. CA 78: 20106.

8.1-11 Granger, R., Passet, J., and Teulade-Arbousset, J. 1973. Lavandula stoechas, a widespread Labiatae [in French]. Trav. Soc. Pharm. Montpellier 33{3}: 355-360. CA 80: 118214.

8.1-12 Haralenneyavar, S. 1973. Downy jasmine (kakada). Lal-Baugh J. 18{2}: 48-51. AGRICOLA.

8.1-13 Igolen, G. 1971. Lavenders and lavandins. SPC. Soap Perfum. Cosmet. 44: 781-794.

8.1-14 Jarvis, C. 1979. A fragrant crop: lavender farming. Ctry. Life 166{4287}: 718-719. AGRICOLA.

8.1-15 Jones, B. 1975. Jasmine. Soaps, Deterg. Toiletries Rev. 6{5-6}: 25-26. CA 84: 126631.

8.1-16 Makovkina, A.I. 1972. Nepeta transcaucasica, a source of geraniol, citronellol and citral [in Russian]. Pages 97-98 in P.V. Naumenko et al., eds. Mezhdunarodnyi kongress po efirnym maslam, 4th, Tiflis, 1968, [Materialy], v. 2. Pishchevaya Promyshlennost', Moscow, USSR. HA 44: 4209.

8.1-17 Mathieu, R.F. 1976. Natural ingredients in potpourri. Herbarist 43: 36-44.

8.1-18 Modignani, C.L. 1972. Lavender, industrial flower [in Italian]. Rilancio Agric. Vet. Zootec. 4{1}: 24-25. AGRICOLA.

8.1-19 Mukhortova, T.G., and Mashanov, V.I. 1972. Morphological and economic characteristics of lavandin in different districts of the Crimea [in Russian]. Byull. Gos. Nikitsk. Bot. Sada 1972{1}: 27-33. HA 43: 4740.

8.1-20 Nambisan, K.M.P., and Krishnan, B.M. 1980. Gundumalli — the romantic jasmine. Indian Hortic. 24{4}: 23, 25. HA 51: 2821.

8.1-21 Nikolov, N., Bojkov, G., Ivanov, I., Doganova, L., and Tzoutzoulova, A. 1972. Researches on the quality and yield of lavender essence from various regions of Bulgaria [in French]. An. Acad. Bras. Cienc. 44(Suppl.): 247-250.

8.1-22 Paulet, M., and Felisaz, D. 1972. Mountain savory [in French]. Parfums Cosmet. Savons Fr. 2: 20-22. CA 76: 131366.

8.1-23 Polak, E.H. 1973. Recent progress in jasmine research. Cosmet. Perfum. 88{6}: 46-48. CA 79: 118253.

8.1-24 Pomini, L. 1972. The Roman chamomile (Anthemis nobilis L.). Riv. Ital. Essenze Profumi Piante Off. Aromi Saponi Cosmet. Aerosol 54: 627-630.

8.1-25 Rabha, L.C., Baruah, A.K.S., and Bordoloi, D.N. 1979. Search for aroma chemicals of commercial value from plant resources of North East India. Indian Perfum. 23{3-4}: 178-183. CA 93: 79858.

8.1-26 Rao, P.S., Sethi, H., Randhawa, G.S., and Badhwar, R.L. 1977. Aromatic plants of India, Part XVIII. Indian J. Hortic. 34: 323-333.

8.1-27 Sacco, T., and Nano, G.M. 1971. Contribution to the botanic and chemical study of Mentha genus, group arvensis [in Italian]. Riv. Ital. Essenze Profumi Piante Off. Aromi Saponi Cosmet. Aerosol 53: 325-327 AGRICOLA.

8.1-28 Schweisheimer, W. 1974. Jasmin in the perfume industry [in German]. Kosmetika (Zurich) 2{4}: 91-92. CA 86: 47191.

8.1-29 Sobti, S.N., Pushpangadan, P., and Atal, C.K. 1977. Ocimum species as a natural source of thymol. Indian Perfum. 21{1}: 11-14. CA 88: 158272.

8.1-30 Van Brunt, E.R. 1973. Lemon-verbena. Plants Gard. (New Ser.) 28{4}: 56-57.

8.1-31 Yankulov, I., and Stoeva, T. 1980. Mint with a new scent [in Bulgarian]. Priroda (Sofia) 29{3}: 85-86. CA 94: 61747.

8.1-32 Zobenko, L.P., Nazarenko, L.G., and Romanenko, L.G. 1979. Varieties of the essential oil-bearing rose, lavender, and clary sage and promising selection of the plants. Int. Congr. Essent. Oils, [Pap.], 7th, 1977. 7: 112-113. CA 92: 64510.

8.2 Compounds of Aromatic Value

8.2-1 Allured, S.E. 1975. R.J. Reynolds' essential oils. Cosmet. Perfum. 90{4}: 69-70, 72.

8.2-2 Asaturova, V.N., and Chkhenkeli, B.N. 1971. Essential oil of large-blossom jasmine [in Russian]. Tr. Gruz. Nauch.-Issled. Pishch. Prom. 5: 191-192. CA 78: 47642.

8.2-3 Bedoukian, P.Z. 1980. Perfumery and flavor materials. Perfum. Flavor. 5{2}: 1, 3-6, 8-10, 13-16, 18-22. CA 93: 191872.

8.2-4 Bedoukian, P.Z. 1976. The jasmine odor in perfumery. Perfum. Flavor. 1{1}: 17-18, 35.

8.2-5 Belik, M.A., Skopintseva, I.S., and Chipiga, A.P. 1978. Accumulation and preservation of esters in lavender and sage oils [in Russian]. Maslo-Zhir. Prom-st. 1978{8}: 23-25. CA 89: 152567.

8.2-6 Bhagat, S.D., Upadhyay, D.N., and Singh, K.K. 1975. Oil of bergamot mint (Mentha citrata Ehrh.). Indian Perfum. 18(pt. 2): 31-33. CA 87: 106638.

8.2-7 Bukhbinder, A.A. 1974. The content of essential oil in leaves of geranium grown on the alluvial soils of the Kolkhida lowland [in Russian]. Subtrop. Kul't. 1974{1}: 92-94. HA 45: 12256.

8.2-8 Bukhbinder, A.A. 1973. Qualitative indices of essential oil of geranium growth in the Kolkhida lowland [in Russian]. Subtrop. Kul't. 1973{4}: 89-91. HA 44: 4212.

8.2-9 Cafaggi, S., Panaro, A., Ranise, A., Gastaldo, P., and Profumo, P. 1977. Studies on the composition of essential oils obtained from hybrid lavender cultivated in Liguria [in Italian]. Riv. Ital. Essenze Profumi Piante Off. Aromi Saponi Cosmet. Aerosol 58: 505-512. HA 48: 10817.

8.2-10 Carro de de la Torre, P., and Retamar, J.A. 1972. Essential oils of the Tucuman Province. Essential oil of Pelargonium hortorum Bailey (Malvon) [in Spanish]. An. Acad. Bras. Cienc. 44(Suppl.): 168-169.

8.2-11 Cheng, Y., and Chao, Y. 1977. Absolute of siu-eng flower (Jasminum odoratissimum L.). Perfum. Flavor. 2{5}: 81 (Abstr.). HA 48: 5802.

8.2-12 Cheng, Y.-S. 1979. Chemical composition of Jasminum grandiflorum L. and Siu-eng flowers [in Chinese]. K'o Hsueh Fa Chan Yueh K'an 7{2}: 140-146. CA 90: 200320.

8.2-13 Conan, J.-Y., Dadant, R., and Michellon, R. 1976. The so-called "Bourbon geranium" essential oils [in French]. Riv. Ital. Essenze Profumi Piante Off. Aromi Saponi Cosmet. Aerosol 58: 556-560. HA 47: 11744.

8.2-14 Conan, J.Y. 1977. Defining a Bourbon standard for some Reunion essential oils [in French]. Riv. Ital. Essenze Profumi 59: 544-549. CA 88: 41537.

8.2-15 Damjanic, A., and Grzunov, K. 1976. Study of the composition and contents of decanted and extracted rosemary oil from water distillates [in Serbo-Croatian]. Arch. Farm. 26: 1-6. CA 85: 99019.

8.2-16 De Pascual Teresa, J., Sanchez Bellido, I., Carames Varela, L., Ruiz Gallego, B., Urones, J.G., and Cuadrado, A.S. 1976. Components of Lavandula penduculata Cav. I. Essential oil [in Spanish]. An. Quim. 72: 545-547. CA 85: 166479.

8.2-17 Gogiya, V.T., and Ivanova, L.N. 1973. Investigation of the composition of the essential oils of Pelargonium capitatum AIT. and Pelargonium radula L'herit. Appl. Biochem. Microbiol. (Engl. Transl.) Translation of Prikl. Biokhim. Mikrobiol. 9: 120-125, 1973.

8.2-18 Granger, R., Passet, J., and Lamy, J. 1975. Essences of marjolain (marjoram) [in French]. Riv. Ital. Essenze, Profumi, Piante Off., Aromi, Saponi, Cosmet., Aerosol 57: 446-454. CA 84: 79580.

8.2-19 Grundschober, F. 1979. Literature review of pulegone. Perfum. Flavor. 4{1}: 15-17. HA 49: 6969.

8.2-20 Gulati, B.C., Shawl, A.S., Garg, S.N., Sobti, S.N., and Pushpangadan, P. 1977. Essential oil of Ocimum canum Sims. (linalooel type). Indian Perfum. 21{1}: 21-25. CA 88: 158273.

8.2-21 Gulati, B.C. 1979. Ocimum basilicum Linn. - methyl chavicol type. Int Congr. Essent. Oils, [Pap.], 7th, 1977. 7: 148-152. CA 92: 64520.

8.2-22 Gulati, B.C., and Duhan, S.P.S. 1976. Essential oils of Mentha citrata Ehrh. (bergamot mint oil) [in German]. Riechst. Aromen Koerperpflegem. 26: 180-182, 184-185. CA 86: 60392.

8.2-23 Hassan, M.M.A., Habib, A.A.M., and Muhtadi, F.J. 1976. Investigation of the volatile oil of Saudi Lavandula dentata. Pharmazie 31: 650-651. HA 47: 5876

8.2-24 Hefendehl, F.W. 1972. Contributions on the biogenesis of essential oils. The composition of the essential oil of Pelargonium tomentosum [in German]. Planta Med. 22: 378-385. HA 43: 5501.

8.2-25 Hosokawa, H., and Shibamoto, T. 1978. Odor tenacity of perfumery materials. Perfum. Flavor. 2{7}: 29-30, 32. CA 89: 30582.

8.2-26 Kaiser, R., and Lamparsky, D. 1977. New mono- and sesquiterpenoid components of lavender, with respect to lavandin oils [in German]. Tetrahedron Lett. 1977{7}: 665-668.

8.2-27 Karawya, M.S., Hashim, F.M., and Hifnawy, M.S. 1974. Oils of jasmin, rose and cassie of Egyptian origin. Bull. Fac. Pharm., Cairo Univ. 13{1}: 183-192. CA 86: 60396.

8.2-28 Karetnikova, A.I., and Kustova, S.D. 1972. Hydrocarbon composition of Soviet lavender oil. J. Appl. Chem. USSR (Engl. Transl.) 45: 1349-1351. Translation of Zh. Prikl. Khim. 45: 1305-1307.

8.2-29 Karetnikova, A.I., Kustova, S.D., and Tsvetkova, E.V. 1974. Composition of secondary oils of clary sage [in Russian]. Maslo-Zhir. Prom. 7: 29-30. CA 81: 111394.

8.2-30 Koedam, A., and Gijbels, M.J.M. 1978. Isolation and identification of 3-octanone in the essential oil of Rosmarinus officinalis L. Z. Naturforsch. Sect. C. Biosci. 33: 144-145.

8.2-31 Lawrence, B.M. 1979. Progress in essential oils. Perfum. Flavor. 4{2}: 53-56.

8.2-32 Lawrence, B.M. 1977. Recent progress in essential oils. Perfum. Flavor. 2{6}: 36-41. HA 48: 5862.

8.2-33 Lawrence, B.M., Hogg, J.W., and Harney, P.M. 1975. Essential oils and their constituents. XIII. The chemical composition of some Pelargonium species. Int. Flavours Food Addit. 6: 42-44.

8.2-34 Lawrence, B.M. 1976. Recent progress in essential oils. I. Perfum. Flavor. 1{4}: 31-34. HA 47: 7756.

8.2-35 Lawrence, B.M. 1976. Recent progress in essential oils. II. Perfum. Flavor. 1{5}: 11-15. HA 47: 7757.

8.2-36 Lawrence, B.M. 1978. Recent progress in essential oils. Perfum. Flavor. 2{7}: 44-50. CA 89: 30555.

8.2-37 Lawrence, B.M. 1978. Progress in essential oils. Perfum. Flavor. 3{3}: 46-50. HA 49: 3708.

8.2-38 Lawrence, B.M. 1978. Progress in essential oils. Perfum. Flavor. 3{4}: 54-58. HA 49: 2827.

8.2-39 Lawrence, B.M. 1978. Progress in essential oils. Perfum. Flavor. 3{5}: 36-41. CA 90: 61062.

8.2-40 Lawrence, B.M. 1979. Progress in essential oils. Perfum. Flavor. 4{5}: 9-10, 12-13. HA 50: 4549.

8.2-41 Lawrence, B.M. 1980. Progress in essential oils. Perfum. Flavor. 5{1}: 55-58. HA 50: 8426.

8.2-42 Lawrence, B.M. 1980. Progress in essential oils. Perfum. Flavor. 5{2}: 33-38. HA 51: 597.

8.2-43 Lawrence, B.M. 1980. Progress in essential oils. Perfum. Flavor. 5{4}: 29-35. HA 51: 3895.

8.2-44 Lawrence, B.M. 1980. New trends in essential oils. Perfum. Flavor. 5{4}: 6, 8, 10, 12-16. HA 51: 3894.

8.2-45 Lawrence, B.M. 1980. Progress in essential oils. Perfum. Flavor. 5{6}: 27-32. HA 51: 4870.

8.2-46 Lawrence, B.M. 1980. Progress in essential oils. Perfum. Flavor. 5{7}: 49-50, 52, 54-55. CA 94: 71177.

8.2-47 Lawrence, B.M. 1977. Recent progress in essential oils. Perfum. Flavor. 2{3}: 53-56. CA 88: 141468.

8.2-48 Lawrence, B.M. 1977. Recent progress in essential oils. Perfum. Flavor. 2{4}: 32-35. CA 88: 126164.

8.2-49 Lawrence, B.M., Hogg, J.W., and Harney, P.M. 1975. Essential oils and their constituents. XIII. Chemical composition of some Pelargonium species. Int. Flavours Food Addit. 6{1}: 421-44. CA 83: 32910.

8.2-50 Lawrence, B.M. 1977. Recent progress in essential oils. Perfum. Flavor. 2: 32-35.

8.2-51 Lawrence, B.M. 1977. Recent progress in essential oils. Perfum. Flavor. 2{2}: 29-32. CA 88: 141527.

8.2-52 Lawrence, B.M. 1977. Recent progress in essential oils. Perfum. Flavor. 1{6}: 31-34. CA 88: 141469.

8.2-53 Lawrence, B.M. 1979. Progress in essential oils. Perfum. Flavor. 4{4}: 49, 52-55. HA 50: 6521.

8.2-54 Martin Mesonero, M., and Cabo Torres, J. 1971. Comparative study of several types of essences from Spanish lavender [in Spanish]. Ars Pharm. 12: 427-435. CA 79: 45625.

8.2-55 Mashanova, N.S., Zavatskaya, I.P., and Koksharov, A.S. 1977. Characteristics of the essential oil in the lavender calyx [in Russian]. Maslo-Zhir. Prom-st. 1977{4}: 33-34. CA 87: 28844.

8.2-56 Misra, S.C., and Chandra, G. 1971. Chemical constituents of peppermint oil and their synthetic uses. Indian Perfum. 15{1}: 32-38. CA 76: 158200.

8.2-57 Murray, M.J. 1972. Extraction of new essential oils from Mentha citrata hybrids showing interest for perfumery [in Russian]. Pages 103-106 in P.V. Naumenko et al., eds. Mezhundarodnyi kongress po efirnym maslam, [Materialy], 4th, Tiflis, 1968, v. 2. Pishchevaya Promyshlennost', Moscow, USSR. CA 81: 68328.

8.2-58 Nagaswara, T., Umemoto, K., Tsuneya, T., and Shiga, M. 1974. Essential oil of Mentha spicata var. crispa grown in Japan. 3. Component of peculiar odor in Japanese spearmint oil [in Japanese]. Koryo 108: 45-50. CA 82: 129171.

8.2-59 Nigam, M.C., Datta, S.C., Garg, S.N., and Duhan, S.P.S. 1976. Essential oil of Mentha citrata: a potential source of linalooel in India. Parfuem Kosmet. 57{6}: 163-165. CA 85: 99022.

8.2-60 Nikolov, N., Tsutsulova, A., Apostolova, B., and Ivanov, I. 1979. Bulgarian lavender oil. Int. Congr. Essent. Oils, [Pap.], 7th, 1977. 7: 155-159. CA 92: 82199.

8.2-61 Nizharadze,   A.N.,   Bagaturiya,   N.Sh.,   Bokuchava,   S.Ch.,
Sepashvili, A.Z., Peitrishvili, M.I., and Kikolashvili, E.Z. 1980.
Change in the content of geraniol and citronellol in essential oils of
geranium [in Russian]. Maslo-Zhir. Prom-st. 1980{2}: 24-25. CA 92:
169034.

8.2-62 Opdyke, D.L.J. 1979. Monographs on fragrance raw materials. Food
Cosmet. Toxicol. 17: 241-275.

8.2-63 Opdyke, D.L.J. 1975. Monograhs on fragrance raw materials. Food
Cosmet. Toxicol. 13: 91-112.

8.2-64 Opdyke, D.L.J. 1979. Monographs on fragrance raw materials.
cis-Jasmone. Food Cosmet. Toxicol. 17(Suppl.): 845. CA 92: 220538.

8.2-65 Opdyke, D.L.J. 1979. Monographs on fragrance raw material. Fennel
oil, bitter. Food Cosmet. Toxicol. 17{5}: 529. CA 92: 82181.

8.2-66 Opdyke, D.L.J. 1976. Monographs on fragrance raw materials. Spike
lavender oil. Food Cosmet. Toxicol. 15{5}: 453. CA 86: 145615.

8.2-67 Opdyke, D.L.J. 1976. Monographs on fragrance raw materials.
Marjoram oil sweet. Food Cosmet. Toxicol. 14{5}: 469. CA 86: 145623.

8.2-68 Opdyke, D.L.J. 1976. Monographs on fragrance raw materials.
Lavender oil. Food Cosmet. Toxicol. 14{5}: 451. CA 86: 145614.

8.2-69 Opdyke, D.L.J. 1976. Monographs on fragrance raw materials. Food
Cosmet. Toxicol. 14(Suppl.). 234 pp. CA 87: 172712.

8.2-70 Opdyke, D.L.J. 1976. Monographs on fragrance raw materials.
Lavender absolute. Food Cosmet. Toxicol. 14{5}: 449. CA 86: 145613.

8.2-71 Opdyke, D.L.J. 1975. Monographs on fragrance raw materials. Food
Cosmet. Toxicol. 13: 449-457.

8.2-72 Opdyke, D.L.J. 1976. Monographs on fragrance raw materials.
Lemongrass oil, West Indian. Food Cosmet. Toxicol. 14{5}: 457. CA 86:
145617.

8.2-73 Opdyke, D.L.J. 1976. Monographs on fragrance raw materials.
Lemongrass oil, East Indian. Food Cosmet. Toxicol. 14{5}: 455. CA 86:
145616.

8.2-74 Opdyke, D.L.J. 1976. Monographs on fragrance raw materials.
Marjoram oil, Spanish. Food Cosmet. Toxicol. 14{5}:   467. CA 86:
145622.

8.2-75 Opdyke, D.L.J. 1976. Monographs on fragrance raw materials.
Laurel leaf oil. Food Cosmet. Toxicol. 14: 337-338. CA 86: 145708.

8.2-76 Opdyke, D.L.J. 1976. Monographs on fragrance raw materials.
Jasmine absolute. Food Cosmet. Toxicol. 14{4}: 331. CA 86: 145705.

8.2-77 Opdyke, D.L.J. 1973. Monographs on fragrance raw materials. Food
Cosmet. Toxicol. 11: 1011-1081.

8.2-78 Opdyke, D.L.J. 1975. Monographs on fragrance raw materials. Food
Cosmet. Toxicol. 13: 545-554.

8.2-79 Opdyke, D.L.J. 1974. Monographs on fragrance raw materials. Food Cosmet. Toxicol. 12(Suppl.): 807-1016.

8.2-80 Opdyke, D.L.J. 1975. Monographs on fragrance raw materials. Food Cosmet. Toxicol. 13(Suppl.). 243 pp. CA 85: 45172.

8.2-81 Opdyke, D.L.J. 1973. Monographs on fragrance raw materials. Food Cosmet. Toxicol. 11: 477-495.

8.2-82 Opdyke, D.L.J. 1976. Monographs on fragrance raw materials. Fennel oil, bitter. Food Cosmet. Toxicol. 14{4}: 309. CA 86: 145699.

8.2-83 Opdyke, D.L.J. 1976. Monographs on fragrance raw materials. Lavandin oil. Food Cosmet. Toxicol. 14{5}: 447. CA 86: 145612.

8.2-84 Opdyke, D.L.J. 1974. Monographs on fragrance raw materials. Food Cosmet. Toxicol. 12: 703-736.

8.2-85 Opdyke, D.L.J. 1973. Monographs on fragrance raw materials. Food Cosmet. Toxicol. 11: 855-876.

8.2-86 Opdyke, D.L.J. 1978. Monographs on fragrance raw materials. Food Cosmet. Toxicol. 16(Suppl. 1). 637 pp. CA 90: 156988.

8.2-87 Osman, A.E. 1973. Study of the citronellol and geraniol contents of Egyptian geranium oil. Flavour Ind. 4: 225, 229.

8.2-88 Pecout, W. 1972. Essential oils of the Comores. Soap, Perfum. Cosmet. 45: 223-229. CA 77: 105504.

8.2-89 Pesnelle, P., Corbier, B., and Teisseire, P. 1971. Geranium oils [in French]. Parfums Cosmet. Savons Fr. 1: 637-640. CA 76: 131367.

8.2-90 Pesnelle, P., Corbier, B., and Teisseire, P. 1972. Geranium essence [in Italian]. Riv. Ital. Essenze, Profumi, Piante Off., Aromi, Saponi, Cosmet., Aerosol 54: 92-95. CA 77: 66096.

8.2-91 Pesnelle, P., Corbier, B., and Teisseire, P. 1971. Comparison between the levels of the sesquiterpene constituents of the essential oils of the Bourbon geranium and the African geranium [in French]. Recherches 1971{18}: 45-52.

8.2-92 Peyron, L. 1972. Some remarks on the composition of essential oils from leaves and flowers of lavender and lavandin [in French]. Plant. Med. Phytother. 6: 7-10. AGRICOLA.

8.2-93 Peyron, L. 1974. Leaf essential oils of Lavandula [in French]. Riv. Ital. Essenze, Profumi Piante Off. Aromi, Saponi, Cosmet., Aerosol 56{11}: 672-680. CA 83: 25039.

8.2-94 Peyron, L. 1971. Composition of essential oils and flowers of lavender and lavandins [in French]. C.R. Seances Acad. Agr. Fr. 57: 1368-1374. CA 77: 24762.

8.2-95 Reynolds, C.H. 1972. Portuguese geranium oil. Soap Perfum. Cosmet. 45: 481-482.

8.2-96 Rojahn, W., and Klein, E. 1977. Citronellyldiethylamine, a new constituent of Reunion geranium oil (Pelargonium graveolens) [in German]. Dragoco Rep. (Ger. Ed.) 24{6}: 150-152. CA 87: 156990.

8.2-97 Sabetay, S. 1971. Pro Lavandula vera naturale; in defence of natural lavender. SPC Soap Perfum. Cosmet. 44{11}: 701-703. AGRICOLA.

8.2-98 Virmani, O.P., Srivastava, R.,, and Datta, S.G. 1979. Oil of lemongrass. Part 1. East Indian. World Crops 31: 72-74.

8.2-99 Virmani, O.P., Srivastava, R., and Datta, S.G. 1979. Oil of lemongrass. Part 2: West Indian. World Crops 31: 120-121.

8.2-100 Vlakhov, R., Ivanov, D., Ognyanov, I., and Chorbadzhiev, S. 1972. Composition of Bulgarian lavender oil [in Russian]. Pages 58-60 in P.V. Naumenko et al., eds. Mezhdunarodnyi kongress po efirnym maslam, 4th, Tiflis, 1968, [Materialy]. v. 1. Pishchevaya Promyshlennost', Moscow, USSR. CA 79: 83393.

8.2-101 Yllera Camino, A. 1971. Rosemary essence in Spain and Mediterranean countries [in Spanish]. Ion 31: 217-228. Bib.Ag. 35: 92667.

8.2-102 Zoilkowsky, B. 1978. Lavender and lavandin oils from Haute Provence [in German]. Seifen, Oele, Fette, Wachse 104{15}: 421-423. CA 89: 185892.

8.2-103 Zola, A., and Vanda, J.-P. Le. 1975. Some essential oils from Corsica [in French]. Plant. Med. Phytother. 9: 211-223. HA 46: 7941.

8.2-104 Zola, A., and Garnero, J. 1973. European-type basil essences [in French]. Parfums, Cosmet. Savons Fr. 3{1}: 15-19. CA 78: 115116.

8.2-105 Zola, A., and LeVanda, J.P. 1979. Grosso lavandin [in French]. Parfums, Cosmet., Aromes 1979: 60-63. CA 90: 174496.

8.3 Extraction, Identification, and Synthesis

8.3-1 Adamski, R., and Dobrucki, R. 1974. Stability of vitamin A palmitate in selected ointment substrates. V. Influence of some ointment emulsion components on vitamin A stability [in Polish]. Farm. Pol. 30{1}: 25-29. CA 81: 68466.

8.3-2 Adzet, T. 1972. Gas chromatographic study of the essence of Lavandula angustifolia [in Spanish]. Rev. Real Acad. Farm. Barcelona 1972{5}: 17-24. CA 79: 9752.

8.3-3 Ahmed, A.Y.B.H., Meklati, B.Y., Guermouche, H.M., Abdeddaim, K., and Richard, H.M.J. 1980. Quantitative analysis of essential oils of lavender grown in Algeria [in French]. Riv. Ital. Essenze, Profumi, Piante Off., Aromat., Syndets, Saponi, Cosmet., Aerosols 62: 293-296. CA 94: 52676.

8.3-4 Anisimova, M.A., Trusova, A.M., Gurinovich, L.K., Kustova, S.D., and Filipenkova, V.S. 1978. Improved method for the treatment of geranium oil [in Russian]. Maslo-Zhir. Prom-st. 1978{11}: 34-35. CA 90: 61066.

8.3-5 Asaka, Y., Kamikawa, T., and Kubota, T. 1972. Total synthesis of (-)-4-hydroxy-2-hydroxymethyl-3, alpha-dimethylcyclopentaneethanol, the iridane part of jasminin. <u>Jasminum</u> <u>primulinum</u> Hemsl. Tetrahedron Lett. 1972{16}: 1597-1599.

8.3-6 Asaka, Y., Kamikawa, T., and Kubota, T. 1974. Synthetic studies of jasminin. Tetrahedron 30: 3257-3262.

8.3-7 Belafi-Rethy, K., Kerenyi, E., and Kolta, R. 1975. Composition of domestic and imported essential oils. V. Composition of lavender oil and muscatel sage oil [in German]. Acta Chim. Acad. Sci. Hung. 87: 105-119. CA 84: 35193.

8.3-8 Belafi-Rethy, K., Kerenyi, E., and Kolta, R. 1975. Composition of domestic and imported essential oils. IV. Composition of Hungarian lavender oil [in German]. Acta Chim. Acad. Sci. Hung. 87: 91-103. CA 84: 35192.

8.3-9 Berezhiani, L.V., and Kachakhidze, T.G. 1979. Study of the acid composition of geranium oil by a gas-liquid chromatographic method [in Russian]. Tr. Gruz. Politekhn. In-t. 1979{2/212}: 85-88. CA 92: 135102.

8.3-10 Bernal, A.A., Cuquerella Cayuela, J., and Santos Caffarena, J. 1976. Results of the first experiments in obtaining essential oil from lavender and lavandin growing in the Valencia region [in Spanish]. Ann. Inst. Nac. Invest. Agrar. Ser. Tecnol. Agrar. (Spain) 3: 153-175. HA 47: 9755.

8.3-11 Bonadeo, I., Lodi, V., and Ghidinis, D. 1980. Hydrophilic properties of aromatics. Int. J. Cosmet. Sci. 2: 215-229. CA 94: 71208.

8.3-12 Briggs, C.J., and McLaughlin, L.D. 1974. Low-temperature thin-layer chromatography for detection of polybutene contamination in volatile oils. J. Chromatogr. 101: 403-407. CA 82: 89983.

8.3-13 Carro de de la Torre, P.C. 1977. Study of the essential oil of <u>Lavandula</u> <u>officinalis</u> (Chaix-Villars) [in Spanish]. Rev. Agron. Noroeste Argent. 14: 209-215. AGRICOLA.

8.3-14 Casahoursat, L., Bidet, J., Palancade, P., Quilichini, R., and Guere, J.M. 1977. Determination of different toilet water constituents by gas phase chromatography [in French]. Ann. Falsif. Expert. Chim. 70{752}: 233-244. CA 87: 172708.

8.3-15 Chatterjee, A., and Banerjee, A. 1978. A simple synthesis of jasminol. Indian J. Chem. Sect. B 16B: 416-417.

8.3-16 Chen, C.C., Yang, K.H., and Wan, F.P. 1980. Analysis of the composition of lavender oil [in Chinese]. Fen Hsi Itva Hsueh 8: 499-503. CA 95: 138377.

8.3-17 Chistiakova, L.M. 1978. Technology for preparaing concentrates of mint and rose aromatic waters [in Ukrainian]. Farm. Zh. 1978{3}: 39-40. CIM 19{13}: 9665.

8.3-18 Ciola, R., and Kurmeier, K.H.D. 1979. Quantitative analysis of mint oil. Int. Congr. Essent. Oils [Pap.], 7th, 1977. 7: 319-323. CA 92: 82202.

8.3-19 Conan, J.Y., Dadant, R., and Michellon, R. 1977. Tests on improving geranium bourbon essential oil [in French]. Parfums. Cosmet. Aromes 15: 55-58. AGRICOLA.

8.3-20 D'Aubigne, J.M., Jacques, M., and Guiochon, G. 1971. Analysis of essential oils by gas phase chromatography at a programmed temperature [in French]. Recherches 1971{18}: 53-68. CA 76: 117424.

8.3-21 Damjanic, A., Grzunov, K., and Krstulovic, A. 1972. Separation of aromatic components by adsorption. II. Isolation of aroma constituents from Flores lavandulae hybridae [in Croatian]. Farm. Glas. 28{9}: 309-313.

8.3-22 Damjanic, A., and Grzunov, K. 1973. Separation of aromatic components by adsorption. III. Isolation of aromatic constituents from Rosmarinus leaves [in Croatian]. Farm. Glas. 29: 203-207. CA 79: 129065.

8.3-23 De Clercq, P, and Mijngheer, R. 1978. The total synthesis of fragrant compounds from jasmine oil. Bull. Soc. Chim. Belg. 87{6}: 495-496. CA: 179789.

8.3-24 Dimitrov, D., and Ivanov, K. 1976. Determination of the essential oil content in distillation water [in Bulgarian]. Kranit. Prom-st. 25{4}: 26-28. CA 86: 78546.

8.3-25 Dotsenko, V.D. 1971. Distillation of the essential oil from lavender and mint [in Russian]. Tr. Vses. Nauchno-Issled. Inst. Efirnomaslichn. Kul't. 4{2}: 58-61. CA 80: 19373.

8.3-26 Dubs, P., and Stussi, R. 1978. Synthesis of three jasmin constituents via a central intermediate. Helv. Chim. Acta 61: 990-997.

8.3-27 Dubs, P., and Stussi, R. 1978. Partial synthesis of methyl dehydrojasmonate and tuberolactone. Helv. Chim. Acta 61: 998-1003.

8.3-28 Dyakov, G., and Balinova, A. 1975. Investigations on two types of cooler for a 100 1 still for essential oil raw material [in Bulgarian]. Rastenievud. Nauki 12{7}: 19-24. HA 46: 6062.

8.3-29 Dzhashiashvili, M.Sh. 1978. Chromatographic analysis of rose and geranium hybrid oils [in Russian]. Pages 117-123 in Sb. St. po Efiromaslich. Kul'turam i Kul'turam i Efir. Maslam 1978. CA 90: 209940.

8.3-30 Georgiev, E., and Ganchev, G.P. 1972. Fragrant extraction products from distilled Lavandula vera inflorescences [in Bulgarian]. Nauchni Tr., Vissh Inst. Khranit. Vkusova Prom-st., Plovdiv 19{3}: 297-301. CA 83: 168310.

8.3-31 Georgiev, E., and Balinova-Tsvetkova, A. 1979. A comparative study of some solvents for the extraction of lavender racemes. Int. Congr. Essent. Oils, [Pap.], 7th, 1977. 7: 232-233. CA 92: 64526.

8.3-32 Georgiev, E., and Balinova-Tsvetkova, A. 1978. A comparative study of some solvents for the extraction of lavender racemes. Riv. Ital. Essenze, Profumi, Piante Off., Aromat., Syndets, Saponi, Cosmet., Aerosols. 60{5}: 324-326. CA 89: 135666.

8.3-33 Georgiev, E., Dimitrov, D., and Balinova-Tsvetkova, A. 1973. Extraction of aromatic substances from lavender racemes [in Bulgarian]. Nauchni Tr. Vissh Inst. Khranit. Vkusova Prom-st., Plovidiv 20{3}: 219-224. CA 85: 148978.

8.3-34 Gerlach, H., and Kuenzler, P. 1978. Michael-addition of carbothioates application to the synthesis of racemic jasmine ketolactone [in German]. Helv. Chim. Acta 61: 2503-2509.

8.3-35 Granger, R., Passet, J., and Arbousset, G. 1973. Essential oil of Rosmarinus officinalis. Influence of the manner of treatment of the vegetal material [in French]. Parfums Cosmet. Savons Fr. 3: 133-138. CA 79: 35038.

8.3-36 Greene, A.E., and Crabbe, P. 1976. A short efficient synthesis of methyl dl-jasmonate and related compounds. Tetrahedron Lett. 1976{52}: 4867-4870.

8.3-37 Hadorn, H., and Zurcher, K. 1973. Experiences with a new kinetic method for determining the diastase [in German]. Apidologie 4{1}: 65-80. AA 25: 675.

8.3-38 Heide, R. Ter., Valois, P.J. de, Wobben, H.J., and Timmer, R. 1975. Analysis of the acid fraction of Reunion geranium oil (Pelargonium graveolens L'Her. ex Ait). J. Agric. Food Chem. 23: 57-60.

8.3-39 Herisset, A., Jolivet, J., and Rey, P. 1971. Differentiation of some essential oils showing similar constitution especially by examination of their UV, IR, and Raman spectra. III. Oils of common lavender (Lavandula vera), aspic lavender (L. latifolia) and lavandin (L. hybrida) [in French]. Plant. Med. Phytother. 5: 305-314. CA 76: 144747.

8.3-40 Hoffmann, W. 1979. Lavender components and selected syntheses [in German]. Seifen, Oele, Fette, Wachse 105: 287-291. CA 91: 128884.

8.3-41 Ho, T.-L., Ho, H.C., and Wong, C.M. 1973. A synthetic route to dihydrojasmone; sulfuric acid as dethio-acetilization agent. Can. J. Chem. 51: 153-155.

8.3-42 Ho, T.L., and Wong, C.M. 1973. A facile approach to dihydrojasmone. Exper ientia 29: 1195.

8.3-43 Hussain, G. 1973. Quantitative analysis of Rosemarinus [sic] officinalis oil from the locally grown plant. Pak. J. Sci. Ind. Res. 16: 215.

8.3-44 Ijima, A., Mizuno, H., and Takahashi, K. 1972. Synthesis of delta lactones. III. Alkenyl 6-delta lactones or alcoyl-6-delta lactones from cyclopentanone. Chem. Pharm. Bull. (Tokyo) 20: 197-201.

8.3-45 Ille, K. 1971. Gas-chromatographic analysis of some essential oils used in perfumery [in Russian]. Pages 112-123 in P.V. Naumenko, et al., eds. Mezhdunarodnyi kongress po efirnym maslam. [Materialy], 4th, Tiflis, 1968. Pishchevaya Promyshlennost, Moscow, USSR. CA 78: 115110.

8.3-46 Ishikawa, H., Uehara, Y., and Takenaka, T. 1971. Basic research

in regulating stable compound perfumes for aerosols. The relations
between perfume materials and certain bases for aqueous aerosols
Aerosol Rep. 10: 187-193. CA 78: 47655.

8.3-47 Jannin, B., and Baron, C. 1980. Microanalytic study of extracts
from Jasminum officinale flowers [in French]. C. R. Seances Soc. Biol.
174: 1060-1066. HA 51: 79789.

8.3-48 Kachakhidze, G.G., Berezhiani, L.B., and Kandelaki, B.S. 1971.
Rapid method for the determination of menthone in geranium oil [in
Russian]. Tr. Gruz. Politekh. Inst. 1971{2}: 34-38. CA 78: 47647.

8.3-49 Kachakhidze, T.G., and Berezhiani, L.B. 1972. Improving menthone
type geranium oil [in Georgian]. Tr. Gruz. Politekh. Inst. 1972{1}:
59-62. CA 78: 101863.

8.3-50 Kaiser, R., and Lamparsky, D. 1974. New cyclopentanoid
constituents from jasmine oil [in German]. Tetrahedron Lett. 1974{38}:
3413-3416. CA 82: 111637.

8.3-51 Kamalam, N., Subbiah, S., Francis, H., and Krishnamoorthy, K.K.
1972. A note on the extraction of jasmine oil from jasmine flowers.
Madras Agric. J. 59: 405-406. HA 43: 5497.

8.3-52 Karawya, M.S., Hashim, F.M., and Hifnawy, M.S. 1972. Colorimetric
and GLC assay of linalooel in volatile oils. An. Acad. Bras. Cienc.
44(Suppl.): 165-167.

8.3-53 Karawya, M.S., Hashim, F.M., and Hifnawy, M.S. 1972. Colorimetric
assay of citral and citronellal in volatile oils. An. Acad. Bras.
Cienc. 44(Suppl.): 161-164.

8.3-54 Kharebava, L.G., and Bukhbinder, A.A. 1979. Study of volatile
compounds in essential-oil geranium by means of capillary gas-liquid
chromatography [in Russian]. Subtrop. Kul't. 1979{1}: 78-88. PBA 51:
652.

8.3-55 Kondo, K., Saito, E., and Tunemoto, D. 1975. Sulfonyl carbanions
in synthesis III. A new method for the synthesis of delta lactols.
Tetrahedron Lett. 1975{27}: 2275-2278.

8.3-56 Kotlyarova, M.V., Ivanova, L.N., and Kviviniya, D.V. 1973.
Determination of menthone in geranium oils [in Russian]. Maslo-Zhir.
Prom-st. 1978{11}: 30. CA 80: 87404.

8.3-57 Kubelka, V., Mitera, J., and Zachar, P. 1972. Analysis of spike
oil chromatography—mass spectrometry. J. Chromatogr. 74: 195-196. CA
78: 688656.

8.3-58 Kulesza, J., and Podlejski, J. 1972. New process for obtaining
angelica and lovage root oils [in German]. Riechst., Aromen,
Koerperpflegem. 22: 333-334. CA 78: 20097.

8.3-59 Kustova, S.D., Kruglova, M.V., Filipenkova, V.S., Khomenko, I.A.,
Bliznyuk, V.I., and Vlasenko, D.S. 1971. Quality of mint reprocessed
at the Zolotonosha plant [in Russian]. Maslo-Zhir. Prom. 37{12}: 36-37
CA 76: 89937.

8.3-60 Luedde, K.H. 1971. Dielectric and refractodensimetric behavior of essential oils during aging [in Russian]. Pages 205-210 in P.V. Naumenko, et al., eds. Mezhundarodnyi kongress po efirnym maslam, 4th, Tiflis, 1968, [Materialy]. v. 1. Pishchevaya Promyshlennost', Moscow, USSR. CA 78: 140346.

8.3-61 Malacria, M., and Roumestant, M.L. 1977. Vinylallenes. VI. Synthesis of ketones of the jasmone series [in French]. Tetrahedron 33: 2813-2817.

8.3-62 Manzoor-I-Khuda, M. 1971. Constituents of Lavandula stoechas Linn. Part III - Spectral studies of lavanol. Pak. J. Sci. Ind. Res. 14: 488-489.

8.3-63 Martin Mesonero, M., Cabo Torres, J., and Villar del Fresno, A. 1974. Comparative study of the different types of essences of Spanish lavender. II. Determination of their components by thin-layer chromatography [in Spanish]. Boll. Chim. Farm. 113{2}: 131-136. CA 82: 34951.

8.3-64 Mezentseva, E.V., Belik, M.A., Levchenko, I.V., and Moskalenko, L.M. 1975. Effect of admixtures of the given plant on the quality of essential oil of lavender [in Russian]. Tr. Vses. Nauchno-Issled. Inst. Efirnomaslichn. Kul't. 8: 230-234. AGRICOLA.

8.3-65 Mookherjee, B.D., and Trenkle, R.W. 1978. Generation of aroma compounds by photo oxidation of unsaturated fatty esters. ACS Symp. Ser. 75: 56-59

8.3-66 More, T.A. 1980. Extraction of essential oil from Jasminum. Sci. Cult. 46: 428-429.

8.3-67 Muthuswami, S., and Sayed, S. 1980. Preliminary note on the extraction of lemongrass oil. Indian Perfum. 24: 226-227.

8.3-68 Muthuswamy, S., Mohammed Ali Khan, W., and Sayed, S. 1972. The extraction of jasmine concrete from Jasminum auriculatum, Vahl. Curr. Sci. 41: 194.

8.3-69 Naoshima, Y., Nishimoto, K., Wakabayashi, S., and Hayashi, S. 1980. Synthesis of(z)-jasmone and methyl jasmonate. Agric. Biol. Chem. 44: 687-688.

8.3-70 Ognyanov, I., and Panaiotova, L. 1973. Gas-chromatographic relative analysis of linalooel and linalyl acetate in lavender essential oil [in German]. Riv. Ital. Essenze, Profumi, Piante Off., Aromi, Saponi, Cosmet., Aerosol [in German]. CA 80: 124569.

8.3-71 Ohloff, G., and Rode-Gowal, H. 1978. Groups of structurally related perfumes, their sensorial properties and perfume use [in German]. Kosmet., Riechst. Lebensmittelzusutzst. 39-60: 219-223. CA 89: 220731.

8.3-72 Persidskaya, K.G., and Kravets, T.I. 1973. Effect of ways to extract several oils on their physicochemical indexes [in Russian]. Tr. Vses. Nauchno-Issled. Inst. Efirnomaslichn. Kul't. 6: 160-163. CA 83: 65315.

8.3-73 Peyron, L., and Acchiardi, J. 1976. Determination of benzyl acetate in jasmine concretes and absolutes [in French]. Riv. Ital.

Essenze, Profumi Piante Off., Aromi, Saponi Cosmet. Aerosol 58{1}: 2-5. CA 84: 169548.

8.3-74 Peyron, L. 1972. Pesticides in fragrant natural products [in Italian]. Riv. Ital. Essenze Profumi Piante Off. Aromi Saponi Cosmet. Aerosol. 54: 166-175. CA 77: 97703.

8.3-75 Peyron, L., Senaux, S., Acchiardi, J., and Broua, M. 1972. Recent fraud of Reunion type basil essences [in French]. Ann. Fals. Expert. Chim. 65{701}: 247-254. CA 77: 138434.

8.3-76 Piliev, Z.G., Khargeliya, L.Sh., and Zaichik, Ts.R. 1976. Factors effecting distillation emulsion separation [in Russian]. Maslo-Zhir. Prom-st. 1976{10}: 40-41. CA 87: 28839.

8.3-77 Ponomarev, E.D., and Naidenova, V.P. 1975. Effect of steam parameters on the yield and quality of essential oil from lavender [in Russian]. Tr. Vses. Nauchno-Issled. Inst. Efirnomaslichn. Kul't. 8: 255-261.

8.3-78 Prager, M.J., and Miskiewicz, M.A. 1979. Gas chromatographic-mass spectrometric analysis, identification, and detection of adulteration of lavender, lavandin, and spike lavender oils. J. Assoc. Off. Anal. Chem. 62: 1231-1238.

8.3-79 Prikhod'ko, L.S., Kurchenko, L.S., Besklinskaya, L.A., and Dumcheva, L.I. 1977. Fire hazards of some medicinal aerosols [in Russian]. Khim.-Farm. Zh. 11{8}: 72-74. CA 88: 177081.

8.3-80 Raguenaud, R. 1972. Development of the physicochemical properties of Bourbon geranium oil during distillation [in French]. Parfums, Cosmet. Savons Fr. 2: 297-301. CA 77: 143731.

8.3-81 Raja, M.I., Devarajan, L., and Kanakabhushani, K. 1976. Studies on the extraction of essential oils from flowers. Madras Agric. J. 63: 253-254. CA 87: 106636.

8.3-82 Rasmussen, K.E., Rasmussen, S., and Baerheim Svendsen, A. 1972. Quantitative determination of the various compounds of the volatile oil in small amounts of plant material by means of gas-liquid chromatography. Terpenes and related compounds. XVIII. Pharm. Weekbl. 107: 277-284. Bib.Ag. 36: 82230.

8.3-83 Rothbaecher, H., and Sutue, F. 1975. Change of limonene contained in caraway oil into carvone [in German]. Parfuem. Kosmet. 56{9}: 258-261. CA 84: 44378.

8.3-84 Rovesti, P. 1972. Ethoxylated essential oils. An. Acad. Bras. Cienc. 44(Suppl.): 341-342.

8.3-85 Salakaya, V.K. 1978. Use of gas-liquid chromatography for analyzing jasmine essential oil [in Russian]. Pages 123-127 in Sb. St. po Efiromaslich Kul'turam i Efir. Maslam. CA 90: 209942.

8.3-86 Sasu, C., and Comanescu, B. 1971. Obtaining of extracts from lavender (Lavandula vera) and establishing of the general characteristics [in Romanian]. Bul. Inst. Politeh. Brasov Ser. B Econ. For. 13: 291-296. CABF 73129761.

8.3-87 Shavgulidze, V.V., Kokorashvilik, I.R., and Giunashvili, E.G. 1974. Polarographic determination of rose, geranium, and sweet basil oils [in Russian]. Soobsch. Akad. 76: 629-632. CA 83: 65307.

8.3-88 Shlaypnikov, V.A., Shlyapnikova, A.P., and Tseitlina, I.I. 1972. Evaluating the efficiency of technological processes for the production of essential oils [in Russian]. Maslo-Zhir. Prom. 38{3}: 25-27. CA 77: 24764.

8.3-89 Shlyapnikov, V.A., and Shlaypnikova, A.P. 1972. Qualitative and quantitative changes of essential oils in plants under the influence of organic solvents [in Russian]. Prikl. Biokhim. Mikrobiol. 8{4}: 488-494. CA 78: 20098.

8.3-90 Srivastava, D.N. 1977. Isolation and identification of constituents of Jasminum auriculatum leaves. J. Appl. Chem. Biotechnol. 27{2}: 55-57. CA 87: 18958.

8.3-91 Swaminathan, K.R., Muthuswamy, S., and Rao, V.N.M. 1979. Pilot plant for extraction of jasmine essential oil from Jasminum grandiflorum. Indian Hortic. 24{1}: 20-21. Bib.Ag. 45: 17605.

8.3-92 Tanasienko, F.S., Pavlikova, N.V., and Zeiskaya, N.P. 1971. Quality improvement of cohobation lavender oil [in Russian]. Tr. Vses. Nauchno-Issled. Inst. Efirnomaslichn. Kul't. 4{2}: 62-63. CA 78: 47650.

8.3-93 Tearo, E., Uus, E., Siirde, E., Shlyapnikov, V.A., and Kochubei, Yu.V. 1978. Isolation of essential oils from extracts of essential oil raw materials [in Russian]. Maslo-Zhir. Prom-st. 1978{12}: 22-24. CA 90: 61071.

8.3-94 Thoma, K., and Pfaff, G. 1978. Solubilization of essential oils with polyethylene glycol glyceric acid esters. Perfum. Flavor. 2{7}: 27-28 CA 89: 11953.

8.3-95 Timmer, R., Heide, R. Ter, Valois, P.J. de, and Wobben, H.J. 1971. Qualitative analysis of the most volatile neutral components of Reunion geranium oil (Pelargonium roseum Bourbon). J. Agric. Food Chem. 19: 1066-1068.

8.3-96 Timmer, R., Heide, R. Ter, Valois, P.J. de, and Wobben, H.J. 1975. Analysis of the lactone fraction of lavender oil (Lavandula vera D.C.). J. Agric. Food Chem. 23: 53-96.

8.3-97 Togano, S., Hayashi, K., Yomogida, K., and Ohta, S. 1979. A study on the residual components of jasmine absolute. Int. Congr. Essent. Oils, [Pap.], 7th, 1977. 7: 469-473. CA 92: 99431.

8.3-98 Tsvetkova, R., and Balinova-Tsvetkova, A. 1976. Studies on the extraction of essential oil from Salvia sclarea in Bulgaria]. Rastenievud. Nauki 13{5}: 26-37. HA 47: 5881.

8.3-99 Ubertis, B., Zanforlin, A., and Benzi, N. 1972. Oxidation of total mint essential oil [in Italian]. Riv. Ital. Essenze Profumi Piante Off. Aromi Saponi Cosmet. Aerosol 54: 878-885. AGRICOLA.

8.3-100 Van der Gen, A. 1972. Compounds with a jasmin odor [in French]. Parfums, Cosmet., Savons Fr. 2{8-9}: 356-370. CA 78: 7735.

8.3-101 Velchev, Kh., Rangelov, P., and Dimitrov, D. 1976. Study of the temperature-pressure relation at the saturation point and determination of the boiling point in some Bulgarian essential oils [in Bulgarian]. Nauchni Tr., Vissh Inst. Khranit. Vkusova Prom-st., Plovdiv 23{2}: 263-269. CA 88: 110367.

8.3-102 Velchev, Kh., Georgiev, E., Kerezieva, M., and Dimitrov, D. 1977. Solubility of some essential oils in water in relation to temperature [in Bulgarian]. Khranit. Prom-st. 26{2}: 19-21. CA 88: 27671.

8.3-103 Vig, O.P., Bari, S.S., and Rana, S.S. 1979. Terpenoids: Part CXXXV - A new synthesis of acetate of P-mentha-1,8 {10}-dien-9-ol. Indian J. Chem. Sect. B 17B: 171-172.

8.3-104 Voitkevich, S.A. 1972. On the synthesis of fragrant substances. Principle constituents of essential oils [in French]. An. Acad. Bras. Cienc. 44(Suppl.): 328-331.

8.3-105 Wakamatsu, T., Akasaka, K., and Ban, Y. 1974. A new synthesis of 1,4-diketones: Application to a synthesis of dihydrojasmone and cis-jasmone. Tetrahedron Lett. 1974{44}: 3883-3886.

8.3-106 Wisneski, H.H. 1976. Determination of bergapten in fragrance preparations by thin layer chromatography and spectrophotofluorometry. J. Assoc. Off. Anal. Chem. 59: 547-551.

8.3-107 Zamureenko, V.A., Klyuev, N.A., Dmitriev, L.B., and Grandberg, I.I. 1979. Chromato-mass-spectrometric method of identifying the essential oil components of Pelargonium roseum [in Russian]. Izv. Timiryazevsk. S-kh. Akad. 1979{1}: 156-162. HA 49: 5260.

8.4 Cosmetics, Perfumes, Fumigants, and Incenses

8.4-1 Alexander, P. 1973. Use of natural products in cosmetic and toiletry preparation. Cosmet. Perfum. 88{9}: 35-42.

8.4-2 Fujii, T., Furukawa, S., and Suzuki, S. 1972. Compounded perfumes for toilet goods. Nonirritative compounded perfumes for soaps [in Japanese]. Yukagaku 21: 904-908. CA 78: 75786.

8.4-3 Goldschmiedt, H. 1973. Herbal bath preparations. Cosmet. Perfum. 88{3}: 89-90, 92.

8.4-4 Heath, H.B. 1977. Herbs - their use in cosmetics and toiletries. Cosmet Toilet. 92{1}: 22, 24.

8.4-5 Mehra, K.L., Kanodia, K.C., and Srivastava, R.N. 1975. Folk uses of plants for adornment in India. Econ. Bot. 29: 39-46.

8.4-6 Munzig, H.P., and Schels, H. 1974. Essential oils as possible preservatives in cosmetics [in Polish]. Tluszcze, Srodki. Piorace, Kosmet. 18{8-9}: 355-361. CA 82: 129170.

8.4-7 Nishi, H., and Morishita, I. 1971. Components of licorice root

used for tobacco flavoring. 1. Fractionation of the substances in
licorice root effective in improving the tobacco smoking quality [in
Japanese]. Nippon Nogei Kagaku Kaishi 45: 507-512. CA 76: 151016.

8.4-8 Paris, M., Bercht, C.A.L., Unger, J., and Clair, G. 1974.
Bergamot-mint. Its importance in essential oil applications [in
French]. Riv. Ital. Essenze, Profumi, Piante Off., Aromi, Saponi,
Cosmet., Aerosol 56{11}: 655-659 CA 83: 39208.

8.4-9 Rovesti, P. 1971. A study of the use of ginseng extracts in
cosmetics [in Italian]. Riv. Ital. Essenze Profumi Piante Off. Aromi
Saponi Cosmet. Aerosol 53: 203-207. AGRICOLA.

8.4-10 Sakagami, H., and Morishita, I. 1972. Studies on the components
of licorice root used for tobacco flavouring. II. Spectrophotometric
determination of glycyrrhizic acid in the tobacco shreds [in
Japanese]. Nippon Nogei Kagaku Kaishi 46: 443-446. AGRICOLA.

8.4-11 Sakagami, H. 1973. Behavior of glycyrrhizic acid and
glycyrrhetinic acid added to tobacco on smoking. Studies on the
components of licorice root used for tobacco flavoring. III [in
Japanese]. Nippon Nogei Kagaku Kaishi 47{10}: 623-626. CA 80: 93264.

9.0 NATURAL DYES AND ORNAMENTAL APPLICATIONS

9.1 Dye Plants and Pigments

9.1-1 Alkamper, J. 1972. Cultivation of Capsicum in Ethiopia as spice
and dye plant [in German]. Bodenkultur 23{1}: 97-107. AGRICOLA.

9.1-2 Haspelova-Horvatovicova, A., Horikova, B. 1976. Time saving method
for the determination of yellow and red dyestuffs contents in paprika
[in Slovak]. Prum. Potravin 27: 233-234. AGRICOLA.

9.1-3 Kasumov, M.A. 1972. Certain dye plants of Azerbaijan suitable for
dying carpet wool [in Russian]. Rastit. Resur. 8: 416-420. HA 43:
3943.

9.1-4 Martin-Leake, H. 1975. An historical memoir of the indigo industry
of Bihar. Econ. Bot. 29: 361-371.

9.1-5 Rembert, D.H., Jr. 1979. The indigo of commerce in colonial North
America. Econ. Bot. 33: 128-134.

9.1-6 Rosebrook, D.D. 1971. Collaborative study of a method for
extractable color in paprika and paprika oleoresin. J. Assoc. Off.
Anal. Chem. 54: 37-41.

9.1-7 Zakirov, P.K., and Karimov, G. 1977. Tugai dye plants potamophyta
of Uzbek-SSR, USSR [in Russian]. Uzb. Biol. Zh. 5: 47-50.

9.1-8 Zavatskaia, I.P., Mashanova, N.S. 1978. Content of some plastic
substances in leaves of Indigofera tinctoria [in Russian]. Byull. Gos.
Nikitsk. Bot. Sada 1978{2}: 73-76.

9.2 Ornamentals

9.2-1 Angiboust, A. 1977. Ornamental horticulture in Belgium: crops destined for export [in French]. Pepinier. Hortic. Maraichers 1977{182}: 53-59. HA 48: 4142.

9.2-2 Blomme, R., and Vanwezer, J. 1978. Some observations on the examination of the pH and salt concentration of some potting soils for the container production of woody nursery stock [in Flemish]. Verbondsnieuws voor de Belgische Sierteelt 22: 315-316. HA 48: 10024.

9.2-2 Blomme, R., and Vanwezer, J. 1980. Substrates for the container culture of woody nursery crops [in Flemish]. Verbondsnieuws voor de Belgische Sierteelt 24: 21-24. HA 50: 6465.

9.2-3 Bose, T.K., Mukherjee, D., Bose, T., and Chatterjee, A.K. 1975. Dwarfing of ornamentals by using ethrel. Pages 130-131 in V.S. Motial, ed. Seminar on recent advances in plant sciences. Abstracts of papers. Association for Advancement of Plant Sciences, Kalyani, India.

9.2-4 Bosse, G. 1972. Lobelia fulgens as a cut flower [in German]. Gartenwelt 72: 104, 106, 108. HA 43: 2215.

9.2-5 Clausen, G. 1976. Healthy plant material from variety trials with outdoor flower crops [in Danish]. Gartner Tidende 1976{50}: 748-749. HA 48: 4712.

9.2-6 Fiertz, G.B. 1971. Our much-maligned native goldenrod. Gard. J. 21: 115-116

9.2-7 Hawk, R.L. 1976. Peppers for ornament. Org. Gard. Farming 23{11}: 104-105.

9.2-8 Kiermeier, P. 1980. Survey of semi-dwarf and dwarf woody plants [in German]. Dtsch. Baumsch. 32: 280-285. HA 51: 2814.

9.2-9 Lent, J.M. 1972. A purple-leaved basil. Plants Gard. (n.s.) 28{1}: 39. AGRICOLA.

9.2-10 Lloyd, C. 1976. From lace to lovage. Ctry. Life 159{4107}: 668-669. AGRICOLA.

9.2-11 Manivel, L., and Syed, S. 1978. Effect of growth regulators on keeping quality of jasmine flowers. Madras Agric. J. 65: 763-764.

9.2-12 McKenzie, E. 1971. The uses of herbs in English gardens. Herbarist 37: 27-30.

9.2-13 Narasimhan, V.S., Jayaraj, M.S., Selvaraj, P., Balasubramanian, A., and Kombairaju, S. 1976. Flower cultivation and marketing in the environs of Madurai City. South Indian Hortic. 24: 14-17.

9.2-14 Reisaeter, O. 1975. Winter flowers [in Norwegian]. Nor. Hagetid. 91: 76-77 AGRICOLA.

9.2-15 Seregina, M.T. 1974. The effect of seed irradiation on the ornamental qualities of chives [in Russian]. Byull. Gl. Bot. Sada 1974{92}: 79-81. AGRICOLA.

9.2-16 Yang, L. 1979. Urban herbs. Am. Hortic. 58: 21, 33.

10.0 COMMERCE

10.1 Marketing

10.1-1 Anonymous. 1977. Global production of paprika and trade in pepper [in German]. Int. Fruit World 35{3}: 82, 85-88. AGRICOLA.

10.1-2 Anonymous. 1975. 23,500 tons of sesame in 1975 [Columbia] [in Spanish]. Rev. Nac. Agric. (Bogota) 68{813}: 10-13. AGRICOLA.

10.1-3 Boning, K. 1971. Horseradish trade, its history and folk peculiarities [in German]. Bayer Landwirtsch. Jahrb. 48: 960-970. AGRICOLA.

10.1-4 Bowser, W.C., Jr. 1974. U.S. mint oil usage down, overseas sales remain high. Foreign Agric. 12{51}: 9.

10.1-5 Czanik, S. 1977. Export possibility of paprika [in Hungarian]. Hajtat as Korai Termesztes Kert. Egy. Zoldsegtermesztesi Tansz. 8{3}: 26-27. AGRICOLA.

10.1-6 Hannah, B. 1980. Buyers outlook. Proc. Annu. Meet. Oreg. Essent. Oil Grow. League 31: 79-81.

10.1-7 Laszlo, K. 1977. Domestic marketing of paprika [in Hungarian]. Hajtat as Korai Termesztes Kert. Egy. Zoldsegtermesztesi Tansz. 8{3}: 24-25. AGRICOLA.

10.1-8 Marks, S.C. 1971. Mint oil market situation. Oreg. Essent. Oil Growers League Proc. 22: 59-63.

10.1-9 Marks, S.C. 1972. Mint oil market situation. Oreg. Essent. Oil Growers League Proc. 23: 17-24.

10.1-10 Mattoso, M.J., Rezende, A.M., Neto, A.A., Sousa, A.F. de, and Brandt, S.A. 1974. Integration of garlic marketing in the State of Minas Gerais [in Portuguese]. Rev. Ceres 21{113}: 30-37. WAERSA 17: 3290.

10.1-11 Patty, G.E. 1976. Orient prizes quality U.S. ginseng exports. Foreign Agric. 14{20}: 12.

10.1-12 Patty, G.E. 1978. U.S. mint oil exports continue at high level. Foreign Agric. 15{13}: 10-11.

10.1-13 Patty, G.E. 1978. U.S. ginseng exports hit record in 1977. Foreign Agric. 15{37}: 6-7.

10.1-14 Patty, G.E. 1974. Demand spurs U.S. exports of ginseng to Asia. Foreign Agric. 12{46}: 11, 16.

10.1-15 Robbins, S.R.J., Greenhalgh, P. 1979. The markets for selected herbaceous essential oils. Trop. Sci. 21: 63-70.

10.1-16 Rojas, M.B., Teixeira Filho, A.R., Penna, J.A., and Barbosa, T. 1975. Analysis of garlic supply in Minas Gerais, 1948-1970 [in Portuguese]. Rev. Ceres 22{121}: 159-177. WAERSA 18: 4718.

10.1-17 Schickel, W. 197 3. Market analysis for vegetable paprika [in German] Ind. Obst.- & Gemuseverwert. 58: 339-340. AGRICOLA.

10.1-18 Seitz, P. 1975. The market decides. A discussion on unusual vegetables for commercial growing [in German]. Dtsch. Gaertnerboerse 75: 656-658, 660-662. HA 46: 3172.

10.1-19 Sundaresh, I. 1977. Export potential of medicinal plants and their derivatives from India. Pages 411-434 in C.K. Atal and B.M. Kapur, eds. Cultivation & utilization of medicinal and aromatic plants. Regional Research Laboratory, Jammu-Tawi, India.

10.1-20 Vashist, V.N., and Atal, C.K. 1977. Prospects of less known essential oils in India. Pages 392-398 in C.K. Atal and B.M. Kapur, eds. Cultivation & utilization of medicinal and aromatic plants. Regional Research Laboratory, Jammu-Tawi, India.

10.1-21 Wang, I. 1972. The production and marketing of Panax roots (ginseng) around the world. Nung Chan Sai Hsiao Shih Ch'ang (Foreign Mark. Inf. Agric. Prod., Taiwan) 185: 14-15. AGRICOLA.

10.1-22 Yoshioka, S. 1975. Production and marketing of red peppers, Capsicum annuum [in Japanese]. Nogyo Oyobi Engei 50{1}: 181-186.

10.2 Economics

10.2-1 Ali, N. 1973. Economics of saffron cultivation. East. Econ. 73: 184-185, 187. AGRICOLA.

10.2-2 Baslas, B.K., and Baslas, R.K. 1972. Occurrence and economic use of essential oils in India [in German]. Riechst., Aromen, Koerperpflegem. 22{12}: 421-422, 424, 426, 428. CA 78: 75764.

10.2-3 Dzur, M. 1973. The development of cost-profit relations in seasoning paprika production [in Hungarian]. Gazdalkodas 17{10}: 41-51. AGRICOLA.

10.2-4 Erickson, R.E. 1976. The industrial importance of monoterpenes and essential oils. Lloydia 39{1}: 8-19.

10.2-5 Fisher, H.M. 1976. Comparison of economic returns from grain crops. J Agric. West. Aust. 17: 64-68.

10.2-6 Gerasimenko, A.M. 1975. Economics of the production of bay-leaves (Laurus nobilis) in the moist subtropics zone of the Krasnodar region [in Russian]. Subtrop. Kul't. 1975{6}: 101-105. FA 38: 1363.

10.2-7 Gupta, R. 1976. Mentha brings money to Indian farmers. Financ. Agric. 7{4}: 21-24. AGRICOLA.

10.2-8 Mikhailov, S., Aleksandrova, V., and Lulcheva, D. 1976. Economic problems of lavender growing in Plovidiv region [in Bulgarian]. Selskostop. Nauka 14{14}: 38-42.

10.2-9 Mishra, R.S., Marothia, D.K., and Mattoo, M.S. 1977. Economics of saffron cultivation in Kashmir Valley. JNKVV Res. J. 11: 59-66.

10.2-10 Schiavo, G. 1975. The cost of producing fennel, leeks and lettuce [in Italian]. Informatore Agrario 31: 19159-19162. HA 46: 2098.

10.2-11 Singh, R.P. 1975. Economics of fertilizer use under dryland conditions. Indian J. Agron. 20: 140-146. FCA 29: 10112.

10.2-12 Tyl, M. 1973. The economics of growing true chamomile in relation to mechanization [in Czech]. Nase Liecive Rastliny 10: 161-163. HA 44: 7023.

Part 3: Other References

11.0 BOOKS ON HERBS

11.1-1 Adrosko, Rita J. 1971. Natural dyes and home dying. (Formerly titled: Natural dyes in the United States). Reprinted. Dover Pub., New York, N.Y. 154 pp. NUC 1968-72{1}: 457.

11.1-2 Ajtay, Zsuzsanna. 1979. Paprikatermesztes. Mezogazdasagi Kiado, Budapest, Hungary. 374 pp. AGRICOLA.

11.1-3 Akademiia na Selskostopanskite Nauki. 1976. Poppy-Papaver somniferum L. (Trans. from Bulgarian by Franklin Book Programs, Cairo). U.S. Dep. Agric., Agric. Res. Serv. TT 75-58072. 275 l.

11.1-4 Alavi, Ahmad. 1974. The opium poppy. Ministry of Agriculture and Natural Resources, Tehran, Iran. 306 pp. NALC.

11.1-5 Altschul, S.v.R. 1973. Drugs and foods from little-known plants. Harvard University Press, Cambridge, Mass.

11.1-6 American Spice Trade Association. 1972. Paprika manual. The Association, Englewood Cliffs, N.J. 80 pp.

11.1-7 American Spice Trade Association. 1976. ASTA microbiological methods. The Association, Englewood Cliffs, N.J. 82 pp.

11.1-8 Anonymous. 1972. Chung i ch'ang yung ts'ao yao, Chung yao, fang chi shou ts'e [Handbook of common Chinese herbs, drugs, and prescriptions]. I yao wei sheng ch'u pan she. Hong Kong. 6, 98 pp. NLMCC 1971-75.

11.1-9 Anonymous. 1973. Wakan'yaku [Japanese and Chinese herbs] (Taisha maki 10, suppl.), [Nakayama, Tokyo, Japan.] 346, 26 pp. NLMCC 1971-75: 1962.

11.1-10 Anonymous. 1974. A barefoot doctor's manual. D.H.E.W. Publication No. (NIH) 75-695. U.S. Dep. Health, Education, and Welfare. Public Health Service. National Institutes of Health. Superintendent of Documents, U.S. Government Printing Office, Washington, D.C. 960 pp.

11.1-11 Ashur, S.S. 1972. Nitrogen retention of adult human subjects who consumed combinations of wheat and rice supplemented with chickpea, sesame meal, milk or whey. Ph.D. Thesis. Purdue University. 222 pp. University Microfilms, Ann Arbor, Mich. Order no. 73-15, 766. DAI-B 34: 299-B.

11.1-12 Atal, C.K., and Kapur, B.M. 1977. Cultivation & utilisation of medicinal and aromatic plants. Regional Research Lab, Jammu- Tawi. Leipzig Press, New Delhi, India. xvi, 568 pp.

11.1-13 Bae, Hyo-Won, ed. 1978. Korean ginseng. Korea Ginseng Research Institute, Seoul, Korea. 317 pp.

11.1-14 Barbosa, M.A. de L.P. 1976. Aspectos da producao e comercializacao de alho [Aspects of production and commercialization of garlic]. Estudos diversos-Fundacao Centro de Pesquisas Economicas e Sociais do Piaui. Governo do Estado do Piaui, Secretaria de Planejamento, Fundacao Centro de Pesquisas Economicas e Sociais do Piaui, Teresina, Brazil. 55 1. LC-S 10-12/1980{4}: 767.

11.1-15 Bowers, W.S. 1980. Chemistry of plant/insect interactions. In Insect biology In the future, Academic Press, New York, N.Y.

11.1-16 Brar, Gurdip Singh. 1979. Inheritance of oil composition in sesame (Sesamum indicum L.). Ph.D. Thesis. University of California-Riverside. 105 pp. University Microfilms, Ann Arbor, Mich. Order no. 77-14, 375. DAI-B 38: 60-61-B.

11.1-17 Brenneker, Vitus. 1976. Geneeskrachtige kruiden van de Antillen. Brenneker, [s.l.]. 60 pp. LC-S 1979{9}: 518.

11.1-18 British Herbal Medicine Association. Scientific Committee. 1971.D British herbal pharmacopoeia. [The Association], London, G.B. 1 v. (loose-leaf). NLMCC 1971-1975.

11.1-19 Brzeski, M.W. 1974. Wegorek niszcyk cebuli i czosnku [Stem nematode on onion and garlic]. Instytut Warzynictwa, Skierniewice, Poland. 16 pp. HELM AB-B 44: 324.

11.1-20 Carter, G.T. 1976. Structures of oligomycin A and C. II. Structures of three isomeric octadecadienoic acids possessing divalent cation ionophoretic activity. III. Insecticidal components of dill and anise plants. Ph.D. Thesis. University of Wisconsin-Madison. 248 pp. University Microfilms, Ann Arbor, Mich. Order no. 76-15,982. DAI-B 37: 766.

11.1-21 Central Council for Research in Indian Medicine and Homeopathy. 1978. Preliminary techno-economical survey of national resources and herbal wealth of Ladakh. 2nd ed. K. Raghunathan, ed. (CCRIMH pub. 21). The Council, New Delhi, India. 184 pp. NLM CC 1979{1}: 825.

11.1-22 Centro Italiano fitofarmacoterapia. Sexione studi, richerche, bibliografia, stampa e propaganda. 1977. Archivio de erboristeria e delle piante officinali utili alimurgiche industriali, velenose, fitotecnica, farmacognostica, cure vegetali, ecc. il Centro, Vercelli, Italy. 58 pp. LC-S 1979{9}: 520.

11.1-23 Chevrenidi, S.Kh. 1978. Ekologo-biologicheskie osobennosti vazhneishikh syr'evykh rastenii v kul'ture [Ecological and biological characters of the imported roughage plants introduced into cultivation]. "Fan", Tashkent, Uzbek SSR. 292 pp. [on Geranium spp. and Glycyrrhiza spp.]. HERB AB 49: 3920.

11.1-24 Chiang-hsi Chung i hsueh yuan. 1978. Chung ts'ao yao [Chinese herbs] (Ch'ih chiao i sheng ho ch'u hsueh Chung i jen yuan ts'an k'ao ts'ung shu). Jen min wei sheng ch'u pan she [Peking, China]. 368 pp. NLM CC 1979{1}: 825.

11.1-25 Chiang-su hsin i hsueh yuan. 1977. Chung yao ta ts'u tien

[Encyclopedia of Chinese drugs]. Shang-hai jen min ch'u pan she, Shanghai, China. 2 v., 2754 pp. NLM CC 1979{1}: 825.

11.1-26 Chuang, Chao-hsiang, and Li, Ning-han. 1978. Hsian-kang Chung ts'ao yao [Chinese medicinal herbs of Hong Kong]. Commercial Press, Hong Kong. v. 1. LC-S 1979{9}: 520.

11.1-27 Chung-kuo i hsueh k'o hsueh yuan, Peking. Yao wu yen chiu so. 1978. Po ts'eng ts'eng li chi ch'i tsai Chung ts'ao yao fen hsi chung ti yingyung [thin-layer chromatography and its application in the analysis of traditional Chinese medicinal plants]. K'o hsueh ch'u pan she, Peking, China. 487 pp. NLM CC 1979{1}: 825.

11.1-28 Darrah, Helen H. 1980. The cultivated basils. Buckeye Print. Co., Independence, Mo. 40 pp. LC-S 10-12/1980{7}: 978.

11.1-29 Debray, M., Jacquemin, H., and Razafindrambao. 1971. Contribution a l'inventaire des plantes medicinales de Madagascar. (Travaux et documents de l'O.R.S.T.O.M., no. 8) [O.R.S.T.O.M., Paris, France]. 150 pp. NLMCC 1971-75: 1962.

11.1-30 Demidovskaia, L.F., et al. 1976. Nouye lekarstvennye i efirnomaslichnye rasteniia Kazakhstana (Trudy Instituta Botaniki; t. 35). Nauka, Alma-Ata, USSR. 210 pp. NLM CC 1977: 489.

11.1-31 Diaz, Jose Luis. 1976. Usos de las plantas medicinales de Mexico (Monografias cientificas - Instituto Mexicano para el Estudio de las Plantas Medicinales 2). The Instituto, Mexico City, Mexico. NLM CC 1979{1}: 826.

11.1-32 Dixon, Pamela. 1976. Ginseng. Duckworth, London, U.K. 103 pp.

11.1-33 Dyer, Anne. 1976. Dyes from natural sources. Bell, London, G.B. 88 pp.

11.1-34 Eastmond, R.J. 1971. Response of four plant communities to eroded soils and smelter smoke in northern Utah. Ph.D. Thesis. University of Utah. 92 pp. University Microfilms, Ann Arbor, Mich. Order no. 72-504. DAI-B-32: 3209-B.

11.1-35 Emboden, William A., Jr. 1972. Narcotic plants. Macmillan Company, New York, N.Y. 206 pp.

11.1-36 Epenhuijsen, C.W. van. 1974. Growing native vegetables in Nigeria. FAO, Rome, Italy. 113 pp. FCA 28: 6168.

11.1-37 Eshtiaghi, H. 1975. Effects of the northern root-knot nematode (Meloidogyne hapla Chitwood, 1949) on Mitcham peppermint (Mentha piperita L.) and Scotch spearmint (Mentha cardiaca Baker). Ph.D. Thesis. Oregon State University. 83 pp. University Microfilms, Ann Arbor, Mich. Order no. 75-13,051. DAI-B 35: 5734-5735-B.

11.1-38 Estes, J.W. 1979. Hall Jackson and the purple foxglove. University Press of New England, Hanover, N.H.

11.1-39 Fenaroli, G. 1975. Fenaroli's handbook of flavor ingredients, 2nd ed., ed.,trans., rev. by T. E. Furia and N. Bellanca. CRC Press, Cleveland. vol. 1. 551 pp.

11.1-40 Fischer, Horst. 1972. Effect and characterization of virus inhibiting principles in paprika plants [in German]. Bonn Universitat. Landwirtschaft Fakultat. Inaugural Dissertation. 90 pp.

11.1-41 Fluek, Hans. 1976. Medicinal plants and their uses: medicinal plants, simply described and illustrated with notes on their constituents, actions and uses, their collection, cultivation and preparations [translation of Unsere Heilpflanzen, 4th ed.]. Foulsham , London, G.B. 188 pp. NLM CC 1978: 505.

11.1-42 Foster, G.B., and Louden, R.F. 1980. Park's success with herbs. Geo. W. Park Seed Co., Inc., Greenwood, South Carolina. 192 pp.

11.1-43 Frohne, ·D., and Jensen, U. 1979. Systematik des Pflanzenreichs: unter besonderer Bedruecksichtigung chemischer Merkmale und pflanzlicher Drogen, 2nd ed. Fisher, New York. 308 pp. NLM CC 1979{1}: 825.

11.1-44 Gammerman, A.F., and Grom, I.I. 1976. Dikorastushchie lekarstvennye rasteniia SSSR. Meditsina, Moscow, USSR. 285 pp. NLM CC 1977: 489.

11.1-45 Garofalo, Francesco. 1971. Red pepper [in Italian] 2nd ed. Edizioni Agricole, Bologna, Italy. 80 pp.

11.1-46 Gavina Mugica, M. de, and Torner Ochoa, J. 1974. Contribution al estudio de los aceites esenciales espanoles. II. Aceites esenciales de la provincia de Guadalajara [Contribution to the study of Spanish essential oils. II. Essential oils of the Guadalajara province]. Instituto Nacional de Investigaciones Agrarias, Madrid, Spain. 431 pp. HA 46: 11651.

11.1-47 Gerhardt, Ulrich. 1973. Gewuerze und Wuerzstoffe sowie ihre Anwendung zur Herstellung von Fleischwaren (Fleischforschung und Praxis: Schriftenreihe; Heft 9). Verlag der Rheinhess. Druckwerkstaette, Alzey, Germany. 150 pp. LC-S 1970-74{86}: 217.

11.1-48 Goock, Roland. 1977. Das Buch der Gewurze: das umfassende Standardwerk der Gewurze, Krauter und Wurzemittel [The book of spices], rev. ed. Mosaik-Verlag, Munich, Germany. 318 pp. LC-S 1979{9}: 519.

11.1-49 Greenwald, S.M., Sr. 1972. Some environmental effects on the growth and monoterpene production of Pinus taeda L. and Ocimum basilicum L. Ph.D. Thesis. Duke University. 97 pp. University Microfilms, Ann Arbor, Mich. Order no. 73-13,003 DAI-B 33: 5695-5696-B.

11.1-50 Grieve, Maud. 1971. A modern herbal: the medicinal, culinary, cosmetic and economic properties, cultivation and folk-lore of herbs, grasses, fungi, shrubs and trees with all their modern scientific uses. Reprint of 1931 ed. Dover Pub., New York, N.Y. 2 vol. LC-S 1975{8}: 153.

11.1-51 Grime, W.E., comp. 1976. Botany of the Black Americans. Scholarly Press, St. Clair Shores, Mich. 230 pp.

11.1-52 Gubanov, I.A., Krylova, I.L., and Tikhonova, V.L. 1976. Dikorastushchie poleznye rasteniia SSR. Mysl', Moscow, USSR. 360 pp. NLM CC 1977: 489.

11.1-53 Guerra, Nonete Barbosa. 1975. Acao antioxidante de algumas espaciarias em diferentes atividades de agua [Antioxidant action of some spices in different water activity]. Universidade de Sao Paulo, Conjunto das Quimicas, Sao Paulo, Brazil. 62 pp.

11.1-54 Guzman, David J. 1974. Especies utiles de la flora salvadorena: medico-industrial con aplicacion a la medicina, farmacia, agricultura, artes, industria y comercio, 2nd ed. (Coleccion Biblioteca del Maestro no. 6). Ministerio de Educacion, Direccion de Cultura, Direccion de Publicaciones, San Salvador, El Salvador. NLM CC 1977: 488.

11.1-55 Hammad, S.M. 1978. Pests of grain legumes and their control in Egypt. Pages 135-137 in S.R. Singh, H.F. van Emden and T.A. Taylor, eds. Pests of grain legumes: ecology and control. Academic Press, New York, N.Y. RAE-A 67: 5038.

11.1-56 Hang-chou yao wu shi yen ch'ang. 1977. Yao yung chih wu tsai pei [Cultivation of medicinal plants]. Shang-hai jen min ch'u pan she, Shanghai, China. 495 pp. NLM CC 1979{1}: 825.

11.1-57 Harding, Arthur Robert. 1972. Ginseng and other medicinal plants: a book of valuable information for growers as well as collectors of medicinal roots, barks, leaves, etc. Emporium Publications, Boston. [reprint of 1908 ed.]. 367 pp. LC-S 1970-74{38}: 314.

11.1-58 Hauke, G., and Paetzold, R. 1978. Photophysikalische Chemie indigoider Farbstoffe (Nova Acta Leopoldina: Supplementum Nr. 11). Deutsche Akademie d. Naturforscher Leopoldina, Leipzig, East Germany. LC -S 1979{10}: 246.

11.1-59 Hawthorn, W.R. 1973. Population dynamics of two weedy perennials, Plantago major L. and P. rugelii Decne. Ph.D. Thesis. University of Western Ontario (Canada). Microfilm obtainable from the National Library of Canada, Ottawa. DAI-B 34: 1470-B.

11.1-60 Heath, H.B. 1978. Flavor technology: profiles, products, applications. AVI Pub., Westport, Conn. CA 89: 213857.

11.1-61 Hillier, H.G. 1973. Hillier's manual of trees and shrubs. A.S. Barnes Co., San Diego, CA.

11.1-62 Hills, L.D. 1974. Comfrey report: the story of the world's fastest protein builder. Henry Doubleday Research Association, Bocking, Braintree, Eng. 110 pp.

11.1-63 Hills, L.D. 1976. Comfrey: past, present and future. Faber and Faber, London, U.K. 253 pp.

11.1-64 Hou, Joseph P. 1978. The myth and truth about ginseng. A.S. Barnes, South Brunswick, N.J. 245 pp. BIP-A 1981-82: 2020.

11.1-65 Hsu, Hong-Yen, Chen, Yuh-Pan, and Hong, Mina. 1975. Chemistry of Chinese herb drugs. Chinese Herb Medicine Committee, National Health Administration, Republic of China.

11.1-66 Hsu, Hon-Yen, and Peacher, William G. 1976. Chinese herb medicine and therapy. Oriental Healing Arts Institute of U.S.A., Hawaiian Gardens, Calif. 223 pp. NLM CC 1978: 300.

11.1-67 Hutchens, A.R., Tretchikoff, N.G., and Tretchikoff, N.K. 1974. Indian herbalogy of North America. Merco, Ontario, Canada. 382 pp.

11.1-68 Hu-pei sheng Chung yao ts'ai kung ssu. 1976. Chung yao ts'ai tsai p'ei chi shu [Techniques of cultivation of traditional Chinese medicinal plants]. Hu-pei jen min ch'u pan she, [Wuchong, China]. 216 pp. NLM CC 1979{1}: 825.

11.1-69 Imamura, Tomo. 1971. Ninjinshi [History of ginseng]. Reprint of 1934-40 ed. Shibunkaku, Kyoto, Japan. 7 v. NLMCC 1971-75: 1959.

11.1-70 Indian Council of Medicinal Research. 1976. Medicinal plants of India. The Council, New Delhi, India. 487 pp.

11.1-71 Indian Institue of Foreign Trade. 1976. Commodity study on crude drugs & herbs. The Institute, New Delhi, India. 271 pp. NLM CC 1979{1}: 477.

11.1-72 Indian Institute of Foreign Trade. 1980. Export prospects of selected medicinal herbs in West Germany, USA and Japan. The Institute, New Delhi, India.

11.1-73 International Trade Centre, UNCTAD/GATT. 1974. Markets for selected essential oils and oleoresins. The Centre, Geneva, Switz. 297 pp.

11.1-74 International Trade Centre, UNCTAD/GATT. 1974. Markets for selected medicinal plants and their derivatives. The Centre, Geneva, Switz. 192 pp.

11.1-75 International Trade Centre, UNCTAD/GATT. 1977. Spices: a survey of the world market, vol. I. The Centre, Geneva. 281 pp.

11.1-76 International Trade Centre UNCTAD/GATT. 1977. Spices: a survey of the world market, vol. II. The Centre, Geneva, Switz. 234 pp.

11.1-77 Juscafresa, Baudilio. 1975. Enciclopedia illustrada flora: medicinal, toxica, aromatica, condimenticia [Illustrated dictionary of plants: medicinal, poisonous, aromatic, condiment]. Editorial Aedos, Barcelona, Spain. 542 pp. LC-S 1976{1}: 882.

11.1-78 Kakbaz-Nejad, M.S. 1972. Versuch zur chemisch-biologischen Unwandlung von Sozialbrache- und Kahlsschlagflachen in wintergrune Futterpflanzenbestande. Dissertation. Justus Liebig-Universitat. Landwirtschaftliche Fakultaet. Giessen, W. Germany. NALC.

11.1-79 Kariyone, Tatsuo. 1971. Yakuyo shokubutsu gafu [Atlas of medicinal plants]. Takeda Yakuhin Kogyo Kabushiki Kaisha, Osaka, Japan. 150 pp. NLMCC 1971-75: 1960.

11.1-80 Keys, John D. 1976. Chinese herbs, their botany, chemistry, and pharmacodynamics. C.E. Tuttle Co., Rutland, Vt. 388 pp. LC-S 1977{7}: 222.

11.1-81 Khokhlov, S.S., ed. 1976. Apomixis and breeding. Amerind, New Delhi, India. 346 pp. PBA 47: 3864.

11.1-82 Khudaibergenov, Enverbek Bekovich. 1979. Solodki Kazakhstana: khoziaistvenno-tsennye vidy. "Nauka", Alma-Ata, USSR. 126 pp. [on licorice]. NALC

11.1-83 Kim, H.J., Nam, S.H., and Fukura, Y., eds. 1977. Korean ginseng studies (chemistry, pharmacology). Ilhwa Co., Seoul, Republic of Korea. v. 1. LC-S 1980{2}: 360.

11.1-84 Kim, Jung Yun. 1974. Saponin and sapogenin distribution in American ginseng plants. Ph.D. Thesis. University of Minnesota. 155 pp. University Microfilms, Ann Arbor, Mich. Order no. 74:26,203. DAI-B 35: 2615-16.

11.1-85 Kirtikar, K.R., and Basu, B. 1975. Indian medicinal plants, 2nd ed. Bishen Singh Mahendra Singh Pal, Dehra Dun, India. 4 vol. 2793 pp. INB 1/77: 24.

11.1-86 Klein, H. 1977. Untersuchungen ueber die genotypische und umweltbedingte Variabilitaet bei Qualitaetseigenschaften der Samen von Sinapis alba, Brassica juncea und Brassica nigra [Investigations on genotypic and environmentally caused variation in seed quality of Sinapis alba, Brassica juncea and Brassica nigra]. Thesis. Justus Liebig-Universitaet, Giessen, German Federal Republic. 189 pp. FCA 34: 3660.

11.1-87 Klokov, M.V. 1973. Race evolution in the genus thyme Thymus L. in the Soviet Union [in Russian]. Kiev, "Naukova Dumka", Kiev, USSR. 188 pp. AGRICOLA.

11.1-88 Krochmal, A., and Krochmal, C. 1973. A guide to the medicinal plants of the United States, Times Bks, New York, N.Y. 512 pp.

11.1-89 Krochmal, Arnold, and Krochmal, Connie. 1974. The complete illustrated book of dyes from natural sources. Doubleday & Co., Inc., New York, N.Y. 272 pp. NUC 1973-77{64}: 242.

11.1-90 Krochmal, A., Walters, R.S., and Doughty, R.M. 1971. A guide to medicinal plants of Appalachia (U.S. Dep. Agric. Handbk. 400). U.S. Superintendent of Documents, Washington, D.C. 291 pp. NMLCC 1971-75: 1959.

11.1-91 Krohn, V.F. 1980. Hawaii dye plants and dye recipes. University Press of Hawaii, Honolulu, HI. 136 pp.

11.1-92 Kudinov, M.A., and Kukhareva, L.V. 1980. Solodka - novoe tsennoe rasteniedlia Belorussii [licorice - a new valuable crop for Byelorussia]. Nauka i Tekhnika, Minsk, USSR. 116 pp. AGRICOLA.

11.1-93 Kudinov, M.A. 1976. Prianoaromaticheskie rasteniia v bytu [Spice plants in our life]. "Uradzhai", Minsk, USSR. 159 pp. NALC 5581-78.

11.1-94 Lawrence, B.M. 1979. Essential oils 1978. Allured Publishing Corporation, Wheaton, Illinois. 192 pp. HA 50: 9400.

11.1-95 Leung, Albert Y. 1980. Encyclopedia of common natural ingredients used in food, drugs and cosmetics. John Wiley & Sons, New York, N.Y. 409 pp.

11.1-96 Lewis, Walter H., and ELvin-Lewis, M.P.F. 1977. Medical botany: plants affecting man's health. John Wiley & Sons, New York, N.Y. 515 pp.

11.1-97 Li, C.P. 1974. Chinese herbal medicine. U.S.D.H.E.W. Pub. No. (NIH) 75-732, U.S. Government Printing Off. Washington, D.C. 120 pp.

11.1-98 Li, Hsiao-Ming. 1978. Mo li ti tsai p'ei [The culture of jasmine]. Fuji An Shinghua Books. Fuzhou, China. 49 pp.

11.1-99 Liu, Edwin H. 1971. The isozymic forms of peroxidase found in the horseradish plant (Armoracia lapathifolia). Ph.D. Thesis. Michigan State University. 218 pp. University Microfilms, Ann Arbor, Mich. Order no. 72-16, 468. DAI-B 32: 6819-B.

11.1-100 Liu, Shao-p'eng. 1975. Mo li hua ti tsai p'ei bo chia kung [The culture and processing of the jasmine and large jasmine flowers]. Light industry publishing house. Beijing, China. 58 pp. LC-S 1976{9}: 331.

11.1-101 Lust, J. 1974. The herb book. Bantam Books, New York, N.Y. 659 pp.

11.1-102 Maarse, Henk. 1971. Semensteiling van de vluchtige olie van Origanum vulgare L. spp. vulgare gedurenda de ontwikkeling van de plant. Elinkwijk, Utrecht, Neth. 104 pp.

11.1-103 Maghami, Parviz. 1979. Culture et cueillette des plantes medicinales [Culture and harvesting of medicinal plants]. Hachette, Paris, France.

11.1-104 Makabe, Jin. 1979. Beni to ai. Heibron Pub., Tokyo, Japan. 144 pp. LC-S 4-6/1980{2}: 884.

11.1-105 Malyshev, A.A. 1978. Zhen'shen': Biologiia i razvedenie [ginseng]. "Lesnaia Promyshlennost'", Moscow, USSR. 151 pp.

11.1-106 Maurais, J., and Brodeur, P., eds. 1976. Lexique des epices et assaisonnements: anglais-francais. Regie de la langue francaise, Quebec, Canada. 72 pp. LC-S 1978{17}: 301.

11.1-107 McGrath, Judy Waldner. 1977. Dyes from lichens and plants. Van Nostrand Reinhold, Toronto, Canada. 144 pp.

11.1-108 McReynolds, W.D. 1972. Alterations in chloroxuron selectivity induced by chemical and environmental factors. Ph.D. Thesis. Michigan State University. 100 pp. University Microfilms, Ann Arbor, Mich. Order no. 72-30,011. DAI-B 33: 1879-1880-B.

11.1-109 Meinert, Georg. 1972. Contributions to distribution, biology and control of field mint (Mentha arvensis L.) [in German]. Dissertation , Hohenheim Universitat. Hohenheim, Germany. 113 pp. AGRICOLA.

11.1-110 Mikhailova, V.P., ed., et al. 1978. Lekarstvennye i technicheskie rasteniia iuzhnogo Kazakhstana (Trudy Instituta Botaniki, t. 38). D Nauka, Alma-Ata, USSR. 143 pp. NLM CC 1979{1}: 826.

11.1-111 Miki, Yokichiro. 1971. Awaai fu [on indigo]. [Mikisangyu], Matsushige Chyo, Japan. 554 pp. LC-S 1978{9}: 513.

11.1-112 Mir, P. 1976. La salade [Green salad]. Centre Technique Interprofessionnel des Fruits et Legumes, Paris, France. 176 pp. WAERSA 19: 6491.

11.1-113 Moerman, Daniel E. 1977. American medical ethnobotany: a reference dictionary. Garland Pub., New York, N.Y. 527 pp.

11.1-114 Morton, Julia. 1978. Major medicinal plants: botany, culture and uses. Charles C. Thomas, Springfield, Ill. 431 pp.

11.1-115 Moule, C. 1972. Special plant techniques. 3. Field and miscellaneous crops [in French]. La Maison Rustique, Paris, France. 252 pp. FCA 28: 4194.

11.1-116 Mueller-Stock, Anneliese. 1972. Untersuchungen uber die Inhaltsstoffe von Fructus capsici deren Struktur und Gehaltsbestimmung (Eidgenossische Technische Hochschule. Diss. no. 4909). Juris, Zurich, Switz. 188 pp. AGRICOLA.

11.1-117 Mustyatse, G.I. 1973. The accumulation of essential oil and menthol in peppermint leaves [in Russian]. Pages 79-85 in Poleznye svoistva dikorastushchikh rastenii Moldavii. Stiinca, Kishinev, Moldavian SSR. HA 44: 9939.

11.1-118 Nagashio, Yasunobu. 1978. Shojobetsu, byokibetsu minkan'yaku ryoho = [Drug therapy of folk medicine by symptoms and diseases]. Shufu no Tomo Sha, Tokyo, Japan. NLM CC 1979{1}: 826.

11.1-119 Negri, Giovanni. 1976. Erbario figurato: descrizione e proprieta della piante medicinali e velenose della flora italiana: con cenni sulle principali specie dell'Africa settentrionale ed orientale, 5th ed. Hoepli, Milan, Italy. 459 pp. NLM CC 1978: 505.

11.1-120 Nishino, Kaemon. 1971. Awaai enkakushi, reprint of 1940 ed. Chimonkaku , Kyoto, Japan. 574,30,33 pp. Note: On history of indigo dye. LC-S 1978{9}: 514.

11.1-121 Omura, Shigemitsu. 1978. Chugoku Nihon Yakuyo shokubutsu shoyaku = [Medicinal plants and crude drugs in China and Japan]. Hirokawa Shoten, Tokyo, Japan. 311 pp. NLM CC 1979{1}: 825.

11.1-122 Opdyke, D.L.J. 1979. Monographs on fragrance raw materials. Pergamon Press, Oxford, Eng. 804 pp. CA 92: 11094.

11.1-123 Perrot, Emile, and Paris, Rene. 1971. Les plantes medicinales, new ed. Presses unversitaires de France, [Paris], France. 2 v. NLM CC 1971-75: 1959.

11.1-124 Perry, Lily M., and Metzger, Judith. 1980. Medicinal plants of East and Southeast Asia: Attributed properties and uses. The MIT Press, Cambridge, Massachusetts and London, England. 620 pp.

11.1-125 Popov, Pavel. 1971. Mak, Papaver somniferum L. [in Bulgarian]. Izd-vo. na Bulgarskata Akademiia na Naukite, Sofia, Bulgaria. 234 pp.

11.1-126 Pruthi, J.S. 1980. Spices and condiments: chemistry, microbiology, technology. Academic Press, New York, N.Y. 449 pp.

11.1-127 Rai, B.K. 1976. Pests of oilseed crops in India and their D control. Indian Council of Agricultural Research, New Delhi, India. 121 pp. RAE-A 65: 2760

11.1-128 Rosengarten, Frederic, Jr. 1973. The book of spices. Pyramid Books, New York, N.Y. 480 pp.

11.1-129 Salmeron Salmeron, Pascual. 1973. El color en los procesos de elaboracion del pimenton. Centro de Edafologia y Biologia Aplicada del Segura, Murcia, Spain. 246 pp.

11.1-130 Schauenberg, Paul. 1977. Guide to medicinal plants [translation of Guide des plantes medicinales]. Lutterworth, Guilford, U.K. NLM CC 1978: 505

11.1-131 Schultes, R.E. 1976. Hallucinogenic plants. Golden Press, New York, N.Y. 160 pp.

11.1-132 Shreter, Aleksei Ivanovich. 1975. Lekarstvennaia flora sovetskogo Dal'nago Vostoka. Meditsina, Moskva, Moscow, USSR. 327 pp. NLMCC 1971-75: 1962.

11.1-133 Singh, Thakur Balwant, and Chunekar, K.C. 1972. Glossary of vegetable drugs in Brhattrayi (Chowkhamba Sanskrit Studies vol. LXXXVII). D Chowkhamba Sanskrit Series Office, Publishers and Oriental & Foreign Book-Sellers, Varanasi, India. 537 pp.

11.1-134 Smolianov, A.M., ed., and Ksendza, A.T. 1976. Efiromaslichnye kul'tury [Volatile oil bearing crops]. "Kolos", Moscow, USSR. 334 pp. NALC 5515-78.

11.1-135 Soares, Francisco Amilton Cavalcante. 1971. Programa para a introducao da cultura do gergelim no Noerdeste [Program for the introduction of sesame in the Northeast]. Cetrede, Fortaleza, Brazil. 2 v. LC-S 1978{16}: 522.

11.1-136 Spoerke, D.G., Jr. 1980. Herbal medications. Woodbridge Press Pub. Co., Calif. 192 pp.

11.1-137 Staikov, V.M. 1975. Bulgaria, the country of roses and essential oils. National Center for Scientific and Technical Information in Agriculture, Food Industry, and Forestry, Sofia, Bulgaria. 78 pp. LC-S 1976{1}: 882.

11.1-138 Swain, Tony, ed. 1972. Symposium "Plants in the Development of Modern Medicine", Cambridge, Mass, 1968. Harvard Univ. Press, Cambridge, Mass. 367 pp. NLMCC 1971-75: 1961.

11.1-139 Swain, T., and Waller, R., eds. 1979. Topics in the biochemistry of natural products. Plenum Press, New York, N.Y. 253 pp.

11.1-140 Szucs, Kalman. 1975. A fuszerpaprika termesztese es feldolgozasa. D Ezogazdasagi Kiado, Budapest, Hungary. 281 pp. AGRICOLA.

11.1-141 Szujkone Lacza, Julia. 1976. Az anizs, Pimpinella anisum L. Magyarorszag Kulturfloraja v. 4 no. 8, also Kulturflora 42. Akademiai Kiado, Budapest, Hungary. 95 pp.

11.1-142 Taiwan, Food and Fertilizer Technology Center for the Asian and Pacific Region. 1974. Multiple cropping systems in Taiwan. [The Center], Taipei, Taiwan. 77 pp. HA 46: 772.

11.1-143 Thurston, Violetta. 1975. The use of vegetable dyes, 14th ed. Reeves-Dryad Press, Leicester, G.B. 48 pp.

11.1-144 Tucker, A.O. 1975. Morphological, cytological, and chemical evaluation of the Mentha X gentilis L. s.l. hybrid complex. Ph.D. Thesis. Rutgers University. 99 pp. University Microfilms, Ann Arbor, Mich. DAI-B 36: 2042.

11.1-145 Turchi, Antonio. 1974. La coltivazione del finocchio. Edizioni Agricole, Bologna, Italy. 43 pp. AGRICOLA.

11.1-146 Tutin, T.G., Heywood, V.H., Burges, N.A., Moore, D.M., Valentine, D.H., Walters, S.M., and Webb, D.A., eds. 1972. Flora Europaea. Cambridge Univ. Press, Cambridge, G.B. 5 vols.

11.1-147 Tyler, V.E., Brady, L.R., and Robbers, J.E. 1976. Pharmacognosy, 7th ed. Lea & Febiger, Philadelphia, Pa. 537 pp. NUC 1973-77{120}: 167.

11.1-148 Urdaneta Urdaneta, Rosigne Ramon. 1980. Estudio de algunos hongos que afectan al ajonjoli (Sesamum indicum L.) en diferentes regiones de Mexico, con enfasis en Macrophomina phaseoli. Thesis. Escuela Nacional de Agricultura. Colegio de postgraduados, secretaria agricultura y recursos hydraulicos, rama de fitopatologia, Chapingo, Mexico 90. AGRICOLA.

11.1-149 UK Ministry of Agriculture, Fisheries and Food. 1980. Culinary and medicinal herbs. Reference Book, Ministry of Agriculture, Fisheries and Food, No. 325. Her Majesty's Stationary Office, London, U.K. 70 pp. HA 51: 7216.

11.1-150 Vassiliou, G. 1979. Untersuchungen ueber die Ursachen der unterschiedlichen Empfindlichkeit von Kulture-Umbelliferen gegen Metoxuron [Studies on the causes of the crop differential susceptibility of crop umbellifers to metoxuron]. Thesis. Universitaet Hohenheim, Stuttgart-Hohenheim, German Federal Republic. 127 pp. WA 30: 304.

11.1-151 Veselvovskaia, M.A. 1976. The poppy: its classification and importance as an oleiferous crop = Mak i ego klassifikatsiya i znachenie, kak maslichnoi kultury (Transl. from Russian) TT-74-52053. Available National Technical Information Service PB-257 858-T. GRAI 76{24}: 28. 200 pp.

11.1-152 Watanabe, Takeshi. 1976. Wakariyasui kampoyaku [understanding Chinese drugs and herbalism]. Kokusai Shogyo Shuppan, Tokyo, Japan. 271 pp. NLM CC 1977: 286.

11.1-153 Weigle, P., Rodriguez, M.H., McGourty, F., Jr., and Dietz, M.J., eds. 1973. Natural plant dyeing. Plants Gard. 29{2}. 64 pp. HA 44: 9934.

11.1-154 Weiner, Michael A., Weiner, Janet, and Farnsworth, N.R. 1980. Weiner's herbal. Stein and Day Publishers, New York, N.Y.

11.1-155 Weiss, E. 1971. Castor, sesame and safflower. Barnes & Noble, New York, N.Y. 901 pp. LC-S 1970-74{82}: 31.

11.1-156 White, Alan. 1976. Hierbas del Ecuador: plantas medicinales = Herbs of Ecuador: medicinal plants. ZIKR Publications, Quito, Ecuador. 315 pp. LC-S 1977{7}: 222.

11.1-157 Wittop Koning, Dirk Arnold, and Leroux, Alain. 1972. La chicoree dans l'histoire de la medecine et dans la ceramique pharmaceutique (Supplement to the Revue d'histoire de la pharmacie, no. 215). [Societe d'histoire de la pharmacie, Paris, France.] 30 pp. NLMCC 1971-75: 1960.

11.1-158 Wong, W. 1972. The changes that occur in peppermint oil during aging, including the relationship between changes in chemical composition and flavor characteristics. Ph.D. Thesis. Rutgers University. 174 pp. University Microfilms, Ann Arbor, Mich. Order no. 72-27, 612. DAI-B 33: 1605.

11.1-159 Worku, Zemedu. 1971. Developing increased color in paprika pepper (Capsicum annuum L.). Ph.D. Thesis. Michigan State University. 91 pp. University Microfilms, Ann Arbor, Mich. Order no. 72-16, 541. DAI-B 32: 6769-B.

11.1-160 Wu, Chin-ch'ang. 1977. T'ai-wan yao ts'ao p'u = The medicinal plants of Taiwan. Wei ch'eng wen hua shih yeh, Taipei, Taiwan. NLM CC 1979{1}: 826.

11.1-161 Yamada, Kentaro. 1979. Koryo hakubutsu jiten [Dictionary of aromatics]. Dohosha, Kyoto, Japan. 559 pp. LC-S 1980{10}: 130.

11.1-162 Yamada, Kentaro. 1976. Toa koryo shi kenkyu [A study of the history of perfumery and spices in the Far East]. Chuokoronbijutsu Shuppan (Pub), Tokyo, Japan. LC-S 1977{13}: 965.

11.1-163 Yermanos, D.M. 1980. Sesame. Pages 549-563 in W.R. Fehr and H.H. Hadley, eds. Hybridization of crop plants. American Society of Agronomy and Crop Science Society of America, Madison, Wis.

11.1-164 Zarghami, N.S. 1971. The volatile constituents of saffron (Crocus sativus L.). Ph.D. Thesis. University of California, Davis. 107 pp. University Microfilms, Ann Arbor, Mich. Order no. 71-7959. DAI-B 31: 5235.

12.0 BIBLIOGRAPHIES ON HERBS

12.1-1 Anonymous. 1974. Annotated bibliography on cultivation of opium poppy, 1958-1972. Papaver somniferum. Query File Commonw. Bur. Hortic. Plant. Crops 29/74. 7 pp. AGRICOLA.

12.1-2 Anonymous. 1974. Annotated bibliography on liquorice (Glycyrrhiza glabra), 1946-1973. Query File Commonw. Bur. Hortic. Plant. Crops 55/74. 4 pp. AGRICOLA.

12.1-3 Anonymous. 1974. Annotated bibliography on nitrogen nutrition of Mentha spp. 1955-1972. Query File Commonw. Bur. Hortic. Plant. Crops 24/74. 5 pp. AGRICOLA.

12.1-4 Anonymous. 1975. Annotated bibliography on fenugreek (Trigonella foenum-graecum), 1969-1975. Query File Commonw. Bur. Hortic. Plant Crops 17/75. 4 pp. AGRICOLA.

12.1-5 Anonymous. 1976. Annotated bibliography on chives, 1970-1975. Query File Commonw. Bur. Hortic. Plant. Crops 11/76. 2 pp. AGRICOLA.

12.1-6 Anonymous. 1976. Annotated bibliography on watercress, 1967-1974. Query File Commonw. Bur. Hortic. Plant. Crops 2/76. 2 pp. AGRICOLA.

12.1-7 Anonymous. 1978. Oilseed poppy (Papaver somniferum) bibliography 1966-1977. Annot. Bibliogr. Commw. Bur. Pastures Field Crops G478. 8 pp. AGRICOLA.

12.1-8 Chonmae Kisul Yon'guso. 1975. Abstracts of Korean ginseng studies, 1687-1975: world-wide collected bibliography, citations, and abstracts. Research Institute, Office of Monopoly, Republic of Korea. 254 pp. LC-S 1979{8}: 958.

12.1-9 Commonwealth Bureau of Horticulture. 1973. Annotated bibliography on valerian (Valeriana spp.) 1965-1971. Commonw. Bur. Hortic. Plant Crops Query File 60/78(S). 2 pp. AGRICOLA.

12.1-10 Duke, J.A. 1973. Annotated bibliography on opium and oriental poppies and related species. (U.S. Agricultural Research Service ARS-NE-28). U.S. Dep. Agric. Agricultural Research Service, Beltsville, Md. 349 pp. LC-S 1970-74{72}: 13.

12.1-11 Gilbertson, G., and Koenig, R.T. 1979. Essential oils and related products. Anal. Chem. 51{5}: 183-196R.

12.1-12 Guenther, E., Gilbertson, G., and Koenig, R.T. 1971. Essential oils and related products. Anal. Chem. 43{5}: 45-64R.

12.1-13 Guenther, E., Gilbertson, G., and Koenig, R.T. 1973. Essential oils and related products. Anal. Chem. 45{5}: 45-67R.

12.1-14 Guenther, E., Gilbertson, G., and Koenig, R.T. 1975. Essential oils and related products. Anal. Chem. 47{5}: 139R-15 7R.

12.1-15 Guenther, E., Gilbertson, G., and Koenig, R.T. 1977. Essential oils and related products. Anal. Chem. 49{5}: 83-98R.

12.1-16 Gupta, B.K., and Jain, N. 1979. Contribution to the bibliography of Cymbopogon grasses. Indian J. For. 2{1}: 71-96. Bib.Ag. 44: 74142.

12.1-17 Gupta, B.K., and Jain, N. 1979. Contribution to the bibliography of Cymbopogon grasses. Indian J. For. 2{2}: 99-117. Bib.Ag. 44: 66460.

12.1-18 Heath, H. 1973. Herbs and spices - a bibliography. Part I. Flavour Ind. 4: 24-26.

12.1-19 Heath, H. 1973. Herbs and spices - a bibliography. Part II. Flavour Ind. 4: 65-68.

12.1-20 Heath, H. 1973. Herbs and spices - a bibliography. Part III. Flavour Ind. 4: 169-172.

12.1-21 Heath, H. 1973. Herbs and spices - a bibliography. Part IV. Flavour Ind. 4: 217-218, 220.

12.1-22 Heath, H. 1973. Herbs and spices - a bibliography. V. Flavour Ind. 4: 263-266.

12.1-23 Heath, H. 1973. Herbs and spices - a bibliography. VI. Nutmeg and mace; onion; origanum/oregano; paprika. Flavour Ind. 4: 346-348, 351.

12.1-24 Heath, H. 1973. Herbs and spices - a bibliography. VII. Parsley; pepper; pimento; rosemary. Flavour Ind. 4: 394-396.

12.1-25 Heath, H. 1974. Herbs and spices - a bibliography. VIII. Saffron and safflower; sage; savory. Flavour Ind. 5: 79, 81.

12.1-26 Heath, H. 1974. Herbs and spices - a bibliography. IX. Tarragon; thyme; turmeric. Flavour Ind. 5: 123-124.

12.1-27 Instytut Przemyslu Zielarskiego. 1974. A bibliographical review of research on medicinal plants; concerned with the works of employees of the Institute of Medicinal Plants in years 1947-1973. A teamwork edited by Jan Kozlowski. [The Institute], Poznan, Poland. NLMCC

12.1-28 Iyengar, M.A. 1976. Bibliography of investigated Indian medicinal plants (1950-75). Iyengar, Manipal, India. 144 pp. NLM CC 1978: 505. 1971-75: 1960.

12.1-29 Khristov, K.D., Breskovska, T.E., and Stalkov, V. 1978. Bibliografiia na bulgarskite eterichnomasleni rasteniia i eterichni masla = Bibliography on Bulgarian aromatic plants and essential oils, 1779-1976. Inst. po Rozata Eterichnomaslenite i Lekarstvenite Kulturi, Kazanlik, Bulgaria. 180 pp. LC-S 4-6/1980{1}: 207.

12.1-30 Kim, Jung Yun. 1975. The ginseng bibliography. Kim, Seoul, Korea. 166 pp. LC-S 1977{6}: 819.

12.1-31 Lynas, Lothian. 1972. Medicinal and food plants of the North American Indians; a bibliography. Library of the New York Botanical Garden, New York, N.Y. 21 pp. NUC 1973-77{70}: 369.

12.1-32 Tamson, R. 1974. Bibliography on medicinal plants and related subjects (South Pacific Commission Technical paper no. 171). South Pacific Commission, Noumea New Caledonia. 145 pp. NLMCC 1971-75: 1960.

12.1-33 Tennessee Valley Authority. 1977. Fertilizing chili 1970-1974. Tennessee Valley Authority. Bibliography 1559. 2 pp. SF 42: 1352

13.0 REPORTS, CONFERENCES, AND SYMPOSIA

13.1-1 Abeysinghe, Ariya. 1975. Mustard, Brassica nigra L.: cultivation, processing, and marketing in Sri Lanka (Crop study series; [no. 30]). Planning Division, Ministry of Plantation Industries, Colombo, Sri Lanka. 8 pp. LC-S 1979{14}: 86.

13.1-2 Abeysinghe, Ariya. 1974. Sesame (gingelly): cultivation, processing and marketing (Crop studies; no. 5). Planning Division, Ministry of Plantation Industry, Colombo, Sri Lanka. 8 pp. LC-S 1976{14}: 877.

13.1-3 Alderman, D.C. 1976. Native edible fruits, nuts, vegetables, herbs, spices, and grasses of California. IV. Herbs, spices, and grasses. D Leaflet, Division of Agricultural Sciences, California University 2895. 13 pp. HA 47: 10731.

13.1-4 American Herbal Pharmacology Delegation. 1975. Herbal pharmacology in the People's Republic of China: a trip report of the American Herbal Pharmacology Delegation: submitted to the Committee on Scholarly Communication with the People's Republic of China. National Academy of Sciences, Washington, D.C. LC-S 1976{7}: 961.

13.1-5 American Spice Trade Association. 1976. Cleanliness specifications for unprocessed spices, seeds, and herbs. The Association, Englewood Cliffs, N.J. 9 pp.

13.1-6 American Spice Trade Association. 1977. The nutritional composition of spices. The Association, Englewood Cliffs, N.J. 2 pp.

13.1-7 Americanos, P.G. 1976. Weed control in peppers, eggplants, beans, squash, melons and watermelons. Technical Paper, Agricultural Research Institute, Nicosia, Cyprus. 11 pp. WA 26: 2917.

13.1-8 Anahosur, K.H. 1978. Alternaria burnsii. C.M.I. Descr. Pathog. Fungi Bact. Commonw. Mycol. Inst. 59 {581}. 2 pp.

13.1-9 Anonymous. 1971. Paprikateelt onder glas. [= Paprika cultivation under glass]. Proefstation voor de groenten- en fruitteelt onder glas te Naaldwijk. Informatiereeks no. 5. 56 l. AGRICOLA.

13.1-10 Anonymous. 1973. Chemical weed control in carrots, parsnips, parsley and celery. Short-Term Leaflet, Ministry of Agriculture, Fisheries and Food, England and Wales 83 (Rev. Ed.). 2 pp. WA 23: 1257.

13.1-11 Anonymous. 1973. Technical information, experimental herbicide HCS 3438. Development Bulletin, Velsicol Agricultural Chemicals. 4 pp. WA 22: 2674.

13.1-12 Anonymous. 1975. Federal specification, EE-S-631H. Spices, ground and whole, and spice blends. U.S. Army Natick Development Center, Natick, Mass.

13.1-13 Anonymous. 1975. Garlic [in Spanish]. Serie de Cultivos 20. 22 pp. HA 47: 368.

13.1-14 Anonymous. 1978. Rose geranium. Outlook for breeding [in French]. IRAT Informations 10. PBA 50: 1428.

13.1-15 Anonymous. 1979. Willow-carrot aphid. Advisory Leaflet, Ministry of Agriculture, Fisheries and Food 603. 6 pp. RAE-A 68: 5110.

13.1-16 Aquino, M. de L.N. de, and Sena, R.C. de. 1973. A new disease of coriander (Coriandrum sativum) caused by Glomerella cingulata (Ston.) in the State of Pernambuco [in Portuguese]. Bol. Tecn. Inst. Pesqui. Agron. Pernambuco 63. 12 pp.

13.1-17 Benoit, F., and Cuestermans, N. 1979. Feeltgegevens tot het bekomen van venkel vanaf Juni tot November [= Cultural methods of obtaining fennel from June to November]. Proefstation voor de Groenteteelt, St. Katelijne-Waver, Belgium. 8 pp. HA 50: 8417.

13.1-18 Berry, R.E., Fisher, G., Capizzi, J., Retan, A., Homan, H., and Todd, J. 1977. Insects on mint. PNW Oreg. State Univ. Coop. Ext. Serv. 82. 15 pp.

13.1-19 Berry, R.E., and Robinson, R.R. 1973. Mint flea beetle in Oregon. Oreg. State Univ. Ext. FS 196. 2 pp.

13.1-20 Boawn, L.C., and Rasmussen, P.E. 1971. Zinc fertilization trials with peppermint, spearmint, and asparagus. Circ. Washington Agric. Exp. Stn. 534. 10 pp. AGRICOLA.

13.1-21 Brett, C.H., and Sullivan, M.J. 1974. The use of resistant varieties and other cultural practices for control of insects on crucifers in North Carolina. Bulletin, Agricultural Experiment Station, North Carolina 449. 31 pp.

13.1-22 Bruns, V.F., Demint, J., Frank, P.A., Kelly, A.D., and Pringle, J.C., Jr. 1974. Responses and residues in six crops irrigated with water containing 2,4-D. Bulletin, College of Agriculture Research Center, Washington State University 798. 10 pp. WA 24: 2825.

13.1-23 Burns, J.J., and Tsuchitani, P.J., eds. 1980. United States-China Pharmacology Symposium, National Academy of Sciences, 1979, proceedings. Committee on Scholarly Communications with the People's Republic of China, Washington, D.C. 354 pp. Available: NAS Pub. Off. NUC 1980{16}: 472.

13.1-24 Cespedes Torres, E. 1979. Sesame growing in Southern Tamaulipas and Northern Veracruz [in Spanish]. Desplegable Ciagon Cent. Invest. Agric. Golfo Norte 7. 6 pp. AGRICOLA.

13.1-25 Chalfant, R.B. 1978. Chemical control of insect pests of greens in Georgia. Res. Bull. Ga. Agric. Exp. Stn. 216. 21 pp.

13.1-26 Charles, W.B. 1976. Shallot growing. Ext. Bull. Univ. West Indies 15. 7 pp. AGRICOLA.

13.1-27 Clevenger, T.S., and Taylor, D.M. 1976. New Mexico's vegetable processing industry. Res. Rep. N.M. Agric. Exp. Stn. 322. 8 pp. WAERSA 18: 6258

13.1-28 Cochran, J.H., and Harness, J. 1975. Pepper weevil control on hot pepper. Inf. Sheet Coop. Ext. Serv. Miss. State Univ. 743. 2 pp.

13.1-29 Conference on Spices, London, 1972. 1973. Proceedings of the conference on spices, Apr. 10-14, London School of Pharmacy, 1972. Tropical Products Institute, London, G.B. 261 pp. LC-S 1975{16}: 355.

13.1-30 Crop Science Society of America. 1975. Registered field crop varieties: 1926-1974. The Society, Madison, WI. 49 pp. PBA 47: 4955.

13.1-31 Croteau, R., ed. 1980. Fragrance and flavor substances. Proceedings of the 2nd international Haarman & Reimer symposium on fragrance and flavor substances. New York City, 1979. D & PS. Verlag, Pattensen, Germany.

13.1-32 Dempsey, A.H., and Fretz, T.A. 1973. New herbicides for weed control in peppers. Ga. Agric. Exp. Stn. Res. Rep. 53. 10 pp.

13.1-33 Devisch, N., and Kempenaers, A. 1972. Comparison of chicory production costs in Belgium, France and the Netherlands [in French]. Notes, Institut Economique Agricole, Ministere de l'Agriculture, Belgium 32. 20 pp. WAERSA 15: 3691.

13.1-34 Doll, C.C., Courter, J.W., Acker, G., and Vandermark, J.S. 1973. Illinois horseradish: a natural condiment. Circ.-Univ. Ill. Coop. Ext. Serv. 084. 8 pp. AGRICOLA.

13.1-35 Eid, M.N., and Rofaeel, I.S. 1980. Geranium oil as influenced by application of IAA. Research Bulletin, Faculty of Agriculture, Ain Shams University 1239. 11 pp. HA 51: 2879.

13.1-36 Eid, M.N., and Rofaeel, I.S. 1980. Effect of B-9 and CCC on the growth and essential oil of geranium (Pelargonium graveolens L.). Research Bulletin, Faculty of Agriculture, Ain Shams University 1238. 15 pp. HA 51: 2878.

13.1-37 El-Kholy, S.A., and Saleh, M.M. 1980. Effect of thiamine and ascorbic acid on the yield, essential oil and chamazulene formation in Matricaria chamomilla L. Research Bulletin, Faculty of Agriculture, Ain Shams University 1409. 19 pp. HA 51: 6480.

13.1-38 El-Tahawi, B.S., El-Shahat, N., and El-Naggar, H.A. 1979. Chromatographic studies on fennel fixed oil. Research Bulletin, Faculty of Agriculture, Ain Shams University 1060. 22 pp. HA 50: 9399.

13.1-39 Emmett, B.J. 1978. Onion fly. Advisory Leaflet, Ministry of Agriculture, Fisheries and Food 163. 5 pp. RAE 67: 1554.

13.1-40 Espinet Colon, G.R., Gonzalez Villafane, E., Muler Manzanares, L., and Chavarria de Gracia, O. 1973. Economic analysis of the production and marketing of plantain at the producer level, Puerto Rico, 1971-72 [in Spanish]. Pub. P.R. Ag. Exp. Stn. 82. 24 pp.

13.1-41 Flengmark, P. 1976. Cultivars of yellow mustard, 1972-1975 D [in Danish]. Meddelelse, Statens Forsoegsvirksomhed i Plantekultur, 78{1283}. 2pp. FCA 31: 4379.

13.1-42 Flengmark, P. 1977. Varieties of caraway, 1974-1976 [in Danish]. Medd. Statens Forsogsvirksomhed. Plantekult. 352. 1 pp. AGRICOLA.

13.1-43 Franz, C., ed. 1978. First international symposium on spices and medicinal plants, July 31-August 4, 1977, Freising-Weihenstephan, Fed. Rep. Germany. International Society of Horticultural Science, The Hague, The Netherlands. 341 pp.

13.1-44 Friesen, O.H. 1976. Grain drying. Publication, Agriculture Canada 1497. 4 pp. FCA 30: 4943.

13.1-45 Ganpat, Roop. 1973. Cultivation of hot peppers. Ministry of Agriculture, Lands and Fisheries, Trinidad and Tobago, Trinidad. 4 pp. AGRICOLA.

13.1-46 Gaylor, M.J., Sterling, W.L., and Eddy, C.D. 1976. Effects of temperature and host plants on population dynamics of the cotton fleahopper, Pseudatomoscelis seriatus. Tex. Agric. Exp. Stn. Bull. B-1161. 8 pp.

13.1-47 Gilbert, N.W. 1977. Opium poppy research in the southwestern United States 1945-1966. U.S. Agric. Res. Serv. Western Region [Rep] ARS W. 44. 24 pp. MC 78-8574.

13.1-48 Gommers, F.J. 1973. Nematocidal principles in Compositae. Meded. Landbouwhogesch. Wageningen 73-17. 71 pp.

13.1-49 Gray, F.A., and Hine, R.B. 1973. Diseases of chili pepper. Q. Coop. Ext. Serv. Univ. Ariz. 253. 3 pp. AGRICOLA.

13.1-50 Gray, F.D. 1972. Spice trends in the United States. USDA Econ. Res. Serv. NFS-142: 34-38. AGRICOLA.

13.1-51 Greenhalgh, P. 1979. The market for culinary herbs. Report of the Tropical Products Institute G121. 171 pp. HA 50: 7313.

13.1-52 Greenhalgh, P. 1979. The markets for mint oils and menthol. Report of the Tropical Products Institute G126. 171 pp. HA 50: 3626.

13.1-53 Guillou, J.P. 1975. Chemical weed control in vegetable crops in Tunisia [in French]. Documents Techniques, Institut National de la Recherche Agronomique de Tunisie 70. 17 pp. HA 46: 11204.

13.1-54 Gutierrez A., Oscar. 1971. Sesame culture in the Apatzingan valley [in Spanish]. Centro de Investigaciones Agricolas del Bajio. Circular CCIAB 38. 14 pp. NALC.

13.1-55 Hand, Wayland D., ed. 1976. American folk medicine: a symposium. UCLA conference on American folk medicine, 1973. University of California Press, Berkeley, Calif. 347 pp. NUC 1973-77{120}: 197.

13.1-56 Hensley, D.L., Alexander, S., and Roberts, C.R., eds. [n.d.].ProceedingsD of the first national ginseng conference, 1979. University of Kentucky, Lexington, KY. 124 pp.

13.1-57 Hruschka, H.W., and Wang, C.Y. 1979. Storage and shelf life of packaged watercress, parsley, and mint. Mark. Res. Rep. U.S. Dep. Agric. 102. 19 pp. HA 49: 5831.

13.1-58 Huhtikangas, A. 1976. Biosynthetic aspects of lipophilic excretion in Carum carvi and Dryopteris ferns. Ann. Acad. Sci. Fenn. Ser. A2 177. 44 pp. HA 46: 11644.

13.1-59 International Ginseng Symposium, Seoul, 1974. 1975. Proceedings of international ginseng symposium. Central Research Institute, Office of Monopoly, Republic of Korea, Seoul, Korea. 152 pp.

13.1-60 International Ginseng Symposium, 2nd, Seoul, 1978. Korea Ginseng Research Institute. 1978. Proceedings of the 2nd international ginseng symposium, September 7-11, 1978. Korea Ginseng Research Institute, Seoul, Korea. 157 pp.

13.1-61 International Ginseng Symposium, 3rd, Seoul, 1980. 1980. Proceedings of the 3rd international ginseng symposium, 1980. Korea Ginseng Research Institute, Seoul, Korea.

13.1-62 Kalutskii, K.K., and Lishchuk, A.I. 1979. Main results of scientific research and production work at the Nikita Botanical Garden during 1978 [in Russian]. Byull. Gos. Nikitsk. Bot. Sada 1979{1}: 5-10. PBA 50: 6020.

13.1-63 Kapoor, L.D., and Ram Krishnan, eds. 1977. Advances in essential oil industry. Proceedings of a symposium on development of essential oil in Uttar Pradesh, Kanpur, India, Jan. 7-18, 1976. Today and Tomorrow's Printers and Publishers, New Delhi. 252 pp.

13.1-64 Kelleher, J.S., comp. 1977. Candian Agricultural Insect Pest Review 55. Res. Program Service, Agriculture, Canada, Ottawa, Canada. 66 pp. WA 29: 154.

13.1-65 Knoll, J., ed. 1976. Second congress of the Hungarian Pharmacological Society. v. 3: Symposium on pharmacology of catecholaminegic and serotonergic mechanisms, October 1974, Budapest, Hungary. Akademiai Kiado, Budapest, Hungary. 202 pp. NUC 973-77{104}: 206.

13.1-66 Ko, W.W. 1974. A mosaic virus disease of Capsicum annum L. in West Malaysia. MARDI Report 17. 7 pp. HA 46: 3366.

13.1-67 Koivistcinen, P., ed. 1980. Mineral element composition of Finnish foods: N, K, Ca, Mg, P, S, Fe, Cu, Mn, Zn, Mo, Co, Ni, Cr, F, Se, Si, Rb, Al, B, Br, Hg, As, Cd, Pb and ash. Acta Agric. Scand. Suppl. 22. 171 pp.

13.1-68 Kostrinski, J. 1974. Problems in chickpea cultivation and grain crop rotation in Israel [in Hebrew]. Spec. Publ., Agric. Res. Organ. Volcani Cent. (Bet Dagan, Isr.) 34. 51 pp. FCA 29: 7266.

13.1-69 Kosuge, S. 1978. Studies on pungent principles of red pepper. V. Determination of the pungent principles {2} Ultraviolet spectrophotometric method. U.S. Dep. Agric. Res. Serv. TT 76-53497. 16 1. AGRICOLA.

13.1-70 Lacy, M.L., and Meggitt, W.F. 1972. Controlling weeds in mint with terbacil herbicide. Res. Rep. Agric. Exp. Stn., Mich. State Univ. 68. 4 pp.

13.1-71 Lawalree, Andre. 1972. Valerianaceae (Flore d'Afrique centrale: Spermatophytes). Jardin botanique national de Belgique, Bruxelles, Belgium. 5 pp. LC-S 1970-74{96}: 92.

13.1-72 Lee, Young Choo, ed. 1974. Korean ginseng science symposium [in Korean]. Korean Society of Pharmacognosy, Seoul, Korea. 261 pp. AGRICOLA.

13.1-73 Lippold, P.C., Hongtrakula, T., Thongdeetaa, S., Banziger, H., Hillerup, P.E., Kelderman, W., Supharngkasen, P., and Deema, P. 1975. Use of colored sticky board traps in insect surveys. Plant Protection Service Technical Bulletin 29. 60 pp. RAE-A 66: 110.

13.1-74 Loewenfeld, C., and Back, P. 1978. The complete book of herbs and spices. David and Charles, Inc., North Pomfret, Vt. 319 pp.

13.1-75 Marsh, A.C., Moss, M.K., and Murphy, E.W. 1977. Composition of foods: spices and herbs raw, processed, prepared. U.S. Dep. Agric. Agriculture Handbook no. 8-2. var. pp.

13.1-76 McGourty, Frederick, Jr., ed. 1980. Dye plants and dyeing - a handbook. Brooklyn Botanic Garden Record, Plants & Gardens, New York, N.Y. 100 pp.

13.1-77 McGourty, Frederick, Jr., ed. 1980. Handbook on herbs. Brooklyn Botanic Garden Record, Plants and Gardens, New York, N.Y. 93 pp.

13.1-78 Medina, J.P., Vera Cruz, W.C., Atienza, N.R., Salisi, M.M., and

Bagtas, P.M. 978. Garlic production and marketing, Ilocos Region. Study, Special Studies Division, Planning Service, Department of Agriculture, Philippines 78-18. 36 pp. WAERSA 21: 2411.

13.1-79 National Symposium on Recent Advances in the Development, Production and Utilisation of Medicinal and Aromatic Plants, Lucknow, 1975. 1975. Abstracts of papers. Central Indian Medicinal Plants Organisation, Lucknow, India. 46 pp. LC-S.

13.1-80 Nayar, N.M., ed. 1974. Proceedings of the first national symposium on plantation crops. Indian Society for Plantation Crops, Kerala, India. 220 pp. HA 45: 6215.

13.1-81 Nelson, C.E., Early, R.E., and Mortensen, M.A. 1971. Effects of growing method and rate and time of N fertilization on peppermint yield and oil composition. Ciircular, Washington Agricultural Experiment Station 541. 19 pp. HA 43: 6265

13.1-82 Nelson, C.E., Mertensen, M.A., and Early, R.E. 1971. Evaporative cooling of peppermint by sprinkling. Circular, Washington Agricultural Experiment Station 539. 12 pp. HA 43: 6264.

13.1-83 Noort, M.E. van den,, and Wassink, E.C. 1980. On different forms of flowers in the same spike in Digitalis purpurea L., f. heptandra De Chamisso. Meded. Landbouwhog. Wageningen 80-9. 22 pp. HA 51: 2007.

13.1-84 Nordestgaard, A. 1976. Sowing rate and row spacing in mustard, cv. Trico [in Danish]. Meddelelse, Statens Planteavlsforsoeg 78{1313}. 4 pp. FCA 31: 5563.

13.1-85 Nordestgaard, A. 1979. Effect of sowing depth on the emergence of rape, yellow and brown mustard, oilseed flax, caraway and poppy [in Danish]. Meddelelse, Statens Planteavlsforsoeg 81{1482}. 4 pp. FCA 33: 3038.

13.1-86 Nystrom, S. 1974. Yield development in some long-term rotation experiments [in Swedish]. Lantbrukshogsk. Medd. Ser. A 219. 26 pp. FCA 28: 6052.

13.1-87 Ogg, A.G. 1975. Evaluation of herbicides for weed control in Bulletin, College of Agriculture Research Center, Washington State University 810. 10 pp. WA 25: 1570.

13.1-88 Patty, G.E. 1972. U.S. mint oil in the European market. Publication, Foreign Agricultural Service, U.S. Department of Agriculture FASM-244. 29 pp.

13.1-89 Patty, G.E. 1974. U.S. ginseng in the Far East market. U.S. Department of Agriculture, Foreign Agricultural Service FASM-261. 11 pp.

13.1-90 Pelletier, J., Coilier, P., Douet, Y., and Vissonneau, A. 1975. Chemical weed control in egg plant and peppers 1972-1973-1974 [in French]. Publicationl Institut National de Vulgarisation pour les Fruits, Legumes et Champignons 322/93. 10 pp. WA 25: 698.

13.1-91 Peron, J.-Y. 1979. Vegetable crop diversification trials under a large plastic tunnel in a northern zone [in French]. Resultats d'Experimentation et d'Essais 3. 15 pp. HA 50: 7091.

13.1-92 Peters, E.J., and Stritzke, J.F. 1976. Wild garlic: life cycle and control. U.S. Agricultural Research Service, Agriculture Information Bull. 390. 22 pp.

13.1-93 Poldini, L., Sancin, P., and Sciortino, T. 1971. Contenuto in olii essenziali della Salvia officinalis nel Carso triestino. Universita degli studi di Trieste. (Facolta di farmacia. Instituto di chimica farmaceutica e tossicologica. Publicazioni n. 5). The Universita, Trieste, Italy. 31 pp. LC-S 1970-74{79}: 424.

13.1-94 Pressman, E., and Negbi, M. 1980. Comparative physiology of wild and cultivated varieties of Apium graveolens L. with special reference to flowering [in Hebrew]. Pamphlet, Volcani Center, Bet Dagan 222. 132 pp. HA 51: 7876.

13.1-95 Price, D.W. 1973. Demand and supply of U.S. mint oil. Bulletin, Washington Agricultural Experiment Station 782. 30 pp. WAERSA 16: 4314.

13.1-96 Pruidze, V.G. 1976. Changes in plastid pigments during the process of drying and storage of bay laurel (Transl. from Russian). U.S. Dep. Agric. TT 76-58076. Translation of Tr. Gruz. Nauchno-Issled. Inst. Pishch. Prom-sti. 4: 316-319,1971. AGRICOLA.

13.1-97 Putievsky, E., Chizer, D., Ron, R., and Fleisher, A. 1978. Experiments with sweet basil (Ocimum basilicum L.). Spec. Publ. Agric. Res. Organ. Volcani Cent. (Bet Daga, Isr.) 113. 26 pp. HA 49: 1455.

13.1-98 Ranatunga, A.S., and Izumi, K. 1974. Production of other corps in paddy fields in Yala 1972. A case study based on record keeping farmers in two special projects (Elahera and Dewahuwa). Research Study Series, Agrarian Research and Training Institute 4. 38 pp. WAERSA 6: 6071.

13.1-99 Rasulpuri, M.L., Lin, K.G., and Sedky, A. 1972. Utilization of Malaysian produce. Drying of red chillies. Working Paper, Food Technology Research and Development Centre of Malaysia 88. 13 pp. WAERSA 17: 2666.

13.1-100 Rheenen, H.A. van. 1973. Major problems of growing sesame (Sesamum indicum L.) in Nigeria. Meded. Landbouwhogesch. Wageningen 73-12. 130 pp.

13.1-101 Richardson, W.G. 1979. The tolerance of fenugreek (Trigonella foenumgraecum L.) to various herbicides. Technical Report Agricultural Research Council Weed Research Organization [U.K.] 58. 31 pp.

13.1-102 Rizk, T.Y., Fayed, M.T., and El-Deepah, H.R. 1978. Effect of some promoters on weed seed germination. Research Bulletin, Faculty of Agriculture, Ain Shams University 818. 30 pp. WA 28: 3685.

13.1-103 Robbins, S.R.J. 1973. Essential oils: a study of production economics. Publ. United Nations Industrial Development Organization 61. 52 pp. HA 44: 8911.

13.1-104 Robbins, S.R.J., and Greenhalgh, P. 1979. The markets for selected herbaceous essential oils. Report of the Tropical Products Institue G120. 60 pp. HA 50: 7314.

13.1-105 Roberts, C.R., and Richardson, J. 1980. Kentucky wild ginseng survey, 978-79. Prog. Rep. Ky. Agric. Exp. Stn. 247. 23 pp. AGRICOLA.

13.1-106 Robinette, S.L. 1974. Checkerberry wintergreen. U.S. For. Serv. Gen. Tech. Rep. N.E. 9: 20-22.

13.1-107 Ryden, P. 1974. Investigation of oilcrops in the Chilalo D awraja. Publication, Chilalo Agricultural Development Unit (Addis Ababa, Ethiopia) 94: 36-54. FCA 29: 5131.

13.1-108 Sadowska, A. 1975. Effect of gamma ionizing radiation upon the yield of peppermint (Mentha piperita L.) and on the quantity and quality of its essential oil [in Polish]. Zeszty Naukowe Akademii Rolniczy Warszawie Rozprawy Naukowe 50. Dzial Wydawnictw, Warsaw, Poland. 75 pp.

13.1-109 Saite, M., comp., Saito, M., and Singh, R.B. 1976. Reports on study of mycotoxins in foods in relation to liver diseases in Malaysia and Thailand [in Japanese and English]. Institute of Medical Science, University of Tokyo, Tokyo, Japan. 85 pp. RMVM 12: 1070.

13.1-110 Sant, L.E. van't, Bethe, J.G.C., Vijzelman, H.E., and Freriks, J.C. 1975. Observations on miners (Napomyza spp., Diptera, Agromyzidae) on chicory, carrots and chamomile [in Dutch]. Versl. Landbouwk-d. Onderz. 840. 44 pp. HA 46: 6685.

13.1-111 Schreier, J. 1980. Stabilization of poppy seed yields at large-scale cultivation technology [in Czech]. Metody Zavadeni Vysledku Vyzk. Praxe (Czech. Ustav Vedeckotech. Inf. Zemed.) 8. 16 pp. AGRICOLA.

13.1-112 Schuurman, J.J., and Schaffner, B.E. 1974. The root development of some horticultural crops in sandy soil [in Dutch]. Rapp.Inst. Bodemvruchtbaarbeid 11-74. 62 pp. HA 46: 7533.

13.1-113 Shacklette, H.T. 1980. Elements in fruits and vegetables from areas of commercial production in the conterminous United States. Geol. Surv. Prof. Pap. (U.S.) 1178. 149 pp.

13.1-114 Simposio Nacional de Farmacobotanica, 1st, Alicante, Spain, 1971. 1972. Simposio nacional de farmacobotanica, 23, 24, y 25 de abril de 1971. Consejo General de Colegios Oficiales de Farmaceuticos, Madrid, Spain. 59 pp. NLMCC 1971-75: 1961.

13.1-115 Stanger, C.E., and Twombly, R. 1980. Weed control in furrow irrigated mint. Pages 49-77 in Spec. Rep. Oreg. Agric. Exp. Stn. 592.

13.1-116 Stange, L.A. 1978. Evania appendigaster (L.), a cockroach egg parasitoid (Hymenoptera: Evaniidae). Entomology Circular, Division of Plant Industry, Florida Department of Agriculture and Consumer Services 191. 2 pp. RAE-B 67: 275.

13.1-117 Stokes, D.E. 1979. Some plant symptoms associated with Aphelenchoides spp. in Florida. Nematology Circular. Division of Plant Industry, Florida Department of Agriculture and Consumer Services 49. 1 pp.

13.1-118 Symposium on Spice Industry in India, 1974, Mysore. 1974. Symposium on spice industry in India, Feb. 28, Mysore, 1974.

[Association of Food Scientists and Technologists, Mysore, India.] 36 pp. LC-S 1975{16}: 355.

13.1-119 Tanaka, J.S., Romanowski, R.R., Jr., and Crozier, J.A., Jr. 1973. Herbicide evaluation studies with solanaceous crops in Hawaii. Res. Rep. Ha. Agric. Exp. Stn. 90. 20 pp. WA 24: 959.

13.1-120 Tetenyi, P., and Mathe, A., eds. 1980. Second international symposium on spices and medicinal plants, July 16-22, 1979, Budapest, Hungary. International Society for Horticultural Science, The Hague, The Netherlands. v. 1. 352 pp.

13.1-121 Tetenyi, P., and Mathe, A. 1980. Second international symposium on spices and medicinal plants, July 16-22, 1979, Budapest, Hungary. D International Society for Horticultural Science, The Hague, The Netherlands. v. 2. 244 pp.

13.1-122 Throneberry, G.O., Booth, J.A., Kasunic, D., and McKinney, H. D 1978. Nitrogen and chlorophyll in crop plants exposed to sulfur dioxide. N.M. Agric. Exp. Stn. Bull. 659. 9 pp.

13.1-123 Tsagareli, K.K. 1976. The application of conductiometry for the rapid measurement of moisture in bay laurel leaves (Transl. from Russian). U.S. Dep. Agric. TT 76-58075. Translation of Tr. Gruz. Nauchno-Issled. Inst. Pishch. Prom-sti 5: 160-162, 1971. AGRICOLA.

13.1-124 United Fresh Fruit & Vegetable Association. 1974. Anise. Fruit Veg. Facts Pointers. 3 pp. AGRICOLA.

13.1-125 United Fresh Fruit & Vegetable Association. 1974. Watercress. Fruit Veg. Facts Pointers. 7 pp.

13.1-126 United Nations. Industrial Development Organization. 1977. Information sources on the coffee, cocoa, tea, and spices industry (UNIDO guides to information sources; no. 28). United Nations Industrial Development Organization, New York. 74 pp. LC-S 1979{18}: 793.

13.1-127 U.S. Fish and Wildlife Service. 1980. Proceedings of the 2nd national ginseng conference. May 19-20, Jefferson City, Mo., 1980. The Department, Jefferson City, Mo. 81pp.

13.1-128 U.S. Dep. Agric. Foreign Agricultural Service. Foreign Agricultural Circulars. Tea, spices, and other tropical products. 1 +. Irregular. Note: includes essential oils, ginseng, and mint oil.

13.1-129 U.S. Sci. Educ. Admin. 1979. Research on cultivated crops and wild plants for dye production in the highlands of northern Thailand: final report, July 1976-June 1979. Highland Agriculture Project, Kasetsart University, Bankok, Thailand. 39 l.

13.1-130 Verdcourt, B. 1971. Flora of tropical East Africa: Plantaginaceae. East African Community, Arusa, Tanzania.

13.1-131 Wagner, H., and Hoerhammer, L., eds. 1971. Symposium on pharmacognosy and phytochemistry, 1st, Munich, 1970. Pharmacognosy and phytochemistry Springer-Verlag, New York, N.Y. 386 pp. NLMCC 1971-75: 1961.

13.1-132 Wahab, Abdul. 1971. A survey of coriander seeds: Pakistan and the world (E.P.B. commodity study series, no. 9). [Karachi, Export Promotion Bureau, Govt. of Pakistan]. 43 pp. LC-S 1970-74{20}: 575.

13.1-133 Williams, L., and Duke, J.A. 1978. Growing ginseng. Farmers' Bull. (U.S. Dep. Agr.) 2201. 8 pp.

13.1-134 World Health Organization. 1977. Seminar on the use of medicinal plants in health care, Tokyo, 1977. Final report. Regional office for the Western Pacific of the World Health Organization, Manila, Philippines. 179 pp. ICP/DPM/001. NLM CC 1978: 505.

13.1-135 Wyk, B.J. van. 1971. An enterprise analysis of farming in the Eastern Cape coastal region with special references to pineapples, chicory and fresh milk. Economic Series, Division of Agricultural Production Economics, South Africa 77. 65 pp. HA 43: 5640.

14.0 GENERAL REFERENCES

14.1-1 Anonymous. 1967. Watercress growing. Bull. Min. Agric. Fish. Food (G.B.) 136. 35 pp.

14.1-2 Arctander, S. 1960. Perfume and flavor materials of natural origin. Steffen Arctander, Elizabeth, N.J. 736 pp.

14.1-3 Bailey, L.H. 1949. Manual of cultivated plants. Macmillan Pub., New York, N.Y. 1116 pp.

14.1-4 Bailey, L.H. and Bailey, E.Z. 1976. Hortus third. Macmillan Pub., New York, N.Y. 1290 pp.

14.1-5 Bourke, D.O'D. 1974. French-English horticultural dictionary, with English-French index. Commonwealth Agricutural Bureaux, Slough, G.B.

14.1-6 Calpouzos, L. 1954. Botanical aspects of oregano. Econ. Bot. 8: 222-233.

14.1-7 Courter, J.W. and Rhodes, A.M.. 1969. Historical notes on horseradish. Econ. Bot. 23(2): 156-164.

14.1-8 Guenther, E. 1949. The essential oils. Vol. III. Individual D. Van Nostrand Co., New York, N.Y. 777 pp.

14.1-9 Guenther, E. 1952. The essential oils. Vol. IV. D. Van Nostrand Co., New York, N.Y. 752 pp.

14.1-10 Guenther, E. 1952. The essential oils. Vol. V. D. Van Nostrand Co., New York, N.Y. 507 pp.

14.1-11 Guenther, E. 1952. The essential oils. Vol. VI. D. Van Nostrand Co., New York, N.Y. 481 pp.

14.1-12 Harrison, S.G., Masefield, G.B. and Wallis, M. 1969. The Oxford book of food plants. Oxford University Press, London, G.B. 206 pp.

14.1-13 Hartwell, J.L. 1968. Plants used against cancer. A survey. Lloydia 31(2): 71-170.

14.1-14 Hartwell, J.L. 1969. Plants used against cancer. A survey. Lloydia 31(1): 79-107.

14.1-15 Hartwell, J.L. 1969. Plants used against cancer. A survey. Lloydia 31(2): 153-205.

14.1-16 Hartwell, J.L. 1969. Plants used against cancer. A survey. Lloydia 32(3): 247-296.

14.1-17 Hartwell, J.L. 1970. Plants used against cancer. A survey. Lloydia 33: 97-194.

14.1-18 Hartwell, J.L. 1970. Plants used against cancer. A survey. Lloydia 33(3): 288-392.

14.1-19 Johnson, A.J. 1955. Indigoid dyes. Pages 551-576 in H.A. Lubs, ed. The chemistry of synthetic dyes and pigments. (Amer. Chem. Soc. Mono. Ser., no. 127). Reinhold Pub. Corp., New York, N.Y.

14.1-20 Kang, J.W. and Chung, I.C. 1970. Effects of ginseng extract on the stratified squamous epithelia of normal and stressed rats [in Korean]. Kalullik Taehak Uihakpu Nonmunjip 18: 1-13.

14.1-21 Karawya, M.S., Abdel Wahhab, S.M., and Zaki, A.Y. 1969. A study of the lawsone content in henna. Lloydia 32(1): 76-78.

14.1-22 Macchi, V., ed. 1970. Dictionary of the Italian and English languages. Sansoni Editore, Florence, Italy. 4 vols.

14.1-23 Muenscher, W.C. and Rice, M.A. 1955. Garden spice and wild pot-herbs. Cornell University Press, Ithaca, N.Y. 211 pp.

14.1-24 Nijdam, J. and DeJong, A. 1970. Elsevier's dictionary of horticulture in nine languages: English, French, Dutch, German, Danish, Swedish, Spanish, Italian. Elsevier Pub. Co., Amsterdam, Neth. 561 pp.

14.1-25 Ohwi, J. 1965. Flora of Japan. Smithsonian Institution, Washington, D.C. 485 pp.

14.1-26 Oss, J.F. van. 1972. Chemical technology: An encyclopedic treatment Vol. V: Natural organic materials and related synthetic products. Barnes and Noble, New York, N.Y. 35 pp.

14.1-27 Patty, G.E. 1980. Ginseng. U.S. Dep. Agric. Foreign Agric. Serv. Foreign Agriculture Circular FTEA 1-80. 13 pp.

14.1-28 Sievers, A.F. 1930. American medicinal plants of commercial importance. Misc. Publ.-U.S. Dep. Agric. 77. 74 pp.

14.1-29 Sievers, A.F. 1948. Production of drug and condiment plants. U.S. Dep. Agric. Farmers' Bull. 1999. 99 pp.

14.1-30 Springer, O., ed. 1962. Langenscheidt's new Muret-Sanders encyclopedic dictionary of the English and German languages, rev. ed. Barnes and Noble, New York, N.Y. 4 vols.

14.1-31 Stockberger, W.W. 1935. Drug plants under cultivation. U.S. Dep. Agric. Farmers' Bull. 663. 37 pp.

14.1-32 Tetenyi, P. 1970. Infraspecific chemical taxa of medicinal plants. Chem. Pub. Co., Inc., New York, N.Y. 225 pp.

14.1-33 U.S. Office of the Federal Register. 1982. Code of Federal Regulations. U.S. Government Printing Office, Washington, D.C. Title 21.

14.1-34 Velazquez de la Cadena, M. 1967. New pronouncing dictionary of the Spanish and English languages, rev. ed. Appleton-Century-Crofts, New York, N.Y.

14.1-35 Windholz, M., ed. 1976. The Merck index. An encyclopedia of chemicals and drugs. Merck and Co., Inc. Rahway, N.J.

AUTHOR INDEX

Numbers reference listings in the bibliography.

1.1-36, 1.1-37, 1.1-38, 1.1-39,
1.1-40, 1.1-41, 1.1-42, 2.9-26,
2.9-27, 3.3-16, 3.3-214
Brigati, S. 5.6-17
Briggs, C.J. 5.9-4, 8.3-12
Briggs, D. 3.4-132, 3.4-133,
3.4-134
Brighton, C.A. 2.7-19, 2.9-64
Bristol, J.C. 2.2-30
Brit. Herbal Med. Assoc. 11.1-18
Britten, E.J. 1.6-20
Brnic, I. 1.5-113
Brochmann-Hanssen, E. 1.7-20,
1.7-21, 1.7-22, 1.7-23, 1.7-24,
7.2-8, 7.3-17, 7.5-10
Brockie, W.B. 3.3-17
Brodeur, P. 11.1-106
Brodnitz, M.H. 6.4-7
Broertjes, C. 4.2-27
Bromfield, A.R. 3.5-5
Bromstein, A.C. 1.2-114, 3.3-115
Bronshtein, B.D. 4.2-155
Brooks, C.J.W. 1.7-8, 5.6-4
Broua, M. 8.3-75
Brovdii, V.M. 5.4-15, 5.4-16
Brown, C.E. 1.4-23
Brown, G.N. 5.2-52
Brown, J.F. 5.8-23
Brown, R.H. 1.1-185
Brown, S.A. 1.7-25, 1.7-132
Brown, S.O. 1.6-43
Brown, T. 6.5-103
Bruckert, S. 3.4-51
Bruckner, K. 5.5-39
Bruhn, J.G. 7.1-43
Bruins, A.P. 1.5-54
Brun, R. 7.8-11
Bruni, A. 1.6-3
Bruns, V.F. 13.1-22
Brunt, A.A. 5.5-40
Bryant, T.G. 6.1-13
Brykin, A.I. 4.2-123
Bryson, P. 7.8-59
Bryzgalova, N.V. 2.5-13, 2.5-14
Brzeski, M.W. 5.7-32, 11.1-19
Bubarova, M. 1.5-23, 1.5-24,
2.9-29, 4.1-60, 4.1-61, 4.4-179,
4.2-180,
Bublova, J. 1.2-22
Bucci, B.T. 1.2-28
Buchanan, G.A. 5.3-10
Buchanan, R.A. 3.3-18, 3.3-19
Buchanan, R.L. 7.8-12
Buchberger, L. 1.1-41
Buchecker, R. 1.4-14, 2.1-14
Buck, S.H. 7.6-27
Buckingham, G. 5.7-173
Bucko, A. 6.4-8

Buckova, A. 7.2-9
Bucur, E. 5.8-26, 5.9-7, 6.3-26
Budai, C. 5.6-12
Budai, C.S. 5.6-13
Budkevich, T.A. 2.1-63
Budowski, P. 1.7-85, 6.4-54,
6.4-55, 6.4-56
Budryunene, D.K. 3.4-20
Buechi, J. 7.3-97
Buffa, M. 1.1-44, 1.1-154
Bugaenko, L.A. 2.7-20, 4.1-18,
4.2-28, 4.2-29, 4.2-30, 4.2-266
Bugrim, N.A. 7.4-56
Bui, N.-S. 2.8-25
Bui Tkhi Bang 1.7-26, 3.3-20
Buiko, R.A. 3.2-77
Buil, P. 1.2-19, 1.2-110, 1.3-43
Buishand, T. 4.1-19
Bukhbinder, A.A. 1.1-45, 2.3-25,
4.4-16, 5.1-9, 8.2-7, 8.2-8,
8.3-54
Bukin, V.P. 3.2-31, 3.2-59
Bukina, N.V. 5.8-15, 5.8-24,
5.8-182, 5.8-183, 5.8-184,
5.9-51
Bukreyeva, T.V. 7.5-7
Buldeo, A.N. 5.5-41, 5.6-28
Bulgakov, S.V. 4.2-174
Bulhoes, G.C. 7.5-11
Bulinski, R. 5.9-5, 6.5-17
Bulmer, G.S. 7.6-53
Bumbu, I.V. 5.7-203
Bunce, J.A. 3.4-21
Bunduq, A.Z. 2.3-234
Burachyns'kaya, N.S. 3.2-66
Burawanuti, T. 7.8-24
Burbott, A.J. 1.3-26 1.5-25,
1.7-35, 1.7-48, 2.4-22, 2.4-25,
2.4-89
Burduja, C. 3.3-21
Burenin, V.I. 4.2-310
Burges, N.A. 11.1-146
Burgett, M. 1.8-38, 2.5-15
Burghardt, G.M. 7.6-73
Burgis, D.S. 5.8-25, 5.8-146,
5.8-190
Burkholder, W.E. 1.8-184
Burks, T.F. 7.6-27
Burl, P. 8.1-9
Burmeister, G. 4.9-78
Burnham, M. 4.3-139
Burns, E.E. 6.4-47, 6.5-93
Burns, J.J. 13.1-23
Burr, R.J. 5.8-61
Burrell, J.W.K. 1.4-9
Burrows, F.M. 2.5-100
Burtea, O. 6.3-12
Burth, U. 5.9-6

Dutta, S.K. 7.2-23
Duvigneaud, J. 2.8-17
Dvorak, S. 4.1-23
Dvorak, V. 6.5-105
Dwivedi, K.K. 7.6-188
Dwivedi, R. 1.8-56, 1.8-57
Dwivedi, R.P. 5.5-239
Dwivedi, R.S. 1.8-56, 4.5-48
Dworecki, E. 4.3-41
Dworschak, E. 6.2-36
Dwyer, J.E. 6.1-22
Dwyer, W. 1.6-20
Dyakov, G. 8.3-28
Dyduch, J. 2.3-241, 2.3-242
Dye, D.W. 5.5-374
Dyer, A. 11.1-33
Dyke, S.F. 7.4-10
Dyuban'kova, N.F. 1.5-7, 1.5-97
Dzadzijeva, M.F. 7.6-28
Dzevaltovs'ky, A.K. 2.5-31
Dzevaltovs'kyi, A.K. 2.7-101
Dzhakupova, N.U. 2.3-1, 2.4-3,
    4.3-115, 5.3-1
Dzhashi, V. 5.6-22, 5.7-57,
    5.7-58, 5.7-59
Dzhashiashvili, M.Sh. 8.3-29
Dzhugeli, R.I. 2.1-17
Dzhumamuratova, A. 1.1-61
Dzhumrko, V.A. 3.3-199
Dzhuraev, I.N. 3.2-47
Dzhurmanski, G. 2.5-32
Dziuba, N.P. 7.3-34
Dzizenko, A.K. 1.4-86, 1.4-89,
    1.5-134, 1.5-140, 1.6-16,
    7.3-134
Dzur, M. 10.2-3
Dzyuba, N.P. 1.5-37, 7.3-35
Eagles, J. 1.1-78
Eakin, M.A. 7.2-51
Earl, F.L. 7.8-22
Earle, F.R. 1.2-8, 4.1-112
Early, R.E. 13.1-81, 13.1-82
Eastman, C. 5.4-11, 5.4-12
Eastman, C.E. 5.7-65
Eastmond, R.J. 11.1-34
Easwaramoorthy, S. 5.4-27, 5.7-61
Ebel, J. 4.9-69, 4.9-74
Eberspacher, J. 4.9-96
Ebrahimi, A.G. 5.7-60
Ebrahimzadeh, H. 2.5-33
Echim, T. 4.8-51
Eckard, A.N. 2.4-68
Eckert, D.J. 1.4-6
Eckhardt, L. 2.3-181
Eddy, C.D. 13.1-46
Eder, A. 2.4-137
Edgar, J.A. 7.2-11, 7.8-16
Edgar, W.M. 7.6-47

Edmiston, J. 5.2-18, 5.2-19
Edner, G. 7.2-26
Edrees, M. 1.4-1
Edwards, R.H. 6.4-76
Eenink, A.H. 2.5-34, 4.1-32,
    4.2-59, 4.2-60
Efendieva, L.G. 7.6-121
Eferdieva, L.G. 7.6-98
Efimova, F.V. 2.6-3
Efimova, T.P. 3.4-124
Efimova, V.N. 5.8-15, 5.8-182,
    5.9-51
Eggens, J.L. 2.3-60
Egin-Buhler, B. 4.9-74
Egler, F.E. 2.1-23
Egorova, L.V. 7.6-115
Egorova, V.I. 7.4-18, 7.4-19,
    7.4-28, 7.4-29
Ehrendorfer, F. 2.9-39
Ehrenstein, W. 7.6-138
Ehrt, M. 6.5-12
Eichenberger, M.D. 3.4-33
Eichholz, E. 5.8-135, 5.8-138,
    5.8-139
Eid, M.N. 13.1-35, 13.1-36
Eid, M.N.A. 2.3-62, 2.4-7, 2.4-33
Eiden, F. 6.3-36, 7.3-37, 7.3-38
Eifrig, H. 2.8-18
Eijsinga, J.P.N.L.R. van 5.6-23
Eisenbraun, E.J. 1.4-23
Eisenreichova, E. 7.2-9
Eisner, M. 2.5-35
Eisner, T. 2.5-35
Ejsmond, J. 6.4-22
Ek, B.S. 1.7-125
Ekbote, A.P. 4.2-61
Eklund, A. 1.1-62, 6.2-18
Ekpenyong, T.E. 6.2-19
Ekstrom, G. 6.5-110
Eksuzyan, A.A. 2.1-24
Ekundayo, O. 1.7-3, 1.7-9
El Ahmar, B.A. 4.2-316
El Alfy, K.A. 5.7-1
El Badry, D.El-D. 5.3-25
El Hindawy, S. 6.5-1
El Khatib, A. 5.7-169
El Kheir, Y.M. 7.2-15
El Motaz, M.B. 4.3-42
El Nadi, A.H. 5.1-19, 5.1-46
El Shiaty, M.A.
El'kin, Yu.N. 7.3-134
El'yashevich, D.G. 7.7-10
Elbanowska, A. 4.6-96, 6.3-30,
    7.3-39, 7.4-11, 7.4-12
Elberse, W.T. 5.3-42
Elena, E.T. 7.3-69, 7.3-70, 7.4-41
Elena-Rossello, J.A. 2.9-40,
    4.2-62, 4.2-63

676

690

706

714

Muhtadi, F.J. 8.2-23
Muinova, S.S. 4.3-4
Mujumdar, A.S. 1.7-108
Mukai, N. 4.9-175
Mukerjee, S.K. 1.1-55, 1.8-166, 7.3-128
Mukerji, K. 1.8-176
Mukerji, K.G. 5.5-297
Mukerji, M.K. 5.4-3
Mukhamedova, Kh.S. 1.1-170
Mukharji, S.P. 5.4-68
Mukherjee, D. 9.2-3
Mukherjee, P. 2.9-100
Mukherji, S.K. 4.5-175
Mukhopadhyay, A.N. 5.5-223, 5.6-69
Mukhopadhyay, S. 5.5-15
Mukhopadhyay, S.K. 5.8-51
Mukhopadhyay, T.P. 4.6-59
Mukhortova, T.G. 2.3-155, 2.6-49, 2.6-50, 3.2-62, 5.3-34, 8.1-19
Mukminova, F.Z. 4.4-10, 4.4-11
Muler Manzanares, L. 13.1-40
Mulevich, V.M. 7.1-42
Mullenberg, M. 4.3-145
Muller, C.H. 3.4-15
Muller, F. 2.4-101, 5.9-50
Muller, F.P. 5.4-90
Muller, H.M. 5.5-224
Muller, J.C. 7.8-5
Muller, P.A. 6.1-70
Muller, W.H. 1.8-92, 1.8-93
Muller-Haslach, W. 4.3-146
Mulligan, G.A. 2.2-61, 2.7-87
Mullin, W.J. 1.6-31, 6.4-103
Mullner, E. 2.3-138
Mumladze, M.G. 1.5-154
Mummery, R.S. 1.7-137
Munakata, K. 1.8-182
Munakata, M. 2.5-85
Mungikar, A.M. 4.3-37, 4.5-146
Munjal, K. 6.5-89
Munjal, R.L. 5.5-292
Munoz de Con, L. 4.3-147
Munoz Burgos, M.S. 5.1-56
Munshi, G.H. 5.4-91
Munshi, G.K. 7.3-98
Munshi, S.R. 7.5-76
Munzig, H.P. 8.4-6
Mupawose, R.M. 6.1-71
Murach, M. 7.2-67
Murai, F. 1.1-241
Murakashi, S. 1.8-109
Muraki, S. 1.1-255, 1.2-111, 1.4-57, 2.1-136
Muralia, R.N. 1.8-39, 2.2-11
Muralidharan, V. 4.2-206
Murant, A.F. 5.4-28, 5.4-92,

5.5-71, 5.5-72, 5.5-73, 5.6-59, 5.6-60 5.6-61, 5.6-62
Murany, E. 4.6-63, 6.5-90
Muraoka, T. 7.4-1
Murari, R. 1.1-22, 1.1-26, 1.1-27, 1.3-3
Murata, G. 3.3-148
Murata, M. 1.4-31
Murata, T. 2.4-42
Murav'ev, I.A. 1.1-30, 1.1-135, 1.3-29, 1.3-30, 3.2-63, 3.3-185, 6.4-91, 7.2-83, 7.3-99, 7.4-35, 7.4-36, 7.4-37, 7.4-38, 7.5-77
Murav'eva, D.A. 3.2-58
Muraviev, I.A. 7.3-100, 7.4-39
Murin, A. 2.7-88, 2.8-64
Murko, D. 5.2-53, 6.5-91
Muroi, T. 6.5-141
Murphy, E.W. 6.2-45, 13.1-75
Murray, B.G. 2.9-76
Murray, M.J. 2.9-68, 4.2-98, 4.2-101, 4.2-103, 4.2-168, 4.2-168, 4.2-169, 4.2-207, 4.2-208, 4.2-209, 4.2-210, 4.2-211, 4.2-212, 4.2-213, 4.2-214, 4.2-216, 4.6-60, 4.6-61, 5.7-140, 8.2-57
Murray, R.D.H. 1.1-171
Murthy, G.S.R. 2.6-35
Murthy, N.B.K. 1.8-110
Murthy, P.K. 5.9-31
Murty, A.S. 2.7-89, 4.5-102
Murty, D.S. 4.2-216, 4.2-217, 4.2-218
Murty, G.S.S. 4.2-219, 4.2-220
Murugesan, M. 4.2-221, 4.2-222, 5.6-1
Murusidze, G.E. 5.7-141
Murzov, Zh. 2.3-231
Musaev, I.F. 3.1-49
Musaev, M.A. 3.4-88
Mush, N.N. 1.8-144, 4.8-75
Mushinskaya, S.Kh. 7.3-124
Mushynskaya, S.Kh. 7.3-101
Musim, M.N. 7.6-139
Mussa, A.E.A. 1.8-139
Mustiatse, G. 4.4-65
Mustiatse, G.I. 4.2-223, 4.5-89, 5.5-81
Mustich, G. 7.3-14, 7.3-15
Mustyatse, G.I. 4.5-147, 11.1-117
Muthukhrishnan, C.R. 4.2-12
Muthukrishnan, C.R. 4.2-354, 5.8-148
Muthukrishnan, T.S. 5.4-27
Muthuswami, S. 2.3-156, 2.5-86, 4.2-351, 4.2-354, 4.5-148, 8.3-67

756

DATE DUE

FEB 2 2 1989			
APR - 5 1989			
DEC 1 3 1989			
FEB 2 0 1991			
APR 2 8 1992			
DEC 2 2 1997			
DEC 2 1 1998			